Third Edition

ACCOUNTING AND INFORMATION SYSTEMS

Third Edition

ACCOUNTING AND INFORMATION SYSTEMS

Joseph W. Wilkinson

Arizona State University

John Wiley & Sons, Inc.

New York   *Chichester*   *Brisbane*   *Toronto*   *Singapore*

To Sharon Rochelle

Recognizing the importance of preserving what has been
written, it is a policy of John Wiley & Sons, Inc. to have
books of enduring value published in the United States
printed on acid-free paper, and we exert our best efforts
to that end.

Library of Congress Cataloging-in- Publication Data

Wilkinson, Joseph W.
    Accounting and information systems / Joseph W. Wilkinson. — 3rd
    ed.
        p.   cm.
    Includes bibliographical references and index.
    ISBN 0-471-61561-7 (cloth)
    1. Accounting—Data processing. 2. Management information
    systems.   I. Title.
HF5679.W52   1991
657.0285--dc20   90-28936
                                                                        CIP

ISBN 0-471-61561-7

Printed in the United States of America

10 9 8 7 6 5 4 3 2

PREFACE

Accountants interact with information systems of business and governmental enterprises as users, evaluators, and designers. They **use** information systems when they retrieve information to prepare reports for managers and financial statements for external parties. They **evaluate** information systems when they review internal controls during audits. They **design** information systems when they devise charts of accounts or propose the addition of specific controls within transaction processing systems.

This textbook is primarily intended for advanced undergraduates or graduates who will soon be assuming the responsibilities of professional accountants. Most of these students are currently majoring in accounting, but some may be majoring in computer information systems or another business discipline and/or minoring in accounting. Presumably the students using this textbook will have completed courses in (1) elementary financial and managerial accounting and (2) fundamentals of computer hardware, software, and applications.

The purpose of this textbook is to provide students with a body of knowledge that includes

1. Broad awareness of the concepts of information systems, especially those pertaining to systems, information, managerial decision making, organizational structures, accounting models, and computer technology.

2. Familiarity with the basic components of information systems, such as inputs, outputs, processing procedures, files, and controls.

3. Introduction to a wide range of systems analysis and design techniques, with particular attention to systems flowcharts.

4. Understanding of the steps involved in comprehensive systems development, as

well as the ability to apply the appropriate techniques in conducting a reasonably complex systems development project.

In compiling the body of knowledge from which the aforementioned results should accrue, I have drawn heavily upon such authoritative sources as the 1986 *Report of the American Accounting Association Committee on Contemporary Approaches to Teaching Accounting Information Systems*. Since the discussion is reasonably comprehensive with respect to all topics, the entire contents cannot be absorbed during a single semester or quarter. Thus, certain topics may be omitted or skimmed, according to the individual instructor's inclinations. Alternatively, the textbook can serve as the primary source for a two-course sequence.

This third edition reflects several significant changes:

1. The major transaction cycles have been moved from study cases into five chapters. By placing this material in separate chapters and by inserting the chapters into the middle portion of the book (Part III), the transaction cycles are accorded the prominence that they merit.

2. Less emphasis is given to manual processing systems in favor of greater attention to computer-based systems of all sizes and architectures. For instance, the initial coverage of computer technology has been moved from Chapter 7 in the second edition to Chapter 5 in this edition.

3. The concepts related to control systems have been more fully and logically developed (in Chapter 6) prior to the discussion of specific controls (in Chapter 9 and the chapters involving transaction cycles).

4. The components of a computer-based information system are grouped into a series of chapters that immediately precede those pertaining to the transaction cycles.

Thus, the components described (documents, screens, processing procedures, files, controls, reports) can be illustrated while the material is fresh in students' minds.

5. The specialized and more advanced topics, such as data base systems and communications networks, are grouped in Part IV. Each of these chapters represents a separate module that can be flexibly assigned at any point during the course.

6. The systems development chapters are grouped into still another part (Part V) following the transaction cycle chapters. These chapters may likewise be assigned as desired during the course.

7. The analysis and design chapters within the systems development sequence have been expanded to include structured techniques and user-developed applications.

8. Additional comprehensive cases have been included in Part VI for use as assigned term projects on system design. Most of these cases provide practice in developing transaction processing systems through the design phase of the systems development cycle. However, one of the cases provides practice in applying spreadsheet and data base packages on microcomputers.

Each chapter includes the following learning aids:

1. A brief introductory statement of objectives and a concluding summary.

2. A variety of figures and diagrams to clarify the concepts and techniques described.

3. Review questions, discussion questions, and one or two problems that review the important points covered in the chapter.

4. A range of problems, of varying difficulty, that can be assigned as homework or can be the basis of class discussions. Certain

of the problems, marked by the figure of a microcomputer, are suited for use in the application of a microcomputer-based software package.

5. A list of suggested readings.

Two major support systems are available to contribute to the learning experience:

1. A **Study Guide** (prepared by Severin Grabski of Michigan State University) contains clear summaries, glossaries, and exercises relating to covered topics in all of the chapters.

2. A **Laboratory Manual** (prepared by James P. Borden of Villanova University and W. Ken Harmon of Arizona State University) provides microcomputer-based assignment problems and cases that familiarize students with meaningful applications of electronic spreadsheets and data base management systems. Included are both a student workbook and a template disk.

An **Instructor's Manual** is also available from the publisher. It contains chapter outlines, suggested answers to discussion questions, solutions to assignment problems and comprehensive cases, a test bank of numerous multiple-choice questions, and figures from which to make transparencies.

I wish to acknowledge the very helpful suggestions made by reviewers James P. Borden of Villanova University, Robert Bromley of Central Michigan University, John S. Chandler of the University of Illinois, Severin Grabski of Michigan State University, Cynthia Heagy of the University of Houston, Donald Jones of the University of Utah, James Mandel of Rice University, and Gemma Welsch of De Paul University. In addition, numerous students have provided considerable assistance in the class testing of new problems and cases that appear in this edition. Furthermore, I appreciate the continuing assistance of my Wiley editor, Karen Hawkins, as well as the diligent craftsmanship of copy editor Judy Burke of Falletta Associates, Inc.

Four professional accounting groups have graciously permitted the use of problem materials from past professional examinations: the American Institute of Certified Public Accountants, the Institute of Management Accounting of the National Association of Accountants, the Institute of Internal Auditors, and the Society of Management Accountants of Canada.

In addition to my gratidute to these organizations and individuals, I extend my thanks to my family for its support. Any errors and omissions (which I hope number fewer than in past editions) must, as always, rest on my doorstep.

Joseph W. Wilkinson
Tempe, Arizona

CONTENTS

Part II
INFORMATION SYSTEM FUNCTIONS 215

Part *I*

BASIC CONCEPTS AND FUNDAMENTALS

Accounting and information systems rest on a foundation of varied concepts. The six chapters in this part set the stage for the study of information systems by surveying selected concepts in the areas of accounting, information, systems, communication, decision making, organizational structures, and controls.

Certain fundamental knowledge is also needed before we explore specific information systems. Since most present-day information systems are computerized, we look at basic aspects of computer technology. Since accounting information systems are greatly affected by controls, we examine internal control systems. In addition, we explore the two major purposes of accounting information systems: transaction processing and information processing.

Chapter **1**

OVERVIEW OF INFORMATION SYSTEMS AND ACCOUNTING

Information is a vital commodity to all enterprises. How is it generated and provided to various users, such as managers, customers, and creditors? How do accountants help to provide and evaluate information, as well as make effective use of information? Questions such as these are discussed in this and the remaining chapters of this textbook.

What Is an Information System?

In order to understand what an information system is, we need to define the terms *information* and *system*.

Information

The "product" of the information system is generated information. Information should be distinguished from data. **Data** are raw facts, figures, and even symbols. Together they comprise the inputs to an information system. In contrast, **information** consists of data that have been transformed and made more valuable by processing. Ideally, information is knowledge that is meaningful and useful for achieving objectives. Figure 1-1 shows the relationship of data to information.

System

A **system** is an integrated framework that has one or more objectives. It coordi-

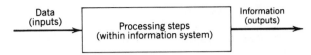

FIGURE 1-1 Information derived from data.

nates the resources needed to convert inputs into outputs. Resources may range from materials to machines to solar energy, depending on the type of system involved.

Definition of an Information System

An **information system** is therefore a framework by which resources (people, computers) are coordinated to convert inputs (data) into outputs (information), in order to achieve the objectives of an enterprise.

Characteristics of Information Systems

The preceding definition presents only the bare bones of an information system. To put flesh on the skeleton, let us view an example information system within a typical (though fictitious) enterprise or firm.[1] This example will illustrate both the functioning and the characteristics of information systems.

Consider the Shinewell Shoe Store, owned and managed by Eric Peterson. As owner-manager, Eric has his fingers in everything. He opens the mail, greets customers, oversees sales made by his sales clerk, makes cash deposits, and negotiates bank loans. To provide time for such a variety of activities, he keeps operations as simple as possible. For instance, he sells shoes on cash terms and rents his store and fixtures. He also employs the simplest possible

formal information system, physically consisting of a checkbook, merchandise order forms, deposit slips, stationery, a cigar box, a cash register, a pocket calculator, and a typewriter.

Witness a typical day at the Shinewell Shoe Store. Eric opens the morning's mail, puts all bills in the cigar box, and answers several letters on his typewriter. He prepares a merchandise order form for those shoe sizes and types in short supply. When previously ordered shoes arrive by parcel post, he checks their receipt against packing slips. Before noon he removes unpaid bills from the cigar box, writes checks for the amounts indicated, and mails the checks. (Since it is payday, he also writes a check to pay his clerk.) While his clerk is at lunch, Eric fills in as salesclerk, selling shoes to customers, ringing up sales on the cash register, and giving sales slips to customers. At the end of the day Eric counts the cash from sales, reconciles the count with the totals in the cash register, and prepares a deposit slip. He totals the deposit on his pocket calculator. Throughout the day Eric receives and initiates calls on the telephone—calls from and to his supplier, customers, bank, insurance agent, and others.

From time to time Eric computes basic ratios (such as the ratio of purchase costs to sales amounts) and prepares basic financial statements (such as balance sheets that support requests for bank loans). However, much of the information that Eric needs to manage is not developed on paper. Because he personally partakes in or observes all operations, Eric usually has the needed information in his head. Thus, he makes quick decisions, which are as quickly transmitted to his clerk and carried out.

[1]For the sake of conciseness, the term *firm* will be used hereafter in place of *enterprise*. However, *firm* should be understood to represent not-for-profit enterprises as well as business enterprises or organizations.

Eric's firm does well. In fact, after a few years it grows into a large department store, renamed Peterson's Emporium. During this growth several significant changes occur. The firm adds a variety of products, which it sells on credit as well as cash terms to a vastly larger number of customers. It expands the number of suppliers from whom it acquires these products. It also attracts the attention of certain outside parties, such as various governmental agencies interested in the affairs of larger firms. Eric gives up his sole ownership rights. To obtain more capital, he sells stock to several stockholders. Although Eric remains the top manager, he gives up his personal involvement in all of the firm's affairs. Instead, he delegates responsibilities for daily operations and much of the decision making to several hired managers.

These changes in Eric's firm are echoed in the information system. Additional documents and records, such as sales invoices and merchandise inventory records, supplement the basic merchandise order forms and checks. File drawers, ledger trays, magnetic tapes, and magnetic disks replace the cigar box and checkbook as repositories of stored data. New bookkeeping machines and small computers reside in back rooms, and sophisticated cash registers dot the sales areas. Prescribed procedures govern the flows of paperwork pertaining to sales, purchases, and payrolls. A greater variety of outputs, such as printed sales analyses and payroll reports, emerge from these procedures; some of these outputs go to managers to assist in decision making, while others go to parties outside the firm such as the Internal Revenue Service.

In other words, the information system tends to expand and become more formalized as the firm grows and becomes more complex. By this means a manager such as Eric is able to integrate his firm's activities and to manage as effectively as he could when the firm was much smaller.

Now let us examine several characteristics of the information systems of Eric's two firms that are common to every firm. These common characteristics are arrayed in Figure 1-2.

Communication Network

An information system resembles a communication network in that it provides paths for information to many points. It enables information to flow to all points of the firm and even to points outside the firm. In Eric's shoe store the communication network was quite simple, since the information generally flowed between Eric and only a few other parties (e.g., his clerk, his supplier). In the department store the network is much more complex. Information now flows among the various managers and employees internally and flows to the greater number of interested parties outside the firm.

This communication network has an informal as well as a formal aspect. Managers and employees communicate informally among themselves and with outside parties. For instance, gossip, hunches, and opinions conveyed to Eric via a telephone conversation (and stored in his head) have been acquired courtesy of the **informal information system**. Conversely, purchase orders prepared according to preestablished procedures represent elements of the **formal information system**.

Data Conversion Stages and Functions

An information system converts inputs into outputs. Three stages are involved in this conversion or transformation: an input stage, a processing stage, and an output stage. Related to these stages are **data collection, data processing,** and **information-generation** tasks or functions. Other functions, such as **data management** and **data control,**

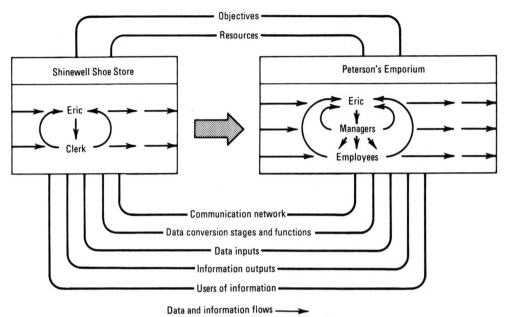

FIGURE 1-2 Characteristics common to the information systems of Eric's two firms.

also are typically performed during data conversion.

Figure 1-3 shows input, processing, and output stages and functional steps pertaining to Eric's shoe store. For instance, in the input stage sales were rung up on the cash register and recorded on sales slips. In the process stage Eric (in effect the data processor) reconciled cash and sales with the aid of his calculator. He then prepared the deposit slip on the typewriter. In the output stage he personally delivered the deposit slip, along with

the cash, to the bank teller. As noted earlier, more elaborate steps and information flows are necessary in the case of the department store. However, the number of stages has not increased.

Data Inputs and Information Outputs

Items of data are entered for processing during the input stage, whereas information is provided during the output stage. By anal-

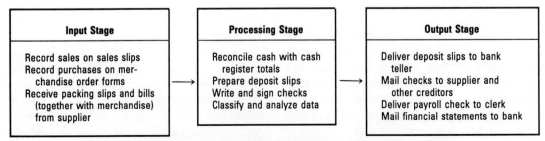

FIGURE 1-3 Data conversion stages in Shinewell Shoe Store's information system.

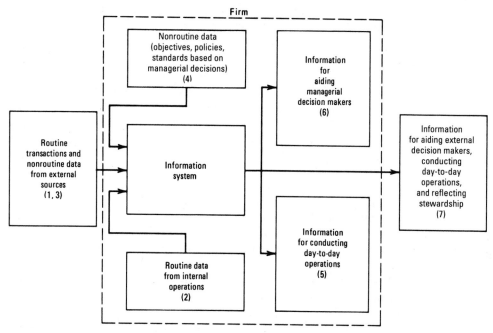

FIGURE 1-4   Data entering and information leaving a firm's information system.

ogy, data items are the raw materials that are converted into informational products or finished goods.

Data originate in differing ways, and information is generated for differing purposes and users. Figure 1-4 displays these several types of data and information. Examples are as follows:

1. Dollar amounts of sales and quantities of merchandise received from suppliers represent data arising routinely from external transactions.

2. Hours worked by the sales clerk and quantities of shoes ordered represent data arising routinely from internal operations.

3. Nationwide shoe sales and levels of personal income represent data arising nonroutinely from such external sources as trade associations and governmental agencies.

4. Shoe prices and the clerk's salary represent data arising from internal management decisions.

5. Quantities of shoes on hand (by style and size) represent information for day-to-day operations.

6. Sales analyses and financial ratios represent information for managerial decision making.

7. Purchase orders for suppliers and financial statements for the bank represent information for external users.

Information and data are often difficult to distinguish. For example, the amounts of individual sales may be viewed as useful information to sales order clerks and salespersons, even though to the sales manager they represent data from which sales summaries are prepared.

Users of Information

Information is generated by the firm's information system for use by either internal users or external users. **Internal users** consist of the managers and employees of the firm.

External users include interested parties outside the firm, such as creditors, suppliers, customers, stockholders, governmental agencies, and labor unions.

The shoe store's information system had only a limited number of users. Eric and the clerk were the internal users. Eric needed such information as the total cash received each day and the inventory of shoes on hand; his clerk needed to know his work schedule and shoe prices. External users included the customers, supplier, and bank personnel. Customers needed to know the descriptions and prices of shoes. The supplier needed to know the quantities of shoes ordered. The bank personnel (when asked to lend money to the store) needed to know the financial status and earnings prospects of the store. Furthermore, the clerk also became an external user in his role as paid contractor of labor services; as such, he needed to know his salary level and take-home pay.

In addition to the users mentioned earlier, the department store's information system must serve many new users. Now the internal users include the added employees and managers, who need information concerning their budgets, the firm's credit policies, and a host of other matters. New external users include stockholders, potential investors, labor unions, governmental agencies, and investment analysts. They all desire financial information concerning the firm's status, earnings, and prospects. Stockholders also are very interested in the dividend rates. Governmental agencies also need to know the amounts of taxes withheld from paychecks, the taxable income of the store, and so on. Moreover, the previously existing users need new information. For instance, those customers who now buy on credit need information concerning their account balances.

Objectives

The information system of a firm in the world of business and government has three major objectives: (1) to provide information that supports decision making, (2) to provide information that supports day-to-day operations, and (3) to provide information that pertains to stewardship. Both internal users and external users are served by decision support and operational support information, while only external users are the targets of stewardship information. Most of the information for the last two objectives, and some of the information for the first objective, are produced through the processing of transaction data. Figure 1-4, noted earlier, links the information outflows that are generated to serve these purposes with the transaction data and the other types of data inflows.

Although the specific information flows vary from firm to firm, these three purposes remain constant for every firm. Thus, Eric needed financial ratios and other information to aid him in deciding whether or not to request a bank loan for the shoe store. Although more financing alternatives are available to the department store and more managers are involved, the same types of decisions must be made and the same categories of information are needed. Similarly, day-to-day operational information (e.g., checks, purchase orders) was and is needed in both situations. Finally, the stewardship purpose remains unaffected when the firm becomes a department store, although the number of stewards increases. In addition to the bank, stewardship information must be provided to stockholders, governmental agencies, and certain other external users.

Resources

An information system requires resources in order to function. Resources may be classified as data, supplies, equipment, personnel, and funds. Resources employed by the shoe store's information system included data on such forms as sales slips, merchandise order forms, and checks; supplies such as stationery and blank-form stocks; and equipment such as a telephone, typewriter, calculator, and cash register. Both Eric and his clerk constituted the personnel resource, since they spent part of their working hours processing data. Bank loans and earnings were the sources of the funds resource. The department store's information system requires the same classes of resources, but in greater variety and size.

Information systems are generally described in terms of their resources. An information system in which the personnel resource is dominant is known as a **manual information system**. An information system that emphasizes the use of equipment is known as an **automated information system**. If the information system incorporates computers and related equipment, it is known as a **computer-based information system**.

Similarities and Distinctions among Information Systems

These common characteristics are portrayed in Figure 1-5. They are arrayed in three dimensions—stages, users, and resources—for each of the three key objectives of an information system.

Although the figure illustrates the variety of similarities among information systems, we should note that each individual system is customized. That is, it consists of its own unique set of detailed features. A primary aim in system design is to determine which specific details suit a particular firm's information system at a particular time. This becomes more challenging as the firm increases in size and complexity.

Functions Performed by Information Systems

Let us examine the working mechanism of an information system more closely. Figure 1-6 shows that this mechanism or framework consists of five major tasks or functions: data collection, data processing, data management, data control and security, and

information generation. These functions, in turn, consist of a series of steps, often called the **data processing cycle,** that transform data from various sources into the information needed by the varied users.

Data Collection

Several steps are typically needed in the collection of data. A *data capture* step draws data into the system. (When the events being captured are quantitative in nature, a *measurement* step may also be necessary.) Upon being captured the data are usually *recorded* by being written onto forms known as source documents. Captured data may also be *validated* to assure their accuracy and *classified* to allow their assignment to preestablished categories. Furthermore, the data may be *transmitted,* or moved from the points of capture to the point where they are to be processed.

Consider the steps employed by the MAW Company in collecting data concerning sales events or transactions. The data are captured by a salesperson (the *data collector*) via a telephone call from a customer. At the same time the salesperson records the data (which consist of identifying items, such as the customer's name and product descriptions, and quantitative items, such as the quantities of products ordered) on a sales order document. He or she then transmits the order by telegraph to the firm's home office. There a clerk validates the name and address of the customer, by reference to a file, and classifies the product data by listing the product codes alongside the product descriptions.

Data Processing

Collected data usually undergo a series of processing steps in being transformed into usable information. Additional validation and classification steps may take place. The collected data might be summarized by aggregating individual transaction quantities. Sometimes the data are *transcribed* (i.e.,

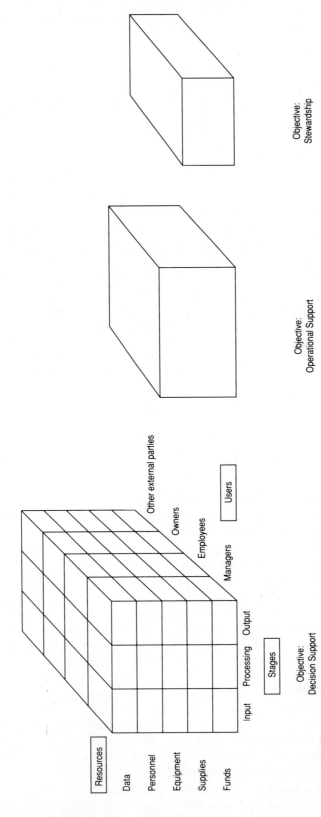

FIGURE 1-5 Dimensions of an information system.

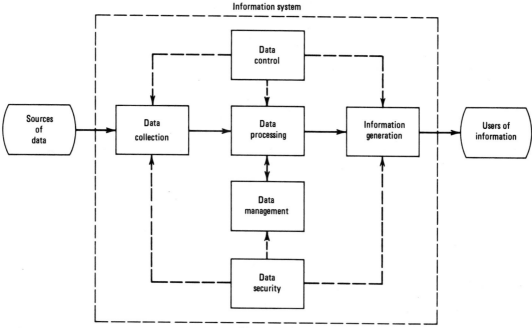

FIGURE 1-6 Information system functions. Adapted with permission from "Report of the Committee on Accounting and Information Systems," in *Committee Reports: Supplement to Vol. XLVI of the Accounting Review* (Evanston, Ill.: American Accounting Association, 1971), p. 290.

copied or reproduced) onto another document or medium. Also, the data may be *batched* by being gathered together in groups of documents pertaining to transactions of a similar nature. In turn, batched data are usually *sorted* to arrange data items according to one or more characteristics. When quantitative data are involved, *calculating* and *comparing* steps are often performed; as a consequence, new data may be "created."

Sales transactions are processed within the MAW Company as follows: A sales clerk transcribes the sales data onto a formal multiple-copy sales order-invoice form. At the end of each day he or she batches the orders and sorts them by customer name. He or she then calculates the total quantity of each product ordered. These totals, which summarize the results of the day's sales, are listed on a sales recap sheet. Then the clerk compares today's totals with yesterday's to-

tals and records the increases or decreases in an analysis column.

Data Management

The data management function consists of three key steps: storing, updating, and retrieving. *Storing* involves placing data in repositories called *files* or *data bases*. Stored data provide a history of events, reflect the status of an entity, and serve as an aid to planning. Data may be stored either (1) on a relatively permanent basis or (2) on a temporary basis to await further processing. *Updating* consists of adjusting stored data to reflect recent events, operations, and decisions. As a result of updating, the adjusted data reflect the current status of entities or events (e.g., the current amounts owed to suppliers). *Retrieving* consists of accessing and extracting stored data. Retrieved data are used in further processing or are converted into information for users.

In the MAW Company, the sales clerk stores data concerning sales by removing one copy from each sales order-invoice and placing it into an open sales-order file. After the order products have been delivered to a customer, the clerk calculates the amount the customer owes. Then he or she updates the customer's account in a customer accounts receivable file; that is, the clerk adds the sales amount to the previous balance in the customer's account, thereby deriving the current, or updated, balance owed by the customer. At the end of each month the clerk retrieves all of the copies of sales invoices and the balances of all customers' accounts; using these data, he or she prepares statements for customers and an aged accounts receivable report for the credit manager.

Data Control and Security

Data being entered for processing may be in error, data may be lost or stolen during processing, records may be falsified during processing, and so on. Thus, an important function of the information system is to safeguard and ensure the accuracy of data (and hence information). Steps that help carry out this function, as Figure 1-6 suggests, are applicable in conjunction with all of the major tasks and stages of an information system. The step of validation, noted earlier, is also a control step that is applicable during data collection and processing. Other control steps and security measures include authorization, locked cash drawers, reconciliations, verifications, and reviews.

Information Generation

The final function of the information system, placing information in the hands of users, may involve one or more steps. *Reporting* involves preparing reports from processed data, from stored data, or from both.

Often the preparation of reports requires the analysis and interpretation of the underlying data. *Communicating* consists of (1) rendering the reports more understandable and usable by the users and (2) physically delivering the reports to the users.

Let us refer one last time to the MAW Company. As we noted when illustrating data management steps, the clerk prepares statements for customers and a report for the credit manager at month's end. Other reports, such as sales analyses, are also prepared upon request of the sales manager. These sales analyses are prepared in graphical as well as tabular form, in order to render them more understandable to the sales manager. After being prepared, the statements are mailed to the customers, while the reports are hand-carried to the managers.

Procedures

A **procedure** is a specific sequence of steps encompassed within the data processing cycle. It may be performed solely by humans, may be fully computerized, or may involve a mixture of human and computerized steps. Usually, but not always, a procedure involves more than one major task. Figure 1-7 diagrams the steps that might comprise a typical procedure.[2] The overall data processing cycle of a firm consists of a variety of procedures, each differing from the others with respect to the number and sequence of steps. For instance, an alternative procedure to the one pictured in Figure 1-7 might omit the data transcription step and place the calculation step before the sort step.

Design Questions

A number of questions arise when designing task and procedural details for a spe-

[2]The circled *A* connects the flow shown in the two rows of boxes.

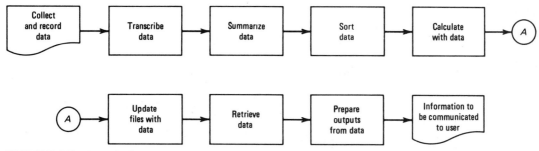

FIGURE 1-7   A typical procedure.

cific information system. Among the questions that require answers are the following:

1. Which data are to be collected and which are to be filtered out (rejected) by the information system?
2. How much data concerning each event, operation, or management decision should be collected?
3. On what media should data be recorded and stored?
4. How should stored data be structured?
5. What should be the sequence of steps in each procedure?
6. What equipment should be used in performing the various task steps?
7. What set of controls and security measures are adequate to safeguard and ensure the accuracy of data?
8. How often and in what form should information go to users?

Devising sound answers to such questions requires much thought, effort, and experience. However, system designers have a variety of design principles and precepts to guide them.

Development of an Information System

As we have observed, an information system evolves during the life of a firm. In effect, a new (or at least significantly improved) information system replaces the current system when it can no longer fully meet the needs of a growing and changing firm. Since each information system has a limited life cycle, systems development is thus a cyclical activity. A **systems development cycle** consists of several phases, beginning with systems planning and concluding with systems implementation.

Systems planning consists of laying the foundation for a new or revised information system. It includes the preparation of a master systems plan as well as proposals for systems projects by which the plan is to be carried out.

Systems analysis consists of surveying and analyzing the present information system. It leads to a determination of the information that users need from a new or improved system as well as the technical requirements of the system itself.

Systems design consists of deriving a set of specifications (i.e., answers to the design questions stated in the foregoing section) that fulfill the needs and requirements determined during systems analysis. Often alternative designs are devised and evaluated. The phase concludes with complete design specifications that best fit the firm's current and expected circumstances.

Systems justification and selection involves a detailed analysis of the benefits and costs pertaining to the selected system design. It also often includes the evaluation of proposals from manufacturers of processing equipment, in order that the most suitable equipment may be selected to implement the design.

Systems implementation consists of such steps as completing the details for the new design (e.g., writing the computer programs), hiring and training new employees, installing and testing newly acquired equipment, converting files to new media, and "turning on the engine" of the new or improved system.

Following these systems development phases comes the period of systems operations. While not a part of the systems development cycle, it represents the longest phase of a system's life. This operational period includes such activities as routine operation, maintenance, and management of the new or improved system. Another activity performed during systems operation is the periodic or continuous evaluation of the system's performance and the reliability of its information outputs.

Accounting Information Systems

Accounting and information systems are closely related. This relationship is well described by one authoritative body as follows:

Essentially, accounting is an information system. More precisely, it is an application of the general theory of information to the problem of efficient economic operations. It also makes up a large part of the general information expressed in quantitative terms. In this context accounting is both a part of the general information system of an operating entity and a part of the basic field bounded by the concept of information.[3]

[3]Committee to Prepare a Statement of Basic Accounting Theory, *Statement of Basic Accounting Theory* (Evanston, Ill.: American Accounting Association, 1966), p. 64.

This close relationship is also acknowledged by the widespread use of the term **accounting information system** (AIS).

Definition and Scope

An accounting information system is a formal information system in every sense of the word. It embraces all of the characteristics described earlier, including purposes, stages, tasks, users, and resources. Moreover, a particular firm's accounting information system has an all-pervasive scope. It extends to all activities of the firm and provides information to all of the firm's users.

On the other hand, the accounting information system of a firm exhibits features that distinguish it from the firm's overall information system. These features stem from the accounting function's concern with the economic impact of events on a firm's activities and well-being. Thus, an accounting information system accepts only economic data arising from external events (transactions) or internal operations. Most of these items of data are expressed in financial terms (e.g., amounts of sales to customers), although data may be nonfinancial (e.g., hours worked by employees) if they are finally converted into financial terms (e.g., gross pay earned). On the output side, an accounting information system generates documents, reports, statements, and other information outputs expressed solely, or at least primarily, in financial terms. These financially oriented outputs provide *scorekeeping* information (e.g., how much profit has been made, how much is owed to whom), *attention-directing* information (e.g., how much more has been spent than was budgeted), and *decision-making* information (e.g., what the benefits are, versus the costs, of introducing a new product).

Accounting Models

A model is a representation of reality. An accounting information system employs

two types of models, financial accounting models and managerial accounting models, to represent financially oriented realities within a firm.

Financial accounting models. The key relationship underlying all financial accounting models is

$$Assets = Equities$$

The major purpose of financial accounting models is to generate scorekeeping information pertaining to firms for use by persons outside the firms. Usually the information appears in the form of such financial statements as balance sheets, income statements, and funds-flow statements. All financial statements prepared by financial accounting models are based on generally accepted accounting principles, as specified by authoritative bodies such as the Financial Accounting Standards Board.

Managerial accounting models. Managerial accounting is that branch of accounting concerned with providing financial information to the internal users within firms. Although the resulting information may, and often does, include versions of the financial statements just noted, it also includes other types of reports and analyses. A wide variety of managerial accounting models may be employed by a single firm to produce these outputs. Examples of managerial accounting models are cost–volume–profit models, cost-variance analysis models, and cash-flow forecasting models. Such models provide managers with attention-directing and decision-making information, in order to aid them in controlling and planning their firm's activities.

Managerial accounting models are not constrained by generally accepted accounting principles. Thus, the data that appear in the models may be predictive (e.g., sales forecasts) or normative (e.g., standard labor

costs) in nature. Also, the financial statements may be arranged to suit the managers' needs. For instance, income statements may appear in direct-costing rather than absorption-costing formats; assets in balance sheets may be based on current rather than historical cost valuations if desired.

Accounting Processing

Accounting models accommodate two forms of processing: transaction processing and information processing. Transaction processing provides both scorekeeping and attention-directing information, whereas information processing focuses on information for decision making.

Transaction processing. Transactions are economic events that can be measured in financial terms, that affect a firm's assets and equities, and that are reflected in the firm's accounts and financial statements.[4] External transactions arise from exchanges between the firm and external parties. Internal transactions arise from the internal operations of a firm.

Although each firm encounters a wide variety of transactions, several basic types of transactions are common to most firms. Basic external transactions include:

1. The sale of products or services to customers.
2. The purchase of merchandise, materials, and fixed assets from suppliers.
3. The receipt of cash from customers and others.
4. The disbursement of cash to suppliers and others.

---

[4]A relatively few transactions do not arise directly from events but represent allocations or accruals over time; depreciation of equipment is an example. Conversely, events such as changes in depreciation methods are not transactions.

A basic internal transaction is the payroll transaction, which arises from operations and services performed internally by a firm's employees.

Certain types of transactions are peculiar to firms in particular lines of endeavor. For instance, the conversion of raw materials into finished goods involves types of internal transactions peculiar to manufacturing firms. Demand deposit accounting involves types of external transactions peculiar to banking and savings firms.

Transactions are processed by standardized procedures that involve such components as source documents, files, processing steps, controls, and outputs. These procedures for the various types of transaction are performed by **transaction processing systems** (TPS). They merge into a common general ledger system and lead to the preparation of financial statements for a firm. Since the financial statements are prepared periodically, the collective process is known as the **accounting cycle**.

Information processing. Information processing involves the use of decision-making models, such as the managerial accounting models. Some of the needed inputs are obtained as by-products of transaction processing. However, many of the inputs must be processed from other sources, both internal and external to a firm. Figure 1-8 shows the relationships between transaction processing and information processing.

The primary users of the outputs from information processing are the managers of a firm, who must carry out both its strategic and its tactical planning. Other users are the professional employees, such as accountants and engineers, and various outside parties, such as stockholders and creditor banks.

Information provided through information processing can be extremely useful. It can provide firms with a competitive edge. For instance, it has helped firms such as General Electric to develop and market successful new products. It has enabled firms to provide better customer service, as when

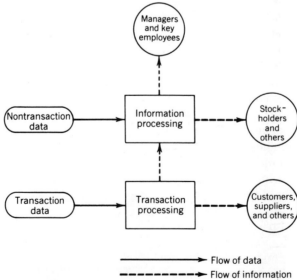

FIGURE 1-8 Relationship of transaction processing to information processing.

American Express helps its cardholders locate the lowest airplane fares.[5]

Relation to the Management Information System

The accounting information system is one of the most important information systems in a firm. However, it is not the whole of even the formal information system.[6] A firm's overall information system includes, besides the informal system, a variety of formal functional information systems. Examples are the marketing information system and the personnel information system. These functional systems provide managers, employees, and parties outside the firm with information not available through the accounting information system. For instance, they may generate reports of market share and personnel skill profiles.

Perhaps the most important information system in a firm, other than the accounting information system, is the **management information system** (MIS). Its purpose is to provide decision-making and attention-directing information, nonfinancial as well as financial, to managers. Since the management information system does not serve users other than managers, and since the accounting information system serves all users but only with financial information, the two systems overlap. Figure 1-9 illustrates this overlapping.

By now you may well be wondering whether you really need to understand exactly how all these overlapping systems and models relate to each other. In fact, you do not, since in reality all these overlapping sys-

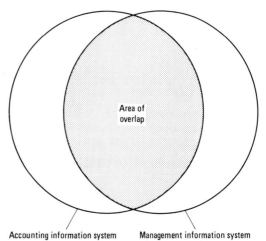

Accounting information system   Management information system

FIGURE 1-9 Overlapping information systems within a firm.

tems comprise only *one* integrated and coordinated information system. A firm simply could not afford a variety of separate systems.

The two major ideas that should be retained from this section are the following:

1. Scorekeeping, attention-directing, and decision-making types of information are generated via the information system with the aid of accounting models.

2. The information system (including both the AIS and the MIS) performs two levels of processing: transaction processing and information processing.

These types of information and levels of processing provide frameworks for later discussions in this textbook. For instance, transaction processing and information processing are the topics of Chapters 3 and 4, respectively.

Current Developments

Rapid changes and developments are currently affecting information systems (including accounting information systems). These changes and developments are ap-

[5]Michael E. Porter and Victor E. Millar, "How Information Gives You Competitive Edge," *Harvard Business Review* (July–August 1985), pp. 149–160.

[6]"Report of the Committee on Accounting and Information Systems," in *Committee Reports: Supplement to Vol. XLVI of the Accounting Review* (Evanston, Ill.: American Accounting Association, 1971), p. 344.

pearing in managerial needs and perceptions, in the business environment, and in information technology.

Many managers are recognizing that they need more relevant and timely information for decision making. In some firms they are perceiving that the financial information provided by their accounting information systems is not adequate to meet all their needs. In other firms (and perhaps most of the preceding firms), they are observing that the financial accounting model is unduly influencing decision making. For example, historical cost values may be employed, rather than current replacement values, in making decisions concerning long-lived assets. Managers in such firms are increasingly demanding more responsive information systems.

The environment facing business firms is becoming more complex and demanding. Populations are growing rapidly; markets are expanding, often to the multinational level; customer expectations are rising and diversifying; government demands are multiplying; social responsibility, ecological concerns, and public institutions are growing. As might be expected, these changes are creating intense competitive pressures, requiring substantial capital outlays, and squeezing available resources. Firms are responding in various ways: diversifying goods and services; rearranging organizational structures; incorporating new technology; participating in community action programs; and, last but not least, reexamining information systems.

New developments in information-related equipment, techniques, and concepts— collectively called **information technology**— are occurring at a breathtaking pace. New versions of computers, terminals, and other devices are announced almost daily in business periodicals. New techniques for solving business problems, based on such disciplines as communications theory and operations research, are described in various technical journals. New concepts, such as the view that information is a resource requiring effi-

cient and effective management, are proposed by systems thinkers. Many of these technological developments are being incorporated into the information systems of progressive business firms and governmental organizations.

American Airlines provides an example of how to use information technology effectively. When computer networks became feasible in the 1970s, it developed the Sabre airline reservation system. Terminals were linked to centralized records of data pertaining to all the airline's flights. Although American Airlines was not the only airline to develop an on-line reservation system, it was the first to place terminals in the offices of numerous travel agencies. Travelers could make reservations more conveniently than ever before. Although the cost of this extensive network was extremely high, American Airlines was able to outstrip its competitors and become one of the world's largest carriers.

Accountants and Information Systems

Accountants may be broadly described as information specialists. They perform a variety of roles with respect to the information systems of firms. In those firms in which accounting information systems are still the only formal information systems, accountants are often the exclusive information brokers. On the other hand, in firms that have added functional information systems, accountants must share information-related roles with such specialists as systems analysts, management scientists, and industrial engineers. When firms add computers, other specialists such as programmers and computer scientists may enter the picture.

Regardless of the business setting, accountants typically perform these four major roles with respect to information systems or their information products: (1) *users,* (2) *evaluators,* (3) *controllers,* and (4) *builders.* The ways in which these roles are performed differ, depending largely on the positions held by accountants. Six familiar positions assumed by accountants are financial accountant, managerial accountant, tax specialist, accounting manager, auditor, and systems designer or consultant. The close relationships between these positions and the roles are portrayed in Figure 1-10 and described in the following paragraphs.

Financial Accountants

Financial accountants use the accounting information system to aid in transaction processing. They also draw upon data stored

within the system to perform such interpretive functions as financial ratio analysis. In addition, they evaluate the accounting information system, in order to ascertain that the financial statements are prepared in accordance with generally accepted accounting principles. On occasion, they may become involved in the design of the accounting information system. For example, they may recommend that the valuation procedure be changed from the first-in, first-out method to the last-in, first-out method.

Tax Specialists

Tax accounting involves the preparation of the returns that reflect tax obligations and

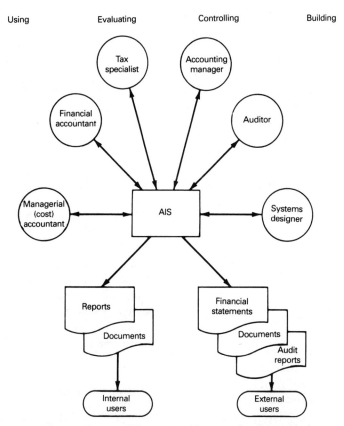

FIGURE 1-10 Accountant positions and roles and the accounting information system.

the making of decisions having tax implications. On the one hand, tax accounting provides income, property, sales, and other types of tax returns to external taxing authorities such as the Internal Revenue Service. On the other hand, it provides reports and analyses to the managers who must make decisions.

Tax specialists may be employees of the firm incurring the taxes or may be public accounting consultants. In either case they make use of the firm's accounting information system to prepare the tax returns and to obtain data for tax planning. Like financial accountants, they may occasionally need to evaluate the accounting information system with respect to data that it collects and processes. When tax laws change, they need to recommend revisions to the accounting information system, in order to enable it to process the information needed for compliance.

Managerial Accountants

Managerial accountants use the accounting information system to develop the information for decision making. They frequently must evaluate and recommend revisions to the system, particularly concerning the structures of the decision models and the formats of the reports and analyses. In doing so they are primarily guided by the information needs of the managers they serve.

Accounting Managers

Generally, the chief accounting manager in a firm is known as the controller. Managers reporting to the controller may include a head financial accountant, a head cost accountant, and a budget manager. In turn, these managers supervise the various aforementioned accountants. They use the accounting information system to obtain information for controlling accounting activities, for evaluating the performances of the staff accountants, and for guiding the direction of the firm's accounting function.

Auditors

Auditing has the purposes of evaluating the reliability and integrity of information produced by the accounting information system, the adequacy of the internal controls used in transaction and information processing, and the efficiency and effectiveness in using system-related resources.

Auditors fall into two categories: external and internal. External auditors are generally members of public accounting firms or of governmental agencies. They serve as independent reviewers of the accounting information systems of clients or regulated firms. Typically they express opinions concerning the adequacy of the internal control system and the fairness of the financial statements. Auditors from public accounting firms issue their reports to the owners of the firm being audited. Governmental auditors issue their reports to the overseeing agency of the firm being audited. Internal auditors, by contrast, are employees of the firm being audited. They express opinions that focus on the efficiency and effectiveness with which system-related resources are being used. Their reports are issued to the top management of the firm being audited.

While auditors are primarily concerned with evaluations, they must make extensive use of the accounting information system in doing so. Moreover, they may recommend changes to the design of the accounting information system, particularly with respect to the internal controls.

Systems Designers

Accountants whose primary duties involve systems development may also be subdivided into external and internal categories.

Those in the external category are generally described as management consultants or advisory services specialists. Often they are colleagues of external auditors and tax specialists within public accounting firms. Internal systems designers or consultants are employees of the firms whose systems they service.

Both categories of systems designers are continually involved in building or developing activities. In these activities they must also use and evaluate (analyze) the accounting information system and its outputs.

Implications for Accounting Students

The foregoing summaries of accounting positions show that most if not all accountants are involved in the use, evaluation, and design of accounting information systems. Thus, all accounting students should acquire a *common body of knowledge* related to information systems. Since information systems are increasingly being computerized, that body of knowledge should include an understanding of computers and their use in accounting applications.

Summary

Information aids day-to-day operations and decision making. Information needed by an enterprise (firm) is produced by an information system. An information system can be defined as a framework of coordinated resources that collects, processes, controls, and manages data through successive stages in order to furnish information via a communication network to varied users for one or more purposes.

An information system performs the five major tasks or functions of data collection, data processing, data management, data control and security, and information genera-

tion. Each function consists of one or more steps. For instance, data management consists of storing, updating, and retrieving data. Developing new or improved information systems is a cyclical activity. Each cycle consists of such phases as planning, analysis, design, justification, selection, implementation, operation, and evaluation.

Accounting meets all the qualifications of an information system. An accounting information system extends to all activities of a firm and provides information to all users. It is limited, however, in that the information provided is primarily or solely in financial terms. (In contrast, the management information system provides nonfinancial as well as financial information to managerial users.) An accounting information system employs two types of models: a financial accounting model and a managerial accounting model. The latter is not constrained by generally accepted accounting principles. These accounting models accommodate transaction processing and information processing. Basic transactions processed by a typical firm include sales, purchases, cash receipts, cash disbursements, and payroll transactions. Through a process known as the accounting cycle they are merged into a general ledger, from which financial statements are periodically prepared. Information processing involves the use of models to produce information for decision making. Ongoing changes in managerial needs and perceptions, as well as new developments in the business environment and in information technology, are affecting all accounting information systems.

Accountants perform roles in such activities as financial accounting, tax accounting, managerial accounting, accounting management, auditing, and systems development. In all these roles they use, evaluate, and design accounting information systems. Therefore, all accountants and accounting students should acquire a common body of knowledge relating to information systems.

Review Problems with Solutions

Problem 1 Statement

The Sun Office Company has served the Phoenix area for a number of years. Its products range from printed business cards and forms to pegboard systems and accounting machines. Although the firm has only a dozen employees, it competes effectively with larger office supply firms because of two strategies: excellent service and attention to specialized groups of customers. For instance, it promises 24-hour delivery on all orders, and it caters to the needs of small professional firms that provide accounting and legal services.

The firm occupies a single building in downtown Phoenix. It acquires merchandise, which it displays on the sales floor, from two suppliers on credit. Its printing press is operated in a back room. Many sales are made on a cash basis to walk-in customers; however, larger sales are generally made on account.

Most of the tasks related to accounting and data processing are performed by an accounting clerk, a secretary, and a cashier. Aiding them in these tasks are such business machines as a posting (accounting) machine, a typewriter, a calculator, and a cash register. The owner-manager performs such tasks as opening the mail, preparing deposit slips, signing checks, reconciling the monthly bank statement, and analyzing key reports.

Required

a. Identify several of the basic types of transactions, as well as key resources and other elements comprising the accounting information system.

b. Describe the procedural steps that might be employed in processing one type of transaction you listed in **a**.

c. Briefly denote the accounting cycle for the same type of transaction you selected in **b**.

d. Discuss information that the accounting information system should provide to (1) a supplier, (2) a customer, and (3) the owner-manager.

Solution

a. The basic types of transactions include cash and credit sales, merchandise purchases, cash receipts from credit customers, cash disbursements to suppliers, and payroll. Key resources include source documents (e.g., purchase orders, checks, and sales invoices); records and files (e.g., accounts receivable ledger, merchandise ledger, general ledger, checks to suppliers and employees, monthly statements to customers, and financial statements to the owner-manager); equipment (e.g., posting machine, typewriter, calculator, and cash register); personnel (e.g., accounting clerk, secretary, cashier, and owner-manager); and funds (e.g., from revenues).

b. The cash disbursements transaction consists of paying a supplier for merchandise previously ordered on a purchase order. A procedure for this transaction might be as follows: When the invoice is received from the supplier, it is filed by due date, together with a copy of the purchase order and the listing of merchandise received. On the due date these documents are retrieved by the accounting clerk, who verifies that the amount owed is correct, deducts any discount allowed, prepares a check for the supplier, and enters the amount of the check in the checkbook. She then submits the check and three supporting documents to the owner-manager. After comparing the check with the supporting documents (as a control over improper payments), he signs and mails the check. At the end of each week all cash disbursements are posted from the checkbook to the cash account and offsetting accounts in the general ledger.

c. The accounting cycle pertaining to cash disbursements begins with the preparation of the check. It continues with the entry of the check in the checkbook (which serves as a journal) and the posting of the check amount to the general ledger. The cycle is completed with the drawing of the trial balance and the preparation of the financial statements each month.

d. The accounting information system will likely provide a variety of information.

(1) To a supplier it should provide (via purchase orders) the quantities of the various items of merchandise needed, the dates needed, and the acceptable unit prices.

(2) To a credit customer it should provide information concerning transactions and current status. When each sale is completed, the customer should receive (via a sales invoice) the quantities of the various items of merchandise ordered, their unit prices, the sales amount, the allowable discount, and the due date. Monthly the customer should receive (via a statement form like the one shown) the dates and amounts of transactions during the month, as well as the current account balance.

(3) To the owner-manager it should provide (via monthly financial statements) the results of operations and the financial status of the firm and (via other timely reports) the status of merchandise inventory on hand, the level of sales made to various groups of customers, the profitability of sales of the major lines of merchandise, the level of bad debts, and so on.

Problem 2 Statement

Sparky Electric Utility Company provides electrical energy to residential and commercial consumers on Long Island. The procedure for billing consumers and reporting sales is as follows: Meter readers drive to the premises of consumers, read the electrical meters, and record the kilowatt-hour readings on meter-reading cards. At the end of each day they return to the main office and turn the cards over to billing clerks. These clerks first refer to consumer (i.e., customer) reference file cards to determine the classification of each customer and to ascertain the correct customer code and rate. Then they sort the meter-reading cards by customer code number and class (i.e., type). The clerks also compute batch totals by summing the customer codes and kilowatt-hours on all the cards they have received that day; these totals are later compared with similar totals computed throughout the processing, in order to detect cards that may be lost or errors that may be committed.

Other clerks in the billing department carry on the processing. For each customer whose meter was read, the clerks calculate the amount to be billed, transcribe the amount and other identification data onto a new billing blank form, and then post the amount of the bill to the customer's record card in the customer master file. Next they mail the bills to the customers. Then they recompute the totals by type of customer, list the totals on a summary sheet, and verify the totals by comparing against the previously computed batch total. Finally, they store the daily summary sheets together with the meter-reading cards and copies of the bills.

At the end of each month the billing supervisor takes the daily billing total summary sheets from the billing data file and gives them to an accountant. The accountant prepares a report of monthly sales by type of customer, analyzes the monthly sales by computing ratios (e.g., proportion of the total monthly sales made to residential customers), and submits the results to appropriate managers.

Required

Prepare a block diagram that portrays the billing and sales reporting procedure described above. Use as many of the terms as possible that represent steps in the conversion of data to information, and underline each such term. Show each file as a separate box or block that is linked to a processing block by a flowline.

Solution

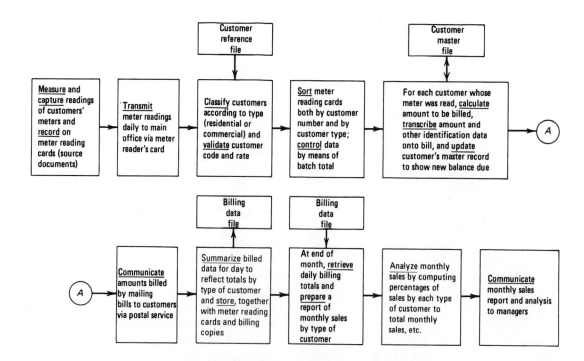

Review Questions

1-1 What is the meaning of each of these terms?

Information
Data
System
Formal information system
Informal information system
Internal user
External user
Manual information system
Automated information system
Computer-based information system
Data processing cycle
Data collection
Data processing
Data management
Data control
Information generation
Procedure
Systems development cycle
Accounting
Accounting information system
Management information system
Financial accounting model
Managerial accounting model
Transaction processing
Information processing
Transaction
Transaction processing system
Accounting cycle
Information technology
Financial accountant
Tax specialist
Managerial accountant
Accounting manager
Auditor
Systems designer

1-2 What are the relationships among information, data, and system?

1-3 List several characteristics that are common to all information systems.

1-4 Identify the differing types of data and information.

1-5 Who are the users of information from the information system of a firm?

1-6 What are three general purposes of accounting information systems?

1-7 Identify the major tasks or functions of an information system and the likely steps within each task.

1-8 What questions must be answered when designing a new or improved information system?

1-9 Describe the major phases comprising an information system development cycle.

1-10 What is the scope of an accounting information system?

1-11 Distinguish between financial accounting models and managerial accounting models.

1-12 Distinguish between transaction processing and information processing.

1-13 List several basic transactions common to most firms.

1-14 How does the accounting information system of a firm relate to the management information system?

1-15 Discuss current changes and developments affecting accounting information systems.

1-16 Identify the several roles and positions of accountants, and discuss how these roles relate to the accounting information system.

Discussion Questions

1-17 All information systems have been seen to have a common set of basic characteristics. Particular information systems, however, may differ greatly with respect to specifics. Identify the similarities and differences likely to exist between the information systems employed by General Motors and by an individual physician; between the information systems employed by your university and IBM.

1-18 Accounting has been defined as "the art of recording, classifying, and summarizing in a significant manner and in terms of money, transactions and events which are, in part at least, of a financial character, and interpreting the results thereof."[7] Compare and contrast this definition with the one given in the chapter. Is it consistent with the chapter discussion?

1-19 How would a managerial accounting cycle differ from the accounting cycle described in the chapter?

1-20 Describe the information system of your campus bookstore in terms of the following characteristics: purposes, users of information, tasks and steps, and resources.

1-21 In what ways might financial statements prepared for the management of a firm differ from financial statements published in annual reports? Can financial statements based on historical information be useful to either internal managers or external parties in their decision making?

1-22 To what extent must a manager rely on intuition and the informal information system, rather than the formal information system, when making decisions? Does the level of the manager within the firm and the type of decision influence the answer?

1-23 What topics should be studied by accountants so that they can acquire a common body of knowledge relating to information systems?

1-24 Assume that you hold each of the following positions. How would you make use of information systems and participate in their development?

a. Managerial accountant in a firm's accounting department.
b. Auditor in a public accounting firm.
c. Management services specialist (with an accounting degree) in a public accounting firm.
d. Financial accountant in a firm's accounting department.
e. Industrial engineer in a firm's production department.

1-25 You are a managerial accountant in a medium-size manufacturing firm. Your superior, the controller, has just assigned you to be a member of a team that is to study and redesign the production information system. What can you contribute to the study?

Problems

1-1 Financial statements are a key output of an accounting information system. Describe the ways in which the balance sheet and income statement for a corporate wholesaler can be helpful to each of the following users:

a. Stockholders.
b. Managers.
c. Prospective investors.
d. Securities and Exchange Commission.
e. Creditor banks.
f. Labor union.

1-2 List in order the specific data processing steps that you, an inventory clerk for an appliance dealer, would perform to transform the indicated inputs into the desired output.

Inputs. Documents that contain the code numbers and quantities of merchandise items received from suppliers and sold to customers. Each individual document refers *either* to a receipt *or* to a sale, although some

---

[7]Committee on Terminology, "Review and Resume," *Accounting Terminology Bulletins,* No. 1 (American Institute of Accountants, 1953), p. 9.

of the documents may contain the code number and quantity for more than one item of merchandise. About 100 documents are given to you daily in unsorted batches.

Outputs. A daily report that shows the *dollar amounts* of merchandise received and sold, in terms of both (a) individual merchandise items *and* (b) totals of merchandise items involved in the day's transactions. The merchandise items should be arranged in code number order, and each should be identified on the report by its descriptive title.

Note: You have available a reference file that lists the descriptive titles and unit prices for all coded merchandise items.

1-3 Draw a block diagram that portrays the indicated procedure for each of the small firms listed below.

    a. Service station (sales procedure based on credit card sales transactions).

    b. Department store (sales procedure based on credit card sales transactions).

    c. Branch bank (demand deposit procedure).

    d. Auto service garage (cash sales procedure).

    e. Home appliance shop (purchases procedure).

    f. Independent retail grocer (purchases procedure).

    g. Furniture dealer (cash receipts procedure).

    h. Building materials retail supplier (cash disbursements procedure).

    i. Public school district (payroll procedure).

Hint: For the details of the designated procedures, refer to such reference books available in your library as *Encyclopedia of Accounting Systems,* rev. ed., Jerome K. Pescow, ed. (Englewood Cliffs, N.J.: Prentice-Hall, Inc., 1976), and *Portfolio of Ac-*

counting Systems for Small Business, rev. ed., by National Society of Public Accountants (Englewood Cliffs, N.J.: Prentice-Hall, Inc., 1977).

1-4 As a graduating accounting major, you are considering two job offers: one from a Big Eight public accounting firm and one from a member of the Big Three automobile manufacturers. It happens that the automobile manufacturer is a client for all the services offered by the public accounting firm.

    a. Assume that you accept the offer of the public accounting firm.

        (1) Describe the area of responsibility that you personally would be assigned, and the interactions that you would likely have with the AIS of your firm and the client firm.

        Note: The choice of the area of responsibility depends on your personal desires and qualifications and may differ from the choices of your classmates.

        (2) Describe the remaining major areas of responsibility within the public accounting firm, and the interactions that individuals in those areas would likely have with the AIS of your firm and the client firm.

    b. Assume that you accept the offer of the automobile manufacturer.

        (1) Describe the area of responsibility that you personally would be assigned, and the interactions that you would likely have with the AIS of your firm and with the accountants from the public accounting firm.

        (2) Describe the areas of responsibility that other accountants would have within the firm, and the interactions that they would likely have with the AIS of your firm.

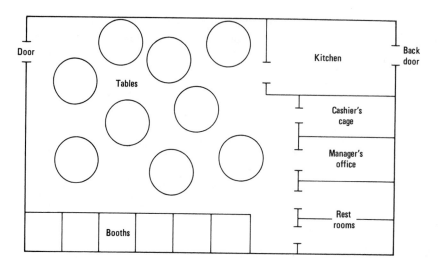

1-5 For several years the Tasty Restaurant of Baltimore, Maryland, has served customers in a choice downtown location. Although everyone says that the food is excellent, the manager, Alvin Scott, has become uncomfortably aware that serious problems exist. Numerous complaints from customers have reached his ears. In essence, the customers are dissatisfied with the service, particularly with the lengthy waits during peak meal periods. In addition, there is antagonism between the chefs and the employees who wait on tables.[8] Finally, the profits and cash receipts appear to be unsatisfyingly small, in spite of the fact that prices are comparable with those of other "fancy" restaurants in town.

Briefly, the restaurant operates as shown in the accompanying layout. Customers enter and seat themselves. A waiter writes their orders on a blank check form, departs and enters the kitchen, and calls out (loudly, because of the noise) the orders to the chefs. When the food has been prepared, the waiter brings the food from the kitchen and serves the customers. When the meal is completed, the waiter takes the payment to the cashier and returns with any change.

[8]Chefs rank higher in a restaurant hierarchy than waiters.

The chefs (two in number) handle the food purchasing tasks, although on a rather unorganized basis. For instance, because of separate preferences, the two chefs may purchase the same items from two different food vendors. In fact, both of the chefs—although good, experienced cooks—are opinionated and take orders only from Alvin. Unfortunately, he must frequently be away from the kitchen because of his many duties, including being gracious to regular customers.

Alvin learns that you, a close relative, are taking a course in information systems at a nearby university. He calls and asks you for help in resolving his problems.

Required

a. Analyze the current weaknesses at the Tasty Restaurant.

b. Briefly describe the phases of the system development cycle (other than the planning and analysis phases) as they might apply to the Tasty Restaurant.

c. Suggest improvements to the procedures, physical layout, and other operational aspects. Indicate which improvements pertain to the information system.

d. Describe information that Alvin needs to manage the Tasty Restaurant.

1-6 The Campus Bookstore is located in a building adjacent to the campus of a large state university. It sells textbooks, books other than textbooks, school supplies, clothing, and sundries. All sales are made on a cash basis. Merchandise for resale and store supplies are acquired on credit from a variety of suppliers. Textbooks are bought subject to return privileges, since estimated course sizes do not always materialize. Used textbooks are bought from students for cash at the end of each semester.

Although the building occupied by the bookstore is leased, the furniture, fixtures, vehicles, and equipment have been purchased. Most disbursements are made from revenues. However, a short-term bank loan is needed at the beginning of each semester; it is repaid before the end of the semester.

The bookstore is owned by Donald Thump. He personally directs the activities of several managers, who in turn supervise operations and the employees who report to them.

Required

a. Describe the purposes of the bookstore and its information system.

b. Identify key transactions conducted by the bookstore.

c. Identify the various users of the bookstore's accounting information system.

d. Identify the resources of the bookstore's accounting information system.

e. Describe several useful reports that might be generated by the bookstore's accounting information system.

1-7 Select a small firm in your locality, such as a florist shop, building contractor, delivery service, or bank branch. After visiting the selected firm, prepare a report that contains the following:

    a. A brief description of the firm's background and environment, such as the products or services that it provides, the industry of which it is a part, its physical facilities and other key assets, and its employees.

b. A listing of its key accounting transactions.

c. A narrative description of one of the key transactional procedures such as sales or purchases.

d. A copy of a source document used in the procedure that you have described.

e. A brief description of one file used by the described procedure, including the data contained in the file and the way that the file is affected by processing steps.

f. A brief description of one device or item of equipment (other than a computer) used in the processing of data.

g. Copies or sketches of outputs from the selected procedure, such as generated documents, reports, and financial statements.

Note: Assignments concerning this selected firm will appear in several following chapters of this textbook.

Suggested Readings

American Accounting Association. "Report of the Committee on Accounting and Information Systems." In *Committee Reports: Supplement to vol. XLVI of the Accounting Review*. Evanston, Ill.: 1971, pp. 287–350.

———. "Report of the Committee on Contemporary Approaches to Teaching Accounting Information Systems." *Journal of Information Systems* (Spring 1987), pp. 127–156.

Applegate, Lynda M.; Cash, James I., Jr.; and Mills, D. Quinn. "Information

Technology and Tomorrow's Manager." *Harvard Business Review* (Nov.–Dec. 1988), pp. 128–136.

Bodnar, George H., and Hopwood, William S. *Accounting Information Systems.* 4th ed. Boston: Allyn and Bacon, 1990.

Butterworth, John E. "The Accounting System as an Information Function." *Journal of Accounting Research* (Spring 1972), pp. 1–27.

Cushing, Barry E., and Romney, Marshall B. *Accounting Information Systems and Business Organizations.* 5th ed. Reading, Mass.: Addison-Wesley, 1990.

Davis, Gordon B. "Computer Curriculum for Accountants and Auditors—Present and Prospective." In *Education for Expanding Computer Curriculums,* edited by Daniel L. Sweeney, pp. 12–21. New York: American Institute of Certified Public Accountants, 1976.

Roussey, Robert S. "The CPA in the Information Age: Today and Tomorrow." *The Journal of Accountancy* (October 1986), pp. 94–107.

After studying this chapter, you should be able to do the following:

Identify the characteristics and classifications of systems.

Describe the environmental settings of firms.

Identify several operational functions within a typical firm, as well as their relationships to the information system.

Recognize and diagram sound organizational structures for a firm and its accounting function, as well as identify relationships between the organization and the information system.

Chapter **2**

ENVIRONMENTS OF INFORMATION SYSTEMS

An information system does not exist in a vacuum; rather, it is an integral part of the firm it serves. As such, it has close relationships with the firm's physical operations and organization. Furthermore, as we have seen, an information system reaches out beyond the firm to customers and others who have dealings with the firm. Collectively, these surroundings have a tremendous influence on the design and use of an information system.

In this chapter we examine the key components of an information system's environment and their relationships to the information system and to each other. Before examining these matters, however, we need to build a foundation by surveying basic systems concepts.

Systems Concepts

What do a football team and Eric's shoe store have in common? The members of a football team act as a unit to strive toward the common purpose or objective of winning games. Eric and his sole employee acted together with the common objective of selling the firm's products at profitable prices. Each example reflects the essential ingredients of a **system,** as defined by a recognized dictionary:

A complex unity formed of . . . often diverse parts subject to a common plan or serving a common purpose . . . objects joined in regular interaction or interdependence; . . . an orderly working totality.[1]

Concepts such as these form the nucleus of general systems theory. By surveying systems concepts we can gain an understanding of systems in general, and information systems in particular. If we can better predict how systems will behave under various conditions, we should be able to design better information systems.

Common Characteristics of Systems

Understanding systems—whether they be business firms, sports teams, or information systems—consists largely of recognizing their common characteristics. Several characteristics of information systems were introduced in Chapter 1: objectives, resources, communication networks, data conversion, data inputs, information outputs, and information users. Now we will redefine these characteristics to pertain to all systems. We will also introduce additional characteristics.

Objectives. Every system attempts to achieve one or more **objectives;** that is, objectives are the motivating force that drive a system. As we noted, the prime objective of a football team is to win games by compiling higher scores than opposing teams. In Eric's shoe store the "bottom-line" objective was to earn profits. If the total dollar value of the sales exceeded the total costs incurred during the same period of time, Eric's firm achieved its objective.

Inputs–process–outputs. Inputs consist of all the tangible inflows to a system as well as the intangible impacts on the system; outputs consist of all generated outflows or results; and the process consists of the method by which the inputs are converted into outputs.

System objectives influence and often control the conversion of inputs into outputs. Consider this influence in the case of the football team. The inputs are the team's facilities, its uniforms, and such player attributes as energy, skills, and knowledge of the opposing team. To achieve its prime objective, the team must expend these inputs in a process lasting 60 playing minutes. If the team "processes" its inputs more effectively than its opponent does, it will reap valued outputs. These outputs may include fame for the team, glory for individual players, and perhaps greater future ticket sales for the school or the owner of the team.

Environment. Every system (except perhaps the universe) is physically limited. The surroundings that lie beyond a system comprise its **environment.** A football team's environment includes the opposing team and the viewing public. The environment of Eric's shoe store included customers, the supplier, and competitors. A **boundary** fixes the limits of a system and separates it from its environment. Although boundaries of certain systems are not visible and may be difficult to "fix" with precision, every system is circumscribed by a boundary.

Subsystems. Every system, no matter how small, contains subsystems. Each **subsystem** performs a specialized role within the larger system of which it is a part. At the same time, each subsystem incorporates all of the characteristics of a complete system. As small as it was, Eric's shoe store contained a clerk, a cash register, and a variety of other subsystems (i.e., systems in their own right). The clerk's role in the store's activities differed from the role of the cash register. (What were their respective roles?)

[1]*Webster's Third New International Dictionary of the English Language—Unabridged* (Springfield, Mass.: G. & C. Merriam, 1981).

Interdependencies. Every system has multiple interdependencies. In addition to possessing tightly related subsystems, a system in turn constitutes an integral part of a larger system. Thus, while the shoe store possessed the cash register as a subsystem, it was a subsystem of the business community within which it resided. Relationships of subsystem to system to supersystem form a **system hierarchy.**

A **system network** represents another type of interdependency. A network is formed when a system is coupled to other systems on the same hierarchical level. The systems comprising a network interact with each other through couplings or shared boundaries called **interfaces.** Interfaces enable resources to flow among the interacting systems. In the case of Eric's shoe store, an interface between the supplier (one system)

and the store (another system) was the parcel service that delivered the ordered shoes.

The interdependent subsystems within a single system also form a network, since they are coupled. **Resources** flow among the subsystems, with outputs from one subsystem becoming inputs to one or more interfacing subsystems. Figure 2-1 shows a network of coupled subsystems within a manufacturing firm. Outputs from the marketing function, for instance, become inputs to the production, personnel, and finance/accounting subsystems; in turn, the marketing function receives inputs from the firm's environment, the personnel subsystem, and the finance/accounting subsystem.

The concept of system interdependencies is useful to the study of information systems. It reminds the analyst that a system or a subsystem should not be viewed in isola-

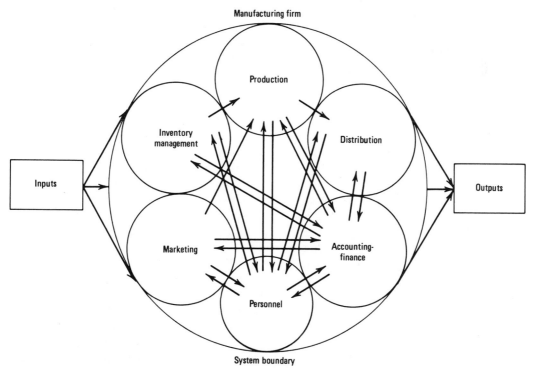

FIGURE 2-1 Coupled subsystems in a manufacturing firm.

tion from the other systems or subsystems to which it is linked. It also suggests that the analyst can move to lower levels in the system hierarchy in order to narrow the scope under scrutiny. For instance, the analyst might begin by surveying the entire information system for improvement; next he or she may select the marketing function as a particular area of concern; then he or she might focus on a subsystem of the marketing function, such as the order-filling activity. By doing so the analyst has in effect opened the "black box" labeled "order-filling activity," while treating the remaining activities and also the other functions of the information system as interconnected but closed "black boxes."

Constraints. Every system encounters **constraints,** internal or external restrictions that define the configuration or capability of the system. A boundary, for example, represents a physical constraint that defines the size and shape of a system. Other constraints imposed on a football team include the rules of the game and the limited skills of the players. The growth of Eric's shoe store was constrained by the demand for shoes, the actions of competitors, and the availability of funds from the bank.

In some cases constraints can be reduced or eliminated. For instance, Eric's shoe store was able to grow to the size of a department store in part because he sold stock to the public. A commonly employed means of reducing constraints affecting operations is known as *decoupling*. Thus, the finished-goods inventory warehouse in a manufacturing firm serves as a decoupling mechanism, or buffer, between the production of goods and their distribution; that is, it reduces the constraint or necessity for extremely close coordination between production and distribution operations.

Controls. Every system must regulate its subsystems if it is to achieve its objectives.

Controls are the regulatory processes by which a system corrects any deviations from a course that leads to the desired objectives. Budgetary control, quality control, credit control, and inventory control are typical control processes employed by firms.

Effective control depends on **feedback.** By means of feedback the outputs of a system are measured against standards to determine deviations, which are then corrected by changing the inputs or the process. Feedback will be discussed further in Chapter 4.

Effective control within the context of a system is also specified by the **law of requisite variety.** According to this law, a viable system must have available one or more control mechanisms or variations to counteract each possible out-of-control state. Consider, for instance, that a firm might experience two out-of-control states: (1) an increasing rate of bad-debt losses and (2) an increasing number of errors per document prepared. To exert effective control, the firm must counteract both states. Thus, it might (1) require prior approval of credit before each sale is accepted and (2) require each document to be proofread before issuance.

Users. Every system has users, although the term must be interpreted broadly. The users of a business firm include its owner, customers, and all others who interact with it. A football team's most numerous "users" are the spectators, although the opposing team can also be viewed as a user.

Business Firms as Systems

We can summarize these system characteristics by means of the business firm diagramed in Figure 2-2. Guiding the firm are such objectives as maximizing profit and maintaining a high level of customer service. Three of its most important subsystems are the organization, the operational system, and the information system. Each of these subsystems can be subdivided or factored into

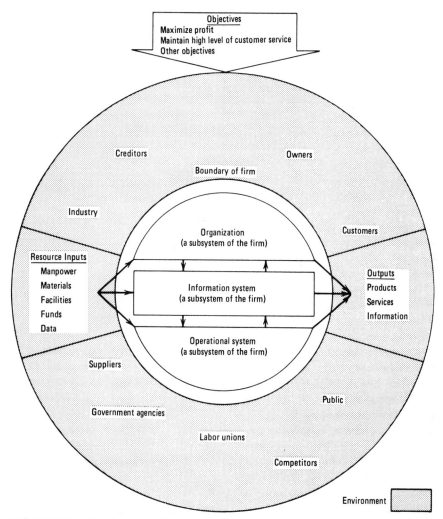

FIGURE 2-2 The business firm as a system.

numerous sub-subsystems. Inputs to the firm consist of resources classified as manpower, materials, facilities, funds, and data. Through complex processes the firm converts these resource inputs into products (and/or services) and information. In the environment beyond its boundary the firm interfaces with competitors and owners as well as customers and suppliers. Although not shown in the figure, the firm encounters constraints such as government regulations and employs controls such as supervision over employees and checks on the quality of products.

A firm's information system shares much in common with the firm, although it also exhibits certain distinct differences. Thus, while it faces the same environment beyond the firm's boundary, it also interfaces with such other firm subsystems as the organization and the operational system. While its objectives (e.g., to provide decision-making information and to aid daily operations) are coordinated with those of the firm, they

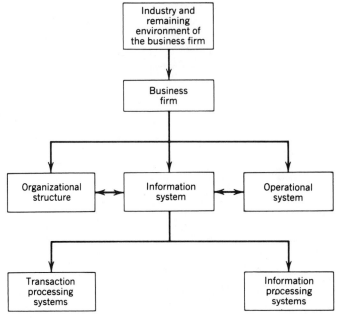

FIGURE 2-3 A hierarchy of systems.

differ in that they only represent a means of achieving the firm's objectives. While the information system accepts the same types of resource inputs, it produces only information as an output. While it is subject to the same types of constraints and controls as the firm, the information system is often the vehicle by which these constraints and controls are measured, managed, or applied.

Figure 2-3 illustrates the hierarchy of systems formed by a business firm, its environment, its three major subsystems, and key subsystems of the information system.

Classifications of Systems

The world is brimming with systems. While each system is unique, it may conveniently be classified according to one or more key modes or attributes. Several modes of classification, together with examples, are as follows:

Classification	Example
Natural systems	Mississippi River system
Human-made systems	Interstate highway system
Simple systems	Bicycle
Complex systems	Human brain
Closed systems	Automatic process control system in an oil refinery
Open systems	Elementary school system
Deterministic systems	Clock
Probabilistic systems	Roulette wheel

Based on these classifications, firms and their information systems can be described as human-made, open, complex, and probabilistic systems. They are **human-made systems** in that they are designed and operated by humans. They are **open systems** in that they receive inputs and provide outputs to their environments. Thus, they can react to changes in their environments in order to maintain stable conditions. They are **complex systems** because they represent social organizations—webs of intricate relationships among humans and other subsystems. Finally, they are **probabilistic systems** since their future conditions cannot be forecast with complete certainty.[2]

The Systems Approach

In addition to clarifying the nature of systems, general systems theory offers a useful framework for solving problems and designing information systems. The approach, called the **systems approach,** encourages a holistic viewpoint—that is, any system (or problem) is best viewed as a whole having interrelated parts. The systems approach reminds us that any system works best when it is guided by clear objectives and is well suited to its environment. Finally, the term implies that a systematic (i.e., carefully planned, step-by-step) development procedure leads to the soundest result.

Consider the application of the systems approach to a community development project. The developer first establishes the overall purpose of the community, for example, to provide good living conditions for its residents. He or she therefore gives due attention to the community's relationships with such aspects of its environment as neighboring communities and nearby businesses. Throughout the planning stage he or she is ever mindful of the interactions among the residential sections, parks, shopping centers, schools, and other parts comprising the community. Each part is assigned its appropriate role within the whole, so that the result is a pleasing unity. Designing follows a careful procedure, each part in turn being the focus of attention while its details are developed within the broad framework. In time a complete, detailed blueprint and timetable emerge. Finally the construction takes place. After the new community is functioning, it is evaluated to see that the residents are served as planned.

The information systems of many firms can be rendered more effective by means of the systems approach. For instance, the objective of providing useful decision-making information might be clarified and stressed. Additional information may be collected concerning the firm's competition and other aspects of the environment. Information flows among the marketing, inventory management, and accounting functions could be more closely coordinated.

The Environment beyond the Firm

We have noted that a firm is influenced by its environment, an environment that is economic, technical, social, and political in nature. Environmental influences may appear in many guises. On the one hand, the environment may provide opportunities, such as entry into a new market or a chance to buy materials on a long-term fixed-price contract. On the other hand, the environment may present constraints and challenges, such as a shortage of critical materials, a rapid rise in interest rates, or the appearance of a new competitor.[3]

If we are to design an information system that is to be responsive to its firm's particular environment, then we should identify significant influences on the firm. Three categories of influences worth noting are those stemming from needed resources, those stemming from the industry of which the firm is a member, and those stemming from the legal obligations of the firm.

Resources

Among the various resources needed by a typical firm are raw materials, employees, funds, electric power, plants, trucks, legal

---

[2]However, certain portions of firms and their information systems, such as transaction processing systems, may be fairly described as deterministic.

[3]C. Roland Christensen, Kenneth R. Andrews, and Joseph L. Bower, *Business Policies: Text and Cases,* 5th. ed. (Homewood, Ill.: Richard D. Irwin, 1982).

Resource	Examples	Factors affecting availability and cost of acquiring	Factors affecting cost of using
Manpower	Unskilled employees Skilled employees Managers	Locations of firm's facilities Skill levels required Strength of labor unions General economic conditions	Labor productivity Wage rates Fringe benefits
Materials	Merchandise Raw materials Parts Supplies	Suppliers' stocks Suppliers' prices Delivery lead times Levels of demand Costs of ordering Size of orders General economic conditions	Control of waste Control of spoilage Cost of storing
Facilities	Land Buildings Machines Furnishings	Locations desired Technology level Interest rate level Market for used facilities Labor rates for construction employees General economic conditions	Maintenance policy Replacement policy Alternative uses Depreciation methods

Funds	Via operations
	Via bank loans
	Via mortgage notes
	Via bond issues
	Via stock issues
		Credit rating of firm
		Profitability of firm
		Interest rate level
		Money-market conditions
		General economic conditions
			Financing mix
			Dividend versus
			  "plowing back"
			  policy

FIGURE 2-4 Factors affecting the acquisition and use of physical resources.

advice, and data concerning economic conditions. To acquire these resources efficiently and effectively, the firm should be aware of specific conditions affecting their availability and cost. Figure 2-4 lists several factors pertaining to each of the four types of physical resources.

Consider the manpower (i.e., labor or human) resource, for example. Availability and cost will differ widely for (1) a high-technology firm whose main plant is located in a highly industrialized, heavily unionized urban area and (2) a sugar beet producer located in a nonunionized rural area. The former needs skilled laborers as well as technical and professional employees; it will likely have to search widely beyond its urban area to find the required specialties, and it will have to pay the specialists well. The latter needs only unskilled labor, which it can probably acquire from nearby farms and towns; also, the wage rates will be considerably lower.

Information systems facilitate the acquisition, use, and status reporting of resources. Let us see how this pertains to the materials resource. An information system can collect data indicating which suppliers are willing to provide specific needed materials, at what prices, and with what lead times. It can record and report the levels of materials on hand and when they are likely to be depleted if the demands for their use continue at the same rates. It can indicate the optimal quantities of materials to order and can process the paperwork to place the orders.

When the materials arrive, the information system can record their receipts and issue checks to pay the suppliers. It can also keep track of waste and spoilage in the storage and use of materials, and then report that information to the appropriate managers.

Information systems should reflect the diversity of their firms' resource needs. For example, an electronics manufacturer needs thousands of parts, which typically are acquired from a variety of suppliers. Thus, its information system would likely maintain voluminous files related to the parts inventory and to the suppliers' accounts. Conversely, a discount furniture store may buy only a few basic items from a single manufacturer in Grand Rapids. Its information system would therefore contain just a few inventory records and a single supplier account.

Industry

A firm identifies with at least one industry, whose members sell similar products or services. Industries tend to differ significantly in certain respects; these differences are reflected in the structure and operating conditions of the member firms. For instance, the firms in the automobile and steel industries can be described as capital intensive and integrated, whereas firms in the garment and insurance industries are labor intensive and relatively unintegrated. Firms in certain industries face rapidly changing environments, while firms in other industries enjoy relatively stable environments. Thus, firms that produce jogging gear and microcomputers are experiencing explosive market growth, while firms that provide electrical and transportation services are growing rather slowly; firms in high-technology industries must cope with rapid changes in technology, whereas firms that produce basic staples such as soap and food encounter less-rapid technological change.

Firms in all industries can benefit by employing their information systems to collect data concerning markets, technology, and other firms in their industry. Those firms facing very dynamic conditions need such data

on a very timely basis, in order to respond to new opportunities and challenges.

Legal Obligations

Firms often receive welcome assistance from legally established public bodies, such as economic data from the U.S. Department of Commerce. More often, however, the contacts between firms and public bodies concern the satisfying of legal obligations. Payments of various taxes to the Internal Revenue Service (and other taxing agencies) and payments to employee benefit programs represent two examples of typical legal obligations.

Legal obligations often take the form of heavy reporting requirements. Many firms must employ their information system resources to generate a variety of reports for public bodies at local, state, and national levels. These reports concern such matters as payroll taxes, workmen's compensation, and new issues of capital stock. Certain firms, such as public utilities, are especially burdened by such reporting requirements. For instance, they must prepare reports and other data to state commissions in support of requests for rate increases. However, almost all firms have seen their reporting loads increased in recent years. New laws concerning pollution and a host of other matters are passed each year, and most of these laws contain reporting requirements.

The Operational System

The **operational system,** one of a firm's major internal subsystems, is the work system.[4] It is the arena of action that includes such daily tasks as buying materials, running machines, and shipping goods. In systems

---

[4]The terms *system* and *subsystem* are used in a relative sense. Hence, the operational system is a system in its own right but a subsystem within the firm.

terms, the operational system is the process or network that transforms physical resources into the products or services provided by a firm. Hence, it is the connecting link between resources flowing into a firm and the products or services flowing out to the firm's customers.

Operational systems vary appreciably from firm to firm. Figure 2-5 illustrates the operational systems for a bus line, a manufacturing firm, and a hospital. The flowlines in the figure link selected resource inputs to the major products or services that are generated via the operational system.

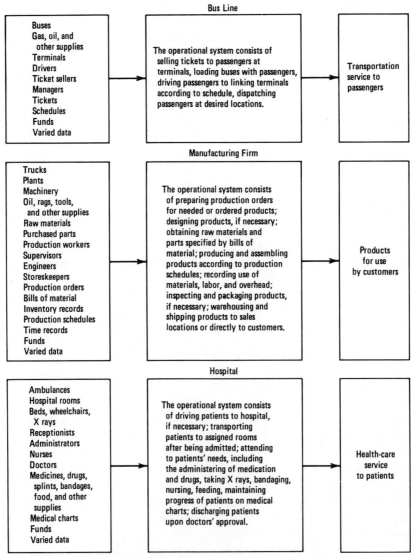

FIGURE 2-5 Operational systems for three types of firms.

Operational Functions

An operational system is generally segmented in order to reduce its complexity and to gain the advantages of specialization. The most popular method of segmenting is according to function.

An **operational function** is a related sequence of physical or paperwork operations within the operational system of a firm. All of the operational functions of a firm comprise an interlocking set of subsystems, akin to those portrayed in Figure 2-1. In turn, each operational function encompasses subsystems (i.e., subfunctions) of its own.

Figure 2-6 depicts a variety of operational functions and subfunctions found within the Tractors Manufacturing Company, a hypothetical manufacturer of farm vehicles. (In effect, the figure diagrams the operational system for a manufacturing firm described in Figure 2-5.) These functions and subfunctions together transform the varied resources (shown entering at the left) into the outputs (such as the products shown leaving at the right). Subfunctions appearing within the dashed lines represent the *primary* subfunctions, those subfunctions that directly participate in the prime role of transforming materials into delivered products. The remaining functions and subfunctions shown in the figure play *supporting* roles. Let us look at the typical objectives and subfunctions relating to several of the key functions in this firm.

Inventory management. The objective of inventory management is to manage the materials resource efficiently. Included within this function for the Tractors Manufacturing Company are such primary and supporting subfunctions as purchasing materials, receiving materials, and storing materials. Other subfunctions such as inventory requirements planning and inventory control (not shown in Figure 2-6) are often added to enhance further the management of the inventory resource.

Production. The objective of the production function is to create *form utility* by converting raw materials into finished goods. Aside from raw materials, resources such as production manpower, production facilities (including electrical energy), funds, and data are required in the production process. Primary production subfunctions in the Tractors Manufacturing Company consist of parts production and assembly of parts and subassemblies. Supporting subfunctions include engineering design (to develop product specifications), production planning and control (to develop production schedules and control mechanisms and to generate necessary production-order paperwork), maintenance (to keep facilities in working order), and quality control (to maintain product quality). Facilities management may also be included, or it may be attached to a separate engineering or administration function.

Marketing/distribution. The objectives of the combined marketing/distribution function are to obtain orders from customers and to fill the orders efficiently. Getting orders involves such subfunctions as advertising, sales promotion, and selling. (In the case of the Tractors Manufacturing Company, sales may be made directly to customers or through outlets such as retail stores.) Filling orders requires such subfunctions as order entry, credit checking, warehousing, and shipping. Resources required in marketing and distribution typically include salespersons, warehouse personnel, delivery truck drivers, sales outlet stores, delivery trucks, funds, and data.

Marketing and distribution functions tend to vary considerably from firm to firm. Service-oriented firms, for instance, do not require distribution subfunctions such as warehousing and shipping. Very large manu-

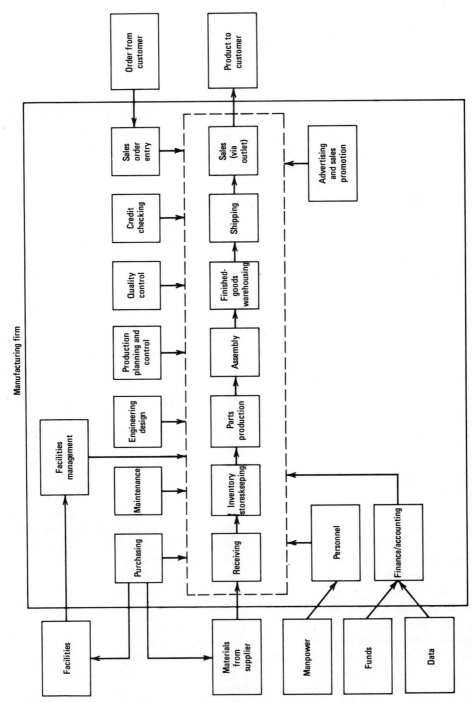

FIGURE 2-6 Primary and supporting operational subfunctions in the Tractors Manufacturing Company.

42

facturing firms, on the other hand, require not only warehousing and shipping but also such marketing subfunctions as market research, product planning, sales forecasting and analysis, and customer relations.

Personnel. The objectives of the personnel function are to assure that the firm's manpower needs and the job-related needs of each employee and manager are met. Managing the manpower (i.e., human) resource usually requires such subfunctions as employment (to recruit and test prospective personnel), training (to develop personnel skills through planned programs), benefits and safety (to administer pension plans, suggestion plans, plant cafeterias, safety programs, medical facilities, and related services), compensation (to establish and administer wage rates and salary scales), and labor relations (to deal with employee grievances and labor unions).

Finance/accounting. The objectives of the finance function are to obtain funds at lowest costs and to disburse funds efficiently. The objectives of the accounting function (often combined with the finance function) are to monitor the physical operations, to report financial status and results of operations, and to provide documents that support daily operations.[5] Thus, the finance function manages the funds resource, whereas the accounting function manages (together with other information systems) the data resource. Operational subfunctions within the finance function usually include cash receipts, cash disbursements, and credit checking. Operational subfunctions within the accounting function typically include those concerned with record keeping, such as accounts receivable and accounts payable; those that prepare necessary opera-

tional documents, such as payroll and billing; and those that aid in coordinating operations, such as operational budgeting.

Relationships to Other Systems

The operational system and the information system are related in two significant ways. First, the transaction processing systems monitor and record the actions of the various operational functions and subfunctions. For instance, the cost accounting system, a key subsystem within a manufacturing firm's information system, records the accumulated costs of materials, labor, and overhead as work orders move through production operations. Second, the information system provides inputs to the operational system. In some cases these inputs trigger physical operations and resource flows. Thus, purchase orders prepared by a purchasing system result in goods being delivered by suppliers to the receiving dock. In other cases these inputs constitute physical resources. For instance, paychecks prepared during payroll processing represent funds as well as employee earnings information.

The operational system also has close ties to the organization, the other major subsystem within a firm. Each operational function is related to the other functions through the formal organizational structure. Furthermore, managers who head the units comprising the organizational structure make the decisions concerning the resource flows, physical operations, and paperwork operations. Expressed another way, the managers direct and coordinate the firm's work through the organization.

The Organization: A Task-Oriented Structure

The organization of a firm has both formal and informal components. The **formal**

[5]These objectives pertain to the operational level. Accounting also has objectives pertaining to decision making.

organization is the structured management system, while the **informal organization** is the network of social relationships and groupings of the firm's managers and employees. We will focus on formal organizations and their relationships to the information systems of firms.

Formal Organizational Structures

A **formal organizational structure** can be defined as a hierarchical arrangement of the tasks of a firm and the authority to see that they are carried out. That is, it specifies the relationships among the various tasks and the authority that is delegated to the respective managerial positions and levels. Figure 2-7 portrays a formal organizational structure, with the tasks grouped by the functions and subfunctions that appeared in Figures 2-1 and 2-6. (The structure is incomplete in that the credit checking and other finance/accounting and personnel subfunctions are omitted.) The diagram or model that portrays the units comprising the structure is called an **organization chart.**

Organizational precepts. Formal organizations are structured according to accepted principles or precepts. One currently favored precept, called **contingency theory,** states that every firm is subject to a unique set of conditions; therefore, the organizational structure of every firm is contingent on the specific conditions (industry, legal obligations, internal processes, etc.) faced by a firm. Most of the time-honored precepts, however, are based on the classical or traditional theory of organizations. These precepts include authority, unity of command, span of management, and division of work.

Authority is a manager's power to invoke compliance. It is delegated to lower managerial levels, such as the three levels of management below the president in Figure 2-7. The degree of authority delegated should be equal to the assigned responsibility for achieving specific objectives. Thus, if a pro-

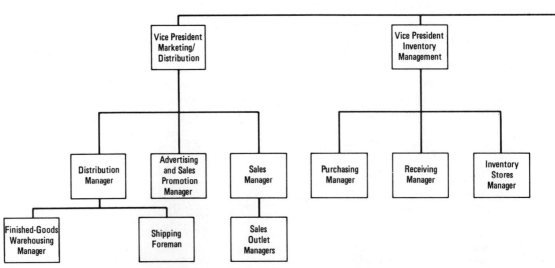

FIGURE 2-7 A partial organizational structure for the Tractors Manufacturing Company.

duction manager has responsibility for maintaining the quality of products, she or he should have complete authority over the administering of quality control. The organizational unit over which a manager has specified responsibility and authority is called a **responsibility center.**

Unity of command refers to clear lines of authority, with each person reporting to only one superior. Figure 2-7 reflects unity of command throughout. When this precept is violated, confusion is likely to follow. Consider a clerk who reports to two managers and receives conflicting instructions. The clerk does not know which instruction to follow, and hence follows one at the expense of the other or follows neither.

Span of management, also called span of control, refers to the number of subordinate managers reporting to a superior. In Figure 2-7 the span of management for the president as well as the vice-president of production is five.

The span of management varies widely

in practice. Broad spans reduce the number of managerial levels. The resulting flat organizational structures can increase the speed and accuracy with which communications can move upward to higher-level managers. If the spans are excessively broad, however, the higher-level managers may receive more information than they can reasonably absorb and respond to.

Division of work refers to the segmentation of operations. In Figure 2-7 the work is divided among five functions at the higher level; in turn, the work of inventory management is divided among three units at the middle level. By dividing its work a firm gains two advantages: (1) It enables the employees and managers to specialize, and (2) it helps the firm to achieve more effective control over a variety of operations and activities.

It should be noted that a problem known as **suboptimization** can occur when work is divided among units. Suboptimization, which results in a firm falling short of its desired overall objectives, is caused by con-

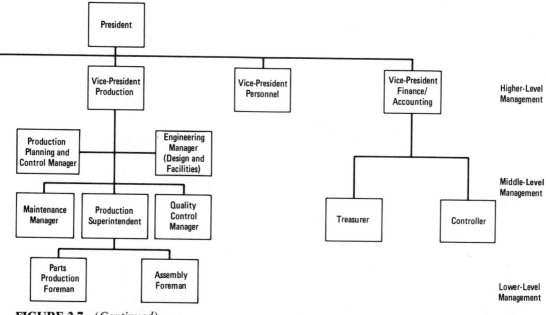

FIGURE 2-7 (*Continued*).

flicting work-unit objectives and poor communication among the work units. It occurs, for example, when the finance function refuses to borrow money at a high rate of interest in order that the marketing function can establish new showrooms "as needed." Although the overall profit of the firm could be improved by establishing the showrooms and thereby increasing sales, the finance function is being governed by its own functional objective: to conserve funds by minimizing financial costs.

The application of these precepts should be clarified by further reference to the organizational structure of a manufacturing firm and its accounting function.

Organizational structure of a manufacturing firm. The organizational structure appearing in Figure 2-7 pertains to the hypothetical Tractors Manufacturing Company. As we noted earlier, five organizational functions report directly to the president. Each function is headed by a vice-president. Reporting to each vice-president are managers of subfunctions that are logically related to the major function and its objectives. For example, reporting to the vice-president of inventory management are managers of purchasing, receiving, and stores. The purchasing manager, in turn, directs buyers who deal with suppliers and perform the necessary paperwork operations to obtain materials. The receiving manager has the responsibility for counting and moving the materials to stores. The stores manager maintains physical custody over the materials and issues them to the production function as needed.

Certain of the organizational units provide support in the form of specialized advice and assistance. Such units, which exercise functional authority rather than command, or **line,** authority, are known as **staff** units. For instance, the vice-president and production superintendent, who have line authority, receive staff assistance from the production planning and control manager and the other three managers mentioned earlier.

In accordance with contingency theory, the organizational structure should fit the unique needs of a firm. Therefore, the organizational structure shown in Figure 2-7 is not suitable for every manufacturing firm. In some firms the inventory management activities, for instance, may be more suitably placed under the production function. The personnel function may be placed under a larger function, called administration, that might include such supporting activities as insurance administration, office management, and information systems management.

Organizational structure of the accounting function. Figure 2-8 portrays the organizational structure of the accounting function for Tractors Manufacturing Company. Although not applicable to all firms, the structure shown is broadly representative of manufacturing firms.

The organizational structure appearing in Figure 2-8 contains two managerial levels below the controller. Reporting directly to the controller are two main-line subfunctions, cost accounting and general accounting, and four supporting subfunctions. In turn, three units report to the chief cost accountant and six units report to the chief general accountant.

The three units under cost accounting are concerned with the records and cost elements related to the products. The inventory control unit maintains records concerning the status and costs of raw materials, work in process, and finished goods. In effect, these records provide accounting control over the physical inventories, which are under the custody of the stores, production, and warehousing units. The timekeeping unit maintains control over the time records concerning production and other nonmanagerial employees. The cost distribution unit maintains records that reflect the detailed costs

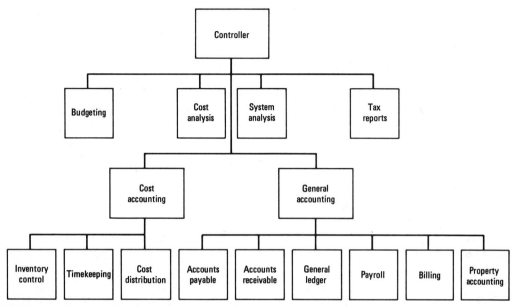

FIGURE 2-8 Organization chart of the accounting function at the Tractors Manufacturing Company.

incurred in the production and distribution of the products.

The six units under general accounting process the basic accounting transactions, maintain the general accounting records, and generate the key accounting documents. The accounts payable unit authorizes and disburses payments to suppliers and other creditors; it also maintains the suppliers' account records. The accounts receivable unit maintains the account records of customers and sends statements to customers. The billing unit prepares and mails invoices to credit customers. The payroll unit prepares paychecks for employees, maintains the payroll records, and prepares required payroll-related reports for governmental agencies. The general ledger unit maintains the ledger of all accounts, both permanent and temporary. The property accounting unit maintains records pertaining to facilities.

The supporting subfunctions or units provide advice and assistance to the controller. As the portrayed units indicate, this ad-

vice and assistance generally pertain to the preparation of budgets, cost analyses, tax returns, and reports, as well as the design of improvements to the accounting information system. Another supporting unit that has traditionally reported to the controller, and still does in some firms, is the internal audit unit. It performs control tasks such as preparing bank reconciliations, reviews controls and security measures built into the information system, checks the accuracy of financial records, recommends improvements in procedures, and appraises the performance of managers and employees. Because these tasks are so important to a firm's well-being, the internal audit unit often reports to a manager at a higher level than the controller. In certain firms this top-level manager is the chief financial officer; in other firms it may be the executive vice-president or even a member of the board of directors.

Certain subfunctions within the finance function are closely related to accounting subfunctions. Thus, the cashier unit maintains records pertaining to the receipts and disbursements of cash, endorses and deposits cash receipts, and reviews disbursement checks that are to be signed by the treasurer or cashier. The credit unit grants credit to customers according to the firm's credit policies and follows up on delinquent accounts.

Alternative organizational structures.

The organization of the Tractors Manufacturing Company is structured according to functions. This organizational approach has several advantages. It fosters technical specialization and thus promotes operational efficiencies. It also helps to harmonize objectives by grouping compatible units and separating incompatible units. For instance, a functional organization facilitates the separation of the credit checking and sales activities. Since the objective of credit checking (minimizing losses from bad debts) is in conflict with the objective of sales (maximizing dollar sales), their organizational separation enables each objective to be given due attention. A functional organizational structure can cause problems, however. Managers tend to become provincial and rigid in their thinking and less attuned to results. Coordination among functions and desired productivity are therefore more difficult to achieve and sustain.

Consequently, organizations are frequently structured or segmented according to product lines, geographical territories, projects, or markets served. For instance, operations in Peterson's Emporium could be segmented according to shoes, suits, and dresses. Organizational structures such as these represent viable alternatives to functional structures in many situations. They tend to integrate the key functional activities in each segment. Therefore, they reduce coordination problems and hence improve responsiveness to changing conditions and opportunities. They also focus on results, such as profits on each product sold, sales to each

market served, and progress on each project under way. On the other hand, such alternative structures do tend to duplicate functional support services and thus tend to be more costly to maintain. In order to gain the best overall set of advantages, many firms employ more than one organizational approach. For instance, public utilities generally employ a functional structure at the second managerial level but segment the marketing function according to industrial and residential markets.

The **matrix organizational structure** blends the functional and project-oriented structures. Thus, the organizational structure in Figure 2-7 can be converted into a matrix structure by overlaying projects A and B (visualized as horizontal strips) across the five major functions (visualized as vertical columns). Each intersection of a project and a function forms the cell of a matrix. Since each project has access to all of the functional skills and resources of the organization, duplication is minimized. However, confusion can arise because the precept of unity of command is violated; that is, each employee and subordinate manager has two or more superiors, his or her functional manager and the project manager(s).

Another way of viewing organizational structures is according to the degree of authority that is delegated. If relatively little authority is delegated to middle and lower managerial levels, the organizational structure is described as **centralized.** Conversely, if considerable authority is delegated, the organizational structure is **decentralized.**

Each type of structure offers relative advantages. A centralized structure enables a firm to control its overall activities and resources more easily and to maintain more uniform decision making. A decentralized structure trains and motivates the managers at lower and middle levels to perform effectively. It tends to produce decisions that are more timely and accommodating to local and rapidly changing conditions. It also reduces the information "overload" on the managers at the higher managerial levels.

Firms that employ centralized decision making are generally organized according to function. Such firms often provide homogeneous products or services to uniform markets. By contrast, firms that employ decentralized decision making are generally organized according to products, services, markets served, or other segments. Decentralization is generally most beneficial to diversified and geographically widespread firms.

Relationships to the Information System

The organization of a firm is related to the information system by several close ties:

1. Both are guided by the objectives of the firm.
2. Each coexists with an informal counterpart. The informal organization, defined earlier, has the purpose of meeting those needs of managers and employees that are not satisfied by the formal organization; these needs include the need to "belong" and to associate socially. The **informal information system,** also known as the grapevine, provides useful channels of communication apart from those available via the formal system. These informal counterparts are intimately related.
3. The organization defines the structure of the centers of responsibility, and hence the locations of the managerial decision makers. Since these managers need reports to aid decision making, the organizational structure determines in large part the routing of information within a firm. Thus, much of the key information in a functionally organized firm flows vertically upward to the various managerial levels of the respective functions. Furthermore, the responsibilities that have been assigned to each center of responsibility in the organization dictate the content of many of the reports.
4. The information system defines the transaction processing procedures, whereas employees within the various organizational units perform some or all of the data entry and processing steps. In turn, the processing steps affect the flows of physical resources within the operational system. Figure 2-9 shows these relation-

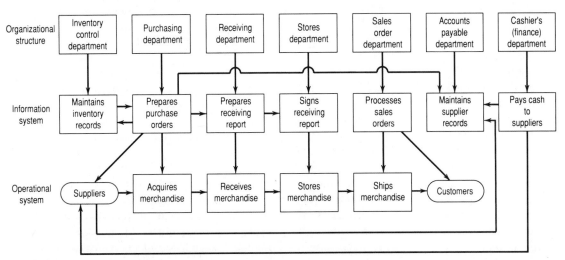

FIGURE 2-9 Relationships among the organizational structure, the information system, and the operational system.

ships with respect to the merchandise (materials) resource.

Summary

A system is an entity composed of interrelated parts that have one or more common objectives. All systems also possess such characteristics as environments, boundaries, inputs, outputs, subsystems, constraints, and controls. Both firms and their information systems exhibit these characteristics. Systems may be classified as natural or human-made, closed or open, simple or complex, deterministic or probabilistic. Business firms are human-made, open, complex, and probabilistic systems. Each firm operates within an environment that provides resources and opportunities and that presents challenges and constraints. In tailoring an information system to a firm, knowledge is needed concerning the firm's resource flows, industrial situation, and legal obligations.

Three major subsystems of every firm are its operational system, its organization, and its information system. The operational system is the network of operational tasks that converts physical resources into the products or services provided by the firm. An operational system is generally segmented into such operational functions as marketing, distribution, inventory management, personnel, and finance/accounting. The organization is the management system that directs and coordinates the tasks of the firm in accordance with assigned responsibilities and authority. Formal organizational structures are hierarchical arrangements of organizational units, connected by lines of authority that reflect responsibilities and their relationships among the various managerial levels and work task subdivisions. Organizations may be structured according to operational functions, product lines, geographical territories, markets served, projects in progress, or some combination of these. They may also be centralized or decentralized with respect to decision-making authority. The three major subsystems of a firm are closely related through the firm's objectives, informal counterpart systems, transaction processing systems, recordings of physical operations, and information flows to responsibility centers.

Review Problem with Solution

Statement

The Aggie Sand and Gravel Company of Sacramento, California, produces a variety of sand, rock, and aggregate products for industrial and home customers. Raw materials are dredged from river bottoms, conveyed to a nearby plant, crushed, screened, mixed, and otherwise processed. Finished products are checked for quality and stored until sales orders are received. Ordered products are then dispatched by truck to the customers' sites.

Aggie's facilities consist of an office building, an adjacent plant, varied production equipment, storage bins, a shop and warehouse, delivery trucks, and a sales office in a nearby city.

Aggie's organization is headed by a president; reporting to him are the sales manager, treasurer, controller, administrative services manager, chief engineer, inventory manager, and production manager. Under each of these higher-level managers are the following middle- and lower-level managers, among others: manager of consumer sales, manager of industrial sales, advertising manager, cashier, credit manager, general accountant, cost accountant, billing manager, inventory control manager, personnel manager, office manager, information systems manager, construction superintendent, applications engineer, purchasing agent, receiving manager, stores manager, plant maintenance engineer, plant superintendent, truck fleet superintendent, quality control manager, dredging foreman, crushing foreman, and aggregates processing foreman.

Required

a. Describe Aggie in terms of its system characteristics.

b. Discuss the environment that extends beyond the boundary within which Aggie conducts its operations.

c. Diagram the key operational functions and subfunctions and resource flows.

d. Prepare an organization chart that structures Aggie's managers according to the precepts of the classical theory of organizations. When necessary, make reasonable assumptions concerning the allocation of responsibilities.

Solution

a. Objectives consist of selling products at a profit, providing good customer service, and so on. **Inputs** include raw materials from the river bottom, other materials and supplies acquired from suppliers, manpower such as crusher equipment operators and truck drivers and managers, facilities such as dredging equipment and trucks and data processing equipment, funds from such sources as sales and bank loans, and data such as orders from customers. **Processing** consists of the primary functions and subfunctions involved in converting basic raw materials into delivered products and includes such supporting functions as sales and administration. **Outputs** include products and invoices to customers and paychecks to employees. The **boundary** encompasses the river bottom, the plant, and all primary and supporting activities. Within the boundary are such **subsystems** as dredging operations, individual employees and managers, and stores of products. Beyond the boundary are such **environmental factors** as customers, suppliers, and prospective employees. **Controls** include checking customers' credit before accepting orders and testing the quality of the products after processing.

b. Three key environmental influences consist of resources, industry, and legal obligations. **Resources** needed by Aggie include the varied inputs (i.e., manpower, materials, facilities, funds, and data) described in the solution to requirement **a.** These resources largely dictate the characteristics of the information system needed by Aggie. For instance, the facilities such as dredging equipment and trucks require that Aggie maintain detailed fixed-asset, depreciation, and maintenance records. The sand and gravel **industry,** of which Aggie is a member, consists typically of numerous small, localized firms. These firms tend to cluster around river bottoms near a large market such as Sacramento. They are capital intensive and seasonal. Major customers are construction firms; however, certain products such as play sand are sold to retail stores for resale to homeowners. Technology affects Aggie only through the heavy equipment that it must use; moreover, this technology changes rather slowly. The **legal obligations** faced by Aggie are not unduly severe. Like all firms, it must pay its fair share of taxes. Also, it must acquire a license from the city to operate on municipal land and must pay fees based on the quantities of materials extracted. However, the reporting requirements are not excessive. The only other strict legal obligation relates to the safety rules that must be followed to comply with standards established by OSHA.

c.

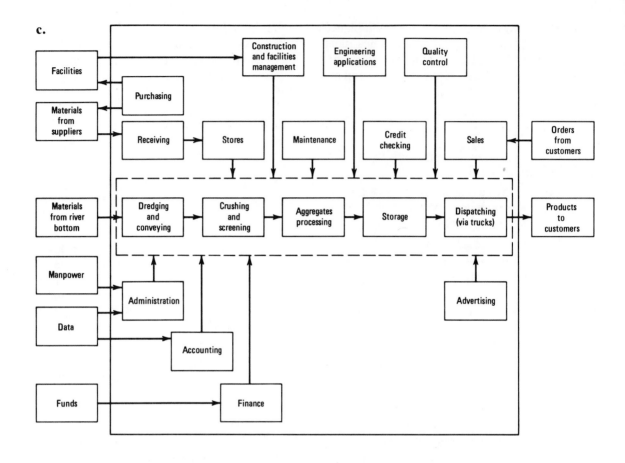

d.

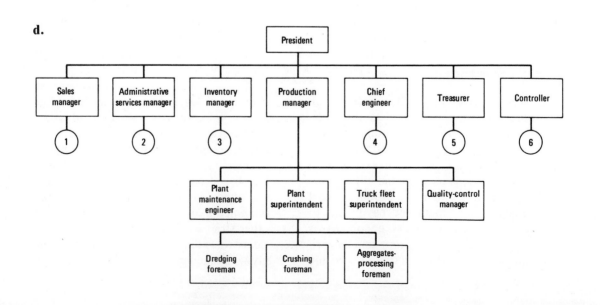

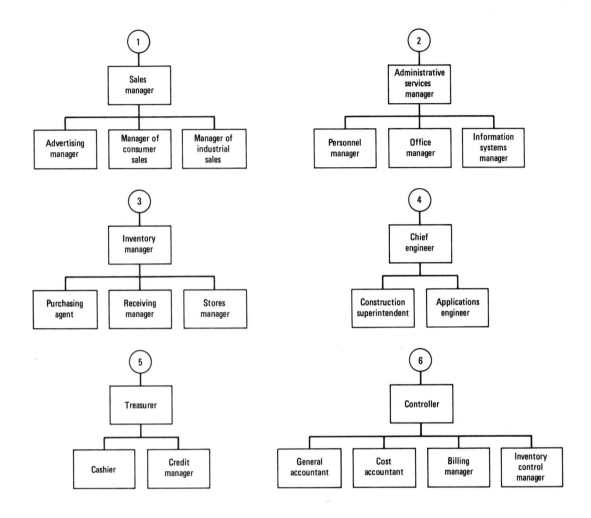

Review Questions

2-1 What is the meaning of each of the following terms?

System
Objective
Input–process–output
Environment
Boundary
Subsystem
System hierarchy
System network
Interface
Resource

Constraint
Feedback
Law of requisite variety
Open system
Human-made system
Complex system
Probabilistic system
Systems approach
Operational system
Operational function
Formal organizational structure
Formal organization
Informal organization
Organization chart

Contingency theory
Authority
Responsibility center
Unity of command
Span of management (span of control)
Division of work
Suboptimization
Line and staff (organizational units)
Matrix organizational structure
Centralized organizational structure
Decentralized organizational structure
Informal information system

2-2 What characteristics are common to all systems?

2-3 Contrast the concept of a system hierarchy with the concept of a system network.

2-4 Compare the specific system characteristics of a business firm with those of its information system.

2-5 Identify the various system classifications that apply to a business firm.

2-6 Describe the systems approach and apply it to a problem of your choice.

2-7 How is a firm influenced by its environment?

2-8 What factors affect the availability, cost of acquiring, and cost of using each of the physical resources needed by a business firm?

2-9 Describe the ways that an information system facilitates the acquisition, use, and reporting of resources.

2-10 What are some of the major ways by which an industry and its firms may be differentiated?

2-11 How can such factors as markets, competition, technology, and legal obligations affect the information systems of firms?

2-12 Diagram in broad terms the operational system for a type of firm of your choice.

2-13 Briefly describe the objectives and subfunctions of five major operational functions of a manufacturing firm.

2-14 What are the major relationships between a firm's operational system and its information system?

2-15 Describe the organizational structure of a typical manufacturing firm.

2-16 Describe the organizational structure of a typical accounting function within a manufacturing firm.

2-17 Identify several precepts based on the classical theory of organizations.

2-18 Identify several alternative ways by which organizations can be structured, and list the relative advantages of each.

2-19 What are the relationships between the organization and the information system of a firm?

Discussion Questions

2-20 Discuss the following types of firms with respect to their system characteristics:

   a. An electric utility.
   b. An electronics manufacturer.
   c. A paper-product manufacturer.
   d. A bank.
   e. A wholesale grocer.
   f. A college bookstore.
   g. A brokerage house.

2-21 Rank these systems in order of complexity: humans, static frameworks (e.g., crystals), simple moving systems (e.g., clocks), social organizations, genetic-societal systems (e.g., plants), animals.

2-22 A business firm is an example of a very complex system. One reason for this complexity is the presence of a variety of subsystems that are linked to and overlay one another. Figures 2-1 and 2-2 picture two sets of such interfacing subsystems. Describe other sets.

2-23 Discuss the way in which each of the following might act as a decoupling mechanism or buffer within a firm:

a. Inventory of raw materials.
b. Unused capacity in a computer.
c. Extra change in a cash register.
d. Temporary file basket on a clerk's desk.

2-24 Describe the application of the systems approach to the design of an information system.

2-25 The "black box" approach involves the study of unknown processes by examining their inputs and outputs. Discuss how the "black box" approach may be applied to the analysis and design of an information system.

2-26 How does an understanding of a firm and its environment aid in the design of an information system?

2-27 Indicate how differences in their firms' environments may lead to differences in the information systems of the following pairs:

a. A grocery chain versus an integrated steel producer.
b. A retail jeweler versus a passenger airline.
c. An oil refiner versus a bank.
d. A toy manufacturer versus a public utility.
e. A governmental agency versus a public accounting firm.

2-28 Describe the ways in which an information system can facilitate the acquisition, use, and reporting of the following types of resources:

a. Personnel (manpower).
b. Funds.
c. Facilities.

2-29 Discuss the concept of the organization as a management system.

2-30 Discuss the ways that segmentation within an organizational structure can aid in decision making and control.

2-31 Why should an accurate and comprehensive organization chart be prepared before beginning the design of a new information system?

2-32 What informational problems can arise when an organizational structure exhibits each of the following weaknesses?

a. Unclear or overlapping assignments of responsibility to the respective organizational units.
b. Excessive spans of management.
c. Excessive number of management levels.
d. Fuzzy lines of authority (e.g., a manager who reports to two superior managers).

2-33 A merchandising firm whose organization is structured according to sales territories sells several product lines in all of the territories. Discuss the needed changes to its information system if the firm decides to add:

a. A new sales territory.
b. A new product line.
c. A new budget control function.

2-34 Discuss the similarities and differences between the physical processing of materials and the paperwork processing of data.

2-35 To what extent should the informal organization and information system affect the design of the formal information system of a firm?

Problems

2-1 Keepwell Association, a health maintenance organization (HMO), provides medical services to a large number of subscribers in metropolitan Minneapolis. The subscribers (patients) call for appointments and enter the reception room at the appointed time. When they check in, their files are "pulled" and they are assigned to available physicians on the staff.

When a particular subscriber sees the assigned physician, several options are possible: (1) he or she may be treated and sent home; (2) he or she may be treated and also given a prescription to be filled at Keepwell's pharmacy; (3) he or she may be given a written authorization to receive medical tests and/or X rays at Keepwell's laboratory; (4) he or she may be referred, via a written authorization, to a specialist such as a surgeon or allergist. In all cases the attending physician notes the action in the subscriber's file.

In addition to general medical services, Keepwell also provides preventive dental services and eye examinations. Subscribers call those offices directly for appointments. Separate dental and eye examination files are maintained for subscribers who make use of such services.

Payments for services take two forms. Each subscriber pays a flat fee of $3.00 at the time of each visit. He or she also pays a monthly charge, consisting of a predetermined base amount plus added charges for services not covered in the contract. A billing department prepares and mails monthly statements to all subscribers; it ascertains the amount of each statement by reference to the subscriber's contract and to notices received from the various service areas concerning uncovered services.

Required

Identify all significant system characteristics in Keepwell's operations.

2-2 Dandy Dining consists of several restaurants located in the state of New Jersey. Each restaurant is individually managed, with profits being shared by the restaurant manager and the stockholders of the chain. A central office is maintained in Trenton for the purposes of providing centralized purchasing of all nonperishable foods, menu planning, and general management guidance.

Dandy Dining as a group has shown outstanding growth in recent years, thanks in part to good locations, high-quality cuisine, and experienced managers. The individual restaurants have generally been quite profitable also, although a few restaurants have not been nearly as profitable as the others.

However, problems have arisen with regard to reporting. Each manager is responsible for employing accounting assistance in the preparation of monthly financial statements and managerial reports. (The central office prepares all tax returns, except for those related to payrolls.) As a result, financial statements are often late in arriving at the central office; also, their formats tend to differ from restaurant to restaurant.

Required

Discuss how the systems approach may be applied to the solution of Dandy Dining's reporting problems. Indicate how its application can benefit Dandy Dining. Do not attempt, however, to develop details of statement and report formats.

2-3 Prepare diagrams of operational functions, similar to Figure 2-6, for the following types of firms:

    a. An electronics manufacturer whose activities include design, parts production, subassembly, assembly, test, packing, and shipping.

    b. An integrated oil company that is involved in such activities as oil exploration, drilling and production, refining, storage, and marketing.

    c. An electric utility whose activities include generation, transmission, and distribution of electricity, as well as the construction of new facilities.

    d. A logging and milling company whose activities include logging, rough sawing, drying (in a kiln), planing, storage, and shipping.

2-4 Bluesky Corp. is a manufacturer of electronics components located in Jacksonville, Florida. It has grown rapidly since its founding 20 years ago as a small, two-man shop. Now it has three divisions and is currently commencing a fourth. The new division will produce sophisticated components for electronic computers, a market that the firm has not served up to now. The president of Bluesky has selected one of the firm's old-timers as manager of the new division. However, although the new division manager has had considerable experience with electronics, he is not acquainted with the computer industry. Therefore, he calls upon a firm of management consultants to help him get under way. You are selected by the consulting firm to work with the new division manager.

Required

a. What initial steps should now be taken in getting under way, if the facilities have already been installed but nothing further has been done?

b. What relationships should be established among the organizational structure, the operational system, and the information system of the new division?

c. To what extent should this new information system be identical to and linked with the information system already being employed by Bluesky?

Hint: Consider such factors as relative developmental costs and the information concerning the new division needed by the president of Bluesky.

d. Assuming that you decide to include an accounting department within the new division, what should be its relationship to (1) the division manager, (2) the company controller at the corporate level, and (3) the divisional information system?

2-5 The Tod Manufacturing Company produces roller bearings in a single plant. The firm is organized functionally, with vice-presidents in charge of marketing, production, finance, and administration. Third-level

managers include a controller, a cashier, a chief engineer, a purchasing director, a sales manager, an advertising manager, an office manager, a production superintendent, a production control manager, a personnel manager, a director of information systems, a credit manager, and a quality control manager. Reporting to these managers are fourth- and fifth-level managers of accounts receivable, accounts payable, billing, budgets, sales analysis, receiving, timekeeping, finished-goods warehousing, cash receipts, materials storeskeeping, cash disbursements, machining, assembly, cost accounting, financial accounting, general ledger, inventory control, payroll, mailroom, plant maintenance, shipping, sales branches, recruitment, employee services, product design, and plant design.

Required

Draw an organization chart for the Tod Manufacturing Company, using sound organizational principles. For instance, group subfunctions should have compatible objectives under the same function (e.g., the credit subfunction under the finance function). Do not allow too large a span of management (e.g., no more than six managers reporting to a single higher-level manager). Furthermore, do not allow a manager to report to more than one higher-level manager.

Hint: The organizational functions at the second level in this firm differ somewhat from those in the chapter example, even though both pertain to manufacturing firms. Differences in structures are to be expected, as a result of differences in circumstances and preferences. However, all of the basic responsibilities must be located somewhere within the structure. In order to cope with the differences in this case, it is suggested that the inventory management responsibilities be included within the production function and the personnel and information systems responsibilities within the administration function.

2-6 The current organization chart for the Smithers Merchandising Corp. of Kansas City appears in the accompanying diagram. Since the firm has grown rapidly from a small, family-owned enterprise to a large corporate distributor of high-quality electronics components, the president is concerned that the organization is in need of an overhaul. Accordingly, he asks you to *analyze the chart and the firm's activities and then to prepare a new chart that reflects sound organizational standards.* The new chart can include additional organizational units that you feel are needed.

In the course of your analysis of Smithers' activities, you discover the following facts:

    a. Credit losses have been high.
    b. Merchandise for resale has often been acquired because of its ease in handling and its accessibility to warehouses, rather than with the considerations of purchasing economy or marketability in mind.
    c. The distribution manager and sales manager have often complained that they do not receive the reports that they need in order to manage.
    d. Customers' bills are not mailed until a couple of weeks after orders are shipped, since the sales manager insists on approving prices charged to each customer.
    e. Cash shortages have been detected from time to time.
    f. Employee turnover has been rather high; terminating employees have indicated that salaries and employee benefits are below par and that paychecks are frequently a day or so late.

2-7 Accunav Company of San Antonio, Texas, was started in 1980 by Margo Muray and John Carter. Muray and Carter developed Accunav's first product, which applies microchip technology to the LORAN-based navigation system. Accunav's product makes LORAN equipment smaller and more compact. As a consequence, Accunav is a pioneer in the new market, and the company is growing rapidly.

Muray and Carter are electrical engineers; however, they also share the administrative duties of Accunav. Muray is the president of the company, and Carter holds the

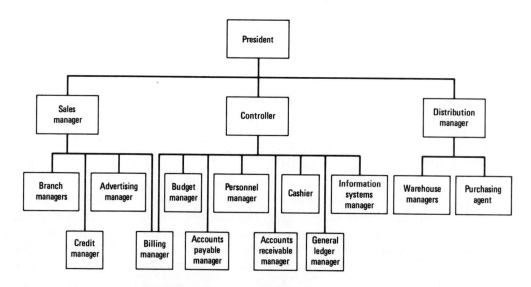

position of vice-president of finance. Accunav follows a simple staffing pattern; when the company's growth overwhelms a position, another person is hired to assume some of the responsibilities. In this manner, Accunav has created the positions of vice-president of marketing and vice-president of manufacturing.

Until recently, Carter has been reluctant to relinquish control over some key positions and currently has ten people reporting directly to him. Now, in order to free some of his time for research and development activities that interest him, Carter is proposing the creation of two new positions, treasurer and controller. The ten people reporting to him

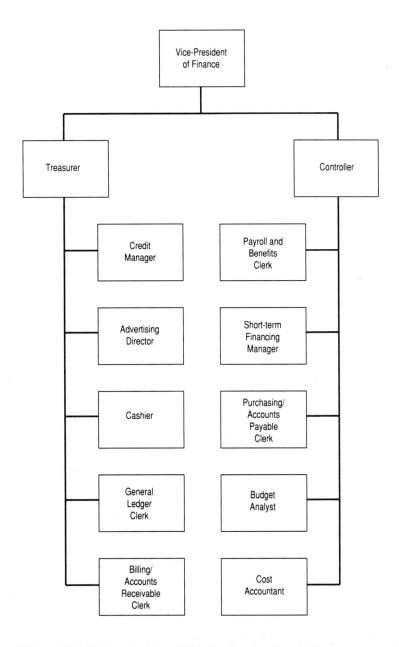

would maintain their present duties and responsibilities but would report to the controller and treasurer, as shown in the proposed reorganization on page 59.

Required

a. Explain how the present organizational structure might benefit upward and downward communication between the vice-president and his subordinates; and discuss the communication problems that have likely resulted.

b. Discuss the strengths and weaknesses of the proposed reorganization of the finance function.

c. Propose an improved reorganization plan. Include any additional personnel who would be beneficial in conducting the firm's finance/accounting activities.

(CMA adapted)

2-8 The Hooper Co. of Springfield, Massachusetts, is considering a reorganization. The company's current organizational structure is represented by the chart shown in Exhibit 1.

The company recently hired a new vice-president for metal products. The new vice-president has an extensive background in sales, which complements the background of the vice-president for plastic products, which has been in production. The new vice-president for metal products believes that Hooper Co. would be more effective if it were reorganized according to the organizational chart presented in Exhibit 2.

Required

a. Identify the two types of organizational structures depicted by the two charts.

b. Compare the two organizational structures by discussing the advantages and disadvantages of each.

c. Discuss the circumstances that would favor one form of organizational structure over the other.

(CMA adapted)

2-9 The Jerment Company is a growing manufacturer of modular office furniture. The company has been experiencing internal problems because of its failure to keep pace

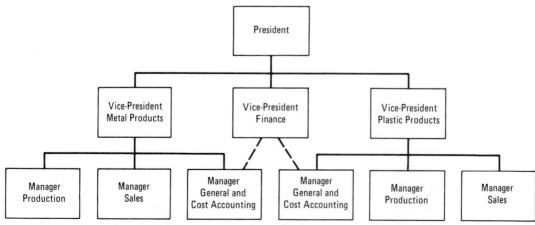

EXHIBIT 1 Current organizational structure.

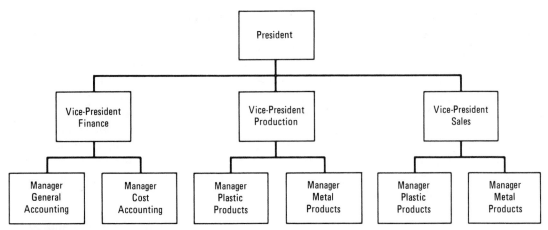

EXHIBIT 2 Proposed organizational structure.

with the rapid growth of its segment of the industry. The company began as a small, one-plant operation but has since expanded into four adjacent states. Now there are seven branch offices in addition to the Detroit home office, each branch having a sales force and a manufacturing plant.

The condensed organization chart presented below shows six functional departments at the home office level: finance, marketing, administrative services, research and development, manufacturing, and personnel. Each of the seven branch offices has a

branch manager of sales and a branch manager of manufacturing, each of whom reports to the vice-president of marketing and the vice-president of manufacturing, respectively, at the home office. Services for the other four functional areas are carried out at the home office.

Every manufacturing plant produces the complete catalog of Jerment products. The 12 product lines are somewhat complementary. There is very little, if any, brand awareness in this segment of the office furniture industry. Some of the sales force find certain

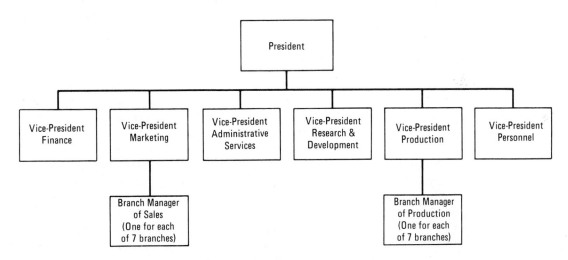

products more difficult to sell and, thus, do not push them in their sales calls.

The home office management has insisted over the years that control be maintained at the home office. However, there has been increasing conflict between the home office and the branches. Branch managers insist they need more flexibility and autonomy to deal with differing local environments. Home office management believes a change in autonomy would damage its efforts to keep up with industry growth. Branch managers believe that the home office is reluctant to modernize and streamline the company. The branch managers' attempts to make some autonomous decisions have conflicted with home office directives. This has led to ambiguous communications and delays in shipments of parts to the plants.

Required

a. The Jerment Company currently employs an organization structure that is departmentalized by function.

   (1) Discuss why Jerment Company probably selected this type of departmentalization when it started operations.

   (2) Explain the behavioral consequences of a functional type of organization structure.

b. Identify two alternative methods of departmentalizing a company's organization structure and, for each alternative method:

   (1) Explain why a company would select this type of organization structure.

   (2) Discuss the strengths and weaknesses of this type of organization structure.

c. Explain how Jerment Company might change the current organization structure to improve its efficiency and effectiveness.

(CMA adapted)

2-10 Ned Gabler has been in the shoe business for 23 years and operates Quality Footwear, a 15-store chain in New York, New Jersey, and eastern Pennsylvania. Quality Footwear has grown steadily from the first store in Manhattan to the current level. Conservative styles, quality shoes, moderate pricing, and attentiveness to customer needs have characterized the operation of Quality Footwear from the beginning.

Gabler's operations manager, Chuck Staub, keeps in touch with each of the 15 stores in the chain in order to respond to any needs or emergencies that arise and to be sure each has enough inventory on hand. There is relatively little problem in maintaining the proper assortment of shoes in stock because each store stocks the same limited assortment of shoe styles and colors. The demands on store managers are relatively few, and each manager is given latitude in running the store as long as the firm's basic policy of quality service to customers is followed. Staub's job is made easier as well by the standardization among stores due to limited offerings and stability in the customer base.

Quality Footwear is structured around five equal general manager levels as shown by the organizational chart at the top of the next page. The staff is well established except for the position of general manager—facilities, which Gabler has intended to fill for the past year. Unfortunately, the acquisition of the 22 stores that make up the Twentieth Century Shoes (TCS) chain has occupied most of his time. The purchase recently was finalized and has expanded Gabler's geographic sales area along the Atlantic coast into the south and southeast.

Prior to concluding an acquisition agreement, Gabler had carefully surveyed the entire organization of TCS and visited every store in the chain. The prior owners had more than doubled the number of outlets in the last three years, and Gabler believed that the haste showed in the way the stores were being operated. There were inconsistencies

ORGANIZATIONAL STRUCTURE BEFORE TCS ACQUISITION

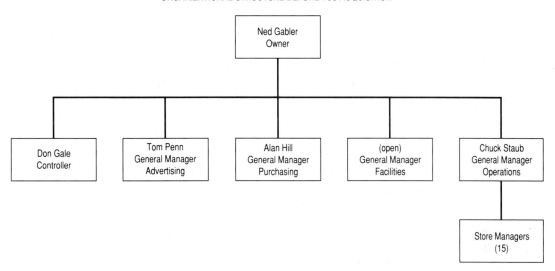

among stores in customer service, cleanliness and neatness, and the adequacy of shoe styles in stock. Store management seemed to vary widely from very courteous and efficient to indifferent and lackadaisical. Each store manager enjoyed a great deal of autonomy. The TCS general manager was strained to keep up with operations.

PROPOSED ORGANIZATIONAL STRUCTURE

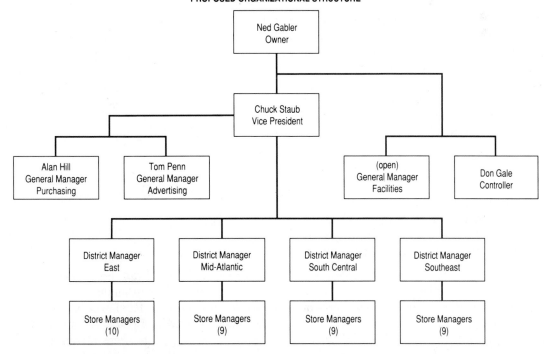

TCS serves a larger area with more stores but has lost money in two of the last three years. In addition, TCS serves a slightly different market. TCS's customers are five to ten years younger and tend to be more fashion conscious; thus, the TCS market segment is more competitive and will require more promotion. TCS also carries a range of accessories that includes socks, shoelaces, polish, and some novelty items, none of which are found in the Quality stores. However, Gabler believed that the increased market area and the attractive acquisition price made up for the losses and other problems. Gabler intends to retain his conservative product line as the core of his new stores and supplement it with the best-selling lines and accessories of the TCS units in all 37 stores.

Gabler asked Staub to prepare an organizational chart that would integrate the two chains and bring the total organization to a level of profitability that Quality Footwear has experienced. Staub submitted the chart that appears at the bottom of page 63.

District managers will assume responsibilities similar to those previously covered by Staub, and store managers would have the same responsibilities that had been carried by the managers of the original Quality stores. In addition, each store manager would be responsible for stocking accessories, advising central purchasing of the stock, and recommending shoe lines to meet regional differences in style and demand.

Required

a. Compare and contrast the organizational responsibilities and reporting relationships under the original and proposed organizational structures for each of the following:

(1) Chuck Staub.

(2) Alan Hill, general manager—purchasing.

(3) Don Gale, controller.

(4) District managers.

b. Discuss whether each of the following functions are either more centralized or more decentralized under the proposed organizational structure:

(1) Quality Footwear store managers.

(2) TCS store managers.

(3) Purchasing function.

c. Review the proposed organizational structure that Chuck Staub has prepared.

(1) Discuss the strengths of the proposed organizational structure.

(2) Identify the weaknesses of the proposed organizational structure and explain how you would change the proposed structure to eliminate each identified weakness.

(CMA adapted)

2-11 *Selected Small Firm (A Continuing Case)* For the small firm that you selected in Chapter 1 (see Problem 1-7), complete the following requirements:

a. Describe the industry of which the firm is a part, as well as the needed resources, technological developments, and legal obligations.

b. Prepare a diagram of the operational functions.

c. Draw an organization chart.

Suggested Readings

Ackoff, Russell L. "Towards a System of Systems Concepts." *Management Science* 17 (July 1971), pp. 661–671.

Baker, Frank. *Organizational Systems: General Systems Approaches to Complex Organizations.* Homewood, Ill.: Richard D. Irwin, 1973.

Boulding, Kenneth E. "General Systems Theory—The Skeleton of Science." In *Management Systems*. 2d ed. Edited by Peter P. Schoderbek. New York: John Wiley, 1971.

Churchman, C. West. *The Systems Approach*. New York: Dell, 1968.

Davis, Gordon B., and Olsen, Margarethe. *Management Information Systems: Conceptual Foundations, Structure, and Development*. 2d ed. New York: McGraw-Hill, 1985.

Galbraith, Jay R. *Organizational Design: An Information Processing View*. Reading, Mass.: Addison-Wesley, 1973.

Gordon, Lawrence A., and Miller, Danny. "A Contingency Framework for the Design of Accounting Information Systems." *Accounting, Organizations and Society* (No. 1, 1976), pp. 59–69.

Hay, Leon E. "What Is an Information System? The Legal, Conventional, and Logical Constraints." *Business Horizons* (Feb. 1971), pp. 65–72.

Hopwood, Anthony G. "Towards an Organizational Perspective for the Study of Accounting and Information Systems." *Accounting, Organizations and Society* (No. 1, 1978), pp. 3–13.

Murdick, Robert G.; Fuller, Thomas C.; Ross, Joel E.; and Winnermark, Frank J. *Accounting Information Systems*. Englewood Cliffs, N.J.: Prentice-Hall, 1978.

Schoderbek, Peter P.; Kefalas, Asterios G.; and Schoderbek, Charles G. *Management Systems: Conceptual Considerations*. Rev. ed. Dallas: Business Publications, 1980.

Ullrich, Robert A., and Wieland, George F. *Organization Theory and Design*. Homewood, Ill.: Richard D. Irwin, 1980.

CHAPTER OBJECTIVES

After studying this chapter, you should be able to do the following:

Describe the network of operations and information subsystems within a typical business firm.

Identify several transaction processing cycles common to most business firms.

Discuss the key components employed in the processing of accounting transactions.

Describe the application of the preceding components to the processing of basic accounting transactions.

Chapter 3

TRANSACTION PROCESSING

One major purpose of an information system is to support the day-to-day business operations of a firm. This purpose is fulfilled by (1) processing transactions arising from both external and internal sources and (2) preparing outputs such as operational documents and financial reports. In a collective sense, these activities are known as **transaction processing**. Accountants are deeply concerned with transaction processing, since much of the data and information are financial in nature. Thus, they often participate in designing the components of systems that perform transaction processing.

Framework of Transaction Processing

Firmwide Network

Transaction processing takes place concurrently with the operations of a firm. The combined set of **transaction processing systems** resembles a complex network of interdependent physical operations, paperwork processes, and data/information flows. Physical operations, such as receiving ordered merchandise, intertwine with such paperwork processes as maintaining the accounts that reflect payments due to suppliers. Paperwork processes, such as those involved with the disbursement and receipt of cash, trace and record the flows of the funds resource. Information generated by transaction processing systems, such as the amount of cash on hand, flows to managers for use in planning and controlling operations.

Figure 3-1 portrays this network of interactions for a typical merchandising firm. We can better understand the flows of data and information if we trace through one of the procedures, portrayed by a series of modules in the figure. As our example we choose the sales transaction procedure,

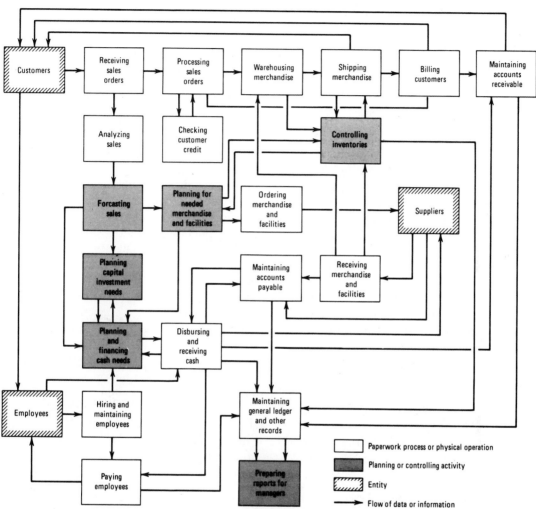

FIGURE 3-1 Network of daily operations and related planning and control activities for a merchandising firm.

which begins at the upper left-hand corner of the diagram.

Customers initiate sales orders to the merchandising firm. These sales orders are a data resource which triggers such operational tasks as receiving and recording the sales orders, checking the customers' credit standings, processing the sales orders, and picking the ordered merchandise from the warehouse. As the sales orders move along this operational sequence, they are modified to

provide new information, so that the outputs differ from the inputs. Thus, after being checked against customers' credit standings, the sales orders are stamped either "Credit approved" or "Credit disapproved." Also, as items are picked from warehouse bins, the sales orders are initialed by the pickers.

After the merchandise items have been picked, they are delivered with the sales orders to the shipping area. From there the merchandise items are shipped to the customers and the sales orders are routed to the billing department. The sales orders are examined by billing clerks for the stamps and initials denoting that all processing has been completed and that the merchandise has been shipped. Then bills (sales invoices) are prepared to trigger payments from customers.

This procedure also provides data to update records and generate key reports. The sales amounts are posted to the accounts receivable and sales records, while the quantities shipped are posted to the inventory records. Sales analyses, sales forecasts, and inventory status reports—which aid the firm's managers in planning and control—are based in part on the sales and shipping data.

Before leaving Figure 3-1, we might again observe the extent to which the various processing systems are interrelated. For instance, both the sales transaction system and the purchases transaction system feed data to the inventory control system. The former provides data concerning shipments, while the latter provides data concerning receipts of ordered goods. Based on both sets of data, plus the prior inventory balances, the inventory control system produces the inventory status report mentioned earlier.

Functional Information Systems

As described in Chapter 2, the operational system and organization of a firm are generally subdivided on a functional basis. To provide effective and efficient control of operations and coordination of managerial activities, its information system should be subdivided according to the same functions.

The information system of a manufacturing firm, for instance, may be subdivided into the following subsystems (which can be regarded as systems):

1. Marketing information system.
2. Distribution information system.
3. Production information system.
4. Resource management information system.
5. Personnel information system.
6. Accounting information system.
7. Finance information system.

The specific array of **functional information subsystems,** of course, varies from industry to industry and even from firm to firm within the same industry. A bank, for instance, might have a personal loan information system, a commercial loan information system, and a demand deposit information system, plus the last four systems in the foregoing list for the manufacturing firm. A different manufacturing firm than the one described might split the resource management information system into inventory management and fixed-asset management information systems; a third manufacturing firm may group its inventory management and production information systems, together with part of its marketing information system, into a logistics information system.

Each functional information subsystem closely associates with, and provides significant control over, one or more transaction processing systems. For example, the marketing information system is involved with the sales transaction processing system, the personnel information system with the payroll transaction processing system, and the accounting information system with all of the transaction processing systems.

Equally important, however, are the linkages maintained by each functional information subsystem between the operational level and the managerial levels. A functional information subsystem thereby aids the flows of transactional information to the functional managers. Using such information, these managers can make necessary decisions to plan and control the activities of their functions. Figure 3-2 shows the upward flows of such information; the triangle indicates that the information is increasingly summarized

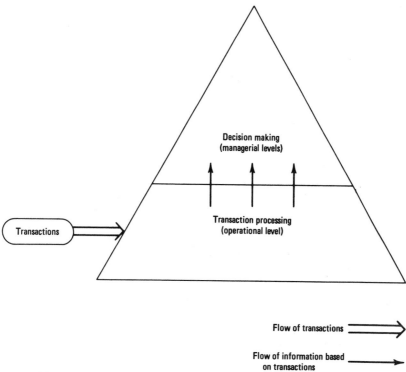

FIGURE 3-2 Flows of information derived from transactions to managerial levels.

as it rises to successively higher managerial levels.

Transaction Processing Cycles

Transaction processing systems are organized around the various transactions that a firm encounters. Thus, a typical merchandising firm may employ transaction processing systems that are focused on such transactions as sales, cash receipts, purchases, cash disbursements, and payroll. Accountants have traditionally viewed the overall transaction processing of a firm in terms of these processing systems.

In recent years, however, transaction processing cycles have been used to portray transaction processing within a firm. A **transaction processing cycle** (often called a trans-

action cycle) groups one or more transactions having common features or similar objectives. The four cycles shown in Figure 3-3 are typical of merchandising firms. Let us briefly examine each of these cycles.[1]

Revenue cycle. Two key transactions are encompassed by the **revenue cycle:** the sales transaction and the cash receipts transaction. In the sales transaction a customer's order for merchandise or services gives rise to a sales invoice. If merchandise is involved, it is shipped to the customer. In the cash receipts transaction a check or currency is received from the customer. If the sale is

[1]For a detailed discussion of cycles, see Arthur Andersen & Co., *A Guide for Studying and Evaluating Internal Accounting Controls* (Chicago: 1978), pp. 9–33.

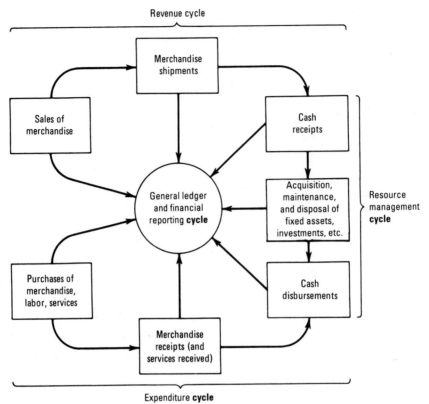

FIGURE 3-3 Transaction processing cycles for a merchandising firm.

on a credit basis, the sales amount is reflected in an accounts receivable ledger until paid.

Expenditure cycle. Two key transactions are encompassed by the **expenditure cycle:** the purchases transaction and the cash disbursements transaction. The purchases transaction consists of acquiring resources or services (e.g., merchandise, parts, supplies, utility services). In the cash disbursements transaction a check voucher is prepared and delivered to the supplier. If the purchase is on a credit basis, the amount of the purchase is reflected in an accounts payable ledger until paid.

Resource management cycle. The **resource management cycle** consists of those events related to the physical resources utilized by a firm. Thus, it includes such events as (1) acquiring, investing, and disbursing funds, (2) acquiring, maintaining, and disposing of facilities (fixed assets), (3) acquiring, storing, and selling materials (finished goods or merchandise), and (4) acquiring, maintaining, and paying personnel (i.e., employees, managers, outside services).

Since each type of resource has its own cycle, the resource management cycle is in reality a collection of cycles. Certain of these cycles overlap with the revenue and expenditure cycles. To avoid double counting, we might delete materials from the resource management cycle. On the other hand, we might delete the personnel resource from the expenditure cycle and retain it as a resource management cycle. Furthermore, we can define the funds resource to include only those acquired from bank loans, bond issues, stock issues, and disposal of fixed assets.

General ledger and financial reporting cycle.

At the center of the aforementioned cycles is the **general ledger and financial reporting cycle**. It is unique, in that the processing of individual transactions is not its sole or even its most important function. Instead, it primarily accepts flows from a variety of transaction processing systems and then generates periodic outputs. The relatively few transactions processed by this cycle are typically the end-of-period adjustments, such as those pertaining to depreciation, and the closing entries.

Other transaction cycles.

The characteristics of other types of firms and specific industries dictate the need for additional specialized transaction cycles. For example, manufacturing firms require a **product conversion cycle**. This transaction cycle includes such steps as (1) preparing and scheduling production jobs, (2) issuing materials into production, (3) moving work through the production process, (4) assigning labor time and overhead costs to the respective jobs, (5) completing work-in-process, and (6) temporarily storing the finished goods.

Components of Transaction Processing

Transaction processing takes place within a standardized process that is based on the double-entry concept. This process, known as the accounting cycle, is pictured in Figure 3-4.

The accounting cycle begins with the preparation of a source document that contains the amount involved in a specific transaction. In the case of a sales transaction, for instance, the source document that begins the accounting cycle is the sales invoice, since it reflects the amount of the sale. Then the source document is classified and coded to show the ledger accounts that are affected by the transaction. Next the transaction data are summarized in a journal. The debits and

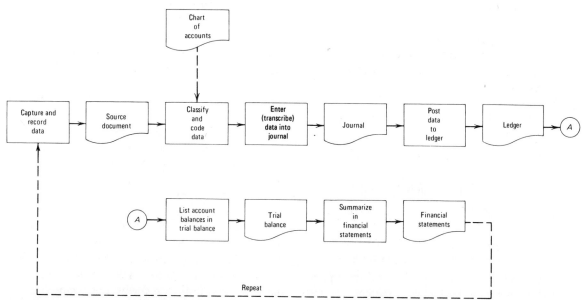

FIGURE 3-4 The accounting cycle.

credits in the summarized journal entry are then posted to a ledger; in other words, the affected ledger account balances are updated. Periodically (e.g., at the end of each month), the balances of all ledger accounts are summarized in a trial balance, to verify that the total of debit balances equals the total of credit balances. Adjusting journal entries are then processed and an adjusted trial balance is prepared. Finally, the financial statements are prepared. This cycle is repeated each accounting period.

As this description suggests, the accounting cycle requires a variety of building blocks or components. These components include source documents, journals, and registers, ledgers and files, reports and other outputs, charts of accounts and other codes, audit trails, processing methods and devices, and controls.

Source Documents

Most transactions are recorded on **source documents.** Figure 3-5 displays a check voucher on which a payment to a supplier is recorded. Other source documents commonly prepared by firms are sales orders, sales invoices, purchase orders, receiving reports, employee time cards, and deposit slips. Source documents received from other firms for processing include invoices from suppliers, remittance advices and checks from customers, and debit memos from banks.

In addition to providing written records, source documents serve to

1. Trigger or authorize physical operations. For instance, sales orders authorize the shipments of merchandise to customers.
2. Monitor physical flows. For instance, sales orders are notated to show the movements of ordered goods from the warehouse to the shipping area.
3. Reflect accountability for actions taken. For instance, suppliers' invoices are initialed to show that they have been checked for accuracy.
4. Maintain an up-to-date and complete data base. For instance, sales invoice copies are used to update balances in the inventory and customer records and then are filed to provide a sales history.
5. Provide data needed for outputs. For instance, data in sales orders are used to prepare sales invoices and sales summaries.

Journals and Registers

Journals and registers are accounting records that list data in chronological order. A **journal,** the formal accounting record of original entry in manual systems, summarizes transaction data in financial terms. Each entry in a journal reflects the key data concerning one transaction. It shows the debit and credit amounts involved, as well as the accounts to which the debit and credit amounts apply. A **register** serves either (1) as an alternative to a journal or (2) as a chronological record or log of nonfinancial data or events.

The two main categories of journals are the general journal and the special journal. A **general journal** contains a series of columns in a generalized format, so that any accounting transaction may be recorded. A **special journal** employs a specialized format tailored to a commonly recurring, relatively high-volume type of transaction. Special journals enable like transactions (e.g., sales, purchases) to be recorded, totaled, and posted to ledgers in an efficient manner. They generally accommodate most of the transaction load of a firm, leaving for the general ledger only the seldom encountered transactions and end-of-period adjustments.

When firms become sufficiently large to need a large accounting department or several accounting departments, a single bound general journal becomes inconvenient. **Journal vouchers,** unbound forms containing one

INVOICE NUMBER	INVOICE DATE	INVOICE DESCRIPTION	GROSS AMOUNT	DISCOUNTS, RETENTIONS, PAYMENTS TO DATE	NET AMOUNT THIS CHECK
2505	2/28/--	CLEAR & GRADE	3,500.00	350.00	3,150.00
2648	3/10/--	CLEAR AND GRADE	2,007.00	200.70	1,806.30

CHECK NO. 000011   DATE 4/10/--
VENDOR   DICKERSON

TOTALS →   GROSS AMOUNT 5,507.00   550.70   NET AMOUNT 4,956.30

NORTH CREEK CONTRACTING

CHECK DATE 4/10/--   CHECK NUMBER 000011

FOUR THOUSAND NINE HUNDRED FIFTY SIX DOLLARS AND 30 CENTS

TO THE ORDER OF:
DICKERSON EXCAVATING
731 LOCUST STREET
ANY TOWN, STATE3 61019

PAY THIS AMOUNT
$ ******4,956.30

AUTHORIZED SIGNATURE

AUTHORIZED SIGNATURE

SE61CA-MSI

FIGURE 3-5 An example of a source document. Courtesy of International Business Machines Corporation.

Journal Voucher No. 688		Date 12/31/91			
Account titles	Codes	Debit		Credit	
Amortization of patent costs	88	15000.00	√		
Patents	29			15000.00	√

To amortize the costs of patents held by the firm, by 1/17 of the original costs, during 1985.

Written by: Sylvia Brown	Approval: Ted Johnson	Auditor: John Eweb

FIGURE 3-6 A journal voucher with sample entry.

transaction per form, are replacing general journals in such firms. Figure 3-6 shows a journal voucher containing a sample transaction. As we can see, it is prenumbered and has spaces for reflecting the accountability of those persons who prepare and approve the transaction entry. These features represent controls that enhance its usefulness.

Many firms employ a variety of registers in addition to journals. For instance, a merchandising firm may use a shipping register to list the shipments of ordered merchandise and a receiving register to list the incoming deliveries of merchandise.

Ledgers and Files

A **ledger,** also a formal accounting record, summarizes the status of accounts in financial terms. The transaction amounts that appear in the journals are transferred or posted to appropriate ledger accounts. Through this **posting process** the status of each affected account is updated by either raising or lowering the level (balance) of the account to reflect the transaction amount. Thus, while a journal emphasizes transaction activity, a ledger emphasizes account status (i.e., the balance of the account).

A **general ledger** is a collection of ledger records (i.e., an accounting "book"). In essence, it contains summary financial data concerning all of the asset, liability, revenue, and expense accounts established by a firm.

A **subsidiary ledger** provides detailed records pertaining to a particular account in the general ledger. A typical merchandising firm maintains subsidiary ledgers that support such general ledger accounts as accounts receivable, accounts payable, merchandise inventory, and fixed assets.

Each general ledger account that is supported by a subsidiary ledger is called a **control account.** Since the sum total of balances in the subsidiary ledger accounts should equal the balance in the corresponding general ledger account, the latter can be said to control the former. That is, the general ledger account helps to control posting accuracy, since the balances in the subsidiary ledger are posted independently and their total is periodically checked against the general ledger account balance.

The close relationship between journals and subsidiary ledgers is shown in Figure 3-7. An entry concerning XYZ Co. in the amount of $375.00 appears in the cash receipts journal. It is then posted to the ac-

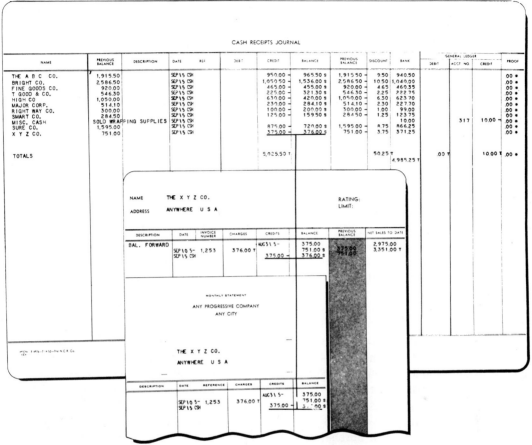

FIGURE 3-7 A cash receipts journal, accounts receivable subsidiary ledger, and monthly statement. From *A Study of Machine Accounting Methods*. Copyright 1955 by National Cash Register Company, Dayton, Ohio.

counts receivable ledger record for XYZ Co., and thereby the balance of the customer's account is decreased. (If desired, it may also be recorded on a monthly statement that will later be mailed to the customer.)

An alternative to the use of a subsidiary ledger is the use of copies of source documents to support a general ledger account. For example, copies of sales invoices may replace a formal accounts receivable subsidiary ledger. As payments are received, the corresponding sales invoice copies are removed from the file of unpaid copies and

marked "Paid." At any time the total of the unpaid invoices should equal the balance in the accounts receivable control account. This alternative is known as **ledgerless bookkeeping.**[2]

Although ledgerless bookkeeping reduces posting costs, it does have drawbacks. Monthly statements cannot easily be prepared for customers, for instance. Inquiries often cannot be quickly answered, since the

[2]Bookkeeping without journals also is possible. For instance, copies of checks can be used in place of a check register.

copies are not cross-referenced to the journals. Partial payments must be deducted from the pertinent copies and the copies refiled, a tedious procedure when partial payments are numerous.

A **file** is typically a repository of data within the overall data base of a firm. Four major types of files are known as master files, transaction files, reference files, and history files. Most of the data stored in these files arise from transactions or are used in the processing of transactions. A **master file** contains the relatively permanent records concerning a firm's entities and activities. All of the ledgers described earlier are master files. A **transaction file** contains the relatively temporary records pertaining to specific transactions. Typically the transaction records are used to update one or more master files. Copies of source documents often comprise transaction files in manual systems. Journals and registers also can be viewed as summary transaction files. A **reference file** contains data, often in tabular form, for use in processing. Examples of reference files are tables of freight rates and lists of merchandise selling prices. A **history file** contains historical data pertaining to sales, purchases, and so forth.

Reports and Documents

A variety of reports generally result from the processing of transactions. One major type of report output is known as a **financial statement.** The three basic financial statements prepared by a business firm are the balance sheet, income statement, and statement of changes in financial position. The balance sheet presents the overall financial condition of the firm as of a given date. The income statement presents the results of the firm's operations for a given accounting period. The statement of changes in financial position, also known as the funds-flow statement, shows the sources and uses of funds during the accounting period (i.e., a month). In other words, the funds-flow statement shows why the funds (i.e., working capital) have increased or decreased during the period.

Managerial reports represent another major type of output. Certain managerial reports, such as sales analyses and accounts receivable aging schedules, can be prepared from transaction data. Sales analyses enable managers to examine closely the significant trends and patterns in sales activity; accounts receivable aging schedules help managers to monitor the collection of amounts due from customers and hence to reduce losses for uncollectible accounts. Other managerial reports, however, cannot be prepared solely or directly from transaction data. They require data drawn from other sources, such as external economic forecasters and managerial opinions. Examples of such reports are sales forecasts, cash budgets, and cost variance reports. Managerial reports are comprehensively discussed in Chapter 10.

Numerous **operational documents** are also generated by transaction processing systems. Some of these documents are produced to trigger actions. Thus, purchase orders are prepared and sent to suppliers to order merchandise. Other documents are produced to record completed actions. Paychecks, for instance, complete the payroll actions for employees for a pay period, since they reimburse the employees for services rendered. Certain of the operational documents prepared by a firm's transaction processing systems become source document inputs to further processing. Consider, for instance, sales invoices, which are mailed to customers to trigger payments of amounts due; these documents also represent the sources of data for processing sales transactions through the accounting journals and ledgers.

Charts of Accounts and Other Codes

Accounting transactions must be classified and coded before being posted to ledgers. A **chart of accounts** is a coded listing of the accounts contained in the general ledger of a firm. In essence, it represents the financial data structure of the firm. Not only does a chart of accounts enable transaction data to be classified and coded, but it also provides the detailed data elements from which information can be assembled and presented in financial statements.

In most firms the accounts are organized according to asset, equity, revenue, and expense categories. Within these broad categories the accounts are subdivided into major groupings. Figure 3-8 presents a summary chart of accounts in which major account groups are aligned with their related blocks of code numbers. Individual accounts, in turn, are assigned specific codes within each major account group. For instance, the accounts receivable account (code number 12) appears within the current assets group, while the sales account (code number 50) appears within the revenue group. A credit sales transaction can therefore be recorded by a debit to account 12 and a credit to account 50.

The chart of accounts represents only one application of codes within the typical firm. Coding systems are so vital to effective and efficient transaction processing that they are universally employed. They are discussed further in Chapter 8.

Audit Trails

An **audit trail** is a set of linkages formed by key transaction processing elements. In effect, it ties accounting transactions to their ultimate dispositions. Consequently, an audit trail provides a means of tracing from source documents through journals and ledgers to summary totals in the financial statements or other financial outputs, and vice versa.

Apart from aiding the audit of transaction processing systems, audit trails enable

1. Detected errors to be corrected. For instance, a difference between the sum total of balances in the accounts receivable subsidiary ledger accounts and the balance in the accounts receivable control account is detected, indicating the presence of one or more errors; these errors can be traced via the audit trail back to their source(s), such as incorrectly transcribed amounts from sales invoices into the sales journal.

2. Inquiries to be answered. For instance, a customer inquires about her current account balance; the source documents affecting the account can be located via the audit trail.

3. Files to be reconstructed. For instance, several sales journal pages are accidentally lost or destroyed; new pages can be recreated via the audit trail.

An audit trail is maintained through the presence of elements ranging from source documents and journals to ledgers and summary outputs. However, the trail is flagged by means of various reference codes, for example, source document numbers and posting reference codes.

Processing Approaches

The two fundamental transaction processing approaches currently in use are (1) manually based processing and (2) computer-

Account Codes	Major Account Groupings
10–19	Current assets
20–22	Investments
23–29	Fixed assets
30–39	Current liabilities
40–44	Long-term liabilities
45–49	Owners' equity
50–54	Revenues
55–59	Cost of sales
60–69	Selling expenses
70–79	Administrative expenses
80–84	Financial management expenses
85–89	Other revenues and expenses

FIGURE 3-8   A summary chart of accounts.

based processing. Many variations of each approach can be discerned.

Manually based processing systems range from simple pen-and-ink clerical systems to rather elaborate equipment-assisted systems. A very rudimentary system was presented in the Shinewell Shoe Store illustration in Chapter 1. A somewhat more developed, though still simple, system would likely consist of a set of handwritten source documents, journals, ledgers, and summary outputs. Data from the source documents would be transcribed into the journals and then posted by hand to the ledgers. The most fully developed manually based processing systems employ a wide variety of processing equipment and devices, short of those that involve computerization.

A representative manually based system for a small business firm might employ the variety of data-related equipment and devices shown in Figure 3-9. Their uses are described in Figure 3-10. Taken together, they enable the full range of processing steps to be performed.

Most manually based transaction processing systems employ **batch processing.** Batch processing consists of accumulating groups of source documents pertaining to similar transactions and entering them into the special journals. Then the source documents are posted to subsidiary ledgers. Total amounts from the batches of transactions entered into the journals are compared with the totals of amounts posted to the ledgers. If they agree, the totals are later posted to the general ledger control accounts and the balances are updated. The batch processing method is pictured in Figure 3-11a.

An alternative processing method is known as **one-write processing.** It consists of performing the entering and posting steps at the same time as the preparation of the source documents and/or outputs. Carbons interleaved between the various records enable the written or printed data to appear simultaneously on all. Periodically, the general ledger is updated. The one-write method was employed in processing the records shown in Figure 3-7. It also is illustrated in Figure 3-11b. An accounting machine, described in Figure 3-10, applies the one-write processing

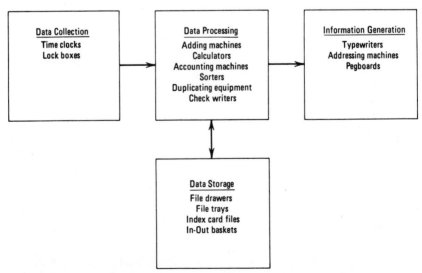

FIGURE 3-9 Equipment and devices employed in a manually based transaction processing system.

Type of Equipment or Device	Typical Uses	Type of Equipment or Device	Typical Uses
Time clock	Stamps times that employees begin and complete work shifts or jobs; stamps time and date on pieces of correspondence received.	Sorter	Facilitates the arrangement of records, source documents, or reports in desired order. (Types of sorters employed include leaf sorters and paper-collating machines.)
Lock box	Receives remittances from customers. (*Note*: The lock box is actually a post office box from which a bank retrieves the cash receipts daily, prepares a listing of the amounts received and from whom, deposits the receipts, and delivers the listing to the firm.)	Duplicator	Reproduces (via "ditto" or mimeograph processes) source documents (such as suppliers' invoices) and reports (such as income statements).
Adding machine	Accumulates columns of figures in journals; prepares totals from batches of source documents; and prints results on paper tapes.	Check writer	Signs checks and "protects" amounts on checks.
		Typewriter	Transcribes reports and correspondence into neat final form.
Calculator	Verifies extensions of amounts on suppliers' invoices by multiplying unit prices times quantities of goods ordered and delivered.	Addressing machine	Prints names and addresses from embossed metal plates onto employee time cards, paychecks, and customer monthly statements.
Accounting machine	Transcribes data from transactions (e.g., sales, purchases) onto batches of source documents, such as sales invoices; performs calculations as needed, then simultaneously posts data to ledger records and journal; also accumulates totals of amounts posted and proves the accuracy of posted amounts.	Pegboard	Facilitates the analysis of weekly sales reports that are written on hole-punched paper and arrayed side by side.
		File drawer	Stores archival copies of source documents and reports.
		File tray	Stores ledger sheets comprising the accounts receivable and accounts payable subsidiary ledgers.
		Index card file	Stores inventory records, which can be rotated by a mechanized wheel for easy retrieval by clerks.
		In-out basket	Stores documents currently awaiting processing by clerks.

FIGURE 3-10 Uses of equipment and devices.

method to batches of transactions. Another device, known as a writing board, enables the one-write method to be applied when the entries are handwritten. For instance, small firms may use writing boards in preparing handwritten paychecks.

Computer-based processing systems automate the processing steps. As in the case of manually based processing systems, many transactions are processed in batches. Another manner of processing transactions in a computer system environment is called online processing. This type of processing consists of entering individual transactions into computer systems via terminals or microcomputers. They may thereby be posted more quickly to records in the master files. Both types of computer-based processing are discussed extensively in Chapter 7.

Controls and Security Measures

Sound transaction processing requires the presence of a variety of controls and security measures. Examples of controls already described include the chart of accounts, control accounts (together with subsidiary ledgers), audit trails, and one-write processing methods.

Controls such as these should be supported by adequate documentation, including (1) procedure manuals and (2) descrip-

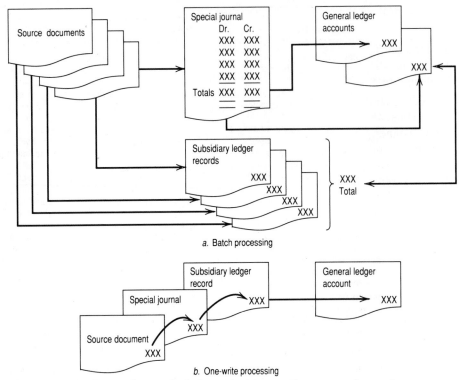

FIGURE 3-11   Processing methods in manual transaction processing systems.

tions of responsibilities assigned to those involved in transaction processing.

Other controls and security measures are described in Chapter 9. However, one additional control—the trial balance—should be noted at this time, since its preparation represents an integral step in the accounting cycle. A **trial balance** is a listing of all account balances in the general ledger. It aids the closing process, which takes place at the end of each accounting period, by providing a convenient format for verifying that the debit account balances equal the credit account balances. Often, two trial balances are prepared: (1) a preclosing trial balance that lists the temporary income and expense accounts as well as the permanent asset and equity accounts, and (2) a postclosing trial balance that lists only the permanent accounts remaining after the temporary accounts have been closed.

Design Considerations

Among the questions that must be answered when designing a transaction processing system are the following:

1. What specific outputs are needed, and which specific account classifications should be established?
2. In what sequence should the components be designed?
3. Which special journals and subsidiary ledgers, if any, should be employed?
4. Which processing methods should be selected?
5. What processing equipment and devices should be acquired?
6. Which accounting controls and security measures should be incorporated?

Although we are not ready to consider answers to most of these questions at this point, a few general guidelines can be proposed:

1. Examine the particular circumstances of the firm in question before deciding on specific design features.

2. With respect to sequence, design the outputs first. Thus, the financial statements should be designed before the chart of accounts, ledgers, journals, and source documents. If this order is followed, the users should be assured that the system will be capable of supplying the desired information via the outputs.

3. Standardize the processing steps whenever feasible. For instance, establish standard journal entries, including adjusting and closing and reversing entries, in order to streamline the posting and closing processes.

4. Incorporate special journals and subsidiary ledgers in the system design as soon as the volume of transactions justifies their use. For instance, a sales returns journal and a notes receivable subsidiary ledger should be added when the volume of sales returns and of notes receivable becomes sufficiently large. Furthermore, if the firm grows quite large, consider splitting subsidiary ledgers into related

groups of accounts. For example, the accounts receivable subsidiary ledger for a public utility may be subdivided between residential customers and commercial customers.

Transaction Flows through the Accounting Cycle

Each transaction processing system combines the previously mentioned components as its transactions flow through the accounting cycle. In this section we trace the flows of sales, cash receipts, purchases, cash disbursements, and payroll transactions. While we will not discuss the various controls at this time, our survey will selectively cover the other components. More detailed coverage of all components and of additional types of transactions is provided in Chapters 11 through 15.

Sales Transactions

Figure 3-12 shows the flow of credit sales transactions through the accounting cycle. For the purposes of the accounting cycle, the flow begins with the source document known as the sales invoice. (Even

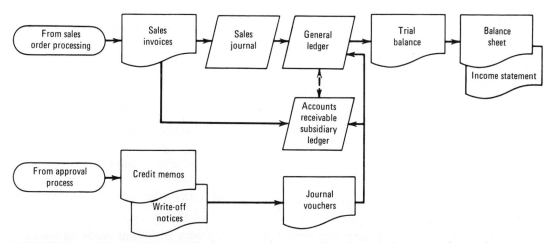

FIGURE 3-12 Diagram showing the flow of sales transactions through the accounting cycle.

though the sales invoice is prepared from the sales order in most cases, the sales order does not contain the amount of the sale. Thus, it cannot be viewed as the relevant source document *within the accounting cycle.* However, we will examine its preparation in Chapter 12, when we discuss the full data processing procedure.)

Data from each sales invoice are (1) entered into a sales journal and (2) posted as debits to individual customer accounts in the accounts receivable subsidiary ledger. Periodically the totals in the sales journal are posted to the general ledger accounts as follows:

Dr. Accounts Receivable	XXX	
Cr. Sales		XXX

If the inventory is maintained on a perpetual basis, the following entry would be recorded on a journal voucher to accompany each daily sales entry:

Dr. Cost of Goods Sold	XXX	
Cr. Merchandise		
(or Finished-Goods)		
Inventory		XXX

To record the costs of those goods sold during this date.

As necessary, journal vouchers are prepared to reflect sales returns and allowances or write-offs:

Dr. Sales Returns and		
Allowances	XXX	
Cr. Accounts Receivable		XXX

To adjust customer account balances to reflect returns and allowances on previous sales.

Dr. Bad-Debt Expenses (or		
Allowance for Doubtful		
Accounts if the reserve		
method for establishing		
bad-debt expenses is		
used)	XXX	
Cr. Accounts Receivable		XXX

To write off those customers' account balances that are deemed to be uncollectible.

After being approved, these journal vouchers are posted both to the general ledger and to customers' accounts in the subsidiary ledger.

Periodically the accounts receivable control account balance is compared with the total of the balances in the subsidiary ledger. At the end of each accounting period the balances in the accounts receivable and sales accounts are listed in the trial balance and then transcribed into the balance sheet and income statement.

Cash Receipts Transactions

Figure 3-13 shows the flow of cash receipts transactions through the accounting cycle. Checks received from customers are the source documents that initiate the recording of most cash receipts transactions. However, since checks represent cash, they should not be used in the processing. Instead, documents called remittance advices are prepared.[3] Amounts appearing on these remittance advices are then (1) entered into a cash receipts journal and (2) posted as credits to individual customer records in the accounts receivable subsidiary ledger.

Periodically, the totals from the cash receipts journal are posted to the general ledger as follows:

Dr. Cash	XXX	
Cr. Accounts Receivable		XXX

The balance of the accounts receivable control account should then agree with the total of balances in the individual accounts receivable records.

Cash may be received from sources other than customers. For example, cash receipts may result from loans, from payments on notes receivable, from the sales of fixed assets, and from income investments. Figure 3-13 shows that the amounts of such re-

[3] Alternatively, the checks might be listed on remittance sheets and journal vouchers prepared from totals of these listings.

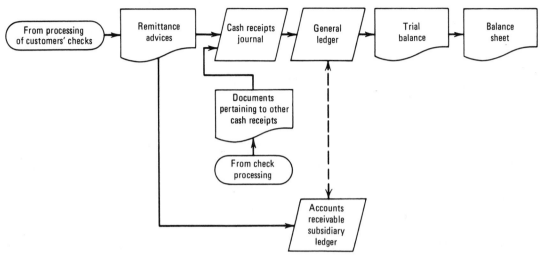

FIGURE 3-13 Diagram showing the flow of cash receipts transactions through the accounting cycle.

ceipts, which generally appear on special documents, are entered into the cash receipts journal. Alternatively, these receipts may be recorded on one or more journal vouchers by an entry such as the following:

Dr. Cash	XXX	
Cr. Notes Payable		XXX
Cr. Notes Receivable		XXX
Cr. Fixed Asset (net value)		XXX
Cr. Interest (or Dividend)		
Income		XXX

To record cash received from sources other than credit customers.

Since these receipts do not involve payments from customers, they are not posted to the accounts receivable subsidiary ledger.

At the end of each accounting period the balances in the accounts receivable and cash control accounts are listed in the trial balance and then transcribed to the balance sheet.

Purchases Transactions

Figure 3-14 shows the flow of purchases transactions through the accounting cycle. Merchandise, raw materials, and supplies typically are acquired on credit. Shortly after the ordered resources have been received, therefore, the suppliers' invoices arrive. These invoices, which reflect the obligations incurred, may be handled in either of two ways: (1) They may be used as the direct sources of amounts entered into a purchases journal or invoice register; (2) they may be first transcribed onto a disbursement voucher, from which the amounts of the obligations are entered into a voucher register.[4]

Periodically, the totals from the journal or register are posted to the general ledger. If the periodic inventory method is employed, the posting is as follows:

Dr. Purchases	XXX	
Cr. Accounts Payable		XXX

If the perpetual inventory method is used, the posting is as follows:

Dr. Raw Materials (or		
Merchandise Inventory)	XXX	
Cr. Accounts Payable		XXX

[4]Source documents such as purchase requisitions and purchase orders actually initiate purchases transactions. However, these documents cannot serve as the source of journal entries or the media for posting, since they do not contain the amounts of the obligations.

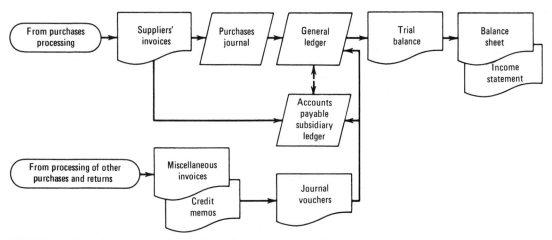

FIGURE 3-14   Diagram showing the flow of transactions arising from purchases through the accounting cycle.

Under either method, the balance in the accounts payable control account should then agree with the total of balances in the individual accounts payable records.

Amounts from suppliers' invoices (or disbursement vouchers) are also posted to individual supplier records in the accounts payable subsidiary ledger. In addition, they may be posted to a raw materials inventory subsidiary ledger if the perpetual inventory method is used.

Obligations may be incurred for resources other than merchandise, raw materials, or supplies. Services and fixed assets, for instance, are usually acquired on credit. Moreover, purchases may be returned, so that the corresponding obligations must be reduced. The journal entry for a purchase return or allowance is as follows:

Dr. Accounts (or Vouchers)
    Payable   XXX
  Cr. Purchases Returns and
    Allowances   XXX
To adjust supplier account balances to reflect returns and allowances on previous purchases (assuming that the periodic inventory system is in use).

When the periodic inventory system is in use, the following adjusting journal entry is needed at the end of each accounting period:

Dr. Merchandise Inventory,
    Ending   XXX
Dr. Cost of Goods Sold   XXX
  Cr. Purchases   XXX
  Cr. Merchandise Inventory,
    Beginning   XXX
To adjust the ending merchandise inventory to its proper amount and to record the cost of goods sold for the accounting period.

Figure 3-14 shows amounts pertaining to such transactions being entered from miscellaneous invoices and suppliers' credit memos onto journal vouchers, which are then posted to the general ledger and (when appropriate) to the accounts payable ledger.[5]

---

[5]Alternative treatments are often employed. For instance, vouchers may be used for recording all resources acquired on credit; expense subsidiary ledgers may be used to reflect the details of various types of resources acquired, with expense control accounts being maintained in the general ledger.

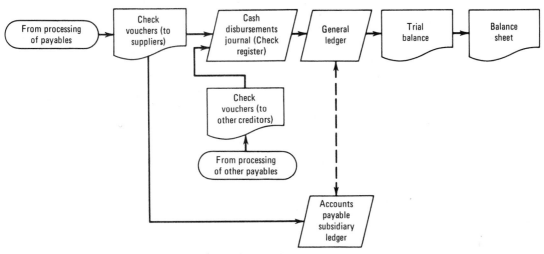

FIGURE 3-15 Diagram showing the flow of cash disbursements through the accounting cycle.

Cash Disbursements Transactions

Figure 3-15 shows the flow of cash disbursements transactions through the accounting cycle. Checks are prepared for suppliers from the suppliers' invoices or disbursement vouchers. Copies of such checks, called check vouchers, provide the amounts and other details to be (1) entered into the cash disbursements journal and (2) posted to the individual supplier records in the accounts payable subsidiary ledger.

Periodically, the totals from the cash disbursements journal are posted to the general ledger as follows:

Dr. Accounts Payable   XXX
    Cr. Cash   XXX

The balance in the accounts payable control account should then agree with the total of balances in the individual accounts payable records.

Cash may be disbursed for other reasons than to pay suppliers. For instance, cash payments are made to distribute dividends, to meet payrolls, to acquire fixed assets, to discharge obligations for utility services, and to repay loans. In Figure 3-15 the check vouchers pertaining to such disbursements are shown being entered separately into the cash disbursements journal. They would not be posted to the accounts payable subsidiary ledger, since in the situation portrayed that ledger contains records of suppliers only.

Payroll Transactions

Figure 3-16 shows the flow of payroll transactions through the accounting cycle. The transactions begin with records reflecting times worked by employees. These source documents, when expressed in dollar terms by applying rates of pay, are used in the two phases comprising payroll processing.

In the first phase the data from these source documents are entered onto a summary that distributes the labor costs to such activities as producing goods, selling goods, and performing administrative tasks. The totals from this summary are posted to such general ledger accounts as follows:

Dr. Work-in-Process Inventory   XXX
Dr. Manufacturing Overhead
    Applied   XXX

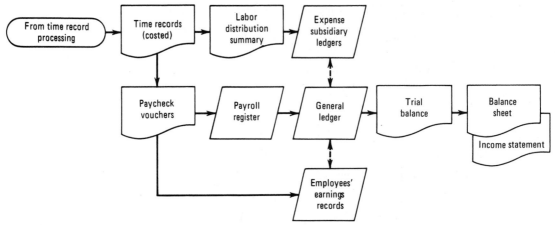

FIGURE 3-16 Diagram showing the flow of payroll transactions through the payroll cycle.

```
Dr. Administrative Expense    XXX
Dr. Selling Expense           XXX
   Cr. Payroll Clearing
      (or Wages and Salaries
      Payable)                        XXX
```

The details are also posted to the appropriate expense subsidiary ledgers for manufacturing overhead, selling expense, and so forth—if such ledgers are maintained.

In the second phase the time data are used to prepare payroll checks. Copies of these paychecks, together with attached earnings statements, are the source documents from which pay data are entered into the payroll register. They are also used as the basis for posting the same data to the earnings records of individual employees.

Totals from the payroll register are posted to the general ledger as follows:

```
Dr. Payroll Clearing
   (or Wages and Salaries
   Payable)                   XXX
   Cr. Federal Income Taxes
      Withheld                        XXX
   Cr. Other Deductions               XXX
   Cr. Cash                           XXX
```

The debit to the Payroll Clearing account in the preceding entry clears the account of labor costs for the pay period. The Payroll Clearing account in effect serves as a control account over the employees' earnings records, since the amount being cleared through the account should equal the total of the gross amounts of pay for all employees.

Other Accounting Transactions

Most firms also process additional transactions that are inherent in their activities. Manufacturing firms, for instance, encounter events relating to the conversion of raw materials into finished goods. Thus, a manufacturer employing a standard cost system will likely make the following entry to reflect the daily accumulation of costs arising from production events:

```
Dr. Work-in-Process Inventory   XXX
   Cr. Raw Materials Inventory          XXX
   Cr. Direct Labor                     XXX
   Cr. Manufacturing Over-
      head—Applied                      XXX
```

As production orders are completed, the firm will make the following entry to transfer the total accumulated production costs into the finished-goods inventory account:

    Dr. Finished-Goods Inventory   XXX
      Cr. Work-in-Process
          Inventory   XXX

Summary

Transaction processing describes the functions involved in supporting the daily operations of a firm. Transaction processing systems resemble a complex network of interdependent physical operations, paperwork processes, and data/information flows. For convenience the network may be subdivided into transaction processing cycles or functional information subsystems.

Basic transaction cycles include the revenue, expenditure, resource management, and general ledger and financial reporting cycles. The revenue cycle includes the sales of merchandise and related cash receipts transactions. The expenditure cycle includes the purchases of merchandise and/or materials and related cash disbursements transactions. The resource management cycle includes transactions related to funds (except for sales and cash receipts from customers), to fixed assets, and to personnel. The general ledger and financial reporting cycle accepts flows from the transaction processing systems that operate within the aforementioned cycles. In addition, it includes the adjustment and closing processes. Among the nonbasic or specialized transaction cycles, perhaps the most frequently encountered is the product conversion cycle within manufacturing firms.

Since transaction processing systems transform transaction data into desired outputs, they require the services of several components. These include source documents, journals and registers, ledgers and files, reports and output documents, charts of accounts, audit trails, processing methods, and controls and security measures. When designing components for a particular transaction processing system, a number of questions must be resolved.

Review Problem with Solution

Statement

Searing Distributors of Reading, Massachusetts, sells a variety of automotive parts and supplies to automobile repair shops, garages, and supply houses. It currently utilizes a manual AIS that includes such components as source documents (e.g., sales invoices, purchase orders, employee time cards, checks), journals (e.g., general, sales, cash receipts, purchases, cash disbursements), ledgers (e.g., general, accounts receivable, accounts payable), financial statements (e.g., income statement, balance sheet), and such controls as trial balances and a coded chart of accounts.

Required

Design a set of documents and accounting records and related elements that illustrate each of the categories listed in the Problem Statement. Include sheets from a general journal, sales journal, cash receipts journal, general ledger, and accounts receivable ledger. The sales journal should provide a single amount column, together with columns for the date, customer name and account number, and sales invoice number (the audit trail reference). The cash receipts journal should provide two columns for debits (cash and sales discounts) and two columns for credits (accounts receivable and other), together with columns for the date, recipient, and remittance number (the audit trail reference). Illustrative data should be shown in these accounting records, as well as in a multicopy sales invoice document. Also include an income statement and a trial balance.

Solution

Exhibit 1 shows a sales invoice with an original and five copies.

Exhibit 2 shows the general journal, with two sample entries. An audit trail is established by listing the numbers of the ledger accounts in the Posting Reference column; the numbers are based on the summary chart of accounts shown in Figure 3-8.

Exhibit 3 shows the sales journal. Its

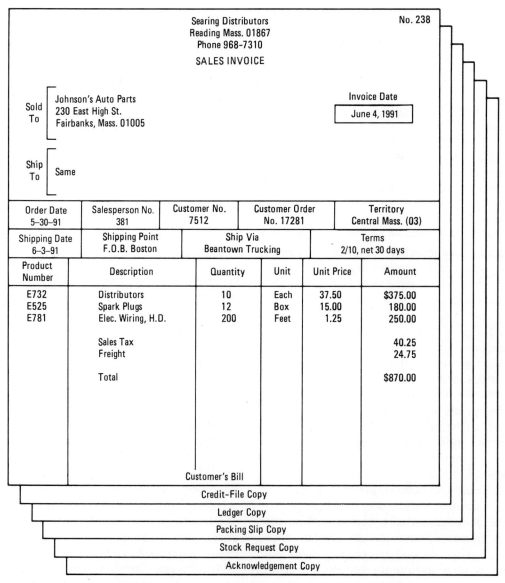

Searing Distributors				No. 238
Reading Mass. 01867				
Phone 968-7310				
SALES INVOICE				

Sold To: Johnson's Auto Parts, 230 East High St., Fairbanks, Mass. 01005

Invoice Date: June 4, 1991

Ship To: Same

Order Date 5-30-91	Salesperson No. 381	Customer No. 7512	Customer Order No. 17281	Territory Central Mass. (03)
Shipping Date 6-3-91	Shipping Point F.O.B. Boston	Ship Via Beantown Trucking		Terms 2/10, net 30 days

Product Number	Description	Quantity	Unit	Unit Price	Amount
E732	Distributors	10	Each	37.50	$375.00
E525	Spark Plugs	12	Box	15.00	180.00
E781	Elec. Wiring, H.D.	200	Feet	1.25	250.00
	Sales Tax				40.25
	Freight				24.75
	Total				$870.00

Customer's Bill
Credit-File Copy
Ledger Copy
Packing Slip Copy
Stock Request Copy
Acknowledgement Copy

EXHIBIT 1   A sales invoice.

General Journal				Page 75
Date	**Account Names and Description**	**Posting Reference**	**Debit**	**Credit**
June 17	Note receivable Land To record the exchange of an unimproved lot for a note from John Broder.	11 23	4000.00	4000.00
June 30	Depreciation expense Accumulated depreciation—office equipment and furniture To record depreciation expense for the month.	76 25C	300.00	300.00

EXHIBIT 2 A general journal.

Sales Journal				Page 32
Date		**Customer Name and Account Number**	**Sales Invoice Number**	**Amount**
June	4	Johnson's Auto Parts #7512	238	870.00
	4	Royal Auto Parts #6158	239	567.50
	4	Automotive Sales #4779	240	1009.00
	4	B & S Auto Supply #5211	241	223.75
	4	Parts Mart #3835	242	818.00
	4	Thomas Motor Exch. #4138	243	1351.25
	4	Fox Auto Service #2816	244	654.50
			Posted 12/50 ✓ ✓	5494.00

EXHIBIT 3 A sales journal.

single amount column is sufficient for all postings, since each credit sales transaction gives rise to one amount, representing a debit to accounts receivable and an equal credit to the sales account. For instance, the amount of $870 is entered from the sales invoice in Exhibit 1. Only the total amount of $5494, however, is posted to the accounts receivable (account number 12) and to the sales account (account number 50) in the general ledger. The check marks indicate that the posting has actually been performed.

Exhibit 4 shows the cash receipts journal. It requires multiple amount columns, since it accommodates cash received from all sources and since sales discounts are possible. As in the case of the sales journal, only the column totals are posted to the general ledger accounts (except for the Other Credits).

Exhibit 5 shows the general ledger page for the accounts receivable account. The postings from the sales and cash receipts journals, in the amounts of $5494 and $4591, appear. Note that the Post. Ref. contains the page numbers of the journals as audit trails. The final amount in the Balance column shows the current status of the account.

Exhibit 6 shows the detailed record for one customer's account in the accounts re-

			Cash Receipts Journal				Page 41
Date	**Received from**	**Remittance Number**	**Other Credits**		**Accounts Receivable (credit)**	**Sales Discount (debit)**	**Cash (debit)**
			Acct. No.	**Amount**			
June 4	Fox Auto Service #2816	520			520.00	10.40	509.60
4	A-1 Auto Parts #1913	521			989.00		989.00
4	Republic Sales Co. #7008	522			450.00	9.00	441.00
4	Dividend-West Corp.		86	2000.00			2000.00
4	Del's Auto Electric #3496	523			1230.00	24.60	1205.40
4	Flint's Distributors #4653	524			652.00		652.00
4	Johnson's Auto Parts #7512	525			750.00	15.00	735.00
				2000.00	4591.00	59.00	6532.00
	Posted			✓	12 ✓	51 ✓	10 ✓

EXHIBIT 4 A cash receipts journal.

		General Ledger				
Account Accounts Receivable				**Account Number 12**		
Date 1991		**Description**	**Post. Ref.**	**Debits**	**Credits**	**Balance**
June	1	Balance forward				41214.00
	1	Sales	SJ31	4828.00		46042.00
	1	Cash receipts	CR40		5132.00	40910.00
	4	Sales	SJ32	5494.00		46404.00
	4	Cash receipts	CR41		4591.00	41813.00

EXHIBIT 5 A general ledger record.

Name Johnson's Auto Parts				Account Number 7512		
Address 230 East High St. Fairbanks, Mass. 01005						
Date		**Explanation**	**Document Number**	**Debits**	**Credits**	**Balance**
June	1	Balance forward				750.00
	4	Sale	S238	870.00		1620.00
	4	Payment	R525		750.00	870.00

EXHIBIT 6 A customer's account in an accounts receivable subsidiary ledger.

```
                    Searing Distributors
                    Income Statement
              For the Month Ended June 30, 1991

Sales                                                   $96,000
Less: Sales discounts, returns, and allowances            1,900

Net sales                                               $94,100
Less: Cost of goods sold                                 38,300

Gross profit on sales                                   $55,800
Operating expenses
   Selling expenses                       $28,600
   Administrative expenses                 19,100
   Financial management expenses            1,300

      Total operating expenses                           49,000

Net operating income                                    $ 6,800
Plus: Nonoperating revenues                               2,000

         Net income                                     $ 8,800
```

EXHIBIT 7   An income statement.

ceivable subsidiary ledger. The amount from the sales invoice in Exhibit 1 ($870) appears in the debits column; the number of the sales invoice serves as the audit trail. Likewise, the amount from remittance advice R525 appears in the credits column. The current balance after all postings is $870.

Exhibit 7 shows an income statement for the month ended June 30.

Exhibit 8 shows a trial balance as of June 30. It is an unadjusted trial balance, since the adjusting entries shown in the general journal have not been posted. Each account name in the trial balance is accompanied by the account number. The total of the accounts having debit balances is shown to equal the total of the accounts having credit balances.

Review Questions

3-1   What is the meaning of each of the following terms?

Transaction processing
Transaction processing system
Functional information subsystem
Transaction processing cycle
Revenue cycle
Expenditure cycle
Resource management cycle
General ledger and financial reporting cycle
Product conversion cycle
Source document
Journal
General journal
Special journal
Journal voucher
Register
Ledger
Posting process
General ledger
Subsidiary ledger
Ledgerless bookkeeping
Control account
File
Master file
Transaction file
Reference file
History file
Financial statement
Managerial report
Operational document
Chart of accounts

Searing Distributors
Trial Balance
June 30, 1991

Account Number	Account Title	Debit	Credit
10	Cash	$ 7,717.00	
11	Notes receivable	4,000.00	
12	Accounts receivable	2,838.00	
13	Merchandise inventory	12,337.00	
14	Supplies inventory	1,260.00	
18	Prepaid insurance	300.00	
20	Investment in long-term securities	3,000.00	
23	Land	1,500.00	
24	Building	90,000.00	
25	Accumulated depreciation—building		$ 22,500.00
26	Office equipment and furniture	18,000.00	
27	Accumulated depreciation—office equipment and furniture		8,400.00
30	Notes payable		2,500.00
31	Accounts payable		6,710.00
33	Taxes payable		4,320.00
40	Long-term notes payable		5,000.00
45	Capital stock		60,000.00
46	Retained earnings		23,650.00
50	Sales of merchandise		96,000.00
51	Sales discounts	1,246.00	
52	Sales returns and allowances	654.00	
55	Purchases	40,020.00	
56	Purchase returns and allowances		1,268.00
57	Freight-in	1,376.00	
61	Sales salaries	22,087.00	
62	Travel expense	3,842.00	
63	Freight-out	2,671.00	
71	Administrative salaries	17,925.00	
72	Utilities expense	200.00	
74	Office supplies expense	75.00	
81	Interest expense	840.00	
82	Bad-debt expense	460.00	
86	Dividend revenue		2,000.00
	Totals	$232,348.00	$232,348.00

EXHIBIT 8 A trial balance.

Audit trail
Batch processing
One-write processing
Trial balance

3-2 In what ways does the information system interact with the physical operations and resources of a firm?

3-3 Describe two bases by which transaction processing and related aspects of the information system may be subdivided, and indicate the logical rationale for each.

3-4 Name several functional information subsystems that are suitable for a manufacturing firm.

3-5 Name several transaction cycles within a manufacturing firm.

3-6 How are functional information subsystems related to the transaction cycles of a firm?

3-7 Identify the components involved in transaction processing.

3-8 Identify several functions performed by source documents.

3-9 What role does a journal play in transaction processing?

3-10 What are the advantages of special journals?

3-11 Name several special journals used in transaction processing.

3-12 What are the basic features of a general ledger?

3-13 Describe the relationship between the general ledger and subsidiary ledgers.

3-14 What are the advantages and drawbacks of ledgerless bookkeeping?

3-15 Distinguish among four types of files used in transaction processing.

3-16 Identify several types of outputs derived from transaction processing.

3-17 Why is the chart of accounts important to transaction processing?

3-18 What functions does an audit trail perform?

3-19 Why is a one-write device useful in transaction processing?

3-20 List several questions that must be answered when designing transaction processing systems.

3-21 Identify several guidelines useful in designing the components of transaction processing.

3-22 Describe the flows of the following transactions through the accounting cycle:

    a. Sales.
    b. Cash receipts.
    c. Purchases.
    d. Cash disbursements.
    e. Payroll.

3-23 List the source documents and special journals suitable to each of the above types of transactions.

Discussion Questions

3-24 What advantages do students gain when they begin their study of transaction processing systems by focusing on manual (i.e., noncomputerized), rather than computerized, elements and settings?

3-25 When designing the elements that comprise the transaction processing of a firm, why should the design process *begin* with the financial statements?

3-26 Describe each of the following in terms of systems characteristics:

    a. Marketing information subsystem.
    b. Financial/accounting information subsystem.
    c. Revenue transaction cycle.
    d. Sales transaction processing.

3-27 Why do specific sets of transaction cycles and types of transactions differ from firm to firm?

3-28 Can a single transaction, such as a sales transaction, be a complete transaction cycle in certain firms?

3-29 Discuss the types of transactions required in the following types of organizations:

    a. Bank.
    b. Hospital.
    c. Construction company.
    d. Municipality.
    e. University.
    f. Insurance company.

3-30 Compare the terms used by accountants in describing transaction processing steps with those used in Chapter 1 to describe the steps in the data processing cycle. For instance, accountants use the term *posting to the ledger,* whereas systems analysts would normally use the term *updating a file.*

Problems

3-1 List the items of data that should appear on each of the following source documents, if the documents are the sources of entries into special journals and if postings are to appropriate subsidiary ledgers:

    a. Sales invoice.
    b. Remittance advice.
    c. Disbursement voucher.
    d. Check voucher.
    e. Employee paycheck.

3-2 Special journals may be designed in differing formats, as the examples in the Review Problem illustrate. Design a purchases journal in two formats:

    a. A format having a single amount column, from which totals are posted to the accounts payable and purchases general ledger accounts.
    b. A format having amount columns for accounts payable, merchandise purchases, freight-in, supplies, and other debit amounts.

In both designed formats include additional needed columns, such as a column for the supplier's invoice number. Also mark each amount column as pertaining to a credit or debit account.

3-3 A check register and a cash disbursements journal, though serving essentially the same purpose, generally have somewhat different formats.

    a. Design a check register for use in a voucher system that employs disbursement vouchers. Include columns for the amount paid, the payee, check number, disbursement voucher number, and date.
    b. Design a cash disbursements journal that provides amount columns for cash (credit), accounts payable (debit), other debit amounts, and purchase discounts (credit). Include other needed columns.

3-4 Design a multiple-column sales journal that reflects all sales made by the Easyway Co., which maintains its records manually. The firm makes both credit and cash sales. It needs to record freight, which is prepaid, and a sales tax. Credit sales are to be entered from numbered sales invoices, whereas daily cash sales are entered in total from a cash register tape. Totals are to be posted to the appropriate general ledger accounts on a daily basis.

3-5 Design a customer's accounts receivable ledger record, post the following data, and reflect the balance after each posting:

Mary Anderson   Credit limit: $1,000
1385 West Fairway Drive
Dallas, Texas 75262

Credit sales: $200 on May 5, posted from sales invoice S558.
    $150 on June 16, posted from sales invoice S731.
    $180 on August 12, posted from sales invoice S942.
Receipts: $200 on May 13, posted from remittance advice CR318.
    $100 on June 25, posted from remittance advice CR487.

The beginning balance on May 1 was zero.

3-6 Design a supplier's accounts payable ledger record, post the following data, and reflect the balance after each posting:

Larry's Supply Mart   Terms: 2/10, n/30
  (No. 37285)
39873 South Plymouth Ave.
Cleveland, Ohio 44101

Credit purchases: $2,000 on October 10, posted from invoice 2191.
    $3,400 on November 19, posted from invoice 3374.
Debits: $2,000 on October 19, posted from check CD5832.
    $1,600 return of goods on November 23, posted from credit memo CM638.

The beginning balance on October 1 was zero.

3-7 Design a raw materials inventory ledger record for a manufacturing firm that maintains a perpetual inventory system. The firm desires to reflect balances both in terms of quantities and dollar amounts for each inventory item. The record should also contain columns that show quantities received from suppliers and issued into production, as well as the unit price of the item in each transaction.

Post data for item number M2389, connecting rod, which has a reorder point of 100 units. On March 1 the quantity on hand is 170 units, at a unit price of $10. Issues for the month were as follows: 80 units on requisition I432, dated March 3; 100 units on requisition I476, dated March 14; 90 units on requisition I497, dated March 23; and 150 units on requisition I525, dated March 28. Receipts for the month were as follows, all at a unit price of $10: 200 units on receiving report RR3462, dated March 10; and 200 units on receiving report RR3503, dated March 27.

3-8 Set up appropriate T-accounts for each of the following situations. Show the effects of the given transaction data as they flow through both the general ledger and subsidiary ledgers, and compute the ending balances. Treat each part of the problem independently of the other parts. All beginning account balances are zero, except as follows: $5000 debit balance in the cash account; $200 balance in the account for Susan Pope and also in the accounts receivable control account.

  a. Sales of $550 to Paul Murphy, $730 to Sally Dawson, and $390 to Jose Quintero; cash receipts of $200 from Susan Pope (based on a previous sale), $400 from Sally Dawson, and $390 from Jose Quintero; sales return of $250 by Paul Murphy.
  b. Purchases of $800 from Plentiful Providers and $660 from Sunny Services; cash disbursements of $660 to Sunny Services; purchase return of $360 to Plentiful Providers.
  c. Payroll of $4800 (at gross), representing $1000 paid to Jim Tabor, $1000 to Nancy Omes, $800 to Dave Custer, $800 to Sam Brister, and $1200 to Jane With. Forty percent of each person's gross salary represents deductions. Jim and Nancy are salespersons, Dave and Sam are administrative assistants, and Jane is general manager.

3-9 Design the components of a payroll one-write system: a paycheck, employee earnings record (ledger), and payroll register (journal). Place them on the same sheet of paper, from top to bottom, in the order stated. The paycheck should appear the same as any check, except that it contains an earnings statement, or "stub," attached at the bottom of the check and separated by a perforation. The check is first to be completed manually by a payroll clerk. Then the clerk will enter data into provided spaces on the earnings statement. By means of carbons this data will be copied onto the ledger and journal.

Use the data given below to determine the needed columns on the forms, and then enter these data onto the drawn forms:

The Progressive Company pays Pamela V. Bush on check number 1243 for 44 hours worked during the pay period ending November 16, 1990. The hourly rate is $8.50, with time and a half for all hours over 40. FICA tax is deducted from gross pay at a rate of 7.1 percent, and federal taxes are withheld at a rate of 14 percent. Other deductions amount to 20 percent of gross pay. (Include columns for employee name, ending date of period, gross pay, the various deductions, and net pay. Be sure to align the columns on all three forms.)

 3-10 *Note:* This problem can be solved by means of an electronic spreadsheet package on a microcomputer.

Bellevue Repair Service was organized by Charles Bellevue on August 1, 199X. Following are its account balances, listed in random order, as of August 31. Assume that adjustments have already been made.

Advertising expense	$ 600
Cash	8,500
Rent expense	1,000
Service trucks	28,800
Tax expense	200
Accounts receivable	9,600
Insurance expense	460
Revenue from repairs	44,000
Salaries and wages payable	2,600
Accounts payable	3,700
C. Bellevue, Capital	55,000
C. Bellevue, Drawing	1,000
Accumulated depreciation—equipment	400
Accumulated depreciation—service trucks	800
Utilities expense	700
Miscellaneous expense	540
Parts and supplies on hand	9,900
Prepaid insurance	1,500
Depreciation expense	1,200
Parts and supplies expense	6,700
Salaries and wages expense	11,800
Equipment	24,000

Required

a. Prepare a trial balance from the given account balances.

b. Prepare an income statement for the month of August and a balance sheet as of August 31.

 3-11 *Note:* This problem can be solved by means of an accounting software package on a microcomputer.

Co-op Sales of Dayton, Ohio, was established on June 1. Merchandise will be sold on credit, with payment due in 15 days. Inventory will be recorded by the periodic inventory method. The accounting records will consist of a general journal, sales journal, purchases journal, cash receipts journal, check register, general ledger, accounts receivable subsidiary ledger, and accounts payable subsidiary ledger. Within the general ledger will be the following accounts: cash, accounts receivable, allowance for bad debts, merchandise inventory, supplies, prepaid expenses, furniture and fixtures, accumulated depreciation, accounts payable, notes payable, accrued expenses payable, FICA taxes payable, income taxes payable, capital stock, retained earnings, sales, purchases, purchase discounts, cost of goods sold, salaries expense, depreciation expense, utilities expense, supplies used, rent expense, taxes expense, interest expense, advertising expense, and miscellaneous expense.

Co-op's June transactions are as follows:

June 1 Capital stock is issued and sold for $50,000.

1 Rent on a building for a year is paid in advance to the Monoco Realty Co., $2400. (Check no. 1 is issued.)

1 Furniture and fixtures are acquired in exchange for a 60-day, 15-percent note in the amount of $16,000.

2 Merchandise inventory is acquired on 2/10, net/30 terms from Tenny's Wares; invoice 283 shows an amount payable of $8000.

3 Supplies amounting to $800 are bought for cash from Vicor's Supply House. (Check no. 2.)

4 Merchandise is sold to Loman's Outlet on invoice number S1, $1200.

5 Merchandise is purchased on 2/10, net/30 terms from Simon Manufacturing; invoice 101 shows an amount payable of $4500.

8 Bill is received from the city for building inspection, $50.

9 Merchandise is sold to Rustic Retailer, $2800. (Invoice no. S2.)

10 Bill is received from the Bugle News for advertising, $220.

11 Check no. 3 is mailed to Tenny's Wares for amount due.

12 Merchandise is sold to Sam's Stores, $4200. (Invoice no. S3.)

15 Salaries are paid for the first half of June, $1600, less income taxes withheld of $240 and FICA taxes withheld of $110. (The payroll transaction is entered in the general journal, since special checks are issued to the employees. Normally a payroll register would support a payroll transaction, but it is omitted in this problem to avoid excessive details.)

18 Remittance is received from Loman's Outlet for amount owed. (Remittance advice no. R1 is prepared.)

19 Checks numbered 4 and 5 are mailed to the city and the newspaper for bills owed.

22 Merchandise is sold to Loman's Outlet, $3600. (Invoice no. S4.)

24 Remittance is received from Rustic Retailer in the amount of $1000 (Remittance no. R2.)

26 Merchandise is sold to Polly's Parlors, $1900. (Invoice no. S5.)

29 Bill is received for utilities, $300.

30 Salaries are paid for the second half of June, $1600, less income taxes withheld of $240 and FICA taxes withheld of $110.

30 Adjustments are made based on the following:

a. The ending merchandise inventory amounts to $3800. (The adjusting entry should involve debits to the merchandise inventory, cost of goods sold, and purchase discounts accounts, with an offsetting credit to the purchases account.)

b. The interest on the note payable has accrued for one month.

c. One month's prepaid rent has expired.

d. The depreciation rate on furniture and fixtures is 12 percent per year, and the depreciation method to be used is straight-line.

e. The amount of unused supplies at the end of the month is $200.

f. The employer's contribution to payroll taxes must match the amount of the employees' contributions to FICA taxes.

g. The losses due to bad debts are estimated to be 2 percent of the balance of accounts receivable at the end of the month.

Required

a. Assign codes to the accounts that comprise the current chart of accounts.

b. On ruled ledger paper write the codes and names of the general ledger accounts on the respective sheets. (Alternatively, draw T-accounts and label with codes and names.)

c. Draw formats for a general journal, sales journal, purchases journal, cash receipts journal, and check register. The formats should allow all sales and cash receipts to appear in the related journals, all cash disbursements except payroll transactions to appear in the cash disbursements journal, and *only* merchandise purchases (based on individual supplier invoices) to appear in the purchases journal.

d. Draw formats for accounts receivable and accounts payable ledgers.

e. Enter all transactions for June (including adjusting journal entries) into the appropriate journals and post to the ledgers.

f. Prepare an adjusted trial balance from the general ledger account balances, and reconcile the control accounts to the subsidiary ledgers.

3-12 Ellen Ether is the information systems manager of the Herson Manufacturing Company of La Crosse, Wisconsin. She has decided to develop an overall view or model of the firm's information system. Her approach will consist of identifying the various subsystems comprising the information system and then linking them together by means of data and information flowlines. The resulting summary block diagram should aid the information systems function when communicating with users and planning future information system development projects.

Thus far she has identified the following information subsystems or subfunctions:

> Sales order processing
> Credit
> Accounts receivable
> Accounts payable
> Billing
> Sales forecasting and analysis
> Inventory control
> Purchasing

> Receiving
> Storeskeeping
> Finished-goods warehousing
> Shipping
> Production planning and control
> Design engineering
> Quality control
> Parts and subassembly fabrication
> Product assembly
> Cash receipts
> Cash disbursements
> Cost accounting
> Payroll
> Production maintenance
> General ledger
> Financial reporting
> Personnel administration
> Cash planning
> Facilities planning

Required

Using these subfunctions, develop a summary block diagram (similar to Figure 3-1) showing the network of operations and related planning and control activities.

3-13 *Selected Small Firm (A Continuing Case)* For the small firm that you selected in Chapter 1 (see Problem 1-7), complete the following requirements:

a. Draw a block summary diagram of daily operations and related planning and control processes.

b. List the chart of accounts; assign suitable account codes if none are used at present.

c. Obtain copies of all source documents.

d. Sketch the formats of all journals and ledgers; list other files in use.

e. List all transaction cycles.

f. Describe all processing equipment and devices in use.

g. Obtain copies of key outputs, including documents and managerial reports.

Suggested Readings

Bodnar, George H., and Hopwood, William. *Accounting Information Systems.* 4th ed. Boston: Allyn and Bacon, 1990.

Page, John, and Hooper, Paul. *Accounting and Information Systems.* 3rd ed. Englewood Cliffs, N.J.: Prentice-Hall, 1987.

CHAPTER OBJECTIVES

After studying this chapter, you should be able to do the following:

Identify the various types of decisions made by managers.

Describe the basic decision process by which effective managers make decisions.

Discuss the essential characteristics of planning and control processes.

Trace the major flows of information within a typical firm.

Describe the value, content, and properties of information.

Identify the varied information needs of managers.

Chapter **4**

INFORMATION PROCESSING

Perhaps the most important purpose of an information system is to support managerial decision making. This purpose is fulfilled by (1) collecting and storing relevant data, (2) processing the data via decision models, and (3) reporting the resulting information to managers. Collectively, these activities are known as **information processing.** Accountants are as concerned with information processing as they are with transaction processing. On the one hand, they have direct responsibility for providing analyzed information to managers. On the other hand, they are involved (with others) in helping to manage the information resource.

Managerial Decision Making

In order to design information processing systems, we must understand managerial

decision making. Therefore, we begin this chapter with a survey of decision making in business firms. Our survey includes broad managerial decision-related activities, specific types of managerial decisions, steps in a logical decision process, and characteristics of key planning and control decisions.

Managerial Decision-Related Activities

The managers of a firm initially are responsible for setting its objectives. Then they must make decisions to achieve the established objectives. These decisions relate to such activities as

1. Organizing the tasks and delegating authority.
2. Hiring the employees and acquiring the other resources.

Classification Plan	Types of Decisions and Examples
1. Managerial activity	*Strategic planning decision:* market a new product *Tactical planning decision:* schedule production *Management control decision:* evaluate a manager for promotion *Operational control decision:* select the quantity of inventory to reorder
2. Problem structure	*Programmed decision:* approve a customer's credit *Semiautomatic decision:* set prices on products *Nonprogrammed decision:* initiate an advertising campaign or begin a foreign subsidiary
3. Resource	*Manpower decision:* hire employees *Materials decision:* raise quality of materials *Facilities decision:* build a new plant *Financing decision:* issue stock *Data decision:* acquire economic data
4. Nature of problem	*Recurring decision:* prepare the annual budget *One-time decision:* merge with another firm *Routine decision:* determine the pay of employees *Complex decision:* establish the location of a new warehouse *Short-range decision:* borrow by issuing a note *Long-range decision:* acquire a new machine
5. Operational function	*Accounting decision:* select a depreciation method *Production decision:* route a production order *Marketing decision:* assign a salesman to a territory *Materials decision:* establish the safety stock level

FIGURE 4-1   Array of managerial decisions.

3. Allocating the resources to the respective tasks and scheduling their use.

4. Coordinating and supervising the work of employees and subordinate managers.

5. Detecting and correcting problems as they arise.

Accountants generally describe these activities by two key words: *planning* and *control.*

Types of Managerial Decisions

Figure 4-1 lists several dimensions by which decisions may be classified. Under each dimension or classification plan categories by which decisions may be typed are suggested.

One very useful way of classifying decisions is in accordance with the two key managerial activities of planning and control. Thus, planning takes place on two levels: strategic and tactical. Similarly, control is maintained on the management control level and the operational control level.[1]

A quite different, but also very useful, way to classify decisions is according to the degree of structure in the problem situation. Certain problems are well structured. That is, they are based on clear logic, so that the underlying relationships among the key factors are clearly apparent to the decision maker. Therefore, explicit sets of instructions can be given to clerks (or programmed for computers), and clear-cut decision results will be derived. An example is the decision of when to reorder an item of merchandise for resale.

[1]This breakdown is based on research reported by Robert N. Anthony in *Planning and Control Systems: A Framework for Analysis* (Boston: Division of Research, Graduate School of Business Administration, Harvard University, 1965). Anthony's plan, however, does not include tactical planning; the author of this text bears responsibility for its addition.

Decisions of this type are known as **programmed,** or **structured, decisions.** In contrast, certain other problems are poorly structured. They are difficult to define, and the relationships among their relevant factors are not well understood. Considerable judgment, as well as trial-and-error approaches, must be exercised in making the decisions that are to deal with such ill-structured problems. Since explicit sets of instructions or computer programs cannot be devised to handle these problems, the decisions derived in such situations are called **nonprogrammed,** or **unstructured, decisions.** An example of an unstructured decision concerns whom to hire as the key managers of a firm.

Between these two extremes are the partially structured problems, which can be partially expressed in clearly stated sets of relationships (i.e., partially expressed by explicit decision models). Decisions related to such problems are known as **semiautomatic,** or **semistructured, decisions.**

Each specific decision may be classified according to both of the preceding dimensions or classification plans. For instance, a decision concerning the quantity of inventory to reorder can be categorized as an operational control decision and also as a programmed decision. In fact, each decision may be classified according to all the dimensions shown in Figure 4-1. Thus, a decision concerning whether to promote a production manager may be categorized as a management control, personnel, recurring, complex, long-range, nonprogrammed production decision.

Decision Process

Each problem situation, with its related decision, is unique. Each decision maker is unique. Nevertheless, the process by which all decisions are made follows a relatively standardized series of steps. While theorists differ somewhat concerning the number and

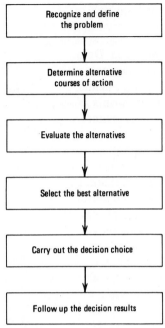

FIGURE 4-2 Steps in a decision process.

descriptions of these steps, most would accept the basic **decision process** portrayed in Figure 4-2. All of the steps shown are followed by effective decision makers.

In order to accommodate the variety of problems and decision makers, however, each step within this process may vary widely from decision to decision. As suggested in the foregoing section, some problems are defined very clearly and objectively, and the decision alternatives are evaluated with a great deal of certainty. Other problems, and hence the steps in the decision process, are characterized by much vagueness, subjectivity, and uncertainty. Some decision makers employ a reasoned approach and seek to develop the most explicit decision model possible in each problem situation; others employ an intuitive approach and habitually depend on implicit decision models. With these differences in mind, we will discuss and illustrate the decision process shown in Figure 4-2.

1. **Recognize and Define the Problem.** The initial step begins with a search and a recognition. By means of information concerning the firm's activities and environment, the decision maker explores his or her firm's current situation. Upon encountering telltale evidence, the decision maker recognizes that a problem exists and that a decision is necessary. In some cases this recognition dawns when the decision maker observes that objectives are not being achieved. For instance, the president of a firm sees in a monthly report that actual sales are below planned sales and that profits are shrinking. Sometimes recognition occurs because adverse changes have been spotted, as, for example, when a sales manager notes that a competitor has lowered prices. In other cases recognition may appear in the guise of opportunities perceived: Thus, a vice-president of finance may learn of an opportunity to acquire a smaller firm with a complementary product line.

   Upon recognizing that a problem exists, the decision maker then defines the problem. This task involves stating clearly the objectives, key problem factors, constraints, assumptions, and planning horizon. To the greatest extent possible, these items should be stated in quantitative terms. Thus, the objectives should be translated into **criteria,** measures by which to judge each alternative course of action. Problem definition generally requires the gathering of much data.

2. **Determine Alternative Courses of Action.** The second major step in the decision process is to search for possible problem solutions or courses of action. All alternatives except those that clearly are not feasible should be listed.

   It should be noted that this step often blends with the previous step of defining the problem. That is, the process of listing alternatives usually brings to light new data that should be gathered. This phenomenon occurs also in later steps of the process, so that continual recycling takes place during the entire decision process.

3. **Evaluate the Alternatives.** Each of the alternative courses of action must be compared against the others. This step requires the factors pertaining to each alternative to be organized in a manner that renders the alternatives comparable. In decision terminology, the decision maker must develop (to the extent possible) a **decision model** that (a) describes the relationships and the behavior of the relevant and significant factors and (b) enables the results of their interactions to be computed in terms of the criteria.[2] When data concerning each alternative are in turn fed into this model, the resulting criteria values enable each alternative to be ranked in relation to the others.

4. **Select the Best Alternative.** The climactic step consists of "making the decision"— choosing the alternative that is best in the circumstances. In the absence of other considerations, the alternative that best satisfies the criteria stated in the decision model should be chosen. In the organizational climate of the firm, however, broader considerations often temper the choice. For instance, other objectives may be in conflict with those on which the stated criteria are based. Selecting the alternative that best meets the stated criteria may result in the suboptimization of the firm's key objectives; another one of the alternatives may actually lead to a greater harmony among these objectives

---

[2]However, this does not mean that a decision maker will in every instance write down a number of mathematical equations; often the model will be roughly developed inside his or her head and used without benefit of precise computations.

and represent a sounder application of the systems approach. Managerial judgment is necessary to resolve such problem situations.

5. **Carry Out the Decision Choice.** After an alternative course of action is selected, it must be implemented. This phase of the decision process consists of planning, executing, and controlling all of the activities necessary to put the decision fully into effect.

6. **Follow Up the Results.** The aftermath of a decision should not be ignored once it has been put into effect; rather, the results should be monitored. By comparing the results achieved with those anticipated, the decision maker can learn of the decision's effectiveness. He or she will then be able to improve future decisions. Moreover, when significant differences appear between anticipated and actual results, the decision maker is alerted to take corrective actions.

To reinforce your understanding of the decision process, you might examine Review Problem 1 at the end of this chapter before reading the following sections.

Planning Processes

Planning consists of deciding (a) which alternative courses of action should be followed in resolving a problem situation and (b) how to put the selected courses of action into effect. Planning processes lead to specific decisions, with the decision making taking place at several managerial levels throughout a firm. Strategic and tactical decisions are two types of specific decisions generated from planning processes. These decisions and related processes are discussed next.

Strategic planning. **Strategic planning** is the process of deciding on the strategies and resources necessary to achieve a firm's ob-

jectives. It reflects a long-range perspective. It also focuses on the firm's major strengths and weaknesses as well as on the problems and opportunities in the environment. Generally, managers at the highest level in a firm make the key decisions related to strategic planning.

Determining the firm's **objectives** is the initial concern of strategic planning, since objectives provide overall guidance in establishing strategies and in making plans at lower levels. To provide effective guidance, objectives should be clearly stated, compatible with each other (to the greatest extent possible), congruent with the personal objectives of managers and employers, and broad in scope. Objectives should be easily divided into subobjectives that are narrower in scope and related to specific areas of responsibility. For instance, objectives may concern a firm's overall market share and profits, whereas subobjectives may pertain to sales quotas and cost levels in particular operational functions. Both objectives and subobjectives should be stated in quantitative terms and for definite time periods. A market-share objective of 10 percent for the next year and a production level of 12,000 units for next month are examples of a useful objective and production subobjective, respectively.

Strategies, often called policies, flow from objectives and provide more specific guidelines and constraints concerning the operations of a firm. In order to achieve the market-share objective, for instance, a firm might select a low-price, high-volume strategy. Another firm in the same market might select a strategy of selling higher-quality products, with the expectation of receiving higher prices on a smaller volume of sales.

Key *strategic decisions* allocate resources in an established framework of objectives and strategies. Most decisions of this type are high impact, complex, long range, broad in scope, and nonrecurring in nature. Often they must be derived from unstruc-

What new products should be introduced?
What new markets should be developed?
What changes are desirable in the product mix?
What levels and types of customer services should be provided?
Where shall the new plant and warehouse be located?
What is the most suitable means of advertising and promoting the products?
What channels of distribution should be used?
How should the prices for products be established?
What types of research should be performed?
How can the quality and design of the present products be improved?
How should the production capacity be expanded, and when?
Should an existing department or product be discontinued?
What new equipment should be acquired, and when?
What approach is most suitable for plant and equipment maintenance?
Should the firm grow by merging with another, similar firm?
How should growth be financed?
How should the actions of competitors be offset in order to retain or increase our
   share of the market?
How can the most suitable employees and managers be hired and retained?
How should the organization be structured to be most effective and adaptable to
   changes?

FIGURE 4-3 Problems requiring decisions related to strategic planning.

tured problem situations. The decision in Review Problem 1 on page 126 provides an example of a strategic decision that displays many of these characteristics. Figure 4-3 lists several other problem situations leading to strategic decisions.

Tactical planning. **Tactical planning** is the process of translating strategic decisions into specific operational programs, plans, and instructions. For example, strategies and broad decisions concerning advertising are translated into more detailed advertising programs and budgets.

Decisions arising from the tactical planning process therefore tend to make choices among alternative programs and to allocate resources among the various activities and functions within a firm. These *tactical decisions* are, of course, related to problem situations that are more routine and shorter term than those with which strategic decisions must deal. Usually they are narrower in scope and better structured; hence, they are more clearly understood. Middle-level man-

agers are responsible for making most tactical decisions, although lower-level managers may be involved in making certain tactical decisions that are very short term in nature. Figure 4-4 lists problems that typically lead to tactical decisions.

Control Processes

Control consists of (1) measuring and evaluating the performance of planned and implemented activities and (2) taking corrective actions when necessary. Thus, control is essentially a regulatory process. Control is related to planning, since it incorporates planned criteria within the process. However, whereas planning is future oriented, control is present oriented.

A central feature of the control process is feedback. In fact, control processes are often referred to as feedback control systems. **Feedback** is the information output of an operation that returns ("feeds back") to the operation (or its regulator) as an input. Feedback therefore provides the means for

What should be the specific advertising program for next year?
Where should new product Y be test-marketed during the spring season?
How should the working capital needs be met?
How should department D be organized for maximum productivity?
What prices should be estabished for the respective products?
What steps should be taken to improve production efficiency next month?
At what points and how often should the quality of products be checked?
What new research projects should be started this year?
What should be the maximum and minimum inventory levels and reorder point for
  item Q?
What should be the plant maintenance schedule for next month?
What should be the production schedule for this month?
Which special orders for products at below the usual price should be accepted?
Should product X be manufactured or purchased from an outside supplier this
  year?
Which orders should be shipped the rest of this week?

FIGURE 4-4   Problems requiring decisions related to tactical planning.

deciding when corrective actions (i.e., control-oriented decisions) are necessary.

A typical control process or system consists of six elements: (1) a factor being controlled, called the characteristic or performance measure, (2) an operation or operating process that gives rise to the characteristic, (3) a sensor element that detects the actual state of the operating process, (4) a criterion or benchmark against which the actual state of the characteristic is to be compared, (5) a planner who sets the benchmark, and (6) a regulator or control element that compares the actual state of the characteristic against the benchmark and feeds back corrections to the operating process.

Consider a household heating system containing thermostatic control, as portrayed in Figure 4-5. The purpose of the system is to control the temperature, which is the characteristic or performance measure. Thus, the home owner (the planner) sets the thermostat reading for the desired temperature (the benchmark). The setting that he chooses depends on the relative strength of his objectives (comfort and economy) as well

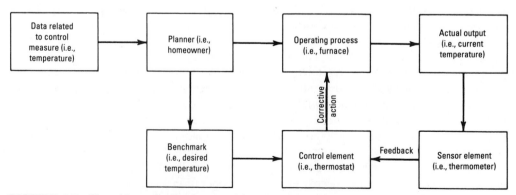

FIGURE 4-5   Closed-loop feedback control in a heating system.

as on such factors as the known cost of maintaining each added degree of temperature. Then the control process takes over. As the furnace (the operating process) generates heat, the thermometer in the thermostat (the sensor element) detects the actual temperature. Next the thermostatic mechanism (the control element) compares the actual temperature (fed to it by the sensor element) with the benchmark temperature. When the actual temperature rises above the preset temperature, the control element notifies the activating mechanism in the thermostat to shut down the furnace. Later, when the actual temperature drops below the preset temperature, the information feedback leads to the furnace being turned on again.

Control processes in business firms employ the same set of elements. Consider a production cost control process in which the factor being controlled is the production cost per unit of production. Production personnel (planners) set standard production costs (benchmarks) for the respective units of product. As products are completed in production operations (the operating process), the data processing department (the sensor element) determines the actual costs. Periodically, the cost accounting department (the control element) compares these actual costs (feedback) with the standard costs. Cost variances (analyzed feedback) are then delivered to the production decision maker, who takes corrective actions as necessary.

Control processes vary in complexity. The two control processes just described are examples of first-order feedback control systems, since we have assumed that the single benchmark (e.g., standard cost) remains unchanged. In the case of a second-order feedback control system, the benchmark changes to adjust to environmental conditions. An example of a second-order feedback control system in a business firm is the budgeting system; the budget values are revised periodically during the budget year to reflect

changes in sales estimates, material prices, labor rates, and so on. A still more complex control process is the third-order feedback control system. This type of control process, also known as a **feedforward control system** or a planning control system, attempts to predict future conditions and output values (e.g., future values of budget variances). On the basis of such predictions, these control systems anticipate future problems and suggest corrective actions before the problems occur. Examples of feedforward control systems are cash planning systems and materials requirements planning systems.

Control processes also differ in accordance with (1) the managerial levels at which related decisions are made and/or (2) the objectives they aim to achieve. Three control processes that can be so differentiated are management control, operational control, and internal accounting control. Characteristics of the first two of these control processes are described next. The internal control process, or system, is discussed in Chapter 6.

Management control.   The control process by which managers ensure that resources are acquired and used effectively and efficiently is known as **management control.** Control is most frequently exercised by middle-level managers, who when necessary make control decisions that lead to corrective actions. The process is called management control because the corrective actions relate to managers who direct lower-level responsibility centers.[3] Thus, management control (1) follows the organizational structure and (2) achieves its aims by influencing the behavior of key personnel within the firm.

[3]The domain of management control actually extends to all levels of the organizational structure. Higher-level managers exercise control over middle-level managers, and lower-level managers exercise control over departmental employees. However, the major arena of management control is located at the middle management level.

Management control can be viewed as the counterpart process to tactical planning, since both are concerned with the allocation and use of resources by the various organizational units of a firm. These two processes also overlap with respect to a key factor: the criterion, or benchmark. This key factor, often called a **performance standard** in management control situations, has its origins jointly in the planning process and in the first phase of the control process. It is then employed during the control process as the basis for evaluating the performances of the subordinate managers.

A commonly cited example of management control is drawn from the production function of a manufacturing firm. Production managers (middle-level managers) have the responsibility for controlling production-related resources. Following the objectives, strategies, and strategic plans established by higher-level managers, production managers develop a production budget that reflects volume and cost targets (performance standards). The budget is broken down by production departments (responsibility centers). Each lower-level manager, such as a department head or a foreman, is evaluated (at least in part) on the basis of variances from the budgeted volumes and costs. When a significant variance is detected, and subsequent investigation leads to the conclusion that the responsible manager's performance is inadequate, a control decision must be made. Often the control decision leads to a corrective action, such as (1) advising the lower-level manager to reassign employees, (2) admonishing the lower-level manager, or (3) transferring the lower-level manager.

Operational control. In contrast to management control, **operational control** is the process that promotes efficiency in operational tasks—that is, it focuses on technical operations rather than on managerial performances. It also differs from managerial control in that responsibility for its application primarily rests with lower-level managers.[4] On the other hand, the operational control process consists of three phases that are similar to those comprising the management control process: (1) setting standards based on tactical plans, (2) evaluating performances, and (3) making, when necessary, decisions that lead to corrective actions. Operational control is also similar to tactical planning in certain respects; that is, it deals with problems that are relatively routine, short term, highly structured, and well understood.

Examples of operational control decisions can be drawn from activities throughout a firm. For instance, a production maintenance department head learns that the rate of rejects on the production line has suddenly jumped, indicating that planned product quality is "out of control" and production operations have become ineffective. After determining the cause to be faulty machines, she makes the decision to schedule machine overhauls. Other examples of problems requiring decisions related to operational control processes appear in Figure 4-6.

Information Flows

To understand more fully the role of decision making within a business firm, we next survey the decision-oriented flows of information. With this knowledge we will be prepared to consider the complex relationships between (1) the broad array of decisions that must be made within a typical firm and (2) the information needed from the formal information system.

[4]Middle-level managers may become involved in the control of technical operations at times. Lower-level managers, on the other hand, must also evaluate the performance of their employees and hence become involved in management control. However, lower-level managers are much more involved with operational control than with management control, whereas middle-level managers are more concerned with management control than with operational control.

What should be done to reduce the usage of raw material *M* in the production process?

What should be done to improve the low labor productivity in the warehousing operations?

Which of the customers who have become delinquent in paying their accounts should not be granted additional credit?

Which employees should be reassigned to new tasks or retrained?

What changes are necessary to speed up a behind-schedule production order?

Which machine should be assigned tomorrow to complete job *X* on schedule?

FIGURE 4-6   Problems requiring decisions related to operational control.

The network in Figure 4-7 shows that the major information flows consist of (1) horizontal flows within the organizational structure, the operational system, and the information system; and (2) vertical flows among the three subsystems. Included within this network are both formal and informal information flows.

Formal Horizontal Flows

Three separate but related formal information flows have an essentially horizontal orientation. These flows connect action centers within the operational system, processing centers within the information system, and decision centers within the organizational structure.

Many of the horizontal flows carry operational information between **action centers,** centers within the operational system where physical or paperwork actions take place. A major purpose of such flows is to trigger specific actions. For instance, a sales order carries information to action centers in the production and shipping functions and gives rise to such actions as the manufacture, packing, and shipment of the ordered products.

Other horizontal flows carry information between **processing centers,** centers within the information system where data are processed and outputs generated. These flows have the purposes of monitoring actions, processing transactions, and coordinating

operations. As Figure 4-8 suggests, these flows often are generated by the accounting function and include diagonal as well as horizontal flows. For instance, the cost accounting department monitors the costs required to produce and ship the abovementioned

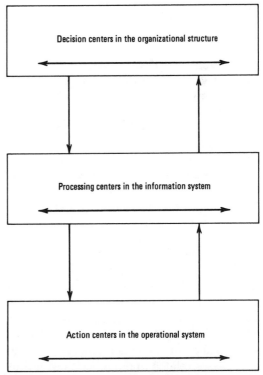

FIGURE 4-7   A simplified view of flows among action, information, and decision centers.

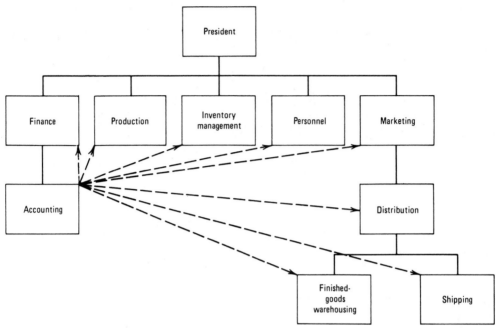

FIGURE 4-8 Horizontal and diagonal flows of information from the accounting function. Adapted with permission from Ronald M. Copeland and Paul E. Dascher, *Managerial Accounting,* 2nd ed. (New York: John Wiley, 1978), p. 9.

products, while the accounts receivable department coordinates the records concerning amounts owed by customers for such products.

Information also flows between **decision centers,** or centers within the organizational structure where managerial decision makers reside. Although not numerous, these information flows are quite important to the effective management of a firm. Strategic planning decisions, such as those that lead to annual operating budgets and to capital expansion projects, usually involve the circulation of decision-making information to managers across the organization. Certain tactical planning decisions are based on information that flows horizontally among functional managers. For instance, both marketing and production managers are involved in decisions related to the scheduling of production.

It should be emphasized that this discussion of separate horizontal information flows is for expository convenience only. As we have noted elsewhere, information flows are inextricably intertwined with physical flows and actions.

Formal Vertical Flows

Information flows both upward and downward within business firms, linking the action centers at the operational level with the numerous decision centers throughout the organizational hierarchy. Information flows upward to provide the basis for making planning and control decisions, whereas it flows downward to translate the decisions into actions. We can view these vertical flows as being three in number: an upward flow for planning decisions, a downward flow for initiating operations, and another upward

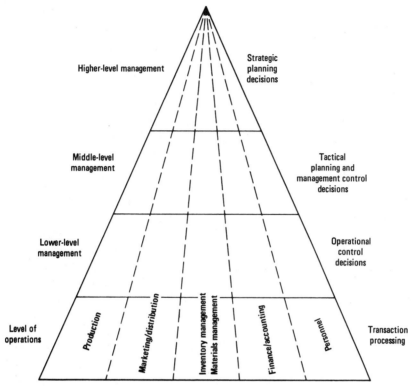

FIGURE 4-9 Levels of managerial decision making and operational functions.

flow for control decisions. As in the case of horizontal flows, we will consider each vertical flow separately. Figure 4-9, which portrays the various managerial levels, should aid us in visualizing these flows.

Upward flow for planning decisions. Much of the information used in planning decisions originates as data from transactions and internal operations. At the operational level the data may be used by lower-level managers without the need for processing. For instance, data concerning a shipment of a particular order comprise information to the shipping department manager. However, the data usually must be summarized before flowing upward to middle and higher managerial levels. Thus, data concerning ship-

ments may be summarized into a report of shipments made this week; the report is then transmitted to a higher-level distribution manager.

Information needed for tactical planning flows to the middle-level managers, whereas information needed for strategic planning flows to the higher-level managers. In some cases the same information flows to all three managerial levels, although it might be more summarized for the higher levels. Much of the information in these flows tends to be grouped by operational function. However, certain information, such as inventory on hand, cuts across functions.

After reaching the respective managerial levels, this information is available for use in decision making. As needed, it is used with information drawn from external sources and the data base in the decision process.

Downward flow. Planning decisions must be implemented throughout the organization. Therefore, decision results and plans are transmitted downward through the successive managerial levels. At each level they are translated by subordinate managers into narrower and more detailed decisions, detailed instructions, and orders. With the aid of the information system they are recorded on documents. When received at the operational level, they initiate and guide operations.

As an example of a downward flow, consider the chain of decisions for producing and shipping goods diagrammed in Figure 4-10. On the basis of information received from the operational level, from files, and from other sources, the production vice-president and other managers decide how much to produce of which products for how many dollars.[5] These decisions then flow downward to the middle managerial level. At that level, production managers and their staff planners schedule production by deciding (1) dates to begin and complete production orders and (2) quantities of materials to acquire. In turn, these decisions flow downward to the lowest managerial level. Department heads and shop foremen at that level decide on specific assignments of machines and employees within the action centers of production departments. Later, other managers at that level make decisions pertaining to the shipment of completed orders. Each of these production and shipment decisions generally triggers the issuance of appropriate instructions and orders, as well as specific operational actions.

[5] A growing number of firms are employing the participative budgeting approach. In such firms some of the information used in setting overall budget amounts would be developed at the lower- and middle-management levels and would flow upward.

Upward flow for control decisions. The third flow feeds information back to managers at the several managerial levels; it consists of summarized operational results compared with standards. In the foregoing example, differences between scheduled and actual shipping dates might appear in one of the reports communicated upward. Using such information, managers make decisions that control operations within their areas of responsibility.

Both management and operational control are maintained on the basis of this feedback information. Consider the control loops diagramed in Figure 4-11. The production manager exerts management control over the performance of the purchasing agent on the basis of comparative budget information fed back to him. At the lower level the purchasing agent exercises operational control over the processing of purchase orders; he achieves this control by reviewing each order prepared by the buyers before he authorizes its issuance by his signature. If he finds errors or violations of policy, he does not sign until they are corrected.

Numerous interrelationships exist among the information flows described in this section. For instance, both of the upward information flows are based in large part on summarized results of actual operations. Moreover, control decisions often lead to revised plans, which trigger new downward flows of instructions and orders.

Informal Flows

Not all information flows are carried by the formal information system. Managers also base decisions on information that they acquire through informal communication channels. Sources of informal information include subordinates, colleagues, employees, friends in other firms, magazines, newspapers, and suggestion boxes. For instance, a casual conversation at a business convention might yield otherwise unavailable facts.

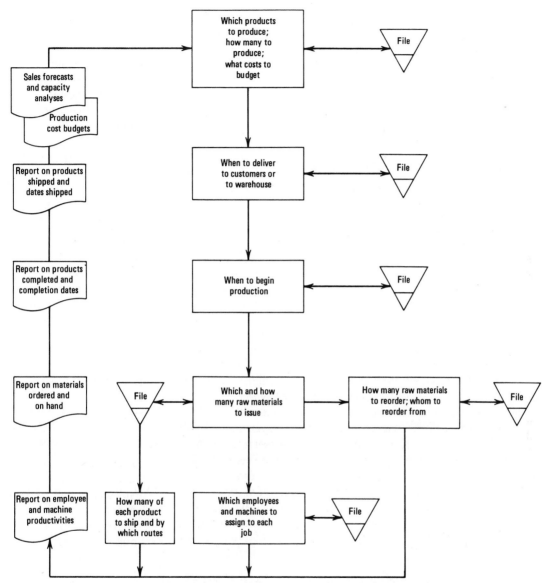

FIGURE 4-10 The chain of decisions for producing and shipping goods.

Informal information items can be critical when making certain decisions, especially those of a strategic type. For instance, the planned routes of freeways can be extremely important information when deciding where to locate facilities.

Informal flows are not always useful or dependable, however. Often the information is unstructured and not clearly understandable. It may be biased by the personal attitudes of the sources. For instance, information from an employee may be colored by the employee's feelings about his or her supervisor. Even information received from a man-

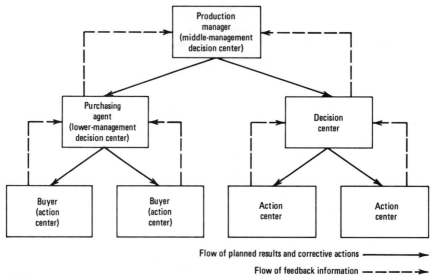

FIGURE 4-11 Multiple control loops within a firm.

ager's subordinate managers may be distorted to make them "look good" or to keep unfavorable results from being exposed.

Information Needs

The foregoing sections have emphasized that

1. Managers within any firm make a variety of decisions.
2. Information for managerial decision making generally flows by complex routes to the various decision makers located throughout the organizational structure.

In this section we are concerned with the nature of the information needed by the managerial decision makers.

Communication of Valued Information

If a firm's information processing system is to fulfill its most critical purpose, it must communicate needed information to all decision makers. *Communication* has several meanings. On one level it means that all information transmitted from the information system must arrive at the manager's office in accurate and complete form. On another level communication means that the information must be in a form that the manager can clearly understand and interpret. Furthermore, if communication is to be ultimately effective, the received information should stimulate the manager to make decisions that help achieve the firm's objectives. Communication theory is discussed more fully in an appendix to this chapter.

When communicated on the various levels just described, information clearly has value for managers and their firms. It can be viewed as a resource that provides definite benefits. If properly managed, this information resource should yield benefits that exceed the costs required to process, generate, and communicate the information.[6]

---

[6]Information values are examined within the area of study known as information economics. See the discussion in Chapter 24.

The value, and hence the benefits, of information cannot be easily expressed in quantitative terms. Nevertheless, we can specify information values on an ordinal (i.e., relative) scale. Thus, if one piece of information provides a great amount of intelligence (i.e., considerably reduces a manager's *uncertainty* concerning a particular decision situation), it has potentially high information value. If a second piece of information provides little or no new intelligence to a manager, or if it has little relevance to a decision for which the manager is responsible, this second piece has low information value. For instance, consider a situation in which a purchasing manager must choose among suppliers when ordering needed merchandise. If she receives information concerning their past performance, her uncertainty about the most suitable supplier is appreciably lessened. If this received information also leads her to place an order with the most suitable supplier, its value has been significantly high.

Information value varies not only among different pieces of information and different decision situations; it also varies among users of the information. A manager with technical background may find the specifications of a machine to be very valuable information, whereas another manager with similar responsibilities may find the same information to be incomprehensible and hence of no value.

From the foregoing comments we can see that information value and information needs are closely related. In determining the decision-making information needed from the information system, it is desirable to maximize the value of the information communicated to each manager throughout the firm. This relationship should underlie every analysis of information needs; however, it is too broad to guide the selection of specific pieces of information. To compile a detailed list of needed information, we can perform a systematic analysis and synthesis that (1)

factors information value into information content and properties, (2) structures specific information needs according to several key dimensions, and (3) assigns the needed information to each manager on an individual basis.

Information Content

Content denotes substance, such as number of units sold last week and expected number of units to be demanded next week. **Information content** is valued in relation to its usefulness in making specific decisions. For instance, a forecast of next month's sales has considerable potential value in the production planning and inventory control decisions of a manufacturer; the same forecast, however, has relatively little value in relation to decisions concerning the issuance of new capital stock.

Information content is as important to control-related decisions as to planning decisions. Therefore, a key example of information content is the benchmark, or performance measure, discussed earlier. Since performance measures are used in management control processes to reflect the performance of managers, specific measures vary from manager to manager. For instance, employee turnover might be employed as a performance measure of the personnel manager, while the materials price variance might be used in the case of the purchasing manager.

An especially critical example of information content is the **key success factor,** a measure of the overall performance of the firm (and hence of its chief executive officer, the president). Although specific key success factors vary from firm to firm, two commonly employed factors are share of the market and return on total assets.

Properties of Information

Apart from specific content, information exhibits attributes or properties affecting the quality of decision making. Significant **properties of information** include the following:

1. **Relevance,** the relationship of the information to the decision situation, as well as to the firm's objectives.
2. **Quantifiability,** the degree to which numeric values can be assigned to the information.
3. **Accuracy,** the reliability and precision of the information.
4. **Conciseness,** the degree to which the information is aggregated or summarized.
5. **Timeliness,** the currency of the information.
6. **Scope,** the span encompassed by the information.

The appendix at the end of the chapter discusses these properties more fully.

An example might clarify these properties. The rate of return on total assets has been mentioned as a key success factor. Since it is directly related to critical objectives of the firm, perhaps its outstanding property is relevance. If we observe that last year the rate of return on the total assets of the Friendly Corporation was 10.25 percent, we note that it also has quantitative and concise properties. The rate of return gives information that is broad in scope, in that it spans the financial results of the entire firm. However, it is not very timely, since the computed value was not available until a month after the end of last year and the next value will not be reported until a year later. With respect to accuracy, its preciseness is high as a result of the two decimal places in its value; however, its reliability may be somewhat questionable because of the necessity of estimating certain underlying figures.

Dimensions of Information Needs

Information needs, with respect to properties as well as content, vary significantly along such dimensions as managerial activities, managerial levels, organizational structures, and operational functions. By analyzing information needs along these dimensions, an accountant or systems analyst gathers clues concerning the information needs of individual responsibility centers and related managers.

Managerial activities. Planning emphasizes the comparison of alternatives, whereas control emphasizes the comparison of planned results (benchmarks) against actual results. Because of these different emphases, the information content needed for planning decisions differs from the information content needed for control decisions.

The key information for a planning decision pertains to the possible alternative courses of action and is future oriented. More precisely, it consists of the *differences* in *expected* consequences among alternatives, usually expressed in financial terms. For example, a decision concerning whether or not to accept a special order requires information that compares the added revenues expected from the order against the expected added costs to fill the order. If the added revenues exceed the added costs, the preferable decision based on the quantitative analysis is to accept the order. Otherwise, the preferable alternative is to reject the order.

The key information for a control decision consists of benchmarks, such as performance standards and actual operating results. More precisely, it consists of *variances* between the benchmarks and actual operating results, measured in terms that best relate to performance.[7] For instance, if the performance standard for Division A of a

---

[7]A variance arising in this process really consists of two separable variances, a performance variance and a forecasting variance, where the latter is computed as the difference between the planned result (performance standard) and the result that would have been established as the planned result if conditions at the end of the control period could have been foreseen.

firm is $100,000 in profits, and actual profits are $90,000, the variance in profits (and hence the divisional performance) is $10,000 below standard.

Apart from information content, the properties of information needed for making decisions related to strategic planning differ from those needed for making decisions related to tactical planning. Similarly, the properties of information needed for making decisions related to management control differ from those needed for making decisions related to operational control.

Strategic planning and related decisions require information that is broad in scope and qualitative as well as quantitative. For example, market share and status of customer service represent strategic information. Because the strategic planning process involves the "big picture" and the long-term future, the information should be highly summarized. Thus, estimates of total sales over the next several years are often needed. While the information should be as reliable as possible, precision is relatively unimportant. Consequently, the estimates of total sales may be rounded to the nearest hundred or thousand units. Because the process involves high-impact decisions made with due deliberation on an irregular basis, relevance is likely more important than timeliness. Thus, a measure of last year's return on total assets could be critical to a strategic decision and worth waiting for, even though it may not be available until the end of January.

Information for strategic planning is often drawn more from external sources than from internal sources. Externally obtained information may include competitors' prices and new products, industry trends, product life cycles, population shifts, economic statistics such as interest rates and income levels, technological developments, availability of resources, and governmental policies and regulations. For instance, a decision involving the addition of needed production capacity may be based on expected sales, new

plant construction costs, subcontracting prices, interest rates, availability of construction labor and materials, and anticipated actions of competitors. Seldom can the formal information system provide all of the external information needed for strategic planning.

Tactical planning and related decisions deal with problem situations that are narrower in scope, more structured, more recurring, and shorter term than those encountered in strategic planning. Information needed for tactical planning is therefore relatively narrow, reliable, quantitative, and timely. Most of the information comes from internal sources and should be available in considerable detail on a regular basis. For example, determining when to schedule a newly received rush order for production depends on accurate and up-to-date information concerning production dates already scheduled and the availability and costs of specific resources. This needed information arises mainly in the production function, except for the facts of the customer order and the promised delivery date of the ordered products; it may flow to the production schedulers on regularly prepared production schedules, inventory status reports, machine loading charts, and labor assignment sheets. The distinctions in information needs between the two types of planning decisions are profiled in Figure 4-12.

Management control requires information that focuses the major responsibilities assigned each manager. For instance, a manager might have responsibility for customer service and related costs. Consequently, he or she should receive performance measures pertaining to customer service (e.g., the number of actual complaints received) together with cost variances concerning costs incurred by his or her department. Information not needed for control should be omitted or clearly labeled. For example, the maintenance expense for equipment used in the manager's department is not needed if the

Information Property	Distinctive Aspect of Needed Information	
	Strategic Planning Decision	**Tactical Planning Decision**
Quantifiability	Qualitative as well as quantitative factors (the latter being mainly financial)	Mainly quantitative factors, nonfinancial as well as financial
Accuracy	Reflects considerable uncertainty	Relatively reliable
Conciseness	Relatively summarized	Relatively detailed
Timeliness	Time delay relatively long	Time delay relatively short
Time frame	Long-term future	Short-term future
Scope	Broad, often cutting across several functions	Narrow, usually confined to one function
Source	Largely external	Largely internal

FIGURE 4-12 Profile of information needs of two types of planning decisions.

manager does not make decisions pertaining to the maintenance or disposal of the equipment. Normally, information for management control need not be provided more often than monthly or weekly, since managerial performance is unlikely to lapse into an "out-of-control" state overnight.

In contrast, *operational control* requires information to pinpoint operations that may suddenly veer out of control. Thus, timely, detailed, and relatively accurate information is needed. Generally, the information should be quantitative, although it often will be nonfinancial in nature. For instance, the percentage of rejected parts (a quality measure) may be gathered hourly at each large production machine and compared with a standard rejection percentage. Alternatively, the number of late deliveries (a time measure) and the number of units produced (a productivity measure) might be compared daily against standards.

Additional information is needed for making a decision when either control process appears to be in an out-of-control state. This information should relate to the cause and possible decision choices or corrective actions. Excessive rejected parts, for example, may be found to be caused by a blunt cutting tool. If replacement tools are found to be out of stock, then the appropriate cor-

rective action might be to reorder tools and to reschedule production to other machines.

Managerial levels. Managers at the several managerial levels have widely varying needs for information. Figure 4.13 provides pictorial profiles of the contrasting needs between the lower and higher levels of management.

Managers at lower levels make decisions related to operational control and planning. Thus, they need detailed, accurate, timely, and quantitative information of rather narrow scope. For example, a production supervisor needs information concerning yesterday's scrap rate and worker productivity plus the current status of production orders in progress. Before leaving each day he also needs detailed instructions pertaining to tomorrow's scheduled production orders as well as information concerning available workers, machines, and materials for his area of operations.

Higher-level managers make the strategic planning decisions for the firm. Therefore, they need relatively summarized information that has a broad scope and a long-range perspective. While they need a wide variety of information—qualitative as well as quantitative, external as well as internal—these managers generally have little need for highly detailed or especially timely

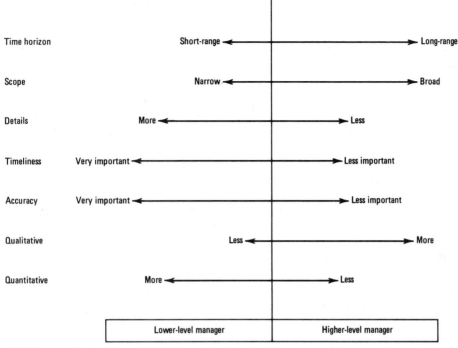

Time horizon	Short-range ◄─────────────────────► Long-range
Scope	Narrow ◄─────────────────────► Broad
Details	More ◄─────────────────► Less
Timeliness	Very important ◄─────────────────────► Less important
Accuracy	Very important ◄─────────────────────► Less important
Qualitative	Less ◄─────────────► More
Quantitative	More ◄─────────────► Less

Lower-level manager	Higher-level manager

FIGURE 4-13 Profiles of the information needs of two managers.

information. For instance, the president needs information pertaining to his or her firm's industry, competitors, market trends, sources and availability of resources, new products, key managerial performances, and current problems. Summarized statements of long-term operating results (e.g., the firm's income statement for last month and funds forecast for next quarter), key success factors and financial indicators better fit his or her needs than voluminous figures concerning yesterday's results.

Managers having middle-level responsibilities need information whose properties fall between the two extremes cited. Thus, as an aid in making decisions related to management control, a sales manager may receive fairly summarized and quantitative monthly reports concerning the performance of branch managers. To aid decision making for tactical planning, a plant manager may re-

ceive information concerning the upcoming week's production work load and availability of resources.

Organizational structures. Organizations may be structured according to operational functions, product lines, geographical areas served, and so forth. Information needs vary in accord with such structures. While few generalizations are possible, comparability is a paramount concern. Thus, in an organization structured according to product lines, the manager who is to evaluate performance should receive the same basic information concerning each product line.

Furthermore, managers in centralized organizations have information needs that differ from those of managers in decentralized organizations. Such informational differences appear especially at the middle management levels. In centralized firms middle-level managers generally have cost-centered responsibilities; thus, they need cost-oriented information. In decentralized firms middle-level managers, such as divisional managers, often have profit-centered responsibilities. Such managers may therefore make decisions concerning pricing, product development, capital investment, and financing. Thus, they have information needs that approximate those of higher-level managers.

Operational functions. Each operational function needs a distinctive set of information that accords with its assigned responsibilities. Thus, the finance/accounting function needs information to aid in raising capital, granting credit, managing working capital, and monitoring financial status and operating results. For instance, the average collection period for accounts receivable is useful information to the credit department, since it reflects on the judgment used in granting credit and the efficiency in collecting outstanding credit amounts.

On the other hand, two or more operating functions often share information needs in common. The sales forecast, for instance, is the basic item of information in preparing the budgets of several functions. It also is used in decisions concerning production scheduling, reordering of materials, and advertising. To take another example, shipment information is needed by the accounting function to prepare invoices for customers and by the inventory management function to determine the levels of inventories on hand.

Information for Individual Managers

Each manager in a firm has a unique set of information needs. The needed information depends largely on the types of decisions that he or she makes, the managerial level at which he or she resides, and the operational function to which he or she is assigned. Information needs are also affected,

however, by such personal characteristics as education, experience, attitudes, and personality.

These personal characteristics have a significant impact on information needs, since they influence the *behavior* of a manager with respect to decision making. That is, they determine the manager's cognitive style, the way the manager perceives and processes information in arriving at a decision. An area of study known as **human information processing** (HIPS) has revealed that cognitive styles vary widely among managers. One manager may employ a *perceptive* view (concern with the "big picture" and intolerance with details), whereas another may be *receptive* (attentive to details). With respect to processing, one manager may emphasize an *analytical* (logical) decision-making approach, whereas another manager may prefer an *intuitive* (heuristic) approach.

As an illustration of the preceding, consider the cases of two middle-level divisional managers within the same firm. Susan has an accounting background and enjoys solving complex problems in a methodical manner. Not surprisingly, she prefers detailed financial and cost reports. She also likes to develop and experiment with financial planning models on her office microcomputer; these models require a wide variety of data drawn from the firm's data base. Mike has a marketing background and enjoys "dreaming up" new sales concepts. He prefers highly summarized information, displayed in graphical formats. Much of the information he desires is qualitative and drawn from sources external to the data base.

Another finding of HIPS is that the quality of decisions made by human decision makers can be significantly affected by the characteristics of information systems. Thus, changing the format of information can alter the decision choice. For instance, a manager may be provided with information in graphical (rather than tabular) form. Because the manager understands the information better when it is conveyed by the graph, he or she may make a better decision choice.

Information Processing Systems

Definition

Information systems that perform information processing in order to support decision making may be called **information processing systems.** As noted in Chapter 1, the outputs from information processing flow primarily to the managers of a firm, although others, such as accounting employees and stockholders, may be recipients. Information processing systems are closely related to systems traditionally called management information systems. In recent years other labels, such as *decision support system* and *expert system,* have been applied. These various forms of information processing systems are fully discussed in Chapter 20. Furthermore, the close relationships between transaction processing and information processing systems are examined in all the chapters pertaining to transaction cycles.

Limitations

Current information processing systems exhibit limitations. Certain limitations are inherent in all processing systems. Thus, information processing systems are not capable of fully replacing managers nor of assuming their responsibilities. Other limitations are due to inadequate development procedures. Limitations of this type include

1. Poorly constructed decision models.
2. Incomplete or illogical decision processes.
3. Unsuitable or insufficient performance measures and decision criteria.
4. Omitted information (e.g., qualitative factors) needed in decision processes.

5. Overly detailed or largely unanalyzed output information, which may lead to information overload.
6. Untimely or misdirected flows of output information.

Concepts introduced in this chapter and its appendix provide the guidelines by which most of these limitations may be overcome. Applying the concepts involves techniques drawn from measurement theory, decision theory, information analysis, and organizational analysis. Computer technology, which is discussed in Chapter 5, also contributes greatly to the improvement of information processing systems.

Summary

Information processing is concerned with providing information for managerial decision making. In order to design information processing systems, accountants and information analysts must be familiar with managerial activities.

Managers are responsible for setting a firm's objectives and then making decisions to achieve these objectives. Their two major activities are planning and control, each involving the making of decisions. Among the variety of decisions made by managers are programmed, nonprogrammed, and semiautomatic decisions, resource-oriented decisions, and function-oriented decisions.

Most business decisions can be made via a systematic process that consists of recognizing the existence of a problem, defining the problem, determining alternative courses of action, evaluating these alternatives by means of a decision model, selecting the best alternative, converting the decision choice into action, and following up.

Planning consists of deciding what courses of action (plans) should be followed and how to put the plans into effect. Strategic planning involves the establishment of objectives and strategies, as well as making decisions concerning broad, nonroutine, complex, and long-term problems. Tactical planning follows from strategic planning and deals with problems that are relatively routine and short term in nature.

Control consists of regulating the operations of a firm and its use of resources in accordance with established plans. A typical control process includes six elements: a factor being controlled, an operating process, a sensor, a planner, a benchmark, and a regulator. The control process within a firm usually involves feedback loops, although feedforward systems are also employed. Management control evaluates the performance of managers to determine that resources are being efficiently and effectively utilized. Operational control focuses on operations in which technical procedures rather than managerial performance are important.

Information flows horizontally within a firm among operational functions, processing centers, and decision centers. It also flows vertically upward from the action centers at the operational level to the several managerial levels and downward from the decision centers to lower-level decision centers and finally to the action centers. Upward-flowing information aids in making planning decisions and in feeding back the comparative results for use in control decisions. Downward-flowing information implements the decisions by providing instructions and orders. Informal flows supplement the formal flows of information.

Managers of a firm need information to aid in making planning and control decisions. In determining specific information needs, an information analyst attempts to maximize the value of information communicated to every manager in the firm.

Information processing systems perform information processing in order to support decision making. Current information processing systems exhibit certain limitations, many of which can be overcome by computer technology and techniques pertaining to measurement, decisions, information, and organizations.

APPENDIX TO CHAPTER 4

Communication and Information Theory

Information must be communicated to users if it is to be employed effectively for some purpose. To be useful, it must also possess certain desirable properties. This appendix briefly examines the underlying theory of communication and several key properties of information.

Communication Theory

The foundation of information theory rests essentially on the mathematical theory of communication.[8] **Communication** consists of conveying information from a source via a channel to a receiver or user.

Communication has three levels: a technical level, a semantic level, and an effectiveness level. On the **technical level** the objective is to transmit accurately the symbols by which information is expressed. On the **semantic level** the objective is to convey the

---

[8]Claude E. Shannon and Warren Weaver, *The Mathematical Theory of Communication* (Urbana, Ill.: The University of Illinois Press, 1949).

precise meaning to the user of the information. On the **effectiveness level** the objective is to stimulate desired actions or behavior via the information conveyed.

Achieving perfect communication is difficult, however. One of the most significant problems is **noise,** or undesired effects. At the technical level noise is usually caused by interference or insufficient capacity of the transmission channel, and it may result in inaccurate, garbled, or lost symbols. At the semantic level noise may be caused by distorted, biased, or incomplete reports; it may lead to confusion or lack of complete understanding.

Noise may be overcome in various ways. At the technical level the grade of transmission channel may be improved. At the semantic level the information may be presented in a more understandable mode; for instance, graphs may be used instead of statistical tables and account titles instead of account codes. **Redundancy,** the repetition of key portions of messages and reports, may be used at both levels to counteract noise. The following telegraphic message sent home by a college student contains an example.

Dear Dad. Please send $100. Repeat $100.
Love, Junior.

Properties of Information

Information and information systems exhibit a wide variety of properties, as reflected in a list compiled by an authoritative group of accountants.

1. Relevance/mutuality of objectives.
2. Accuracy/precision/reliability.
3. Consistency/comparability/uniformity.
4. Verifiability/objectivity/neutrality/traceability.
5. Aggregation.
6. Flexibility/adaptability.

7. Timeliness.
8. Understandability/acceptability/motivation/fairness.[9]

This list includes some properties, such as verifiability and objectivity, that are of primary concern to external users. Since the emphasis in this book is on such internal users of information as managers, we have modified the list somewhat.

Relevance

Relevance relates to the objectives of a firm and depends on the use to which information is to be put. Thus, relevance is a fundamental criterion that governs the usefulness of other information properties. For instance, the information concerning sales for the past week is relevant to a sales manager because it relates to the sales growth objective of the firm and is summarized (i.e., has the property of conciseness). Relevant information usually has predictive value. By comparing the weekly sales total with next week's sales target, the sales manager can make decisions concerning sales.

Quantifiability

Quantifiability is the property that assigns numeric values to events and objects. Quantification is normally employed within a measurement process consisting of four steps: (1) deciding what to measure, (2) selecting a suitable measurement scale, (3) ascertaining the state of an event or object, and (4) using the resulting measure. For example, supervisor Jack Dawkins decides to evaluate the productivity of his typists by measuring their typing rates and comparing the actual rates to average rates compiled during this

[9]Report of the Committee on Concepts and Standards—Internal Planning and Control," in *Committee Reports: Supplement to Vol. XLIX of the Accounting Review* (Sarasota, Fla.: American Accounting Association, 1974), p. 83.

year. He observes (via his information system) that Mary Jones types 3200 words during a one-hour stint (the event). Upon learning that this typing performance is 200 words per hour above the average, Jack commends her for excellent productivity.

The degree of quantifiability depends on the measurement scale that is employed. Arranged in ascending order of measuring capabilities (and hence quantification), four levels of scales are (1) the **nominal scale,** which classifies information concerning an event or object (e.g., a fire caused damage to our home; John is intelligent); (2) the **ordinal scale,** which provides a relative comparison (e.g., a fire caused more damage to our home than to the home down the block; John is more intelligent than Mary); (3) the **interval scale,** which assigns a numeric value (e.g., a fire caused $10,000 damage to our home; John has an IQ measure of 130); and (4) the **ratio scale,** which provides computed values (e.g., a fire caused damage valued at one-fourth the cost of our $40,000 home; John has an IQ measure 10 points above the average of his class). On the basis of these definitions, it is now clear that Jack used the interval scale in measuring the observed typing rate and the ratio scale in evaluating the typing performance.

The typing example may be described as a **fundamental measurement** process, since the actual typing rate of 3200 words per hour was determined by direct observation of the typing event. Fundamental measurements may be contrasted with **derived measurements,** which are determined only through the processing of other measurements. Derived measurements, such as sales forecasts, standard costs, real estate appraisals, and accounting profits, are very necessary to business operations, although they are beset with measuring problems. For instance, projections such as sales forecasts usually contain forecast errors caused by uncertainties in the future and biases of the forecasters. Moreover, certain derived measures (e.g., ac-

counting profits) used as surrogates for desired events or objects (e.g., "business success") often are not fully satisfactory measures.

Information not capable of being measured is labeled as qualitative in nature. Many decisions made by managers, especially at the higher levels, are based in part on qualitative information. Sometimes information that appears to be qualitative in nature, such as employee morale and the public reputation of a firm, can be measured on nominal and ordinal scales.

Accuracy

Information that is free from errors and precise is described as accurate. Information is more useful to managers if they have faith in its accuracy (that is, its quality).

A variety of errors can easily occur, however, when data are being measured and processed. Measuring errors may occur when inventory is being counted; forecast errors may occur when future values are estimated. Errors may also occur with respect to qualitative information, as when an employee mixes up the facts in reporting a breakdown or when an employee enters an incorrect product name on a sales order. Finally, errors may occur when measurements normally made are omitted, such as when a sale is not recorded.

Accuracy can be increased through greater care in gathering and processing data and in transmitting information to users. Controls and security measures built into the information system represent one effective way to obtain more accurate information. Redundancy in messages and reports represents another way to reduce errors.

Conciseness

A variety of details concerning numerous individual events and operations is captured and processed by the information system of a typical firm. However, humans are limited in the quantities of information they can use effectively. Therefore, information must often be reduced (made more concise) before being presented to human users. The greater the reduction of information, the greater the saving in space needed to present the information and the time required to digest its meaning.

Conciseness can be achieved by various methods. One method employs the use of summarizing accounts within the framework of the accounting cycle. This method leads to the preparation of financial statements and accompanying summaries. Another method employs the managerial levels within the organizational structure as a summarizing mechanism. Reports are prepared for each higher level by summarizing the information contained in like reports for the level just below. A third method consists of drawing inferences from a body of opinions. For instance, a consensus figure concerning the expected rate of inflation for the coming year may be drawn from the results of questionnaires submitted to a large group of economists.

Conciseness is not always a desirable property of information. Because it blurs the identifiability of individual events, conciseness causes an information loss that may limit the uses of the available information. Thus, summarized sales and payment information is not sufficient for evaluating the creditworthiness of individual customers.

Timeliness

Information that is too old may be of little use and value. In the fast-paced situations faced by most modern business firms, users of information often need to be aware of very recent events.

Timeliness has two related facets: frequency and delay. Both are governed essentially by the design of the information system. Frequency indicates how often information is updated and is measured as the interval of time between two successive reportings of like information. For example, information needed in a volatile product-quality-control situation may require a reporting frequency of one hour. By contrast, the frequency of information summarizing a firm's overall operating results may be as seldom as a month or even a quarter. Delay is the length of time that expires after an event until the related information reaches the user.[10] Information generated by a firm's information system might have delays ranging from a few seconds to several weeks. A chemical firm, for instance, may employ automated gauges and meters that receive open or shut signals from process control computers within seconds, whereas its managers and owners may wait several weeks after the end of a year until accounting statements arrive.

The **age** of a particular item of information is related to both frequency and delay if the item appears in periodic reports. For instance, with a weekly reporting frequency and a delay of three days in issuing the report, an item could be as much as 10 days old when a user receives the information. To be useful, information must be received soon enough for needed corrective actions to be effective. Although time limits are difficult to set, it is clear that in no case should the delay exceed the reporting frequency.

Another time-related property is the **time frame** of information, the point in time or period of time with which an item of information can be identified. For instance, at the close of business on November 1, 1989, the cash balance was $10,000; for the year ended December 31, 1989, the net income was $100,000. Time frames such as months or years allow comparisons to be made between like items of information.

---

[10]**Response time** (the length of time from an event until some response is made by the recipient of information) is often used instead of delay time.

Scope

The span of activities or responsibilities encompassed by an item of information denotes its scope. Information may be broad or narrow in scope. A firm's overall sales would be broad in scope compared to the sales of any of its 12 product lines. Information becomes more discriminating as its scope narrows.

Related to the concept of scope is the concept of **information correlation.** Just as units within an organizational structure combine at higher managerial levels to form broader spans of management, items of information combine to form items having broader scopes. The sales of each sales office within a territory, for instance, combine to yield the total sales for the territory; in turn, each territory's sales combine to yield the sales for the entire firm. The concepts of scope and correlation underlie the variety of segmented reports prepared by the information systems of many firms.

Other Properties of Information

Among other properties of an item of information are source and mode of presentation. The **source** of an item of information is its point of origination. With respect to a firm, an item originates at a point either internal or external to the firm. The **mode** of presenting items of information concerns their form of appearance. Typical modes include narrative, tabular, and graphical presentations.

Review Problems with Solutions

Problem 1 Statement

Hippo Co. is a large department store in downtown Denver. Ms. Carlene Franks, the treasurer, receives a phone call from the president, who says, "We have a problem. Our fleet of delivery trucks is no longer ade-

quate, because of our continued growth in sales and the flight of many of our customers to outlying suburbs. Roger, our marketing manager, feels we should take prompt action. We've discussed the possibility of acquiring new trucks. I'd like you to look into the problem, including the financing aspects."

Ms. Franks begins the definition of the problem by reviewing relevant objectives. The Hippo Co. stresses customer service. Part of this service consists of prompt customer deliveries. Another objective emphasizes economy in all activities, including the delivery of customer packages and the financing of capital acquisitions. She concludes, therefore, that the decision should (1) minimize total delivery costs while (2) ensuring prompt deliveries. These two measures represent the overall criteria by which the decision choice will be judged. (Note that she does *not* narrowly state the criteria to be the acquisition of funds promptly and at the lowest interest rate. Therefore, she widens the range of possible actions beyond the acquisition of new delivery trucks.)

Next Ms. Franks considers constraints, assumptions, and the planning horizon. The first constraint pertains to the decision deadline, which, because the matter is urgent, she sets at one week. Next she eliminates the possible solution of issuing common stock. Company policy forbids this method of financing, since Hippo Co. is family owned. Then she ascertains that available garage space is limited to only one dozen more trucks. Any additional trucks would have to sit unprotected or would require additional garage space. Her assumptions are that sales will grow at the same rate as in recent years and that interest rates will remain at about the same level for the foreseeable future. Finally, she specifies the planning horizon to be three years, the estimated life of delivery trucks.

As the final aspect of problem definition, she gathers relevant data (with the aid of the accounting department). The facts gathered include the acquisition cost of each truck, the terms of sale, the operating costs of similar trucks, the availability of drivers in the labor market, the current financial status of the store, the current interest rate, and the rates charged by commercial delivery services in the area.

Ms. Franks next lists the following courses of action:

a. To purchase trucks by borrowing funds from the local bank on a long-term note.

b. To lease trucks and pay out of current revenues.

c. To contract with a commercial delivery service.

She also considers briefly the alternative of factoring accounts receivable, but discards it as involving too high a cost for funds.

She then determines that a decision model can be developed in explicit terms, since most of the factors are quantitative in nature. Therefore, Ms. Franks sets to work and has a completed model in a matter of hours. Her model relates the financing costs, the initial and operating costs pertaining to the trucks, the costs of added garage rental, and other relevant costs. Although none of the alternatives will incur all of these costs, the model is sufficiently general to apply to all. That is, it enables all of the alternatives to be compared on the basis of the first criterion—minimized total delivery costs (expressed at present values).

Furthermore, it enables the second criterion, prompt delivery service, to be incorporated in the decision model via the values of key factors. That is, the operating costs of acquired trucks in the first and second alternatives and the contract price for a commercial delivery service in the third alternative can be computed under the assumption that one-day delivery service is provided.

Thus, Ms. Franks uses the newly developed decision model to determine the total delivery costs, at present values, for the four alternatives. She finds that contracting with a commercial delivery service involves the least cost over the three-year planning horizon. The purchase of trucks involves the next lowest cost. She then meets with the president and marketing manager, since all three managers must agree on the final decision. After considerable discussion, in which nonquantitative factors are added to the quantitative results, they reach this decision: The commercial delivery service alternative should be rejected and the alternative involving the purchase of trucks should be selected.

Their reasoning in reaching this decision is as follows: In spite of incurring the lowest cost and providing a contractual guarantee of prompt service, the commercial delivery service alternative is not suitable. Its acceptance would conflict with objectives relating to the store's public image and control over its activities. On the other hand, purchasing and using its own labeled trucks enhances both these objectives while incurring only relatively small added costs. By means of the latter alternative the store preserves its image as a personalized messenger service as well as a merchandiser of goods. It also retains control over the truck drivers, so that instances of discourtesy and unreliability can be corrected easily.

With the concurrence of the president, Ms. Franks prepares a schedule of all required activities. For instance, the first activity she lists is to notify all managers and employees of the decision, the next step is to contact the bank officials, and so on. Beside each activity she notes the expected completion date. As each activity is executed, she inserts the actual date of completion.

After the delivery trucks are acquired, the appropriate managers receive periodic reports. Ms. Franks receives reports concerning loan repayments. The marketing manager receives reports indicating the level of operating costs and the number of complaints about delivery service. If the actual level of operating costs rises significantly above predicted costs, the marketing manager will investigate and take necessary cost-reduction steps.

Required

Identify the several steps of the decision process that are illustrated in this problem situation.

Solution

STEP	PARAGRAPH
1. Problem recognition and definition.	1, 2, 3, 4
2. Determination of alternative courses of action.	5
3. Evaluation of alternatives	6, 7, 8
4. Selection of best alternative.	8, 9
5. Implementation of decision choice.	10
6. Follow-up of decision results.	11

Problem 2 Statement

George Morrill is the purchasing manager for Tolliver Electronics, Inc., an Amherst, Massachusetts, manufacturer of high-quality electronics products. Before becoming purchasing manager, he was an electronics technician and quality control supervisor.

Among decisions made by George are the following:

a. Selecting the suppliers from whom to buy parts and subassemblies (tactical planning decisions).

b. Establishing purchasing policies (strategic planning decisions; to be made together with higher-level managers within the firm).

c. Hiring and evaluating supervisors, buyers, and other purchasing department personnel (management control decisions).

d. Negotiating purchase contracts (tactical planning decisions).

Required

a. Describe briefly how George would determine his information needs.

b. For one of the foregoing decisions, list needed items of information and required properties.

c. Note any other information that should be provided to George.

d. Describe a key report that George should receive.

Solution

a. Together with one of the firm's accountants or systems analysts, George would first list the decisions that he makes. Then they would develop information specifications for each decision, add other information needs, and design suitable reports to provide the information.

b. With respect to the selection of suppliers, George needs such information concerning each potential supplier as the expected unit prices of the parts or subassemblies, the expected lead times (time periods between the order dates and receipt dates), the quality of the parts or subassemblies, and the current availability of the parts or subassemblies. He needs this information in a summarized form at least weekly. Although some of the items, such as unit prices and availability, are subject to change, they should be as reliable as possible and thus based on up-to-date facts. The quality of parts or subassemblies should be expressed quantitatively if possible; perhaps an index rating based on a top score of 10 could be used.

c. Because of George's technical background, he also might desire key technical information concerning critical subassemblies. For instance, he may want to know the allowable tolerances between the various parts within such subassemblies, as reflected in the manufacturer's specifications. If he has this kind of information for the subassemblies available for each potential supplier, he may feel that he has a better basis for comparing quality.

To help spot upcoming supplier problems, George should receive information that shows trends in (1) the unit prices charged by each supplier for critical subassemblies and (2) the expected lead time for each supplier.

d. One key report George might receive would be a weekly report that summarizes on a single page the important factors pertaining to each potential supplier of critical subassemblies. In addition to showing the up-to-date status of unit prices, lead time, quality, and availability, the report should reflect percentage changes in unit prices and lead times.

Review Questions

4-1 What is the meaning of each of the following terms?

> Information processing
> Programmed decision
> Nonprogrammed decision
> Criteria
> Decision process
> Decision model
> Planning
> Control
> Strategic planning
> Tactical planning
> Objective
> Strategy
> Feedback
> Feedforward control system
> Management control
> Operational control
> Performance standard
> Action center
> Processing center
> Decision center
> Communication
> Information value
> Information content
> Information property
> Key success factor
> Human information processing
> Information processing systems

4-2 What are the major activities performed by managers?

4-3 In what ways may managerial decisions be classified?

4-4 Name several types of decisions under each classification plan.

4-5 Discuss the steps in the decision process, using a decision of your choice for illustration.

4-6 What are the fundamental characteristics of a planning process within a firm?

4-7 Contrast the characteristics of strategic planning and tactical planning.

4-8 Name several problems requiring planning decisions and classify each as either strategic or tactical.

4-9 Describe the elements of a control process.

4-10 Give examples of feedback control loops within a typical firm, and identify the various elements of each.

4-11 Contrast the characteristics of management control and operational control.

4-12 Name several problems requiring control decisions and classify as either management control or operational control problems.

4-13 In what ways are tactical planning and management control similar, and how do they differ?

4-14 What are the implications of planning and control processes to the design of information systems?

4-15 Describe the horizontal flows of information within a firm.

4-16 Describe the vertical flows of information within a firm.

4-17 How are managerial levels, managerial decision-making activities, and operational functions related within a firm?

4-18 What are typical characteristics of information derived from informal flows?

4-19 Identify three levels of communication.

4-20 Discuss the relationships between the value of information and the information needs of managers.

4-21 How does information content relate to decision making, and what are key examples of information content?

4-22 Discuss such information properties as relevance, quantifiability, accuracy, conciseness, timeliness, and scope. (See the appendix to Chapter 4.)

4-23 Contrast the basic information needed for planning versus control decisions.

4-24 Contrast the properties of information needed
  a. For strategic planning versus tactical planning.
  b. For management control versus operational control.
  c. For higher-level managers versus lower-level managers.
  d. For decentralized organizations versus centralized organizations.
  e. For accounting managers versus production managers.

4-25 What types of information does a firm typically need to acquire from its environment for strategic planning?

4-26 Why might two departmental managers who have identical responsibilities receive different sets of information?

4-27 Are information processing systems related to management information systems?

4-28 What are the limitations of information processing systems?

4-29 Describe a suitable approach for developing the information needs of the managers within a firm.

4-30 Why are accountants suited to serve as information analysts in analyzing information needs and in providing decision-making information to managers?

Discussion Questions

4-31 Name two or more alternative courses of action that should be considered during the decision process pertaining to each of the following problems:
  a. How to expand plant capacity.
  b. How to promote products.
  c. How to generate a firm's growth.
  d. How to reduce costs in production operations.

4-32 Describe the steps in the decision process pertaining to each of the following problem situations:
  a. Whether to buy or make a part used in a final product.
  b. Whether or not to replace a delivery truck.
  c. Whether to introduce new product A or new product B.

4-33 Discuss the control process and suitable performance measures in each of the following areas:
  a. Inventory control.
  b. Quality control.
  c. Budgetary control.
  d. Production control.
  e. Credit control.

4-34 What corrective actions (control decisions) are likely to be suitable in each area listed in question 4-33 if the operations appear to be "out of control"?

4-35 Suggest three overall objectives and three key success factors for each of the following types of firm:

- **a.** Automobile manufacturer.
- **b.** Bank.
- **c.** Public utility.
- **d.** Wholesale grocer.
- **e.** Contractor.
- **f.** Jobbing printer.
- **g.** Commercial airline.
- **h.** Hardware manufacturer.
- **i.** Life insurance company.
- **j.** Department store.
- **k.** Cosmetic goods manufacturer.
- **l.** Food manufacturer.
- **m.** Computer manufacturer.
- **n.** Hospital.

4-36 Describe a chain of decisions related to the acquisition and sale of merchandise by a retailer.

4-37 Information has been defined as data made meaningful through processing. Discuss how such information properties as relevance, accuracy, timeliness, and conciseness may modify this definition. Especially consider cases where these properties are negatively represented in an item of information (e.g., where an item is inaccurate).

4-38 Does the existence of an informal information system suggest that the formal information system should be expanded? Can certain kinds of information be better supplied by an informal information system?

4-39 Discuss the extent to which a formal information system can be expected to provide information for making the typical strategic planning decision and for making the typical tactical planning decision.

4-40 A manufacturing firm experiences a sudden drop in the level of orders from customers. However, the production manager does not receive word of this drop for two weeks. Discuss the likely impact of this delayed feedback.

4-41 What are the possible drawbacks of providing too much information to a manager? Too little information?

4-42 A firm's financial statements may be said to measure the flow and levels of resources. Explain.

4-43 The published financial statements of many firms no longer show amounts to the nearest cent (e.g., net income of $76,727.66). If the underlying accounting records provide this degree of preciseness, why not reflect the same degree of preciseness in the published statements?

4-44 Appropriate performance measures can assure that management's concerns are followed. If management was concerned about plant safety, what additional measure might be used to evaluate the safety performance of the plant manager?

4-45 The rate of return on investment, computed as net income after income taxes divided by the total assets, is one possible measure of the effectiveness with which a firm's management uses its total resources. Discuss the benefits and difficulties in employing this measure.

4-46 Discuss the trade-offs between the accuracy and timeliness of an item of information.

4-47 Describe the control loops that may be established with respect to a sales manager, the two branch managers that report to the sales manager, and the salespersons assigned to the two branches.

4-48 How do the information needs of external users differ from those of managers?

4-49 Describe the properties of each of the following items of information:

- **a.** Direct labor cost incurred in production department A last week.
- **b.** Estimated sales of product Y by competitor X next year.

4-50   Contrast the properties of information needed to make the following pairs of decisions:

a. A decision to locate a new warehouse versus a decision concerning which machine to assign a production employee tomorrow.

b. A decision concerning the possible elimination of a product line versus a decision concerning the possible promotion or reprimand of a department manager who has cost responsibilities.

4-51   For the following managers of a typical firm, describe (1) decisions for which each is primarily responsible, (2) suitable performance measures by which each decision may be evaluated, and (3) information needed by each to make decisions and to carry out assigned responsibilities:

a. President.
b. Controller.
c. Production manager.
d. Sales manager.
e. Personnel manager.
f. Treasurer.
g. Materials manager.
h. Advertising manager.
i. Credit manager.
j. Production foreman.

4-52   For each of the following problems, indicate the type of decision (by managerial activity) and the items of information needed to resolve the problem:

a. What additional productive capacity to acquire.

b. Whom to hire as the new department manager.

c. How to advertise the firm's products for the coming year.

d. How many of each product to produce during the coming month.

e. When and in what quantities to acquire materials for inventory.

f. Which machines to use in producing special orders received from customers.

g. Which sources of added financing to use.

h. Which warehouses to use in shipping special customers' orders.

i. Where to establish new sales branches.

j. How to achieve 10 percent added production this week (e.g., through overtime, second shift, hiring new employees).

Problems

4-1   Arment Co. has sales in the range of $25 million to $30 million, has one manufacturing plant, and employs 700 people, including 15 national account salespersons and 80 traveling sales representatives. The home office and plant are in Philadelphia, and the product is distributed east of the Mississippi River. The product is a line of pumps and related fittings used at construction sites, in homes, and in processing plants. The company has total assets equal to 80 percent of sales. Its capitalization consists of: current liabilities, 30 percent; long-term debt, 15 percent; shareholders' equity, 55 percent. In the last two years sales have increased 7 percent annually, and income after taxes has amounted to 5 percent of sales.

Required

List the strategic decisions that must be made or confirmed during the preparation of the annual profit plan or budget.

(CMA adapted)

4-2   The Brown Company of Coral Gables, Florida, is a medium-size regional distributor. Over the past 10 years its sales have increased more than 100 percent; however, its profits have not kept pace with the growth in sales. The lag in profits began about the time the founder died, five years ago. He had managed largely on instinct, or "by the seat of his pants," as he put it. His successors apparently have not had his intuitive sense about the business, and they have blamed the slower growth of profits upon inflation.

Other ominous signs have recently appeared. For instance, the firm borrowed funds at high rates of interest two years ago to build a warehouse. The intentions were to obtain higher sales penetration in the area surrounding the warehouse and to reduce shipping costs. However, inventory costs and operating costs at the warehouse have been higher than expected; also, the monthly payments on the loan have proved to be quite burdensome. Furthermore, the firm has been paying its suppliers immediately upon receipt of invoices, apparently because of pride rather than necessity. As a result, the firm is currently encountering a cash squeeze in addition to the profit decline mentioned earlier.

Required

Describe specific information that, if more accurate and available in a timely manner, would have helped to avert the firm's current problems.

4-3 Marval Products of the Bronx, New York, manufactures and wholesales several lines of luggage in two basic types: soft-side and molded. Each luggage line consists of several different pieces, each of which is available in a variety of sizes. At least one line is a complete set of luggage designed to be used by both men and women; however, most of the lines are designed specifically for either men or women. Certain of the lines also include matching attaché cases. Luggage lines are discontinued and introduced as

tastes change or as product improvements are developed.

The firm also manufactures luggage for large retail firms, in accordance with each firm's unique specifications. Luggage in this category is marketed under the retail firms' private labels, rather than under the Marval label.

Marval has been in business for 10 years and has increased its annual sales volume manyfold.

Required

a. Identify strategic decisions that must be made periodically by Marval with respect to new and/or existing products.

b. Identify in detail the information that Marval needs during its annual review of long-term product strategy.

c. Identify in detail the information that Marval needs to prepare its sales forecast for the annual budget.

d. Describe in detail the process involved in the decision concerning whether or not to discontinue a particular luggage line.

e. Describe the information flows that occur in relation to the development of product strategy and the preparation of the sales forecast.

(CMA adapted)

4-4 The Lippmann Manufacturing Company of Charlotte, North Carolina, manufactures two products: bingles and bangles. At the beginning of each month the production manager must decide how many of each to produce that month. Both products must undergo a two-stage manufacturing process. Each of the two stages requires the use of machines that are limited in number: that is, only so many machine-hours are available to each stage each month during the normal one-shift operations. Each bingle that is sold contributes twice as much toward covering fixed costs and generating profits as does each bangle. Each bingle requires the same number of machine-hours in the first stage as each bangle; however, each bingle requires more time in the second stage than each bangle.

Required

Describe the decision process under each of the following assumptions. Use diagrams if helpful.

a. Demand for each product is unlimited, but the firm has a policy of not producing beyond the capacity of the manufacturing process.

b. Demand for bingles is limited to a level that is less than the capacity of the manufacturing process, whereas the demand for bangles is unlimited.

c. Demand for each product is limited, although the combined demand is greater than the capacity of the manufacturing process; the firm has a policy of attempting to satisfy demand fully, even if arrangements must be made for additional production.

4-5 A regional governmental agency located in Iowa serves a nine-county area with a small office located in each county. Each office is responsible for the acquisition and storage of operating supplies used in the respective county. Therefore, each office has leased warehouse space and has one employee in charge of purchasing, warehousing, and record keeping for operating supplies.

The services provided by the governmental unit have increased substantially over the past 10 years. Consequently, the use of supplies has increased greatly. Total acquisition cost of supplies reached $5.2 million during fiscal 1989. Because the activity related to operating supplies has become so large, the agency management is considering the establishment of a central purchasing and warehousing function for the nine-county area.

Currently the total inventories for all nine county warehouses total $600,000 during an average month. The offices pay from $2.10 to $3.25 per square foot for warehouse space. The total expenditures for warehouse facilities for fiscal 1990 amounted to $275,000. Utilization of warehouse space averaged 60 percent of leased space for all offices and ranged from 45 percent to 70 percent in the individual cases.

The office in the extreme southwest portion of the nine-county region appears at this time to be the most likely choice for the location of the central warehouse and purchasing function. The greatest volume of operating supplies of all offices is used in this county. Warehousing space that should be adequate for the entire nine-county region is available because the present facility for this county, only partially leased at present, can be leased in its entirety. In addition, the rental fee would drop from $2.85 per square foot to $2.40 per square foot.

Required

a. The agency is preparing a detailed analysis to be used to reach the decision whether to continue with the present system or to centralize the purchasing and warehousing functions. Identify and briefly justify the specific economic information needed for this analysis.

b. In addition to the economic data, what qualitative factors should the governmental unit consider before the decision is made?

(CMA adapted)

4-6 Tavil Corporation has been manufacturing high-quality wood furniture for over 50 years. Tavil's five product lines are Mediterranean, Modern, Colonial, Victorian, and the recently introduced Country. Business has been very good for Tavil recently.

Part of the reason for Tavil's recent success has been the ability of Sally Grant, chief executive officer. Grant has assembled a first-rate top management team, which has now been together for four years. All major decisions are made by this centralized top management team after thorough study and review. Many members of top management were not expecting Grant's suggestion at a regular staff meeting that management should consider dropping the Victorian line—Tavil's oldest furniture line.

Grant indicated that Victorian sales had dropped in total and as a percentage of Tavil's total sales during the last three years. This conclusion was supported by the schedule shown below, which shows sales percentage by line for the last three years.

Sam Mills, vice-president of sales, commented that the data did not reflect important regional differences in the market. Total 1990 sales of Victorian, $413,000, were almost entirely in New England and New York. In fact, Victorian sales constituted over one-half of all Tavil sales in some of these locations. He indicated that more Victorian could be sold if the production department could produce it. He believes that he will lose at least two top salespersons in New England to competitors if the Victorian line is dropped.

However, Mills also conceded that many sales have been lost in other sales regions because of the long lead time on Country. Furthermore, Colonial had obviously benefited from the popularity of Country. In fact, sales in Colonial were dangerously ahead of supply.

Bob James, vice-president of production, pointed out that production of all lines was possible in existing facilities. However, he also identified several problems with the Victorian line. Victorian is the least mechanized of Tavil's lines, in part because of the high degree of detailed workmanship required. Furthermore, the equipment is old and outdated, requiring increased amounts of maintenance in recent years. The artisans needed to maintain the Victorian quality that had become Tavil's greatest asset are just not available in the labor market anymore, so it is difficult to support increased production. Several of Tavil's artisans would need special training on their new production assignments if the Victorian line were eliminated. James also indicated that margins on the Victorian line had dwindled because of the relative labor-intensiveness on that line and the high union wages of the skilled workers. Dropping the Victorian line would also cause $80,000 worth of fabric in inventory to become totally obsolete.

Grant asked Jack Turner, chief financial officer, to collect and assimilate the necessary data to aid in the evaluation of whether to keep or drop the Victorian line. As she closed the staff meeting, she stated, "Even-

| | Product-Line Sales Percentage | | | | | |
	Mediter-ranean	Modern	Colonial	Victorian	Country	Total
1988	31%	26%	21%	20%	2%	100%
1989	28	28	21	14	9	100
1990	24	26	23	10	17	100

tually we might consider expansion, but currently we must consider our present markets and resources.''

Required

Discuss the type and nature of information that Jack Turner should provide to the rest of Tavil Corporation's top management to assist in the decision to keep or drop the Victorian line. As part of your discussion, give specific examples of information that Turner should prepare and present.

(CMA adapted)

4-7 An analysis of information needs does not stop with individual managers. All of the information needed by a firm's managers must be specified. The following quotation illustrates the variety of information needed in a flour mill at the Pillsbury Co.:[11]

Each car of wheat received at one of our flour mills results in an entry which discloses the cost per unit, an official classification, an official grade, a total weight, a protein analysis, a bin location in our elevator where it is stored, a freight transit credit in most cases and several other bits of data. All of these pieces of data are collected in our central data bank.

In the course of processing this data, we derive an inventory of our wheat. Since each shipment loses its identity in the bin in which it is placed, the inventory of each bin is an average of the type, grade, protein, cost and so forth of its contents. We derive accounts payable in favor of the seller. A transit credit account and other fascinating offal of the milling accounting process also result. So by processing these data into like or related classes, we begin their transformation into information.

[11]Terrance Hanold, ''Accounting versus Management Information Systems,'' speech given to the American Accounting Association Annual Convention, August 1971. Used with permission.

Concurrently, it is hoped, sales of flour are being made. As orders are received, they are scheduled for production. The central production department allocates orders among the mills by means of a program which employs inventory data, data respecting the location of each mill, the character of wheat supply tributary to each mill, the delivery point of the order, the availability of transit billing suitable for application to its further shipment, the specifications of the flour ordered, the capacity and load balance of our mills and so on. This determination rests on data which have reciprocal as well as consecutive relationships and hence are handled best through computer-administered programs. These programs employ raw data from the data bank, as well as information derived from the accounting system. So information at one level of use is merely data at the next.

On receipt of its production schedule, the wheat committee at the mill uses another computer program to determine the optimum cost and quality of wheat mixes to be used to produce these orders. It is based on data respecting its wheat inventories and the array of orders directed to be placed on the mill. It also uses subjective data in our data bank respecting many functional characteristics of various types of wheat, their several milling qualities, yield and so forth. This program, of course, serves also to indicate the specified order in which these shipments will be manufactured.

The wheat procurement department is advised of the planned depletion of stocks by kind, grade and amount. So having a view both of the kinds and qualities of wheats consumed, of the future orders received or anticipated for milling at that location and the destination points, it makes plans for purchasing wheats in the market of the predicted type, grade, protein, origins, destinations, etc. Again, in making this decision, accounting information is used in combination with a great deal of historical crop and sales data.

Through these processes, an immense amount of market data accumulates respecting the total and seasonal uses of present and potential customers by product and by delivery point. Employing models of several kinds, the marketing department can determine the most profitable mix of products to sell, to whom and at what destinations and by sales periods. In consequence, it is able to assign specific targets by time period, by customer and by product.

Finally, the general management in flour milling is able to make medium term forecasts, taking into account estimates of wheat supplies by origin, type, cost, estimates of the effect of these elements on prices, margins, volumes and product mix by market area. By varying the data and assumptions, they derive alternative strategies to fit changes in wheat supplies, transportation costs, competitive action and other contingencies. Necessary capital investments, distribution networks, sales force assignments, and personnel requirements are also indicated.

What we see here briefly and simplistically is the transformation of data to information for use in immediate departmental actions through the injection of the functional intelligence of that department. As each informational component is successively woven into other data processed through further functional methods and intellectual disciplines, we ultimately reach a system complexity and a volume and variety of informational flows which begin to match the needs of the general or executive management. Only at that point do we begin to justify the label of a managerial information system.

Required

a. Identify all decisions noted in the foregoing quotation, and classify each as related to strategic planning, tactical planning, or operational control.

b. Discuss the difficulties likely to be encountered in the foregoing situation with respect to decision making.

4-8 SharpEdge, Incorporated, is a manufacturer of cutlery and hand tools that are sold to retail hardware stores. SharpEdge also manufactures a line of industrial-quality tools that are sold to commercial establishments. The company's single manufacturing plant and corporate headquarters are located in the midwest. Regional sales offices and company-owned warehouses are located on the east and west coasts and in the south.

SharpEdge initiated a new monthly closing and reporting procedure for calendar year 1990. The books are always closed on a Friday. In addition, each quarter consists of two four-week months and one five-week month; the five-week month is always the middle month of the quarter. Thus, each month for internal reporting purposes is not necessarily the end of the calendar month, and each four- or five-week reporting month may include days from two calendar months. The monthly reports and schedules are to be prepared and ready for the executive management meeting, which is held on the Friday following the monthly closing date. Prior to these changes, SharpEdge closed its books on the last day of each month, and the executive management meeting was not scheduled until all data were compiled. This frequently resulted in the executive management meeting being held as late as three weeks after the closing date.

When the new closing procedure was implemented, SharpEdge's accounting department had to implement some artificial cutoffs in order to assure that the monthly reports would be completed for the executive management meeting. The schedule that was implemented is outlined as follows:

- Sales data from the regional offices are telexed to headquarters on the Monday morning following the closing date. Rather than wait for data regarding returned sales as was previously done, gross sales data are submitted by the regional offices. The gross sales are adjusted for returns during the closing procedures for the next month.

- Cash receipts are deposited daily. However, a lock-box system is employed for the eastern, western, and southern regional sales offices, and this lock-box report is not received at corporate headquarters until Monday afternoon for the preceding week. Thus, the last week's cash receipts from these three regions are estimated. The cash receipts for the midwestern region are available through the Thursday immediately preceding the Friday closing date.

- Hourly personnel (all manufacturing and clerical support in the administrative offices) are paid weekly. The payroll is run on Wednesday and distributed on Thursday for the prior week. Thus, actual payroll data for these people are not available for the last week of each month. Administrative personnel are paid monthly on the last calendar day of the month; however, monthly salary is known and is included as of the monthly closing even if the payment date is after the designated monthly closing.

- The manufacturing records are updated on Thursday of each week after the payroll is completed. Thus, the actual manufacturing data are not available for the last week of the monthly period.

- All payments on account are paid out of corporate headquarters. All payables are entered into the accounting system each week on Wednesday. The payables represent all transactions that have been received from Wednesday of the prior week through the following Tuesday. Thus, three days of payables are not recorded during the last week of each monthly period.

Required

a. SharpEdge has elected a quarterly reporting period consisting of two four-week periods and one five-week period. Discuss the advantages of this type of schedule.

b. The accounting department of SharpEdge, Incorporated, must make several adjustments to accommodate the new monthly reporting and closing procedures. Explain why SharpEdge's top management is likely to accept these limitations in the monthly operating reports and results.

c. For each of the data constraints described in the question, discuss how errors in the estimates implemented by SharpEdge's accounting department could affect the current asset and/or current liability account balances on the company's Statement of Financial Position.

(CMA adapted)

4-9 *Selected Small Firm (A Continuing Case)* For the small firm that you selected in Chapter 1 (see Problem 1-7), complete the following requirements:

a. List key objectives, strategies, and decisions; classify each decision according to managerial activity and responsible manager.

b. Diagram a decision chain.

c. Diagram the major flows of information throughout the firm, including those that form control loops.

d. List the content and key properties of information needed for making the decisions listed in **a** and for detecting problem areas.

Suggested Readings

Aaker, David A. "Organizing a Strategic Information Scanning System." *Califor-*

nia Management Review (Jan. 1983), pp. 76–83.

American Accounting Association. "Report of the Committee on Concepts and Standards—Internal Planning and Control." In *Committee Reports: Supplement to Vol. XLIX of The Accounting Review.* Sarasota, Fla.: 1974, pp. 79–94.

Berdine, W. R., and Brickner, W. H. "Strategic Planning and Attributes of External Information." *Managerial Planning* (Jan.–Feb. 1976), pp. 17–21.

Carr, Arthur. "Accounting Information for Managerial Decisions." *Financial Executive* (August 1977), pp. 40–44.

Davis, Gordon B., and Olsen, M. *Management Information Systems: Conceptual Foundations, Structure, and Development.* 2d ed. New York: McGraw-Hill, 1985.

Demski, Joel S. *Information Analysis.* 2d ed. Reading, Mass.: Addison-Wesley, 1980.

Eilon, Samuel. "What Is a Decision?" *Management Science* (Dec. 1969), pp. B172–B189.

Fredericks, Ward A. "A Manager's Perspective of Management Information Systems." *MSU Business Topics* (Spring 1971), pp. 7–12.

Gorry, G. Anthony, and Scott-Morton, Michael S. "A Framework for Management Information Systems." *Sloan Management Review* (Fall 1971), pp. 55–70.

Helbriegel, Don, and Slocum, John W., Jr. "Managerial Problem-Solving Styles." *Business Horizons* (Dec. 1975), pp. 29–37.

King, William R., and Cleland, David I. "The Design of Management Information Systems: An Information Analysis Approach." *Management Science* (Nov. 1975), pp. 286–297.

Libby, Robert. *Accounting and Human Information Processing: Theory and Applications.* Englewood Cliffs, N.J.: Prentice-Hall, 1981.

Lin, W. Thomas, and Harper, William K. "A Decision-Oriented Management Accounting Information System." *Cost and Management* (Nov.–Dec. 1981), pp. 32–36.

Mintzberg, Henry. *Impediments to the Use of Management Information.* New York: National Association of Accountants, 1975.

Pakrul, Herbert A. "A Decision Maker's Perspective on How the Accounting System Can Meet User-Needs." *Cost and Management* (Sept.–Oct. 1977), pp. 12–19.

Radford, K. J. "Information Systems and Managerial Decision Making." *Omega* (No. 2, 1974), pp. 235–242.

Rockart, John F. "Chief Executives Define Their Own Data Needs." *Harvard Business Review* (Mar.–Apr. 1979), pp. 81–93.

Wilkinson, Joseph W., and Kneer, Dan C. *Information Systems for Accounting and Management: Concepts, Applications and Technology.* Englewood Cliffs, N.J.: Prentice-Hall, 1987.

Wilkinson, Joseph W. "Specifying Management's Information Needs." *Cost and Management* (Sept.–Oct. 1974), pp. 7–13.

After studying this chapter, you should be able to do the following:

Identify the impacts of computers on information systems, managerial decision making, organizations, and accounting.

Describe the functional components of various computer hardware.

Describe the functions and relative advantages of various computer software, particularly systems software and application software.

Identify several trends with respect to computer hardware, software, and applications.

Chapter **5**

COMPUTER TECHNOLOGY

Computers are becoming increasingly indispensable to an increasing number of business firms. Although they do no more than manipulate bits and digits, computers greatly enhance the capabilities of information systems. Most managements believe that computers provide ample value, in spite of computer-related costs that may approach 10 percent of sales.

In this chapter we briefly explore the roles of computers in business information systems. Then we examine the computer **hardware** (physical equipment) and **software** (instructions directed to computers) that comprise today's computer-based information systems. Finally, we review the traditional and emerging **applications** (uses) for computers in business settings.

Impacts of Computerization

Very few aspects of a firm remain unaffected when computers enter the picture. In addition to affecting the processing and storage of data, computers significantly influence the ways that a firm organizes, makes decisions, and utilizes its accounting function.

Impact on Information Systems

For centuries the information systems of firms have been dominated by human processors. Although assisted by such devices as adding machines and cash registers, clerks and bookkeepers have performed the various system tasks manually. During the late 1940s and early 1950s, however, these manual or human-oriented information systems began to be transformed into **computer-based,** or **human–machine,** systems. Machines such as computers began to work together with humans in many firms to perform data processing tasks. Since that time period, computers increasingly have taken over those information and data processing tasks for which they are better fitted than humans. On the other hand, humans have continued to perform those tasks for which they are better suited than computers.

Advantages of computers.   Computers are able to process data more effectively than humans. Not only can they perform computations with lightning speed, but they also are extremely accurate and expansive processors. By comparison, humans are very slow, error-prone, and limited processors. Thus, a computer may process hundreds of transactions in the time that a human requires to process a single transaction. A computer can process transactions all day without making a single error; a human may make an error in processing the first transaction of the day. A computer can process, without pause, complex transactions or problems involving tens or hundreds of numbers and other symbols; a human cannot easily deal with more than nine symbols (e.g., numbers) or groups of symbols at one time.[1] That is, a human is very subject to information overload.

Under certain conditions, computers are able to process transactions less expensively than humans. Although a typical computer requires a large investment as compared to a human, its speed allows it to process each transaction at a very small incremental cost. A human, on the other hand, is inexpensive to hire but much more costly in processing each additional transaction. Therefore, beyond a certain break-even volume the pro-

cessing cost per transaction is less for a computer than for a human.

Computers are more dependable processors than humans. Instead of becoming fatigued, bored, emotional, or "hung over" from late parties, computers can work tirelessly around the clock. They automatically follow sets of detailed coded instructions, called **programs,** in an exact and consistent manner. Moreover, they can flawlessly execute quite complex programs, involving comparisons and choices as well as computations.

Computers can store data more compactly than humans. Information systems that use computers can therefore consolidate much of the stored data. In the absence of computers a firm's data are scattered in file folders and drawers throughout various departments; consequently, many of the data tend to be less accessible or to be duplicated.

Computers can be more operationally efficient than humans. They can integrate transaction processing cycles and files. They can perform numerous operations in parallel, thereby minimizing peak loads. They can control complex physical processes requiring split-second timing. Together with communications networks they can tie together data and files at physically distant points. By comparison, humans are unable to handle large sequences of operations and have difficulty in dealing with complex processes, with widely scattered operations, and with peak periods.

Finally, computers together with humans can meet the information processing needs of managers better than can humans alone. Computers can help to provide reports on a more timely basis. Because of their computational power, computers can facilitate the preparation of reports. These reports may be as detailed or as selective as desired. For instance, foot-thick inventory status reports can be generated easily, as can one-page exception reports. Furthermore, computers can aid in keeping information up

[1]George A. Miller, "The Magical Number Seven, Plus or Minus Two: Some Limits on Our Capability for Processing Information," *The Psychological Review* 63 (No. 2, March 1956), p. 81.

to date. Thus, budgets can be frequently revised and analyzed for better control.

Advantages of human processors. Humans do outshine computers in three traits: flexibility, intelligence, and personality. We can perform a wide variety of tasks, changing from one to the other with relative ease. We can cope with ill-structured problems because we can perceive improbable relationships, deal with illogical facts (e.g., a million-dollar paycheck), recognize intricate patterns, and evolve imaginative solutions. Our personalities enable us to interact effectively with other humans, such as customers. Computers, on the other hand, are inflexible and unintelligent. They work well only when concentrating on a single task. They must be given fully explicit instructions and carefully formatted data. They are helpless when faced with unanticipated conditions. Only

computers in science fiction movies (such as HAL in the film *2001: A Space Odyssey*) have been known to have personalities.

Also, as suggested above, we humans have certain economic advantages over computers. Not only are our salaries less than the purchase prices or rental fees of many computers, but we can be taught fairly inexpensively to deal with complex situations and exceptional conditions. Thus, we are generally less expensive processors when transaction volumes are low and when complex situations and exceptional conditions arise.

Information-related tasks and computers. On the basis of these relative advantages and disadvantages, we can expect to find computers having large impacts on certain tasks and slight impacts on others. Figure 5-1 summarizes these impacts for a vari-

Task	Impact of Computer
Collecting and processing large volumes of routine data such as basic transactions	Large impact, because computers operate with more speed, fewer errors, more consistency, and a greater degree of integration
Storing collected and processed data	Large impact, because computers store data more compactly and generally with less duplication (Although the stored data is invisible to humans, it can be retrieved via computer instructions and reported in readable form.)
Monitoring and controlling continuous processes, such as steel cold-rolling, oil refining, and credit checking	Large impact, because computers operate without fatigue and with more rapid responses to routine problems
Answering inquiries and providing needed reports	Large impact, because computers can provide information in a timely manner and in accordance with precise specifications
Making routine decisions involving well-structured problems	Large impact, because computers can follow structured rules precisely and consistently
Processing exceptional (nonroutine) transactions	Slight impact
Setting objectives and making nonroutine decisions	Slight impact
Finding new problems requiring solution	Slight but growing impact
Designing information systems and programming computers	Slight impact

FIGURE 5-1 Information-related tasks and the possible impact of computers on each.

ety of tasks.[2] Of course, the suggested impacts apply to the average firm. For any particular task the impact will vary from firm to firm, depending on the conditions faced by a firm and the adequacy of its information system design. The impacts may also change over time. Thus, as technology leads to improved capabilities in computers, the impact on a particular task may increase.

In later chapters we shall note specific ways and instances in which computers have altered data collection, data processing, data management, data control and security, and information generation.

Impact on Organizations

The presence of computers affects a firm's organizational structure as well as its information system.[3] As we have seen, computers can process data quickly and transmit the resulting information without delay. Thus, information may be shared more widely and effectively throughout an organization. As a consequence a firm's management gains more flexibility in selecting and changing organizational structures. It may select a centralized structure, with the benefits of centralized decision making and improved coordination, without sacrificing timely information. Alternatively, it may select a decentralized organizational structure, with the consequent advantages of "flatness" and localized decision making. More

extensive use may be made of project-oriented and other transitory organizational structures; these structures can be quickly created and then easily disbanded when the projects are completed.

Computers also may affect the organizational responsibility for managing transaction and information processing. Often these activities are unified under an information systems function. This function is likely to be newly established and assigned a relatively high status within the organizational structure.

Computers are likely to have diverse effects on individual employees within firms. Many employees must learn new skills related to the use of computer technology. New types of knowledge-oriented employees, such as information analysts and modelers, may be needed. On the other hand, middle-level managers may see their job security weakened when computers are installed. For instance, some firms have thinned their ranks of middle management through firings and forced retirements. Certain duties of the released managers, such as those relating to communication and control functions, have been assumed by the firms' computer systems.[4]

Impact on Managerial Decision Making

Computers can greatly aid managerial decision making. Because of their processing speeds, they can perform extensive analyses of data in a very timely manner. When connected to computer networks, thereby forming numerous information channels, they provide managers who must make decisions with easy and direct access to the analyzed information.

Decision making and control are facilitated at all managerial levels by computers.

[2]For a clear discussion of the advantages and impacts of computers in accounting information systems, see R. Keith Martin, "The Financial Executive and the Computer: The Continuing Struggle," *Financial Executive* 45 (March 1977), pp. 26–32.

[3]See, for instance, John F. Rockart and Michael S. Scott-Morton, "Implications of Changes in Information Technology for Corporate Strategy," *Interfaces* (January–February 1984), pp. 84–95; also Lynda M. Applegate, James I. Cash, Jr., and D. Quinn Mills, "Information Technology and Tomorrow's Manager," *Harvard Business Review* (November–December 1988), pp. 128–136.

[4]See Applegate et al., pp. 128, 132, and 135.

At the lower levels managers are aided in making operational decisions and providing operational control. For instance, computers can generate timely exception reports that inform department managers when parts or supplies need to be requisitioned and in what quantities; they then can aid purchasing managers in deciding which suppliers to select and can even prepare the purchase orders for signature. At the middle levels managers are aided in making tactical planning decisions and in performing their coordinating functions. At the higher levels managers are aided in making strategic decisions and in controlling the major activities of their firms. For instance, computers can assist the president and vice-presidents of a firm in developing timely and well-analyzed budgets and in controlling the performance of the various operational functions.

The impact of computers should not be overstated, however. As we observed in Chapter 4, managerial decision making is primarily supported by information processing systems. Sound decision models, logical decision processes, and relevant information items are critical to sound decisions. Computers serve as tools to increase the effectiveness of information processing systems.

Impact on Accounting Functions

Accounting functions in many firms have also been significantly affected by the arrival of computers. The effects have been both traumatic and beneficial.

On the negative side, accounting functions have lost or been forced to share key responsibilities. Thus, the accounting functions in many firms no longer have sole jurisdiction over data processing. As mentioned earlier, this responsibility increasingly is being transferred to information system functions, as accounting functions primarily become users of information. Consequently, accounting functions are losing control over

processing resources. In fact, the ranks of accounting clerks thin when computers appear. Such accounting departments as billing, accounts receivable, accounts payable, inventory control, payroll, cost distribution, and general ledger therefore shrink, consolidate, or even disappear.

On the positive side, computers have provided considerable support to accounting functions and accounting managers. Consider these comments by one manager:

For example, I used to worry about our overdue accounts receivable. Now we have a report which indicates accounts receivable for each customer by billing date. We send a copy of this report to each of our customers every month. This eliminates a lot of calls we used to have to make.

In addition, my subordinates now follow up on routine cases so that I only have to handle the exceptional ones.[5]

Computers also are helping accountants to provide better information for managerial decision making. Furthermore, the presence of computers has not affected two key accounting responsibilities: reporting to outside parties and evaluating the performances and results of information systems.

On balance, these negative and positive effects have tended to offset each other thus far. The future net effect can be positive, however, if accountants

rise to the challenge and opportunity of the developing information technology and take the lead in information management.[6]

To become leaders in information management, accountants must become knowledge-

[5]Charles W. Hofer, "Emerging EDP Patterns," *Harvard Business Review* 48 (March–April 1970), p. 26.

[6]"Report of the Committee on Accounting and Information Systems," *Committee Reports: Supplement to Vol. XLVI of the Accounting Review* (Evanston, Ill.: American Accounting Association, 1971), p. 344.

able in the analysis and design of computer-based information systems.

Computer Hardware

Computer hardware includes the physical equipment that performs the various activities of a computer-based system. As Figure 5-2 illustrates, numerous types of mechanisms and devices and storage media comprise the hardware useful to present-day computer-based information systems. However, the essential components needed in every computer can be reduced to five: a primary storage unit, a control unit, an arithmetic–logic unit, an input unit, and an output unit. These components are depicted in Figure 5-3. A sixth component that frequently accompanies these essential components is a secondary storage unit. Our discussion of computer hardware centers around these six

components. Other hardware components are discussed in Chapters 16 and 19.

Processors

Components. As Figure 5-3 indicates, the first three of the five essential components constitute the **central processing unit** (CPU). They form the nucleus of a computer, since together they coordinate all its components, interpret and execute (perform) instructions, store data as well as instructions, and move data from one component to another. In fact, the central processing unit is often called the processor or computer because of its critical functions.

The functions of these three units are as follows:

1. The **control unit** coordinates the actions of the components within the entire computer system. While it interprets the in-

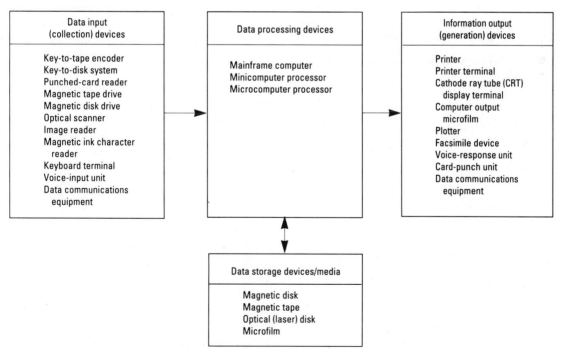

FIGURE 5-2 Computer hardware arranged by major activity.

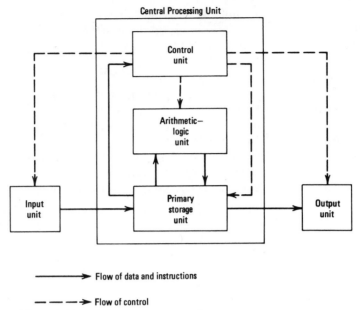

FIGURE 5-3 Major components of a computer.

structions in computer programs (software), the control unit directs other components to execute the processing steps according to such instructions.

2. The **primary storage unit,** also known as the memory unit, is the "staging area" of the CPU. Data received from input devices and program instructions are temporarily brought together in primary storage before execution. The primary storage unit later stores the processed results until the control unit specifies their destination, such as an output unit.

3. The **arithmetic–logic unit** performs basic arithmetic computations, such as addition, subtraction, multiplication, and division. It also performs such logical operations as comparing two numbers to determine whether one is equal to, greater than, or less than the other.

Primary storage features. Data and instructions are stored in the primary storage unit at specific locations. Each location has a permanently assigned **address** for reference purposes.

Data are represented at the elemental level by means of binary digits, or **bits.** A bit is capable of reflecting two values, usually either 0 or 1 (or on or off). In turn, a group of bits (usually 6 or 8) forms a **byte.** Each byte generally represents a numeric, alphabetic, or special character.

Data may be coded, with the use of bits, according to several alternative formats. Although a detailed survey of these formats is beyond the scope of this textbook, three available formats are: (1) **binary coded decimal** (BCD), (2) **extended binary coded decimal interchange code** (EBCDIC), and (3) **American Standard Code for Information Interchange** (ASCII). For instance, a zero in BCD is 100 1010, in EBCDIC is 1111 0000, and in ASCII is 011 0000. Still another format, called packed decimal, compresses two decimal numbers into a single byte. Unfortunately, these formats are essentially incompatible among different computers.

Processors move and manipulate data in

the form of **words.** A word is a unit or block of one or more bytes, although it is expressed in terms of bits. The word size of a processor is determined by the capacities of the registers used in computations and the conduits (called buses) that carry the data between components. Word sizes for current processors range from 16 to 128 bits, and even larger word sizes are expected to be in use soon.

Capacities of primary storage units are generally expressed in kilobytes (thousands of bytes) or megabytes (millions of bytes). They range widely in current processors from 640 kilobytes (K) to numerous megabytes (M).

Two major types of storage or memory are employed in primary storage units. Most of the capacity of a primary storage unit is devoted to random-access memory (RAM). Data and instructions are temporarily stored in RAM, then erased when no longer needed. Read-only memory (ROM), on the other hand, generally cannot be altered by users or programmers. (Certain types of ROM may be erased and reprogrammed, but only by means of special techniques.)

Microprograms, also known as microcodes or firmware, consist of microinstructions that are permanently fixed ("burned" or "hardwired") on a ROM chip. When a program located in RAM is being executed, the control unit initiates the appropriate microinstructions. Microprograms replace electronic circuits and/or system software routines; they have gained in favor, since they tend to reduce execution times and system costs while increasing system security.

In physical terms current primary storage units typically consist of **semiconductors,** which are on–off circuits mounted on silicon chips. Semiconductors have replaced the traditional magnetic cores of earlier computers, since they are smaller, provide faster access times, and are competitive in cost. Other storage technologies, however, are appearing on the horizon. **Bubble memory,** consist-

ing of tiny magnetic fields in a crystalline or semiconductor material, has been installed on a selective basis. This type of memory permits data to be stored with extremely high density and retains data even when power failures occur. **Charge-coupled storage devices** hold promise of providing high-density storage together with very rapid access to data.

Processing operations and times. Each instruction in a computer program is executed by a sequence of steps. First, the control unit accesses and interprets the instruction and then directs the arithmetic–logic unit to perform the processing. The period during which these steps occur is known as the **instruction time.** Second, the arithmetic–logic unit actually performs the steps specified by the instruction. This period is known as the **execution time.** Taken together, the instruction time and execution time comprise the **machine cycle time.**

Separate steps within these periods can also be associated with times. Thus, the time required to retrieve data from primary storage is called **access time;** the time required to move data from one place to another within the primary storage unit, or from one component to another, is called **transfer time** or **transfer rate.**

Times such as the foregoing may be measured in fractions of a second. A relatively slow time would be measured in milliseconds, or thousandths of a second, while faster times might be measured in microseconds (millionths of a second), nanoseconds (billionths of a second), or picoseconds (trillionths of a second). Alternatively, the speed of executing instructions may be measured as millions of instructions per second (MIPS).

Hierarchy of processors. Processors may be classified in accordance with their performance and capability. Measures generally used to classify processors include processing speed, primary storage capacity, word size, and roles within computer systems. The following set of categories suggests the current hierarchy of processors (computers):

1. **Large-scale computers,** also known as mainframe computers. These computers generally serve as the flagship computers of organizations. They can perform multiple processing tasks concurrently, and hence they also may be described as multitasking computers. Often they are host computers for networks containing a variety of medium and small computers. In some cases they are used as massive research tools for organizations having needs for extremely high processing speeds and storage capacities.

   The largest of the large-scale computers are known as supercomputers. Because they can perform from several hundred to a thousand MIPS and have machine cycle times of a few nanoseconds, supercomputers are mainly assigned to research and mathematical modeling projects. Part of their power derives from the fact that they incorporate parallel processors, so that they can process several parts of a computer program simultaneously. They also may have primary storage capacities that approach a gigabyte (one billion bytes). The most powerful supercomputers cost several million dollars.[7]

   At present, however, most firms do not own a supercomputer. Instead, a typical large or medium-sized organization might have a less powerful mainframe computer that can perform dozens of MIPS and have machine times of several dozen nanoseconds. They generally have word sizes of 64 bits and offer primary storage capacities that measure in the

dozens of megabytes. Their prices may range up to $1 million.

2. **Minicomputers,** or medium-scale computers. These can serve a variety of roles. They may, for instance, be the main computer for a smaller firm or serve as the second-level computers in large computer networks. Like large-scale computers, minicomputers are multitasking computers and can control a variety of attached input–output devices. A typical minicomputer may perform a dozen MIPS, allow a machine cycle time of dozens of nanoseconds, provide a primary storage capacity of several megabytes, and employ a word size of 32 bits. Its cost will be in the hundreds of thousands of dollars.

3. **Microcomputers,** or small computers. Included in this category are home or personal computers and small business-oriented computers. In turn, the business-oriented microcomputers can be classified as single tasking or multitasking. A single-tasking microcomputer is dedicated to one processing task during any period of time, whereas a multitasking microcomputer may be concurrently devoted to several tasks (e.g., transaction processing and word processing). Business-oriented microcomputers are suitable as the sole computers for small business firms. Alternatively, they may serve as key elements in the computer networks of somewhat larger firms.

   A wide variety of microcomputers is currently in use. However, typical microcomputers may have processing speeds of up to one MIPS or more, may provide primary storage capacities of 640 kilobytes or more, and may employ word sizes of 16 or 32 bits. Chapter 16 discusses microcomputers at length.

4. **Portable computers.** Included in this category are the full-function portables,

[7]Karen Gullo and Willie Schatz, "The Supercomputer Breaks Through," *Datamation* (May 1, 1988), pp. 50–63.

the "attaché-case-size" or "lap-top" portables, and the hand-held portables. A full-function portable, which may weigh up to 20 pounds, is equipped with all the features and capabilities of a single-tasking microcomputer. However, the display area is significantly smaller and the weight is less. An "attaché-case-size" portable typically weighs only a few pounds. Its display area, also smaller than that of a microcomputer, is a liquid crystal display (LCD); its primary storage is comprised of bubble memory. A hand-held portable, also known as a micromicrocomputer, weighs less than 2 pounds, employs a word size of 4 or 8 bits, and provides a primary storage capacity of at least 16 kilobytes. It is suitable for such dedicated applications as route accounting, inventory taking, point-of-sale transactions, and time and appointment management. All portable computers may be attached to various input and output devices and to secondary storage units.

5. **Programmable calculators.** These hand-held devices are often used simply as traditional calculators; however, because they can be programmed, programmable calculators can in effect serve as limited micromicrocomputers.

Processor enhancements. Most of the processors we have described are likely to be used in multitasking environments and to control varied computer system components. These processors need features that enhance their capabilities. Commonly employed enhancements include overlapping, multiprogramming, partitioning, virtual storage, parallel processing, multiprocessing, time-sharing, and multithreading.

1. **Overlapping.** Overlapped processing consists of performing processing, input, and output operations simultaneously within a computer system. The capability generally improves the performance and throughput of the system and its processor. The improvement may be quite significant, since without overlapping the processor often remains idle during much of the so-called processing time. If it is not waiting for data to be entered, the processor is bound by output operations or by an internal transfer of data.

Overlapping, also called buffering, is achieved through the use of such devices as channels and controllers and buffers. **Channels** are, in effect, small computers that serve as data pipelines between input–output units and the processor. They relieve the processor of the need to communicate directly with the input–output devices; they also make adjustments for differences in transfer speeds between the processor and the input–output devices, as well as take other steps to ensure that the devices are efficiently utilized. Linked to each channel are one or more **controllers.** Each of these control mechanisms maintains direct contact with a particular type of input–output device, translating and routing coded signals from the processor to each individual device, and vice versa. **Buffers** are storage areas that hold small quantities of data for processing; in effect, they serve as the "anterooms" within primary storage for the processor. Although the exact relationships among these devices differ among computer systems, Figure 5-4 portrays a typical arrangement.

2. **Multiprogramming.** The concurrent execution of two or more application programs within the same processor is known as **multiprogramming.** Programs are allotted specific intervals of time called time slices; at regular intervals a hardware clock **interrupts,** or suspends, the execution of one program, so that execution can begin or resume on another program. If the execution speed of the

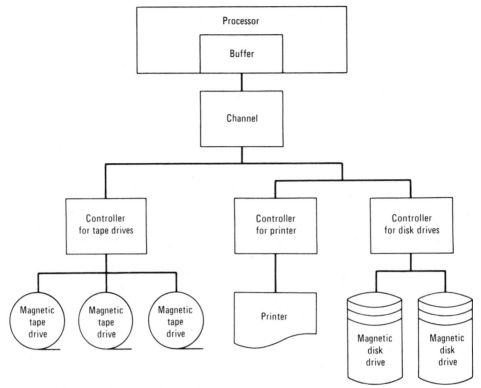

FIGURE 5-4 Devices used in overlapped processing.

processor is sufficiently fast, the processor can execute several programs and keep the attached input–output devices fully utilized. Multiprogramming is a software feature that can greatly improve the throughput and response time of a computer system. Its effect is multiplied when employed in conjunction with overlapping.

3. **Partitioning.** Considerable activity may take place in the primary storage unit of a processor. This is especially true if such features as overlapping and multiprogramming are employed. To provide adequate protection from interference, partitions or modules may be established within primary storage. Each program or data set may reside within its own partition, with strict **boundary protection** be-

tween partitions. By means of a technique known as **interleaved storage access,** each partition may be controlled separately. Thus, the processor may access and retrieve data from one partition while data are being entered into another partition from an input device.

4. **Virtual Storage.** A feature that artificially expands primary storage is known as **virtual storage.** This feature is needed when all of the programs being processed cannot fit into primary storage, a situation frequently encountered when multiprogramming is employed. By means of this feature, programs are divided into segments (called **pages**), which are stored in secondary storage. Pages of programs, and related data, are moved into primary storage as needed for execution. When a

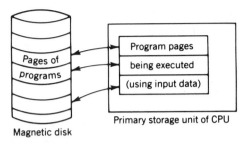

FIGURE 5-5 Virtual storage feature.

page has been executed, it is swapped with the next page needed for execution. The virtual-storage feature therefore enables programmers and users to view primary storage as virtually unlimited. It also enables the processor, especially the primary storage unit, to be used more efficiently. Figure 5-5 illustrates this feature of virtual storage.

5. **Parallel Processing.** When multiple segments of a program (or two or more separate programs) are being simultaneously executed within a single processor, the activity is called **parallel processing.** This feature allows faster processing than serial processing, in which the instructions of a single program are executed one after the other. It is also an improvement over multiprogramming, in which only one program or program segment can be processed at a single point in time. The parallel-processing feature is found primarily in supercomputers, although it is currently being incorporated into certain other large-scale computers.

6. **Multiprocessing.** Like parallel processing, **multiprocessing** enables two or more programs or program segments to be processed simultaneously. However, multiprocessing involves the use of two or more processors that share a common primary storage unit. Figure 5-6 shows a multiprocessing arrangement. Although this feature is relatively expensive, it can provide "built-in backup." If one of the

processors fails, another in the system can take over the processing tasks.

7. **Time-sharing.** A processor feature known as **time-sharing** involves the concurrent servicing of two or more independent users, each of whom is generally connected to the processor via a terminal. Each user views the computer system as serving him or her alone, and thus expects fast response times. As in the case of virtual storage, time-sharing typically is employed in a multiprogramming environment. Time-sharing is also a necessary feature of systems that provide on-line commercial computing service to subscriber firms.

8. **Multithreading.** When a processor allows multiprogramming and processes transactions promptly as they arise, it is possible for two programs to need to update the same files or to use the same data in processing. The **multithreading** feature enables two or more programs to refer to the same file or data in the same time period (although not simultaneously); thus, one program does not have to suspend processing until another program has completed its use of the data. This feature therefore improves the operational efficiency of the processor and tends to re-

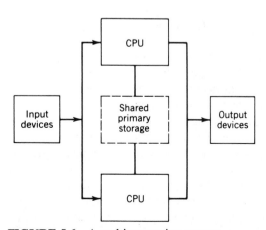

FIGURE 5-6 A multiprocessing system.

duce the average processing time per transaction.

Input–Output Devices

A large modern computer system can accept data from a wide variety of input devices and deliver information on an equally wide variety of output devices. Input data and output information handled by these devices appear on various media or in various forms, ranging from paper documents to spoken words. In addition, data are stored on various media within the computer system, either for later use in processing or for the preparation of outputs.

Input–output devices can be critical components in the design of effective computer-based information systems. For instance, transaction processing and other business applications involve large volumes of inputs and outputs but relatively little processor activity. If the processor is too powerful, it is likely to sit idle much of the time waiting for the input–output devices to complete their tasks. In such situations the computer system is said to be **input–output bound.** The remedy, of course, is to match the input–output devices and the processor carefully when designing computer-based applications.

Figure 5-7 displays an array of input–output devices (plus storage media) that are available to computer systems. When these devices are connected directly and continuously to the CPU by means of electrical conduits (e.g., cables), they are described as **on-line devices.** When the devices are used to prepare input–output media while disconnected from the CPU, they are called **off-line devices.** Terminals and magnetic disk drives are designed to be on-line devices, whereas character recognition devices and magnetic tape drives may function in either on-line or off-line modes. (Other devices not shown in the figure, such as keypunch machines and

key-to-tape encoders, can be used only in the off-line mode.) The input–output devices (including several not explicitly shown in Figure 5-7) are discussed next.

Punched-card devices. Devices known as **punched-card readers** accept input on punched cards that have been prepared by keypunch machines. **Card-punch units** are output devices that emit punched cards for use in further processing, for data storage, or for use in preparing printed outputs. Although widely used in an earlier period, these devices are employed infrequently today. An application for which they are still suitable involves **turnaround documents,** output documents that are returned to the system as input documents. An example is a customer's bill in punched-card form, which is mailed to the customer and later returned to the firm with the payment.

Terminals. The devices known as terminals include keyboard/printers, video display terminals, telephone-oriented terminals, intelligent terminals, and specialized terminals. Each type is briefly discussed next.

Keyboard/printer terminals, also known as teleprinters, have typewriterlike keyboards for entering data. Each entered item of data appears on hard copy; likewise, each item of information received from the processor appears on hard copy.

Video display terminals, also known as cathode ray tube (CRT) terminals, employ the same type of keyboards as do keyboard/printer terminals. Instead of printing data or information on hard copy, however, the basic video display terminal displays data and information in soft-copy form, that is, on a screen.

Video display terminals have become widely used because of several significant advantages over keyboard/printer terminals. They are versatile with respect to both data entry and display. For instance, certain

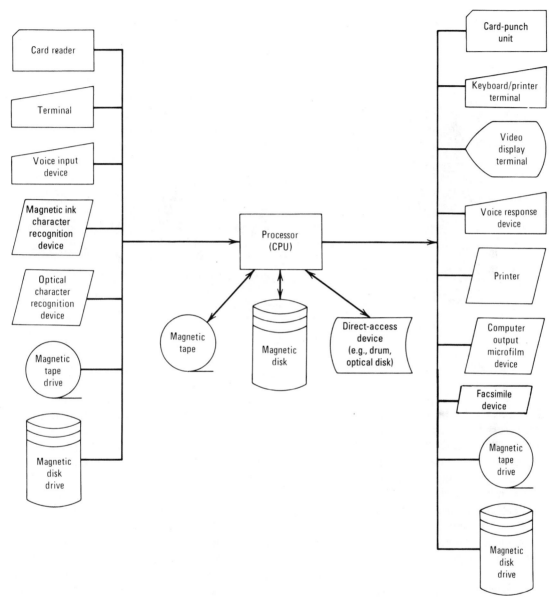

FIGURE 5-7 Input–output devices and storage media employed within computer systems.

models enable data to be entered directly on the face of the screen, by means of either light pens or fingertip touches. Other models, known as graphics terminals, allow graphs and charts to be displayed in color. Since no mechanical parts are involved, the displays are produced for the viewers very quickly. When fitted with suitable attachments (as shown in Figure 5-8), video display terminals can provide hard copy as desired. In addi-

FIGURE 5-8 A video display terminal with hard-copy attachment. Courtesy of Tektronix, Inc.

tion, they enable persons entering data to detect errors and then to correct these keying errors immediately. On the other hand, these added features cause video display terminals to carry price tags generally higher than those on keyboard/printer terminals.

Telephone-oriented terminals are terminals that connect through ordinary telephones to computer systems. Two examples of telephone-oriented terminals are portable terminals and voice-response terminals.

Portable terminals are lightweight terminals, video display or keyboard/printer type, that are easily transported to points remote from the computer systems to which they will be connected. For instance, an accountant may carry a portable terminal to a client's remote warehouse, from which he or she connects via telephone to the CPA firm's computer system.

Audio input-response terminals are terminals that use ordinary telephones to transmit either keyed-in or voice input to computer systems. Responses to such inputs are provided by the computer systems in the form of voice outputs. For example, a farm equipment dealer may key in needed part numbers and learn of the availability of such parts through simulated voice responses.

Intelligent terminals are, essentially, visual display or keyboard/printer terminals to which small processors have been added. These "smart" terminals thus can process data without assistance from larger central processors, to which they are often connected via data communication lines. For instance, an intelligent terminal located at a warehouse, with magnetic tape or disk storage attached, can process inventory and shipping transactions. If attached to a central processor, the terminal can also transmit the processed data to the central location and can receive messages and output from the central location.

Specialized terminals are on-line devices that essentially have single functions relating to particular types of organizations. Four commonly encountered examples of specialized terminals are

1. **Data collection terminals,** such as those used at production workstations and in the vehicles of police officers, route salespersons, construction supervisors, and delivery persons. For instance, a data collection terminal at a production workstation will typically be used to collect labor hours worked on production jobs. The data may be entered by alternative methods. Thus, the job number may be keyed in, the number of the employee performing the labor may be entered by inserting the employee's badge into a reader slot in the device, and the time may be entered by pressing a special function lever.

2. **Point-of-sale terminals,** such as those used at checkout counters in retail stores. The method of entering sales data may be keying the item numbers of the merchandise and sales quantities via keyboards on the terminals. More likely, however, the data entry method involves the use of an optical scanner (either a hand-held wand or a fixed device) that "reads" the bar codes or price tags on the merchandise items.

3. **Automated teller machines,** such as those found mounted outside banks.

4. **Reservation terminals,** such as those found in airports and motels.

Character recognition devices. Three types of character recognition devices in fairly wide use are optical character recognition (OCR), magnetic ink character recognition (MICR), and image-reading devices.

OCR devices read documents containing typed or handwritten characters and enter the data directly into computer systems or onto machine-readable storage media. Since they eliminate the need for added preparation of data by typists or keypunchers, data preparation errors and labor costs are reduced.

However, most OCR devices currently available can read only limited numbers of rigidly specified character styles called **fonts.** If the characters are not carefully printed or typed according to these font specifications, or if smudges appear on the documents, often the documents are rejected. Certain OCR devices can read wider ranges of font styles plus handwriting, and are less affected by poor-quality characters, but these devices are more expensive.

OCR devices vary widely in size, setting, and applications. Some models are as large as cabinets, whereas others are small hand-held wands. Some models are used alone; others are used in mixed-media arrangements that may include MICR devices, keyboard-to-disk devices (discussed later), and small processors.

Two heavy users of OCR devices are public utilities and credit card issuers. Meter readers employed by public utilities enter the usage by consumers of gas or electricity, for instance, on meter reading forms. These penciled entries (e.g., 4520) are then read by OCR devices in the processing centers of the utilities.[8] Holders of credit cards from such issuers as Visa and Sears present their cards when making credit purchases at service stations or department stores. Attendants or salespersons imprint the identification data from the presented cards onto sales forms by means of data recording or imprinting devices. Copies of the sales forms are then forwarded to the issuers' processing centers, where they are read by OCR devices.

MICR devices accept documents on which characters have been encoded with a magnetic ink. Banks have used MICR devices for several decades to read and sort checks for processing.

---

[8]Meter readings are recorded by some utilities on hand-held devices.

Both OCR and MICR devices are suited to applications involving the use of turn-around documents. For instance, when customers' bills are mailed by public utilities, the portion returned with each remittance can be read by the appropriate device. Thus, if the identifying data are printed with magnetic ink, the returned remittance advices would be read by an MICR device.

Image-reading devices convert images into electronic impulses and then either (1) store them on suitable media or (2) transmit them to remote facsimile devices. The typical image reader consists of a photocopying device with an attached scanner. It can scan a wide variety of images, ranging from handwritten source documents to photographs and blueprints. Scanned images may be stored on microfilm or magnetic disk. In most applications, however, they are stored on optical disks. Alternatively, the images may be transmitted to remote points and then reproduced as facsimiles of their original forms.

Other character recognition devices include mark sense readers, which read marks from such forms as examination coding sheets, and tag readers, which read such forms as price tags used by department stores.

Devices related to magnetic media.   Magnetic media devices such as **magnetic tape drives** and **magnetic disk drives** are widely used in current computer systems. These are the on-line devices by which data from magnetic tapes and magnetic disks are entered into the primary storage of a computer. They also enable information to be transferred (1) from primary storage onto magnetic tapes and magnetic disks for temporary or permanent storage and (2) to output devices such as printers for the preparation of reports and documents.

Often data are not captured directly onto magnetic media. Hence, off-line devices are needed to transcribe the captured data onto magnetic tapes and disks. As mentioned earlier, one type of off-line device is a **key-to-tape encoder.** This device provides a keyboard by which a data entry clerk transcribes data from source documents directly onto magnetic tape. In most encoder models a CRT screen is available, so that the clerk can visually view the data being recorded on tape. Key-to-tape encoders may be used as stand-alone units or be grouped into a key-to-tape system that includes several keyboards ("stations"), several tape recorders, and a small computer processor. The processor enables transaction data to be validated immediately as they are entered, as well as to be formatted for entry onto each magnetic tape. An alternative off-line device is a **key-to-disk system.** It is similar to the key-to-tape system, except that it temporarily stores the transaction data on a magnetic disk during the validating and editing process. Consequently, a key-to-disk system has a greater storage capacity than a key-to-tape system. The data entered via a key-to-disk system may end up on either magnetic tapes or magnetic disks.

Printers.   These output devices provide hard copy on paper stock. They are either (1) **impact printers,** which print one line or character at a time, or (2) **nonimpact printers,** most of which print a page at a time. Impact printers trace their origins to punched-card tabulator machines. However, nonimpact page printers have developed rapidly during the past two decades. Figure 5-9 shows a nonimpact printer. A number of nonimpact printing technologies have emerged, including thermal, laser, electrophotographic, ion deposition, and ink-jet printing.

Nonimpact printers are gaining at the expense of impact printers for two major reasons. First, they combine high-quality printing with high-speed, noiseless outputs. Second, they increase flexibility. For instance, certain sophisticated nonimpact printers (called **electronic printing systems**) permit a

FIGURE 5-9   A nonimpact printer. Courtesy of International Business Machines Corporation.

selection from a variety of type fonts and character sizes and enable report formats as well as variable information to be printed directly onto blank paper stock. On the other hand, impact printers will be in existence for years to come, since they are less costly than nonimpact printers and can provide multiple copies during one printing run.

Computer output microfilm devices. Computer output microfilm (COM) devices produce outputs on various microfilm forms (e.g., cartridge, microfiche). The COM technique involves the transfer of data in digital form. Data may be transferred in an on-line mode from the primary storage unit of a processor or from a magnetic disk. Alternatively, data may be transferred in an off-line mode from magnetic tapes. Central to this technique is a microfilm recorder (the image reader) that photographs the data onto microfilm and then develops the exposed film by a dry or wet chemical process. The developed microfilm can then be displayed on microfilm readers or the screens of specially designed terminals. Figure 5-10 pictures a microfilm automated retrieval terminal that

enables files stored on microfilm to be searched and the desired records to be quickly displayed. Other special equipment enables paper copies of the microfilmed data to be printed if desired.

COM devices provide two significant benefits. First, they produce microfilm at an extremely high rate of speed, in some cases ranging up to 50,000 lines per minute. Second, they store data on an output medium that has several important advantages: Microfilm is very compact; one 4×6 inch microfiche can contain roughly 207 pages of computer printouts. Moreover, microfilm is relatively inexpensive and data stored on it can be retrieved more quickly than from paper printouts. It is therefore suitable for copying documents and nonactive accounting records. One main drawback to the use of microfilm is that the COM devices and related equipment can be quite expensive.

Other input–output devices.   Several devices having specialized uses deserve brief mention. **Plotters** produce various types of graphs on paper. They may employ either ink pens or electrostatic processes. **Facsimile**

FIGURE 5-10 A microfilm retrieval terminal. Courtesy of Eastman Kodak Company

(fax) devices reproduce transmitted images of source documents and other materials back into facsimiles of their original hard-copy forms. In effect, facsimile devices are printer terminals that can precisely reconvert electronic impulses into the images from which they were created. These devices are rapidly increasing in popularity, since they enable needed documents to be speedily and accurately dispatched to distant points in an inexpensive manner. **Cellular telephones** allow voice inputs and responses to and from moving vehicles. A **punched-paper-tape reader** reads characters from punched paper tape, either for entry into a computer system or for conversion to another medium. A **paper tape punch** emits punched paper tape, which may then be read into a computer system or converted to a medium such as magnetic tape or a hard-copy report. Because of their relatively slow reading and punching

speeds, plus such disadvantages of paper tape as a tendency to tear, paper tape devices are seldom employed in modern computer systems. A **sensing device** accepts data, such as temperatures and rates of flow, in analog (continuous) form. By means of a **transducer** the device converts these analog measurements into digital form for computer processing. Sensors are used in the automatic monitoring and control of industrial processes such as steel making and oil refining.

Secondary Storage Devices and Media

The primary storage unit does not have the capacity to store most of the data needed for modern computer applications. In addition to the limited size of the central processing unit, the physical medium used for primary storage is relatively expensive. Thus, auxiliary or secondary storage devices are usually attached to the system to provide the additional capacity needed. These devices control various types of storage media. Files containing data and programs may be stored on secondary storage media. When needed for processing or for outputs, the files or portions of the files are transferred from their secondary storage locations to the primary storage unit. Because of this required transfer step, files on secondary storage media are not as quickly available to users as files and data already in the primary storage unit. However, secondary storage capacity can be increased as needs dictate.

Secondary storage media that may be employed on-line to a modern computer system include magnetic tapes, magnetic disks, magnetic drums, magnetic cards, data cells, magnetic bubbles, and optical disks. Off-line storage media that can be converted to secondary storage include punched cards, punched paper tape, and optically scannable documents. Microfilm forms are usually stored in off-line devices but can be stored on-line for retrieval. The three main secondary storage media currently in use are magnetic tape, magnetic disk, and optical disk.

Magnetic tape. The **magnetic tape** medium stores data as magnetic spots or bits. Each tape reel is controlled by a magnetic tape drive. Although this drive is attached on-line, individual reels of magnetic tape are generally stored off-line until needed for processing. Magnetic tape has long been a popular storage medium for the following reasons:

1. Large storage capacity: a reel of magnetic tape can contain over 100 million characters of data.
2. Fast transfer rate: data can be read into primary storage from magnetic tape for processing many times faster than from such media as punched cards or optically scanned documents. Magnetic tape trans-

fer rates vary from 40,000 to 1,200,000 characters per second.

3. Relatively low cost: a magnetic tape is about one-tenth as costly as a magnetic disk, the other currently popular secondary storage medium.
4. Reusability: one tape can be used over and over again.
5. Reliability: magnetic tape stores and transfers data with very few errors or losses of data.
6. Flexibility and efficiency: data records may have either fixed or variable lengths and may be stored with little wasted space.

Physical features of magnetic tapes and the means of coding data thereon are as follows:

1. Tape widths range from $\frac{1}{2}$ inch to 1 inch, and lengths range from 2400 feet to 3600 feet.
2. Characters—letters, numbers, and special symbols—are coded as columns of bits (bytes) that are arrayed side by side along the tape.
3. Data densities range upward from 1600 bytes to several thousand bytes per inch, so that a single reel of tape may typically contain 4 million bytes or more.
4. **Tracks** or **channels,** which provide positions for the magnetic bits comprising each coded character, range from 7 to 10 in number.[9]
5. One track provides bit positions for check or **parity bits,** bits that are used to check the accuracy of the characters.
6. Groups of characters form **data items** or **elements,** which generally represent words and/or numbers; in turn, groups of data elements form **records,** and one or more records form **blocks** of data.

[9]Nine appears to be the most popular number of tracks at the present time.

7. Blocks are separated by **interblock gaps**, which allow the tape drive to stop and then start again when it is in the process of reading from or writing onto the tape.

Figure 5-11, which illustrates most of these features, portrays a seven-track tape, with two records comprising a block and gaps separating blocks. Within the left-most record appear the first two characters on the tape. Each character is represented by a seven-bit code. The left-most character is the letter *U,* made up of the A zone bit plus the 4 numeric bit; the character to its right is the number *8,* represented simply by the 8 numeric bit. Other characters, if shown, would be represented by other combinations of bits. The parity position is denoted by the *C* to the left of the tape. A check bit appears in the parity position of the code representing the letter *U,* for instance. It has been added by the computer system to provide an odd number of bits in the column. If the computer system somehow loses a needed bit or adds an extraneous bit, the system can detect the error; it does so by counting the bits in each character position and noting whether the total count is even or odd. In this example an erroneous character would be denoted by a total count that is even. (In certain other computer systems an erroneous character would be denoted by a total count that is odd.)

How does a computer system accept data stored on magnetic tape? First, a reel of tape is mounted on a tape drive and started into motion. Identifying data from its **header label** are then displayed, so that the operator can verify that the proper tape is being used. Then, upon proper instructions from the application program, a **read–write head** transfers data either to or from the tape as the tape is moved past the head. Data being written onto the tape are transferred from primary storage onto the tape; conversely, data being read from the tape are transferred into primary storage. One block of records is transferred by each instruction, with the gap serv-

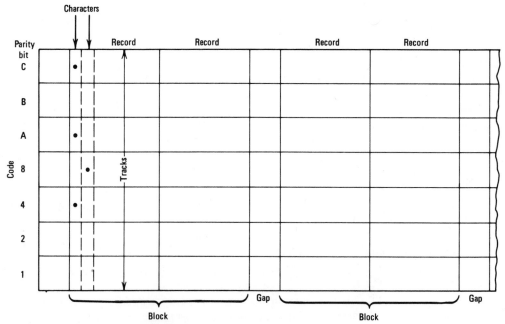

FIGURE 5-11   Features of a magnetic tape.

ing as a means of detecting the end of the block. When the last block has been transferred, a **trailer label** is encountered (or written, if a new tape is being prepared). Then an end-of-file character is detected (if the transfer involves reading data from the tape) or is inserted (if the transfer involves the writing of data onto the tape).

As the preceding description suggests, magnetic tape is a **sequential storage medium** in that it can be read and written on only in sequence—one record after another. To reach a particular record within a file of data stored on tape, for instance, it is necessary to read every block, starting with the first block, into primary storage. On the average, one-half of a file must be searched before a desired record is located. The time in searching and locating a desired record (**access time**) may involve several minutes when a file is lengthy and the desired record is near the end of the file.

Magnetic disk.

The **magnetic disk** is also a secondary storage medium that contains data in magnetized form. In recent years it has been replacing magnetic tapes in more and more applications. One reason for such replacements is the relatively large capacity of a magnetic disk. Another reason is that data transfer for a magnetic disk is often even faster than for magnetic tape.

The increasing popularity of magnetic disks, however, rests principally on one outstanding advantage: the ability to provide direct access to stored records. With magnetic disks it is possible to instruct a computer system to move directly to a desired record. Searching through all of the preceding records in a file is not necessary, as is the case when the file is stored on magnetic tape. Thus, the time to access most records is significantly reduced. Consequently, a magnetic disk is generally the appropriate storage medium for applications that require on-line processing and situations that require the prompt retrieval of stored data.

Because of the aforementioned capability, a magnetic disk is called a **direct-access storage medium** or **device.** The feature that enables direct access to occur is a set of permanent addresses assigned to the various physical storage locations on the disk.

Other physical features of magnetic disks appear in Figure 5-12. This figure portrays a group or pack of magnetic disks. In large computer systems the number of individual circular disks forming such a pack may reach 100, although many disk packs contain from 5 to 20 disks.

Each magnetic disk platter has two magnetizable recording surfaces. **Read–write heads** attached to **access arms** move in and out among the disks, which continually rotate at high speeds. Data transfers between the recording surfaces and primary storage are effected via these read–write heads. Thus, data transfers to and from magnetic disks take place in a manner similar to data transfers to and from magnetic tapes.

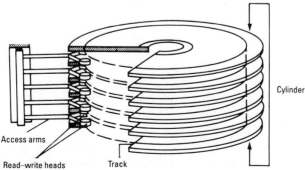

Cylinder

Access arms

Read–write heads   Track

FIGURE 5-12   Features of a magnetic disk pack.

Each recording surface is divided into concentric **tracks,** whose number may range from 200 to 800. The data are actually recorded on these tracks. In turn, the corresponding tracks of all the disk-recording surfaces of a disk pack form a **cylinder.** For instance, a single cylinder in a disk pack having 10 disk platters will consist of all tracks numbered 001 on disk-recording surfaces 1 through 20. If the recording surfaces contain 200 tracks, the disk pack contains 200 cylinders. Further, if each track can store 7294 bytes of data, the disk pack itself can contain about 29 million bytes of data (7294 bytes/track $\times$ 200 tracks/surface $\times$ 20 surfaces = 29 million bytes). Larger disk packs can store 200 million bytes or more of data.

Data records can be stored on magnetic disks in much the same way as on magnetic tape, but with certain interesting differences. Records can be blocked for more efficient storage. Interblock gaps separate blocks of data, as in the case of magnetic tape. One difference, however, is that the disk pack does not pause at each gap. Another difference is that track labels, as well as block header labels, appear with blocked data on magnetic disks. A third difference concerns the manner of storing data. Not only are data records stored in a concentric track on a magnetic disk, but after one track is filled, the additional records are stored on another track *within the same cylinder.* Since all of the data within a cylinder can be accessed without the need to move the read–write heads, this pattern of storage minimizes the data transfer times when processing a sequential file on a magnetic disk.

Data may be transferred to and from magnetic disks at rates which depend on the time necessary to move the read–write head to the proper track, the rotational speed of the drive, the density of the recorded data, and the size of each block of data. (The first two factors are, of course, not relevant to magnetic tape transfer rates; instead, the speed of the magnetic tape drive is a main factor in the case of magnetic tapes.) Magnetic disks can exhibit transfer rates that exceed one million bytes per second.

Some magnetic disk packs are removable from the disk drives with their read–write heads, whereas others are not; by contrast, every reel of magnetic tape is removable from the tape drive on which it is mounted.

Magnetic disks have two drawbacks that tend to inhibit their use as a universal storage medium in computer-based systems. First, they are several times as expensive as magnetic tapes having equal storage capacity. Second, they employ the **overlay approach,** by which updated records are written back into the same physical locations. The overlay approach is most suitable when individual records are being updated by the on-line processing approach. However, overlaid values destroy the prior contents of records. Therefore, special procedures are necessary, in order both to guard against accidental losses of valuable records and to provide audit trails.

A **magnetic diskette,** also known as a floppy disk, is a circular, flexible magnetic film. It is covered by a square-shaped jacket of black polymer for protection. A hole in the center of the jacket allows access by the read–write mechanism of the drive. Data may be recorded on both sides of ''double-sided'' diskettes, but only on one side of ''single-sided'' diskettes. Data are recorded in concentric tracks on the surface of the diskette. A typical diskette might store from 200 K bytes to 20 M bytes per side and transfer data at the rate of roughly 31,000 bytes per second. While this capacity and transfer rate are several magnitudes below those of hard magnetic disks, they are considerably larger than the capacity and transfer rate for cassette tape. Also, the storage capacity can be increased by packing data via the use of ''double-density'' or ''quad-density'' modes.

Optical disk. The **optical disk** is a secondary storage device that has transparent, rigid optical recording surfaces. It is also called a laser disk, since laser beams burn microscopic spots onto the surfaces. These spots are electronic representations of data characters or images, which can be read and retrieved by the laser beams as needed. Most currently available optical disks do not allow burned spots containing data to be erased or modified. Such disks are thus called WORM (write once, read many) storage devices. They generally store data and images pertaining to a firm's transactions and activities, such as source documents, narrative reports, schedules, maps, and engineering blueprints.

Optical or laser disks can contain massive quantities of data at a much lower cost than can magnetic disks. For instance, a single 12-inch optical platter can store over 2 gigabytes (2 billion bytes). They also are easily removable from their optical disk drives, so that other disks can be inserted as needed. Moreover, erasable optical disks are beginning to be available. The main drawback of optical disks (apart from the WORM limitation) is that data cannot be retrieved as quickly as from magnetic disks. Depending on the size and power of the optical-disk system and its retrieval software, the access time ranges from 10 to 40 seconds. The necessary hardware for optical disk systems is also relatively expensive in comparison to magnetic tape and microfilm.

Developments in optical technology are occurring rapidly. Optical disks using a high-density recording film called "digital paper," soon to be available, allow data and images to be accessed almost as fast as from magnetic disks. Digital paper can store even greater quantities of data than their rigid optical disk counterparts.[10]

The future of optical disks, however, is tied most closely to image-processing applications. An increasing number of firms are concerned about the voluminous flows of paper documents throughout their departments. As the technology improves and becomes more affordable, many such firms will capture images of documents, via image-reading devices, onto optical disks or digital paper. These stored document images will be available for retrieval through terminals or microcomputer workstations as the need arises. In most cases at present they are simply used as reference copies. However, certain firms are beginning to link these stored document images to critical business applications. Thus, a retailer can use the images of remittance advices in processing its cash receipts; an airline can use images of turned-in tickets in verifying passenger revenues.

Hardware Configurations

The **hardware configuration** of a computer system is the arrangement of hardware devices utilized. It can be represented by a diagram that portrays the relationships of the hardware devices to the processor or processors. Figure 5-13 shows a hardware configuration diagram for a relatively basic on-line computer system.

Hardware configuration diagrams can contain a variety of specific data concerning the computer systems they portray. For instance, Figure 5-13 indicates which devices are used for inputs and which for outputs. They may include notations concerning the organizational or physical locations of devices, as shown in Figure 5-14. They may also specify the particular makes and models of the devices, such as an IBM 7090 processor. Finally, they may include off-line devices such as magnetic tape encoders. If shown, however, such devices should appear as disconnected from the computer processors.

Hardware Evolution and Trends

Generations of computer hardware. Computers had their beginnings in the difference machines of Charles Babbage, the punched-card tabulating machine of Herman Hollerith, and the adding machine of William

[10]Fisher, Marsha J., "Digital Paper Promises Cost, Storage Gains for Optical Media," *Datamation* (May 15, 1988), p. 32.

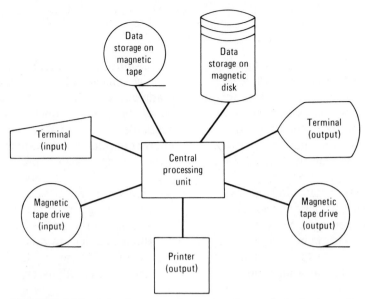

FIGURE 5-13 A hardware configuration diagram of a basic on-line computer system.

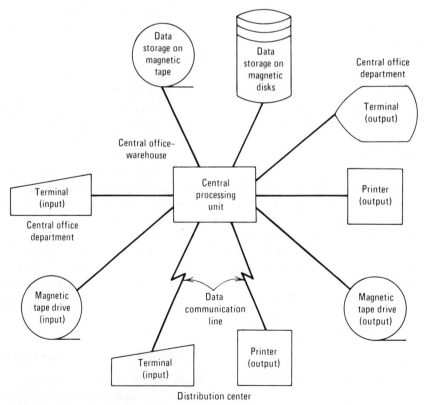

FIGURE 5-14 A hardware configuration diagram of an on-line computer system having multiple locations.

Burroughs. The first generation of computers, however, began in the 1940s with such vintage models as Mark I, ENIAC, and EDVAC. In the 1950s the first commercial general-purpose computers—the UNIVAC I and IBM 650—appeared. These were able to perform useful applications, since they were stored-program computers; that is, they stored instructions internally in the same manner that they stored data. However, these first-generation computers had serious limitations. In performing internal operations they used huge numbers of vacuum tubes, which were large and heat-producing. They also tended to be input–output bound. Thus, these computers were not well suited for performing business applications involving large volumes of inputs and outputs.

In the late 1950s the second generation of computers was introduced. These computers contained transistors rather than vacuum tubes. Since transistors are less expensive, faster, more reliable, and smaller than vacuum tubes, they brought dramatic improvements in computer cost, speed, reliability, and size. Second-generation computers also incorporated such developments as **buffers,** devices that enable data to be read and reports to be printed concurrently with processing operations.

The mid-1960s witnessed the introduction of integrated circuits and hence the third generation. **Integrated circuits,** solid-state technology incorporated on miniaturized printed circuits, further reduced the size and cost of computers while increasing their speed and reliability.

The fourth and current generation, which began in the 1970s, is marked by large-scale integrated circuits and very-large-scale integrated circuits. Other developments during this generation include virtual storage and microprocessors.

Computer hardware trends. To summarize the foregoing, computer hardware has dramatically improved over the past 40 years

with respect to size, speed, storage capacity, reliability, cost, and options. Whereas the early day ENIAC was the size of a moving van, a present-day microchip with even greater computational capability is half the size of a dime. The time required by a first-generation computer to perform a single computation was 20 milliseconds; the time required by a fourth-generation computer to perform the same computation is 100 nanoseconds or less. The capacity of the primary storage unit of an early computer was a few thousand characters; the corresponding capacity for certain fourth-generation computers is tens of millions of characters. Reliability has so improved that computers can now be said to be essentially error free (except for errors introduced by humans). Processing costs have declined from over one dollar per million instructions to less than one cent. Options have expanded from early basic central processing units with punched-card input and paper output to wide-ranging choices. Current computer systems may employ central processing units having such features as multiprogramming, overlapping, and virtual storage; input units that include terminals, magnetic tape drives, and magnetic disk drives; output units that include the preceding input units plus voice response units and several types of printers; and data communications equipment of extreme complexity.

Future hardware developments.[11] During the upcoming decades computer hardware should become ever faster, smaller, more reliable, and more user friendly. The speed dimension should illustrate these trends. By the turn of the century the least-expensive microcomputers should be able to process about 10 MIPS, while supercomputers are likely to process 4 billion floating-point oper-

[11]Most of the views expressed in this section are based on a series of five columns by James Martin entitled "Modeling Technology," which appeared in *PC Week* from October 17 through November 21, 1988.

ations per second. By the year 2010 these speeds are likely to reach 90 MIPS and 8 trillion floating-point operations per second. Processing speeds of these magnitudes will be possible for two reasons. Parallel processing will become increasingly employed as the processing mode, and processing chips will be designed to contain many millions and even billions of components.

Storage capacities should also increase dramatically. Optical disks, which are likely to be the dominant secondary storage medium, will be able to store billions of bits of data.

Input–output devices will become more convenient and user friendly. Terminals will be developed that are cellular, so that (like cellular phones) users can access their computer systems without needing to plug into a wired network. Users will normally enter data by speaking into voice-input terminals. Speech will be converted into computer-readable text, which can then be processed and stored by the computer systems. Presentation graphs or voice responses should replace printed text as the preferred modes of output.

The fifth generation of computers should arrive in the early 1990s. In addition to the higher performance levels just described, this new generation of computers should exhibit a limited degree of artificial intelligence. They will be able to perform logical inferences, recognize patterns, and adapt to new or changing situations (i.e., "learn"). For instance, the recognition and conversion of speech patterns will require such capabilities. Those fifth-generation computers that are particularly designed to apply artificial intelligence, and hence to mimic human brain processes, may be called by such names as neurocomputers.

Computer Software

Computers collect, process, store, and retrieve data; maintain control over data ac-

curacy; provide security for stored data; and generate information. While they sometimes are directed by humans, more often they perform these tasks under the direction of computer software. As Figure 5-15 shows, the term *computer software* describes a variety of languages and instruction sets (programs) prepared from such languages.[12] This section discusses the categories of software portrayed in the figure.

Machine and symbolic languages. Each computer follows (executes) instructions expressed in a **machine language** unique to its type of computer. While machine languages vary, they all employ a binary code comprised of zeros and ones. During the era of first-generation computers only machine languages were available. Thus, humans were required to write instructions for computers directly in machine language. As many discovered, programming in machine language is a slow, tedious, and error-prone task.

By the time second-generation computers arrived on the scene, new languages employing symbols had been developed. **Symbolic languages,** also known as assembly languages, enable machine instructions (as well as locations in primary storage) to be represented by mnemonic symbols rather than by binary codes. For instance, the instruction to add might be represented by ADD rather than 010. Symbolic languages are thus easier to use than machine languages; consequently, programs are written faster and with fewer errors.

Procedure-oriented languages. A new class of **procedure-oriented languages** was developed during the eras of the second- and third-generation computers. These languages enable entire sets of machine instructions to be represented by single algebralike or Englishlike statements. For instance, an in-

---

[12]Software also includes documentation and other aids related to the use of computer systems. Documentation is discussed in Chapter 9.

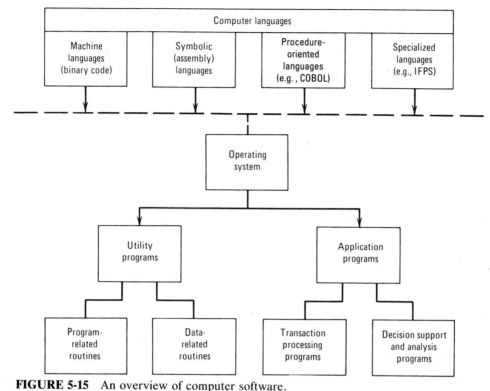

FIGURE 5-15   An overview of computer software.

struction in the language known as FOR-
TRAN might appear as

$$D = (A * B)/C$$

An instruction in the language known as CO-
BOL might appear as:

COMPUTE COMMISSION EQUALS
SALES-AMOUNT * TEN-PERCENT.

In addition to FORTRAN and COBOL,
the most popular procedure-oriented languages are BASIC, C, and PASCAL. Of
these, the one of greatest interest to accountants is likely to be COBOL (*CO*mmon *Business O*riented *L*anguage). As the name implies, it is designed specifically for
business-oriented applications. Not only

does it facilitate the writing of transaction
processing programs, but it also provides excellent documentation of input data, files,
and output reports.[13]

Furthermore, all procedure-oriented
languages provide several advantages over
symbolic or machine languages:

1. They employ simpler instructions and are
   hence easier to learn.

2. They enable programs to be written much
   more quickly.

3. They are generally machine independent;
   that is, programs in such languages can be
   used on a wide variety of computers without the need for significant changes.

On the other hand, programs written in
procedure-oriented languages are generally

---

[13]Chapter 25 provides an example of a COBOL program.

less efficient than the same programs written in symbolic or machine languages. Since they are not written to take advantage of the features peculiar to a particular computer, programs in procedure-oriented languages tend to execute more slowly. They also are likely to consume more primary storage.

Specialized languages. The languages just discussed are general purpose, in that they may be employed to write any of the several types of programs noted in the lower portion of Figure 5-15. A body of languages has also been developed to serve specialized purposes. Certain of these languages, known as financial modeling and simulation languages, aid managers in decision making. Other such languages assist auditors in performing financial audits and system analysts in designing information systems. Examples of specialized languages are Simscript, Interactive Financial Planning System, STRATA, UFO, and Easytrieve.[14]

Specialized languages are relatively high level—that is, they are even easier to learn and use than procedure-oriented languages. In fact, specialized languages are ''friendly'' even to those users who have absolutely no computer background. Instead of requiring that procedures be specified in programs, they allow users to describe the problems (i.e., what needs to be done). Thus, they are often called *problem-oriented* or nonprocedural languages. They also allow users to write instructions *interactively,* by direct interaction with the computer system through terminals. Consequently, users receive immediate feedback. (Furthermore, users can generally receive guidance from stored explanations by simply typing HELP on the terminal.) Finally, the instructions are typically expressed in natural language (i.e., English words and phrases).

Application programs. The data conversion tasks of a firm are performed in a computer-based system by **application programs.** One category of application programs concerns routine transaction processing, while a second category pertains to decision support and analysis activities.

Application programs that are concerned with transaction processing may be organized around particular types of transactions. For instance, a set of related application programs may pertain to the sales transaction. Perhaps the first program verifies and edits the sales transaction data when entered for processing. A second program may update the accounts receivable file to reflect the sales data. A third program may print the sales invoices and related reports. Alternatively, application programs may focus on certain tasks for a variety of transaction types. Thus, a file maintenance program may be employed to post data from all transactions to the relevant master files. Further, this same program may be used to post any changes (such as changes in customers' addresses) to the appropriate master files. Another program may be applied to the retrieval of data from any of the files within the computer system, in order to prepare reports demanded (specified) by users.

Application programs in the second category span a wide range of activities related to problem solving, decision making, and accounting. A typical firm might maintain programs that provide time series analyses, sales forecasts, regression analyses, linear programming analyses, cash budgets, breakeven analyses, critical-path analyses, and inventory reorder quantities. One recent program that has gained enormous popularity, the electronic spreadsheet, is discussed in Chapter 16.

In recent years numerous commercial software firms have blossomed. These firms collectively market hundreds of software packages, many consisting of application programs. Thus, those user firms that decide

[14]Specialized languages, also known as fourth-generation languages, are illustrated in Chapter 20.

not to develop their programs internally currently have considerable latitude when acquiring software.

Utility programs. Another class of programs, broadly called **utility programs,** performs functions or routines necessary in the operation of every computer-based system. These routines are closely related to the system hardware and are frequently encountered in the body of application programs.

One category of utility programs is data oriented. Examples include routines for transferring data from one medium to another, sorting data, merging data, and managing data within a sophisticated data base. While these routines often handle transaction data, they differ to a degree from application programs. For instance, a routine for transferring data from one medium to another might be used to convert transaction data from magnetic tape to magnetic disk, prior to further transaction processing. However, the same routine may be used to "dump" master files from magnetic disk to magnetic tape, in order to provide a backup copy. Utility routines are designed to operate efficiently with a particular computer system; thus, they are generally written in symbolic language and provided by the manufacturer of the particular computer system.

The other category of utility programs may be described as program oriented. One such routine familiar to everyone who has written programs is the diagnostic, which helps programmers to find programming errors, or "bugs." Other routines in this category translate programs into the machine language of the computer on which they are to be executed. (Computers can only understand and execute programs expressed in their own machine languages.) Thus, a routine called a **compiler** translates a program written in a procedure-oriented language (the *source program*) into a machine language program (the *object program*).

Operating systems. The software that manages the computer system, including all the hardware and software, is known as the **operating system.** In effect, a modern operating system automates and expedites many of the control, coordinating, and "housekeeping" tasks performed by human computer operators in earlier computer systems. The term *operating system* is a bit misleading, since this systems software package actually consists of a collection of programs. Utility programs, just discussed, generally comprise one major group. The other group may be called control programs. Riding herd over both groups is a supervisory program, also called the *supervisor* (executive, manager), which resides in the primary storage unit during system operations.

Although operating systems differ in specifics, the following list of control programs (and stated tasks) is reasonably typical:

1. The supervisor, which controls the movement of data and programs within and between the primary and secondary storage units and coordinates the execution of all the other programs.

2. The load program, which initially loads or "boots" the computer system and then passes control to the supervisor.

3. The job control program, which accepts and interprets instructions written in a job control language and issued by human operators or users. (A **job control language** (JCL) is a special language by which users can specify, usually via terminals, aspects concerning the execution of application programs. For instance, a user might specify the particular input–output units, file devices, and memory spaces to be employed. Furthermore, the user could indicate the sequence in which multiple programs—jobs—are to be executed.)

4. Input–output programs, which assign the particular input and output devices to the

various jobs being performed by the computer system.

5. The scheduling program, which determines the sequence and schedules the data processing jobs involving application and utility programs.

6. The monitor program, which maintains logs and statistics pertaining to jobs and equipment performance.

7. The library/memory manager program, which assigns primary storage locations to data and programs and "remembers" the locations of all application and utility programs that are stored on secondary storage devices.

Operating systems are designed to operate in either batch mode or interactive mode. Batch-oriented operating systems place jobs in a waiting line to await execution. When time becomes available in the computer system for executing a job, the operating system selects a job on the basis of a priority. The priority may be provided by a JCL instruction or by a multiprogramming interrupt, for example. Interactive operating systems enable users to provide directions via an interactive terminal. Thus, a user may interrupt the execution of a program to enter a transaction for editing and posting to a master file.

Computer software trends. Software has become more "friendly," specialized, and machine independent over the past 40 years. In the early days computer programming languages were very difficult to use, employed mainly to produce application programs, and usable only with specific computers. Today's software tends to be user friendly, in that programmers and even nonprogrammers can construct programs easily and relatively quickly. Hundreds of programming languages are currently available, from which an extremely wide range of software is developed. In addition to application programs, currently developed software includes complex operating systems, sophisticated data management software systems, and comprehensive decision-making and planning software systems. Furthermore, these languages tend to be relatively machine independent, in that they are compatible with a wide variety of computers.

During the first generation of computers the hardware was much more costly than the software. Today the reverse is true: The cost of software for a computer system exceeds the cost of all the hardware. Because of the rising cost of software, due in large part to its growing complexity, firms are increasingly acquiring software packages from commercial software firms. On those occasions when firms decide to develop their own programs internally, they tend to employ higher-level languages.

Future software developments. These computer software trends are likely to continue. Software will be even easier to develop and use. Automated software development tools such as CASE (Computer-Assisted Software Engineering) will enable program instructions to be generated automatically from system-design diagrams. Natural language packages will enable users to use everyday English (or another language) to request needed information or to modify application programs. Software will be even more specialized, with application software packages being developed almost on a custom basis (e.g., by specific industry, size, and inventory method). An increasing number of application software packages will aid in making decisions by incorporating the knowledge and logical processes of experts.

Business-Oriented Applications of Computers

Upon acquiring computer hardware and software, a firm typically progresses through several stages of applications development. Figure 5-16 portrays three major applications

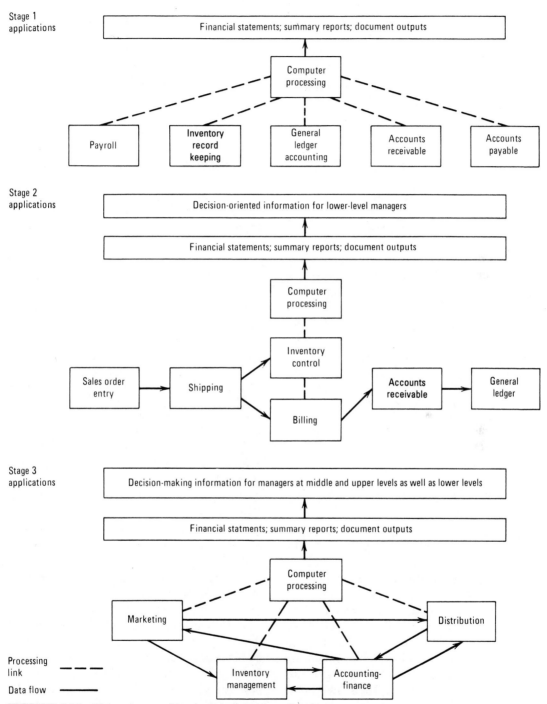

FIGURE 5-16 Three stages of business-oriented applications.

stages. This stage-by-stage progression has tended to occur irrespective of the year of acquisition. Thus, a small retailer that acquires a microcomputer system in 1990 should experience roughly the same types of application stages that were encountered 30 years ago by a large wholesaling chain. To simplify our discussion, therefore, we will focus on one hypothetical example: the Stuart Merchandising Company (SMC). SMC is a regional merchandiser that supplies retailers through several distribution centers.

First-stage computer-based applications.

SMC acquired its first computer in 1960, near the beginning of the second generation of computer hardware. Among the applications for which SMC developed programs were payroll, inventory recordkeeping, and general ledger accounting. It focused on these narrow applications because of their relative simplicity. They could be converted on an as-is basis—that is, the source documents and processing sequences and outputs employed on the previous system could be left essentially unchanged. The major objective was efficient processing of transactions.

First-stage applications are generally characterized by this somewhat unintegrated approach. Each application is relatively independent from other applications. Not only does it process data via its own programs, but it also maintains its own set of files. The primary outputs of each application consist of historical information, rather than information for managerial decision making.

As noted, those firms that acquire their first computer this year will likely select the same types of applications as SMC did. The key differences are that currently acquiring firms will generally (1) purchase software packages rather than write their own computer programs, (2) employ terminals rather than punched-card devices for handling data and information, and (3) keep files on magnetic disk storage rather than magnetic tape storage.

Second-stage computer-based applications.

In 1970 SMC replaced its initial computer system with a third-generation computer. By the time of the change it had installed almost all of its transaction processing applications on the computer system. With the receipt of the new computer system it decided to take bold new steps with respect to applications; by doing so it entered the second stage of applications development.

Second-stage applications are relatively integrated. SMC therefore reorganized its applications around its key operational functions, broad transaction flows, and even transaction cycles. The firm combined its cash receipts and cash disbursements applications to create a financial function application. It combined its accounts receivable, inventory record keeping, sales order entry, and related applications to create an integrated credit sales processing application.

Second-stage applications generally provide decision support information to lower-level managers. For instance, SMC's financial function application provided information concerning current and expected cash flows to the cashier; based on this information she was able to plan and manage the cash resource more effectively. Similarly, the sales processing application provided information concerning inventory needs to the inventory and purchases managers, thereby enabling them to achieve better inventory control.

Certain second-stage applications may involve a limited degree of decision making by the computer system itself. Thus, the inventory control application of SMC required the computer to calculate and print the economic reorder quantities (EOQ) for those inventory items needing to be reordered. To perform such routine decision making, the computer system needed to store nontransactional data. With respect to the above EOQ calculations, the system needed the expected demand, carrying cost, and reorder cost for each item.

Third-stage computer-based applications. In 1980 SMC changed computer systems for a second time. In this change the computer system extends via communication lines to the various distribution centers. (Previously it was confined to the central office and warehouse, with manual processing being performed at the centers.) Although individual pieces of equipment have been replaced by newer and more powerful models, this configuration exists today.

Third-stage applications have been designed for and installed on this current computer system.[15] Applications in the third stage are highly integrated. Thus, SMC has linked together applications that cut across such functions as marketing, inventory management, accounting/finance, and distribution. The files related to such applications are stored together within a sophisticated data base, so that they may be managed by a data base software package and shared by the various applications. These files are kept up to date, since many of the transactions are processed without delay. To assure timely processing, transactions are generally captured at their sources and promptly entered for processing. For instance, those transactions arising at the distribution centers are entered via terminals and transmitted to the computer at the central office-warehouse. As a result of this timely processing, the sales manager of SMC is able to obtain the up-to-date status of a customer's order whenever he wishes.

Another feature of third-stage applications is the support that they provide to middle-level and higher-level decision making. This support is provided by means of decision models that are developed and stored for use by various managers. Among the models developed by SMC are those that aid in managing working capital, in selecting the best suppliers from whom to buy specific products, in matching the skills of employees and applicants against the requirements of open jobs, and in evaluating the performances of managers and employees. An especially important model being currently developed should aid higher-level managers in budgeting capital resources. Much of the data needed in such models must be drawn from external sources. For instance, the working-capital model requires data concerning interest rates.

Computer-based business application trends. In moving through the application stages, two trends are dominant: (1) greater integration and (2) more emphasis on decision-making information. First-stage applications are segmented and narrow, whereas third-stage applications integrate a variety of processing sequences and/or functions. First-stage applications focus on efficient processing of transactions, whereas third-stage applications serve managers at all levels with information for planning and control.

These two application trends have been fostered by such system-related developments as integrated data bases, timely data processing approaches, and financial modeling languages. Other emerging developments in computer hardware, software, application approaches, and management should reinforce these application trends. Furthermore, they should extend computer-assisted activities to most aspects of the commercial and business world.

Summary

When computers have been introduced into firms, they have had significant impacts on information systems, organizational structures, managerial decision making, and functions such as accounting. Most of these

---

[15] A change from one application stage to the next does not *necessarily* coincide with a major change in computer hardware. However, since the computer software is often rewritten to fit a newly acquired computer system, the changeover represents a logical point at which to review and modify a firm's applications.

impacts have been beneficial, although certain adverse effects have been experienced.

Computer hardware includes such physical equipment as the central processing unit, input–output devices, secondary storage devices, and data communications lines. The central processing unit consists of a control unit, a primary storage unit, and an arithmetic–logic unit. In turn, the primary storage unit contains both read-only memory and random-access memory. Processors range from large-scale computers to small, portable computers. Enhancements to processors include overlapping, multiprogramming, memory partitioning, virtual storage, time-sharing, and multithreading. Input–output devices include punched-card devices, terminals, character recognition devices, magnetic tape drives, magnetic disk drives, printers, and computer output microfilm devices. Secondary storage media include magnetic tapes, magnetic disks, optical disks, and microfilm forms. Hardware devices for a particular computer system may be represented by a hardware configuration diagram. Computer hardware has progressed through four generations. Today the typical computer processes much faster and more reliably than computers of earlier generations, provides much greater storage capacity and many more options, and costs much less per processing operation. Tomorrow's computers are likely to continue these trends and to incorporate a degree of artificial intelligence.

Computer software encompasses machine and symbolic languages, procedure-oriented languages, specialized languages, application programs, utility programs, and operating systems. The trend in computer software development is toward more "user-friendliness" and specialization. However, it has also become much more costly in relation to hardware. These trends are likely to continue.

Computer-based business-oriented applications also undergo changes over time. They have generally moved from independent accounting applications to applications that are more integrated and that provide decision-making information.

Review Problem with Solution

Statement

Computers Aplenty, Inc. (CAI), is a recently established computer retail store in Abilene, Texas. It merchandises and services four makes of microcomputers and related components such as terminals, printers, magnetic tape cassettes, diskettes, and so forth. It also carries a variety of business application software packages. Currently the store is managed by its owner, Jay Sparks, and employs 12 sales and service personnel.

Jay has high hopes that the store will grow rapidly in revenues and that more stores will be established. He recognizes the importance of an efficient and effective accounting information system in achieving these hopes. Thus, he decides to utilize a microcomputer from his stock as the heart of the system. With the aid of a microcomputer, he believes, the various transactions will be processed promptly, the files will be kept up to date, and needed information may be easily and quickly retrieved.

Required

a. Draw and label a hardware configuration diagram that reflects a suitable microcomputer system for CAI.

b. List several applications that would likely be suitable for CAI's microcomputer system.

c. Briefly describe software that would likely be suitable for use by CAI's microcomputer system.

d. Assume that CAI does grow rapidly, so that two additional stores are established and a total of 50 employees comprise the work force. Discuss alternative ways that the microcomputer system described in **a**

might feasibly be augmented or replaced to accommodate this growth.

Solution

a. A suitable microcomputer system hardware configuration would likely consist of a microcomputer, plus a nonremovable hard disk drive, one diskette drive, a cassette tape drive, one video display terminal, and one printer. A labeled configuration diagram appears below.[16]

b. Applications that would be suitable for the microcomputer system include

  (1) General ledger accounting.

  (2) Accounts payable processing.

  (3) Accounts receivable processing.

  (4) Cash disbursements processing.

  (5) Cash receipts processing.

  (6) Payroll processing.

  (7) Service order processing.

  (8) Inventory record keeping and control.

  (9) Sales analysis and forecasting.

  (10) Cash forecasting and management.

  (11) Budgetary planning and control.

  (12) Capital investment analysis.

c. Software that would be suitable for the microcomputer system includes

  (1) An operating system.

  (2) Utility programs such as text editors and directories.

  (3) Compilers for BASIC and COBOL.

  (4) An integrated package that includes an electronic spreadsheet, a data manager, and a word processor.

  (5) Application packages for general ledger accounting and for the remaining applications listed under **b.**

d. When CAI consists of three stores and 50 employees, a single microcomputer system is not sufficient. Alternative systems that might be considered include

  (1) Separate microcomputer systems for each store.

  (2) A minicomputer system located at the main store, with terminals located at

[16]The symbols employed in the diagram are based on computer system flowchart symbols appearing in the Appendix to Chapter 7, on page 253.

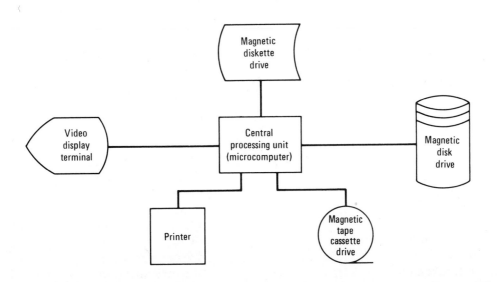

the other stores and tied by communications lines to the minicomputer.

(3) A supermicrocomputer system located at the main store, with terminals located at the other stores and tied by communications lines to the supermicrocomputer.

(4) An enhanced or larger microcomputer at the main store, accompanied by the utilization of a commercial computer service bureau or time-sharing service.

Variations of these alternatives might also be considered. The choice should be based on a comparison of the benefits provided by each alternative with the costs required for the alternative.

Review Questions

5-1 What is the meaning of each of the following terms?

Hardware
Software
Application
Human–machine system
Program
Central processing unit
Control unit
Primary storage unit
Arithmetic–logic unit
Address
Bit
Byte
Binary coded decimal (BCD)
EBCDIC
ASCII
Word
Random-access memory
Read-only memory
Microprogram
Semiconductor
Bubble memory
Instruction time
Execution time
Machine cycle time
Access time
Transfer rate
Overlapping
Channel
Buffer
Multiprogramming
Partitioning
Boundary protection
Interleaved storage access
Virtual storage
Parallel processing
Multiprocessing
Time-sharing
Multithreading
Input–output bound
On-line device
Off-line device
Punched-card reader
Card-punch unit
Turnaround document
Terminal
Optical character recognition device
Magnetic ink character recognition device
Image-reading device
Key-to-tape encoder
Key-to-disk system
Impact printer
Nonimpact printer
Computer output microfilm device
Facsimile (fax) device
Plotter
Magnetic tape
Parity bit
Block of data
Magnetic disk
Interblock gap
Sequential storage medium
Direct-access storage medium
Read–write head
Access arm
Header label
Track
Cylinder
Overlay approach
Magnetic diskette

Optical disk
Hardware configuration diagram
Integrated circuit
Machine language
Symbolic language
Procedure-oriented language
Application program
Utility program
Operating system
Job control language

5-2 What are the relative advantages of computers?

5-3 What are the relative advantages of humans as data processors?

5-4 Which information-related tasks are significantly affected by the introduction of computers?

5-5 What are the impacts of computers on the organizational structures of firms?

5-6 What are the impacts of computers on the decisions made by managers at the several managerial levels?

5-7 What are the impacts of computers on the accounting function?

5-8 Describe the five hardware components of any computer system.

5-9 Describe how data and instructions are stored and located within a computer processor.

5-10 Identify two types of computer storage or memory.

5-11 Identify several materials from which primary storage may be constructed.

5-12 Identify measures by which the performance of a computer processor may be evaluated.

5-13 Rank computer processors in order of size.

5-14 Describe each of the following features or capabilities, which may be associated with computer processors: overlapped processing, interleaved storage access, multiprogramming, program swapping, time-sharing, and multithreading.

5-15 Enumerate the array of input–output devices and storage media that may be found in large computer system.

5-16 Briefly contrast keyboard/printer terminals, video display terminals, data collection units, portable terminals, audio response terminals, and intelligent terminals.

5-17 Describe two types of character recognition devices.

5-18 Indicate the purposes of magnetic tape drives, magnetic disk drives, key-to-tape encoders, and key-to-disk systems.

5-19 Compare the relative advantages of impact printers and nonimpact printers.

5-20 Describe computer output microfilm devices.

5-21 Discuss the basic features of magnetic tape.

5-22 How does a computer system accept data stored on magnetic tape?

5-23 Contrast the basic features of a magnetic disk and magnetic tape.

5-24 Name one important advantage of a magnetic disk and two important advantages of magnetic tape as computer-related media.

5-25 Describe the developments and trends in computer hardware from the time of the earliest computers to the present.

5-26 Describe and contrast the major classes of computer software.

5-27 What are the significant trends in the development and use of computer software?

5-28 What tasks are performed by an operating system employed within a large computer system?

5-29 Contrast the three stages of computer-based business applications.

Discussion Questions

5-30 Which of the following system-related tasks can best be performed by computers, which by humans, and which by both computers and humans? Why?

a. Setting the objectives of a firm.
b. Making routine decisions concerning inventory management.
c. Making decisions concerning the promotion of employees and managers.
d. Finding problems needing solutions.
e. Processing large volumes of transactions.
f. Processing exceptional types of transactions.
g. Preparing income tax returns.
h. Answering inquiries concerning the status of customers' orders.
i. Answering inquiries concerning income tax laws.
j. Designing information systems.
k. Opening and closing valves regulating the flows of petroleum products through a pipeline system.
l. Evaluating the performances of managers.
m. Analyzing stocks and making investment recommendations.

5-31 Will information systems ever be completely computerized? Why or why not?

5-32 To what degree should accountants understand computer hardware and software?

5-33 Discuss the variety of effects on transaction processing (e.g., the processing of sales transactions) that are likely when a computer is first introduced into a firm.

5-34 What specific improvements in reports are most easily achieved when computers are incorporated within information systems?

5-35 The double-entry method of recording transactions has been employed by the accounting departments of most firms for a number of years. Should the double-entry method be retained when computers are incorporated into the information systems of such firms?

5-36 Discuss the possible effects that a newly incorporated computer might have on the scope and complexity of an information system.

5-37 Discuss the arguments by the owner of a small firm that a computer system would never pay for itself and that she would lose control of the firm if a computer was installed to process the firm's transactions.

5-38 On the basis of past trends and emerging developments, discuss the likely features of an information system in a large progressive firm in 1995.

Problems

5-1 Heathcliff Thornski is a buyer for the Screw-Up Tool and Die Company of Columbia, South Carolina. On August 1 he received a requisition from the materials control department pertaining to part number XTPO311K34. The firm had just received a contract, due to begin January 1, that would require a quantity of these parts. Since the parts were not needed for five months, Heathcliff put the requisition in his "to be done in the future" file. After all, the part was a fairly common steel gadget that could be obtained from a dependable supplier on very short notice; ordering early would unduly increase the investment in inventory. Besides, Heathcliff was very busy at the moment.

In fact, Heathcliff was busy during the rest of the year. His "to be done in the future" file grew and grew.

Suddenly, on December 15, several steel-fabricating firms were struck by their unionized employees. Among the struck firms were Screw-Up's principal suppliers of steel parts.

When January arrived and work began on the contract mentioned above, usage of part number XTPO311K34 jumped from 100 units per month to 1000 units per month.

Naturally, the available supply of the parts was soon exhausted. Heathcliff tried to obtain the parts, but he could locate only a few for a premium price. Production thus stalled on the contract. As a result of failing to complete the contract by the scheduled date, the company suffered a very substantial loss.

Required

Describe the ways that a computer-based information system could help prevent such catastrophies as that described, as well as improve other purchasing-related activities.

5-2 Mason's Department Store, Inc., owns a large store in Jackson, Mississippi. It recently acquired a computer system of the following configuration: (a) a medium-size central processor having 262,000 bytes of primary storage, (b) one image-reading device, (c) four magnetic tape drives, (d) four magnetic disk drives with removable disk packs, (e) one plotter, (f) two printers, (g) two keyboard/printer terminals, and (h) four visual display terminals.

Required

Draw two diagrams that reflect the preceding configuration, assuming that the computer system

a. *Does not* have overlapped processing capabilities.

b. *Does* have overlapped processing capabilities.

5-3 Visit a computer retail store and survey the computer hardware available for sale. On the basis of the visit, prepare a report that compares the key characteristics of each microcomputer and major component (such as terminal) on display. Include such characteristics as the capacity of primary storage, the word size, the processing speed, and the price.

5-4 Visit a computer retail store and survey the software packages available for sale.

On the basis of the visit, prepare a report that lists one dozen software packages. Describe briefly what each package does, how much it costs, which operating system it functions under, and in what languages the programs are written.

5-5 Prepare a hardware configuration diagram for each of the following computer systems. Label each of the symbols to reflect the type of hardware item; if components are situated in more than one location, indicate the location of each.

a. A microcomputer located in the office of a small public accountant, with attached components consisting of one video display terminal, one printer, and two diskette drives.

b. A minicomputer located in the main office of a merchandising firm, with on-line components consisting of one magnetic disk drive, two printers, ten video display terminals, one computer output microfilm device, and two magnetic tape drives.

c. A mainframe computer located in the main office area of a manufacturing firm, with on-line components consisting of two magnetic disk drives, three printers (two impact type, one nonimpact type), five video display terminals, and four magnetic tape drives. Additional components located elsewhere and connected on-line to the same computer are: six data collection terminals on the production floor, one video display terminal in the warehouse and production office, one printer in the warehouse, and one microcomputer in the executive office.

5-6 Specify the most suitable input or output device for each of the following situations:

a. A public utility needs to employ a specialized means of handling turnaround documents returned by customers with their payments.

b. An insurance company having numerous branches needs to transmit policy data from its regional offices for timely processing by a mainframe computer located at its home office.

c. A bank needs to employ a specialized means of inputting its large volume of checks for processing each day.

d. A grocery store chain desires to capture bar-coded data on groceries and other merchandise and to transmit these data to a central computer so that each sales transaction can be automatically and immediately completed.

e. A stock exchange desires to provide the latest stock prices to security representatives in brokerage offices, who enter requests via special telephones with keyboard attachments.

f. A construction firm desires to process its weekly payroll from time records in which the hours worked have been mark-sensed in pencil.

g. A university desires to employ a specialized means of handling registration forms filled in by students and returned for computer processing.

h. An automobile salvage dealer (one who buys old or wrecked automobiles and salvages key parts) is tired of answering numerous telephone inquiries every day concerning the availability of parts for specified models; instead, he wishes personalized answers to be provided by a computerized system.

i. A large transportation firm having more than 3000 prime and subsidiary accounts desires to post batches of journal vouchers each month to the general ledger, which is maintained on magnetic tape.

j. A wholesaler desires to record its numerous sales of merchandise on media that can be quickly entered in batches for processing by its computer system.

k. An automobile manufacturer desires to receive from its dealers orders that have been directly entered into a computer system and transmitted immediately to the manufacturer's order department at its home office.

l. A steel manufacturer prefers to eliminate the use of time cards for recording attendance times of employees; instead, it plans to assign badges containing employee numbers as bar codes, which would interface with an input device to the computer system.

m. A small business proprietor needs to obtain cash on Saturday to pay for emergency repairs to the company vehicle.

n. A management consultant desires to include high-quality colored graphics in her report to a client firm.

5-7 Identify the type of software for each of the following computer-based functions. If a programming language is indicated, specify the level.

a. Coordinating the actions of the hardware components of a computer system.

b. Preparing sales invoices on the basis of shipped orders.

c. Performing merges of data located in two or more files.

d. Compiling COBOL programs into machine language.

e. Constructing and using financial models for budget planning.

f. Processing the payroll.

5-8 Assume the availability of these computer-based storage media: magnetic tape, magnetic disk, optical disk, microfilm, primary storage, and punched cards. Indicate which storage medium (or media, if more than one) is preferable for each of the following situations. Briefly state why the selected medium is preferable.

a. A brokerage firm desires to retain records of the complete daily stock quotations as taken from the financial newspapers.

b. A credit card company desires to keep its members' account records readily available, so that updates can be made and inquiries can be quickly answered.

c. A private research institute needs to retain files concerning its completed projects; the files are not subject to updating, but they need to be frequently referenced in a timely manner.

d. A bank needs to keep available a series of amortization tables; these tables require relatively little storage space, but they need to be frequently accessed by a computer program that determines interest payments due from debtors.

e. A railway company needs to record transactions pertaining to movements of its freight cars, so that it can update the master file (which contains 10,000 records) on a daily basis.

f. A department store needs to record the amounts owed by customers on bills, which are mailed to the customers and returned by them (with payments) for processing.

g. A telephone company desires to retain copies of all checks and drafts that it issues, for occasional reference by accounting clerks.

h. A hospital needs to back up all its patient-related records, which are stored on magnetic disk.

5-9 The Ute Savings and Loan Association of Salt Lake City has over 50 branches throughout Utah at which members' savings are deposited or withdrawn. It also has a mortgage department that converts the deposited funds into mortgage loans to home buyers and builders. Currently the firm uses a small computer system located at the main office to prepare payroll, to update savings and loan accounts, and to prepare routine accounting reports. However, the controller of Ute believes that the computer system is not adequate for the current and future needs of the firm.

Required

Propose in broad terms a new computer system that might better serve Ute's needs. Include in your proposal the following:

a. A description of the system, including a hardware configuration diagram.

b. A description of desirable applications, both those that involve transaction processing and those that aid managerial decision making.

c. A list of needed software other than application packages.

5-10 The Gripper Brake Company is a small New Orleans manufacturer of brakes, brake linings, and other parts of braking systems. It sells approximately 100 different sizes and varieties of brake products to garages and retail outlets of motor vehicle products in 10 states. With a work force of 30 employees and three managers, Gripper generated sales revenues last year of $8 million. Moreover, John Hartley, the owner and manager of Gripper, foresees rapid growth in sales during the coming years.

Mr. Hartley, however, has become aware that the firm is already suffering growing pains. For instance, it is having difficulty in processing the increasing number of sales orders and in delivering orders to customers by promised dates. When customers inquire about the status of their orders, clerks often must spend hours tracking down the answers. Critical parts and materials needed in manufacturing the ordered products are frequently out of stock. Losses from bad debts have been increasing at an alarming rate.

These problems lead Mr. Hartley to seek help from Jeff Harris, the firm's public accountant. After a careful investigation Jeff recommends that the firm acquire its own computer system. Upon agreement from Mr. Hartley, he investigates further and proposes two alternatives: (a) a minicomputer system, or (b) three stand-alone microcomputer systems.

Required

a. Describe the hardware components that appear to be suitable for each of the foregoing alternative computer systems, and draw hardware configuration diagrams.

b. List the types of software that should be acquired by Gripper, regardless of the alternative selected.

c. After installing the selected computer system, Gripper acquires software application packages that perform general ledger accounting and that process sales orders. Briefly describe other software application packages that would aid Gripper in solving its current and future problems.

5-11 *Selected Small Firm (A Continuing Case)* For the small firm that you selected in Chapter 1 (see Problem 1-7), complete the following requirements:

    a. If it currently uses a computer-based information system, de-

scribe the hardware configuration, software, and applications. Also suggest further developments of the computer-based system that appear useful and feasible.

    b. If it does not currently use a computer-based information system, describe the hardware configuration, software, and applications that appear useful and feasible.

Suggested Readings

Ahlers, David M. "Management Information Systems, From Spyglass to Pocket Calculators." *Financial Executive* (July 1976), pp. 44–52.

American Accounting Association. "Report of the Committee on Accounting and Information Systems." In *Committee Reports: Supplement to Vol. LXVI of the Accounting Review.* Evanston, Ill.: 1971, pp. 288–350.

Bohl, Marilyn. *Information Processing.* 3d ed. Palo Alto, Calif.: Science Research Associates, 1980.

Bruns, William J., and McFarlan, F. Warren. "Information Technology Puts Power in Control Systems." *Harvard Business Review* (Sept.–Oct. 1987), pp. 89–94.

Burch, John G., and Grudnitski, Gary. *Information Systems: Theory and Practice.* 5th ed. New York: John Wiley, 1989.

Coleman, Raymond J., and Riley, M. J. "The Organizational Impact of MIS." *Journal of Systems Management* (March 1972), pp. 13–19.

Dearden, John. "Will the Computer Change the Job of Top Management?" *Sloan Management Review* (Fall 1983), pp. 57–60.

Dykeman, John. "Optical Disk: A Technology on the Move." *Modern Office Technology* (June 1988), pp. 81–88.

Evans, Sherli. "Let's Look at the Fax." *Modern Office Technology* (May 1986), pp. 55–62.

Grant, F. J. "Twenty-First Century Software." *Datamation* (April 1, 1985), pp. 123–130.

Gullo, Karen, and Shatz, Willie. "The Supercomputer Breaks Through." *Datamation* (May 1, 1988), pp. 50–63.

Mandell, Steven L. *Computers and Data Processing Today*. 2d. ed. St. Paul, Minn.: West Publishing, 1987.

McLeod, Raymond, Jr. *Management Information Systems*. 3rd. ed. Chicago: Science Research Associates, 1986.

Nofel, Peter J. "40 Million Hits on Optical Disk." *Modern Office Technology* (March 1986), pp. 84–88.

Ogdin, Carol A. "The Many Choices in Development Languages." *Mini-Micro Systems*. (August 1980), pp. 81–84.

Paddock, Harold E. "Voice Input a Reality." *Internal Auditor* (December 1983), pp. 23–26.

Pirani, Judith. "On the Beam with Laser Printing." *Modern Office Technology* (March 1986), pp. 47–54.

Rockart, J. F., and Scott-Morton, M. S. "Implications of Changes in Information Technology for Corporate Strategy." *Interfaces* (Jan.–Feb. 1984). pp. 84–95.

Rochchild, Edward S. "An Eye on Optical Disks." *Datamation* (March 1, 1986), pp. 73–74.

Runyan, Linda. "Hot Technologies for 1989." *Datamation* (January 15, 1989), pp. 18–24.

Strassman, Paul A., and Willard, Charles F. "The Evolution of the Page Printer." *Datamation* (May 1978), pp. 167–170.

Takeuchi, Hirotaki, and Schmidt, Allan H. "New Promise of Computer Graphics." *Harvard Business Review* (Jan.–Feb. 1980), pp. 122–131.

Verity, John W. "A New Slant on Parallel Processing." *Datamation* (February 15, 1987), pp. 79–84.

Withington, Frederic G. "Winners and Losers in the Fifth Generation." *Datamation* (December 1983), pp. 193–209.

After studying this chapter, you should be able to do the following:

Identify the objectives of the internal control structure of a firm.

Describe the exposures to risk that a firm faces with respect to assets and data.

Identify the impact of computers upon the controls needed by firms.

Discuss the especially severe impact of computer crime.

Describe major classifications of controls and security measures within the internal control structure.

Survey and illustrate design considerations pertaining to controls.

Discuss the considerations that affect the feasibility of controls and control systems within firms.

Identify the forces that are instrumental in the improvement of control systems within firms.

Chapter **6**

RISK EXPOSURES AND INTERNAL CONTROL CONCEPTS

A control framework is an integral part of a firm's information system. Consisting of a wide variety of controls and security measures, this framework spans all transactions as well as the firm's organization, operations, and even management practices. Because the controls and security measures are internal to the firm, the framework is often called an **internal control structure.**

A weak and unsound internal control structure can lead to serious repercussions. Information generated by the information system is likely to be unreliable, incomplete, and perhaps untimely. Moreover, the firm's resources may be used ineffectively and may become vulnerable to loss or damage. Consequently, a firm's management should be very

concerned with the adequacy of the controls and security measures that comprise the internal control structure.

Accountants often take active roles in the development and review of control frameworks. They work closely with system designers during the development of information systems, in order to assure that the planned controls and security measures are adequate and auditable. For instance, they make sure that totals will be balanced and reconciled properly and that audit trails are clearly established. As auditors they determine the adequacy of internal accounting control procedures and security measures, so that they can assess the reliance to be placed thereon during subsequent auditing procedures. Developing and evaluating control structures are considered to be relative strengths of accountants.

Internal Control Objectives

Broad Objectives

The major objectives of internal control, as stated by the American Institute of Certified Public Accountants, are as follows:

1. To safeguard the firm's assets (i.e., resources, including data and information).
2. To ensure the accuracy and reliability of the accounting data and information (i.e., to keep the data and information free from errors and to provide consistent results when processing like data).
3. To promote efficiency in all of the firm's operations.
4. To encourage adherence to management's prescribed policies and procedures.[1]

Many of the controls that further these objectives are applied within the context of the control process. That is, they consist of comparing actual measures against benchmarks. For instance, the actual cash on hand is compared with the amount shown in the cash ledger account; the customer number on a remittance advice is compared to the number of the account listed in the accounts receivable master file; the date an order is actually shipped is compared to the scheduled date; the signature on a check may be verified by reference to the names of authorized signers in a management policy.

Other controls, such as the use of locked cash registers and safes, are physical in nature. These controls are often called security measures.

[1]American Institute of Certified Public Accountants, Committee on Auditing Procedure, *Internal Control—Elements of a Coordinated System and Its Importance to Management and the Independent Public Accountant* (New York: AICPA, 1949).

Difficulties in Achieving Internal Control Objectives

The aforementioned control objectives are difficult to achieve fully. One difficulty is due to the complexity and rapid changes faced by a typical firm. It is bombarded by confusing and ever-changing tax laws, new technology, competitive actions, and so on. Complexities and changes such as these affect the benchmarks on which many of the controls are based. Another difficulty is the array of risks to which the internal control structure and its firm are exposed. For instance, data may be accessed by unauthorized persons. A third difficulty, related to the first, concerns the use of computer technology within the control structure. A fourth difficulty may be traced to the human factor, since control objectives are accomplished through people. For example, employees may not follow procedures consistently. A final difficulty relates to the costs of controls. When would a firm be unwise to add a costly control, for instance? Most of these difficulties are discussed in following sections of this chapter.

Risk Exposures

A firm is exposed to a variety of risks. Certain risks, for instance, are encountered through competition in the market place. **Risk exposures** are the threats to a firm's assets and information quality due to lapses or inadequacies in controls.

Types of Risks

Among the system-related risks to which a firm is exposed, other than those due to poor decision making and inefficient operations, are the following:

1. **Unintentional errors.** Errors may appear in input data, such as customer names or numbers. Alternatively, they may appear

during processing, as when clerks incorrectly multiply quantities ordered (on customers' orders) by the unit prices of the merchandise items. These errors may occur on an occasional basis, or they may occur consistently. For instance, an incorrectly written computer program may cause computational errors to occur each time the program is executed. In any of these situations, the erroneous data damage the accuracy and reliability of a firm's files and outputs. Unintentional errors often occur because employees are inadequately trained or supervised, or when they become tired and careless.

2. **Deliberate errors.** These errors constitute fraud, a deception practiced in order to secure unfair or unlawful gain. These, like unintentional errors, may appear in input data or during processing. For instance, a clerk may increase the amount on a check received from a customer or underfoot a column of cash receipts. Either type of error damages the accuracy and reliability of files and/or outputs. However, deliberate errors may also conceal thefts (and hence losses) of assets. For example, a manager may enter a misstatement in a report or financial statement. In addition to affecting the accuracy of the outputs, this error could mislead and thereby possibly defraud stockholders and creditors.

3. **Unintentional losses of assets.** Assets may be lost or misplaced by accident. For example, newly received merchandise items may be put into wrong warehouse bins, with the result that they are not found by pickers when filing orders. Data as well as physical assets may be lost. For instance, the accounts receivable file stored on a magnetic disk may be wiped out by a sudden power surge.

4. **Thefts of assets.** Assets of a firm may be stolen by outsiders, such as professional thieves who break into a storeroom in the dead of night. Alternatively, assets may be misappropriated through embezzlement or defalcation; that is, they may be taken by employees who have been entrusted with their care. For example, a cashier may pocket currency received by mail, or a production employee may carry home a tool. Employees who embezzle often create deliberate errors in order to hide their thefts.

5. **Breaches of security.** Unauthorized persons may gain access to the data files or other assets of a firm. For instance, a "hacker" may break into a firm's computerized files via a distant terminal, or an employee may peek at a salary report in an unlocked file drawer. Security breaches can be very damaging in certain cases, as when competitors gain access to a firm's confidential marketing plans.

6. **Acts of violence and natural disasters.** Certain violent acts can cause damage to a firm's assets, including data. If sufficiently serious, they can interrupt business operations and even push firms toward bankruptcy. Examples of such acts are the sabotage of computer facilities and the malicious destruction of customer files. Although violent acts are sometimes performed by outsiders such as terrorists, they are more often performed by disgruntled employees and ex-employees.

Great losses can also occur from natural disasters. In May 1988, for instance, a fire swept through the headquarters building of First Interstate Bank in Los Angeles. Before being brought under control, the fire destroyed the twelfth through the sixteenth floors. Smoke and water damage throughout all 62 floors was so severe that the entire building was closed for several months. Two thousand employees had to be relocated, and phone lines had to be rerouted.

Degrees of Risk Exposure

In order to combat the aforementioned risks effectively, exposures to each type of risk should be assessed and then controlled.

Exposure to risk is affected by such factors as

1. **Frequency.** The more frequent an occurrence, the greater the exposure to risk. A merchandising firm that makes numerous sales is highly exposed to errors in the transaction data. A contractor that bids on custom projects is exposed to calculation errors. A department store with numerous browsing shoppers has a significant exposure to merchandise losses from shoplifting.

2. **Vulnerability.** The more vulnerable an asset, the greater the exposure to risk. Cash is highly vulnerable to theft, since it is easily hidden and fully convertible. A telephone may be highly vulnerable to unauthorized use for long distance calls, especially if it is left untended in a remote office.

3. **Size.** The higher the value of a potential loss, the greater the risk exposure. An accounts receivable file represents a high risk exposure, since it contains essential information concerning amounts owed

and other matters that affect credit customers.

When two or more of the foregoing factors act in unison, the exposure to risk is multiplied. Thus, an extremely high exposure occurs in the case of a firm that conducts numerous sales for sizable amounts of cash. As might be imagined, this situation requires more extensive controls than one in which the exposure to risk is slight.

Computer Crimes

The increasing use of computer-based information systems has broadened the exposure to risks. Figure 6-1 lists a variety of errors, frauds, and security lapses that have been documented by newspapers and other sources.

In particular, those offenses known as **computer crimes** represent an increasingly serious class of risk exposure. Computer crimes pose very high degrees of risk, since all three of the risk factors mentioned earlier tend to be accentuated. A computer-based

---

- A customer received a bill for $1 million instead of $100, because of an error in the invoicing program.
- A supervisor added fictitious employees to the payroll, so that the payroll program would cause their paychecks to be sent to a friend's address.
- A programmer who was employed by a bank changed an interest calculation program to have it credit the fractional cents to his account.
- Another bank programmer modified a withdrawal program so that withdrawals against her personal account would be charged to an inactive account.
- A purchasing agent entered unauthorized purchase transactions via a terminal and had the merchandise delivered to his home.
- A disgruntled employee erased several reels of magnetic tape by the use of a small magnet.
- A salesperson carried away in her briefcase a magnetic tape containing a publishing firm's list of customers.
- A rookie computer operator accidentally wrote over the records in a customer master tape file and thus destroyed the account balances and related data.
- A fire in a firm's tape library destroyed thousands of reels of magnetic tape.
- A failure in an essential component of a computer caused the system to break down and the data to be lost.

FIGURE 6-1 Reported errors, frauds, and security lapses involving computer-based information systems.

system can process hundreds of transactions per hour, each transaction being subject to errors and fraudulent activity. A computer and its stored data are often vulnerable to damage and unauthorized access. A loss from computer fraud tends to be several times larger than the average loss when a manual system is involved. In fact, individual losses from computer crimes often exceed $1 million. To make matters worse, computer crimes are seldom detected and even less often prosecuted.

The following sampling of reported computer crimes suggests the dimensions of the problem:

1. A self-employed computer expert discovered the daily code that authorized funds to be transferred from a large bank to other banks. One day, five minutes before closing time, he called the wire room, gave the correct authorization code, and transferred $10 million into a bank account opened under his alias.

2. A technician who helped design the computerized ticket system for a major league baseball club stayed around the office one day to show staff workers how to operate the system. Later, club officials discovered that he had also used that day to print 7000 tickets, which he illegally sold through ticket brokers.

3. Automated teller machines (ATMs) installed by a large New York bank were the means of an ingenious fraud. Persons posing as bank employees would stop depositors in the middle of ATM transactions and direct them to other ATMs, explaining that the ATMs being used were inoperative. Then these persons would withdraw funds from the abandoned ATMs which had been opened (but not closed) by the depositors.

4. A number of unauthorized persons obtained the password into the files of the largest credit bureau in the country. From home computers they were able thereby to view the credit reports of millions of credit card users.

5. In a case similar to the preceding one the "414 gang" (a group of young computer "hackers") broke into the highly sensitive files of the Los Alamos National Laboratory.

Impacts of Computers on Internal Control

Computer-based information systems manipulate and transcribe data with impeccable accuracy. However, they tend to heighten the exposure to risks. These increased risk exposures are due to several inherent problems:

Concentrated Processing

In manual systems the processing of transactions is divided among clerks in several departments. This approach provides a means of cross-checking the work of others. Computer-based processing, however, largely takes place within self-contained computer facilities. Often these facilities include centralized data bases. Concentration of the processing bypasses or shortens the flows of data among organizational units. Consequently, less opportunity exists for detecting fraudulent activities, such as unauthorized transactions and thefts of assets.

Non-Human-Oriented Data Storage

Data stored in computer-based systems are oriented to the characteristics of magnetic or optical media. These characteristics differ from the paper-oriented media that are familiar to users of manual systems.

First, the data are invisible and hence incomprehensible to humans. The data can be printed or displayed, but it is necessary to request the computer or computer system personnel to do so. This additional data retrieval step increases opportunities for errors to occur. It also often frustrates such users as managers and accountants.

Second, the data are often erasable. For example, a customer's account can be erased from a magnetic disk without a trace remaining. A new invoicing program can be superimposed on a current program, which thereby is wiped out. Either of these situations can occur as planned or can happen accidentally or fraudulently.

Third, the data are extremely compressed. A single reel of magnetic tape can hold as much data as several file cabinets. Thus, vast quantities of data can be easily destroyed, damaged, or accessed by unauthorized users.

Fragmented Audit Trail

Portions of the audit trail are more likely to be eliminated in computer-based processing systems than in manual systems. Source documents may not be used, for instance, when sales orders are received via telephone and entered directly into the computer system through terminals. Journals may be omitted, since transactions can be posted directly to ledger accounts. Alternatively, journals may be retained but printed out infrequently or only when requested. This fragmentation of the audit trail hinders the detection of errors and irregularities.

Bypassed Human Judgment

Computers perform programmed instructions blindly; that is, they exercise no judgment. Thus, fewer opportunities exist in computer-based systems for humans to spot errors or questionable data. For instance, a time record that shows 400 hours worked by an employee this week is clearly erroneous; unless the computer is so informed by special editing instructions, it will accept and process the quantity as valid.

Added Complexity

Physical and logical features of computer-based systems are relatively complicated. Computers are difficult for most persons involved in the production or use of information to understand. Furthermore, they are designed to process large volumes of transactions within integrated procedures, often affecting multiple files.

One consequence of this complexity is the added possibility of introducing errors. Some errors may become implanted in computer programs, and this can lead to losses or embarrassments. Generally, such program errors are accidental, but sometimes they are deliberately inserted by programmers with fraudulent purposes. In either case they may be difficult to uncover. Other errors may be introduced by users, such as clerks, who are careless or not fully trained to use the equipment to which they have access. Most of these errors are also accidental. However, users occasionally enter intentional errors or attempt to gain unauthorized access to data within a system. They may perform these malicious acts either because of frustration with the system, because of a perverse desire to "beat the system," or because of unrestrained curiosity.

Another consequence of complexity is the mushrooming effects of errors, especially in those computer-based systems that employ on-line processing and large data bases. An incorrect product number on a sales order, if processed on-line, may quickly lead to errors in the records reflecting the quantity on hand, the ordering customer's account balance, and the balances of the related general ledger accounts. If the ordered product is to be manufactured by the firm, even more files would be affected.

Added Vulnerability of Stored Data and Equipment

Although data stored in computer-based systems may appear to be relatively inaccessible to users, the data actually may be quite accessible to skilled trespassers. Persons who understand computer systems and who have personal computers or terminals can break past inadequate security barriers to peer at confidential data. Moreover, when the computer system encompasses a widespread network, such intruders can access the data from thousands of miles away.

As noted earlier, computers are subject to a variety of possible ills. They have been struck by floods, fires, power outages, and vandals. They have broken down from lack of proper maintenance. As a firm becomes more dependent on its computer system, such breakdowns tend to cause greater degrees of inconvenience and even chaos.

A particularly disastrous breakdown occurred in May 1989. American Airline's Sabre reservation system was felled by a programming error that eliminated access to reservation data stored on 1080 hard disks. For about 13 hours the entire reservation system was inoperable; as a result American lost millions of dollars in potential revenue from bookings.[2]

Figure 6-2 summarizes the various control problems caused by computerization. It is generally arranged according to the major information system activities, but it also includes a category for equipment. The characteristics of computer-based systems are contrasted with those of manual systems. In addition, key risk exposures are identified and compensating controls are suggested. Specific controls are discussed in more detail in the following section and in Chapter 9.

Classifications of Controls

An effective internal control structure for a typical firm may consist of numerous and varied controls (including security mea-

sures). These controls may be classified according to objectives, intended uses, system architectures, and settings.

Classification by Objectives

The American Institute of Certified Public Accountants (AICPA) has defined two major categories of control as follows:[3]

Accounting control comprises the plan of organization and the procedures and records that are concerned with the safeguarding of assets and the reliability of financial records and consequently are designed to provide reasonable assurance that:

a. Transactions are executed in accordance with management's general or specific authorization.
b. Transactions are recorded as necessary (1) to permit preparation of financial statements in conformity with generally accepted accounting principles or any other criteria applicable to such statements and (2) to maintain accountability of assets.
c. Access to assets is permitted only in accordance with management's authorization.
d. The recorded accountability for assets is compared with the existing assets at reasonable intervals and appropriate action is taken with respect to any differences.

Administrative control includes, but is not limited to, the plan of organization and the procedures and records that are concerned with the decision processes leading to management's authorization of transactions. Such authorization is a management function directly associated with the responsiblity for achieving the objectives of the organization and is the starting point for establishing accounting control of transactions.

---

[2]Steinberg, Don, "Rare Software Glitch Costs American Millions," *PC Week* (May 29, 1989), p. 61.

[3]American Institute of Certified Public Accountants, *Statement on Auditing Standards No. 1,* "Codification of Auditing Standards and Procedures" (New York: AICPA, 1973), p. 20. Copyright 1973 by the American Institute of Certified Public Accountants, Inc.

Element or activity	Manual system characteristics	Computer-based system Characteristics	Risk exposures	Compensating controls
Data collection	Data recorded on paper source documents	Data sometimes captured without use of source documents	Audit trail may be partially lost	Printed copies of source documents prepared by computer system
	Data reviewed for errors by clerks	Data often not subject to review by clerks	Errors, accidental or deliberate, may be entered for processing	Edit checks performed by computer system
Data processing	Processing steps performed by clerks who possess judgment	Processing steps performed by CPU "blindly" in accordance with program instructions	Errors may cause incorrect results of processing	Outputs reviewed by users of computer system; carefully developed computer processing programs
	Processing steps spread among various clerks in separate departments	Processing steps concentrated within computer CPU	Unauthorized manipulation of data and theft of assets can occur on larger scale	Restricted access to computer facilities; clear procedure for authorizing changes to programs
	Processing requires use of journals and ledgers	Processing does not require use of journals	Audit trail may be partially lost	Printed journals and other analyses
	Processing performed relatively slowly	Processing performed very rapidly	Effects of errors may spread rapidly throughout files	Editing of all data during input and processing steps
Data storage and retrieval	Data stored in file drawers throughout the various departments	Data compressed on magnetic media (e.g., tapes, disks)	Data may be accessed by unauthorized persons or stolen	Security measures at points of access and over data library
	Data stored on hard copies in human-readable form	Data stored in invisible, erasable, computer-readable form	Data are temporarily unusable by humans, and might possibly be lost	Data files printed periodically; backups of files; protection against sudden power losses
	Stored data accessible on a piecemeal basis at various locations	Stored data often readily accessible from various locations via terminals	Data may be accessed by unauthorized persons	Security measures at points of access
Information generation	Outputs generated laboriously and usually in small volumes	Outputs generated quickly and neatly, often in large volumes	Inaccuracies may be buried in impressive-looking outputs that users accept on faith	Reviews by users of outputs, including the checking of amounts
	Outputs usually in hard copy form	Outputs provided in various forms, including soft copy displays and voice responses	Information stored on magnetic media is subject to modification (only hard copy provides permanent record)	Backups of files; periodic printing of stored files onto hard copy records
Transmission of data and information	Usually transmitted via postal service and hand delivery	Often transmitted by communications lines	Data may be accessed or modified or destroyed by unauthorized persons	Security measures over transmission lines; coding of data; verification of transmitted data
Equipment	Relatively simple, inexpensive, and mobile	Relatively complex, expensive and in fixed locations	Business operations may be intentionally or unintentionally interrupted; data or hardware may be destroyed; operations may be delayed through inefficiencies	Backup of data and power supply and equipment; preventive maintenance of equipment; restrictions on access to computer facilities; documentation of equipment usage and processing procedures

FIGURE 6-2 Control problems caused by computerization.

Accounting controls are therefore concerned with achieving the first two objectives of internal control; **administrative controls** are concerned with the latter two. Accounting controls can be viewed as comprising an accounting control system, one key component of the internal control structure. Administrative controls, on the other hand, are implemented via the operational control and management control systems described in Chapter 4. Figure 6-3 portrays these relationships among the component systems and control objectives.

Classification by Intended Uses

Controls may also be classified according to intended uses. **Preventive controls** are intended to prevent an adverse event, such as an error or loss, from occurring. **Detective controls** are intended to determine when adverse events occur. **Corrective controls** are intended to provide the information needed to correct the effects of adverse events. These controls also may be differentiated according to degrees of activism. Preventive controls are passive, detective controls are active, and corrective controls are very ac-

tive. Most accounting controls are preventive or detective in nature, whereas many administrative controls are corrective in nature.

Classification by System Architectures

Information systems may be differentiated according to such architectures as manually based processing systems, computer-based batch processing systems, computer-based on-line processing systems, centralized data base systems, and distributed networks. Each architecture tends to require a unique set of specific controls, even though many of the controls overlap among the various architectures.

Classification by Settings

The control framework centers around the transactions to which the routine activities of an information system are applied. Controls related to these transaction flows are called **transaction** or **application controls.** The overall objectives of transaction controls are to provide reasonable assurance that all transactions are properly authorized

	Name	Objective(s)	Type of controls employed
Internal control structure	Management control system	To encourage compliance with management's policies and procedures	Administrative
	Operational control system	To promote efficiency in operations	Administrative
	Accounting control system	To safeguard assets and ensure the accuracy and reliability of data and information	Accounting

FIGURE 6-3 Three component systems comprising the internal control structure.

and accurately recorded, classified, processed, and reported. Hence, transaction or application controls may be divided into input, processing, and output controls. The remainder of the control framework pertains to the environmental setting in which the transaction flows take place. Within this environmental setting is a broad collection of controls relating to the firm's organization, operations, management practices, documentation procedures, security measures, asset accountability procedures, and policies (such as authorization policies).

The control framework is pictured in Figure 6-4. In addition to showing the transaction controls, it identifies the various controls within the environmental setting as being either accounting controls of a general nature or administrative controls. The figure also shows that certain control categories may be classified as either **general accounting controls** or administrative controls.

Design Considerations Pertaining to Controls

While classification plans provide conceptual frameworks for visualizing internal control structures, they cannot show the specific controls that must be designed into such structures. In this section we survey specific controls and the principles or considerations on which they are based. For convenience the survey is arranged in accordance with the framework shown in Figure 6-4. Since the

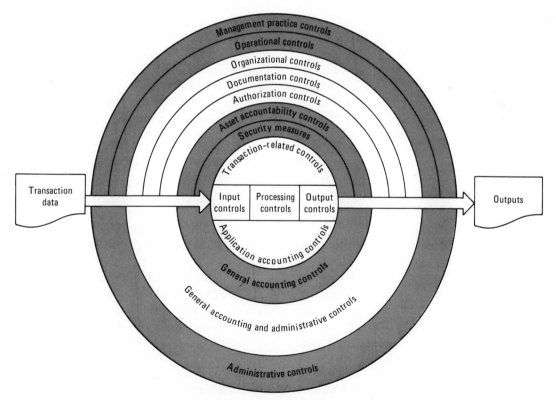

FIGURE 6-4   A control framework for information systems.

underlying control principles and procedures are emphasized, the illustrated controls are pertinent to both manually based and computer-based processing systems. Controls that pertain to specific computer-based architectures are discussed in Chapter 9 or in the chapters describing the various architectures. Operational controls are omitted in the following survey, since they were discussed in Chapter 4.

Management Practice Controls

Sound management policies and procedures, here called management practices, are essential to an effective internal control system. Such practices encompass the organization and documentation controls noted previously. Practices relating to planning and personnel also are important to control systems.

Sound planning practices include the preparation of budgets. A budget quantifies the financial objectives of a firm. That is, it establishes both the revenue levels that the firm expects to achieve and the cost levels within which it desires to constrain its operations. Through comparisons with actual revenues and costs, the budgeted values can help to detect inefficiencies, losses, and even fraudulent activities.

Planning practices extend beyond routine operations to cover system development projects. When the information system needs to be changed or further developed in some manner, careful procedures should be followed. If the development is to be substantial, project budgets should be prepared as a basis of control.

With respect to personnel practice, employees should be carefully selected and trained to fulfill all positions of responsibility. Each employee should have his or her performance evaluated periodically, with merit raises based on the results of such reviews. Employees having access to cash and other negotiable assets should be bonded. (Fidelity bonds indemnify a firm in case it suffers losses from defalcations committed by employees.) Also, employees in key positions of trust should be required to take periodic vacations; any irregularities are likely to be detected by their substitutes. Finally, all employees should be well supervised, so that they are encouraged to follow established policies and avoid irregularities.

Organizational Controls

Organizational controls are designed in accordance with the principle of **organizational independence.** This principle states that there should be a clear and logical division of assigned duties and responsibilities. Hence, two or more organizationally separated employees should be involved in processing each transaction. No single employee should be allowed to handle all aspects of any transaction. Thus, clerks in the sales order department, warehouse, shipping department, and billing department should be involved in the processing of sales orders. With effective organizational independence, no single employee should be able to commit an error or fraudulent act and then hide the act. To take an example from cash disbursements processing, clerks who are responsible for checking the validity of suppliers' invoices should be organizationally separated from the person who signs and mails the checks to suppliers. When responsibilities are so divided, the check signer should detect errors or omissions of the vouching clerks. Also, if either the vouching clerks or the check signer attempts to obtain funds by means of a fictitious supplier's invoice, the fraudulent act should be detected.

Organizational independence provides most effective control when the authorizing, record-keeping, and custodial functions are organizationally separated. For instance, employees in separate organizational units

Transaction	Authorization Units	Record-keeping Units	Custodial Units
Sales	Sales order Credit	Billing Accounts receivable	Warehouse Shipping
Cash receipts	(None, since cash receipt is dependent on prior sale transaction)	Mailroom Accounts receivable	Cashier
Purchases	Inventory management Purchasing	Inventory control Accounts payable	Receiving Stores
Cash disbursements	(None, since cash disbursement is dependent on prior purchase transaction)	Accounts payable	Cashier
Payroll	Personnel Timekeeping	Payroll	Paymaster or cashier
Fixed-assets acquisition	Management (or asset manager)	Property	Using department
Production	Production planning	Inventory control Cost accounting	Stores Production operations Warehouse

FIGURE 6-5 Examples of organizational independence.

should (1) authorize a transaction, (2) physically handle the assets involved in the transaction, and (3) maintain the records that reflect the transaction. In fact, an employee who has access to assets should not have access to the records, and vice versa. Examples of effective organizational independence are listed in Figure 6-5.

The principle of organizational independence also applies within individual functions or departments. For instance, within the purchasing department the purchasing manager should approve purchase orders prepared by buyers; within the accounting function an accounting manager should approve journal vouchers prepared by accountants.

While effective organizational independence influences the behavior of most employees, it unfortunately does not guarantee the absence of fraud. If **collusion** (a conspiracy among two or more persons to commit fraud) exists, even a well-designed division of responsibilities can be negated. Fortunately, the probability of collusion occur-

ring in a specific situation is generally quite low.[4]

Documentation Controls

All components of a firm's information system, as well as the related organization and policies, should be fully documented. Complete and understandable documentation aids control in several ways. Not only does it (1) help employees to interpret the policies correctly and (2) help them to visualize the relationships among organizational

[4] Several behavioral assumptions underlie internal control. For instance, people are viewed as having inherent mental, moral, and physical weaknesses. However, it is assumed that an effective internal control system will deter most (if not all) persons from committing fraud, since it poses the threat of prompt exposure. Furthermore, a situation that requires collusion introduces an added deterrent. Most persons (it is assumed) abhor the possibility of being socially rejected for suggesting that irregularities be committed. For more details, see D. R. Carmichael, "Behavioral Hypotheses of Internal Control," *The Accounting Review* (April 1970), pp. 235–245.

functions, but it also (3) ensures that procedures will be performed more reliably, consistently, and efficiently. Examples of useful documentation are policy statements, organization charts, job descriptions, procedure manuals, charts of accounts, computer program manuals, and audit trail reference codes.

Authorization Controls

Authorizations serve as a bridge between administrative and accounting controls. They represent a key means by which management meets its responsibility for safeguarding the firm's assets and assuring that transactions are proper. Also, as we have seen, the addition of an authorizing function enhances organizational independence.

Authorizations may be classified as either general or specific. A **general authorization** establishes standard conditions under which transactions are approved and executed. For instance, management sets general criteria by which credit sales are to be approved. When a customer applies for credit, the credit department either approves or disapproves the application according to the criteria of the general authorization. A **specific authorization** pertains to a particular event, with the conditions and parties specified. For example, a cashier who has general authorization to sign checks paying valid obligations may need specific authorization to write and sign a $100,000 check repaying a bank loan.

Authorizations are generally reflected through transaction documents. Thus, copies of a sales order prepared by a clerk in the sales order department authorize goods to be released from the warehouse and to be shipped. Their power to authorize derives from management's general authorization granted through the established sales order procedure. To take another example, the write-off notices signed by a designated manager authorize amounts owed by certain customers to be cleared from their accounts. The power of such notices to authorize derives from management's general authorization embodied in the established bad-debt write-off procedure.

Asset Accountability Controls

For adequate protection, assets should be properly reflected in the accounting records. Controls that provide asset accountability include accounting ledgers, acknowledgment procedures, reconciliations, and reassessments.

Accounting subsidiary ledgers. As described in Chapter 3, accounting ledgers consist of detailed records that are controlled by accounts in the general ledger. Assets for which subsidiary ledgers are typically maintained include accounts receivable, inventory, and fixed assets.

Acknowledgment procedures. Employees and outside persons such as customers should be asked to acknowledge their receipt and hence accountability for assets. For instance, when merchandise is received from suppliers, a clerk in the receiving department counts the items and prepares a receiving report. He or she thereby acknowledges accountability for the items counted.

Reconciliations. Reconciliations are comparisons of values computed independently. For example, all items of the physical inventory should be counted periodically. These physical counts can then be compared or reconciled with the counts shown in the inventory records. Discrepancies, due to such causes as pilferage and miscounting, flag the need for adjustment. An adjustment might consist of reducing the counts in the records to equal the physical counts. (Other examples of reconciliations are discussed under the transaction control categories.)

Reassessments. Reassessments are reevaluations of asset values, with a view toward making adjustments if necessary. As noted above, physical counts may raise the need to adjust downward the counts reflected in the inventory records, in order to allow for breakage and losses. Such adjustments in counts translate into adjustments to values, since the inventory balances shown in the records are computed as the products of quantities and unit prices.

Security Measures

A variety of controls are needed to safeguard a firm's assets, such as cash and data. Those that provide physical protection are called **security measures.** Many security measures provide protection by restricting access to the assets. That is, only those persons who are authorized by management should be allowed to handle the assets personally; all others should be denied access. In the case of data, unauthorized persons should not even be allowed to see the data records. Examples of physical restriction measures include security guards, locked cash registers and computer terminals, and read-only memory in computer processors. Another type of security measure provides protection against environmental hazards. Examples range from fire alarm systems to backup equipment and copies of records.

Transaction Input Controls

Transactions should be recorded accurately, completely, and promptly. The proper amounts should be reflected in the proper accounts and within the accounting periods during which the transactions occur.

Specific controls employed to achieve these input objectives include visual checks, well-designed source documents, document registers, controlled tapes, and account codes.

1. *Visual checks* are reviews or edits by clerical employees of inflowing data. For instance, sales order clerks normally review orders received from customers, checking for all needed items of data and for the validity of merchandise or product codes.

2. *Well-designed source documents* encourage the recording of complete and accurate transaction data by providing clear instructions and labels, adequate spacing, and so forth. One feature of critical importance is sequential prenumbering. Prenumbered documents, such as prenumbered sales invoices, enable transactions to be identified quickly. Prenumbering therefore aids in establishing clear audit trails. Also, by checking all numbers in sequence, it is possible to detect the loss or delayed processing of particular transaction documents. Another important feature of many source documents is space for authorizing signatures.

3. *Document registers,* on which incoming source documents are listed and then checked off after processing, reinforce the prenumbering feature of source documents. Examples of document registers are cash receipts journals and supplier invoice registers.

4. *Controlled tapes,* such as those that are locked within cash registers, constitute a tamperproof record of all transactions. Since controlled tapes are usually checked against the actual cash received, they encourage careful handling of cash transactions by salesclerks or cashiers.

5. *Account codes,* established via the chart of accounts, simplify the recording of transactions and route the data into the appropriate processing procedures.

Transaction Processing Controls

Transaction data should enter a processing procedure without loss and should be processed accurately and completely. Specific processing controls include documented actions, verifications, batch totals, and reconciliations.

1. **Documented actions** consist of actions that acknowledge accountability for performance. The sales order procedure, for instance, may require the shipping clerk to prepare a shipping notice for each shipment. Upon signing the notice, the clerk acknowledges accountability for any impropriety in the shipment. To take another case, the procedure pertaining to the expenditure cycle may specify that a vouching box is to be stamped on each incoming supplier's invoice. After checking each invoice, an accounting clerk is expected to place his or her initials in the box; by this action the clerk acknowledges accountability for undiscovered errors or discrepancies.

2. **Verifications** are checks by one or more persons on work performed by others. For instance, one clerk in the billing department may check the computations appearing on sales invoices before they are mailed to customers. The supervisor in the general ledger department may verify the postings performed during the day by the general ledger clerks. Verifications may also be performed by automated equipment. For instance, accounting machines are equipped with proofing features, by which they check the accuracy of transaction postings.

3. **Batch totals** are indispensable controls when transactions are processed in batches. To initiate this type of control, key values pertaining to a batch of newly recorded transaction documents are accumulated prior to processing. Then, during or after each batch processing step, the same key values are again totaled. If the totals agree, there is reasonable assurance that all recorded transactions have been accurately processed and that no transaction records have been lost.

4. **Reconciliations** are performed in order to spot omissions or processing errors. One type of reconciliation, illustrated by the batch total procedure, involves the comparison of two independently computed totals. Other examples in this category include (1) the use of trial balances to compare total debit account balances against total credit account balances and (2) the reconciliation of the total of all balances in a subsidiary ledger against the balance in the corresponding control account.

Another type of reconciliation involves the comparison of documents obtained from separate sources. An example is the comparison of copies of the sales invoices held in an open order file with notices of goods shipped.

A third type of reconciliation consists of comparing the level of a resource against records pertaining to the resource. Examples are a bank reconciliation and an inventory count–reconciliation. In fact, a thorough bank reconciliation actually involves four reconciliations:

1. A reconciliation of the balance in the bank account with the cash balance in the general ledger, as of the beginning of the accounting period.

2. A reconciliation of all deposits made to the bank account during the period with the total receipts entered into the cash receipts journal.

3. A reconciliation of all withdrawals from the bank account during the period with the total amount of checks entered into the cash disbursements journal.

4. A reconciliation of the balance in the bank account with the cash balance in the general ledger, as of the end of the accounting period.

In accordance with the principle of organizational independence, reconciliations should be prepared only by employees or managers not otherwise responsible for the processing of related transactions. For instance, no employee involved in the processing or handling of cash receipts or cash disbursements should prepare a bank reconciliation. Instead, it should be prepared by an accounting manager or an internal auditor.

Transaction Output Controls

The outputs provided by an information system should be complete and reliable and be distributed to the proper users. Output controls consist mainly of reviews and distribution logs.

Reviews are similar to verifications except that they are typically performed by persons other than those involved in transaction processing. In some cases the reviewers are managers or employees of the firm. Thus, the treasurer may review the deposit slips that have been prepared by the cashier before the day's cash receipts are taken to the bank. An internal auditor may review the bank statement and checks when they have been returned by the bank. In other cases the reviewers are persons outside the firm. For instance, customers normally review the monthly statements they receive before remitting the amounts due. Creditors review the financial statements and key accounts before extending credit. External auditors also review the financial statements, as well as all aspects of the internal control system, before releasing their written professional opinions.

Distribution logs are lists of persons who have been designated to receive reports. They are therefore useful in directing reports to the proper recipients. Entries made in the logs provide written records pertaining to the actual distribution of the reports.

Example of Controls in a Small Firm

A small firm often lacks certain requisites for sound internal control. Its employees may be too few for an effective division of duties and responsibilities, and its funds may be too scanty to allow the preparation of sufficient documentation. Nevertheless, a small firm can overcome such deficiencies. The key to an effective control structure is the manager–owner. He (or she) should closely supervise the employees and even perform such tasks as opening mail, depositing cash, writing checks, signing purchase orders, and reconciling the bank statements. He should also carefully distribute tasks among the available employees, creating as many cross-checks and segregations of incompatible duties as possible.

The typical small retail firm can also gain a significant measure of control from the familiar cash register. In addition to being the focal point for cash receipts transactions, it can contribute to the system of controls in several ways:

1. By providing a printed receipt that the customer can compare with the total displayed in a window at the top of the register.

2. By ringing a bell that alerts the manager or supervisor to the fact that a sales transaction is taking place.

3. By transcribing the amount of each sale onto a tape that is locked in the register (and thus safe from possible tampering by a sales clerk). At the end of the day the tape can be removed by the manager and the totals reconciled with the cash in the drawers.

Optional control features for cash registers include separate cash drawers for each sales employee using the register; several internal accumulators that provide totals by such classifications (for a food store) as groceries, meats, and produce; and an attachment that automatically dispenses the correct amount of change.

Considerations of Feasibility

Building an effective and feasible internal control structure is not a simple task. It involves more than assembling all of the controls and security measures that come to mind. Audit, cost, and human factors need to be considered.

Audit-Effectiveness

The controls in an information system should not only be adequate to achieve the objectives stated above; they should also be capable of being evaluated or audited. In addition, they should actually be audited. All of these qualifications can fully be met only with the involvement of both the internal and external auditors.

Auditors can play a significant role in the selection of suitable controls. In fact, they should serve as consultants *during* the systems development phases. Expert advice is needed, since control frameworks must be adapted to the particular circumstances of individual firms and their information systems. Auditors also understand the auditability of control frameworks, since they are aware of the available audit techniques. In those areas or types of processing applications where auditability is relatively low, the auditors may recommend the insertion of additional controls. Finally, every control framework requires ongoing reviews and evaluations by auditors. These reviews will likely include bank statements and other financial records, plus statistical reports and related outputs. The evaluations should include the controls as well as the general ledger. Approaches to and techniques for audits are discussed in Chapter 17.

Cost-Effectiveness

Incorporating a control or security measure into a system involves a cost. Certain types of controls—such as corrective controls, documentation controls, and most security measures—are quite expensive. One question to be answered when designing a control structure may be stated as follows: Will the addition of a specific control provide a benefit, in reduced risk or increased reliability, at least as great as its cost? If the answer is yes, the control is likely to be a desirable (i.e., cost-effective) addition. In some cases, even controls that complement other controls may be found to be cost-effective, since they increase reliability by detecting errors that may be missed by the other controls. On the other hand, certain complementary controls may not improve reliability or reduce risks to a significant degree, and hence may not be desirable additions.

In most control situations this concern can be expressed as the following trade-off between processing efficiency and reliability: To what extent does transaction processing become less efficient, and hence more costly, when a specific control is added for the purpose of increasing reliability? If the addition of the control will appreciably degrade processing efficiency without significantly enhancing reliability, the control should not be employed.

Since controls form an interlocking framework, all controls should be reviewed and assessed by means of a **cost–benefit analysis.** Preferably, this review and assessment should take place during a systems development activity; however, it may be performed at any time.

A cost–benefit analysis begins with a thorough assessment of the risks to which the firm is exposed, such as losses of vital data records. The second step is to measure the extent of each risk exposure in dollar terms. For instance, if the exposure is the possible loss of an asset, the amount needed to replace the asset would represent the extent of the exposure. The third step is to multiply the estimated effect of each exposure by the estimated frequency of occurrence over a reasonable period (e.g., a year). The resulting product is the potential loss that can be incurred by not avoiding a particular risk. Alternatively, it is the benefit to be gained by avoiding the risk or improving the reliability of the information system. The fourth step is to determine the cost of installing and maintaining a control (or controls) to improve reliability with respect to each particular risk exposure. The fifth step is to compare the benefit from improved reliability against the cost of the related control. When the benefit due to a particular control exceeds its cost, the added control can be said to be desirable. A final step, when suitable, would be to sum the benefits attained by all controls and compare this total against the total cost of the internal control structure.

Cost–benefit analyses should incorporate transaction processing systems as well as general internal control environments. In such cases each source of data and processing point should be assessed for its exposure to risk. For instance, the risk exposure at the point of receiving cash receipts transactions may be assessed as very high, whereas the risk exposure during the posting step may be assessed as quite low.

A cost–benefit analysis is difficult to apply. None of the factors is easily measured. Moreover, the added degree of reliability provided by each control is hard to assess. However, new techniques are being developed. For instance, a technique known as **reliability analysis** calculates reliability by measuring the probabilities related to a process such as transaction processing. Thus, it measures the probability of executing the process without error, the probability of an error arising that will be detected by a specific control, and so on. These probabilities are then employed in a formula to compute the reliability when a specified set of controls is employed. While still in the experimental

stage, reliability analysis is a promising technique for use in a cost–benefit analysis.[5]

Behavioral Reactions of Employees

Employees are a critical element in any control structure. In the last analysis, any structure is only as good as the people who operate it and function within it. One of the primary purposes of controls, therefore, is to influence the behavior of employees and others who interface with the system. Consequently, designers of control structures must be concerned with the reaction of employees to controls. If controls are perceived by affected employees as being punitive or unnecessary, the employees may circumvent the controls. Thus, it usually is desirable to clarify the usefulness of controls and security measures when adverse reactions are noted. For instance, it can be pointed out that measures restricting access to cash are useful in that they remove temptation from honest employees.

Forces for the Improvement of Controls

During earlier periods many an information system was deficient with respect to controls and security measures. Often the system was intended primarily to provide the needed day-to-day documents and reports and to satisfy legal obligations. In recent decades, however, various forces have arisen to encourage the improvement of internal control systems. Perhaps the most influential of these forces have been management, professional associations, and governmental bodies.

---

[5]For details of this technique, see George Bodnar, "Reliability Modeling of Internal Control Systems," *The Accounting Review,* Oct. 1975, pp. 747–757.

Needs of Management

The managers of most firms have recognized their vital stake in adequate internal control structures. On the one hand, they have become aware of the huge losses and damages that can occur to the costly assets entrusted to their care. Newspapers and the other media have publicized the increasing instances of "white collar" crime, as well as overt thefts of merchandise and other portable assets. Managers have noted that the average loss from each crime has also been rising dramatically. On the other hand, they have grown concerned about the accuracy and reliability of the information they receive. Being primary users of information from their information systems, they appreciate the potential for making poor decisions because of inaccurate and incomplete information. Furthermore, as dependence on computer systems has increased, they have come to realize the seriousness of security breaches.

Concerns of Professional Associations

Professional accounting associations such as the American Institute of Certified Public Accountants (AICPA) and the Institute of Internal Auditors (IIA) have established codes of ethics. These codes are self-imposed and self-enforced rules of conduct. Included are rules pertaining to such matters as independence, technical competence, and suitable practices during audits of information systems.

The codes of ethics have been expanded and clarified by various pronouncements, such as Statements on Auditing Standards issued by the AICPA. Particular attention has been given to internal controls, as the following excerpts illustrate:

- A professional standard of field work for auditors specifies ". . . a proper study and evaluation of the existing internal controls as a basis for reliance thereon . . . ."[6]

- The Statement on Auditing Standards (SAS) No. 3 requires that the computerized portions of an information system be included in an auditor's study and evaluation of the internal control system (now called structure).[7]

- A study issued by the AICPA provides lists of control objectives and a step-by-step procedure for analyzing controls in computerized systems.[8]

- A set of standards issued by the IIA pertains to the responsibilities of internal auditors for evaluating control and otherwise conducting the practice of internal auditing.[9]

- SAS No. 48 amends SAS No. 3 with respect to the effects of computerized systems on accounting controls, as well as the need for specialized auditing skills when evaluating such systems.[10]

- SAS No. 55 supersedes SAS No. 1 in order to restate the need for obtaining a thorough understanding of the internal control structure (formerly called system) before undertaking audits of financial statements.[11]

[6]American Institute of Certified Public Accountants, *Statement on Auditing Standards No. 1* (New York: AICPA, 1973), Section 640.

[7]American Institute of Certified Public Accountants, *Statement on Auditing Standards No. 3* (New York: AICPA, 1974).

[8]American Institute of Certified Public Accountants, *The Auditor's Study and Evaluation of Internal Control in EDP Systems* (New York: AICPA, 1977).

[9]The Institute of Internal Auditors, *Standards for the Professional Practice of Internal Auditing* (Altamonte Springs, Fla.: IIA, 1978).

[10]American Institute of Certified Public Accountants, *The Effects of Computer Processing on the Examination of Financial Statements* (New York: AICPA, 1984).

[11]American Institute of Certified Public Accountants, "Consideration of the Internal Control Structure in a Financial Statement Audit," *Statement on Auditing Standards No. 55* (New York: AICPA, 1988).

Acts and Rulings of Governmental Bodies

Investigations by such governmental agencies as the Securities and Exchange Commission (SEC) have revealed illegal activities within American firms that were not detected by their internal control structures. As a result, Congress passed the **Foreign Corrupt Practices Act** in 1977. In addition to prohibiting certain types of bribes and hidden ownership, this act requires subject corporations to devise and maintain adequate internal control structures. Managers of those corporations that do not comply are liable to large fines and imprisonment. Consequently, many have taken suitable actions to strengthen the internal control structures of their corporations.

Section 102 of the act, pertaining to internal control structures, echoes Statement on Auditing Standards No. 1 (quoted on page 190). It states that corporations subject to the Securities Exchange Act of 1934 shall:

(A) make and keep books, records, and accounts, which, in reasonable detail, accurately and fairly reflect the transactions and dispositions of the assets of the issuer (corporation); and
(B) devise and maintain a system of internal accounting control sufficient to provide reasonable assurance that
> *(i) transactions are executed in accordance with management's general and specific authorization*
> *(ii) transactions are recorded as necessary (I) to permit preparation of financial statements in conformity with generally accepted accounting principles applicable to such statements, and (II) to maintain accountability for assets*
> *(iii) access to assets is permitted only in accordance with management's general or specific authorization*
> *(iv) the recorded accountability for assets is compared with the existing assets*

at reasonable intervals and appropriate action is taken with respect to any differences.

Subsequent to the Foreign Corrupt Practices Act, the SEC has issued rulings pertaining to internal control structures. In time it may issue a ruling that requires auditors to make formal reports concerning their evaluations of the internal control structures of client firms.

Summary

The internal control structure is a framework consisting of a wide variety of controls and security measures. Its major objectives are to safeguard assets, to ensure the accuracy and reliability of data and information, to promote operational efficiency, and to encourage adherence to management's prescribed policies and procedures. These objectives are difficult for a firm to achieve fully, because of environmental changes, risk exposures, the presence of computers, the human factor, and costs of controls. Risks to which a firm's information system is exposed include unintentional errors, deliberate errors, unintentional loss of assets, theft of assets, breaches of security, and acts of violence. The degree of exposure to risk depends upon the frequency of occurrence, vulnerability of the assets, and size of potential loss. Exposure to risk of crime increases dramatically when computers are integrated into the internal control structure. Computer-based information systems cause control problems because they concentrate processing, store data in invisible, erasable, and compressed forms, heighten complexity, tend to fragment audit trails, bypass human judgment, and increase the vulnerability of stored data and facilities.

Controls within an internal control structure may be classified according to objectives, intended uses, system architectures, and settings. Needed controls include those relating to organizational independence, security measures, asset accountability, documentation, sound management practices, required authorizations, transaction inputs, transaction processing, and transaction outputs.

Building an effective and feasible internal control structure requires that audit, cost, and human factors be considered. Internal control structures are undergoing improvements, partly because of such forces as the needs of management, the concerns of professional associations, and the acts and rulings of governmental bodies.

Review Problem with Solution

Statement

The Campus Bookstore of Tacoma, Washington, is considering the acquisition of a new computer system. The bookstore's manager believes that a computer system will aid the processing of data and possibly reduce the risks to which the bookstore's assets (including data and information) are currently exposed. Before making a final decision, however, he asks its public accountant–consultants to review the internal control structure. Among other concerns, the manager wonders what changes in controls might be necessary.

Required

a. Identify the three component systems comprising the bookstore's internal control structure, and illustrate by means of the cash control system, budgetary control system, and general ledger control system.

b. Discuss the risks to which the assets of the bookstore are currently exposed, giv-

ing examples of each type of risk as well as of high-risk and low-risk exposures.

c. Describe the impacts that the computer system will likely have on the bookstore's operations and internal control structure.

d. Identify key categories of controls that should be incorporated into the bookstore's internal control structure, and provide examples of certain specific controls that should be added when the change is made from manually based processing to computer-based processing.

Solution

a. The first of the component control systems is the operational control system, which promotes efficiency in operational tasks. An important operational task is to maintain an adequate supply of cash to meet operational needs. In order to control cash, the bookstore manager (planner) first sets a minimum bank balance (benchmark) with respect to the level of cash (performance measure). This benchmark is set at a level that is (1) sufficiently high to prevent the bookstore from depleting its funds and entailing bank charges and (2) sufficiently low to minimize idle cash deposits. Periodically the cash control system compares the actual amount of cash on hand with the minimum balance. When the actual amount on hand falls to or below the minimum balance, the system takes corrective action by borrowing an amount to replenish the account balance. Conversely, when the actual amount on hand rises significantly above the minimum, the system either repays a previous loan or invests the excessive amount. This cash control system, which is operated manually by the bookstore manager or the bookkeeper, may be aided by means of third-order feedback mechanisms such as cash forecasts.

The second component control system is the management control system, which encourages compliance with the bookstore's policies and procedures. An important tool of management control is a budgetary control system. The process begins with the setting of policies and of revenue and cost benchmarks by the bookstore manager (planner). These policies and benchmarks are embodied in annual operating budgets for the major responsibility areas. During the budget year revenues are accumulated and expenses are incurred. Monthly budget control reports are prepared that compare these actual results against the budgeted amounts and computed variances. The area managers are evaluated on the basis of the feedback provided by these reports. When necessary, corrective actions are taken.

The third component control system is the accounting control system, which has the objectives of safeguarding the bookstore's assets and ensuring the accuracy and reliability of the bookstore's data and information. An important technique for providing accounting control is the general ledger system. A key device in this system is the trial balance, which helps to ensure posting accuracy by verifying that total debit account balances equal total credit account balances. Another feature of the system that helps to ensure posting accuracy is the reconciliation of control accounts in the general ledger with the accounts in subsidiary ledgers. A feature that helps to safeguard assets is the reconciliation of physical counts of assets on hand (e.g., inventory) with the balances in general ledger accounts. Other control features include the use of coded accounts and the audit trail.

b. The bookstore is subject to risks with respect to its assets, including information. Among these risks are the following:

(1) Unintentional errors can be made in recording and processing transactions and related events such as sales, purchases, merchandise receipts, payroll, and cash disbursements. For instance, a clerk might enter an incorrect quantity to be ordered on a purchase order, or might incorrectly multiply the number of hours worked by an employee by the hourly rate of pay.

(2) Deliberate errors can be made in counting assets or in preparing reports or records. For instance, a clerk might deliberately undercount a receipt of merchandise and keep some of the items. A sales manager might inflate the sales amounts on a sales report.

(3) Assets may be accidentally lost. For instance, a clerk may lose a box of office supplies received from a supplier.

(4) Assets may be stolen by outsiders or employees. For instance, a shopper may shoplift a textbook; a stock clerk may carry merchandise out the back door. [See the example in item (2).]

(5) Security may be breached. For instance, a stock clerk may see a budget sheet on the bookkeeper's desk and repeat the key amounts to a friend.

(6) An act of violence may be committed. For instance, a customer may deface textbooks on a shelf.

High-risk exposures faced by the bookstore include theft and damage of merchandise, which is easily accessible on shelves and racks, and the theft of cash by the cashiers. Low-risk exposures include accidental errors. Although they may occur fairly frequently, they are not likely to be sizable. Breaches of security are also likely to be low-risk exposures, since information is not often easily available to unauthorized persons, especially when the system involves manual processing.

c. The planned computer system should provide faster and more accurate processing of transactions and other data while concentrating the processing overall. Much of the data will be stored in invisible, erasable, and more compressed forms. The audit trail could have gaps unless care is taken to prepare source documents for all transactions and to provide journal listings of all transactions. Errors in transaction input data and processing will be less likely to be detected by clerks, in part because transaction data may be entered directly into computer processing and in part because the processing will be performed by complex programs within the computer itself. Data may be more subject to access by unauthorized persons. Breakdowns or damage to the computer system will likely have a greater adverse effect on data processing than the loss of a clerk in the manual system.

d. Key categories of controls that will be needed in the internal control structure if a computer is acquired include

(1) Organizational controls to provide adequate segregation of duties and responsibilities, in light of the added concentration of processing caused by the computer. An example is to separate the unit involved in computer processing from the areas that provide transaction inputs.

(2) Security measures to prevent unauthorized access by employees or outsiders to computer facilities and data records and to provide physical protection over assets. For instance, the door to the computer room should be kept locked, and backups of computerized records should be maintained.

(3) Asset accountability controls to monitor assets, such as periodic reconciliations of the merchandise inventory with the computerized records pertaining to inventory.

(4) Documentation controls to describe fully aspects of the information system, such as procedure manuals that show the computerized transaction processing procedures.

(5) Management practices to ensure efficient and effective processing, such as adequate training of computer operators.

(6) Authorization controls to enable management to exercise its oversight responsibilities, such as required authorization before checks are mailed to suppliers.

(7) Transaction input controls to ensure the accuracy and completeness of input data, such as checks built into computer programs that handle input data from purchases transactions.

(8) Transaction processing controls to ensure accurate and complete processing of transactions, such as the use of batch totals over batches of purchase transaction documents.

(9) Transaction output controls to ensure that outputs are complete and distributed to the proper persons, such as a distribution log.

Review Questions

6-1 What is the meaning of each of these terms?

Internal control structure
Risk exposure
Computer crime
Accounting control
Administrative control

Preventive control
Detective control
Corrective control
Transaction control
General control
Organizational independence
Security measure
Asset accountability control
Documentation control
Management practice control
General authorization
Specific authorization
Reconciliation
Batch total
Reassessment
Acknowledgment procedure
Documented action
Verification
Review
Distribution log
Audit-effectiveness
Cost–benefit analysis
Reliability analysis
Foreign Corrupt Practices Act

6-2 Why is the internal control structure so important to the proper functioning of the information system?

6-3 Identify four objectives of the internal control structure.

6-4 What difficulties are likely to be encountered in attempting to achieve the objectives of the internal control structure?

6-5 Identify several system-related risks confronting a typical firm.

6-6 What are three factors that influence the degree of risk exposure?

6-7 Identify several types of computer crimes.

6-8 What are several problems posed by computer-based systems that affect internal control structures?

6-9 Identify categories into which controls may be classified according to objectives, in-

tended uses, system architectures, and settings.

6-10 Describe design considerations of internal control structures and identify example controls under each of the following categories:
    a. Organization.
    b. Security measures.
    c. Asset accountability.
    d. Documentation.
    e. Management practices.
    f. Authorizations.
    g. Transaction inputs, processing, and outputs.

6-11 What are proper roles for auditors with respect to the internal control structure?

6-12 Describe the steps in a cost–benefit analysis.

6-13 Why is it necessary to consider the behavioral reactions of employees when designing the internal control structure?

6-14 Describe three forces for the improvement of controls.

6-15 What are the significant requirements imposed by the Foreign Corrupt Practices Act with respect to internal control structures?

Discussion Questions

6-16 What are examples of high-risk exposures and low-risk exposures within a typical firm?

6-17 Which errors, either accidental or deliberate, are most likely to be eliminated or reduced when an information system is converted from manually based processing to computer-based processing?

6-18 Respond to a manager who says that her firm does not need accounting controls over the assets, since the firm has only one employee, who is well trusted.

6-19 Discuss the costs that a particular accounting control might impose on a firm, including the possible adverse effects on processing efficiency.

6-20 Can certain controls compensate for the omission of others? Give examples if such controls exist and indicate whether the compensatory effect is full or partial.

6-21 A designer or evaluator of an information system must analyze the entire set of controls comprising the internal control structure. Unless a sufficient number of effective controls are present, the internal control structure may be judged to be inadequate. Discuss the implication of such a judgment and the value of controls needed to raise the structure to a level of adequacy.

6-22 An effective internal control structure should deter persons from committing fraudulent acts by removing opportunities or by promptly exposing such acts where opportunities do exist. However, certain behavioral tendencies may undercut this presumption. Discuss.

Problems

6-1 Jane Huston opens a shoe store and hires two employees. She also asks you, a public accountant, to prepare financial statements for her at the end of each month. You agree, but you suggest that she needs an adequate internal control structure to make the venture a success. She replies that she cannot afford more costly outlays and that she does not want to offend the two employees with elaborate precautions.

Required

a. Explain the benefits to Jane of an internal control structure.

b. Present the response that you would offer to her argument that controls would be too costly.

c. Point out the difficulties in establishing an effective internal control structure in her shoe store.

6-2 Jiffy Express is an overnight airfreight delivery service. It guarantees delivery of letters and packages to points throughout the United States by 10 A.M. the day following pickup. The reputation of Jiffy is directly related to the reliability of this service. Thus, it maintains pools of vans for local pickup and delivery as well as a large fleet of planes. Because time is of the essence, Jiffy has installed an on-line computer-based information system, with terminals located at its offices in all metropolitan centers. In addition to owning its various offices, the firm has its own garages for overnight parking. Moreover, it services both its vans and its planes in rented facilities.

Required

Assess the various risk exposures faced by Jiffy, and specify the factors that affect the risk in each case.

6-3 Colleges and universities have installed complex networks of computers and microcomputers in recent years. Although the specifics of the networks differ from university to university, they generally serve two major purposes: academic and administrative. They also are subject to a variety of abuses.

Required

Identify at least a dozen abuses and crimes to which a typical university computer network is subject. Assume that a single network, involving one mainframe and numerous microcomputers, serves *both* academic and administrative purposes.

6-4 Hot & Shot, CPAs, have just installed a new minicomputer system. This system includes eight terminals that are directly connected to the minicomputer, as well as an online magnetic disk unit, one magnetic tape cartridge unit, two printers, and one plotter. The firm intends to use the system to perform internal applications, such as billing and budgeting, as well as to prepare tax returns and financial analyses for clients. Each of these applications involves the use of software packages that are to be acquired from an outside software firm. It is anticipated that most of the packages will need to be modified by the single programmer that the firm employs.

Required

Discuss the several control problems that are introduced by the new minicomputer system, assuming that the firm has never used computers before. Illustrate these control problems, where suitable, by reference to the billing and financial analysis applications.

6-5 Identify a risk exposure that each of the following control procedures or practices is intended to prevent or detect. For each item give an example of what might occur if the control were not in place, and list one or more factors that could cause the risk exposure to be relatively high.

- **a.** Assigning one employee to handle the merchandise in the warehouse and another employee to maintain the inventory records.
- **b.** Storing the inventory within a fenced area that is kept locked.
- **c.** Requiring all disbursements (except petty transactions) to be made by check.
- **d.** Counting the inventory on hand periodically and comparing the count of each item to the inventory records.
- **e.** Requiring all returns of sold merchandise to be listed on a special credit memorandum form that is prepared and signed by a manager.
- **f.** Mailing a monthly statement to each customer, showing the details

of all transactions and the balance owed.

6-6 Identify a risk exposure that each of the following control procedures or practices is intended to prevent or detect. For each item give an example of what might occur if the control were not in place, and list one or more factors that could cause the risk exposure to be relatively high.

- **a.** Preparing reconciliations of all bank accounts upon receipt of the bank statements.
- **b.** Maintaining comprehensive manuals that show detailed steps of all the accounting procedures.
- **c.** Requiring a clerk who receives ordered merchandise to prepare and sign a form that separately lists all the items and quantities received.
- **d.** Listing all the cash remittances received daily by mail and comparing the total to the deposit slip.
- **e.** Depositing all cash received daily intact in the bank.
- **f.** Having auditors examine the financial statements once a year.

6-7 What accounting control(s) or security measure(s) would be most effective in preventing or detecting each of the following errors or undesirable practices?

- **a.** A storeroom clerk discovers that a particular part is out of stock, even though the accounting records show that 90 units are on hand.
- **b.** A petty cash custodian removes $100 from the petty cash fund for personal use but replenishes the amount with cash received from customers that day.
- **c.** A general ledger clerk posts to the accounts receivable control account a credit pertaining to a return of merchandise from a customer; however, the clerk forgets to post the debit to the sales return account.
- **d.** A firm's bank prepares a debit mem-

orandum for an NSF (Not Sufficient Funds) check, but the bank clerk forgets to mail a copy of the memo to the firm.

e. A general ledger clerk forgets to post Wednesday's total cash receipts, amounting to $2,397.

f. An accounts receivable clerk pockets $100 in currency received by mail from a customer but nevertheless posts the amount of the receipt to the customer's accounts receivable account.

6-8 What accounting control(s) or security measure(s) would be most effective in preventing or detecting each of the following errors or undesirable practices?

a. A production line employee walks into the tool room just before quitting time one day, puts a small precision tool in his jacket pocket, and takes it home.

b. A clerk in the personnel department lists a fictitious employee in the personnel records; when the signed paychecks are received from the cashier for distribution, this clerk takes the paycheck for the fictitious employee, cashes it, and keeps the proceeds.

c. A purchasing manager orders goods that are not needed from a supplier firm, of which he happens to be an owner.

d. A storeskeeper takes inventory items home at night; when the shortages become apparent during physical inventory, he claims that the receiving department did not deliver the goods to the storeroom.

e. A cashier steals $50 in currency received by mail from a customer; she conceals the theft by preparing a credit memorandum that reduces the balance of the customer's account by $50.

f. A cashier prepares and submits an invoice from a fictitious supplier having the name of her mother, writes a check to the "supplier," and mails the check to her mother's address; the daughter and mother later split the proceeds.

6-9 The Y Company of Hanover, New Hampshire, has asked your help with a problem. It has three clerical employees who must perform the following functions:

a. Maintain general ledger.

b. Maintain accounts payable ledger.

c. Maintain accounts receivable ledger.

d. Prepare checks for signature.

e. Maintain cash disbursements journal.

f. Issue credits on returns and allowances.

g. Reconcile the bank account.

h. Handle and deposit cash receipts.

The company requests that you assign these functions to the three employees in such a manner as to achieve the highest degree of internal control. It may be assumed that each employee is able to perform any of the functions, that these employees will perform no accounting functions other than the ones listed, and that any accounting functions not listed will be performed by persons other than these three employees.

Required

State how you would distribute the listed functions among the three employees. Assume that with the exception of the nominal jobs of bank reconciliation and issuance of credits on returns and allowances, all functions require an equal amount of time.

(CPA adapted)

6-10 Aqua Valves and Fittings Company of Laramie, Wyoming, sells plastic pipes, copper tubing, brass and cast-iron valves, and assorted other items to contractors. In addition to Sid Center, the general manager, the firm employs a salesperson (Nolan Kobb), a bookkeeper (Rita Records), and two yard workers (Phil Stone and Fred Bass).

Sales are made by phone, with later pickup. When a customer places an order, an unnumbered sales order is prepared. It lists the descriptions of the ordered items, the quantities ordered, and the unit prices, as well as a notation of whether the sale is for cash or credit. One copy of the sales order is filed in the office, and the second copy is taken to the yard. On the basis of the second copy, either Phil or Fred assembles the ordered items and tapes the copy of the sales order to the assembled order.

When a customer arrives to pick up an order, if the sale is cash and carry, he or she first stops in the office and pays. Otherwise, he or she goes directly to the yard and picks up the order. Whether the sale is for cash or on credit, the customer receives the second copy of the sales order.

At the end of each month Rita prepares monthly statements from the file of open credit sales orders and mails them to the customers.

Each morning Rita or Nolan opens the mail and segregates the remittances from customers. Rita then removes the sales orders against which remittances have been received and files them in a closed orders file. She then prepares a deposit slip, listing cash received both from credit sales and from yesterday's cash sales, and carries the deposit to the bank. At the end of each month she prepares the bank reconciliation.

Required

List the control weaknesses in the foregoing sales and cash receipts procedure and recommend improvements. Assume that Aqua cannot afford to hire any additional employees.

6-11 After undertaking a data security review, a firm adopts plastic cards that are needed for accessing the computer terminals owned by the firm. These cards are then given to those employees whose duties require them to use the terminals. The cost of the cards is $100,000. The probability that unauthorized data will be entered into the system or that unauthorized persons will be able to access the system is thereby reduced from 25 percent to 5 percent. What reasons have likely been used by management to justify the $100,000 investment?

6-12 Aidbart Company has recently installed a new on-line, data-base computer system. CRT units are located throughout the company, at least one being located in each department. James Lanta, vice-president of finance, has overall responsibility for the company's management information system, but he relies heavily on Ivan West, director of MIS, for technical assistance and direction.

Lanta was one of the primary supporters of the new system because he knew it would provide labor savings. However, he is concerned about the security of the new system. Lanta was walking through the purchasing department recently when he observed an Aidbart buyer using a CRT unit to inquire about the current price for a specific part used by Aidbart. The new system enabled the buyer to have the data regarding the part brought up on the screen as well as each Aidbart product that used the part and the total manufacturing cost of the products using the part. The buyer told Lanta that, in addition to inquiring about the part, he could also change the costs of parts.

Lanta scheduled a meeting with West to review his concerns regarding the new system. Lanta stated, "Ivan, I am concerned about the type and amount of data that can be accessed through the CRTs. How can we protect ourselves against unauthorized access to data in our computer file? Also, what happens if we have a natural disaster such as a fire, a passive threat such as a power outage, or some active threat resulting in malicious damage—could we continue to operate? We need to show management that we are on top of these things. Would you please outline the procedures we now have, or need to have, to protect ourselves.''

West responded by saying, ''Jim, there are areas of vulnerability in the design and implementation of any EDP system. Some of these are more prevalent in on-line systems such as ours—especially with respect to privacy, integrity, and confidentiality of data. The four major points of vulnerability with which we should be concerned are the hardware, the software, the people, and the network.''

Required

For each of the four major points of vulnerability identified above by Ivan West,

a. List at least one risk exposure to the system, and give your assessment of the degree of possible risk exposure.

b. Describe a control procedure that should protect the system from each risk exposure.

(CMA adapted)

6-13 The Arcade Co. of Orlando, Florida, has established a new division that will manage a chain of video-game arcades in 40 locations throughout several southern states. The locations will be divided into two regions under regional managers. Each location will be assigned a local manager. As many as 60 machines will be available at certain locations, although the average per location will be 35 machines.

Management intends to minimize the number of operating and accounting employees in order to reduce costs. However, it plans to hire sufficient maintenance personnel to minimize downtime of machines. The resident manager will be required to collect and deposit the coins from machines in a local bank. Access to the game counter and coins in each machine will be by means of a master key. Validated deposit slips are to be mailed to the corporate office by the resident manager. Bank statements are to be mailed by the bank directly to the corporate office.

Required

Identify the specific risk exposures that are inherent in the operations of the new division. Group the risk exposures according to the four activities with which accounting controls are concerned (i.e., execution of transactions, recording of transactions, access to assets, and recorded accountability for assets); for each risk exposure suggest one or more offsetting accounting controls.

(CIA adapted)

6-14 The XYZ Company of Monterey, California, has identified certain control and security weaknesses. Its data processing department does not have physical security over access to the computer room and the magnetic tape library. Further, the firm does not keep duplicate tape files stored off site. Among other functions, the computer maintains the general ledger, accounts receivable ledger, perpetual inventory records, and payroll records. Average accounts receivable and inventory balances are $50 million (10 percent of total assets) and $75 million (15 percent of total assets), respectively.

The identified risks related to the firm's conditions are as follows:

a. The magnetic tape records could be lost, stolen, or destroyed (either accidentally or intentionally). This would necessitate the very difficult, time-consuming, and costly task of re-creating (to the extent possible) the information stored on them. As a consequence:

(1) Collection of accounts receivable would be inhibited, at best, and in some cases the inability to follow up adequately might result in collections not being made.

(2) A special physical count might be necessary to determine the inventory.

(3) The ability to operate the business efficiently probably would be inhibited during the period when the records were being re-created.

b. Because of the lack of security over access to the computer, someone could circumvent controls that otherwise exist and cause false information to be entered into the financial records; such false information might be used to cover up the embezzlement of certain of the firm's assets, to pad the payroll, or for other fraudulent activities. The estimated identifiable costs to install controls that would, in management's opinion, adequately reduce the risks related to this weakness are as follows:

Initial costs:

Cost of installing a security system (written procedures for authorized access, coded employee badges, system of locks, etc.) that would ensure access to the computer room and magnetic tape library by authorized personnel only	$ 5,000
Cost of duplicating 144 magnetic tapes (12 months' tapes retained)—including cost to purchase tapes ($15 each) and cost to process on the computer ($25 each)	6,000
	$11,000

Annual costs:

Cost to maintain the security system	$ 500
Cost to update 144 magnetic tapes (oldest month's tapes erased and data for current month duplicated)	3,600
Cost related to off-site storage	2,000
	$ 6,100

The benefit expected to be derived from installing the controls is the reduction of the risks mentioned. Although it is difficult, if not impossible, to quantify all the risks accurately, the following can be estimated:

Estimated manpower costs to re-create the information stored on the magnetic tapes:

5000 man-hours @ $6.50	$ 32,500
Taxes and fringe benefits @ 20%	6,500
200 computer-hours @ $25	5,000

Estimated costs related to the delay in re-creating or inability to re-create certain accounts receivable information:

Slower collections, assuming 10% of the accounts are collected 30 days later than normal ($5,000,000 at 9% interest × 30 days)	37,000
Lost collections ($50,000,000 × .2%)	100,000

Estimated costs to conduct a special physical inventory:

2000 man-hours @ $6.50	13,000
Taxes and fringe benefits @ 20%	2,500
20 computer-hours @ $25	500
Quantifiable risk per occurrence	$197,000

Estimated annual probability of occurrence:

Without the controls	5%	
With the controls	—	5%
Annual benefit of risk elimination		$9,850

Additional risks include interruption of the business, inability to operate the business efficiently, possible cover-up of embezzlement or fraud, and possible effect on employees' attitudes and productivity because of payroll difficulties that may occur. Since these costs are not subject to estimation, they cannot be quantified. Although insurance coverage would offset some of the loss from business interruption and embezzlement or fraud, the reduction in the risk that these events would occur is still a benefit.

Required

Discuss the desirability of installing the controls and security measures pertaining to the computer room and data tapes.[12]

6-15 *Selected Small Firm (A Continuing Case)*
For the small firm that you selected in Chapter 1 (see Problem 1-7), complete the following requirements:

a. Describe the operational, management, and accounting control systems.
b. Identify several high-risk exposures.
c. Discuss the control problems that have been introduced by the computer system the firm now owns or that would be introduced by a proposed new computer system.

---

[12]Courtesy of Arthur Young & Co., CPAs. Reprinted with permission from *Evaluating Accounting Controls: A Systematic Approach,* Copyright Arthur Young & Company 1980.

Suggested Readings

Alderman, Tom. "Computer Crime." *Journal of Systems Management* (Sept. 1977), pp. 32–35.

Baird, Bryon N., and Michenzi, Alfred R. "Impact of the Foreign Corrupt Practices Act." *The Internal Auditor* (June 1983), pp. 20–22.

Campitelli, Vincent A. "Is Your Computer a Soft Touch?" *Financial Executive* (February 1984), pp. 10–14.

Cerullo, Michael, and Shelton, F. A. "Analyzing the Cost-Effectiveness of Computer Controls and Security." *The Internal Auditor* (October 1981), pp. 30–37.

Comptom, Ted R. "A Cost-Effective Internal Control System—Management's Dilemma." *Journal of Systems Management* (May 1985), pp. 21–25.

Computer Services Executive Committee. *The Auditor's Study and Evaluation of Internal Controls in EDP Systems.* New York: AICPA, 1977.

Cushing, Barry E., and Romney, Marshall B. *Accounting Information Systems and Business Organizations.* 5th ed. Reading, Mass.: Addison-Wesley, 1990.

Hooper, Paul, and Page, John. "Internal Control Problems in Computer Systems" *Journal of Systems Management* (December 1982), pp. 22–27.

Nash, John F. *Accounting Information Systems.* 2d ed. New York: Macmillan Publishing Co., 1989.

Part *II*

INFORMATION SYSTEM FUNCTIONS

Information systems perform several critical tasks or functions. The four chapters in this part focus on these functions, with emphasis on their performance in computer-based information systems. Chapter 7 describes the two principal methods of collecting and processing data. Chapter 8 discusses the storage and retrieval of data from files. Chapter 9 enumerates the various controls and security measures, as well as the means of correcting errors. Chapter 10 describes the managerial reports and other outputs needed for operations and decision making. Each chapter emphasizes the objectives, alternative methods, documentation techniques, and design considerations with respect to the function being discussed. Knowledge of the topics covered in this part is essential to an understanding of transaction cycles, the subject of the third part.

Chapter **7**

DATA ENTRY AND PROCESSING

Data conversion consists of entering collected data and performing appropriate data processing steps to generate needed information. Computer-based systems are increasingly becoming the preferred means for converting data (although they may never be the best choice in all situations).

Accountants have considerable interest in data conversion systems. Their responsibilities encompass all accounting transactions, which comprise most of the data collected and processed by a firm. They are also involved in preparing the reports and analyses that result from data conversion. If accountants are to have significant impacts on data conversion systems, however, they must become aware of the array of options in computer-based data conversion. They need to be able to distinguish among the alternative approaches to data entry and process-

ing. Furthermore, they should be able to evaluate the relative merits of alternative approaches in specific situations.

Overview of Data Conversion

Our study of data conversion begins with a survey of objectives. Then we examine the benefits of and approaches to data conversion.

Objectives

Figure 7-1 arrays eight objectives or criteria relating to data conversion.

Relevance. An information system has limited processing capacity. Thus, only data that are relevant to current or future needs of the firm should be collected.

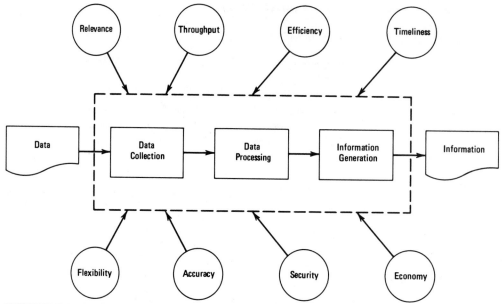

FIGURE 7-1 Design objectives pertaining to data conversion.

Throughput. One measure of a data conversion system is its **throughput,** the quantity of data that a system converts during a period of time. Increasing throughput therefore improves the performance of the system.

Efficiency. The term **efficiency** refers to the results achieved by a given set of resources. An efficient data conversion system generally provides high throughput at a reasonable cost. It also often provides ease of use.

Timeliness. When data conversion is performed in a timely manner, the records in the data base can be kept up to date. Thus, more useful information can be provided to users.

Flexibility. Most firms encounter very frequent changes. Therefore, it is important that a data conversion system be able to respond smoothly and effectively to such changes and to the varying needs of users.

Accuracy and security. To ensure that data are reliable, a data conversion system requires adequate controls and security measures.

Economy. Converting data at the lowest reasonable cost is the last objective. It is also the broadest objective, since economy is related either directly or inversely to the other objectives. For instance, efficiency directly contributes to economy, while timeliness generally has an inverse effect on economy.

Advantages of Computer-Based Data Conversion

Computer-based data conversion enables business firms to fulfill the foregoing objectives more satisfactorily in most business applications. Computer-based transaction processing systems enhance throughput and efficiency, especially when transaction volumes are relatively large. They are more economical in such applications, since the incremental cost per transaction is quite small. They also can provide up-to-date information in a timely and flexible manner.

Furthermore, computer-based systems used either for transaction processing or information processing can do the following as desired:

- Enter automatically-generated data (e.g., dates, times, serial numbers) onto accounting records and source documents.
- Print source documents and transaction listings as the by-products of updating files.
- Verify the accuracy of identification numbers (such as customer numbers) entered from transaction data.
- Compare identification numbers against lists of valid numbers.
- Extract descriptive names (such as inventory item descriptions) that match entered codes (such as inventory item numbers).
- Quickly generate complex reports and analyses based on collected or stored data.

This last capability of computer-based data conversion systems is extremely useful, since producing such reports and analyses manually is time consuming and tedious. As an illustration of this capability, two sales analyses—sales by territory and sales by product—might be desired by a sales manager. A computer-based information processing system can easily sort the data by territory, tabulate the results, and print the first analysis; then it can quickly re-sort the data by product, tabulate the results, and print the second analysis. In fact, it could produce several other analyses from the same data with little added effort.

Approaches to Computer-Based Data Conversion

Two basic methods employed in manually based systems are batch processing and one-write processing. These methods or approaches were briefly described in Chapter 3.

Because of their overwhelming advantages, computer-based systems are being selected for an ever-increasing number of data conversion applications. As noted earlier, they are particularly suited to applications involving large volumes of transactions. Thus, we shall focus in this and the next several chapters on computer-based data conversion approaches.

Computer-based systems, like manually based systems, can differ significantly. Transactions may be entered in batches or individually, and they may be processed in batches or individually. These separate data entry (i.e., input) and processing approaches generally appear in the following combinations:

1. Batch data entry and batch processing.
2. On-line data entry and on-line processing.
3. On-line data entry and batch processing.

Each of these combinations embodies a variety of options. For instance, data may be entered on-line from written documents or from other sources.

In the following sections we contrast the two data entry approaches, focus separately on each of the data processing approaches, and illustrate various approaches and options.

Data Entry Approaches

Batch Input Approach

Characteristics. The batch input approach represents the traditional mode of entering transaction data for processing. It consists first of capturing the data concerning each transaction on a source document. The source documents from like transactions are then gathered into batches, validated by various checks, and transcribed (if necessary) onto a medium that is readable by the computer system. Periodically these batches of transactions are thrust into the processing phase. Certain of the data collection steps may be performed by clerks, although the clerks may be aided by data entry devices.

Batching transactions is an application of the division-of-work concept. Developed during the era when most firms processed transactions manually, the batch input approach often resembles a job order production process. That is, the process is highly organized and centralized. Trained data entry clerks occupy rows of stations within data preparation rooms. They spend all their working hours preparing batched transactions for processing.

Input media. In addition to ordinary paper documents, input media available for use with the batch input approach are optical character recognition (OCR) documents, magnetic ink character recognition (MICR) documents, magnetic tapes, magnetic disks, and diskettes. Punched cards and punched paper tape may be used on rare occasions.

OCR documents have become increasingly popular as an input medium. This popularity stems from the fact that they embody the concept of **source data automation.** That is, they capture data in computer-readable form at the points where transactions originate. Data are typed or handwritten onto each OCR document, by means of a special type font or carefully formed characters. A batch of documents is then fed into a reader or scanner, which can directly transfer the data into the computer system at speeds ranging up to 2400 documents per minute. Larger OCR input systems can also validate and edit the transaction data.

OCR documents are suited for high-volume applications. For instance, they are widely used as credit card transaction documents. In addition, they are employed in applications in which they serve as turnaround documents. Figure 7-2 shows a customer statement. It was printed by the retailer's computer system from credit sales invoices generated during the month as OCR documents and then mailed to the customer (who happens to be the author). When the top portion was returned to the retailer, together with the payment, it served as a preprinted OCR document and was entered into the cash receipts procedure.

OCR documents are often the preferred medium when data can be mark-sensed or prepared as the by-product of other processing. Thus, (1) course registration forms that are mark-sensed by college students and (2) cash register tapes that are generated during cash transactions are frequently designed to be read as OCR documents.

Being computer readable, OCR documents eliminate the need for keying operations. They therefore can enhance the efficiency of a batch processing application. OCR documents do have two drawbacks, however. They generally are not suited for low-volume applications because the required readers or scanners are relatively expensive. Moreover, current scanner models tend to reject fairly high percentages of documents, since they are often confused by slight imperfections in the typed or printed characters. These drawbacks are being gradually overcome.

MICR documents are best illustrated by means of bank checks. Each check contains magnetic ink characters that have been standardized by the American Banking Association (ABA). Characters on the check shown in Figure 7-3 list the check-routing code (1221), the ABA transit code (170), and the depositor's account number (1-1937). As the check is processed, the amount will also be encoded with magnetic ink characters. Since the magnetic ink characters are directly readable by input devices known as MICR readers, checks are also documents that illustrate the source data automation concept.

MICR documents are increasingly being used in nonbanking applications. Many public utilities use MICR-encoded customer bills, and mortgage firms use MICR-encoded payment coupons. Applications such as these enable the MICR-encoded forms to serve as turnaround documents.

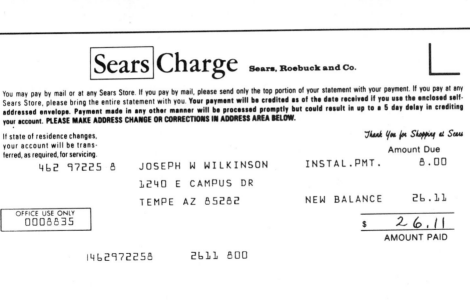

FIGURE 7-2 An OCR turnaround document.

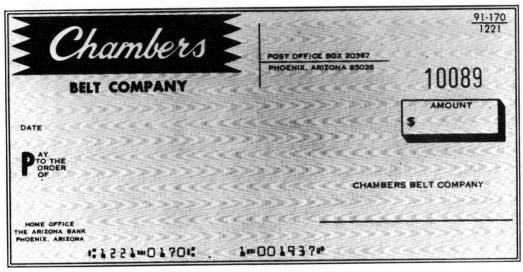

FIGURE 7-3 An MICR document.

Magnetic tapes are not source documents, of course. However, magnetic tape is a widely used medium for transferring batched data directly into computer systems. Transaction data captured on source documents are often transcribed onto magnetic tape before the entry of data. Three reasons justify this added step. First, data on magnetic tape can be transferred into and out of computer systems much faster than data on such media as OCR and MICR documents. Faster transfer rates improve the throughput of computer systems. Second, a magnetic tape can contain a large volume of data. Third, data can be transferred from magnetic tape very reliably and without loss.

Transaction data are transcribed to magnetic tape by various means. Data captured on OCR or MICR documents may be transcribed by means of OCR or MICR scanning devices. Data on non-OCR source documents may be transcribed using a key-to-tape encoder or key-to-disk system. Alternatively, data can be transcribed as a by-product of a document preparation step; for instance, when sales invoices are being prepared from sales orders on an accounting computer, the data can be simultaneously transferred, via a special attachment, to a magnetic tape. In some applications the data may be transcribed from another magnetic medium. For example, a grocery chain takes inventory in individual stores on portable key-to-tape cassettes; later the data are transmitted by specially equipped telephones to the main computer location, where the data are recorded on magnetic tape before entry into the computer system.

Figure 7-4 depicts the transcription of data to magnetic tapes using a key-to-disk system. (The symbols in the flowchart are described in the appendix to this chapter; see Figure 7-23.) This type of off-line data preparation system consists of a number of video display terminals tied to a common magnetic disk and a special data input computer processor. First the source documents (e.g., sales invoices) are batched and batch totals are computed. Then the transaction data are keyed by data entry clerks at the keyboard stations. As each data entry clerk keys in data, he or she sees the data displayed on the video screen. Many keying errors can be detected and corrected immediately. Generally this visual verification reduces the need for extensive key verification, a process whereby other clerks rekey selected items of data. The entered data are temporarily stored on the magnetic disk within the system, in order to undergo editing and validation by the processor.[1] For instance, the data are formatted and blocked according to magnetic tape specifications; also, the batch control totals are computed and automatically checked against the previously computed totals. The edited transactions are then entered onto the magnetic tape, ready for computer processing.

Magnetic disks and diskettes may serve as batch input media instead of magnetic tapes. For example, data prepared by means of a key-to-disk system may be entered onto a magnetic disk (rather than magnetic tape) as the final depository. Also, data captured on OCR or MICR documents may be transferred to a disk. However, magnetic disks and diskettes are used mostly with the on-line input approach, which is described next.

On-Line Input Approach

Characteristics. On-line input is the entry of data via some type of on-line data entry or input device. This approach, also known as the direct or interactive input approach, typically refers to the entry of individual transactions as they arise. Generally these transactions are entered by employees with primary duties other than data entry. Such employees are often located in operational departments

---

[1]Invalid transactions are corrected and resubmitted for processing. See Chapter 9 for a discussion of an error correction procedure.

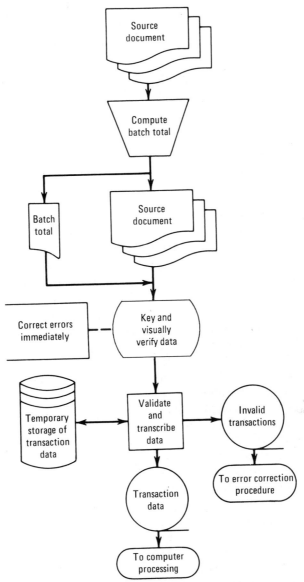

FIGURE 7-4 A station within a key-to-disk system.

(e.g., purchasing, shipping, stores) or accounting departments (e.g., accounts receivable, accounts payable).

In some applications the data pertaining to transactions are initially recorded on source documents; in other applications transactions are entered without the prior preparation of source documents. However, all devices employed in the on-line input approach enter the data directly into the computer system in computer-readable form. Since in most applications the data are also entered at the point where captured, most on-line input devices embody the source data automation concept.

On-line input devices fall into two main categories: (1) those that involve the keying of data by humans, and (2) those that function without the need for keying.

Keyed data entry. Many transactions are entered via the keyboards of terminals. For example, salespersons may enter orders through portable terminals in their motel rooms, at branch offices, or even on customers' premises. Alternatively, order clerks located in central sales departments enter sales into video display terminals. Data pertaining to the sales may be provided to the clerks (1) by salespersons on written sales order forms or (2) by customers through telephone calls.

A familiar example of on-line data entry is found in a savings and loan institution. When a depositor wishes to deposit or withdraw funds, he or she prepares a slip at a branch office. By reference to this source document, a teller keys the transaction data via the keyboard of a terminal. As the transaction data enter the computer system, each item of data is checked by an edit program. When errors are found, the clerk is notified by a display or printout on the terminal. When the computer system finishes validating the transaction data, it prints the transaction data and new account balance in the depositor's passbook and on the on-line record. It also logs the transaction on magnetic disk storage. Figure 7-5 shows this process.

Entering data via keying is a meticulous and deadening task for humans. In order to reduce the load on data entry clerks and other system users, the computer system can be designed to provide memory aids. Two such aids are preformatted screens and dialogue prompts.

Preformatted screens are displays of structured formats on the screens of video display terminals. These formats may be replicas of blank source documents, or they may consist of rows and columns of labeled blank boxes. Figure 7-6 displays a screen preformatted to aid an order clerk when entering a sales transaction; its appearance resembles the format of the sales order document that the salesperson had previously completed when taking the order. Figure 7-7 shows a preformatted screen that would aid the teller of a savings and loan branch in entering a deposit transaction. The notes with the figures indicate that the computer system can aid the entry process by automatically displaying (and even computing) data based on items keyed in.

Dialogue prompts consist of questions or suggestions that are displayed to a user. For instance, the following question might be displayed to a sales order clerk who takes an order by telephone or over the counter:

IS THE PERSON PLACING THE ORDER A NEW CUSTOMER? >

If the clerk answers Yes, a series of questions will follow to acquire information concerning the customer's creditworthiness. If the answer is No, the next question might read

---

WHAT IS THE CUSTOMER'S NUMBER? >

When the number is entered, the system may display the customer's name, address, and credit standing. After this information is verified with the customer, the system would ask questions pertaining to the specific order.

Another aid when entering data is the **menu screen.** Figure 7-8 shows a master menu screen that enables users to select the desired preformatted screen or prompts from a variety of options. (The preformatted

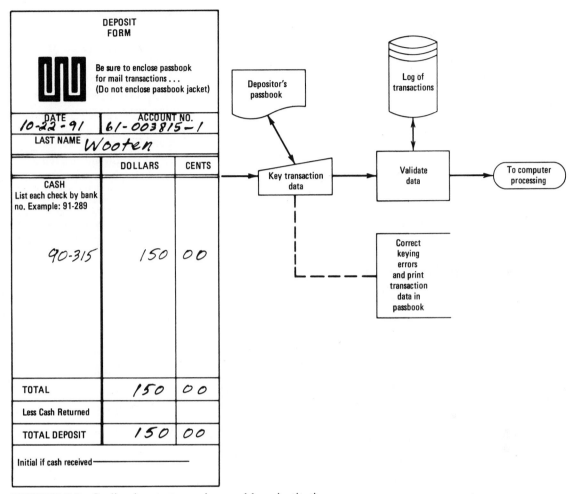

FIGURE 7-5 On-line input at a savings and loan institution.

screen in Figure 7-6 resulted from selecting option 1.) Certain of the options can relate to actions (e.g., inquiries) other than data entry.

Nonkeyed data entry. Keyed entry of data is slow, error prone, and costly. A variety of devices have been developed, therefore, that eliminate or reduce the keying process.

Scanning devices or readers capture data by recognizing characters or codes. Retailers employ optical scanners, together with point-of-sale terminals, to read bar codes affixed to products or tags. Figure 7-9 shows a typical bar code. Railroads employ track-side scanners to read mounted bar codes as freight cars pass by, in order to monitor the movements of the cars. Manufacturing firms use similar devices—called card or badge readers—to keep track of job orders and labor times. As each work step is completed on a job, the reporting employee enters the data into a reader by inserting (1) a prepunched card containing the job number

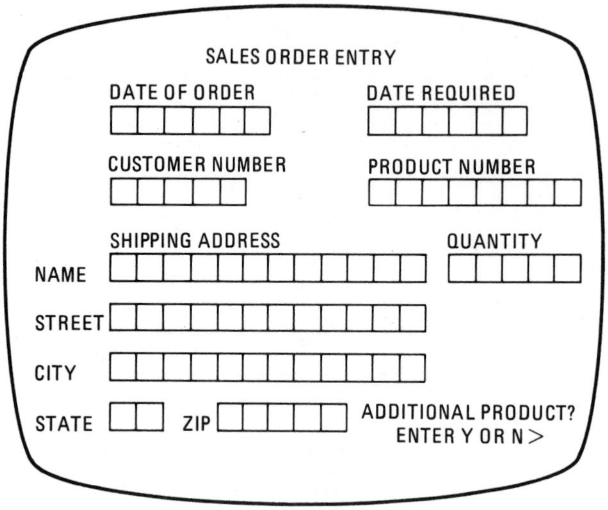

FIGURE 7-6 A preformatted screen for sales orders.

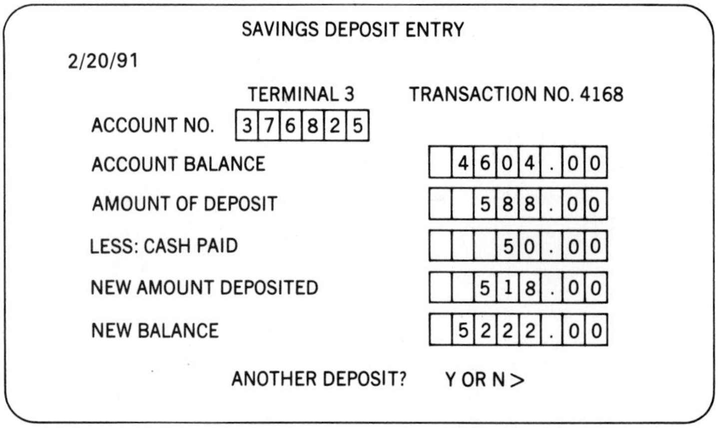

Notes: 1. If more than one product is ordered, product number and quantity boxes will clear after data for each product is accepted.
2. The shipping address data do not need to be entered unless the customer is new. If a record is already stored concerning the customer, the computer system can automatically provide the name and address in the record after the customer number is entered. The clerk would then compare the address that appears with the address on the sales order. If it is different, the clerk could then override the system-entered address.

FIGURE 7-7 A preformatted screen for entering data pertaining to one cash-deposit transaction. Note that the date, terminal number, transaction number, and prior account balance are entered automatically by the computer system after the account number is entered manually. In addition, the net amount deposited and the new account balance are computed automatically after the amount of deposit and amount of cash paid are entered manually.

and (2) his or her employee badge. When the employee also strikes the appropriate function key (e.g., the job setup function), the data are immediately entered into the computer system.

Voice-input devices enable clerks, sales-persons, and others to enter transaction and status data rapidly (50,000 characters per hour) and conveniently.[2] For example, a

[2]Harold E. Paddock, "Voice Input a Reality," *The Internal Auditor* (December 1983), p. 23.

```
                  MASTER MENU

           1. SALES ORDER ENTRY

           2. SHIPPING ENTRY

           3. CASH REMITTANCE ENTRY

           4. PURCHASE ORDER ENTRY

           5. RECEIPT OF GOODS ENTRY

           6. GENERAL LEDGER ENTRY

           7. INQUIRY

           8. DEMAND REPORT GENERATION

           9. EXIT FROM SYSTEM

         ENTER DESIRED NUMBER >
```

FIGURE 7-8   A menu screen.

voice-input terminal may be used by a receiving clerk to enter coded data concerning received goods.

Most transactions entered by nonkeyed means (as well as some entered by keying) are not initially recorded on source documents. However, computer systems may be designed to produce source documents as by-products of on-line processing. In such cases they enhance audit trails and improve data control.

Contrasts between Data Entry Approaches

The main advantages of the batch input approach are economy and productivity.

FIGURE 7-9   A scannable bar code.

Batch-oriented hardware and software are less expensive than the array of input devices and complex programs usually required by the on-line input approach. The handling of large batches of transactions by well-trained clerks is inherently more productive than the intermittent handling of transactions by clerks who may also have other tasks.

The on-line input approach offers greater timeliness, flexibility, and simplicity. Timeliness is achieved because transactions are generally captured and entered as they arise. Even transactions containing errors can usually be corrected immediately by the entry clerk and then entered for processing. In the case of the batch input approach, transactions containing errors are typically suspended and reentered at a later date. Flexibility is enhanced because transactions can be easily captured wherever they arise. Moreover, there is a greater variety of input devices from which to choose when designing the system. Simplicity results because transcription is not necessary.

Each input approach provides means of assuring data accuracy. The batch input approach can use batch totals for control. Preformatted screens, dialogue prompts, and nonkeyed devices reduce the likelihood of errors when data are entered via the on-line input approach. In addition, both approaches employ programmed edit checks, which will be described in Chapter 9.

Batch Processing Approach

Characteristics

Batch processing involves the processing of data in like groups. Data are collected and stored until a sufficiently large batch is accumulated or until a designated time arrives. This approach is most frequently employed to process routine transactions that occur in relatively large volumes. Typical candidates for batch processing include sales order and invoicing applications, inventory record-keeping applications, cash receipts and disbursements applications, payroll applications, fixed-asset accounting applications, cost accounting applications, and general ledger accounting applications. The batch processing approach is also suitably employed to extract information from a file. For instance, the account balances of all customers stored within an accounts receivable master file can be scanned by a specially devised computer program; based on instructions in the program, the name of each customer having a balance in excess of $1000 might be retrieved and listed in a report for the credit manager.

Since time is required to collect transactions into batches or to search files of batched data, batch processing is marked by delays. Periods of time—such as days, weeks, or months—elapse between successive processings. Hence, batch processing is sometimes referred to as **delayed,** or **periodic, processing,** with the periods of time between successive processings called **processing cycles.**

The length of a processing cycle depends on such factors as the volume of in-

flowing transactions, the desired batch size, and the available processing capacity. For example, if inventory transactions are accumulating at the rate of 25 per hour and the desired batch size is 100 transactions, the processing cycle for inventory transactions may suitably be established as four hours. If processing capacity is limited, the processing cycle may be established as 24 hours, with processing to take place at the off-peak hour of 2:00 A.M. In some cases, the reporting needs determine the processing cycle. Payroll transactions, for instance, need be processed only at the end of each pay period. On the other hand, inventory transactions may be processed four times daily, since a longer delay could adversely affect the value to users of information about inventory status.

Most batch transaction processing applications involve **sequential processing.** In other words, the transactions are processed one after the other, according to the order in which they have been arranged or sorted. Sequential processing is more efficient than random (unsorted) processing when the transactions are accumulated into large batches.

Batch processing traditionally has been associated with the batch input approach. However, in many current applications batch processing is performed after transactions have been entered by the on-line approach. In these applications the transactions are stored temporarily, generally in a file on magnetic disk, until a batch has been accumulated. Then batch control totals are computed and the batch is processed.

Typical Computer-Based Batch Processing Runs

A computer-based batch processing application can be viewed as a series of *runs*. Each run, under the control of a computer program, performs one or more processing steps with respect to each transaction in the batch. Each run is generally completed without pause before the next run begins. After each run is completed, a human computer operator will set up the files needed for the next run.

Six basic batch processing runs are shown as flowchart segments in Figure 7-10.

In conformity with generally accepted terminology, they are labeled the conversion run, edit run, sort run, file maintenance run, file extraction run, and report generation run. These runs perform virtually all of the steps required in processing transactions. The

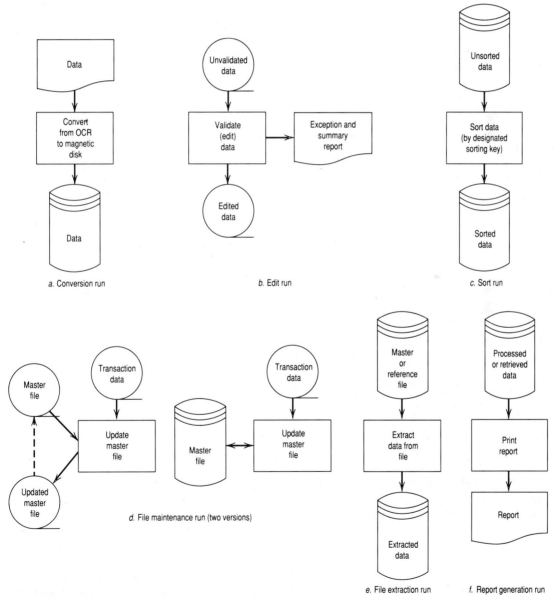

FIGURE 7-10 Basic batch processing runs.

storage medium may be magnetic tape, as indicated by the circular symbol with the tail, or magnetic disk, as indicated by the cylinder.[3] Magnetic tape has customarily been used in batch processing applications, although magnetic disks are increasingly being selected for such applications.

Conversion run. Run *a* in Figure 7-10 denotes the conversion or transcription of data from one medium to another. A **conversion run** is needed to transfer data to a medium that is best suited for entry into computer-based processing. The rectangular symbol indicates that the conversion is performed by means of a computer, rather than an off-line device such as a key-to-tape encoder. The conversion shown is from OCR documents to magnetic disk. The conversion run often takes place in combination with the edit run.

Edit run. Run *b* is an **edit run,** during which data received by a computer-based system are edited or validated. Each transaction within a batch is checked for completeness, accuracy, and validity by a special editing program. Those transactions containing errors, omissions, or exceptional conditions are listed for investigation on an exception and summary report (also called an error listing, edit report, or edit and balance report). The valid transactions are shown being recorded on a so-called edited tape for use in processing. (This edited tape is a new magnetic tape, since it is not possible or desirable to write the validated data back on the same tape from which data have been read.)

Sort run. Run *c* depicts a **sort run,** in which data have been sorted by reference to a **sorting key.** Sorting is needed either (1) to prepare the transactions for sequential processing against a master file or (2) to arrange the data in appropriate order for preparing a desired report or other output.

If the former is the case, the transaction file is to be sorted into the same sequence as the records in the master file. For example, cash receipts transactions that are to be processed sequentially against an accounts receivable master file, in which the master file records are sequenced by customer numbers, would also be sorted according to customer numbers. (Hence, customer number is the sorting key.)

When a prepared report or other output is the aim, the data are sorted in a manner to facilitate the use of the output. For example, data that are to appear in customers' monthly statements may be sorted by zip codes before the statements are mailed. Statements sorted in this manner may be mailed more expeditiously. Similarly, data that are to report sales results may be sorted by product codes (or other codes) in order to provide useful sales analysis information for sales management.

In some cases the sort run may be accompanied by a **merge run** (not shown in Figure 7-10). For instance, records reflecting materials and labor used in various production jobs may initially be transcribed onto two magnetic tapes, one containing materials transactions and the other labor transactions. At some point in the processing it may be necessary to update production order records, which are arranged by job order numbers. Before doing so, it is necessary simultaneously (1) to sort the transactions on both tapes according to job order numbers and (2) to merge (combine) them on a single new magnetic tape or disk.

File maintenance run. Run *d* shows transaction data being processed against a master file, thereby bringing the data in the master file records up to date. For example, if a transaction involves a sale in the amount of $100 to Mary Rogers, the $100 would be added to the balance in her account receiv-

---

[3]As mentioned earlier, all system flowcharting symbols are described in Figure 7-23, which appears in the appendix to this chapter.

able ledger record. When performed sequentially, a file update run involves a pass through all the records in the master file.

Transactions that update the balances in master files represent one type of transaction employed in maintaining the status of customers' accounts and other entities within a business firm. Other types of transactions needed for file maintenance include (1) transactions that cause new records to be added, (2) transactions that cause currently maintained records to be deleted, and (3) transactions that cause file data other than balances to be changed or adjusted. Consider, for example, the accounts receivable master file. Sales transactions and cash receipts transactions update customers' balances; transactions pertaining to new credit customers cause new records to be created; discontinued credit customers cause records to be deleted; and revisions in the credit limits or new addresses lead to nonbalance changes in the records of affected customers.

When a master file is maintained on magnetic tape, all of the master file records (both updated and unchanged) are written onto a new magnetic tape during a **file maintenance run.** The prior, or "old," file can therefore be retained as backup; thus, if the updated file were accidentally erased, its contents could be reconstructed from the prior file. The dashed line connecting the two files indicates that the updated file will become the prior file in the next processing cycle.

When a master file is maintained on a magnetic disk, all of the master file records are written back into the same locations during the file maintenance run. Thus, only one magnetic disk symbol is shown, with a double-headed arrow as a connector. Occasionally an application may employ two removable magnetic disk packs in a manner similar to magnetic tapes. In that case the file would be written onto a new magnetic disk, and the two disks would appear in the flowchart with the connecting dashed line.

File extraction run. Run *e* reflects the processing steps involved in searching a file, retrieving desired items of data, and writing the retrieved items onto a new magnetic tape. **File extraction runs** are employed when (1) data that are to appear in reports must be rearranged before printing, (2) data must be temporarily stored because the available printers are busy, and (3) data are needed in succeeding file maintenance runs. For instance, someone may need a report that shows the inventory quantities on hand at three warehouses maintained by the firm. If these data are stored in a file arranged by inventory item number, it is necessary (1) to extract the inventory items from the file and then (2) to re-sort the data by warehouse code before preparing the report.

Report generation run. Run *f* consists of a **report generation run,** in which one or more printed outputs are produced. Often this type of run is combined with a file maintenance run. Assume, for instance, that an inventory status report, listing the up-to-date quantity on hand of each inventory item, is desired as an output from the run that updates the inventory master records. The file maintenance program could include instructions that send the data concerning each inventory item to the printer after the program updates the balance of the item.

Batch Processing Illustration

A computer system flowchart of a batch processing application is simply a compilation of several processing runs, together with inputs, files, and outputs. The sales order and invoicing application of a drug wholesale firm will serve as an illustration.

Initial steps. This application begins when sales order clerks receive orders phoned in by drugstores. The clerks capture the order data on order forms using typewriters; the keys on the typewriters have special fonts, so that the characters can be read by OCR devices. Recorded data include the customer name, customer number, code numbers of products ordered, and quantities of each. Between telephone calls they look up and enter the product descriptions, unit prices, and unit costs. Then the orders are sent for credit checks; if approved, they are filled from the warehouse and shipped. Quantities shipped are carefully entered on the orders in pencil by the shipping clerk.

Copies of the orders are batched in the shipping department, and a batch total of quantities shipped is computed. The batch of orders and total are then forwarded to the computer data processing department. This batching step and the following processing runs appear in the system flowchart in Figure 7-11.

Processing runs. Run 1 reads the data from the orders and performs programmed edit checks. Because they are OCR documents, the orders are read by an OCR device and converted to magnetic tape with the aid of the computer. Run 2 merges the order records with transaction records pertaining to new customers, discontinued customers, and nonbalance changes with the records of current customers. The run also sorts all of the data records according to customer numbers. Run 3 updates (posts) the customer accounts receivable master file, which is also arranged according to customer numbers.[4] It also prints sales invoices (in three copies) and prepares an invoice register (in effect a journal or transaction listing).

Details of file maintenance run. Figure 7-12a presents a detailed portrayal of the processing performed by the file maintenance program (run 3). The prior accounts

[4]The master file is shown to be on removable magnetic disks, with an entire new file being written onto a separate disk (or into a separate area on the same disk). The processing details would be unchanged if the master file were stored on magnetic tape.

receivable master file and the sorted sales transaction file provide inputs to the run, while the newly created accounts receivable master file is the single output file. In order to simplify the following discussion, we will assume (1) that the records in the files are unblocked and (2) that no more than one transaction affects a particular customer.

The customer program begins the file maintenance procedure by reading the first transaction record into primary storage. It then reads each record in turn from the master file, comparing the customer number from the transaction file record with the customer number from the master file record. When a match occurs, the first master record to be updated has been located. After updating this record, the computer program continues the matching procedure until all the transactions have been processed. Concurrent with the updating procedure, new customer records are inserted at appropriate places in the master file and discontinued customer records are deleted.

In Figure 7-12a the first master record contains the same customer number, 11050, as the first transaction record. Since the numbers match, the master record is updated. (Assume that the transaction record indicates a sale in the amount of $100. The balance in the customer's account would therefore be increased by $100.) Then the next transaction record, pertaining to customer 11055, is read. The program then sequentially searches the master records for the one containing 11055. As it does so, it places the checked master records onto the updated file. Thus, master record 11050 (which has just been updated) and master record 11051 (which remains unchanged) are placed on the updated file, as shown in figure 7-12a. When the program finds master record 11055, it "destroys" the record in accordance with the record deletion transaction. It next matches the records for customer number 11058, updates the master record, and then places the updated record on the up-

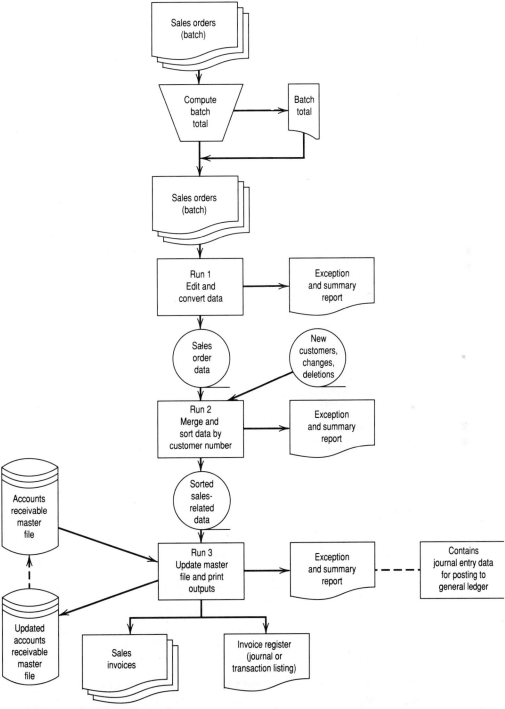

FIGURE 7-11 System flowchart of computer-based processing of sales transactions.

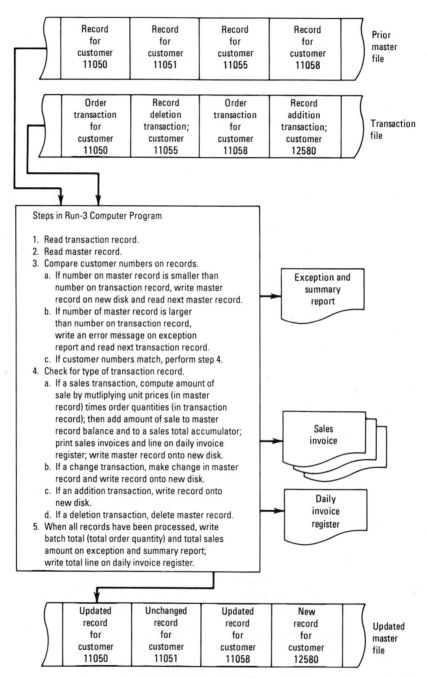

Record for customer 11050	Record for customer 11051	Record for customer 11055	Record for customer 11058	Prior master file

Order transaction for customer 11050	Record deletion transaction; customer 11055	Order transaction for customer 11058	Record addition transaction; customer 12580	Transaction file

Steps in Run-3 Computer Program

1. Read transaction record.
2. Read master record.
3. Compare customer numbers on records.
   a. If number on master record is smaller than number on transaction record, write master record on new disk and read next master record.
   b. If number of master record is larger than number on transaction record, write an error message on exception report and read next transaction record.
   c. If customer numbers match, perform step 4.
4. Check for type of transaction record.
   a. If a sales transaction, compute amount of sale by mutliplying unit prices (in master record) times order quantities (in transaction record); then add amount of sale to master record balance and to a sales total accumulator; print sales invoices and line on daily invoice register; write master record onto new disk.
   b. If a change transaction, make change in master record and write record onto new disk.
   c. If an addition transaction, write record onto new disk.
   d. If a deletion transaction, delete master record.
5. When all records have been processed, write batch total (total order quantity) and total sales amount on exception and summary report; write total line on daily invoice register.

Exception and summary report

Sales invoice

Daily invoice register

Updated record for customer 11050	Unchanged record for customer 11051	Updated record for customer 11058	New record for customer 12580	Updated master file

a. Detailed processing steps pertaining to run 3

FIGURE 7-12 Details of the updating run for the illustrative sales order and invoicing application.

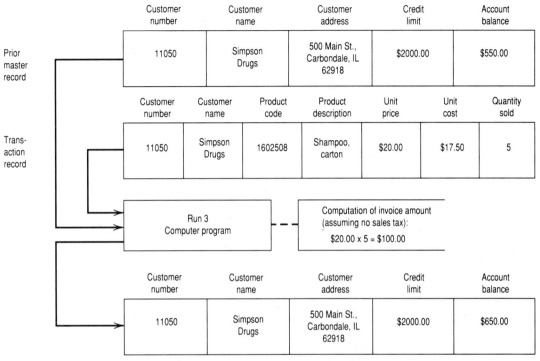

	Customer number	Customer name	Customer address	Credit limit	Account balance
Prior master record	11050	Simpson Drugs	500 Main St., Carbondale, IL 62918	$2000.00	$550.00

	Customer number	Customer name	Product code	Product description	Unit price	Unit cost	Quantity sold
Trans-action record	11050	Simpson Drugs	1602508	Shampoo, carton	$20.00	$17.50	5

Run 3
Computer program

Computation of invoice amount
(assuming no sales tax):

$20.00 x 5 = $100.00

	Customer number	Customer name	Customer address	Credit limit	Account balance
	11050	Simpson Drugs	500 Main St., Carbondale, IL 62918	$2000.00	$650.00

b. Effects of updating an accounts receivable master record in run 3.

FIGURE 7-12 (*Continued*)

dated master file. Finally, it adds a record for customer 12580 to the master file.

Figure 7-12*b* shows the details of the master record for customer number 11050 and a transaction record that reflects an order amounting to $100.00. The updated record for the customer displays a new balance of $650.00 ($550.00 + $100.00). This example is simplified, in that all data needed for preparing a sales invoice are not shown. Additional data would need to be included in the master file and perhaps in a separate reference file. However, the example stresses that a major purpose of the file maintenance run is to update the balance field.

Outputs from processing. **Exception and summary reports** are shown as outputs from all the computer processing runs in Figure 7-11. Although this report is especially neces-

sary with respect to an edit run, it also may be needed if errors are detected in later runs. For instance, if a transaction record is out of sequence during the file maintenance run, this erroneous condition should be noted. Also, the exception and summary report lists the batch total computed during each successive run; these computed totals will be compared with the batch total previously computed in the shipping department. Still another reason for exception and summary reports is to reflect summary data needed in journal entries. For instance, the exception and summary report in run 3 will list the total sales value of the products shipped, which will provide the basis for an entry debiting the accounts receivable account and crediting the sales account in the general ledger.

Two other outputs are generated from the file maintenance run in Figure 7-11. Sales invoices are prepared and mailed to customers. An invoice register is prepared to show the key data pertaining to each sales invoice. It serves as an important link in the audit trail of a computer-based system.

Other scheduled reports could be provided as desired by special print runs. For example, the customer monthly statements are prepared at the end of each month from data stored in each customer's master record. Sales analyses and accounts receivable aging schedules are also likely candidates.

Simplifications. The system flowchart in Figure 7-11 has been simplified. For instance, the comparisons of batch totals are not shown, nor are the sources and dispositions of the various documents and reports. The appendix to this chapter shows how these features may be included.

The procedure described has also been simplified. For example, an inventory master file is normally updated to reflect quantities sold. More complete sales procedures are described in Chapter 12, "The Revenue Cycle."

Contrasts with Manual Batch Processing

Computer-based batch processing can be better understood when compared to batch processing by manual means. Figure 7-13 shows a system flowchart that depicts the way processing would appear if the sales order and invoicing illustration were performed by a manual system.

Certain similarities are apparent: Most of the same steps are required in both systems, the processing cycles are identical in length, and the contents of the sales invoices are identical. Moreover, the files are likely to be identical in number and contents.

Several significant differences appear, however. The files are stored on paper sheets rather than magnetic media. Editing is performed by a clerk who reviews the sales or-

der and prepares the sales invoice, rather than by a computer edit program. Thus, no computer-printed exception and summary reports are produced. The processing steps follow a somewhat different sequence. For instance, the sales invoices are prepared manually at a fairly early stage, since they represent the posting medium. The journal is integrally involved in the processing, rather than being a by-product of the posting step. A batch total of sales amounts (based on sales invoices) is at least as important as a batch total taken from sales orders; it verifies the accuracy of the posting to the subsidiary ledger, which is performed by someone other than the clerk who prepares the sales invoice and makes the journal entry. Finally, the system flowchart for manual processing has mainly horizontal flows, while its counterpart for computer-based processing shows mainly vertical flows. This difference is a matter of convention, rather than logic.

Processing Options

A variety of options are available within the batch processing approach. As a result, many alternative batch processing system designs are possible.

Direct-access storage. One option is to avoid creating a new master file when the records are updated by a batch of transaction records. The reason for employing this option is to allow individual records to be directly accessed. Thus, a credit manager could retrieve the record for customer 11055 quickly when desired, rather than having to wait while the system sequentially scans all records from the beginning of the file.

The direct access option can be employed only when the master file is stored on a direct-access storage medium, such as magnetic disk. Since the less expensive magnetic tape cannot be used, this option is relatively costly.

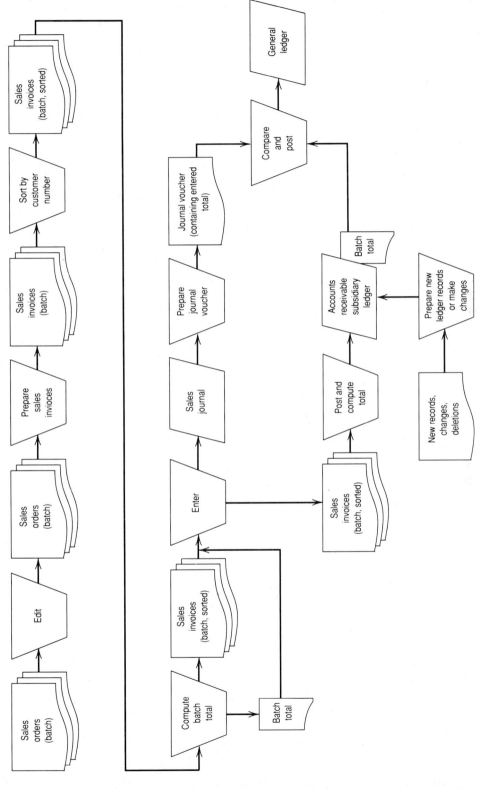

FIGURE 7-13 Document flows of a manually based sales order and invoicing system.

Direct processing. Even when stored on a direct-access storage medium, so that individual records may be accessed directly, files may still be updated sequentially by batches of transactions. Figure 7-11, which shows an accounts receivable master file being updated by sorted transactions, illustrates this option. Alternatively, the files may be updated by **direct processing,** also known as random processing. Under this option the batch of transactions need not be sorted. Each transaction in the unsorted batch is processed directly; that is, the system retrieves the appropriate master record from its location within the file, updates the record, and returns the updated master record to the same location on the storage medium. Since sequential processing is inherently more efficient than direct processing, the latter option is best suited to small batches.

Separate file maintenance processing. Another option is to process the file maintenance changes (e.g., new records, record deletions) in a procedure apart from the updating procedure. If this option is selected, the file maintenance computer programs will be simplified. On the other hand,

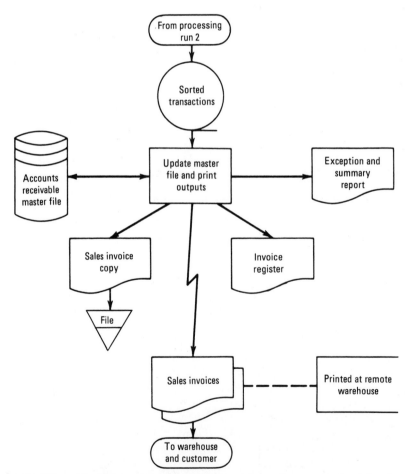

FIGURE 7-14 The remote processing portion of computer-based sales transaction processing.

separating the file maintenance will result in more lengthy overall processing times.

Remote processing. Batch processing may be performed at sites that are geographically remote to the central processor, rather than solely at the central site. Assume, for instance, that the drug wholesaler in our illustration has warehouses in several locations that are physically remote from its central location. In each warehouse a batch terminal with printing capability might be installed. Then, as batches of orders are processed, the sales invoices could be printed at the warehouses where the items are to be picked and shipped.

Figure 7-14 portrays this **remote batch processing** portion of the sales order procedure. In order to show the effect of another processing option, we have also assumed that the accounts receivable master file is stored on magnetic disk. The batch of transactions is processed sequentially as before, but now a user such as the credit manager can directly access customers' records. Note that the disk symbol is connected to the processing run symbol by a double-headed arrow. This indicates that the master records are read from the disk into primary storage, updated, and then placed back onto the disk in the same locations from which they were read.[5]

Output Options

Spooling. An output option is to spool data rather than to print the results of processing immediately. **Spooling** consists of temporarily storing the results of processing on a secondary storage medium such as magnetic tape or disk. At a later time the data are transcribed from the magnetic medium onto the desired hard-copy forms. For instance, the data for the sales invoices in run 3 might be spooled onto magnetic tape, with the in-

voices being printed later. Often the printing of spooled data is performed off-line, that is, without the direct involvement of the central processing unit. Thus, the sales invoices might be printed off-line by connecting the printer to a magnetic tape drive. Spooling is employed either (1) when insufficient printers are available for the needed outputs or (2) when the printing operation would significantly increase the overall processing time of the application.

Combination processing-extraction runs. Another output option pertains to the data extraction run. In the illustrative batch processing procedure we noted in run 3 that updating and printing functions were combined. It is also feasible to combine updating and data extraction in the same run. If, for instance, an inventory analysis report is needed, it is more efficient to extract the data from the inventory master file during the inventory file update run than to extract the desired data by means of a separate run.

On-Line Processing Approach[6]

Characteristics

On-line processing consists of processing each transaction as soon as it is captured.[7] Each transaction is posted immediately to the affected files. Therefore, the stored data concerning the status of events and entities (e.g., the progress of a production job, the balance of a customer's ac-

---

[5]This overlay method of restoring updated master records on magnetic disks is discussed in Chapter 8.

[6]On-line processing is also called real-time processing by some authors. However, real-time systems are considered in this textbook to be special cases of on-line processing systems. See page 242.

[7]In rare cases transactions may be entered for on-line processing in batches rather than individually. For instance, a firm that receives sales orders and/or cash remittances in batches by mail might effectively employ the on-line/batch approach. A clerk first keys the transaction data via the terminal keyboard. After all the data are entered and validated by the edit program, the processing programs directly update the on-line files. Since this approach involves the entry of data in batches, batch totals may be employed to aid data control.

count) are continuously current. This approach is used in dynamic situations when up-to-date information is needed on short notice.

On-line processing is not a new concept. It has been applied for centuries in very small firms by managers who could nimbly handle and process each event as it arose. What is new is the capability of applying this approach to not-so-small firms through the use of computer-based hardware and software. Transactions of differing types can be captured, processed, and stored by on-line processing systems.

The savings and loan institution mentioned earlier can illustrate the approach. In a short time span one morning a teller received and entered a deposit at 10:33, paid out a withdrawal at 10:37, and accepted and applied a loan payment at 10:40. She entered the data for each transaction via her counter terminal, which connects through the institution's central computer to on-line magnetic disk files located at the main office. The account balance of each person initiating a transaction was updated immediately to reflect the transactions.

On-line processing systems are also called **interactive processing systems,** since on-line processing generally involves direct interactions between humans and a computer-based system. The interacting humans, usually employees or managers of a firm operating a computer-based system, initiate the processing via terminals or other input-output devices. As in the case of the teller, they often enter transaction data that will update files. However, they may also initiate processing to change the permanent data in records or to perform other file maintenance actions. Equally important, they initiate processing to retrieve desired up-to-date information from the files.

Typical On-Line Processing Steps

On-line processing involves discrete steps rather than separate batch runs. Typi-

cal steps include data entry and edit, file update or maintenance, file inquiry, and report generation. Each step is performed under the control of a computer program stored on-line. In turn, each program required in on-line processing is directed and coordinated by the operating system.

Data entry and edit. As noted earlier, data that are to be processed on-line are entered via the on-line approach. During the entry process the data are edited for errors and omissions.

File update or maintenance. When entering transaction data the entry clerk informs the computer system of (1) the type of transaction (e.g., a sale) and (2) the type of action (e.g., an update). The appropriate application program is then called from secondary storage and employed to perform the processing. In on-line processing systems often more than one file is affected by transaction data.

File inquiry. When information is desired immediately from the data base of an on-line processing system, the inquirer (e.g., a manager) enters a request via an input device. The information is retrieved by inquiry software; it is then presented within seconds or minutes to the inquirer in the form specified.

Report generation. An on-line processing system can generate the same types of documents and periodic reports that are provided by batch processing systems. Upon a request from the appropriate person, the computer system prints the documents or reports under the control of a report generation program.

On-Line Processing Illustration

Assume that the drug wholesale firm redesigns its sales order and invoicing application. As the computer system flowchart in Figure 7-15 shows, sales orders are now en-

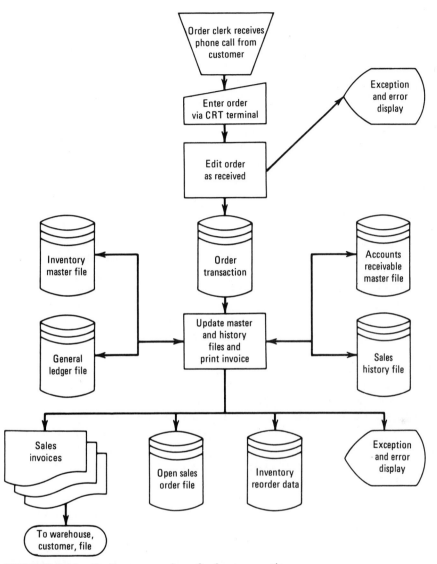

FIGURE 7-15 On-line processing of sales transactions.

tered and processed by an on-line processing system. Order clerks located in a central department sit in front of video display terminals. As orders are phoned in by drugstores, the clerks key the data into the terminals. During the keying process the clerks visually review the entered data on their screens. The order data are verified by an edit program, with errors being displayed on the screens. These detected errors are corrected by the clerks. If data in the accounts receivable master file show a customer to be credit-

worthy, the computer system then accepts his or her order.

Accepted orders lead to a host of actions. Three master files (inventory, accounts receivable, and general ledger) are updated. Data concerning the order are added to an open sales order file and a sales history file.

In addition to updating several files, this on-line processing application is likely to generate more outputs than its batch processing counterpart. For instance, it can easily produce an inventory reorder list and a log of transactions as well as the invoice register. Furthermore, it can promptly retrieve requested data from files, such as the current account balance of a particular customer.

The system flowchart in Figure 7-15 is simplified, as was Figure 7-11, to focus on the key features of the on-line processing approach. A more complete on-line sales processing system, together with detailed system flowcharts, is described in Chapter 12.

Processing Options

As in the case of batch processing, various options are available within the on-line processing approach. Two such options, remote processing systems and real-time systems, are briefly discussed below.

Remote processing. On-line processing may be performed at sites which are geographically remote from the central processor. Moreover, data may be entered at remote terminals, transmitted to a central processor, and processed against on-line files.

Real-time systems. Another option is to apply on-line processing in the service of a real-time system. A **real-time system** is a computer-based support system that provides information in a sufficiently timely manner to control a process or operation. Figure 7-16 portrays the structural components of a real-time system.

Since the purpose of a real-time system is to control a process or operation, the emphasis is on **response time.** The allowable response time, the length of time from an inquiry or event until a response is produced by the system, varies from situation to situation. Continuous physical processes, such as steel-rolling and oil-refining processes, may require fractional-second response times for adequate control. By contrast, several seconds or even minutes may be sufficient to control such transaction-oriented business processes as credit checking, production control, and motel reservations.

Real-time systems often involve remote processing as well as on-line processing. Complex support systems of this type are extensively discussed in Chapter 20.

Output Options

Soft-copy displays. An output option is to display responses to inquiries on CRT screens, rather than to print the results on hard copy. Terminal technology enables the displays to include color graphics if desired.

Voice responses. Another output option consists of simulated voices that provide

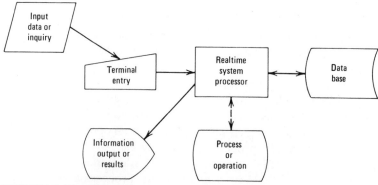

FIGURE 7-16 Components of a real-time system.

"humanized" responses. On-line systems that handle transactions with the public are increasingly using the voice-response option. Examples include point-of-sale systems of grocery chains, automated teller systems in banks, and automatic operator systems of telephone companies.

Design Considerations

This chapter has surveyed approaches and options pertaining to the input, processing, and output stages. Designing a computer-based data conversion system consists of selecting the most suitable approaches and options for the respective applications of a firm. These choices should refer to the several design objectives and address the particular circumstances of each application. In this section we propose guidelines for selecting the most suitable data conversion approaches, for improving throughput and efficiency, for designing input forms, and for optimizing the mix of data conversion systems.

Selecting the Best Data Conversion Approach

The two basic choices for each application are between batch processing (with batch input) and on-line processing (with on-line input). Figure 7-17 compares the relative advantages of these two choices, including those discussed earlier with respect to date entry approaches.

Batch processing applications are suited to present-day real-world firms in many industries. Examples range from banks (check and credit card transactions) to cities (water billing transactions). Almost all firms employ

	Batch Processing	On-line Processing
Advantages	1. Requires less complex and expensive hardware and software. 2. Normally employs more efficient sequential processing mode. 3. Provides added control through such mechanisms as batch totals.	1. Provides up-to-date information in a timely manner. 2. Provides early and thorough validation of data to assure accuracy and completeness. 3. Eliminates sorting and transcribing of data. 4. Provides added flexibility to changing needs of users.
Disadvantages	1. Allows records in master files to become out-of-date. 2. Inhibits the timely retrieval of data from records (when magnetic tape storage media are used). 3. Normally requires sorting and transcribing activities. 4. Requires more manual handling of files, programs, and source documents (especially when magnetic tape storage is used).	1. Requires more complex and expensive hardware and software. 2. Normally inhibits use of batch totals for control. 3. Employs less efficient random processing method.

FIGURE 7-17 Batch processing versus on-line processing.

APPLICATION OF AN ON-LINE PROCESSING SYSTEM
Helene Curtis Industries, Inc.[a]

A Chicago-based cosmetics maker, Helene Curtis, recently changed its strategy of being a low-cost manufacturer to being a supplier with excellent service to retailer customers. To foster this new strategy, the firm developed transaction processing systems for on-line order entry and finished-goods inventory. It also added a 300,000-square-foot automated warehouse. The on-line transaction process-

ing is performed by a dedicated Stratus computer system which is designed to accommodate on-line applications very efficiently and reliably. Also supporting the processing is a DB-2 relational data base system. Tom Gildea, vice-president of business information services, feels that the new system provides "quick response" to its retailer customers. When the new warehouse is fully tied into the on-line processing systems, the firm's shipping costs are expected to decrease by 25 percent.

[a]Leila Davis, "On-Line Applications Grow Up," *Datamation*, January 1, 1990, pp. 61–63.

---

batch processing in the preparation of paychecks for employees.

On-line processing applications are likewise suited to most firms. An early application still vitally important to airlines and motels is the reservation system. Firms in manufacturing, retailing, and banking industries are rapidly adding on-line processing applications.

In sum, the batch processing approach should be selected when processing efficiency and economy are paramount. Conversely, the on-line processing approach should be selected when timely and up-to-date information is necessary to achieve adequate service and effective decision making. Because timeliness and up-to-dateness have become increasingly important in the modern business world, on-line processing systems are being selected more frequently. However, batch processing is not on the verge of extinction. In fact, most present-day accounting application software packages are based on the batch processing approach.

Improving Throughput and Efficiency

Two objectives that are related and important to data conversion are throughput

and efficiency. A designer must be concerned with means of enhancing these objectives in order to gain the greatest possible productivity from a given computer system. Choices such as the following tend to enhance throughput and efficiency:

1. Processing large batches of transactions in sequential fashion.
2. Eliminating data transcription whenever feasible (for example, by capturing data in computer-readable form).
3. Capturing data in as condensed a form as possible (for example, by using codes to the fullest extent and by prepunching cards).
4. Minimizing the outputs produced by the system (for example, using exception reports whenever feasible).
5. Providing computer assistance (for example, preformatted screen forms) when data are entered via on-line terminals.
6. Employing high-speed input and output media, such as magnetic tapes and disks and a sufficient number of input–output devices, in order to match the processing capacity of the computer system.
7. Blocking data records in transaction files, in order to have a larger quantity of data

transferred into primary storage during each input command from the processing program.

8. Acquiring such software and hardware features as overlapping, multiprogramming, and added primary storage buffers.

9. Scheduling processing runs and jobs to minimize peaks and backlogs.

Designing Forms

A **form** is a vehicle for capturing and recording data in a structured manner. Examples of forms are source documents, preformatted screens, microfilm images, and op-

tical disk images. Good design of forms enables data needed in applications to be entered quickly and accurately. It also enables clerks and others to use the forms efficiently and effectively. Thus, it minimizes the combined costs of devising, entering, and using forms.

Sound design of forms consists of applying a comprehensive set of guidelines. Figure 7-18 provides a checklist of guidelines that are applicable to hard-copy source documents. This checklist may be employed when designing new forms or when revising forms currently in use. It may be used in conjunction with a Forms Analysis Sheet, such as the example shown in Figure 7-19.

What is the purpose of the form?

What is the source of the information?

Who are the users of the form?

Has a title been established?

Has an identification number been assigned for control purposes?

Are the information items adequate to meet the purpose, with all unnecessary items omitted?

Are clear but brief instructions provided, when necessary, for use by the preparer?

Is a space provided for the date?

Is related information grouped together?

Is there a logical flow of the information items (e.g., from left to right and from top to bottom) to minimize backtracking?

Is the quantity of information to be entered kept at a minimum by such devices as check boxes and preprinted descriptions?

Is adequate space provided for entering needed information?

Are key information items stressed by heavy type or distinctive color?

Are the margins adequate?

Is standard-size paper ($8\frac{1}{2}'' \times 11''$) used?

Is the vertical spacing appropriate for the machines used to enter the items?

Are such technical features as perforations, scoring, type size, and paper weight suited to the intended use?

Are adequate copies prepared for distribution and filing, and are they prebound in multicopy sets?

Are copies color-coded to reduce mistakes in distribution?

FIGURE 7-18   A checklist for design of forms involving source documents.

The HIJ Company

Sales Order   No. 2653

Date Received 3-14-91	Customer's Order Number 1738-6	Salesperson K. Brown

Sold to	Handy Warehousing Co. 718 South Desert Phoenix, Arizona 85208

Ship to	Handy Warehouse No. 5 6100 No. College Drive Tempe, Arizona 85282

F.O.B. Destination	Routing Via Western Rail Lines	Terms Net 30 Days

Product number	Quantity ordered	Unit of measure	Description	Unit price
26-B	10	50 gal. dr.	Cleaning Solvent	76.50
75-A	5	Unit	Steel Brush	8.75
106-D	50	Yard	Heavy Duty Hosing	5.07

Form No.	HIJ162		

Form Analysis Sheet

Title: Sales order   Form Number HIJ162

Purpose: To record on a company form the receipt of an order, so that shipment of the order can be assured.

Point of origin: Sales order department when customer's order received
Source of data: Customer's order by letter, telegram, or call; salesperson's order slip.

Method of preparing: Typed

Average lines of data: 11   Frequency of use: Daily

Annual quantity used: 2500   Peak weekly volume: 130

Size of form: $6\frac{1}{2}'' \times 8\frac{1}{2}''$ Cost of preparing 100 forms: $145.00

Disposition—   Original: Sales order department
                  Copy 1 : Shipping department
                  Copy 2 : Billing department
                  Copy 3 : Acknowledgement to customer
                  Other copies: None

Other forms using data: Sales invoice, shipping order

Transcription onto machine-readable media: Magnetic tape
Files affected: Inventory, customer, open orders, various reference files
Volume of errors per week: 20   Approval signatures required: None
Data added after form originated: Back order number, if any; unit costs; freight cost
Use of form for internal checking and control: Initialed by clerks who review for completeness and who enter
   in register; compared with shipping report.
Remarks: No spaces for priority, delivery date scheduled, unit costs, special instructions

FIGURE 7-19   A sales order document and related form analysis sheet.

As the figure indicates, a filled-in copy of the form is also helpful to the analysis. While the example is largely self-explanatory, we might note that the sample sales order document is reasonably well designed. For instance, it has a clearly defined heading section (the top portion), plus a well-arranged body (the columnar portion). However, it does not provide certain desirable data, such as delivery date scheduled in the heading or unit costs in the body. Furthermore, it does not contain instructions, which generally appear at the bottom or on the back side. Certain documents, such as sales invoices, would also include totals or approval signatures in a foot section.

Transactions increasingly are being entered into on-line computer systems via preformatted screens, such as the example in Figure 7-7. As in the case of a hard-copy form, a preformatted screen should have a clear purpose and logical arrangement. Boxes or highlighted areas should guide the data entry clerk in entering each item. In order to reduce fatigue, the number of data items should be minimized. For instance, the data entry software can be programmed to enter standard data (e.g., date of transaction) and to perform needed computations (e.g., totals). It can also be designed to respond with clarifying data (e.g., depositor name) upon the clerical entry of codes (e.g., depositor number); such response is sometimes called echoing. Clear instructions should guide the data entry clerk in completing the entry (e.g., the question at the bottom of the screen in Figure 7-7). When a variety of input screens are employed, all of the screens should present consistent formats to avoid confusing users.

Optimizing the Mix of Data Conversion Applications

The data conversion systems within a typical modern firm are likely to include a mix of computer-based batch processing applications, on-line processing applications, and partially or wholly manual processing applications. Achieving an optimal overall set of data conversion systems requires **trade-offs** among objectives: sacrifices of certain objectives to attain greater advantages from others.

Although intelligent trade-offs are dependent on specific circumstances, a general principle can be stated: Do not too readily sacrifice the objective of economy; in other words, do not design and acquire a system whose added costs exceed its added benefits. An adequate manual system should not be replaced by a computer-based system unless the latter's added benefits exceed its added costs. Similarly, an on-line processing system is not an automatic replacement for a computer-based batch processing system. If the current batch processing system is indeed outdated, a better replacement may be a new batch processing system with on-line data input.

Summary

Data conversion systems are involved in entering processing data. Since computers offer several advantages over manual systems, an increasing number of data conversion systems are computer based. Objectives that guide the design of such systems relate to relevance, throughput, efficiency, timeliness, flexibility, accuracy and security, and economy.

Data may be collected and entered by the batch input or the on-line input approach. The batch input approach involves the collection of data on source documents and the accumulation of documents into batches. Source documents may consist of ordinary paper documents, or they may appear as OCR or other special documents. Data are often transcribed onto magnetic tape or disk before being entered for processing. The on-line input approach does not require that data be collected on source documents, although in some applications they are. It involves the entry of data either by keying via an input device or by using a nonkeyed technique such as voice input or optical scanning. The batch input approach offers greater processing efficiency and economy, whereas the on-line input approach provides greater timeliness, flexibility, and simplicity.

In computer-based systems data may also be processed by a batch approach or by an on-line approach. The batch processing approach consists of periodic processing runs that perform edit, conversion, sorting, updating, reporting, and extracting functions. It may be combined with either the batch input approach or the on-line input approach, may employ magnetic tape or disk files, and allows other options such as spooling. The on-line processing approach generally involves the processing of transactions as soon as they are captured, so that the on-line files are kept continually up to date. This approach also accommodates a variety of options, such as on-line inquiries, soft-copy displays, voice responses, and real-time control. The batch processing approach is best suited to applications where processing efficiency and economy are paramount. The on-line processing approach is preferable when timely and up-to-date information is essential.

In addition to selecting the most suitable input and processing approaches, a designer of data conversion systems should be capable both of preparing effective forms and input screens and of choosing options that enhance throughput and efficiency and that optimize the mix of data conversion applications.

APPENDIX TO CHAPTER 7

Flowcharting

Introduction

Flowcharts are diagrams that pictorially portray the sequential flows of data and/or operations. Accountants and systems analysts use flowcharts extensively in the analysis, design, and evaluation of information systems. No technique is used more widely by accountants than flowcharting when depicting transaction processing systems. Our discussion in this appendix covers the levels of flowcharts, types of system flowcharts, and construction of system flowcharts.

Levels of Flowcharts

Flowcharts may be classified according to three broad levels of detail:

1. A summary or overview level of detail. An example of an overview diagram is shown in Figure 3-1. At this level only the major flows among activities, processes, and/or physical locations are portrayed. The purpose of an overview diagram, as the name implies, is to provide a bird's-eye view, or integrating perspective, of a

system. It is useful to designers, evaluators, and even users. For instance, the managers of a firm can more easily grasp the nature of a new system design via an overview diagram than through a detailed flowchart.

2. A middle level of detail, as represented by system flowcharts. A flowchart at this level can be employed to portray key details of one of the activities or processes appearing in an overview diagram. System flowcharts typically include inputs, outputs, processing sequences, files, and/or controls.

3. A highly detailed level, as represented by program flowcharts or block diagrams. A program flowchart portrays a logical sequence of operations performed by computers or humans. In effect, it provides a "blowup" of a single processing step (e.g., sorting of invoices, updating of the accounts receivable master file) pictured in a system flowchart. Program flowcharts in turn may be subdivided into macro and micro levels. (They are discussed in Chapter 25.)

Figure 7-20 illustrates these three broad levels, including the subdivided detailed level. It also shows that the levels form a hierarchical structure. Note that the levels can be linked to each other through coded references (located in the striped boxes).

Types of System Flowcharts

System flowcharts hold the greatest interest for accountants because they highlight relationships among components of transaction processing systems. In other words, they provide answers to such questions as

1. What inputs (e.g., source documents) are received and from what sources?

2. What outputs (e.g., reports) are generated and to whom?

3. What are the approaches to processing and what steps comprise the data conversion sequence?

4. What files (including accounting records) are affected, and on what media are they stored?

5. Which accounting controls are employed (to the extent that they can be pictorially displayed)?

System flowcharts can be adapted to emphasize one or more components of transaction processing systems. A **process flowchart** stresses basic procedural steps and incorporates symbols such as those shown in Figure 7-21. A **document flowchart** emphasizes the inputs and outputs and their flows through organizational units. Document flowcharts are generally used to portray manual transaction processing systems; however, they are also useful in showing transaction processing systems that involve a mixture of manual and computer-based data conversion. A **computer system flowchart** emphasizes the computer-based portions of transaction processing systems, including computer runs or steps and accesses of on-line files. A **control-oriented flowchart** emphasizes the control points within a transaction processing system, especially as they relate to the accounting documents and records. Figure 7-22 displays the basic structure of a control-oriented flowcharting approach called Seadoc.

A flow diagram that resembles the flowchart in certain respects is the **data flow diagram.** Rather than tracing the flows of specific documents by physical processing devices, though, the data flow diagram traces the *logical* flows of data through transaction processing procedures. Thus, a data flow diagram designates only essential data sources, data destinations, processing steps, and stores of data. Examples of data flow diagrams are provided in Chapters 11, 12, and 22.

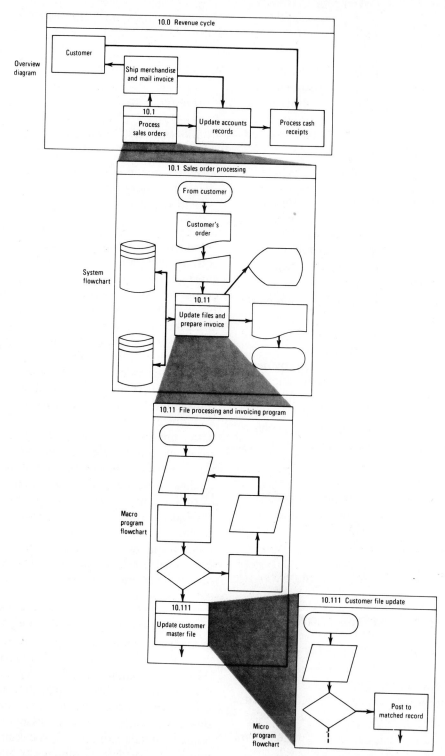

FIGURE 7-20 A flowchart hierarchy.

| Operation | Transportation | Inspection | Delay | Storage |

FIGURE 7-21   Process flowchart symbols.

Construction of System Flowcharts

In order to construct sound system flowcharts, a preparer must be aware of all available symbols, follow a careful step-by-step approach, and apply consistent guidelines.

Flowcharting Symbols

The building blocks for a system flowchart are a set of symbols, most of which are generally accepted by accountants and analysts. Figure 7-23 displays the set of symbols to be used in this textbook. These may be grouped as input–output symbols, processing symbols, storage symbols, flow symbols, and miscellaneous symbols. All of the symbols in the figure can be drawn with the assistance of a flowcharting template, which is available at most university bookstores.

Input–output symbols.   The top symbol in the left-most column represents data on source documents or information on output documents or reports. The second and third symbols reflect the entry of data by keyboards or other on-line means and the display of information on CRT screens or other on-line devices. The last two symbols in the column, involving punched cards and punched paper tape, are seldom used in modern-day systems.

Processing symbols.   Symbols are available to indicate the processing of data by clerks, noncomputerized machines, and computers. Clerical processing may take place in computer-based as well as manual systems. Two

symbols pertain to processing by noncomputerized devices used in off-line operations. The square symbol is used to represent such auxiliary processing operations as transcribing, sorting, and printing. Examples are sorting checks by MICR devices, transcribing from OCR documents to magnetic tapes or disks by means of OCR devices, and printing data from magnetic tape or disks to microfilm by means of COM devices. The rectangular symbol with rounded sides is used to represent keying operations by such devices as key-to-tape encoders and key-to-disk systems.

Storage symbols.   The top symbol is used to show documents or records being stored in an off-line storage device, such as a file cabinet or hold-basket. The remaining symbols are available to show data being stored on computerized media. The bottom symbol pertains to any on-line storage device, including a magnetic disk. However, it may be employed to indicate that data are being stored on a temporary basis.

Data and information flow symbols.   The five symbols in the right-most column provide direction throughout a flowchart. The oval terminal symbol marks a beginning or ending point within the flowchart being examined, such as the receipt of an order from a customer. Often a beginning or ending point is also a link to an adjoining procedure. The flowline shows the flow of data or information, usually in written form. The communication link symbol (the one that looks like a lightning bolt) represents the flow of

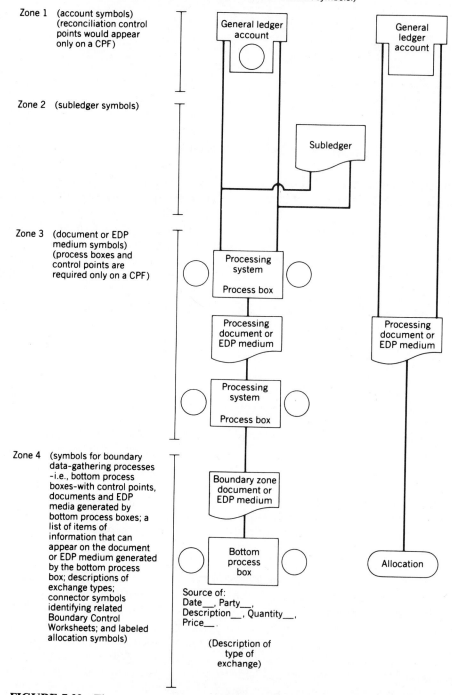

Illustration of the Four Zones and Their Contents
(Note that this is not a completed SEADOC flowchart; it is intended only to illustrate the appropriate location of the flowchart symbols.)

Zone 1 (account symbols) (reconciliation control points would appear only on a CPF)

General ledger account

General ledger account

Zone 2 (subledger symbols)

Subledger

Zone 3 (document or EDP medium symbols) (process boxes and control points are required only on a CPF)

Processing system

Process box

Processing document or EDP medium

Processing system

Process box

Processing document or EDP medium

Zone 4 (symbols for boundary data-gathering processes –i.e., bottom process boxes–with control points, documents and EDP media generated by bottom process boxes; a list of items of information that can appear on the document or EDP medium generated by the bottom process box; descriptions of exchange types; connector symbols identifying related Boundary Control Worksheets; and labeled allocation symbols)

Boundary zone document or EDP medium

Bottom process box

Allocation

Source of:
Date__, Party__,
Description__, Quantity__,
Price__.

(Description of type of exchange)

FIGURE 7-22 The structure of a control-oriented flowchart. Adapted with permission from Peat, Marwick, Mitchell & Co., 1985.

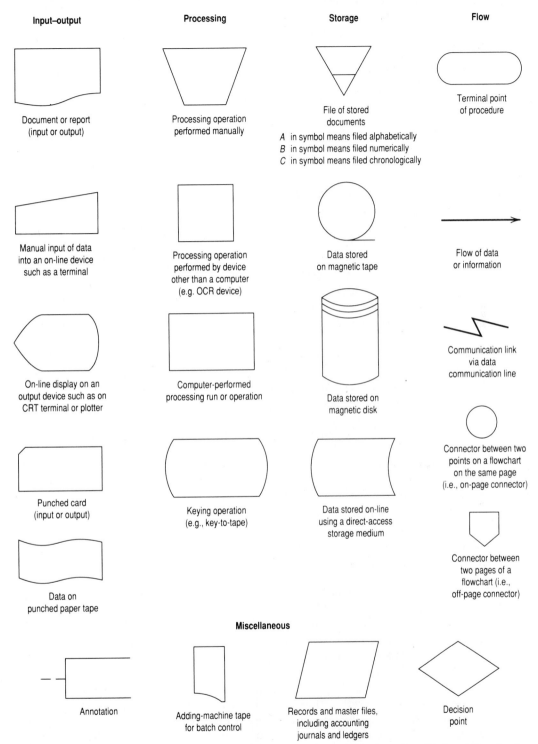

Input–output	Processing	Storage	Flow

Input–output

Document or report
(input or output)

Manual input of data
into an on-line device
such as a terminal

On-line display on an
output device such as on
CRT terminal or plotter

Punched card
(input or output)

Data on
punched paper tape

Processing

Processing operation
performed manually

Processing operation
performed by device
other than a computer
(e.g. OCR device)

Computer-performed
processing run or operation

Keying operation
(e.g., key-to-tape)

Storage

File of stored
documents

A in symbol means filed alphabetically
B in symbol means filed numerically
C in symbol means filed chronologically

Data stored
on magnetic tape

Data stored on
magnetic disk

Data stored on-line
using a direct-access
storage medium

Flow

Terminal point
of procedure

Flow of data
or information

Communication link
via data
communication line

Connector between two
points on a flowchart
on the same page
(i.e., on-page connector)

Connector between
two pages of a
flowchart (i.e.,
off-page connector)

Miscellaneous

Annotation

Adding-machine tape
for batch control

Records and master files,
including accounting
journals and ledgers

Decision
point

FIGURE 7-23 A set of symbols for system flowcharting. Based on American National Standards Institute, *Standard Flowchart Symbols and Their Use in Information Processing (X3.5)* (New York: ANSI, 1971) and on other sources.

data from one physical location to another. Finally, two connector symbols are available to provide further linkages. The on-page connector is used within a single page of a flowchart, and the off-page connector links two pages of a multipage flowchart.

Miscellaneous symbols. The annotation symbol can be connected to any symbol within a flowchart; its purpose is to provide space for a note concerning the procedure. For instance, it could indicate how often a particular processing step takes place or who performs it. The adding-machine tape symbol is appropriate mainly to reflect the computing and recording of batch control totals, in either manual or computer-based systems. The parallelogram represents accounting records when stored in off-line storage in hard-copy form. The decision symbol can be used when two or three alternative processing paths can be followed. For instance, in a flowchart showing sales transaction processing, a decision symbol may be placed at the point just after a credit check. If an ordering customer's credit is found to be satisfactory, one path may lead to continued processing of the order. Alternatively, if the credit is not satisfactory, another path might lead to the writing of a rejection letter.

Step-by-Step Development

The developmental process can best be seen through examples. The three following examples pertain to a document flowchart for a purchasing procedure involving manual processing and two computer system flowcharts pertaining to the same procedure.

Document flowchart of manual processing. The following narrative describes the purchasing procedure for the Easybuy Company:

A clerk in the accounting department periodically reviews the inventory records in order to determine which items need reordering. When she notes that the quantity on hand for a particular item has fallen below a preestablished reorder point, the clerk prepares a prenumbered purchase requisition in two copies. The original is sent to the purchasing department, where a buyer (1) decides on a suitable supplier by reference to a supplier file and (2) prepares a prenumbered purchase order in four copies. The original copy of the purchase order is signed by the purchasing manager and mailed to the designated supplier. The second copy is returned to the inventory clerk in the accounting department, who pulls the matching requisition copy from a temporary file (where it had been filed chronologically), posts the ordered quantities to the inventory records, and files the purchase requisition and order together. The third copy is forwarded to the receiving department, where it is filed numerically to await the receipt of the ordered goods. The fourth copy is filed numerically, together with the original copy of the purchase requisition, in an open purchase order file. When the invoice from the supplier arrives, this last copy will be entered into the accounts payable procedure.

Several features of this procedure should be noted. It involves manual processing of transactions, it moves among three departments, and it generates documents having several copies. To present all of these features clearly, a system flowchart must blend characteristics of a document flowchart with those of a process flowchart. Let us see how this can be done.

We begin by identifying the relevant organizational units (i.e., accounting department, purchasing department, and receiving department). Next we select those symbols from Figure 7-23 that pertain to manual processing. These symbols are then combined in strict accordance with the sequence of the narrative. For convenience we subdivide our work into four key steps or functions.

1. **Preparation of the purchase requisition.** As the segment headed by the words "Accounting Department" shows, the flowcharted procedure begins in the accounting department with a terminal symbol. This symbol is connected by a flowline to a clerical or manual processing symbol. Inserted inside this second symbol is a notation that briefly states the actions taken by the inventory clerk. In order to explain the basis on which the clerk prepares the document labeled "Purchase requisition," an annotation symbol is also attached to the manual processing symbol. Another flowline connects an accounting record symbol, labeled "Inventory records," to the manual processing symbol. This connection *from* the inventory records *to* the manual processing symbol denotes that inventory data are used during the preparation of the purchase requisition. A flowline *from* the manual processing *to* the document symbol indicates that a purchase requisition, in two copies, is an output from the processing step. Note that when multiple copies of a form are prepared, they are numbered and shown by means of overlapping symbols.

   The final function of this flowchart segment is to show the disposition of the two copies of the purchase requisition. A flowline pointing to the right directs copy 1 to the purchasing department, and a downward flowline indicates that copy 2 is filed in a folder. The letter C in the file symbol means that copy 2 is placed chronologically (by date) within the file.

2. **Preparation of a purchase order.** The activity in the second segment also centers on a manual processing symbol. Two flowlines lead *to* this processing symbol, one from the first copy of the purchase requisition and the other from the supplier file. On the basis of data from these two sources, a buyer in the purchasing department prepares a purchase order in four copies. Again, a flowline pointing from the processing symbol to the document symbol(s) designates the latter as an output. Another "output" flowing from the processing symbol is copy 1 of the purchase requisition. Since this output entered the processing symbol, as noted by the flowline from the accounting department, it must also leave the processing symbol. As the segment shows, it is then deposited in the open purchase order file. (An important rule of flowcharting is to show the final disposition of every copy.)

   The remainder of this flowchart segment depicts the disposition of the four purchase order copies. Copy 1 is mailed to the supplier. Since this mailing ends our treatment of copy 1 (as far as the flowchart is concerned), we indicate this final disposition by means of a terminal symbol. (Alternatively, we could have added a column on the flowchart labeled "Supplier" and shown the flow of copy 1 to that column.) Copy 2 terminates with an on-page connector labeled "1." The next segment will continue the disposition of copy 2. Copy 3 is directed to the receiving department. Copy 4 is filed together with copy 1 of the purchase requisition. The terminal symbol below the file indicates that the filed copies will be used in the accounts payable procedure (shown on a separate flowchart).

   One additional flowcharting convention is illustrated in this segment. When flowlines cross, a "jumper" (⌐∩⌐) denotes the cross-over.

3. **Updating of the inventory records.** This flowchart segment, like the first segment, is located organizationally in the accounting department. Two inputs, copy 2 of the purchase requisition and copy 2 of the purchase order, enter into the processing. The former is pulled from the file folder; the latter arrives from the purchasing de-

Accounting department

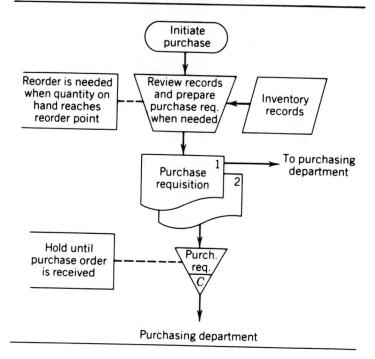

Initiate purchase

Reorder is needed when quantity on hand reaches reorder point

Review records and prepare purchase req. when needed

Inventory records

Purchase requisition 1 2

To purchasing department

Hold until purchase order is received

Purch. req. C

Purchasing department

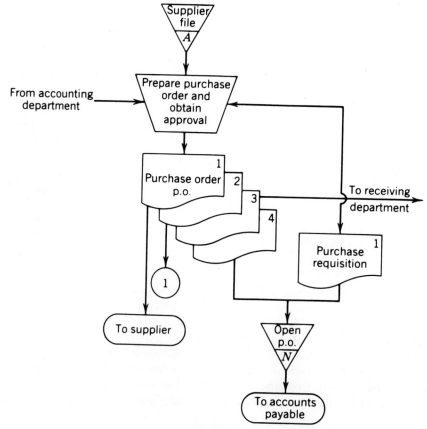

Supplier file A

From accounting department

Prepare purchase order and obtain approval

Purchase order p.o. 1 2 3 4

To receiving department

Purchase requisition 1

1

To supplier

Open p.o. N

To accounts payable

Accounting department

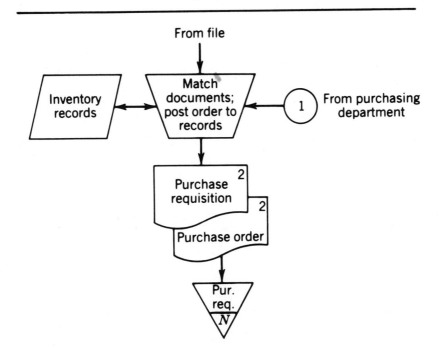

Receiving department

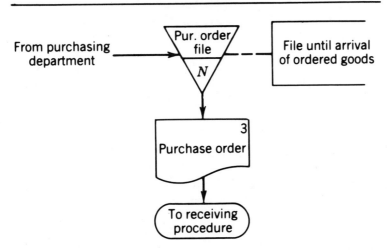

partment. (Note that the on-page connector is, in effect, a link to the on-page connector shown in the previous segment.)

Processing is performed by the in-

ventory clerk, who matches the documents, accesses the proper inventory records, posts the ordered quantities, and then replaces the posted inventory records within the inventory file. A bidirectional flowline (i.e., one with arrowheads on both ends) symbolically represents these accessing, posting, and replacing actions. As the last step in this segment, the two documents leave the processing symbol and flow into a file. Note that when two or more documents move together, a single flowline is sufficient.

4. **Filing of receiving department's copy of the purchase order.** In this brief segment

copy 3 of the purchase order is placed temporarily into a file maintained in the receiving department. Upon the arrival of the ordered inventory goods, the copy is withdrawn (pulled) and entered into the receiving procedure. Since the receiving procedure is shown on a different flowchart, a terminal symbol is employed to denote the interface with that procedure.

Figure 7-24 combines the four segments just described into a document flowchart of

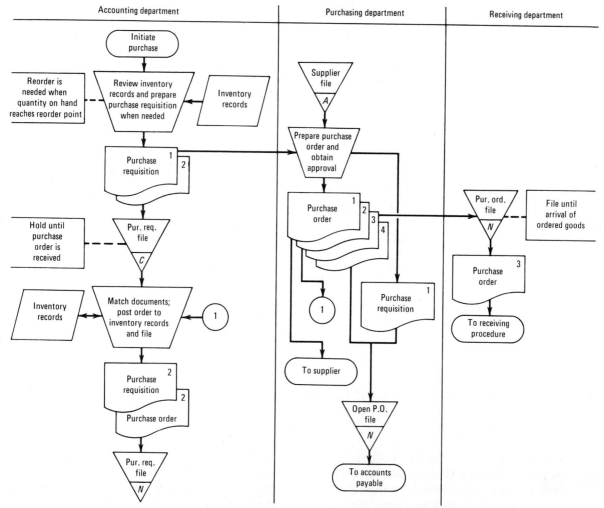

FIGURE 7-24 A document flowchart of a manually performed purchases procedure.

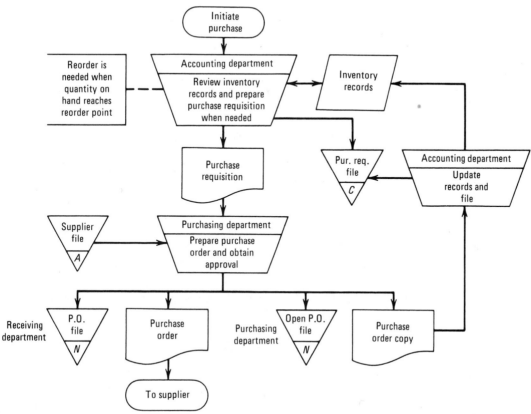

FIGURE 7-25 A variation of the document flowchart shown in Figure 7-24.

the purchases procedure. A variation of this flowchart, which omits the columns for organizational units, appears in Figure 7-25. Still another variation, which retains the columns for organizational units but omits most symbols, appears in Figure 7-26.

Computer system flowcharts. A system flowchart of a computer-based procedure uses special symbols pertaining solely to computer processing, input–output, and data storage. It also employs most of the symbols needed for a manual procedure, since certain steps are likely to be performed manually in even the most computerized system.

Figure 7-27 shows a computer system flowchart of a batch processing system which parallels the purchasing procedure described in the previous section. It is somewhat more detailed than the chapter example of batch processing shown in Figure 7-11 (although it ignores the use of batch totals and most of the needed exception and summary reports for simplicity's sake). Six computer runs form the backbone of the input and processing operations.

Run 1 consists of extracting data from the inventory master file (on magnetic tape) concerning those inventory items whose on-hand quantities have fallen below their reorder points. Such items are listed on an inventory reorder list, which in effect replaces the purchase requisitions. After being approved by an accounting manager, this list is for-

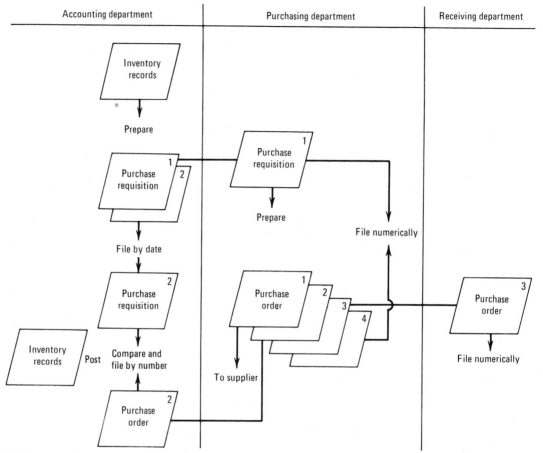

FIGURE 7-26 A second variation of the document flowchart shown in Figure 7-24.

warded to the purchasing department. One or more buyers select suitable suppliers and enter the necessary data on drafts of purchase orders. Then these purchase order drafts are sent to the data processing department, where clerks key the data onto magnetic tape and verify the keyed data.

Run 2 consists of editing the keyed and verified purchase order data. An exception and summary report is shown as the means of recording detected errors.

Run 3 consists of sorting the purchase order data into supplier number sequence, in order to be able to update the supplier master file sequentially.

Run 4 involves the printing of the purchase orders. Each purchase order is printed in two copies and is automatically assigned a sequential identification number by the computer processing program. Third and fourth copies are not needed, since a "copy" is stored on magnetic tape in the open purchase order file. A purchase order listing, in effect a journal of the entered purchase orders, is also printed.

As noted earlier, another purpose of this run is to update the supplier master records, which are maintained on magnetic disk to allow quick retrieval.

Run 5 consists of re-sorting the purchase order transaction tape into inventory item

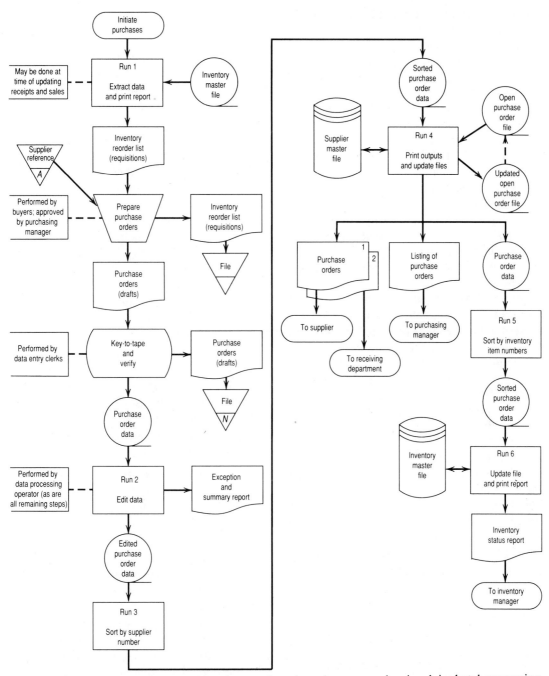

FIGURE 7-27   A system flowchart of a computer-based purchases procedure involving batch processing.

number sequence. It is a necessary step prior to updating the inventory master file.

Run 6 involves updating the affected inventory master records, so that the quantity of each ordered inventory item is recorded. As each inventory master record is accessed during the sequential run, a line of an inventory status report is printed to show the quantity on hand and on order.

Figure 7-28 shows a computer system flowchart; it assumes the use of the on-line input and processing approach. Three major steps are needed.

Step 1 corresponds to run 1 in the batch processing system, except that the data are extracted from an on-line file.

Step 2 illustrates the on-line entry and editing of reorder data. On the basis of the inventory reorder list, plus data extracted from an on-line supplier reference file, the buyers enter the data needed for preparing purchase orders. Entered data are edited by an on-line purchasing program, which displays all detected errors on the terminal screen. After the errors are corrected and all data for a transaction are validated, the data are stored on a transaction file.

Step 3 occurs immediately after the previous step. It involves both the updating of two files and the creation of a new record in the open purchase order file. Several reports are generated as a result of the previous file processing, although they are likely to be printed only at the end of the processing day.

Figure 7-29 shows the on-line computer processing procedure in the form of a document flowchart. Thus, it highlights the organizational units where the input and processing steps take place. This type of hybrid flowchart is particularly useful in the case of a procedure that involves both manual and computer-based processing in several organizational units.

Guidelines for Preparing Flowcharts

Good flowcharts result from sound practices consistently followed. Sound practices can be grounded on such guidelines as the following:

1. Carefully read the narrative description of the procedure to be flowcharted. Determine from the facts the *usual* or *normal* steps in the procedure, and focus on these steps when preparing the flowchart.

2. Choose the size of paper to be used. Use either letter size ($8\frac{1}{2}'' \times 11''$) or an extra-large size. Then gather such materials as pencils, eraser, and flowcharting template. (The template, which contains the symbols shown in Figure 7-23, is typically available in campus bookstores.)

3. Select the flowcharting symbols to be used. Generally, the symbols should be drawn from those listed in Figure 7-23. Other symbols are available and may appear on the template you purchase, but the variety of symbols used should be limited for the sake of clarity.

4. Prepare a rough flowchart sketch as a first draft. Attempting to draw a finished flowchart during the first effort usually results in a poorer final product.

5. Review your sketch to be sure that the following have been accomplished:

    a. All steps are clearly presented in a sequence, or a series of sequences. No obvious gaps in the procedure should be present.

    b. Symbols are used consistently throughout. Thus, the symbol for manual processing (an inverted trapezoid) should appear each time a clerk performs a step in the procedure.

    c. The dispositions of all documents and reports are shown. In fact, the final "resting place" of every copy of every prepared document should be specified. Typical dispositions include placing documents in files, sending documents to outside parties such as customers, forwarding documents to connecting procedures (such as a general ledger procedure), and distribut-

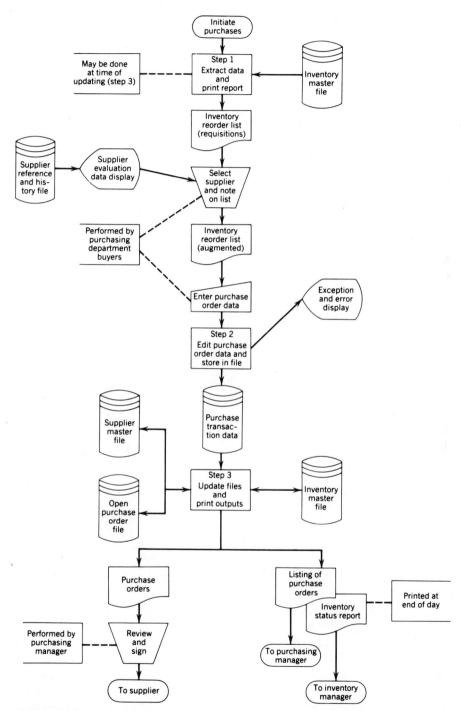

FIGURE 7-28 A system flowchart of a computer-based purchases procedure involving on-line processing.

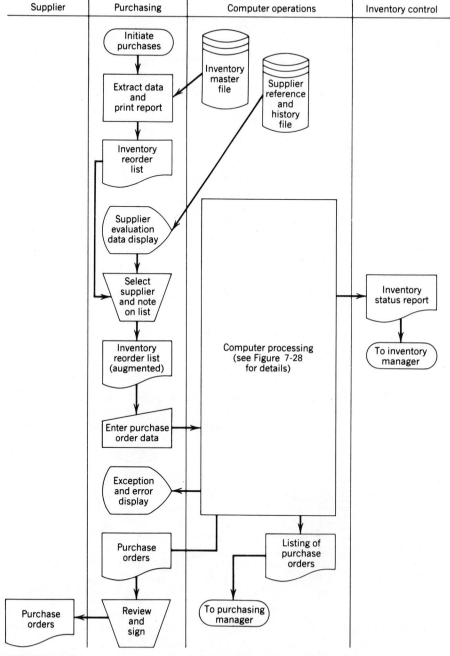

FIGURE 7-29 A computer system flowchart similar to Figure 7-28 but in columnar form.

ing reports to managers. If the disposition consists of destroying a document, this action may be represented as shown at the right.

From prior processing → Source document A → Destroy

d. The "sandwich" rule is consistently applied. This rule states that a processing symbol should be sandwiched between an input symbol and an output symbol, as shown at the right.

From prior processing → Input document → Manual process → Output document

e. The flows generally begin in the upper left-hand corner of the sheet and move from left to right and from top to bottom.

f. All symbols contain brief but specific labels written inside the symbols. For instance, "Sales invoice" might appear inside a document symbol. (Do not simply write "Document" inside a document symbol, since the shape of the symbol indicates its nature.) When it is necessary to use lengthy labels, draw the symbols large enough to contain the labels completely; the size of a symbol may vary without affecting its meaning.

g. Multiple copies of documents are numbered in the upper right-hand corners, and these numbers remain with the copies during their flows through the procedure.

h. Added comments are included within annotation symbols and attached to appropriate symbols, such as the processing symbols to which the comments relate.

i. Persons and departments performing processes or steps are specified by the use of either column headings or annotations.

j. Ample connections (cross-references) are provided. The symbols used in forming the connections depend on the situation. Thus, if two sheets are needed to contain the flowchart, the flows between pages are formed by off-page connector symbols. In those cases where the procedure being flowcharted is linked to an adjoining procedure, the connection can be formed by a terminal symbol as follows:

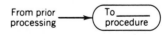

From prior processing → To procedure

k. Exceptional occurrences, such as back orders, are clearly noted. They may appear (1) as comments within annotation symbols, (2) as separate flowcharts, with references to the main flowchart, or (3) as decision branches. The last alternative may be illustrated as shown on the next page.

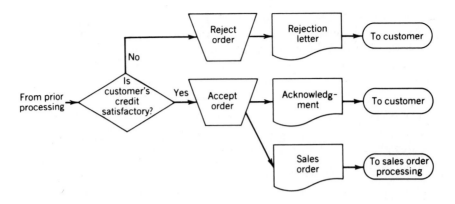

l. Special presentation techniques are adopted when their use increases both the content and clarity of the procedure. An apt illustration of this rule is the portrayal of batch control totals in computer-based batch processing systems. As described earlier, batch control totals are generally computed from key data in each batch of transactions prior to processing runs. Then during each processing run the totals are recomputed and compared to the precomputed totals. These run-to-run comparisons may be performed at the direction of the computer processing programs, and the results may be shown on printed exception and summary reports. If the results show differences in the totals, the differences must be located before processing can continue. This batch control procedure may be diagramed as shown at the right, where the dashed lines indicate the run-to-run comparisons with the precomputed totals.

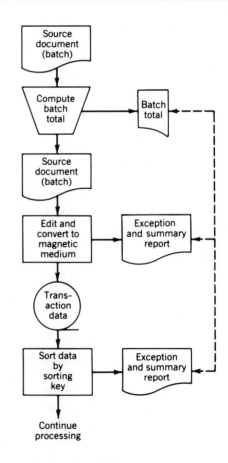

6. Complete the flowchart in final form. A finished flowchart should be neatly drawn and uncrowded. Normally it also should contain a title, a date, and the name(s) of the preparer(s).

Notes: **(1)** Batch total(s) are computed when the batch of sales orders has been accumulated on a temporary storage disk.

(2) Batch total(s) are checked from run to run, as indicated by the dashed connectors to the exception and summary reports.

(3) Since the on-line input approach typically employs a magnetic disk for storing transactions, the master file is also likely to be stored on a magnetic disk.

Review Problem with Solution

Statement

Wunder Drug Wholesale Company, the firm whose sales order and invoicing application was described in the chapter, is undecided concerning the new on-line processing system design. It believes that a modified design, such as on-line input and batch processing, might be more suitable.

Required

a. Identify the advantages of an on-line input and batch processing system for the sales orders and invoicing application.

b. Draw a computer system flowchart of this data entry and processing combination.

Solution

a. The on-line input of sales orders enables the sales transaction data to be captured and entered as soon as the orders are received. The data may be edited as entered, with any errors being corrected immediately. Since the data are entered via terminals, no transcription is necessary.

The batch processing of the sales orders enables batch totals of order quantities (and other data, if desired) to be computed and used to control the accuracy of processing. It also employs the more efficient sequential processing mode.

b. A system flowchart of the on-line input/ batch processing system is as shown on the following page.

Review Questions

7-1 What is the meaning of each of the following terms?

Throughput
Efficiency
Timeliness
Flexibility
Economy
Batch input approach
Source data automation
OCR document
MICR document
On-line input approach
Interactive input approach
Preformatted screen
Dialogue prompt
Menu screen
Batch processing approach
Processing cycle
Sequential processing
Conversion run
Edit run
Sort run
Sorting key
Exception and summary report
Direct processing
Remote batch processing
Spooling
On-line processing approach
Interactive processing system
Data entry and edit step

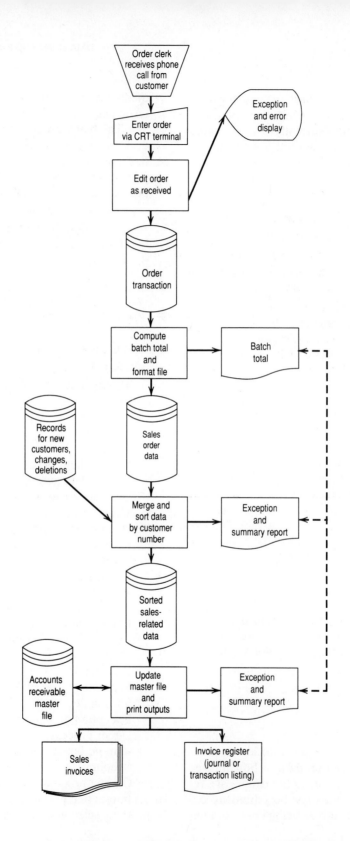

File inquiry
Real-time system
Response time
Form
Trade-off
Merge run
File maintenance run
File extraction run
Report generation run

7-2 Discuss the design objectives by which data entry and data processing systems may be judged.

7-3 In what ways can a data conversion system be improved by changing from a manual to a computer-based system?

7-4 What are three combinations of data entry and processing approaches that form practical computer-based data conversion systems?

7-5 Describe the characteristics of the batch input approach.

7-6 What options are available with respect to a computer-based batch input system?

7-7 Describe the characteristics of the on-line input approach.

7-8 What aids are available when keying data into an on-line computer system?

7-9 What nonkeying options are available when entering data into an on-line computer system?

7-10 Contrast the advantages of the batch input and on-line input approaches.

7-11 Describe the characteristics of the batch processing approach.

7-12 Briefly describe several typical processing runs used by tape-oriented batch processing systems.

7-13 What are the uses of the exception and summary report?

7-14 Describe the steps in a file maintenance run in which the sequential processing method and the magnetic tape medium are used.

7-15 What processing, input, and output options are available when using the batch processing approach?

7-16 Describe the characteristics of on-line processing.

7-17 Identify several steps or programs that are likely to be employed in a typical on-line processing application.

7-18 What processing, input, and output options are available when using on-line processing?

7-19 Compare the relative advantages of batch processing and on-line processing.

7-20 Describe several applications within a typical firm for which each of the three practical data conversion systems are likely to be most suitable.

7-21 Identify several means by which processing throughput and efficiency may be enhanced.

7-22 Describe several features that a well-designed form is likely to possess.

7-23 Identify several guidelines for designing an effective preformatted screen.

7-24 Discuss key trade-offs that should be considered when developing the overall data conversion system of a firm.

Discussion Questions

7-25 Why might the acquisition of a computer system for use in processing payroll transactions result in several months of extra work on the part of the payroll clerks?

7-26 Discuss the two choices offered to a manager of receiving an estimate of monthly sales revenue (e.g., $80,000) on the first day of the following month versus receiving the precise value of monthly sales revenue (e.g., $80,761.56) on the fifth day of the following month.

7-27 Discuss the value of the on-line processing approach in relation to the frequency of reporting.

7-28 Discuss the impact of computerization upon the collection and processing of nontransaction data as compared with transaction data.

7-29 A variety of reports can be easily provided to managers as by-products of computer-based data conversion; such reports would be quite time consuming to prepare if manual data conversion methods were employed. Discuss and illustrate with respect to a business function.

7-30 Suggest two applications for which on-line input but delayed batch processing would be appropriate.

7-31 Most applications involving on-line data entry do not permit the use of batch control totals. Describe two situations in which batch totals may feasibly be computed from data entered by the on-line input approach.

7-32 Describe the trade-offs involved in choosing between alternatives in each of the following pairs of situations.

    a. (1) Inputting transaction data via a terminal at a sales office and transmitting the data to a central sales order department via data communications facilities.

    (2) Collecting transaction data by clerks at a sales office and mailing the data to a central sales order department.

    b. (1) Processing transactions one by one against relevant files as soon as they are captured.

    (2) Processing transactions in batches once each day.

    c. (1) Preparing a desired managerial report each Friday.

    (2) Preparing a desired managerial report one-half hour after it is requested.

Problems

7-1 The Hooper Department Store of Fullerton, California, has been in existence for only a few years. It sells a wide variety of merchandise; almost all sales are for credit. When a sale is made, the sales clerk imprints the customer's identification from his or her credit card onto the sales document. Merchandise is acquired from numerous suppliers, also on credit. In order to concentrate on marketing, its management decided to use an outside service bureau to process its basic transactions. However, it has reached a sufficient volume of sales and purchases so that management feels these transactions should be processed internally by a data processing center. (Payroll will still be handled by the service bureau.) Because of their high volume, the batch input approach is selected for the sales, cash receipts, purchases, and cash disbursements transactions. Batches of each of the four types of transactions will be recorded on magnetic tape for entry into batch processing systems.

Required

a. Identify the most suitable input device for initially handling the charge sales documents and cash remittance forms (i.e., upper portions of monthly statements). Describe the steps that lead to the transcription to magnetic tape.

b. Identify the most suitable input device for initially handling documents involved in purchases and cash disbursements (purchase orders and disbursement vouchers). Describe the steps that lead to the transcription to magnetic tape. Explain why the input device identified in **a** is not suitable for these transactions.

7-2 You have recently been involved in consulting engagements involving a retailer and wholesaler. The retailer has a large number of outlets, each of which has numerous sales daily. The average sale is of relatively low value. The wholesaler has three warehouses. Only a few sales are made daily from each warehouse, although the value of each sale is relatively large. Each warehouse is also responsible for maintaining inventory records and performing other data processing activities.

Required

If the on-line input approach is economically feasible in both cases, should the same input device be employed? If so, what is the device and how would it function in each case? If not, identify a suitable input device for each case and describe how each would function. (For the purposes of this problem, regard the various types of terminals as different devices.)

7-3 Which data processing approach and related input approach would best suit each of the following data conversion situations? Why?

a. Large volumes of transactions, with weekly reports prepared from data stored in the records of master files.

b. Numerous inquiries concerning the current status of individual entities and events.

c. Fluctuating quantities of transactions received, with high peak volumes occurring randomly.

d. Frequent needs by managers for demand reports provided on a timely basis.

e. Small volumes of transactions, with infrequent data requests by users

who can tolerate lengthy response times.

f. Small volumes of transactions, with numerous requests for up-to-date data from the records of master files.

g. Highly integrated physical operations requiring close monitoring.

h. Geographically dispersed activities, with a need to provide documents and reports at remote sites promptly at the end of each day.

7-4 Would batch processing or on-line processing better suit each of the following applications? Explain.

a. Weekly preparation of payrolls.

b. Seat reservations on scheduled airlines.

c. Maintenance of records at a central credit bureau.

d. Monthly preparation of financial statements.

e. Production of goods to fill customers' special orders on tight schedules.

f. Processing and shipment of orders received by mail and filled from a stock of 200 standard products.

g. Preparation of monthly utility bills.

h. Provision of patient care in a large metropolitan hospital.

i. Preparation of monthly responsibility reports.

j. Production of cement for inventory.

k. Daily preparation of checks to be disbursed to suppliers.

7-5 *Note:* This requirement may be performed by the use of a microcomputer-based data base software package such as dBase or RBase.

a. Design a suitable format of a form for entering the courses that you request to take next semester at your university or college. The form should show all necessary information concerning you and the courses, including your name, your ID number, your major department, the course numbers and descriptions, the times of the courses, and the room locations of the courses. Space should be provided for a signature by your adviser.

b. Design the format of a preformatted data entry screen to aid a clerk at an on-line campus computer site in entering the data from the form in **a**. Assume that the computer system stores descriptive information concerning students and courses. Thus, only the key identification numbers need be entered, and the system can ''echo'' the descriptive information on the screen.

7-6 Design a suitable format of a form to be used by a depositor of Thrift Savings and Loan. The form should accommodate either a deposit or a withdrawal of funds from a savings account. When filled in, it is given to the teller together with the depositor's passbook. The form should allow checks or currency to be deposited and allow cash to be returned to the depositor from the total of deposited checks if desired.

 7-7 *Note:* This problem can be solved with the aid of a microcomputer-based data base software package such as dBase or RBase.

Refer to Problem 7-6. Assume that Thrift Savings and Loan employs an on-line depositor transaction processing system with video display terminals.

Required

a. Design a suitable preformatted data entry screen to aid the tellers in entering deposit and withdrawal transactions. Provide for the ''echo'' of the depositor's name and current account balance on the screen upon the entry of the depositor's account number.

b. Revise the input screen in **a** to include explicit dialogue prompts, in the forms either of questions or of directions. Assume that a separate screen is used for new depositors.

7-8 The Good Shepherd Hospital employs an on-line patient transaction processing system, including video display terminals.

Required

Design a preformatted data entry screen to aid the receptionist in admitting a patient to the emergency room. Data to be entered include the patient's name, address, age, medical insurance plan; the means by which the patient was delivered to the hospital; the code for the suspected type of injury or illness; the attending physician; the time of arrival; and so on. Allow space for the description of the injury or illness to be ''echoed'' upon the entry of the code.

7-9 A recently employed systems analyst of the Newhall Company prepared the sales invoice shown on the next page. The invoice has been designed for computer preparation from data provided on shipping notices. It is to be printed in three copies, with the original and one copy to be sent to the customer and the other copy to be placed into a customer file (arranged alphabetically in file folders). The accounts receivable master file, on magnetic tape, is to be updated during the invoicing run.

The sales invoices currently in use are prepared manually. About 3000 sales invoices are prepared annually, although as many as 800 are prepared during the busiest week. Roughly 2 percent of the sales invoices this year have been found to contain errors; with the use of the computer, the firm expects to reduce the errors by 75 percent. The cost of preparing each invoice, now averaging \$3, is expected to be cut in half. Three separate products are shipped on a typical order.

Required

As a forms consultant, you have been asked to examine the newly designed sales invoice and the related processing prior to its adoption. Prepare a form analysis sheet, including remarks pertaining to possible weaknesses and needed improvements.

Newhall Company	
New Haven, Connecticut	

Amount due:　　　　　Date:

Ship to:　　　　　Salesperson:

Sold to:　　　　　Ship via:

Product number	Quantity sold	Unit price	Amount	Description

Total

Terms:　　　Freight charge:　　Sales tax:

Notes: **1.** Actual size is 7″ × 10″.
　　2. All copies are white.
　　3. Weight of paper: 20-pound bond.

7-10　A partially completed document flowchart appears on page 274. The flowchart depicts the charge sales activities of the Bottom Manufacturing Corporation of Lansing, Michigan.

A customer's purchase order is received and a six-part sales order is prepared therefrom. The six copies are initially distributed as follows:

Copy no. 1—Billing copy: to billing department.

Copy no. 2—Shipping copy: to shipping department.
Copy no. 3—Credit copy: to credit department.
Copy no. 4—Stock request copy: to credit department.
Copy no. 5—Customer copy: to customer.
Copy no. 6—Sales order copy: file in sales order department.

When each copy of the sales order reaches the applicable department or destination, it calls for specific internal control procedures and related documents. Some of the procedures and related documents are indicated on the flowchart. Other procedures and documents are labeled with the letters *a* to *q*.

(CPA adapted)

7-11　The computer system flowchart depicted on page 275 reflects the sales and cash receipts procedures for the Boomer Sales Corporation of Charlottesville, Virginia. Unfortunately, the accountant who was preparing the flowchart was suddenly called to another assignment.

Required

Complete the flowchart.

(CPA adapted)

7-12　Before beginning the annual audit you review the narrative description of the Tenney Corporation's factory payroll system. A portion of that narrative goes as follows:

Factory employees punch time-clock cards each day when entering or leaving the shop. At the end of each week the timekeeping department collects the time cards and prepares duplicate batch control slips by department showing total hours and number of employees. The time cards and original

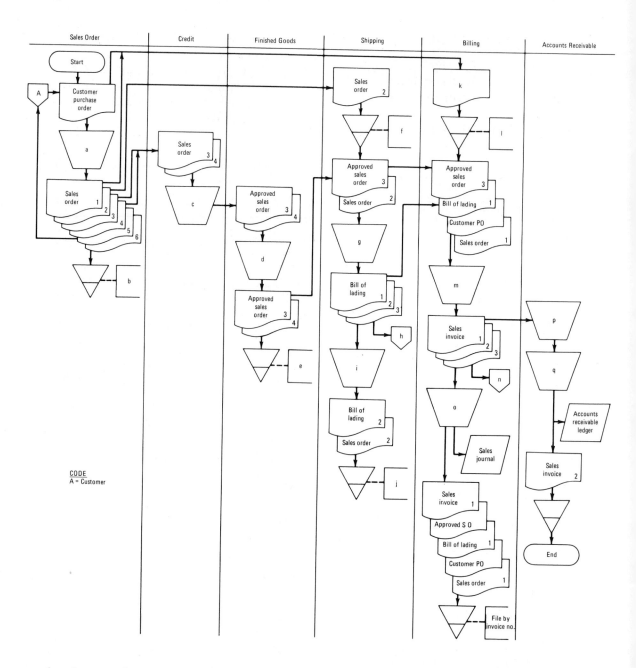

batch control slips are sent to the payroll accounting section. The second copies of the batch control slips are filed by date.

In the payroll accounting section, payroll transaction cards are keypunched from the information on the time cards, and a batch total card for each batch is key-punched from the batch control slip. The time cards and batch control slips are then filed by batch for possible reference. The payroll transaction cards and batch total card are sent to data processing, where they are sorted by employee number within batch. Each batch is edited by a computer program

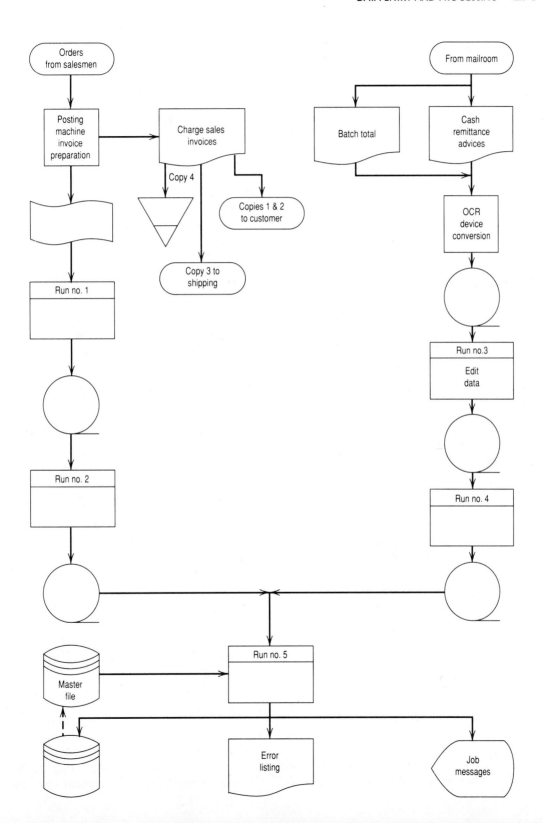

that checks the validity of employee numbers against a master employee tape file and the total hours and number of employees against the batch total card. A detail printout by batch and employee number is produced which indicates batches that do not balance and invalid employee numbers. This printout is returned to payroll accounting to resolve all differences.

In searching for documentation you found a flowchart of the payroll system that included all symbols but was only partially labeled. The portion of this flowchart described by the foregoing narrative appears on page 277.

Required

a. Identify the appropriate labels (document name, process description, file, etc.) applicable to each numbered symbol on the document flowchart.

b. Revise the document flowchart to correct the symbols and flows. Assume that (1) the time cards are first batched and batch control totals are computed, (2) the data from the time cards are then transcribed using a key-to-disk system, so that payroll transaction records are stored on magnetic tape, (3) the batch control totals are also transcribed in the previous step, so that an initial record on the magnetic tape includes the batch control totals, (4) the batch of payroll preparation records is sorted in a computer run, (5) next the batch of payroll preparation records is edited in a second computer run, and (6) a detailed printout (labeled an exception and summary report) is then returned to payroll accounting to resolve all differences. Note that an exception and summary report should also be generated during the sort run and checked against the edit run for differences. (All steps not mentioned remain the same.) Note also that certain symbols may need to be cor-

rected to correspond to those provided in the Appendix to Chapter 7.

(CPA adapted)

7-13 Peabock Co. is a Carbondale, Illinois, wholesaler of softgoods. The inventory is composed of approximately 3500 different items. The company employs a computerized batch processing system to maintain its perpetual inventory records. The system is run each weekend so that the inventory reports are available on Monday morning for management use. The system has been functioning satisfactorily for the past 15 months, providing the company with accurate records and timely reports.

The preparation of purchase orders has been automatic as a part of the inventory system to ensure that the company will maintain enough inventory to meet customer demand. When an item of inventory falls below a predetermined level, a record of the inventory item is written. This record is used in conjunction with the vendor file to prepare the purchase orders.

Exception reports are prepared during the update of the inventory and the preparation of the purchase orders. These reports identify any errors or exceptions identified during the processing. In addition, the system provides for management approval of all purchase orders exceeding a specified amount. Any exceptions of items requiring management approval are handled by supplemental runs on Monday morning and are combined with the weekend results.

A system flowchart of Peabock Co.'s inventory and purchase order procedure appears on page 278.

Required

a. The illustrated system flowchart of Peabock Co.'s inventory and purchase order system was prepared before the system was fully operational. Several

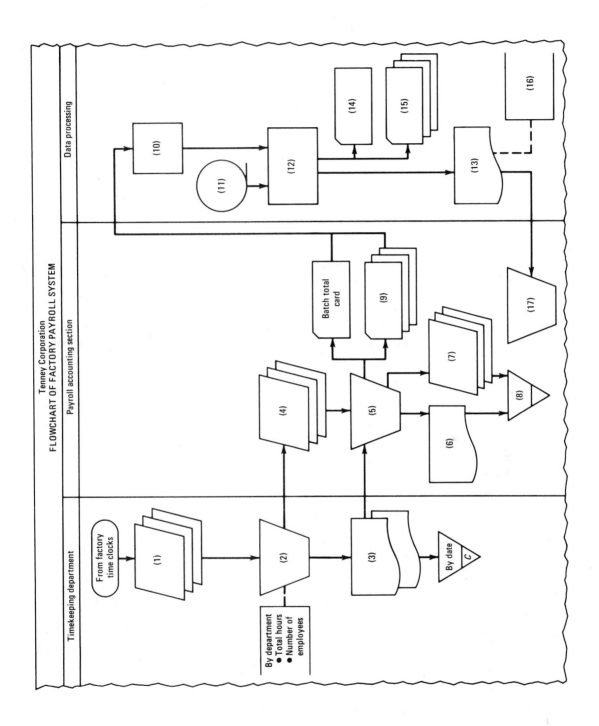

Tenney Corporation
FLOWCHART OF FACTORY PAYROLL SYSTEM

Timekeeping department

Payroll accounting section

Data processing

From factory time clocks

(1)

(2)

By department
• Total hours
• Number of employees

(3)

By date

C

(4)

(5)

(6)

(7)

(8)

Batch total card

(9)

(10)

(11)

(12)

(13)

(14)

(15)

(16)

(17)

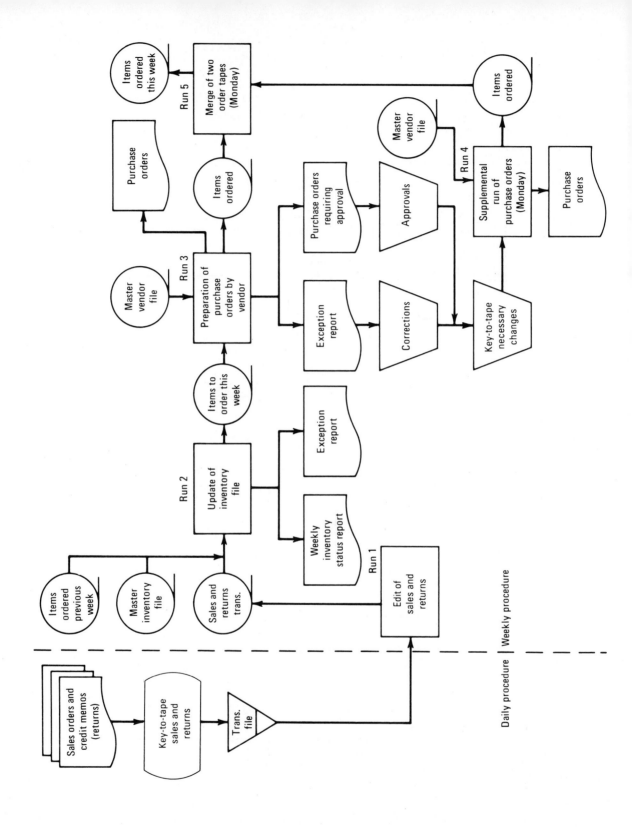

278

steps important to the successful operations of the system were inadvertently omitted from the chart. Now that the system is operating effectively, management wants the system documentation complete and would like the flowchart corrected. Describe the steps that have been omitted and indicate in narrative terms where the omissions occur. Also indicate where symbols should be added or changed to improve the clarity and accuracy of the flowchart. The flowchart does not need to be redrawn.

b. After the passage of a couple of years, management decides to redesign the inventory and purchase order system. Sales orders and credit memos are to be entered by the on-line approach and accumulated daily. Then, the daily batch of sales and returns is to be processed by the batch processing approach to update the inventory master file and generate purchase orders. All files are to be stored on magnetic disks, so that (1) inquiries can be made concerning individual inventory items and purchase orders and (2) vendor records can be accessed directly when preparing purchase orders. Purchase orders requiring management approval are identified on the exception report, approved, and reprocessed the following day. Redraw the system flowchart in proper form to reflect these changes. Add notes where needed to explain modifications.

(CMA adapted)

7-14 The computer system flowchart shown on page 280 depicts a newly proposed procedure pertaining to the receipts of ordered goods for the Frost Company of Fargo, North Dakota. Your supervisor, the chief accountant, has completed the symbols for the procedure. Now she asks you to enter the labels into the respective symbols.

7-15 Draw segments of system flowcharts that depict each of the activities described:

a. Manually prepares invoices in five copies by reference to a customer's order and pricing file.

b. Manually sorts purchase orders by assigned numbers and then files.

c. Manually compares the purchase order and receiving report with the pertinent supplier's invoice, marks the invoice approved, and files all documents together in chronological order in an open-to-pay file.

d. Manually posts a batch of check vouchers to the accounts payable subsidiary ledger, re-sorts the batch by suppliers' names, and files in suppliers' folders.

e. Processes by computer a batch of sorted sales transactions (on magnetic tape) to update a customer master file (on magnetic tape).

f. Processes by computer a batch of cash receipts transactions (on magnetic tape) to update a customer master file (on magnetic disk).

g. Processes by computer in order to extract data from an employee earnings file and an employee personal history file (both on magnetic disks) onto a report file (on magnetic disk), and then to print a personnel report from the extracted data.

h. Converts sales data from a batch of OCR documents to magnetic tape by means of an off-line OCR device.

i. Enters data concerning shipments from documents by means of CRT terminals, the data being checked upon entry by an edit program, and stores the edited data in a temporary file on an on-line magnetic disk.

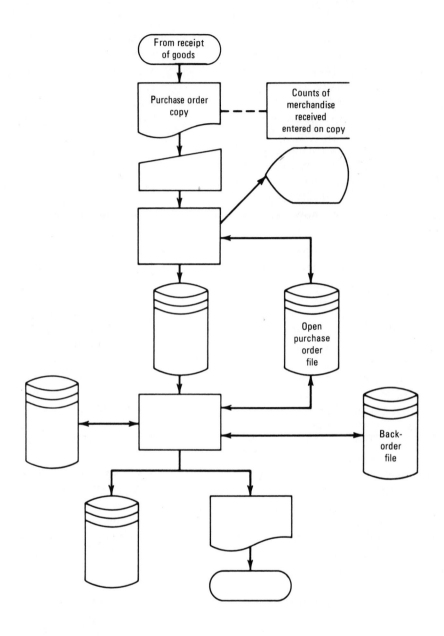

7-16 The SEADOC flowchart shown in Figure 7-22 is characterized as a type of control-oriented flowchart. Contrast the features of this type of flowchart with the type of system flowchart appearing in Figure 7-24. Describe the ways in which the SEADOC flowchart aids in the evaluation of accounting controls relating to a transaction processing system such as cash disbursements, and identify the specific documents, subledgers, and so on for the system on the SEADOC flowchart.

7-17 Academy State University maintains an on-line computer system for the registration of its students. Each student brings a completed and approved course-request sheet to an on-line registration site. There a registration clerk enters the student's identification number, plus the schedule line numbers (e.g., 12369) that identify the particular sections of courses being requested by the student. The course-request data are edited upon entry and then stored in an on-line course-request file (on a magnetic disk). On course-assignment day the computer operator processes the course-request data to produce confirmed course-schedule listings. (In preparing these listings the computer program refers to a course-schedule file that contains descriptive data concerning the courses, to a class status file that shows the number of vacancies remaining in each course section, and to the student file, which contains descriptive data—name, address, and so on—concerning students. It also increases the count by one in each course section to which the student is added.) The course schedule listings are then mailed to the students' addresses.

Required

Prepare a system flowchart of the registration procedure described.

7-18 The following four firms are located or headquartered in Atlanta. Each sells products and handles inventory, but each operates under circumstances that might well be served by a transaction processing system that significantly differs from those of the others. Describe for each firm the essential features (e.g., hardware, data entry approach, data processing steps) that would characterize the desired new type of system.

    a. The Cardinal Book Store sells textbooks, college classroom supplies, and clothing to students and the community near one of the large universities in the area. It currently is experiencing difficulty in controlling its large and varied inventory. For instance, textbooks and supplies often are out of stock. Also, certain items are in oversupply at the end of each school year. This firm appears to need a *real-time system* with special terminals.

    b. Dad's Bakery manufactures and distributes bakery products throughout the metropolitan area. It employs route salespeople who obtain orders from retail stores, deliver the ordered baked goods, and return the unsold goods. These salespeople also write the invoices for each order and compute the total amounts due. Several problems in the present procedure cause continual concern. The salespeople spend too much time each day in writing invoices and computing returns, discounts, and so on; they also make numerous errors. In addition, the accounting clerks must take time to key the invoice data for entry into the firm's computer system. Furthermore, the bakers often do not receive information concerning the sizes of the orders for the next day until it is too late; thus, they must judge volume from the orders for today, and consequently bake too much or too little. This firm seems to need a system involving *remote data entry and processing* plus subsequent *on-line processing of batched data.*

    c. Rochelle Fashions is a woman's wear chain with approximately 12 stores in cities throughout the Southeast. A buyer in each store mails orders for merchandise to the home office, where they are received several days later. Purchase orders are then prepared by buyers in the home office, and the merchandise is routed directly to the requesting stores. Since styles vary among the cities and change very rapidly, this procedure is not sufficiently responsive. Moreover, fast-selling merchandise items are often sold out, and sales are lost before replenishments can be obtained via the procedure. Buyers in the stores could largely overcome these problems by purchasing directly from garment makers in their own or nearby cities. However, company policy insists that all proposed amounts for purchases be approved beforehand by the treasurer in the home office; this policy is not subject to change. This firm appears to need a *remote batch processing system* with a central computer.

d. Neatfeet and Company imports and distributes footwear from its Atlanta distribution center warehouse to retail shoe stores throughout the Eastern states. Shoes are delivered from the ports of entry to the warehouse in ocean containers, which contain cases of shoes based on various separate purchase orders. Each shoe is identified by style, width, size, and color. Receiving these incoming containers is a formidable task. Hundreds of cases must be sorted onto pallets by purchase order number and style. Then a receiving clerk records each case on a special receiving form. The clerk next summarizes the data for each purchase order and keys the data into a receiving department terminal, so that the computer system can match the received goods against purchase orders on file. These operations usually require more than 8 hours per ocean container. Furthermore, errors are often made in the counts or recorded numbers, and these lead to mismatches with the stored purchase orders. When mismatches occur, recounts must be made by a second clerk. The received inventory cannot be distributed until the mismatches are resolved. Thus, inventory may remain in the receiving area for a week in some cases, and so it is relatively unprotected and open to pilferage. Finally, the various cases of shoes are not easily identified during warehousing because they contain only the markings of the off-shore shoe manufacturers. The firm needs a system that enables the receiving clerks to perform *hands-free (no writing) data entry* on the warehouse floor and *automatic identification* of the merchandise during distribution operations.

Hint: In **d,** the firm's engineering research department has been investigating speech synthesizers and radio mobile units.

7-19 Auto Barn is an automotive parts retailer in a midwestern city with three outlets. It supplies the outlets from a central warehouse that is adjacent to its office building. The firm sells about 5000 types of parts for cash only. Because it buys in large quantities, it is able to sell the parts at relatively low prices. The firm also takes care to maintain adequate stocks, so that the customers can usually find the items they want. Thus, its sales volume has been growing rapidly. However, its investment in inventory has been growing even more rapidly. In addition, its costs of performing the necessary paperwork manually have been rising sharply. Consequently, the management is considering the acquisition of a computer system.

Required

a. Describe three alternative computer-based data conversion systems which Auto Barn might install to maintain its inventory records and control the level of inventory. Identify the relative advantages of each system.

b. Draw hardware configuration diagrams that illustrate the hardware components needed for each of the systems identified in **a**. If off-line devices, such as key-to-tape encoders, are used, they should be included in the diagrams but not shown as directly connected to the computer processor.

7-20 The Tangier Company is a construction company in a western state. Currently the firm uses a computer system with a single mainframe computer to help it keep track of construction jobs, to maintain inventory status, to bill customers, and to prepare payrolls. Two key documents employed in the system are time sheets and materials requisitions, which are filled in by the foremen in charge of the various jobs and turned in to the office at the end of each week. Appropriate data from these documents are keyed onto magnetic tapes by data entry clerks using key-to-tape encoders. Data from these tapes are then read into the computer system, and transaction listings are printed. By reference to these listings the clerks correct errors in the data on the transaction tapes and, if necessary, generate new magnetic tapes containing corrected data. Then the transaction data from the corrected tapes are sorted and processed to update the master files (on magnetic tapes) containing job records, materials inventory records, customer billing records, and employee time records. During each update run one or two outputs, such as a customer bill and invoice register, are printed.

The present computer system has several weaknesses. Separate transaction tapes are prepared daily for updating each master file, since the sorting keys are different and differing data items are needed. (This means that each document must be handled several times.) Correcting the transaction tapes is a time-consuming process, and certain trans-

actions must be "suspended" for a day until foremen can be contacted to correct erroneous documents. Moreover, the records containing the current status of jobs, bills, materials inventory, and accumulated labor hours cannot be accessed quickly; instead, an interested user must wait until hard copies of the records are printed during the weekly processing activity.

Required

a. Draw a computer system flowchart based on the procedure described. Assume that batch control totals are not computed.

b. Draw a hardware configuration diagram of the computer system currently employed by the Tangier Company to perform the applications. Indicate on the diagram the minimum number of magnetic tape drives and printers required; assume that spooling is not employed. Include off-line as well as on-line devices, but do not show the off-line devices to be connected directly to the computer processor.

c. Draw a computer system flowchart of an on-line input and processing system that should eliminate the described weaknesses.

d. Draw a hardware configuration diagram of the hardware components required in the system flowcharted in **c**.

7-21 The Mobile Insurance Co. of Birmingham, Alabama, issues automobile insurance policies. Currently the firm has about 20,000 policies in force. Transactions affecting these policies are processed on a relatively small card-oriented computer system with magnetic tape storage.

Policy processing involves several steps. Transaction data pertaining to billing, payments, renewals, new policyholders, canceled policyholders, and changes in status are first recorded on standardized source documents. These documents are forwarded by the initiating departments to the input preparation section, where the data therein are keypunched and key verified. The punched cards containing transaction data are edited in a computer run and then sorted by policyholder number. Then they are processed against the policyholder master file in order to update the records. During this updating run a transaction listing (journal) is prepared. Also, data are extracted from the policyholder records concerning those policyholders who are due to pay premiums or to renew policies. A tape containing these extracted data is then processed to print premium notices and renewal notices.

Required

a. Draw a computer system flowchart of the policy processing procedure described.

b. Draw computer system flowcharts that reflect the following changes made in the aforementioned procedure:

  (1) Eliminate the use of punched cards; instead, key the data from the source documents directly onto magnetic tape.

  (2) Eliminate the use of punched cards; instead, key the data from the source documents directly onto magnetic tape. Also, substitute magnetic disks as the storage medium for the policyholder master file.

  (3) Eliminate the use of punched cards; instead, enter the transaction data individually via video display terminals (located in the initiating departments) directly into the computer system. Also, substitute magnetic disks as the storage medium for the policyholder master file, and have the computer system update the affected record directly as soon as the data are entered and edited.

Note: In the batch processing procedures described above, use batch totals plus run-

to-run comparisons if specified by your instructor.

c. Enumerate benefits that would be achieved in each of the revised computer systems in **b.**

7-22 The controller of Kensler Company of Denver has been working with the data processing department to revise part of the company's financial reporting system. A study is under way on how to develop and implement a data entry and data retention system for key computer files used by various departments responsible to the controller. The departments involved and details on their data processing related activities are as follows:

General Accounting

- Daily processing of journal entries submitted by various departments.
- Weekly updating of file balances with subsystem data from areas such as payroll, accounts receivable, and accounts payable.
- Sporadic requests for account balances during the month with increased activity at month-end.

Accounts Receivable

- Daily processing of receipts for payments on account.
- Daily processing of sales to customers.
- Daily checks to be sure that credit limit of $200,000 maximum per customer is not exceeded and identification of orders in excess of $20,000 per customer.
- Daily requests for customer credit status regarding payments and account balances.
- Weekly reporting to general accounting file.

Accounts Payable

- Processing of payments to suppliers three times a week.

- Weekly expense distribution reporting to general accounting file.

Budget Planning and Control

- Updating of flexible budgets on a monthly basis.
- Quarterly rebudgeting based on sales forecast and production schedule changes.
- Monthly inquiry requests for budget balances.

The manager of data processing has explained the concepts of the following processing techniques to the controller's staff and to the appropriate staff members of the departments affected:

- Batch processing.
- On-line processing.
- Real-time processing.
- On-line inquiry.

The manager of data processing has indicated to the controller that batch processing is the least expensive processing technique and that a rough estimate of the cost of each of the other techniques would be as follows:

Technique	Cost in Relation to Batch Processing
On-line processing	1.5 times
Real-time processing	2.5 times

Required

a. Define and discuss the major differences between the input options of the following processing approaches:

(1) Batch processing.

(2) On-line processing.

(3) Real-time processing.

b. Identify and explain (1) the type of input approach and (2) the type of file processing that probably should be employed by Kensler Company for each of the four departments responsible to the controller.

(1) General accounting.

(2) Accounts receivable.

(3) Accounts payable.

(4) Budget planning and control.

Assume that the volume of transactions is not a key variable in the decision.

(CMA adapted)

Suggested Readings

Bower, James B.; Schlosser, Robert E.; and Newman, Maurice S. *Computer-Oriented Accounting Information Systems.* Cincinnati: South-Western, 1985.

Burch, John G., and Grudnitski, Gary. *Information Systems: Theory and Practice.* 5th ed. New York: John Wiley, 1989.

DeMars, Norman A. "Computer Voice Data Entry for Warehouse Receiving Improves Customer Service." *Industrial Engineering* (May 1988), pp. 26–30.

Kumar, Vijay. "Current Trends in Transaction Processing Systems." *Journal of Systems Management* (January 1990), pp. 33–37.

Litecky, Charles R., and Rittenberg, Larry E. "Systems Flowcharting: Principles for Uniform Practice." *EDP Auditor* (December 1979), pp. 17–29.

Moscove, Stephen A., and Simkin, Mark G. *Accounting Information Systems: Concepts and Practice for Effective Decision Making.* 4th ed. New York: John Wiley, 1990.

Nash, John F. *Accounting Information Systems.* 2d ed. New York: Macmillan, 1989.

PMI SEADOC Guide. New York: Peat, Marwick, Mitchell & Co., 1985.

Walsh, Myles E. "The Fictional Demise of Batch Processing." *Infosystems* (March 1981), pp. 64–68.

Whitten, Jeffrey L.; Bentley, Lonnie D.; and Ho, Thomas I. M. *Systems Analysis and Design Methods.* St. Louis: Times Mirror/Mosby, 1986.

After studying this chapter, you should be able to do the following:

Identify fundamental functions, objectives, and approaches to data management.

Describe the key types and characteristics of files and records.

Contrast logical and physical records.

Identify the methods of organizing and accessing records within files.

Describe several useful and contrasting file structures.

Discuss the major considerations pertaining to the design of file and record structures for manual and computer-based systems.

Devise codes that facilitate the storage and processing of transaction data.

Chapter *8*

FILES AND DATA MANAGEMENT

A firm's **data base** is its repository of stored data. In a broad sense it includes all of a firm's collected data, whether stored on magnetic media or in file drawers. However, in firms having computer-based information systems, the term *data base* generally refers to the subset of logically arranged data stored on media accessible by the computer.

The management of data and the data base becomes more complex when a firm converts to a computer-based information system. System designers are faced with a variety of difficult questions, such as

What data should be stored in the data base, and which data should be excluded?

How should the data be organized and accessed within the data base?

Which physical media should be employed for storing the data?

How should the data be classified and coded for storage?

How often, and by what methods, should files be updated?

How should desired data be retrieved from the data base?

Accountants are deeply involved in data management. On the input side, they are concerned with the transactional data that flow into the ledger accounts. On the output side, accountants are concerned with devising reporting systems that provide a wide array of reports. These reports are based on stored data.

To fulfill these responsibilities, accountants need to understand data management fundamentals. For instance, they should be able to distinguish between the major types of files and data structures. They should definitely be aware of the alternative approaches

287

to managing data in computer-based information systems, as well as the factors underlying critical design choices.

Overview of Data Management

Functions

Data can be viewed as a resource. Even though this resource does not appear on the balance sheet of a firm, it nevertheless is extremely valuable. Managing data is therefore a vital activity of the information system.

Data management encompasses three functions: (1) creating a data base, (2) maintaining the stored data within the data base, and (3) retrieving needed data from the data base. Figure 8-1 portrays these three functions. Creating a data base consists of such steps as defining the logical data structures and the physical media on which they are to be stored, classifying and coding the data, and establishing the means for managing data on the physical storage media. Maintaining the data base involves updating values in the data structures (e.g., master files). It also includes other types of file and data maintenance, such as adding records for new entities and deleting records of discontinued entities. Retrieving data from the data base consists of clearly specifying the desired data, searching for the data by an appropriate method, and presenting the data to the requester.

Objectives

Figure 8-2 displays seven design objectives. A foremost objective is to assure that the data base contains *sufficient* and *relevant*

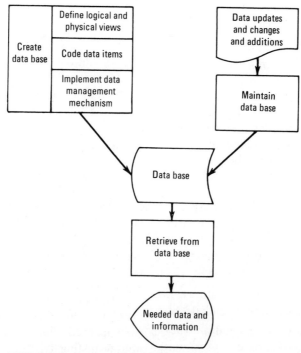

FIGURE 8-1 Functions of data management.

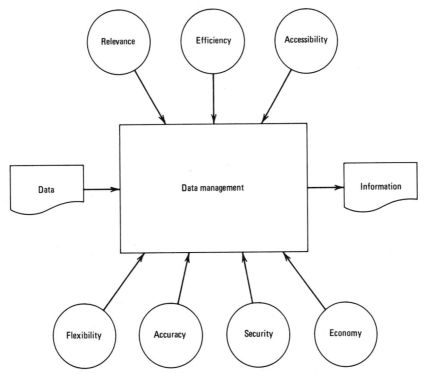

FIGURE 8-2 Design objectives pertaining to data management.

data to meet the expected needs of users. In a typical firm relevant data pertain essentially to transactions and decision making. The relevant data should be processed and stored *efficiently,* so that processing time and storage space are minimized. Moreover, up-to-date data should be *accessible* to users in a timely manner upon request. Data based on past events should be *accurate,* while estimates should be based on reasonable forecasting techniques. Another objective is *flexibility,* so that the data base can satisfy a wide variety of ever-changing informational needs. In addition, the data should be *secure* from access by unauthorized persons and from irretrievable loss. Finally, all of the data management functions should be achieved in as *economical* a manner as possible.

Advantages of Computer-Based Data Management

In a manual information system the data are generally stored in folders, tubs, in/out baskets, and file drawers throughout the departments of a firm. Often the same data are duplicated on several copies and stored in several places. Certain data may be abbreviated or even omitted on forms, since such "shortcuts" are understandable to experienced clerks. In general, an air of informality permeates the management of data.

In computer-based information systems the management of data requires formalized procedures that are strictly followed. The identity and location of each item of data stored in a computer system must be precisely specified. Each step in the storage, maintenance, and retrieval of data must be carefully programmed. In addition, the needed hardware and software are relatively costly to acquire and maintain.

In return for this inconvenience and costliness, however, computer-based data management enables most of the foregoing objectives to be more fully achieved. Large quantities of relevant data can be stored very compactly on magnetic media. Data can also be stored efficiently, since the number of needed copies can be reduced. Furthermore, stored data are very accessible, assuming the presence of suitable hardware and software. Not only can data be provided to users more quickly, but a greater variety of information needs can be satisfied.

A brief example should emphasize a couple of these benefits. Prior to computerization, many police departments could not easily answer urgent inquiries from police officers. With the conversion of motor vehicle license records to magnetic disk storage, the situation has changed dramatically. Now an officer in a patrol car may radio in this request: "Tell me who owns the car with license AJQ 748." After a delay of a few seconds, during which the dispatcher queries the files via her terminal, the answer comes back: "The owner is John Q. Blue, and he lives at 95 Fair Drive, Tucson, Arizona."

Approaches to Computer-Based Data Management

As in the case of data conversion, two alternative approaches to computer-based data management are available. The traditional approach is known as the file-oriented approach, while the modern approach is known as the data base approach.

The **file-oriented approach,** also known as the application approach, focuses on individual applications. Each application, such as the sales transaction processing application, has its own set of files and application programs. The file is the primary structure for storing data used in the application. While more than one file is often employed by an application, each file is physically separate from the others.

The **data base approach,** by contrast, emphasizes the integration of data. It allows a variety of applications to access a wide range of data stored within the data base. Though files are generally retained, additional data structures are also available. The data base approach offers several significant benefits, but it also introduces design complexities.

Both approaches are widely employed by business firms today. This chapter introduces files and data management concepts and examines their applicability to file-oriented systems. Chapter 18 focuses on systems that employ the data base approach.

Characteristics of Files

As a first step we distinguish among the various types of files needed by firms. Then we examine the array of data-related characteristics possessed by the most prevalent types of files. These files are discussed in the context of computer-based information systems.

Types of Files

Data files. Earlier a **file** was described as typically being a repository of data. That is, most files employed by firms exist for the purpose of containing data. These data files consist of collections of key components known as records. Chapter 3 identified four types of data files:

1. **Master files,** which contain records pertaining to entities (i.e., people, places, or things) such as customers, offices, and products.

2. **Transaction files,** which contain records pertaining to events currently being processed, such as sales or receipts of goods.

3. **History files,** which contain records pertaining to completed transactions, such as past sales.

4. **Reference files,** which contain records or tables of data needed for making calculations or checking the accuracy of input data, such as product prices or customer lists.

Figure 8-3 displays the array of these four types of files that might be employed by a typical merchandising firm. Note that several master files are duplicated between two major functions within the firm.

A variety of data files are derivative in nature. As in the case of the history file, an **open document file** is derived from the transaction file. It consists of transaction records whose amounts or quantities have been posted to the master files but which are still not fully processed. An example is the open purchase order file, which comprises records from purchase order transaction files that have not yet been fully processed with respect to corresponding supplier invoices. A **report file** is derived from records within master or transaction files. It consists of data that have been arranged into the format of a needed report. For instance, data may be periodically extracted from the inventory master file to prepare an inventory analysis report. A **backup file** is a copy of a current file,

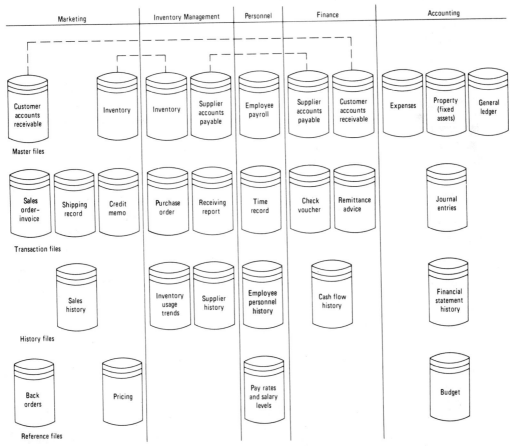

FIGURE 8-3 Groups of files maintained to support the major functions.

usually a master file. It is generated so that the original file can be recreated in case of loss. A **suspense file** is a collection of those records of a transaction file which appear to contain erroneous or questionable data. Both backup and suspense files are discussed in Chapter 9.

Nondata files.   Several types of files contain information that is not intended to be used in processing or to be summarized in reports. A **program file,** also known as a command file, consists of instructions needed to direct computer hardware in processing transactions. A **text file** consists of narrative material. An example of a text file is the description of an accounting procedure. An **index file** contains cross-references that relate identifying codes for records and the locations of the records on direct-access storage media. It serves the same purpose as an index that appears at the end of a book.

Logical Records

Each record in a master or transaction file is similar to the remaining records in the file. From the point of view of the users of the file, a record contains data pertaining to one logical focus of interest. For instance, each record in an inventory master file contains data concerning a particular inventory item. Thus, to users these key components of a data file represent **logical records.**

Data hierarchy.   Logical records incorporate groups of data items. Figure 8-4 lists data items that might be found in typical records for an accounts receivable master file and a sales transaction file. A **data item** is the smallest unit or element of data that has intrinsic meaning. Comprising each data item, in turn, are bytes of data representing **characters.** The data hierarchy within a file-oriented application therefore moves downward from file to record to data item to character.

Accounts Receivable Master Record	Sales Transaction Record
Customer account number	Sales document number
Customer name	Customer account number
Customer address	Date of order
Credit limit	Date shipped (or to be shipped)
Balance beginning of year	Customer name
Current account balance	Customer purchase order number
	Salesperson number
	Sales territory number
	Product number[a]
	Quantity sold[a]
	Amount of sale

[a] These items will be repeated to reflect each product sold in the transaction.

FIGURE 8-4   Data items within the records of two types of files.

Attributes, values, and modes.   Data items within a record reveal relevant facets or **attributes** concerning the entity or event being represented. A customer's number and current account balance are two attributes usually found in the accounts receivable master file; the sales amount is the critical attribute of a sale.

Data items also have values. The **value** of a data item is its specific content in one occurrence. For instance, the value of a particular customer number might be 23861, whereas the value of the account balance for that customer may be $1550.00. The former value provides identification, while the latter value reflects current status.

Individual data values may be classified according to degree of permanence. A *fixed value* is relatively permanent and thus changes only rarely. Examples are a particular customer's number, name, and address. A *variable value* tends to change fairly frequently. For instance, a customer's account balance changes every time that the master record is updated to reflect a transaction.

In addition to attributes and values, data items express modes. The **data mode** is the type of data represented by its value. Data modes include numeric, alphabetic, and alphanumeric characters. The values for the customer number and account balance assumed earlier are numeric in mode. The name of the customer, Jack Bow, is alphabetic in mode; alternatively, the code for a product purchased by the customer, C-8452-3, is alphanumeric in mode.

Keys. Certain data items within a record can serve as sorting keys. Two types of keys found in each record are primary keys and secondary keys.

A **primary key,** also called a record key, is the attribute that uniquely identifies each particular record. It therefore provides the most suitable way in which to sequence the records within the file of which they are a part. In master files the primary keys are generally numeric codes, such as customer numbers. However, they may alternatively be alphabetic, such as customer names. In transaction files they are often numeric codes, such as source document numbers; since documents are sequentially numbered, sorting a transaction file according to source document numbers also arranges it in chronological order.

Occasionally the primary keys of logical records are composed of two or more related data items. Such combined primary keys are called **concatenated keys.** For instance, the primary key in an employee record may consist of the employee number plus the department to which the employee is assigned.

A **secondary key** is an attribute within a record other than the primary key. It represents an alternative way in which to sequence the records within the file. However, it does not necessarily identify a record uniquely. For instance, assume that the primary key in a sales transaction record is the sales invoice number. A secondary key in the same record might be the number of the sales territory where the sale was made or the date of the sale.

As noted before, either type of key may be employed in sorting the records. The primary key is used more frequently for this purpose, since it renders possible the sequential processing method of updating master files. However, secondary keys can also assist file processing. For instance, suppliers' invoices may be sorted by the payment dates to form a "tickler file."[1] Secondary keys can, in addition, enable data to be sorted in a manner that aids the retrieval of data needed to answer complex inquiries. This use of secondary keys is discussed in Chapter 18.

Figure 8-5 illustrates the foregoing features of a file.

Formats. A logical record is organized or formatted into a series of fields. Each **field** encompasses an established number of *character positions* and provides the location for the value of a data item. Figure 8-6 displays the format of a record stored on a punched card.[2] Four fields comprise this record (which has been simplified in this illustration). The first field is the customer number field, which provides five numeric character positions. The value of the customer number in the occurrence shown (i.e., for the customer named Eric Peters) is 23861.

The format of every record within a file is identical. Thus, each field has a specified position within the record. For example, all records in the file of which Figure 8-6 is a member have the following order of fields: The customer number is the first field, the name is the second field, and so forth. Four subfields (street, city, state, and zip code) appear as components of the address field. None of the other fields have subfields.

---

[1] A "tickler" file derives its name from the fact that the invoices are arranged so that those due to be paid earliest appear at the front of the file; hence, they "tickle" the memory of the payables clerk.

[2] Although punched cards are infrequently used at present, their tangible nature helps to clarify record format concepts.

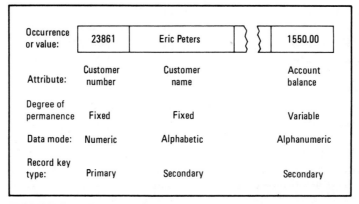

Occurrence or value:	23861	Eric Peters		1550.00
Attribute:	Customer number	Customer name		Account balance
Degree of permanence	Fixed	Fixed		Variable
Data mode:	Numeric	Alphabetic		Alphanumeric
Record key type:	Primary	Secondary		Secondary

FIGURE 8-5 Features of an accounts receivable record.

Lengths. The length of a logical record is determined by the number of fields it contains and the number of characters in each field. The record in Figure 8-6 is 80 characters in length, with the number of characters in the first field consisting of 5 characters. Record lengths vary considerably from file to file, with some logical records being hundreds of characters in length.

Logical records in many files are **fixed length.** Each record in such a file contains exactly the same number of fields. Also, each field within the record contains the same number of character positions as the corresponding files in all other records of the file. The record in Figure 8-6 is a fixed-length record if all other records in the file of which it is a member are 80 characters in length and all corresponding fields are identical in length. A file consisting of fixed-length rec-

Customer Number	Name	Address				Balance Due
		Street	City	St.	Zip	

FIGURE 8-6 A record in an accounts receivable master file.

ords is called a **flat file.** Because its logical records are relatively easy to visualize and simple to handle by computer programs, flat files are commonly selected for computer-based systems. Furthermore, a flat file is the prototype for a table employed by a relational model, as we shall see in Chapter 18.

Variable-length records, in which the number of fields vary from record to record, are preferable to fixed-length records in some applications, however. Consider, for example, the sales transaction record shown in Figure 8-4. Within the record format is a subset of two fields relating to a product sold. This subset of fields is known as a **repeating group,** since it will be repeated to reflect all products involved in a particular sale. The number of repeating groups will vary from sale to sale, depending on the number of products sold. If fixed-length records are used, each record will need to be sufficiently lengthy to accommodate the sale having the largest number of products that are likely to be sold. Assuming that this number is 20, considerable space will be unfilled in most sales records comprising the file. By using variable-length records, in which only the needed number of repeating groups are employed for each sale, the wasted space will be minimized.

Variable-length records often can be converted into fixed-length records by re-moving the repeating groups. For instance, the repeating group in the sales transaction record can be eliminated by creating a new type of record. Each occurrence of this new record, which may be called a line-item record, would contain the number of a product sold in a sales transaction and the quantity sold. It would also include the number of the sales document, in order to provide a cross-reference to the sales transaction record.

Fields within records may also be variable. *Variable-length fields* are primarily employed in alphabetic fields. For instance, the customer name field may be a variable-length field in accounts receivable master records.

When variable-length records or fields are used, their endings must be denoted. One suitable method is to place a special symbol at the end of each affected record or field.

Documentation. Two types of documentation commonly employed with respect to records and the data therein are record layouts and data dictionaries. **A record layout** shows the respective fields comprising a record in a file. It also shows the size of each field and data item contained therein, as well as the sequence of the fields. Figure 8-6 is a record layout for a customer record stored on a punched card. Figure 8-7 shows a record layout for a stockholder record stored on a magnetic medium such as magnetic tape or

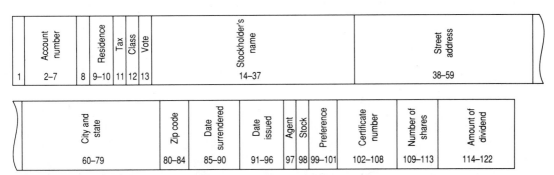

FIGURE 8-7 A layout for a logical record in a stockholder master file.

disk. A **data dictionary** is oriented to individual data items rather than to records. It provides such additional information concerning each data item as its mode (character type) and source. Because it usually lists the records in which a particular data item appears, the data dictionary provides a cross-reference to record layouts.

Logical Versus Physical Data Storage

Data contained in logical records must be stored on tangible or physical media. As we have seen, physical storage media include hard-copy forms (such as paper documents, file cards, and punched cards), microfilms, magnetic tapes, magnetic disks, magnetic drums, data cells, magnetic cards, and optical disks.

Similarities.   Logical data storage and physical data storage have certain similarities. We have described the several fields in Figure 8-6 as comprising a logical record. The punched card itself represents a **physical record,** since all of the fields are contained on a single tangible form. Similarly, a source document such as a purchase order represents a physical record as well as a logical record. This one-to-one correspondence is typical of records used in manual systems.

Differences.   Logical records, however, often do not coincide with physical records in computer-based systems. Assume that the logical customer record shown in Figure 8-6 were 240 characters in length. A record of this length would require three punched cards; in other words, one logical record would require three physical records.

The physical arrangement of data depends on the medium employed. Consider the effects of converting the record in Figure 8-6 to magnetic tape storage. Each logical record would be unaffected by the conversion. Physically, however, several changes

can be observed. First, the physical length of the record is significantly reduced. Magnetic tape can compress several inches of data from a punched card into a fraction of an inch. Second, the data are invisible to the human eye, since magnetized spots rather than holes represent the data values. Third, the physical record is denoted by the interval between two adjacent interblock gaps, rather than by a discrete card. Typically, a physical record on magnetic tape contains several logical records. Fourth, a physical file, represented by a reel of magnetic tape, is rigidly fixed at a specified length (e.g., 2400 feet). Thus, it seldom exactly matches a collection of logical records. It is either too long or too short, depending on the number of logical records and the length of each.

Logical and physical storage also differ in purpose. Logical records are intended to serve the informational needs of users, since users view data in logical terms. Physical storage arrangements of records, on the other hand, are selected to make best use of the capabilities of the physical storage medium.

Conclusion.   Logical records differ from physical records in certain respects. However, we should be aware that under the file-oriented approach these distinctions are not always sharp. For instance, the fields of a record contain data items. The lengths of the fields are physical in nature, whereas the contents of the data items are logical. Nevertheless, the collective fields of a record are viewed as comprising a logical record. As we shall see, the logical versus physical contrast is much sharper under the data base approach.

File Storage and Retrieval

Storing records of data and retrieving records from files are closely intertwined functions. The ways in which records are organized on a storage medium can affect the ease and timeliness of accessing and retrieving the records. They also affect the maintenance of records within files. With contrasts between logical and physical storage in mind, we are ready to survey the storage and retrieval of files and records.

Organization of Stored Records

Methods. The arrangement of the stored records of a file on a physical storage medium is known as **file organization.** Two file organization methods are (1) according to some specified sequence or (2) according to no sequence (i.e., randomly). The sequential file organization method is particularly suited to the magnetic tape medium, which stores records one after another along the tape. Alternatively, records may be stored sequentially along the tracks of a magnetic disk. In contrast, the nonsequential (random) file organization method is suited only to magnetic disks and other storage media possessing direct-access capabilities.

Blocking. Two objectives when storing records on magnetic media are (1) to store the logical records with as little wasted space as possible and (2) to update the stored records as fast as possible. Both objectives can be aided by **blocking**—grouping blocks of sequentially organized records between two interblock gaps. The blocks represent physical records. As the examples in Figure 8-8 demonstrate, blocking both reduces needed storage space dramatically and increases processing speed.

Although the examples in Figure 8-8 pertain to magnetic tape, they could also be adapted to a magnetic disk. Figure 8-9 shows the blocking of two logical stockholder records on a magnetic disk. We might note in passing that these records are arranged within tracks on a surface containing 200 tracks. Since the records are arranged sequentially, they are preceded by a block header record (similar to the first identifying record in a file on magnetic tape).

Blocking does have an upper limit, however. Since a physical record is read into primary storage as a unit, its size cannot exceed the buffer capacity of primary storage. Thus, even with large processors, blocks do not usually exceed several thousand bytes or characters.

File maintenance. To paraphrase the discussion in Chapter 7, four effects of the file maintenance function are

1. To update variable values within records of a file.
2. To add new records to a file.
3. To change fixed, or relatively permanent, values within records of a file.
4. To delete records from a file.

Master files require the greatest attention with regard to file maintenance, since they contain the most-current and most-valued data. However, other types of files, such as price reference files and sales history files, also must be continually maintained. Files of transaction and change records provide the data involved in the maintenance activity.

The file organization method affects the approach to file maintenance. Sequentially organized files are generally maintained through the batch processing approach, whereas files with randomly located records are normally maintained via a direct approach.

Access and Retrieval of Stored Records

File access refers to the method by which each record in a file is physically located. Records are accessed in order to be retrieved, either (1) to update or change the records or (2) to provide the data for reports or displays. Records may be accessed either (1) by following a specified sequence or (2) by means of a more direct search method.

Sequential-access method. The method that requires each record in a file to be ac-

Assume that a magnetic tape has these characteristics:

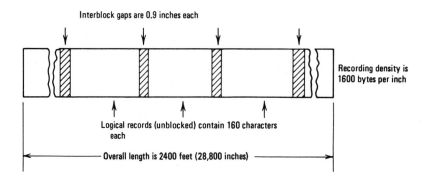

Interblock gaps are 0.9 inches each

Recording density is 1600 bytes per inch

Logical records (unblocked) contain 160 characters each

Overall length is 2400 feet (28,800 inches)

CASE I. *Number of records that can be stored on above tape when records are unblocked (i.e., when logical records and physical record are identical)*

Length of each physical record =

$$160 \text{ characters}/1600 \text{ characters per inch} = 0.1 \text{ inch}$$

Combined length of a physical record plus gap =

$$0.1 \text{ inch} + 0.9 \text{ inch} = 1.0 \text{ inch}$$

Number of records on tape =

$$28.800 \text{ inches}/1.0 \text{ inch} = 28.800 \text{ records}$$

CASE II. *Number of records that can be stored on above tape when 20 logical records are blocked to form one physical record*

Length of each physical record =

$$160 \text{ characters}/1600 \text{ characters per inch} \times 20 \text{ logical records} = 2.0 \text{ inches}$$

Combined length of a physical record plus gap =

$$2.0 \text{ inches} + 0.9 \text{ inch} = 2.9 \text{ inches}$$

Number of physical records (blocks) on tape =

$$28.800 \text{ inches}/2.9 \text{ inches per block} = 9931 \text{ blocks}$$

Number of logical records on tape =

$$9931 \text{ blocks} \times 20 \text{ records per block} = 198.620 \text{ records}$$

CASE III. *Transfer rate for unblocked records, assuming a tape drive speed of 100 inches per second*

Transfer rate =

$$\text{number of logical records per inch times tape drive speed}$$

Transfer rate =

$$1 \text{ record}/1.0 \text{ inch} \times 100 \text{ inches per second} = 100 \text{ records per second}$$

CASE IV. *Transfer rate for blocked records, assuming a tape drive speed of 100 inches per second*

Transfer rate =

$$20 \text{ records}/2.9 \text{ inches} \times 100 \text{ inches per second} = 690 \text{ records per second}$$

FIGURE 8-8 Examples of the effects of blocking on storage space and processing speed.

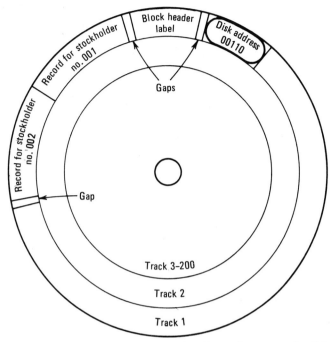

FIGURE 8-9 Data stored on the face of a magnetic disk.
Note: The records, as well as the tracks, are greatly magnified
in the figure. Many more records than shown, for instance,
would fit around one track.

cessed, beginning with the first record and
continuing in sequence until the desired record is reached, is known as the **sequential-
access method** (SAM). Generally, this
method is employed with respect to master
files that are maintained by means of batch
sequential processing. Its choice also depends in part on the physical medium used to
store the file being accessed. If the medium is
magnetic tape, SAM is the only feasible
method. SAM may also be selected when the
medium is magnetic disk, although a direct-
search method is often more suitable to a
direct-access storage device such as a magnetic disk.

Direct- or nonsequential search methods.
Direct access is the capability of accessing
individual records without the need for a sequential search. Any direct-access method
should therefore enable individual records to

be accessed more quickly. Four direct-access search methods are the binary search
method, the index search method, the randomizing method, and the embedded pointer
method. All of the direct-access methods are
made possible by the permanent address feature of direct-access physical storage devices. For instance, the disk address 00110
shown in Figure 8-9 is a permanent fixture of
the magnetic disk.

The **binary-search method** begins by determining the value of the primary key of the
record at the midpoint of a sequentially organized file. This value is then compared to the
key value of the desired record. If the value
of the middle record is less than the desired
value, the search is narrowed to the upper
half of the records in the file. The middle
record of the upper half is then checked. On
the basis of the result, the search moves to
the indicated half of that half. The search

continues until the desired record is pinpointed.

The **index-search method** employs an index in which a key of each record in a file is cross-referenced to its address on a direct-access storage device. Often the cross-referenced key is the primary key of the record, although secondary keys are used in a particular type of index.

The **randomizing method** consists of performing computations to generate the address of an individual record. This access method can only be used in conjunction with randomly organized files.

The **embedded-pointer method** involves the insertion of pointers into special fields within the records of a file. **Pointers** are data items that provide *direction* rather than *content*. They usually consist of the addresses on a physical storage medium where related records being "pointed to" are located.[3]

File Structures

File organization and access methods can be combined to form physical file structures. Three widely used physical file structures are sequential files (sequential organization–sequential access), indexed sequential files (sequential organization–direct access), and random (random organization–direct access). Each of these structures represents an alternative means of storing all the logical records of a master file on a physical storage medium and retrieving them from this medium. Two additional file structures, inverted files and linked lists, do not directly incorporate the records of a file. Instead, they consist of indexes and embedded pointers that allow access through the secondary keys of the records.

One key distinction might be kept in mind during this discussion. Although the physical aspects of a particular file are altered if the file is converted from one to another of the structures, its logical content remains unchanged. Thus, a typical end user of an accounts receivable master file would view the file in the same manner, regardless of its physical structure. On the other hand, the user would likely be aware of changes in such performance measures as updating efficiency and speed in accessing records if the physical structure is changed.

Sequential Files

The records in a **sequential file** are organized sequentially, usually in ascending order, according to a primary key. For instance, a sequentially organized master file may consist of records whose primary key values are arranged as follows: 102, 131, 176, 218, 220. Each record immediately follows the preceding record, all locations being filled up. No spaces appear except interblock gaps. Thus, sequential organization makes efficient use of storage space. Also, since the records are in order, it is not necessary for a computer updating or retrieval program to know exactly where a particular record is located on the storage medium. Instead, all that is necessary is to scan all records, beginning with the first record. In this sequential-accessing process the key value of the record to be updated or retrieved is compared with each record key value until a match is found.

Two brief examples should illustrate the sequential-access procedure. First, assume that data from a batch of transactions will be processed to update the records in the preceding file of five records. These transactions consist of four records having key values of 102, 176, 220, and 131. After sorting these records in ascending order, our program can process the sequential file records very efficiently. It begins by matching the first transaction record (102) with the first file record (102). Then it proceeds to the second transaction and master records (131) and matches

---

[3]Pointers alternatively can refer to key values rather than to storage addresses; however, it is then necessary to search for the storage addresses in an index that associates storage addresses and key values.

them. It continues this process until it reaches the transaction record 220, which it attempts to match with the file record 218. Since there is no match, it then moves to the next file record, 220, and makes the match. In our second illustration, assume that our task is to retrieve data from file record 218. To access this record, our program begins with file record 102. It then compares the value on each record against the desired value, until it reaches the next-to-last record and makes the match.

As our first example shows, sequential files are efficient in processing sizable batches of data. Unfortunately, however, sequential files are less suited for accessing individual records. Unless the desired records are located near the beginning of the file, they cannot be accessed in a timely manner.

Indexed Sequential Files

An **indexed sequential file** (often called an ISAM file) provides one remedy for this deficiency. This type of file retains the sequential organization, and hence the updating efficiency, of batch processing. However, it adds a means of direct access known as a directory or **index.** An individual record can therefore be retrieved more quickly for a user by this method than by the sequential or binary search method.

Figure 8-10 shows a blowup of an index used to access records stored sequentially on a magnetic disk. Corresponding to each block of nine records (e.g., 102 through 235) is the disk address at which the block is located. Retrieving a record involves the following steps:

1. Accessing the index, which is usually stored on the disk with the records. (Alternatively, it may be stored in primary storage, in order to reduce the lookup time.)

2. Searching the index to locate the key value of the desired record. Assume that the desired record is number 176. Since

176 is greater than 102 and less than 235, it is within the first block of records.

3. Locating the disk address that corresponds to the key value of the desired record. The disk address in the index corresponding to the first block of records is 00103.

4. Accessing, with the aid of the disk address, the record block (often called a *bucket*) within which the desired record resides.

5. Searching sequentially through the bucket until the key value of the desired record is located.

Indexed sequential files represent a viable compromise between sequential files and direct-access random files. That is, they provide both processing efficiency and timely retrieval of records. They also make efficient use of storage space, since records are placed one after the other and blocked. Not surprisingly, therefore, they have gained widespread popularity.

However, an indexed sequential file does have several drawbacks. First, it must be stored on a direct-access storage medium such as a magnetic disk rather than on less expensive magnetic tape. Second, the index occupies added storage space and the disk addresses it contains must be updated when records are moved or added. Third, the index is a relatively ponderous means of providing direct access, since it requires two mechanical movements of the read–write head. The head must first move to the location of the index; after the desired disk address is determined from the index, the head must then move to that location. Fourth, new records cannot be easily accommodated by an indexed sequential file. Because the overlay approach must be employed with this file structure, the current records comprising the file are returned to their previous locations during updating runs—that is, they are not reordered on a new disk, as are sequential files maintained on magnetic tape. Thus, new records cannot be inserted into

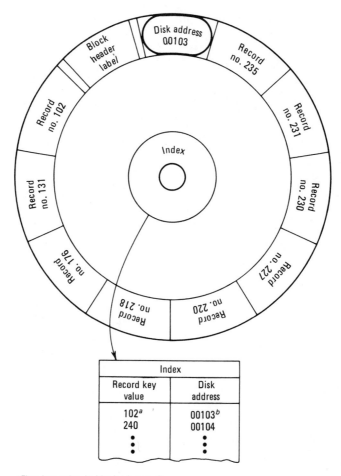

[a]First key value in block of records.
[b]001 is the track number; 03 is the record surface number.

FIGURE 8-10 An index used to access records stored sequentially on a magnetic disk.

the locations within the file designated by their primary keys. Instead, they must be put into overflow areas, with pointers to their proper places within the file. Periodically the file must undergo a special maintenance procedure in order to rearrange all records physically into sequential order and to eliminate the linkages.

Several variations of the indexed sequential-access method are used. The virtual-storage access method (VSAM), for instance, employs a hierarchical index to access records that are not arranged sequentially on tracks. Although the advantage of

sequential processing is lost, VSAM enables records to be accessed more quickly.

Random Files

In **random files** the records are stored throughout a direct-access storage medium in no apparent order; that is, the primary key values of the records are not physically sequenced. Figure 8-11 shows several records of a random file on a magnetic disk, together with their disk addresses. The records of a random file, however, are directly accessible at all times, since the addresses at which

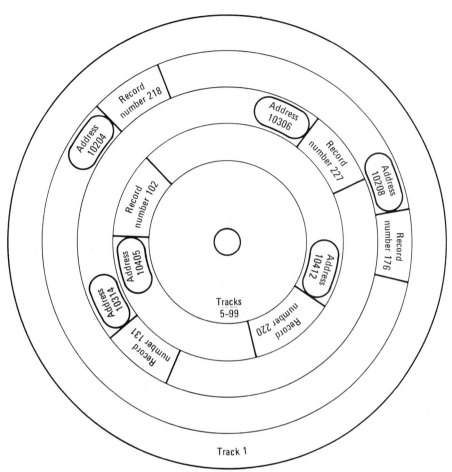

FIGURE 8-11 Records stored by the random method on a magnetic disk. *Notes:* (1) For simplicity, the disk is assumed to have only one recording surface and 99 tracks. (2) The records, as well as the tracks, are greatly magnified in the figure. Many more records than shown, for instance, would fit around one track.

they are located may be easily generated by the randomizing method.

Randomizing involves a procedure, often called a **hashing scheme,** that transforms the primary key of each record into a randomized number.[4] This randomized number,

[4]Randomizing is not necessary if the key values match the addresses of the direct-access storage medium. In such cases the *direct-addressing* approach could be used. However, key values and addresses seldom match; thus, direct-addressed files are a rarity in the real world.

in turn, is converted into the storage address at which the record is stored. Randomizing procedures are mathematical algorithms and generally involve dividing record key values by prime numbers and saving certain digits of the quotient's remainder as the randomized number. An ideal randomizing procedure generates a different randomized number (and hence a different storage address) for each record key value.

As an example of a randomizing procedure in action, consider the record in Figure

8-11 having a primary key value of 176. The disk address 10208 is generated by the procedure for the first time when the key value of 176 is assigned to the record. At this time the contents of the record are stored at the generated address. Then, each time that the record is to be accessed—either to update the record or to retrieve data from the record—the randomizing procedure is repeated to generate the storage address.

The most important advantage of random files is access speed. Since the randomizing procedure utilizes the computer's computational ability, it enables individual records to be accessed more quickly than by alternative methods. Whereas the table lookup method employed by indexed sequential files requires two head movements, the randomizing procedure requires only one head movement to reach the disk address where the record is located. In addition to access speed, random files provide flexibility. That is, new records can be easily added and obsolete records deleted without regard for physical sequencing. Also, special resorting procedures are unnecessary. Another aspect of flexibility pertains to updating. Random file structures (as do other direct-access file structures such as those that employ indexes) enable more than one file to be updated simultaneously in an on-line processing procedure. For instance, both an accounts receivable master file and inventory master file can be updated simultaneously to reflect a sales transaction, if at least one of the master files provides direct access.

Random files, like the other file structures, do have severe drawbacks. Large batches of transactions cannot be processed efficiently, since the records are not organized sequentially. Equally important, the available storage space is inefficiently used. This latter drawback arises from the imperfect nature of known randomizing procedures. Any currently available randomizing procedure produces two undesirable results:

(1) Many of the available storage locations remain blank because they are not generated from the collection of record key values. (2) Many of the available storage locations overflow because the same addresses are generated by more than one record key value. As a consequence, a significant part (usually about 30 percent) of the total available storage space remains unoccupied, while a large number of records must be placed in overflow areas and linked to the generated addresses.

Inverted Files

A sequential file is typically arranged according to the primary key of its records. An **inverted file,** by contrast, is arranged by one of the secondary keys within the record of a file. It is in essence an index that is created *in addition to* the file to which it relates. Each value of the secondary key within an inverted file is cross-referenced to one or more pointers. Each pointer provides an address where a record within the file is located on the physical storage medium.

Assume that the records in Figure 8-12*a*, which are arranged sequentially by customer number, comprise an accounts receivable file. The other attributes within the records (customer name, credit limit, and current balance) represent secondary keys. Thus, three inverted files could be generated. Figure 8-12*b* shows the inverted file for the credit limit attribute. Using this inverted file, the records of customers having a particular credit limit value (e.g., 2, representing $2000) may be obtained very quickly. The computer program that accesses the inverted file would first scan the disk addresses of 1000, 1300, and 1600. Then it would retrieve the records at those addresses and display them for an interested user such as the credit manager.

Inverted files are particularly useful in answering inquiries involving several attributes within a record, known as *multiple-key inquiries*. Assume, for example, that an employee record contains the skill code, work location, and years of experience for each employee in a nationwide firm. If these three attributes are structured into inverted files, answers can be quickly provided to such in-quiries as which employees having two or more years of experience as a project cost accountant are located in the firm's Los Angeles facility.

If inverted files are formed from all the secondary keys within a record, the file is said to be *fully inverted*. This condition enables the broadest range of multiple-key inquiries to be quickly answered. However, a fully inverted file exacts heavy penalties. Each additional inverted file consumes storage space, and pointers must be changed in each whenever records are added to or deleted from the sequential file that it supports. Consequently, partially inverted files are more common than fully inverted ones.

Disk address	Customer number	Customer name	Credit limit (000$)	Current balance ($)
1000	100	Waters, John	2	715.00
1100	101	Jacobs, Paul	4	3010.00
1200	104	Adams, Steve	3	0.00
1300	106	Trimble, Shirley	2	1497.50
1400	107	Baker, Trevor	4	50.00
1500	110	Early, Kristin	3	882.75
1600	112	Malcolm, Doris	2	100.00

a. Records arranged in sequence by primary key

Credit limit	Disk addresses
2	1000, 1300, 1600
3	1200, 1500
4	1100, 1400

b. Inverted file based on a selected secondary key

FIGURE 8-12 An accounts receivable master record and an inverted file based on a single secondary key.

Linked Lists

A **linked list** is a chain of embedded pointers that tie together records containing logically related data. Each pointer in a linked list appears within a **pointer field** that is contiguous to the fields of a record that contain content data. Thus, a linked list is a structure that is appended to an existing file structure. Its major purpose, like that of inverted files, is to enable needed information to be accessed and retrieved in a very timely manner.

Figure 8-13 provides a simple example of a linked list. In the figure are record lay-

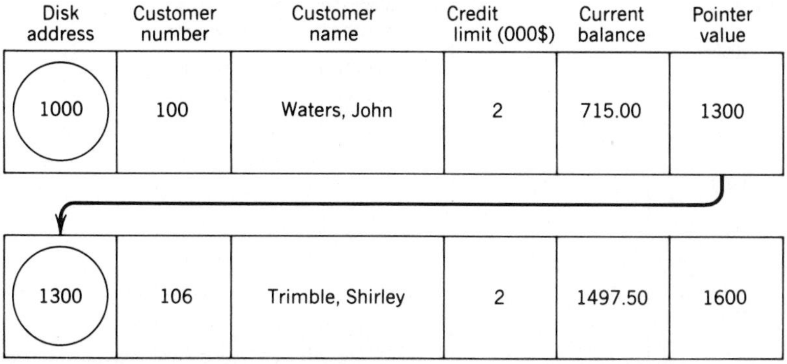

Disk address	Customer number	Customer name	Credit limit (000$)	Current balance	Pointer value
1000	100	Waters, John	2	715.00	1300
1300	106	Trimble, Shirley	2	1497.50	1600

FIGURE 8-13 Pointers within accounts receivable master file records.

outs for two of the records in the accounts receivable file that appears in Figure 8-12. A pointer field has been added to the records, and thus the structure for a linked list has been created. The pointer value of 1300 has been inserted in the record for John Waters. An arrow in the figure indicates that this pointer value specifies, or "points to," the record for Shirley Trimble, which is located at disk address 1300. In turn, the value of the pointer in Shirley Trimble's record is 1600. As we recall from an example concerning inverted files, these disk addresses store records whose credit limit value is 2, representing $2000. Thus, Figure 8-13 shows a portion of a linked list involving the credit-limit attribute.

Attribute chains. Linked lists that chain together identical values of secondary keys or attributes such as credit limits are known as **attribute chains.** Since most attributes can have numerous values, multiple chains are likely to be formed for each attribute within a file. Figure 8-14 shows a flat file with pointer fields containing the three chains needed for the credit limit. (Asterisks mark the ends of chains.) One chain links the record at disk address 1000 to records at addresses 1300 and 1600, while other chains link records at addresses 1200 and 1500 and records at ad-

dresses 1100 and 1400. By comparison with Figure 8-12, we can see that attribute chains involve the same groups of addresses as the records in an inverted file. Thus, attribute chains and inverted files represent alternative means of achieving an identical purpose.

Like inverted files, linked lists can be formed with respect to more than one attribute or secondary key within a file. These multilist structures require additional pointer fields within each record. Thus, linked list structures have the same drawbacks as inverted files. That is, they consume additional storage space and increase the maintenance burden.

Linked lists, however, are more versatile than inverted files. In addition to forming chains based on secondary keys, linked lists can be used (1) to reorder records in any desired sequence and (2) to tie together the records of two or more files. Linked lists used for reordering are discussed next, and linked lists involving two or more files are considered in Chapter 18.

List reordered by primary key. The records in a file are not organized when a random file structure has been employed. Thus, a linked list is necessary to provide the ordering for any desired reports. Consider, for instance, the case of an open sales order file in which

Disk Address	Customer Number	Remainder of Record Content	Pointer Field
1000	100		1300
1100	101		1400
1200	104		1500
1300	106		1600
1400	107		*
1500	110		*
1600	112		*

FIGURE 8-14   A linked list based on the credit-limit attribute.

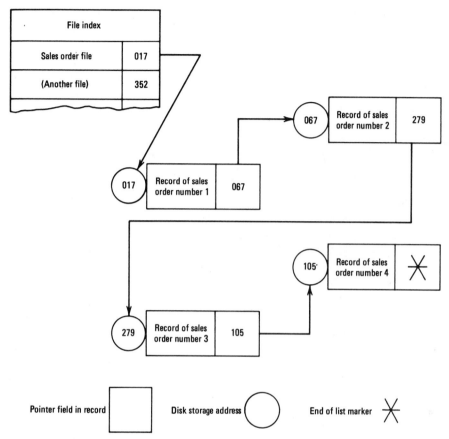

FIGURE 8-15 A list of sales order records stored randomly on a magnetic disk.

the records are stored by means of a random-izing procedure. A daily report of open sales orders, arranged by sales order number (the primary key), is needed to provide a handy reference and to augment the audit trail. Figure 8-15 indicates how a linked list can facilitate the printing of this report. The computer program for report preparation would first access a file index (i.e., a directory). From this index it would ascertain the disk address (017) of the record containing the data for the first sales order to be printed. (This first record is called the **head record**). After retrieving and printing the first sales order, the program refers to its pointer field to determine that the address of the second sales or-

der to be printed is 067. After printing the data for the last sales order in the report, the program encounters an end-of-list marker in the last (or tail) record.

List reordered by secondary key. Often information is needed from a sequential file that is ordered according to a secondary key. A linked list can enable a report to be quickly prepared without the need for time-consuming re-sorts. For example, the records of an employee file are arranged sequentially by employee number. Periodic reports are needed in which the employee data are arranged by skill code numbers, a secondary key. Included in the reports should be the names and department numbers of employees or managers possessing the respective skills. Each report will begin with the smallest skill code, 01 (for general management), while the last line will contain the largest skill code, 40 (for janitor). Figure 8-16 presents an abbreviated flat file containing the employee number, skill code, and pointer fields for a sampling of employees. When preparing the desired report the computer program would be directed via a file index to the record containing skill code 01. After the first line is printed, then the program is "pointed to" 107, the address of the second record to be printed. This process continues until the end-of-list mark is encountered in the record at address 112.

Ring-linked lists. All of the linked lists thus far described have been **simple linked lists** or chains, since they have ended with marks in the last records comprising the lists or chains. Simple lists, however, provide only one access path, generally from the head record to the tail record.

In order to enhance accessibility, additional pointers may be inserted into the records containing the linked lists. One possibility is to add a pointer value in the last record of a simple list, thereby creating a **ring list.** Consider the three simple lists or chains in Figure 8-14. Ring lists can be formed by adding the values 1000, 1200, and 1300 in the pointer fields of the last three records in the flat file. These values "point to" the ad-

Employee Records

Disk Address	Employee Number	Skill Code	Remainder of Record Content	Pointer Field
100	10	30		111
101	20	37		112
102	30	15		103
103	40	20		110
104	50	33		106
105	60	09		102
106	70	35		101
107	80	02		105
108	90	15		108
109	100	12		109
110	110	24		114
111	120	30		115
112	130	40		*[b]
113	140[a]	01		107
114	150	25		100
115	160	32		104

[a] Head record, since 01 is the smallest skill code.

[b] End of list record.

FIGURE 8-16 A linked list of skill codes within a sequential file.

dresses of the first records in each of the three chains pertaining to the credit limit attribute. Ring lists allow a searching program to enter a chain at any record and to follow the chain all the way around. Thus, they increase the accessibility of data within a linked list. Other enhancements of simple lists are described in Chapter 18.

Design Considerations Pertaining to Records and Files

Managing the files and records of an information system and devising their structures involve a number of choices. In making these choices designers can refer to the objectives listed at the beginning of this chapter. They should also consider the particular circumstances of each application.

File and Records Management

Sound **file management** depends primarily upon suitable tradeoffs between the various objectives. In particular, efficiency in file maintenance should be balanced against the accessibility of data within the files. In turn, data accessibility should be balanced against costs related to file management (i.e., the costs of creating and maintaining files and retrieving data from them). Data accessibility can be improved by such techniques as storing data on direct-access storage media in disaggregated form. For instance, data concerning each sale may be coded and stored according to several dimensions, such as sales territory and products sold. Economy and efficiency can be improved by storing data in coded forms, minimizing duplicate files, processing transaction data sequentially, employing magnetic tape when feasible, and practicing effective records management.

Records management pertains to the creation, maintenance, and retention of the records arising from transactions and other business activities. The records may range from hard-copy source documents to records on magnetic or optical media. Effective records management consists of such actions as

1. Approving the creation and design of each new record or form, such as a new credit memo.
2. Determining the point at which each record should be transferred from an active file, such as a sales record in the sales invoice transaction file, to an inactive file, such as the sales history file.
3. Establishing the length of time that a record should be retained in an inactive file before being destroyed.
4. Establishing the manner of storing inactive and backup files.

Records retention is an important concern. Inactive records are often needed for reference and for the satisfaction of legal requirements. Backup records are needed for security, as described in Chapter 9. With respect to inactive records, the optimal approach is to store them for as long as needed and in a manner that is inexpensive but reasonably accessible. For instance, many records might be stored on microfilm or magnetic tape in a record storage center, with each container clearly marked and catalogued. As each scheduled disposal date arrives, the affected records would be pulled and destroyed.

Record Structures

Among the choices that a designer must make with respect to a logical record are

1. The content of the data items comprising the record.
2. The arrangement of these data items.
3. The sizes and modes of the fields that are to contain the values of the respective data items.

4. The data item that is to represent the primary key.

5. The length of the record, and whether it is to be fixed or variable.

The best option for each of these choices depends in large part on the particular situation. However, certain generalizations are possible. With respect to the arrangement of data items, for instance, the primary key usually appears as the left-most field and a quantitative item (such as a quantity of units or an amount balance) appears as the right-most field. The content of the record is related to both data inputs and information outputs. Relative to inputs, a record must provide fields for all data items to be posted from relevant transactions. Relative to outputs, it should provide descriptive information in addition to codes and quantitative values. Thus, it should include the name of a customer or account or inventory item as well as the number of the account or customer or inventory item. These names improve the readability of reports by users. (Note, however, that names often do not need to be entered as a part of transaction data if they are already in the records. By entering only the more concise identifying numbers, the data input clerk can minimize the volume of input characters per transaction.)

Another choice open to the designer concerns whether to consolidate or split records. Consider again the records shown in Figure 8-4 on page 292. The accounts receivable record is shown to be separate (split) from the sales record. However, data in the two records are logically related, if one record pertains to a particular customer and the other to a sale made to him or her. Logically, therefore, the two record types shown in Figure 8-4 could be consolidated, so that a customer and his or her sales history are maintained in physical proximity. Consolidated records aid the preparation of more complete reports concerning entities of importance, such as customers. On the other

hand, sales analysis needs are based on all sales records being maintained together in a sales history file. Moreover, file processing efficiency is improved when records are shortened. Thus, it may be preferable to keep the sales records separate from the customer records. The designer must weigh arguments such as these for each option and then make a choice.

File Structures

Choices among the three major file structures, as well as physical storage media, are best considered in the light of several relevant measures. By means of these measures we can develop those sets of conditions that most favor the use of each file structure.

File size. The number of records in a file times the length of each record yields the size of a file. Files range in size from very short to tremendously long. For instance, a file of policyholder accounts maintained by an insurance company might number several hundred thousand records and occupy several reels of magnetic tape.

The larger the size of a file, the more desirable is the use of a relatively inexpensive storage medium. Thus, magnetic tape is often employed for very large files. This choice in turn dictates the use of sequential files.

Activity ratio. The proportion of the records in a file affected by some type of maintenance action indicates the busyness or activity of the file. A measure of this busyness is the **activity ratio,** the number of records affected (i.e., updated, changed, deleted and added) during a file maintenance run, divided by the total number of records in a file. If 1000 records are affected in a file of 10,000 records, the activity ratio would be 10 percent.

Generally, the higher the activity ratio, the greater the benefits gained from the efficiencies of processing batches of data against sequential files. Since the payroll application has a very high activity ratio, it typically employs sequential employee files and processes batches of employee time transactions. Conversely, the lower the activity ratio, the less advantageous are sequential files and batch processing. Thus, a low activity ratio (e.g., 2 percent) suggests that random files, which employ direct processing, should be given favorable consideration.

Up-to-dateness. The up-to-dateness, or currency, of stored data depends on the promptness with which transactions are processed against the files that they affect. Data in sequential files are generally up to date only just following each file processing run. Data in random and indexed sequential files will be continually up to date if the transactions that affect them are processed by the on-line approach.

Response time. The response time is the time that elapses between the request for information and the receipt of that information. In some applications, such as airline and motel reservation systems, the response time must be held to just a few seconds. For such applications the needed data should be stored in random files on a direct-access storage medium such as magnetic disk.

File volatility. **File volatility** refers to the frequency with which records are added and deleted over a period of time, such as a week. The records in the guest file of a motel

are very volatile, for instance. Applications that encounter high file volatility require frequent access to individual records. Hence, sequential files stored on magnetic tape are not satisfactory for such applications. Of the two major direct-access file structures, random files are preferable. Response times are faster than when indexed sequential files are used.

Conclusions. Figure 8-17 lists those conditions favorable to the use of the three major file structures. In summary, a random file (on a direct-access storage medium) is most suitable when up-to-dateness and fast response times are important, the activity ratio is low, the file volatility is high, and the file is relatively limited in size. A sequential file (on magnetic tape) is most suited to the opposite set of conditions. An indexed sequential file (on a direct-access storage medium) is a good choice when both processing efficiency and rapid accessibility are important.

Classification and Coding of Data

Coding is critical to the efficient storage and processing of data. Thus, an important step when creating a data base is to devise codes suited to the various types of data needed by a firm in its transaction and information processing activities. This section examines the relationships of coding to classification, the major coding systems, and the attributes of sound codes.

Measure	Sequential file (on magnetic tape)	Indexed sequential file	Random file
Size of file	Very large	Large	Limited
Activity ratio	High	Moderate	Low
Up-to-dateness	Relatively unimportant	Important	Very important
Fast response time	Relatively unimportant	Important	Very important
File volatility	Low	Moderate	High

FIGURE 8-17 Comparison of conditions favorable to the use of the respective file structures.

Classification Versus Coding

Classification is the act of grouping into classes. In the context of an information system, classification refers to the grouping of data and information. For instance, transaction data may be grouped according to the accounts to which they pertain, such as the sales account. Sales data may be classified or grouped according to the sales offices making the sales, the product lines sold, and the dates of the sales.

Classification plans or schemes are designed with certain objectives in mind. Consider, for example, a chart of accounts, the basic financial classification plan of every organization. As we briefly noted in Chapter 3, the chart of accounts has the primary purpose of satisfying key internal and external information needs. If it is well designed, a chart of accounts enables useful financial statements and other reports to be prepared. Not only should such financial statements and reports aid managers in controlling operations, but they should assist external parties in making investment decisions.

Coding is the assignment of symbols, such as letters and numbers, in accordance with a classification plan. A coding system provides unique identities for specific events and entities. For instance, the coding system of a firm may assign the letter code CS to identify a credit sales transaction; the number code 711 to identify the sales invoice issued in a particular credit sales transaction; the number code 1346 to identify the customer John Henry Johnson of Akron, Ohio; and the alphanumeric code XQ7 to specify a particular type of transmission that it sells. As we can see, codes are much briefer than the events or entities for which they stand. A coding system can therefore ease the entry of data, enhance processing efficiency and accuracy, speed the retrieval of data from files, and aid the preparation of reports.

Coding Systems

A variety of coding systems have been devised. Familiar examples are (1) bar codes, such as those used to identify merchandise items, (2) color codes, such as those used to distinguish copies of multicopy forms, and (3) cipher codes, such as those used to protect confidential messages. However, the codes most widely useful to business firms are based on alphabetic, numeric, and alphanumeric characters. Four coding systems that use these characters are mnemonic, sequence, block, and group coding systems.

Mnemonic coding system. A code of this type provides visible clues concerning the objects it represents. For instance, AZ is the code for Arizona and WSW-P175R-14 represents a white sidewall radial tire of a specific size. Thus, a **mnemonic code** is relatively easy to remember. On the other hand, its applications are more limited than those of the other three coding systems.

Sequence coding system. The simplest type of code is the **sequence coding system,** which assigns numbers or letters in consecutive order. Sequence codes are applied primarily to source documents such as checks and sales invoices. A sequence code can facilitate document searches, such as a search for a particular sales invoice. Furthermore, a sequence code can help prevent the loss of data, since gaps in the sequence signal missing documents.

Sequence codes are inflexible, however. New entities or events can be added only at the end of the sequence. Moreover, a sequence code generally is devoid of logical significance. For instance, a specific sequence code assigned to a customer does not identify the sales territory within which he or she resides, nor the customer class to which he or she belongs.

Block coding system. A second coding system partially overcomes these drawbacks. A **block coding system** assigns blocks of numbers within a sequence to entities or events having common features. Consequently, a block code designates the classification of an individual entity or event.

Block codes have varied applicability within a firm. Customer numbers, for instance, may be blocked by sales territory. To illustrate, customers in the southern sales territory may be assigned numbers ranging from 1 to 4999, whereas customers in the northern sales territory may be assigned numbers from 5000 to 9999. In other applications, products may be blocked by product line, employees by department, and accounts by major type.

While a block is reserved for individual codes, it is not necessary to assign every possible number within a block. In fact, one advantage of a block code is that unassigned numbers are usually available to be assigned to new objects (e.g., products) as they are added to the firm's scope of activity.

Group coding system. The group code is a refinement of the block code in that it provides more meaning to the users. In effect, a **group coding system** reveals two or more dimensions or facets pertaining to an object. Each facet is assigned a specific location, called a field, within the code format. Code segments (i.e., subcodes) appear within the respective fields, thus identifying the facets pertaining to a particular object.

An example of a group code for an entity should clarify this description. Raw materials stored for use by a metal products manufacturer may be coded according to the following format:

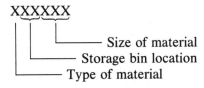

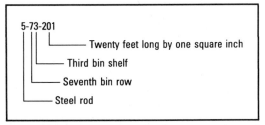

FIGURE 8-18 An example of a group code used to identify raw materials.

A particular raw material item could therefore be coded 573201 (or 5-73-201 for greater clarity), as explained in Figure 8-18.

Group codes are extremely versatile. They may be expressed as hierarchical structures. For instance, the left-most field in the code of a fixed asset may designate the major or broad classification, the fields to the right designating increasingly detailed classifications. They may include block, sequence, or other types of codes. For instance, the employee code may be assigned sequentially as each employee is hired, with the department code being added as a suffix.

Although this combinational feature of group codes tends to make them relatively lengthy and cumbersome, it also packs such codes with much useful information. For instance, a code that captures relevant features of a transaction can provide the basis for key analyses and reports. Thus, a variety of sales analyses can be prepared when a group code of the following format is employed to record sales transactions:

ABBBBCCDDDE

where A represents the class of customer to whom a sale is made,
BBBB represents the account number of the customer,
CC represents the sales territory where the sale is made,
DDD represents the code of the salesperson making the sale,

E represents the type of product (product line) sold.

Attributes of Codes

A sound coding system furthers the primary purpose of a classification plan, which is to satisfy certain informational needs of users. In addition, each of its codes

1. Uniquely identifies objects, such as customers and sales.

2. Is concise and simple, so it is easy to remember and apply and economical to maintain.

3. Allows for expected growth, so that it will not need to be changed in the foreseeable future. For instance, a growing firm with nine product lines should allow two digits (assuming a numeric code) for the product line coding system.

4. Is standardized throughout all functions and levels within a firm, so that reporting systems can be fully integrated.

Computer-based systems also dictate certain attributes. For example, they require that codes be fixed in length. In addition, they encourage the use of numeric codes, since numeric sorting can be performed more easily. On the other hand, the presence of computers should not discourage the application of sound design principles. Thus, alphabetic codes provide 26 choices for each character position of a code. Their use can therefore aid the attribute of conciseness.

Certain codes are peculiar to computer-based systems. Two such codes, the user code and the cipher, relate to security and are discussed in Chapter 9. Two other computer-oriented codes are the transaction code and the action code.

APPLICATION OF A CODING SYSTEM
Bell Communications Research, Inc.[a]

A large organization such as Bell Communications requires a consistent coding system for identifying its extensive array of equipment. Two separate group codes identify the specific items of equipment and the locations of the items.

A CLEI code, for specific items, has four segments: a four-character field for the basic function of the equipment, a four-character field for one or more key features, a single-character field for reference, and a two-character field for complementary data. An example of this code is

DLMO 52B B RA

where DLMO represents a miniaturized dial, long-line circuit,
52B indicates that the item has interrupted-ringing supply capability, a particular power-supply arrangement, and no motor start lead,

B (in position 8) specifies the source drawing,
RA refers to computer-based operations support systems using the item.

The location code has three segments: a four-character field for place, a two-character field for state, and a five-character field for building and other location identifiers. An example is

DNVR CO MAF24

where DNVR stands for Denver,
CO stands for Colorado,
MAF24 specifies a main distributing frame on the second floor of the main building

[a]Germain Boer, *Classifying and Coding for Accounting Operations* (Montvale, N.J.: National Association of Accountants, 1987), pp. 57–63. The term "CLEI" is a trademark of Bell Communications Research.

Transaction codes identify types of transactions to the computer system. Such codes designate the specific application programs to be used in processing the various transactions entered into the system. By specifying a particular transaction code, a user informs the computer system which accounts to debit and credit and which data items to update in which files. In effect, a transaction code is a concise replacement for the familiar journal entry format used in manual processing systems.

Action codes identify specific actions pertaining to file maintenance or data retrieval. For instance, they may specify the addition of new master records, the deletion of current master records, or the display of stored records. Action codes are employed primarily with on-line processing systems. Often they are entered with the aid of menu screens.

Summary

Data management consists of creating and maintaining a firm's data base—its repository of stored data—for the primary purpose of retrieving data and information as needed. The objectives applicable to data management include relevance, efficiency, accessibility, flexibility, accuracy and security, and economy. Computers affect data management by requiring careful specification of data when stored or retrieved; on the other hand, they allow great quantities of data to be stored compactly and needed data to be accessed easily and quickly by users. Two alternative approaches to data management are available. The file-oriented, or application, approach is discussed in this chapter, and the data base approach is discussed in a later chapter.

Files are the traditional vehicles for organizing and storing data. They may be classified as master, transaction, reference, open document, history, report, backup, suspense, program, index, and test files. Several of these file types comprise logical records, which in turn contain data items and characters. Logical records, which can be either fixed or variable in length, are divided into fields that contain the values of the data items. In addition to values, data items can reflect attributes, degrees of permanence, and modes. Certain data items serve as primary or secondary keys.

Logical records and data items can be documented through record layouts and data dictionaries. Logical records are related to physical records, but they also exhibit significant differences. These differences are apparent in the use of blocking and the selection of physical storage media.

Files may be organized sequentially or randomly. Records within files may be accessed sequentially or by means of such direct methods as binary search, index search, randomizing procedure, and embedded pointers. File structures consist of collected records that are organized and accessed by certain of these methods. Three major file structures are (1) sequential files, which are organized and accessed sequentially; (2) indexed sequential files, which are organized sequentially and accessed directly via indexes; and (3) random files, which are organized randomly and accessed directly by a randomizing procedure. Sequential files, which are generally stored on the less expensive magnetic tape, provide processing and storage efficiency; they are best employed when large batches of transactions are to be processed against voluminous files. Random files, which must be stored on a direct-access storage medium, are most suitable when up-to-dateness and rapid accessibility are very important, the activity ratio is low, the file volatility is high, and the file is relatively small. Indexed sequential files, which also must be stored on a direct-access storage medium, are most suitable when both processing efficiency and timely retrieval of data are important.

Review Problem with Solution

Statement

Excitement Magazine (EM) has 10,000 subscribers. It uses several files relating to subscribers: (1) a master file of all current subscribers, (2) a daily transaction file of billings, payments, renewals, new subscribers, cancellations, and changes in status (e.g., changed addresses), (3) a history file that summarizes past years' activities, (4) a reference file of subscription rates, (5) a report file of analyzed subscriber activity and financial information for the current month, and (6) a suspense file of subscriber transactions that require correction of errors or addition of missing data.

EM operates a computer-based information system that incorporates magnetic tape and disk storage, video display terminals, printers, and off-line key-to-disk systems.

Required

a. Prepare a layout for a fixed-length record in the subscriber master file, incorporating a reasonable set of data items and including the mode of each data item. Identify the primary key.

b. Describe needed data items for a variable-length record in the daily transaction file, including optional data items for all the various types of transactions.

c. Compare the advantages of storing the subscriber master file on magnetic tape with those of storing on magnetic disk.

d. Describe three alternative file structures that could be selected for the subscriber master file, assuming that the magnetic disk storage medium is employed.

e. Describe and illustrate codes that identify (1) each type of transaction, (2) each specific transaction, and (3) each specific subscriber. The subscriber code should be a combinational group code that incorporates both sequence and block code fields.

Solution

a. The primary code for the subscriber master file is the subscriber number. A suggested record layout appears on page 317; the order of the data items is arbitrary, except that the primary key normally appears as the first item and the balance as the last item. With respect to modes, *A* means alphabetic, *N* means numeric, and *AN* means alphanumeric.

b. Needed data items for the variable-length transaction record include those below. All except the first two are optional, in that their appearance depends on the type of transaction.

Transaction code (which shows the type of transaction, such as a payment transaction, or an action, such as deletion of a subscriber record)

Subscriber number (to identify the record being affected)

Amount (relating to billing or payment transactions)

Subscription rate code (relating to new customer or renewal transactions)

Subscriber name (relating to new customer and change of status transactions)

Subscriber billing address and mailing address (see the answer to **a**, relating to new customer and change of status transactions)

Class of customer (relating to new customer and change of status transactions)

Date of last issue (relating to new customer or renewal transactions)

Reason for cancellation code (relating to cancellation transactions)

Note: A transaction sequence number and date will be automatically generated by the computer program and attached to the beginning of each transaction.

c. If the subscriber master file were stored on a magnetic tape, the sequential processing approach would be employed.

Data item	Subscriber code	Subscriber name	Street address (billing)	City and state (billing)	Zip code (billing)	
Character positions	9	28	30	26	9	
Mode	AN	A	AN	A	N	

Street address (mailing)	City and state (mailing)	Zip code (mailing)	Date of initial subscription	Class of subscriber[a]	
30	26	9	6	1	
AN	A	N	N (date)	A	

Subscriber rate code[b]	Date of last issue	Number of times renewed	Renewal or new but not yet billed	Balance due on account[c]
2	6	2	1	6
A	N (date)	N	N	N (amount)

[a]Corporate, personal (regular), personal (discount offer), school, student/faculty, complimentary.

[b]Related to length of subscription and class of subscriber.

[c]Decimal point assumed to be two places from right.

Because the batches of transactions are likely to be large, sequential processing should be relatively efficient. Moreover, magnetic tape is considerably cheaper than magnetic disk.

If magnetic disk were used as the storage medium, individual subscriber records could be directly accessed. Thus, users could quickly obtain information as needed, instead of waiting until the next sequential processing cycle. In addition, the records could be kept completely up to date, since each transaction could be processed as soon as received. If this on-line processing approach is employed, the sorting run (by subscriber number) would be eliminated. On the other hand, the use of magnetic disk allows the designer to retain the sequential processing approach if it appears to be more suitable.

d. The three alternative file structures available to a designer are sequential, indexed sequential, and random. If a magnetic disk is to be the storage medium for the subscriber master file, the sequential file structure would probably be discarded. Instead, the designer might select the indexed sequential file structure, since (1) it enables the efficient processing of batched transaction records and (2) it also allows users to access individual subscriber records quickly as desired. Alternatively, the random file structure might be selected if the need to access individual records is much more important than the desire to process transactions efficiently.

e. Suggested codes are as follows:

(1) The type of transaction code would be alphabetic, with BIL for billing transactions, PAY for payment transactions, REN for renewal transactions, NEW for new customer transactions, CAN for cancellation transactions, and STA for change-of-status transactions. The transaction type code would be added to a sequential number for a specific transaction. For instance, transactions might be 3238BIL and 5765CAN.

(2) Each specific transaction would be assigned the next number in sequence by the data entry computer program; in addition, each transaction could be identified by the date it occurs.

(3) Each subscriber would be assigned a group code comprising two fields; the first field of three letters would represent the last name of the subscriber, while the second field of six numbers would be a sequence code within the three letter field. For instance, a subscriber code for the author might be WLK 280157, where the WLK is one item within the W--block.

Note: A subscriber code appears on the label of each magazine issue. Other portions of the subscriber's records will also appear on the label, including the subscriber's name, mailing address, zip code, date of last issue, and class of subscriber.

Review Questions

8-1 What is the meaning of each of the following terms?

Data base
File-oriented approach
Data base approach
Data set
File
Master file
Transaction file
History file
Reference file
Open document file
Report file
Backup file
Suspense file
Program file
Text file
Index file
Logical record
Data item
Character
Attribute
Data value
Data mode
Primary key
Secondary key
Concatenated key
Field
Fixed-length record
Flat file
Variable-length record
Repeating group
Record layout
Data dictionary
Physical record
File organization
Blocking
File access
Sequential-access method
Binary-search method
Index-search method
Randomizing method
Embedded-pointer method
Pointer
Random file
Sequential file
Indexed sequential file
Index
Randomizing procedure
Hashing scheme
Inverted file
Multiple-key inquiry
Linked list
Pointer field
Attribute chain
Head record
Simple linked list
Ring list
File management
Records management
Activity ratio
File volatility
Classification
Coding
Mnemonic code

Sequence coding system
Block coding system
Group coding system
Transaction code
Action code

8-2 What are the three functions of data management?

8-3 What questions need to be answered when designing the data management functions of an information system?

8-4 Discuss the objectives pertaining to data management.

8-5 What are the effects of computers on the management of data within an information system?

8-6 What are the two alternative approaches to computer-based data management?

8-7 How may files be classified?

8-8 What is the hierarchy of data elements within a typical file?

8-9 What are several characteristics of a data item?

8-10 Contrast primary, secondary, and concatenated keys.

8-11 What is the feature that differentiates fixed-length and variable-length records, and what are their respective advantages?

8-12 Describe two types of documentation commonly employed with respect to files.

8-13 What are two differences between logical records and physical records?

8-14 List the similarities and differences (other than those pertaining to hardware characteristics) between magnetic tape and magnetic disks as physical storage media.

8-15 In what ways may files be organized and accessed?

8-16 What factors are involved in determining the number of records that may be stored on a magnetic tape and the speed of processing the records?

8-17 Describe four direct or nonsequential search techniques.

8-18 Contrast the characteristics and advantages of sequential, indexed sequential, and random file structures.

8-19 Describe how inverted files can facilitate the answering of multiple-key inquiries.

8-20 Describe how an attribute chain facilitates the retrieval of records having a specified value for an attribute.

8-21 Describe how linked lists enable reports based on secondary keys to be prepared without the need for re-sorting.

8-22 What tradeoffs are necessary in order to optimize file management in an information system?

8-23 What steps are necessary to achieve effective management of records?

8-24 Discuss the choices that must be made in the design of record formats.

8-25 Discuss conditions that are favorable to the use of sequential, indexed sequential, and random files.

8-26 What is the relationship between a classification plan and a coding system?

8-27 Contrast four types of systems for coding data using numeric and alphabetic characters.

8-28 List several attributes of a sound code.

Discussion Questions

8-29 Identify the type of file and describe the contents suggested by each of the following terms:

    a. Stockholder.
    b. Standard overhead rates.
    c. Job order costs.
    d. Sales trends.
    e. Economic statistics.

8-30 Why is microfilm better for storing canceled checks than for storing the records of active customers?

8-31 What are the trade-offs involved in designing a classification plan and coding system?

8-32 Discuss the trade-offs between processing efficiency and rapid retrieval of data.

8-33 It has been suggested that a data base is the heart of an information system. Discuss.

8-34 Discuss the advantages of maintaining the general ledger on a magnetic disk.

8-35 The steps involved in updating records in files appear to be the same, regardless of whether the records pertain to customers or to suppliers or to general ledger accounts. Can one general-purpose updating program therefore be used?

8-36 Identify the type of list or data structure that is preferable and describe how it employs pointers to answer each of the following inquiries:

    a. How many employees in plant 2 who have five or more years of seniority earn $12.00 or more per hour?

    b. Who were the top five salespersons in sales territory 10 in terms of gross sales last month?

    c. Which employees have the best qualifications, with respect to experience, education, and sales achievements, to head the new sales branch in Terre Haute?

Problems

8-1 Draw record layouts and enter the indicated values for the accounts payable, finished-goods inventory, and employee payroll earnings records below. Assign reasonable field sizes.

    a. Morris Winston, a supplier whose address is 20 Tern Street, Boise, Idaho 83702, and whose number is 735, is due on May 18 an amount of $568.27 for a purchase initiated by purchase order number 2381, dated April 19. His invoice number is 723, dated April 28.

    b. A quantity of 50 camshafts, product 76A, is on hand in the warehouse (bin location L81B) on September 30. During the month of September, 30 were received from production and 15 were issued. The unit cost of product 76A is $75.25.

    c. George Briscoe, employee number 93565 in department 56, is salaried (code 1) and thus does not earn overtime premium. As of March 15 he had earned gross pay of $2000, with deductions of $700. He was employed in 1971 (code 71) and was born in 1929 (code 29). His occupational code is 536.

8-2 Design a record layout for a student master file. Include at least 10 data items, beginning with the student identification number. Do not include transcripts. Arrange the data items within the record, specifying field lengths and modes for the respective items. (Limit the modes to numeric, alphabetic, or alphanumeric, i.e., a combination of letters and numbers and special characters such as decimal points.)

8-3 Lockspar National Bank serves a state in the northeast. It maintains separate master files pertaining to checking accounts, savings accounts, and installment loans. It serves both personal and business customers.

Required

a. Prepare a record layout for the checking account master file, including the mode as well as the size of each field. Identify the primary key.

b. List ten data items that should appear in the savings account and installment loan master records. Identify a suitable primary key and several secondary keys for each.

c. Identify the types of transactions needed to maintain the file of checking accounts.

d. If the checking accounts are sequentially updated at the end of each day but data in the individual accounts must be immediately available during the day, which types of file structures may be employed? If more than one structure is suitable, indicate whether the selection of one over another will affect the use of the system by tellers, and if so, how.

e. If the checking accounts are to be updated as transactions occur, how would the answer to part **d** be changed?

8-4 A master file is stored on a magnetic tape as a sequential file. The file comprises 100 fixed-length records with primary key values ranging from 100 to 199. These records are not blocked. An identical file is stored on a magnetic disk. Its sequentially organized records are grouped into blocks of four and located at disk addresses 0820 through 0844.

Required

a. Describe the procedure by which the computer system accesses the record stored on magnetic tape whose key value is 163.

b. What advantages are provided by the file stored on the magnetic disk?

c. Describe the procedure by which the computer system accesses the same numbered record stored on magnetic disk, using the binary search method.

d. Prepare an index to convert the file on magnetic disk to an ISAM structure, using the key value of the first record in each block to represent the block of logical records. Then describe the procedure by which the computer system accesses the same numbered record.

e. Assume that the file on magnetic disk is changed to a random structure. The hashing scheme consists of dividing the key

value of a record by 13 and using the first four digits of the remainder as the disk address. For instance, the disk address for the record having the key value of 100 is 6923. Describe the procedure by which the computer system would access the record having the key value of 163. Include the computed disk address.

8-5 If a standard reel of tape is 2400 feet, each interblock gap is 0.55 inches, a logical record consists of 200 characters, and the tape is to be written at a density of 800 characters per inch, how many records will fit on a reel if

a. The records are unblocked?

b. The records are blocked with 16 records to a block?

(Round to the nearest full block).

8-6 The Becker Baking Company of London, Ontario, has 5500 employees. It maintains an extensive personnel record, requiring 5000 characters of storage, for each employee. The firm presently uses 2400-foot magnetic tapes to store employee records. Each tape blocks data at a density of 1000 characters per inch; gaps one inch in width separate blocks of logical records.

Required

a. Explain the desirability of using as few interblock gaps as possible.

b. Identify the factor that limits the number of records that may be included in one block.

c. If a blocking factor of two records per block is established, how many feet of tape are needed to contain the employee master file? How many tape reels are required?

d. If the blocking factor is increased to 20, how many feet of tape and reels are needed?

(SMAC adapted)

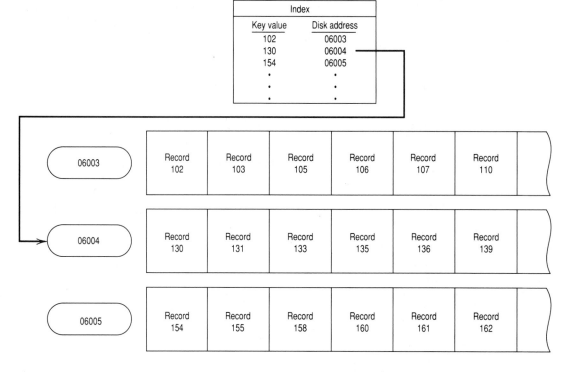

8-7 The diagram above illustrates a type of file structure for a master file.

Required

a. What is the name of the illustrated file structure?

b. Describe the procedure for accessing the record with a key value of 133.

c. Describe the procedure for processing, by the direct method, a batch of transactions affecting records with key values of 155, 103, 131, 161, 107, 153, 110, and 135.

d. Describe the procedure for processing the transactions in **c** by the sequential method.

e. A new record with the key value of 134 is to be added to the master file. Describe in general terms where the record would be located and how it would be accessed.

8-8 In each of the following situations select the file structure (sequential, ISAM, or random) that seems to be most suitable. Justify your selections.

a. A large life insurance company with approximately 2 million policyholders maintains a single policyholder master file, which is updated twice weekly to reflect premium payments, to add new policyholders, to delete canceled policyholders, to reflect changes to permanent data, and to print overdue premium notices. Approximately 1 million records are affected during each processing run.

b. An automotive and truck parts supplier maintains a 10,000-record inventory master file. An average of 2500 records are updated daily to reflect sales and receipts, and approximately 30 parts are either added or deleted daily. An inventory reorder list is printed daily to notify buyers when parts on hand have declined to their reorder points; however, parts clerks need to be able to check the status of parts on hand at any time during the day, since customers often want to know how many units of particular parts are available when they call to place orders.

c. A manufacturing firm produces goods on orders received from customers. Approximately 100 orders are in production on any given day, and these orders are maintained as records in a work-in-process master file. Each record must be accessed frequently in order to post data concerning production steps completed and to enable managers and planners to discover current order status. A five-second response time is considered tolerable. On the average, about 10 orders are begun and 10 completed daily.

d. The water department in a city with approximately 75,000 residents maintains a resident account master file. Once a month all the records in the file are updated to reflect water usage; bills are also prepared at that time, as well as a listing of residents and amounts billed.

e. A motel chain employs a room reservation system, in which all rooms of each member motel represent the available inventory. Each time a room is reserved, a new record is created in the name of the person making the reservation. This record is then changed to reflect occupancy on specific dates, to add food and phone charges, to prepare the bills, and then to delete the records when occupants leave. On the average, travelers occupy a room for one and one-half nights.

8-9 Insert the appropriate pointer values in the pointer field illustrated at the bottom of the page, if the purpose of the resulting simple linked list is to enable the preparation of a report arranged by date of most recent purchase, with the latest date listed first.

8-10 The Metropolitan Trust Company of Toronto is in the process of converting its personal loans application. All of the records in the loan master file are being loaded onto a

		Supplier Records		
Disk Address	Supplier Number	Date of Most Recent Purchase	Remainder of Record Content	Pointer Field
010	1000	10/3		
020	1001	9/6		
030	1002	9/17		
040	1003	8/30		
050	1004	10/7		
060	1005	9/21		
070	1006	9/14		
080	1007	10/2		
090	1008	9/11		
100	1009	9/28		
110	1010	9/5		

magnetic disk by means of a randomizing procedure. The first four records are stored at the following disk addresses:

Disk Address	Loan Number	Name	Loan Amount	Interest Rate (%)	Due Date
6	0100	Dawson	$5,000	15	7/91
4	0200	Cannon	20,000	10	10/91
8	0300	Baker	10,000	15	1/91
2	0400	Ames	15,000	12	1/91

After loading these records, linked lists will be formed.

Required

a. Label five columns as Loan Number Pointer, Amount Pointer, Name Pointer, Interest Rate Pointer, and Due Date Pointer. Relist the disk addresses to the left of these columns. Then enter in each of the five columns the pointers needed to create linked lists for retrieving attribute values in the following sequences: (1) loan number, from lowest to highest; (2) amount, from highest to lowest; (3) name, alphabetically; (4) interest rate, from lowest to highest; (5) due date, chronologically. For example, the pointers that form the loan number list would appear as follows:

Disk Address	Loan Number Pointer
6	4+
4	8
8	2
2	*

Note: + marks head record; * marks tail of list.

b. Prepare inverted files for all secondary keys in the loan records except name.

c. Explain how the linked lists can be employed by the DBMS to provide an answer to the following inquiry: What loan amounts are due in January 1991?

(SMAC adapted)

8-11 The Elk Construction Co., Ltd., intends to computerize its payroll system. The company produces paychecks every two weeks for its average employee force of 2000. This work force varies in size from 1750 in the winter months to more than 3000 during the peak summer months. In addition to preparing paychecks, the payroll system must also prepare, in employee number sequence, the payroll and deduction registers. It must also post pay data to the earnings records and prepare quarterly reports.

The configuration acquired by Elk consists of a central processor with a 500,000-byte storage capacity, eight tape drives, five disk drives, one printer, and one video display terminal.

Required

a. Identify two alternative file structures that would be suitable for Elk. List the advantages of each identified file structure and the physical storage devices that it would use.

b. Assume that the firm is aware of two impending changes: (1) a likely increase in the turnover rate of employees during a season and (2) regulations that will require each terminating employee to be paid immediately and the payment to be recorded in his or her records. Which of the alternative file structures identified in **a** thereby becomes the preferable choice? Why?

(SMAC adapted)

8-12   The Phoenix Board of Realtors' Multiple Listing Service (MLS) maintains a listing of houses for sale in the Phoenix metropolitan area. The listing for each house includes the data in the collection of 10 records shown at the bottom of the page. To provide faster service to buyers, MLS has decided also to maintain inverted files. Then, when buyers ask to see houses having certain desired features, the computer system can quickly retrieve the requested data.

Required

a. Prepare inverted files based on the four attributes that can serve as secondary keys. The records shown are stored on a magnetic disk and located at consecutive disk addresses, beginning with 250. (Thus, the record having MLS number 10 is located at address 259). In preparing the inverted file for asking price, use a range that begins from $95,000 to (but not including) $100,000.

b. Describe the procedure for obtaining the answers to the following inquiries, and show how the answers might appear on a video display screen.

   (1) What are the addresses of the houses for sale in Tempe?

   (2) Which houses in Mesa, identified by address, are priced below $100,000?

   (3) Which houses in Phoenix, identified by address, have four bedrooms and were constructed in the 1980s?

c. List three more inquiries, involving at least two inverted files, that can be answered by the set of inverted files.

8-13   Specify the most suitable type of coding system for each of the following situations:

   a. Numbering payroll checks.
   b. Identifying airports on baggage claim checks.

MLS Number	Address	Area	Asking Price (000$)	Number of Bedrooms	Date of Construction
1	2340 Cricket Dr.	Tempe	101	4	1982
2	1504 Indian St.	Phoenix	119	4	1977
3	4328 Sunset Rd.	Mesa	104	4	1976
4	2264 Robson Dr.	Mesa	98	3	1981
5	1720 Terrace Ave.	Tempe	110	5	1987
6	116 Mountain Dr.	Phoenix	130	5	1978
7	3101 Gilbert Rd.	Mesa	106	3	1980
8	1730 Brown St.	Phoenix	132	4	1983
9	2525 College Ave.	Tempe	115	5	1988
10	5150 Vista Dr.	Mesa	127	4	1985

c. Identifying categories of expenses incurred during business operations.

d. Identifying key aspects (e.g., salesperson) of a sales transaction.

8-14 Devise block codes for the following situations:

a. The courses at a university which has both undergraduate and graduate programs. (Each course is to be identified by the department prefix, such as ACC, followed by a number within the block code.)

b. The jersey numbers to be assigned to football players for a university (e.g., 10–19 for quarterbacks).

c. The major groups of accounts (e.g., assets) in a chart of accounts.

8-15 Devise combinational group codes for the following entities that contain at least three fields:

a. A checking account depositor in a national bank.

b. A patient admitted to a hospital.

c. A consumer of a gas and electric utility.

d. A project undertaken by a construction firm that builds highways, bridges, airports, apartment buildings, and so on.

8-16 Longevity Life Insurance Company of Omaha has 30,000 policyholders, each of whom has one life insurance policy type (e.g., term, ordinary life, endowment). It maintains a master file of policyholders on magnetic disk. Weekly it processes an average batch of 800 transactions (including both billings and payments) against the policyholder master file, in order to update the account balances. During the week policy clerks process via on-line terminals an average of 500 renewals, new policyholders, cancellations, and changes in policy type or status of policyholder data.

Required

a. Prepare a layout for a fixed-length record in the policyholder master file, incorporating a reasonable set of data items and including the mode of each data item. Identify the primary key and three secondary keys. Also specify the length of each field.

b. List needed data items in a fixed-length record that services both billing and payment transactions.

c. Describe the relative advantages of using ISAM versus random file structures for the master file.

d. Describe and illustrate codes that identify (1) each type of transaction and (2) each policy.

e. Briefly describe the data that might be contained in the following types of files useful to this application: (1) reference file, (2) history file, (3) report file, and (4) suspense file.

8-17 J. B. Means, a retail chain based in Buffalo, uses the following fixed-length master records to retain data concerning its charge customers:

Data Item	Field Size (Characters)
Account number	10
Customer name	35
Customer address	40
Customer zip code	5
Credit limit	10
Account balance, beginning of month	10
Account balance, current	10

These records are maintained in a sequential file on magnetic disk. Each day, the account balances are updated from sales and cash receipts transaction tapes; any customer whose balance exceeds the credit limit is listed on a credit notification report. At the end of each month the daily transaction tapes are merged and re-sorted; then they are used, together with the master records, to print the monthly statements to customers.

Required

a. Identify the likely primary key and at least three secondary keys in the foregoing master record.

b. Describe, with the aid of a system flowchart, the steps required to produce a report that lists customers, arranged alphabetically within zip codes; also, draw the report format.

c. Draw a monthly statement for a customer and enter sample data.

d. Draw a record layout for the master record. Key each data item in the master record to the printed item in the monthly statement. For instance, enter a circled A under the account number field in the record layout, and also a circled A next to the assumed value for the account number (e.g., 01234567) in the statement.

e. Draw a record layout for the transaction record, beginning with a transaction code field. Include in the record layout at least those data items that are to reflect the monthly account activity in the customer's monthly statement. Key each data item from the record layout to a like item in the monthly statement.

8-18 Resort Hotels, a luxury hotel chain in the Virgin Islands, recently computerized its front desk operations. It installed a software package that provides "management by exception" reports. These reports reflect only those activities that vary significantly from established plans. One report shows the variation of the actual room rates charged to guests from standard room rates. The columns in this report are, from left to right: room number, guest's name, type of room,

number of guests (adults, children), room rate (charged, standard), and comments. This particular report would be used by the front desk manager to be aware of pricing practices by the front desk personnel, and to approve or disapprove of specific cases.

Required

a. Two files that are needed to produce the described report are the guest master file and the guest/room cross-reference file. Name and briefly describe the contents of one or two other files that are needed.

b. Prepare record layout for the guest master file and guest/room cross-reference files, including the data items, assumed size of each field, and mode of each data item.

c. For the guest master file, specify a likely primary key and several secondary keys. Describe the use of a report that can be prepared by arranging the file data according to each identified key.

(SMAC adapted)

8-19 Down and Out is a not-for-profit organization in Victoria, British Columbia. Its accounting information system uses the general ledger to summarize and report variances between actual and budgeted amounts. The general ledger master file is actually split into two files: (1) a header file that contains relatively permanent data concerning each account in the chart of accounts and (2) a balance file that contains the total outstanding commitment, the budgeted amount, and the actual amount for each account. In addition, a general ledger transaction file contains transaction data pertaining to commitments and actual expenditures.

The following steps are involved in the expenditures procedure: When a purchase order is issued, the committed amount of the expenditure and the appropriate numbered general ledger account that it affects are recorded. After purchase orders have been batch processed, summary amounts for the accounts involved in the purchases are computed and entered onto the general ledger transaction file. Then the commitment balances in the general ledger master file are updated.

When supplier invoices are received, they are vouched and marked to reflect the accounts against which the amounts apply. Then the invoices are batch processed, and the summary amounts affecting each account are posted to the general ledger balance file. This updating step reduces the commitment balance and increases the actual expense balance.

For each of the 13 periods in the organization's fiscal year, the accounting manager receives a report summarizing each of the following: (1) the total commitment amount, (2) the actual expense amount, (3) the budgeted expense amount, and (4) the variance for each project in progress. Furthermore, another report is provided that shows a detailed breakdown of the expenses pertaining to each project.

Required

a. Prepare record layouts for the general ledger header file and balance file. Specify the primary key and two or more secondary keys for each.

b. Prepare a format of the summary report described.

(SMAC adapted)

Suggested Readings

Bodnar, George H., and Hopwood, William. *Accounting Information Systems*. 3rd. ed. Boston: Allyn and Bacon, 1987.

Boer, Germain. *Classifying and Coding for Accounting Operations*. Montvale, N.J.: National Association of Accountants, 1987.

Johnson, Mina M., and Kallaus, Norman F. *Records Management*. Cincinnati: South-Western, 1982.

Kroenke, David M. *Business Computer Systems: An Introduction*. 2nd ed. Santa Cruz, Ca.: Mitchell Publishing, 1986.

After studying this chapter, you should be able to do the following:

Describe the array of general controls and security measures that pertain to information systems, with particular emphasis on computer-based systems.

Describe the array of controls and security measures that pertain to the various application areas within a firm, with particular emphasis on computer-based systems.

Contrast the differences in controls and error-correction procedures needed for such alternative types of systems as batch processing systems and on-line processing systems.

Chapter **9**

ACCOUNTING CONTROLS AND SECURITY MEASURES

Built into a firm's information system and its environment is a control framework. This framework, introduced in Chapter 6, is often called the internal control structure. It has several objectives: to provide security for the firm's resources; to ensure the accuracy and reliability of the firm's data and information; to promote efficiency, including timeliness and economy, in the firm's operations; and to encourage adherence to management's prescribed policies and procedures. These objectives pertain whether processing is performed manually or by means of computers.

As we observed in Chapter 6, a control framework comprises numerous controls and security measures. Certain controls, such as good supervision, are unaffected by the mode of processing. However, "the nature of the internal accounting control procedures," including security measures, is influenced when the processing mode is changed from manual to computer-based.[1] New types of controls and security measures are necessary, and certain controls are altered.

Those accountants who serve as auditors and designers of computer-based information systems require specific knowledge. They should understand the impact of computer hardware and software on control frameworks. They should be aware of the

[1]AICPA, Statement on Auditing Standards No. 3, *The Effects of EDP on the Auditor's Study and Evaluation of Internal Control*, Sec. 321.09, as amended by SAS No. 48.

array of controls and security measures suitable to particular computer-based information systems. They also should be able to analyze complete transaction cycles, following transaction data as they progress (1) from source documents to summary reports and statements and (2) from manual processing steps to computerized processing steps.

Consequently, in this chapter we emphasize computer-based controls and security measures. When they differ significantly from manual controls and security measures, we note the differences. We further distinguish controls and security measures needed in batch processing systems from those applicable to on-line processing systems.

The following sections cover controls relating to the organizational structure, asset accountability, documentation, computer hardware and software, management practices, and transactions. Also included are sections pertaining to security measures and error-correction procedures. Most of the sections parallel the discussion under "Design Considerations Pertaining to Controls" in Chapter 6. As we recall, that arrangement corresponds with the broad classifications of (1) general accounting and administrative controls and (2) application or transaction controls.[2]

Organizational Controls

Because of the concentrated nature of computer-based processing, organizational independence is critical to a computer-based control framework. Organizational independence in computer-based information systems has two facets.

1. The segregation of responsibilities between user departments and the computer-based information systems function.
2. The segregation of responsibilities within the computer-based information systems function.[3]

Segregation of Responsibilities between Departments

The information systems (IS) function has responsibility for such tasks as processing data and controlling data during the processing activity. It should be organizationally independent of all departments that use data and perform the various operational activities of a firm. Thus, the information systems function likely would report to an independent manager such as an administrative vice-president, rather than to a functional manager such as the financial vice-president or marketing manager.[4]

Several activities should be performed *apart from* the computer-based data processing department and its parent information systems function. First, all transactions and changes to master records should be initiated and authorized by user departments, never by the data processing department, programmers, or related personnel. For instance, sales transactions should be initiated by the sales order department, even though the sales orders are processed and the sales invoices are printed within the data processing department. Second, the function involving the custody of assets (except data processing assets) should reside with designated operational departments. Thus, the merchandise

[2]These categories in turn correspond with the general controls and application controls proposed by the American Institute of Certified Public Accountants in *Statements on Auditing Standards (SAS) No. 1*, Section 320.34, as amended by SAS No. 48.

[3]Computer Services Executive Committee of the American Institute of Certified Public Accountants, *The Auditor's Study and Evaluation of Internal Control in EDP Systems* (New York: AICPA, 1977), p. 26.

[4]Possible locations of the information systems function within a firm are considered in Chapter 21.

to fill customers' orders should be stored within a warehouse department and transferred to a shipping department for delivery. Third, all transactional errors (except those originating during processing) should be corrected by user departments. Fourth, all new systems, changes to existing systems, and controls should be initiated by those managers or departments who will benefit and should be authorized by higher authority.

In some cases it may appear that complete segregation of these functions is not possible. For instance, when a computer-based system automatically approves an order from a customer, on the basis of credit guidelines built into a computer program, it may seem that the information systems function is performing the authorizing function. However, since the credit guidelines were established by credit management, rather than by information systems personnel, segregation can be viewed as adequate.

To summarize, the information systems function (which includes the data processing function) should *not* be assigned the following functions: the initiation and authorization of transactions or changes to master records; the initiation and authorization of new systems; and the custody of assets.

Segregation of Responsibilities within the IS Function

The information systems function has the overall purpose of providing information-related services to other departments within a firm. In many firms it has taken over the array of record-keeping and processing activities traditionally performed by the accounting function. To enhance organizational independence, it is therefore necessary to segregate several key responsibilities *within* the organizational structure of the information systems function. Figure 9-1 presents an organization chart that suggests a plan of segregation. Although each firm must tailor the organization of its information systems function to meet its particular needs and resources, Figure 9-1 is reasonably typical of medium-size firms.

The major segregation of responsibilities is between the systems development function and the computer-based data processing

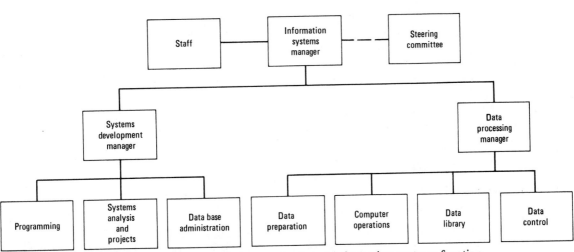

FIGURE 9-1 Organization chart for a typical computer-based information systems function.

function.[5] The **systems development function** is concerned with analyzing, designing, programming, and documenting the various applications needed by user departments and the firm as a whole. Not only is it responsible for new computer-based applications, but it must also make changes in existing applications as needed. Furthermore, systems development in a growing number of firms includes a data base administration function, which is responsible for the design and control of the firm's data base. A **data base administrator** (DBA) maintains the data dictionary, the data base management system, the utility programs that load data into the data base, and the controls related to the data base. On the other hand, the **data processing function** has responsibility for ensuring that transaction data are processed and controlled and the related files are properly handled.

The systems development function must be segregated from the data processing function for a very sound reason. If the same individuals had both (1) detailed knowledge of programs and the data base and (2) access to them, they could make unauthorized changes. In fact, the two functions must not only be segregated organizationally but also be separated physically. Systems analysts, programmers, and data base administrators should not be allowed to operate the computer or to have access to programs or the data base; computer operators and other data processing personnel should not have access to the documentation concerning programs or the data base. Preferably, the latter should not even understand programming.

Organization for Batch Processing

Figure 9-1 shows the organizational units within the data processing function that

are needed for computer-based batch processing applications.

The **data preparation function** prepares and verifies input data for entry into processing. The **computer operations function** processes data to produce outputs. It usually includes loading data into input devices, mounting secondary storage devices such as magnetic tapes and magnetic disk packs, and performing operations as prescribed by run manuals and computer console messages.[6] Although not strictly incompatible, these activities often are organizationally segregated in order to achieve greater efficiency and throughput.

The **data control function** or group serves as an interface between the various user departments and computer operations. It records input data (including batch totals where applicable) in a control log, follows the progress of data being processed, and distributes outputs to authorized users. Furthermore, the data control group maintains control totals pertaining to master files as well as transaction files and reconciles these totals to updated totals shown on exception and summary reports. Finally, it monitors the correction of detected errors by user departments. It is imperative for effective control that this data control group be organizationally independent of computer operations, since it helps to ensure that processing is performed correctly and data are not lost or mishandled. For instance, the data control group makes sure that computer operators do not attempt to correct detected errors or to balance to control totals. If the firm is suffi-

---

[5]The relationships between the information systems manager and (1) the staff and (2) the steering committee are discussed in Chapter 21.

[6]A *console* is the portion of the computer that allows communication between the operators and the computer (as well as between the maintenance engineers and the computer, when necessary). For instance, it logs jobs currently being processed, provides instructions to the operators for mounting tapes, and accepts instructions and responses from operators. Physically, the console generally consists of a visual display screen and keyboard; often, it also includes a hard-copy printout of the messages for review by the data control group and auditors.

ciently large, other data control groups may also be established within user departments or the accounting department to provide independent checks on the data processing function.

The **data library function** maintains a storage room, called the library, where the data files and programs are kept. A librarian issues these files and programs to computer operators or other authorized personnel when needed for processing activities and keeps records (often called logs) of file and program usage. The essential role of the data library function is to separate the custody of the information assets from those who process them and to prevent access by unauthorized persons. Thus, the function should be organizationally and physically segre-

gated from computer operations and other functions. Figure 9-2 shows the flow that takes place among these units when a batch of transactions is received from a user department by a data control section.

Organization for On-Line Processing

The organization for on-line processing applications tends to differ in two respects from that needed for batch processing. Since on-line processing applications often involve an integrated data base, the data base administrator becomes more important. On the other hand, the data control and data library tasks are often performed by the computer system hardware and software in the case of on-line processing applications, while data

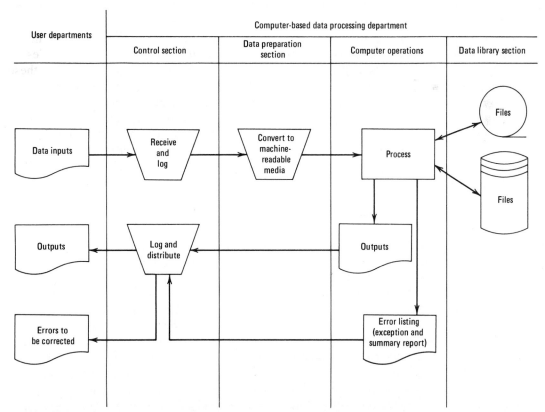

FIGURE 9-2 Flow of batched data within a computer-based processing organization.

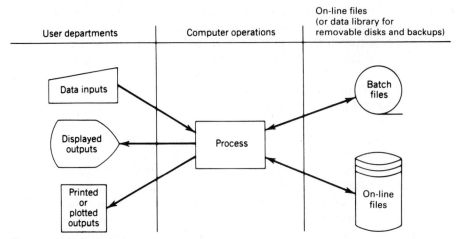

FIGURE 9-3 Simplified organizational separation in a computer-based system using on-line processing.

preparation is the responsibility of user departments. As Figure 9-3 suggests, the user departments enter the transactions via departmental terminals or microcomputers. The transactions are checked by edit programs for accuracy and then processed against on-line files. Outputs may be printed or displayed on printers, plotters, or terminals located in the departments of the recipients.

Organizational Controls in Manual Systems

In manual systems both transaction processing and operational activities are entirely performed by employees. Thus, organizationally separating the authorizing, record-keeping, and custodial functions is critically important. Chapter 6 provides several illustrations of this principle of organizational independence.

Two points worth remembering are (1) that almost all information systems involve a significant degree of manual processing and (2) that the organizational separation of the authorizing, record-keeping, and custodial functions is also important when processing is performed by computer-based systems.

Documentation and Asset-Accountability Controls

Documentation and asset-accountability controls are related, since they involve written evidence pertaining to the use and control of resources. Documentation controls are more heavily influenced by the mode of processing than are asset-accountability controls, since the former directly pertain to the information system facilities and the data they process.

Documentation

Documentation consists of narrative descriptions, flowcharts, lists, printouts, sample documents, and other explicit means of defining the objectives and features of an information system, as well as the manner in which it should perform. Standardized documentation aids the control framework, since it serves as a reliable source of information for those who must operate, improve, and evaluate the information system. Thus, it helps new employees to learn how to operate the information system, it enables systems analysts and programmers to establish a sound starting point when undertaking the design of a new system, and it provides reference materials for auditors during their examinations of the internal accounting control systems. Adequately documented systems or programs also can save a firm much time when a systems analyst or programmer leaves the firm. A new but experienced analyst or programmer can resume the project of the departed professional without starting over if documentation is up to date and up to standard.

Documentation of computer-based systems.

The categories of documentation that pertain directly to a computer-based information system are procedural, systems, program, operations, data, and user documentation. The contents within these categories tend to overlap, as the following descriptions indicate. Moreover, many variations are found in practice.

Procedural documentation defines the overall or master systems plan, operations performed by the system, documentation standards, systems analysis standards, programming standards, testing procedures, file labeling and handling procedures, computer operating standards, data definition standards, security standards, and so forth.

Systems documentation describes the purpose of a processing system and includes computer system flowcharts, input descriptions, output descriptions, file descriptions, error messages, and lists of controls. In addition, it assigns responsibility for performing each control and processing procedure and specifies error-correction procedures. Systems documentation is of primary interest to systems analysts, systems users, and auditors. For instance, documentation pertaining to the production processing system would be useful to systems analysts who are responsible for redesigning the production system and to such users as production control analysts. It would also be useful to auditors who are to evaluate controls within the production processing system.

Program documentation, such as the *program run manual,* describes the purpose of a program and includes program flowcharts, decision tables, program listings, control features, record layouts, input and output formats and samples, test data, testing results, operating instructions, and notations of program changes. Program documentation is of primary interest to programmers who are responsible for revising the program. In a data base environment, however, the DBA is also concerned about adequate program documentation. One responsibility of the DBA is to document the verbs in the data manipulation language (DML) that are allowed to alter data within the data base.

Operations documentation, such as the *console run book,* provides the operating instructions for a program, including required input and output files and units on which they are to be mounted, setup procedures, lists of program halts and messages and required actions, recovery and restart procedures after hardware or software malfunctions, estimated run times, and procedures for disposing of the outputs. Operations documentation is of primary interest to computer operators.

Data documentation, such as the *data dictionary,* defines data items contained within the data base. Data documentation is of primary interest to DBA's and auditors. It is also of interest to application programmers—but only insofar as it relates to the data items required by the programs that they write.

User documentation, such as the *user manual,* describes the purpose of a transaction processing system, procedures for entering data onto source documents, procedures for checking the accuracy of entered data, formats and uses of reports and other outputs, possible error messages, and error-correction procedures. User documentation, of course, is of primary interest to clerks, accountants, and others who directly use the inputs and outputs of a transaction system.

Sometimes it is combined with systems documentation.

Documentation should be accessible only to those who have legitimate needs. For instance, program run manuals should *not* be available to computer operators; data dictionaries should *not* be fully available to systems analysts, programmers, users, or operators.

Documentation of manual systems. Documentation for manual systems relates to the components described in Chapter 3: source documents, journals, ledgers, reports, document outputs, chart of accounts, audit trail references, processing device manuals, procedure manuals, and control lists. Because of the importance of organizational independence, formal organization charts and written job descriptions are desirable.

Since every information system includes portions that involve manual processing, it is apparent that every firm should include the preceding items in its collection of documentation. The majority of systems that employ computer-based processing would also incorporate the categories previously listed. In addition, every firm should prepare clear statements of management's policies.

Asset-Accountability Controls

As noted in Chapter 6, the controls that provide asset accountability include accounting subsidiary ledgers, acknowledgment procedures, reconciliations of physical assets with accountability records, and reassessments of asset values. These controls are as applicable to manual systems as to computer-based systems. However, computer-based systems can more easily maintain a variety of subsidiary ledgers. They can also perform quantitative reconciliations quickly and accurately. Thus, it is reasonable to expect the asset accountability controls to be applied more thoroughly and frequently in computer-based systems.

Hardware and Software Controls

Modern computer hardware and system software are equipped with a variety of built-in controls. These hardware and software controls or checks detect malfunctions of the equipment. Therefore, they assure the reliability of computations, manipulations, and transfers of data within a computer-based information system.

Hardware Checks

Typical built-in hardware checks such as the **parity check, echo check, read-after-write check, dual read check,** and **validity check** are described in Figure 9-4.

Other hardware controls also deserve brief recognition. **Duplicate circuitry** allows the arithmetic unit within the CPU to perform calculations twice and to check the results. **Scheduled preventive maintenance** programs provide periodic servicing of the computer system and hence reduce the likelihood of an unexpected system failure. **Diagnostic test routines** enable the computer system to be checked thoroughly for hardware weaknesses; when built into the hardware, such routines can automatically signal the impending failure of a component.

Software Checks

Among the controls generally incorporated in operating systems are the label check and the read–write check. The **label check** automatically notifies the computer operator of the contents of internal labels on such storage media as magnetic tapes and disks. (Internal labels are discussed in the following section.) The **read–write check** automatically halts a program when reading or writing is inhibited (e.g., when a printer runs out of paper) or initiates an end-of-file routine when no further processing of a file medium is possible (e.g., when the end of a magnetic tape reel is reached).

Type of Check	Description of Check in Use	Purpose of Check
1. Parity check	An added bit, called a parity or check bit, is attached when necessary to each binary coded character or message that enters or arises from computations within a computer system. As a result, all characters or messages contain either an even or an odd number of bits (depending upon whether the particular computer system is designed for even or for odd parity). For instance, the number 2 (a character having one bit in binary form) would have a bit added in an even parity system, whereas the number 3 (a character having two bits in binary form) would *not* have a bit added in the same system. Each time that characters or messages are moved within the system (e.g., from CPU to magnetic tape or disk storage, or from terminal via data communication lines to CPU), the parity of the characters or messages at the new location are compared with those at the original location. A difference in parity between the two locations indicates an incorrect transfer of data.	To verify each binary coded character or message when the character or message is moved within a computer system, in order to detect the loss or addition of bits.
2. Echo check	The CPU signals an input or output device concerning the appropriate mechanism to activate. An echoing signal is returned from the device to the CPU. For instance, the CPU signals a printer to activate the appropriate print hammers as each character is ready to be printed; the printer sends back a signal that the hammers in the proper print positions are activated.	To verify that the proper input/output device (e.g., card reader, printer, magnetic tape unit) is operating satisfactorily when needed.
3. Read-after-write check	A two-gap dual read/write head first writes data onto the storage medium and then immediately reads what was just written. If a comparison shows that the data written onto the storage medium differ from the data at the source of the transfer (e.g., the CPU or an input device such as optical scanner), the dual head backs up and rewrites. A read-after-write check is better than an echo check because recorded data, rather than an activating impulse, are checked.	To verify the accuracy of data written onto magnetic tape or magnetic disk storage.
4. Dual read check	An input device, such as a punched-card reader or magnetic tape drive, reads data from an input medium twice; it then compares the results of both read operations.	To verify that data have been accurately read.
5. Validity check	A device used to send or receive data within a system compares the bits of each coded character against a list of valid possibilities. For instance, the combination of holes read by a card reader is checked against those combinations of holes that comprise valid characters; bit configurations received via data communication lines are checked against valid bit combinations.	To verify that data are validly coded.

FIGURE 9-4 Typical hardware checks built into computer systems.

Operating systems and other system software are generally developed by computer manufacturers and software supply firms. Most computer-using firms purchase such software as packages. Accountants and systems analysts in computer-using firms can reasonably assume that the built-in software controls, like the built-in hardware controls, are sound and adequate. However, any changes made to system software after purchase may invalidate this assumption. Such changes should therefore follow the same change procedures as application programs.

Security Measures

Security is a very broad and complex area when a computer-based information system is involved. It encompasses not only the day-to-day protection of the computer hardware and software, but also the integrity of data, the privacy of data, the safeguarding of all physical facilities, and the avoidance of disastrous losses. Many of the security measures (also called security controls) attempt to prevent or detect unauthorized access to data, computer equipment, or other physical facilities. Other security measures are corrective in nature, since they enable losses of data or facilities to be recovered or reconstructed. Certain security measures are directed against accidents of nature, while others are intended to inhibit human acts. Some security measures are highly technical and sophisticated, especially when providing security for centralized data bases and data communications networks.

Security measures may be catalogued in a variety of ways. Our approach is to separate the measures into three categories: (1) those that provide security over all physical assets except the computer hardware, (2) those that provide security primarily for computer hardware facilities, and (3) those that provide security over data. Within each section the security measures are organized according to their main purposes. All of the security measures apply to computer-based systems. In a final section we consider differences among manual systems, computer-based batch processing systems, and computer-based on-line processing systems.

Security for Physical Assets

Most of the security measures in this category have the purpose of restricting access to unauthorized persons, generally to circumvent theft or acts of violence. The unauthorized persons might be nonemployees or employees of the firm that possesses the assets. Restrictive security measures include security guards, fenced areas, burglar alarms, closed-circuit television monitors, safes, locked cash registers, locked file cabinets, and lockboxes in post offices. Another measure that protects the *value* of physical assets is adequate insurance coverage. Employees having access to cash and negotiable assets, for instance, should be bonded. **Fidelity bonds** indemnify a firm in case it suffers loss from defalcations committed by covered employees. Still another measure is close supervision of employees who handle assets, such as mailroom clerks who open mail containing currency and checks.

Other security measures protect physical assets from disasters due to natural causes. Sprinkler systems are available to put out fires that may break out in the merchandise warehouse, for instance. A fireproof vault protects cash and valuable papers from fire and also serves to restrict access to unauthorized persons.

A third type of security measure protects assets from breakdowns and business interruptions. Preventive maintenance of such assets as automobiles, typewriters, production machinery, and other fixed assets is a prime example. When breakdowns occur (in spite of such maintenance or in its absence), business interruption insurance and backup equipment can provide support.

Security for Computer Hardware Facilities

The computer system and related equipment, such as off-line input–output devices, require protection from the same causes that afflict noncomputer physical assets. Many of the same types of security measures are useful, so some overlap is unavoidable.

Protection from unauthorized access. Physical access to the computer facilities should be restricted to authorized persons. Normally only such personnel as computer operators, librarians, supervisors, and information systems management should have authorized access to computer facilities.

Unauthorized persons, such as accountants, clerks, and visitors, should not have access to the computer facilities; otherwise, the hardware will be needlessly exposed to the risk of possible damage. Even systems analysts, programmers, and the DBA should be denied access. Although they might be less likely to damage the hardware accidentally, they would have the opportunity to alter programs and data with which they are familiar.

Among the available means of restricting access to computer facilities are (1) locked doors to the computer room, (2) security guards at strategic points, (3) closed-circuit television monitors at strategic points, (4) magnetic-coded cards that open doors to the computer room, (5) badges that identify personnel, and (6) alarms that sound illegal entry. As many of these may be employed as circumstances warrant.

When terminals are employed as a part of the information system, the restrictions on physical access must be modified. As we will see when discussing data security, it is necessary to allow data clerks, accountants, and others to have access to the system via terminals. However, it is feasible to limit their use to authorized activities, to specified terminals, and to designated time periods. For instance, programmers may be allowed only to use terminals to test programs, and they may be assigned specific test terminals to do so.

Terminals may also be physically restricted to nonclerical employees and non-employees. They should be disconnected and locked at the end of each working day, to render them secure against night custodial employees. They can be placed behind counters or locked doors, to keep them out of reach of visitors and unauthorized employees. In addition, they can be controlled by security software that detects all attempts to access the system and that locks a terminal after a specified number (say, three) of unsuccessful attempts; this measure should deter hackers and others who try to guess the passwords.

Protection from disasters due to nature. Computer facilities should be environmentally controlled and protected from fires, floods, power outages, sabotage, and so on. Sites that house the major facilities should be air conditioned and humidity controlled. They should be constructed of fireproof materials and contain a fireproof vault to serve as the data library. Smoke detectors and fire alarm systems should be installed, together with gas-based automatic extinguisher systems. Uninterruptible power systems are also very desirable. These auxiliary power supplies ensure that electrical power is continuously available and maintained within tightly regulated voltage limits.

Other measures may also be employed to protect against the adverse effects of disasters, whether due to nature or to human violence. Computer facilities can be constructed on high terrain that minimizes threats of floods. They can be placed in inconspicuous locations that are not inviting to possible vandalism or sabotage. Insurance coverage can be acquired to enable financial recovery in case of fire, flood, sabotage, and accidental error.

This array of protective security measures can be made more effective by careful planning, which entails the development of a **disaster contingency and recovery plan.** A plan of this type identifies potential threats to the computer system, specifies the needed preventive security measures, and outlines the steps to be taken in case each type of disaster actually strikes. The disaster plan also identifies the resources that must be protected and the available resources to minimize the disaster. Furthermore, the plan should assign responsibility for its implementation and provide for follow-up reviews.

The disastrous fire in the First Interstate Bank building (described in Chapter 6) offers a good example of planning. First Interstate had previously developed a business crisis/resumption plan. After conducting a risk analysis, senior management decided to allocate sufficient funds to planning for disasters. Each operating unit was required to prepare its own business resumption plan; however, a unit of six professionals was organized to provide assistance. Consequently, the firm was able to function effectively after the fire. Even though the securities trading floor was destroyed, for instance, traders were able to operate in temporary quarters the very next day.

Protection from breakdowns and interruptions. As in the case of the noncomputer facilities, the computer hardware facilities should be protected from breakdowns and interruptions. The disaster plan, if well developed, will specify the steps to take in case of emergencies. However, it must be implemented to be effective. The person who is to administer the plan should ascertain that a preventive maintenance program is put into effect and that adequate insurance coverage is acquired. In addition, he or she should make arrangements for backup system components (besides the backup power supply noted earlier). Thus, it might arrange with another firm having the same type of computer to use its facilities in case of breakdown. Alternatively, it might contract with a service bureau to obtain services in case of emergency. Another possibility, although an expensive one, is to maintain duplicate computer facilities on the premises. A less expensive approach is to acquire a computer system having the capability of "soft fallback" or "graceful degradation" in the face of hardware troubles—that is, it would be able to operate at lowered efficiency but with no loss of data until recovery is possible.

Security for Data

Data security refers to maintaining the integrity and privacy of data, a key resource of any firm. With respect to a computer-based information system, the data of primary concern include the data contained within (1) files stored off-line or on-line, (2) data structures stored in on-line data bases, and (3) the data dictionary. Data also include the application programs themselves, which are either (1) stored on magnetic tapes in the data library maintained by the librarian or (2) stored in an on-line library maintained by special data base software or by the operating system.

Data security measures in computer-based systems provide three types of protection: protection from unauthorized access to data, protection from undetected access and changes, and protection from loss or alteration of data. The measures providing these protections are thus preventive or detective in nature. Other measures are corrective, in that they enable lost data to be recovered.

Protection from unauthorized access to data. Restricting the access to data to authorized persons is extremely important. In addition, access restrictions help to achieve adequate separation of responsibilities among the various employees of a firm. The actual prevention of unauthorized accesses requires a wide variety of security measures, particularly when the accesses occur via terminals. Numerous barriers are needed because (1) the unauthorized persons may be either employees or outside parties and (2) the techniques for penetrating security are numerous and varied. For instance, a phone company needs not only to prevent outside private detectives and "hackers" from accessing its private telephone conversations and unlisted phone numbers but also prevent its own programmers or clerks from accessing confidential salary files. One such unauthorized person may use a random-number generator to search for codes that permit entry to the data base; another may "tap" the communications lines to gain access to transmitted data.

Two additional factors complicate the task of devising measures to control access to data. First, most persons granted access rights are authorized to access only a portion of the data base. For example, a bank may allow depositors to access their checking account balances, but will not want the depositors to browse within the data base for the balances of other depositors. The same bank may allow bank tellers to access account balances of depositors but will likely not want the tellers to access the loan accounts of the same depositors. The second complication exists because of the various types of accessing actions. Among the actions that might be taken are reading a record, changing data within a record, adding a new record, and deleting a current record. For instance, the bank may authorize its tellers to read and change data within a depositor's record but not to add or delete depositors' records.

Access restrictions with respect to data may be applied by such means as isolation, identification of authorized users, limitations on terminal usage, encryption, and destruction.

1. Isolation. Data that are confidential or critical to a firm's operations should be physically isolated in order to discourage unauthorized access. Thus, key reference files, confidential files, programs, and program documentation should be kept in a secured off-line or on-line data library when not in active use. In on-line processing systems the master files and the data sets of various users should be maintained in separate partitions on direct-access storage media and provided boundary protection. The data dictionary should be maintained, either off-line or on-line, under the control of the DBA; it should remain inaccessible to all others except high-level systems managers and auditors. Stocks of blank forms, such as blank checks, should be kept under lock and key.

Programs that are concurrently being executed in primary storage should also be isolated from one another in order to prevent intentional or accidental modifications. Program isolation is achieved by means of the memory protect feature of multiprogramming.

Programs being tested should be isolated from both the live programs currently in use (i.e., the production programs) and the live data base. This isolation may be achieved, without harm to testing effectiveness, by generating a separate copy of the data base for program testing.

2. Identification of authorized users. Authorized use and modification of data should be precisely established by key designated managers. Lists of authorized persons and the extent of their authorizations should be maintained by the DBA. Figure 9-5 shows a table of authorizations, broken down by user, file, and type of access.

Authorizations should be authenticated by sound identification techniques. When requesting access to data via on-line terminals, users may be required to enter passwords, badges, magnetic striped cards, or "smart" (e.g., chip or optical-scannable) cards. For instance, when a production employee is ready to record her time spent on a job, she inserts her badge into a badge reader (a type of terminal) to identify herself to the security system. More personalized techniques may be employed if the foregoing are abused, for example, when employees tape their current passwords to terminals or lend their badges to others. For example, users might be asked to answer prearranged sets of personally oriented questions (e.g., birthplace, spouse's middle name). Alternatively, users might be identified on the basis of electronic fingerprints or voice patterns.

Upon receiving identification data, the security software performs the authentica-

User number	User name	Inventory master file	Accounts payable master file	Purchase order file
1234	B. White	R		W
1286	P. Dane		RW	
1302	R. Rogers	RWCD		
1355	H. Powers		W	

Action codes:
R   Display (i.e., read) only
W   Write (e.g., update) only
RW Display and write
C   Create new record
D   Delete current record

FIGURE 9-5 An authorization table.

tion step by comparing the entered data against a stored authorization list, for example, a list of authorized passwords. In order to thwart hackers and other outside parties who may discover passwords and attempt to gain access from outside, the system may also employ a **callback procedure**—that is, the security software would automatically break the connection and dial back in order to verify that the person signing on is accessing the system from a terminal with an authorized number.

Of the available techniques for restricting access, the password technique is the most frequently employed. A **password** is a user authorization code. Usually at least two passwords are required to access desired data. The user first enters a unique user identification code, which allows him or her access to the system. Next, the user enters a password to gain access to a particular file. The security software then verifies, by reference to a stored authorization table (similar to Figure 9-5), that the user having the unique code first entered is authorized to use the designated file. If so, the user is allowed by the software to undertake the types of

actions (e.g., read, update) indicated in the table.

A password procedure is most effective when it provides precise and tight security. Both of these attributes can be enhanced by the tiered approach, that is, by increasing the number of levels of password protection. Figure 9-6 illustrates a three-level password system that can identify authorized users

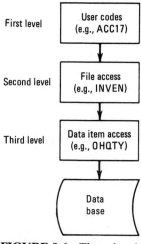

FIGURE 9-6 Three-level password security.

down to the level of data items. Gaining access to particular data items requires the use of three passwords in a specific sequence. Users who do not know all three passwords cannot gain access, that is, are locked out. (If they know the first two passwords, however, they will gain access in most such systems to all data in the file except the specially protected data items.) Security locks on individual data items are normally reserved for the most sensitive items (e.g., salary levels of individual employees or sales forecasts of individual product lines).

Passwords may be employed to restrict access to processing programs as well as data. For instance, a password assigned to an inventory control clerk may enable him to access the inventory updating program as well as the inventory master file. His supervisor, the inventory control manager, may be assigned a password that enables him to access the inventory adjustment program for the purpose of writing down the values of inventory items when necessary. While both passwords allow access to the same file, they restrict each user to the program related to his responsibilities.

Password secrecy can be tightened further by changing passwords frequently and by not displaying passwords as they are entered at the terminals by users.

3. Usage limitations. Devices as well as users may be restricted in various respects as to usage. Thus, terminals may be equipped with lockable keyboards so that they may be locked after working hours. Also, a particular terminal might be authorized to access data from certain files, to enter specified types of transaction data for processing against those files, to read but not to update files, and so on. Limitations such as these may be implemented by (1) assigning a number to each device (e.g., terminal) and (2) placing a device authorization table in online storage. Each time a user employs a particular terminal, the security software checks the device authorization table; if the termi-

nal's number appears in the table, the terminal is permitted to access the specified files and undertake the specified actions.

When used together, device authorization tables and user authorization tables provide an added degree of security. For instance, a warehouseman might learn the passwords for accessing the payroll master file from a friend in the accounting department. However, he cannot access the file from the warehouse terminal if adequate usage limitations are in effect.

4. Encryption. To counteract unauthorized tapping of communications lines, sensitive and confidential data may be protected by **encryption.** That is, data being entered at a remote terminal may be encoded, transmitted in coded form, and then decoded upon their arrival at the firm's home office. Being in coded form, the data would not be understandable to a wiretapper. Data may also be stored in coded form. Since coded data require time to be decoded before use, coding should be performed only on a selective basis.

5. Destruction. To counteract unauthorized browsing, confidential data should be destroyed deliberately after use. For instance, hard-copy printouts might be fed to paper shredders or disintegration machines before being discarded. Confidential data on magnetic tapes or disk packs should be erased after the results have been recorded elsewhere (unless the data include active account balances.) Moreover, nonconfidential data in records and master files should be purged when no longer needed.

Protection from undetected access and changes. Preventing unauthorized access is not sufficient. All attempts to access the computer system and all authorized access should be monitored. Unwarranted activity can thus be investigated and perhaps halted before security breaches are effected. Two types of logs facilitate this monitoring process. An **access log,** generally a component of the data base security software, records all attempts to access the data base. This log reflects the time, date, code of person attempting access, type of inquiry or mode of access, and data accessed (if the access is successful). The access log should be reviewed frequently by the DBA or internal auditor, in order to detect any unauthorized or excessive accesses. A **console log** records, through the assistance of the operating system, all actions of the computer system and its operators. For instance, it shows the requests and responses made by the computer operator during processing runs or activities. When displayed on a video display screen located near the CPU, the log can be helpful to the operator in determining the causes of program halts and in entering instructions or data to resume processing. A console log, in the form of a hard-copy printout, also enables a computer supervisor to determine when an operator may have made an unwarranted intervention during processing.

Changes to programs, files, and controls can be monitored by a **system and program change log.** A systems development manager would enter onto this log all unauthorized changes or additions to data, application programs, and data controls. These entries should be reviewed by an internal auditor for adherence to prescribed procedures for change.

Protection from loss or alteration of data.

A variety of logs, devices, hardware features, and software techniques are useful in preventing data loss or alteration.

Two logs provide monitoring controls over data and programs. A **data library log** is used by the data librarian to enter the files and programs checked out to computer operators for use in applications processing. This log traces the movements of the files and programs. It aids the librarian in reclaiming the files and programs from the operators promptly after processing, so that they can be returned to their fireproof repository. Another library log that monitors the on-line files and programs can be maintained by the computer system. A **transaction log** maintained by the system software in an on-line processing system records individual transactions as they are entered for processing. This log reflects all entered and edited data; it also provides a key part of the audit trail in an on-line processing system, especially if the data have not been previously recorded on source documents. Included in the log would be the number of the terminal through which the transaction is entered, the time entered, the identification number of the person entering the data, the identification number of the person or entity affected by the transaction, the transaction code, and the amount involved. For added identification the system software generally assigns a number to each transaction. Furthermore, a hard-copy listing of the transaction log should be obtainable at any time.

A **tape file protection ring** provides protection to a reel of magnetic tape. Only when it is inserted into the reel can the magnetic tape be written on; when the ring is removed, the data on the tape are protected from accidental writeovers.

External and internal file labels provide protection to either a reel of magnetic tape or a disk pack. An **external file label** is a gummed-paper label attached to a physical storage unit, such as a tape reel, to identify its contents. An **internal file label** is a message stored on a physical storage medium in computer-readable form. An *internal header label,* the first record in a file stored on magnetic tape or a direct-access storage device, contains the name and number of the file, the date it was created, and other identifying data. Before allowing a computer program to use data from the file in processing steps, the operating system checks the header label to be sure that the file is specified by the program. If not, the operating system alerts the computer operator via the computer console. An *internal trailer label,* the last record in a file, contains an end-of-file code plus control totals and record counts that pertain to data in the file. These totals and counts can be checked by the program to assure that all data have been processed and that none have been lost.[7] The details of internal labels should be described in program documentation.

Read-only memory (ROM), a type of storage from which data can only be read, provides security to the operating system, key programs, and critical data sets. Any software and data stored in ROM cannot be altered by new instructions, nor can new data be added. Thus, instructions stored in ROM are safe from unauthorized tampering by a programmer, operator, or other person who might access the system.

Special protective measures are needed in the presence of a data base, since multiple users and programs often access the stored data simultaneously. One necessary measure, called **lockout,** prevents two programs from accessing the same data concurrently. In effect, one of the programs is held in abeyance until the other program has completed its action (e.g., updating a record). If both of the programs were allowed to update the same record at the same time, it is likely that one set of data would be written over and lost.

Reconstruction of lost data. In spite of sound security measures, abnormal events sometimes occur. Perhaps the hardware malfunctions, a fire or other natural disaster sweeps through the computer-based data

[7]Header and trailer labels are most suitable for sequential files. When data are stored in a nonsequential manner on direct-access storage devices such as magnetic disks, only internal file labels similar to the header label are employed.

processing facility, or a computer operator makes a serious error. When such events cause data to be lost, there must be a means of prompt reconstruction. Therefore, it is necessary to maintain **data backup** (i.e., duplicate copies of data files, data bases, programs, and documentation). These backup copies should reflect all changes made in program and documentation, as well as the up-to-date status of the files. At least one set of backup copies should be stored at a location that is physically removed from the computer facilities. There also should be a definite policy concerning how long such data backup is to be retained.

Since files and data bases are changed frequently by newly received data, their backup and reconstruction require the most attention. Various data file and data base backup plans have been devised, depending on whether the data are stored on magnetic tape or magnetic disks.

The backup procedure generally used with magnetic tape files is known as the **grandfather-father-son approach.** Figure 9-7 pictures this approach for the situation in which the processing cycle is one day in length. Over a three-day period three generations of master files would be generated. All three generations of master files would be retained during this period, together with the transaction files. Furthermore, one generation would be kept at a site remote from the computer facility. If the ''son'' file were destroyed or if during later use it was found to contain errors, it could be reconstructed by rerunning the ''father'' file against the transaction file for today. If both the son and father files were destroyed, they could still be reconstructed by use of the ''grandfather'' file and the last two days of transaction files. Note that during tomorrow's processing run the grandfather file may be released to create tomorrow's son file.

A different backup procedure is necessary for a data base stored on magnetic

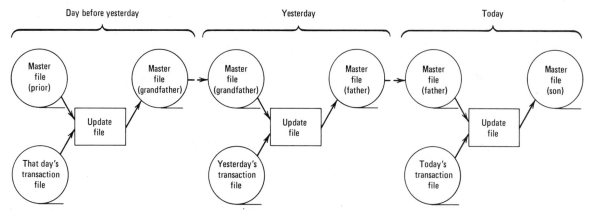

FIGURE 9-7 Grandfather-father-son approach to magnetic tape file backup. From Robert McLeod, *Management Information Systems* (Science Research Assoc., 1979). Reprinted by permission of the publisher.

disks.[8] The contents of the data base are duplicated (dumped) periodically onto a backup medium. As Figure 9-8*a* illustrates, the data base may be dumped at the end of each workday onto magnetic tape. (In an increasing number of computer installations, magnetic tape is used solely as a backup medium). In addition, an activity log is maintained on a continuous basis. The activity log contains images ("snapshots") of the items in the data base that are changed by each transaction, plus the time of the transaction, the files affected, and other useful data. For each item changed it shows both the value *before* the change and the value *after* the change. Since a single transaction may change (e.g., update) more than one file or data structure, an activity log is needed to provide links from the backup file to the current status of the "live" data base.

The backup file of the data base and the activity log are stored at a site remote from the computer facility. If the data base is later discovered to contain erroneous data, if data are lost, or if the storage media are damaged

---

[8]One exception to this statement should be noted. In those relatively rare cases where removable magnetic disk packs are employed with batch processing applications in lieu of magnetic tapes, the grandfather-father-son backup procedure may be used.

or shut down, these two backups generally enable the data base to be reconstructed. The transaction log, discussed earlier, also can be employed in the reconstruction process if errors are found in the activity log.

Reconstructing a data base depends on the damage incurred. If all or part of the data base is lost, its recovery involves a **rollforward** procedure. As shown in Figure 9-8*b*, this procedure begins with the most recent backup version being loaded onto a new magnetic disk. Then the images from the activity log (and the transaction log data, if necessary) are processed against the backup version. When all intervening transactions have been processed, the data base should be restored to its proper current state.

On occasion certain data in a data base may become invalid, perhaps because an updating program containing "bugs" has been used. In such cases the recovery of a valid data base involves a rollback procedure. **Rollback** consists of removing the effects of erroneously processed transactions from the affected records and files in the data base. Then the activity log is used to restore the data base to its proper current state.

A recovery procedure useful for application programs involves the use of checkpoints. **Checkpoints** are points in a batch pro-

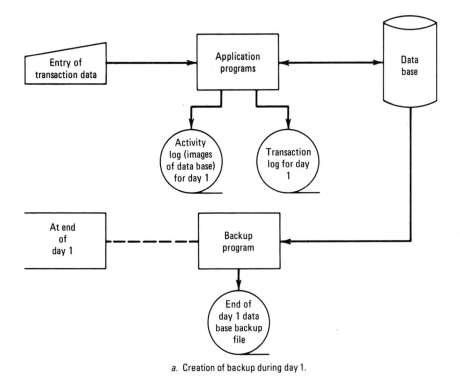

a. Creation of backup during day 1.

b. Reconstruction of data base after failure in day 2.

FIGURE 9-8 A backup and reconstruction file for a data base system.

cessing program at which snapshots are taken of the values of all data items and program indicators. For instance, snapshots might be taken every 10 minutes during the running of an inventory processing program and transcribed onto a backup magnetic tape. If a temporary hardware failure occurs during the run, the processing can be resumed at the last checkpoint. Thus, recovery from a failure can be achieved in a shorter time than if the program had to be restarted at the beginning.

This concludes the lengthy list of security measures. Figure 9-9 summarizes the identified security measures for the major

categories of physical assets, computer hardware facilities, and data. The measures are grouped according to the several purposes that they serve.

Differences among processing modes. Security measures for manual systems are

Purpose of Security Measures	Physical Assets in Both Manual and Computer-Based Systems	Hardware Facilities of Computer-Based Systems	Data in Computer-Based Systems
1. Protect from theft or access by unauthorized persons	Security guards Fenced areas Burglar alarms Television monitors Safes and vaults Locked cash registers Lockboxes Close supervision Insurance coverage Logs and registers	Security guards Television monitors Locked doors Locked terminals Inaccessible terminals Employee badges Passwords Segregated test terminals	Locked doors, terminals, blank checks Off-line data library On-line data and program storage partitions Encoded data Paper shredders Passwords Limited terminal functions Automatic lockouts Callback procedures
2. Protect from natural environment or disasters	Sprinkler systems Fireproof vaults	Air conditioning Humidity controls Fireproof vaults Halon gas spheres Auxiliary power supplies Insurance coverage Prudent locations Disaster contingency plans	
3. Protect from breakdowns and business interruptions	Preventive maintenance Backup equipment Insurance coverage	Preventive maintenance Backup hardware systems Graceful degradation Insurance coverage	
4. Protect from loss or alteration			Read-only memory Tape file protection rings External file labels Internal file labels Transaction logs Data library logs Lockouts
5. Detect attempted access or change			Access logs Control logs System and program change logs
6. Reconstruct lost files			Backup procedures Rollback and recovery procedures

FIGURE 9-9 List of selected security measures for physical assets, computer facilities, and data.

considerably fewer in number than those needed for computer-based systems. The same measures apply both to the physical assets and to data in manual systems, and of course no computer hardware facilities exist in manual systems.

The security measures that are particularly suited to computer-based batch processing systems include the data library log, system and program change log, console log, tape file protection ring, internal file labels, external file label, grandfather-father-son backup procedure, and checkpoint recovery procedure.

The security measures that are unique to computer-based on-line processing systems include the on-line transaction log, on-line data library log, lockout feature, memory protection and boundary protection features, lists of authorized users, passwords, computer-readable badges, usage restrictions on terminals, and data base backup procedure.

Management Practice Controls

Management practice (procedural) controls were described in Chapter 6. Because of their importance, we focus in the following sections on sound procedures relating to computer-based information systems.

Procedures for Change

Changes in a computer-based information system generally pertain to application programs or to the schema of the data base. Both types of changes should follow clearly defined and sound procedures to prevent unauthorized and undesirable manipulations.

If the change pertains to an application program, it should be initiated by a user-department manager, who explains the needed change in writing. The requested change should next be approved by an appropriate management committee or individual manager. Systems development personnel then

undertake the redesign of the program. (Changes should never be made by the DBA or by data processing personnel such as computer operators.) They should use a working copy of the program rather than the "live" version currently in use. Then they should revise the documentation. Each change should be tested jointly by (1) the user, (2) a member of the systems function who is independent of the person making the change, and (3) an internal auditor. Finally, the documented change and test results should be approved by a manager within the information systems function and formally accepted ("signed off") by the user who initiated the change.

If the change involves the data base, the preceding segregation of responsibilities is even more important. Moreover, approval should be required by all major users who will be affected by the change. Documentation concerning the change should be reviewed by the DBA prior to submission to the user-managers for approval.

Procedures for New System Development

The design and development of new computer-based applications require controls similar to those needed for program and data base changes. Each request for a new development should either be initiated by a user-department manager or higher-level manager, depending on its scope, and authorized by an appropriate management committee. Assume, for instance, that a new automated credit approval system is desired. The credit manager could initiate the request, which would then be authorized by a computer-system steering committee. The user-department and systems development personnel next work together to clarify information needs, to define system requirements, and then to develop necessary system design specifications. After implementing the designed system, they should jointly test all portions of the system, manual as well as computerized. Finally, the documentation concerning the design and tests should be reviewed and approved by the manager of the user department.

Project controls should be employed during the course of each system change and new development. These controls, as well as additional details concerning system development controls, are described in Chapters 21 and 25.

Computer Operating Procedures

Sound computer operations are based on close supervision, careful planning, and ongoing control procedures. Therefore, supervisory personnel, such as the manager of data processing and shift supervisors, should actively observe and review the actions of computer operators. Procedural manuals concerning all aspects of computer operations, part of the overall documentation, should be provided to the computer operators together with the appropriate console run books. *Data processing schedules* should be prepared as far in advance as feasible and revised as necessary. A variety of control reports should be prepared daily or weekly. Suggested reports include: (1) computer facilities *utilization reports,* which reflect the productive and nonproductive uses of equipment; (2) employee *productivity reports,* which reflect the activities of computer operators and other data processing personnel; and (3) computer *processing run-time reports,* which reflect the throughput. To be most effective, these control reports should compare actual times against standard times. For instance, the last-named report can compare actual run times, as shown in the console log, against standard times shown in the data processing schedule.

Routine computer operating procedures should include control aspects whenever possible. For instance, computer program runs should minimize the number of operator actions and interventions in order to reduce the chance of human errors. A start-up routine should be run daily in order to locate possible data errors in the data base. Preventive diagnostic programs should be employed to monitor the hardware and software functions, so that existing or potential problems may be detected.

Personnel Procedures

Sound personnel procedures can significantly help to achieve and maintain data integrity. As noted in Chapter 6, employees should be carefully selected, well trained in their responsibilities, and imbued with a concern for adequate control and security. Operations personnel such as computer operators should be rotated among jobs and shifts and required to take vacations. Two operators should be on duty in the computer facility during processing. If this is not feasible, supervision should be especially close and fidelity bonds perhaps required. When employees leave the firm, for whatever reason, their passwords should be immediately invalidated, their badges taken up, and so on.

Managerial and Evaluative Procedures

Higher-level management must participate in the establishment of controls and security measures. To assure that the controls and security measures remain adequate and are followed, management should establish several key monitors.

Two important monitors are (1) an information systems steering committee and (2) an internal audit group. Both should be organizationally independent of the information systems function. Their composition and responsibilities are discussed in Chapters 21 and 17, respectively.

Other monitors should function within the information systems function. The DBA represents an increasingly important monitor to many firms, since the DBA's responsibilities typically include review and approval of (1) additions of data items to the data base, and (2) modifications to data base software. Another monitor worth considering is a security administrator. The responsibilities of this person would include (1) devising a plan for security of data and facilities, including provisions for backup, and (2) investigating security lapses and violations.

Differences between Computer-Based Processing Modes

In batch processing systems the emphasis is placed on data processing schedules and various processing control reports. Other than users, the programmer is the key person involved in the change procedure.

In on-line processing systems the emphasis is placed on reports concerning such matters as terminal usage. In addition to users and programmers, the DBA is likely to be a key person in change procedures.

Transaction Controls

Transaction controls, often called application controls, have the overall objective of providing reasonable assurance that transactions are legitimately authorized and accurately recorded, classified, processed, and reported. They are generally grouped according to input controls, processing controls, and output controls. This subdivision is illustrated in Figure 9-10.

Figure 9-10 also identifies **control points,** junctures within a transaction processing system where specific controls are needed. For instance, the point at which a transaction is first recorded represents a control point. Each type of transaction has a unique pattern of control points. Thus, the control points for a cash receipts transaction differ in certain

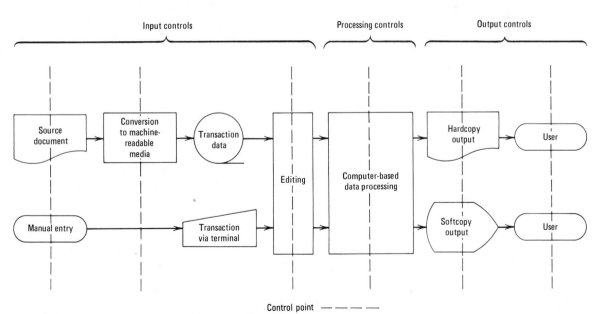

FIGURE 9-10 The categories of transaction (application) controls and typical control points.

specifics from those for a purchases transaction.

Input Controls

The purposes of **input controls** are the same for computer-based processing systems as for manual processing systems: to ensure that valid transaction data are completely and promptly recorded and that all erroneous data are detected, corrected, and resubmitted for processing. Thus, sound input controls should detect such errors as omitted employee time records, omitted customer numbers and order quantities on sales orders, and unreasonable order quantities on sales orders. Input controls also ensure, where necessary, that all captured data are accurately transmitted over communication lines and converted into computer-sensible form.

Input controls are important to all computer-based information systems. Errors can be corrected more easily in the input stage. Also, by correcting errors at the point of entry, the data used in processing and stored in files should be error free. These considerations are especially critical for systems employing on-line processing, since errors are quickly spread throughout such systems and can be quite difficult to detect after leaving the input stage. A single erroneous transaction, for instance, can affect several files and cause both output documents and managerial reports to be incorrect. It might also cause undesired actions. For example, an erroneously large quantity on a sales order may cause the quantity on hand for that item to drop below the reorder point. If an automatic purchasing procedure is built into the firm's information system, this situation will lead to the preparation of a purchase order—even though sufficient goods may actually be on hand.

Input controls are logically grouped according to the data collection steps. Thus,

we will discuss controls pertaining to authorizing, recording, batching, converting, editing, and transmitting data.

Authorization of transactions. Although authorization controls are based on the concept of organizational independence, they may also be included within the input control group. Two types of authorizations are employed: general and specific. The two types were contrasted in Chapter 6.

Authorizations are typically given early in the input stage. In the case of manual and computer-based batch processing systems, authorizations may appear as signatures, initials, or stamps on transaction source documents.[9] In the case of on-line processing systems, they may assume such forms as codes (e.g., passwords).

Authorizations should be verified before processing proceeds. When transactions are entered in batches for computer processing, the data control clerks would review the batched documents. When transactions are entered on-line via terminals, perhaps without the support of source documents, authorizations should be verified by the computer system. The generally adopted computer verification procedure involves the use of passwords. If a user provides the proper passwords, he or she is assumed by the system to be authorized to enter the forthcoming transactions, changes, or other data. As mentioned earlier, this general authorization procedure can be tightened by (1) restricting the types of data that each particular terminal is authorized to accept and (2) logging all attempted accesses by users into the system.

New variations of computer verification are becoming available. One familiar example involves credit checking. A customer's

---

[9]In some cases, such as disbursement checks, the authorization signature is applied near the end of the processing stage.

credit card is inserted into a scanning device, which reads and transmits the credit card number to a credit data center. The center responds by returning a signal. If the customer is within his or her credit limit, the signal turns on a green light at the device. If the credit limit is exceeded, however, the signal turns on a red light.

Recording of transactions. Transaction data are recorded onto source documents in all manual systems and most computer-based processing systems. To minimize errors in recording data, the source documents should provide carefully structured formats. Block spaces should be provided for key data items. Codes, such as account numbers and transaction codes, should be widely employed in order to reduce the quantity of input data. Furthermore, turnaround documents, bar codes, and other computer-readable inputs should be used whenever feasible.

In certain applications the transaction data are entered directly via on-line terminals. For instance, a sales clerk in an auto brake service firm may enter a work order at the counter, on the basis of data supplied verbally by a customer. Among the features that can be used to minimize input errors are

1. Menu screens that allow the data entry clerk to select the appropriate transaction screen by simply entering a number or letter code.

2. Preformatted screens that display formats of input documents or a series of prompting questions.

3. Scanners, badges, or prepunched cards that enter product codes, employee numbers, and so on.

4. Automatic entry of certain data items by the computer system. In the entry of a sales order, the data entry program can assign the number of the sales order and can insert the transaction date. When the clerk enters the number of the customer, the program can retrieve and enter the customer's name and billing address from the customer master file.

5. Printed documents that reflect the entered transactions. These documents provide visual verification of the entered data and serve as key links in the audit trail.

Batching of transaction data. Control totals should always be computed and maintained for transactions processed in batches. The batching procedure is detailed in Figure 9-11. First, a clerk runs batch totals on an adding machine tape. Next the clerk prepares a prenumbered batch transmittal sheet, such as appears in Figure 9-12. Then the clerk forwards the batched documents and transmittal sheet to the data control section. There a control clerk logs the batch number and control totals on a **batch input-output control log.** This log enables transactions to be traced from their point of receipt or preparation into the computer operations area; its use helps to prevent unauthorized data from being introduced, to prevent authorized transactions from being lost, and to foster the audit trail.

After the transaction data from the source documents have been keyed and verified, the newly computed totals are checked against the batch control totals originally calculated. (This comparison should either be made by a supervisor or a control clerk.) The transaction file is then processed in computer operations.

All outputs from processing are returned to the control section, which enters the batch in the control log as completed. It also verifies that the totals derived from computer operations agree with the batch control totals originally calculated. This verification consists of checking the exception and summary report, on which the computer will have printed the control totals. If a discrepancy exists, the control section must investigate

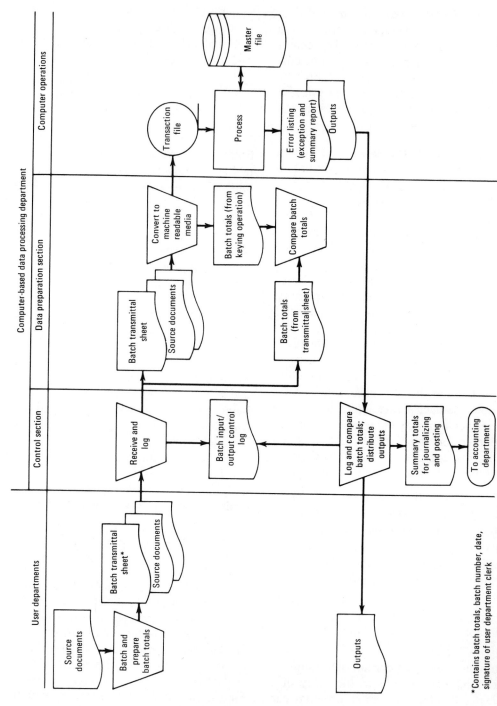

FIGURE 9-11 A document flowchart showing the uses of batch controls within a computer-based data processing system.

*Contains batch totals, batch number, date, signature of user department clerk

BATCH TRANSMITTAL SHEET

Batch No. 175

Date _____

Originating Dept. Code

Transaction data type

Number of documents

Name of field	Type of total	Control total

Prepared by:	Approved by:	Logged by:	Verified with totals from data preparation by:

FIGURE 9-12 A batch transmittal sheet.

for unprocessed or incorrectly processed transactions.

Often a computer is programmed to print the difference between the two sets of totals.[10] A nonzero difference would then indicate a discrepancy. For example, assume that the precomputed total is 362589, and the following appears at the bottom of the exception and summary report:

```
BATCH TOTAL FROM TRANSMITTAL SHEET    362589
TOTAL COMPUTED DURING PROCESSING      361076
          DIFFERENCE                     1513
```

[10]In addition to comparing differences between the two sets of totals, the computer can be programmed to check the sequence of batch numbers and to print out numbers of missing batches.

The difference of 1513 must be resolved before the outputs can be released.

When differences have been resolved, the control section distributes the outputs to the user departments. It also transmits summary transaction totals for posting to the general ledger. For instance, several payroll and labor distribution registers are generated during payroll and labor time processing. The originals of these registers are forwarded to the payroll and timekeeping departments, the user departments in this application. In addition, copies of these registers are also sent to the general ledger department for posting.

The three types of totals used in the control of batches are

1. An **amount control total,** the total of the values (e.g., dollars, hours, units) in an

amount or quantity transaction data field.

2. A **hash total,** the total of the values (e.g., employee numbers, transaction codes) in an identification data field.

3. A **record count,** the total of the source documents, and hence transactions, being processed in a batch.

The amount control total and record count have intrinsic meanings. Thus, an amount control total drawn from the hours-worked field of employee time records reflects the total hours worked by the employees represented in the batch. On the other hand, a hash total (e.g., the total of all employee numbers in a batch of time transactions) has no intrinsic meaning; it is simply the total of a "hash" of identification numbers.

Several batch control totals should normally be computed for each batch of transactions. For a batch of sales transaction documents, for example, five totals might be computed: the total quantity of items ordered, the total dollar sales amount, the total of the customers' numbers, the total of the unit prices of all items ordered, and the total count of sales transaction documents. On the other hand, batch control totals should be limited in number. They should be applied only to those data items whose undetected errors could cause serious control problems.

As Figure 9-11 illustrates, totals for a batch of transactions are recomputed during successive processings of a batch. Thus, they assure that transactions are not lost. In addition, during an updating run they ensure that the amounts from all the transactions in the batch are posted correctly. However, they *cannot* assure that the amounts are posted to the proper records (e.g., to the proper general ledger accounts). The latter function can be performed only by means of an appropriate programmed edit check, to be discussed later.

Batch control totals need not be limited to transaction documents. They may also be applied to master files. Thus, in the customer accounts receivable master file the total of all account balances represents an amount control total. In addition, the total of all customer account numbers is a hash total, and the total number of master records in the file is a record count. Batch control totals pertaining to a master file are normally stored in the trailer label of the file.

Batch control totals are generally not applicable to on-line processing systems. However, balance controls, akin to batch control totals, should be developed whenever possible. In a savings and loan firm, for instance, the daily deposits and withdrawals entered from a particular terminal or branch can provide balance controls. Thus, the amounts deposited today via terminal 45 can be accumulated by a computer program and the total printed out at the end of the day. This balancing total can then be reconciled to today's total deposits shown on deposit slips (the application's source documents) collected by the terminal's teller.

Conversion of transaction data. In batch processing systems the transaction data are converted off-line. In on-line processing systems the data are generally "converted" by keying directly from source documents into the computer system. Whichever process is employed, conversion is often a major source of errors.

Converted transaction data therefore need to be verified. One type of verification is visual in nature. **Visual verification** may consist of comparing printed listings of the keyed transaction data or visual displays of the entered transaction data against the source documents. Another type of verification, called **key verification,** consists of re-keying the data and comparing the results of the two keying operations. Preferably, key verification is performed on special verifying keyboards by operators other than those who do the original keying. Errors are indicated by lights or some other means of signaling.

Since key verification is an expensive and nonproductive process, only critical fields (e.g., customer numbers, sales amounts) are typically verified.

Editing of transaction data. The numerous transactions entering a computer-based system normally do not undergo the close scrutiny of trained clerks. In fact, many of the transactions are likely to be originated by persons for whom data entry is not a primary duty. For instance, a storeskeeper in a remote warehouse may enter shipping transactions, or a nurse in a remote hospital ward may enter data based on readings of patients' conditions. Hence, some of the entered transactions may be presumed to contain errors or omissions.

Fortunately, the logical capabilities of computer systems enable a wide variety of input errors to be detected. Thus, each computer-based transaction processing system should incorporate logical data error-detecting edit tests. The editing procedure has the purpose of screening *all* incoming data against established standards of validity. Those data that pass all edit tests are viewed as being valid and are then admitted to processing. Those data that fail one or more edit tests are viewed as being invalid and are diverted into the error-correction procedure.

Because of the severe problems caused by errors reaching the processing stage and beyond, edit tests should be applied as early as possible. In batch processing systems an edit program is generally run, often in combination with a conversion run, just after the data are batched. In on-line processing systems each transaction is generally edited as soon as it is entered at a terminal. However, not all edit tests can be applied in the input stage. Certain tests must be deferred until immediately after a required step has been performed. For instance, a test for correct sequence must wait until after the transaction data have been sorted. A test to determine that the correct master record has been updated cannot be applied until after updating occurs.

Edit tests are often called **programmed checks** because they are validation programs built into application and system software. A variety of programmed checks are applied in a typical transaction processing system, such as the internal label and control total checks already noted. The **validity check** is a test to see that an entered code (e.g., customer number, transaction code) appears in a stored list of authorized and valid codes. The **field check** is a test to see that the characters entered into a particular field (e.g., a product code field) all consist of the mode assigned to that field (e.g., numeric). The **limit check** is a test to see that an entered quantity (e.g., hours worked this week) does not exceed a preestablished limit. The **relationship or logical check** is a test to see that entered items of data (e.g., a sales territory number and salesperson number) are compatible or in a logical relationship. Additional programmed checks include the sign check, matching check, cross-foot balance check, and check digit. These checks and others are specifically described and applied in Chapters 11 through 15, which concern the various transaction cycles.

However, because of its usefulness and relative complexity, we might examine the check digit at this point. The check digit, or **self-checking digit,** is a redundant digit added to an identification number for the sole purpose of detecting incorrectly recorded numbers. Assume, for instance, that a sales order clerk transposes two digits in a customer number, writing 3758 instead of 3578. If a self-checking digit were incorporated into the number, the error should be detected by the edit program when the number is entered into the computer system.[11]

[11]As in the case of batch control totals, the self-checking digit should be applied sparingly. It is normally used only with those data items (e.g., customer numbers) whose accuracy is critical, since it requires additional computations and storage space.

An illustration involving employee numbers should clarify the mechanics of the self-checking digit. At present all employee numbers in our firm are four digits in length. To each employee number we are to add one self-checking digit so that it becomes a five-digit number. To determine the value of the self-checking digit for each particular employee number, we apply an algorithm based on the digits in the employee number itself. (For instance, we might multiply the digits in 8463 by separate weighting factors of 5, 4, 3, and 2, respectively, and then sum the products. Next we might subtract the sum, 80, from the next-higher multiple of 11—88—to obtain a self-checking digit of 8.) The original employee number with the added digit now becomes the new employee number (e.g., 84638). Each time this new number is entered into the computer system, it is validated by the edit program. Validation consists of *recomputing* the self-checking digit, using the same algorithm by which it was predetermined, and then comparing the result to the keyed-in value. If the algorithm is sound, this procedure should detect most types of keying errors.[12]

Numerous variations of programmed checks are employed by real-life firms. One variation combines the concepts of the self-checking digit and the relationship check. Thus, each customer number may include a digit that represents the sales territory within which he or she resides. If the customer were assigned the number 37216, the 6 might represent the sales territory. Each sales order received from this customer would be checked to see that the last digit of the entered customer number agreed with the sales territory number entered elsewhere in the transaction data.

---

[12]Some algorithms are more efficient than others, however. See Ron Weber, *EDP Auditing: Conceptual Foundations and Practice*, 2d ed. (New York: McGraw-Hill, 1988), pp. 385–387.

Transmission of transaction data. Transaction data must often be transmitted from the point of origin to the processing center. Increasingly, transmission involves the use of data communications facilities. In these cases, all of the programmed checks noted earlier are necessary. Certain additional programmed checks, such as those described in the following paragraphs, should also be considered.

The **echo check** consists of transmitting data back to the terminal for comparison with the transmitted data. For instance, a sales transaction just entered at a branch sales office terminal would be displayed on the CRT screen for the sender to verify visually. Additional data could be provided to aid the verification. For instance, if the customer number is entered, the system could be programmed to retrieve the customer's name and address from the master file and display them on the screen.

The **redundancy check** requires that the sender enter additional items of data to enable the accuracy of the transmitted data to be checked. In the case of a sales transaction, the sender might enter the first few letters of a customer's last name in addition to the customer number. The system could then be programmed to verify that the two data items match; if not, a signal could be flashed to the sender.

The **completeness check** consists of verifying that all required data have been entered. If the sender of a sales transaction, for instance, omitted the number of an ordered item of merchandise, the system could be programmed to notify the sender. A related transmission control consists of identifying each message transmitted from a terminal with a message number, the terminal number, and the date. This transmission control allows a sequence of messages to be checked for completeness and summary totals to be accumulated for each terminal.

Processing Controls

Controls over computer-based processing of transactions should assure that the data are processed accurately and completely, that the proper files and programs are involved, and that all transactions and records can be easily traced. **Processing controls** can be grouped under the categories of processing logic checks, run-to-run controls, file and program checks, and audit trail linkages.

Processing logic checks. Several of the programmed checks already listed are applicable to the processing phase. The **sequence check** is appropriate when sequential processing is performed. The limit and relationship checks may be applied during the processing as well as the input phase. For instance, the limit check may be applied as an input control with respect to the field for hours worked on input time records. It may also be applied as a processing control with respect to the computed gross earnings amount for each employee.

Run-to-run controls. As was noted earlier, batched data should be controlled during processing runs so that no records are omitted from or unauthorized records are inserted into a transaction file. The processing programs thus should generate totals *during each run*; these totals then should be balanced after each run against the predetermined batch totals. When data are processed on-line, proof account activity listings, also called file change reports, should be prepared at the end of each day. These reports show, for each general ledger account, the beginning account balance, all transaction activity, and the ending account balance. The change in each account balance should be reconciled to the total of the transactions, as determined from source documents or other sources. For instance, cash receipts that are entered on-line and posted to the cash account can be balanced against totaled listings of remittance advices.

File and program checks. To ensure that transactions are posted to the proper master files, the processing programs should include label checks. If an incorrect file is mounted with respect to either the input file or output file, a warning message should be displayed on the computer console for the operator. (Alternatively, the program could be prevented from processing data if an incorrect file is mounted or accessed.) To ensure that transactions are posted to the proper record within a master file, the processing program should employ a matching check.

Processing programs should be periodically checked for validity. One approach by which this can be done is to employ test data in order to see that expected results are obtained. Another approach is to reprocess actual data with the program and to compare the results against previously generated reports. Both of these approaches are discussed in Chapter 17.

Audit trail linkages. Fostering the audit trail is an important objective of processing controls. A clear audit trail is needed to enable individual transactions to be traced, provide support to changes in general ledger account balances, prepare financial reports, and correct transaction errors or losses.

Among the records needed to provide a clear audit trail for users are input–output control logs, transaction logs, and transaction listings. Processing procedures should require that a printed transaction listing be prepared (1) during each file-updating run by batch processing systems and (2) at the end of each day by on-line processing systems. In addition, each transaction in a listing should be identified by a unique and sequentially assigned transaction reference number; these transaction numbers should be posted to the general ledger account records and also recorded on source documents pertaining to the transactions. (In on-line systems the input terminal numbers and transaction entry times should also appear.)

Output Controls

Output controls are designed to determine that the results of processing are complete, accurate, and distributed to the proper users. These objectives are fulfilled mainly by reviews of the outputs and related registers.

Reviews of processing results. An important output control consists of verifying that the changes made to master records are correct. Thus, the proof account activity listings generated daily should be sent to the appropriate user departments for review. These listings should contain all changes to the accounts, including changes due to file maintenance runs. A particular listing, for instance, should reflect the effects in finished-goods inventory master records of changes to selling prices. In its review of such price changes the sales department could trace the changes back, via the audit trail, to the price change documents.

Another important output control consists of reviewing exception and summary reports, also known as error, or suspense, listings. The control group should personally remove these reports from the printer, review the errors and exceptional items listed thereon, investigate where necessary, and submit the errors to the user departments for correction. A control clerk should reconcile the final totals reflected in the outputs to the precomputed batch control totals. In addition, the clerk should balance the new control totals of key fields in the master records, as shown in the trailer label of each updated file, against the control totals of these fields before updating. To balance the totals of the accounts receivable balance field, for instance, the clerk would (1) add the amounts of the day's sales transactions to the total of the accounts receivable balance field before updating and then (2) compare the sum to the total of the accounts receivable balance field after the sales transaction updating run.

Other control-oriented reports should also be reviewed. For instance, the console log and other logs (e.g., change log) should be reviewed by the internal audit group. Such reviews should detect attempts to override controls, to change programs without proper authorization, and so on.

Controlled Distribution of Outputs

The outputs generated during processing should be distributed only to proper users. Distribution can be controlled by means of **distribution registers.** By reference to the registers, the control group should distribute the outputs directly and in a timely manner, recording the distribution in the control log. Upon receiving the outputs, the users should carefully review their contents by comparing the computed results against the input data and assessing their reasonableness.

Alternative Control Categories

Error-Correction Procedures

Although most errors are detected during the input phase, errors can occur during any of the phases. Moreover, the error-correction procedure is sufficiently important to warrant a separate section. Thus, we have deferred its discussion until this point.

Carefully prescribed and formalized procedures are needed to ensure that detected errors are corrected and that corrected data are reentered for processing. Separate procedures should be prescribed for batch processing applications and on-line processing applications.

Error correction in batch processing applications. A sound error-correction procedure for batch processing applications would consist of the following steps:

1. Flagging erroneous transactions and suspending their processing.
2. Recording the erroneous transactions by fully explanatory error messages on exception and summary reports.
3. Entering the erroneous transactions on a file of suspended transactions—called a **suspense file**—and adjusting the batch control totals accordingly.
4. Recording the suspended transactions—that is, the contents of the suspense file—on periodic printed listings.
5. Returning the erroneous transactions, together with the reasons for rejection, to the user departments for correction by a supervisor.
6. Reentering corrected transactions for *re-editing* and processing.
7. Deleting each corrected transaction from the suspense file.
8. Periodically investigating any erroneous transactions that have not been reentered for processing within a specified period of time.
9. Periodically printing statistical reports that reflect the number of times each type of error has occurred, the average lengths of time to correct the various types of errors, and so on.

Steps 1, 2, 3, 4, and 7 can be performed by the edit or processing programs; step 9 can be performed by system software. Steps 5, 6, and 8 would be monitored by the control group. Thus, a control clerk, upon obtaining the exception and summary reports, would enter each erroneous transaction in an error log. Dates would be entered in the log as each transaction is returned to the user and then later resubmitted for processing.

Error correction in on-line processing applications. Input errors are generally corrected by the data entry clerk at the time of entry. When the input edit program detects an error in a data item, it notifies the clerk by an error message. This message is typically displayed on a CRT screen. The clerk must immediately correct the error before the program will accept additional data. Then the data item is again edited. This procedure is followed until all individual data items have been edited and accepted by the program. At that point the program might ask the clerk to confirm the transaction by striking a function key. When the clerk does so, the program enters the transaction into the system.

Some errors are not detected until after the data are stored in the data base. Changes to data already in the data base should be made only by authorized persons; such changes can be controlled by the restrictive use of passwords that enable changes to be made. In addition, the proof account activity listings (mentioned earlier) should clearly identify every change that affects an account balance. All changes should also be recorded on change logs and reviewed by user departments and the internal auditors.

Preventive, Detective, and Corrective Controls

Application controls have the broad purposes of preventing, detecting, or correcting various errors and omissions. In a sound application control framework, each stage (input, processing, output) is likely to be represented by controls having all three purposes. Figure 9-13 provides a matrix in which application controls are listed under both classification schemes.[13]

---

[13]Krish N. Bhaskar, W. Thomas Lin, and Richard Savich, "An Integrated Internal Control Framework to Prevent and Detect Computer Frauds," *The EDP Auditor Journal* (Vol. II, 1987), pp. 42–49.

Control stage \ Control purpose	Preventive	Detective	Corrective
Input	Properly authorized transactions Well-designed and controlled source documents, e.g., prenumbered forms Sound conversion control techniques, e.g., key verification of input data	Batch control totals Adequate input edit tests (programmed checks), e.g., field checks	Sound error correction procedures Complete audit trail
Processing	Sound file maintenance procedures Adequate preventive-type programmed checks, e.g., label checks, sequence checks, matching checks	Run-to-run verifications Adequate detective-type programmed checks, e.g., limit checks, sign checks	Complete audit trail
Output	Distribution log of authorized users	Reconciliation of computed totals with predetermined control totals Reviews of outputs and tests to source documents by users	Reviews of logs and procedures by internal auditors Reviews of error-correction statistics

FIGURE 9-13 Application controls arranged by two classification plans.

Summary

The internal control structure, which has several important objectives appropriate to both manual and computer-based processing systems, comprises numerous controls and security measures. Controls of a general nature include organizational controls, documentation and asset-accountability controls, hardware and software controls, and management practice controls. The latter relate to procedures for change, procedures for new system development, procedures for computer operations, personnel procedures, and managerial and evaluative procedures. Security measures provide protection for physical assets, including computer hardware facilities, and for data. The measures with respect to assets and facilities provide protection from unauthorized access, from disasters due to nature, and from breakdowns and interruptions. The data security measures provide protection from unauthorized access, from undetected access and changes, and from loss or alteration of data; a fourth group of measures facilitates the reconstruction of lost data. The transaction controls consist of input, processing, and output controls, including an important group of controls known as programmed checks. Errors that are detected during the input stage should be corrected according to a sound procedure. The appropriate controls and security measures differ in certain respects among manual processing systems, computer-based batch processing systems, and computer-based on-line processing systems.

Review Problems with Solutions

Problem 1 Statement

Barbara Eagle is a cost accountant for the Tech-High Co. of Culver City, California. She is responsible for monitoring the costs incurred in developing and marketing a new product. In addition to her, two top managers are authorized to access these confidential costs. Tech-High maintains a computer system with on-line inquiry capability. The accounting department has several terminals available for making inquiries and entering data as necessary.

Required

Describe several security measures and general controls that can help to assure (a) privacy of the cost data, (b) on-line availability of the data at all times, and (c) reliability of the cost data.

Solution

The following are some of the security measures and general controls that can help to assure:

a. *Privacy of cost data.*
  (1) Assign passwords to Barbara and other authorized users that provide precise access to cost data.
  (2) Lock accounting terminals at the end of each business day.
  (3) Establish usage limitations that prohibit terminals other than those in the accounting department from access into cost data records.
  (4) Maintain an access log of all persons attempting to gain access into the system; provide for a terminal to lock automatically after three unsuccessful attempts via its keyboard.
  (5) Establish a policy that prohibits programmers and other nonaccounting personnel from using accounting department terminals; enforce the policy by placing terminals in secure areas to which outsiders are denied entrance.
  (6) Consider storing cost data in encrypted (encoded) form.
  (7) Shred printouts of cost data after use.

b. *Availability of cost data at all times.*
  (1) Dump cost data from on-line files onto backup magnetic tape at least daily.
  (2) Prepare a log of all cost data transactions (together with other transactions) and also of the status of costs before and after each update.
  (3) Maintain copies of backup tapes and transaction logs at a site separate from the main office of the firm.
  (4) Provide adequate protection for computer equipment against fires, floods, power losses, etc.

c. *Reliability of cost data.*
  (1) Maintain an authorization list within the computer system that specifies those persons authorized to change data; have system software verify that each person gaining access is authorized to perform updates.
  (2) Employ an edit program to verify the accuracy of input data.
  (3) Employ auditors to perform continuous checks of system controls.

Problem 2 Statement

McGlynn Distributors of New Rochelle, New York, processes transactions relating to sales orders by means of a computer-based batch processing system. Sales order documents are batched, batch control totals are computed, and the data are keyed onto magnetic tape. The transaction file is then edited, sorted by customer account numbers, and used to update the accounts receivable master file. Errors may be detected during the first and third of these computer runs. Examples of errors are invalid customer account numbers, out-of-sequence transaction records, and discrepancies in the batch total amounts.

Required

Describe the procedure for correcting errors pertaining to the sales order transactions and for adjusting batch control totals.

Solution

The error-correction procedure is portrayed in the flowchart on page 365. Steps shown in the flowchart may be described as follows: Transactions having detected errors are flagged during the edit or updating runs. They are also listed on the exception and summary reports applicable to the runs in which the errors are detected. Later, the order transaction tape is processed against the outstanding suspense file, so that the file is updated to reflect the newly detected erroneous transactions. During this run a listing of the newly detected errors is prepared. The listing is then obtained by the control group and logged, and afterward the erroneous transactions are returned to the sales department for correction. Upon correction, the transactions are reentered for editing and processing. During the next processing run of sales order transactions against the suspense file, the transactions (previously flagged as needing correction) are deleted from the file.

The presence of erroneous transactions slightly complicates the run-to-run comparison of batch control totals; that is, when flagged transactions are removed from an order transaction file, the batch totals of the remaining transactions are changed. Thus, to make a valid comparison it is necessary to add the totals from the listing of suspended transactions to the remaining transactions, in order to obtain totals that equal the precomputed batch totals. Or it is necessary to adjust the precomputed batch totals by deducting the amounts represented by the suspended transactions. Either approach can be incorporated into the processing programs, so that the computations are automatically performed.

Review Questions

9-1 What is the meaning of each of the following terms?

Systems development function
Data processing function
Data base administrator
Data preparation function
Computer operations function
Data control function
Data library function
Documentation
Procedural documentation
Systems documentation
Program documentation
Operations documentation
Data documentation
User documentation
Duplicate circuitry
Parity check
Echo check (hardware control)
Read-after-write check
Dual read check
Validity check (hardware control)
Scheduled preventive maintenance
Diagnostic test routine
Label check
Read–write check
Fidelity bond
Disaster contingency and recovery plan
Callback procedure
Password
Encryption
Access log

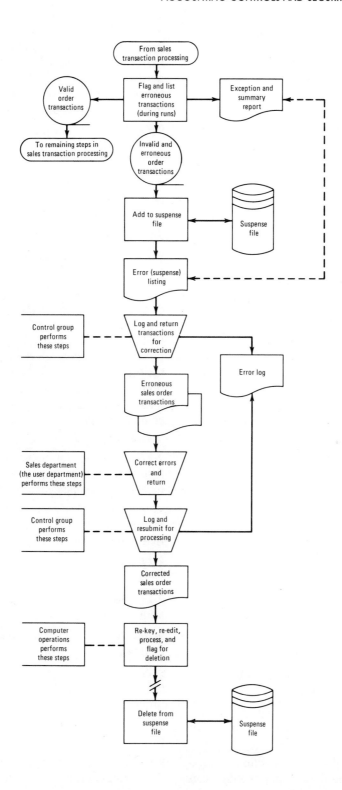

Console log
System and program change log
Data library log
Transaction log
Tape file protection ring
External file label
Internal file label
Read-only memory (ROM)
Lockout procedure
Data backup
Grandfather-father-son approach
Rollforward
Rollback
Checkpoint
Control point
Input control
Batch input-output control log
Amount control total
Hash total
Record count
Visual verification
Key verification
Programmed check
Validity check
Field check
Limit check
Relationship (logical) check
Self-checking digit
Echo check
Redundancy check
Completeness check
Processing control
Sequence check
Output control
Distribution register
Suspense file

9-2 What are the objectives of the internal control structure?

9-3 What knowledge should accountants possess concerning the control frameworks of computer-based information systems?

9-4 Identify several subdivisions of controls within the broad category of computer-based general controls.

9-5 Describe appropriate functional segregation of organizational units within firms having computer-based information systems.

9-6 Contrast the organizational functions that are involved in applications processed manually with those involved in computer-based batch processing applications and on-line processing applications.

9-7 Discuss several levels of desirable documentation for computer-based information systems.

9-8 Are asset accountability controls as important to computer-based systems as to manually based systems?

9-9 Identify several commonly employed hardware and software controls.

9-10 What are the purposes of security measures in computer-based information systems?

9-11 Identify several security measures that are useful in providing protection (1) for physical assets, (2) for computer hardware facilities, (3) from breakdowns and interruptions, (4) from unauthorized accesses of data, (5) from undetected accesses and changes of data, and (6) from loss or alteration of data.

9-12 Contrast the means of reconstructing lost data from magnetic tape files and from magnetic disk files.

9-13 Describe procedures for system change and development that provide effective control.

9-14 Identify several suitable control procedures pertaining to computer operations.

9-15 Identify basic control procedures pertaining to personnel.

9-16 Identify several suitable monitors or evaluators of control procedures.

9-17 What are the broad objectives of transaction controls? Of input controls? Of processing controls? Of output controls?

9-18 Identify several ways in which transactions may be authorized.

9-19 What means are available for minimizing input errors when data are entered by the on-line input approach?

9-20 Explain how batch control totals help to prevent the loss of data during the processing of batches of transactions.

9-21 Contrast the various types of batch control totals.

9-22 Describe two types of verification that may be performed during the conversion of data.

9-23 Identify a variety of programmed checks that help to detect errors in computer-based processing systems.

9-24 Identify three programmed checks that are important when transmitting data over data communications facilities.

9-25 Describe how a self-checking digit validates the accuracy of identification numbers.

9-26 Discuss several controls that are pertinent to the processing phase.

9-27 Describe the linkages necessary to establish a clear audit trail in a computer-based information system.

9-28 Discuss several controls that are pertinent to the output phase.

9-29 Describe a suitable procedure for correcting the errors detected in a batch processing system. Then describe a procedure suitable for an on-line processing system.

Discussion Questions

9-30 What depth of knowledge should be possessed by accountants concerning (a) computer hardware controls, (b) organizational controls, (c) data security measures, (d) physical facility security measures?

9-31 Which errors, either accidental or deliberate, are most likely to be eliminated when an information system is converted from manual processing to computer-based processing?

9-32 A firm has just converted from a manual information system to an on-line process-

ing system. Discuss any ways in which this change might (a) help and (b) hinder each of the following: (1) an accounting employee who is intent on embezzling funds, (2) a competitor who is intent on pilfering confidential files and records, (3) a disgruntled ex-employee who is intent on disrupting data processing operations.

9-33 Discuss the likely effects of magnetic disk storage on data control and security.

9-34 What security measures should be employed to

    a. Prevent the malicious destruction of data on magnetic disks?

    b. Ensure the privacy of confidential files?

    c. Ensure that only authorized use is made of data within the information system?

9-35 Contrast the security measures needed in a tape-oriented batch processing system with those needed in an on-line processing system.

9-36 What steps should be taken to locate an error when totals computed during a processing run do not match the predetermined batch control totals?

9-37 Contrast the set of programmed checks suitable to batch processing systems with the set suitable to on-line processing systems.

9-38 Discuss the features of on-line processing systems that create difficulties in maintaining an effective control framework.

9-39 How can the audit trail be maintained when source documents are not used in a specific application?

9-40 Is it possible to incorporate too many programmed checks into an application program?

9-41 Preventive controls are capable of preventing errors from entering a computer system and of preventing access by unauthorized persons; detective controls are able to detect errors during processing. Give examples of each type of control that are suitable to an on-line processing system.

Problems

9-1 What general control(s) or security measure(s) would be most appropriate for preventing, detecting, or minimizing the adverse effects from each of the following occurrences?

   a. A fire in an office area spreads to the computer center of a firm. All the computer facilities and many files are destroyed.

   b. A computer hardware component malfunctions during a processing run, causing many of the accounts receivable records to be lost. The records must be reconstructed manually from stored transaction documents and past monthly statements.

   c. A severe storm causes the computer system to be shut down for several days. As a result, confusion reigns, many of the firm's operations are crippled, and employee paychecks are delayed.

   d. A five-minute power failure causes the computer system to cease functioning, thus resulting in the loss of data being transmitted from several terminals.

   e. A payroll clerk accesses her salary records from a terminal and increases her salary level.

   f. An industrial "spy" taps the communications lines of a high-technology firm, acquires confidential product information, and sells it to a competitor.

   g. A computer printout of confidential personnel data is sent by mistake to the production manager.

   h. A programmer for a local bank modifies the program that computes interest amounts on savings account balances. His modification, known as the "salami fraud," consists of transferring to his account the fraction of a cent from each interest computation (which previously had been rounded in the depositor's favor). This type of programming modification is very difficult to detect.

9-2 What general control(s) or security measure(s) would be most appropriate for preventing, detecting, or minimizing the adverse effects from each of the following occurrences?

   a. A magnetic tape containing yesterday's sales transactions is accidentally moved to the scratch-tape rack and cannot be located.

   b. A visitor to the computer center of a nationwide publication carries away a diskette containing a list of subscribers. After using a service bureau to prepare a hard-copy printout, she sells the list to direct mail advertisers.

   c. A disgruntled computer operator accesses several master files through the main computer console and alters data in their header labels.

   d. A programmer for a small firm assists the computer operator during rush periods. One day during the processing of checks he substitutes bogus vouchers and overrides the control in the program designed to prevent the payment of unauthorized vouchers.

   e. A warehouseman accesses the confidential salary file in the data base via a terminal located in the warehouse.

   f. An inexperienced computer operator mounts the accounts receivable master file (on a magnetic tape reel) for the daily updating run. However, he inadvertently designates the tape drive on which it is mounted as an output drive and erases many of the customers' records.

g. A firm which performs batch processing runs on a regular basis frequently has difficulty in assuring that erroneous transactions are corrected and resubmitted for processing and that batch totals are verified after each processing run.

9-3 What general control(s) or security measure(s) would be most appropriate for preventing, detecting, or minimizing the adverse effects from each of the following occurrences?

a. A teenaged hacker breaks into the data base of a military contractor from a home computer which is emulating a terminal. He views classified specifications of a new fighter plane.

b. A cashier who receives currency and checks over the counter from customers keeps a portion of the receipts for her own use.

c. A repairman from an equipment servicing firm accesses a teller's terminal one weekend at a bank branch office where he is servicing typewriters and other office machines. He enters a fictitious deposit of $1000.00 to his personal checking account.

d. A programmer modifies the operating system of her firm's computer-based system, thereby accidentally eliminating password protection over certain confidential files.

e. The throughput of a firm's main computer system drops sharply for three consecutive weeks, although the computer operators seem to be continually busy.

f. Two accountants post adjusting journal entries concurrently from separate terminals to accounts in the firm's on-line general ledger file. Both entries affect a common general ledger account, so that one of the entries is written over and the account balance is not updated to reflect that entry.

g. The controller discovers that a newly prepared consolidated financial statement contains several errors, which apparently are due to "bugs" in the computer program that processed and printed the statement. However, the programmer who developed the consolidation program recently resigned and no one else can understand the logic of the program.

9-4 Draw a sound organization chart for the information systems function of a moderate-sized firm, if it includes the following managers and employees:

Harry Snell, director of information systems.

May Wilks, systems analyst.

Jack Dierks, programmer.

Paul Miller, computer operator.

Bill Parks, data processing manager.

Susan Aspen, data librarian.

Barry Naylor, systems development manager.

Jane Hibbler, data control clerk.

Mary Jackson, data entry clerk.

Dave Johns, systems analyst.

Laura Meyers, data base administrator.

Kirsten Hanes, data entry clerk.

Jarvis Cline, computer operator.

9-5 You have just been assigned to review the documentation pertinent to the computer-based information system of your firm.

Required

a. List three advantages of adequate documentation.

b. Match each of the elements of documentation below with the category in which it is likely to be found. Use every element given, but do not use any element more than once.

Categories	Elements
A. Systems documentation	1. Flowcharts showing the flow of information.
B. Program documentation	2. Procedures needed to balance, reconcile, and maintain overall control.
C. Operations documentation	3. Contents of data to be stored.
D. Data documentation	4. Record layouts.
E. User documentation	5. Data relationships.
	6. Logic diagrams and/or decision tables.
	7. Report distribution instructions.
	8. Messages and programmed halts.
	9. Data formats.
	10. Source statement listings.
	11. Instructions to show proper use of each report.
	12. Descriptions of files.
	13. Restart and recovery procedures.
	14. Instructions to ensure the proper completion of all input forms.
	15. List of system controls.

(CIA adapted)

9-6 You are performing an operational audit on the management information system (MIS) department which integrates planning, development, and computer operations. The MIS department has a staff of eighty people.

The data center is located on the main floor of the head office building so that visitors can observe, through the glass walls, the impressive computer installation. The location also allows the visitors to view the computer operators mounting the tapes or disk packs and removing computer reports.

One morning in the cafeteria you overhear the following conversation between the payroll system supervisor and his manager.

"Russell did it again! The payroll checks had to be ready by 6 o'clock this morning, but the payroll system went down last night. Operations notified Russell, our super programmer, who came in at 3:00 A.M. Fortunately, the tape librarian had not locked the door to the library while he was taking a short break. This enabled Russell to pick up the right tape, mount it onto the computer himself and fix the problem in 25 minutes with some changes to the program. Earlier, I had guaranteed the controller of the corporate accounting department that the system would be working like a charm. I am glad that the problem has been rectified, so that no one needs to be informed of the change. Documentation for the change will be made when Russell can free himself from his tight work schedule."

When you talk to the director of MIS, you note the following:

- Many of the production systems have been in place for 10 or more years. Maintenance and enhancements have been made where required. Users are still receiving reports produced by the same programs used since system implementation. Some of the reports which are produced monthly for management decision-making purposes are over 100 pages in length.

- A disaster recovery plan has been set up for the MIS department. However, because of the high costs involved, it has not been tested.

• The corporation has a backup site one block away, where documentation and backup tapes are stored in duplicate. The backup site was selected for its proximity, which allows quick access by authorized staff and provides nearby storage.

Required

Identify the risks inherent in the operations of the MIS department, and for each risk recommend a compensating internal control.

(SMAC adapted)

9-7 The Landers Corporation has established the following procedures pertaining to its information systems function:

   a. Access to the computer room is limited to the firm's employees.
   b. The vault door of the tape library is locked at night and opened each morning by the data processing manager or his assistant. The combination is known only to information systems personnel.
   c. The grandfather-father-son retention cycle is used for files, with ancestors stored in the vault.
   d. The function has an administrative manager who authorizes the development of applications, approves run schedules, and supervises the work of programmers, analysts, and operators. Another of his responsibilities is to review all program modifications.
   e. The programmers and analysts have flexible work requirements and frequently work into the evening or come in at night to debug and test programs on the computer.
   f. All systems development is initiated by the data processing manager. An informal mechanism exists to assess users' needs and to prioritize application requests. Priorities are determined by the data processing man-

ager according to a long-range master plan initiated last year. The information systems function absorbs all costs of development work.
   g. Structured programming (a standardized and efficient method of writing programs) is required when developing all new programs.
   h. Each program is assigned to a programmer who is responsible for coding, testing, and documenting that program.

Required

For each of the eight preceding procedures, identify the strengths and/or weaknesses present. For each strength, indicate why it is a strength; for each weakness, suggest a procedure to correct the deficiency.

(CIA adapted)

9-8 Simmons Corporation is a retailing concern with stores and warehouses throughout the United States. The company is in the process of designing a new integrated computer-based information system. In conjunction with the design of the new system, the management of the company is reviewing data processing security to determine what new control features should be incorporated. Two areas of specific concern are (1) confidentiality of company customer records and (2) safekeeping of computer equipment, files, and EDP facilities.

The new information system will be employed to process all company records, which include sales, purchases, financial, budget, customer, creditor, and personnel information. The stores and warehouses will be linked to the main computer at corporate headquarters by a system of remote terminals. This arrangement will permit data to be communicated directly to corporate headquarters or to any other location from each location throughout the terminal network.

At the present time certain reports have restricted distribution, either because not all levels of management need to receive them or because they contain confidential information. The introduction of remote terminals in the new system may provide access to this restricted information by unauthorized personnel. Simmons' top management is concerned that confidential information may become accessible and may be used improperly.

The company is also concerned with potential physical threats to the system, such as sabotage, fire damage, water damage, power failure, and magnetic radiation. Should any of these events occur in the present system and cause a computer shutdown, adequate backup records are available to enable the company to reconstruct necessary information at a reasonable cost on a timely basis. However, with the new system, a computer shutdown would severely limit company activities until the system could become operational again.

Required

a. Identify and briefly explain the problems Simmons Corporation could experience with respect to the confidentiality of information and records in the new system.

b. Recommend measures Simmons Corporation could incorporate into the new system that would ensure the confidentiality of information and records in the new system.

c. Identify safeguards that Simmons Corporation can develop to provide physical security for its (1) computer equipment, (2) files, and (3) computer-related facilities.

(CMA adapted)

9-9 Refer to Problem 6-12.

Required

Ivan West realizes that a contingency plan for the new system must be developed in or-der to be prepared for a natural disaster, passive threat, or active threat to the system.

a. Discuss why a contingency plan is necessary.

b. Outline and briefly describe the major components of a contingency plan that could be implemented in the case of a natural disaster, passive threat, or active threat to the system.

(CMA adapted)

9-10 The Department of Taxation of one state is developing a new computer system for processing state income tax returns of individuals and corporations. The new system features direct data input and inquiry capabilities. Identification of taxpayers is provided by using the Social Security number for individuals and federal identification number for corporations. The new system should be fully implemented in time for the next tax season.

The new system will serve three primary purposes:

- Data will be input into the system directly from tax returns through cathode ray tube (CRT) terminals located at the central headquarters of the Department of Taxation.

- The returns will be processed using the main computer facilities at central headquarters.
  The processing includes:
  Verification of mathematical accuracy.
  Auditing the reasonableness of deductions, tax due, etc., through the use of edit routines; these routines also include a comparison of the current year's data with the prior years' data.
  Identification of returns which should be considered for audit by revenue agents of the department.
  Issuing refund checks to taxpayers.

- Inquiry service will be provided to taxpayers upon request through the assistance of

Tax Department personnel at five regional offices. A total of 50 CRT terminals will be placed at the regional offices. A taxpayer will be allowed to determine the status of his or her return or get information from the last three years' returns by calling or visiting one of the department's regional offices.

The state commissioner of taxation is concerned about data security during input and processing over and above protection against natural hazards such as fire and floods. This includes protection against the loss or damage of data during data input or processing or the improper input or processing of data. In addition, the tax commissioner and state attorney general have discussed the general problem of data confidentiality which may arise from the nature and operation of the new system. Both want to have all potential problems identified before the system is fully developed and implemented so that the proper controls can be incorporated into the new system.

Required

a. Describe the potential confidentiality problems that could arise in each of the following areas of processing and recommend the corrective action(s) to solve the problem(s):

   (1) Data input.

   (2) Processing of returns.

   (3) Data inquiry.

b. The State Tax Commission wants to incorporate controls to provide data security against the loss, damage, or improper input or use of data during data input and processing. Identify the potential problems (apart from natural hazards such as fire and floods) for which the Department of Taxation should develop controls, and recommend the possible controls for each problem identified.

(CMA adapted)

9-11 Tempo Retailers of Durham, New Hampshire, processes its payroll by means of a small computer system. The following table presents sorted transaction data pertaining to the first several employees for a recent pay period.

Employee Number	Employee Name	Department Number	Hours Worked
13251	Smith, John	1	40
13620	Black, Charles	1	40
13543	Adams, Steve	1	48
13658	Brown, Rodney	1	40
13752	Jones, 8aul	2	42
24313	Krause, Ken	2	44
25001	Tingey, Sharon	2	84

The first digit of the employee number indicates the employee's department, and the last digit is a nonzero self-checking digit.

Required

Assuming that the above data represent the entire group of employees to be paid:

a. Compute three types of batch control totals.

b. Identify errors in the data and the specific type of programmed check that should detect each error.

9-12 Self-checking digits are employed by a firm to validate its identification numbers. The algorithm used is known as the modulus-11 system and involves the following steps:

   a. Assign weights to each digit in the number, using 2 as the weight for the lowest-order (right-most) digit, 3 for the next-lowest-order digit, and so on.

   b. Multiply each digit by its weight.

   c. Sum the products.

   d. Divide the sum by 11.

   e. Subtract the remainder from 11; the result is the self-checking digit.

(If there is no remainder or if the result is 10, the self-checking digit is zero.)

Required

a. Verify the correctness of the self-checking digit for each of the following employee numbers:

(1) 45675   (2) 33693

Solution to (1):

$$2 \times 7 = 14$$
$$3 \times 6 = 18$$
$$4 \times 5 = 20$$
$$5 \times 4 = \underline{20}$$
$$72$$

$$\begin{array}{r} 6 \text{ R6} \\ 11\overline{\smash{)}72} \end{array}$$

$11 - 6 = 5$

Thus, 5 is the self-checking digit.

b. Verify that the following five-digit product number, recorded by a salesperson, contains an incorrect self-checking digit: 73256. What is the correct self-checking digit for this number, assuming that the remainder of the digits were recorded correctly?

c. Determine the digit that should be attached to customer number 28346__ in order to provide the self-checking feature.

d. Each of the following customer numbers (all of which contain self-checking digits) were entered via a salesperson's terminal as a part of sales order data. Which should be rejected by the computer system as invalid?

(1) 357920.

(2) 186212.

(3) 243760.

9-13 Recently, the Central Savings and Loan Association of Jefferson City, Missouri, installed an on-line computer system. Each teller in the association's main office and seven branch offices has an on-line terminal. Customers' mortgage payments and savings account deposits and withdrawals are recorded in the accounts by the computer from data input by the teller at the time of the transaction. The teller keys the transaction code and proper account by account number and enters the information in the terminal keyboard to record the transaction. The accounting department at the main office also has terminals. The computer is housed at the main office.

In addition to servicing its own mortgage loans the association acts as a mortgage servicing agency for three life insurance companies. In this latter activity the association maintains mortgage records and serves as the collection and escrow agent for the mortgagees (the insurance companies), who pay a fee to the association for these services.

Required

List specific general controls, transaction controls, and security measures needed to provide an adequate control framework for this system. Relate any programmed checks you describe to specific items of data being entered by the tellers.

(CPA adapted)

9-14 Gosse Hotels of Reno, Nevada, utilizes an on-line computer system to maintain room reservations. Operators key data concerning each reservation into on-line terminals. Included in each entry are the name of the person making the reservation, the code of the hotel for which the reservation is being made, the reservation dates, the expected time of arrival, and special requests (e.g., a roll-away bed). The system then updates the room master file and creates a new record for the traveller. All files are maintained on magnetic disks.

Required

Give specific descriptions of general controls, transaction controls, and security measures needed to provide an adequate control framework for this system. Relate any programmed checks you describe to specific items of data being entered by the operators.

9-15 The Johnson Insurance Company of Providence, Rhode Island, maintains its policy file on a direct-access storage device. In order to update the files, a policy clerk first gains access to the system by entering a password and then her name. Once access is obtained, the transaction data are entered on easy-to-read preformatted screens. The system immediately edits the data and requests corrections if errors are detected. When the data have passed all edits, they are stored on a file temporarily. At a scheduled time they are entered into a batch run that updates the insurance policy master file. Verification notices that identify the changes made to the policies are printed during the updating process; after the run they are delivered to the underwriters, who compare and match the notices to the source documents.

Required

Specify the transaction controls and security measures that should be employed to ensure that (a) unauthorized persons do not gain access to the policy file, (b) transactions are authorized, and (c) transactions are accurate and complete.

(CIA adapted)

9-16 Babbington-Bowles is a Toronto advertising agency. It employs 625 salespersons whose responsibilities require them to travel and entertain extensively. Salespersons, who earn both salaries and commissions, receive paychecks at the end of each month. Formerly, the paycheck for each salesperson included reimbursement for expenses. These expense reimbursements were based on expense reports submitted by the salespersons, approved by supervisors, and computer-processed in batches.

Although this procedure was satisfactory to the firm, it displeased the salespersons. They were forced to wait a month (sometimes two) for the reimbursement, which often amounted to several thousand dollars. Thus, they requested permission to submit expense reports with receipts directly to the accounting department, and to receive reimbursement very promptly thereafter.

To provide this service, the accounting department would need a video display terminal and small on-line printer. The accounting clerk would enter the salesperson's name into the terminal, together with the requested expense amounts and account numbers to which the amounts would be charged. An on-line program would process the data and, if valid, print a check on presigned blank-check stock kept in the printer.

Required

Identify the general and transaction controls that are needed for this proposed expense reimbursement procedure.

(SMAC adapted)

9-17 Contrast the controls and security measures needed in the following three situations:

    a. A fast-food restaurant that has installed a microcomputer together with several terminals located at the order counter to compute amounts of sales and change from payments as well as to accumulate sales totals by food items.

    b. A local grocery chain that has installed a centralized medium-size computer, which is linked to point-of-sale terminals located at the checkout counters of several stores throughout a metropolitan area.

    c. A statewide bank that has installed a centralized large-size computer, which is linked to visual display terminals located at the teller windows of its several dozen branches and to automated teller terminals located in stores, airports, etc.

Suggested Readings

Allen, Brandt. "The Biggest Computer Frauds: Lessons for CPA's." *The Journal of Accountancy* (May 1977), pp. 52–63.

Auditing Standards Committee, American Institute of Certified Public Accountants. *The Effects of EDP on the Auditor's Study and Evaluation of Internal Control.* Statement on Auditing Standards No. 3. New York: AICPA, 1974.

———. *The Effects of Computer Processing on the Examination of Financial Statements.* Statement on Auditing Standards No. 48. New York: AICPA, 1984.

Bhaskar, Krish N.; Lin, W. Thomas; and Savich, Richard S. "An Integrated Internal Control Framework to Prevent and Detect Computer Frauds." *The EDP Auditor Journal* (Vol. II, 1987), pp. 42–49.

Buss, M. D. J., and Salerno, L. M. "Common Sense and Computer Security." *Harvard Business Review* (March–April 1984), pp. 112–121.

Cerullo, Michael. "Application Controls for Computer-Based Systems." *Cost and Management* (June 1982), pp. 18–23.

Davis, Gordon.; Schaller, Carol A.; and

Adams, Donald L. *Auditing & EDP.* 2d ed. New York: AICPA, 1983.

Davis, Keagle, and Perry, William E. *Auditing Computer Applications: A Basic Systematic Approach.* New York: Ronald Press, 1982.

Li, David H. "Preventive Controls and Detective Controls in a Computer Environment." *The EDP Auditor* (Spring 1983), pp. 21–28.

Moscove, Stephen A., Simkin, Mark G., and Bagranoff, Nancy A. *Accounting Information Systems: Concepts and Practice for Effective Decision Making.* 4th ed. New York: Wiley, 1990.

Nash, John F. *Accounting Information Systems,* 2d ed. New York: Macmillan, 1989.

Porter, W. Thomas, and Perry, William E. *EDP Controls and Auditing.* 5th ed. Boston: Kent Publishing Co., 1987.

Rushinek, Avi, and Rushinek, Sara F. "Audit Trail Controls in an EDP Information System." *The EDP Auditor Journal* (Vol. II, 1986), pp. 20–30.

Wilson, Glenn T. "Computer Systems and Fraud Prevention." *Journal of Systems Management* (September 1984), pp. 36–39.

Wood, Charles C. "Countering Unauthorized Systems Accesses." *Journal of Systems Management* (April 1984), pp. 26–28.

Wu, Frederick H., and Safran, Ronald A. "A Practical Approach for Evaluating EDP Controls." *The CPA Journal* (October 1987), pp. 58–69.

CHAPTER OBJECTIVES

After studying this chapter, you should be able to do the following:

Describe the variety of reports needed by the managers of a firm.

Design reports that effectively present needed information to managers for support of operations and decision making.

Identify the characteristics of integrated reporting systems.

Develop integrated reporting systems, such as cost, responsibility, and profit-planning reporting systems.

Chapter *10*

REPORTS FOR OPERATIONS AND DECISION MAKING

An information system generates a wide variety of outputs. Many of these outputs are vital to the recipients. Consider the importance of messages received by a mission control center concerning the progress of a spaceship, or, on a more mundane level, consider the importance of paychecks to employees. Among the varied outputs provided by the information system of a firm, none are more vital than managerial reports. As vehicles of structured information, these reports provide the basis for sound decision making. Furthermore, integrated reporting systems communicate meaningful and useful information throughout a firm to all its managers and employees.

As noted in Chapter 4, managerial reports should contain information identified by an information needs analysis. This information is largely generated and formatted by the information processing system of a firm. Some of the information in managerial reports, however, is provided by a firm's transaction processing systems.

Accountants actively participate in designing many such managerial reports, especially those that present financial information for planning and control. For example, accountants are generally involved in the design, application, and interpretation of budgetary reports and analyses.

Types of Reports

A typical firm of moderate size may generate hundreds of managerial reports. If

Classification Plan	Typical Categories	Examples
1. Purpose	Operational report Planning report Control report Stewardship report Legal compliance report	Work-order status report Operational budget Cost variance analysis Annual report to stockholders Income tax return
2. Scope	Firmwide report Divisional report Departmental report Sales territory report	Balance sheet Income statement for Division A Budget versus actual costs for Department D Analysis of product sales in Territory X
3. Conciseness	Detailed report Summary report Exception report	Cash disbursements listing Daily cash received summary List of inventory items below reorder point
4. Occurrence	Scheduled or periodic report Demand report Event-triggered report	Weekly production report Request for best sales performers Power outage flash report
5. Time frame	Historical report Short-range forecast report Long-range forecast report	Cash flow statement Sales forecast for next month Sales forecast for next two years
6. Mode	"Hard-copy" report "Soft-copy" display	Inventory status printout Display of cumulative costs on Project Y
7. Format	Narrative report Graphical report Tabular report	Report of goals for next year Sales trend, past five years Price comparisons for "basket" of grocery items
8. Operational function	Financial or accounting report Production report Marketing report Inventory management report Personnel report	Accounts receivable aging schedule Cost of goods manufactured statement Sales by products and territories Back-order report Staffing requirements report

FIGURE 10-1 Types of reports.

these were collected together, the resulting stack would defy description. Figure 10-1 attempts to organize the stack by grouping reports according to plans (and categories within plans). Three of the classification plans should illustrate the overall organization scheme.

Useful Classification Plans

Perhaps the most useful way to classify reports is according to their *purposes*. **Stewardship reports** are intended to disclose the custodianship of the resources entrusted to management. Thus, they are prepared for the eyes of stockholders, prospective investors, creditors, and securities analysts. The best-known example of a stewardship report is the annual report of a corporation. **Legal compliance reports** are intended to fulfill legal obligations. Examples are financial statements (Form 10-K reports) filed with the Securities and Exchange Commission and income tax returns filed with the Internal Revenue Service. Operational, planning, and control reports are prepared to aid managers in performing their activities and fulfilling their decision-making responsibilities.

Figure 10-2 portrays the relationships among the categories of reports described

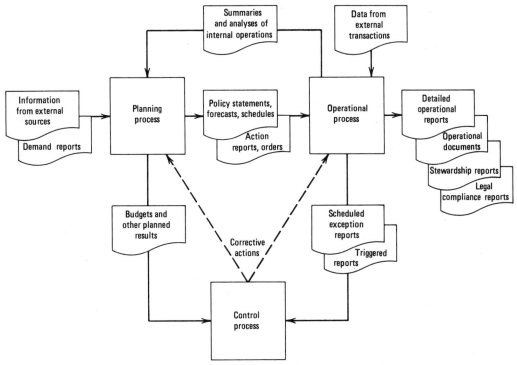

FIGURE 10-2   Reports related to the planning, control, and operational processes.

above. A variety of information, arising both internally and externally, flows into the planning process. Policy statements, orders, and various reports issue from the planning process as decisions are made. Many of the planning outputs flow into the operational process, which in turn gives rise to various reports and documents. Certain of these reports and documents are used internally, whereas stewardship and legal compliance reports flow to outside users. Other of the reports arising out of the operational process serve as feedback for use in the control process. By reference to control-oriented reports, managers make control-oriented decisions and take corrective actions affecting *either* the planning process *or* the operational process.

Another way to classify reports is according to *conciseness*. **Detailed reports** are the least concise, since they provide details

concerning events or entities. **Summary reports** are more concise, since they summarize details of multiple events or entities. **Exception reports** are also quite concise, since they eliminate irrelevant or less significant data concerning events or entities; that is, they highlight exceptional circumstances that warrant managerial attention. For instance, Figure 10-3 lists only those machines for which the actual down-hours differ from the standard down-hours by at least one hour.[1]

A third way to classify reports is according to *occurrence*. **Scheduled reports** are issued at predetermined intervals of time, such as daily or weekly. **Demand reports,** on the other hand, appear only when requested

[1]Reprinted with permission from Joseph W. Wilkinson, "Effective Reporting Structures," *Journal of Systems Management* (Nov. 1976), p. 39.

Allan Products Co.			
Machine Downtime Control Report			
Machining Department			Week of June 18–22
Machine identification	Down-hours over (under) standard	Percent of production time down	Cause
123B	2.0	5.0%	Operator injured; no immediate replace-ment
268D	(1.5)	0.6%	
477C	1.5	4.4%	Extra maintenance required
491B	8.0	12.5%	Broken clutch; slow delivery from supplier
602F	(1.2)	1.0%	
753A	5.8	9.7%	Worn pin; trouble difficult to locate
928G	(2.0)	0%	

Notes: 1. Production time per week = 80 hours.
2. Standard downtime per week = 2 hours or 2.5 percent.
3. Significant standard deviation = ±1 hour.
4. Of the 95 machines in above department, 56 had a favorable deviation (under standard); 39 had an unfavorable deviation (over standard) during reported week.

FIGURE 10-3 An exception report.

("demanded") by managers; they generally are intended to answer specific inquiries or to provide analyses pertaining to ad hoc problems. **Event-triggered reports,** as the term implies, are triggered by events such as outages on power lines, shortages of inventory, or breakdowns of machines.

Reports That Support Operations

Because of their direct relationships to managerial decision making, operational, planning, and control reports deserve close attention. As noted, managers need reports from all three categories in order to direct, plan, and control operations.

Operational reports reflect past events and/or current status. Information contained in such reports is obtained from day-to-day operations conducted by a firm. In fact, most

of the reports are prepared from accounting transactions processed and summarized by the firm's general ledger system.

The major purpose of operational reports is to support operations. They achieve this purpose in two ways. First, they initiate actions and implement decisions arising from the planning process. For example, production schedules and orders initiate actions and implement decisions made in the production function. Second, they support operations by providing scorekeeping-type information for ready reference. For instance, balance sheets, listings of outstanding purchase orders, and accounts receivable aging reports reflect the current status of resources; income statements, cash receipts journals, production cost and volume summaries, employee payroll registers and labor distribution summaries show the results of recent

Toddlers', Inc.
Inventory Status Report
for October 1991

Item Description	Item Number	Quantity Received	Quantity Shipped	Ending Quantity on Hand
Rubbers	2861	375	205	815
Diapers	3765	2100	1280	8646
Sleepers	5617	—	120	424
Cribs	7311	72	98	338

FIGURE 10-4 An operational report.

operations. Figure 10-4 depicts an operational report showing the status of various inventory items; it also reflects past activity with regard to quantities received and shipped during a particular month.

Although designed primarily to support operations, certain operational reports can nevertheless support decision making. They can help managers spot problems and analyze trends that lead to decisions. For example, banks prepare summaries of the daily volumes of deposits and withdrawals for use by bank managers. If a particular summary reveals deposits to be declining relative to withdrawals, it may signal the need to adjust loan policies. Alternatively, operational reports can provide the building blocks for developing information useful in the planning process. Figure 10-5 illustrates the computation of the inventory turnover from information in the finished-goods inventory status report and the income statement of a firm. The inventory turnover is one factor considered by marketing and production managers when setting production rates.

Reports That Aid the Planning Process

A variety of **planning reports** aid managers in planning and making decisions concerning the future. Perhaps the most widely

employed planning reports are sales forecasts and budgets; the latter appear in such formats as projected income statements, projected balance sheets, and projected funds statements. Planning reports of narrower scope include those that compare the current availability of such resources as raw materials to the expected demand for those resources. Other planning reports analyze performance differences among segments or

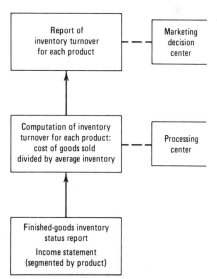

FIGURE 10-5 Decision-making information derived from operational reports.

entities. Examples of such reports are analyses of sales and contribution margins achieved by the respective product lines of a firm, analyses of costs incurred on each of several ongoing projects, and analyses of the relative merits of a firm's principal suppliers. Still other planning reports explicitly compare the economic consequences of two or more alternative courses of action, such as making a part or buying it from an outside supplier.

All of the foregoing planning reports have two features in common: they look to the future and they provide comparisons. Thus, the sales, costs, and other values are either (1) estimates of future values or (2) past values that can serve as estimates of future values. The comparisons often consist of explicit matchups of alternative courses of action, alternative segments of a firm, and so on. However, in some cases the comparisons are less apparent. For instance, an approved budget usually appears with a single set of values. However, this approved version is geared to a particular set of assumptions, including the forecast of sales. In the budget planning process, alternative sets of budget values based on other assumptions have also been developed for comparison.

Planning decisions often follow on the heels of planning reports. Sales forecasts may lead to changes in prices, entries into new markets, or increases in the advertising expenditures. Budgets may lead to such resource-related decisions as the acquisition of new production capacity, the hiring of new employees, the issuance of new stock, and the scheduling of production and deliveries. Analyses may result in decisions to expand one product line or sales branch while discontinuing another product line or closing another branch. Resource-demand reports, by projecting shortage conditions for a resource such as raw materials, may prompt decisions to increase purchases or to revise production schedules. A make-or-buy analysis may lead to a decision to make the part.

Let us look at two specific planning reports. Figure 10-6 analyzes sales by the salespersons within a particular sales territory and the product lines sold by each salesperson. A series of reports similar to Figure 10-6 would provide an overall analysis of sales made by the Eastern Manufacturing Co. They could aid in (1) planning the assignment of salespersons and territory sales managers and (2) determining the need for changes in commission rates or other incentives on low-selling products. If the analyses also included sales by types of customers, they could help to detect shifts in consumer tastes. Figure 10-7 analyzes two prospective products that have been developed by the Marpark Corporation. If the estimated demands and sales prices and costs are realistic, and if production capacity is available, the report provides sound support for a decision. It suggests that a decision to introduce product 1 will contribute an *added* $2500 ($6000 − $3500) toward covering the common fixed costs and providing a profit for the firm. Unless qualitative factors suggest otherwise, introducing product 1 would be the appropriate decision.

As we might expect, planning reports that aid strategic planning generally differ significantly from those that aid tactical planning. Reports for strategic planning cut across several operational functions, incorporate information drawn from external as well as internal sources, involve projections that extend more than a year into the future, and often are prepared on an ad hoc basis. Reports that fall into this category include market survey reports (to aid in selecting areas in which to expand), analyses of new warehouse locations (to aid in selecting warehouse sites), and capital budgets (to aid in selecting among competing investment opportunities). On the other hand, reports that aid tactical planning usually span relatively narrow ranges of activity, draw mainly from internal sources, span fairly short-range time periods, and tend to be issued on a recurring

Eastern Manufacturing Co.
Analysis of Sales by Salesperson, Product, and Territory
For the Month of August 1991
Central Massachusetts Territory (03)

Salesperson Name	No.	Product Line	Current Month Quota ($)	Current Month Actual ($)	Current Month Variance ($) Over (Under)	Year-to-date Quota ($)	Year-to-date Actual ($)	Year-to-date Variance ($) Over (Under)
Comden, K. J.	325	A	4,000	5,000	1,000	32,000	34,600	2,600
		B	3,000	2,500	(500)	24,000	24,300	300
		C	1,000	800	(200)	8,000	7,100	(900)
		D	6,000	7,400	1,400	48,000	50,700	2,700
		E	10,000	12,100	2,100	80,000	83,200	3,200
		F	8,000	8,400	400	64,000	62,800	(1,200)
		G	2,000	1,700	(300)	16,000	15,300	(700)
		All	34,000	37,900	3,900	272,000	278,000	6,000
George, M. P.	381	A	5,000	4,800	(200)	40,000	39,200	(800)
		B	4,000	4,100	100	32,000	31,800	(200)
		C	1,000	900	(100)	8,000	6,900	(1,100)
		D	7,000	6,200	(800)	56,000	54,800	(1,200)
		E	12,000	11,800	(200)	96,000	96,500	500
		F	9,500	9,900	400	76,000	78,100	2,100
		G	2,500	3,200	700	20,000	25,300	5,300
		All	41,000	40,900	(100)	328,000	332,600	4,600
Totals		A	50,000	53,300	3,300	400,000	410,700	10,700
		B	35,000	34,700	(300)	280,000	281,500	1,500
		C	10,000	8,900	(1,100)	80,000	77,700	(2,300)
		D	65,000	69,100	4,100	520,000	528,100	8,100
		E	108,000	111,800	3,800	864,000	891,000	27,000
		F	86,000	84,700	(1,300)	688,000	679,300	(8,700)
		G	23,000	24,000	1,000	184,000	183,900	(100)
		All	377,000	386,500	9,500	3,016,000	3,052,200	36,200

FIGURE 10-6 A sales analysis report.

basis. Production schedules, sales analyses, machine utilization analyses, special-order analyses, and expected stock-out reports are examples.

However, strategic planning reports may be closely related to tactical planning reports. For instance, reports that help to select the means of adding productive capacity are related to reports that help to schedule production, establish inventory levels, and determine the suppliers from whom to buy raw materials.

Reports That Aid the Control Process

Control reports help to control the acquisition and use of resources by comparing actual performances against benchmarks.[2]

[2] A rather different type of control report reflects errors and exceptions encountered in processing data, thus helping to maintain the accuracy of information. This type of report was discussed in Chapter 7.

	Introduce Product 1[a]		Introduce Product 2[b]	
MARPARK CORPORATION **Analysis of Alternative Products** **May 15, 1991**	**Per Unit**	**Amount**	**Per Unit**	**Amount**
Sales	$10.00	$100,000	$6.00	$120,000
Direct materials	$4.00	$40,000	$2.50	$50,000
Direct labor	2.50	25,000	1.50	30,000
Variable manufacturing overhead	1.00	10,000	.70	14,000
Variable selling expenses	1.50	15,000	.90	18,000
Total variable expenses	9.00	90,000	5.60	112,000
Contribution margin	$1.00	$10,000	$0.40	$8,000
Direct fixed selling expenses		4,000		4,500
Contribution after all direct expenses		$6,000		$3,500

[a]Projected demand is 10,000 units.

[b]Projected demand is 20,000 units.

FIGURE 10-7 A planning report.

The following examples indicate the variety of control reports used by firms:

Production-cost-center control reports, which compare actual costs with standard costs.

Profit-center control reports, which compare actual profits achieved with planned profits.

Project control reports, which compare actual costs and progress with budgeted costs and time schedules.

Delivery (or shipment) control reports, which compare actual deliveries with scheduled deliveries.

Inventory control reports, which compare the actual quantities on hand with established reorder-point quantities.

Quality control reports, which compare the actual and expected numbers of rejects.

Equipment utilization reports, which compare the percentages of the total times that equipment was in service with planned percentages.

Capital budgeting performance reports, which compare the projected cash flows or returns on invested capital with actual cash flows or returns.

As these examples suggest, control reports consist of actual performances, benchmarks, differences, and centers or objects of concern. *Actual performances,* expressed in such terms as costs and time spans, reflect operating results or current status. *Benchmarks* provide the bases for comparison. Several types of benchmarks are commonly used: (1) actual performances in previous time periods, such as last year; (2) actual performances of similar operational centers, such as plants or divisions; (3) ratios based on such industry averages as return on investment; and (4) performance standards, such as standard cost per unit produced. Differences of actual performances from benchmarks, often called **variances** or deviations, provide warnings of possible problems. For instance, a significantly unfavorable materials-usage variance suggests the presence of a materials-related problem. Perhaps materials of poor quality are being used, machines used to work the materials are not properly adjusted, or employees are careless in using materials. *Centers* and *objects* focus the concern for control. Centers and objects in the foregoing examples include production cost centers, profit centers, projects, sales orders, inventory items, production units, pieces of equipment, and capital investments.

In general, the usefulness of control reports increases as they become more discriminating, more timely, more concise, and more understandable. A report that (1) focuses on the productivity of individual employees and machines of a department, (2) appears daily or weekly, and (3) highlights exceptional productivities likely will be more useful than a report in the same circumstances that (1) shows only the productivity for the department as a whole, (2) appears monthly, and (3) reflects production levels with no emphasis on exceptions. The exception report in Figure 10-3 illustrates a useful report: not only does it exhibit the desirable attributes just listed, but it also enhances understandability by providing explanations in the right-hand column. Figure 10-8 shows that another way to enhance understandability is by the use of a graphical format.[3]

Of course, differing purposes and circumstances affect reporting needs, especially with regard to timeliness. Thus, reports that aid the control of operations, such as those that show labor efficiency and materials availability, must be very timely. Since the factors can change frequently and require prompt corrective actions, they should be issued weekly, daily, or even hourly. Moreover, they should reach the responsible managers with relatively short delay. Thus, a report of today's events should be in managers' hands tomorrow. On the other hand, those reports that aid in the evaluation of managerial performances need not be so timely. Not only may they be issued less frequently—say, once a month—but they may be delayed for several days without serious consequences.

Budgetary Reports

Certain key reports aid in both planning and controlling operations. Most such reports fit into the budgetary process, where they perform several roles. First, the sales forecast, reports of economic and market conditions, and other broad reports and policy statements establish the firm's activity levels. Then, a variety of integrated reports called component budgets allocate resources and provide detailed plans for every activity, project, and responsibility center of the firm. Next, as Figure 10-9 shows, these component budgets are condensed into summary statements of operating results, cash flows, and financial status. Once approved by top management, the budgetary reports become the performance standards against which actual performances are to be evaluated. As the period covered by the budget unfolds, budgetary (management) control reports reflecting variances from budgeted values are issued at equal intervals. The variances in such reports prove to be most useful if the budgeted values are issued at equal intervals. These variances also prove to be most useful if the budgeted values are adjusted to reflect the actual levels of activity achieved using the flexible budgeting technique.[4] When the

---

[3]From Anker V. Andersen, *Graphing Financial Information: How Accountants Can Use Graphs to Communicate,* Exhibit 10. Copyright © 1983 by National Association of Accountants, Montvale, N.J. All rights reserved. Reprinted by permission.

[4]For a discussion of flexible budgeting, see Shane Moriarity and Carl P. Allen, *Cost Accounting,* 2d ed. (New York: Harper & Row, 1987), pp. 317–319. Note that flexible budgeting requires budgeted costs to be classified into their fixed and variable components, with variability being related to reasonable measures of activity.

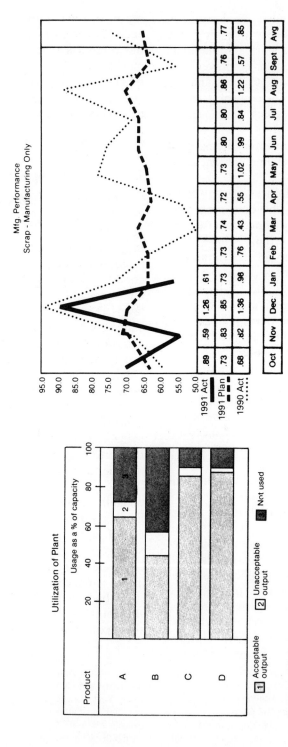

FIGURE 10-8 Control reports using graphical formats.

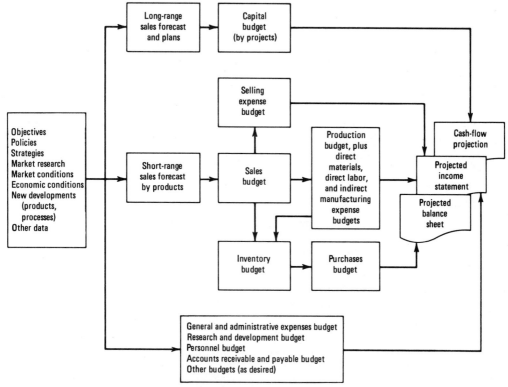

FIGURE 10-9 Development of budget reports.

time arrives for the next budgetary planning process, the results reflected in the control reports become part of the input data affecting future expectations.

For sound results budgetary reports should involve the participation of managers at all levels within an organization. In brief, higher-level managers first provide budget guidelines. Middle- and lower-level managers then prepare budgets for their areas of responsibility. After review and consolidation of these component budgets, higher-level managers give final approval to the master budget. Budgets prepared on the basis of such involvement motivate managers at all levels to perform more effectively and efficiently.

Design Considerations for Reports

Attributes

To be effective, a report should possess attributes such as relevance, conciseness, adequate discrimination, appropriate scope, understandability, timeliness, reliability, and consistency with other reports.

1. **Relevance.** An effective report aids one or more managers in fulfilling major responsibilities pertaining to directing, planning, or controlling operations and the use of related resources. If feasible, a report should be tied to the decision processes of the manager(s). Thus, a report showing

the status of work orders is more effective if it also shows the number of days that each work order is ahead or behind schedule. This added information signals the manager(s) when corrective decisions are necessary.

2. **Conciseness.** An effective report omits all unnecessary and irrelevant details. A busy manager simply does not have time to read massive reports consisting of many pages and buried facts. Instead, managers appreciate reports that filter the mass of data and highlight the key facts on one or two pages. Exception reports, such as the example presented in Figure 10-3, emphasize this attribute of conciseness.

3. **Adequate Discrimination.** While a report should be concise, it should not hide needed details. Rather, an effective report discriminates sufficiently to allow meaningful comparisons. For instance, a report to aid in profit planning should show profits broken down by segments (i.e., products, sales territories), rather than merely showing the overall profits for the firm.[5]

4. **Appropriate Scope.** An effective report spans a scope that is related to the responsibilities of the managers for whom it is prepared. Managers with broader areas of responsibility require reports of broader scope than do managers with narrower areas of responsibility. Thus, whereas a report for a department head should focus on the activities and performance of his or her department, a report for the president may span the overall activities of the firm. (However, in order to satisfy the conciseness attribute, the information in the report to the president would be more sum-

marized than in reports to lower-level managers.)

5. **Understandability.** An effective report provides information in a clear and readily usable format. For many managers, reports in graphical format are more easily understood than reports in tabular format. Financial statements are often more useful to managers if they include interpreted information, for example, financial ratios, dollar changes from one year to the next, and so forth.

6. **Timeliness.** An effective report is issued in a timely manner, in order to allow the manager to take effective action. This attribute received attention in the discussion of control reports, for which it is often critical.

7. **Reliability.** An effective report meets a high standard of accuracy. As noted in Chapter 6, this attribute is enhanced by an adequate internal control structure.

8. **Consistency with Other Reports.** If a report fits into a system of reports, its information should be consistent with that presented in all of the related reports. For example, if detailed sales reports are to be prepared for each of the regional sales branch managers, the formats of all the detailed reports should be identical and their information should correlate with the sales report for the top sales manager.

Output Modes

Reports may appear in either hard-copy or soft-copy mode. Hard-copy reports appear on traditional paper stock, whereas soft-copy reports appear on the screens of video display terminals. Though all of the attributes just described generally pertain to both modes, certain attributes are emphasized when applied to soft copy reports.

Soft-copy reports, frequently called **screen displays,** should be designed for maxi-

---

[5]A detailed chart of accounts and related coding system is necessary to provide highly discriminating reports and analyses. Coding systems were discussed in Chapter 8.

mum understandability. An effective screen display arranges the information items logically and meaningfully for the user. Figure 10-10, which shows a screen display that responds to a purchase order inquiry, meets this standard. Key descriptions appear at the top of the display. Details are balanced throughout and organized into columnized groupings. Labels are expressed in bold letters. An effective screen display also stresses conciseness, although brevity should not be permitted to reduce understandability. In Figure 10-10, for instance, certain words are abbreviated when their meanings are clear to the user.

Screen displays should be easily accessible to users. If they are responses to on-line inquiries, screen displays can be accessed by means of menus. If they are demand reports, screen displays should be built with user-friendly assistance via a report generator

software package, such as Easytrieve Plus (from Pansophic System).

Reporting and Budgetary Systems

Although individual reports can be very helpful, they nevertheless provide limited information. Thus, varied reporting systems have evolved, especially during the years since World War II. Their development has been particularly fostered by the analytical capabilities of computers.

Certain reporting systems encompass numerous firms and even industries. For example, Industry Ratios, published by Dun's Review, and the Survey of Current Business, published by the Department of Commerce, cut across the entire American economy. At the level of a single firm, reporting systems

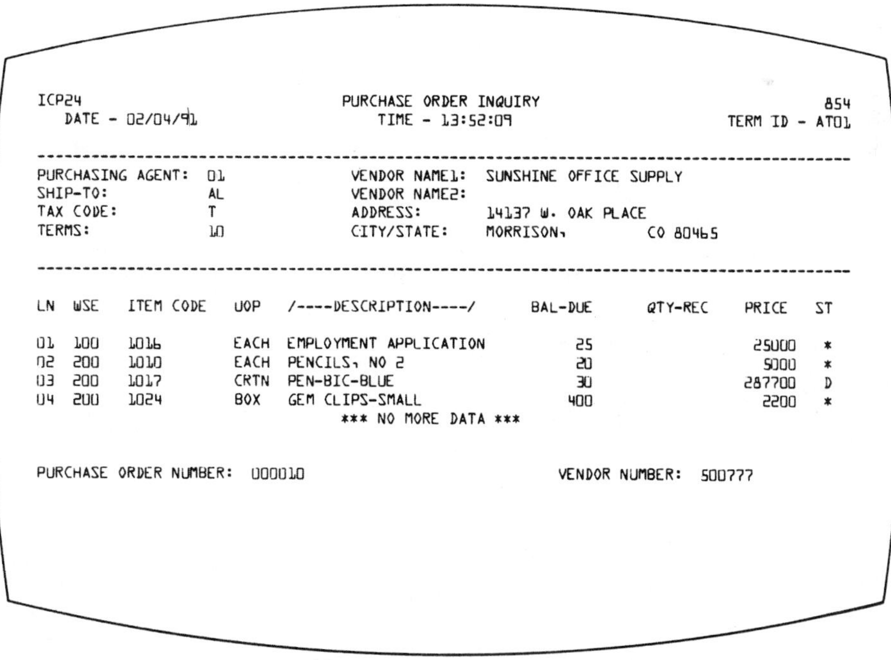

```
  ICP24                        PURCHASE ORDER INQUIRY                              854
      DATE - 02/04/91              TIME - 13:52:09               TERM ID - AT01

  -------------------------------------------------------------------------------
  PURCHASING AGENT:  01        VENDOR NAME1:  SUNSHINE OFFICE SUPPLY
  SHIP-TO:           AL        VENDOR NAME2:
  TAX CODE:          T         ADDRESS:       14137 W. OAK PLACE
  TERMS:             10        CITY/STATE:    MORRISON,         CO 80465

  -------------------------------------------------------------------------------

  LN   WSE    ITEM CODE   UOP   /----DESCRIPTION----/    BAL-DUE    QTY-REC    PRICE   ST

  01   100    1016        EACH  EMPLOYMENT APPLICATION       25                25000    *
  02   200    1010        EACH  PENCILS, NO 2               20                 5000    *
  03   200    1017        CRTN  PEN-BIC-BLUE                30               287700    D
  04   200    1024        BOX   GEM CLIPS-SMALL            400                 2200    *
                                *** NO MORE DATA ***


  PURCHASE ORDER NUMBER:  000010                      VENDOR NUMBER:  500777
```

FIGURE 10-10 A display screen in response to an inquiry. Courtesy of Management Science America, Inc. (MSA), a division of Dun & Bradstreet Software, Inc.

are related to the horizontal and vertical flows of information within the firm. Well-integrated horizontal and vertical reporting systems can greatly strengthen a firm's planning and control processes. In addition, they coordinate and reduce the volume of information flows.

Horizontal reporting systems link together the activities and operations within related operational functions and generate varied summaries, analyses, and projections. Figure 10-11 traces the portion of the horizontal reporting system relating to sales and purchases transactions within a merchandising firm. As orders flow in from customers and are entered in the sales register, they form the data base for analyzing sales by such segments as products and sales territo-

ries. The sales analyses, in turn, assist in the preparation of the sales forecast, the budgets, and the resource requirements reports for upcoming periods. These reports then give birth to other planning, operational, and control reports used by accounting and other functions.

Vertical reporting systems link together the several managerial levels within the organizational structure, thus helping to assure that managers receive information suitable to their needs and responsibilities. An effective vertical reporting system, which is dependent on a sound organizational structure, filters and summarizes information as it flows upward from the operational level through the respective managerial levels. Figure 10-12 presents reports that comprise several

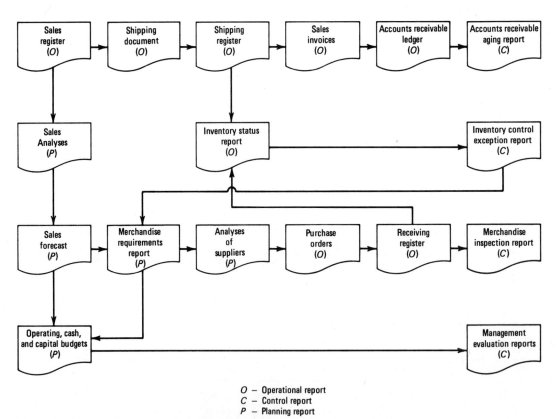

O – Operational report
C – Control report
P – Planning report

FIGURE 10-11 A horizontal reporting structure.

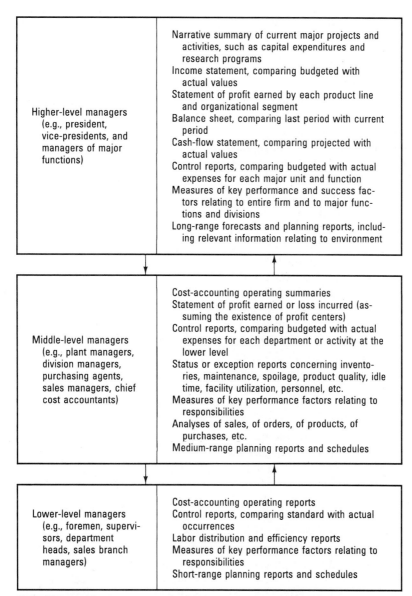

FIGURE 10-12 Reports typically found in vertical reporting systems of manufacturing firms. From Joseph W. Wilkinson, "Effective Reporting Structures," *Journal of Systems Management* (November 1976), p. 41.

vertical reporting systems among the three managerial levels of a typical manufacturing firm.[6]

[6]Wilkinson, "Effective Reporting Structures," *Journal of Systems Management* (Nov. 1976), p. 41.

Because of its concern for sound reporting and its comprehensive perspective, the accounting discipline has been instrumental in the development of integrated reporting systems found in modern firms. In addition to financial and cost reporting systems, it has given birth to and fostered responsibility reporting systems and profit planning systems.

Financial Reporting Systems

Every firm requires a basic **financial reporting system** that produces a wide variety of financial reports and statements. This reporting system draws on the transactions collected and processed by the general ledger system.

Numerous reports and statements, as noted earlier, are prepared according to financial accounting standards and serve users outside the firm. Certain of these reports and statements may be highly summarized. Income statements provided to stockholders via annual reports fall into this category. Other reports and statements for external users are relatively detailed and tailored. For instance, income statements required from some firms by the Securities and Exchange Commission provide revenue and cost information that is detailed by appropriate segments (e.g., products or services).[7]

Most of the reports and statements provided by the financial reporting system, however, are intended for use by managers and employees. Generally these outputs focus on specific activities or entities within a firm; in many cases they have no counterparts in reports intended for external users. However, certain financial reports and statements span the entire activities of a firm and appear to be quite similar to outputs intended for external users.

Nevertheless, significant differences frequently exist between financially oriented outputs intended for internal and external users, even when the outputs span the same scope. First, reports and statements for internal users tend to contain more details. For example, an income statement intended for

internal use usually provides even more detail than the segment information required by the Securities and Exchange Commission. Second, reports and statements for internal users are not constrained by generally accepted accounting principles. Thus, alternative formats of income statements are often provided to managers. One format will likely be prepared according to the full-absorption-costing format used for externally directed statements. Another format may be prepared according to the direct-costing format, with the costs grouped into variable and fixed categories. Third, financial reports and statements destined for internal users are mainly intended to serve managerial planning and control aims. Since budgets and budgetary control reports effectively serve both of these purposes, they constitute the major component of the typical internal financial reporting system.

Cost Accounting Systems

Numerous firms employ cost accounting systems in addition to financial reporting systems. Among those finding cost accounting systems to be especially useful are manufacturing firms, construction firms, publishers, vehicle repair services, banks, hospitals, and professional service firms.

In effect, a **cost accounting system** is a specialized data collection and processing system that is embedded within the more comprehensive financial reporting system. It summarizes costs according to some object and then generates cost-focused reports by means of the financial reporting system. Depending on the specific operations conducted by the firm, the object around which costs are summarized may be job, product, project, process, cost center, or some combination of these.

The most familiar type of cost accounting system is the job order cost system of a manufacturer that converts raw materials into finished goods. As we recall, a particular

[7]For examples see Arthur Andersen & Co., *Segment Information: Disclosure of Segment Information in 1977 Annual Reports* (Chicago: 1978).

JOB ORDER COST SHEET

Job Number 76A

Number of Units 100
Product Folding chairs

Date Started Feb. 25, 1991

Date Completed Feb. 28, 1991

Materials		Direct Labor		Manufacturing Overhead		
Requisition Number	Amount	Job Time Ticket Number	Amount	Hours (based on direct labor)	Rate	Amount
2365	$525	225-3	$100	50	$5	$250
2381	350	226-2	180			
2402	125	227-2	200			
	$1000	227-6	60			
			$540			

Cost Summary:

Materials	$1,000
Direct labor	540
Overhead	250
Total cost	$1,790

FIGURE 10-13   A completed job order cost sheet.

cost accounting system of this type accumulates three cost components: raw materials costs, direct labor costs, and manufacturing overhead costs. Each actual instance of a cost incurred for materials, labor, or overhead is assigned to the particular job order to which it applies. When a particular production job is completed, the costs of these three components are totaled; the result is the completed cost of the job and hence the inventory value of the batch of finished products (goods). An example of a completed job order cost sheet appears in Figure 10-13.

While numerous variations of job order cost systems have been adopted, the one most useful for operational control is the *standard cost system*.[8] In this variation standard unit costs are established for the raw materials, direct labor, and manufacturing

overhead components. As units of material and labor are put into production, they are charged to the affected job order on the basis of the standard unit costs. Manufacturing overhead is also applied to the job by multiplying the predetermined standard overhead rate by the selected activity base (e.g., direct labor hours incurred on the job). Meanwhile, all of the actual costs incurred with respect to each job are recorded from suppliers' invoices and pay records; all actual manufacturing overhead costs, pertaining to all jobs, are recorded from utility bills, depreciation journal vouchers, and so forth.

As noted, the standard cost system aids the operational control process. To be specific, it pinpoints inefficiencies in the production process. These inefficiencies are flagged by means of cost variances, that is, differences between the actual costs incurred for the three components and the standard costs charged into production. (Cost variances re-

[8]Standard costs are also usefully employed with other types of cost accounting systems.

veal efficiencies as well as inefficiencies, but we will focus on the latter.) Among the cost variances typically computed by a standard cost system are the following:

1. Materials price variance, which reveals possible inefficiencies in the purchasing of raw materials.

2. Materials usage variance, which reveals possible inefficiencies (e.g., excessive spoilage) in the use of raw materials during the production process.

3. Labor rate variance, which reveals possible inefficiencies in the assignment of employees to jobs (e.g., the assignment of more highly skilled, and hence higher-paid, employees than needed for particular jobs).

4. Labor efficiency variance, which reveals possible inefficiencies in the use of employees in the production process (e.g., excessive times to complete operations).

5. Overhead spending variance, which reveals possibly excessive spending for overhead items.

Production costs and variances are provided to production managers periodically—usually daily, weekly, or monthly.[9] The financial reports that contain these costs and variances may assume a variety of formats. Thus, one report could focus on individual jobs, showing for each job the actual and standard costs for the three components, together with the separate variances just described. For example, in the case of Job No. 76A (see Figure 10-13) it might show that standard costs for materials, direct labor, and overhead are $900, $600, and $300, respectively; that the total variance is $10 unfavorable ($1790 − $1800); that the materials price variance is $20 unfavorable; that the

---

[9]Nonfinancial reports are also needed by production managers. Examples are production schedules and reports of production jobs behind schedule.

Clopper Corp. Product Cost Analysis as of April 30, 1991			
Product Name	Type of Cost	Actual Cost	Variance (Over) Under Standard
Arches	Material	$ 650	($ 20)
	Labor	800	100
	Overhead	1200	90
	Total	$2650	$170
Beams	Material	$1725	$ 85
	Labor	2000	(150)
	Overhead	3000	30
	Total	$6725	($ 35)

FIGURE 10-14 An analysis of production costs by product.

materials usage variance is $80 unfavorable; and so on. Another report might focus on the manufactured products, analyzing for each product the actual costs and variances pertaining to the three components. Figure 10-14 presents a product cost analysis for the Clopper Corporation. Still other financial reports might focus on the production departments. Reports having this focus generally fit into reporting structures known as responsibility reporting systems.

Many current cost accounting systems employ computerized processing of transactions, as we shall see in Chapter 15. However, most are still designed with earlier modes of physical production in mind. For instance, they assign overhead costs on the basis of direct labor hours, even though direct labor generally represents only a small portion of product costs. They often collect overhead costs into large pools, thus reducing the possibility of controlling those increasingly important costs. They do not provide needed unit cost and productivity measures, such as overhead costs per unit of product and throughput time per work order.

A few progressive firms are attempting to correct such deficiencies; in the years ahead the typical cost accounting system should reflect an array of improved measures.[10]

Responsibility Reporting Systems

While standard cost accounting systems provide information useful to operational control processes, **responsibility reporting systems** provide information for management control. In essence, responsibility reporting systems, also known as responsibility accounting systems, consist of a set of correlated reports prepared for managers in the various responsibility centers of a firm. These reports feed accountability information upward through the managerial levels of the organizational structure. At each managerial level the reports summarize or filter the results of lower managerial levels; thus, the entire set of reports forms a pyramid linking together all managerial levels and organizational units of a firm. Because the reports focus on the financial performances of the respective responsibility centers, the reporting system is critically dependent on clearly established lines of responsibility and authority within the organizational structure.

As an element within a firm's management control process, each responsibility report contains performance standards. Since the system is financially oriented, the performance standards consist of the amounts budgeted for the responsibility center to which the report pertains. Thus, a responsibility reporting system may be described as a budgetary control system that follows the organizational structure of a firm.

The nature of the budgeted amounts depends on the category into which the respon-

sibility center fits. If the responsibility center is cost oriented, the performance standards consist of budgeted costs. For example, the performance standards for the cost center having the name "accounts payable department" include budgeted salaries and supplies. If the center is profit oriented, the performance standards consist of revenues and profits as well as costs. Thus, a profit center such as the sales department might have such performance standards as budgeted sales, budgeted sales salaries and commissions, and budgeted contribution margins.

To be effective, a responsibility report should trace inefficiencies to individual components and motivate the manager who heads the responsibility center to take corrective actions. Assuming the responsibility center to be a cost-oriented production department, the report would list such costs as direct materials, direct labor, supplies, and so forth. However, it would list *only* **controllable costs**—those that the manager heading the cost center can directly and significantly influence within the reporting period. For each controllable cost the report should provide one or more variances, based on differences between the actual and budgeted costs. For instance, it might include a labor rate variance and a labor efficiency variance, computed from information concerning actual and standard labor rates and hours worked on jobs. (As we recall from the managerial accounting course, the labor standards developed for use in the cost accounting system are utilized in computing budget values and labor cost variances.)

An example of a set of responsibility reports appears in Figure 10-15. The cost-oriented reports pertain to responsibility centers at four management levels. In Figure 10-16 these centers, all within the production function, appear as shaded organizational boxes. Each report links to (articulates with) the one above by means of "rolled-up" total

[10]See, for instance, Robert S. Kaplan, "One Cost System Isn't Enough," *Harvard Business Review* (Jan.–Feb. 1988), pp. 61–66.

Cost Summary for President

| Month: October | This Month | | Year-to-Date | |
Cost	Budget	(Over) Under Budget	Budget	(Over) Under Budget
President's office[a]	$ 36,600	$200	$ 366,000	$1,000
V.P.–finance and accounting	52,700	300	527,000	(600)
V.P.–engineering	25,300	(100)	253,000	(900)
V.P.–production	244,000	(3,860)	2,440,000	(45,659)
V.P.–marketing	120,000	(850)	1,200,000	(7,640)
V.P.–industrial relations	12,600	–	126,000	500
Total controllable costs	$491,200	$(4,310)	$4,912,000	$(53,299)

[a] Includes insurance, taxes, staff, salaries, depreciation (other than factory equipment), and miscellaneous items.

Cost Summary for Vice-President–Production

| Month: October | This Month | | Year-to-Date | |
Cost	Budget	(Over) Under Budget	Budget	(Over) Under Budget
Vice-President's office[b]	$ 30,800	$(200)	$ 308,000	$500
Purchasing[c]	3,500	310	35,000	(878)
Production planning and control	3,200	(480)	32,000	(4,280)
Production superintendent	192,430	(3,855)	1,924,300	(45,161)
Receiving, shipping, and stores	3,370	(85)	33,700	(660)
Quality control and maintenance	10,700	450	107,000	3,820
Total controllable costs	$244,000	$(3,860)	$2,440,000	$(45,659)

[b] Includes employee benefits, overtime premium payroll taxes, staff salaries, and miscellaneous items.

[c] Includes material price variance.

Cost Summary for Production Superintendent

| Month: October | This Month | | Year-to-Date | |
Cost	Budget	(Over) Under Budget	Budget	(Over) Under Budget
Superintendent's office[d]	$ 20,500	$200	$ 205,000	$(500)
Production unit 1	57,200	(1,650)	572,000	(14,855)
Production unit 2	21,760	710	217,600	(1,960)
Production unit 3	36,930	1	369,300	(696)
Finishing	15,240	(376)	152,400	(2,050)
Assembly	40,800	(2,740)	408,000	(25,100)
Total controllable costs	$192,430	$(3,855)	$1,924,300	$(45,161)

[d] Includes depreciation–factory equipment, staff salaries, and miscellaneous items.

Controllable Costs for Foreman, Production Unit 3

| Month: October | This Month | | Year-to-Date | |
Cost	Budget	(Over) Under Budget	Budget	(Over) Under Budget
Direct materials	$16,000	$150	$160,000	$1,210
Direct labor[e]	17,500	(276)	175,000	(3,172)
Supervision and staff salaries	1,500	–	15,000	–
Supplies	300	10	3,000	100
Setup for jobs	560	(35)	5,600	(318)
Rework	420	52	4,200	490
Heat, light, and power	200	15	2,000	(55)
Maintenance	350	(20)	3,500	117
Other costs	100	5	1,000	(68)
Total controllable costs	$36,930	$1	$369,300	$(696)

[e] Labor rate variance = $18; labor efficiency variance = $(294).

FIGURE 10-15 Four levels of responsibility reports.

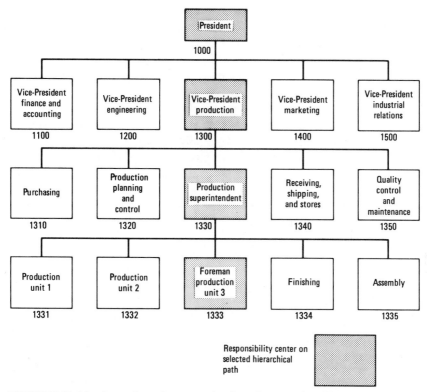

FIGURE 10-16 A portion of an organization chart used to illustrate responsibility reporting.

controllable costs.[11] (Arrows in Figure 10-15 trace these "roll-ups.") Since every cost is controllable at some level within an organization, the report to the president contains all of the costs incurred by the firm. However, the report to the president is as concise as the other three reports, since the costs it contains are more highly summarized or aggregated.

A sound coding system is critical to the success of a responsibility reporting system.

Since the system must gather and report costs (and possibly revenues) by responsibility center, each actual cost must be coded by center as well as by object of expenditure. Figure 10-16 illustrates responsibility center codes based on a hierarchical scheme. The resulting coding system enables (1) costs to be effectively accumulated for each separate report and (2) the managerial level and organizational function of each center (and hence report) to be identified. For instance, all costs coded 1333 will be compiled for the report to be received by the foreman of production unit 3. Thus, the code 761-1333 attached to a direct labor cost of $200 would cause the amount to be assigned to cost center 1333 and added to other direct labor costs already assigned there.

Responsibility reports vary widely in

[11]The foreman at the department level is responsible for all the variances listed in his report, including the two component labor variances and the materials usage variance (amounting to $250). However, the purchasing manager (and not the production department foreman) is responsible for the materials price variance; thus, it would appear in the responsibility report to the purchasing manager.

format from the example shown in Figure 10-15. Although almost all show variances, some also include actual amounts as well as (or instead of) budget amounts. Others include noncontrollable costs (e.g., allocated administrative costs) in a separate section of the report, even though the manager does not have responsibility for such costs. As suggested earlier, responsibility reports often include revenue and profit variances where appropriate (e.g., in the president's report). In addition, the reports may include key items that are relevant to each manager, for example, average labor productivity, percentage of orders shipped on time, and value of shipments for the vice-president of production.[12] At the other extreme, some reports only include those cost items for which the variances are significant.

Profit Planning (Profitability) Reporting Systems

Profit planning is the process of allocating resources in order to achieve desired profit objectives. Profit planning is embodied in budgets, as described earlier, that parallel a firm's organizational structure and span all of its segments and activities. The various component budgets or profit plans are generally summarized in projected income statements, also known as *profitability reports*.

The reports of a **profitability reporting system** employ several fundamental concepts of managerial accounting to aid the overall planning and decision making of a firm. These concepts are illustrated by Figure 10-17, a profitability report for a hypothetical manufacturing firm. First, revenues and costs are segmented by the products that the firm sells. This segmentation enables operating margins (also called segment margins) to be computed for the respective products, so that the relative performances of the prod-

ucts may be analyzed. (It also enables the return on invested capital to be computed for each product.) Second, costs are separated according to their variable and fixed natures. This separation enables contribution margins to be computed for each product, so that the effects of changes in activity levels may be analyzed. Third, only those fixed costs are allocated that can be directly traced to the respective products. Joint fixed costs are *not* arbitrarily allocated to the respective products. Instead, the joint fixed costs are included only in the computation of planned net income for the entire firm. Thus, an improper (and possibly dysfunctional) matching of product revenues and cost is avoided.

Other reports in the profitability reporting system of the above hypothetical firm might segment revenues and costs according to sales territories, markets, and so forth. In fact, certain of the reports may segment according to two or more dimensions. An example of a report segmented according to three dimensions—classes of customers, products, and sales territories—appears in Figure 10–18. Thus, the left-most column of the report would display the planned operating margin or profit based on sales of product 1 (e.g., full keyboard calculators) to customer class 1 (e.g., banks) within sales territory A (e.g., southwestern United States.)[13]

Profitability reports show the impact of each segment's contribution to a firm's fixed costs and overall profits. Therefore, they enable managers to make decisions concerning the retention of segments (e.g., sales territories or products), the pricing of products, the advertising effort to devote to each product, the acceptance of special orders, and the allocation of resources (e.g., salespersons) to the respective sales territories and customer classes. Furthermore, profitability reports aid the budgetary control process. Actual

[12]Howard G. Johnson, "Key Item Control," *Management Services* (Jan.–Feb. 1967), p. 25.

[13]Stephen L. Busby and L. E. Heitger, "Profit Contribution by Market Segment," *Management Accounting* (Nov. 1976), p. 45.

	Total	Products		
		1	2	3
Net sales	$1,575,000	$500,000	$850,000	$225,000
Less variable costs				
Direct materials	$525,000	$172,000	$290,000	$63,000
Direct labor	360,000	100,000	215,000	45,000
Variable indirect manufacturing expenses[a]	83,000	26,000	45,000	12,000
Variable selling expenses[b]	79,500	25,000	42,500	12,000
Variable administrative expenses[c]	5,500	2,000	2,500	1,000
Total variable costs	$1,053,000	$325,000	$595,000	$133,000
Contribution margin	$522,000	$175,000	$255,000	$92,000
Less fixed costs				
Committed costs assignable to products	$160,000	$55,000	$80,000	$25,000
Managed costs assignable to products	158,000	50,000	85,000	23,000
Total assigned fixed costs	$318,000	$105,000	$165,000	$48,000
Planned operating margin	$204,000	$70,000	$90,000	$44,000
Operating margin percentage		14.0%	10.6%	19.5%
Unallocated joint fixed costs	44,000			
Planned net income	$160,000			
Income taxes	83,200			
Planned net income after income taxes	$76,800			
Planned return on total assets[d]	5.1%			

[a]Schedule *A* details expenses (not shown).
[b]Schedule *B* details expenses (not shown).
[c]Schedule *C* details expenses (not shown).
[d]Expected average total assets = $1,500,000.

FIGURE 10-17   A report of planned profits by product for a manufacturing firm.

revenues, costs, and profits for each segment may be compared with planned revenues, costs, and profits. The resulting variances provide the means of evaluating the performances of the segments, so that responsible managers may take corrective actions when necessary.

Coding systems are as important to the preparation of profitability reports as they are to the preparation of responsibility reports. Since profitability reporting focuses on segments, a code for capturing transaction data must accommodate all of the relevant segments. Thus, in addition to the account number identifying the transaction, the code might include codes for the product, customer class, and sales territory. A sales transaction for the hypothetical manufacturing firm may therefore be coded 700-1-A-1, where 700 is the sales account, 1 is the product number, A is the sales territory code, and the last 1 is the customer class. Furthermore, an added code field may be needed to reflect the fixed or variable status of costs. For example, 1 might indicate a fixed cost, whereas 2 might denote a variable cost.

Relationships Among Reporting Systems

The four reporting systems just described are closely related. Each provides re-

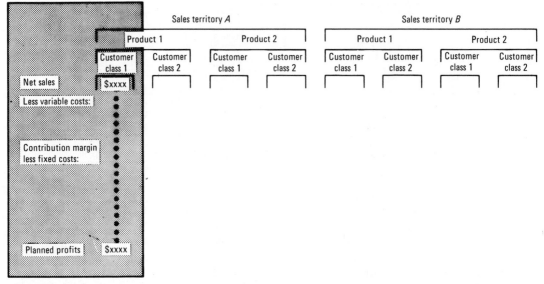

FIGURE 10-18 Profitability report segmentation by class of customer within products within sales territories. *Note:* (1) the shaded area denotes the scope of a report that would show the planned profits of product 1 within sales territory A for customer class 1. (2) Customer classes are within products, which are within sales territories. Thus, sales territories are the major classification, products the intermediate classification, and customer classes the most detailed classification.

ports that are (1) expressed in financial terms. (2) geared to a firm's chart of accounts, and (3) used to aid managers in fulfilling planning and control responsibilities. The financial reporting system is the most comprehensive in that it provides reports for external as well as internal users and serves the greatest variety of purposes. In fact, the financial reporting system can be viewed as incorporating the other three financially oriented reporting systems within the framework of the accounting information system.

Consequently, the cost accounting, responsibility reporting, and profitability reporting systems represent specialized reporting subsystems designed to aid managers in coping with the several decisions related to planning and control. The cost accounting system focuses on the costs of operations and provides reports useful for operational control. The responsibility reporting system focuses on costs and revenues incurred by responsibility centers; thus, it provides reports useful for management control. The profitability reporting system focuses on the profitability of products and other segments; hence, it provides reports useful primarily for tactical and strategic planning.

Additional reporting systems exist within a modern firm. Certain of these reporting systems are oriented to specific operational functions. For instance, some firms employ product planning systems that comprise a part of marketing information systems, quality control systems that comprise a part of production information systems, and capital budgeting systems that comprise a part of finance information systems. Others of these reporting systems are oriented to other activities, such as projects. However, few, if any, of these reporting systems are as highly developed and structured as the financially oriented reporting systems.

As the scheduled reports of a firm become more numerous, the reports themselves should be clearly identifiable. Each report can be coded to indicate the reporting system of which it is a member, the frequency of the report, the key manager or other party who is to receive the report, and so on. These codes thus aid distribution of the reports as well as facilitate administrative control over the totality of reports generated by a firm.

Decentralized Reporting Systems

In firms with decentralized organizational structures the division is often the major organizational unit. Most reports are division oriented in order to accommodate the heavy decision-making responsibilities of divisional managers. Division-level reports generally include profitability reports, since divisional managers typically have revenue and even investment responsibilities. Responsibility and production-cost reporting systems may also be geared to individual divisions.

Relatively few reports may flow from the divisional level to the corporate level of a decentralized firm. Those reports that do, however, should be comparable among divisions in terms of format and performance measures. For instance, if divisional managers have responsibility for the invested capital of their divisions, their performance reports should reflect the actual rates of return on invested capital achieved by the respective divisions. In addition, such reports should reflect variances from budgeted values for both segment revenues and segment costs.

Behavioral Considerations in Reporting Systems

Reports influence behavior—that is, they cause recipients such as managers to make decisions and to take actions. Some-

times the decisions and actions are in the best interests of the managers' firms, but sometimes they are not. When the latter occurs, a manager is acting dysfunctionally.

Various factors may cause managers to act dysfunctionally. Two prominent factors are information overload and inadequate performance measures.

A person's memory is limited. One cannot digest and remember more than about seven comparisons in a single report.[14] **Information overload** occurs when managers receive more information than they can digest. For instance, a materials manager may receive a thick listing of the status of all material items on hand, with no information concerning which items have reached dangerously low levels; or a personnel manager may receive a complex, poorly arranged report in which appear numerous comparisons of manpower needs and availabilities. A manager's reaction to information overload may take one of the following forms.[15]

1. Omission (not processing and using some of the information).
2. Error (processing and using information incorrectly).
3. Filtering (using only selected information as determined by a priority scheme).
4. Approximation (responding in a general but less precise way to the information than he or she would if the information input were reduced).
5. Queuing (delaying use of the information until a lull occurs).
6. Multiple channels (having one or more assistants help in processing and using the information).

[14]Frank Collins and Robert Seiler, "Perceptual Limitations: Their Effect on Financial Reports," *The Internal Auditor* (June 1978), pp. 24–25.

[15]Robert H. Ashton, "Behavioral Implications of Information Overload in Managerial Accounting Reports," *Cost and Management* (July–August 1974), p. 38.

Inadequate performance measures usually cause managers to manipulate the results that appear in control reports. Their decisions and actions are designed to make their reported results look as favorable as possible in the short run, even though those decisions and actions may be detrimental to their firm in the long run. For instance, divisional managers who are judged solely by return on invested capital will attempt to increase divisional net contribution and decrease divisional net investment. Thus, a manager might defer repairs, slight employee training, charge expenses to incorrect accounts, and refuse to approve feasible capital investments.

A sound reporting system can help to reduce such dysfunctional behavior. Reports should communicate effectively. Not only should they be based on reliable information, but they should take into account the personal limitations and specific information needs of the recipients. As noted earlier, reports should be as concise and understandable as possible. Also, they should include information in the most useful form, for example, graphically. Furthermore, while individual reports should not produce information overload, the reporting system should not slight needed information. Thus, besides providing relevant planning information, the financial reporting system should provide sufficient information for the sound evaluation of managerial performance. For example, divisional managers might be provided with more performance reports than those concerning profit variances. Other performance reports may reflect residual income, level of customer service, and so forth.

Of course, an effective reporting system is not sufficient in itself to ensure desired motivation and behavior of managers. Sound managerial practices such as participative budgeting and interdepartmental coordination are also necessary.

Summary

Needed information becomes useful and accessible when communicated via reports. Reports can be typed according to purpose, scope, conciseness, occurrence, time frame, format, and operational function. For instance, reports may be differentiated according to such purposes as supporting operations, aiding planning, assisting control, fulfilling stewardship, and complying with legal obligations. Operational reports initiate actions and record the results of operations and the status of resources. Planning reports, which contain future-oriented and comparative information, provide the basis for deciding among alternative courses of action. Control reports reflect comparisons of actual results against such benchmarks as established performance standards. Effective reports for use in managerial decision making provide information that is relevant, concise, discriminating, appropriate with respect to scope, understandable, timely, reliable, and consistent with the other reports of the firm. Screen displays should be user friendly.

Horizontal and vertical reporting systems link together the activities and managerial levels of a firm. Several financially oriented reporting systems are found within the modern firm. The financial reporting system provides financial reports to external and internal users; many of the reports intended for internal users are budgetary reports. The cost accounting system summarizes results of operations and aids the operational control process. The responsibility reporting system aids in evaluating performances within responsibility centers throughout a firm. The profitability reporting system provides reports that focus on the profitability of various segments (e.g., product lines); it aids in tactical and strategic planning. All of these reporting systems mesh to provide an integrated network of reports to aid overall planning and control, and are appropriate to decentralized as well as centralized organizations. Sound reporting systems are also helpful in reducing dysfunctional behavior on the part of managers.

Review Problems with Solutions

Problem 1 Statement

The Oregon Paper Company of Eugene, Oregon, was recently incorporated.[16] Although the company was founded by sawmill operators in western Oregon, its stock is publicly owned and traded on the major stock exchanges. Its main facility consists of a paper mill and adjoining offices and warehouse.

The purpose of the firm is to transform wood chips into pulp and then into kraft paper by a process consisting of more than 80 steps. Excess pulp is sold separately as an unfinished by-product.

Resources used in the production of these products include wood, cooking and bleaching chemicals, paper additives, machine wires, and other direct materials; supplies, boiler feedwater chemicals, fuel oil, and other indirect materials; direct and indirect labor; purchased electric power, specialized equipment, and other overhead items.

One of the first concerns of the new managers was the need for a sound reporting structure. Accordingly, they established the firm's objectives, policies, organizational structure, lists of responsibilities, and lists of needed decisions. Then they employed a consulting firm to develop the details of a reporting structure geared to the foregoing.

---

[16]This case is roughly based on Karl Patrick's "The Concept and Development of a Total Business Information System, Part 2: The Delta Pulp and Paper Company Limited," *Cost and Management* (Jan. 1969), pp. 10–16. Reprinted with permission of the Society of Management Accountants of Canada.

Required

Outline the reporting structure that you, as the consultant, would design for the Oregon Paper Company.

Solution

The overall framework for the reporting structure will consist of four reporting systems: an operational control reporting system, a management control reporting system, a tactical reporting system, and a strategic reporting system.

The **operational control reporting system** focuses on the processes at the operational level. Its cycle ranges from an hour to a week. Reports in the system will be expressed in nonfinancial as well as financial terms. Among the key reports will be

Weekly production summaries, actual versus scheduled.

Hourly quality control reports.

Daily labor productivity reports.

Weekly machine utilization reports.

Weekly labor distribution reports.

Weekly cost accounting summaries.

Most of the reports pertain to such objects of concern as individual processes, employees, machines, and orders.

The **management control reporting system** focuses on departmental performances and has a monthly cycle. The key reports will be responsibility reports for all departments; each report will show variances for the respective controllable costs, with the materials variances separated into price and usage variances and the labor variances separated into rate and efficiency variances.

The **tactical reporting system** focuses on plantwide activities. Its cycle ranges from a month to a year. As in the case of the operational control reporting system, reports will be expressed in nonfinancial as well as financial terms. Among the key reports will be

Monthly production schedules (revised weekly or as necessary).

Monthly inventory status reports.

Monthly plant efficiency reports.

Monthly product shipment reports.

Monthly maintenance schedules.

Monthly sales analyses.

Monthly accounts receivable aging schedules.

Monthly purchase analyses.

Monthly idle-time and productivity analyses.

Monthly production cost analyses.

Annual profit plan, by product.

Annual cash budget.

The **strategic reporting system** focuses on long-range corporate plans. Although it is not cyclic in nature, its time horizon extends five or more years into the future. The key reports will be a capital or strategic budget, plus annual reports on competitors and markets. Other reports will be prepared on an ad hoc basis to aid managers in making specific long-range resource allocation decisions. Most reports will be expressed in financial terms.

Problem 2 Statement

The Maxy Sales Corporation of San Antonio, Texas, sells two lines of products (line A and line B) throughout three sales regions. One day the sales manager calls your superior, the head of the management reports department, for assistance. You and a fellow management accountant are assigned to interview the sales manager concerning her problem. During the ensuing discussion you learn that she needs information to help her judge how well the respective product lines and regional sales offices are performing.

Required

Describe the steps that you and your colleague should take to satisfy the request of the sales manager. Also, prepare a suitable report format, complete with illustrative information.

Solution

Our first step is to recognize that the needed report is related to the management control process. Thus, it should measure and compare performances. Since each sales office is a profit center, we decide that sales volume and profit contribution are suitable performance measures. Budgeted values of these measures will serve as performance standards.

Having established the relevant information to be provided, we turn to the other attributes. We first observe that the scope of the report should span *all* regional sales offices, since all sales activities are the responsibility of the sales manager. To provide suitable discrimination, we decide to segment the results both in accordance with product lines and in accordance with sales offices. On the other hand, we decide not to show the *actual* values of sales and profit contributions in the interest of conciseness. Therefore, the report will emphasize budgeted values and variances, which are likely to be of most interest to the sales manager.

Next we consider the attribute of timeliness. After discussing the matter with the sales manager, we decide that the report will be issued monthly and will be available within three days after the end of each month. The manager is satisfied that monthly reports will be sufficiently timely to allow her to make necessary control decisions. However, she leaves open the possibility of increasing the frequency to once a week during the peak selling season. With respect to format, we decide on a tabular arrangement by which to display the information; it allows all of the information to be presented concisely on a single page. In addition, we plan to present the variances in graphical form, using a bar-type chart.

Finally, we consider the attribute of reliability. In order to collect and report sales accurately and completely, we require a sound internal control structure. One key feature of this structure is a code for identifying sales-oriented transactions. To be adequate, the code should identify the general ledger account affected by the transaction, plus the product line and the regional sales office involved in the transaction.[17] For instance, the code for a sales transaction (account 700) pertaining to produce line A and

---

[17]If additional sales analyses are to be prepared, other facets might be added to the code, for example, the salesperson making the sale and the customer to whom the sale is made.

the northern sales office (assigned number 3) might appear as 700-A-3. The code for a sales commission relating to a sale of product B by the eastern regional sales office (assigned number 2) could appear as 810-B-2.

An example of the resulting tabular report appears below. Several points of the report are worth noting:

1. All of the information is neatly typed or printed.

2. The format includes identifying information such as the name of the firm, the name of the report, the period covered, and the units of measure.

3. Headings appear across the top and down the left side, whereas totals are at the bottom and the right side.

4. Labeling is clearly descriptive of the contents. For instance, the label "Variance Over (Under) Budget" indicates that the

Maxy Sales Corp.
Sales Report
(Thousands of Dollars)
July 1991

| Regional Sales Office | Product Line | | | | | | | | | |
| | A | | | B | | | Total | | |
	Budget	Variance Over (Under) Budget	Percent Variance	Budget	Variance Over (Under) Budget	Percent Variance	Budget	Variance Over (Under) Budget	Percent Variance
Western: sales	$6,000	($500)	(8.3)	$10,000	$400	4.0	$16,000	($100)	(0.6)
contribution	2,000	(167)	(8.3)	1,000	40	4.0	3,000	(127)	(4.2)
Eastern: sales	$9,000	($200)	(2.2)	$14,000	($100)	(0.7)	$23,000	($300)	(1.3)
contribution	3,000	(67)	(2.2)	1,400	(10)	(0.7)	4,400	(77)	(1.8)
Northern: sales	$7,500	$100	1.3	$12,000	$600	5.0	$19,500	$700	0.8
contribution	2,500	33	1.3	1,200	60	5.0	3,700	93	2.5
Total: sales	$22,500	($600)	(2.7)	$36,000	$900	2.5	$58,500	$300	0.5
contribution	7,500	(201)	(2.7)	3,600	90	2.5	11,100	(111)	(1.0)

figure $500 without parentheses represents a favorable variance, whereas the same number within parentheses represents an unfavorable variance.

5. Percentage variations from budgeted amounts are added in order to suggest significance and to increase the meaningfulness of the information. For example, they reveal that the two most significant variances are (a) the variance of product line A in the western sales office territory and (b) the variance of product line B in the northern sales office territory. They also suggest that the western sales office is significantly below budget in its contribution to profits. Furthermore, the overall 1.0 percent variance of contribution below budget points to a generally unfavorable performance in spite of an overall favorable sales volume.

6. Other information could be included in the report. For instance, year-to-date variances, units sold, and major costs incurred would each add to the meaning. However, they would also increase the clutter of the report and might overload the manager with information.

7. If a larger number of product lines or sales offices were to be compared, the format would need to be modified. In the case, for example, of 10 product lines and the identical three sale offices, the product lines could be listed down the side rather than across the top. In the case of 10 product lines and 10 sales offices, sales offices might be grouped into a summary report, with the details of individual sales offices shown in supporting schedules.

Review Questions

10-1 What is the meaning of each of the following terms?

    Stewardship report
    Legal compliance report

    Operational report
    Planning report
    Control report
    Summary report
    Exception report
    Scheduled report
    Demand report
    Event-triggered report
    Benchmark
    Screen display
    Horizontal reporting system
    Vertical reporting system
    Financial reporting system
    Cost accounting system
    Responsibility reporting system
    Controllable cost
    Profitability reporting system
    Information overload

10-2 List eight ways in which reports may be classified, and note several categories of reports under each classification plan.

10-3 Identify two uses of operational reports.

10-4 Identify several examples of planning reports.

10-5 What are the key features of planning reports?

10-6 How do planning reports that aid in strategic planning differ from those that aid in tactical planning?

10-7 Describe several examples of control reports.

10-8 Why must a report contain benchmarks if it is to serve as a control report?

10-9 What types of benchmarks are commonly used in control reports?

10-10 Identify several centers or objects that provide focuses of concern for control reports.

10-11 What are the attributes of a useful control report?

10-12 Discuss the attribute of timeliness in control reports.

10-13 Discuss the roles of reports in the budgetary process.

10-14 Discuss the general attributes and special features of effective reports.

10-15 What attribute is critical in screen displays?

10-16 Contrast horizontal and vertical reporting systems.

10-17 What are several differences between financial reports intended for external users and those intended for internal users?

10-18 Describe the major features of a standard job order cost accounting system.

10-19 Identify several cost variances that are provided by a standard job order cost accounting system.

10-20 Describe the features of a responsibility reporting system.

10-21 Describe the features of an effective profitability report.

10-22 How can profitability reports aid in decision making?

10-23 Describe the distinguishing features of codes that are needed for responsibility and for profitability reporting systems.

10-24 Describe the relationships and distinctions among cost, responsibility, and profitability reporting systems.

10-25 What are desirable features of reports in decentralized organizational structures?

10-26 What are examples of reporting inadequacies that may cause managers to act dysfunctionally?

Discussion Questions

10-27 Briefly describe several reports that reflect certain of the general ledger or subsidiary ledger account balances.

10-28 In what respects can reports be said to determine the design of an information system?

10-29 Why are reports expressed in financial terms more useful for making strategic decisions and other planning decisions than reports expressed in nonfinancial terms?

10-30 Which level of management would likely receive each of the following reports and what type of decision would the reports help the managers to make?

   a. Profitability report.
   b. Analysis of purchases made from various suppliers.
   c. Production schedule for the next quarter.
   d. An inventory activity and status report.
   e. A market survey report pertaining to the feasibility of new product lines.
   f. A monthly budgetary control report reflecting cost variances pertaining to the various operations departments.
   g. A report of the number of units of product rejected for poor quality in the machining department.

10-31 For each of the following reports, (1) identify several key items of information likely to be included, (2) suggest questions that likely will be answered by the information contained therein, and (3) indicate decisions that they can aid responsible managers to make:

   a. Production schedule.
   b. Maintenance schedule.
   c. Production labor productivity report.
   d. Accounts receivable aging report.
   e. Cash flow projection.
   f. Labor distribution summary.
   g. Inventory status report.
   h. Sales analysis by salespersons within customer classes.

i. Sales analysis by products within sales territories.

j. Expected inventory stock-out report.

k. Supplier evaluation analysis.

l. Distribution-by-value report, which lists products sold by a firm, arranged by amounts of sales dollars.

m. Scrap report.

n. Production cost control report.

o. Project control report.

p. Report of outstanding purchase orders.

q. Report of orders shipped and payments received.

r. Employee overtime report.

s. Quality control report.

t. Equipment utilization report.

u. Spoilage control report.

v. Report of actual versus planned production.

10-32 Each of the following could generate event-triggered reports. What decision might follow the receipt of each report by the responsible manager?

a. Reorder points.

b. Credit limits.

c. Overdue payments.

d. Behind-schedule shipments.

e. High level of rejects.

f. Low inventory turnover rate.

g. Low current ratio.

h. Low employee productivity.

i. High level of customer complaints.

j. Insufficient machines to handle workload.

10-33 Each of the following items of information appears in a report received by a manager having appropriate responsibility. What additional information, if any, might the manager desire and what control decisions (corrective actions) might be considered?

a. Ten percent of the total employees are absent today.

b. Product line B generates 80 percent of total sales revenue.

c. Five percent of the inventory items comprise 70 percent of the value of total inventory.

d. Fifteen percent of credit sales cost more to process than they generate in profits.

e. Eight percent of the customers are responsible for 90 percent of past-due accounts.

f. Two of the 10 sales branches generate 75 percent of total sales revenue.

g. Department 7 had labor turnover of 50 percent last year, whereas the average departmental turnover rate was 12 percent.

h. Twenty percent of customers' orders are delivered late.

10-34 Describe the content of a suitable report to aid in each of the following control processes:

a. Controlling the level of inventory items.

b. Controlling the quality of products.

c. Controlling the credit of customers.

d. Controlling the productivity of employees.

e. Controlling the on-time shipments of customers' orders.

f. Controlling the costs of production orders.

10-35 Describe one operational report, one planning report, and one control report that would be useful to each of the following managers:

a. President.

b. Treasurer.

c. Controller.

d. Personnel director.

e. Production manager.
f. Sales manager.
g. Credit manager.
h. Purchasing manager.
i. Inventory manager.
j. Distribution manager.

10-36 A number of variances may be provided by a standard job order cost accounting system. While such variances are useful in the operational control process, they may also be used in the evaluation of managerial performances. For each of the following variances, indicate the responsible manager and possible corrective actions:

a. Materials price variance.
b. Materials usage variance.
c. Labor rate variance.
d. Labor efficiency variance.
e. Overhead spending (budget) variance.
f. Overhead volume variance.
g. Selling price variance.
h. Sales volume variance.

10-37 A cost control report for this week shows that the materials usage variance is $100 over standard, and the labor efficiency variance is $200 over standard. Comment on the relative significance of each of these variances, if the weekly budgeted materials and labor costs are $10,000 and $25,000, respectively, and variances in the past have averaged 1 percent for materials usage and 3 percent for labor efficiency. Should this additional information be included in the control report?

10-38 Discuss the feature of effective reporting that is illustrated by a delinquent notice to a customer, a red-light pressure gauge, a list of absent employees, and a list of jobs behind schedule.

10-39 Why is each of the following generally an inappropriate reporting practice?

a. Providing hourly reports to the president.

b. Providing complete listings of the status of all production jobs and inventory items to the production manager.
c. Providing the income statement and balance sheet for last period to the sales manager when she requests information that will enable her to plan the sales activities for the coming year.
d. Providing information concerning Monday's employee productivity to the assembly production foreman on Wednesday.
e. Providing responsibility reports to the respective production foremen that include allocations of plant depreciation and other overhead costs and cost variances related to these allocated costs.
f. Providing responsibility reports to a foreman that omit all favorable cost variances, even if they are quite large.

10-40 Is it possible to issue reports too frequently to managers? Discuss.

10-41 Managerial accountants generally are responsible for designing responsibility reporting and other control reporting systems. However, the technical accounting aspects underlying such reporting systems are part of a broader fabric, which includes organizational relationships, behavioral patterns, and corporate philosophies. Discuss the implications of this situation on the design approach to be taken by accountants.

Problems

10-1 Identify the strengths and weaknesses (if any) of each of the following reports and describe how each report could be of use to the responsible managers:

a.

Assembly Department July 26, 1991			
Employee Number	Employee Name	Percent of Standard Productivity	
		Today	This Week
8236	Brown, G.	94	90
7113	Dalton, M.	86	88
5263	Green, R.	93	93
6879	Lightner, P.	98	99
7325	Newstrom, L.	100	100
4731	Stuart, T.	88	94
8512	Walker, B.	79	76
	Average	91.1	91.4

b.

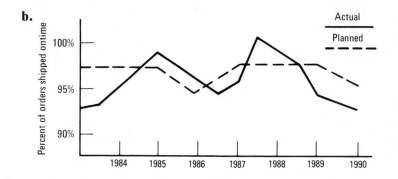

c.

Product	Projected Out-of-Stock			
	Next Week	Two Weeks Ahead	Three Weeks Ahead	Four Weeks Ahead
A			X	X
B	X	X	X	X
C				X

10-2 Design reports that will provide needed information to enable the responsible managers to achieve the purposes stated below.

   a. Review the activity and status of each merchandise item.

   b. Analyze sales by product, sales-man, and sales territory. Assume that two products—Alpha and Beta—are sold by all salespersons. Salespersons A, B, C, and D are assigned to territory 1, and salespersons E, F, G, and H are assigned to territory 2.

   c. Analyze this month's profitability

to decide whether products A, B, C, and D should be retained or discontinued.

d. Evaluate the weekly performance of a salesperson who sells products A and B on a quota, is paid on a commission basis, and is required to reimburse the firm for any expenses in excess of a weekly budget.

e. Analyze the collectibility of accounts receivable from all the customers having balances.

f. Evaluate the performances of alternative suppliers relative to price, quality, and reliability of promised delivery dates.

g. Evaluate direct material, direct labor, and overhead costs incurred in production, with respect to both prices and usages.

h. Project the expected requirements for cash during the four quarters of the coming year.

i. Evaluate the daily usage of materials by employees in key production operations, where the intent is to enable the foremen to control waste caused by carelessness and inefficiency. Assume that two materials (Delta and Omega) and four operations (I, II, III, and IV) are involved in the production process.

10-3 Super-Snap, Ltd., of San Juan, Puerto Rico, provides a variety of photographic services. In planning its operations for 1991 the owner estimates that total revenues will amount to $70,000, broken down according to the major services as follows:

Photo posters,	60%
Photofinishing,	30%
Copywork,	10%

The owner also estimates that the major

costs and cost groupings will be as follows:

	Photo Posters	Photo-finishing	Copywork
Labor	$10,500	$7,000	$2,100
Supplies	7,000	4,000	1,300
Outside services	5,000	3,000	1,500
Other variable costs	1,500	1,000	400
Direct fixed costs	1,100	800	200

Joint fixed costs should amount to $17,000. The income tax rate may be assumed to be 34 percent.

Required

Prepare a profit planning report for Super-Snap, Ltd.

10-4 The Arguay Corporation of St. Petersburg, Florida, prepares a weekly comprehensive inventory control report, such as the example shown on page 412. The report was developed by the firm's data processing department from a sketch prepared by the plant manager. The report is sent regularly to the production manager, purchasing manager, and cost accounting manager.

Required

Based upon the displayed segment of the inventory control report and the circumstances described above, discuss why the report is not an effective communication vehicle.

(CMA adapted)

10-5 The Mecom Co. of Las Cruces, New Mexico, produces sports equipment. Each manager in charge of a department or higher responsibility center receives a monthly performance report. Last month (June) the costs pertaining to the fabricating depart-

Arguay Company
Comprehensive Inventory Control Report
Week Ended August 9, 1991

Part Number	Inventory on Hand	Used	Purchased	Standard Cost Per Unit	Total Actual Costs	Variance
...						
53 Series						
...	...	...	...	...	...	...
5397	175	8,433	8,556	$1.0325	$9,033	$ (199)
5398	215	9,717	9,810	.0786	765	6
...	...	...	...	...	...	...
Total 53 Series	12,387	647,305	649,077	.6438	· 423,068	(5,192)
54 Series						
...	...	...	...	...	...	...
5401	1,191	15,448	16,352	.3597	5,723	159
5402	1,723	37,236	35,897	.5500	19,815	(72)
...	...	...	...	...	...	...
Total 54 Series	42,786	1,437,233	1,435,865	.7490	1,074,173	1,290
Total inventory	708,113	10,797,828	10,872,560	1.4350	15,657,100	(54,976)

Note: The series of dots (i.e., ...) represent other data omitted from the report to simplify presentation.

ment within the production function were as follows:

	Actual	Budgeted
Raw materials	$ 5,600	$ 6,000
Direct labor	12,800	12,000
Supplies	650	700
Utilities	1,680	1,500
Depreciation of departmental equipment	1,000	1,000
Depreciation of plant—allocated	6,000	6,000
Production administration cost—allocated	5,200	4,000
Indirect labor	3,400	3,000
Salary—department head	2,000	2,000

Each department manager is responsible for decisions concerning equipment needed in his or her department.

Required

Using the data provided, prepare June's report for the fabricating department in good form and in accordance with the concepts of responsibility reporting.

10-6 The report on page 413 was prepared to reflect the operating results of the Tyler Manufacturing Corporation of Oklahoma City.[18]

Required

a. Identify the specific weaknesses of the report if the users are the firm's top managers.

b. Why might the report cause information overload for a busy high-level manager, and what behavioral reactions might follow from this information overload?

c. Revise the side headings of the report to reflect production cost behavior that is

[18]From Frank Collins and Robert Seiler, "Perceptual Limitations: Their Effect on Financial Reports," *The Internal Auditor* (June 1978), p. 31. Copyright © 1978 by The Institute of Internal Auditors, Inc., 249 Maitland Avenue, Altamonte Springs, Fla. 32701. Reprinted by permission.

	This Year		Last Year	This Year to	Last Year to
	April	March	April	Date	Date
Gross sales	$13,675,657.40	$12,991,874.53	$11,624,308.45	$67,154,494.43	$65,796,769.33
Less					
Returns and allowances	88,664.10	84,230.89	75,364.44	471,692.93	448,107.47
Cash discounts	102,820.20	97,679.19	87,397.02	547,002.47	519,650.22
Freight and express allowed	93,961.43	89,263.36	79,867.41	499,874.82	474,880.24
	$285,445.73	$271,173.44	$242,628.87	$1,518,570.22	$1,442,637.93
NET SALES	$13,390,211.67	$12,720,701.09	$11,381,679.58	$65,635,924.21	$64,354,131.40
Cost and expenses					
Cost of products sold					
Inventory at beginning of period	$12,680,496.09	$12,546,471.20	$10,768,421.60	$11,000,237.64	$10,697,213.44
Purchased material	3,432,208.27	3,180,597.62	3,097,376.82	17,271,343.24	16,502,458.93
Direct labor	2,877,356.73	2,753,488.21	2,645,753.52	14,307,532.89	13,591,876.24
Indirect labor	2,657,832.40	2,583,549.74	2,359,157.22	13,299,874.46	12,634,849.23
Supervision	943,494.80	916,320.06	841,975.54	5,019,307.72	4,768,924.64
Other employee benefits	474,820.13	451,080.23	403,597.76	2,473,264.55	2,349,811.11
Small tools and shop supplies	87,430.26	83,058.75	73,155.62	465,124.87	441,897.62
Heat, light, and power	76,764.19	72,925.98	52,494.77	408,385.48	387,949.73
Traveling	30,124.30	28,618.09	25,605.47	160,260.81	152,441.18
Telephone and telegraph	13,086.87	12,431.70	11,123.49	69,617.84	66,124.98
Royalties	487.21	462.85	413.95	2,591.96	2,460.60
Property taxes	102,680.72	97,546.66	87,278.36	506,257.61	480,771.52
Payroll taxes	75,749.40	71,961.93	64,382.81	402,394.72	261,387.94
Maintenance and repairs	570,280.00	574,162.37	484,501.11	3,047,307.21	2,894,076.53
Rent	23,455.20	23,455.20	19,947.62	131,348.01	124,782.44
Insurance	39,000.82	38,056.29	33,150.22	213,113.67	202,349.98
Miscellaneous	782,378.08	743,259.10	455,021.48	3,662,209.74	3,478,949.67
Scrap sales	48,766.29[a]	46,327.97[a]	41,452.23[a]	259,391.62[a]	246,874.22[a]
	$24,818,879.18	$24,131,118.01	$21,381,905.13	$72,180,780.80	$68,791,451.56
Less inventory at end of period	12,977,200.03	12,680,496.09	11,030,601.49	12,977,200.03	11,030,601.49
TOTAL COST OF PRODUCTS SOLD	$11,841,679.15	$11,450,621.92	$10,351,303.64	$59,203,580.77	$57,760,850.07
TOTAL SELLING AND ADVERTISING EXPENSE	$473,796.02	$450,118.66	$402,776.33	$2,519,947.93	$2,392,767.93
Administrative and general expense					
Administrative expense	$45,505.64	$43,230.57	$38,671.92	$242,088.97	$229,987.69
General office expense	187,949.32	178,551.45	159,732.44	999,605.62	949,876.22
Data processing	21,677.24	20,593.72	18,425.61	115,320.04	109,324.67
Legal	3208.71	3048.27	2726.66	11,468.72	10,868.69
Public relations	27,480.20	26,106.21	23,359.14	146,130.82	138,764.77
TOTAL ADMINISTRATIVE & GENERAL EXP.	$285,821.11	$271,530.22	$242,915.77	$1,514,614.17	$1,438,822.04
TOTAL COSTS AND EXPENSES	$12,601,296.28	$12,172,270.80	$10,996,995.74	$63,238,142.87	$61,592,440.04
NET OPERATING EARNINGS	$788,915.39	$548,430.29	$384,683.84	$2,397,781.34	$2,761,691.36
Other income					
Dividends	$37,082.00	$39,230.00	$31,450.00	$79,620.00	$75,051.00
Gain on sales of securities	46.25	0	0	46.25	24.80
Gain on disposal of property, plant, and equipment	3127.08	5820.10	5207.08	32,592.04	30,960.21
Interest	1180.00	1121.00	1003.00	6446.00	6123.70
Royalties	8027.50	8027.50	7846.00	47,614.00	45,220.00
TOTAL OTHER INCOME	$49,462.83	$54,198.60	$45,506.08	$166,318.29	$157,379.71
Other expense					
Interest	$108,233.33	$102,826.66	$91,982.67	$575,825.64	$547,621.42
Amortization of bond discount	17,301.00	15,469.00	14,762.00	86,626.42	82,267.41
TOTAL OTHER EXPENSE	$125,534.33	$118,295.66	$106,744.67	$662,452.06	$629,888.83
NET EARNINGS BEFORE TAXES ON INCOME	$712,843.89	$484,333.23	$323,445.25	$1,901,647.57	$2,289,182.24
Federal taxes on income	377,000.00	254,000.00	168,000.00	1,051,000.00	1,280,000.00
NET EARNINGS	$335,843.89	$230,333.23	$155,445.25	$850,647.57	$1,009,182.24

[a] Credit Item

useful for the purpose of planning. Assume that royalties, heat, light, power, maintenance, repairs, and rent are fixed production costs. All other production costs are variable.

 10-7 *Note: This problem can be solved with the aid of a microcomputer-based data base software package such as dBase or RBase.* Canyon Technical Institute maintains an on-line computer system that allows authorized faculty and staff to obtain needed information concerning students. Responses to coded inquiries are displayed on screens of video display terminals and microcomputers tied to the computer network and located in administrative offices.

Required

Design screen displays that represent responses to the following inquiries. In each of the responses the student(s) should be identified by both name(s) and Social Security number(s). Enter assumed information into each screen display.

a. The grades earned by an individual student during a past semester, including the grade point average (GPA) and cumulative GPA.

b. The students presently enrolled in a specific class, including the location of the class, time of the class, major of the students, class standing of the students, and total number of students. Assume a limit of 10 students.

c. The current status, in amounts, of an individual student's loans, parking fines, library fines, and tuition fees. Show the fines to be overdue and payable.

10-8 The Brown Printing Company of Fairfax, Virginia, accounts for the services it performs on a job-cost basis. Most jobs require a week or less to complete and involve two or more of Brown's five operating departments.

Actual costs are accumulated by job. To ensure timely billing, however, the firm prepares sales invoices based on cost estimates.

Recently, several printing jobs have incurred losses. To avoid future losses, management has decided to focus on cost control at the department level. Since labor is a major cost element, one proposal is to develop a departmental labor cost report. This report is to be issued by the payroll department as one of the biweekly payroll outputs. The report is to be sent to an accounting clerk for comparison with the labor cost estimates of each department. If the actual total department labor cost in a payroll period is not significantly more than the estimated amount, the accounting clerk is to send the report to the department foreman. However, if the accounting clerk concludes that a significant variance exists, the report will be sent to the assistant controller. She will investigate the cause, if time is available, and will recommend corrective action to the production manager.

Required

a. List the key aspects of management control, as discussed in Chapter 4, that are supported by the proposed report and related procedure.

b. List the key aspects of management control that are violated by the proposed report and related procedure.

(CIA adapted)

10-9 George Johnson was hired on July 1, 1988, as assistant general manager of the Botel Division of Staple, Inc. It was understood that he would be elevated to general manager of the division on January 1, 1989, when the then current general manager retired, and this was duly done. In addition to becoming acquainted with the division and the general manager's duties, Mr. Johnson was specifically charged with the responsibility for development of the 1989 and 1990 budgets. As general manager in 1990 he was, obviously, responsible for the 1991 budget.

The Staple Corporation, headquartered in Rochester, Minnesota, is a highly decentralized multiproduct company. Each division is quite autonomous. The corporation staff approves division-prepared operating budgets but seldom makes major changes in them. The corporate staff actively participates in decisions requiring capital investment (for expansion or replacement) and makes the final decisions. The division management is responsible for implementing the capital program.

The major method used by the Staple Corporation to measure division performance is contribution return on division net investment. The budgets presented below

were approved by the corporation. Revision of the 1991 budget is not considered necessary, even though 1990 actually departed from the 1990 budget.

Required

a. Identify Mr. Johnson's responsibilities under the management and measurement program described above.

b. Appraise the performance of Mr. Johnson in 1990 as reflected in the report below.

c. Recommend to the president any changes in the responsibilities assigned to managers or in the measurement methods used to evaluate division management based upon your analysis.

(CMA adapted)

Botel Division[a]

Accounts	Actual			Budget	
	1988	1989	1990	1990	1991
Sales	1,000	1,500	1,800	2,000	2,400
Less division variable costs:					
Material and labor	250	375	450	500	600
Repairs	50	75	50	100	120
Supplies	20	30	36	40	48
Less division managed costs:					
Employee training	30	35	25	40	45
Maintenance	50	55	40	60	70
Less division committed costs:					
Depreciation	120	160	160	200	200
Rent	80	100	110	140	140
Total costs	600	830	871	1,080	1,223
Division net contribution	400	670	929	920	1,177
Division investment:					
Accounts receivable	100	150	180	200	240
Inventory	200	300	270	400	480
Fixed assets	1,590	2,565	2,800	3,380	4,000
Less: accounts and wages payable	(150)	(225)	(350)	(300)	(360)
Net investment	1,740	2,790	2,900	3,680	4,360
Contribution return on net investment	23%	24%	32%	25%	27%

[a]$ and 000 omitted.

10-10 The National Association of Trade Stores is located in Columbus, Ohio. Each month the department heads receive a financial report of the performance of their departments for the previous month. The report is generally distributed around the 16th or 17th of the month. Although the association is a not-for-profit trade and educational association, it does attempt to generate revenues from a variety of activities to supplement the member dues. The association has several income-producing departments: research, education, publications, and promotion consulting services. As a general rule, each department is expected to be self-supporting, and the department head is responsible for both the generation of revenue and the control of costs for the department.

As an example of the monthly department report, the March 1991 report of the education department is presented below with the comments of the accounting department.

The annual revenue target, which becomes the revenue budget, is established by the executive director and the association's board of directors. The annual and monthly expense budgets are then developed at the beginning of the year by the department heads for all costs except rent, utilities, and janitorial services; equipment depreciation; and allocated general administration. The

National Association of Trade Stores
Education Department
Report for the Month of March 1991

	Budget			Actual			Variance		Variance as a % of Budget	
	Person Days or Units	$	%	Person Days or Units	$	%	Person Days or Units	$	Person Days or Units	$
Revenue										
Week-long courses	1500	$225,000	71.4%	1250	$187,500	66.4%	(250)	$(37,500)	(16.6)%	(16.6)%
One-day seminars	50	15,000	4.8	17	5,100	1.8	(33)	(9,900)	(66.0)	(66.0)
Home-study courses	1000	75,000	23.8	1100	89,700	31.8	100	14,700	10.0	19.6
Expenses		$315,000	100.0%		$282,300	100.0%		$(32,700)		(10.4)%
Salaries		$174,000	55.2%		$167,000	59.1%		$7,000		4.0%
Course material		35,500	11.3		34,670	12.3		830		2.3
Supplies, tele. & tele.		4,000	1.3		4,200	1.5		(200)		(5.0)
Rent, utilities & janitorial serv.		7,000	2.2		7,000	2.5		—		—
Equipment depreciation		700	.2		700	.2		—		—
Allocated gen. admin.		5,000	1.6		5,000	1.8		—		—
Temporary office help		5,000	1.6		3,750	1.3		1,250		25.0
Contract employees		15,000	4.8		18,500	6.6		(3,500)		(23.3)
Travel		12,000	3.8		11,500	4.1		500		4.2
Dues & meetings		500	.2		500	.2		—		—
Promotion & postage		32,000	10.1		36,500	12.9		(4,500)		(14.1)
Total expenses		$290,700	92.3%		$289,320	102.5%		$1,380		0.5%
Contribution to the Association		$24,300	7.7%		$(7,020)	(2.5)%		$(31,320)		(128.9)%

Note: The department did not make its budget this month. There was a major short-fall in the week-long course revenues. Although salaries were lower than budget, this saving was entirely consumed by overexpenditure in contract employees and promotion. Further effort is needed to increase revenues and to hold down expenses.

amounts for these accounts are supplied by the accounting department. The monthly budget figures for revenues are also determined by the department heads at the beginning of the year. The monthly budget amounts for revenues and expenses are not revised during the year.

For example, the following changes in operations have taken place but the monthly budgets have not been revised: (1) a new home-study course was introduced in February, one month earlier than scheduled; (2) a number of the week-long courses were postponed in February and March and rescheduled for April and May; and (3) the related promotion effort—heavy direct-mail advertising in the two months prior to a course offering—was likewise rescheduled.

Required

Identify and briefly discuss the good and bad features of the monthly report presented for the education department as a means of communication in terms of

a. Its format for presenting data concerning the operating performance of the education department, and

b. Its content in providing useful information to the education head for managing the education department.

Include in your discussion the changes you would recommend to improve the report as a communication device.

(CMA adapted)

10-11 Jessica Allison, Inc., of Evanston, Illinois, manufactures sailboats and canoes. Founded by Jessica Allison, a water-sports enthusiast, the firm has grown rapidly because of its high-quality products. Last year the firm sold 20,000 boats and had a payroll of 250 production employees, 10 salespersons, and 45 clerks and others involved in administrative tasks.

However, Jessica Allison, Inc., has had severe difficulties. Most important, profits have declined dramatically in the last couple of years and cash shortages have occurred at critical times.

Several symptoms point to the causes of such difficulties. Salespersons complain that the lead times on orders have become quite excessive and shipping delays have become commonplace. Storeskeepers ask for more space to store the ever increasing inventories.

On the other hand, production foremen complain that certain key materials are often out of stock when they submit requisitions to the storeskeeper. The controller adds that materials and labor costs, on which prices are based for special orders, seem to be sloppily recorded by production personnel. He wonders if certain charges have been omitted or roughly estimated. The treasurer completes the litany by stating that she has no "feel" for cash needs. In spite of the fact that she tries to keep excess cash reserves on hand, during certain rush periods the cash just seems to disappear.

Required

Describe several reports that could aid Jessica Allison, Inc., in overcoming its difficulties.

10-12 The Amos Company of University, Alabama, employs a responsibility reporting system. Each manager who heads a responsibility center receives a report monthly concerning his or her controllable expenses. A typical monthly report to the president is shown on page 418. Also shown is a list of jumbled expenses and expense variances for selected responsibility centers within the production function.

Required

Reconstruct the responsibility reports for the head of the machining department, factory

The Amos Company Report to the President February 1991

Item	Total	Cost of Sales	Selling	Adminis-trative	(Over) Under Budget
President's office[a]	$21,876			$21,876	$(1,101)
Sales manager	31,174		$31,174		(167)
Production manager	102,018	$102,018			932
Head designer	5,749	5,749			(921)
Treasurer	10,565			10,565	(478)
Subtotal	$171,382	$107,767	$31,174	$32,441	$(1,735)
Expenses not control-lable elsewhere	18,435	11,325	2,435	4,675	
Productive labor	48,078	48,078			1,949
Totals	$237,895	$167,170	$33,609	$37,116	$ 214

[a]Includes salaries of principal managers.

Item	Actual Expense	(Over) Under Budget
Production manager's office	$ 4,048	$ (301)
Factory office	3,921	(79)
Inspection	532	32
Rough milling (labor)	9,019	901
Machining (labor)	11,718	496
Assembly (labor)	17,465	(517)
Finishing (labor)	9,876	1,069
Factory superintendent (total, except productive labor)	89,962	1,625
Rough milling department (other than productive labor)	35,597	1,669
Machining department (other than productive labor)	22,112	(156)
Shipping and receiving department	4,576	(124)
Machine setups	876	(24)
Idle time	134	(16)
Assembly department (other than productive labor)	15,612	923
Production control department	3,432	(268)
Finishing department (other than productive labor)	9,002	(631)
Maintenance department	3,718	(101)
Preventive maintenance routines	434	34
Employee benefits	1,565	65
Tools and supplies	415	(17)
Other costs	283	15
Direct materials	17,873	(245)

superintendent, and production manager from the listed figures. The factory superintendent reports to the production manager, as do two other department heads; the rough milling, machining, assembly, maintenance, and finishing department heads report to the factory superintendent. Detailed expenses (except for productive labor) are included only for the machining department. Productive (direct) labor expenses are listed separately from the remaining controllable expenses in each report to production function management.

Hint: Prepare the report for the machining department last.

10-13 Wright Company of Princeton, New Jersey, employs a computer-based data processing system for maintaining all company records. The present system was developed in stages over the past five years and has been fully operational for the last 24 months.

When the system was being designed, all department heads were asked to specify the types of information and reports they would need for planning and controlling operations. The systems department attempted to meet the specifications of each department head. Company management specified that certain other reports be prepared for department heads. During the five years of systems development and operation there have been several changes in the department head positions, because of attrition and promotions. The new department heads often made requests for additional reports according to their specifications. The systems department complied with all of these requests. A report was discontinued only on request by a department head, and then only if it was not a standard report required by top management. As a result, few reports were in fact discontinued. Consequently, the data processing system was generating a large quantity of reports each reporting period.

Company management became concerned about the quantity of information that was being produced by the system. The internal audit department was asked to evaluate the effectiveness of the reports generated by the system. The audit staff determined early in the study that more information was being generated by the data processing system than could be used effectively. They noted the following reactions to this information overload:

a. Many department heads would not act on certain reports during periods of peak activity. The department head would let these reports accumulate, with the hope of catching up during a subsequent lull.

b. Some department heads had so many reports that they did not act at all on the information or they made incorrect decisions because of misuse of the information.

c. Frequently, action required by the nature of the report data was not taken until the department head was reminded by someone who needed the decision. These department heads did not appear to have developed a priority system for acting on the information produced by the data processing system.

d. Department heads often would develop the information they needed from alternative independent sources, rather than utilizing the reports generated by the data processing system. This was often easier than trying to search among the reports for the needed data.

Required

a. Indicate, for each of the observed reactions, whether they are functional or dysfunctional behavioral responses. Explain your answer in each case.

b. Assuming one or more of the foregoing were dysfunctional, recommend procedures the company could employ to eliminate the dysfunctional behavior and to prevent its recurrence.

(CMA adapted)

10-14   Music Teachers, Inc., is an educational association for music teachers that had 20,000 members during 1990. The association operates from a central headquarters but has local membership chapters throughout the United States. Monthly meetings are held by the local chapters to discuss recent developments on topics of interest to music teachers. The association's journal, *Teachers' Forum*, is issued monthly with features about recent developments in the field. The association publishes books and reports and sponsors professional courses that qualify for continuing professional education credit. The statement of revenues and expenses for the current year is as follows:

Music Teachers, Inc.
Statement of Revenues and Expenses
for the Year Ended November 30, 1990
($000 omitted)

Revenues	$3,275
Expenses	
Salaries	$ 920
Personnel costs	230
Occupancy costs	280
Reimbursement to local chapters	600
Other membership services	500
Printing and paper	320
Postage and shipping	176
Instructors fees	80
General and administrative	38
Total expenses	$3,144
Excess of revenues over expenses	$ 131

The board of directors of Music Teachers, Inc., has requested that a segmented statement of operations be prepared showing the contribution of each revenue center (i.e., membership, magazine subscriptions, books and reports, continuing education). Mike Doyle has been assigned this responsibility and has gathered the following data prior to statement preparation:

• Membership dues are $100 per year, of which $20 is considered to cover a one-year subscription to the association's jour-

nal. Other benefits include membership in the association and chapter affiliation. The portion of the dues covering the magazine subscription ($20) should be assigned to the magazine subscriptions revenue center.

• One-year subscriptions to *Teachers' Forum* were sold to nonmembers and libraries at $30 each. A total of 2500 of these subscriptions were sold. In addition to subscriptions, the magazine generated $100,000 in advertising revenue. The costs per magazine subscription were $7 for printing and paper and $4 for postage and shipping.

• A total of 28,000 technical reports and professional texts were sold by the books and reports department at an average unit selling price of $25. Average costs per publication were as follows:

Printing and paper	$4
Postage and shipping	$2

• The association offers a variety of continuing education courses to both members and non-members. The one-day courses cost $75 each and were attended by 2400 students in 1990. A total of 1760 students took two-day courses at a cost of $125 for each course. Outside instructors were paid to teach some courses.

• Salary and occupancy data are as follows:

	Salaries	Square Footage
Membership	$210,000	2,000
Magazine Subscriptions	150,000	2,000
Books and Reports	300,000	3,000
Continuing Education	180,000	2,000
Corporate staff	80,000	1,000
	$920,000	10,000

The books and reports department also rents warehouse space at an annual cost of

$50,000. Personnel costs are 25 percent of salaries.

- Printing and paper costs other than for magazine subscriptions and books and reports relate to the continuing education department.
- General and administrative expenses include all other costs incurred by the corporate staff to operate the association.

Doyle has decided he will assign all revenues and expenses to the revenue centers that can be

- Traced directly to a revenue center.
- Allocated on a reasonable and logical basis to a revenue center.

The expenses that can be traced or assigned to corporate staff as well as any other expenses that cannot be assigned to revenue centers will be grouped with the general and administrative expenses and not allocated to the revenue centers. Doyle believes that allocations often tend to be arbitrary and are not useful for management reporting and analysis. He believes that any further allocation of the general and administrative expenses associated with the operation and administration of the association would be arbitrary.

Required

a. Prepare a profitability report that is segmented according to the respective sources of revenue (i.e., revenue centers).

b. In what ways can this profitability report be used by the association?

(CMA adapted)

10-15 Stratford Corporation is a diversified company whose products are marketed both domestically and internationally. The company's major product lines are pharmaceutical products, sports equipment, and household appliances. At a recent meeting of Stratford's board of directors, there was a lengthy discussion on ways to improve overall corporate profitability without new acquisitions as the company is already heavily leveraged. The members of the board decided that they required additional financial information about individual corporate operations in order to target areas for improvement.

Dave Murphy, Stratford's controller, has been asked to provide additional data that would assist the board in its investigation. Stratford is not a public company and, therefore, has not prepared complete income statements by segment. Murphy regularly has prepared an income statement by product line through contribution margin. However, Murphy now believes that income statements prepared through operating income along both product lines and geographic areas would provide the directors with the required insight into corporate operations. Murphy has the data shown at the top of page 422 available to him.

Murphy had several discussions with the division managers for each product line and compiled the following information from these meetings:

- The division managers concluded that Murphy should allocate fixed factory overhead on the basis of the ratio of the variable costs expended per product line or per geographic area to total variable costs.
- Each of the division managers agreed that a reasonable basis for the allocation of depreciation on plant and equipment would be the ratio of units produced per product line or per geographical area to the total number of units produced.
- There was little agreement on the allocation of administrative and selling expenses, so Murphy decided to allocate only those expenses that were directly traceable to the segment being delineated (i.e., manufacturing staff salaries to prod-

| | Product Lines | | | |
	Pharmaceutical	Sports	Appliances	Total
Production/Sales in units	160,000	180,000	160,000	500,000
Average selling price per unit	$8.00	$20.00	$15.00	
Average variable manu- facturing cost per unit	4.00	9.50	8.25	
Average variable selling expense per unit	2.00	2.50	2.25	
Fixed factory overhead excluding depreciation				$500,000
Depreciaton of plant and equipment				400,000
Administrative and selling expense				1,160,000

uct lines and sales staff salaries to geographic areas). Murphy used the following data for this allocation:

• The division managers were able to provide reliable sales percentages for their product lines by geographical area.

Manufacturing Staff		Sales Staff	
Pharmaceutical	$120,000	U.S.	$ 60,000
Sports	140,000	Canada	100,000
Appliances	80,000	Europe	250,000

| | Percentage of Unit Sales | | |
	U.S.	Canada	Europe
Pharmaceutical	40%	10%	50%
Sports	40%	40%	20%
Appliances	20%	20%	60%

Stratford Corporation
Statement of Income by Product Lines
for the Fiscal Year Ended April 30, 1991

| | Product Lines | | | | |
	Pharmaceutical	Sports	Appliances	Unallocated	Total
Sales in units	160,000	180,000	160,000		
Sales	$1,280,000	$3,600,000	$2,400,000	—	$7,280,000
Variable manufacturing and selling costs	960,000	2,160,000	1,680,000	—	4,800,000
Contribution margin	$ 320,000	$1,440,000	$ 720,000	—	$2,480,000
Fixed costs					
Fixed factory overhead	$ 100,000	$ 225,000	$ 175,000	$ —	$ 500,000
Depreciation	128,000	144,000	128,000	—	400,000
Administrative and selling expense	120,000	140,000	80,000	820,000	1,160,000
Total fixed costs	$ 348,000	$ 509,000	$ 383,000	$ 820,000	$2,060,000
Operating income (loss)	$ (28,000)	$ 931,000	$ 337,000	$(820,000)	$ 420,000

Murphy prepared the product line income statement shown at the bottom of page 422 on the basis of the preceding data.

Required

a. Prepare a segmented income statement for Stratford Corporation based on the company's geographic areas of sales. The statement should be in good form and show the operating income for each segment.

b. As a result of the information disclosed by both segmented income statements (by product line and by geographic area), recommend areas where Stratford Corporation should focus its attention in order to improve corporate profitability.

(CMA adapted)

Suggested Readings

Andersen, Anker V. *Graphing Financial Information: How Accountants Can Use Graphs to Communicate.* New York: National Association of Accountants, 1983.

Ashton, Robert H. "Behavioral Implications of Information Overload in Managerial Accounting Reports." *Cost and Management* (July–August 1974), pp. 37–42.

Benke, Ralph L. Jr., and Caster, Bruce. "Information Systems and Fixed Costs in Multidivisional Companies." *Cost and Management* (March–April 1983), pp. 21–25.

Böer, Germain. *Direct Cost and Contribution Accounting: An Integrated Management Accounting System.* New York: John Wiley, 1974.

Busby, S. L., and Heitger, L. E. "Profit Contribution by Market Segment." *Management Accounting* (Nov. 1976), pp. 42–46.

Clancy, Donald K. "The Management Control Problems of Responsibility Accounting." *Management Accounting* (March 1978), pp. 35–39.

Dykeman, Francis C. *Financial Reporting Systems and Techniques.* Englewood Cliffs, N.J.: Prentice-Hall, 1969.

Enrick, Norbert L. "Be Mean About Management Reporting." *Computer Decisions* (Sept. 1970), pp. 28–31.

Ferrara, William L. "Accounting for Performance Evaluation and Decision-Making." *Management Accounting* (Dec. 1976), pp. 13–19.

Floyd, Herbert F., and Zmud, Robert W. "Daily Information Reporting." *Business Horizons* (Feb. 1976), pp. 39–44.

Hindman, William R., and Kettering, Floyd F., Jr. "Integrated MIS: A Case Study." *Management Accounting* (August 1973), pp. 20–27.

Joplin, Bruce, and Pattillo, James W. *Effective Accounting Reports.* Englewood Cliffs, N.J.: Prentice-Hall, 1969.

Kaplan, Robert S. "Accounting Lag: The Obsolescence of Cost Accounting Systems." *California Management Review* (Winter 1986), pp. 174–199.

Leivian, Gregory M. "How to Communicate Financial Data More Effectively." *Management Accounting* (July 1980), pp. 31–34.

Martin, Merle P. "Making the Management Report Useful." *Journal of Systems Management* (May 1977), pp. 30–37.

Mills, William B. "Drawing Up a Budgeting System for an Ad Agency." *Management Accounting* (Dec. 1983), pp. 46–51.

Snoball, Doug. "Information Load and Accounting Reports: Too Much, Too Little or Just Right?" *Cost and Management* (May–June 1979), pp. 22–28.

Walker, Charles W. "Profitability and Responsibility Accounting," *Management Accounting* (Dec. 1971), pp. 23–30.

Part III

TRANSACTION CYCLES

Transaction processing is one of the major purposes of a firm's information system. The first four chapters in this part examine transaction processing in terms of the transaction cycles employed by most business firms: the general ledger and financial reporting cycle, the revenue cycle, the expenditure cycle, and the resource management cycle. The final chapter explores transaction processing within the conversion cycle, which is employed by an important group of firms that encompasses those involved in manufacturing and construction. Coverage of each transaction cycle includes its purposes and functions, relationships, data sources and inputs, data flows and processing, data base, accounting controls, and reports and other outputs.

CHAPTER OBJECTIVES

After studying this chapter, you should be able to do the following:

Identify the objectives and functions of the general ledger and financial reporting cycle.

Describe the interrelationships among the various transaction cycles.

Identify the data sources, inputs, data flows, files, outputs, and accounting controls pertaining to the general ledger system.

Construct a coded chart of accounts for a business firm.

Contrast the general ledger systems for various types of firms.

Chapter *11*

GENERAL LEDGER AND FINANCIAL REPORTING CYCLE

Transaction processing represents a critical concern to accountants. Consequently, it occupies a central place in this textbook. We will focus in the next five chapters on the transaction processing systems that are basic to many firms. For the sake of clarity our survey will be organized according to transaction cycles. This initial chapter pertains to the general ledger and financial reporting cycle, since it provides an integrating view of the remaining transaction cycles.

Cycle Objectives and Functions

The **general ledger and financial reporting cycle,** which for brevity will be called the general ledger system, provides information for an array of financial reports concerning an accounting entity (e.g., a business firm, a government agency). A sound general ledger system (1) records all accounting transactions promptly and accurately, (2) posts these transactions to the proper accounts, (3) maintains an equality of debit and credit balances among the accounts, (4) accommodates needed adjusting journal entries, and (5) generates reliable and timely financial reports pertaining to each accounting period.

In order to achieve these objectives, a general ledger system performs several functions. The manner in which these functions are performed depends in part on the extent and type of computerization employed. However, all general ledger systems must perform the following:

1. **Collect Transaction Data.** Transactions arise from a variety of sources, such as sales and purchases. The more numerous types of transactions are grouped by component transaction processing systems. These component systems then interface with and feed their summarized data to the general ledger system. Other transactions are recorded individually, generally on specially designed forms and journal vouchers.

2. **Process Transaction Inflows.** Collected transaction data undergo several processing steps before coming to rest in the general ledger. First, they are checked to see that debit amounts equal credit amounts, that eligible account names are used, and so on. Individual transactions may also be verified to see that they conform with generally accepted accounting principles. Then the transactions are posted to the general ledger accounts. If the posting is performed sequentially, the transactions are sorted beforehand. Proof listings of the posted transactions may be prepared.

3. **Store Transaction Data.** The general ledger, as well as varied subsidiary ledgers, reflect account balances. Thus, they represent master files within a firm's data base. If the balances in the accounts of the general ledger "master file" are to be kept current, they must be updated through the posting of transaction data.

   In addition to updating the general ledger accounts, the system generally accumulates the details of the transactions into transaction files for backup and ready reference. Linkages between these transactions and the postings to the general ledger are provided by an audit trail. The audit trail in turn is enhanced by journals and journal listings, which include cross-references between the transactions and their postings.

4. **Maintain Accounting Controls.** Since the general ledger system is an integral part of the accounting information system, it incorporates certain accounting controls. As we are well aware, the structure of the general ledger itself provides a fundamental control. That is, the total of the credit account balances must constantly equal the total of the debit account balances. Checks of this equality are made periodically by means of trial balances. Other controls range from (1) checks or edits of the transaction data as they are entered into the system to (2) reviews of the financial reports by managers and other recipients. Organizational independence represents yet another type of essential control.

5. **Generate Financial Reports.** The most familiar financial reports generated by the general ledger system are the income statement and balance sheet. However, a wide variety of other beneficial reports may be prepared. Certain of these reports aid in the verification of the general ledger accounts themselves. Other reports, such as financially oriented operating budgets, aid managers in planning and control responsibilities.

6. **Classify and Code Transaction Data and Accounts.** Underlying the maintenance of the general ledger system are adequate classification and coding systems. Classification is necessary in assigning the various accounts within the general ledger. Coding is desirable for identifying accounts, transactions, files, and other elements that impinge upon the general ledger.

Each of the aforementioned functions will be explored more thoroughly in the following sections. We then conclude the chapter by contrasting the differences exhibited by the general ledger systems of varying types of organizations.

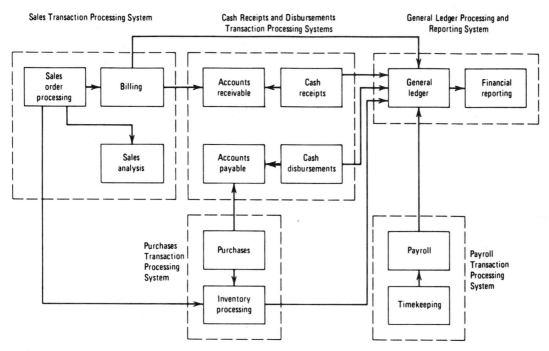

FIGURE 11-1 Relationships among transaction processing systems.

Transaction-Oriented Relationships and Cycles

Before examining the various functions, we might consider an overview of transaction processing. As Figure 11-1 shows, the various component **transaction processing systems** of a typical firm form several distinct though highly interrelated groupings. For instance, the sales transaction processing system involves the processing of sales orders as well as the preparation of bills (invoices) and sales analyses. It also interrelates with cash receipts through the accounts receivable records and with purchases through the inventory records. Of particular interest is the general ledger system and its financial reporting activity. Not only does it interrelate with the sales transaction processing system (through the billing activity), but it also interrelates with *all* of the remaining

component transaction processing systems. Consequently, the general ledger system serves as the final repository of all transaction data entering the accounting information system.

The pivotal and unique role of the general ledger system can be more clearly seen in Figure 11-2. This figure, an example of a data flow diagram, also provides more details concerning the flows of documents and the accounting records.[1] It shows that the process of updating the general ledger is based on journal vouchers from processes involving sales—shipping, purchases—payables, cash receipts, cash disbursements, fixed assets, and payroll. In turn the various processes giving rise to the journal vouchers are

[1]In a data flow diagram a process is represented by a circle, a file or data store by an open-ended rectangle, an entity by a closed-ended rectangle, and a data flow by an arrow.

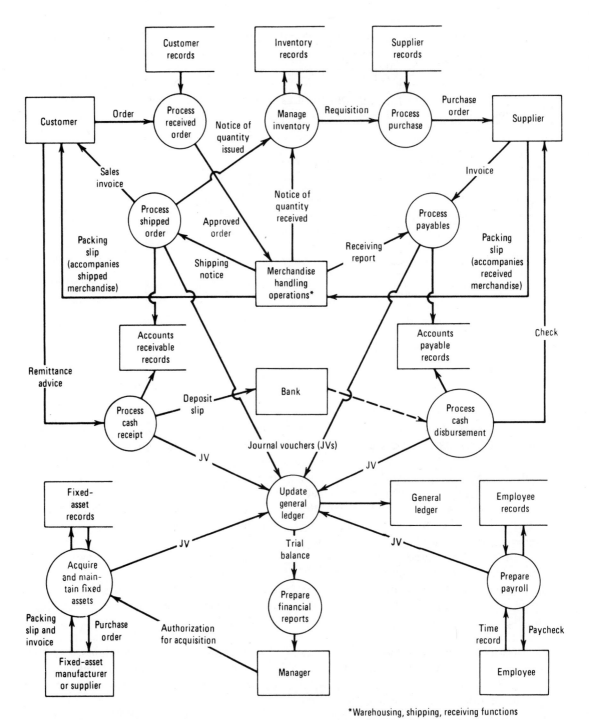

FIGURE 11-2 An overview data flow diagram of basic transaction processing systems.

Cycle	Typical Included Events
Revenue	Sales of products or services Cash receipts from products or services sold
Expenditure	Purchases of materials or services Cash disbursements in payment of acquired materials or services
Resource management	Acquisition, maintenance, and disposal (or disbursement) of funds, facilities, and human (e.g., employee) services
Product conversion	Conversion of raw materials into finished goods through the use of labor and overhead
General ledger and financial reporting	Compilation of accounting transactions from the remaining transaction cycles Generation of financial reports

FIGURE 11-3 Common transaction cycles.

fed by source documents ranging from sales orders to checks and are supported by files ranging from customer records to accounts payable records.

The component transaction processing systems may be grouped and viewed by reference to the cycles of business activity. Figure 11-3 lists several common transaction cycles used by business firms, together with the major events that are typically included in each cycle. Since the cycles were introduced in Chapter 3 and will be discussed fully in following chapters, no further details are necessary here.

Data Sources and Inputs

Sources

The general ledger system receives inputs from a wide variety of sources. Figure 11-4 emphasizes this variety. It shows the source documents of the various component transaction processing systems being entered into special journals. Summary totals from these entries are posted to the general ledger, as well as to any subsidiary ledgers that are maintained. Most transactions that affect the general ledger arise from such sources.

Other sources of general ledger inputs are financial transactions that traditionally have been entered into the general journal. Included in this group are

1. **Nonroutine transactions** that occur during the accounting period, such as a transaction that records the exchange of a fixed asset for capital stock.

2. **End-of-period adjusting transactions** that (a) are recurring, such as the depreciation of fixed assets and the expiration of insurance, and (b) are nonrecurring, such as a change of inventory valuation methods.

3. **Reversing transactions** that are entered at the beginning of accounting periods, such as an entry that reverses the accrual of payroll expense at the end of the previous period.

Forms of Input

Manual systems. The primary source document to the general ledger system is the general ledger **journal voucher,** which has generally replaced the general journal sheet. A journal voucher is typically prepared for each nonroutine, adjusting, and reversing transaction. (Figure 3-6 illustrated a manually prepared journal voucher containing a standard adjusting transaction.) A journal voucher is also often prepared to summarize the results of a batch of routine transactions that have been manually entered into special journals. For instance, after today's checks have been written and entered into the check register, a clerk may prepare a journal voucher that reflects the total of the cash disbursements.

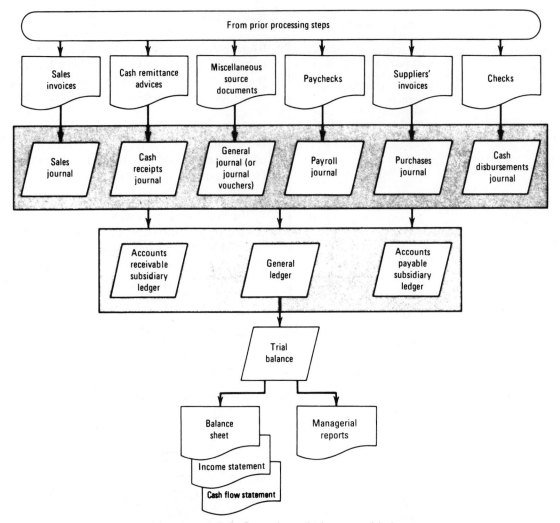

FIGURE 11-4 Sources of inputs and their flows through the general ledger system.

Computer-based systems. Although the journal voucher remains the primary input to the general ledger in computer-based systems, its form will likely vary from that employed in manual systems. Three variations worth noting are the individual journal entry form, the batch entry form, and the on-line screen.

The journal voucher for entering individual transactions may be similar in appearance to Figure 11-5. It likely contains columns for entering account descriptions and numbers, as well as columns for debit and credit amounts. After the data pertaining to an individual transaction have been manually written onto this form, the data are keyed by data entry clerks onto transaction files stored on magnetic tape or disk.

The **batch entry form** may have an appearance that resembles the journal voucher form. It is used to replace the special journal in computer-based systems, or to record the

JOURNAL VOUCHER			No. 6212	
			Date June 14, 1991	
Account Code	Account Titles	Amounts to Be Debited	Amounts to Be Credited	
204	Accounts payable— control	64,720 | 50		
101	Cash		64,720 | 50	
	Explanation of entry: To record the daily total of cash disbursed.			
Prepared by: *Jean Nelson*	Approved by: *Shirley Hagen*		Posted by: *Audrey Rule*	

FIGURE 11-5 A journal voucher.

entry of miscellaneous transactions. Data are entered manually onto the batch entry form and then keyed onto tape or disk transaction files. Often the entered data are then listed on a hard-copy printout, in order to provide a permanent record of the journal. Figure 11-6 depicts a batch entry journal form. Note that it includes details concerning the batch itself, so that the system can verify the completeness of the entered data.

A **data entry screen** can be used to record transactions when the general ledger

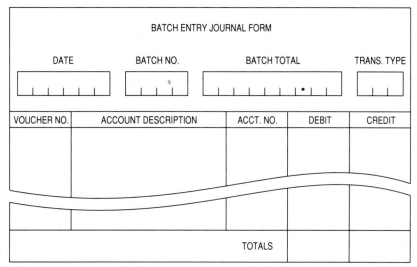

FIGURE 11-6 A batch entry journal form. *Note:* More than one sheet is often needed to contain a batch of journal entries; hence, the totals at the bottom of a sheet generally differ from the batch total.

system employs on-line files. Transactions are entered interactively with the aid of a CRT screen that is preformatted to exhibit a journal voucher. Either individual transactions or batches of transactions may be entered in this manner. Figure 11-7a exhibits a preformatted journal voucher screen for an individual transaction.

Data Entry Codes

Codes are extremely useful for the entry of transactions. As Figure 11-7a shows, data entry is simplified by the use of account codes. Later in this chapter the development and expansion of coded charts of accounts are discussed in detail.

In computer-based systems transaction codes can further simplify the entry of data. Consider, for instance, the transaction entry screen shown in Figure 11-7a. A general ledger clerk has likely accessed this screen via a menu that includes the option "Data entry." Figure 11-7b shows this main menu and the related detailed menu. Alternatively, the clerk could enter the transaction code EXCN, which has been assigned to the type of transaction appearing in the figure. As a

```
               GENERAL LEDGER JOURNAL ENTRY

   DATE   4/12/91

                    DEBIT                        CREDIT

  J V NO.    ACCT. NO.     AMOUNT       ACCT. NO.     AMOUNT
  |7|1|6|5|   |1|1|4|   | |1|5|0|0|.|0|0|   |1|1|0|   | |1|5|0|0|.|0|0|
  DESCRIPTION
  TO EXCHANGE ACCOUNT RECEIVABLE FOR NOTE RECEIVABLE, 30 DAYS AT 10%

        TO ACCEPT TRANSACTION, ENTER A
        TO POST ANOTHER DEBIT, ENTER D
        TO POST ANOTHER CREDIT, ENTER C
        TO CANCEL TRANSACTION, ENTER X
```

a. A journal entry screen

```
   GENERAL LEDGER MAIN MENU              GENERAL LEDGER DATA ENTRY

  1. DATA ENTRY                        1. JOURNAL ENTRY
  2. RECORD INQUIRY                    2. ADJUSTING ENTRY
  3. ACCOUNT ANALYSIS                  3. CLOSING ENTRY
  4. END-OF-PERIOD LISTING             4. CORRECTION TO PREVIOUS ENTRY
  5. REPORT PREPARATION                5. CHANGE IN ACCOUNT INFORMATION
  6. EXIT FROM GENERAL LEDGER SYSTEM   6. EXIT TO MAIN MENU

      ENTER DESIRED OPTION >               ENTER DESIRED OPTION >
```

b. Two menus used to access journal entry screen

FIGURE 11-7 Screens relating to journal entries.

result, the transaction entry screen would be displayed with the account numbers and partial description already filled in. All that the clerk would need to provide is the transaction amount and specific details concerning the note receivable.

Data Flows and Processing

In the traditional manual system, transaction data flow into journals (both special and general), then are posted to subsidiary ledgers, and finally are posted to the general ledger. Figure 11-8 depicts this process.

In computer-based systems, the transaction data are entered from the forms previously described and temporarily stored either on magnetic tapes or on magnetic disks. Periodically the individual transactions are processed to update the master files known as subsidiary ledgers, and their summarized amounts are processed to update the general ledger. If the transactions are stored on magnetic tapes, the summary data are extracted, sorted by account numbers, and then processed sequentially against the general ledger accounts. If the transaction data are stored on magnetic disks, they will likely be processed directly to the general ledger accounts.

Figure 11-9 shows a system flowchart of the latter situation. During the accounting period transaction data are drawn from sales, cash receipts, purchases, cash disbursements, payroll, fixed assets, and other types of events. Processing computer programs for the component transaction processing systems perform such steps as summarizing the transaction amounts and generating prenum-

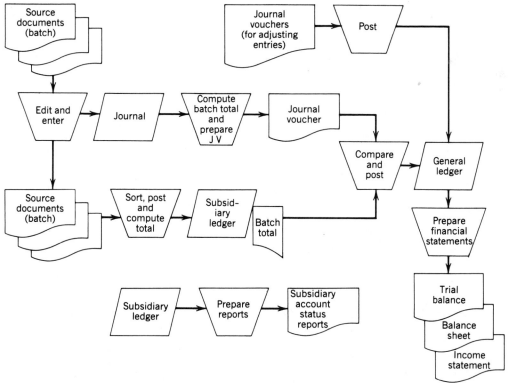

FIGURE 11-8 Batch processing of transactions by manual system.

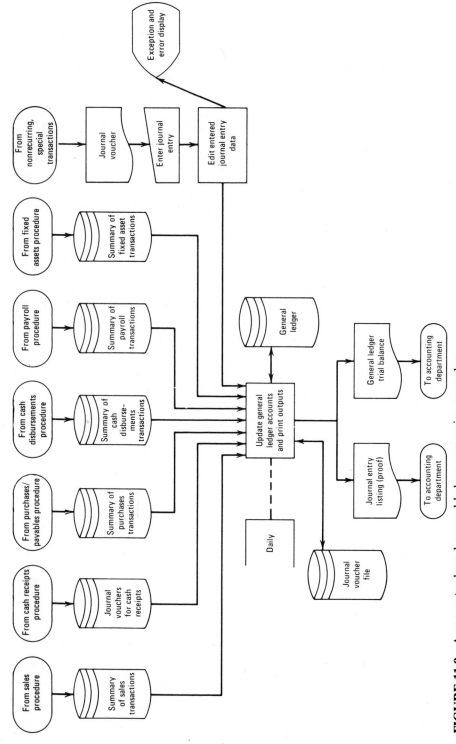

FIGURE 11-9 A computer-based general ledger processing procedure.

bered journal vouchers. Since the general ledger is on line, these processing programs may also post the summary amounts to the general ledger accounts. In fact, the general ledger postings can be done concurrently with, and as a by-product of, the updating of the various subsidiary ledgers (master files).

As nonrecurring special transactions arise, they are entered by accountants via CRT terminals from manually prepared journal vouchers. Each day the general ledger system generates a journal entry listing and a trial balance, so that the accountants can verify the correctness and accuracy of the processing.

At the end of each accounting period the journal entries for adjusting transactions must be recorded and processed. Figure 11-10 portrays the processing of standard and nonrecurring adjusting journal entries, assuming an accounting period of one month. **Standard** (recurring) **adjusting journal entries** are stored in an on-line file from month to month. **Nonrecurring adjusting journal entries** are entered via a CRT terminal from a manually prepared journal voucher coding form. The two types of adjusting journal entries are merged and next sorted into general ledger account number sequence. Then the general ledger accounts are updated and the printed outputs are generated.

Since the general ledger is stored on a magnetic disk, the steps described in the flowchart could be modified. For instance, if the general ledger records are organized as an indexed sequential file, the adjusting journal entries could be processed directly to the accounts.

Data Base

The data base pertaining to the general ledger and financial reporting system contains a variety of master, transaction, and history files. In addition to financial data concerning past events and current status, the data base often contains budgeted data that relate to planned future operations and status.

Although their exact contents and composition will vary from firm to firm, the following set of files is representative:

- **General Ledger Master File** Each record of the **general ledger master file** contains data concerning one general ledger account. Figure 11-11 displays a suggested layout of a general ledger record. Taken together, the records in the general ledger master file constitute the complete chart of accounts for the firm and the current status of all account balances.

- **General Ledger History File** The general ledger history file contains the actual balances of general ledger accounts for each month for several past years. It is used to provide financial trend information.

- **Responsibility Center Master File** The responsibility center master file contains the actual revenues and costs for the various divisions, departments, work centers, and other profit and cost centers within the firm. It is used in the preparation of responsibility reports for managers.

- **Budget Master File** The **budget master file** contains the budgeted values of assets, liabilities, revenues, and expenses for the various responsibility centers of the firm. The budgeted values may be broken down on a monthly basis for the following year, and they may extend for five or more years into the future. Together with the responsibility center master file, the budget file provides the basis for the preparation of responsibility reports.

- **Financial Reports Format File** The financial reports format file contains the information necessary for generating the formats of the various financial reports. Included are such factors as the headings of each report, all needed column head-

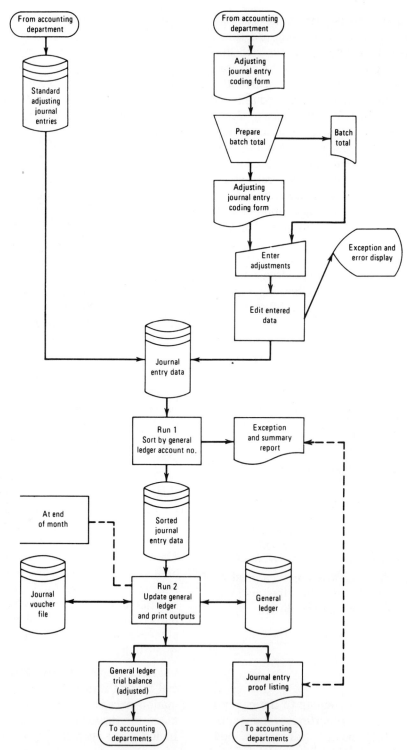

FIGURE 11-10 A month-end general ledger processing procedure.

Account number	Account description	Account classification (asset, liability, revenue, expense)	Account balance, beginning of year	Total debits, year-to-date	Total credits, year-to-date	Total debits, current month	Total credits, current month	Current account balance	Dr. or cr.

FIGURE 11-11 A record layout for the general ledger master file. *Note:* Lengths of fields and modes of data items are omitted for simplicity, although they are necessary for complete documentation.

ings, all side labels (such as descriptions of accounts and subtotal and total lines), spacing and totaling instructions, and so on.

- **Current Journal Voucher File** This file contains all significant details concerning each transaction that has been posted to the general ledger during the current month. Included for each voucher would be the journal voucher number, date of the transaction, accounts debited and credited and the corresponding amounts, and description of the transaction. In effect this file is a summary of all journals for the current month.

- **Journal Voucher History File** The journal voucher history file contains journal vouchers for previous months.

In addition to the aforementioned files, a firm will need detailed transaction files that support the journal voucher file. These de-

tailed transaction files are discussed in Chapters 12–15, which deal with component transaction processing systems. Certain firms also need various reference files, such as a cost allocation file that contains factors for allocating incurred costs (e.g., administrative costs) to responsibility centers, to products, and to other segments within the firm. Those firms that employ the data base approach need files that contain "pointers," which link together the data in two or more of these files. (The data base approach is discussed in Chapter 18.)

Certain of the aforementioned files are involved in transaction processing programs, as we have seen. Almost all of the files provide data needed in the preparation of listings, analyses, financial statements, and managerial reports. Figure 11-12 portrays the variety of outputs that are generated from the files. While several processing programs may actually be required to produce the dis-

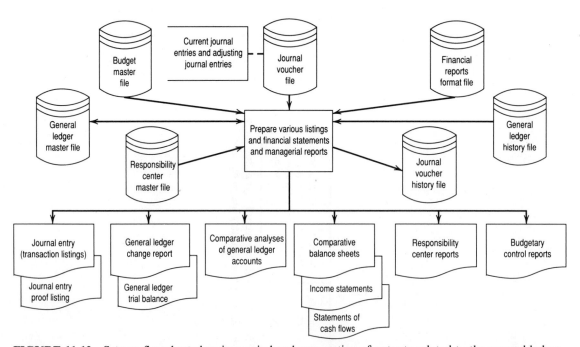

FIGURE 11-12 System flowchart showing period-end preparation of outputs related to the general ledger.

played outputs, the figure describes the essential printing activity. It also previews the outputs that are discussed in a later section.

Accounting Controls

The general ledger system is expected to provide reliable financial reports for a variety of users. In order to do so, it must independently check on the component transaction processing systems, carefully monitor the array of nonroutine transactions that it accepts, and accurately record and post data from all transactions.

Risk Exposures

A first step in providing reliable reports is to determine the risks to which the general ledger system is exposed. Among the risks that exist in the maintenance of the general ledger are the following:

1. Journal entries may be improperly prepared.
2. Journal entries may be left unposted.
3. Total debit balances and total credit balances in the accounts in the general ledger may become out of balance.
4. Control account balances in the general ledger may become out of balance with the totals of balances in subsidiary ledgers.
5. Unauthorized persons may gain access to data in the general ledger.
6. The audit trail that links the general ledger with source documents may become obscured.
7. Data pertaining to the general ledger and source documents may be lost or destroyed.

These risks lead to such exposures as inaccurate financial statements and related reports. For instance, assets may be overstated and liabilities understated. They also can lead to "leaks" of important financial data to competitors and added expenses in locating or reconstructing needed transaction data. Adequate general and transaction controls must be established in order to counteract such exposures to the inherent risks.

General Controls

Suitable general controls are as follows:

1. Organizationally, the function of posting journal vouchers to the general ledger should be separated from the functions of preparing and approving journal vouchers and from the function of preparing the trial balances from the general ledger.
2. Documentation should consist at least of a fully descriptive chart of accounts, plus a manual of general ledger procedures.
3. Operating practices, including period-end schedules and the preparation of control reports, should be clearly established. Figure 11-13 presents an example of a general journal listing, which serves as a proof for verifying that posted journal entries are in balance and as an audit trail aid. Figure 11-14 shows a screen display that summarizes the status of the various journals, indicating those needing corrections, those that have been posted, and so on.
4. Security should be maintained (in the case of on-line systems) by such techniques as (a) requiring that clerks enter passwords before accessing the general ledger file, (b) employing special terminals for the sole entry of journal voucher data, (c) generating audit reports (access logs) that monitor entries, and (d) dumping the general ledger onto magnetic tape backups.

Northcreek Industries Journal—GJ001 Batch—1		General Journal Time 15:52:00 Date 4/30/91 Page 1 37402 Posting date 4/30/91			
Reference Date	Reference number	Description	Account number	Debit	Credit
4/05/91	JV4-01	Deposits	1010	3,556.52	
4/05/91	JV4-01	Deposits	1110		3,056.52
4/05/91	JV4-01	Deposits	1140		123.00
4/05/91	JV4-01	Deposits	1130		377.00
4/05/91	JV4-02	Travel advances	1010	10,000.00	
4/05/91	JV4-02	Travel advances	1560		10,000.00
4/12/91	JV4-03	City power	6110	1,675.42	
4/12/91	JV4-03	City water	6120	30.00	
4/17/91	JV4-04	Central loan	2030	1,200.00	
4/17/91	JV4-04	Central loan	1010		1,200.00
4/19/91	JV4-05	Trash collection	6260	47.25	
4/19/91	JV4-05	Security service	6270	237.00	
4/19/91	JV4-05	Utility bills	1010		1,989.67
4/30/91	JV4-06	FET Transfer to bank	1010		3,250.00
4/30/91	JV4-06	FET Transfer to bank	2150	3,250.00	
4/30/91	JV4-07	Dep land improve	1720		318.54
4/30/91	JV4-07	Dep land improve	6020	318.54	
4/30/91	JV4-08	Dep buildings	1730		1,500.00
4/30/91	JV4-08	Dep buildings	6030	1,500.00	
4/30/91	JV4-09	Dep machinery & equip	1750		309.39
4/30/91	JV4-09	Dep machinery & equip	6050	309.39	
4/30/91	JV4-10	Dep auto & truck	1760		153.23
4/30/91	JV4-10	Dep auto & truck	6060	153.23	
4/30/91	JV4-11	Dep office equip	1740	150.00	
4/30/91	JV4-11	Dep office equip	6040		150.00
				22,427.35	22,427.35

FIGURE 11-13   A general journal listing. Courtesy of IBM Corporation.

Transaction Controls

The following controls and control procedures relating directly to general ledger accounts and processing are generally adequate:

1. Prenumbered journal vouchers are prepared in the appropriate accounting or finance departments. For instance, a journal voucher that reflects the declaration of a dividend may be prepared in the treasurer's office. These prepared journal vouchers are then approved by responsible managers.

2. The data in journal vouchers, such as the account numbers, are checked for accuracy:

   a. In the case of manual systems general ledger clerks perform the checks, referring if necessary to the chart of accounts and procedure manuals.

   b. In the case of computer-based systems the checks are mainly performed by computer edit programs. Figure 11-15 lists several suitable programmed edit checks pertaining to transaction data.

3. Detected errors in journal entries are corrected before the data are used in posting to the general ledger.

4. Approved journal vouchers are posted by specially designated persons who are not involved in their preparation or approval:

   a. In the case of manual systems the journal vouchers are posted by general ledger clerks directly to the general ledger sheets.

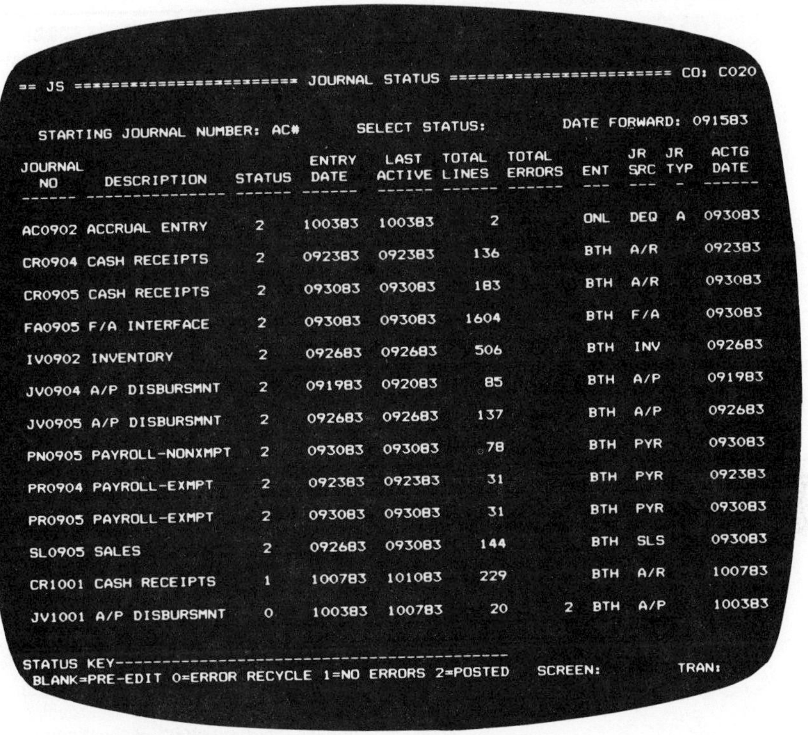

== JS ======================== JOURNAL STATUS ======================== CO: C020

STARTING JOURNAL NUMBER: AC#   SELECT STATUS: DATE FORWARD: 091583

JOURNAL NO	DESCRIPTION	STATUS	ENTRY DATE	LAST ACTIVE	TOTAL LINES	TOTAL ERRORS	ENT	JR SRC	JR TYP	ACTG DATE
AC0902	ACCRUAL ENTRY	2	100383	100383	2		ONL	DEQ	A	093083
CR0904	CASH RECEIPTS	2	092383	092383	136		BTH	A/R		092383
CR0905	CASH RECEIPTS	2	093083	093083	183		BTH	A/R		093083
FA0905	F/A INTERFACE	2	093083	093083	1604		BTH	F/A		093083
IV0902	INVENTORY	2	092683	092683	506		BTH	INV		092683
JV0904	A/P DISBURSMNT	2	091983	092083	85		BTH	A/P		091983
JV0905	A/P DISBURSMNT	2	092683	092683	137		BTH	A/P		092683
PN0905	PAYROLL-NONXMPT	2	093083	093083	78		BTH	PYR		093083
PR0904	PAYROLL-EXMPT	2	092383	092383	31		BTH	PYR		092383
PR0905	PAYROLL-EXMPT	2	093083	093083	31		BTH	PYR		093083
SL0905	SALES	2	092683	093083	144		BTH	SLS		093083
CR1001	CASH RECEIPTS	1	100783	101083	229		BTH	A/R		100783
JV1001	A/P DISBURSMNT	0	100383	100783	20	2	BTH	A/P		100383

STATUS KEY--
BLANK=PRE-EDIT 0=ERROR RECYCLE 1=NO ERRORS 2=POSTED   SCREEN: TRAN:

FIGURE 11-14 A journal status screen display. Courtesy of Data Design Associates.

b. In the case of batch computer-based systems the journal vouchers are keyed by data entry clerks onto a magnetic medium; then the batches of entries are sorted by general ledger account numbers and posted during computer runs to the accounts. Figure 11-16 lists various checks that should be made during the posting run.

c. In the case of on-line computer-based systems the journal vouchers are entered directly into the system, with the aid of preformatted screens on CRT terminals; then the entries are posted by the computer system, usually in a direct manner, to the accounts.

5. The equality of debits and credits for each posted journal entry is verified.

6. The totals of amounts posted from batched journal entries to general ledger accounts are compared to precomputed control totals. Figure 11-17 shows a display screen of such compared totals; a difference of $1000 is detected. Note that the posted totals of both debits and credits are compared to precomputed control totals in this example, thereby performing the verification described in item 5.

7. Adequate cross-references are included to provide a clear audit trail. For instance, the journal voucher number and general ledger numbers are shown in printed listings of the general journal

Type of Edit Check	Typical Transaction Data Items Checked	Assurance Provided
1. Validity check	General ledger account numbers; transaction codes	The entered numbers and codes are checked against lists of valid numbers and codes stored within the computer system
2. Field check	Transaction amounts	The amount fields in the input records are checked to see if they contain the proper mode of characters for amounts (i.e., numeric characters). If other modes are found, such as alphabetic characters or blanks, an error is indicated.
3. Limit check	Transaction amounts	The entered amounts are checked against preestablished limits that represent reasonable maximums to be expected. (A separate limit is set for each account.)
4. Zero-balance checks	Transaction amounts	The entered debit amounts are netted against the entered credit amounts, and the resulting net amount is compared to zero. (A non-zero net amount indicates that the debits and credits are unequal.)
5. Completeness check[a]	All entered data items	The entered transaction is checked to see that all required data items have been entered.
6. Echo check[a]	General ledger account numbers and titles	After the account numbers pertaining to the transaction are entered at a terminal, the system retrieves and "echoes" back the account titles; the person who has made the entry can visually verify from reading the titles that the correct account numbers were entered.

[a]Applicable only to on-line processing systems.

FIGURE 11-15 Programmed edit checks that validate journal entry data. *Note:* When entered data do not match or otherwise meet the expected conditions or limits, alerting messages are displayed by the edit program on the CRT screen.

(see Figure 11-13) and the source page number of the general journal or journal voucher number is shown in each posting to the general ledger. Also, transaction numbers on source documents may be carried to transaction listings and into such proof reports as listings of account activity (see Figure 11-18).

8. Journal vouchers are filed by number, and periodically the file is checked to see that the sequence of numbers is complete.

9. Standard adjusting journal entries (including accruals and reversing entries) are maintained on preprinted sheets (or on magnetic media), in order to aid postings at the end of the accounting period.

10. Trial balances of general ledger accounts are prepared periodically, and differences between total debits and total credits are fully investigated.

11. General ledger control account balances are reconciled periodically to totals of balances in subsidiary ledger accounts.

12. Special period-end reports are printed for review by accountants and managers before the financial statements are prepared. Figure 11-19 shows a general

Type of Edit Check	Typical Transaction Data Items Checked	Assurance Provided
1. Internal label check[a]		The internal header label of the file to be updated (posted to) is checked before processing begins to ascertain that the correct general ledger master file has been accessed for processing.
2. Sequence check	General ledger account numbers	The transaction file, which has been sorted so that the amounts in the various journal vouchers are ordered according to account numbers, is checked to see that no transaction item is out of sequence.
3. Redundancy matching check[b]	General ledger account numbers and titles	Each transaction debit and credit is checked to see that its account number matches the account number in the general ledger record it is to update. Then the account titles in the transaction record and master file record are also matched, thus providing double protection against updating the wrong file record.
4. Relationship check[b]	Transaction amounts and account numbers	The balance of each general ledger account is checked, after the transaction has been posted, to see that the balance has a normal relationship to the account. If the balance in an account balance that normally exhibits a debit balance (e.g., accounts receivable) appears as a credit, the abnormality will be flagged by the check.
5. Posting check[b]	Transaction amounts	The after-posting balance in each updated account is compared to the before-posting balance, to see that the difference equals the transaction amount.
6. Batch control total checks	Transaction amounts	The amounts posted are totaled and compared to the precomputed amount total of the batch being processed; also, the total number of transaction items processed is compared to the precomputed count of the transaction.

[a]While not true edit checks, these listed checks are programmed, and they help to assure that updated data will be accurate.

[b]These checks are also applicable to the posting step in on-line computer-based systems.

FIGURE 11-16 Programmed edit checks that validate batched data during posting (updating) runs.

ledger change report that reflects beginning and ending account balances, plus various control totals.

13. Periodic reviews of journal entries and financial reports are performed by managers, and when feasible, general ledger procedures are reviewed by internal auditors.

Financial Reports

The financial reports generated by the general ledger system may be classified as general ledger analyses, financial statements, and managerial reports. A wide variety of examples are found in each of the above categories.

```
                    JOURNAL CONTROL TOTALS

ENTITY:   15              JOURNAL TYPE:   STANDARD JOURNAL
JOURNAL: 051              JOURNAL DESC:   STANDARD RECURRING JE
YEAR:     90              TRAN CODE:      05
PERIOD:   04              BATCH NUM:      A240


                   USER ENTERED      CALCULATED
                   CONTROL TOTALS    CONTROL TOTALS    DIFFERENCE
     LINE COUNT:        0003             0003              0
     TOTAL DEBITS:   10,000.00        11,000.00       1,000.00
     TOTAL CREDITS:  10,000.00        10,000.00           0.00


MANUAL PROCESSING OPTION (Y/N): N


- - - - - - - - - - - - - - - - - - - - - - - - - - - - - - - - - - - -

ACTION:        NP=NEXT PAGE    CA=CANCEL    FI=FILE    FT=FILE TO TEF
```

FIGURE 11-17 A display screen used to verify batch control totals relating to entered journal entries. Courtesy of American Software.

General Ledger Analyses

Most **general ledger analyses** are prepared to aid accountants in verifying the accuracy of postings. Two examples already presented are the general ledger proof listing and the change report. Other general ledger analyses:

1. List all transactions posted during an accounting period, arranged by account number.

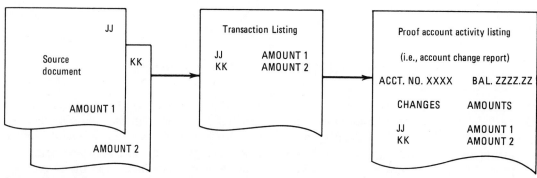

FIGURE 11-18 An audit trail for a computer-based system.

SAMPLE COMPANY   GENERAL LEDGER   CLIENT 00125   PAGE 14   DECEMBER 31, 19xx

MO DAY YR	ACCT.	DESCRIPTION	REFERENCE	DEBITS	CREDITS	NET CHANGE	NEW BALANCE
11-30-xx	5130	ACCOUNTING & LEGAL	BALANCE	4750.00			
12-05-xx	5130	DEC. RETAINER	10131	450.00			
				450.00		450.00	5200.00
11-30-xx	5140	SALARIES	BALANCE	20769.83			
12-20-xx	5140	DEC. PAYROLL	12332	1885.12			
				1885.12		1885.12	22654.95
11-30-xx	5150	INSURANCE	BALANCE	1125.00			
12-15-xx	5150	ALLTOWN INSURANCE	652	105.10			
				105.10		105.10	1230.10
11-30-xx	5160	OFFICE RENT	BALANCE	3323.33			
12-15-xx	5160	CORRECT NOVEMBER ERROR	J12		23.33		
12-31-xx	5160	DEC. RENT	0012	300.00			
				300.00	23.33	276.67	3600.00
11-30-xx	5170	OFFICE SUPPLIES	BALANCE	895.26			
12-02-xx	5170	K & C FORMS	6736	33.75			
12-17-xx	5170	JACKS STATIONERY	J211A	51.25			
				85.00		85.00	980.26

******************** CONTROL TOTALS ************************

PRIOR PERIOD BALANCE TOTALS	523,721.12	523,721.12	.00
CURRENT PERIOD TRANSACTIONS	33,968.22	33,968.22	.00
TRIAL BALANCE TOTALS	557,689.34	557,689.34	
TRANSACTION COUNT CURRENT PERIOD	453		

FIGURE 11-19 A general ledger change report. Courtesy of the American Institute of Certified Public Accountants, Inc.

447

2. Show allocations of expenses to various cost centers.

3. Compare account balances for the current period with those for the same period last year, and compare year-to-date account balances for this year with those for last year.

Financial Statements

The most visible financial statements are the balance sheet, income statement, and statement of cash flows. These statements, which are based directly on the general ledger, are provided to various parties outside the firm that they represent. In addition to stockholders or other owners, the financial statements are made available to governmental agencies, to creditors, to prospective owners, and to financial analysts. Often the financial statements are accompanied by additional information that is useful to the recipients. For instance, they may be accompanied by comparative statements for previous years, by ratio analyses, and by detailed schedules. In special cases they may be altered to suit reporting requirements. An example is the income tax return.

Managerial Reports

The greatest number of reports based on the general ledger are prepared for the use of the firm's managers. Most of these managerial reports are derivatives of the financial statements. However, the financial statements for managers tend to be much more detailed than those provided to outside parties. For instance, **analyses** based on individual general ledger accounts are often prepared. Examples are (1) analyses of sales, broken down by products or sales territories or markets; (2) analyses of cash, broken down by types of receipts and expenditures; and (3) analyses of receivables, broken down by customers and ages of amounts due.

Financial statements prepared for managers often involve budgetary amounts. Since a firm's budget represents expected results, such statements reflect the quality of performance achieved by actual results. Figure 11-20 shows a balance sheet and income statement for the United Industries Company, with columns that compare budget and actual amounts. In the case of the income statement variances have been computed for both the current month and year-to-date.

Financial reports can also be based on comparisons of budget and actual amounts for responsibility centers and segments. As we saw in Chapter 10, reports of this nature are provided when responsibility and profitability reporting systems have been established. Figure 11-21 presents screen displays of data drawn from the files that underlie such reporting systems.

Coded Charts of Accounts

The general ledger is built upon the foundation known as the chart of accounts. As described in Chapter 3, a **chart of accounts** is a coded listing of the asset, liability, equity, revenue, and expense accounts pertaining to a firm. Of the coding systems described in Chapter 8, the block and group coding systems are most suitable for coding charts of accounts.

Block Codes

Block codes are often used to form the broad coding frameworks. For instance, assets may be assigned the block of numbers from 100 through 199. Each broad block may contain subordinate blocks. Thus, operating expenses may be blocked from 600 through 899. Within this broad block could be subordinate blocks representing the functional categories of expenses. Figure 11-22 lists typical expense accounts comprising the administrative category.

Balance Sheet

UNITED INDUSTRIES   COMPANY CO20 GLRO100 REQ 8   BALANCE SHEET CORPORATION   AS OF 12/31/90 PAGE 1   RUN DATE 01/04/91 21:35:49

BEGINNING OF YEAR	PCT CHG	PRIOR MONTH	PCT CHG		CURRENT BALANCE	CURRENT BUDGET	PRIOR YR BALANCE
				ASSETS:			
				CURRENT ASSETS:			
1,044,500	46.4	1,028,899	48.6	CASH	1,529,480	598,000	1,044,500
922,000	-15.7	841,020	-7.6	ACCOUNTS RECEIVABLE	776,580	0	922,000
-117,582	-10.2	-104,122	1.3	ALLOW DOUBTFUL ACCT	-105,542	-2,500	-117,582
908,000	36.2	732,820	68.8	NOTES RECEIVABLE	1,237,180	200,000	908,000
62,100	16.8	58,940	23.1	INTEREST RECEIVABLE	72,580	5,000	62,100
972,000	73.3	1,026,207	64.2	INVENTORY	1,685,259	210,000	972,000
19,645	131.4	28,158	61.4	OFFICE SUPPLIES	45,462	5,000	19,645
113,450	137.6	168,482	60.0	PREPAID INSURANCE	269,578	25,000	113,450
				TOTAL--			
3,924,113	40.4	3,780,404	45.7	CURRENT ASSETS	5,510,577	1,040,500	3,924,113
				FIXED ASSETS:			
8,346,400	72.7	8,368,314	72.3	MACHINERY	14,419,310	2,015,000	8,346,400
-6,513,500	71.0	-6,541,080	70.2	ACC DEPR - MACH	-11,138,600	-1,583,600	-6,513,500
1,560,000	100.0	1,560,000	100.0	BUILDINGS	3,120,000	0	1,560,000
-50,000	220.0	-80,000	100.0	ACC DEPR - BLDGS	-160,000	0	-50,000
891,000	85.5	899,550	83.8	OFFICE EQUIP	1,653,433	250,000	891,000
-256,390	21.6	-273,430	14.1	ACC DEPR - OFF EQUIP	-311,990	-10,000	-256,390
1,175,000	100.0	1,175,000	100.0	LAND	2,350,000	0	1,175,000
				TOTAL--			
5,152,510	92.7	5,108,354	94.4	FIXED ASSETS	9,932,153	671,400	5,152,510
				TOTAL--			
9,076,623	70.1	8,888,758	73.7	ASSETS	15,442,730	1,711,900	9,076,623

LIABILITIES:

857,800							
0							
1,358,800							
164,200							
0							
153,200							
2,534,000							
463,900							
1,500,000							
1,963,900							
4,497,900							
1,010,000							
2,000,000							
0							
3,010,000							
1,568,723							
9,076,623							

Income Statement

UNITED INDUSTRIES   COMPANY CO20 GLRO120 REQ 9   INCOME STATEMENT CORPORATION   AS OF 12/31/90 PAGE 1   RUN DATE 01/04/91 21:35:49

CURRENT MONTH ACTUAL AMOUNT	BUDGET AMOUNT	BUDGET VARIANCE	PCT VAR		YEAR-TO-DATE ACTUAL AMOUNT	BUDGET AMOUNT	BUDGET VARIANCE	PCT VAR
				INCOME:				
				SALES INCOME:				
1,931,600	1,500,000	431,600	22.3	SALES	2,624,650	1,500,000	1,124,650	42.8
-26,860	-22,500	-4,360	16.2	SALES RETURNS & ALL	-34,630	-22,500	-12,130	35.0
				TOTAL--				
1,904,740	1,477,500	427,240	22.4	SALES INCOME	2,590,020	1,477,500	1,112,520	42.9
				OTHER INCOME:				
315,968	300,000	15,968	5.0	INTEREST INCOME	345,994	300,000	45,994	13.2
0	0	0	0.0	DIVIDEND INCOME	0	0	0	0.0
0	0	0	0.0	CURRENCY GAIN/LOSS	1,367	0	1,367	100.0
36,360	30,000	6,360	17.4	MISC INCOME	48,680	30,000	18,680	38.3
				TOTAL--				
352,328	330,000	22,328	6.3	OTHER INCOME	396,041	330,000	66,041	16.6
				TOTAL--				
2,257,068	1,807,500	449,568	19.9	INCOME	2,986,061	1,807,500	1,178,561	39.4
				EXPENSE:				
				COST OF GOODS SOLD:				
-29,052	0	-29,052	100.0	CHANGE IN INVENTORY	-83,081	0	-83,081	100.0
544,160	300,000	244,160	44.8	PURCHASES	974,980	300,000	674,980	69.2
0	0	0	0.0	PURCHASES-I/C	0	0	0	0.0
12,592	15,000	-2,408	-19.1	PURCH RETURNS & ALL	8,126	15,000	-6,874	-84.5
0	0	0	0.0	PURCH RET-I/C	0	0	0	0.0
22,360	15,000	7,360	32.9	FREIGHT	35,780	15,000	20,780	58.0
				TOTAL--				
550,060	330,000	220,060	40.0	COST OF GOODS SOLD	935,805	330,000	605,805	64.7
				OPERATING EXPENSES:				
99,760	75,000	24,760	24.8	DEPR - MACH	146,130	75,000	71,130	48.6
110,000	80,000	30,000	27.2	DEPR - BLDGS	140,000	80,000	60,000	42.8
39,908	37,500	2,408	6.0	INSURANCE	44,474	37,500	6,974	15.6
24,496	15,000	9,496	38.7	MISC OPERATING EXP	42,138	15,000	27,138	64.4
				TOTAL--				
274,164	207,500	66,664	24.3	OPERATING EXPENSES	372,742	207,500	165,242	44.3
				GENERAL EXPENSES:				
789,980	685,500	104,480	13.2	RENT EXPENSE	942,530	685,500	257,030	27.2
581,556	557,000	24,556	4.2	ADMIN SALARIES	614,443	557,000	57,443	9.3
274,736	274,000	736	0.2	OFFICE SUPPLIES	272,178	274,000	-1,822	-0.6
106,000	101,000	5,000	4.7	INCOME TAXES	111,000	101,000	10,000	9.0
23,316	22,500	816	3.5	STATE & LOCAL TAXES	27,968	22,500	5,468	19.5
22,500	22,500	0	0.0	BAD DEBT EXPENSE	22,500	22,500	0	0.0
295,908	284,500	11,408	3.8	INTEREST EXPENSE	309,474	284,500	24,974	8.0
20,960	13,600	7,360	35.1	DEPR - OFF EQUIP	34,480	13,600	20,880	60.5
11,400	10,000	1,400	12.2	DATA PROC EXPENSE	12,800	10,000	2,800	21.8
106,720	92,000	14,720	13.7	MKTG EXPENSE	133,160	92,000	41,160	30.9
477,172	475,500	1,672	0.3	MISC EXPENSE	480,416	475,500	4,916	1.0
-3,666,400	-265,000	-3,401,400	92.7	SUSPENSE	-3,655,260	-265,000	-3,390,260	92.7
				TOTAL--				
-956,152	2,273,100	-3,229,252	337.7	GENERAL EXPENSES	-694,311	2,273,100	-2,967,411	427.3
				TOTAL--				
-131,928	2,810,600	-2,942,528	2230.4	EXPENSE	614,236	2,810,600	-2,196,364	-357.5

FIGURE 11-20 Comparative financial statements. Courtesy of Data Design Associates.

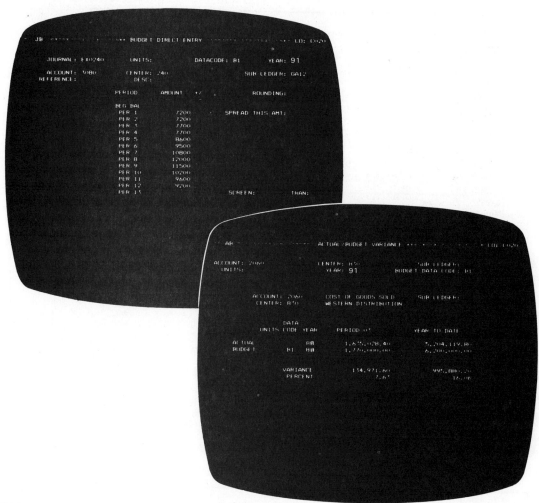

FIGURE 11-21   Screen displays containing budget and actual general ledger data for responsibility centers. Courtesy of Data Design Associates.

Several pertinent features are illustrated by Figure 11-22. First, the particular accounts, and the detail they represent, are based on the various needs of users. These needs in turn derive from the financial statements and reports required by users both inside and outside the subject firm. Second, although the coding of individual accounts must conform to the block code, all possible codes do not need to be used. For instance, codes 853 and 854 are vacant in the figure. They are available to be assigned as needed.

Third, individual accounts within the chart of accounts may serve as control accounts. Thus, account 850 controls the remaining administrative expense accounts; that is, the balance in account 850 should at all times equal the total of the balances in all other administrative expense accounts.

Group Codes

Group codes can provide added meaning to individual account codes. The left-

```
850   Administrative expenses control account
852   Officers' salaries
855   Office salaries
859   Overtime premium
861   Unemployment insurance expense
863   FICA expense
870   Office supplies
871   Office repairs
872   Telephone and telegraph
873   Postage
881   Dues and subscriptions
883   Donations
884   Travel
886   Insurance
888   Taxes
890   Depreciation—office equipment and furniture
891   Insurance—office equipment and furniture
892   Taxes—office equipment and furniture
899   Miscellaneous administrative expense
```

FIGURE 11-22 Expense accounts.

most digit can represent a major category (e.g., asset), the middle digit an intermediate classification (e.g., fixed assets), and the right-most digit a minor classification (e.g., the type of fixed asset). For example, the account code 112 may refer to the type of fixed asset known as buildings.

Additional dimensions can be linked to the general ledger account codes. Frequently useful additions are codes for subsidiary ledgers, organizational units, locations, and products. A group code format encompassing two of these facets might appear as follows:

$$AAA–BBBB–CC$$

where AAA is a general ledger account number, BBBB is a subsidiary ledger account number, and CC is a responsibility center number. A sales transaction coded according to this format could involve a debit to combined account 121-5634-00 and a credit to combined account 820-1738-08. The 121 and 820 refer to the general ledger accounts entitled Accounts Receivable and Sales. The 5634 refers to the customer account against which the credit sale is charged, and the 1738 refers to the salesperson whose account is credited in the commissions payable ledger. The 08 refers to the sales region (responsibility center) where the sale is made. Finally, the 00 indicates that Accounts Receivable are general in nature and not applicable to a particular responsibility center.

Responsibility reporting systems are dependent on group codes that combine gen-

APPLICATION OF A CODED PLANNING SYSTEM
Federal Express [a]

Memphis-based Federal Express, the rapid delivery firm, employs a planning and budgeting system that depends on a carefully constructed coding structure. Called Flex Budgeting, this system consists of a data base, set of planning models, and decision-oriented reports. The coding structure is built around cost centers at four levels: corporate level, division level, department level, and budget unit level. Each cost center is assigned a ten-digit code, with the codes linking from the bottom level to the top. Tied to the cost center codes are general ledger account numbers, subledger account numbers, and associated financial data. A set of financial data consists of last year's actual balance, current account balance, current budget, and two forecasts. All of these financial data, broken down into monthly amounts, are loaded from the general ledger and budget files into the Flex data base. Then, by means of suitable budget models, a variety of reports can be generated. These reports can provide financial planning and control information at several levels of detail. For instance, monthly expense reports, showing budget versus actual values, can be generated for each budget unit in the firm.

[a]David Livingston, "A System to Grow With," *Datamation* (October 1, 1985), pp. 89–96.

eral ledger account codes with responsibility center codes. When a firm decides to employ responsibility reporting concepts, it codes budgeted costs and revenues according to responsibility centers in addition to general ledger accounts. (An example of a suitable responsibility center group coding scheme appears in Chapter 10.) As costs are incurred by the various responsibility centers during accounting periods, responsibility center codes are attached to the costs. Revenues achieved through profit centers are also assigned responsibility center codes. At the end of each accounting period the costs and revenues are sorted by both general ledger accounts and responsibility centers. Then responsibility reports are prepared to reflect budget variances for the respective centers. In order to generate the firmwide income statement, the costs and revenues need only be re-sorted in accordance with the general ledger account codes alone.

Group codes within charts of accounts are extremely flexible to use. They can incorporate added fields to reflect a wide variety of dimensions. For instance, a field can be included in the responsibility reporting system to indicate whether a specific cost is controllable or noncontrollable with respect to a particular responsibility center. This added field facilitates the preparation of reports that accord with the principle that centers should be held responsible only for controllable costs.

Differences among Various Types of Organizations

Organizations as well as data may be classified. Separately identifiable types of organizations include

1. Business firms that merchandise products, such as wholesalers and retailers.
2. Business firms that market services, ranging from professional firms and custodial service firms to universities and hospitals.
3. Business firms that manufacture and distribute products, ranging from automobile manufacturers to electric utilities.
4. Not-for-profit organizations, ranging from governmental agencies to churches.

Each type of organization displays distinctive accounts in its general ledger system as well as unique features in its operating procedures. The wholesalers and retailers focus on merchandise inventory and the activities related thereto. The service firms, in contrast, de-emphasize inventories and focus on the performance and pricing of services. Manufacturers must look to raw materials and work-in-process inventories as well as to finished goods. They also must distinguish between direct labor and indirect labor used in production and decide how to allocate overhead costs to the manufactured products. Not-for-profit organizations focus much more on costs than on revenues; in fact, they may receive allocations of funds rather than revenues. In addition, these varied types of organizations must devote attention to their forms of ownership, which may range from stockholders to individual proprietors.

Although our examples in this chapter have centered on merchandising firms, we will employ examples in later chapters that are drawn from manufacturing and the other types noted earlier.

Summary

General ledger systems are involved in collecting transaction data, classifying and coding transaction data, processing transaction inflows, storing transaction data, maintaining accounting controls, and generating financial reports. The general ledger system is also called the general ledger and financial reporting cycle, which is at the center of such transaction-oriented cycles as the revenue cycle, expenditure cycle, and resource management cycle.

The general ledger system receives inputs from the various transaction processing systems (cycles), from nonroutine transactions, from adjusting transactions, and from reversing transactions. The inputs are normally on general ledger journal vouchers, which in the case of computer-based systems may be transferred to batch entry forms or to data entry screens. The entered data, in journal entry form, are then posted to the general ledger to update the accounts during the accounting period. At the end of each accounting period standard and nonstandard adjusting journal entries are posted. The exact methods of processing vary, depending on whether the processing is performed by manual or computer-based systems. The data base includes such files as the general ledger master file, general ledger history file, responsibility center master file, budget master file, financial reports format file, current journal voucher file, and journal voucher history file. A variety of general and transaction controls are needed to offset a number of risks to which the general ledger is exposed. These controls include adequate documentation, segregation of organization, data security, carefully designed and prepared journal vouchers, and periodic trial balances. Financial reports typically generated by the general ledger system include analyses of general ledger accounts, financial statements, and such managerial reports as sales analyses and responsibility reports. Many of the managerial reports involve comparisons between budget and actual amounts.

The chart of accounts is a coded listing of all the classified accounts of a firm. Sound classification and coding techniques can make a chart of accounts more meaningful to users. Often it embodies such coding schemes as block coding and group coding, and its general ledger account codes are linked to codes relating to organizational units and subsidiary ledger accounts. Charts of accounts vary among different types of organizations, such as merchandising firms, manufacturing firms, and not-for-profit organizations.

Review Problem with Solution

Statement

The Sinclair Appliance Company of Clemson, South Carolina, is a newly formed corporation engaged in merchandising appliances. Its sales categories may be described as major appliances; other merchandise, such as small appliances; parts and accessories; and appliance servicing. Most sales are made on credit; in fact, a large number of major-appliance sales are made on the installment basis.

Sinclair has developed good credit relations. Not only has it obtained a large loan on a note from the local bank, but it has assurances from major suppliers that it will be able to sign notes and contracts for shipments of merchandise acquired from them. Consequently, it intends to finance all installment sales itself.

Sinclair has acquired a large building, the mortgage being held by a local realty mortgage firm. It also pays rent on a nearby building used as a garage and service center, to which certain improvements have been made by the firm. It owns furniture and fixtures, as well as several automobiles and trucks.

Several managers and such employees as sales clerks and bookkeepers are located at the main building. Other employees, such as service personnel, delivery personnel, and a mechanic, are located in the nearby buildings. In addition, several salespersons travel around the metropolitan area to visit retailers and other prospective customers. These salespersons work on a commission basis and on occasion entertain prospective customers.

As a local accountant specializing in accounting system design, you have been retained by the firm's controller to help de-

Sinclair Appliance Company
Income Statement
For the Month Ended _____ 19——

	Major appliances	Other merchandise	Parts and accessories	Appliance Service	Total
Sales.........................	$...........	$...........	$...........	$...........	$...........
Less: Sales discounts.............	$...........	$...........	$...........	$...........	
Sales returns and allowances	....	....	....	....	
Total deductions...........	$...........	$...........	$...........	$...........	$...........
Net sales.......................	$...........	$...........	$...........	$...........	$...........
Less: Cost of sales...............	....	....	....	....	....
Gross profit on sales.............	$...........	$...........	$...........	$...........	$...........
Selling expenses					
Sales salaries................			$...........		
Commissions.................			....		
Travel.......................			....		
Entertainment................			....		
Advertising..................			....		
Trucking and delivery.........			....		
Depreciation—automobiles and trucks...........................			....		
Service......................			....		
Repairs and maintenance.......			....		
Total selling expenses....				$...........	
Administrative expenses					
Office salaries and wages......			$...........		
Rent........................			....		
Taxes.......................			....		
Utilities.....................			....		
Telephone and telegraph.......			....		
Insurance....................			....		
Office supplies................			....		
Stationery, printing, and postage...			....		
Legal and accounting..........			....		
Dues and subscriptions........			....		
Donations...................			....		
Employee welfare			....		
Depreciation—buildings........			....		
Depreciation—furniture and fixtures...			....		
Amortization—leasehold improvements...			....		
Total administrative expenses........				....	
Financial management expenses					
Interest expense..............			$...........		
Bad debts...................			....		
Dividends...................			....		
Miscellaneous expense.........			....		
Total financial management expenses..........				....	
Total operating expenses..........					....
Net operating profit.............					$...........
Other income					
Interest earned...............			$........,...		
Miscellaneous income..........			....		
Total other income...........					....
Net income for the month........					$...........

Sinclair Appliance Company
Balance Sheet
As at December 31, 19——

ASSETS

Current
  Cash in bank and on hand .... $............
  Notes receivable .... $............
  Less: Discounted notes ....
  Accounts receivable... $............
  Contracts receivable... ....
    Total.. ....
  Less: Allowance for bad and doubtful accounts.................... ....
  Inventories:
    Major appliances .... $............
    Parts and accessories.. ....
    Other merchandise.. $............ ....
  Prepaid expenses ....
    Total current assets.. $............
Fixed
  Land .... $............
  Buildings .... $............
  Less: Allowance for depreciation ....
  Furniture and fixtures... $............
  Less: Allowance for depreciation ....
  Automobiles and trucks....................................... $............
  Less: Allowance for depreciation ....
  Leasehold improvements...................................... $............
  Less: Allowance for amortization ....
    Total fixed assets .... $............
      Total assets .... $............

LIABILITIES

Current
  Notes payable—bank.. $............
  Notes payable—others ....
  Merchandise notes and contracts payable ....
  Accounts payable ....
  Taxes payable—sales, payroll, and others....................... ....
  Accrued expenses payable..................................... ....
    Total current liabilities....................................... $............
Long-term
  Mortgage payable... $............
    Total liabilities .... $............

CAPITAL STOCK AND RETAINED EARNINGS

Capital stock: Authorized.. $............
Less: Unissued .... $............
Retained earnings ....
  Total capital and retained earnings .... $............
  Total liabilities and net worth .... $............

velop a suitable system. Your first step is to design the financial statements. After a couple of hours you produce the statements shown on pages 454 and 455. Then you turn to the underlying accounts.

Required

a. Design a coded chart of accounts that will provide appropriate data for the financial statements. Assume that Sinclair uses the periodic inventory method and pays incoming freight on many of its purchases of merchandise.

b. Describe an expanded code format that should be useful if the firm grows in amount of sales, number of employees, and number of outlets. The code should accommodate the use of subsidiary ledger accounts and the accumulation of costs by responsibility centers.

Solution

a. Chart of accounts.

Assets (100–199)

101	Cash in Bank—General Account
102	Cash in Bank—Payroll Account
103	Petty Cash
110	Notes Receivable
111	Discounted Notes
112	Accounts Receivable—Trade
113	Accounts Receivable—Other
114	Allowance for Bad and Doubtful Accounts
115	Contracts Receivable
120	Inventory—Major Appliances
121	Inventory—Parts and Accessories
122	Inventory—Other Merchandise
130	Prepaid Expenses
150	Land
151	Buildings
152	Allowance for Depreciation—Buildings
153	Furniture and Fixtures
154	Allowance for Depreciation—Furniture and Fixtures
155	Automobiles and Trucks
156	Allowance for Depreciation—Automobiles and Trucks
157	Leasehold Improvements
158	Allowance for Amortization—Leasehold Improvements
170	Long-Term Investments
180	Intangible Assets
190	Other Assets

Liabilities and Capital (200–299)

201	Notes Payable—Bank
202	Notes Payable—Other
203	Merchandise Notes and Contracts Payable
204	Accounts Payable
210	Sales Taxes Payable
211	Employee Income Taxes Payable
212	FICA Taxes Payable
213	Federal Unemployment Taxes Payable
214	State Unemployment Taxes Payable
215	Other Taxes Payable
216	Pension Expense Payable
217	Medical Insurance Withholdings Payable
218	Other Withholdings Payable
220	Accrued Wages and Salaries Payable
230	Accrued Interest Payable
231	Accrued Dividends Payable
238	Other Expenses Payable
240	Mortgage Payable
250	Capital Stock
251	Paid-In Capital
252	Retained Earnings

Revenues and Cost of Sales (300–399)

301	Sales—Major Appliances
302	Sales—Other Merchandise
303	Sales—Parts and Accessories
304	Sales—Service
306	Sales Discounts—Major Appliances

307 Sales Discounts—Other Merchandise
308 Sales Discounts—Parts and Accessories
309 Sales Discounts—Service
310 Sales Returns and Allowances—Major Appliances
311 Sales Returns and Allowances—Other Merchandise
312 Sales Returns and Allowances—Parts and Accessories
313 Sales Allowances—Service
320 Interest Earned
321 Miscellaneous Income
331 Cost of Sales—Major Appliances
332 Cost of Sales—Other Appliances
333 Cost of Sales—Parts and Accessories
334 Cost of Sales—Service
341 Purchases—Major Appliances
342 Purchases—Other Appliances
343 Purchases—Parts and Accessories
344 Purchases—Service
345 Purchase Returns and Allowances—Major Appliances
346 Purchase Returns and Allowances—Other Appliances
347 Purchase Returns and Allowances—Parts and Accessories
348 Purchase Allowances—Service
351 Freight In—Major Appliances
352 Freight In—Other Appliances
353 Freight In—Parts and Accessories
354 Freight In—Service

Selling Expenses (400–449)

400 Selling Expenses Control
401 Sales Salaries
402 Commissions
403 Travel
404 Entertainment
405 Advertising
406 Trucking and Delivery
407 Depreciation—Automobiles and Trucks
408 Service
409 Repairs and Maintenance

Administrative Expenses (450–479)

450 Administrative Expenses Control
451 Office Salaries and Wages
452 Rent
453 Taxes
454 Utilities
455 Telephone and Telegraph
456 Insurance
457 Office Supplies
458 Stationery, Printing, and Postage
459 Legal and Accounting
460 Dues and Subscriptions
461 Donations
462 Employee Welfare
463 Depreciation—Buildings
464 Depreciation—Furniture and Fixtures
465 Amortization—Leasehold Improvements

Financial Management Expenses (480–499)

481 Interest
482 Bad Debts
483 Dividends
484 Miscellaneous

Notes: (1) Blocks of numbers have been assigned to each major account group (e.g., assets). Within each block certain numbers remain unassigned. These numbers are available for assignment if new accounts are found to be needed. (2) Accounts 400 and 450 are control accounts in that they control the totals of the detailed sales and administrative expense accounts.

b. An expanded code format might consist of the following three fields:

$$AAA–BBB–C$$

where AAA represents the general ledger account code, BBB is a three-digit code representing a subsidiary detail account (e.g., for a customer or supplier), and C is a numeric or alphabetic code representing an outlet where a sale takes place or a cost is incurred.

Notes: (1) The foregoing format assumes that outlets are the only responsibility centers likely to be established by the firm. An additional field will be needed if responsibility centers are to be established *within* each outlet. (2) The second and third fields will be left blank in the cases of those transactions that do not involve revenues or expenses.

Review Questions

11-1 What is the meaning of each of the following terms?

> General ledger and financial reporting cycle
> Transaction processing system
> Nonroutine transaction
> End-of-period adjusting transaction
> Reversing transaction
> Journal voucher
> Batch entry form
> Data entry screen
> Standard adjusting journal entry
> Nonrecurring adjusting journal entry
> General ledger master file
> Budget master file
> General ledger analysis
> Chart of accounts

11-2 What is the major objective of the general ledger system?

11-3 Identify several functions of the general ledger system.

11-4 Identify four common transaction-oriented cycles of business activity.

11-5 How does the general ledger system relate to the component transaction processing systems within a firm?

11-6 What are several sources of inputs to the general ledger system?

11-7 How are the forms of input likely to differ between manual and computer-based general ledger systems?

11-8 Describe the processing of transactions in an on-line computer-based general ledger system.

11-9 How are processing steps likely to differ in a computer-based general ledger system between (a) transaction data entered during an accounting period and (b) transaction data entered at the end of an accounting period?

11-10 What is the sorting key when the general ledger is to be updated sequentially?

11-11 Identify the various types of files that might be found in a general ledger data base.

11-12 What are the risks to which the general ledger maintenance activity is exposed?

11-13 What general controls are needed to counteract the risks to which the general ledger is exposed?

11-14 What transaction (application) controls are needed to counteract the risks to which general ledger processing is exposed?

11-15 How may the financial reports generated by the general ledger system be classified?

11-16 Describe the application of block codes to the coding of charts of accounts.

11-17 Describe the application of group codes to the coding of charts of accounts.

11-18 What additional dimensions may logically be linked to general ledger account codes?

11-19 Describe several differences among the charts of accounts of organizations in various lines of endeavor.

Discussion Questions

11-20 What are the advantages of having a general ledger that is continually on line?

11-21 Describe the differences in general ledger accounts needed by a not-for-profit organization and those needed by a merchandising firm.

11-22 Discuss modifications that are likely to be needed when a general ledger software package is acquired.

Problems

11-1 Describe transaction-oriented cycle(s) that are unique or special for each of the following types of organizations:

    a. Manufacturing firm.
    b. Bank.
    c. Hospital.
    d. University.
    e. Municipality.
    f. Electric utility.
    g. Insurance company.
    h. Architectural firm.
    i. Brokerage firm.

11-2 Merchandise Unlimited, Inc., records those daily and end-of-period transactions that affect the general ledger on numbered journal vouchers. Each journal voucher is entered by Joan Campbell and approved by Martin Turner. Selected general ledger account codes are as follows: Cash in Bank, 101; Accounts Receivable, 120; Prepaid Rent, 163; Capital Stock, 280; Rent Expense, 547.

Required

Draw journal voucher forms and enter the data to show how each of the following selected transactions would appear after being recorded by Joan Campbell. (Assigned journal voucher numbers appear in parentheses.)

    a. Payments received from credit customers on October 12 and deposited in the bank total $12,435.20. (569)

    b. Additional capital stock is issued and sold at par value for $10,000 on October 27; the full amount in cash is received the same day from several large acquirers. (598)

    c. One month's prepaid rent of $2,400 has expired on October 31. (617)

11-3 Your firm employs an on-line general ledger system. When you sign on to the system, the menu shown below appears on the video display screen. Draw the appearance of the data entry screen after you press the number 1 and then enter the following transaction on August 15, 1990: A dividend of $5.00 per share is declared on the capital stock, payable on September 14 to stock-

---

```
GENERAL LEDGER MAIN MENU
1. INPUT OF JOURNAL ENTRY
2. CORRECTION OF PREVIOUS JOURNAL ENTRY
3. CHANGE OF PERMANENT DATA IN ACCOUNT RECORD
4. INQUIRY INTO ACCOUNT RECORD
5. MONTH-END STANDARD ADJUSTING JOURNAL ENTRIES
6. MONTH-END CLOSING ENTRIES
7. FINANCIAL STATEMENT PREPARATION
8. GENERAL LEDGER LISTING PROOF REPORTS
9. MANAGERIAL REPORTS MENU
10. EXIT FROM GENERAL LEDGER SYSTEM
        ENTER DESIRED NUMBER>
```

holders of record on August 31. (Outstanding shares of capital stock total 10,000; account codes for Dividends Payable and Retained Earnings are 2780 and 2900, respectively.)

11-4 The Deckman Company is a wholesale distributor of beers and wines. It sells on credit to retail establishments such as grocery chains. Merchandise is obtained by credit purchases from bottlers and wineries. Other transactions involve cash receipts and disbursements, payroll, inventories, and fixed assets. Certain of the transactions, such as those involving cash and payroll, are processed in batches. Other transactions are processed by the on-line approach. All master files are maintained on magnetic disk files. The firm has several video display terminals for entering data and obtaining output displays.

Required

Describe a suitable system for entering and processing the various types of journal entries that affect the general ledger. Identify in your description all files that would be useful in storing data relating to journal entries and the general ledger.

11-5 Refer to the Review Problem. Identify each of the following journal entries as pertaining to routine, nonroutine, standard recurring adjusting, nonrecurring adjusting, or reversing transactions.

a. Cash   XXX
     Notes payable—
     bank   XXX
     To record the receipt of cash in exchange for a _____ day, _____ percent note payable to _____ Bank.

b. Amortization-leasehold improvements   XXX
     Allowance for amortization-leasehold improvements   XXX
     To record amortization for (period).

c. Accounts receivable—trade   XXX
     Sales—major appliances   XXX
     Sales—other merchandise   XXX
     Sales—parts and accessories   XXX
     Sales—service   XXX
     To record sales of all lines for (date).

d. Furniture and fixtures   XXX
     Paid-in capital   XXX
     To record the donation of office furniture and fixtures by the president on the first day of incorporation.

11-6 Refer to the Review Problem. Prepare examples of journal entries pertaining to routine, nonroutine, standard recurring adjusting, nonrecurring adjusting, and reversing transactions.

11-7 Refer to Problem 11-4. Design a record layout for the general ledger to be used by Deckman Company. Include field sizes and data modes. Enter assumed data into copies of the layout for two accounts: Cash in Bank—General Account and Accounts Payable.

Note: Use Figure 11-11 as a guide in designing the record layout, but make at least one significant modification.

11-8 Design a five-digit group code for fixed assets. The code should be of the hierarchical type and based on the ledger account codes. Thus, the leftmost digit should designate the broad category of assets, and the remaining digits should specify increasingly narrow categories. Illustrate your code format by coding drill presses owned by a firm, assuming that the firm employs three types of drill presses.

11-9 Assume that each error situation in the following list is independent from the others and that the error occurs in an accounting information system that processes transactions *manually*.

a. The credit portion of a nonroutine transaction is inadvertently omitted when the transaction is entered for processing.

b. The debit amount of a nonroutine transaction contains an inadvertent transposition upon entry of the transaction.

c. A nonroutine transaction is entered twice inadvertently.

d. The cashier forgot to enter the accrual of the interest on the note payable last month.

e. A nonexistent number of an accounts payable account is entered during the posting of cash disbursements, and hence the accounts payable ledger is out of balance with the general ledger account.

f. A nonexistent number of a general ledger account is entered during the entry of a nonroutine transaction, and hence the debits do not equal the credits in the general ledger.

g. A nonstandard adjusting entry is prepared and entered by the cashier to conceal the theft of cash.

Required

Identify one or more transaction controls that should have prevented or detected each of the error situations.

11-10 Refer to Problem 11-9. Identify one or more transaction controls that should have prevented or detected each of the error situations, assuming that they take place in an accounting information system that employs *on-line processing* of transactions.

Hint: Certain of the controls will be identical to those identified in Problem 11-9.

11-11 Refer to Problems 11-4 and 11-7. List the programmed checks that can perform appropriate validations in the following situations, and specify examples of data items that each programmed check is intended to verify. Assume that journal vouchers contain journal voucher (JV) numbers, general ledger account numbers, account descriptions, debit amounts, credit amounts, and debit or credit (i.e., DR, CR) designations. In addition, assume that transaction codes are included when an on-line system is employed.

a. Batches of journal vouchers being posted sequentially to general ledger accounts during batch processing runs.

b. Data on journal voucher forms, pertaining either to summarized transactions or to nonroutine individual transactions, being entered individually via on-line terminals and being posted immediately to the general ledger accounts.

11-12 The Brassila Corporation performs all of its transaction processing on computers by the batch approach. Its sales, purchases/ payables, cash receipts and disbursements, payroll, and fixed assets transactions are gathered into batches, batch-totaled, and then transcribed onto magnetic tapes from the source documents. Then, as the individual transactions are processed daily or weekly to update the subsidiary ledgers, the summary data (i.e., total amounts affecting the various general ledger accounts) are transferred or extracted onto account distribution tapes. These account distribution tapes are merged daily with each other and with a daily tape containing entries for all nonroutine transactions originally recorded that day on journal vouchers. The resulting tape is sorted according to general ledger account numbers and then processed to update the accounts in the general ledger. Batch totals of the account distribution tapes are not computed.

At the end of each month a tape containing all adjusting journal entries is processed to update the general ledger, just after the last day's tapes are processed. Then the firm performs computer processing runs that (1) close all temporary accounts and produce a magnetic tape containing all financial statement data pertaining to actual and budget values for the month and (2) print balance sheets and income statements that compare actual and budgeted values. The subsidiary ledgers, general ledger, and budget are maintained as separate files on magnetic disks throughout the month.

Required

Prepare a system flowchart that reflects the daily and monthly processing of the general ledger.

11-13 Joel Mutt and Anne Jeffers are combining their individual public accounting practices into a two-person partnership. One of the first requirements is to establish a new chart of accounts. Their firm will provide audit, tax, and management consulting services. Each service area is to be headed by a separate manager, who is responsible for the profits of the area. In addition, the firm will have an office manager, who will have responsibilities for secretarial services, the internal accounting information system, insurance, payroll, and so on.

The assets to be owned by the firm include furniture and fixtures, office equipment, microcomputers, short-term investments, receivables from clients, supplies, office building, and land. Liabilities include notes payable to the bank, accounts payable, the various payroll withholdings, and other customary accruals. The major expense is for salaries to the professional accountants and other staff, as well as bonuses to managers. However, travel and entertainment expenses are significant, as are telephone and other utility expenses, taxes, and insur-

ance. Other expenses typical of a service enterprise are also incurred.

Required

Design a coded chart of accounts that will facilitate the preparation of a monthly balance sheet and income statement. Add a set of organizational codes that will enable the preparation of responsibility reports for the three major service areas and the office management activity. The responsibility reports will be profit oriented for the service areas and cost oriented for the office management activity. Expenses that are jointly incurred for the benefit of all areas are not to be included in the responsibility reports.

11-14 The College Bookstore occupies two levels in a building adjacent to the campus of a large Arizona university. On the lower level are textbooks and other books; on the upper level are writing materials, art supplies, clothing, typewriters, cameras, souvenirs, and related items.

Tony Lattimore, the bookstore owner-manager, is in charge of all bookstore operations. Lynn Smythe is in charge of the upper level, and Tricia Danten is the manager of activities on the lower level. The staff consists of a bookkeeper, five merchandise order clerks, four sales clerks, two stock clerks, two cashiers, and a janitor. During peak periods, such as the beginning of each semester, temporary personnel are added. All managers and employees are paid on the first and fifteenth of each month, deductions being made for federal and state income taxes, Social Security tax, federal unemployment tax, pension plan, medical insurance, and various miscellaneous items. Paychecks are written on a special bank account after funds are transferred from the regular checking account.

The building occupied by the bookstore is leased; however, all utilities, including heat, water, electricity, and telephone, must be paid by Tony in addition to the lease payments. Fixed assets owned by the bookstore include four cash registers, store fixtures, desks and related office furnishings, typewriters, desk calculators, dollies, and a small van.

All items of merchandise are purchased on account from over 200 suppliers. Payments made within 10 days from the invoice dates receive 2-percent discounts. Textbooks are bought subject to return privileges, since estimated course sizes do not always materialize. In addition to merchandise, some store supplies, such as janitorial supplies, must be acquired. To finance such acquisitions, the bookstore must obtain a short-term bank loan at the beginning of a school year.

All merchandise is sold on a cash basis. State and city sales taxes are collected on each sale. Each cash register is provided with a change fund. Sales returns are made when merchandise items, including books, are returned in good condition; the payments on such returns are made from a cash register, and records of the amounts involved are retained. All cash receipts, less the amounts paid on returns, are deposited daily in the checking account at the local bank.

The bookstore is currently nearing the end of its first year of operations. It has been recording the foregoing activities and transactions in accounts and records established by the bookkeeper. However, Tony feels that a formal chart of accounts and related records should be established. Therefore, he asks for your suggestions.

Required

Assuming that the bookstore employs the periodic inventory system and takes physical inventory once a year, just prior to the preparation of financial statements, do the following:

a. Prepare formats for the financial statements, including information concerning the two product lines (i.e., the products sold on the upper level and on the lower level).

b. Design a coded chart of accounts needed to provide these financial statements.

c. Draw formats for journals and subsidiary ledgers that would be useful in transaction processing at the bookstore, assuming that transactions are processed manually.

11-15 Refer to Problem 11-14. A transaction code has been selected in the format AAA-B-CCCCC, where AAA is the general ledger account to be debited or credited, B is the responsibility center (1 means upper level, 2 means lower level), and CCCCC is the subsidiary ledger account number. For the purposes of this problem, assume that the only subsidiary ledger is accounts payable, and that only suppliers of merchandise are maintained in the ledger. Assign codes to both the debit and credit portions of the following transactions, using the above format and the chart of accounts provided. When a part of the coding format is not applicable, assign zeros in place of significant digits.

a. A valid and correct invoice is received from supplier number 52179 relating to the purchase of 10 dozen university-inscribed sweatshirts.

b. A check is prepared and mailed to supplier number 64231 relating to the purchase of 200 textbooks for an accounting course.

c. A valid and correct bill is received from the bookstore's accountants for general auditing services, and a check is duly prepared and mailed.

d. A valid and correct bill is received from the electric utility, and a check is duly prepared and mailed. Separate meters are employed to measure usage on each level, so that amounts can be fairly allocated.

11-16 Refer to Problem 11-14. Design a monthly report that shows the profits for the upper and lower levels of the bookstore. The following are joint expenses that cannot be reasonably allocated to separate profit centers: salaries of managers, advertising, heating, water, repairs and maintenance, janitorial supplies, insurance, legal and accounting, donations, taxes, interest, amortization of leasehold improvements, depreciation of motorized vehicles, purchase discounts lost and miscellaneous.

 11-17 *Note: This problem can be solved by using a microcomputer-based spreadsheet software package.* The budgeted and actual values pertaining to the January 1990 income statement for Hargreaves, Ltd., are as follows:

	Budget	Actual
Sales	$10,000	$9,000
Cost of goods sold	6,500	5,600
Gross profit on sales	$3,500	$3,400
Selling expenses	$ 500	$450
Administrative expenses	1,400	950
Total expenses	$1,900	$1,400
Net income before taxes	$1,600	$2,000
Estimated income taxes	240	300
Net income	$1,360	$1,700

Required

Prepare a report for management in good form that reveals the performance of the firm during January.

11-18 The Mountainair Public Service Company of Fort Collins, Colorado, serves approximately 195,000 gas and electric consumers throughout a portion of the state. The firm's operations and maintenance activities are divided into five districts, each headed by a manager. Within each district are from 7 to 20 offices, each headed by a supervisor.

As a public utility, Mountainair employs the uniform chart of accounts prescribed by the Federal Power Commission. Thus, codes in the 100s pertain to assets, in the 200s to liabilities, in the 400s to revenues, in the 500s and 600s to operating expenses associated with electricity, in the 700s and 800s to operating expenses associated with gas, and in the 900s to selling and administrative expenses.

However, the controller of Mountainair feels that the coding system might usefully be expanded. For instance, he would like a coding system that would enable the preparation of the following reports.

> Balance sheet.
> Income statement, by types of revenues.
> Responsibility report for each supervisor, showing the types of expenses charged to his or her office, broken down by those that are controllable by the supervisor and those that are noncontrollable overhead.
> Responsibility report for each district manager, showing the totals of expenses incurred by each supervisor within his or her district.
> Operating statement showing expenses by district and office.

Required

a. Design and illustrate a coding system that will enable the preparation of these reports while retaining the coding prescribed by the Federal Power Commission.

b. Design a customer code that will be useful to the firm in analyzing sales. Note that some customers are residential, others are commercial, and still others fall into special categories such as public street lighting and school lighting; some use gas only, some use electricity only, and some use both.

11-19 Pitman Auto Sales and Service has just been established as a sole proprietorship in Blacksburg, Virginia. It plans to sell three lines of cars: Econs, Meds, and Quals. In addition to new-car sales, it has set up service, parts, and used-car sales departments, each under the supervision of a manager. The firm owns its buildings, land, furnishings, and service equipment. Some of the expenses that it expects to incur are salaries for salespersons and mechanics and for the office force (including managers), utilities, advertising, supplies, taxes, gas and oil, insurance, telephone, and various administrative items. Since it will not handle financing of sales contracts, its receivables will be due from financing agencies. Its inventories of cars and parts, as well as its suppliers, likely will be rather numerous.

Required

Design a coded chart of accounts, together with a group coding format that extends the chart of accounts to include subsidiary ledgers and organizational units. In addition to providing control over inventories and suppliers' accounts, the group code should enable the following reports to be prepared:

a. A balance sheet and income statement for the firm.

b. A report that reflects gross profits on sales related to each line of new cars, used cars, parts, and service.

c. An expense report that shows total expenses, plus a breakdown of the direct expenses chargeable to each department.

11-20 Ollie Mace has recently been appointed controller of a family-owned manufacturing enterprise. The firm, S. Dilley & Co., was founded by Mr. Dilley about 20 years ago and is 78 percent owned by Mr. Dilley. Located in Indianapolis, Indiana, it has served the major automotive companies as a parts supplier. The firm's major operating divisions are heat treating, extruding, small-parts stamping, and specialized machining. Last year, sales from the several divisions ranged from $150,000 to over $3,000,000. The divisions are physically and managerially independent except for Mr. Dilley's constant surveillance. The accounting system for each division has evolved according to the division's own needs and to the abilities of individual accountants or bookkeepers. Mr. Mace is the first controller in the firm's history to have responsibility for over-all financial management. Mr. Dilley expects to retire within six years and has hired Mr. Mace to improve the firm's financial system.

A new chart of accounts, as it appears to Mr. Mace, is essential to getting started on other critical financial problems. The present account codes used by divisions are not standard. They also do not reflect organizational responsibility or product groups.

Mr. Mace sees a need to divide asset accounts into five major categories: current assets, plant and equipment, and so on. Within each of these categories, he sees a need for no more than 10 control accounts. Based on his observations to date, 100 subsidiary accounts are more than adequate for each control account.

Each division now handles five or fewer product groups, such as the radiator group. The maximum number of cost centers Mr. Mace foresees within any product group is six, including operating and nonoperating groups. He views general divisional costs as a non-revenue-producing product group. Altogether, Mr. Mace estimates that about 44 natural expense accounts, such as tools and advertising, plus about 12 cost-of-sales accounts (including variance accounts), would be adequate.

Mr. Mace is planning to implement the new chart of accounts in an environment that at present includes manual records systems and one division using a computer-based system. Mr. Mace expects that in the near future most accounting and reporting for all units will be automated. Therefore, the chart of accounts should facilitate the processing of transactions manually or by computer. Efforts should be made, he believes, to restrict the length of the code for economy in processing and convenience in use. (To achieve this condensation, the same code fields should be used to contain data pertaining to assets, expenses, equities, and revenues. Thus, each coded transaction data should incorporate a separate code field which specifies the type of account.)

Required

a. Design the structure of a chart-of-accounts coding system that will meet Mr. Mace's requirements. Your answer should begin with a layout of the code format. You should explain the type of code you have chosen and the reason for the size of your code fields. Explain your code as it would apply to asset and expense accounts.

b. Use your chart-of-accounts coding system to illustrate the code needed for the following data.

   (1) In the small-parts stamping division, $100 was spent on cleaning supplies by foreman Bill Shaw in the polishing department of the door lever group. Code the expense item, using the code you have developed above.

   (2) A new motorized sweeper has been purchased for the maintenance department of the extruding division for $3450. Code this asset item, using the code you developed above.

(CMA adapted)

11-21 Family Resorts, Inc., is a holding company for several vacation hotels in the northeast and mid-Atlantic states. The firm originally purchased several old inns, restored the buildings, and upgraded the recreational facilities. The inns have been well received by vacationing families, as many services are provided that accommodate children and afford parents time for themselves. Since the completion of the restorations ten years ago, the company has been profitable.

Family Resorts has just concluded its annual meeting of regional and district managers. This meeting is held each November to review the results of the previous season and to help the managers prepare for the upcoming year. Prior to the meeting, the managers have submitted proposed budgets for their districts or regions as appropriate. These budgets have been reviewed and consolidated into an annual operating budget for the entire company. The 1991 budget has been presented at the meeting and was accepted by the managers.

To evaluate the performance of its managers, Family Resorts uses responsibility accounting. Therefore, the preparation of the budget is given close attention at headquarters. If major changes need to be made to the budgets submitted by the managers, all affected parties are consulted before the changes are incorporated. Presented on page 467 and at the top of page 468 are two pages from the budget booklet that all managers received at the meeting.

Required

a. Responsibility accounting has been used effectively by many companies, both large and small.

   (1) Define responsibility accounting.

   (2) Discuss the benefits that accrue to a company using responsibility accounting.

Family Resorts, Inc.
Condensed Operating Budget—Maine District
For the Year Ending December 31, 1991
($000 omitted)

	Region			New England District				Maine District Inns		
	Family Resorts	Mid-Atlantic	New England	Not Allocated[a]	Vermont	New Hampshire	Maine	Not Allocated[b]	Harbor	Camden Country
Net sales	$7,900	$4,200	$3,700	—	$1,400	$1,200	$1,100	—	$600	$500
Cost of sales	4,530	2,310	2,220	—	840	720	660	—	360	300
Gross margin	$3,370	$1,890	$1,480	—	$560	$480	$440	—	$240	$200
Controllable expenses										
Supervisory expense	$240	$130	$110		$35	$30	$45	$10	$20	$15
Training expense	160	80	80		30	25	25		15	10
Advertising expense	500	280	220	$50	55	60	55	15	20	20
Repairs and maintenance	480	225	255	—	90	85	80	—	40	40
Total controllable expenses	$1,380	$715	$665	$50	$210	$200	$205	$25	$95	$85
Controllable contribution	$1,990	$1,175	$815	$(50)	$350	$280	$235	$(25)	$145	$115
Expenses controlled by others										
Depreciation	$520	$300	$220	$30	$70	$60	$60	$10	$30	$20
Property taxes	200	120	80		30	30	20		10	10
Insurance	300	150	150		50	50	50		25	25
Total expenses controlled by others	$1,020	$570	$450	$30	$150	$140	$130	$10	$65	$55
Total contribution	$970	$605	$365	$(80)	$200	$140	$105	$(35)	$80	$60
Unallocated costs[c]	160									
Income before taxes	$810									

[a]Unallocated expenses include a regional advertising campaign and equipment used by the regional manager.
[b]Unallocated expenses include a portion of the district manager's salary, district promotion costs, district manager's car.
[c]Unallocated costs include taxes on undeveloped real estate, headquarters expense, legal fees, audit fees.

```
┌─────────────────────────────────────────┐
│            Family Resorts, Inc.          │
│           Responsibility Summary         │
│             ($000 omitted)               │
│                                          │
│  Reporting Unit: Family Resorts          │
│  Responsible Person: President           │
│      Mid-Atlantic Region          $605   │
│      New England Region            365   │
│      Unallocated costs           (160)   │
│          Income before taxes      $810   │
│                                  ═════    │
│  Reporting Unit: New England Region      │
│  Responsible Person: Regional Manager    │
│      Vermont                      $200   │
│      New Hampshire                 140   │
│      Maine                         105   │
│      Unallocated costs            (80)   │
│          Total contribution       $365   │
│                                  ═════    │
│  Reporting Unit: Maine District          │
│  Responsible Person: District Manager    │
│      Harbor Inn                   $ 80   │
│      Camden Country Inn             60   │
│      Unallocated costs            (35)   │
│          Total contribution       $105   │
│                                  ═════    │
│  Reporting Unit: Harbor Inn              │
│  Responsible Person: Innkeeper           │
│      Revenue                      $600   │
│      Controllable costs          (455)   │
│      Allocated costs              (65)   │
│          Total contribution       $ 80   │
│                                  ═════    │
└─────────────────────────────────────────┘
```

(3) Describe the advantages of responsibility accounting for the managers of a firm.

b. The budget of Family Resorts, Inc., was accepted by the regional and district managers. On the basis of the facts presented, evaluate the budget process employed by Family Resorts by addressing the following:

(1) What features of the budget preparation are likely to result in the managers adopting and supporting the budget process?

(2) What features of the budget presentation shown on page 467 are likely to make the budget attractive to managers?

(3) What recommendations, if any, could be made to the budget preparers to improve the budget process? Explain your answer.

(CMA adapted)

11-22 Forward Corporation of Los Angeles is a progressive and fast-growing company. The company's executive committee consists of the president and the four vice-presidents who report to the president—marketing, manufacturing, finance, and systems.

The marketing department is organized into nine territories and 25 sales offices. The vice-president of marketing wants the monthly reports to reflect those items for which the department is responsible and can control. The marketing department also wants information that identifies the most profitable products; this information is used to establish a discount policy that will enable the company to meet competition effectively. Monthly reports showing performance by territory and sales office also would be useful.

The vice-president of finance has recommended that the accounting system be revised so that reports would be prepared on a contribution margin basis. Further, only those cost items that are controlled by the respective departments would appear on their reports. The monthly report for the manufacturing department would compare actual production costs with a budget containing the standard costs for the actual volume of production. The marketing department would be provided with the standard variable manufacturing cost for each product, so that it could calculate the variable contribution margin of each product. The monthly reports to the marketing department would reflect the variable-contribution approach; the reports would present the net contribution of the department calculated by deducting standard variable manufacturing costs and marketing expenses (both variable and fixed) from sales.

A portion of Forward Corporation's chart of accounts is shown below.

Account Number	Description
2000	Sales
2500	Cost of sales
3000	Manufacturing expenses
4000	Engineering expenses
5000	Marketing expenses
6000	Administrative expenses

The company wants to retain the basic structure of the chart of accounts to minimize the number of changes in the system. However, the numbering system will have to be expanded in order to provide the additional information that is desired.

Required

Devise a group coding structure that would satisfy the needs of the marketing department management. Using the preceding chart of accounts to provide the major ac-

count framework, expand by adding any needed new accounts and other coding dimensions. Explain and illustrate the new coding structure.

(CMA adapted)

Suggested Readings

General Ledger. Atlanta, Ga.: Management Science America, 1989.

General Ledger Financial Control System. Sunnyvale, Ca.: Data Design Associates, 1984.

A Guide for Studying and Evaluating Internal Accounting Controls. Chicago: Arthur Andersen, 1978.

Guidelines to Assess Computerized General Ledger and Financial Reporting Systems for Use in CPA Firms. New York: American Institute of Certified Public Accountants, 1979.

Hicks, James O., and Leininger, Wayne E. *Accounting Information Systems*. 2d ed. St. Paul, Minn.: West Publishing, 1986.

After reading this chapter, you should be able to do the following with respect to the revenue cycle:

Describe its objectives, functions, and relationships to the pertinent organizational units.

Identify its data sources and forms of input.

Identify the files comprising its data base.

Describe the steps and approaches employed in processing its transaction data flows.

List needed accounting transaction controls.

Describe a variety of operational and managerial reports and other outputs that may be generated.

Chapter *12*

THE REVENUE CYCLE

Most organizations depend on revenues for their continued existence. Certain of these revenue-oriented organizations generate revenues through the sales of products, others generate revenues through the provision of services, and still others generate revenues through both product sales and services. The functions related to the generation of revenues comprise the revenue cycle. As we noted in the previous chapter, the **revenue cycle** is one of the principal transaction-oriented cycles that interfaces with and provides key inputs to the general ledger and financial reporting system.

Overview

Cycle Objectives

The major purpose of the revenue cycle is to facilitate the exchange of products or services with customers for cash. Typical objectives within this broad purpose are (1) to verify that the customers are worthy of credit, (2) to ship the products or perform the services by agreed dates, (3) to bill for products or services in a timely and accurate manner, (4) to record and classify cash receipts promptly and accurately, (5) to post sales and cash receipts to proper customers' accounts in the accounts receivable ledger, (6) to safeguard products and cash until shipped or deposited, and (7) to prepare all needed documents and managerial reports related to the product sales or services.

Functions

In the case of product sales, the functions of the revenue cycle generally include obtaining the order from the customer, checking the customer's credit, entering and processing the sales order, assembling the goods for shipment, shipping the goods, billing the customer, receiving and depositing the cash payment, maintaining the receivables record, posting transactions to the general ledger, and preparing the needed financial reports and other outputs. In the case of services, the functions of assembling and shipping goods are replaced by the function of performing the ordered services. In the case of cash sales, the function of maintaining the receivables records is unnecessary. These groups of functions are pictured in Figure 12-1. Each of the aforementioned functions pertaining to a credit sale of a product will be discussed.

Obtain order from customer. Orders from customers may be obtained in various ways. A customer may mail or wire a purchase order; the customer might phone in an order or might enter the merchandising firm's store and buy one or more items from a salesperson; or the salesperson (an employee or an independent broker) may travel to the customer's premises and obtain the order directly. Regardless of the means of receiving the order, it is customarily expressed in writing on some form (e.g., the customer's purchase order or the salesperson's order blank). The final step in obtaining an order is to determine that it is valid. For instance, a sales order clerk may verify that the customer is a reputable firm.

Check credit. When the order pertains to a sale on credit, however, more checking is necessary. Most credit sales, including credit card sales for more than $50, are subject to credit checks. If an order is received from a repeat credit customer, the firm will normally have credit information concerning the customer in its data base. The information will be summarized in the form of a credit rating (e.g., excellent, good, poor) or a credit limit (e.g., a cumulative $5000 of automatic credit). If an order is from a new customer, or if the customer applies for a credit card, the firm may refer to a credit bureau to ascertain the applicant's creditworthiness. Criteria of creditworthiness include the prospective customer's financial status, previous payment record, and future earnings prospects. In the case of a customer (new or old) who has a special situation, the credit manager will typically be expected to make a judgment.

Enter sales order. Orders that have been approved for credit are next entered into the sales processing procedure. Sales order entry usually consists first of preparing a formal sales entry document (unless the salesperson's form is to be used instead). This formal sales entry document may be prepared manually or may be prepared automatically in the case of a computer-based system.

Three types of document preparation

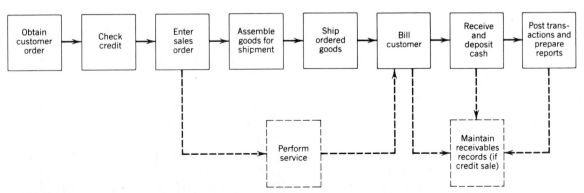

FIGURE 12-1   Typical functions of a revenue cycle.

procedures may be employed: prebilling, incomplete prebilling, and separate order and billing. In the **prebilling procedure** the sales invoice (bill) is completely filled in, including prices and extensions and total, as soon as the order is approved. This procedure reduces the paperwork but is feasible only if all data are known, including the availability of ordered quantities. In the **incomplete prebilling procedure** a sales order-invoice is prepared at the time the order is approved. This document shows quantities but not price extensions, freight charges, and so on. After the order has been shipped, the document is completed and used as the sales invoice. In the **separate sales order and invoice procedure** the invoice is prepared as a separate document only after the goods have been shipped. The sales order is used only as a shipping order. Although this procedure involves more paperwork, it is necessary when ordered goods are often out of stock or frequent back-ordering occurs. Regardless of the procedure used, a copy is generally sent to the customer to acknowledge the order and to confirm the shipping date. Other copies are used to initiate processing steps and to store data concerning the transaction.

Assemble goods for shipment. Goods that are ordered must be physically moved to the shipping dock. Often this function involves picking the goods from a warehouse, using a picking ticket or a copy of the sales order, and moving them to the shipping dock. In the case of expensive goods or of special made-to-order goods, it may consist of acquiring the goods from suppliers or of producing the goods within the firm's manufacturing facilities. Also, any step affecting the firm's inventory of goods for sale must be noted in appropriate records.

Ship ordered goods. Unless the customer is to pick up the ordered goods at the shipping dock, the goods must be physically distributed to the customer. Before being distributed, the goods are generally packaged with a packing slip enclosed. The goods are then shipped by means of the firm's own delivery vehicles, by parcel service, by the U.S. postal service, or by an independent common carrier. In the last case, the carrier is selected (often in accordance with the customer's instructions), the packages are weighed and labeled, the charges are established, and the shipping documents are prepared. The shipping documents must include a bill of lading and often involve a shipping report or order. The freight charges are paid to the carrier either by the selling firm or by the customer, depending on the F.O.B. designation.

Bill customer. The preparation of the invoice has already been discussed under the entry of the order. Billing is not complete, however, until the bill is presented for payment. The terms stated on the invoice specify the due date of the payment; often they allow a cash discount for payment by an earlier date. An alternative type of billing occurs when a retail merchandising firm accepts credit cards serviced by an independent financing firm. In that case the retail firm forwards the sales slip (''flimsy'') to the financing firm and immediately receives cash in return. The financing firm then bills the customer via a monthly statement.

At this point most of the functions involving the sale itself have been completed. The data flow diagram in Figure 12-2 portrays these sales-related functions, plus the interfacing functions (described later) of posting the transaction to the subsidiary and general ledgers.

Receive and deposit cash payment. Cash remitted by customers may be received through the mail or over the counter. Each cash payment is recorded immediately upon receipt. Preferably all remitted amounts are listed on a deposit slip during the same day and delivered intact to the firm's bank. An

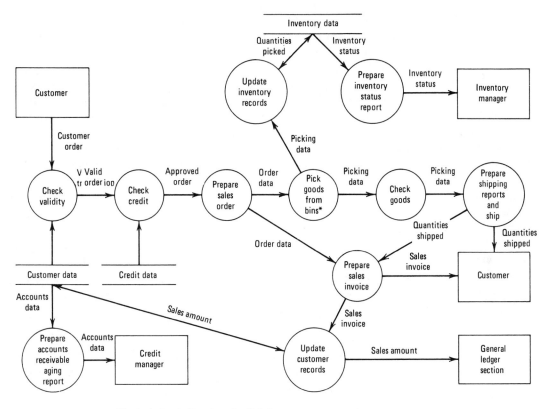

FIGURE 12-2 A data flow diagram of the functions related to credit sales transactions.

alternative means of receiving cash is through a lockbox collection system. Under this type of system customers mail cash remittances to a post office box; the bank opens the box daily, deposits the remittances to the creditor firm's account, and prepares a detailed listing for the firm.

Maintain accounts receivable. A separate accounts receivable record is maintained for each active credit customer. Each billed sale amount is debited to the account, whereas each cash remittance is credited to the account. An outstanding balance appears in the account as long as not all sales have been paid in full. Either of two methods may be employed in adjusting the balance to reflect

payments made by customers. The **balance forward method** applies a payment against the outstanding balance, rather than against a specific invoice. The **open invoice method,** on the other hand, matches each payment with a specific invoice. In the case of the former method the monthly statement, usually mailed to customers, merges all invoice amounts of previous months and simply shows a "balance forward"; in the case of the latter method it continues to show all invoices as "open." Thus, disputed invoices are more easily isolated in the open invoice method.

Post transactions to general ledger. Summarized sales and cash receipts transactions are posted to the general ledger. This function, which represents the interface between the revenue cycle and the general ledger system or cycle, was discussed in Chapter 11.

Prepare needed financial reports and other outputs.

A variety of outputs are generated as by-products of the aforementioned revenue cycle functions. One example already mentioned is the monthly statement for customers. Summaries of sales and cash receipts, akin to journal listings, are also needed. Financial reports ranging from the accounts receivable aging schedule to sales analyses are typically viewed as necessary. If an on-line computer-based system is employed, displays of individual accounts and other specific information are also available.

Other related functions.

Additional functions of interest include salespersons' commissions, product costing, sales returns and allowances, collection procedures, miscellaneous cash receipts, and back orders. Salespersons' commissions are noted in Chapter 14 in the sections involving payrolls; product costing is discussed with production procedures in Chapter 15. The remaining functions are briefly scanned in the following paragraphs, and their relationships (except for back orders) to the revenue cycle are shown in Figure 12-3.

Sales returns arise when unsatisfied customers send back all or part of the ordered goods. Sales allowances are adjustments in prices granted to customers as compensation for damaged goods, shortages, or similar defi-

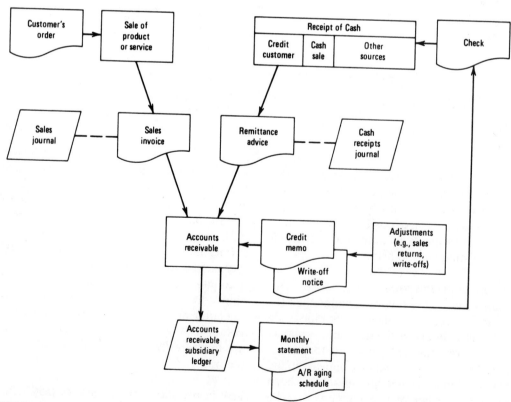

FIGURE 12-3 Relationships within the revenue cycle.

ciencies. In either case credit memoranda are prepared to formalize the agreements reached.

Most customers pay their outstanding balances, or make installment payments, upon receiving statements. Collection procedures are unfortunately necessary, however, in the case of slow-paying customers. Generally these procedures begin with the second notice of a balance due. Then a delinquency notice is likely sent. If payment is still not received, the firm may hire a collection agency, factor the receivables with a financing agency, or eventually write off the balance.

Miscellaneous cash receipts include amounts received from sales of fixed assets, income from investments, and bank loans. These receipts are generally recorded in the cash receipts journal or other daily cash summary. They are further discussed in Chapter 14.

Back orders are necessary when insufficient quantities of inventory are on hand to fill all orders. Back-ordering involves the preparation of a back-order form, showing the customer for whom ordered, the order number, the quantity needed, and the date requested. This form is sent to the selected supplier, and the data are posted to inventory records. When the back-ordered items arrive, they are immediately shipped to the customer and the notation is removed from the inventory records. A new sales invoice is also prepared for the back-ordered items and mailed to the customer.

Relationships to the Organization

The revenue cycle functions are typically achieved under the direction of the marketing/distribution and finance/accounting organizational functions (units) of the firm, as Figure 12-4 illustrates. Thus, the revenue cycle involves the interaction of the marketing information system and the accounting information system. Moreover, the results attained and information generated by the revenue cycle further the objectives of the marketing/distribution and finance/accounting functions.

Marketing/distribution. Marketing management has the objectives of (1) satisfying the needs of customers and (2) generating sufficient revenue to cover costs and expenses, replace assets, and provide an adequate return on investment.

As Figure 12-4 shows, in many firms the top marketing manager is a vice-president, with responsibilities relating to market research, product development and planning, sales, promotion and advertising, customer service, and shipping and transportation. Market research focuses on the markets for the firm's products or services. It studies the customers and potential customers, including their attitudes, preferences, and spending power. Product (or service) development and planning focuses on the product lines (or services), including styling, packaging, and performance. It also plans for the introduction of new products (or services). Sales concentrates on the selling effort, usually through a sales force. It is interested in sales forecasts, in current sales performance (including profitability), and in expenses incurred in selling activities. It also enters sales orders for processing. The promotion and advertising unit deals with such activities as dealer incentive programs, trade shows, and advertising campaigns. Customer service handles customer servicing needs after the sale of the product (or the performance of the service). It may deal with complaints, user training, and maintenance.

The shipping and transportation unit is the distribution arm of the marketing function. In some firms it may be under the direct sales organization, in other firms it may constitute a separate organizational function, and in service-oriented firms it is nonexistent. Its major concern is to assure that or-

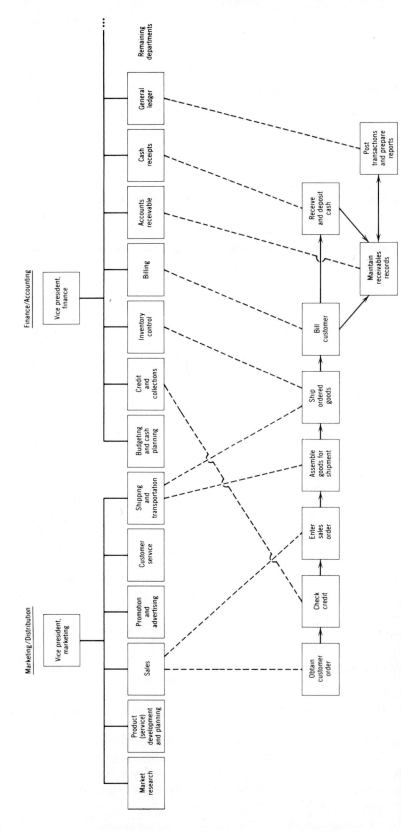

FIGURE 12-4 Relationships of organizational units to revenue cycle functions.

dered goods are delivered to customers promptly, in good condition, and in accordance with customer specifications.

Finance/accounting. The objectives of financial and accounting management relate broadly to funds, data, information, planning, and control over resources. With respect to the revenue cycle the objectives are limited to cash planning and control, to data pertaining to sales and customers' accounts, to inventory control, and to information pertaining to cash and sales and customers. For instance, with respect to cash planning and control the objectives are to maintain an optimal level of cash (neither too low nor too high) and to safeguard cash from loss or theft.

The top financial manager in many firms is the vice-president of finance. Two managers often report directly to this top manager: a treasurer and a controller. The treasurer has such responsibilities in the finance area as budgeting and cash planning, credit and collections, and cash receipts. The controller has such responsibilities in the accounting area as billing, inventory control, accounts receivable, and general ledger. (Both the treasurer and the controller have other responsibilities that are not related to the revenue cycle.) The budgeting and cash planning unit develops short-range and long-range budgets and cash forecasts. The credit and collections unit develops credit and collection policies and administers the policies with respect to individual customers. Cash receipts, an arm of the cashier, deposits cash received and maintains the related records. Billing prepares the sales invoices. Inventory control maintains the records pertaining to inventory balances. Accounts receivable maintains the accounts of individual customers. General ledger, of course, maintains the ledger of all balance sheet and income statement accounts, from which the financial reports are prepared.

Data Sources and Inputs

Sources

Data used in the revenue cycle are mainly based on inputs from customers. Customers initiate both the sales and the cash receipts transactions. In the case of product sales other sources include the salespersons, the customer reference and credit records, the inventory records, the finished-goods warehouse, the suppliers (and/or the firm's production function), the shipping department, and the common carrier. In some cases a financing agency or a bank may also be sources of data.

Forms of Input

Manual systems. The revenue cycle source documents typically found in firms that employ manual processing and make product sales include

1. **Customer order.** Often the **customer order** is the customer's purchase order and thus not a document prepared by the selling firm. However, it may be a form prepared by the salesperson, as shown in Figure 12-5.

2. **Sales order.** Figure 12-6 presents a **sales order.** Although similar to the customer order in Figure 12-5, it has significant differences. First, it is a more formal, multicopy form. (Note the words "Salesman's Copy" at the top right.) Second, it is prenumbered for more effective control. Third, it contains price and extension columns, so that it can be completed as an invoice. Finally, it has a space for the customer's purchase order number. Incidentally, the sales order is sometimes called the shipping order, since it provides authorization for the shipping action.

3. **Order acknowledgement.** Usually the **order acknowledgement** is a copy of the

Sold To:*
No. ☐☐–☐☐☐☐

PRODUCTS / PARTS
CUSTOMER ORDER

Ship To:*
No. ☐☐–☐☐☐☐

Order No:* ______ Date:* ______

Sold-To:
Name: ______ / ______

Address: ______ / ______ Zip: ______

Ship-To:
Name: ______ / ______

Address: ______ / ______ Zip: ______

Sman: (Products) ______ Terms: ______ B/O# ______

Page Qn:* ______ Ship From: (Products) ______ Cust Date: ______

PO# ______ How to Ship:: Date:* ______

: ______ / ______

Item #	Charge Description		Override		Special Instructions
	Quan.*	Model/Part No.*	Price	Disc	
1					
2					
3					
4					
5					
6					
7					
8					
9					
10					
11					
12					
13					
14					

Note: *Denotes Required Entries!

Special Price Approval ______ Order Taken By ______

Computer Form No. T-100 PC-3-76026

FIGURE 12-5 A customer order. Courtesy of Arvin Industries.

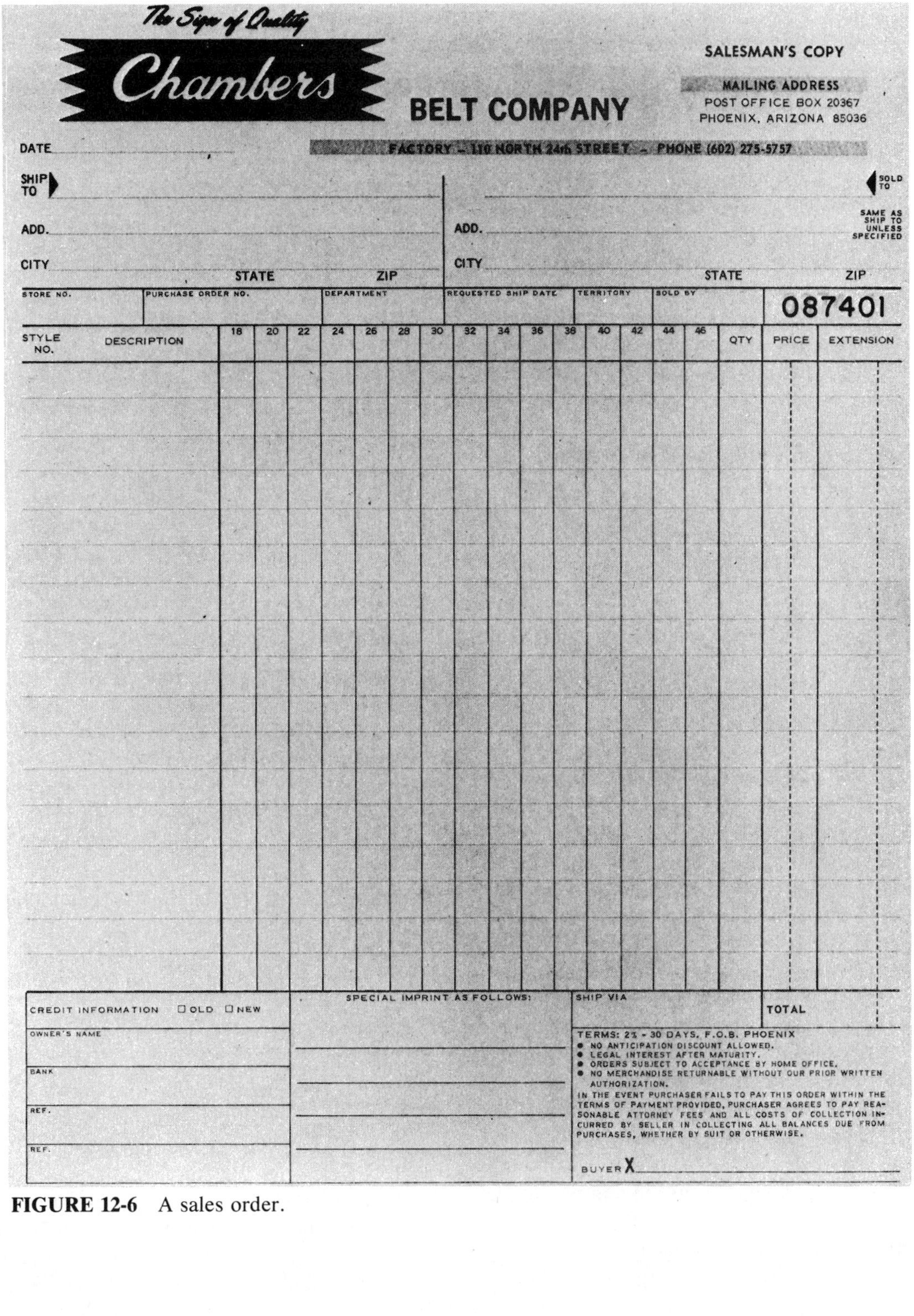

FIGURE 12-6 A sales order.

sales order, although it may be a separate form. (In some cases the customer also requires the selling firm to return a signed acknowledgement that has been prepared by the customer.)

4. **Picking list.** In some cases a copy of the sales order is sent to the warehouse for use in picking the ordered goods from the bins. Alternatively, a separate **picking list** document may be prepared. The ordered product data are arranged in such a list in accordance with the bin locations in the warehouse. Thus, the picking can be done more efficiently.

5. **Packing list.** A **packing list** or slip is enclosed with the goods when they are packaged. It is generally a copy of the sales order or is the picking list.

6. **Bill of lading.** Figure 12-7 displays a straight **bill of lading,** which is relatively uniform from firm to firm. It is intended for the agents of the common carrier that is to transport the products, informing them that goods are legally on board the carrier, that the freight has been paid or billed, and that the consignee is authorized to receive the goods at the destination. In addition to the carrier, the shipping department and the customer receive copies. Another copy may serve as the freight bill (invoice) and be forwarded to the traffic department (if any) of the customer or seller, depending on who is paying.

7. **Shipping notice** (report, order). Often a copy of the sales order, when duly noted by the shipping manager, serves as proof that the goods were shipped. However, a separate **shipping notice** may be prepared by the shipping department (perhaps as one copy within the bill of lading set). This notice is forwarded to the billing department for use in completing the invoice.

8. **Sales invoice.** A **sales invoice** serves as the key sales input to the accounting cy-

cle, since it contains the total amount of the transaction. An example of a multiple-copy sales invoice appears as Exhibit 1 in a Review Problem in Chapter 3.

9. **Remittance advice.** A **remittance advice** is a counterpart to the sales invoice, since it contains the amount of the cash receipt from the customer. An example of a cash remittance is shown in Figure 12-8. This example can be described as a turnaround document, since it represents a portion of the sales invoice that is returned by the customer with the cash. (If the customer does not return a cash remittance, the firm must prepare one for use as the posting medium.)

10. **Deposit slip.** Deposits of cash with the bank must be accompanied by **deposit slips.** Figure 12-9 shows a deposit slip that contains imprints of both the firm name and the bank name. Coding at the bottom of the slip refers to the account number and bank code.

11. **Back order.** A form called a **back order** is prepared when insufficient quantities are in inventory to satisfy sales orders. It should be prenumbered and contain data concerning the customer for whom the back order is being placed, the original sales order number, the quantity needed, and the date requested. If the original order is partially filled and the remaining quantities are back-ordered, the back-order number and relevant data should be entered on the sales invoice. Figure 12-10 depicts a sales invoice showing that back-order number 3128 has been placed with the Universal Supply Company. These back-order data have also likely been posted to the inventory records. When the back-ordered items are received from the supplier, they will be immediately shipped to the customer and the notation will be removed from the inventory records. A new sales invoice will also be prepared for the back-

Straight Bill of Lading - Short Form - Original - Not Negotiable

RECEIVED, subject to the classifications and tariffs in effect on the date of the issue of this Bill of Lading.

DATE _____

From ArvinAir Division   Arvin Industries, Inc.
SOLD TO

(Mail or street address of consignee - For purposes of notification only.) - Agent's No. _____

Phoenix, Az.
CONSIGNED TO:

RTE
DEL
CARRIER

Subject to Section 7 of conditions if this shipment is to be delivered to the consignee without recourse on the consignor, the consignor shall sign the following statement. The carrier shall not make delivery of this shipment without payment of freight and all other lawful charges.

_____
(Signature of Consignor)

If charges are to be prepaid, write or stamp here, "To Be Prepaid".

Charges Advanced
$ _____

AvinAir
(Signature of Consignee)

Received $ _____
to apply in prepayment of the charges on the property described hereon

_____
Agent or Carrier

Per _____
(The signature here acknowledges only the amount prepaid.)

ITEM NO.	ORDER-ED	SHIPPED	MODEL NUMBER	DESCRIPTION	UNIT WEIGHT	TOTAL WEIGHT	B/L NO.	CUST. ORDER NO.	NO. PACKAGES	DESCRIPTION OF ARTICLES, SPECIAL MARKS, AND EXCEPTIONS	WEIGHT (Sub. to Cor.)	CLASS OR RATE CHECK COLUMN
										Air Coolers, water evaporative type, with blowers or fans, with or without heating action.		
										Portable		
										NOI		
										Electric Motors, over 5 lbs.		
										Pumps, Power, NOI		
										Cooler accessory kits or components consisting of articles rated class 85 or lower		
										Stands, NOI, other than furniture—folded flat or KD flat		
										Registers, Air, Nabon, other than cone type, including air louvres, iron or steel		
										Sheet Steel Articles, NOI, Nested		
										Excelsior, Wood, in machine pressed bales		
										Pads Evaporative Cooler, Wood, Excelsior:		
										4 lbs. and over per cubic foot		
										6 lbs. and over per cubic foot		

COLLECTION
DELIVERY $ _____   AND
REMIT TO _____
STREET _____
CITY _____ STATE _____

WEIGHT (SUB TO CORR.)

WEIGHT SHIPPED

TOTAL UNITS

SHIPPER, PER _____
AGENT, PER _____

FORM R103

Arvin
Air

PERMANENT ADDRESS,
500 S 15th ST   PHOENIX, ARIZONA 85034

1

FIGURE 12-7 A bill of lading. Courtesy of Arvin Industries.

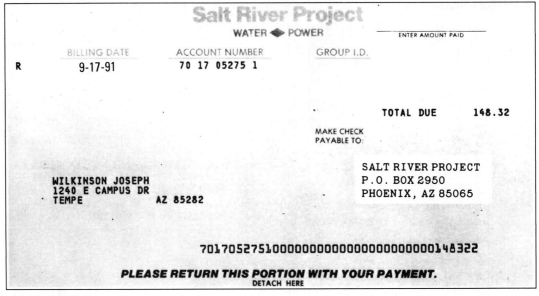

FIGURE 12-8 A remittance advice.

ordered items and mailed to the customer.

12. **Credit memo.** Before ordered goods can be returned or before allowances can be granted, a **credit memo** must be prepared and approved. Figure 12-11 shows a credit memo containing the number 12542. Credit memos should be approved only on the basis of clear evidence, such as a sales return notice that lists the physical count of returned goods by the receiving department.

13. **Other documents.** A new customer *credit application* is useful when customers apply for credit. It should include all the data pertaining to the applicant's current financial condition and earning level. A *salesperson call report* may be

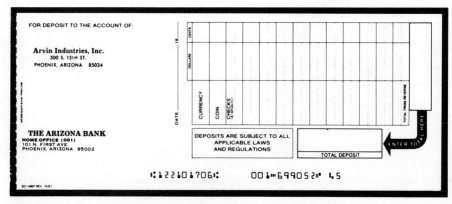

FIGURE 12-9 A deposit slip. Courtesy of Arvin Industries.

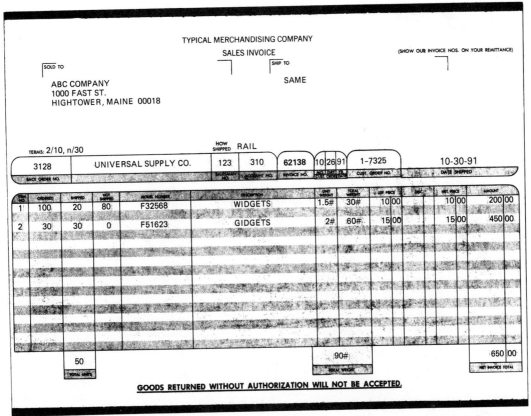

TYPICAL MERCHANDISING COMPANY

SALES INVOICE

(SHOW OUR INVOICE NOS. ON YOUR REMITTANCE)

SOLD TO

ABC COMPANY
1000 FAST ST.
HIGHTOWER, MAINE 00018

SHIP TO

SAME

TERMS: 2/10, n/30   HOW SHIPPED RAIL

| BACK ORDER NO. 3128 | UNIVERSAL SUPPLY CO. | SALESMAN NO. 123 | ACCOUNT NO. 310 | INVOICE NO. 62138 | MO DAY YR CUST COUNT DATE 10 26 91 | CUST. ORDER NO. 1-7325 | DATE SHIPPED 10-30-91 |

ITEM NO.	ORDERED	SHIPPED	NOT SHIPPED	ROUTE NUMBER	DESCRIPTION	UNIT WEIGHT	TOTAL WEIGHT	LIST PRICE	DISC.	NET PRICE	AMOUNT
1	100	20	80	F32568	WIDGETS	1.5#	30#	10 00		10 00	200 00
2	30	30	0	F51623	GIDGETS	2#	60#	15 00		15 00	450 00

| TOTAL UNITS 50 | | TOTAL WEIGHT 90# | NET INVOICE TOTAL 650 00 |

GOODS RETURNED WITHOUT AUTHORIZATION WILL NOT BE ACCEPTED.

FIGURE 12-10 A sales invoice showing back-ordered items. Courtesy of Arvin Industries.

used to describe each call upon a prospective customer and to indicate the result of the call. A *delinquent notice* may be sent to customers who are past due on their credit account balances. A *write-off notice* is a document prepared by the credit manager when an account is deemed to be uncollectible. As described in Chapter 11, a *journal voucher* is prepared as the basis for each posting to accounts in the general ledger. For instance, a journal voucher will be prepared to reflect one or more account write-offs. Finally, in the case of retail firms that make cash sales, receipted *sales slips* or *cash register receipts* are used to reflect cash received.

Computer-based systems. All of the aforementioned hard-copy documents may also be used in computer-based systems. In some cases, however, they may be generated automatically upon the entry of data via terminals or microcomputers. Some of the source documents may also be designed to speed the entry of data into the computer-system with fewer errors. The customer order in Figure 12-5 is one example of a user-friendly form; the sales order form in Figure 12-12 is another.

Preformatted screens may be used to enter data concerning sales orders, sales returns, and cash receipts transactions. These screens, like simplified entry forms, may be designed to handle individual transactions or batches of transactions.

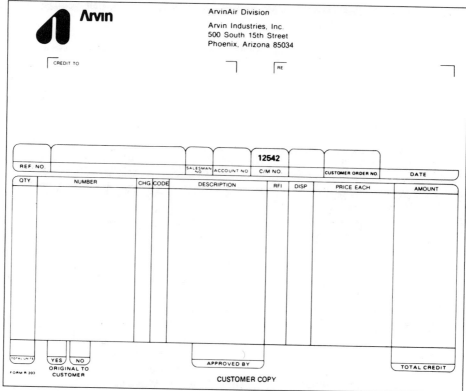

FIGURE 12-11 A credit memo. Courtesy of Arvin Industries.

Figure 12-13 displays the on-line entry of a batch of cash receipts. Note that the blank columns will be filled in when command key number 1 is pressed. The data for these columns, which are stored in the open sales invoice and customer files, will be retrieved by the computer entry program. This program will also compute the total of all payment amounts entered and place the result in the box labeled "Entered Total"; in addition, the program will automatically compare the Entered Total and previously computed Control Total and display the difference. (Although the screen and the described procedure are simplified, they illustrate the essentials of an on-line cash receipts entry.)

Codes

Codes are essential for identifying key aspects of sales and cash receipts transactions. An example in Chapter 8 suggested that codes may be assigned to customers, sales territories, salespersons, and product types when recording sales transactions. When these codes are employed, various sales analyses can be provided to managers. Two such analyses would show (1) amounts of sales made to customers within each sales territory and (2) amounts of sales made of the various products by each salesperson. Other coded data captured about sales transaction could include characteristics of products (e.g., colors) and market channels (e.g., residential customers).

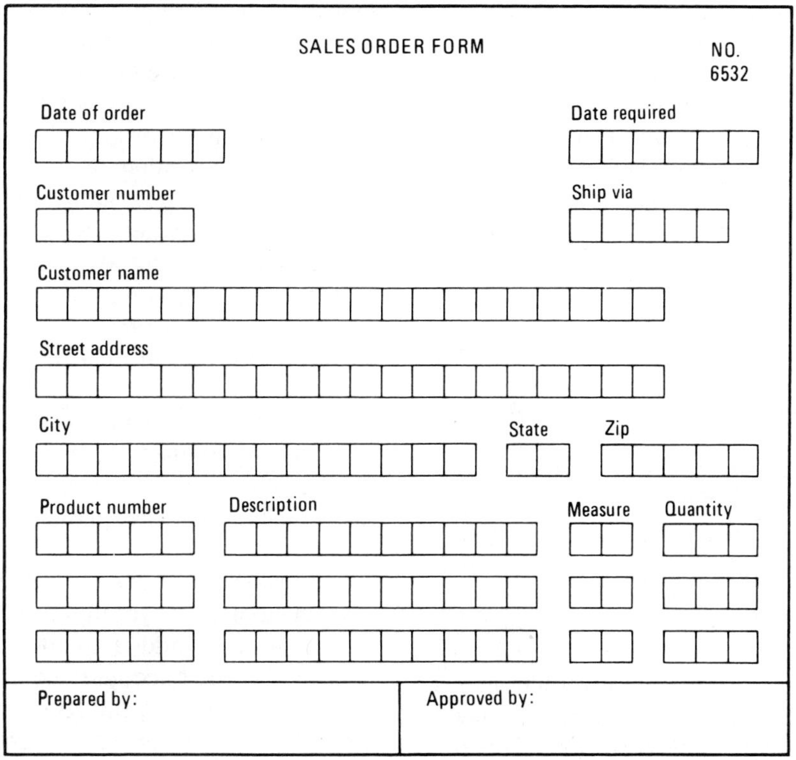

SALES ORDER FORM

NO.
6532

Date of order

Date required

Customer number

Ship via

Customer name

Street address

City

State

Zip

Product number	Description	Measure	Quantity

Prepared by:

Approved by:

FIGURE 12-12 A source document for manually recorded data.

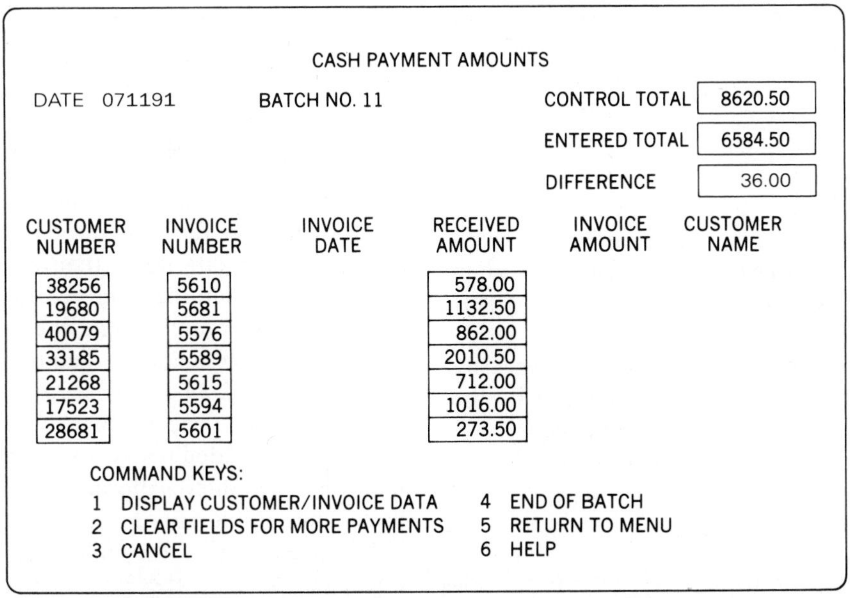

CASH PAYMENT AMOUNTS

DATE   071191   BATCH NO. 11

	CONTROL TOTAL	8620.50
	ENTERED TOTAL	6584.50
	DIFFERENCE	36.00

CUSTOMER NUMBER	INVOICE NUMBER	INVOICE DATE	RECEIVED AMOUNT	INVOICE AMOUNT	CUSTOMER NAME
38256	5610		578.00		
19680	5681		1132.50		
40079	5576		862.00		
33185	5589		2010.50		
21268	5615		712.00		
17523	5594		1016.00		
28681	5601		273.50		

COMMAND KEYS:

1 DISPLAY CUSTOMER/INVOICE DATA   4 END OF BATCH
2 CLEAR FIELDS FOR MORE PAYMENTS   5 RETURN TO MENU
3 CANCEL   6 HELP

FIGURE 12-13 On-line entry of cash receipts.

Codes that describe transactions are group codes, since they encompass several dimensions. As the preceding example emphasizes, two key components of sales transactions are customers and products. Codes for these entities may also be designed as group codes. For instance, a customer code might have the format

ABBCCCCD

where A represents the class or type of customer,

BB represents the year the customer became active,

CCCC represents the specific customer identifier,

D represents a self-checking digit.

Data Base

The following master, transaction, history, and reference files are representative of the revenue cycle data base for a firm that makes product sales. Of course, the exact number and content of the files will vary from firm to firm, depending upon such factors as types of customers and markets, variety of desired managerial reports, degree of computerization, and structure of the data base. For instance, a firm that employs the computer-based data base approach, discussed in Chapter 18, will use a different set of files and data structures. Moreover, certain of the listed files, such as the merchandise inventory master file, will not be needed if the firm is involved solely in offering services.

Our survey of these files is necessarily brief. A more complete description of the data base would include a data dictionary, such as illustrated in Chapter 18.

Customer Master File

A customer master file contains records pertaining to individual customers. It provides useful information to any type of firm and is especially important to firms that sell merchandise on credit terms. Generally, its primary and sorting key will be the customer number. Each record of this file contains such data concerning the customer as the shipping and billing addresses, telephone number, past payment performance, credit rating, trade discount allowed, and sales activity. These data items are useful in preparing sales invoices and monthly statements, as well as in determining the credit limit.

An important concern with this file, as with the other master files, is keeping the records and their permanent data up to date. Each time a customer moves to a new address, for instance, the change must be quickly reflected in the record. Whenever a new customer is granted credit, another record must be added to the file. When a customer's credit account becomes inactive, for whatever reason, the record must be deleted. These changes can be made during the processing of sales orders, although they complicate the processing. Alternatively, they may be made at other times. An advantage of on-line computer-based files is the convenience they afford in making such changes at any time.

Accounts Receivable Master File

The records in an accounts receivable master file also relate to credit customers. There are two data items that are essential: the customer identification (usually the customer account number) and the current account balance. Remaining data items are optional. Figure 12-14 arrays several suggested data items in a record layout. If desired, however, the added items could be moved to the customer file. Alternatively, all data items pertaining to a customer, including all transactions for this year, could be consolidated into the accounts receivable file.

Customer account number	Customer name	Credit limit	Balance, beginning of year	Year-to-date sales	Year-to-date payments	Current account balance

FIGURE 12-14 A layout of an accounts receivable record. *Note:* Although the lengths of fields and modes of data items are necessary for complete documentation, they have been omitted for the sake of simplicity.

Merchandise (or Finished-Goods) Inventory Master File

A merchandise inventory master file is relevant to the revenue cycle for a firm that sells products. If the firm also manufactures the products sold, the file includes the words "finished goods" rather than "merchandise." Data items that might appear in a record layout include the product (inventory item) number, description, warehouse location code, unit of measure code, reorder point, reorder quantity, unit cost, quantity on order, date of last purchase, and quantity on hand. If inventory is maintained on the perpetual basis, the current balance will also be included. The primary and sorting key is usually the product or inventory item number.

Open Sales Order File

An open sales order file consists of copies of sales orders pertaining to sales that have not yet been shipped and billed. In both manual and computer-based systems the printed copies contain data items such as shown in Figures 12-5 and 12-6. In computer-based systems a record of each order is also stored on magnetic media, the primary and sorting key usually being the sales order number. (The record layout should allow for such repeating line items as product numbers and quantities ordered, or they should be placed in a separate line item file and cross-referenced.) Customer names and product descriptions may be omitted in the case of computer-based systems; these data will be drawn from the customer and merchandise inventory files when preparing the sales invoices.

Open Sales Invoice Transaction File

In a manual system an open sales invoice transaction file consists of a copy of each current sales invoice, such as shown in Figure 12-10. Records in this file provide the details of the sales transactions posted to the accounts receivable records; by being maintained in a separate file they enable the size of the accounts receivable records to be reduced. In a computer-based system a printed copy may or may not be filed. The record stored on magnetic media likely omits customer names and product data, since the data are available in other files. The primary (and sorting) key is likely the sales invoice number. Each record remains open until payment is received from the customer (or until the end of the period if the balance forward method is used).

Cash Receipts Transaction File

In a manual system a cash receipts transaction file likely consists of a copy of each current remittance advice. In a computer-based system the record layout on magnetic media may contain the customer's account number, the sales invoice number against which the payment is being applied, the date of payment, and the amount of payment. It also includes a code to identify the record as a cash receipt transaction, and it may be assigned a transaction number.

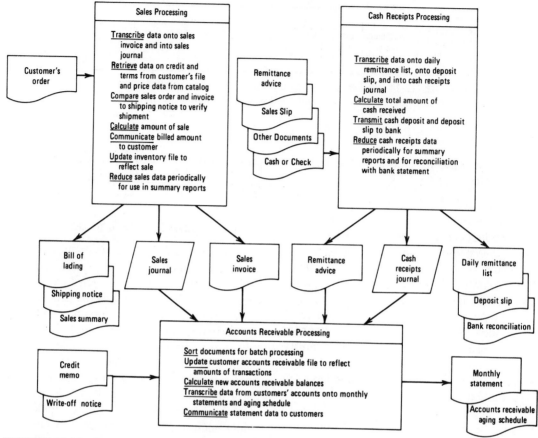

FIGURE 12-15   Processing steps and related documents for the revenue cycle.

Other Transaction Files

In addition to the basic sales and cash receipts files, the revenue cycle data base will likely include a shipping report file, credit memo file, and back-order (or production order) file. Each of the records in these files would contain roughly the data shown in the documents discussed earlier.

Shipping and Price Data Reference File

A shipping and price data file (which may be split into two files) contains freight rates, common carrier routes and schedules, current prices of all products, trade discounts, and so on. (Another reference file often used in manual systems is a credit file, which is used to check and approve the credit of customers.)

Sales History File

A sales history file contains summary coded data from sales order-invoices. In a computer-based system the records pertaining to sales orders and invoices are transferred to this file when they are removed from the open files. These records are retained in the history file for a reasonable period. For instance, a firm may decide to maintain a his-

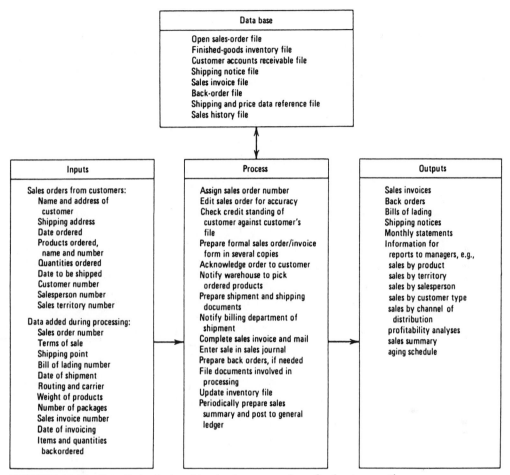

FIGURE 12-16 Detailed relationships in the processing of sales transactions.

tory file for the past five years. Records older than five years would be purged from the file. (However, the firm that employs computer-based processing may retain printed copies of sales orders and invoices for a longer period.) Data from this file are used to prepare sales forecasts and analyses.

Data Flows and Processing

Within the revenue cycle the data flows and processing steps can be divided into three major subsets: processing of sales transactions, processing of cash receipts transactions, and maintenance of the accounts receivable ledger. Figure 12-15 depicts these subsets of processing steps, together with related documents and reports. Each processing subset can be portrayed in more detail, showing specific transaction data and the processes that convert these data into outputs with the aid of a data base. Figure 12-16 portrays these detailed activities for sales transaction data. These diagrams should provide useful springboards as we examine several flowcharts of processing systems in the following sections.

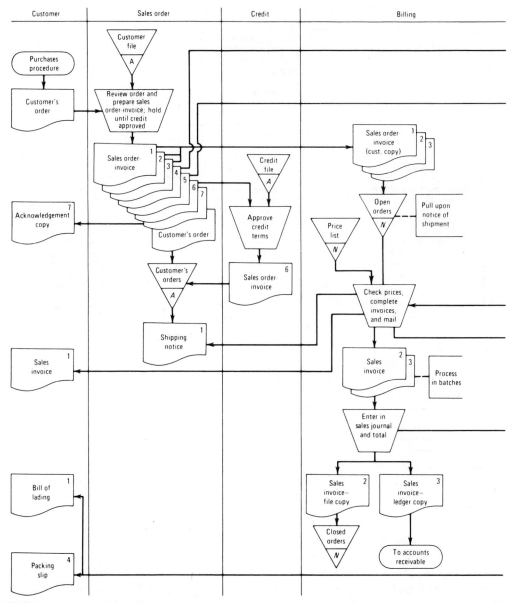

FIGURE 12-17 System flowchart of a manual credit sales transaction processing procedure, with emphasis on document flows.

Manual Processing Systems

Credit sales procedure. Figure 12-17 presents a document system flowchart of a procedure involving the credit sales of prod-

ucts. Since the processing is performed manually, the emphasis is on the flows of source documents and outputs. Thus, the flowchart provides a good introduction to processing within the revenue cycle. If we understand

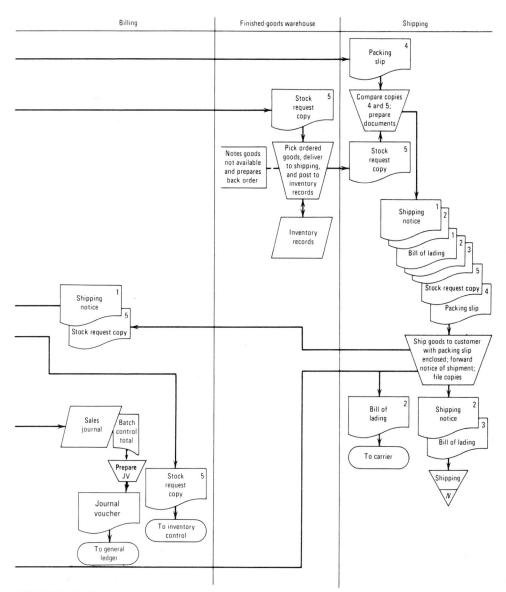

FIGURE 12-17   (*Continued*).

these document flows, we will be able to grasp more easily the processing steps performed by computer-based systems.

The credit sales procedure begins with the receipt of the customer's purchase order in the sales order department. After verifying that the order is valid and accurate, a clerk prepares the sales order-invoice by reference to the customer master file. A copy is sent to the credit department for credit check and approval. If approval is provided, the customer is sent an acknowledgment. The order

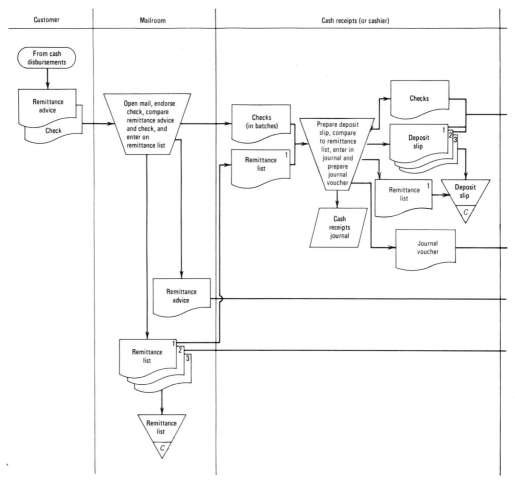

FIGURE 12-18 System flowchart of a manual cash receipts transaction processing procedure, with an emphasis on document flows.

is also entered for processing, with copies distributed to the billing department (to await notice of shipment), to the warehouse (for picking), to the shipping department (as prior notification), and to the customer order file.

In the warehouse a picker is given the stock request copy (or a picking slip); he or she assembles the ordered goods. Then the goods, together with the stock request copy, are forwarded to the shipping department. There a shipping clerk pulls the packing slip copy from the file, checks the goods against the copies, and prepares the shipping-related documents. The goods are packed for shipment, with the packing slip enclosed. The goods are shipped and the documents are distributed as shown.

Upon being notified of the shipment, a billing clerk completes the sales order-invoice set. Other clerks in the department enter the invoice amount in the journal, accumulate sufficient invoices to form a batch, and compute batch totals. A journal voucher is prepared for use in posting to the general ledger. Each sales invoice is mailed to the appropriate customer, with copies distrib-

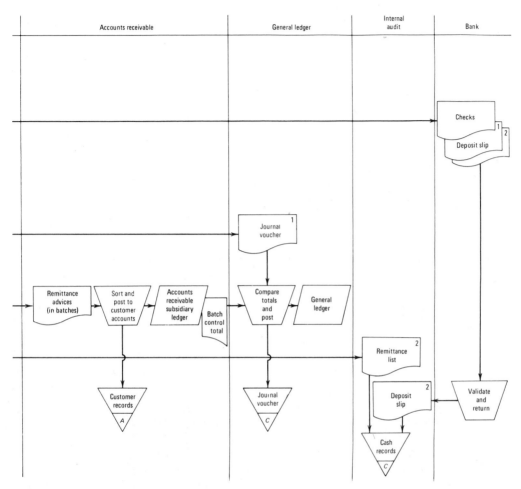

FIGURE 12-18 (*Continued*).

uted to the accounts receivable department and filed. A copy of the sales invoice may also be sent to the inventory control department, in order to reflect the reduction in the quantity of inventory (products) on hand.

Cash receipts procedure. Figure 12-18 shows a flowchart of a procedure involving the receipts of cash related to credit sales. This particular procedure begins with receipts of mailed cash and remittance advices from customers. A mailroom clerk compares the checks with the remittance advices (and prepares advices when none are received).

Then the clerk endorses the checks "for deposit only," enters their amounts on a remittance list, and computes a total of the batch received. One copy of the list is sent to the cashier with the checks; a second copy is sent to the internal audit department (if any) for later reviews; the third copy is filed.

The cashier prepares a deposit slip in triplicate by listing all checks from customers (plus cash received from other sources that day). Then the cashier compares the total with that shown on the remittance list and delivers the deposit intact to the bank. A cash receipts clerk enters the total receipts in the cash receipts journal and prepares a journal voucher, which is sent to the general ledger department for posting.

The internal audit department receives a copy of each deposit slip, stamped and initialed by a bank teller and delivered direct by the bank. This deposit slip is compared to the remittance list, as well as to the deposit slip in the cashier's office and to the general ledger posting.

The steps affecting the accounts receivable and general ledger departments are discussed next.

Accounts receivable procedure. Figure 12-19 illustrates, by means of a simplified diagram, the essence of the accounts receivable procedure. Sales invoices and remittance advices serve as the media from which the transaction amounts are posted to the accounts receivable subsidiary ledger. When verified by comparison to precomputed batch totals, the total amounts are then posted to the general ledger.

A detailed description of the sales postings should clarify the procedure in a manual system. Upon receiving copies of the sales invoices from the billing department, a clerk in the accounts receivable department posts the sales amounts to the customers' accounts in the accounts receivable ledger. Another clerk verifies the posting and obtains a total of the amount posted. This clerk then forwards the batch total to the general ledger department. There a clerk compares the total posted with the precomputed amount shown on the journal voucher. If they agree, the clerk posts the total amount to the accounts receivable and sales control accounts in the general ledger. If they disagree, the clerk locates the discrepancy, corrects the error, notifies the accounts receivable clerk of posting errors, and then completes the general ledger posting. Figure 12-20 shows these steps.

Sales returns and write-off procedure. Figure 12-20 also depicts the adjustments necessary to account for sales returns and allowances and account write-offs.

With respect to sales returns, the undesired goods must first be received in the receiving department. There they are counted by a clerk and listed on a sales return notice. The receiving department then forwards a copy to the credit manager or other designated manager for approval. The approved notice is transmitted to the billing department, where the prices are checked against the original sales invoice and a credit memo is prepared. Copies are sent to the accounts receivable department for posting and to the customer. A clerk in the billing department also prepares a journal voucher for the general ledger department, which posts the sales return transaction by debiting the sales returns account and crediting the accounts receivable control account.

Allowances on sales are granted for damaged goods, shortages, or similar deficiencies. In such cases the sales order department or salesperson settles the amount, which is then approved by the credit manager. Sales allowances are processed in the same manner as sales returns.

Another type of adjustment transaction is the write-off of customer account balances. When an account is deemed to be uncollectible, the credit manager initiates the write-off by preparing a write-off notice. After the action has been approved by the treasurer or other designated manager the write-off transaction is processed in a manner similar to the processing of sales returns transactions.

Computer-Based Processing Systems

When computer-based systems are used, sales and cash receipts transactions may be processed by the batch method, by the on-line method, or by a combination of the two methods. In the batch method the transaction data are keyed onto magnetic tape or disk, sorted according to customer

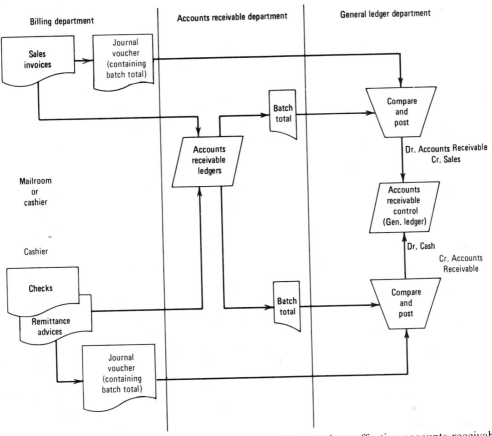

FIGURE 12-19 Diagram showing the processing of transactions affecting accounts receivable.

account numbers, and posted sequentially to the accounts receivable master file. In the on-line method the transaction data are entered via a terminal and posted individually to the master file. In the combined method the transaction data are entered via a terminal; however, they are gathered into a batch before being processed, either sequentially or directly, to the master file. The combined method, described next, is popular since it aids data entry and editing while retaining batch total controls.

Credit sales procedure. Figure 12-21 present a system flowchart of the on-line/

batch sales processing procedure. The flowchart logically divides into three segments: order entry (segment *a*), shipping (segment *b*), and billing (segment *c*).

Each customer's order is entered when received by means of a terminal in the sales order department. The edit program validates the accuracy of the data, performs the credit check, and verifies that adequate merchandise is on hand to fill the order. (If insufficient quantities of goods are available, the sales order clerk may specify to the computer system that a back order is to be prepared.) If the order is accepted, it is placed in the open order file. When the order is ready

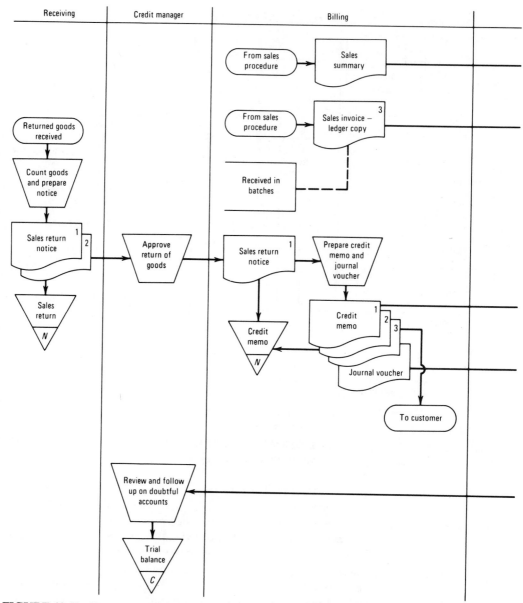

FIGURE 12-20 Document system flowchart of procedures relating to accounts receivable, sales returns and allowances, and write-offs of accounts receivable.

to be filled (which may be immediately), the order entry program prints the acknowledgment to the customer, a picking list, and a backup file copy.

After the ordered goods have been picked in the warehouse, the picking list is initialed by the picker and amended to show any changes (e.g., items out of stock, substitutions). The goods are moved to the shipping department, where a clerk counts the

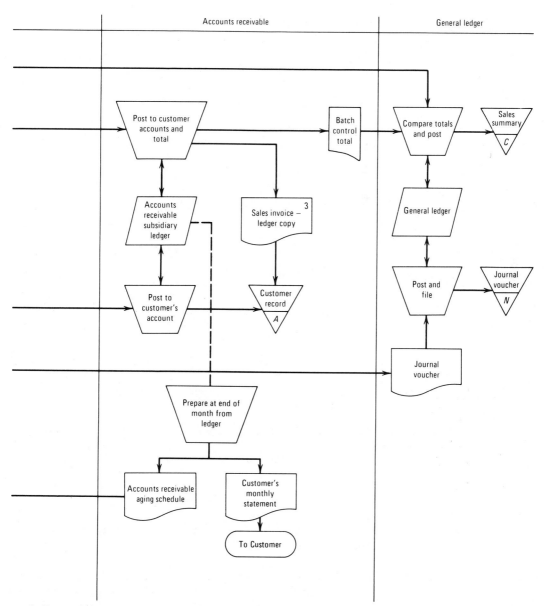

FIGURE 12-20 (*Continued*).

goods and enters the quantities ready for shipment from the picking slip. A shipping program prepares the necessary documents for the shipment. When the goods are packed, they are delivered to the carrier for shipment. A shipping notice (which is in ef-

fect a copy of the bill of lading) concerning the shipment is generated on the billing department's printer. It shows not only quantities shipped but also the shipping routes, freight charges, and other needed shipping data.

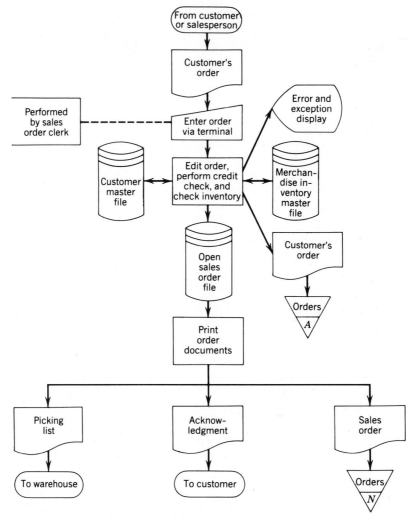

FIGURE 12-21 System flowchart of an on-line/batch computer-based credit sales transaction processing procedure.

Upon receiving the shipping notices for the day, a billing clerk prepares and enters the batch total of quantities shipped. The clerk also converts each order to an invoice by viewing the order on the terminal screen, selecting product prices, and so on. Data for all the readied invoices are stored temporarily until processed, at which time (1) the invoices are printed, (2) each customer's account is debited, (3) the inventory records are reduced by the quantities shipped, (4) the sales order is closed to the sales history file,

(5) a new record is created in the sales invoice file, (6) a sales invoice register and summary of accounts receivable are printed, and (7) the total amounts affecting the sales and accounts receivable accounts are posted to the general ledger accounts. Finally, the accounts receivable clerk verifies that the postings to the accounts receivable ledger agree with the batch total.

Cash receipts procedure. Figure 12-22 presents a system flowchart of the on-line

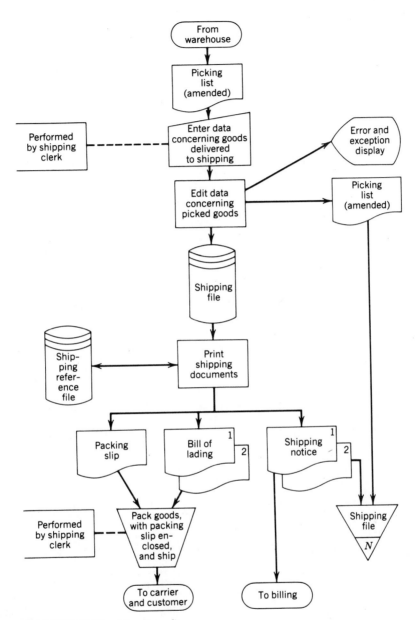

FIGURE 12-21 (*Continued*).

cash receipts procedure. It is divided into two segments: entry and deposit, and end-of-day processing.

As checks and remittances are received, one mailroom clerk endorses the checks and prepares a batch total. Another clerk enters the batch total and the data (amount, customer number, and sales invoice number) for each payment. If the indicated sales invoice pertaining to an amount is unpaid, and if the

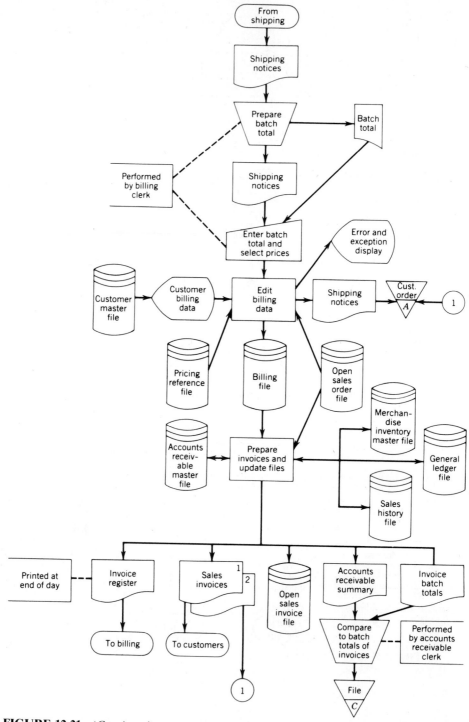

FIGURE 12-21 (*Continued*).

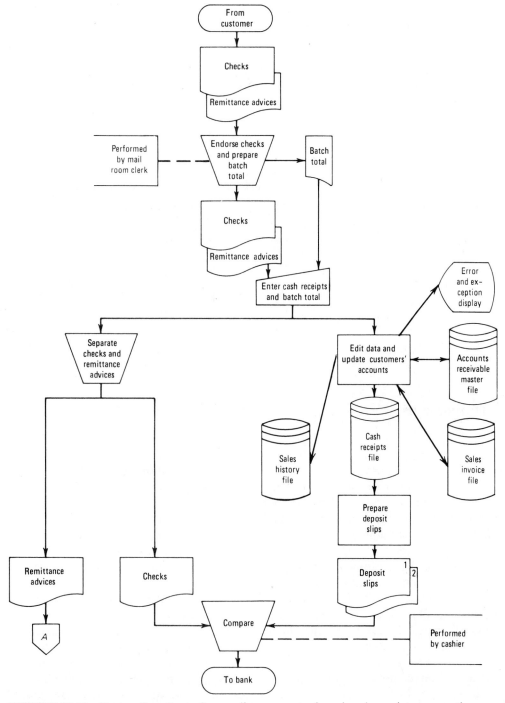

FIGURE 12-22 System flowchart of an on-line computer-based cash receipts processing procedure.

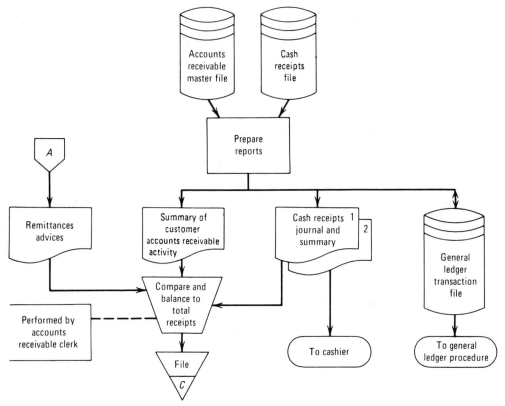

FIGURE 12-22 (*Continued*).

customer number is correct, the amount is accepted. If the total of all the individual amounts entered (as computed by the edit program) is equal to the precomputed batch total, the batch is accepted. Then the processing program credits the accounts receivable records for the remitting customers, records that the affected sales invoices are paid, and closes the sales invoices to the sales history file. After the processing is completed, the mail clerk sends the checks to the cashier and the remittance advices to the accounts receivable department.

The cashier compares the checks with deposit slips prepared by a print program. In order to verify the total being deposited, the cashier may also (1) receive a computer-prepared listing of cash remittances or (2) access

via a terminal the record of cash receipts for the day. When satisfied that the received checks and deposit slips agree, the cashier delivers them to the bank. The remainder of the deposit procedure corresponds to the steps described in the manual system.

At the end of a day several summaries are prepared, mainly for use with respect to the ledgers. A summary of accounts receivable activity, together with a listing of cash receipts, is compared with the remittance advices. This comparison, performed by an accounts receivable clerk, verifies the accuracy of the postings to the accounts. Concurrently with this verification a summary journal entry, reflecting the total receipts for the day, is transferred into the general ledger transaction file.

If the open invoice method is employed for posting payments from customers, the foregoing procedure might be modified as follows: Instead of entering payments into the computer system, the mail clerks would prepare a remittance listing manually. They would then forward a copy to the accounts receivable department. An accounts receivable clerk would then enter the batch total and payment data via an on-line terminal. During the entry of each payment the clerk would match the cash payments directly against specific sales amounts in the appropriate customer's account.

Accounting Controls

Risk Exposures

In attempting to achieve the objectives stated at the beginning of this chapter, the revenue cycle is exposed to a variety of risks. Figure 12-23 lists representative risks and consequent exposures due to these risks.

For example, one risk is that payments from credit customers may be lapped when the accounts receivable records are posted. **Lapping** is a type of embezzlement that involves the theft of cash and its concealment by a succession of delayed postings to customers' accounts. A clerk who undertakes lapping first cashes a check from a customer and keeps the cash. Since the check cannot be recorded, the customer's account is in error. To cover his or her tracks, the clerk credits the customer's account upon receiving a check for an equal or larger amount from another customer. Then the clerk credits the second customer's account with the proceeds from the check of still another customer. This falsifying process must continue indefinitely, unless the clerk decides to return the embezzled funds. The major risk exposure to the firm from lapping is clearly a loss of funds received from customers. Another risk exposure, however, is that certain accounts receivable records will reflect over-

stated account balances; consequently, the accounts receivable total that appears in the balance sheet will be overstated.

Examples of Real-World Exposures

Losses have been sustained by real-world firms from all of the risks listed in Figure 12-23. For instance, an employee of the Union Dime Savings Bank perpetrated a lapping fraud that involved unrecorded transactions, altered transactions, and unauthorized transfers with respect to customer's accounts; the loss to the bank amounted to $1.4 million.[1]

Other risks not listed in the figure also have caused severe losses, as the following cases illustrate:

- Customer service representatives of a large public utility, together with an outside confederate, used computer error correction codes to erase customer receivable accounts from files on magnetic tapes maintained by the utility. In reward they received kickbacks from the affected customers. The total established losses amounted to $25,000, although the probable losses were much greater.

- A vice-president of computer systems with a brokerage house misappropriated $277,000 of the firm's funds by making illegal debits to the interest earned account.

- A director of a publishing subsidiary altered computer programs so that false sales were added to the revenue account and certain expenses were not recorded; the effect was to inflate the operating results by at least $11.5 million.

In order to counteract all of the risks that are inherent within the revenue cycle, a

[1]This and the following fraud cases are based on Brandt Allen, "The Biggest Computer Frauds: Lessons for CPAs," *The Journal of Accountancy* (May 1977), pp. 52–63.

Risk	Exposure(s)
1. Credit sales made to customers who represent poor credit risks	1. Losses from bad debts
2. Unrecorded or unbilled shipments	2. Losses of revenue; overstatement of inventory and understatement of accounts receivable in the balance sheet
3. Errors in preparing sales invoices (e.g., showing greater quantities than were shipped or showing unit prices that are too low)	3. Alienation of customers and possible loss of future sales (when quantities are too high); losses of revenue (when unit prices are too low)
4. Misplacement of orders from customers or unfilled back orders	4. Losses of revenue and alienation of customers
5. Incorrect postings of sales to accounts receivable records or postings to wrong accounting periods	5. Incorrect balances in accounts receivable and general ledger account records (e.g., overstatement of Mary Smith's balance), overstatement of revenue in 1990 and understatement in 1991
6. Excessive sales returns and allowances, with certain of the credit memos being for fictitious returns	6. Losses in net revenue, with the proceeds from subsequent payments by affected customers being fraudulently pocketed
7. Theft or misplacement of finished goods in the warehouse or on the shipping dock	7. Losses in revenue; overstatement of inventory on the balance sheet
8. Fraudulent write-offs of customers' accounts by unauthorized persons	8. Understatement of accounts receivable; losses of cash receipts when subsequent collections on written-off accounts are misappropriated by perpetrators of the fraud
9. Theft of cash receipts, especially currency, by persons involved in the processing; often accompanied by omitted postings to affected customers' accounts	9. Losses of cash receipts; overstatement of accounts receivable in the subsidiary ledger and the balance sheet
10. Lapping of payments from customers when amounts are posted to accounts receivable records	10. Losses of cash receipts; incorrect account balances for those customers whose records are involved in the lapping
11. Accessing of accounts receivable, merchandise inventory, and other records by unauthorized persons	11. Loss of security over such records, with possibly detrimental use made of the data accessed
12. Involvement of cash, merchandise inventory, and accounts receivable records in natural or man-made disasters	12. Losses of or damages to assets, including possible loss of data needed to monitor collection of amounts due from previous sales

FIGURE 12-23   Risk exposures within the revenue cycle.

firm needs to incorporate relevant general and transaction controls.

General Controls

Among the general controls that are particularly useful to the revenue cycle are the following:

1. Within the organization the units that have custodial functions (warehouse, shipping department, cashier) are separate from those units that keep the records (billing department, accounts receivable department, inventory control department, data processing department). Moreover, the sales order and credit departments, whose managers authorize credit sales transactions as well as account adjustments and write-offs, are separate from all the aforementioned units.

2. Complete and up-to-date documentation concerning the revenue cycle, including copies of the documents, flowcharts, record layouts, and reports illustrated in this chapter, is available. In addition, details pertaining to sales and cash receipts edit/processing programs are organized into separate books or "packages" that are directed, respectively, to programmers, computer operators, and system users.

3. Operating practices relating to processing schedules, preparation of control summaries and reports, and other matters are clearly established.

4. Management policies concerning credit approvals, account write-offs, and so forth are in written form.

5. Security is maintained (in the case of on-line systems) by such techniques as (a) requiring that clerks enter assigned passwords before accessing accounts receivable and other customer-related files, (b) employing terminals that are restricted solely to the entry and access of sales and cash receipts transactions, (c) generating audit reports (access logs) that monitor accesses of system files, and (d) dumping the accounts receivable and merchandise inventory master files onto magnetic tape backups. Security measures for manual and computer-based systems include the use of physically restricted warehouses (for protecting goods) and safes (for holding cash receipts). A lockbox collection system may also be considered where feasible.

Transaction Controls

Control points within the revenue cycle include (1) the receipt of the sales order, (2) the credit check, (3) the shipping of ordered goods, (4) the billing for goods shipped, (5) the posting of each transaction to ledgers, (6) the receipt of goods by the customer, (7) the receipt of cash, and (8) the deposit of cash in the bank.

The following controls and control procedures are applicable to revenue cycle transactions and customer accounts:

1. Documents relating to sales, shipping, and cash receipts are prenumbered and well designed.

2. Data on sales orders and remittance advices are validated (and key-verified if suitable) as the data are prepared and entered for processing. In the case of computer-based systems validation is performed by means of such edit checks as listed in Figure 12-24.

3. Errors detected during data entry or processing are corrected as soon as possible by means of an established error correction procedure.

4. Multiple-copy sales orders (and/or invoices) are issued on the basis of valid authorizations, usually including customers' orders and credit approvals.

5. Ordered goods are transferred from the finished-goods warehouse and shipped only on the basis of written authorizations such as picking lists or stock request copies.

6. Customers are billed only upon notification by the shipping department of the quantities shipped, preferably by means of formal shipping documents, and by reference to current price lists.

7. Sales returns and allowances and write-offs of accounts are subject to prior approval by the credit manager and one other manager; in the case of sales returns approval is not granted until the goods being returned have been received.

8. All data items on sales invoices, including computations, are verified by a billing clerk other than the preparer or by a computer program.

Type of Edit Check	Typical Transaction Data Being Checked			Assurance Provided
	Sales	**Cash Receipts**		
1. Validity check	Customer account numbers, product numbers, transaction codes	Customer account numbers, transaction codes		The entered numbers and codes are checked against lists of valid numbers and codes that are stored within the computer system.
2. Self-checking digit	Customer account numbers	Customer account numbers		Each customer account number (e.g., 34578) contains a check digit (e.g., 8), whose value is based on an established mathematical algorithm involving the other digits of the number (e.g., 3, 4, 5, 7). When a customer account number is entered as a part of a sales or cash receipts transaction, the same computation is performed on the digits (e.g., 3, 4, 5, 7). If the value computed at this time (e.g., 2) differs from the attached digit (e.g., 8), the difference signals an input error (e.g., a transposition of 4 and 5) in entering the customer account number.
3. Field check	Customer account numbers, quantities ordered, unit prices	Customer account numbers, amounts		The fields in the input records that are designated to contain the data items (listed at the left) are checked to see if they contain the proper mode of characters (i.e., numeric characters). If other modes are found (such as alphabetic characters or blanks), an error is indicated.
4. Limit check	Quantities ordered	Amounts received		The entered quantities and amounts are checked against preestablished limits that represent reasonable maximums to be expected. (Separate limits are set for each product and class of customer.)
5. Range check	Unit prices	None		Each entered unit price is checked to see that it is within a pre-established range (either higher or lower than an expected value). To find the preestablished range, the edit program must first check the entered product number corresponding to the unit price and then look in a stored table of unit prices arranged by product numbers.

6. Relationship check	Product numbers	Amounts received	When two or more products are involved in a sales transaction, their numbers are checked to a stored table of reasonable combinations of products that appear on the same order; if the entered products do not appear in one of the combinations, the sales transaction is flagged by the edit program. When a payment amount is entered in a cash receipts transaction, together with the number of the sales invoice to which the amount applies, the amount in the sales invoice file is retrieved and compared with the entered amount. If a difference appears, the transaction is flagged.
7. Sign check	Product on-hand balances	Customer account balances	After the ordered quantities of products for a sales transaction are entered and posted to the inventory master file (thereby reducing the on-hand balances of the affected products), the remaining on-hand balances are checked. If any of the balances is preceded by a negative sign, the transaction is flagged. After the amount of a cash receipts transaction is entered and posted to the account in the accounts receivable ledger (thereby reducing the account balance of the customer), the remaining balance is checked. If the balance is preceded by a negative sign (indicating a credit balance), the transaction is flagged.
8. Completeness check[a]	All entered data items	All entered data items	The entered transactions are checked to see that all required data items have been entered.
9. Echo check[a]	Customer account numbers and names, product numbers and descriptions	Customer account numbers and names	After the account numbers for customers relating to a sales or cash receipts transaction (and also the product numbers in the sales transaction) have been entered at a terminal, the edit program retrieves and "echoes" back the related customer names (and product descriptions in the case of sales transactions). The person who entered the data can visually verify from reading the names (or descriptions) on the screen that the correct numbers were entered.

[a]Applicable only to online processing systems.

FIGURE 12-24 Programmed edit checks that are useful in validating transaction data entered into the revenue cycle.

507

9. After preparation sales invoices are compared against shipping notices and open sales orders, in order to assure that the quantities ordered and billed agree with the orders shipped and back-ordered.

10. All cash receipts are deposited intact with a minimum of delay, thus eliminating the possibility of cash receipts being used to pay employees or to reimburse petty cash funds.

11. If processing is performed in batches, control totals are precomputed from sales invoices (or shipping notices) and remittance advices; these batch control totals are compared with totals computed during postings to the accounts receivable ledger and during all other processing runs.[2] In the case of cash receipts, the total of remittance advices is also compared with the total on deposit slips.

12. Accounts in the accounts receivable subsidiary ledger are periodically reconciled with the accounts receivable control account in the general ledger.

13. Monthly statements are prepared and mailed to all credit customers. Since a customer will likely complain if overcharged, this practice provides control over accidental and fraudulent acts.

14. Copies of all documents pertaining to sales and cash receipts transactions are filed by number, and the sequence of numbers in each file is periodically checked to see if gaps exist. If transactions are not supported by preprinted documents, as often is the case in on-line computer-based systems, numbers are assigned to the documents and they are stored in a transaction file.

15. In the case of computer-based systems, transaction listings and account summaries are printed periodically in order to provide an adequate audit trail.

16. All bank accounts are reconciled monthly by someone who is not involved in revenue cycle processing activities, and new bank accounts are authorized by the proper managers.

17. Employees who handle cash are required to be bonded and are subject to close supervision.

Reports and Other Outputs

Outputs generated by the revenue cycle include both financial reports and nonfinancial reports, sales-related and cash-related reports, daily and weekly and monthly reports, hard-copy and soft-copy reports. All these reports may be arbitrarily classified as operational (including operational control) listings and reports, inquiry screens, and managerial reports.

Operational Listings and Reports

The **monthly statement** is a listing of all outstanding sales invoices for a customer. It is based on information in the customer, accounts receivable, sales invoice, and cash receipts files. Figure 12-25 shows a monthly statement, including the total amount due. As added information this particular version also provides an aging of overdue amounts.

The **open orders report** lists those sales orders that are not completely shipped and billed. It may be arranged chronologically, by sales order numbers, or by customers. Figure 12-26 presents a report of open orders by customer. Note that it also indicates back orders. This report thus provides operational control, since it helps to expedite the pro-

---

[2]Three types of batch control totals may be computed. Of these three, the amount total can be computed during processing as either (1) the total of transaction amounts posted to customers' accounts or (2) the difference between the sums of customers' account balances before and after postings.

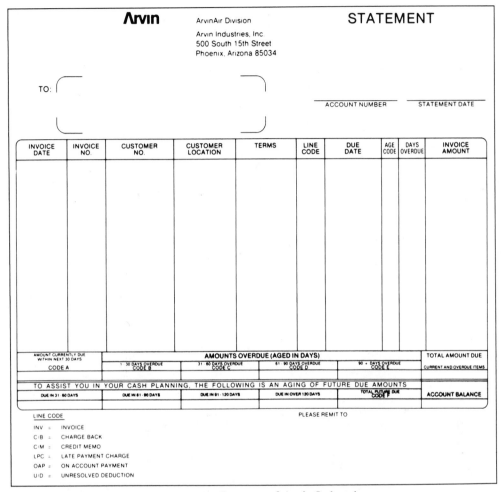

FIGURE 12-25 A monthly statement. Courtesy of Arvin Industries.

cessing of sales orders. Related operational control reports include the *unbilled shipments report,* the *late shipments report,* and the *back-order status report.*

Various registers and journals help to maintain the audit trail. The *sales invoice register* is a listing of all sales invoices, arranged by sales invoice numbers. It is in effect the sales journal. The *shipping register* is a listing of all shipments, arranged by shipping date. The *cash receipts journal* is a listing of amounts received, arranged chrono-

logically. Figure 12-27 shows a cash receipts journal, including a summary of debits and credits distributed to accounts.

The **accounts receivable aging schedule** is based on the same files as the monthly statement. However, it contains data concerning the status of the open balances of all active credit customers. Since it arrays the overdue amounts by time period, it flags those accounts that are urgently in need of collection. Thus, it provides operational control over the collection of open accounts and

OPEN ORDERS BY CUSTOMER
REPRESENTATIVE MERCHANDISING COMPANY

ORDER NO	ITEM NO		W/H LOC'N	ITEM CLASS	VENDOR NO	ORDERED QTY	U/M	UNIT PRICE	U/M	SOURCE SHIPMT	BACK ORDER
CUSTOMER-11111800		BOYER PLUMBING SUPPLY									
25137	77620000000000-1	ALUMINUM PAINT	L-147	07	1630VE	3	CS		CS	0	—
25137	82100000000000-1	RADIAL PIPE CUTTER 1-3	P-112	08	4155RR	2	EA		EA	0	—
25137	89600000000000-1	C12 L D CHAIN WRENCH 4CP	P-116	08	4115RR	1	EA	7.100	EA	0	—
CUSTOMER-11610000		FIELDS APPLIANCES									
80349	33250000000000-1	REFRIGERATOR – 20.7 S/S COPPER	A-120	03	2010AB	1	EA		EA	0	—
80349	33410000000000-1	REFRIGERATOR – 19 S/S GOLD	A-140	03	2010AB	2	EA		EA	0	—
80349	78900000000000-1	LATEX SEMI-GLOSS WHITE	L-169	07	9060LE	2	CS		CS	0	—
80349	78900000000000-1	LATEX SEMI-GLOSS WHITE	L-169	07	9060LE	3	GAL		CS	0	—
CUSTOMER-11750000		FRIED & JONES SUPPLY CORP.									
25111	11110000000000-1	TWO-LIGHT WALL MOUNT	R-119	01	6000AR	10	EA		EA	0	—
25111	56810000000000-1	EVAPORATIVE COOLER	Q-190	05	7710JW	6	EA		EA	0	—
25111	66640000000000-1	BATHTUB FAUCET	F-100	06	7370UN	12	EA		EA	0	—
25111	82100000000000-1	RADIAL PIPE CUTTER 1-3	P-112	08	4155RR	6	EA		EA	0	—
CUSTOMER-11800010		WESTERNWIDE *STORE 1*									
77999	57890000000000-4	AIR FILTER 12 × 14 × 1	033	05	2250SS	32	EA	.900	EA	0	B
CUSTOMER-12780000		HEARN MANUFACTURERS									
5	91200000000000-1	6 OZ COLD CUPS	X-380	09	7960BL	17	CS	6.900	CS	0	B
CUSTOMER-17640000		MADSEN CORPORATION									
75968	95020000000000-1	ROBOT – 3FT	D-181	10	1180AB	27	EA	19.270	EA	0	B
CUSTOMER-21000000		QUINN & ASSOCIATES									
9	77970000000000-1	CALUMET 750	L-160	07	1630VE	19	CS	88.960	CS	0	B
CUSTOMER-25000020		UNIVERSITY CONTRACTORS – APTOS									
80348	68360000000000-1	SINK – LAV	F-124			1	EA	42.500	EA	0	B
CUSTOMER-28000000		XAVIER HARDWARE & PAINT									
77996	22490000000000-1	U-BOLT FOOT MOUNT	M-115	02	6400IC	1	DZ	14.950	DZ	0	B

FIGURE 12-26 A status report of open orders. Courtesy of International Business Machines Corporation.

Representative Merchandising Company   1
Journal - CJ001   Batch - 1

Cash receipts journal

Time 17:35:18   Date 5/31/91   Page 1   35441
Posting date 5/31/91

Date	Customer number	Customer name	Ref number	Inv number	1110 Accts rec CR	1010 Cash DR	8130 Cash disc DR	1150 Adjustment DR	— General Ledger — amount DR	number
5/31/91		Vending machine				15.60			(15.60)	8040
5/31/91		Pay phone				20.80			(20.80)	8040
5/31/91	10400	Anderson Inc.	ck123		100.00			100.00		
5/31/91	10700	Andrus Inc.			150.00	150.00				
5/31/91	10700	Andrus Inc.	adj90		(7.48)		(7.48)			
5/31/91	10800	Angeroth Incorporated			110.76	110.76				
5/31/91	11810	Westernwide *Store 1*		UN	66.76	66.76				
5/31/91	11810	Westernwide *Store 1*		20915	325.99	325.99				

Representative Merchandising Company   1
Journal - CJ001   Batch - 1

Cash receipts journal summary

Time 17:36:55   Date 5/31/91   Page 1   35442
Posting date 5/31/91

Account number	Debits	Credits
8040	.00	36.40
1010	6,917.67	.00
1110	.00	6,976.62
1150	92.52	.00
8130	2.83	.00
Totals	7,013.02	7,013.02

FIGURE 12-27   A cash receipts journal and summary. Courtesy of International Business Machines Corporation.

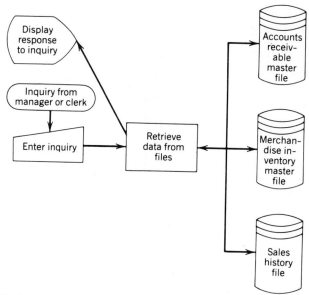

FIGURE 12-28   Response to inquiry of on-line files in revenue data base.

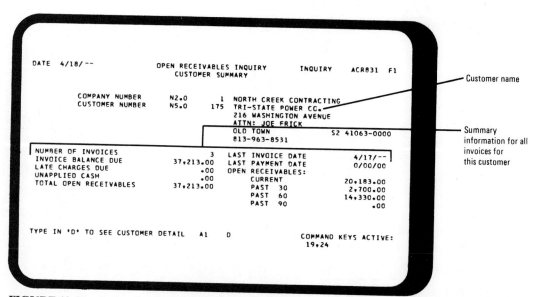

FIGURE 12-29   An inquiry screen relating to an open receivable. Courtesy of International Business Machines Corporation.

aids the credit manager in making collection and write-off decisions.

Inquiry Screens

If the revenue cycle data base is stored in on-line files, a variety of inquiries can be made interactively. Figure 12-28 shows a response from the system to an inquiry by a manager or clerk of key files in the data base.

Figure 12-29 presents a screen display output concerning the status of a customer's account receivable. Note that aging information is included as well as the current balance. Other inquiries might concern (1) the quantity of a particular product on hand, (2) the dates when certain orders are expected to be shipped, and (3) the detail of a single cash remittance or a batch of remittances.

<table>
<tr><td colspan="9" align="center">Eastern Manufacturing Co.
Analysis of Sales by Salesperson, Product, and Territory
For the Month of August 1991
Central Massachusetts Territory (03)</td></tr>
<tr><td colspan="3"></td><td colspan="3" align="center">Current Month</td><td colspan="3" align="center">Year-to-date</td></tr>
<tr><td colspan="2" align="center">Salesperson</td><td rowspan="2">Product
Line</td><td rowspan="2">Quota ($)</td><td rowspan="2">Actual ($)</td><td>Variance
($) Over</td><td rowspan="2">Quota ($)</td><td rowspan="2">Actual ($)</td><td>Variance
($) Over</td></tr>
<tr><td>Name</td><td>No.</td><td>(Under)</td><td>(Under)</td></tr>
<tr><td>Comden, K. J.</td><td>325</td><td>A</td><td>4,000</td><td>5,000</td><td>1,000</td><td>32,000</td><td>34,600</td><td>2,600</td></tr>
<tr><td></td><td></td><td>B</td><td>3,000</td><td>2,500</td><td>(500)</td><td>24,000</td><td>24,300</td><td>300</td></tr>
<tr><td></td><td></td><td>C</td><td>1,000</td><td>800</td><td>(200)</td><td>8,000</td><td>7,100</td><td>(900)</td></tr>
<tr><td></td><td></td><td>D</td><td>6,000</td><td>7,400</td><td>1,400</td><td>48,000</td><td>50,700</td><td>2,700</td></tr>
<tr><td></td><td></td><td>E</td><td>10,000</td><td>12,100</td><td>2,100</td><td>80,000</td><td>83,200</td><td>3,200</td></tr>
<tr><td></td><td></td><td>F</td><td>8,000</td><td>8,400</td><td>400</td><td>64,000</td><td>62,800</td><td>(1,200)</td></tr>
<tr><td></td><td></td><td>G</td><td>2,000</td><td>1,700</td><td>(300)</td><td>16,000</td><td>15,300</td><td>(700)</td></tr>
<tr><td></td><td></td><td>All</td><td>34,000</td><td>37,900</td><td>3,900</td><td>272,000</td><td>278,000</td><td>6,000</td></tr>
<tr><td>George, M. P.</td><td>381</td><td>A</td><td>5,000</td><td>4,800</td><td>(200)</td><td>40,000</td><td>39,200</td><td>(800)</td></tr>
<tr><td></td><td></td><td>B</td><td>4,000</td><td>4,100</td><td>100</td><td>32,000</td><td>31,800</td><td>(200)</td></tr>
<tr><td></td><td></td><td>C</td><td>1,000</td><td>900</td><td>(100)</td><td>8,000</td><td>6,900</td><td>(1,100)</td></tr>
<tr><td></td><td></td><td>D</td><td>7,000</td><td>6,200</td><td>(800)</td><td>56,000</td><td>54,800</td><td>(1,200)</td></tr>
<tr><td></td><td></td><td>E</td><td>12,000</td><td>11,800</td><td>(200)</td><td>96,000</td><td>96,500</td><td>500</td></tr>
<tr><td></td><td></td><td>F</td><td>9,500</td><td>9,900</td><td>400</td><td>76,000</td><td>78,100</td><td>2,100</td></tr>
<tr><td></td><td></td><td>G</td><td>2,500</td><td>3,200</td><td>700</td><td>20,000</td><td>25,300</td><td>5,300</td></tr>
<tr><td></td><td></td><td>All</td><td>41,000</td><td>40,900</td><td>(100)</td><td>328,000</td><td>332,600</td><td>4,600</td></tr>
<tr><td>Totals</td><td></td><td>A</td><td>50,000</td><td>53,300</td><td>3,300</td><td>400,000</td><td>410,700</td><td>10,700</td></tr>
<tr><td></td><td></td><td>B</td><td>35,000</td><td>34,700</td><td>(300)</td><td>280,000</td><td>281,500</td><td>1,500</td></tr>
<tr><td></td><td></td><td>C</td><td>10,000</td><td>8,900</td><td>(1,100)</td><td>80,000</td><td>77,700</td><td>(2,300)</td></tr>
<tr><td></td><td></td><td>D</td><td>65,000</td><td>69,100</td><td>4,100</td><td>520,000</td><td>528,100</td><td>8,100</td></tr>
<tr><td></td><td></td><td>E</td><td>108,000</td><td>111,800</td><td>3,800</td><td>864,000</td><td>891,000</td><td>27,000</td></tr>
<tr><td></td><td></td><td>F</td><td>86,000</td><td>84,700</td><td>(1,300)</td><td>688,000</td><td>679,300</td><td>(8,700)</td></tr>
<tr><td></td><td></td><td>G</td><td>23,000</td><td>24,000</td><td>1,000</td><td>184,000</td><td>183,900</td><td>(100)</td></tr>
<tr><td></td><td></td><td>All</td><td>377,000</td><td>386,500</td><td>9,500</td><td>3,016,000</td><td>3,052,200</td><td>36,200</td></tr>
</table>

FIGURE 12-30 A sales analysis report.

Managerial Reports

The revenue cycle data base can provide a wealth of information to aid managers in making decisions. One example already listed is the accounts receivable aging schedule, which is useful for decision making as well as operational control. Several other useful reports and analyses are worth noting.

Performance reports reflect results in terms of such key measures as average dollar value per order, percentage of orders shipped on time, and the average number of days between the order date and shipping date.

Sales analyses reflect the relative effectiveness of individual salespersons, sales regions, product lines, customers, and markets. Figure 12-30 shows a sales analysis that compares the actual sales for three of these factors against established quotas. Analyses of sales returns are also useful.

Cash flow statements provide the basis for developing cash forecasts and budgets. Hence, they aid the process of managing the cash resource.

Figure 12-31 portrays most of the listings and reports described in the preceding paragraphs. They are shown as outputs produced from data in the various files listed in an earlier section. Certain of the outputs could alternatively have been included in the shipping and billing segments of the flowchart in Figure 12-21. Other outputs are typically generated monthly during special print runs.

Summary

The revenue cycle facilitates the exchange of products or services with customers for cash. Functions of the revenue cycle (for product sales) are to obtain the order from the customer, check the customer's credit, enter the sales order, assemble goods for shipment, ship the ordered goods, bill the customer, receive and deposit the cash payment, maintain accounts receivable records, post transactions to the general ledger, and prepare needed financial reports and other outputs. Related functions involve back orders and sales returns. These functions are achieved under the direction of the marketing/distribution and finance/accounting organizational units.

Most of the data used in the cycle arise from customers. Documents typically employed are the customer order, sales order, picking list, packing list, bill of lading, shipping notice, sales invoice, remittance advice, deposit slip, back order, and credit memo. Preformatted screens may be used in on-line computer-based systems to enter sales and cash receipts data. The data base includes such files as the customer master, accounts receivable master, merchandise inventory master, open sales order, open sales invoice, cash receipts transaction, shipping and price data reference, and sales history files. Data processing consists of processing sales transactions, processing cash receipts transactions, and maintaining accounts receivable records. Processing may feasibly be performed by manual systems, batch computer-based systems, and on-line computer-based systems. A variety of risks exist in the processing of sales and cash receipts transactions. Exposures due to these risks can be counteracted by means of adequate general and transaction controls. Among the outputs generated by the revenue cycle are the customer's monthly statement, open orders report, sales invoice register, accounts receivable aging schedule, customer inquiry screen, performance report, sales analyses, and cash flow statement. Figure 12-32 summarizes many of the system components of the revenue cycle.

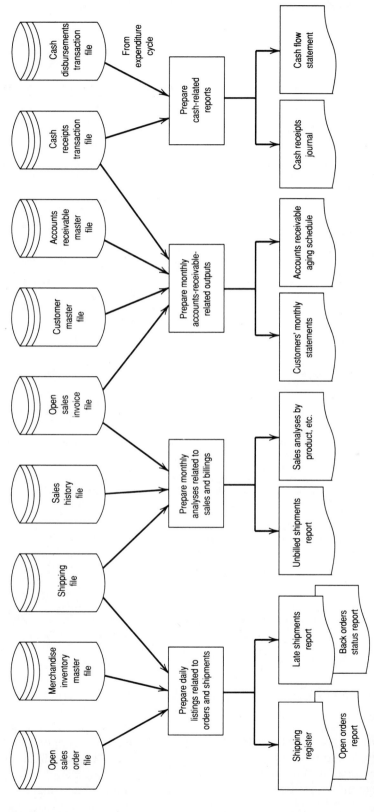

FIGURE 12-31 System flowchart showing daily and monthly listings, statements, and reports in the revenue cycle.

Component	Sales	Cash Receipts	Accounts Receivable	Sales Returns and Write-offs
Source documents	Customer's order Sales order Shipping notice Bill of lading	Remittance advice (with cash or check) Deposit slip	Sales invoice Journal voucher (and/or sales remittance sum- maries)	Credit memo Write-off notice
Processing steps	Receive and process customer's order Check credit Pick and ship mer- chandise Bill customer Enter transaction in sales journal	Receive and list remittance Prepare deposit slip and deliver to bank Enter transaction in cash receipts journal	Post transactions in accounts receiv- able ledger Transmit for posting to general ledger Prepare and mail monthly statements	Receive returned merchandise Prepare and autho- rize credit memo Analyze accounts and prepare and authorize write-offs Prepare journal vouchers
Files	Customer file Credit file Pricing file Inventory file Sales order/invoice file	Customer file Cash remittance file	Accounts receivable (A/R) ledger General ledger	Customer file Inventory file Credit memo file Write-off file
Outputs	Sales summary Sales analysis by product, territory, etc.	Cash remittance list or summary Cash flow statement	Customer monthly statements Accounts receivable aging schedule	Sales returns and write-off summa- ries Sales returns analy- ses
Selective transac- tion controls	Approval of credit Verification of prices, terms, mathemati- cal accuracy Prenumbered sales orders, invoices, etc. Batch totals of in- voice amounts	Prenumbered remit- tance advices or cash receipt forms Prompt deposit of all cash receipts intact Reconciliation of remittance list with deposit slip, and of cash account with bank statement Batch totals of cash receipt amounts	Verification of post- ings Reconciliation of accounts receiv- able control ac- count with A/R ledger	Authorization of sales returns and write- offs Prenumbered credit memos and write- off notices

FIGURE 12-32 Analysis worksheet for the revenue cycle. Based on a technique described in "Systems Procedures and Controls," *Journal of Systems Management* (Sept. 1983), pp. 28–32.

Review Problems with Solutions

Problem 1 Statement

Millsap sells stationery products to department stores, book stores, greeting card stores, and other retailers on credit. It receives orders from these customers by mail.

After validating the orders, checking and approving their credit status, and issuing formal sales orders, the firm ships the ordered merchandise. The shipping clerk amends the shipping notice copies of the sales orders to reflect appropriate data concerning the shipments. Then the shipping department batches these shipping notice copies of the sales orders at the end of each day and arranges them in sequence by sales order number.

Exhibit 1 presents a system flowchart that diagrams the manner in which the batched copies of sales orders are processed by the firm's computer-based system. (However, to simplify the procedure, the updating of the merchandise inventory master file is omitted.) The procedure for correcting errors detected during the entry and processing of the sales orders is identical to the solution shown for Review Problem 2 in Chapter 9, page 364.

Required

a. Identify key data items that appear on the shipping notice copies of the sales orders being entered into processing.

b. Identify and describe the transaction controls and pertinent general controls reflected by the two exhibits. Also, add descriptions of controls that do not explicitly appear in the exhibit but that are needed in the batch processing approach being shown.

c. Briefly discuss the changes that would be needed to the flowchart in order to reflect the updating of the merchandise inventory master file.

Solution

a. Key data items that should appear on each amended sales order are the sales order number, date of order, customer account number, customer name, shipping address, billing address, terms, customer purchase order number, shipping date, salesperson number (if any), method of shipping and carrier, back-order data (if any), product numbers, quantities shipped of each product, unit price of each product, and initials of shipping clerk.

b. The accounting controls involved in the computer-based batch processing system are as follows:

(1) Three batch control totals are computed in the shipping department: an amount total of the quantities ordered, a hash total of the customer account numbers, and a record count of the number of shipping notices. These totals are entered on a prenumbered batch transmittal sheet and forwarded to the control section or group. It logs the batch data on an input–output control log and verifies that the count of the batch is correct. (The dashed line between the batch total and the batch input–output control log reflects this verification.)

(2) Data entry clerks in the data preparation section or group key the data from the documents onto magnetic tape, thereby creating an order transaction file. Each keyed transaction is key-verified, and errors are corrected. The clerks also record the batch control totals within a trailer label on the tape, so that they may be checked at a later point in the processing.

(3) The computer operator mounts the tape containing the transaction file; then he or she removes the tape file protection ring, thereby preventing the tape from being written on and the data destroyed.

(4) If the accounts receivable master file is stored on a magnetic tape or removable magnetic disk, the computer operator obtains the medium from the data library by signing the library log and mounts the master file. (If the file is on line, this step is not necessary.)

(5) The computer operator begins run 1 by opening the run manual, which

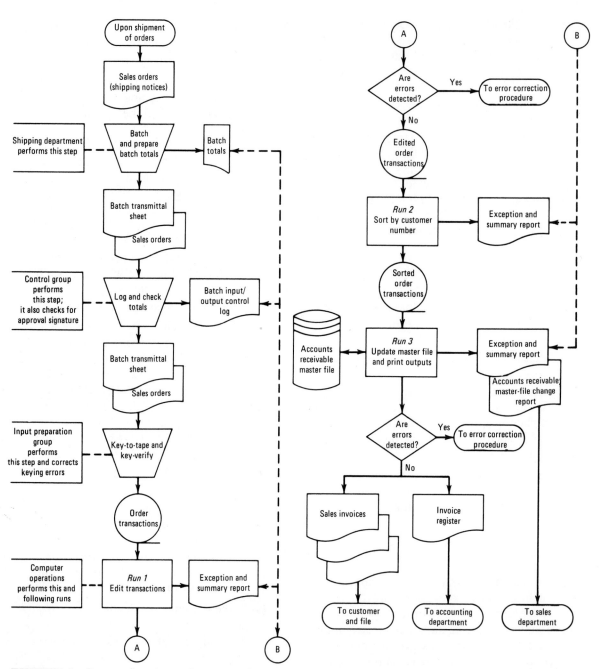

EXHIBIT 1 System flowchart of computer-based batch processing of sales transactions, with emphasis on controls.

contains detailed operating instructions. As the first step, he or she performs internal label checks, that is, verifies that the correct master file and transaction header labels are displayed on the console log.

(6) During run 1 the edit program performs a variety of programmed checks on the data pertaining to each transaction. Among the checks applied are the validity, field, limit, range, relationship, sign, and self-checking digit checks. (See Figure 12-24 for the types of data items checked and descriptions of the checks.)

(7) Errors or exceptional conditions detected by these edit checks are listed on an exception and summary report and entered into the error correction procedure (to be discussed later).

(8) During the edit run the program accumulates transaction totals and counts and then compares the values for the entire batch against the precomputed batch control totals. Any differences are listed on the exception and summary report, and they are investigated by the control group.

(9) Before run 2 begins, the computer operator removes the tape file protection ring from the newly created tape of edited transactions and performs an internal label check on the tape. In addition, the operator removes the exception and summary report and gives to the control group for investigation.

(10) Before run 3 begins, the computer operator performs the same actions as earlier with respect to the files.

(11) During run 3 the updating and invoicing program performs checks to see that the transactions are in correct customer account number sequence and that each transaction is posted to the correct master file record. It assigns sequential numbers to the sales invoices. It updates the data in the header and trailer labels. It reflects any differences in batch totals on the exception and summary report and also includes data for the summary journal entry that is to be posted to the general ledger.

(12) Reports that aid the audit trail and provide the basis for review are printed. Included are the invoice register and the accounts receivable master file change report.

(13) The various outputs from run 3 are logged and distributed by the control group to the appropriate recipients.

The error correction procedure ensures that all detected errors are properly handled:

(1) All detected errors are listed on an exception and summary report during the run.

(2) All transactions containing errors are transferred to a suspense file, which is monitored by the control group so that erroneous transactions are not mislaid.

(3) All detected errors are corrected by user departments, which are most knowledgeable concerning the transactions.

(4) All corrected transactions are re-edited, in order to verify that all errors are corrected and that no new errors have been introduced.

(5) The batch control totals are adjusted to reflect the amounts involved in all suspended transactions.

c. In this batch processing procedure the updating of the merchandise inventory master file will likely take place before the accounts receivable master file is updated. Thus, the edited order transaction file (after run 1) would first be sorted by product numbers. Then the merchandise inventory master file can be sequentially updated.

It should be noted, however, that many orders will likely involve more than one product. Consequently, steps in addition to the preceding are necessary. Before sorting by product numbers, the data comprising the headings of the orders (e.g., customer account number and addresses) must be placed in a separate file from the product line order data (e.g., product number and quantity ordered). Even before this is done, each product in an order must be coded with the sales order number, since it will be detached from the order heading. Then, after the updating run is completed, the heading and product data for each order must be reassembled via a merge run.

Problem 2 Statement

The cashier of the Easy Company intercepted customer A's check payable to the firm in the amount of $500 and deposited it in a bank account that was part of the firm's petty cash fund, of which he was custodian. He then drew on the petty-cash-fund bank account a $500 check payable to himself, signed it, and cashed it. At the end of the month, while processing the monthly statements to customers, he was able to change the statement to customer A so as to show that A had received credit for the $500 check that had been intercepted. Ten days later he made an entry in the cash receipts book that purported to record receipt of a remittance of $500 from customer A , thus restoring A's account to its proper balance but overstating cash in bank. He covered the overstatement by omitting two checks, the aggregate amount of which was $500, from the list of outstanding checks in the bank reconciliation.[3]

Required

Identify the central control weakness in Easy Company's cash receipts procedure and specify control procedures that can improve the internal control structure.

Solution

The central control weakness in this situation is the inadequate division of duties and responsibilities. Not only does the cashier have access to cash as well as to the customers' records, but he is allowed to check on his own work and to handle the petty cash fund in a very loose manner.

The internal control system can therefore be greatly strengthened if the following steps are taken:

1. Assign other persons not in the cashier's office to process the customers' records, to maintain the petty cash fund, to open the incoming mail, and to reconcile the bank account.

2. Do not allow the cashier to have access to incoming mail, to the customers' records, and to the petty cash fund.

3. Instruct the bank to refuse to accept checks made payable to the firm for deposit in the petty-cash-fund bank account.

4. Require the person who opens the mail to make a separate listing in triplicate of all remittances received; one copy is to be sent to the cashier for entry in the cash records, another copy is to be sent to the accounts receivable clerk for posting to the customers' ledger accounts, and the third is to be sent to the treasurer or internal auditor for comparison with the deposit slip returned from the bank.

[3] Adapted from the May 1958 CPA examination. Copyright © 1958 by the American Institute of Certified Public Accountants. Reprinted by permission.

Review Questions

12-1 What is the meaning of each of the following terms?

> Revenue cycle
> Prebilling procedure
> Incomplete billing procedure
> Separate order and billing procedure
> Balance forward method
> Open invoice method
> Customer order
> Sales order
> Order acknowledgement
> Picking list
> Packing list
> Bill of lading
> Shipping notice
> Sales invoice
> Remittance advice
> Deposit slip
> Back order
> Credit memo
> Lapping
> Monthly statement
> Open orders report
> Accounts receivable aging schedule

12-2 What are the objectives of the revenue cycle?

12-3 What are the major functions of the revenue cycle?

12-4 Contrast the three alternative procedures for billing customers.

12-5 Describe the back-ordering procedure.

12-6 Describe the relationships of the marketing and distribution organizational functions to the revenue cycle.

12-7 Describe the relationships of the finance and accounting organizational functions to the revenue cycle.

12-8 What are the sources of data used in the revenue cycle?

12-9 Identify the various documents used in the revenue cycle.

12-10 Identify the various files used in the revenue cycle.

12-11 Describe the credit sales procedure when processing is performed manually.

12-12 Describe the cash receipts procedure when processing is performed manually.

12-13 Describe the accounts receivable procedure when processing is performed manually.

12-14 Describe the revenue cycle procedure when processing is performed by a computer-based system involving a combination of the batch and on-line methods.

12-15 What are the risk exposures that exist in the processing within the revenue cycle?

12-16 Identify various general and transaction controls that concern the revenue cycle.

12-17 Identify various reports and other outputs that may be generated from information provided by the revenue cycle.

Discussion Questions

12-18 In what ways does the revenue cycle procedure differ when performed by computer-based systems (1) using the batch processing approach and (2) using the on-line processing approach?

12-19 What are sources of information for marketing managers other than from revenue cycle processing?

12-20 In what ways does a cash sale differ from a credit sale, especially with regard to documents, files, procedure, and outputs?

12-21 Describe several programmed edit checks, such as the redundancy matching check, that can be applied by the posting programs used in processing sales and cash receipts transactions.

12-22 Why should a bank reconciliation be prepared periodically?

12-23 Which of the transaction controls that are needed in a revenue cycle procedure involving an on-line computer-based system are not suitable when a batch computer-based system is employed, and vice versa?

Problems

12-1 The Flip Shopper sells a variety of merchandise for cash only at a single location. Four cash registers are used for checking out customers. Describe the cash sales procedure—including documents, processing steps, controls, and reports—if this merchandiser does not employ computers. Identify the likely changes if point-of-sale terminals were installed in place of the cash registers. Assume that the terminals are, in effect, stand-alone microcomputers.

12-2 The Overlord Company has just employed a new credit manager. Because the firm has an outstanding total of $3 million in accounts receivable (when last year's sales were $12 million), the credit manager realizes that her most urgent task is to reduce the level of accounts receivable. Credit customers are billed at the end of each month, on the basis of individual accounts receivable records. The credit manager has been assured by the president that a new computer-based system is to be installed within the coming year.

Required

a. List the types of transactions that affect the accounts receivable balance.

b. Describe at least two reports that can aid the credit manager in reducing the outstanding accounts receivable.

c. Discuss the relative advantages of processing the various daily transactions that affect the accounts receivable records by a computer-based system that (1) uses the

batch processing approach and (2) that uses the on-line processing approach.

12-3 Sapphire Department Stores, Inc., has eight locations in a major eastern city. Sales are made on credit to customers who have applied and received credit cards from Sapphire. All other sales are made for cash. Deliveries of purchased merchandise are made upon request, whether the sale is for cash or on credit. Merchandise may be returned by customers, refunds being made in the case of cash sales and credits against account balances being provided in the case of credit sales. Credit customers are billed once a month, on the basis of accounts receivable records. Overdue balances are automatically assessed interest charges.

Required

a. List the data items needed to record and process cash sales, credit sales, payments on account, and sales returns transactions.

b. List the files needed to store the data items you listed in **a.**

c. Describe reports that would be useful to the firm's management in analyzing the sales and cash receipts transactions and the activities related to the credit customers' accounts.

12-4 Antler and Horn, Consultants, bill their clients for services rendered. The invoices, which are sent at the end of each month, itemize the hours worked by the various classes of consultants in the firm. One invoice sent on November 30, 1991, to the Mover Construction Co. showed the following billable hours: 4 hours for a partner, 10 hours for a manager, 85 hours for a senior staff consultant, and 230 hours for staff consultants. Hourly rates charged by the firm are $250 for partner, $180 for manager, $150 for senior staff consultant, and $90 for staff consultant. All taxes are included in the billing rates. Design and complete the invoice to be sent to the above client, whose offices are located at 50 Lark Lane, Prescott, Arizona 86301. The consultants are located at 1000 Woodshire Blvd., Los Angeles, California 90028.

12-5 At the end of each month the Egress Corporation of Andover, Massachusetts 01810, prepares monthly statements for its credit customers, plus an accounts receivable aging schedule. The files on which these reports are based are the accounts receivable master file, the customer master file, the sales invoice file, and the cash receipts file. (The firm does not maintain a sales history file but instead retains all sales data in the invoice file for one year.) The files are all maintained on magnetic disk and can be accessed as needed during the end-of-month printing runs.

Required

a. Design the monthly statement, assuming that it is not intended to be used as a turn-around document.

b. Design the accounts receivable aging schedule, including such columns as customer account number and name, current balance, amount of the receivable balance that is not overdue, and amounts that are 30–60 days old, 60–90 days old, and over 90 days old. Terms are net 30 days.

c. Draw suggested record layouts (omitting field sizes and modes of data items) of the aforementioned files. Be sure that all the information in the two outputs can be derived from one of the files or can be computed or generated by the computer system. (For instance, the date may be computer generated.)

12-6 Computers Unlimited carries two makes of microcomputers, Speedos and Whizbangs, plus software and hardware accessories. Its retail stores are located in three

sales districts, and it sells to individuals and to businesses. Since sales growth has been rather erratic in recent years, the sales manager desires a variety of monthly sales analyses. On the basis of these analyses, he believes, he can better determine where to emphasize sales efforts.

Required

Design formats of sales analyses for Computers Unlimited that show the following:

a. Sales of the four product lines (the two makes of microcomputers, the software, and the accessories).

b. Sales to the two classes of customers, individuals and businesses.

c. Sales in the three sales districts (I, II, and III).

d. Sales of the four product lines within the three districts.

e. Sales to the two classes of customers within the three districts, which in turn are within the four product lines.

Hint: See Review Problem 2 in Chapter 10, page 404.

12-7 What error or fraudulent activity might occur if each of the following procedures is allowed?

a. The person who maintains the accounts receivable records also receives the cash payments from customers.

b. The person who approves the write-offs of uncollectible accounts also carries the cash receipts to the bank.

c. The sales invoices are not prenumbered (or if prenumbered, are not filed in a sequential file that is periodically checked for gaps in the numbers).

d. The accounts receivable ledger is not periodically reconciled to the control account in the general ledger.

e. Incompleted sales order-invoice copies are filed in the billing department but are not accounted for on a periodic basis.

f. After billing is completed, the shipping notices are not marked in some manner, stapled to copies of the invoices, and filed.

12-8 What internal accounting control(s) would be most effective in preventing or detecting each of the following errors or fraudulent practices?

a. The amount of $380 is posted from a sales invoice to a customer's accounts receivable record as $308.

b. A customer is billed for all 100 units ordered, though only 80 units are shipped because of an insufficient quantity on hand to fill the order.

c. A customer is not billed for ordered merchandise shipped.

d. A general ledger clerk posts a debit to sales returns but does not post the credit to the accounts receivable control account.

e. A shipment never reaches a customer, even though it leaves the shipping dock via a common carrier.

f. Goods are shipped to a customer who is delinquent in paying for past sales.

g. Goods are taken from the finished-goods warehouse and knowingly shipped by the shipping clerk to a person who did not place an order.

h. A sale that is billed to a customer is not posted to the accounts receivable record.

i. Certain goods are never returned to the firm, in spite of the fact that

a credit memo is issued and approved.

j. A cash receipt is stolen by the cashier.

k. A computer-prepared sales analysis is mistakenly sent to the personnel manager rather than the sales manager.

l. A computer operator mounts the magnetic tape containing the cash disbursements for the day, rather than the cash receipts, and incorrectly updates the accounts receivable master file.

m. A payment from a customer in the amount of $100.10, properly listed on a remittance advice, is keyed by a data entry clerk onto the transaction tape as $101.00.

n. A sales order clerk accidentally omits the quantity of one of the ordered products when entering sales data via a terminal.

o. A sales order is coded with an incorrect and nonexistent customer number. The error is not detected until the file updating run, when no master is located to match the erroneous number.

p. A sales order clerk accidentally keys the letter o instead of a 0 (zero) as a part of the quantity 30.

12-9 What internal accounting control(s) would be most effective in preventing or detecting each of the following errors or fraudulent practices?

a. An accounts receivable clerk issues fictitious credit memos to a customer (who is also a friend) for goods that were supposedly returned from previous sales.

b. Sales have been sharply rising since salespersons were placed on a commission basis, but uncollectible accounts receivable have risen even more sharply.

c. An accounts receivable clerk improperly writes off the balance in a customer's account to conceal the theft of cash.

d. A billing clerk correctly prepares a sales invoice in the amount of $3800.00, but the invoice is entered as $3008.00 in the sales journal and posted in the latter amount to the general ledger and accounts receivable ledger.

e. The magnetic tape containing the accounts receivable master file is accidentally used as a scratch (output) tape during a processing run for a separate application, with the result that the accounts are wiped out.

f. A mailroom clerk accidentally omits the number of the customer when entering a remittance via a mailroom terminal.

g. A sales order clerk accidentally enters the quantity 2000 when entering an order on her terminal for motorcycles from a small dealer.

h. The cashier, who enters over-the-counter payments from customers directly into the computer system, accidentally enters the name of a nonexistent customer upon receiving a payment; when the cash remittances are later posted to the accounts by an updating program, the amount relating to the erroneously entered customer name cannot be posted.

i. The accounts receivable department prepares 100 remittance advices for transmittal to computer operations for processing; however, two of the advices are accidentally removed before the batch is transmitted, and thus the amounts of only 98 advices are posted to the accounts receivable records.

j. A warehouseman takes merchandise from the warehouse for his personal use and covers the theft by deducting the quantities taken from the inventory records.

k. A programmer misunderstands the sales transaction processing procedure and makes several logic errors when modifying a sales invoicing program.

l. An employee in the cash receipts department accesses her personnel records via a terminal and increases her salary level.

m. A sales invoice is accidentally misplaced just after being prepared and thus not mailed to the affected customer; the omission is never detected.

n. Customers are often charged for merchandise items that they do not order and are not shipped.

o. A firm processes its sales transactions in batches and feels confident that all credit sales are properly billed to customers; however, the head of the accounts receivable department often has difficulty in tracing individual sales transactions.

p. The accounts receivable control account is generally out of balance with the total of the individual customer account records at the end of an accounting period.

12-10 The Tuffy Merchandising Company enters sales orders via on-line terminals as soon as received, and the computer system stores the orders in a file and then generates printed shipping orders. The Duffy Merchandising Company keys batches of sales orders onto magnetic tape and then enters these batches into its computer system, where the sales orders are stored and used at the end of the day to generate shipping orders and to provide data for later processing. Both firms employ the separate sales order and invoice procedure, and both store their sales order records on magnetic disks for reference and use in sales processing. Assume that the key-to-tape encoders used by Duffy's system do not perform any edit functions.

Required

a. List the data items that should appear on the shipping orders of both firms.

b. List the programmed edit checks that should be performed by the computer edit programs of Tuffy's system; include with each check one or more key data items from shipping transactions to which each check pertains.

c. List the programmed edit checks that should be performed by the computer edit programs of Duffy's system; include with each check one or more key data items from shipping transactions to which each check pertains.

d. If Tuffy's system allows a variety of transactions to be entered via the same terminals, what added item of data must be entered before the order data are entered? Give an illustration of this item of data.

12-11 Fast Burger is a chain of fast food establishments. List the control objectives to be achieved during cash sales transactions, as well as the internal accounting controls or security measures needed to achieve the objectives.

(CIA adapted)

12-12 The Jason Department Store of Ann Arbor, Michigan, sells a wide variety of merchandise for cash or credit. It mails account statements to credit customers monthly. Customers then return their payments, including in the envelopes the detached portions of the statements, which serve as remittance advices for the cash receipts proce-

dure. These remittance advices are processed against the accounts receivable master file. Daily listings of cash receipts and monthly accounts receivable aging schedules are prepared.

Each remittance advice contains the customer account number, customer name and address, remittance advice code, type of account, payment date, and amount paid.

Each record in the accounts receivable master file contains the customer number, customer name and address, credit limit, sales amounts and dates for the past six months, cash payment amounts and dates for the past six months, adjustment amounts and dates and codes for the past six months, and current balance.

The daily listing of cash receipts (in effect, the cash receipts journal) reflects customer numbers, customer names, remittance advice codes, cash payment amounts, the daily deposit number, and the date.

The monthly accounts receivable aging analysis reflects customer names, total balances owned, plus portions of balances that are current, 30–60 days old, 60–90 days old, and over 90 days old.

Jason currently processes cash receipts manually, but it has decided to convert to computer-based processing.

Required

a. Specify the source of each item in the two output reports, assuming that the system has been converted to computer processing. Sources may be the master file, transaction document, or a "computer-generated" operation.

b. Prepare a system flowchart of a proposed computer-based cash receipts procedure. Assume that the firm adopts the batch processing approach, that the remittance advices are converted to magnetic tape by means of an OCR device, and that the master file is stored on a magnetic disk.

c. Prepare a record layout of the remittance advice transaction record as it might appear on the magnetic tape medium. Include assumed field sizes and modes of data items.

d. List the transaction controls that are suitable to the computer-based system. In the case of programmed checks indicate the data items being edited.

e. Prepare a data flow diagram of the cash receipts procedure.

12-13 A cash sale procedure in a small department store involves several steps. First, the sales clerk prepares a prenumbered sales slip as a triplicate set. The original and second copy, together with the payment, are presented to the cashier by the sales clerk. The cashier validates the original copy and gives it to the customer. The third copy of the sales slip is retained in the sales book; when the sales book has been depleted of sales slip sets, it is filed in the sales office.

At the end of each day the cashier prepares a sales summary, counts the cash, and prepares a deposit slip in duplicate. He next takes the cash to the bank, where one copy of the deposit slip is retained and the other is validated to reflect the amount deposited. Then the cashier turns over the validated deposit slip, second copies of the sales slips, and the sales summary to the firm's accountant. She compares the above documents and accounts for all numbered sales slips. Then she gives the sales summary to the general ledger clerk, who posts the sales totals to the appropriate accounts and files the sales summary chronologically. The accountant files the sales slips numerically and the deposit slip chronologically.

Required

Prepare a document system flowchart of the foregoing procedure.

12-14 The flowchart on page 528 depicts the activities related to the sales, shipping, billing, and collecting processes used by Newton Hardware, Inc.

Required

Identify the weaknesses in the system of internal accounting control relating to the activities of

a. The warehouse clerk.

b. Bookkeeper A.

c. The collection clerk.

Do not identify weaknesses relating to the sales clerk or to bookkeepers B and C. Do not discuss recommendations concerning the correction of these weaknesses.

(CPA adapted)

12-15 Jersey Wholesalers, Inc., of Athens, Georgia, performs sales order, shipping, and billing procedures as shown in the system flowchart on page 529. All documents used in the procedures are prenumbered. There are numerous partial shipments on customers' orders, since quantities on hand are frequently not sufficient to fill orders completely; however, goods not shipped in such cases are *not* automatically back-ordered.

Required

List the control weaknesses in the flowcharted procedures and recommend improvements.

(CIA adapted)

12-16 The Robinson Company is a small paint manufacturer in Lincoln, Nebraska. Its customer billings and collections are attended to by a receptionist, an accounts receivable clerk, and a cashier who also serves as a secretary. The company's paint products are sold to wholesalers and retail stores.

The following describes the procedure

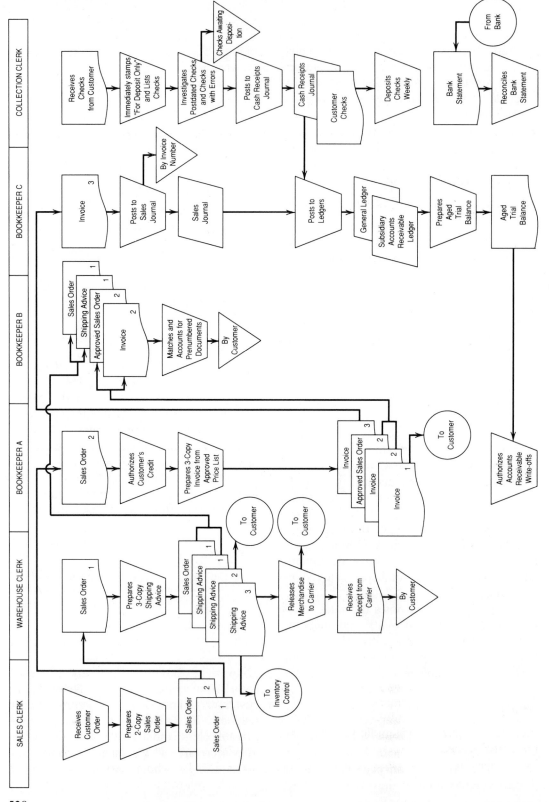

528

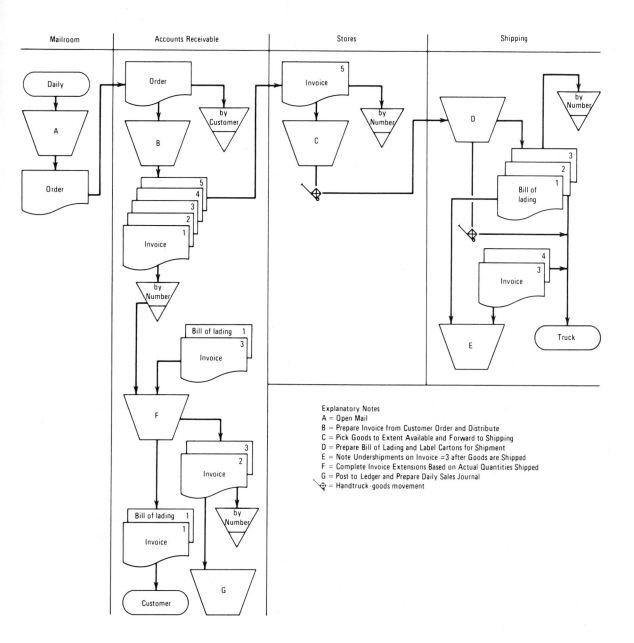

| Mailroom | Accounts Receivable | Stores | Shipping |

Explanatory Notes
A = Open Mail
B = Prepare Invoice from Customer Order and Distribute
C = Pick Goods to Extent Available and Forward to Shipping
D = Prepare Bill of Lading and Label Cartons for Shipment
E = Note Undershipments on Invoice ≠3 after Goods are Shipped
F = Complete Invoice Extensions Based on Actual Quantities Shipped
G = Post to Ledger and Prepare Daily Sales Journal
⊕ = Handtruck-goods movement

pertaining to customer billings and collections:

a. The mail is opened by the receptionist, who gives the customers' purchase orders to the accounts receivable clerk; 15 to 20 orders are received each day. Under instructions to expedite the shipment of orders, the accounts receivable clerk at once prepares a five-copy sales invoice form, which is distributed as follows:

Copy 1, the customer billing copy, is filed alphabetically by the accounts receivable clerk until notice of shipment is received.

Copy 2, the accounts receivable department copy, is held with copy 1 for ultimate posting of the accounts receivable records.

Copies 3 and 4 are sent to the shipping department.

Copy 5 is sent to the storeroom as authority for release of the goods; it then accompanies the goods to the shipping department.

b. After the ordered paint has been moved from the storeroom to the shipping department, the shipping department prepares bills of lading (in three copies) and labels the cartons. Sales invoice copy 4 is inserted in a carton as a packing slip. After the trucker has picked up the shipment and its bill of lading copy, the customer's copy of the bill of lading and copy 3 (on which any undershipments are noted) are returned to the accounts receivable clerk. The company does not back-order in the event of undershipments; customers are expected to reorder the merchandise. The Robinson Company's copy of the bill of lading is filed by the shipping department in numerical order, together with copy 5.

c. When copy 3 and the customer's copy of the bill of lading are received by the accounts receivable clerk, copies 1 and 2 are completed by numbering them and inserting quantities shipped, unit prices, extensions, discounts, and totals. The accounts receiv-

able clerk then mails copy 1 and the original of the bill of lading to the customer. Copies 2 and 3 are stapled together.

d. The accounts receivable clerk posts the individual accounts receivable ledger cards by a bookkeeping machine procedure whereby the sales register is prepared as a carbon copy of the postings. Postings are done from copy 2, which is then filed, along with staple-attached copy 3, in numerical order. Monthly, the general ledger clerk summarizes the sales register for posting to the general ledger accounts.

e. Since the Robinson Company is short of cash, the deposit of receipts is also expedited. The receptionist turns over all mail receipts and related correspondence to the accounts receivable clerk, who examines the checks and determines that the accompanying vouchers or correspondence contains enough detail to permit posting of the accounts. The accounts receivable clerk then endorses the checks and gives them to the cashier, who prepares the daily deposit. The cashier then carries the deposit to the bank and files the duplicate deposit slip. No currency is received in the mail, and no paint is sold over the counter at the factory.

f. The accounts receivable clerk uses the vouchers or correspondence that accompanies the checks to post the accounts receivable ledger cards. The bookkeeping machine prepares a cash receipts register as a carbon copy of the postings. Monthly, the general ledger clerk summarizes the cash receipts register for posting to the general ledger accounts. The accounts receivable clerk also corresponds with customers about unauthorized deductions for discounts, freight or advertising allowances, returns, and so on, and prepares the appropriate credit memos. Disputed items of large amount are turned over to the sales manager for settlement. Each month, the accounts receivable clerk prepares a trial balance of the open accounts receivable and compares the resulting total with the general ledger control account for accounts receivable.

Required

a. Prepare a document system flowchart, using appropriate symbols. Ignore returns, etc.

b. List the control weaknesses in the foregoing procedure and recommend improvements.

(CPA adapted)

12-17 OBrien Corporation is a medium-sized, privately owned industrial instrument manufacturer supplying precision equipment manufacturers in the midwest. The corporation is ten years old and operates a centralized accounting and information system. The administrative offices are located in a downtown St. Louis building; the production, shipping, and receiving departments are housed in a renovated warehouse a few blocks away. The shipping and receiving areas share one end of the warehouse.

OBrien Corporation has grown rapidly. Sales have increased by 25 percent each year for the last three years, and the company is now shipping approximately $80,000 of its products each week. James Fox, OBrien's controller, purchased and installed a computer last year to process the payroll and inventory. Fox plans to integrate the accounting information system fully within the next five years.

The marketing department consists of four salespersons. Upon obtaining an order, usually over the telephone, a salesperson manually prepares a prenumbered, two-part sales order. One copy of the order is filed by date, and the second copy is sent to the shipping department. All sales are on credit, F.O.B. destination. Because of the recent increase in sales, the four salespersons have not had time to check credit histories. As a result, 15 percent of credit sales are either late collections or uncollectible.

The shipping department receives the sales orders and packages the goods from the warehouse, noting any items that are out of stock. The terminal in the shipping department is used to update the perpetual inventory records of each item as it is removed from the shelf. The packages are placed near the loading dock door in alphabetical order by customer name. The sales order is signed by a shipping clerk when the order is filled and ready to send. The sales order is forwarded to the billing department, where a two-part sales invoice is prepared. The sales invoice is prepared only upon receipt of the sales order from the shipping department so that the customer is billed just for the items that were sent, not for back orders. Billing sends the customer's copy of the invoice back to shipping. The customer's copy of the invoice serves as a billing copy, and shipping inserts it into a special envelope on the package in order to save postage. The carrier of the customer's choice is then contacted to pick up the goods. In the past, goods were shipped within two working days of the receipt of the customer's order; however, shipping dates now average six working days after receipt of the order. One reason is that there are two new shipping clerks who are still undergoing training. Because the two shipping clerks have fallen behind, the two

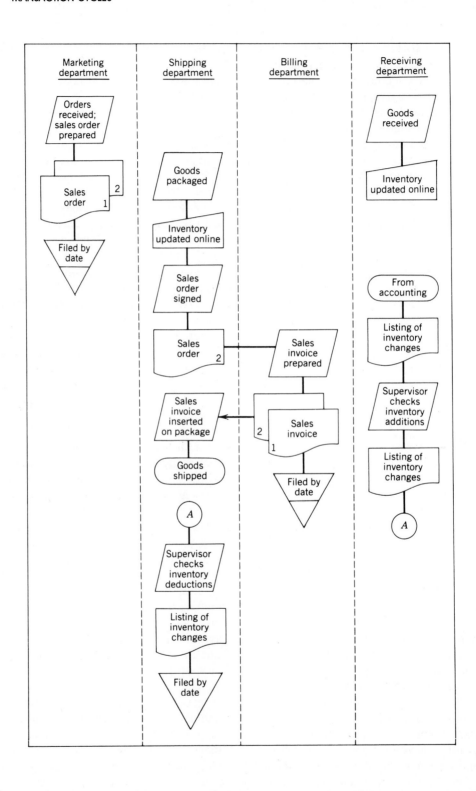

clerks in the receiving department, who are experienced, have been assisting the shipping clerks.

The receiving department is adjacent to the shipping dock, and merchandise is received daily by many different carriers. The clerks share the computer terminal with the shipping department. The date, vendor, and number of items received are entered upon receipt in order to keep the perpetual inventory records current.

Hard copy of the changes in inventory (additions and shipments) is printed once a month. The receiving supervisor makes sure the additions are reasonable and forwards the printout to the shipping supervisor, who is responsible for checking the reasonableness of the deductions from inventory (shipments). The inventory printout is stored in the shipping department by date. A complete inventory list is printed only once a year, when the physical inventory is taken.

The diagram on page 532 represents the document flows employed by OBrien Corporation.

Required

OBrien Corporation's marketing, shipping, billing, and receiving information systems have some weaknesses. For each weakness in the systems:

a. Identify the weakness and describe the potential problem(s) caused by the weakness.

b. Recommend controls or changes in the systems to correct each weakness.

c. List the programmed edit checks that would be suitable when entering data via (1) the shipping department terminal and (2) the receiving department terminal. For each programmed check, specify the data items to which the check pertains.

(CMA adapted)

12-18 VBR Company of Lubbock, Texas, has recently installed a new computer system that has on-line, real-time capability. Cathode ray tube terminals are used for data entry and inquiry. A new cash receipts and accounts receivable file maintenance system has been designed and implemented for use with this new equipment. All programs have been written and tested, and the new system is being run in parallel with the old system. After two weeks of parallel operation, no differences have been observed between the two systems other than keying errors on the old system.

Al Brand, data processing manager, is enthusiastic about the new equipment and system. He reveals that the system was designed, coded, compiled, debugged, and tested by programmers utilizing an on-line CRT terminal installed specifically for around-the-clock use by the programming staff; he has claimed that this access to the computer saved one-third in programming elapsed time. All files, including accounts receivable, are on line at all times as the firm moves toward a full data base mode. All programs, new and old, are available at all times for recall into primary storage for scheduled operating use or for program maintenance. Program documentation and actual tests confirm that data entry edits in the new system include all conventional data error and validity checks appropriate to the system.

Inquiries have confirmed that the new system conforms precisely to the flowchart, part of which appears on page 534. A turnaround copy of the invoice is used as a remittance advice (R/A) by 99 percent of the customers; if the R/A is missing, the cashier applies the payment to a selected invoice. Sales terms are net 60 days, but payment patterns are sporadic. Statements are not mailed to customers. Late payments are commonplace and are not vigorously pursued. VBR does not have a bad-debt program, because

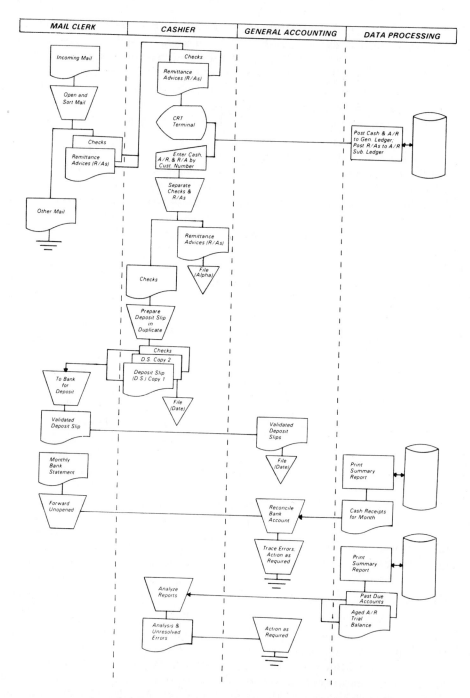

bad-debt losses average only 0.5 percent of sales.

Before authorizing the termination of the old system, Cal Darden, controller, has requested a review of the internal control features that have been designed for the new system. Security against unauthorized access and fraudulent actions, assurance of the integrity of the files, and protection of the firm's assets should be provided by the internal controls.

Required

a. Describe how fraud by lapping of accounts receivable could be committed in the new system, and discuss how it could be prevented.

b. On the basis of the description of VBR Company's new system and the flowchart that has been presented:

  (1) Describe any other defects that exist in the system.

  (2) Suggest how each identified defect could be corrected.

(CMA adapted)

12-19 Until recently, Consolidated Solar Products of Houston employed a batch processing system for recording the receipt of customer payments. The following narrative and the flowchart presented on page 536 describe the procedures involved in this system.

The customer's payment and the remittance advice (a punched card) are received in the treasurer's office. An accounts receivable clerk in the treasurer's office keypunches the cash receipt into the remittance advice and forwards the card to the EDP department. The cash receipt is added to a control tape listing and then filed for deposit later in the day. When the deposit slips are received from EDP later in the day (at approximately 2:30 P.M. each day), the cash receipts are removed from the file and deposited with the original deposit slip. The second copy of the deposit slip and the control tape are compared for accuracy before the deposit is made and then filed together.

In the EDP department, the remittance advices received from the treasurer's office are held until 2:00 P.M. daily. At that time the

customer payments are processed to update the records on magnetic tape and to prepare a deposit slip in triplicate. During the update process, data are read, nondestructively, from the master accounts receivable tape, processed, and then recorded on a new master tape. The original and second copy of the deposit slip are forwarded to the treasurer's office. The old master tape (former accounts receivable file), the remittance advices (in customer number order), and the third copy of the deposit slip are stored and filed in a secure place. The updated accounts receivable master tape is maintained in the system for processing the next day.

The firm has revised and redesigned its computer system so that it has on-line capabilities. The new cash receipts procedures, described next, are designed to take advantage of the new system.

The customer's payment and remittance advice are received in the treasurer's office, as before. A cathode ray tube terminal is located in the treasurer's office to enter the cash receipts. An operator keys in the customer's number and payment from the remittance advice and check. The cash receipt is entered into the system once the operator has confirmed that the proper account and amount are displayed on the screen. The payment is then processed on-line against the accounts receivable file maintained on magnetic disk. The cash receipts are filed for deposit later in the day. The remittance advices are filed in the order they are processed; these punched cards will be kept until the next working day and then destroyed. The computer prints out a deposit slip in duplicate at 2:00 P.M. for all cash receipts since the last deposit. The deposit slips are forwarded to the treasurer's office. The cash receipts are removed from the file and deposited with the original deposit slip; the duplicate deposit slip is filed for further reference. At the close of business hours (5:00 P.M.) each day, the EDP department prepares a record of the current day's cash receipts ac-

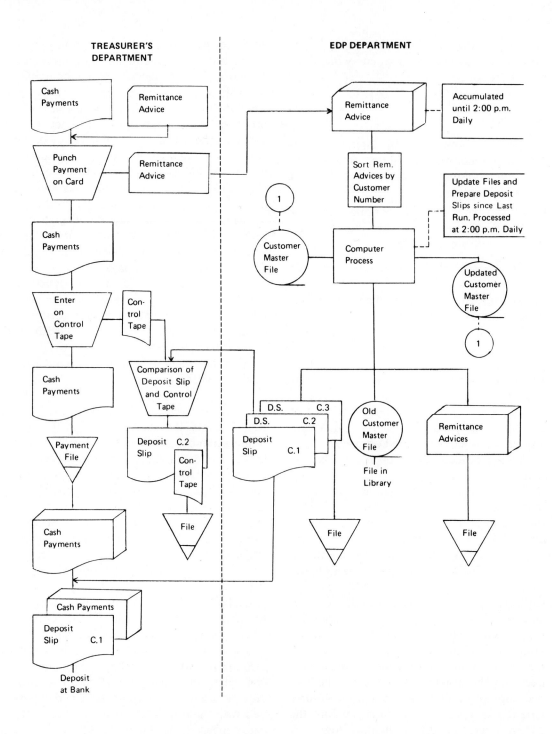

tivity on a magnetic tape. This tape is then stored in a secure place in the event of a systems malfunction; after 10 working days the tape is released for further use.

Required

Prepare a computer system flowchart of the firm's new on-line cash receipts procedure.

(CMA adapted)

12-20 Universal Floor Covering is a manufacturer and distributor of carpet and vinyl floor coverings. The home office is located in Charlotte, North Carolina. Carpet mills are located in Dalton, Georgia, and Greenville, South Carolina; a floor-covering manufacturing plant is in High Point, North Carolina. Total sales last year were just over $250 million.

The company manufactures over 200 different varieties of carpet. The carpet is classified as being for commercial or residential purposes and is sold under five brand names with up to five lines under each brand. The lines indicate the different grades of quality; grades are measured by type of tuft and number of tufts per square inch. Each line of carpet can have up to 15 different color styles.

Just under 200 varieties of vinyl floor covering are manufactured. The floor covering is also classified as being for commercial or residential use. There are four separate brand names (largely distinguished by the type of finish), up to eight different patterns for each brand, and up to eight color styles for each pattern.

Ten different grades of padding are manufactured. The padding is usually differentiated by intended use (commercial or residential) in addition to thickness and composition of materials.

Universal serves over 2000 regular wholesale customers. Retail showrooms are the primary customers. Many major corporations are direct buyers of Universal's products. Large construction companies have contracts with Universal to purchase carpet and floor covering at reduced rates for use in newly constructed homes and commercial buildings. In addition, Universal produces a line of residential carpet for a large national retail chain. Sales to these customers range from $10,000 to $1,000,000 annually.

There is a company-owned retail outlet at each plant. The outlets carry overruns, seconds, and discontinued items. This is Universal's only retail sales function.

The company has divided the sales market into seven territories, with the largest concentration on the East Coast. The market segments are New England, New York, Mid-Atlantic, Carolinas, South, Midwest, and West. Each sales territory is divided into 5 to 10 districts with a salesperson assigned to each district.

The current accounting system has been adequate for monitoring the sales by product. However, there are limitations to the system because specific information is sometimes not available. A detailed analysis of operations is necessary for planning and control purposes and would be valuable for decision-making purposes. The accounting system department has been asked to design a sales analysis code. The code should permit Universal to prepare a sales analysis that would reflect the characteristics of the company's business.

Required

a. Develop a group code for customers, assuming that all sales are for credit.

b. Develop a coding system for Universal Floor Covering which would assign sales analysis codes to sales transactions. For each portion of the code:

   (1) Explain the meaning and purpose of the field.

(2) Identify and justify the number of digits required.

(CMA adapted)

12-21 Thistle Co. of Berkeley, California, manufactures and sells 10 major product lines. About 25 items, on the average, are in each product line. All sales are made on credit, and orders are received by mail or telephone. The firm's transaction processing systems are computer based, with all active files maintained on magnetic disks.

All orders received during regular working hours are entered immediately by sales order clerks via video display terminals. Orders are first edited by an edit program. A second program (a) checks for credit acceptability by reference to the accounts receivable file and (b) checks for product availability by reference to the finished-goods inventory file. Outputs from this program for accepted orders are shipping notices and packing slips plus a sales order transaction file on magnetic disk. (If on-hand quantities are short of the ordered quantities, back-order cards are prepared. These cards are sent to the production planning department to initiate production of needed quantities.) The shipping notices and packing slips are sent to the warehouse.

After the products are shipped, with packing slips enclosed, the shipping notices are initialed (to verify shipments) and forwarded to the billing department. Billing clerks enter the data from the shipping notices via video display terminals. The shipping transaction data—consisting of the customer number, product number, and quantities shipped—are edited and stored temporarily.

At 7 P.M. that evening the shipping transaction data for the day are processed as a batch by a series of runs under the guidance of processing programs. First, batch totals are computed and printed on an exception and summary report. Next the data are

sorted by customer number. Then the transactions are processed to update the records in the accounts receivable file. Sales invoices are generated during this update run; the originals are mailed to customers, and copies are stored in an on-line sales invoice file. Batch totals are verified on an exception and summary report. Next, the same data are re-sorted by product number and processed sequentially to update the records in the finished-goods inventory file. A listing of products shipped and on back order is also generated during this second update run for the sales manager. Batch totals are again verified, and a copy of the exception and summary report is sent to the general ledger clerk.

Inquiries concerning the quantities of products on hand and on back order, as well as those concerning the customers' current account balances, are frequently entered via their video display terminals by sales order clerks and accounting clerks.

At the end of each month a sales summary and analysis is prepared for the sales manager. Monthly statements are also prepared and mailed to customers. Furthermore, an aging analysis of accounts receivable is prepared for the credit manager.

Each record in the accounts receivable master file contains the customer's account number, customer's name and address, credit rating, invoice numbers and dates and amounts of all sales, remittance numbers and dates and amounts of all payments, and account balance.

Each record in the finished-goods inventory master file contains the product number, description, reorder point, units on back order, selling price, and units on hand.

Required

Prepare a computer system flowchart consisting of the following segments:

a. The on-line entry and initial processing of sales orders.

b. The on-line entry and nightly batch processing of shipping data.

c. On-line inquiries.

d. The monthly preparation of reports and statements from the master files.

Hint: The flowchart segments described in **a** and **b** may be prepared in columnar fashion akin to document flowcharts.

12-22 Value Clothing is a large Atlanta distributor of all types of clothing acquired from buyouts, overstocks, and factory seconds. All sales are on account with terms of net 30 days from date of monthly statement. The numbers of delinquent accounts and uncollectible accounts have increased significantly during the last 12 months. Management has determined that the information generated from the present accounts receivable system is inadequate and untimely. In addition, customers frequently complain of errors in their accounts.

The current accounts receivable system has not been changed since Value Clothing started its operations. A new computer was acquired 18 months ago, but no attempt has been made to revise the accounts receivable application, because other applications were considered more important. The work schedule in the systems department has slackened slightly, enabling the staff to design a new accounts receivable system. Top management has requested that the new system satisfy the following objectives:

a. Produce current and timely reports regarding customers which would provide useful information to

    (1) Aid in controlling bad debts.

    (2) Notify the sales department of customer accounts that are delinquent (accounts that should lose charge privileges).

    (3) Notify the sales department of customers whose accounts are considered uncollectible (accounts that should be closed and written off).

b. Produce timely notices to customers regarding

    (1) Amounts owed to Value Clothing.

    (2) A change of status of their accounts (loss of charge privileges, account closed).

c. Incorporate the necessary procedures and controls to minimize the chance for errors in customers' accounts.

Input data for the system would be taken from four source documents: credit applications, sales invoices, cash payment remittances, and credit memoranda. The accounts receivable master file will be maintained on a machine-readable file by customer account number. The preliminary design of the new accounts receivable system has been completed by the systems department. A brief description of the proposed reports and other output generated by the system follows.

a. Accounts Receivable Register. A daily alphabetical listing of all customers' accounts which shows the balance as of the last statement, activity since the last statement, and account balance.

b. Customer Statements. Monthly statements for each customer showing activity since the last statement and account balance; the top portion of the statement is returned with the payment and serves as the cash payment remittance.

c. Aging Schedule, All Customers. A monthly schedule of all customers with outstanding balances displaying the total amount owed with the total classified into age groups: 0–30 days, 30–60 days,

60–90 days, over 90 days; the schedule includes totals and percentages for each age category.

d. **Aging Schedule, Past Due Customers.** A schedule prepared monthly which includes only those customers whose accounts are past due (i.e., over 30 days outstanding), classified by age. The credit manager uses this schedule to decide which customers will receive delinquent notices, temporary suspension of charge privileges, or have their accounts closed.

e. **Activity Reports.** Monthly reports which show:
   (1) Customers who have not purchased any merchandise for 90 days.
   (2) Customers whose account balances exceed their credit limits.
   (3) Customers whose accounts are delinquent yet who have current sales on account.

f. **Delinquency and Write-Off Register.** A monthly alphabetical listing of customers' accounts which are
   (1) Delinquent.
   (2) Closed.
   These listings show name, account number, and balance. Related notices are prepared and sent to these customers.

g. **Summary Journal Entries.** Entries are prepared monthly to record write-offs to the accounts receivable file.

Required

a. Identify the data that should be captured and stored in the computer-based file records for each customer.

b. Review the proposed reports to be generated by the new accounts receivable system.
   (1) Discuss whether the proposed reports should be adequate to satisfy the objectives enumerated.
   (2) Recommend changes, if any, that should be made in the proposed reporting structure generated by the new accounts receivable system.

(CMA adapted)

12-23 The Sunshine Housewares Company of Evansville, Indiana, is organized on a divisional basis, with each division having profit responsibility. The kitchenwares division has three product lines: utensils, ceramic cookwares, and cutlery. Each product line has a separate markup percentage. The division's 80 salespersons sell the three product lines to department stores, hardware stores, and other retail outlets. Groups of 10 salespersons are assigned to each of eight branch offices. At the end of each day the salespersons submit to their branch offices call reports that show, for each call, the type of outlet visited, the time involved, and the result of the call. At the end of each week they submit a report of expenses based on mileage traveled, telephone calls made, and meals and lodging purchased.

Required

a. Design a salesperson's call report.

b. Design a weekly report for a branch manager that will enable him or her to evaluate the performances of all salespersons within the branch and the levels of expenses incurred. Each salesperson is assigned a weekly quota in terms of sales amounts and contributions to profits. Each branch office has an expense budget that includes office salaries, supplies, and miscellaneous expenses in addition to the expense budgets for the salespersons.

c. Design a monthly report for the general sales manager that will enable her to evaluate the performances of all branch offices in terms of sales, contributions to profits, and expenses incurred. The general sales office incurs the same type of expenses as the branches.

d. Design for the marketing vice-president a monthly report that will enable him to evaluate the performances of all major subordinate units. In addition to the sales manager for the kitchenwares division, other managers reporting to the marketing vice-president are the sales manager for the patio division, the sales manager for the general housewares division, an advertising manager, and a manager of marketing planning. The vice-president's office incurs the expenses noted in **b,** plus office equipment expense.

e. Design a code by which to classify costs incurred by salespersons and organizational units within the marketing function.

f. Design codes for salespersons and products.

12-24 The Broadline Manufacturing Company of Cleveland, Ohio, produces an extensive line of industrial supplies, ranging from drill bits and sockets to air compressors and welders. It markets these supplies through a dozen distributors scattered throughout the eastern part of the United States.

Each distributor, with sole rights within its designated area, ships products directly from its own warehouse to customers who place orders. In turn, Broadline replenishes stocks at the various distributor warehouses from its factory, which is located adjacent to its Cleveland office. Furthermore, Broadline bills the customers, based on shipping notices mailed to the Cleveland office by distributors. The following diagram shows the key paperwork flows:

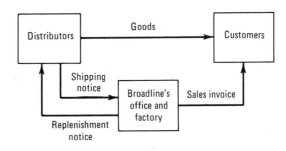

The contents of the documents in the preceding diagram are as follows:

> **Shipping notice,** containing the shipping date; shipping notice number; distributor number; customer number; shipping destination; carrier; freight charges; and, for each item shipped, the item number and quantity.
>
> **Replenishment notice,** containing the date shipped; number of distributor to whom shipped; and, for each item shipped, the item number and quantity.
>
> **Sales invoice,** containing the invoice date; invoice number; shipping date; distributor number; customer number; customer name and address; shipping destination; carrier; terms; and for each item shipped, the item number and quantity and extended amount; freight charges; and total amount.

The files needed to record the inventory flows and to aid in preparing the sales invoices and desired reports are as follows:

> **Inventory master file,** which contains in each record the item number,[4] item description, unit sales price, unit of measure, year-to-date sales, and on-hand quantity.
>
> **Inventory master file by distributor,** which contains in each record the distributor number,[4] item num-

---

[4]Key or keys by which the file is sorted.

ber,[5] replenishment level, year-to-date sales, and on-hand balance.

Accounts receivable master file, which contains in each record the customer number,[5] customer name and address, terms, credit rating, distributor number, year-to-date sales, and current balance. All of these files are maintained in the Cleveland office.

Currently the firm prepares the following reports:

Daily invoice register, which contains columns showing the invoice numbers, invoice date, customer name and address, distributor number, and invoice amount.

Weekly inventory replenishment report, which is arranged by distributor and contains columns showing the distributor number, item number, item description, on-hand balance, and variance above or below the replenishment level.

Monthly inventory status report, which contains columns showing the item number, item description, year-to-date sales, and on-hand quantity.

Processing is performed once each day at the Cleveland office on a tape-oriented computer system. Documents (shipping notices and replenishment notices) are separately batched, totaled, and converted on a key-to-type device; then the transaction data are entered into an edit run, with transactions containing errors or omissions being listed on an exception and summary report, corrected, and reentered the following day. Then the transaction data are sorted as necessary and processed against the master files in successive runs in order to update the records and to prepare the sales invoices and daily invoice register.

[5]Key or keys by which the file is sorted.

Separate report runs are made weekly and monthly to produce the inventory replenishment report and inventory status report, respectively.

This processing procedure has been in existence for several years, but the firm has grown and is currently experiencing troublesome problems. Inventory items are frequently not available at the distributors' warehouses to fill customers' orders. Customers must often wait several days or weeks before the inventory shortages are replenished by the factory. Furthermore, it is necessary to make phone calls and to track down replenishment notices in order to inform customers when they can expect to receive the out-of-stock items. Since competition is severe in the industrial supplies market, customers often turn elsewhere to fill their needs.

Another problem concerns the sheer volume of transactions and the lengths of files. Approximately 2000 transactions are processed daily against files that contain records for 1500 different inventory items and 20,000 customers. Because the processing involves a somewhat complex series of runs, the processing time has become excessive.

Finally, the weekly and monthly reports are outdated much of the time, so that they are generally not useful for control or reference purposes. Moreover, they tend to be so bulky that managers and clerks are discouraged from using them extensively.

Required

a. List all of the items described in the three reports and the sales invoice. Next to each item, list the source (i.e., the specific input document or master file from which it is derived). If the item, such as a date, is produced by the computer system, state "System generated."

b. Prepare a computer system flowchart of the current procedure for processing shipment and inventory transactions. Make the following assumptions: (1) Four items, on average, are involved in each shipment. (2) No inventory is maintained at the Cleveland warehouse. (3) Orders from customers are not filled unless and until sufficient stocks are available at the distributors' warehouses; in other words, partial shipments against orders are *not* made. (4) The three master files are arranged, respectively, by (a) item number, (b) item number within distributor number, and (c) customer number. (It should be noted that the shipping notice, a key transaction document, contains all of these sorting keys. The data contained within the shipping notice must be processed against all three master files. For ease of processing, it is suggested that each shipping notice be split into *two* transaction files. The data in the header portion—from the shipping date through the freight charges—should appear in one of these files. The data in each line of the body—the item number and quantity— should appear in the other file, with the shipping notice number and distributor number "added on." For instance, if there are four items on a shipping notice, four separate segments or records would appear in the latter file, each containing the distributor number, the item number, the shipping notice number, and the quantity.)

c. Design an alternative input and processing approach to replace the current procedure. Include in your design (1) a hardware configuration diagram; (2) a computer system flowchart; (3) formats of several desirable output documents, registers, and reports; and (4) a discussion of the benefits afforded by the newly designed processing system.

Suggested Readings

Accounts Receivable. Atlanta: Management Science America, 1989.

Eliason, Alan I. *Business Information Processing: Technology, Applications, Management*. Palo Alto, Cal.: Science Research Associates, 1980.

Introducing Accounts Receivable. 2d. ed. Atlanta: IBM, 1982.

Nash, John F., and Roberts, Martin B. *Accounting Information Systems*. New York: Macmillan Publishing Co., 1984.

Page, John, and Hooper, Paul. *Accounting Information Systems*. 3rd ed. Englewood Cliffs, N.J.: Prentice-Hall, 1987.

Chapter *13*

THE EXPENDITURE CYCLE

An organization makes expenditures for goods and services. Goods may consist of merchandise, raw materials, parts, subassemblies, supplies, and fixed assets. Services may include those provided by outside parties, such as telephone and legal services, as well as the services provided by the organization's employees. Conceptually all of these goods and services may be encompassed by the **expenditure cycle.** Because the expenditure cycle involves the outflow of funds, it is the counterpoint to the revenue cycle, which provides inflow of funds. The expenditure cycle is necessary to every organization; however, it is especially critical to those, such as many not-for-profit organizations, that have no true revenue cycles.

Most acquired goods and services represent resources to the organization. For instance, merchandise and raw materials and supplies are materials resources, fixed assets

are facilities resources, and hours worked by employees are human service resources. All such resources also fall within the resource management cycle, an activity cycle that is closely related to the expenditure cycle. Because the procedures involving goods and services vary significantly, even within the same firm, we will divide their coverage into two chapters. This chapter focuses on the goods involved in the materials resource, plus outside services; Chapter 14 examines such resources as facilities and employee services.

Overview

Cycle Objectives

The major purpose of the expenditure cycle is to facilitate the exchange of cash with suppliers for needed goods and services. Typical objectives within this broad

544

purpose are (1) to ensure that all goods and services are ordered as needed, (2) to receive all ordered goods and verify that they are in good condition, (3) to safeguard goods until needed, (4) to determine that invoices pertaining to goods and services are valid and correct, (5) to record and classify the expenditures promptly and accurately, (6) to post obligations and cash disbursements to proper suppliers' accounts in the accounts payable ledger, (7) to ensure that all cash disbursements are related to authorized expenditures, (8) to record and classify cash disbursements promptly and accurately, and (9) to prepare all needed documents and managerial reports related to the acquired goods and services.

Functions

In the case of purchases of goods (i.e., merchandise, supplies, or raw materials) the functions of the expenditure cycle consist of recognizing the need for the goods, placing the order, receiving and storing the goods, ascertaining the validity of the payment obligation, preparing the cash disbursement, maintaining the accounts payable, posting transactions to the general ledger, and preparing needed financial reports and other outputs. In the case of services, the functions of receiving and storing the goods are replaced by the function of accepting the or-

dered services. In the case of direct payments by cash (as is done through a petty cash fund), the function of maintaining the payables records is unnecessary. These groups of functions are pictured in Figure 13-1. Each of the aforementioned functions pertaining to the purchase of goods or services is discussed in the following paragraphs.

Recognize the need for goods or services. The need for goods is often triggered by inventory records, which show the on-hand quantity or balance of each inventory item (whether merchandise, supply, or raw material). These records are routinely checked by an inventory clerk or a computer program. When the current balance of an item is seen to have fallen below a preestablished reorder point, the time for reordering has arrived.

Other means of recognizing needs are also employed by most firms. A back-order request from the sales procedure signals the need to place an order for a specific customer. A long-term procurement contract may specify that orders be initiated at regular intervals.

Services may be acquired on a continuing basis (e.g., utilities), on a regular but non-continuing basis (e.g., once-a-year audit service), or on an ad hoc basis (e.g., a systems consulting service). The need for a service is

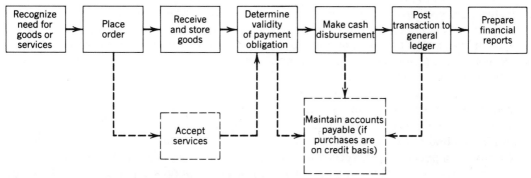

FIGURE 13-1 Typical functions of an expenditure cycle.

generally initiated by the manager of a department, a division, or another organizational unit of the firm. In some cases the need is brought to the attention of such managers by agents who represent the service, such as the salesperson of an office cleaning service.

Place the order for goods or services. When a need is recognized, a legally binding order must be placed with a supplier. Generally the order is not placed by the person or unit that recognizes the need, although exceptions do occur. For instance, a vice-president may sign an agreement with a management consultant concerning an organizational redesign project. Nevertheless, most orders for goods and services are placed through a central purchasing department.

The principal task in placing an order is to select the supplier (also called the vendor). Suppliers of goods are usually selected on the basis of such criteria as comparative unit prices, lead times required before goods are received, and services such as "hot lines." The quality level of goods is an increasingly important consideration in this age of international competition. After the supplier is selected, the specifications concerning unit prices, quality, and other matters are listed in writing.

The tasks of selecting suppliers and stating specifications can be relatively simple. For many items the buyers in the purchasing department search through current catalogs of previously approved suppliers and complete the purchase order forms. However, complications can arise. Consider the situation in which the needed goods are not routinely available and for which there are no established prices. In this situation competitive bids should be obtained. The bidding procedure, which should be set by management policy, usually involves sending a **request for proposal (RFP)** to each of several prospective suppliers. Upon receiving the bids or proposals from those suppliers who respond, the purchasing manager evaluates them by means of a rating procedure. If one of the bids is preferable, it is accepted and the order is placed; if necessary a contract is also signed.

Receive and store goods or accept services. When incoming goods arrive at the receiving dock, they are accepted only if they can be matched to order documents. Next they are unloaded, counted, inspected for damage, and checked to see that all goods conform exactly to specifications in the order. Then they are moved, in accordance with proper controls, to an inventory storeroom or warehouse. (The storeroom as well as the shipping dock should be physically and organizationally separate from the receiving dock.)

If the received goods have been ordered but have certain deficiencies, such as lower-than-specified quality or breakage, they may be accepted on the condition that an allowance be granted by the supplier (vendor). However, if the goods vary so widely from specifications that they are unacceptable, they should be returned.

Received goods and services are generally documented. As goods are counted, they are listed on receiving reports or the receiving department's copy of purchase orders. They also appear on invoices sent by the suppliers. Received services are intangible; thus, they are not reflected on receiving reports. If the service is provided over an extended period of time or if quality is a factor, the receiving firm often prepares a written acceptance or evaluation. If the service is a routine one, such as electrical power service, the bill or invoice from the supplier is sufficient.

Ascertain validity of the payment obligation. Invoices received from suppliers for goods or services are first recorded in a register. This register may be called an invoice register or purchase journal. Each invoice is checked against supporting documents showing that the goods or services were duly ordered and received or accepted. **Vouching,** the term for checking invoices, consists of such steps as (1) tracing all data items (e.g., dates, unit prices, quantities) to the supporting documents, (2) recalculating extensions and totals, and (3) ascertaining payment terms. All questionable items and adjustments are settled with the suppliers. The various charges on invoices are distributed to the proper inventory or expense accounts. Then the invoices are marked "approved for payment" and filed by the dates on which they are to be paid.

Prepare the cash disbursement. In some cases goods and services are payable in cash upon receipt or even in advance. (Payments upon receipt are discussed later.) However, most goods and services are paid on credit terms specified on the invoices, as just suggested. If cash discounts are allowed by the credit terms, the acquiring firm should pay before the end of the discount period. Preferably the firm should also employ the net method of recording purchases. Under this method the invoiced amounts are entered and posted *net* of the allowed purchase discounts; if discounts are missed, they are charged to a "Purchase Discounts Lost" account. Goods and services not subject to discounts should be paid before the due dates stated on the invoices. If goods and services are accepted under contracts calling for progress payments, the conditions specifying the payment points should be carefully monitored.[1]

Checks are prepared on the basis of approved invoices. Then they are given to the person or persons designated by management policy to sign checks. Often these persons are the cashier and/or treasurer. The signer reviews the documents that support each check, signs the check if it is a proper disbursement, and mails the check promptly.

Maintain accounts payable. A firm must keep track of amounts owed to suppliers of goods and services. Two opposing approaches are currently in use.

In the first approach a separate record is maintained for each supplier with which the firm has a credit arrangement. The file containing these records is generally called the supplier or vendor file, although it is in effect the accounts payable subsidiary ledger. Each approved invoice is credited to a supplier's account, and each cash disbursement check is debited to the account. Traditionally the invoices from suppliers have been entered into a purchases journal or invoice register and have been posted directly to the ledger. A variation of this approach is to prepare a disbursement or payment voucher for one or more invoices, to enter it in a voucher register, and to post from the voucher to the ledger.

In the ledgerless approach no formal accounts payable records are maintained during the period. Instead, the unpaid invoices or vouchers are filed and paid when due. At the end of each accounting period all remaining unpaid invoices or vouchers are totaled, and the total amount is posted to the general ledger accounts. A supplier file is kept, but it only contains copies of both the paid and the unpaid invoices (or vouchers).

Post transactions to the general ledger. Summarized payables and cash disbursements transactions are posted to the general ledger. This function represents the interface between the expenditure cycle and the general ledger system or cycle, as discussed in Chapter 11.

Prepare needed financial reports and other outputs. A variety of outputs are gen-

---

[1]Another special situation relates to goods on consignment. When a firm accepts consigned goods, it does not pay for the goods until they are sold. In some cases payments are made by the ultimate customers directly to the supplier and the firm handling the consigned goods receives a fee.

erated as by-products of the aforementioned expenditure cycle functions. Summaries of purchases and disbursements, akin to journal listings, are needed. Useful financial reports include evaluations of suppliers and summaries of open payables. If an on-line computer-based system is employed, displays of individual supplier accounts and other specific information are also available.

Other related functions. Additional functions of interest include payroll disbursements, expense distribution, purchase returns and allowances, miscellaneous cash disbursements, and petty cash disbursements. Payroll disbursements (together with the distribution of employee labor expenses) are discussed in Chapter 14. The remaining functions are briefly discussed in the following paragraphs.

Purchase returns and allowances represent adjustments to the expenditure cycle, as Figure 13-2 shows. They usually arise when the goods are received and inspected or when the invoice is being vouched. Perhaps the supplier sends goods that were not ordered, the goods were damaged en route, or the invoice contains an overcharge. The person who discovers the needed adjustment should notify the purchasing department. A buyer or purchasing manager prepares a prenumbered debit memorandum and forwards it to the accounts payable department. There a clerk pulls the original disbursement voucher (if prepared), the invoice, and supporting documents. After comparing these

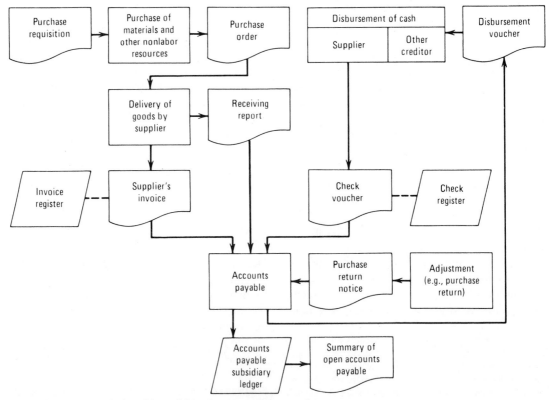

FIGURE 13-2 Relationships within the expenditure cycle.

documents, the clerk prepares a journal voucher to reflect the transaction. Other clerks (or the computer system) post the adjustment to the accounts payable ledger and the general ledger.

In the case of a return copies of the debit memorandum are also sent to the storeroom (or receiving department) and the shipping department. The goods being returned are then released to the shipping department, which counts the goods, notes the count on the debit memorandum, and ships. The shipping department then forwards the debit memorandum to the accounts payable department, which performs the steps just described.

Miscellaneous cash disbursements include amounts paid to acquire fixed assets, to acquire investments or the firm's stock, and to discharge bank loans and mortgages. These disbursements are generally recorded in the cash disbursements journal or check register. They are further discussed in Chapter 14.

Petty cash disbursements consist of payments of currency for small expenses. In effect a petty cash disbursement is a type of miscellaneous disbursement. In order to maintain effective control over these amounts, an **imprest system** is normally used. It begins with the establishment of a petty cash fund at some level (e.g., $500). The fund remains fixed in the general ledger at the established level. However, the currency itself, which is locked in a cash box or drawer, fluctuates in amount during use. One person, who has no other responsibilities related to cash, is assigned to administer the fund. For each disbursement from the fund this petty cash custodian prepares in ink a petty cash voucher, which the payee signs before receiving currency. At all times the total amount of the paid vouchers plus the cash remaining in the box or drawer should equal the established amount of the fund. When the remaining currency reaches a low point, the accounts payable department is re-

quested to prepare a disbursement voucher. The petty cash vouchers are attached to this voucher, together with a prepared check. The authorized check signer reviews the vouchers and signs the check. Then the custodian cashes the check and replenishes the fund. The replenishment check is listed in the check register.

Relationships to the Organization

The expenditure cycle functions are typically achieved under the direction of the inventory management and finance/accounting organizational functions (units) of the firm. Figure 13-3 illustrates these relationships.

The expenditure cycle therefore involves the interaction of the inventory management information system and the accounting information system. Moreover, the results attained and the information generated by the expenditure cycle further the objectives of these organizational functions.

Inventory management. The function of **inventory management,** in the context of a merchandising firm, has the objective of managing the merchandise inventory that the firm acquires for resale. In addition to planning responsibilities, the function is concerned with the physical activities of (1) purchasing, (2) receiving, and (3) storing the merchandise. Figure 13-3 shows corresponding organizational units that report to the vice-president of inventory management. The function of inventory management can be viewed as the major subfunction within the broader logistics function. Also included in the logistics function is the distribution of merchandise to customers, an activity which organizationally may be assigned to the marketing/distribution function.

Purchasing focuses primarily on selecting the most suitable suppliers or vendors from whom to order goods and services. It makes the selections on the basis of such factors as the unit prices charged for the goods

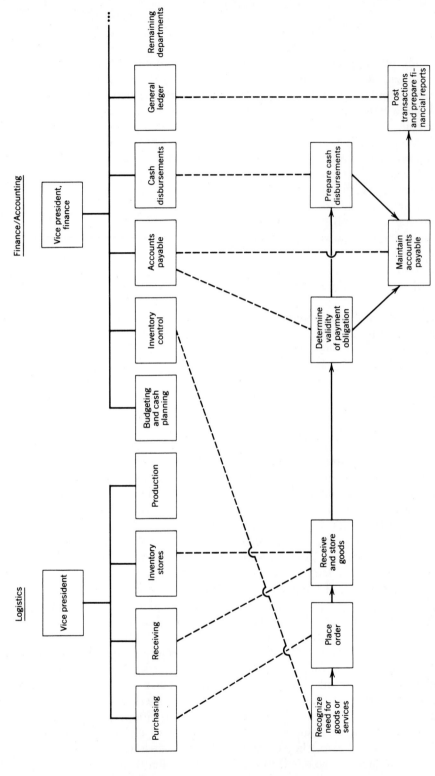

FIGURE 13-3 Relationships of organizational units to expenditure cycle functions.

or services, the quality of the goods or services offered, the terms and promised delivery dates, and the reliability of the supplier. As discussed earlier, it also uses competitive bids when necessary. Together with inventory control, purchasing also ascertains the quantity of goods to acquire. The optimal order quantity is determined by a formula that includes such factors as the expected demand for the goods, the carrying cost, and the ordering cost. However, this formula is normally applied only to the high-cost or high-volume goods. Order quantities for low-cost or low-volume goods are more likely to be determined on a rough basis that seeks to avoid stock-outs. In some cases a good buying opportunity or a price break determines the quantities to order.

Receiving has the responsibilities of accepting only those goods that were ordered, verifying their quantities and condition, and moving the goods to the storeroom. Storing has the responsibilities of safeguarding the goods from theft, loss, and deterioration and of assembling them promptly when proper requisitions or requests are presented. Production's responsibilities are discussed in Chapter 15.

Finance/accounting. The objectives of financial and accounting management relate broadly to funds, data, information, planning, and control over resources. With respect to the expenditure cycle the objectives are limited to cash planning and control, to data pertaining to purchases and suppliers' accounts, to inventory control, and to information pertaining to cash and purchases and suppliers.

As described in Chapter 12, the top financial managers are often the vice-president of finance, the treasurer, and the controller. The treasurer's responsibilities include cash disbursements, whereas the controller's responsibilities include accounts payable. Cash disbursements, an arm of the cashier, prepares checks for disbursement,

and maintains the related records. Accounts payable maintains the records of individual suppliers and approves their invoices for payment. (The other units are described in Chapter 12).

Data Sources and Inputs

Sources

Data used in the expenditure cycle are mainly based on inputs from the inventory records and from suppliers. The inventory records are the primary source of most purchase transactions, whereas supplier invoices are the source of payable/disbursement transactions. Other sources are department heads, buyers, supplier history files, receiving and stores departments, and (in the case of manufacturing firms) the production departments. If payroll disbursements are included within the expenditure cycle, such sources as the personnel and payroll records would be added.

Forms of Input

Manual systems. The expenditure cycle source documents typically found in firms that employ manual processing include

1. **Purchase requisition.** The initiating form in the expenditure cycle is the **purchase requisition.** It provides authorization for the purchasing department to place an order for goods or services. Figure 13-4 shows a prenumbered requisition for goods. Key items of data that it conveys are the quantities and identifications of the goods to be purchased, the date needed, the name of the requestor and department, and the approver's name or initials. Optional data includes the suggested supplier (vendor), suggested unit prices, and shipping instructions. The shaded items in Figure 13-4 are filled in by the purchasing department on the confirmation copy and returned to the requester.

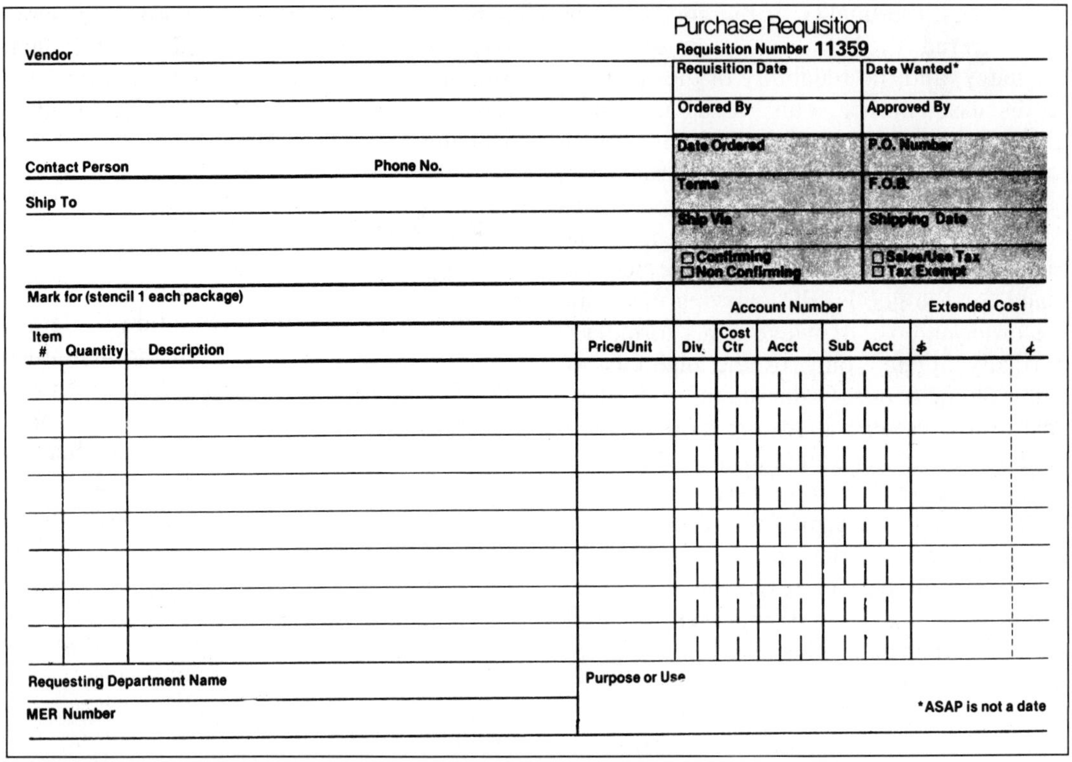

Vendor	Purchase Requisition

Purchase Requisition
Requisition Number **11359**

Requisition Date	Date Wanted*
Ordered By	Approved By
Date Ordered	P.O. Number
Terms	F.O.B.
Ship Via	Shipping Date
□ Confirming □ Non Confirming	□ Sales/Use Tax □ Tax Exempt*

Contact Person   Phone No.

Ship To

Mark for (stencil 1 each package)

Account Number   Extended Cost

Item #	Quantity	Description	Price/Unit	Div.	Cost Ctr	Acct	Sub Acct	$	$

Requesting Department Name

Purpose or Use

MER Number

*ASAP is not a date

FIGURE 13-4 A purchase requisition. Courtesy of Arvin Industries.

2. Purchase order. Figure 13-5 presents a prenumbered **purchase order.** It is a formal document that is signed by an authorized buyer or purchasing manager. If the supplier agrees to all stated terms and conditions on the order, it is binding upon the issuing firm. In addition to the signature area at the bottom of the form, a typical purchase order has two sections: a heading and a body. The heading contains the supplier's name and address, shipping instructions, and reference items. The body contains one or more line items, each of which pertains to a single item of merchandise or material being ordered. Although unit prices for the various line items are included, cost extensions are not normally provided because the unit prices are tentative.

A purchase order is usually prepared as a multiple-copy form, with copies being sent to the supplier, to receiving, to accounts payable, and to inventory control.

3. Receiving report. A prenumbered document prepared by a clerk in the receiving department is called a **receiving report** (or record, memorandum, or ticket). Figure 13-6 shows an example. This document provides proof that the listed quantities of goods have been received and indicates their condition. It is used to reflect the receipt of any goods, such as goods on consignment or goods returned by a dissatisfied customer. However, most receipts of goods—and receiving reports—relate to issued purchase orders. A copy of the receiving report usually accompa-

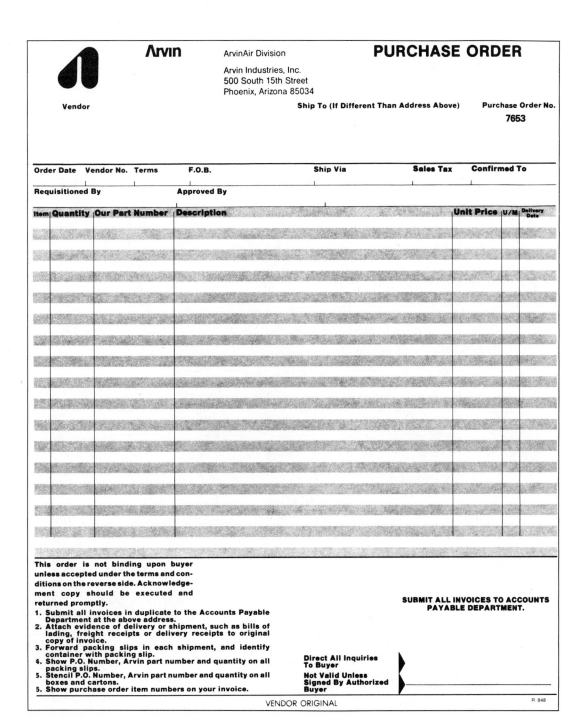

FIGURE 13-5 A purchase order. Courtesy of Arvin Industries.

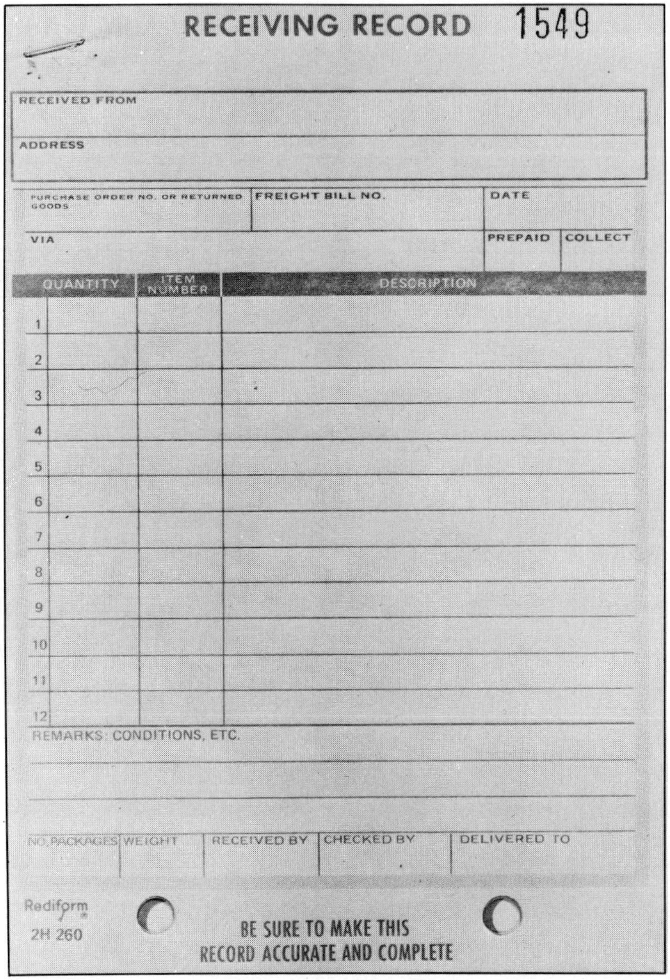

RECEIVING RECORD 1549

RECEIVED FROM

ADDRESS

PURCHASE ORDER NO. OR RETURNED GOODS	FREIGHT BILL NO.	DATE	
VIA		PREPAID	COLLECT

	QUANTITY	ITEM NUMBER	DESCRIPTION
1			
2			
3			
4			
5			
6			
7			
8			
9			
10			
11			
12			

REMARKS: CONDITIONS, ETC.

NO. PACKAGES	WEIGHT	RECEIVED BY	CHECKED BY	DELIVERED TO

Rediform
2H 260

BE SURE TO MAKE THIS
RECORD ACCURATE AND COMPLETE

FIGURE 13-6 A receiving report or record.

nies the goods to the storeroom and then is forwarded to accounts payable.

4. **Supplier's (vendor's) invoice.** To the buying firm, a **supplier's invoice** is a response to a previously issued purchase order. To the supplier, it is a sales invoice akin to the document discussed in Chapter 12. For an example, see Figure 12-10.

5. **Disbursement voucher.** A **disbursement voucher** is prepared when the widely popular **voucher system** is used. As Figure 13-7 illustrates, a voucher is generated when one or more invoices are received from a supplier. It is entered in a **voucher register,** which serves as a journal. Then the voucher may be used as the medium for posting to the accounts payable ledger, if one is maintained. Totals from the voucher register are posted to the general ledger. As the columns in the voucher register indicate, miscellaneous disburse-

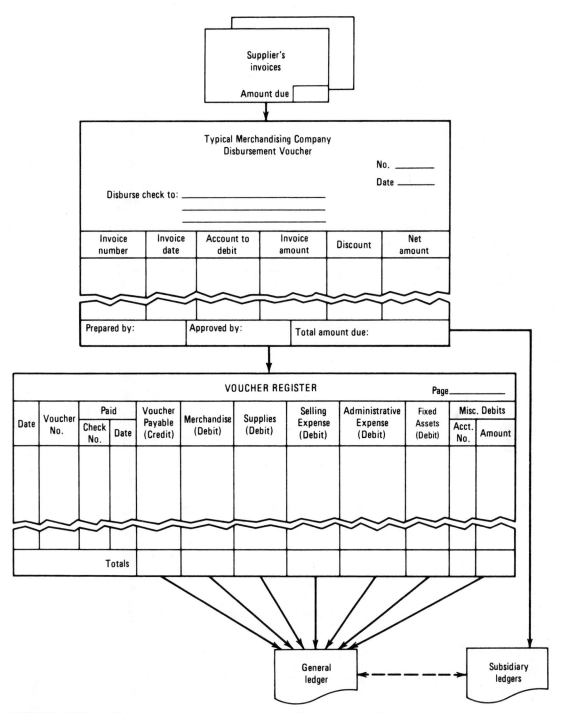

FIGURE 13-7 A disbursement voucher, together with key accounting records used in the voucher system.

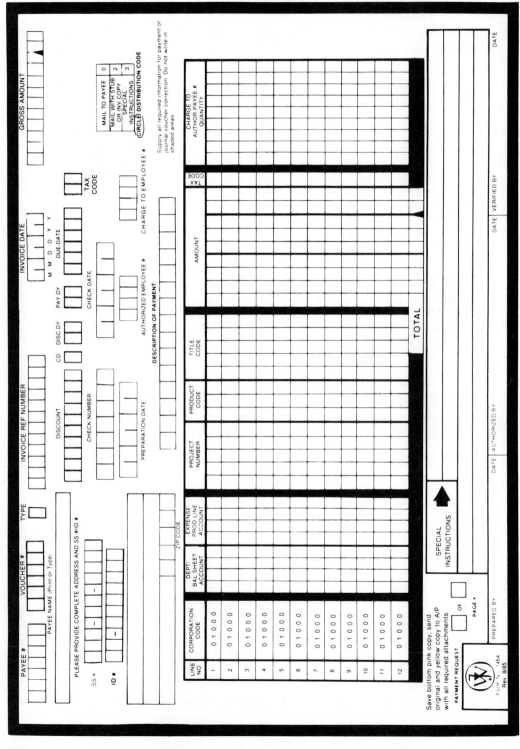

FIGURE 13-8 A voucher or payment request used in a publishing organization. Courtesy of John Wiley & Sons, Inc.

ments as well as disbursements to suppliers may be encompassed within the voucher system.

Vouchers may assume a wide variety of forms, since they must fit the needs of different types of organizations. Figure 13-8 shows a voucher (called a payment request) that is used by a book publisher. Forms that itemize claims for expenses incurred also represent a type of voucher.

A disbursement voucher offers several advantages. It allows several invoices to be accumulated, thereby reducing the number of checks to be written. Because it is prenumbered, the voucher provides numerical control over the payables. Finally, it provides a convenient means for grouping and vouching documents (i.e., the invoices, purchase orders, and receiving reports) together into a package and reflecting the approval for payment.

6. **Check voucher.** A disbursement check is the final document in the expenditure cycle. Usually the check has an attachment, which in effect is a copy or abbreviated version of the voucher. Figure 13-9 shows a check with attached voucher,

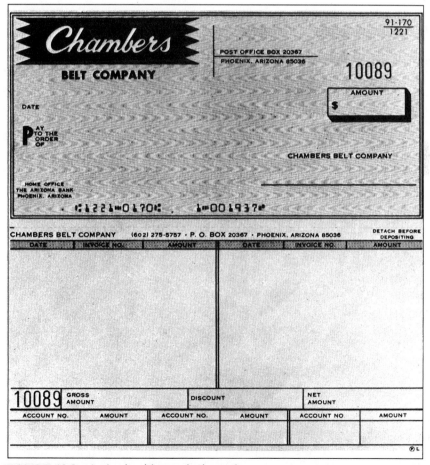

FIGURE 13-9 A check with attached voucher.

called a **check voucher.** (In some systems the check voucher is prepared in lieu of the disbursement voucher.)

The check is signed by an authorized signer. In some cases, as when the amounts are large, it may be countersigned. Then it is entered in a cash disbursements journal or check register.

7. **Other documents.** A *new supplier (vendor) form* is useful in the selection of new suppliers. It contains such data as prices or rates, types of goods or services provided, experience, credit standing, and references. A *request for proposal (or for quotation)* is a form used during a competitive bidding procedure. It lists the various goods or services needed and provides columns into which the bidding suppliers are to enter their proposed prices, terms, and so on. A *bill of lading* generally accompanies received goods. (See Chapter 12 for details.) A **debit memorandum** is prepared when a purchase return or allowance is granted. Finally, a *journal voucher* is prepared as the basis for each posting to the general ledger. For instance, a journal voucher is prepared from the debit memorandum.

Computer-based systems. All of the aforementioned hard-copy documents may also be used in computer-based systems. In some cases, however, they may be generated automatically upon the entry of data via terminals or microcomputers. Moreover, some of the source documents, such as the one shown in Figure 13-8, may be designed to aid the entry of data into the computer system with fewer errors.

Preformatted screens may be used to enter data concerning purchases, payables, purchase returns, and cash disbursement transactions. These screens, like simplified entry forms, may be designed to handle individual transactions or batches of transactions.

Codes

Codes can aid the entry of purchases and cash disbursements transactions. In addition to codes for general ledger accounts, codes can be entered for suppliers, purchase orders, products, buyers, purchase contracts, and so on. When such codes are employed, various purchase analyses can be performed.

Group codes are useful when recording such transactions as purchases, since they encompass several dimensions. They may also be used to represent such entities as products, suppliers, and buyers. A product code for a battery sold by a retail chain, for instance, might include such fields as the following:

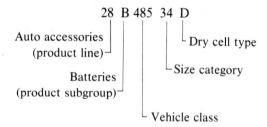

Data Base

The following master, transaction, history, and reference files are representative of the expenditure cycle data base for a firm that purchases merchandise for resale. Of course, the exact number and content of the files will vary from firm to firm, depending on such factors as types of suppliers and sources of services, variety of desired managerial reports, degree of computerization, and structure of the data base. For instance, a firm that employs the computer-based data base approach, discussed in Chapter 18, will use a different set of files and data structures.

Our survey of the data base is necessarily brief. A more complete description would include a data dictionary such as shown in Figure 8-8 and additional record layouts.

Supplier account number	Supplier name	Mailing address	Phone number	Credit terms	Year-to-date purchases, in total	Year-to-date payments, in total	Current account balance

FIGURE 13-10 A layout of a supplier (vendor) record. *Note:* Although the lengths of fields and modes of data items are necessary for complete documentation, they have been omitted for the sake of simplicity.

Supplier (Vendor) Master File

A supplier master file is vital to the expenditure cycle, since it specifies where the checks for suppliers are to be mailed. In many firms it also serves as the accounts payable subsidiary ledger by showing the amount currently owed to each supplier. Figure 13-10 presents a layout of the data items that may usefully appear in a supplier file. Generally the primary and sorting key of the file is the supplier number.

An important concern with this file, as with the inventory master file, is keeping the records and their permanent data up to date. When a supplier obtains a new mailing address, for instance, this change must be quickly reflected in the record. When a new supplier is added to the approved supplier list, a new record should appear in the file; when a supplier is dropped, the corresponding record should be deleted also. These changes can be made during the processing of payables, or they may be made at other times as they arise.

Merchandise Inventory Master File

The merchandise inventory master file is essentially the same file discussed in Chapter 12. If the firm is a manufacturer, the file will be called the raw materials inventory master file. Some firms also maintain a separate file of supplies.

Open Purchase Order File

An open purchase order file consists of copies of issued purchase orders pertaining to purchases that have not yet been approved for payment. In both manual and computer-based systems the printed copies contain data items such as shown in Figure 13-5. In a computer-based systems a record of each order is also stored on magnetic media, with the primary and sorting key usually being the purchase order number. The record layout should allow for such repeating line items as item number, quantity ordered, and expected unit price; alternatively, they can be placed in a separate line-item file and cross-referenced.[2] Such items as supplier names and item descriptions may be omitted, however, since they can be drawn from the supplier and inventory master files when preparing the vouchers and checks.

Open Voucher File

In a manual system an open voucher file consists of copies of the disbursement vouchers. (If vouchers are not prepared, the file would be replaced by an open invoice file.) Thus, the primary and sorting key is normally the voucher number. Most of the data items pertain to the supplier's invoice, although cross-references to the purchase order, requisition, and receiving report may also appear. In a computer-based system only a few key items may be stored on magnetic media, since the hard copies of the invoice and supporting documents are kept in an accessible file. A record in this file is closed when the payment is made.

---

[2] A line-item file is also called a purchase order detail file.

Check Disbursements Transaction File

In a manual system a check disbursements transaction file consists of a copy of each current check voucher, arranged in check number order. In a computer-based system the record layout on magnetic media may contain the supplier's account number, related purchase order number(s), date of payment, and amount of payment. It also includes a code to identify the record as a cash disbursement transaction.

Other Transaction Files

In addition to the basic purchase and cash disbursements files, the expenditure cycle data base will likely include a purchase requisition file, a receiving report file, and a debit memo file.

Supplier Reference and History File

A supplier reference and history file contains summary data pertaining to each active supplier. Included are evaluations based on the relevant factors noted earlier, plus a history of the past purchases. Data from this file are used to select suppliers with which to place orders and to analyze purchasing trends.

Data Flows and Processing

Within the expenditure cycle the data flows and processing steps can be divided into three major subsets: processing of purchases transactions, establishment of accounts payable, and processing of cash disbursements. Each of these subsets can be examined through system flowcharts for manual and computer-based processing procedures.

Manual Processing Systems

Purchases procedure. Figure 13-11 presents a system flowchart of a procedure involving the purchases of goods on credit. Since the processing is performed manually, the emphasis is upon the flows of source documents and outputs. Thus, this flowchart provides a good introduction to processing within the expenditure cycle. However, it is quite detailed and therefore imposing. A simpler version of purchasing steps was offered in Figure 7-24 as an illustration of the flowcharting technique. You might review that flowchart before reading the following paragraphs.

The first step in the procedure for purchasing goods takes place in the inventory control department. There an accounting clerk determines that goods are needed and prepares a purchase requisition. Upon approval of the requisition, perhaps by the inventory manager, copies are sent to the purchasing department and receiving department.

In the purchasing department a buyer is assigned by the purchasing manager to handle the requisition. If the goods or circumstances are nonroutine, competitive bids are obtained. If the needed goods are routine (or after bids have been evaluated), the buyer selects the most suitable supplier and prepares a purchase order. When the purchase order is signed by an authorized person, such as the purchasing manager, two copies of it are mailed to the supplier. Other copies are forwarded to the inventory control, receiving, and accounts payable departments. The copy sent to inventory control (which actually may be an amended copy of the requisition) is used to post ordered quantities to the inventory records. The copy for the receiving department (which has the quantities blanked out, i.e., is "blind") is used later to verify the authenticity of the received goods. The copy sent to accounts payable is to provide prior notification that an invoice is soon to be received. The last copy is filed in the open purchase order file to await the arrival of the invoice.

When the ordered goods arrive at the receiving dock, the "blind" copy of the purchase order is matched to the packing slip (and the bill of lading, if one is received). Next the receiving clerk inspects the goods for damage and counts the quantities received. Then he or she prepares a receiving report upon which the findings are recorded. The original copy of this report accompanies the goods to stores, where the storeskeeper or warehouseman signs the copy (to acknowledge receipt) and forwards it to accounts payable. Other copies of the receiving report are sent to the purchasing department (to update the open purchase order) and to the inventory control department (to update the inventory records).

When the supplier's invoice arrives, shortly after the ordered goods, it is routed to the purchasing department for comparisons with the relevant documents pertaining to the order. If found to be proper and complete, it is forwarded to the accounts payable department and combined with other copies of the relevant documents. (Many firms bypass the purchasing department and route the invoice directly to accounts payable.)

Accounts payable procedure. Whether or not the purchasing department reviews the invoice, a careful vouching by the accounts payable department is highly desirable. Since accounts payable is an accounting department not directly involved in purchasing and receiving goods, its review serves as an independent verification of these activities.

Figure 13-12 illustrates the processing of invoices that lead to payables. Invoices pertaining to services as well as to purchases of goods are included in this processing. However, the former are first routed to the using departments, where they are approved for payment by the managers responsible for incurring the expenditures.

Upon receiving each invoice in the accounts payable department, a clerk pulls the supporting documents from a file and performs various comparisons and checks. These verifications are intended to determine that (1) the purchase has been authorized, (2) the goods or services listed in the invoice have been duly ordered, (3) the goods or services have been received in full, (4) the unit prices are in conformity with the purchase order or are satisfactory to the purchasing department, (5) the terms and other specifications are in agreement with the purchase order, and (6) all computations are correct. After finishing, the clerk initials an audit box (stamped either on the invoice or on another document such as a voucher) to acknowledge that the verifications have been performed. Any differences must be settled before the invoice can be approved for payment. For instance, if only part of the order is received, the purchase order should be so marked and returned to the file.

When the voucher system is used, as described earlier, a disbursement voucher is prepared on the basis of one or more approved suppliers' invoices. Then the voucher is entered in a voucher register. Batch control totals are computed from the columns in the voucher register, including the total amount of payables, the total merchandise cost, the total selling expense, and so on. A journal voucher is prepared from these totals.

A clerk posts the vouchers to the suppliers' accounts in the accounts payable subsidiary ledger. Batch totals of the posted credits are computed. Also, copies of the vouchers are forwarded to accounting departments that maintain the ledgers relating to the various expenditures (labeled in the flowchart as inventory/expense control). Clerks in these departments post debits to inventory, supplies, fixed assets, selling expense, and administrative expense ledgers. Batch totals of the posted debits are computed. Then the batch totals of the posted debits and credits are compared to the journal voucher previously prepared. If all amounts agree, the entry is posted to the accounts in the general ledger.

Finally, the originals of the vouchers, together with the supporting documents, are

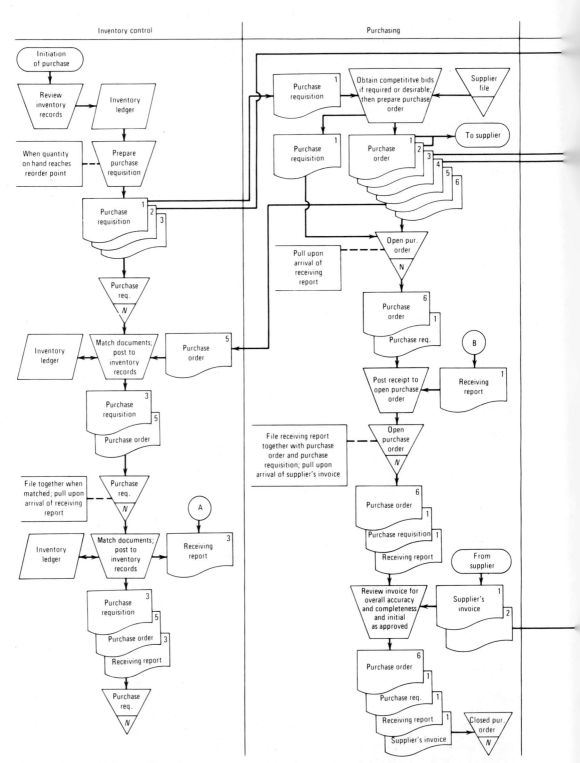

FIGURE 13-11 System flowchart of a manual purchases transaction processing procedure, with an emphasis on document flows.

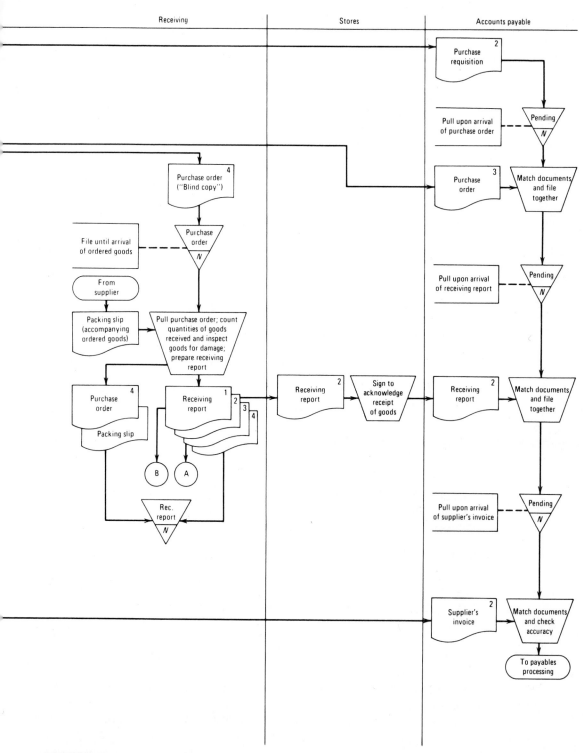

FIGURE 13-11 (*Continued*).

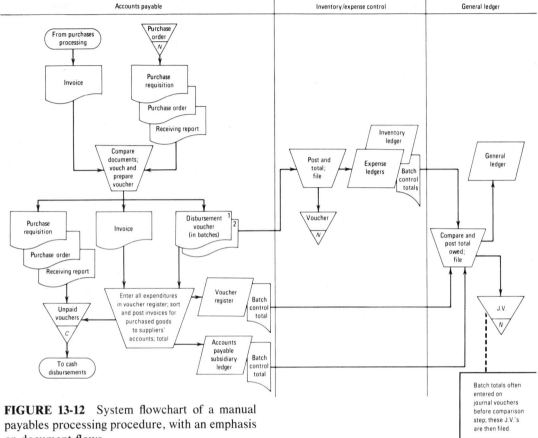

FIGURE 13-12 System flowchart of a manual payables processing procedure, with an emphasis on document flows.

filed in a tickler arranged by payment due dates. There the unpaid vouchers are ready for use in cash disbursements processing.

Cash disbursements procedure. Figure 13-13 shows a flowchart of a procedure involving the disbursements of cash related to purchases on credit. This particular procedure begins in the accounts payable department with the unpaid voucher file. Each day (or at specified periods) a clerk extracts the unpaid vouchers due to be paid that day. After computing the total amount to be paid and posting the amounts of the vouchers to the appropriate suppliers' accounts, the clerk forwards the vouchers and supporting

documents to the cash disbursements department.

A cash disbursements clerk inspects each voucher for completeness and authenticity and then prepares a prenumbered check. When done, the clerk submits the checks to an authorized check signer (e.g., the cashier). This person reviews the supporting documents, signs each check that is properly supported, and routes the checks directly to the mailroom. From the mailroom the checks are delivered to the post office.

Checks are entered in a check register, and the total of the paid amounts is computed. A journal voucher is prepared on the basis of this total and sent to the general ledger department. If the amount in the journal voucher agrees with the total debits posted to the accounts payable ledger, the entry is posted to the accounts in the general ledger.

The cash disbursements clerk stamps all supporting documents as paid and staples them to the disbursement and check vouchers. Then these voucher packages are returned to the accounts payable department, where the number of each check and date are entered in the voucher register. Finally, the voucher packages are filed alphabetically by supplier (or in a closed payables file).

Firms that process large volumes of invoices often find that the bulky voucher packages consume much storage space and are awkward to retrieve for later reference. Thus, they may decide to microfilm the documents after processing and then to destroy the documents. The microfilm images may be arranged by voucher numbers and cross-referenced to supplier names.[3]

Computer-Based Processing Systems

When computer-based systems are used, purchases and cash disbursements transactions may be processed by the batch approach, by the on-line approach, or by a combination of the batch and on-line approaches. In our examples the on-line approach is used for purchases, the combined approach for payables, and the batch approach for cash disbursements.

Purchases procedure. As you may recall, several system flowcharts were presented in Chapter 7 to illustrate the flowcharting technique. For the purchases procedure we will refer to Figure 7-28, which shows the on-line approach to processing. (You may find Fig-

ure 7-27, which shows the contrasting batch approach, useful as well.)

In the first step the inventory records are checked to find those items whose on-hand quantities have been drawn below their reorder points. This step may be performed when batches of sales transactions are being processed to update the inventory master file. If back orders are prepared and processed, they could also be an input to this step.

The output from this first step is an inventory reorder list, which is in effect a batch of purchase requisitions. After being approved by an inventory control manager, the list is sent to the purchasing department. Buyers are assigned the various items on the list. By making inquiries of an on-line supplier reference file, which contains evaluation data, the buyers select suitable suppliers and enter their relevant data (e.g., names and numbers) on the list. Then they enter the data needed to prepare purchase orders into their video terminals. Upon being validated by an edit program, the purchase order data are stored temporarily in a purchase transaction file.

In step 3 a purchase order, based on data from the transaction file as well as the supplier and inventory master files, is printed. The computer system automatically assigns a number to the purchase order and dates it. A copy of the purchase order is placed in the on-line open purchase order file, and a notation of the order is placed in the appropriate record(s) of the inventory master file. The purchasing manager or another authorized signer reviews the purchase order. If he or she approves and signs the order, it is mailed to the supplier. If revisions are necessary, the buyer retrieves the purchase transaction data via the terminal, makes the changes, and prints a revised purchase order.

At the end of the day a listing of the day's purchase orders is printed. Other re-

[3]John F. Guldig, "Redesigning Accounts Payable," *Management Accounting* (September 1983), pp. 42–46.

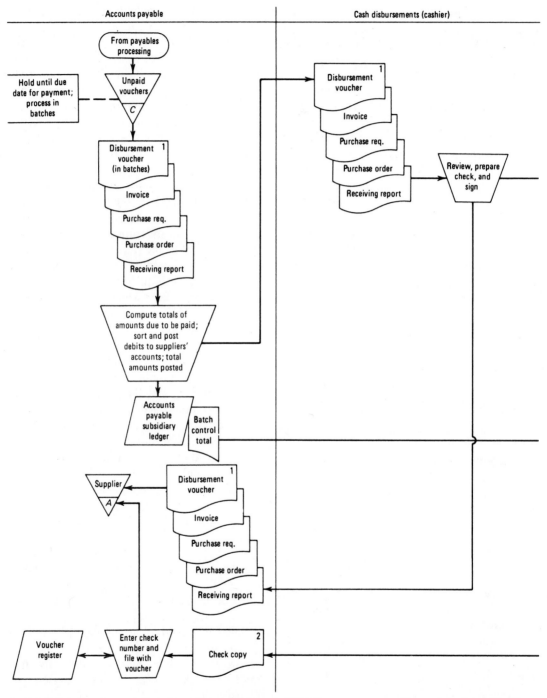

FIGURE 13-13 System flowchart of a manual cash disbursements transaction processing procedure, with an emphasis on document flows.

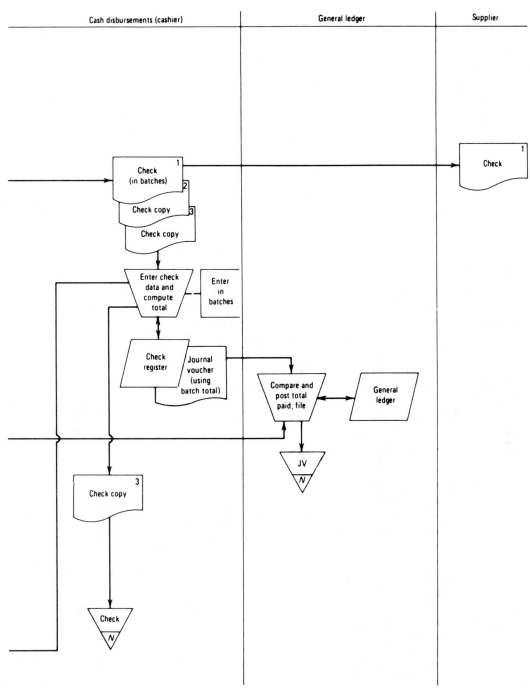

FIGURE 13-13 (*Continued*).

ports, such as an inventory status report, may also be generated.

Receiving procedure. Figure 13-14 shows a system flowchart of an on-line receiving procedure. A clerk in the receiving department first counts and inspects the received goods. Then he or she keys the count and inventory item numbers into a departmental terminal, together with the related purchase order number listed on the packing slip. A receiving program checks the entered data against the on-line open purchase order file. Any differences between the ordered quantities and the counted quantities are displayed on the terminal screen. Also, if no matching purchase order number is found in the on-line file, an alerting message is displayed.

Assuming that the goods are accepted, the program prints a prenumbered receiving report. A copy of this report accompanies the goods to the stores department to be signed and forwarded to the accounts payable department. The receiving program also (1) updates the inventory master file, increasing the on-hand quantity and eliminating the quantity on order, (2) notes the quantity received in the open purchase order file, and (3) notes the date of receipt in the supplier history file. If a back-order is involved, the back order record is flagged.

Inventory maintenance procedure. Figure 13-15 presents a system flowchart that pertains to the maintenance of the inventory records. It draws together the processing activities that affect the inventory master file, namely, purchase ordering, receipts of ordered goods, shipping of goods to customers, and returns of goods. The flowchart also emphasizes the variety of reports that can be provided from several files that are related to inventory processing.

Payables procedure. Figure 13-16 portrays a system flowchart of a combined on-line/batch payables procedure. As invoices are received from suppliers, an accounts receivable clerk performs a visual check for completeness, pulls the related receiving reports, and then computes a batch control total based on the invoice amounts. He or she enters into a terminal the batch total, plus key data items from each invoice. An edit program validates the entered data, checks the quantities against those in the open purchase order file, recomputes the batch totals, and displays any differences. Then the batched transaction data are stored until a designated processing time (e.g., end of the day).

When the processing time arrives, an accounts payable posting program updates each record in the supplier master file (i.e., accounts payable subsidiary ledger) that is affected by an invoice. No sorting is necessary, since the program accesses and retrieves each supplier record directly from its location in the file. Then the program adds the amount of the invoice to the balance in the account. If all of the quantities pertaining to the related purchase order have been received, it also closes the purchase order and transfers its record to the supplier history file.

A variety of outputs are generated during this posting of the supplier master file. Prenumbered disbursement vouchers are printed, one copy being filed together with the supporting documents in an unpaid vouchers file. A voucher register is printed to provide a key part of the audit trail. Summaries of the vouchers are added to the on-line open vouchers file. The debits from the summary vouchers are accumulated by account number; the totals are then compiled by the program into a sequentially numbered journal voucher and added to the journal voucher transaction file (or are posted immediately to the accounts in the general ledger). A total of the invoice amounts is also computed by the program and displayed on a terminal in the

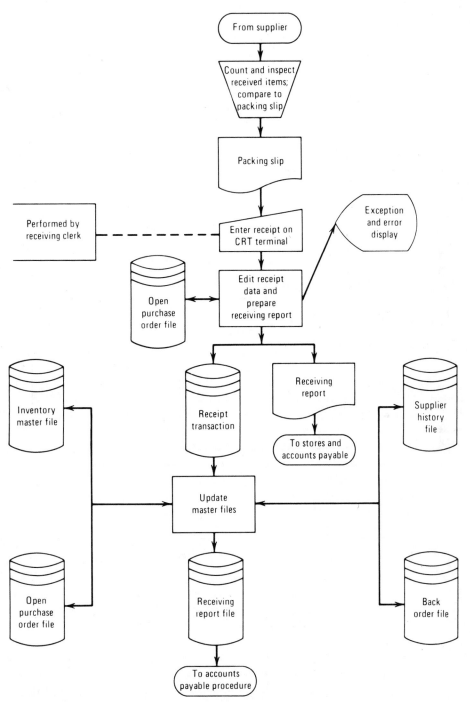

FIGURE 13-14 System flowchart of an on-line computer-based receiving procedure.

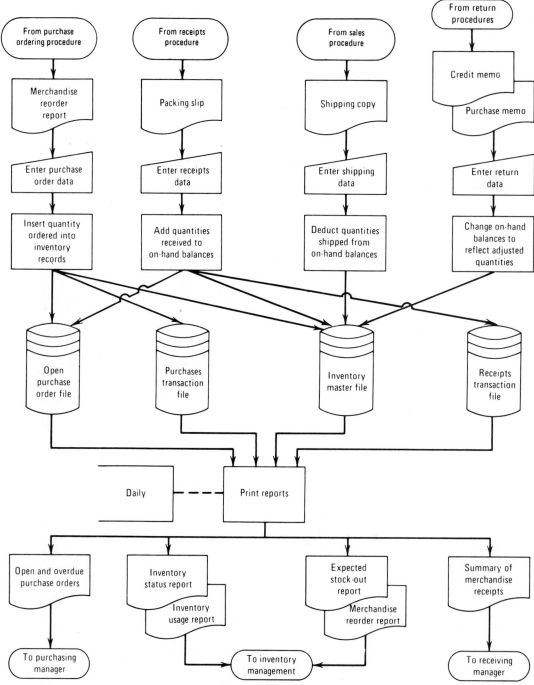

FIGURE 13-15   System flowchart of an on-line computer-based inventory procedure.

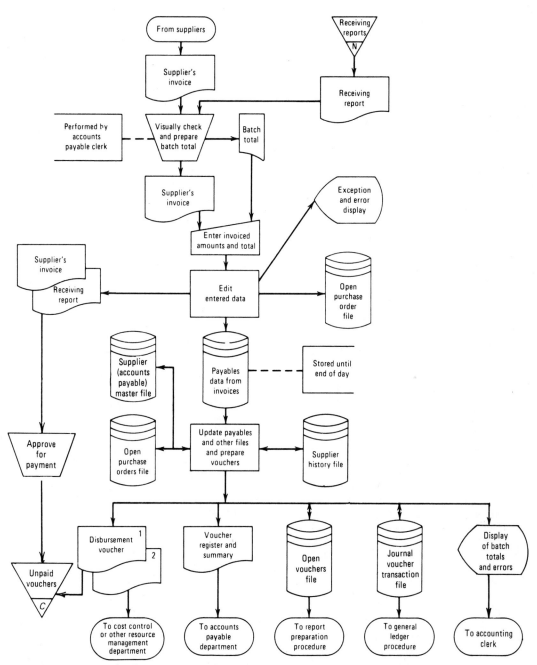

FIGURE 13-16 System flowchart of an on-line computer-based payables procedure.

accounts payable department. A clerk verifies that this total agrees with the precomputed batch total.

Cash disbursements procedure. Figure 13-17 shows a system flowchart of a batch cash disbursements procedure. Our illustrated procedure begins with the approved disbursement vouchers that have been printed during the payables procedure and filed with the supporting documents. We have selected this procedure because it has been widely used and because it provides a contrast to the on-line procedures discussed earlier. It also facilitates the prior computation of batch control totals and the review of documents by the check signer. However, we should recognize that the alternative on-line procedure offers significant benefits. For instance, it can use as transaction data the open vouchers stored in an on-line file, thereby omitting the need to key data from

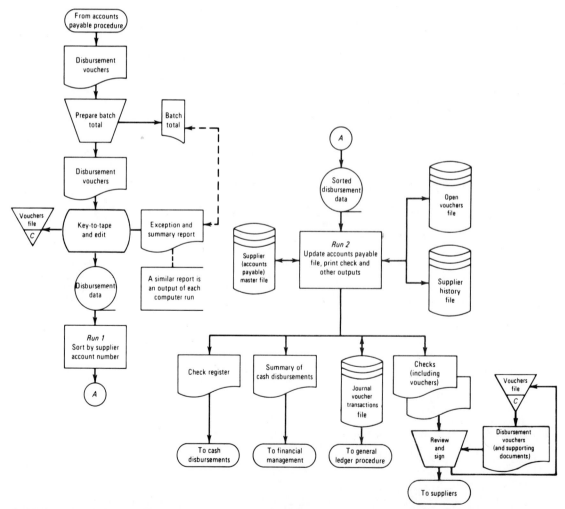

FIGURE 13-17 System flowchart of a batch computer-based cash disbursements procedure.

the vouchers. The vouchers in that file would be sorted by due date at the end of each day, and the vouchers due to be paid on the next payment date would be extracted.

The batch procedure shown in the flowchart can be described as follows. On each payment date the vouchers due to be paid are pulled from the unpaid vouchers file. As in all batch processing procedures, the first step is to compute one or more batch control totals. Then the data needed for preparing checks are keyed from the vouchers onto magnetic tape. The data are edited, either during the keying or during a separate edit run. Next the data are sorted by supplier account numbers. Finally, in run 2 the voucher amounts are posted to the accounts payable ledger. The program also prints the checks and a check register, as well as a summary of disbursements. It removes the paid vouchers from the open vouchers file (if one is maintained on line) and adds the data concerning disbursements to the supplier history file. Finally, it accumulates the amounts disbursed and prepares a sequentially numbered journal voucher, which it adds to the journal voucher transaction file.

The authorized check signer reviews the checks and supporting documents. After signing he or she forwards the checks to the mailroom. Alternatively, the checks may be signed automatically by the program in run 2, using a signature plate. If this is done, the checks are later reviewed to see that they pertain to authorized obligations.

Accounting Controls

Risk Exposures

In attempting to achieve the objectives stated at the beginning of this chapter, the expenditure cycle is exposed to a variety of risks. Figure 13-18 lists representative risks and consequent exposures due to these risks. For instance, goods may be ordered that are not needed or more goods may be ordered

than are needed. Goods that are not ordered may be received, or conversely, goods may be ordered but not received. These risks (the first three listed in the figure) expose the acquiring firm to excessive inventory and storage costs, or to possible losses due to goods being unavailable for sale. Another risk is that checks may be kited. **Kiting** is a type of embezzlement that involves transfers of checks among bank accounts. The purpose is generally to cover cash shortages and/or to inflate the assets. Transfers typically take place near the end of a month, so that float (i.e., delay) causes the checks not to be recorded until the following month. At the least, the result of this kiting activity is an overstated cash balance for the end of the month. Another frequent consequence is a loss of cash.

Examples of Real-World Exposures

All of the risks listed in Figure 13-18 have led to the described exposures in real-world firms. In some cases the exposures have been quite severe. For instance, an organized crime ring, operating through an assistant branch manager, used a check kiting scheme that involved a transfer of $900,000 between accounts in two banks; the same amount was withdrawn from both accounts before discovery, since the insider had the opportunity to alter records in a manner that allowed immediate withdrawals.[4]

Other risks not listed in the figure also have caused severe losses, as the following cases illustrate:

• A clerk in a department store defrauded his employer of $120,000 by issuing unauthorized vouchers that were paid to a fictitious supplier firm (in reality a friend's address).

[4]This and the following fraud cases are based on Brandt Allen, "The Biggest Computer Frauds: Lessons for CPAs," *The Journal of Accountancy* (May 1977), pp. 52–63.

Risk	Exposure(s)
1. Orders placed for unneeded goods or more goods than needed	1. Excessive inventory and storage costs
2. Receipt of unordered goods	2. Excessive inventory and storage costs
3. No receipt of ordered goods	3. Losses due to stock-outs
4. Fraudulent placement of orders by buyers with suppliers to whom they have personal or financial attachments	4. Possibility of inferior or over-priced goods or services
5. Overcharges (with respect either to unit prices or to quantities) by suppliers for goods delivered	5. Excessive purchasing costs
6. Damage of goods en route to the acquiring firm	6. Possibility of inferior goods for use or sale (if undetected)
7. Errors by suppliers in computing amounts on invoices	7. Possibility of overpayment for goods received
8. Erroneous or omitted postings of purchases or purchase returns to suppliers' accounts payable records	8. Incorrect balances in accounts payable and general ledger account records
9. Errors in charging transaction amounts to purchases and expense accounts	9. Incorrect levels (either high or low) for purchases and expense accounts
10. Lost purchase discounts due to late payments	10. Excessive purchasing costs
11. Duplicate payments of invoices from suppliers	11. Excessive purchasing costs
12. Incorrect disbursements of cash, either to improper or fictitious parties or for greater amounts than approved	12. Losses of cash and excessive costs for goods and services
13. Improper disbursements of cash for goods or services not received	13. Excessive costs for goods or services
14. Fraudulent alteration and cashing of checks by employees	14. Losses of cash
15. Kiting of checks by employees	15. Overstatement of bank balances; possible losses of deposited cash
16. Accessing of supplier records by unauthorized persons	16. Loss of security over such records, with possibly detrimental use made of data accessed
17. Involvement of cash, merchandise inventory, and accounts payable records in natural or man-made disasters	17. Loss of or damage to assets, including possible loss of data needed to monitor payments of amounts due to suppliers within discount periods

FIGURE 13-18 Risk exposures within the expenditure cycle.

- A partner in a brokerage house who was in charge of the computer system transferred a total of $81,000 to his account by means of adjusting entries that increased the expense accounts of the firm.
- A claims reviewer who was employed by an insurance company prepared false claims totaling $128,000 that were payable to friends and were automatically paid by the computer system.

In order to counteract all of the risks that are inherent within the expenditure cycle, a firm needs to incorporate relevant general and transaction controls.

General Controls

General controls that particularly concern the expenditure cycle include the following:

1. Within the organization the units that have custodial functions (the stores department or warehouse, receiving department, cashier) are separate from those units that keep the records (the accounts payable department, inventory control department, expense control departments, and data processing department). Moreover, the purchasing department, whose manager authorizes purchase orders and debit memoranda, is separate from all the aforementioned units.

2. Complete and up-to-date documentation is available concerning the expenditure cycle, including copies of the documents, flowcharts, record layouts, and reports illustrated in this chapter. In addition, details pertaining to purchases and cash disbursements edit and processing programs are organized into separate books or "packages" that are directed respectively to programmers, computer operators, and system users.

3. Operating practices relating to processing schedules, reports, changes in programs, and other matters are clearly established.

4. Purchasing policies are established by management to require competitive bidding for large and/or nonroutine purchases and to prohibit conflicts of interest, such as financial interest by buyers in current or potential suppliers.

5. Security is maintained (in the case of online systems) by such techniques as (a) requiring that clerks enter assigned passwords before accessing supplier and inventory files, (b) employing terminals that are restricted solely to the entry and access of purchases and cash disbursement transactions, (c) generating audit reports (access logs) that monitor accesses of system files, and (d) dumping the supplier and inventory files onto magnetic tape backups. Security measures for manual and computer-based systems include the use of physically restricted stores areas (for protecting goods) and safes (for holding stocks of blank checks and signature plates).

Transaction Controls

Control points within the expenditure cycle include (1) the determined need for goods or services, (2) the purchase order, (3) the receipt of goods or services, (4) the movement of goods into storage, (5) the receipt and approval of the supplier's invoice, and (6) the disbursement of cash.

The following controls and control procedures are applicable to expenditure cycle transactions and supplier accounts:

1. Documents relating to purchases, receiving, payables, and cash disbursements are prenumbered and well designed.

2. Data on purchase orders and receiving reports and invoices are validated (and key-verified if suitable) as the data are prepared and entered for processing. In the case of computer-based systems validation is performed by means of such programmed edit checks as listed in Figure 13-19.

3. Errors detected during data entry or processing are corrected as soon as possible by means of an established error correction procedure.

4. Multiple-copy purchase requisitions, purchase orders, disbursement vouchers, checks, and debit memoranda are issued on the basis of valid authorizations.

5. Verifications are performed to ensure that all requisitioned goods and services are ordered, all ordered goods and ser-

Type of Edit Check	Typical Transaction Data Being Checked		Assurance Provided
	Purchases	**Cash Disbursements**	
1. Validity check	Supplier account numbers, inventory item numbers, transaction codes	Supplier account numbers, transaction codes	The entered numbers and codes are checked against lists of valid numbers and codes that are stored within the computer system.
2. Self-checking digit	Supplier account numbers	Supplier account numbers	Each supplier account number contains a check digit that enables errors in its entry to be detected.
3. Field check	Supplier account numbers, quantities ordered, unit prices	Supplier account numbers, amounts paid	The fields in the input records that are designated to contain the data items (listed at the left) are checked to see if they contain the proper mode of characters (i.e., numeric characters). If other modes are detected, an error is indicated.
4. Limit check	Quantities ordered	Amounts paid	The entered quantities and amounts are checked against preestablished limits that represent reasonable maximums to be expected. (Separate limits are set for each product.)
5. Range check	Unit prices	None	Each entered unit price is checked to see that it is within a preestablished range (either higher or lower than an expected value).
6. Relationship check	Quantities received	Amounts paid	The quantity of goods received is compared to the quantity ordered, as shown in the open purchase orders file; if the quantities do not agree, the receipt is flagged by the edit program. When an amount of a cash payment is entered as a cash disbursement transaction, together with the number of the voucher or invoice to which the amount applies, the amount in the open vouchers (or invoices) file is retrieved and compared with the entered amount. If a difference appears, the transaction is flagged.
7. Sign check	None	Supplier account balances	After the amount of a cash disbursement transaction is entered and posted to the supplier's account in the accounts payable ledger (thereby reducing the account balance of the supplier), the remaining balance is checked. If the balance is preceded by a negative sign (indicating a debit balance), the transaction is flagged.
8. Completeness check[a]	All entered data items	All entered data items	The entered transactions are checked to see that all required data items have been entered.
9. Echo check[a]	Supplier account numbers and names, inventory item numbers and descriptions	Supplier account numbers and names	After the account numbers for suppliers relating to a purchase or cash disbursements transaction (and also the product numbers in the purchase transaction) have been entered at a terminal, the edit program retrieves and "echoes back" the related supplier names (and product descriptions in the case of purchase transactions).

[a]Applicable only to on-line processing systems.

FIGURE 13-19 Programmed edit checks that are useful in validating transaction data entered into the expenditure cycle.

vices are received, all received goods are transferred to stores, and all goods and services are recorded as obligations and paid before due dates.

6. All open transactions, such as partial deliveries and rejected goods, are monitored, and all transactions missing one or more supporting documents are investigated.

7. Purchase returns and allowances are subject to prior approval by the purchasing manager.

8. All suppliers' invoices are matched to corresponding purchase orders and receiving reports (in the case of goods), and all data items on the invoices, including computations, are verified by an accounts payable clerk or a computer program.

9. Account balances in the accounts payable subsidiary ledger, the inventory master file, and the expense ledgers (if any) are periodically reconciled with the control accounts in the general ledger.

10. All inventories on hand are verified by physical counts at least once yearly under proper supervision, reconciled with the quantities shown in the inventory records, and adjusted when necessary to reflect the actual quantities on hand.

11. Receiving and payables cutoff policies are clearly established, so that inventory and accounts payable are fairly valued at the end of each accounting period.

12. Budgetary control is established over purchases, with periodic reviews of actual purchase costs and such key factors as inventory turnover rates.

13. Evidence supporting the validity of expenditures and the correctness of amounts is reviewed prior to the signing of checks.

14. Discount periods relating to payments are monitored to ensure that all purchase discounts are taken, or the net method for recording purchases is employed.

15. If processing is performed in batches, control totals are precomputed on amounts in received suppliers' invoices and in vouchers due for payments; these batch totals are compared with totals computed during postings to the accounts payable ledger, as well as during each processing run in the case of computer-based processing.

16. Check protectors are used to protect the amounts on checks against alteration before the checks are presented to be signed.

17. Checks over a specified amount are countersigned by a second person.

18. Balances in monthly statements from suppliers are compared with balances appearing in the suppliers' accounts.

19. Copies of all documents pertaining to purchases and cash disbursement transactions are filed by number, and the sequence of numbers in each file is periodically checked to see if gaps exist. If transactions are not supported by pre-printed documents, as often is the case in on-line computer-based systems, numbers are assigned to generated documents and they are stored in transaction files.

20. In the case of computer-based systems, transaction listings and account summaries are printed periodically in order to provide an adequate audit trail.

21. All bank accounts are reconciled monthly by someone who is not involved in expenditure cycle processing activities, and new bank accounts are authorized by the proper managers.

22. Employees who handle cash are required to be bonded and are subject to close supervision.

23. An imprest system is used for disbursing currency from petty cash funds, with the

Line number	Vendor name	Invoice number	Due date	Balance due	Payment amount	Discount taken	Net amount	Hold	Comments
1	Able Manufacturing Co.	000123	3/04/91	100.00	100.00	.00	100.00		
2		000789	2/28/91	600.00	600.00	.00	600.00		
3		004560	3/29/91	500.00	500.00	.00	500.00		
4		123457	4/29/91	100.50	100.50	10.00	90.50		
	Vendor A1011 Total			1,300.50	1,300.50	10.00	1,290.50		
7	Butler Supply Co.	112	4/29/91	1,567.98	1,567.98	235.20	1,332.78		
5		156710	4/29/91	400.00	400.00	.00	400.00		
	Vendor B2893 Total			1,967.98	1,967.98	235.20	1,732.78		
9	Bishop Brothers	2034	5/06/91	750.00	750.00	37.50	712.50		
	Vendor B4056 Total			750.00	750.00	37.50	712.50		
8	Sanford Stationery Store	10	4/29/91	12.00–	12.00–	.00	12.00–	Debit memo	
	Vendor S3123 Total			12.00–	12.00–	.00	12.00–		
6	Doral, Inc.	32	4/29/91	7,200.00	7,200.00	800.00	6,400.00		Exceeds maximum check amt
	Vendor 0 Total			7,200.00	.00	800.00			

Total debit memo amount		12.00–	12.00–	.00	12.00–
Total check amount		11,218.48	11,218.48	1,082.70	10,135.78

Cash required	10,125.78
Number of checks	4
Number of debit memos	1
Summary totals check	1
Total number of checks	6

FIGURE 13-20 A cash requirements report. Courtesy of International Business Machines Corporation.

funds subject to surprise counts by internal auditors or a manager.

REPORTS AND OTHER OUTPUTS

Outputs generated by the expenditure cycle include financial and nonfinancial reports, purchases-related and cash-related reports, daily and weekly and monthly reports, and hard-copy and soft-copy reports. All these reports may be arbitrarily classified as operational (including operational control) listings and reports, inquiry screens, and managerial reports.

Operational Listings and Reports

Various registers and journals help to maintain the audit trail. *The invoice or voucher register* is a listing of invoices received from suppliers or a listing of the vouchers prepared from the invoices. The *check register* is a listing of all checks written. It may alternatively be called the cash disbursements journal. Each day's listing is accompanied by a summary of the gross amount of payables reduced, the discounts taken, and the net amount paid. A related **cash requirements report,** such as is shown in Figure 13-20, lists the payments to be made on a particular upcoming day.

The **open purchase orders report** is based on one of the key open document files. It shows all purchases for which the related invoices have not yet been approved for payment. The **open payables report** is related to the open purchase orders report, in that it lists all approved invoices or vouchers that are currently unpaid. It may be arranged by invoice or voucher number, by inventory and expense account numbers, or by due date. Those invoices or vouchers that are past their due dates may be highlighted.

Other operational reports may focus on inventory and receiving activities. The **inventory status report** contains quantities received, shipped, and on hand for the respective items of inventory. Figure 13-21 shows a brief inventory status report for a retail infants' goods store. This type of report is based on sales as well as purchases transactions and reflects the balances in the inventory master file. The *receiving register or summary* lists all incoming shipments from suppliers, including those that are rejected. It also contains comments based on the inspection of received goods. The **overdue deliveries report** pinpoints those purchase transactions whose requested delivery dates have passed without shipments having arrived from suppliers.

Inquiry Screens

If the expenditure cycle data base is stored in on-line files, a variety of inquiries can be made interactively. Figure 13-22 presents a screen display output that is based on the open payables file. The display shows the summary of total payables due, aged by due dates. Figure 13-23 shows a screen display of the recent invoices and corresponding vouchers for a particular vendor (supplier). Other inquiries might concern (1) the status of an individual purchase order, (2) the current on-hand balance and other details pertaining to an inventory item, (3) a summary of open purchase orders, and (4) the detail of a single cash disbursement or a batch of disbursements.

Managerial Reports

The expenditure cycle data base contains considerable information that can aid managers in making decisions. Certain of these reports, such as the cash flow statement and the inventory status report, overlap with the revenue cycle. We can identify others, however, that focus on expenditures.

Purchase analyses show the levels of purchasing activity for each supplier, inventory item, and buyer. Thus, they aid in evalu-

	Toddlers', Inc. Inventory Status Report for October 1990			
Item Description	Item Number	Quantity Received	Quantity Shipped	Ending Quantity on Hand
Rubbers	2861	375	205	815
Diapers	3765	2100	1280	8646
Sleepers	5617	—	120	424
Cribs	7311	72	98	338

FIGURE 13-21 An inventory status report.

ating performances. A more detailed evaluation of suppliers is provided by the supplier or **vendor performance report,** such as appears in Figure 13-24. Cash requirement forecasts show expected withdrawals in coming days, perhaps grouped by individual bank accounts.

Figure 13-25 portrays most of the listings and reports described in the preceding paragraphs. They are shown as outputs produced from data in the various files listed in an earlier section. The daily outputs have also been included in the receiving, payables, and disbursements segments of the flowcharts in Figures 13-14, 13-16, and 13-17, or in the inventory segment flowchart shown in

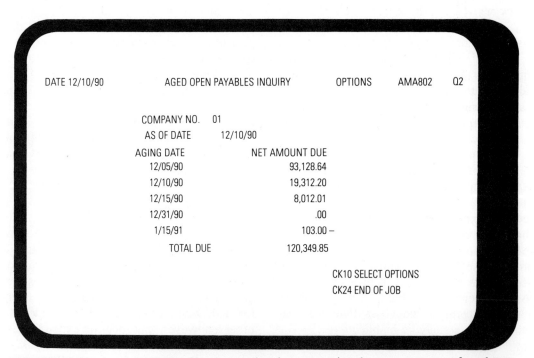

FIGURE 13-22 A screen display based on an inquiry concerning the current status of total payables. Courtesy of International Business Machines Corporation.

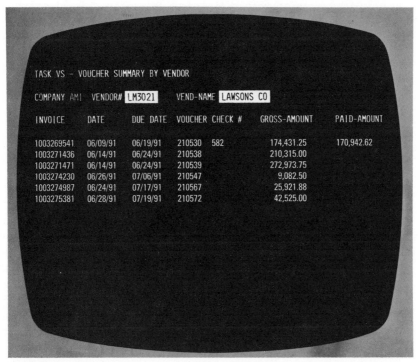

FIGURE 13-23 A screen display based on an inquiry concerning the recent history of an individual vendor (supplier). Courtesy of Data Design Associates.

Figure 13-15. Other outputs are typically generated throughout the month during special print runs. Examples of such inventory-related outputs appear in Figure 13-15.

Summary

The expenditure cycle facilitates the exchange of cash with suppliers for needed goods and services. Functions of the cycle (in the case of goods) are to recognize the need, place the order, receive and store the goods, ascertain the validity of the payment obligation, prepare the cash disbursement, maintain the accounts payable, post transactions to the general ledger, and prepare needed financial reports and other outputs. Related functions include purchase returns and allowances and petty cash disbursements. These functions are achieved under the direction of the inventory management and finance/accounting organizational units.

Most of the data used in the cycle arise from suppliers and inventory records. Documents typically employed are the purchase requisition, purchase order, receiving report, supplier's (vendor's) invoice, disbursement voucher, and check voucher. Preformatted screens may be used in on-line systems to enter purchases and cash disbursements data. The data base includes such files as the supplier (vendor) master, merchandise inventory master, open purchase order, open voucher, cash disbursements transaction, and supplier reference and history files. Data processing consists of processing of purchases transactions, maintaining accounts payable records, and processing cash dis-

REPRESENTATIVE MERCHANDISING COMPANY — VENDOR PERFORMANCE REPORT

COMPANY AMI REPORT APR62-1
REPORT DATE 04/30/91 PAGE 1
RUN DATE 04/30/91

VENDOR NUMBER	NAME		SHIPMENTS TOTAL	SHIPMENTS PCT LATE	SHIPMENTS DEFECTIVE	AVERAGE DAYS LATE	AVERAGE PCT DEFECTS	PRICE VARIANCE AMOUNT	PRICE VARIANCE PCT	VENDOR RATINGS
AT3022	ANDREWS CO	THIS PERIOD	60							IMPORTANCE MEDIUM
		THIS YEAR	222	.9	11	3.5	5.0	7,364	8.0	QUALITY.... AVERAGE
		LAST YEAR								SERVICE... GOOD
LM3021	LAWSONS CO	THIS PERIOD	30	50.0		3.4		8,500		IMPORTANCE HIGH
		THIS YEAR	97	12.1	4	4.6	.2	118,245-	6.0-	QUALITY.... GOOD
		LAST YEAR	130	3.0	13	8.5	3.0	113,920-	3.0-	SERVICE... GOOD
RM3023	RIVERTON	THIS PERIOD	11	70.0	1	4.6		6		IMPORTANCE MEDIUM
		THIS YEAR	22	41.7	2	4.2	.1	436	1.0	QUALITY.... AVERAGE
		LAST YEAR								SERVICE.... AVERAGE
TF1028	TRIANGLE	THIS PERIOD	12							IMPORTANCE HIGH
		THIS YEAR	79							QUALITY.... GOOD
		LAST YEAR	242							SERVICE... GOOD
VI3024	VOLMER IND	THIS PERIOD	2							IMPORTANCE HIGH
		THIS YEAR	12	5.0		.5	1.0			QUALITY.... GOOD
		LAST YEAR								SERVICE... EXCELLENT

FIGURE 13-24 A supplier performance evaluation report. Courtesy of Data Design Associates.

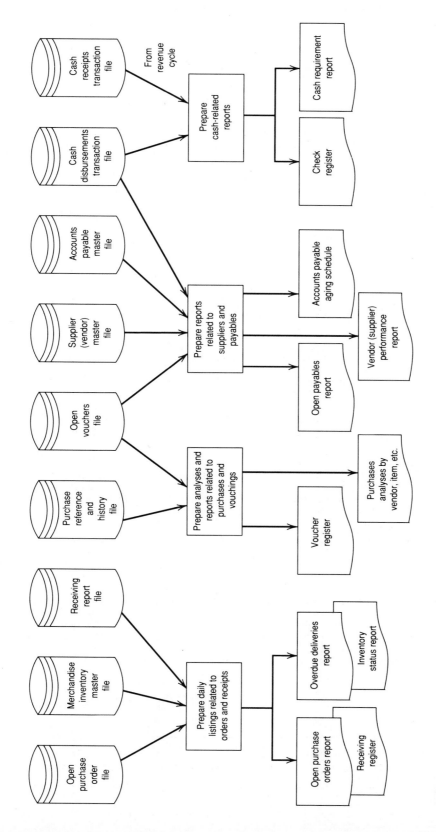

FIGURE 13-25 System flowchart showing daily and monthly listings and reports in the expenditure cycle.

bursement transactions. Processing may feasibly be performed by manual systems, batch computer-based systems, and on-line computer-based systems. A variety of risk exposures exist in the processing of purchases and cash disbursements transactions. Risks due to these exposures can be counteracted by means of adequate general and transaction controls. Among the outputs generated by the expenditure cycle are the voucher reg-

ister, check register, cash requirements report, open purchase orders report, open vouchers or payables report, inventory status report, receiving summary, overdue deliveries report, supplier inquiry screens, inventory item inquiry screens, purchase analyses, supplier performance report, and cash flow statement. Figure 13-26 summarizes many of the foregoing system components.

Component	Purchases	Accounts Payable	Cash Disbursements
Source documents	Purchase requisition Purchase order Receiving report	Supplier's invoice Disbursement voucher	Check voucher
Processing steps	Determine needs and requisition merchandise Prepare purchase order and mail to supplier Receive merchandise Transfer merchandise to storeroom	Receive and vouch supplier's invoice Prepare disbursement voucher Enter transaction in purchases journal Post obligation to accounts payable ledger Transmit for posting to general ledger	Prepare check voucher Enter transaction in check register Mail check Post payment to accounts payable ledger Transmit for posting to general ledger
Files	Supplier file Inventory file Purchase requisition file Purchase order file Receiving report file	Accounts payable (A/P) ledger General ledger Disbursement voucher file	Supplier (A/P) ledger General ledger Check file
Outputs	Open purchase order report Purchase analysis by product, supplier, etc.	Accounts payable aging summary Open and unpaid suppliers' invoices report	Cash disbursement summary Cash requirements statement
Selective transaction controls	Approval of purchase order Prenumbered purchase requisitions, orders, etc. Verification of received merchandise	Prenumbered disbursement vouchers Verification of billed prices, quantities, terms, accuracy Authorization of payment Batch totals of invoice amounts Reconciliation of A/P control account with A/P ledger	Prenumbered checks Signing of checks by authorized managers Reconciliation of cash balance with bank statement

FIGURE 13-26 Analysis worksheet for the expenditure cycle. Based on a technique described by Dan C. Kneer in "System Procedures and Controls," *Journal of Systems Management* (September 1983), pp. 28–32.

Review Problem with Solution

Hartshorn Manufacturing Company

Statement

The Hartshorn Manufacturing Company of Wichita, Kansas, recently engaged a public accountant to review its various transaction processing procedures. During her review of the expenditure transaction cycle, the public accountant made the following notes.

A production foreman initiates a purchase by calling the purchasing department on the phone and stating his request. A buyer then prepares a letter concerning the requested materials, mails the letter to a supplier, and files his copy in the supplier's file folder. As the materials arrive, they are laid in any convenient area until the storeskeeper has an opportunity to store them in their bins or until the production foreman carts them directly to the production line. When the supplier's invoice reaches the accounting department, an accounting clerk enters the invoice in the purchase journal. Near the end of each month the clerk prepares an unnumbered check for the amount of the invoice,

has the treasurer sign the check, and mails the check to the supplier. Then the same clerk enters the amount of the check in the check register, posts the amount to the subsidiary ledger account sheet for the supplier, and files the check copy by supplier's name. Just before the trial balance is prepared, the same clerk totals the various special journals and posts the totals to the general ledger. When the work load is too heavy for this single clerk to perform, another clerk is assigned to handle those invoices from suppliers whose names begin with letters from N to Z. No one at any time counts the materials on hand, compares documents involved in a particular transaction, or reconciles accounting ledgers. When asked why such checks are not made, the accounting clerk replies that there is not enough time in a day and that the more urgent tasks have to be done.

Required

Analyze weaknesses in accounting control and suggest improvements.

Solution

Control Weakness	Suggested Changes
1. Verbal request for materials made by production foreman.	**1.** Prepare a written request on a purchase requisition form; send the requisition to the purchasing department, with a copy to the accounts payable department; assign the preparation of the purchase requisition to the storeskeeper or to an inventory control clerk, who likely would have a better knowledge of inventory needs than the foreman.
2. Letter prepared by buyer, with copy filed in supplier's folder.	**2.** Prepare a formal prenumbered purchase order, which is to be signed by the purchasing manager, and send to the supplier; send copies of the purchase order to a newly organized receiving department and to the accounting department as prior notification; also send a copy to the person who requested the order as verification and file a copy by number in the purchasing department. (*Note:* The copy to the receiving department should be blind. Also, consider requesting bids from suppliers before deciding on the supplier with whom to place the order.)

(Table continued)

Control Weakness	Suggested Changes
3. Arriving materials accepted without use of formal receiving procedure.	**3.** Require arriving materials to be formally accepted by a receiving department, organizationally separate from the stores department, which should perform the following steps: **a.** Verify that the materials were ordered by referring to its copy of the purchase order. **b.** Count the materials and note their condition. **c.** Prepare and sign a prenumbered receiving report, listing the quantities counted and the condition of the materials. **d.** Forward the materials with a copy of the receiving report to the storeskeeper, who should count the materials, sign the receiving report to acknowledge receipt, and then send the receiving report to the accounting department. **e.** Send other copies of the receiving report to (1) an inventory control clerk for entry in inventory records and (2) the purchasing department for verification; also file a copy by number.
4. Materials laid in any convenient area accessible to the production foreman.	**4.** Store materials promptly as received (see 3 above) in a stores area that is physically restricted to authorized stores personnel; issue to production foreman on a prenumbered materials issue slip, which he should sign to acknowledge receipt.
5. Supplier's invoice inadequately verified and approved for payment.	**5.** Perform the following steps: **a.** Compare quantities shown to quantities listed on the receiving report. **b.** Compare unit prices shown to acceptable prices listed on the purchase order. **c.** Check the accuracy of the extensions and the totals. **d.** Initial and date the invoice, in a box stamped on its face, to indicate the completion of these actions. **e.** Prepare a disbursement voucher, attach supporting documents, and file by due date.
6. Cash disbursement not adequately controlled.	**6.** Prepare a prenumbered check and protect the amount; then forward the check to the treasurer, who should review the supporting documents, sign the check, and mail direct from his or her office (instead of returning to the accounting clerk for mailing); stamp "Paid" on all supporting documents and file by check number.
7. Inadequate separation of responsibilities in the accounting department.	**7.** Assign the responsibility for posting to the general ledger to another clerk in the accounting department, so that the work of the accounting clerk will be independently verified.
8. Tardy posting and lack of reconciliations.	**8.** Post daily from the journals to the general ledger and check the accuracy of posting by means of batch control totals; reconcile the accounts payable control account with the subsidiary ledger accounts on a frequent basis; count the materials on hand once or twice a year and reconcile with the perpetual inventory records maintained by an inventory control clerk.
9. Inappropriate assignment of duties during peak periods.	**9.** Assign a second clerk to particular tasks, such as making entries in the check register, filing copies of checks prepared for all suppliers, and totaling special journals. *Note:* This allocation of tasks is preferable to the assignment of a block of suppliers' invoices to the second clerk, since it enables one clerk to verify the work of the other.

Review Questions

13-1 What is the meaning of each of the following terms?

Expenditure cycle
Request for proposal
Vouching
Imprest system
Inventory management
Purchase requisition
Purchase order
Receiving report
Supplier's invoice
Disbursement voucher
Voucher system
Voucher register
Check voucher
Check register
Debit memorandum
Kiting
Cash requirements report
Open purchase orders report
Open payables report
Inventory status report
Overdue deliveries report
Purchase analysis
Vendor performance report

13-2 What are several objectives of the expenditure cycle?

13-3 What are the major functions of the expenditure cycle?

13-4 In what ways may the need for goods and services be established?

13-5 Describe the competitive bidding procedure.

13-6 How is the validity of a supplier's invoice established?

13-7 Describe the procedure for handling purchase returns.

13-8 Describe the imprest basis for handling petty cash disbursements.

13-9 Describe the relationships of the inventory management organizational function to the expenditure cycle.

13-10 Describe the relationships of the finance and accounting organizational functions to the expenditure cycle.

13-11 What are the sources of data used in the expenditure cycle?

13-12 Identify the various documents used in the expenditure cycle.

13-13 Identify the various files used in the expenditure cycle.

13-14 Describe the purchases of goods and services when processing is performed manually.

13-15 Describe the payables procedure when processing is performed manually and accounts payable are maintained.

13-16 Describe the cash disbursements procedure when processing is performed manually and payments are made by check.

13-17 Describe the expenditure cycle procedure when processing is performed by a computer-based system involving a mixture of the on-line and batch methods.

13-18 What are the exposures to risk that exist in the processing within the expenditure cycle?

13-19 Identify various general and transaction controls that concern the expenditure cycle.

13-20 Identify various reports and other outputs that may be generated from information provided by the expenditure cycle.

Discussion Questions

13-21 In what ways does the expenditure cycle procedure differ when performed by computer-based systems (1) using the batch method and (2) using the on-line method?

13-22 What are sources of information for inventory managers other than from expenditure cycle processing?

13-23 Describe several programmed edit checks, such as the redundancy matching check, that can be applied by the posting programs used in processing payables and cash disbursements transactions.

13-24 In what ways is the purchases activity related to the inventory management activity?

13-25 What are the ethical considerations that a purchasing department buyer faces?

13-26 How does information developed during the expenditure cycle aid the preparation of the cash forecast?

13-27 How do logistics activities in merchandising firms differ from logistics activities in manufacturing firms?

Problems

13-1 North Enterprises, Inc., has been experiencing increased difficulties in the accounts payable area. Lateness of numerous payments has caused the loss of a significant amount in purchase discounts. A small minority of suppliers have been overcharging, either by raising their unit prices or by shipping larger quantities than appear on the purchase orders. In some cases it has been found that the same invoices have been paid two or three times. More errors than seem reasonable have appeared in the suppliers' accounts payable accounts. Many checks have been prepared for signing each day. In fact, often three or more checks are prepared for the same supplier during a day. These difficulties have led the accounts payable manager to press for a new computer-based system that will process accounts payable.

Required

a. List the types of transactions that affect the accounts payable balances.

b. Describe several reports that can aid the manager in assessing the extent of the difficulties and achieving success in overcoming them.

c. Describe one or more ways of correcting each of the difficulties raised, other than to install a new computer system.

d. Assuming that a computer-based system is approved for installation, weigh the relative advantages between (1) a system that uses the batch processing approach, (2) a system that uses the on-line processing approach, and (3) a system that uses on-line data entry but batch processing.

13-2 The City of Rockrib is a southern city of 100,000 persons. It has a centralized purchasing department, a receiving department, an accounts payable department, and a cashier's office, among other departments. Routine, widely used supplies are ordered on the basis of reorder reports, which are prepared daily by an inventory search program within the city's computer system. Nonroutine supplies and services are ordered on the requests of the various operating departments, such as the water department. Most of these nonroutine supplies and services are obtained after competitive bidding. Unacceptable receipts of supplies are returned to suppliers, with requests for refunds. Invoices from suppliers are approved via a voucher system. Checks are prepared on the computer system and mailed to suppliers within the discount periods. Balances owed and paid to suppliers are maintained on computer-based records.

Required

a. List the data items needed to record and process purchases on credit, purchase returns, and cash disbursements transactions.

b. List the files needed to store the data items listed in **a.**

c. Describe reports that would be useful to city managers in analyzing the purchase and data disbursements transactions and the activities related to the suppliers' accounts.

13-3 Two recent graduates of Midwest University have decided to start their own firm, which is to sell microcomputer supplies at discount prices. Since one is a graduate in general business, he undertakes the task of designing needed forms. He begins with the purchase requisition and purchase order forms. Believing that the forms should be as simple as possible, he limits the data on each form. Each form begins with the name of the document. Then on the purchase requisition the heading contains labels for supplier name and address, the body contains columns headed "Description" and "Dollar Amount," and the bottom of the "Dollar Amount" column is labeled "Total." On the purchase order the heading contains the firm's address, supplier name and address, shipping address, discount terms, ship via, and freight terms; the body contains columns headed "Description" and "Dollar Amount"; and the bottom contains several Purchase Conditions.

Required

Specify data items that should be added to and deleted from each designed form, and give reasons for their addition or deletion. Indicate the number of copies of each form, the disposition of each copy, and any differences that should appear between copies of the same form.

13-4 Wooster Company is a distributorship for beauty and barber supplies and equipment, servicing a five-state area. Management has generally been pleased with the firm's operations to date. However, the present purchasing system has evolved through use rather than having been formally designed. It may be described as follows: Whenever the quantity of an item is low, the inventory supervisor phones the purchasing department and provides the description and quantity of each item to be ordered. The purchasing department then prepares a purchase order in duplicate. The original is sent to the supplier, and a copy is filed in the purchasing department numerically. When the ordered items arrive, an inventory clerk (under the supervisor) checks off each item on the packing slip that accompanies the shipment. The packing slip is then forwarded to the accounts payable department. When the invoice arrives from the supplier, the packing slip is compared with the invoice by an accounts payable clerk. After any differences between the two documents have been reconciled, a check is drawn for the appropriate amount and is mailed to the supplier together with a copy of the invoice. The packing slip is attached to the invoice and is filed alphabetically in the paid invoice file.

Required

a. Identify all documents that are needed to fulfill the requirements of an adequate expenditure cycle, and the number of copies of each.

b. List each copy of the documents identified in **a** and trace its route through the various departments involved in the expenditure cycle, including its final disposition. Add new departments if they are desirable.

(CMA adapted)

13-5 The National Industrial Corporation uses the form shown on page 590 as its purchase order.

```
                                                              PURCHASE ORDER

                              SEND INVOICE ONLY TO:
                     297 HARDINGTEN DR., BX., NY 10461

  TO _____      SHIP TO _____

     _____              _____

     _____              _____
```

DATE TO BE SHIPPED	SHIP VIA	DISC. TERMS	FREIGHT TERMS	ADV. ALLOWANCE	SPECIAL ALLOWANCE
QUANTITY		**DESCRIPTION**			

PURCHASE CONDITIONS

1. Supplier will be responsible for extra freight cost on partial shipment, unless prior permission is obtained.

2. Please acknowledge this order.

3. Please notify us immediately if you are unable to complete order.

4. All items must be individually packed.

Required

List added data items that should be included on the form and their locations, i.e., in the heading, body, or foot. Also specify a suitable number of copies of the form and the distribution of all copies.

(CPA adapted)

13-6 Mason Pharmaceuticals is a large manufacturer of drugs and other medical products. It receives numerous deliveries of raw materials and supplies at its central receiving dock. As each delivery arrives, a receiving clerk checks, via the receiving de- partment on-line terminal, to ascertain that a related purchase order is on file. Then the clerk counts and inspects the received goods and lists the received items (and their condi- tion) on a receiving form. Next the clerk transfers these receiving data to the com- puter system via the terminal. In doing so the clerk is aided by a preformatted receiving form that appears on the screen of the termi- nal. If the entered data correspond with the ordered data in the open purchase orders file, the transaction is accepted. This entry up- dates the inventory master file, makes a no- tation in the open purchase orders file, and creates a prenumbered formal receiving re- port.

Required

a. Draw a preformatted screen format that shows all the data items to be entered by the receiving clerk and that aids him or her in the data entry process. Include in the screen format those items that would be automatically entered by the computer program, either to identify the transaction or to aid in reducing input errors. Denote these system-generated items by an asterisk (*).

b. Identify the programmed edit checks that should be incorporated into the data entry program and the data item(s) that each is to check, plus all security measures that should pertain to the use and protection of this receiving department terminal.

13-7 The Arrington Wholesaling Co. of Little Rock, Arkansas, services a number of retailers with several thousand grocery and sundry items. In turn it acquires merchandise from a wide range of suppliers across the country. Although it uses a computer system for billing, purchasing, and payroll processing, it has just recently turned to the application of cash disbursements.

Mary Brenner, a systems analyst, has been assigned the task of developing the processing procedure for cash disbursements. She begins by ascertaining the desired outputs from the procedure, as well as the file record layout and input document format. They are as follows:

Outputs

a. Check, which contains the check number, date, payee, accounts debited, invoice numbers, gross amount, discount, net amount.

b. Cash disbursements journal, which contains the date, check numbers, supplier numbers, supplier names, debits to accounts payable, credits to cash, and purchase discounts.

Master File

Accounts payable, which contains in each record the supplier number, supplier name and address, invoice numbers, voucher number, date payment due, invoice amounts, discount, account balance.[5]

Input

Disbursement voucher, which contains the voucher number, date, supplier number and name, invoice numbers and dates, invoice accounts to be debited, discounts, net amounts.

Required

a. Indicate the source (i.e., the input document or master file) from which each item in the outputs is derived. If the item is produced by the computer system, state "system generated."

b. Prepare a computer system flowchart to reflect the batch processing of cash disbursements. Assume that the master file is stored on a removable magnetic disk pack.

c. Draw the outputs and the input, with all of the data items being included within suitable formats.

d. List the accounting transaction controls that are suitable to a computer-based system for entering disbursement vouchers and processing cash disbursements by the batch approach. For each listed programmed check, add the data items to which the check pertains.

13-8 Regal Supply, Ltd., of Windsor, Ontario, maintains the following records pertaining to its vendors (suppliers) and outstanding (unpaid) accounts payable transactions. The general ledger account

[5]This record layout reflects the assumption that only one voucher is unpaid at any time.

number refers to the type of expense incurred through the vendor: for example, purchases of new merchandise, purchases of used merchandise, or purchases of supplies, utility service, insurance service, and custodial service.

Accounts Payable Transaction Record

Data Item	Field Size
Vendor number	7
General ledger account number	4
Invoice number	7
Voucher number	7
Invoice date	6
Due date	6
Invoice amount	10
Discount	5
Net amounts	10

Vendor Master Record

Data Item	Field Size
Vendor number	7
Vendor name	21
Street number	6
Street name	15
City	15
Province/state	15
Country	6
Postal/zip code	6

Required

a. Draw record layouts for both records.

b. Design a report listing the outstanding payables according to account numbers. Reported data concerning each payable should include the vendor name, city, province/state, invoice number, due date, and net amount due.

c. Key each item in the report to a field in one of the record layouts drawn in **a** above. For instance, enter a circled A under the account number column in the report, and also a circled A under the general ledger account number field in the transaction record.

d. Describe, with the aid of a system flowchart, the preparation of the report. Assume that the transaction records are on magnetic tape and the master records on magnetic disk.

(SMAC adapted)

13-9 The Exeter Merchandising Corporation of Iowa City, Iowa, prepares checks daily in payment of obligations that have come due. The basic data processing steps, together with their locations, are as follows:

A (accounts payable): Disbursement vouchers, which had been prepared during the payables processing, are pulled from the payables-due tickler file and forwarded.

B (data control): Disbursement vouchers are reviewed and forwarded.

C (data preparation): Disbursement vouchers are converted to magnetic tape and forwarded.

D (computer operations): Data from the disbursements tape are processed against the accounts payable master file (on magnetic disk) to produce checks, a check register, and a debit distribution tape; all outputs are distributed.

E (cashier): Checks and check register are reviewed and checks are signed.

Required

a. List the possible errors or discrepancies that might occur at each of the preceding processing steps.

b. For each possible error or discrepancy, cite the corresponding control or security measure that should be in effect. Include all programmed checks needed to edit the input data fully.

c. Prepare a document system flowchart that incorporates the manual and computer-based processing steps described (except for the posting of the debit distribution tape to the general ledger).

13-10 Bargains, Inc., a retail firm of Evansville, Indiana, purchases merchandise for resale. A wide variety of merchandise items are acquired from about 200 suppliers. The firm employs an on-line processing system, with terminals located in the purchasing and receiving departments (among others) to handle its purchases procedure.

Purchase orders are prepared by buyers, who select suitable suppliers from which to order needed merchandise specified on purchase requisition sheets received from the inventory control department. (To aid the selection process, they make on-line inquiries via their terminals and obtain displays of suppliers' records on their CRT screens.) A buyer next enters the necessary data into his or her terminal relating to each purchase, including the transaction code, the number of the selected supplier, the numbers of the merchandise items being ordered and corresponding order quantities and expected unit prices, the expected date of arrival of the merchandise, the terms, the method of shipment, shipper, the code of the warehouse to which the merchandise is to be shipped, and the buyer's number. The computer system then generates a printed purchase order, which contains the above data plus a computer-assigned order number, the order date, the supplier name and address, the merchandise descriptions, the units of measure, the shipping address, and so on. (The computer system also posts the number of the purchase order and ordered quantities, plus the expected date of arrival, to all pertinent records of the merchandise inventory master file.) After review, the purchasing manager signs and mails each purchase order.

When ordered merchandise arrives at the receiving dock, it is counted by a receiving clerk and entered on a simplified receiving report containing fields for the date, supplier number, related purchase order number, the merchandise item numbers and corresponding quantities, a space for comments concerning the condition of the received merchandise, and a box for the initials of the receiving clerk. After completing the form, the clerk keys the receiving data into his or her terminal. The computer system then posts the receipt of the quantities to the pertinent records of the merchandise inventory master file. It also posts the date of receipt to the pertinent record in the open purchase order file. Then it generates a printed copy of a prenumbered receiving report, containing the entered data plus the supplier's name and address and the merchandise descriptions. (It also adds a copy of this receiving report to a disk file.)

Required

a. Prepare a preformatted screen for inputting the purchase order data and enter assumed sample data.

b. Draw the simplified receiving report form used by receiving clerks and enter assumed sample data.

c. Prepare record layouts for the following files, using assumed lengths for the various fields and modes for the data items:

(1) Open purchase order file.

(2) Supplier master file.

(3) Merchandise inventory master file.

(4) Receiving report file.

d. Place circled POs by those data items within the foregoing record layouts that provide the sources of data for the printed purchase order (PO) (other than those provided by the screen).

e. Place circled RRs by those data items in the foregoing record layouts that provide the sources of data for the printed receiving report (RR) (other than those provided by input form).

13-11 What error or fraudulent activity might occur if each of the following procedures is allowed?

a. The buyer in the purchasing department owns part interest in a supplier who provides merchandise of the type used by this firm.

b. The person who maintains the accounts payable records also prepares and signs checks to suppliers.

c. Suppliers' invoices are not compared to purchase orders or to receiving reports before payment.

d. Purchasing, receiving, and stores functions are combined into a single organizational unit.

e. Purchasing and accounts payable are combined into a single organizational unit.

f. The purchase orders are not prenumbered (or, if prenumbered, are not filed in a sequential file that is periodically checked for gaps in the numbers).

g. The accounts payable ledger is not periodically reconciled to the control account in the general ledger.

h. After checks are written, the suppliers' invoices are not marked in some manner, stapled to the supporting documents, and filed.

i. The bank statement is reconciled by the person who signs the checks or by the accounts payable clerk.

13-12 What internal accounting control(s) would be most effective in preventing or detecting each of the following errors or fraudulent practices?

a. A supplier sends an invoice showing an amount computed on the basis of $10 per unit. However, the buyer in the purchasing department had listed the expected unit price as $7.

b. A supplier sends an invoice in the amount of $150. However, the goods were never ordered.

c. A supplier sends an invoice showing a quantity of 120 units shipped. However, only 100 units were actually received.

d. The cashier signs two checks, on successive days, to pay the same invoice from a supplier.

e. A firm's bank prepares a debit memorandum for an NSF (Not Sufficient Funds) check, but the bank clerk forgets to mail a copy of the memo to the firm.

f. A cashier prepares and submits an invoice from a fictitious supplier having the name of his neighbor, writes a check to the "supplier," and mails the check to his neighbor's address; the neighbor then cashes the check and splits the proceeds with the cashier.

g. A cashier prepares and signs a check that is not supported by an invoice. She cashes the check and conceals this theft by overfooting the columns of the check register (i.e., intentionally showing totals that are too large).

h. A petty cash custodian removes $80 from the petty cash fund to pay personal debts.

i. A truck driver who delivers goods to an electronics firm extracts for his use several small but expensive items from each delivery. Upon receiving one of these deliveries a receiving clerk signs a bill of lading that shows the number of items leaving the shipping dock and returns a copy to the driver.

j. A storeskeeper takes inventory items home at night; when the shortages become apparent, he claims that the receiving department did not deliver the goods to the storeroom.

k. When preparing a batch of disbursement vouchers for payment, a data entry clerk keys the voucher number as 236544. (Voucher numbers in the firm in question are 5 digits in length.)

l. A purchasing department buyer requests a supplier (who happens to be a friend) to deliver ordered supplies directly to his home address, where he puts the supplies to personal use.

m. A prepared check voucher is accidentally lost; by the time the firm receives the following month's statement from the supplier, showing the continuing balance due, the purchase discount is lost.

n. A receiving clerk posts, via a terminal, the receipt of a quantity of goods that exceeds the quantity ordered.

o. A disbursement voucher is prepared in the amount of $3010, but it is incorrectly posted as $1030 in the accounts payable subsidiary ledger.

p. The expected unit price of a part is listed on a purchase order as $0.21, although the lowest unit price of any ordered part is $2.10.

13-13 What internal accounting control(s) would be most effective in preventing or detecting each of the following errors or fraudulent practices?

a. An accounts payable clerk, to whom a batch of signed disbursement checks is sent by the treasurer, abstracts one of the checks and cashes it after posting the amount to the payee's record.

b. A buyer enters, via her terminal, the number of a part being ordered as 54l48, where the l is the letter l rather than the number 1.

c. An accounts payable clerk mistakenly enters, via her terminal, an account code for an expense as 333, although expense accounts begin at 500.

d. The actual quantity of a particular inventory item on hand in the storeroom is discovered to be zero, even though the inventory records show a quantity of 100 on hand.

e. A supplier's invoice is lost during the processing of a batch.

f. A purchasing department buyer orders unnecessary goods from a supplier firm, of which he happens to be an officer.

g. A receiving clerk posts the receipt of goods, via a terminal, to the incorrect inventory record.

h. During an inventory updating run a receipt transaction is accidentally posted as an issue transaction, and so the on-hand balance in the computerized record is reduced to a negative quantity.

i. A buyer accidentally omits the unit price of one of the ordered products when keying the data for a purchase into a terminal.

j. A purchase order is coded with an incorrect and nonexistent supplier number. The error is not detected until the file updating run, when no master record is located to match the number.

k. Two supplier invoices are lost in transmitting the invoices to the data preparation room.

l. A check is written in the amount of $1000, whereas the disbursement voucher shows the amount to be paid as $100.

m. An error in an inventory transaction is referred by the data control group to the receiving department for correction. A week later the stores department complains that the weekly inventory status report is suspicious with respect to the inventory item in question. However, the data processing department cannot determine whether the error has been corrected and reprocessed.

n. Errors in posting and pilferage have led to a large difference for a particular item between the on-hand quantity shown in the inventory record and the actual physical quantity.

o. A posting error to the accounts payable control account has resulted in a large overstatement of the account.

13-14 The following data pertain to vouchers that have been transmitted from the accounts payable department to the data processing department on May 17, where the data have been keyed onto a magnetic tape file. The vouchers represented by the data are to be used in preparing disbursement checks on this date.

Voucher No.	Supplier No.	Invoice Date	Disc. Pct.	Amount
6673	532	041991	0.00	540.00
6674	321	041991	0.00	892.00
6675	285	041991	0.00	1276.00
6676	502	041991	0.00	773.00
6678	477	041991	0.00	2343.50
6679	331	041991	0.00	390.00
6682	492	041991	0.00	3109.00
6723	294	050891	2.00	582.50
6726	439	050891	2.00	1500.00
6728	588	050891	3.00	668.00
6730	447	050891	1.50	800.00

Required

a. The preceding list of data comprises a batch, for which control totals were precomputed in the accounts payable department. Identify all the possible batch control totals that might have been computed for this batch, and compute their values on the basis of the listed data.

b. Explain why gaps appear in the document numbers.

c. Various edit checks may be applied to the preceding batched data during processing runs. For instance, the sequence of voucher numbers could be checked. If voucher number 6730 appeared ahead of 6728, an error would be listed on the exception and summary report. Identify five additional edit checks that may reasonably be applied, and illustrate each by means of the listed data.

13-15 The Old Missou Manufacturing Company is located in Columbia, Missouri. It has had many difficulties in materials control. Recently a raw materials inventory shortage was discovered. The resulting investigation revealed the following facts: Stock ledger cards are maintained in the storeroom and indicate the recorder point for each item. When the recorder point is reached, or when a special production order is received, the stock ledger clerk calls the purchasing agent and instructs him to order the item or items required. The purchasing agent prepares the purchase order in two copies, sending the original to the supplier and retaining the duplicate as the firm's record. All incoming materials are delivered direct to the storeroom. A receiving report is prepared; it is the basis for posting to stock ledger cards. Invoices are received by the purchasing agent, who verifies price, terms, and extensions. He sends them to the stock ledger clerk, who verifies the receipt of the materials against stock-ledger-card postings. If the materials have been received, the invoice is sent to the cash disbursements section for payment. The stock ledger clerk verifies the balances shown by stock ledger cards with materials actually on hand as filler work. There has been little time recently to check ledger cards, since two clerks have been sick. No annual physical inventory is taken.

Required

List the control weaknesses in the foregoing procedures and recommend improvements.

13-16 The Branden Company of Dover, Delaware, is a medium-size concern manufacturing special machinery to order. Its procedure relating to purchases of materials is as follows.

After approval by manufacturing department foremen, material purchase requisitions are forwarded to the purchasing department supervisor, who distributes such requisitions to the several employees under his control. The latter employees prepare prenumbered purchase orders in triplicate, account for all numbers, and send original purchase orders to vendors (suppliers). One copy of each purchase order is sent to the receiving department, where it is used as a receiving report. The other copy is filed in the purchasing department.

When the materials are received, they are moved directly to the storeroom and issued to the foremen on informal requests. The receiving department sends a receiving report (with its copy of the purchase order attached) to the purchasing department and sends copies of the receiving report to the storeroom and to the accounting department.

Vendors' invoices for material purchases, received in duplicate in the mailroom, are sent to the purchasing department and directed to each employee who placed a related order. The employee then compares the invoice with the copy of the purchase order on file in the purchasing department for price and terms and compares the invoice quantity with the quantity received as reported by the shipping and receiving department on its copy of the purchase order. The purchasing department employee also checks discounts, footings, and extensions, and initials the invoice to in-

dicate approval for payment. The invoice is then sent to the voucher section of the accounting department, where it is coded for account distribution, assigned a voucher number, entered in the voucher register, and filed according to payment due date.

On payment dates, prenumbered checks are requisitioned by the voucher section from the cashier and prepared, except for signature. After the checks are prepared, they are returned to the cashier, who puts them through a check-signing machine, accounts for the sequence of numbers, and passes them to a cash disbursements bookkeeper for entry in the cash disbursements book. The cash disbursements bookkeeper then returns the checks to the voucher section, which notes payment dates in the voucher register, places the checks in envelopes, and sends them to the mailroom. The vouchers are then filed in numerical sequence. At the end of each month one of the voucher clerks prepares an adding machine tape of unpaid items in the voucher register and compares the total thereof with the general ledger balance and investigates any difference disclosed by such comparison.

Required

List the control weaknesses in the foregoing procedure and recommend improvements.

(CPA adapted)

13-17 Masters Merchandising, Inc., acquires and sells a wide variety of housewares. Purchasing, shipping, and inventory management are therefore critical functions. The firm recently analyzed the activities related to these functions. It found that at least six parties are involved: the inventory control clerks, suppliers, customers, purchasing manager, shipping clerks, and inventory manager. Three main stores contain data regarding inventory, suppliers, and purchase orders. Among the activities that take place are preparation of requisitions, receiving reports, purchase orders, inventory aging reports, inventory status reports, supplier evaluation reports, and shipping records; determination of quantities to order; determination of quantities received and moved to storage; shipping of merchandise; mailing of purchase orders; updating of inventory records to show reductions, quantities ordered, and receipts; determination of suppliers from which to order; and matching of receipts with orders.

Required

Prepare a data flow diagram that portrays the logical flows of data through the described activities.

Hint: See Figure 22-15 and the related discussion.

13-18 ConSport Corporation of Chattanooga, Tennessee, is a regional wholesaler of sporting goods. The system flowchart on page 599 and the following description present ConSport's cash disbursements system.

a. The accounts payable department approves for payment all invoices (I) for the purchase of inventory. Invoices are matched with the purchase requisitions (PR), purchase orders (PO), and receiving reports (RR). The accounts payable clerks focus on vendor (supplier) name and skim the documents when they are combined.

b. When all the documents for an invoice are assembled, a two-copy disbursement voucher (DV) is prepared and the transaction is recorded in the voucher register (VR). The disbursement voucher and supporting documents are then field alphabetically by vendor.

c. A two-copy journal voucher (JV) that summarizes each day's entries in the voucher register is prepared daily. The first copy is sent to the general ledger department, and the second copy is filed in the accounts payable department by date.

d. The vendor file is searched daily for the disbursement vouchers of invoices that are due to be paid. Both copies of disbursement vouchers that are due to be paid are sent to the treasury department along with the supporting documents. The cashier prepares a check for each vendor, signs the check, and records it in the check register (CR). Copy 1 of the disbursement voucher is attached to the check copy and filed in check number order in the treasury department. Copy 2 and the supporting documents are returned to the accounts payable department and filed alphabetically by vendor.

e. A two-copy journal voucher that summarizes each day's checks is prepared. Copy 1 is sent to the general ledger department and copy 2 is filed in the treasury department by date.

f. The cashier receives the monthly bank statement with canceled checks and prepares the bank reconciliation (BR). If an adjustment is required as a consequence of the bank reconciliation, a two-copy journal voucher is prepared. Copy 1 is sent to the general ledger department. Copy 2 is attached to copy 1 of the bank reconciliation and filed by month in the treasury department. Copy 2 of the bank reconciliation is sent to the internal audit department.

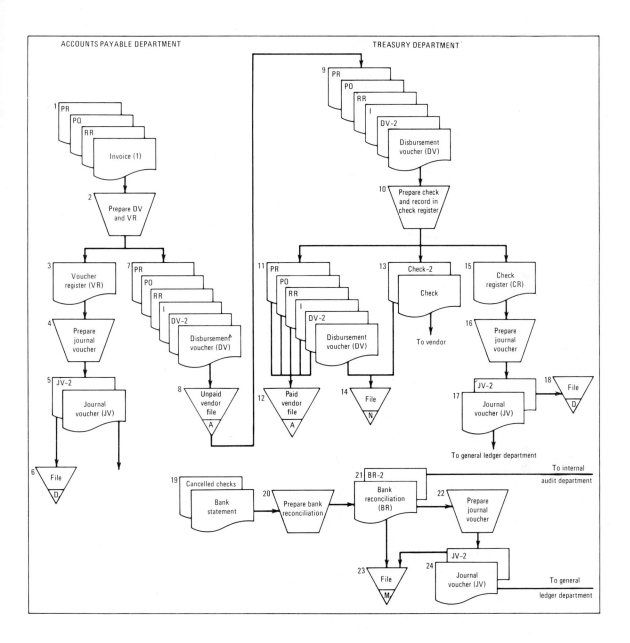

Required

ConSport Corporation's cash disbursements system has some weaknesses. Review the cash disbursements system and then, for each weakness in the system, do the following:

a. Identify where the weakness exists by using the reference number that appears to the left of each symbol.

b. Describe the nature of the weakness.

c. Make a recommendation to correct the weakness.

Use the following format in preparing your answer:

Reference Number	Nature of Weakness	Recommendation To Correct Weakness

(CMA adapted)

13-19 GoodLumber Company of Greensboro, North Carolina, is a large regional dealer of building materials that requires an elaborate system of internal controls. The flowchart of the purchasing activities is presented on page 601.

The activities in the purchasing department start with the receipt of an approved copy of the purchase requisition (PR) from the budget department. After reviewing the purchase requisition, a prenumbered purchase order (PO) is issued in multiple copies. Two copies are sent to a vendor (supplier), one retained in the purchasing department, and the remainder distributed to various other departments. The second copy of the purchase order is to be returned by the vendor to confirm the receipt of the order; this copy is filed according to PO number in the PO file.

A receiving report (RR) is completed in the receiving department when shipments of materials arrive from vendors. A copy of the receiving report is sent to the purchasing department and attached to the purchase order and purchase requisition in the vendor's file.

The accounts payable department normally receives two copies of a vendor's invoice. These two copies are forwarded to the purchasing department for review with various documents related to the order. Purchasing will either institute authorization procedures for the payment of the invoice or recommend exception procedures.

Required

a. A primary purpose for preparing a flowchart is to identify system control points. Explain what a control point is.

b. Control points are not specifically identified in the flowchart presented for the purchasing department of GoodLumber Company. Review the flowchart and identify where control points exist. For each control point:

(1) Identify where the control point exists in the flowchart. Use the reference number that appears to the left of each symbol.

(2) Describe the nature of the control activity required for each control point.

(3) Explain the purpose of or justification for each control activity.

Use the following format in preparing your answer:

Reference Number	Control Activity	Purpose or Justification

(CMA adapted)

13-20 The chart on page 602 illustrates a manual system for executing purchases and cash disbursements transactions.

Required

Indicate what each of the letters A through L represents. Do not discuss adequacies or inadequacies in the system of internal control.

(CPA adapted)

13-21 The Acme Manufacturing Co. employs you as an internal auditor. Your current assignment is to perform an operational audit of the purchasing department, composed of 12 buyers and several secretaries and headed by a purchasing manager. "We run a fairly efficient operation here," the purchasing manager comments to you. "We have established purchasing policies and procedures. The buyers have an average of 12 years of purchasing experience, and all have long tenure with the firm. They have received on-the-job training, and a few have

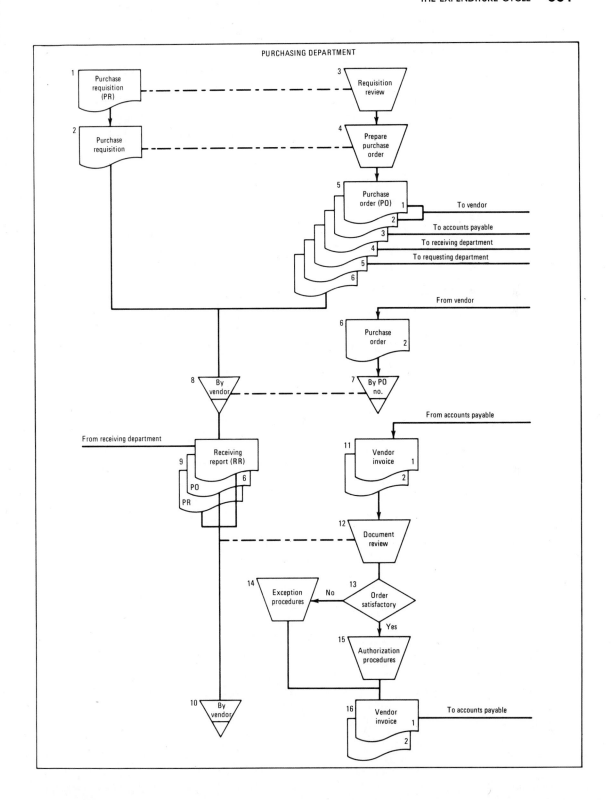

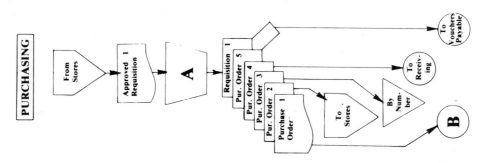

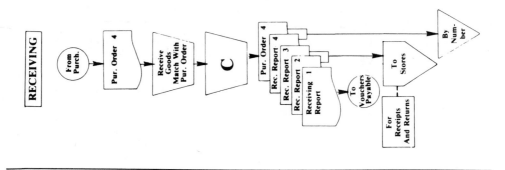

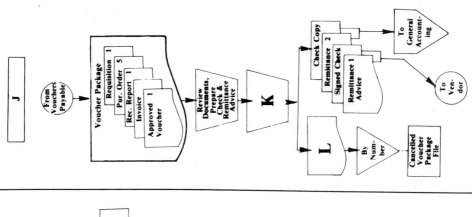

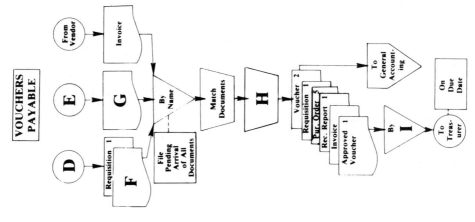

been sent to outside seminars for management training. Our main task is to get the right product in the right quantity to the right department. If you refer to the statistics on the number of purchase orders we handle each year, you will see that in recent years we have processed more purchase orders than ever with no increase in staff. I am pleased with my staff's performance."

During your review of operations you note the following:

1. The firm is spending huge sums on microcomputers and related products. It acquires a variety of different makes from a variety of suppliers. The purchasing department orders the microcomputer that meets the capability requirements and has the lowest possible price. However, some of the suppliers have declared bankruptcy or have stopped producing the product lines the firm purchased.

2. The purchasing department insists on ordering a certain chemical product from a supplier for the production department because the supplier is "stable and reliable and because the firm has always purchased from this supplier in the past." Some competing firms have successfully used a substitute product that has a much lower price.

3. The firm normally purchases from local suppliers. By enquiries you determine that these local suppliers acquire their materials from two major producers in the East; any firm such as yours could order directly from these producers.

4. One reason the number of purchase orders has increased is because of the increased frequency in gasoline purchases. It is possible to negotiate bulk purchases of gasoline.

5. Only one quote is received from a supplier in the case of each product acquired, even though for most products ordered there are several suppliers available.

6. Branch managers can order supplies in amounts less than $500 without following the purchasing department procedures. You note a few instances in which a purchase of an item costing more than $500 was made without the purchasing manager's approval by means of issuing several purchase orders for the item.

7. One buyer is acquiring goods for Acme from a supplier owned by his wife and her brother.

Required

Identify each deficiency in the operations of the purchasing department, discuss the risk(s) related to the deficiency, and recommend controls to compensate for the exposures due to the risk(s).

(SMAC adapted)

13-22 Beccan Company is a discount tire dealer that operates 25 retail stores in the metropolitan area. Both private brand and name brand tires are sold by Beccan. The company operates a centralized purchasing and warehousing facility and employs a perpetual inventory system. All purchases of tires and related supplies are placed through the company's central purchasing department to take advantage of quantity discounts. The tires and supplies are received at the central warehouse and distributed to the retail stores as needed. The perpetual inventory system at the central facility maintains current inventory records, designated reorder points, optimum order quantities, and continuous stocktakings for each type of tire and size and other related supplies.

The documents employed by Beccan in their inventory control system and their use are as follows:

• **Retail Stores Requisition.** This document is submitted by the retail stores to the central warehouse whenever tires or supplies are needed at the stores. The shipping clerks in the warehouse department fill the orders from inventory and have them delivered to the stores.

- **Purchase Requisition.** The inventory control clerk in the inventory control department prepares this document when the quantity on hand for an item falls below the designated reorder point. The document is forwarded to the purchasing department.

- **Purchase Order.** The purchasing department prepares this document when items need to be ordered. The document is submitted to an authorized vendor.

- **Receiving Report.** The warehouse department prepares this document when ordered items are received from vendors. The receiving clerk completes the document by indicating the vendor's name, the date the shipment is received, and the quantity of each item received.

- **Invoice.** An invoice is received from vendors specifying the amounts owed by Beccan.

The following departments are involved in Beccan's inventory control system:

- **Inventory Control Department.** This department is responsible for the maintenance of all perpetual inventory records for all items carried in inventory. This includes current quantity on hand, reorder point, optimum order quantity, and quantity on order for each item carried.

- **Warehouse Department.** This department maintains the physical inventory of all items carried in inventory. All orders from vendors are received (receiving clerk) and all distributions to retail stores are filled (shipping clerks) in this department.

- **Purchasing Department.** The purchasing department places all orders for items needed by the company.

- **Accounts Payable Department.** Accounts payable maintains all open accounts with vendors and other creditors. All payments are processed in this department.

Required

Prepare a document system flowchart to show how these documents should be coordinated and used among the departments at the central facility of Beccan Company to provide adequate internal control over the receipt, issuance, replenishment, and payment of tires and supplies. You may assume that the documents have a sufficient number of copies to assure that the perpetual inventory system has the necessary basic internal controls.

(CMA adapted)

13-23 The Roster Distributing Company of Logan, Utah, employs the following purchasing and cash disbursements procedures:

The purchasing department prepares a four-part purchase order from a verbal request by the plant superintendent or by one of the foremen. Copies 1 and 2 are sent to the supplier. Copy 4 is sent to the receiving department for use as a receiving report. Copy 3 is filed as a control and follow-up copy for open orders.

Goods received are noted on the copy being used as the receiving report. This copy is then sent to the purchasing department, where it is filed with copy 3 of the purchase order and held until the supplier's invoice is received. (No perpetual inventory records are maintained.)

When the supplier's invoice is received, purchase order copies 3 and 4 are pulled from the file and checked against the invoice. The clerical accuracy (including prices) is checked, and the invoice is assigned a number and recorded in the invoice register. The code for the account(s) to be debited is written on the invoice. Copy 3 of the purchase order is filed numerically. The invoice and copy 4 of the purchase order are sent to the accounts payable clerk.

The accounts payable clerk files the invoice and copy 4 of the purchase order by due date. When the invoices are due, the clerk pulls the invoices and purchase orders and prepares checks and check copies; on the check copies she notes the account distribution. From the checks the clerk prepares an adding machine tape of the cash amounts. She then forwards the invoices, purchase orders, checks, check copies, and tape to a clerk in the general accounting department.

The general accounting clerk posts by hand the check copy amounts to the cash disbursements book. The tape forwarded from the accounts payable clerk is compared with the totals in the cash disbursements book; if they agree, the tape is discarded. The clerk then forwards the invoices, purchase orders, checks, and check copies to the treasurer for his signature.

The treasurer reviews the support, signs the checks, and returns all items to the general accounting clerk.

The general accounting clerk "protects" the checks with a protector device, mails the checks to the vendors, files the check copies by number, stamps the invoices "Paid," and forwards the invoices and attached receiving reports to the purchasing department.

The firm's books are not on an accrual basis. The invoice register is used only as a control device. Accounts payable are set up at month's end by a journal entry. The amounts are determined by running a tape of the invoices listed as unpaid in the invoice register.

Required

a. Prepare a document system flowchart, using appropriate symbols.

b. List the control weaknesses in the procedure described and recommend improvements.

13-24 The Alberta Company is a large research institute located in Calgary, Alberta. It employs a mainframe computer for transaction processing and research support. Magnetic disks provide all secondary storage; on-line terminals are located in all of the departments.

The institute allows managers in the various departments to acquire supplies, furniture, equipment, and other items needed and budgeted for. The purchases procedure begins with a requisition prepared by a department manager. Included in the purchase requisition are the description of each item to be purchased, the account number to be charged for the purchase, and the signature of the manager. Upon receipt of the requisition, a buyer in the purchasing department adds a supplier name and number and the estimated price of the item.

The buyer enters the data from the requisition into the computer system via a video display terminal. First, the data are edited via an on-line program. Then a purchases program produces the following outputs: (1) A prenumbered purchase order is printed on a small impact printer in the purchasing department, while a copy of the purchase order is stored in an open purchase order file. (2) A message is displayed on the CRT screen, showing the amount of remaining funds in the department's budget after the estimated amount of the requested purchase. If the amount is within the budget, the buyer gives the purchase order to the purchasing manager for signature. Then the purchase order is distributed as follows: copy 1 to the supplier, copy 2 to accounts payable, copy 3 to receiving, and copy 4 to the requisitioner. (If the amount exceeds the budget, the buyer puts the purchase order in a hold file and notifies the requisitioner by preparing a hold notice.)

When the ordered items arrive at the receiving dock, a receiving clerk pulls the purchase order (on which the quantities have been blanked out) from the file and counts the goods. Then the clerk enters the purchase order number, item numbers, and quantities counted via a video display terminal in the area. A receiving program edits the data, verifies that a purchase order exists, and updates the open purchase order file. It also updates either (1) the fixed-asset master file or (2) the expense control file, depending on the nature of the items received. The program then produces a prenumbered receiving report on a small printer in the receiving area, as well as a copy of the receiving report on a receiving report file (stored on a magnetic disk). The receiving clerk signs the receiving report and sends it, together with the items, to the requisitioning department. He refiles the purchase order copy by number, after stamping it completed.

The requisitioning department receives the items, signs the receiving report, and forwards it to accounts payable. When the supplier's invoice arrives, the payables clerk pulls the purchase order and receiving report from the file (where they have been filed by supplier name). Then the clerk enters the invoice number, purchase order number, receiving report number, item numbers, and quantities invoiced into a video display terminal. A payables program compares the data on the three documents and displays any differences. The clerk approves the invoice for payment if no differences appear (or puts it into a hold basket if differences must be reconciled) and enters the amount to be paid via the terminals. She files the documents by supplier name. The payables program (1) groups all payment data into an accounts payable file, (2) updates the open purchase order file by removing the completed purchase order, and (3) deducts the amount of the payable from the remaining balance in the department's budget.

At the end of each week the checks pertaining to all approved invoices are printed from the accounts payable file; data from the supplier file are also used in this run. A listing of the checks is generated during this run. In addition, a weekly report of open purchase orders is printed, arranged by order date. Finally, summary journal vouchers showing the total amounts of new payables and disbursements for the week are printed; these are sent to the general ledger clerk.

Required

Prepare a computer system flowchart consisting of the following segments:

a. The preparation of purchase requisitions and purchase orders.
b. The processing of receipts of ordered goods.
c. The processing of invoices and recording of accounts payable.
d. The preparation of checks and weekly reports.

(SMAC adapted)

13-25 The Wedge Manufacturing Co. of Cleveland processes purchases and inventory transactions as follows:

The request for purchases begins in the plant operations department. That department prepares a two-part prenumbered inventory materials request, which indicates the description and quantity of inventory items and the date they are needed. The request must be approved by the plant manager. One copy of the request is forwarded to the manager of the purchasing department and the other copy is filed temporarily by inventory item name in the plant operations department.

On receiving its copy of the inventory materials request, the purchasing department prepares a six-part prenumbered purchase order (P.O.). The distribution of the P.O. is as follows:

Original—supplier.

Second copy—plant operations department.

Third copy—receiving department.

Fourth copy—accounts payable department.

Fifth copy—filed temporarily with the inventory materials request by supplier name.

Sixth copy—filed by number for two years.

The plant operations department matches its copy of the P.O. to the inventory materials request, then files and retains for two years the two documents together according to the inventory materials request number.

The receiving department temporarily files its copy (the receiver copy) of the P.O. by supplier name until inventory materials are delivered. The receiving clerk indicates on the receiver the quantity of items received and the date. The clerk then photocopies the receiver and sends the original to the accounts payable department. The photocopy is sent to the purchasing department.

The purchasing department matches its supplier file copy of the P.O. with the receiver returned from the receiving department. When all items ordered are received, the P.O., receiver, and the initial inventory materials request are filed by supplier name for two years.

The accounts payable department matches the receiver with its copy of the P.O. and files the documents by supplier name.

When a supplier's invoice is received, an accounts payable clerk compares the invoice and the related P.O. and receiver for description of material, quantities, and price. The three documents are then stapled together with a prenumbered two-part voucher ticket. The clerical accuracy of the invoice is verified and account distribution is assigned and indicated on the face of the voucher ticket. The voucher ticket also indicates the supplier name and number and the invoice number and date. This set of documents, called the voucher package, is filed by supplier name for seven years.

Before filing, however, the original copy of the voucher ticket is detached from the package and forwarded to another clerk in the accounts payable department, who verifies the clerical accuracy of the voucher ticket. Voucher tickets are accumulated and batched using a batch ticket, which indicates the date, the number of voucher tickets, and the total amount of invoices. From the batch ticket an adding machine tape is prepared of the daily total amount of invoices. The batch ticket and the related batch of voucher tickets are sent to the EDP department for processing.

On receiving the batch ticket and the voucher tickets, the EDP department compares the documents for number of vouchers and the total amount of invoices. At this point, the batch ticket is assigned a number, and the batch is entered in the batch log (batch input control sheet). The voucher tickets are keyed to tape and forwarded for processing within the computer operations room. The voucher tickets are held in the EDP department until all edit errors are corrected, then are forwarded to the accounts payable department. The batch ticket is filed and retained in the EDP department by batch number for two years.

Computer operations performs a report processing run that produces a daily voucher register, together with an error report. The accounts payable master file and the general ledger are the two disk files used in processing. The voucher tickets and error records from previous runs, on magnetic tape, serve as input.

The daily voucher register is returned to

the same person in the EDP department who prepared the batches for input. This person reviews the error report, accounts for the batches and control totals, and corrects errors. No approval is required for error corrections, which are processed the next day.

The accounts payable department receives the daily voucher register, together with the voucher tickets. The tickets and register are compared to ensure that each voucher ticket sequence number is in the daily voucher register. The voucher tickets are destroyed. The adding machine tape of the daily total amount of invoices on the batch ticket is compared to the total of the daily voucher register. The adding machine tape and the daily voucher register are filed separately by date and retained in the department for three years.

Required

a. Prepare a document system flowchart that incorporates the manual and computer-based system operations described.

b. Identify any weaknesses in controls, indicate the possible errors or discrepancies that might occur because of such weaknesses, and recommend improvements.

c. Describe several transaction controls that would be suitable to this processing system and that have not been noted above. For each included programmed check, list the data items to which the check pertains.

Suggested Readings

Accounts Payable. Atlanta, Ga.: Management Science America, 1989.

Accounts Payable and Purchase Control System. Sunnyvale, Cal.: Data Design Associates, 1982.

A Guide for Studying and Evaluating Internal Accounting Controls. Chicago: Arthur Andersen & Co., 1978.

MSA Inventory and Purchasing System. Atlanta, Ga.: Management Science America, 1983.

Nash, John F. *Accounting Information Systems.* 2d ed. New York: Macmillan Publishing Co., 1989.

Robinson, Leonard A.; Davis, James R.; and Alderman, C. Wayne. *Accounting Information Systems: A Cycle Approach.* 3rd ed. New York: John Wiley & Sons, 1990.

CHAPTER OBJECTIVES

After reading this chapter, you should be able to do the following:

Identify the objectives of three cycles involved in the management of resources.

Describe functions, relationships, and components of the cycle involved in the management of the employee services resource.

Describe functions, relationships, and components of the cycle involved in the management of the facilities (fixed assets) resource.

Discuss functions and relationships of the cycle involved in management of the funds resource.

Chapter **14**

THE RESOURCE MANAGEMENT CYCLES

Every organization uses resources that may be categorized as materials, human and technical services, facilities, cash, and data. Each type of resource must be managed. **Resource management** gives rise to inputs, events or transactions, processing steps, and data flows. To provide means of reference, these dynamic facets are recorded, filed, and presented in reports and other outputs. To assure their reliability, controls and security measures are established and maintained.

The process of managing resources necessarily creates the same type of transaction-oriented activity cycles as discussed in the two previous chapters. Cycles related to four basic resources are portrayed in Figure 14-1. Two of the cycles are in effect expenditure cycles. However, they pertain to employee services and facilities rather than to materials and outside services. These two cycles are surveyed in this chapter. A third cycle, pertaining to the management of the funds resource, is given less attention, since cash receipts and cash disbursements transactions have already been examined directly. A fourth cycle, focusing on raw materials and their conversion into finished goods, is considered in Chapter 15. The management of the fifth resource, data, was introduced in Chapter 8 and will be treated more extensively in Chapter 18.

Employee Services Management Cycle

Employee services are the major component of the human services resource employed by organizations. In management

609

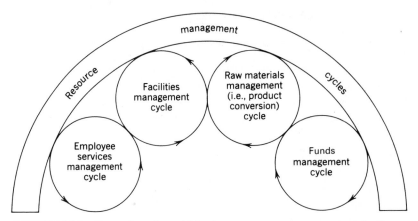

FIGURE 14-1 Several cycles within the resource management umbrella.

textbooks employee services have traditionally been called the labor or manpower resource. In certain organizations, such as service-oriented firms and governmental agencies, this resource consumes the greatest portion of the recurring expenditures. Employee services in such organizations may be encompassed within the expenditure cycle. In other organizations, such as manufacturing firms, this resource is a key cost in the conversion of raw materials into finished goods. Employee services in such organizations may be considered a part of the product conversion cycle. In order to accommodate all types of organizations, we have placed employee services within the resource management cycles.

Cycle Objectives

The major purpose of the **employee services management cycle** is to facilitate the exchange of cash with employees for needed services. (Because it centers upon payments to employees, it is also known as the payroll cycle.) Key objectives within the broad purpose of this cycle are to ensure that the status, pay rates or salaries, and pay deductions of employees are authorized; that payments are made for actual services rendered; and that employee-related costs are promptly

and accurately recorded, classified, summarized, distributed, and reported.

Functions

Functions related to employees include hiring, training, transferring, terminating, classifying, adjusting pay levels, establishing safety measures, preparing payrolls, maintaining employee benefits programs, and reporting to governmental agencies. Although all of these are important concerns within the field of personnel administration, the employee services management cycle focuses primarily on the payroll expenditures. Therefore, a more relevant listing of functions for our use consists of establishing pay status, measuring the services rendered, preparing paychecks, issuing and distributing paychecks, distributing costs for employee services, and preparing required reports and statements.

Establish pay status. Before an employee can be paid, his or her status should be clearly stated in writing. Status is a multifaceted concept. It first implies that the employee has successfully completed the hiring process, which usually consists of filling out a detailed application form and undergoing interviews. When the applicant is hired, the data from the application form become part of the employee's personnel data record. Status also involves classification and type of remuneration. An employee may be classified as an accounting clerk, a salesperson, a production worker, a manager, and so forth. Production, other operational employees (e.g., truck drivers), and many clerks are paid according to hourly rates; professional and managerial employees and certain clerks are generally paid monthly salaries; and salespersons are often paid on a commission basis. Certain classifications are eligible for overtime rates and shift differentials, whereas others are exempt from such premiums. Finally, pay status depends on the types and number of deductions that are to be offset against the amounts payable by a firm. Of two employees who were hired on the same date with the same job classification, one may have a higher "take-home" pay than the other as a result of fewer deductions from his or her gross pay.

Measure the services rendered. The means by which employee services are measured vary according to the type of remuneration. Those employees on hourly wages are expected to record their times on the job rather precisely; each time they enter and leave the job locations, they enter the times on time cards. Salaried employees prepare attendance records of some sort (e.g., time sheets), showing attendance and absences during the various days comprising the pay period. Commission employees prepare vouchers that reflect the amounts of sales made during the period on which commissions are to be computed. Each type of service-related document serves as the legal basis for payment when approved by the employee's supervisor.

Prepare paychecks. Employees are normally paid by checks, since they provide relative safety and written records of the amounts due. In some cases, however, hourly employees may be paid by currency.

As mentioned earlier, the net amount of each paycheck is equal to the gross amount less all deductions. Certain deductions are required by law or contract, such as premiums or dues for social security benefits, unemployment benefits, group medical insurance benefits, pension benefits, and union representation. Other deductions are voluntary, such as payments for U.S. savings bonds and contributions to recognized charities. All approved deductions are withheld by the employees' firm, at which point they become accrued liabilities. These liabilities are removed when the amounts withheld are deposited in designated financial institutions.

As a control procedure, a special payroll-imprest bank account may be established to accommodate paycheck amounts. A firm that follows this practice prepares a disbursement voucher when the total amount of the payroll is known. Next a check is drawn on the firm's regular bank account and given to the person who signs checks. He or she signs the prepared check and delivers it to the bank for deposit in the special account. Then the paychecks can be issued and distributed.

Issue and distribute paychecks. Employees are paid, according to law, on established schedules. A schedule for a particular pay classification may be weekly, biweekly, semimonthly, or monthly. After the paychecks are signed, they are either distributed to the employees at their job sites or at other designated places.

Paychecks may be replaced by other modes of payment. Hourly employees are sometimes paid in currency. In such cases the employees are generally expected to obtain their pay amounts at a cashier's window and to sign receipts. Salaried employees and managers are often encouraged to select a direct-deposit arrangement, under which the firm deposits their pay amounts directly into their personal bank accounts.

Distribute costs for employee services. An employer's costs for employee services include the gross amounts of pay for all employees. In addition, the employer incurs payroll-related expenses pertaining to such benefits as unemployment, pension, vacation, sick leave, and group insurance. Like costs of any type, these costs for employee services must be distributed to various accounts. Most of the employee service costs are likely to be distributed in accordance with the organizational structure of the firm, for example, to marketing, finance, and other functions. If the firm is a manufacturer, production-related costs will be distributed to manufacturing overhead or to direct labor. When employees are directly involved in the development of long-lived assets for the firm, their costs will be capitalized.

The services of those employees directly involved in the production of goods are absorbed in the value of the products. Thus, a record called the job-time ticket is often used to capture the hours of direct labor they expend in the production process.

Prepare required reports and statements. A variety of reports and statements related to payroll must be prepared. Certain of these outputs are specified in detail by a maze of federal and state regulations, since deductions from each employee's paycheck are destined to flow into governmental funds. For instance, the Federal Insurance Contributions Act (FICA) specifies the manner of computing and withholding employee (and employer) contributions for old age, survivors', disability, and hospital insurance benefits. State and federal unemployment compensation laws specify the manner of computing and withholding contributions for unemployment benefits. These laws also detail the manner of reporting on these withholdings at the end of each quarter and year.

Other reports and statements pertain to the remainder of the deductions taken from employees' paychecks.

Relationships to the Organization

These functions are typically achieved under the direction of the personnel and finance/accounting organizational functions (units) of the firm. The employee services management cycle therefore involves the interaction of the personnel information system and the accounting information system. In addition, every department or other organizational unit is involved, since the employees are located throughout the organization. Figure 14-2 shows the relations between key departments and the cycle functions.

Personnel. Personnel management has the primary objective of planning, controlling, and coordinating the employees—the internally employed human resource—within an organization. Among the various functions it performs, those related to the establishment of the employees' pay status are most relevant to the payment for services rendered. The personnel department performs this function by preparing and distributing the necessary paperwork concerning employee pay actions.

Finance/accounting. The objectives of financial and accounting management relate broadly to funds, data, information, planning, and control over resources. Organizational units that lie within this function and are involved in the management of employee services include timekeeping, payroll, accounts payable, cash disbursements, cost distribution, and general ledger. Timekeeping maintains control over the time and attendance records of hourly employees. Payroll prepares paychecks, maintains the payroll records, and prepares required reports and statements. Accounts payable, in the context of this cycle, approves the dis-

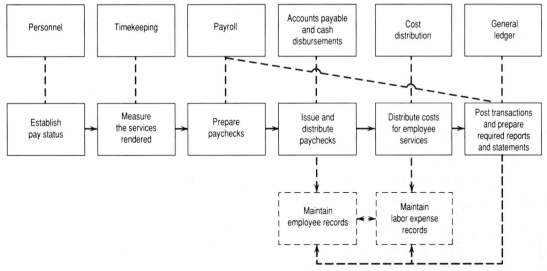

FIGURE 14-2 Typical functions and related organizational units of an employee services cycle.

bursement voucher pertaining to employee services. Cash disbursements, together with the cashier, signs and distributes the paychecks. Cost distribution maintains the records reflecting detailed costs of the products. General ledger maintains control over all asset, equity, expense, and income accounts. Note that the timekeeping and cost distribution units are more typically found in manufacturing firms than in other types of organizations.

Data Sources and Inputs

Data used in this cycle are mainly based on inputs from the time records and from documents provided by the personnel department. Other sources are the payroll files and the departments in which jobs requiring direct labor are performed.

Source documents typically used in the management of employee services include the following:

1. **Personnel action form.** A **personnel action form** serves to notify interested parties of actions concerning employees. These actions may pertain to the notice of

hiring, a change of status, an evaluation of job performance, and so on. Figure 14-3 shows a personnel action form that notifies the payroll department of a situation or change affecting the status of an employee's pay. Another category of personnel actions concerns deductions. Some of these forms are issued by the firm and some by governmental agencies. An example of the latter is the W-4 Form, Employee Withholding Allowance Certificate, which is provided by the Internal Revenue Service.

2. **Time and/or attendance form.** The **time card,** also known as clock card, records the actual hours spent by hourly employees at their work locations. It contains an employee's name and number, plus the dates of the applicable pay period. Each time the employee enters or leaves, he or she "punches" the card in the time clock. At the bottom of the card is a space for the supervisor's signature. Other attendance forms, as noted earlier, include a time sheet for use by salaried employees.

3. **Job-time ticket.** In contrast to the time card, which focuses on attendance at the

PERSONNEL FORM 1174

Distribution:
White, Green, Canary: Personnel
Pink: Originator

PERSONNEL — PAYROLL ACTION NOTIFICATION

Name _____

Effective Date _____ Organization Unit No. _____ Employee Number _____

Address *(Change Only)* _____

Enroll or transfer only — Overtime Exempt ☐   Overtime Non-Exempt ☐

ACTION TO BE TAKEN — CHECK APPLICABLE BOX(ES)

☐ Enroll   ☐ Termination   ☐ Vacation (Specify dates & pay request below)

☐ Transfer   ☐ Leave of Absence   ☐ Other (Explain)

☐ Rate Change   ☐ Cross Charge

Present Status:

Job Title _____   Salary _____

Dept. & Div. _____   Job Class _____

New Status:

Job Title _____   Salary _____

Dept. & Div. _____   Job Class _____

If salary increase, give following information:

Amount of increase as % of present salary _____ .

Midpoint of salary range for job class _____ .

Date of last increase _____; amount of last increase _____ .

(Guidelines per Sec. -0500 must be observed.)

Date of last appraisal _____ summary evaluation _____ .

(Within 6 mos. of requested increase.)

Explanation: _____
_____
_____
_____

Originated by _____ Transmittal date _____

Management Approval _____ Personnel Approval _____

PAYROLL USE ONLY	Pay Period _____	Permanent
	Follow Up Yes _____ No _____	_____ hrs. $ _____
	Action PR# _____	Temporary
	Action Type _____	_____ hrs. $ _____

REMARKS:

FIGURE 14-3 A document relating to personnel actions. Courtesy of John Wiley & Sons, Inc.

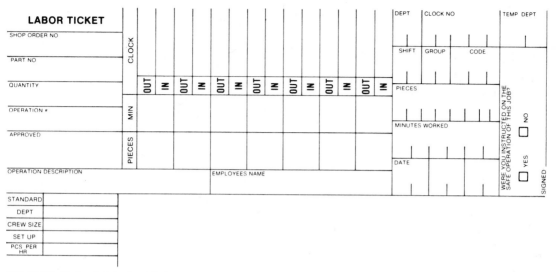

FIGURE 14-4 A job-time (labor) ticket.

work site, the **job-time ticket** focuses on specific jobs or work orders. Each time an hourly employee, such as a production worker, begins and ends work on the job, he or she records the time on the card. As in the case of the time card, the means of entering the times may be a time clock or a terminal. Figure 14-4 pictures a job-time ticket (called here a labor ticket). Note that spaces are provided for entering the productivity in terms of pieces completed during the elapsed periods.

4. **Paycheck.** A **paycheck,** with voucher stub, is the final document in the employee services management cycle. Figure 14-5 presents a typical paycheck prepared by computer. The stub shows all necessary details, including overtime pay and deductions.

Codes are useful for identifying data needed in payrolls and labor cost distributions. In addition to codes for general ledger accounts, codes can identify employees, departments, production jobs, and skills.

An employee code is particularly important, since it will appear on most (if not all) input documents. Some firms use the social security number as the employee code. Other firms use a sequential code to identify employees. Although both of these approaches are easy to apply, a group code would be more useful for analysis. Fields within a group code for employees might include pay category (i.e., hourly or salaried), department number, skill code, date of hire, and self-checking digit. A drawback to a field such as department number, however, is that it may change during the tenure of an employee.

Data Base

Among the files needed in managing employee services are the employee payroll master, personnel reference and history, time record transaction, paycheck transaction, and compensation reference files.

Employee payroll master file. An **employee payroll master file** contains the earnings records of the employees. It is updated to show the amounts received from paychecks at the end of each pay period. Figure

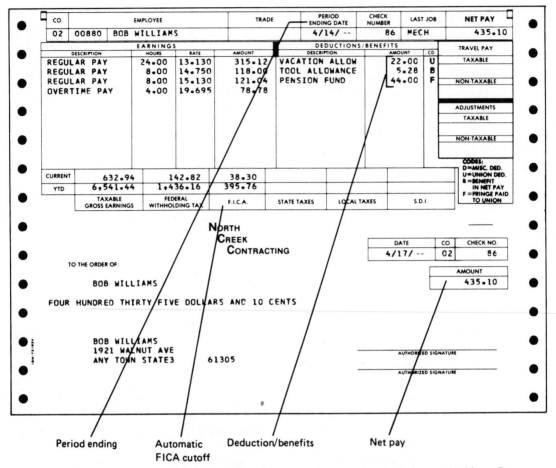

CO.		EMPLOYEE		TRADE		PERIOD ENDING DATE	CHECK NUMBER	LAST JOB	NET PAY
02	00880	BOB WILLIAMS				4/14/ --	86	MECH	435.10

EARNINGS				DEDUCTIONS/BENEFITS				TRAVEL PAY
DESCRIPTION	HOURS	RATE	AMOUNT	DESCRIPTION	AMOUNT	CD		TAXABLE
REGULAR PAY	24.00	13.130	315.12	VACATION ALLOW	22.00	U		
REGULAR PAY	8.00	14.750	118.00	TOOL ALLOWANCE	5.28	B		NON-TAXABLE
REGULAR PAY	8.00	15.130	121.04	PENSION FUND	44.00	F		
OVERTIME PAY	4.00	19.695	78.78					

ADJUSTMENTS
TAXABLE
NON-TAXABLE

CODES:
D=MISC. DED.
U=UNION DED.
B =BENEFIT IN NET PAY
F =FRINGE PAID TO UNION

CURRENT	632.94	142.82	38.30			
YTD	6,541.44	1,436.16	395.76			
	TAXABLE GROSS EARNINGS	FEDERAL WITHHOLDING TAX	F.I.C.A.	STATE TAXES	LOCAL TAXES	S.D.I.

NORTH CREEK CONTRACTING

DATE	CO.	CHECK NO.
4/17/ --	02	86

AMOUNT
435.10

TO THE ORDER OF:

BOB WILLIAMS

FOUR HUNDRED THIRTY-FIVE DOLLARS AND 10 CENTS

BOB WILLIAMS
1921 WALNUT AVE
ANY TOWN STATE3   61305

AUTHORIZED SIGNATURE

AUTHORIZED SIGNATURE

Period ending   Automatic FICA cutoff   Deduction/benefits   Net pay

FIGURE 14-5 A paycheck and voucher stub. Courtesy of International Business Machines Corporation.

14-6 displays a record layout of the variety of data items that might appear in this file. Generally the primary and sorting key is the employee number.

An important concern with this file is keeping the records and their permanent data up to date. When an employee marries and takes a new last name, for instance, this change should appear quickly in her record. When a new employee is hired, a record must be established before the end of the pay period. On the other hand, when an employee is terminated, the record should not be discarded until after the end of the year. Certain year-end reports require data concerning all employees who were active during any part of the year.

Personnel reference and history file. As the main source of personnel data in the firm, the **personnel reference and history file** complements the payroll master. It contains a variety of nonfinancial data as well as financial data concerning each employee. For instance, it might contain the employee's address, skills, job title, work experience, edu-

Employee number	Employee name	Social security number	Department or center code	Pay class-ification	Pay rate or salary	Overtime rate	Marital status	Number of exemptions

Deduction code	Deduction rate or amount per pay period	Year-to-date withheld	Year-to-date gross pay	Year-to-date net pay	Quarter-to-date gross pay	Quarter-to-date net pay

Repeat for each deduction

FIGURE 14-6 A layout of an employee payroll record. *Note:* Although the lengths of fields and modes of data items are necessary for complete documentation, they have been omitted for the sake of simplicity.

cational history, performance evaluations, and even family status.

This file may be consolidated and maintained in the personnel department. Alternatively, it may be split into several reference files, which may be located in the payroll and/or data processing departments as well as the personnel department.

A related file is a *skills file,* which provides an inventory of skills required by the firm and the employees who currently possess each skill. This type of file enables a firm to locate qualified candidates when an opening or new need arises, as well as to establish a sound salary structure.

Time record transaction file.   A **time record transaction file** consists of copies of all the time cards or sheets for a particular pay period. In computer-based systems they are likely stored on magnetic media for use in processing the payroll.

Paycheck transaction file.   In a manual system the **paycheck transaction file** consists of a copy of each current paycheck, arranged in check number order. In a computer-based system the record layout on magnetic media may appear similar to a record in the check disbursements transaction file.

Compensation reference file.   A table of pay rates and salary levels for the various job descriptions within the firm represents a **compensation reference file.**

Data Flows and Processing

Both manual and computer-based processing systems will be described. The emphasis in the former is on the flows of source documents and outputs, whereas the latter focuses on the processing runs.

Manual processing system.   Figure 14-7 presents a system flowchart of a procedure involving the payment of hourly operations-type employees (e.g., production employees) who also work directly on specific jobs. Our discussion of this procedure parallels the functions of the cycle listed earlier.

1. **Establish pay status.** This beginning function takes place in the personnel department, where all of the personnel actions and changes are prepared and then transmitted to the payroll department.

2. **Measure the services rendered.** The time records are prepared in the operational (e.g., production) departments and time-

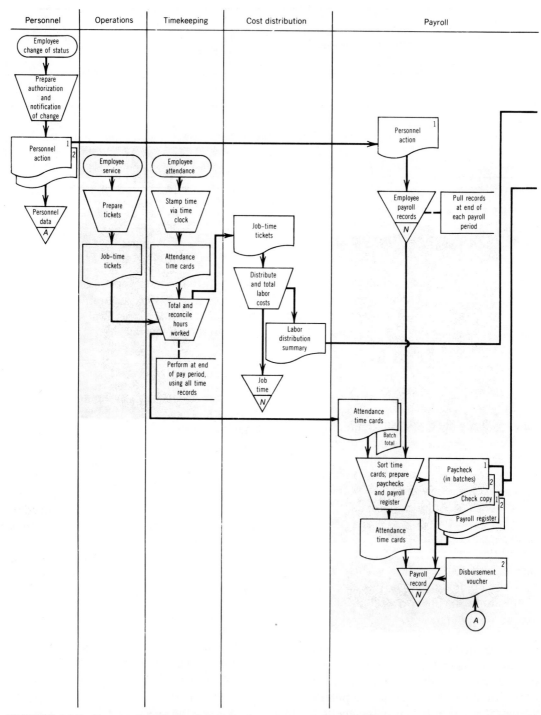

FIGURE 14-7 System flowchart of a manual employee payroll transaction processing procedure, with an emphasis on document flows.

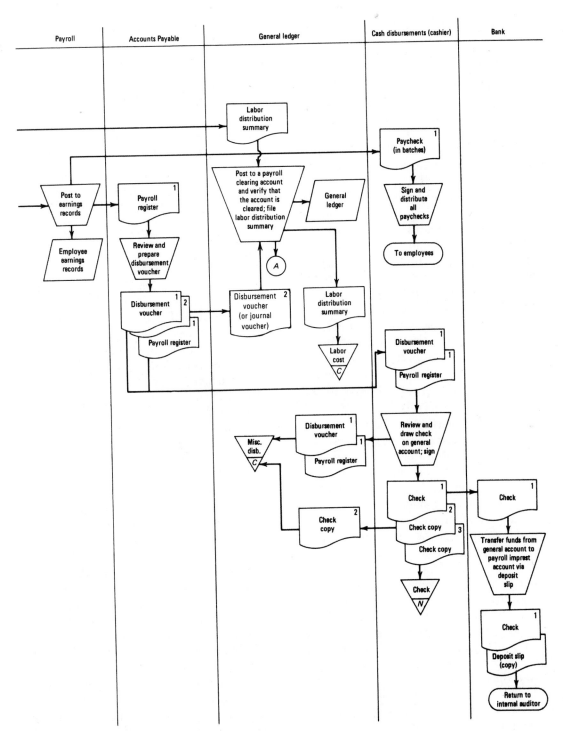

FIGURE 14-7 (*Continued*).

keeping areas. Time cards are maintained in racks near the entrance to the work site. Employees clock in and clock out under the eye of a timekeeper. The job-time tickets are available right at the work site. Employees either punch the tickets on a clock or mark them manually under the eye of their supervisor.

At the end of each day the job-time tickets are collected and approved by the employees' supervisor. Then the supervisor forwards the tickets to the time-keeper. At the end of the pay period the timekeeper compares the total hours shown on the job-time tickets, for each employee, with the total hours shown on his or her attendance time cards. If the two sets of total hours are approximately equal (after allowing for breaks, lunch, etc.), the time records are said to be reconciled. Then the timekeeper sends the attendance time cards to the payroll department (together with the total of hours worked) and the job-time tickets to the cost distribution department.

3. **Prepare the paychecks.** In the payroll department a clerk prepares a paycheck and voucher stub for each employee, on the basis of data from the time card and from the employee's payroll reference file. Next the clerk enters the relevant information from the paycheck and voucher stub (i.e., gross pay, deductions, net pay, overtime premium) into the payroll register. Another clerk then posts the information to the employee's earnings record (i.e., the payroll master). Still another clerk verifies that the hours used in preparing the payroll register equal the total hours on the time cards, and that the total payroll amount entered into the register equals the total amount posted to all employees' earnings records. The paychecks and attached voucher stubs are sent, in a batch, to the cash disbursements department (or cashier).

4. **Issue and distribute paychecks.** Upon receiving a copy of the payroll register, an accounts payable clerk verifies its correctness and then prepares a disbursement voucher. A clerk in the cash disbursements department draws a check on the firm's regular bank account and gives it to the cashier for signing. The signed check is delivered to the bank and deposited in the special payroll account. Then the cashier signs all the paychecks. A paymaster (a designated person not otherwise involved in personnel or payroll procedures) distributes the paychecks.

5. **Distribute labor costs** (i.e., cost of employee services). Meanwhile, a clerk in the cost distribution department distributes the employee labor costs incurred by the operational personnel (e.g., production employees) to the various jobs in progress. The clerk next reports the costs, via a **labor distribution summary** or a journal voucher, to the general ledger department. Then the general ledger clerk debits the amounts to the various labor-related accounts (e.g., direct factory labor) and credits a payroll control account (e.g., accrued payroll).

Subsequently, the general ledger clerk clears the payroll control account by reference to the disbursement voucher (or related journal voucher) prepared by accounts payable. That is, he or she debits the payroll control account and credits the cash account as well as the deductions withheld accounts. Since the totals from both sources (labor cost distribution and disbursement voucher) should be equal, the payroll control account will be cleared to zero if processing has been correct.

It should be noted that this clearing procedure is a partial substitute for the computation of formal batch totals in the timekeeping department. When attendance time records are not accompanied by time records related to jobs, it is highly desirable to compute batch totals at the point where the time records are assembled.

6. **Prepare required reports and statements.** The only report shown in the flowchart is the payroll register. Other reports are discussed in a later section.

Computer-based processing system. Although the on-line approach may be used in computer-based processing, the batch approach is better suited to the payroll procedure. Since all of the records in the employee payroll master file are affected, sequentially accessing and updating the records is the more efficient alternative. Figure 14-8 therefore shows a system flowchart in which the batch approach is applied.

The flowchart begins with the attendance time cards being gathered in a batch by the timekeeper and transmitted to the payroll department. In the system being described the employees do not prepare job-time tickets. Therefore, to enhance control, the timekeeper (or a payroll clerk) computes batch totals on the basis of the time records. One total is based on the hours worked, a second total (of the hash variety) is based on the employee numbers, and a third total is based on a count of the time cards.

The batch of time cards, prefaced by a batch transmittal sheet, is forwarded to the data processing department. There the time data are keyed onto magnetic tape and edited. In the first computer processing run the data are sorted by employee number. In run 2 the time data are processed to produce paychecks (and voucher stubs). The program also updates the employee payroll master file and prints the payroll register. The paychecks and a copy of the register are sent to the cashier, where the paychecks are signed and distributed. (The transfer of funds from the regular account may be included if desired.) The program in run 2 also adds a journal voucher concerning the payroll transaction to the general ledger transaction file.

The flowchart also portrays the establishment of pay status for employees. Clerks in the personnel department enter all personnel actions via departmental terminals. Since the employee payroll master file is stored on a magnetic disk, the actions (e.g., a change in pay rate) can be entered into the affected employee records promptly by direct access. Thus, all actions can be effected during the pay period and before the payroll processing begins.

Accounting Controls

Risk exposures. In the attempt to achieve the objectives stated at the beginning of this chapter, the employee services cycle is exposed to a variety of risks. Figure 14-9 lists representative risks and consequent exposures due to these risks. For instance, an unqualified or larcenous employee is likely to be unproductive, to ignore or circumvent policies and controls, and to be the cause of lost assets. In order to counteract all of the risks that are inherent within the employee services cycle, a firm needs to incorporate relevant general and transaction controls.

General controls. Among the general controls that are particularly relevant to the employee services cycle are the following:

1. Within the organization the persons and units that have custodial functions (cashier, paymaster) are separated from those units that keep time records (timekeeping) and that prepare the payroll documents (payroll department). Also, the persons and units that authorize and approve (i.e., the personnel department, which authorizes personnel actions, and the departmental supervisors, who approve time records) are separated from all the aforementioned units.

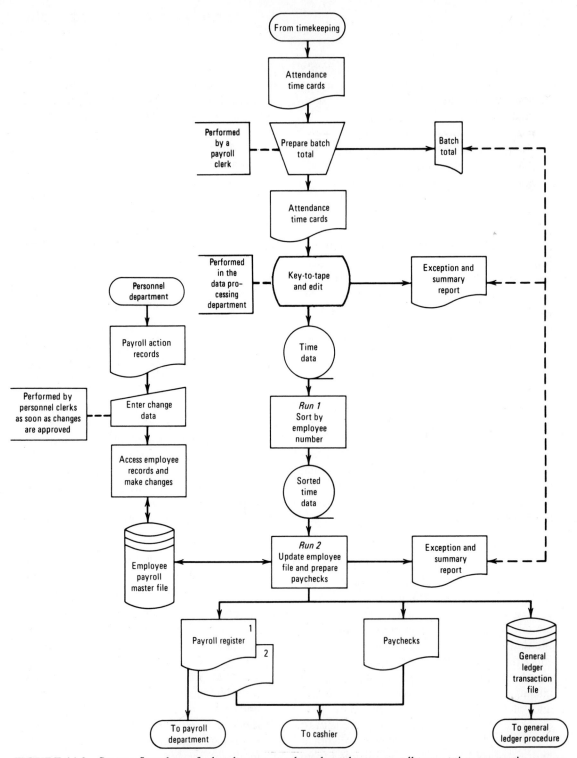

FIGURE 14-8 System flowchart of a batch computer-based employee payroll transaction processing procedure.

Risk	Exposure
1. Employment of unqualified persons	1. Lessened productivity and higher training costs
2. Employment of larcenous persons	2. Possibility of loss of assets and circumvented policies and controls
3. Errors or omissions in time records	3. Incorrect payroll records and labor distribution summaries
4. Errors in payments to employees	4. Possibility of overpayments and/or adverse effects on employee morale; erroneous quarterly statements sent to federal and state agencies
5. Incorrect disbursements of paychecks to fictitious or terminated employees, or diversions of valid paychecks to unentitled employees	5. Excessive wage and salary costs
6. Errors in charging labor expenses or in stating payroll liabilities	6. Incorrect levels for expense and liability accounts
7. Violation of government regulations and laws, with regard to payments or reporting requirements	7. Possibility of penalties and fines being assessed

FIGURE 14-9   Risk exposures within the employee services management cycle.

2. Complete and up-to-date documentation is available concerning the management of employee services.

3. Operating practices related to processing schedules, reports, changes in programs, and other matters are clearly established.

4. Security is maintained (in the case of on-line systems) by such techniques as (a) requiring that clerks enter assigned passwords before accessing employee payroll files, (b) employing terminals that are restricted solely to the entry and access of personnel records, (c) generating audit reports (access logs) that monitor accesses of system files, and (d) dumping the employee files onto magnetic tape backups. Physical security measures include the use of safes for holding stocks of blank paychecks and signature plates.

Transaction controls.   Control points within the cycle involving employee payrolls include (1) the establishment of pay status for each employee, (2) the recording of time-related services, (3) the conversion of time into payments due, and (4) the disbursement of cash.

The following controls and control procedures are applicable to employee services transactions and employee records:

1. Documents relating to payables and cash disbursements are prenumbered and well designed. In addition, time cards, and job-time tickets where applicable, are preprinted with the employees' names and numbers.

2. Data on time records are validated (and key-verified if suitable) as the data are prepared and entered for processing. In the case of computer-based systems validation is performed by means of such edit checks as (a) validity checks on employee numbers, (b) limit checks on hours worked, (c) field checks on key identification and amount data, and (d) relationship checks on employee num-

bers and related departments to which employees are assigned.

3. During payroll processing the results, such as net pay, are validated. In the case of computer-based systems validation is performed by means of such edit checks as the sign check and cross-foot balance check. Thus, the net-pay field of each paycheck is verified by the former to see that the sign is positive and by the latter to see that the amount equals the gross pay less all deductions.

4. Errors detected during data entry or processing are corrected as soon as possible by means of an established error correction procedure. A part of this procedure may involve the printing of suitable exception and summary reports during edit runs. An example of such a report appears in Figure 14-10. In the case of the payroll application, processing of paychecks may be delayed until all transaction data errors and discrepancies have been corrected.

5. Personnel actions (such as new hiring and pay rate changes) and paychecks are issued promptly on the basis of valid authorizations.

6. Time cards, and job-time tickets where applicable, are approved by the employees' supervisors.

7. Where job-time tickets are used, the hours that they reflect for each employee are reconciled with the hours shown on the attendance time cards.

8. Batch control totals are precomputed on hours worked, as reflected by time cards, and on net pay amounts, as shown in the payroll register; these batch totals are compared with totals computed during paycheck preparation and during postings to the employee payroll master file, respectively.

9. Paychecks are drawn on a separate payroll-imprest bank account.

10. Voided paychecks are retained, in order that all paycheck numbers can be accounted for.

11. Unclaimed paychecks are traced back to the time records and employee payroll master file, in order to verify that they belong to actual current employees.

12. In the case of computer-based systems, a preliminary payroll register is reviewed before the paychecks are printed, in order to determine that all errors have been corrected. Payroll account summaries are also printed periodically to enhance the audit trail.

13. All controls pertaining to cash disbursements also apply to the issuance of paychecks. See transaction controls numbered 13, 16, 17, 19, 21, and 22 in Chapter 13.

Reports and Other Outputs

Operational listings, statements, and reports. One of the most used outputs is the **payroll register.** It essentially lists the key payment data concerning each employee for a single pay period, ranging from gross pay to net pay. A related output is the **deduction register,** which provides a detailed breakdown of the deductions for each employee. The cumulative **earnings register** shows amounts earned year-to-date, and possibly quarter-to-date, for each employee and the totals for all employees. Figure 14-11 provides an excerpt from an earnings register. Required governmental reports include those pertaining to withholdings of social security and federal income taxes, plus a variety of others. Some are due at the end of each quarter, while others are due at the end of each year.

Inquiry screens. Most inquiries concern employees, so on-line systems usually enable personnel clerks and other authorized persons to view the data in an individual em-

RECORD NUMBER	CODE MX AC	DESCRIPTION	BADGE	DAY	DATE	–SHIFT– WORK PAID	TIME	ORDER NO.	OPER SEQ.	WORK CTR	DEPT	1st KEY ENTRY	2nd KEY ENTRY	3rd KEY ENTRY

NORTHCREEK IND. CO. 01   LABOR EXCEPTION REPORT   DATE 11/14/90 TIME 09.13.42 PAGE   1 AND30
FOREMAN – MK   OPER DAN   BATCH   6

DAN HANVILLE ___ ___ ___   EMP NO – 00210

1	01 01	TIME/ATT	10012	2	11/14/90	01	1	8:07							
2	01 01	TIME/ATT	10012	2	11/14/90	01	1	11:56							
3	01 01	TIME/ATT	10012	2	11/14/90	01	1	12:30							
4	01 01	TIME/ATT	10012	2	11/14/90	01	1	16:33							
5	38 10	PROD-ON	10012	2	11/14/90	01	1	8:10	M000390	0010	ML025	DP20			
6	11 15	PROD-OFF	10012	2	11/14/90	01	1	13:42	M000390	0010	ML025	DP20	00000004	00000000	00000001

TRAN QTY 0004   SCRAP QTY 0000   COMP CODE 1

| 7 | 11 15 | PROD-OFF | 10012 | 2 | 11/14/90 | 01 | 1 | 13:42 | M000390 | 0030 | OR045 | DP20 | 00000000 | 00000000 | 00000001 |

7 **** E AM-6317 ON RECORD MISSING

| 8 | 12 15 | PROD-OFF | 10012 | 2 | 11/14/90 | 01 | 1 | 16:33 | M000390 | 0030 | DR045 | DP20 | 00000002 | 00000000 | 00000000 |

8 *** E AM-6317 ON RECORD MISSING

CAROL HARRIS ___ ___ ___   EMP NO 00220

9	01 01	TIME/ATT	10063	2	11/14/90	01	1	7:55							
10	01 01	TIME/ATT	10063	2	11/14/90	01	1	11:58							
11	01 01	TIME/ATT	10063	2	11/14/90	01	1	12:29							
12	28 14	INDIR-ON/OFF	10063	2	11/14/90	01	1	7:55	M000390	0010	ML025	DP20			
13	28 14	INDIR-ON/OFF	10063	2	11/14/90	01	1	16:27	M000390	0010	ML025	DP20			

E AM-6271 T/A RECORD MISSING

NORTHCREEK IND. CO. 01   LABOR EXCEPTION REPORT   DATE 11/14/90 TIME 09.13.42 PAGE   2 AMD30
FOREMAN – MK   OPER DAN   BATCH 6

RECORD COUNTS:

A – TOTAL TIME RECORDS _ _ _ _ _ _ _ _ _ = 43
B – TIME RECORDS MARKED AS ERRORS _ _ _ _ = 13
C – RECORDS MARKED FOR DELETION _ _ _ _ _ = 0
RECORDS ACCEPTED (A–B–C) _ _ _ _ _ _ _ _ = 30

FIGURE 14-10 An example of an exception and summary (edit) report for the payroll application. Reprinted courtesy of International Business Machines Corporation.

ployee's payroll or personal data record. Other inquiries may relate to departmental payrolls or to cumulative earnings.

Managerial reports. Various analyses are of interest to managers, such as those pertaining to absenteeism, overtime pay, sales commissions, direct labor costs, and indirect labor costs. Other reports that are often helpful include (1) surveys of average pay rates per occupational category, compared to similar firms, and (2) personnel strength reports, showing levels of staffing and changes during the past month.

Figure 14-12 portrays most of the registers and reports described in the preceding

Emp number	Employee name	Home dept		Gross earnings	Gross taxable	Sick pay	Tips taxed	Tips not taxed	FIT	FICA	EIC	Weeks worked
71500	Thomas C. Ryan	DADM	YTD	4,500.00	4,500.00	.00	.00	.00	784.50	299.25	.00	16
			QTD	562.50	562.50	.00	.00	.00	107.39	37.41	.00	2
75000	Russ A. Stinehour	DADM	YTD	13,800.00	13,800.00	.00	.00	.00	4,303.28	917.70	.00	16
			QTD	1,725.00	1,725.00	.00	.00	.00	511.66	114.71	.00	2
76000	Vince J. Tavormina	DOFC	YTD	2,254.00	2,254.00	.00	.00	.00	234.80	149.89	.00	15
			QTD	304.00	304.00	.00	.00	.00	68.01	20.22	.00	2
	TOTAL YTD			84,472.77	84,472.77	520.98	.00	.00	18,847.16	5,582.81	.00	
	TOTAL QTD			10,844.60	10,844.60	63.28	.00	.00	2,551.13	716.97	.00	
	TOTAL pay period			9,764.60	9,764.60	63.28	.00	.00	2,443.60	645.14	.00	

FIGURE 14-11 A cumulative earnings register. Courtesy of International Business Machines Corporation.

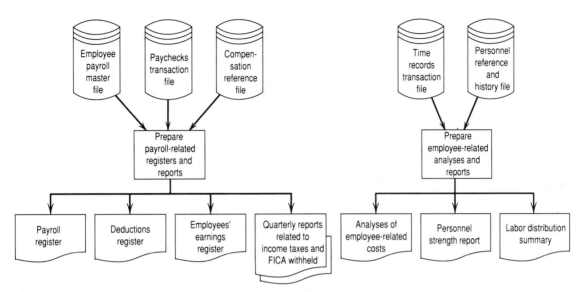

FIGURE 14-12   System flowchart showing pay-period and quarterly registers and reports in the employee services cycle.

paragraphs. They are shown as outputs produced from data in the various files listed in an earlier section.

Facilities Management Cycle

The facilities resource concerns the fixed assets, also known as property, plant, and equipment. Within the wide range of fixed assets are buildings, machines, furniture, fixtures, vehicles, and other items requiring capital expenditures. Because they have lives of longer than one year, fixed assets are subject to depreciation. Another feature of fixed assets is that their dollar value is often a relatively large portion of the total asset value of a firm. Because of these distinctions, we have separated the acquisition of fixed assets from the expenditure cycle, discussed in Chapter 13.

Our view of fixed assets, as described in this section, is that they can be better treated within the facilities management cycle. This cycle encompasses not only capital expendi-

tures but also the transactions that occur during the economic lives of the fixed assets and the disposals of such assets.

Cycle Objectives

The major purpose of the **facilities management cycle,** therefore, is to facilitate the acquisition, economic life, and disposal of needed fixed assets. Typical objectives within this broad purpose are (1) to ensure that all acquisitions are properly approved and recorded and exchanged for cash or equivalents, (2) to safeguard the fixed assets in assigned locations, (3) to reflect depreciation expense properly and consistently in accordance with an acceptable depreciation method, and (4) to ensure that all disposals are properly approved and recorded.

Functions

The three key functions of the facilities management cycle consist of acquiring the fixed assets, maintaining the fixed assets during their economic lives, and disposing of the fixed assets.

Acquire fixed assets. The capital expenditure process begins when a manager perceives that his or her department (or other organizational unit) needs an additional fixed asset or needs to replace an asset. For instance, a shipping manager may learn from his drivers that certain delivery trucks need replacement. This need should be substantiated through formal capital investment analyses. As we recall from managerial accounting, this type of analysis requires that expected benefits and costs be gathered for the economic lives of the new fixed assets, as well as such factors as the expected disposal or salvage values of the assets. Furthermore, these benefits and costs must be discounted to the present time by a factor (i.e., desired rate of return or opportunity cost of capital) specified by management.

The manager places a formal request for the needed fixed assets. Higher-level management must approve such a request. Generally, the larger the amount involved, the higher the request must ascend for approval. Upon receiving approval, the request then follows a procedure similar to the acquisition of merchandise. That is, a copy of the request is sent to the purchasing department (or in the case of highly technical equipment, the engineering department, if any). Bids are requested, a supplier is selected, and a purchase order is prepared. When the fixed asset arrives, a receiving report is completed and the asset is delivered to the requesting organizational unit. Upon the receipt of the supplier's invoice, a disbursement voucher is prepared (if the voucher system is in effect). On the due date a check is written and mailed.

If a firm constructs its own fixed assets, the procedure is closely related to the product conversion procedure. That procedure is discussed in the next major section.

Maintain fixed assets. Fixed assets usually represent valuable property. In order to safeguard and maintain each acquired fixed asset, all relevant details are generally recorded. Included are all acquisition costs, the estimated salvage value, the estimated economic life, and the location. If the fixed asset is transferred to a new location, this move is recorded. If costs are incurred during the life of the asset that increase its value or extend its economic life, these costs are added to the asset's current value.

A fixed asset diminishes in value during use or the passage of time. An allocated portion of the asset's cost, called depreciation expense, must be removed at periodic intervals. The amount of the depreciation expense is determined in part by the method of depreciation that is selected for the asset and in part by the estimated economic life of the asset. These depreciation amounts are included in the record of the individual fixed asset as well as in adjustments to general ledger accounts.

Dispose of fixed assets. When their economic lives have come to an end, fixed assets are either sold, retired, or exchanged for replacement assets. These disposals, like acquisitions, require the approval of management. They also lead to the removal of asset values from the general ledger accounts.

Relationships to the Organization

The facilities management cycle functions are mainly achieved under the direction of the finance/accounting organizational function (unit) of the firm. The key departments involved are budgeting, accounts payable, cash disbursements, property accounting, and general ledger. The budgeting department develops capital expenditures budgets and coordinates these budgets with the short-range and cash budgets. The accounts payable department approves the

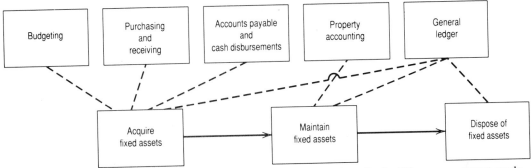

FIGURE 14-13 Typical functions and related organizational units of a facilities management cycle.

suppliers' invoices pertaining to fixed assets for payment. The cash disbursements department, an arm of the cashier, prepares checks for disbursement to suppliers of fixed assets. The property accounting department establishes and maintains the records concerning fixed assets. The general ledger department maintains control over all asset, equity, expense, and income accounts.

Other units of the organization are involved to a degree. Higher-level managers, from various organizational functions (e.g., production) in addition to the finance/accounting function, approve the acquisition and disposal of fixed assets. As in the case of the expenditure cycle, the purchasing and receiving departments are responsible for ordering and receiving the fixed assets. Figure 14-13 shows the relations between key departments and the cycle functions.

Data Sources and Inputs

Data used in this cycle are mainly based on inputs from the managers in departments needing new fixed assets. Other sources are the fixed asset records maintained by accounting departments.

Source documents typically used in the management of facilities include the following:

1. **Capital investment proposal.** The initiating form is the **capital investment proposal,** also called the property expenditure request. Figure 14-14 displays a copy of this form. As the form indicates, it is accompanied by a capital investment analysis form. The latter form lists all future cost and benefit flows that are expected to accrue from the asset investment, the net cash flows being discounted to present values. The proposal package, including both forms, is forwarded to higher-level managers, such as the controller, vice-president, and president, for approval. Upon approval a copy of the proposal is sent to the purchasing department, where it serves as a requisition.

2. **Fixed-asset change form.** A **fixed-asset change form** is used as the basis for (1) transferring fixed assets from one department to another or (2) retiring, selling, or trading in fixed assets. It lists the net book value of the asset and the amount to be received (if disposed of). It also provides spaces for justifying the disposal and for the approval signatures of higher-level managers.

3. **Other source documents.** Since expenditures are involved, additional documents include the request for quotation, purchase order, bill of lading, receiving re-

ARVIN INDUSTRIES, INC.

Division

CAPITAL INVESTMENT PROPOSAL (CIP)

786
CIP Number

Plant/Office

Project Title

Date

CAPITAL ASSET NAME	PLANT/DEPT.	ACCOUNT NO.	AMOUNT
1			
2			
3			
4			
5			
		Total	

PROJECT PURPOSE AND DESCRIPTION (Alternative 1 on Capital Investment Analysis Form)

DESCRIBE ANOTHER ALTERNATIVE REVIEWED (Alternative 2 on Capital Investment Analysis Form)

INVESTMENT CATEGORY

☐ Replacement
☐ Expansion
☐ Cost Reduction/Productivity*
☐ Compliance (OSHA, etc.)
☐ Rebuilding
☐ New Product*
☐ Energy Conservation
☐ Other _____
_____

*Complete Capital Inv. Analysis Form

OTHER INFORMATION

Included in budget?   Yes ☐   No ☐
Has the Corporate Insurance Department been informed?
     Yes ☐   No ☐   N/A ☐   (Refer to para 1.12 in exhibit B)
Is surplus equipment available from other divisions?
     Yes ☐   No ☐   If Yes, provide further details.
For Cost Reduction/Productivity or New Product CIP:
     Alternative 1:   IRR% _____   NPV $ _____
                              Discounted Payback Years _____
     Alternative 2:   IRR% _____   NPV $ _____
                              Discounted Payback Years _____

INVESTMENT REVIEW AND APPROVAL

Division	Signature	Date	Group	Signature	Date
Originator			Controller		
Dept. Mgr.			Vice Pres.		
Plant Mgr.			**Corporate**	**Signature**	**Date**
President			Off. of Pres.		

ID-9099

FIGURE 14-14 A request for fixed-asset acquisition. Courtesy of Arvin Industries.

Fixed-asset number	Description	Asset type code	Location code	Supplier number	Date acquired	Estimated economic life	

	Estimated salvage value	Depreciation method	Depreciation annual rate	Cost basis	Accumulated depreciation

FIGURE 14-15 A layout of a fixed-assets record. *Note:* Although the lengths of fields and modes of data items are necessary for complete documentation, they have been omitted for the sake of simplicity.

port, supplier's invoice, disbursement voucher, check voucher, and journal voucher. See Chapter 13 for a description of these documents.

Codes are also useful for identifying data needed in the management of facilities. In particular, meaningful codes can be developed to identify fixed assets. A group code for fixed assets might include fields to represent the asset class or function, asset subclass, size or capacity, distinctive features, year of installation, and so on. Attached to the integral fixed-asset code might be a location code. For a large firm such as Bell Communications, this location code could identify the city, state, and building (or other site) where a particular fixed asset is currently placed.[1]

Data Base

The distinctive files needed in managing facilities are the fixed-assets master file and the fixed-assets transaction file. Other files are those used in all expenditure transactions, such as the supplier master, open purchase order, open voucher, and check dis-

bursement files. See Chapter 13 for details of these files.

Fixed-assets master file. A key file is the fixed-assets master file, a subsidiary ledger that supports the fixed-asset control accounts in the general ledger. Figure 14-15 portrays the layout of the contents of a typical record for a fixed asset. Included is the fixed-asset number, a unique identifier that generally serves as the primary and sorting key. The asset type code identifies the major classification of fixed assets (e.g., buildings, equipment) to which the individual asset belongs. The location code refers to the department or physical site to which the asset is assigned.

An important concern is keeping the records and their permanent data up to date. When an asset is relocated, for instance, the location code should be promptly changed. When a new fixed asset is approved and acquired, a new record should appear in the file.

Fixed-assets transaction file. A fixed-assets transaction file contains transactions pertaining to new acquisitions, sales of currently held fixed assets, retirements, major additions to asset costs or to economic lives, and transfers between locations. It is needed if

[1]Germain Boer, *Classifying and Coding for Accounting Operations* (Montvale, New Jersey: National Association of Accountants, 1987), pp. 57–61.

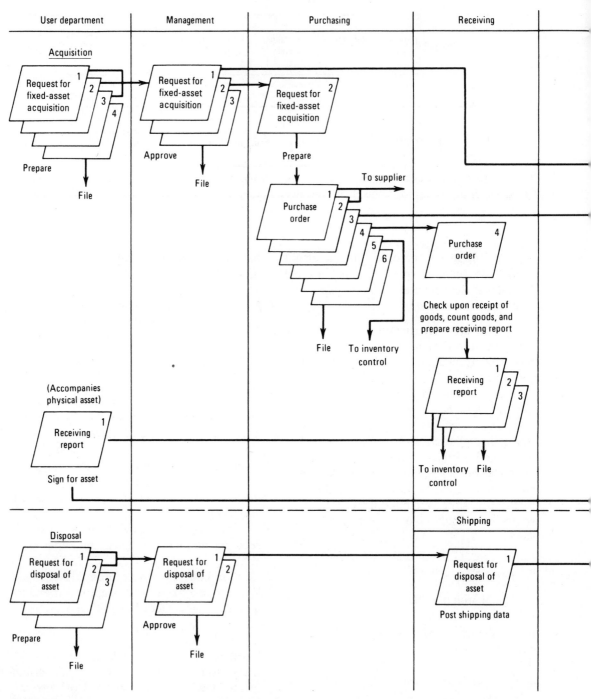

FIGURE 14-16 System flowchart of a manual fixed-assets processing procedure, with an emphasis on document flows.

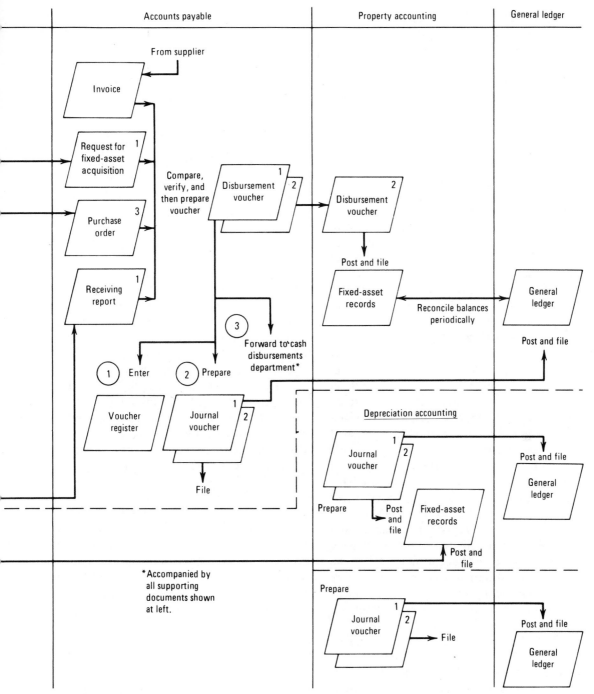

FIGURE 14-16   (*Continued*).

fixed-asset transactions are accumulated for a period of time (e.g., a week) and then processed in a batch. If the transactions are posted to the records as they arise, the file will likely not exist in a physical sense.

Transactions that allocate depreciation expense for each fixed asset are not included in this file. Instead, they are included in the adjusting journal entries at the end of each accounting period.

Data Flows and Processing

Both manual and computer-based processing systems are described. The description of the former emphasizes the flows of source documents; the description of the latter focuses on the processing of the master file.

Manual processing system. Figure 14-16 presents a document-type system flowchart of the procedure for processing fixed-asset transactions. The upper portion of the flowchart pertains to acquisition transactions; the lower portion concerns disposal transactions. Depreciation transactions are included at the lower right.

To begin an acquisition, a manager in a user department prepares a request. This form, together with a capital investment analysis, is forwarded to higher-level management. After the request is reviewed and approved, it is distributed to the purchasing and accounts payable departments. Then the regular expenditure procedure is followed. Finally, the property accounting department prepares a record for the new fixed asset and the general ledger accounts are posted.

The disposal procedure likewise begins with a request. After the request is approved, the fixed asset is shipped for disposal. On the basis of a copy of the approved request form, a property accounting clerk posts and removes the appropriate record from the fixed asset file. Then the clerk prepares a journal voucher that reflects the final depreciation expense, actual salvage value (if any), and the gain or loss on the disposal.

With regard to depreciation, a property accounting clerk prepares a journal voucher at the end of each accounting period. (Alternatively, depreciation entries may be preestablished when the fixed asset is acquired and entered in the file of standard adjusting entries.) Then the clerk posts the amounts to the fixed-asset record and sends the journal voucher to the general ledger department for posting.

Computer-based processing system. Figure 14-17 shows a system flowchart of a procedure involving fixed-assets transactions. The on-line method has been selected for discussion because the number of fixed-asset transactions is relatively small in many firms and the records can be kept up to date. However, the batch method is suitable for firms that have numerous acquisitions.

The flowchart begins at the point when the approved request forms have been received by the property accounting department, as shown in Figure 14-16. A clerk uses the departmental terminal to enter data from each transaction document when received. The entered data are first validated by edit checks. Then the data are immediately posted by an updating program to the appropriate record in the fixed-asset master file. If the transaction affects general ledger accounts, the program also prepares a journal voucher and stores it on the general ledger transaction file. At the end of the accounting period (e.g., the month) a print program generates useful reports. It also prepares journal vouchers that reflect depreciation entries.

Accounting Controls

Risk exposures. In attempting to achieve its objectives, the facilities management cycle is exposed to a variety of risks. Figure 14-18

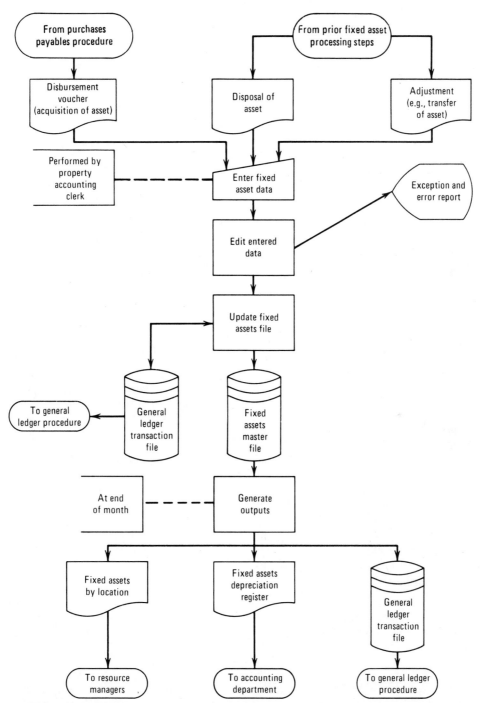

FIGURE 14-17 System flowchart of an on-line computer-based fixed-assets transaction processing procedure.

Risk	Exposures
1. Improper acquisition of fixed assets	1. Excessive costs for fixed assets
2. Improper disposal of fixed assets	2. Loss of productive capability; loss of disposal values
3. Theft or loss of fixed assets	3. Loss in fixed-asset values
4. Errors in billing for ordered fixed assets	4. Possibility of excessive costs for fixed assets
5. Errors in balances in fixed-asset accounts	5. Over- or undervaluation of total assets

FIGURE 14-18 Risk exposures within the facilities management cycle.

lists representative risks and consequent exposures due to these risks. For instance, the improper acquisition or theft of a minicomputer can represent a lost value of tens of thousands of dollars. Incorrect balances in fixed-asset accounts can overstate or understate the balance sheet by many thousands of dollars. In order to counteract the risks that are inherent within the facilities management cycle, a firm needs to incorporate relevant general and transaction controls.

General controls. Among the general controls that are particularly relevant to the facilities management cycle are the following:

1. Within the organization the managers who approve requests relating to fixed assets are separated from the users of the fixed assets and from all units involved in the processing of expenditures and disposals. Otherwise, the organizational segregation described for the expenditure cycle pertains.

2. Complete and up-to-date documentation is available concerning fixed-assets transactions.

3. Operating practices relating to processing schedules, reports, changes in programs, and other matters are clearly established.

4. Security is maintained (in the case of online systems) by such techniques as (a) requiring that clerks enter assigned passwords before accessing fixed-asset files, (b) employing terminals that are restricted solely to the entry or access of fixed-asset transactions, (c) generating audit reports (access logs) that monitor accesses of system files, and (d) dumping the fixed-asset files onto magnetic tape backups.

Transaction controls. Control points within the facilities management cycle include (1) the approval of requests, (2) the purchase order, (3) the receipt (or shipment) of fixed assets, (4) the movement of new assets to an assigned location, (5) the receipt and approval of the supplier's invoice, (6) the disbursement of cash, and (7) the preparation of a fixed-asset record.

The following controls and control procedures are applicable to fixed-asset transactions:

1. Documents relating to requests for fixed-asset acquisitions and disposals are prenumbered and well designed. They are also approved by responsible higher-level managers before being issued.

2. Fixed-asset acquisitions are required to follow the same purchasing, receiving, payables, and cash disbursements procedures employed for merchandise, raw materials, and supplies.

3. A unique identification number is assigned to each fixed asset, and a tag bearing this number is affixed to the asset.

4. Detailed and up-to-date fixed-asset records are maintained.

5. Balances in the fixed-assets subsidiary ledger (master file) are reconciled at least monthly with the balances of the fixed-assets control accounts in the general ledger.

Reports and Other Outputs

Operational listings and reports. The **fixed-asset register** is a listing of all fixed assets, arranged by fixed-asset numbers, and showing book and/or tax values of the assets. The *fixed-asset acquisition listing* shows all assets acquired during an accounting period, including capitalized values and estimated salvage values. The *asset retirement register* shows all assets disposed of during the accounting period. The *fixed-asset depreciation expense report* lists depreciation expense for every fixed asset for the current accounting period, plus related costs and accumulated depreciation amounts. Figure 14-19 provides an example of this report. Certain reports are needed to fulfill information requirements of the Securities and Exchange Commission, the Internal Revenue Service, and local property tax authorities. An example is a summary of all acquisitions, transfers, and retirements during a year.

```
CORP 01   CO.  01   FEDERAL IMPORTS                   FIXED ASSETS  PROPERTY LISTING   FARO5-2   5 PERIODS AS OF 2 QTR 9- PAGE    3
                                    R ACQRD ---------------------------------CORP/TAX---------------------------------       EXPN
ASSET NO.  DIST STOR DEPT      ACCT C INSTL   COST BASIS  ACCUM RESERVE  CURRENT DEPR    YTD DEPR      NET BOOK    RESV    OLDN
---------  ---- ---- ----  ---- ---- ------- ----------  -------------  ------------  ----------   ----------   ------  ------
BUILDINGS                               05/66  165,531.29    141,531.29          .00          .00   24,000.00 910100 BLDG 4

850011     31   41   503                06/59   73,020.00     25,108.75       473.75       568.50   47,911.25 710100
BUILDINGS                               06/59   73,020.00     31,303.87       458.43       550.11   41,716.13 910100 BLDG W3

850012     31   41   503                11/70   83,321.88     13,319.47       520.29       624.35   70,002.41 710100
BUILDINGS                               11/70   83,321.88     19,711.37       671.00       805.20   63,610.51 910100 BLDG 12

CATG
7101
                                      ---COST BASIS---  -ACCUM RESERVE--  --CURRENT DEPR--  -----YTD DEPR----  ----NET BOOK----
CATG 7101                       CORP      1,261,873.17       185,333.31       11,008.22       13,209.88    1,076,539.86
                                TAX       1,261,873.17       585,490.37       31,392.45       37,670.93      676,382.80

810014     31   41   501   7201         11/78   30,000.00      8,000.03     1,250.01     1,500.01   21,999.97 720100
AIR COND                                11/78   30,000.00     12,720.00     1,600.00     1,920.00   17,280.00 920100

810015     31   41   501   7201         11/78    2,000.00        533.33        83.33       100.00    1,466.67 720100
AIR COND                                11/78    2,000.00        848.00       106.67       128.00    1,152.00 920100

810020     31   41   501   7201         11/78      -57.00        -15.20        -2.37        -2.85      -41.80 720100
AIR COND                                11/78      -57.00        -35.29        -2.02        -2.42      -21.71 920100

CATG
7201
                                      ---COST BASIS---  -ACCUM RESERVE--  --CURRENT DEPR--  -----YTD DEPR----  ----NET BOOK----
CATG 7201                       CORP        31,943.00         8,518.16        1,330.97        1,597.16       23,424.84
                                TAX         31,943.00        13,532.71        1,704.65        2,045.58       18,410.29

800016     31   41   501   7800         06/72   80,000.00          .00          .00          .00   80,000.00 780000
LAND                                    06/72   80,000.00          .00          .00          .00   80,000.00 980000 HQL

810016     31   41   501   7800         06/72         .00          .00          .00          .00         .00 780000
LAND                                    06/72         .00          .00          .00          .00         .00 980000 HQL

CATG
7800
                                      ---COST BASIS---  -ACCUM RESERVE--  --CURRENT DEPR--  -----YTD DEPR----  ----NET BOOK----
CATG 7800                       CORP        80,000.00            .00              .00              .00        80,000.00
                                TAX         80,000.00            .00              .00              .00        80,000.00

CO.  01                         CORP     1,507,941.17       213,390.34       21,259.45       24,217.58    1,294,550.83
                                TAX      1,507,941.17       620,186.45       42,620.65       50,035.19      887,754.72

CORP 01                         CORP     1,507,941.17       213,390.34       21,259.45       24,217.58    1,294,550.83
                                TAX      1,507,941.17       620,186.45       42,620.65       50,035.19      887,754.72
```

FIGURE 14-19 A fixed-asset depreciation expense report. Courtesy of Data Design Associates.

Inquiry screens. Most inquiries concern individual fixed assets. A screen displaying this type of inquiry appears in Figure 14-20. Other inquiries may relate to specific fixed-asset transactions or capital budgeting data.

Managerial reports. Various analyses are of interest to managers, such as those showing fixed assets reported by location or by department. Other reports show maintenance schedules and costs and projected depreciation expenses.

Figure 14-21 portrays most of the registers and reports described in the preceding paragraphs. They are shown as outputs produced from data in the various files listed in an earlier section.

Funds Management Cycle

Within a firm the funds resource consists of the working capital and long-term investment assets. The **funds resource,** therefore, extends beyond cash to include receivables, prepaid expenses, short-term marketable securities, and investments in the long-term bonds and stocks of corporations. Even payables and current accrued liabilities are encompassed, since they enter the computation of working capital. In addition, the fixed assets may be considered a part of the funds resource, since presumably they could be sold at any time and hence be converted into cash.[2]

Moreover, the term *funds* can broadly be viewed as including the net capital of the owners of the firm; in the case of a corporation the net capital consists of bonds, common and preferred stock, contributed capital, and retained earnings. Although the net capital is an equity of the firm, rather than a

[2]In a going concern, however, fixed assets are not customarily viewed as a normal source of funds. Thus, they were previously discussed as the focus of the facilities management cycle and receive no further attention under the funds management cycle.

resource, it does give rise to transactions and does need to be managed.

Cycle Objectives

The major purpose of the **funds management cycle,** also known as the treasury or investment cycle, is to facilitate the inflows and outflows of the funds needed to maintain a going concern. Key objectives within this broad purpose are (1) to assure that an adequate quantity of funds is available to meet all legitimate needs, (2) to reflect reasonable values for funds at all times, and (3) to safeguard funds from theft and loss.

Functions

Among the functions related to funds are acquisition of needed funds from suitable sources, use of funds to meet all obligations when due, and maintenance of control over the funds on hand.

Acquire funds. Funds may be acquired from sales to customers, loans from banks, issues of bonds, sales of stock, and miscellaneous sources. One miscellaneous source, already mentioned, is the sale of fixed assets. Other sources include dividends and interest on and sales of investments, interest on notes receivable, factoring of accounts receivable, and even delays in payments on accounts payable.

Procedures for acquiring funds are quite varied, because of the wide range of sources. Two procedures, pertaining to sales of products and fixed assets, have already been described. Most other types of funds are acquired through the intervention of outside parties, such as bank loan officers, investment bankers, securities brokers, and factors. An acquiring firm must follow procedures that have been established by such parties. The key procedural concerns of the acquiring firm should be twofold: (1) to require clear authorization for the acquisition

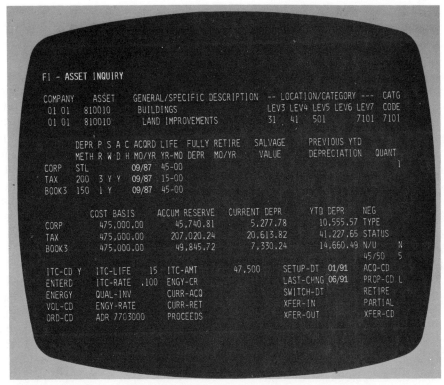

FIGURE 14-20. A screen display that shows a response to a fixed-asset inquiry. Courtesy of Data Design Associates.

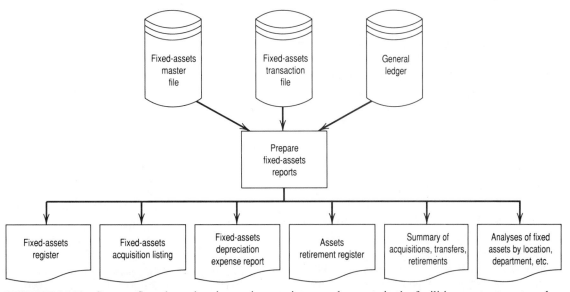

FIGURE 14-21 System flowchart showing various registers and reports in the facilities management cycle.

by a responsible manager, and (2) to ascertain that the intermediaries are qualified and responsive to the best interests of the acquiring firm.

Sound funds management is more dependent on careful planning than on detailed procedures, however. Careful planning consists of employing (1) comprehensive and powerful tools and (2) prudent rules and precepts.

A time-tested tool is the funds-oriented budget. In developing a budget of this type, the first step is to establish desirable values for key criteria (e.g., cash balance and current ratio). For instance, the desired cash balance should be adequate to meet all expected needs; however, it should not be so excessive that earnings on the idle cash would be foregone. The next step is to estimate the expected level of sales and other sources of funds for the coming year, broken down by quarters. For the nearest quarter, the estimates can be further broken down by months. Then the expected uses of funds (to be discussed next) should be estimated for the same period. These estimates can be cast into the format of a **projected sources-and-uses-of-funds statement**. In addition, a **projected cash-flow statement** can be prepared. The desired cash balance and funds-oriented ratios should be compared to the forecasted values, as shown in the statements.

At this point the firm's financial planner is often called upon to make funds management decisions. If a shortfall appears in the desired cash balance, the planner must acquire added cash from a bank loan or some other source. By knowing of this need well in advance, he or she can arrange to obtain such a loan at the lowest feasible rates. Alternatively, the planner can reduce the amount of the needed loan by delaying payments on payables or by factoring certain accounts receivable. If an excess in cash appears to be in prospect, the planner can convert the excess into short-term marketable securities. Again, by knowing

of the need in advance, he or she could look for the most lucrative short-term investments.

Funds management must also include long-term needs and opportunities. The planner thus needs to project income and balance sheet values, and such ratios as long-term liabilities to owners' capital, over the next several years. If these projections indicate a need for additional long-term funding, he or she can consider the relative desirability of issuing new bonds or selling new stock. If they suggest a long-term surplus, the planner can survey long-term opportunities and investments, or possibly the reduction of present long-term debt or capitalization.

Funds management can be greatly aided by computer-based **financial modeling techniques.** These techniques enable the planner to evaluate the consequences of numerous alternative scenarios. The treasurer of Tanner Companies was able to reduce the desired level of cash and the firm's borrowing rate by the use of such techniques.[3] Financial models are discussed in Chapter 20.

Use funds. Funds may be disbursed for purchase of goods and services, conversion into fixed assets or investments, repurchase of the firm's own stock (treasury stock), retirement of loans and bond issues, payment of dividends and interest, and redemption of stock rights or options. Procedures involved in the use of funds were discussed with regard to goods and services and fixed assets. As in the case of acquiring funds, procedures related to using the other types of funds are mainly established by intermediaries.

Planning is also important in the use of funds. For instance, planning is necessary to ensure that all invoices from suppliers are paid within the allowed discount periods and

---

[3]Joseph W. Wilkinson, "Financial Models: Helping Top Managers Plan," *Arizona Business* (First Quarter 1984), p. 10.

that proceeds from credit sales are collected promptly. On a higher level, planning for uses of funds is performed within the same budgeting framework as discussed for the acquisition of funds. An important rule is to require all nonessential expenditures to be fully justified.

Maintain control over funds on hand. Accounting controls are needed to ensure the reliability of financial statement balances and to safeguard the funds from loss or theft. Funds such as cash and marketable securities require strict controls, since they are extremely liquid. Although most of the controls have been listed earlier in discussion of cash receipts and disbursements, we repeat the following selected list of desirable controls for emphasis:

1. Close supervision of all activities involving cash and securities.
2. Adequate separation of responsibilities among the authorization, custodial, and record-keeping functions involving cash and securities.
3. Proper recording of all cash receipts, from whatever sources, in a single journal.
4. Prompt endorsement of all received checks.
5. Deposit of all received cash intact.
6. Adequate physical security over funds:
   a. Use of locked cash registers, safes, and lockboxes for cash.
   b. Use of safe deposit boxes or brokers' facilities for securities.
7. Issuance of all cash disbursements (except those for petty cash but including those for securities) via prenumbered check vouchers.
8. Use of a separate imprest bank account for payroll expenditures.
9. Preparation of a monthly bank reconciliation for each bank account by a person

not otherwise involved in cash transactions.
10. Audit, on a surprise and periodic basis, of all cash and securities.

Relationships to the Organization

The functions of the funds management cycle are mainly achieved within the finance function of the organization, although the accounting function performs bookkeeping activities. Financial planning is largely the responsibility of the treasurer, with assistance from the budgeting department. Other departments involved in the procedures related to the acquisition and use of funds include credit, accounts receivable, cash receipts, accounts payable, cash disbursements, property accounting, and general ledger. In addition, other higher-level managers are also involved in the budgeting process and large acquisitions.

Cycle Components

Key inputs, files, procedures, controls, and outputs that pertain to funds have largely been encompassed within discussions of cash receipts and disbursements. Other funds, such as marketable securities, long-term investment assets, and issued long-term bonds, are often handled by intermediaries. When such funds are maintained by the firm, however, subsidiary ledgers or master files are desirable. Figure 8-8, for instance, shows the layout for a stockholder record. Moreover, status reports of such funds, whether physically maintained within the firm or by an outside party, should be prepared on a regular basis.

Summary

Three important resource management cycles involve employee services, facilities, and funds. Functions within the employee services management cycle include establishing pay status, measuring the services rendered, preparing paychecks, issuing and distributing paychecks, distributing employee service costs, and preparing required reports and statements. This cycle involves the personnel, timekeeping, payroll, accounts payable, cash disbursements, cost distribution, and general ledger units. Key inputs are the personnel action form, time record, job-time ticket, and paycheck. The data base includes the employee payroll master and personnel reference and history files. Outputs include the payroll and other registers, plus analyses of labor cost components.

The facilities management cycle includes the functions of acquiring fixed assets, maintaining the fixed assets, and disposing of fixed assets. This cycle involves such organizational units as budgeting, accounts payable, cash disbursements, property accounting, and general ledger. Key inputs are the capital investment proposal and fixed-asset change form. The data base includes the fixed-assets master and transaction files. Outputs include the fixed-asset register; fixed-asset acquisition, retirement, and depreciation expense registers; reports of fixed assets by location; and inquiry screens concerning individual fixed assets.

The funds management cycle includes the functions of acquiring funds from a variety of sources, using funds to meet all obligations when due, and maintaining control over the funds on hand. This cycle involves such organizational units as finance, credit, budgeting, cash receipts and disbursements, property accounting, and general ledger. Many of the cycle components are those pertaining to cash receipts and disbursements, although other funds such as long-term investments require their own master files.

Review Problem with Solution[4]

Olympia Manufacturing Co.

Statement

The Olympia Manufacturing Company of Seattle, Washington, produces consumer goods by the job order approach. It pays all production employees on the basis of hourly rates, with time and a half for overtime hours. The five organizational units actively involved in the payroll and labor cost determination procedures are timekeeping, factory operating departments, payroll audit and control, data preparation, and computer operations. The basic data collection and processing steps, together with their locations, are as follows:

A   (timekeeping): Employee time (clock) cards are prepared.

B   (factor operating departments): Job-time tickets are prepared and forwarded.

C   (timekeeping): Employee time cards and job-time tickets are compared and forwarded.

D   (payroll audit and control): Preceding source documents are reviewed and forwarded.

E   (data preparation): Preceding source documents are converted to magnetic tape and forwarded.

F   (computer operations): Data on magnetic tape are edited, sorted, and then processed against the employee payroll master file (on magnetic disk) to produce paychecks, a payroll hour summary, a payroll register, and a labor cost distribution sheet.

---

[4]Adapted from the November 1972 CPA examination, with permission of the American Institute of Certified Public Accountants.

Required

a. List the possible errors or discrepancies that might occur at the data collection or processing step.

b. For each possible error or discrepancy, cite the corresponding control or security measure that should be in effect. (Assume that personnel procedures related to hiring, promotion, termination, and pay rate authorization are adequate.)

c. Describe changes in the preceding procedure that would enable a computer-based system to be employed more fully in the data entry and processing steps.

Solution

For requirements **a** and **b**:

Step	Possible Errors or Discrepancies	Controls or Security Measures
A	1. Time improperly reported by employees.	1. Independent timekeeping function; requirement that employees punch time clock; periodic checks of employees on duty.
	2. Payroll padded by timekeeper.	2. Paychecks distributed by payroll function, not timekeeping function.
	3. Employees work unauthorized overtime hours.	3. Overtime authorized by supervisor.
B	4. Employees loaf on duty.	4. Hours worked on each job recorded on time clock on factory floor; job-time tickets approved by supervisor.
	5. Overtime work not charged at premium rate.	5. Hours worked at premium rate marked by timekeeping.
C	6. Total hours on job-time tickets and employee time cards not in balance.	6. Hours checked by timekeeper and differences reconciled.
D	7. Job-time ticket or employer time cards lost in transit from timekeeping to payroll audit and control.	7. Batch control totals computed by timekeeping separately for job-time tickets and employee time cards; totals agreed; batch transmittal sheet prepared to accompany documents.
E	8. Job-time tickets or employee time cards lost in transit from payroll audit and control to data preparation.	8. Batch control totals logged on batch input control log by control group that is independent of computer operations; totals recomputed during keying operation and compared to predetermined totals.
	9. Data incorrectly transcribed from documents onto magnetic tape.	9. Keyed data on tape verified; also, batch control totals compared (in step 8, above).
F	10. Employee number incorrectly recorded or keyed.	10. Self-checking digits used on employee number and verified by programmed check.
	11. Errors in recording or keying time data, in sorting time records, etc.	11. Various programmed checks written into payroll processing program.
	12. Employee time records lost in transit from data preparation to computer operations.	12. Batch control totals computed during processing and printed on exception and summary report; these totals compared to totals logged in batch input control log.
	13. Wrong master file disk mounted for processing.	13. Internal header label check employed at beginning of run.
	14. Employee payroll master file misplaced.	14. File signed out of the data library only when needed for processing, and then returned to library afterwards.

(Table continued)

Possible Errors or Discrepancies	Controls or Security Measures
15. Detected errors not corrected and documents reentered for processing.	15. Logging of errors performed by payroll audit and control and error-correction procedure carefully followed.
16. Outputs lost or diverted in transit to intended destinations.	16. Outputs routed in accordance with distribution log maintained by payroll audit and control; payroll register personally delivered to payroll representative, paychecks to treasurer or cashier or paymaster, and summary totals to the general ledger section.

For requirement **c:**

Function Affected	Data Collection and Processing Steps Subject to Computerization
Data preparation	Instead of recording time data on job-time tickets and employee time cards and later converting these data to magnetic tape, the data could be captured via on-line terminals located in timekeeping and the factory operating departments.
Timekeeping	If data are captured on-line, the computer system could be programmed to zero-balance total hours on job-time tickets with total hours on employee time cards; differences could be printed out on the exception and summary report for investigation by timekeeping and supervisors. The computer system could also be programmed to compute the batch control totals that are to be used for later comparisons.
Payroll audit and control	If data are captured on-line, the computer system could be programmed to perform prompt validity checks of employee numbers.
Computer operations	Regardless of the manner in which the data are captured, the computer system could be programmed to compare the computed batch control totals against predetermined batch control totals and to print any differences for investigation.

Review Questions

14-1 What is the meaning of each of the following terms?

Resource management
Employee services management cycle
Personnel action form
Time card
Job-time ticket
Paycheck
Employee payroll master file
Labor distribution summary
Payroll register
Deduction register
Earnings register
Facilities management cycle
Capital investment proposal
Fixed-asset change form
Fixed-asset register
Funds resource
Funds management cycle
Projected sources and uses-of-funds statement
Projected cash-flow statement
Financial modeling technique

14-2 What are the purpose and related objectives of the employee services management (payroll) cycle?

14-3   Identify the functions that pertain to payroll expenditures.

14-4   Which organizational units are involved in paying employees?

14-5   Identify the source documents used in the management of employee services.

14-6   Which files are related to employees and the payroll?

14-7   Describe the steps in a typical manual payroll procedure.

14-8   Describe the payroll procedure when a batch-oriented computer-based system is used.

14-9   What risk exposures exist in the management of employee services?

14-10   What are several general and transaction controls that can counteract the exposures to risks within the cycle involving employee payrolls?

14-11   Identify several control points within the cycle involving employee payrolls.

14-12   What is the impact of governmental requirements on reports related to employee payrolls?

14-13   What are several listings and reports that may be generated from payroll transactions, other than required reports?

14-14   What are the purposes and related objectives of the facilities management cycle?

14-15   Identify the major functions that pertain to the facilities management cycle.

14-16   Which organizational units are involved in transactions pertaining to facilities (fixed assets)?

14-17   What source documents are used in the management of facilities?

14-18   Identify the major files that relate to fixed assets.

14-19   Describe the procedures for fixed-asset transactions when a manual system is employed.

14-20   How is the processing of fixed-asset transactions changed when an on-line computer-based system is used?

14-21   What risk exposures exist in facilities management?

14-22   Identify several general and transaction controls that can counteract the exposures to risks within the facilities management cycle.

14-23   Identify several listings and reports that may be generated from fixed-asset transactions.

14-24   What is the purpose and related objectives of the funds management cycle?

14-25   Identify the functions of the funds management cycle.

14-26   What are two essential procedural concerns for a firm when acquiring funds from such sources as bank loans and stockholders?

14-27   Describe the steps in developing and using a funds-oriented budget.

14-28   List several sound rules for acquiring needed funds.

14-29   Identify the various uses of funds.

14-30   List rules concerning the prudent use of funds.

14-31   List accounting controls that pertain to cash and marketable securities.

14-32   Which organizational units are involved in transactions and planning pertaining to funds?

Discussion Questions

14-33   Why might the acquisition of a computer system for use in processing payroll transaction result in much extra work on the part of the payroll clerks?

14-34   Describe several programmed edit checks, such as the redundancy matching check, that can be applied by the posting programs used in processing payrolls.

14-35 Discuss the emerging development known as human resource accounting (HRA).

14-36 Discuss the emerging developments in financial modeling, especially as they relate to capital investment analysis.

Problems

14-1 Design an attendance time card which is to be used by production employees to clock in and out of a plant. (Figure 14-3 can be viewed as representing the form used by the employees to clock in and out of jobs.) The time card should provide four spaces for clocking each day for six days. Enter data for Jacob Keeley, No. 45982, week ending 9/7/91. On September 2 his times are 7:52 A, 12:01 P, 12:58 P, and 5:03 P.

14-2 Chambeers Clothiers of Princeton, New Jersey 08540, has 200 employees, including Ms. Peggy Ames Gridley, No. 138. On Friday, April 12, 1991, she receives a weekly paycheck, which is prenumbered 7421. The check has been signed by Morton J. Bottom, Treasurer, and is payable by the Tiger National Bank. Peggy worked 46 hours during the week and receives a regular hourly rate of $10, with time and one half for all overtime hours. Weekly deductions for Peggy are as follows: 7.85 percent of gross pay for FICA (to a limit of $51,300 for year-to-date gross earnings), $30 plus 20 percent of gross pay over $300 for federal income tax withholding (FITW), 3 percent of gross pay for state income tax withholding, $8 for group hospitalization plan, $5 for term life insurance plan, 5 percent for pension plan, and 1 percent for United Way contribution. Before being updated with this week's amounts, the employee payroll master record for Peggy showed year-to-date gross earnings of $6,450, net earnings of $4349.18, and FITW of $832. Assume that all deduc-

tions and withholdings have been computed every week in the same manner as this week. Other relevant facts concerning Peggy are as follows: social security number, 526-99-9966; department number, 04; pay classification, HR; marital status, S; number of exemptions, 1. The bank number on the paycheck (including the ABA transit code) is 18-170, the check routing code is 1001, and the firm's account number is 04-52365.

Required

a. Design a paycheck with attached stub or voucher for Chambeers Clothiers and enter suitable data from the problem statement.

Hint: Use a paycheck received by you or a friend, as well as the sample paycheck in Figure 14-4, to guide you.

b. Design a record layout for the employee payroll master file and enter suitable data for Peggy *after* the paycheck amounts for this week have been added to the record. Draw the fields in the record to scale, allowing sufficient lengths to accommodate data for employees with longer names and larger amounts than Peggy.

c. Design a payroll register (i.e., the journal or transaction listing) and enter Peggy's pay data for this week. The design should include such columns as employee name, number, department, hours worked, regular amount, overtime amount, all deduction amounts, and other relevant amounts.

14-3 Boone and Bower, CPAs, is a public accounting firm in the Northeast. It has two offices and approximately 50 employees. The firm has been very progressive in its use of microcomputers. Recently it acquired a software package that manages the time records of its clerical and professional employees and that also prepares the payroll and related reports. Now the firm is also considering a software package to manage its various fixed assets, such as furniture, office machines, fixed and portable microcomputers, and fixtures.

Required

a. List the data items that are likely needed by the time management–payroll package in order to generate the outputs.

b. List the data items that are likely to be needed by the fixed-asset package in order to manage the fixed assets and prepare outputs.

c. List the files needed by both of the packages.

d. Describe several listings and reports that can be provided by each of the packages and would likely be useful to the partners and office manager. (Do not include reports that are required by governmental agencies.)

14-4 The Shriver Computer Services Company of Pullman, Washington, uses an online processing system to keep its fixed-asset records up to date and available for inquiry. It employs preformatted screens for the entry, modification, and retrieval of data pertaining to fixed assets. In order to access the preformatted screens, a user first specifies the master menu shown on this page. When this menu screen is displayed on the user's CRT terminal, the user enters the desired number. The computer software then presents the requested screen or asks for additional information (e.g., the number of the desired asset). For instance, if the user needs to adjust the depreciation amount of an asset, he or she enters the number *1*; the software then asks the number of the asset to be adjusted.

Assume that the user enters the number *2*. A screen would appear that provides spaces for entering data concerning the acquisition of a fixed asset. Among the data items provided in the preformatted screen

```
╭──────────────────────────────────────╮
│    FIXED ASSETS MASTER MENU          │
│                                      │
│  1. ASSET DATA ENTRY                 │
│  2. ASSET ACQUISITION ENTRY          │
│  3. ASSET DISPOSAL ENTRY             │
│  4. ASSET ACCOUNT STATUS INQUIRY     │
│  5. INDIVIDUAL ASSET STATUS INQUIRY  │
│  6. REPORT DISPLAY                   │
│  7. DEMAND REPORT GENERATION         │
│                                      │
│  ENTER DESIRED NUMBER > _____        │
╰──────────────────────────────────────╯
```

are date of purchase, manufacturer from whom purchased, class of asset, general ledger account number, assigned property number, description of asset, location of asset within firm, method of depreciation, estimated life, cost basis, and estimated salvage value.

Required

Design a preformatted screen that arranges the preceding items in a structured manner, and simulate the action of the data entry clerk by entering sample values for the items. Include in the screen format those items that would be automatically entered by the computer program, either to identify the transaction or to aid in reducing input errors. Denote these system-generated items by an asterisk (*).

14-5 Devise and illustrate numeric group codes as follows:

a. An employee code that has fields to represent pay category, department number, year of hire, and sequential hire within the year. Use not more than eight numeric positions. Assume that 300 employees, on the average, are hired each year. Illustrate with employee Jerry Bell, who was the 57th person hired in 1988, is assigned to department 14, and is paid an hourly rate.

b. A fixed-asset code that has fields to represent the asset block, the fixed-asset category, the subclass within the fixed-asset category, and the specific type and distinguishing feature (e.g., capacity level, size, capability) within the subclass. Use six numeric positions within a hierarchical arrangement. Begin with a block code for assets as the first position. Illustrate with a giant-size drill press, a member of the machinery subclass. Drill presses are a code 2 type of machine, and their sizes range from a midget size coded 01 to a giant size coded 12. Asset accounts within the chart of accounts are assigned codes within the block 100–199.

Note: Assume code values for illustrations when not provided.

14-6 Roadrunner Casinos, Inc., with headquarters in Reno, operates five casinos in Nevada. The firm maintains its employee files on magnetic disks, since numerous personnel changes occur between pay dates. Personnel actions are entered via a video display terminal in the personnel department. To enter a personnel action, a payroll clerk chooses the Personnel Actions menu from the Main Menu. Next the clerk chooses the desired action (e.g., enter a new hiring, change an employee pay rate, add an employee deduction, display an employee record). A preformatted screen then appears, onto which the clerk enters the personnel action data.

a. Design the Personnel Actions menu, which should list at least eight options and also allow for exit to the Main Menu.

b. Design a preformatted screen for the Change an Employee Pay Rate option.

c. Design a record layout for a skills file that Roadrunner Casinos maintains in order to select replacements quickly when employees resign. Include assumed modes for data items and sizes of fields.

Note: Repeating fields will be needed, so the skill record will be variable in length.

14-7 Deake Corporation is a medium-size, diversified manufacturing company located in Norman, Oklahoma. Frank Richards had been promoted recently to manager of the property accounting section. Richards has had difficulty in responding to some of the requests from individuals in other departments of Deake for information about the company's fixed assets. Some of the requests and problems Richards has had to cope with are as follows:

a. The controller has requested schedules of individual fixed assets to support the balances in the general ledger. Richards has furnished the necessary information, but always late. The manner in which the records are organized makes it difficult to obtain information easily.

b. The maintenance manager wished to verify the existence of a punch press which he thinks was repaired twice. He has asked Richards to confirm the asset number and location of the press.

c. The insurance department wants data on the cost and book values of assets to include in its review of current insurance coverage.

d. The tax department has requested data that can be used to determine when Deake should switch depreciation methods for tax purposes.

e. The company's internal auditors have spent a significant amount of time in the property accounting section recently, attempting to confirm the annual depreciation expense.

The property account records that are at Richards' disposal consist of a set of manual books. These records show the date when the asset was acquired, the account number to which the asset applies, the dollar amount capitalized, and the estimated useful life of the asset for depreciation purposes.

After many frustrations Richards has realized that his records are inadequate and he cannot supply the data easily when they are requested. He has decided that he should discuss his problems with the controller, Jim Castle.

Richards Jim, something has got to give. My people are working overtime and can't keep up. You worked in property accounting before you became controller. You know I can't tell the tax, insurance, and maintenance people everything they need to know from my records. Also, that internal auditing team is living in my area and that slows down the work pace. The requests of these people are reasonable, and we should be able to answer these questions and provide the needed data. I think we need an automated property-accounting system. I would like to talk to the information systems people to see if they can help me.

Castle Frank, I think you have a good idea, but be sure you are personally involved in the design of any system, so that you get all the information you need.

Required

a. Identify and justify several major attributes Deake Corporation's computer-based property-accounting system should possess in order to provide the data necessary to respond to requests of information from company personnel.

b. Identify the data that should be included in the record for each asset included in the property account.

(CMA adapted)

14-8 The Kowal Manufacturing Company employs about 50 production workers and has the following payroll procedures:

The factory supervisor interviews applicants and on the basis of the interview either hires or rejects them. The applicant who is hired prepares a W-4 form (Employee's Withholding Exemption Certificate) and gives it to the supervisor. The supervisor writes the hourly rate of pay for the new employee in the corner of the W-4 form and then gives the form to a payroll clerk as notice that the worker has been employed. The supervisor verbally advises the payroll department of rate adjustments.

A supply of blank time cards is kept in a box near the entrance to the factory. All workers take a time card on Monday morning, fill in their names, and note in pencil on the time card their daily arrival and departure times. At the end of the week the workers drop the time cards in a box near the door to the factory. The completed time cards are taken from the box on Monday morning by a payroll clerk. Two payroll clerks divide the cards alphabetically between them, one taking the A to L section of the payroll and the other taking the M to Z section. Each clerk is fully responsible for a section of the payroll. The clerk computes the gross pay, deductions, and net pay, posts the details to the employee's earnings records, and prepares and numbers the payroll checks. Employees are automatically removed from the payroll when they fail to turn in a time card.

The payroll checks are manually signed by the chief accountant and given to the supervisor. The supervisor distributes the checks to the workers in the factory and arranges for the delivery of the checks to the workers who are absent. The payroll bank account is reconciled by the chief accountant who also prepares the various quarterly and annual payroll tax reports.

Required

List your suggestions for improving the Kowal Manufacturing Company's internal controls for the factory hiring practices and payroll procedures.

(CPA adapted)

14-9 You are auditing the Alaska branch of Far Distributing Co. This branch has substantial annual sales, which are billed and collected locally. As a part of your audit you find that the procedures for handling cash receipts are as follows:

Cash collections on over-the-counter sales and COD sales are received from the customer or delivery service by the cashier. Upon receipt of cash, the cashier stamps the sales ticket "paid" and files a copy for future reference. The only record of COD sales is a copy of the sales ticket that is given to the cashier to hold until the cash is received from the delivery service.

Mail is opened by the secretary to the credit manager and remittances are given to the credit manager for review. The credit manager then places the remittances in a tray on the cashier's desk. At the daily deposit cutoff time the cashier delivers the checks and cash on hand to the assistant credit manager who prepares remittance lists and makes up the bank deposit that the manager also takes to the bank. The assistant credit manager also posts remittances to the accounts receivable ledger cards and verifies the cash discount allowable.

You also ascertain that the credit manager obtains approval from the executive office at Far Distributing Co., located in Chicago, to write off uncollectible accounts, and that the manager has retained in custody as

of the end of the fiscal year some remittances that were received on various days during the last month.

Required

a. Describe the irregularities that might occur under the procedures now in effect for handling cash collections and remittances.

b. Give procedures that you would recommend to strengthen internal control over cash collections and remittances.

(CPA adapted)

14-10 Manor Company of Orlando, Florida, operates several manufacturing plants on the East Coast. Its internal audit department performs operational audits of the various procedures in the plants on a regular basis. As an experienced internal auditor you have been assigned to head an audit team at the Galena plant. A major objective of the audit is to review the payroll procedures currently employed.

Various plant personnel were interviewed to ascertain the payroll procedures being used in the department. The findings were as follows:

- The payroll clerk receives the time cards from the various department supervisors at the end of each pay period, checks the employee's hourly rate against information provided by the personnel department, and records the regular and overtime hours for each employee.

- The payroll clerk sends the time cards to the plant's data processing department for compilation and processing.

- The data processing department returns the time cards with the printed checks and payroll register to the payroll clerk upon completion of the processing.

- The payroll clerk verifies the hourly rate and hours worked for each employee by comparing the detail in the payroll register to the time cards.

- If errors are found, the payroll clerk voids the computer-generated check, prepares another check for the correct amount, and adjusts the payroll register accordingly.
- The payroll clerk obtains the plant signature plate from the accounting department and signs the payroll checks.
- An employee of the personnel department picks up the checks and holds them until they are delivered to the department supervisors for distribution to the employees.

Required

Evaluate each finding of the audit team as either a weakness or a strength to the payroll procedures. In the cases of weaknesses, specify improvements that should be effected.

(CMA adapted)

14-11 What error or fraudulent activity might occur if each of the following procedures is allowed?

- **a.** Personnel and payroll are combined into the same organizational unit.
- **b.** Departmental supervisors distribute paychecks to their employees.
- **c.** The same person who prepares paychecks also signs them.
- **d.** The fixed-assets ledger is not periodically reconciled to the control accounts in the general ledger.
- **e.** A bank reconciliation is not prepared when checks against a bank account are returned by the bank.
- **f.** The paychecks are not prenumbered (or if prenumbered, copies are not filed in a sequential file

that is periodically checked for gaps in the numbers).
- **g.** Voided paychecks are destroyed.
- **h.** Fixed assets do not have attached tags or labels showing their assigned numbers.
- **i.** Fixed-asset retirements are not reported.

14-12 What internal accounting control(s) would be most effective in preventing or detecting each of the following errors or fraudulent practices?

- **a.** A payroll clerk computes 40 hours times $6 per hour to equal $250 gross pay.
- **b.** An employee spends four hours in working on job order 782; however, he erroneously enters five hours on the labor job-time ticket.
- **c.** A supervisor does not notify the personnel department when one of his employees quits; the supervisor turns in phony time cards for the employee each week and then keeps the paychecks for the employee when given the paychecks for distribution.
- **d.** An engineering technician employed by a firm removes a complex testing machine from the premises and then reports to the property accounting department that it has been scrapped.
- **e.** A computer programmer modifies the payroll programs so that the deduction for FICA is not made when preparing paychecks.
- **f.** An assistant cashier in the finance function acquires a large amount of high-yield "junk" bonds with excess cash from the firm's account; the bond market suddenly plunges and the bonds become worthless.
- **g.** The number of hours worked by a production employee is incor-

rectly entered into an on-line terminal as 84 hours; it should appear as 48 hours.

h. Ten time cards are accidentally lost in transmitting them to the payroll department.

i. A personnel clerk accidentally omits a deduction code when entering a personnel action change for an employee into an on-line terminal.

j. A data entry clerk accidentally keys the letter l for the number 1 when entering time-card data onto a magnetic tape.

14-13 What internal accounting control(s) would be most effective in preventing or detecting each of the following errors or fraudulent practices?

a. A payroll clerk increases the pay rate for a friend from $7 per hour to $9 per hour and then uses this higher rate to compute the friend's pay amount.

b. A computer-prepared fixed-asset analysis is mistakenly sent to the storeskeeper rather than to the property accounting manager.

c. A computer operator enters a correction to a transaction via the console terminal and accidentally erases part of the employee payroll master file stored on magnetic tape.

d. A programmer obtains the employee payroll master file and increases her salary in her record.

e. A department manager has a large fireproof vault installed in the department, even though company policy is to maintain a centralized vault for use by all departments.

f. An employee is assigned a microcomputer for use in her job; however, she keeps it at home for personal use.

g. One fixed-asset account in the general ledger reflects a considerable overstatement of asset value, since two posting errors were made earlier this year.

h. Cash received from the sale of long-term investments is recorded by a special journal voucher; however, the posting to the cash account was delayed and hence the treasurer borrows funds by means of a short-term note payable at a high rate of interest.

i. A new office copier machine is purchased with cash from the day's receipts by the office manager; however, he reports an incorrect amount to the bookkeeper, which is duly recorded in the accounts.

j. A property accounting clerk accumulates depreciation on a machine in an amount that exceeds the cost of the machine.

14-14 Tempo Retailers of Durham, New Hampshire, processes its payroll by means of a small computer system. The following table presents sorted transaction data pertaining to the first several employees for a recent pay period.

Employee Number	Employee Name	Department Number	Hours Worked
13251	Smith, John	1	40
13620	Black, Charles	1	40
13543	Adams, Steve	1	48
13658	Bró wn, Rodney	1	40
13752	Jones, Paul	2	42
24313	Krause, Ken	2	44
25001	Tingey, Sharon	2	79

The first digit of the employee number indicates the employee's department, and the last digit is a nonzero self-checking digit.

Required

Assuming that the above data represent the entire group of employees to be paid:

a. Compute three types of batch control totals.

b. Identify errors in the data and the specific type of programmed check that should detect each error.

14-15 Royal Payne Cleaners performs janitorial and cleaning services for office buildings and business firms in a large metropolitan area. The firm uses small computers to process its various accounting transactions and to manage its cash. With respect to cash management, the treasurer develops a cash requirements projection at the end of each month for the following month. He refuses to look more than one month ahead, since he believes that the economic and monetary uncertainties are too great. On the basis of the month-ahead projection, he adjusts the cash balance. If it appears to be too low, he borrows from the firm's bank at the prime rate. If the balance seems to be too high, he invests in short-term certificates of deposit (CD's). (These investments safeguard the principal amount, although they do impose a penalty for early withdrawal.)

With regard to sales, the firm bills all credit customers at the end of each month. Most customers receive services on a continuing basis. However, a significant minority of sales each month are to customers who need services only sporadically. For instance, a customer may call five months after the previous service and ask for a cleaning "overhaul." This may occur early in the month. Terms of sale are net 45 days.

Payments on credit sales are received in the form of checks or currency. These cash receipts are first sent to the receivables clerk, who posts the amounts to the accounts on her small accounting computer. Then she sends the cash receipts to the cashier, who makes out the deposit slip and enters the total in the cash receipts journal. She with-

holds about $200 each day for small expenditures. Occasionally cash amounts are received from the sale of fixed assets or from additional investments by the owner; these special receipts are deposited directly by the owner in a bank account in the owner's name. In most cases he informs the cashier orally of the amounts.

Invoices from suppliers are approved for payment. Most specify terms of 2/10, net 30 days. Since supplies are acquired in large quantities from only a few suppliers, the number of invoices received per week is considered too small for efficient check processing. Hence, checks are written on a biweekly basis for all invoices that have been approved during the period. The cashier signs most checks, although the owner signs all checks that pertain to relatively unusual and large transactions (e.g., the acquisition of a new panel truck).

Required

List the weaknesses in Royal Payne Cleaner's cash management system. Provide a recommended improvement for each listed weakness.

14-16 Alichem is a chemical producer that has been in business for three years. Ed Caz was hired as Controller two months ago. Recently, when copies of the completed purchase orders arrived in the accounting department, Caz learned that the processing department was replacing some large machines. Caz had not approved these purchase orders. By questioning Sharon Price, director of purchasing, he learned that the orders had not been forwarded to him for approval. He discovered that, although the purchasing department negotiates and orders all direct materials and processing supplies, the procedure differs for the purchase of fixed assets. When fixed assets are to be acquired, the purchasing department issues and records a blank, prenumbered purchase order to the requesting user department. The user department handles its own purchasing arrange-

Current Procedures	Proposed Procedures
Current Procedures	**Proposed Procedures**
User Department • Need determined, decision and approval to acquire made internally. • Vendor bids requested and obtained for type and model of asset selected. • Blank, prenumbered purchase order requested from Purchasing Department.	User Department • Determine need. • Obtain bids and select best vendor in consultation with purchasing, as necessary. • Prepare purchase request that includes type and model, bids, and justification.
Purchasing Department • Issue and log blank, prenumbered purchase order to user.	Management Review • Review justification. • Assure that asset meets goals and objectives of the business and department. • Verify that request is within existing guidelines. • Approve or reject asset request.
User Department • Select best bid and place order. • Prepare purchase order and distribute copies as follows: —Original and copy to vendor. —File copy for receiving department. —File copy for accounting department. —File copy retained for user department.	Purchasing Department • Receive approved requisition. • Prepare prenumbered purchase order and place order with selected vendor. • Negotiate financing with vendor, if necessary. • Assume responsibility to follow up if delivery is delayed and distribute copies as follows: —Original and copy to vendor. —File copy for receiving department. —File copy for accounting department. —File copy for purchasing department.
Receiving Department • Asset arrives at receiving department's dock. • Receiving notifies accounting so that accounting can verify that correct asset has been received and can issue brass tag number. • Asset delivered to user department after verifications or returned to vendor if there is a problem. • Send invoice to accounting if packed with asset.	Receiving Department • Asset arrives. • Prepare a receiving report including visible condition of asset upon receipt; copy sent to accounting department. • Match original of receiving report with purchase order copy and file. • Deliver asset to user. • Deliver copy of receiving report and invoice, if received with asset, to accounting.
User Department • User receives, installs and tests the asset or receives notification of return. • If asset malfunctions upon or shortly after installation, user deals with vendor and attempts to delay payment.	User Department • Receive, install, and test asset. • Accept or reject asset. • Prepare and send copies of acceptance report to accounting and purchasing indicating acceptance or rejection. • Asset returned to vendor if rejected.
Accounting Department • Verify asset, issue and record brass tag number. • Receive and match invoice to purchase order copy. • Forward invoice to controller for approval. • Payment approved by controller. • Check prepared and asset recorded unless user requests a delay of payment. • Check mailed. • Brass tagging of asset is verified.	Purchasing Department • Receive acceptance report from user department. • Deal with vendor if asset rejected or fails shortly after installation.
	Accounting Department • Match accounting copies of purchase order, receiving report, acceptance report with invoice. • If all reports are acceptable, prepare payment approval or else keep matched documents in open invoice file. • Controller or delegate approves invoice for payment. • Issue and mail check. • Record asset. • Issue brass tagging number and verify that asset is tagged.

ments. Through additional inquiries, Caz was able to identify the current procedures followed for fixed-asset acquisition; these procedures are presented in the first column above.

Caz believes that the acquisition procedure should be more efficiently distributed over the functions, thus providing the automatic implementation of new controls. Furthermore, he believes that a management group should review and approve requests for fixed assets before an order is placed.

In a manner similar to the description of the current procedures, Caz prepared the description of his proposed procedure presented in the second column on page 654.

Required

a. Identify the strengths or improvements of Ed Caz's proposed procedures for fixed-asset acquisition over the current procedures.

b. Identify and explain what further modifications, controls, or applications could be incorporated into the proposed procedures for fixed-asset administration.

(CMA adapted)

14-17 "Whew!" sighed the controller. "It's a good thing you started your audit after we finished the corporate budget. Look at this thick file of papers. My staff worked overtime to ensure all the figures are balanced and correct.

"Senior management likes the idea of the bottom-up approach of preparing budgets to allow participation of lower-level managers in developing the budget. What I hate most is the changes senior management makes to the budget at the very last minute; this causes a lot of extra work because the budget is done manually. My department has to work like crazy to incorporate the new figures into the budget. As far as the lower-level managers are concerned, once their initial budgets are submitted, their jobs are done.

"Preparing budgets, monthly reports, and special assignments keeps my staff busy all the time. It is true that as far as corporate investment goes, it has been a frantic, unorganized rush at times, which frequently results in unplanned borrowing. But I am glad that we are flexible enough to adapt to the changes, and we have been able to meet the challenge of finding short-term capital.

"With regard to monthly reports, because we want to satisfy the needs of all managers in our corporation, we produce one set of reports which show the financial performance of each of the 50 product lines for each of the five divisions.

"We measure the performance of the divisions on the basis of their return-on-investment after all direct or indirect overhead costs are charged to each department. As you know, we suffered a huge loss last year; therefore, the new president stipulated that all product prices will be increased by 20% next year. We were thinking of taking less than the normal 15% depreciation on the microcomputer equipment, but our external auditors said that we have to be consistent with prior years."

You have also noted from your discussion with the controller that, according to the computer services department, the current plan for usage of microcomputer equipment is only 3 years.

Required

Identify the deficiencies in the operations of the financial management department, describe the risk(s) related to each deficiency, and recommend improvements or controls to compensate for the risk(s).

(SMAC adapted)

14-18 Refer to the Review Problem for this chapter.

Required

a. Prepare a system flowchart that portrays both the manual and the computer-based payroll procedures described in the problem. Use a columnar flowchart similar to the manual flowcharts, with columns labeled "Factory operating departments," "Timekeeping," "Payroll audit and control," "Data preparation," "Computer operations," and "Data library." Do not show the computer-based preparation of the labor cost distribution sheet, however.

b. Identify the programmed checks that should be used in Step *F* (substep 11), assuming that the key-to-tape device used in Step *E* cannot perform edit checks. Indicate the data items that each programmed check is intended to check.

14-19 The Superior Co. of Huntington, West Virginia, manufactures automobile parts for sales to the major U.S. auto makers. On the basis of a recent review of the procedures concerning machinery and equipment, the firm's internal auditors noted the following findings in a memorandum:

a. Requests for purchases of machinery and equipment are normally initiated by the supervisor who needs the asset. This supervisor discusses the proposed acquisition with the plant manager. A purchase requisition is submitted to the purchasing department when the plant manager is satisfied that the request is reasonable and when he determines that the balance in the plant's share of the total corporate budget for capital acquisitions is adequate to cover the acquisition cost.

b. Upon receiving a purchase requisition for machinery or equipment, the purchasing department manager looks through the records for an appropriate supplier. A formal purchase order is then completed and mailed. When the machine or equipment is received, it is immediately sent to the requesting department for installation. This allows the economic benefits from the acquisition to be realized at the earliest possible date.

c. The property, plant, and equipment ledger control accounts are supported by lapsing schedules organized by year of acquisition. These lapsing schedules are used to compute depreciation as a unit for all assets of a given type that are acquired in the same year. Standard rates, depreciation methods, and salvage values are used for each major type of fixed asset. These rates, methods, and salvage values were set 10 years ago, during the firm's initial year of operation.

d. When machinery or equipment is retired, the plant manager notifies the accounting department so that the appropriate entries may be made in the accounting records.

e. There has been no reconciliation, since the firm began operations, between the accounting records and the machinery and equipment physically on hand.

Required

Identify the internal control weaknesses in the preceding fixed-assets procedure and recommend improvements.

(CMA adapted)

14-20 The narrative description and document flowchart on page 657 pertain to the payroll procedure of Croyden, Inc., of Fullerton, California.

The internal control system with respect to the personnel department is functioning well and is not included in the accompanying flowchart.

At the beginning of each workweek payroll clerk no. 1 reviews the payroll department files to determine the employment status of factory employees and then prepares time cards and distributes them as each indi-

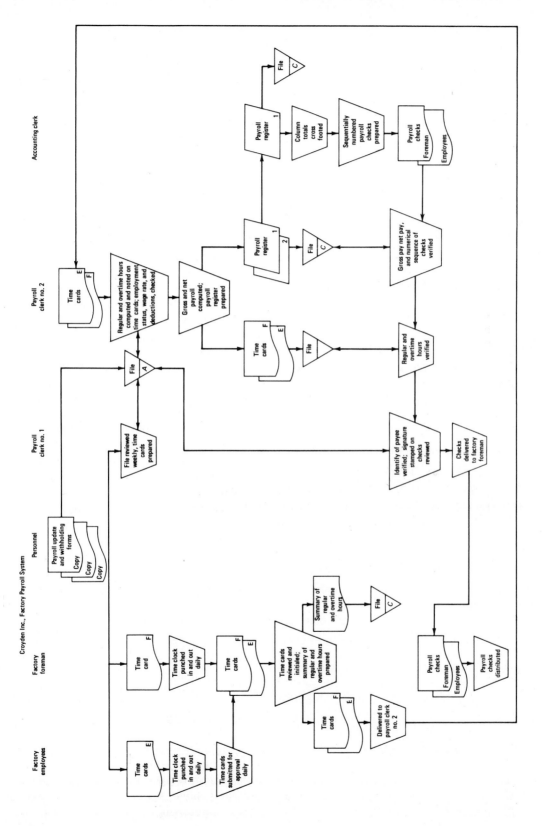

Croyden Inc., Factory Payroll System

657

vidual arrives at work. This payroll clerk, who is also responsible for custody of the signature stamp machine, verifies the identity of each payee before delivering signed checks to the foreman.

At the end of each workweek the foreman distributes payroll checks for the preceding workweek. Concurrent with this activity, the foreman reviews the current week's employee time cards, notes the regular and overtime hours worked on a summary form, and initials the aforementioned time cards. The foreman then delivers all time cards and unclaimed payroll checks to payroll clerk no. 2.

Required

a. On the basis of the narrative and accompanying flowchart, describe the weaknesses in the system of internal control.

b. On the basis of the narrative and accompanying flowchart, what inquiries should be made with respect to clarifying the existence of possible additional weaknesses in the system of internal control?

Note: Do not discuss the internal control system of the personnel department.

(CPA adapted)

14-21 The Vane Corporation of Miami, Florida, is a manufacturing concern that has been in business for the past 18 years. During this period the company has grown from a very small, family-owned operation to a medium-size manufacturing concern with several departments. Despite this growth a substantial number of the procedures employed by Vane Corporation have been in effect since the business was started. Just recently, Vane Corporation has computerized its payroll function.

The payroll function operates in the following manner. Each worker picks up a weekly time card on Monday morning and writes in his name and identification number. These blank cards are kept near the factory entrance. The workers write on their cards their daily arrival and departure times. On the following Monday the factory foremen collect the completed time cards for the previous week and send them to data processing.

In data processing the time cards are used to prepare the weekly time file. This file is processed with the master payroll file, which is maintained on magnetic tape according to worker identification number. The checks are written by the computer on the regular checking account and imprinted with the treasurer's signature. After the payroll file is updated and the checks are prepared, the checks are sent to the factory foremen, who distribute them to the workers or hold them for absent workers to pick up later.

The foremen notify data processing of new employees and terminations. Any changes in hourly pay rate or any other changes affecting payroll usually are communicated to data processing by the foremen.

The workers also complete a job-time ticket for each individual job they work on each day. The job time tickets are collected daily and sent to cost accounting, where they are used to prepare a cost distribution analysis.

Further analysis of the payroll function reveals the following information:

a. A worker's gross wages never exceed $400 per week.

b. Raises never exceed $0.55 per hour for the factory workers.

c. No more than 20 hours of overtime is allowed each week.

d. The factory employs 150 workers in 10 departments.

The payroll function has not been operating smoothly for some time, but even more problems have surfaced since the payroll was computerized. The foremen have indicated that they would like a weekly report indicating worker tardiness, absenteeism, and idle time, so they can determine the amount of productive time lost and the reason for the lost time. The following errors and inconsistencies have been encountered the past few pay periods:

a. A worker's paycheck was not processed properly because he had transposed two numbers in his identification number when he filled out his time card.

b. A worker was issued a check for $2,531.80 when he should have received $253.81.

c. One worker's paycheck was not written, and this error was not detected until the paychecks for that department were distributed by the foreman.

d. Part of the master payroll file was destroyed when the tape reel was inadvertently mounted on the wrong tape drive and used as a scratch tape. Data processing attempted to reestablish the destroyed portion from original source documents and other records.

e. One worker received a paycheck for an amount considerably larger than he should have. Further investigation revealed that "84" had been keyed instead of "48" for hours worked.

f. Several records on the master payroll were skipped and not included on the updated master payroll file. This was not detected for several pay periods.

g. In processing nonroutine changes a computer operator included a pay rate increase for one of his friends in the factory. This was discovered by chance by another employee.

Required

Identify the control weaknesses in the payroll procedure and in the computer processing as it is now conducted by the Vane Corporation. Recommend the changes necessary to correct the system.

(CMA adapted)

14-22 Rose Publishing Company devotes the bulk of its work to the development of high school and college texts. The printing division has several production departments and employs 400 persons, of which 95 percent are hourly rated production workers. Production workers may work on several projects in one day. They are paid weekly on the basis of total hours worked.

A manual time-card system is used to collect data on time worked. Each employee punches in and out when entering or leaving the plant. The timekeeping department audits the time cards daily and prepares input sheets for the computerized functions of the payroll system.

Currently, a daily report of the previous day's time-card information by department is sent to each departmental supervisor in the printing division for verification and approval. Any changes are made directly on the report, signed by the supervisor and returned to the timekeeping department. The altered report serves as the input authorization for changes to the system. Because of the volume and frequency of reports, this report-changing procedure is the most expensive process in the system.

Timekeeping submits the corrected hourly data to general accounting and cost accounting for further processing. General accounting maintains the payroll system, which determines weekly payroll, prepares weekly checks, summarizes data for monthly, quarterly, and annual reports, and generates W-2 forms. A weekly and monthly payroll distribution report that shows the labor costs by department is prepared by the cost accounting department.

Competition in college textbook publishing has increased steadily in the last three years. Although Rose has maintained its sales volume, profits have declined. Direct labor cost is believed to be the basic cause of this decline in profits, but insufficient detail on labor utilization is available to pinpoint the suspected inefficiencies. Chuck Hutchins, a systems consultant, was engaged to analyze the current system and to make recommendations for improving data collection and processing procedures. Excerpts from the report that Hutchins prepared appear in the accompanying box.

Required

a. Compared with the traditional time-card system, what are the advantages and dis-

advantages of the recommended system of electronically recording the entry to and exit from the plant?

b. Identify the items to be included in the individual employee's master file.

c. The TALC system allows the employee's departmental supervisor and the personnel department to examine the data contained in an individual employee's master file.

   (1) Discuss the extent of the information each should be allowed to examine.

   (2) Describe the safeguards that may be installed to prevent unauthorized access to the data.

d. The recommended system allows both the departmental supervisors and the project managers to obtain current labor distribution data on a limited basis. The limitations mentioned can lead to a conflict

---

. . . An integrated time and attendance labor cost (TALC) system should be developed. Features of this system would include direct data entry; labor cost distribution by project as well as department; on-line access to time and attendance data for verification, correction, and update; and creation and maintenance of individual employee work history files for long-term analysis.

. . . The TALC system should incorporate uniquely encoded employee badges that would be used to electronically record entry to and exit from the plant directly into the data system.

. . . Labor cost records should be maintained at the employee level, showing the time worked in the department by project. Thus, labor cost can be fully analyzed. Responsibility for correct and timely entry must reside with the departmental supervisors and must be verified by project managers on a daily basis because projects involve several departments.

. . . On-line terminals should be available in each department for direct data entry. Access to the system will be limited to authorized users through a coded entry (password) system. Departmental supervisors will be allowed to inspect, correct, verify, and update only time and attendance information for employees in their respective departments. Project managers may access information recorded for their projects only, and exceptions to such data must be certified outside the system and entered by the affected supervisor.

. . . Appropriate data should be maintained at the employee level to allow verification of employee personnel files and individual work-history by department and project. Access to employee master file data should be limited to the personnel department. Work-history data will be made available for analysis only at the project or departmental level, and only to departmental supervisors and project managers for whom an employee works.

between a departmental supervisor and a project manager.

(1) Discuss the reasons for the specified limitations.

(2) Recommend a solution for the possible conflict that could arise if a departmental supervisor and a project manager do not agree.

(CMA adapted)

14-23 Precision Tillers, Inc. (PTI), of Arlington, Texas, is a small manufacturer of rototillers. PTI's business is very seasonal, requiring careful attention to cash management.

The controller of PTI begins the cash management task with an annual projection of unit sales that is converted into dollar sales. Production is scheduled for the month prior to sale. Materials must be ordered two months before they are scheduled for use, received a month after they are ordered, and paid for a month after receipt. Materials costs average 30 percent of the product's selling price.

Labor and the variable overhead requiring the expenditure of cash average 25 percent of sales. These amounts are paid for during the month of production.

Fixed costs requiring the expenditure of cash total $3000 per month. This figure includes all fixed costs other than those specifically mentioned below.

Half of PTI's sales are for cash; the other half are on account. Receivable collections normally occur as follows:

During month after sale	80%
Two months after sale	15%
Three months after sale	3%
Uncollectible	2%

PTI pays royalties to the designer of its rototiller. The royalty amounts to 2 percent of sales. The total royalty for each quarter is

paid during the first month of the next quarter.

PTI pays a regular cash dividend of $0.25 per share per quarter on each of its 100,000 outstanding shares. This dividend is paid during the first month of each quarter.

Monthly depreciation charges amount to $1500. Planned capital expenditures of $25,000 in June and $25,000 for August of the next year will not affect this amount. PTI must make a $60,000 payment to a bank to settle the balance due on a note payable in September.

The controller is aware that PTI's investment tax credit carry-forwards will eliminate any tax obligations for the next year.

To assist in the cash management task for next year, the controller wants to develop a model. The model should permit the controller to determine the cash inflows and outflows for each component and the net cash flow for each month. The model is to be stated in terms of sales using the following notation:

$$S = \text{sales for a month}$$
$$t = \text{time}$$

For example, S_t would stand for sales during month t. If a cash flow in month t depended on a sale made in the second prior month, the appropriate notation would be S_{t-2}.

Required

a. For each of the items enumerated in the table on page 662, develop the appropriate notation for use in the controller's cash flow model. The notation should include an algebraic sign (+, −) and be stated in terms of S and t where applicable. Indicate whether the item is used each month or is used only for specific months (i.e., if an item is used for all months, show $t = 1$–12; if an item is used for a specific month(s), such as June, show the number of the month, such as $t = 6$). Use the following format for presenting your answer:

Estimated Cash Flow Item	Notation	Applicable Months
1. Materials		
2. Labor and variable overhead		
3. Fixed costs		
4. Cash sales		
5. Collections of accounts receivable		
6. Royalties		
7. Regular dividend		
8. Capital expenditures		
9. Debt repayment		

b. Describe how the cash-flow model can be used to aid the controller (and the treasurer) in financial planning and funds management.

(CMA adapted)

Suggested Readings

Cushing, Barry E., and Romney, Marshall B. *Accounting Information Systems and Business Organizations*. 5th ed. Reading, Mass.: Addison-Wesley, 1990.

Fixed Assets System. Sunnyvale, Cal.: Data Design Associates, 1982.

Payroll/Personnel. Atlanta: Management Science America, 1989.

CHAPTER OBJECTIVES

After reading this chapter, you should be able to do the following with respect to the product conversion cycle:

Describe its objectives and functions, as well as its relationships to pertinent organizational units.

Identify its data sources and forms of input.

Identify the files comprising its data base.

Describe the steps and approaches employed in processing its transaction data flows.

List needed accounting transaction controls.

Describe a variety of operational and managerial reports and other outputs that may be generated.

Chapter *15*

THE PRODUCT CONVERSION CYCLE

The previous four chapters have considered transaction cycles and systems that are basic to the large majority of organizations. This chapter examines the product conversion cycle, which is found mainly in firms undertaking manufacturing, construction, and repair and maintenance activities. A similar conversion cycle that involves services rather than products is found in health care, systems consulting, and certain other service-oriented firms. Although all conversion cycles have several common threads, this chapter focuses on the product conversion cycle, also known as the production cycle, within manufacturing firms.

Overview

Cycle Objectives

The major purpose of the **product conversion cycle** is to facilitate the conversion of raw materials into products or finished goods. Because this cycle emphasizes the raw materials resource, it may also be called the raw materials management cycle. Key objectives within the broad purpose are to ensure that

1. Adequate raw materials and other resources are available for production, while the investment in such resources is minimized.

2. Production costs are minimized through high labor productivity, full utilization of production equipment, low levels of scrap and rework, and optimal design of production layouts and processes.

3. Finished goods are completed and warehoused or shipped on schedule.

4. Established levels of product quality and after-sales service are attained.

5. Costs for each order or process are accumulated fully and accurately.

6. Information for sound decision making is gathered, stored, and provided to managerial decision makers as needed.

Functions

In the case of product conversion, the functions related to these objectives include undertaking strategic production planning, obtaining and managing the raw materials inventory, initiating production processes, maintaining and controlling production operations, accumulating work-in-process costs, completing and transferring finished goods, and preparing financial reports and other outputs. These functions, shown in Figure 15-1, involve a mind-boggling number of decisions and planning and control techniques.

Undertake strategic production planning. Strategic planning extends years into the future. Strategic decisions that must be made by a manufacturing firm include the following:

Which products and product components should be manufactured?

How much production capacity should be acquired in each year for the next several years?

What method of physical production should be employed?

What should be the means of initiating the production process?

What materials are to be included in each unit product, and what steps should be followed in manufacturing the product?

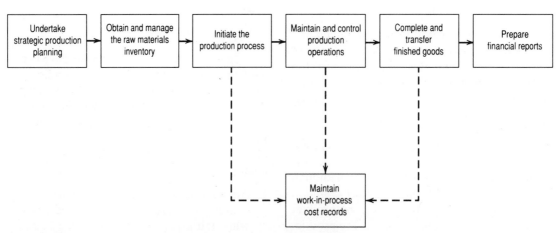

FIGURE 15-1 Typical functions of a product conversion cycle.

How should work centers be arranged within the production area?

From what sources should resources, such as raw materials and direct labor, be obtained?

Each of these decisions, and others not listed, preferably should be made well in advance of the actual production activity. Since the decisions are strategic in nature, they should be made by higher-level managers. Most of the decisions typically involve the participation of managers who are in charge of directing the product conversion (i.e., production) operations. To provide a foundation for the product conversion cycle, let us briefly consider each of these decisions and the key information needed for their resolution.

Which products to manufacture is largely a marketing decision, since it is based on such information as customer preferences and degree of competition. However, it also is affected by production capabilities.

Which product components to manufacture is in effect the classic "make-or-buy" decision, since presumably the product components (such as subassemblies and parts) are available from suppliers. The decision depends mainly on a comparison of the relevant costs. If a firm decides to acquire most of its components from suppliers, its main task is the assembly of such components.

How much production capacity to maintain can be decided only after the product demands are forecast over the next several years. A related decision is how to acquire the capacity (e.g., to build new plants, to lease currently available plants, or to use subcontractors).

Which method of physical production to employ is a decision that depends on the nature of the products being manufactured. Four major patterns are

1. Process production, which involves the continuous production of standardized products (e.g., petrochemicals, cement, margarine, steel).

2. Mass production, which involves the production of discrete and relatively similar products on assembly lines (e.g., automobiles, television sets).

3. Batch production, which involves the production of batches or job lots of distinctly differing products; an example is found in a metal products firm that might manufacture bearings in one batch and gears in another.

4. Custom production, which involves the production of uniquely individual products, often of a complex nature (e.g., a special machine tool).

What means to employ in initiating the production process is a decision that depends on the method of physical production as well as the nature of the product. The production process may be initiated either (1) to replenish inventory levels or (2) to fill firm customer orders. Products manufactured by the process production method generally are initiated to replenish finished-goods inventory levels, which are set in part on the basis of their forecast demand. Products manufactured by the custom production method are, of course, initiated by customers' orders. Mass- or batch-produced goods may be initiated in either way, depending partly on industry practice.

What materials and manufacturing steps to employ are technical decisions made by the engineering function. Needed information includes the capabilities of various types of material and manufacturing equipment.

What work center arrangement to employ is also an engineering decision, which depends in part on the normal sequence of required manufacturing steps.

Where to obtain the needed resources can be decided on the basis of information concerning raw materials suppliers and skilled labor pools.

After decisions such as these are made, the manufacturing firm can develop long-range production schedules, as well as production and inventory budgets. They provide important inputs into the shorter-term planning schedules, control reports, and operational documents.

Obtain and manage the raw materials inventory. Raw materials consist of basic building materials (e.g., metal rods, wood boards, plastic screws), finished parts, and subassemblies used directly in finished goods or products. Of course, a basic material or part to one manufacturer may represent a finished good to another manufacturer. Nevertheless, the finished goods of most manufacturers contain a variety of the components broadly labeled as raw materials.

Raw materials, like merchandise for resale and fixed assets, traverse all the functions of the expenditure cycle. Thus, they are ordered, received, stored, and paid for. Because of their importance, raw materials and all other inventories (including supplies) also warrant careful management. A broad activity known as inventory management is therefore often superimposed. **Inventory management** encompasses the receipt, storage, and disposition of all inventories, together with related planning and control activities. Inventory management may be conducted through an organizational unit with that name, or its responsibilities may be spread among several units (e.g., production planning, inventory control).

A major aim of inventory management is to minimize the total cost of each type of inventory. In the case of raw materials inventory, the total cost consists of the *sum* of ordering, storing, and out-of-stock costs for *each raw material item*. Ordering costs include mainly the costs of processing purchase orders and freight on incoming orders; they tend to vary with the number of orders.

Storing (carrying) costs include interest on the investment in inventory, insurance, taxes, space utilized, and losses through spoilage, breakage, and so on. Out-of-stock costs for raw materials consist of losses in production efficiency and timeliness, which lead to higher unit costs for products and possible losses in customer goodwill.

Numerous decisions must be made in managing these three types of costs. Most of the decisions are relatively minor, though important. For instance, storage locations and control procedures must be determined, as well as the amounts of insurance coverage to carry. Four decisions are critical to the management of raw materials: (1) when to reorder, (2) how many to reorder, (3) whom to order from, and (4) how many to issue into production (i.e., to dispose of). The fourth decision is discussed under the next function.

The decision concerning *when to reorder a raw material item* depends on the level of inventory on hand, the expected requirements for the raw material in production, a desired reserve or safety level of inventory, and the lead time needed to receive the item from the supplier after an order is placed. When these factors are known or estimated, a reorder point can be computed. Then (as described in Chapter 13) the reorder point is compared with the current level or balance of inventory; when the balance falls below the reorder point, the time for reordering has arrived.

The decision concerning *how many to reorder* can be based on the economic order quantity (EOQ) formula. The EOQ formula includes the key factors of reorder costs, storage (carrying) costs, and expected future requirements. The resulting EOQ is then provided to the purchasing department as the needed quantity to reorder. In a manufacturing firm where hundreds and even thousands of raw materials are used, the EOQ is likely to be computed only for those items that are heavily used or relatively costly. Other raw materials items would be ordered in sufficient quantities to assure their continuous availability.

In fact, in certain manufacturing environments the EOQ approach is modified for all raw materials because of the greater need posed by production requirements. Raw materials are ordered in such environments to meet the requirements of planned production for the upcoming weeks or months. This alternative approach is called **materials requirements planning** (MRP). Even if quantities ordered under the MRP approach exceed those specified by the EOQ approach, the overall cost savings due to production efficiencies should outweigh the added costs of inventory management.

The decision concerning *whom to order from* relates to the selection of suitable suppliers (vendors). As noted in Chapter 13, the decision for each raw material item depends on such factors as the suppliers' reliability, unit price, lead time, and quality. If a prime supplier is selected for a raw material, the supplier's number should be noted in the raw material records. However, usually secondary suppliers should also be selected, so that they may be contacted quickly in case the primary supplier is out of stock, struck by a labor union, or faced by some other emergency.

A recent development concerning inventory management is the **just-in-time** (JIT) system. The objective of a JIT system is to eliminate or at least minimize the need for all inventories, including raw materials. A JIT system involves very tight scheduling of inventory deliveries, so that the raw materials arrive "just in time" to be used in the production process. Usually the needed materials are delivered in small batches and at relatively frequent intervals. The JIT concept provides such advantages as greatly reduced costs of materials storage and handling. To be effective, however, the system must be accompanied by accurate planning for materials requirements, precise production coordination, and highly dependable suppliers. Firms with successful JIT systems employ on-line computer systems, often with direct communications links to the primary suppliers.

All of the inventory management decisions concerning raw materials are reflected in suitable inventory records. A record for each raw material item is posted to show quantities ordered, receipts of ordered quantities, quantities issued into production, and current balance (i.e., level of quantity on hand). Related records for suppliers are posted to show amounts of purchases, while the general ledger is posted to reflect debits to raw materials inventory and credits to accounts payable.

Initiate the production process. The production process begins with a recognized need for finished goods. In custom manufacturing firms an order from a customer creates the need. In other manufacturing firms the need arises when the quantity of finished-goods inventory on hand falls below a determined replenishment level. This replenishment level, similar in concept to the raw materials reorder point, is based on such factors as expected future demands from customers and production lead times.

Upon recognizing the need, two decisions must be made:

What quantity of goods should be produced?

When should production be scheduled?

Production size is based either on the special order (in the case of custom manufacturing) or on set-up costs, direct production costs, and level of expected demand (in the case of job lot inventory replenishment). The scheduled start date depends upon the other production orders or jobs already scheduled and the relative priority of the order or job in question.

After scheduling the production order or job, the materials requirements are determined. When the start date arrives, the materials are issued to the job and labor and machines are assigned.

Maintain and control production operations. Each scheduled production order or job follows a physical flow through production operations. It moves either (1) from process to process (in the case of process production), or (2) from work center to work center or department to department (in the case of batch, mass, or custom production). As the order or job flows through the operations, it is monitored and controlled with respect to time, costs, and quality. The time control is based on the scheduled duration for the production order or job, as shown in the production schedule. The cost control is based on standard product costs, as established by industrial engineers. The quality control is based on specified capabilities of the product, as established by product design engineers.

Each type of control is administered during the production operations by means of comparing the actual achievements against the standards. Time comparisons are made by work center supervisors or department foremen; cost comparisons are made by cost accountants; quality comparisons are made by quality control inspectors.

Maintain work-in-process cost records. Product costs consist of direct materials costs, direct labor costs, and overhead costs. Included as overhead are costs of indirect labor, supplies, utilities, small tools, depreciation of machines, plant insurance, and so on. These product costs are accumulated to reflect the value of the orders or jobs flowing through production operations. They are recorded on work-in-process records; in total they equal the work-in-process inventory balance in the general ledger. The journal entry that summarizes the cost accumulations has the following form:

```
Dr. Work-in-Process Inventory   XXX
    Cr. Raw Materials Inventory         XXX
    Cr. Direct Labor                    XXX
    Cr. Manufacturing Overhead          XXX
```

Cost accounting systems vary widely. However, they can broadly be classified as either actual cost systems or standard cost systems. In pure actual cost systems the actual dollar amounts incurred for the three cost components are accumulated in the work-in-process records. In pure standard cost systems the standard costs are accumulated in the records. As suggested in the previous function, a standard cost system provides a better basis for cost control. It enables a variety of cost variances to be computed and reported.[1]

Complete and transfer finished goods. When a production order or job has flowed through all required production operations and thus is completed, the consequent finished goods are transferred to a warehouse or to the shipping dock. Then the product costs are totaled and the following journal entry is prepared:

```
Dr. Finished Goods Inventory
(or Cost of Goods Sold)         XXX
    Cr. Work-in-Process Inven-
        tory                            XXX
```

Prepare financial reports and other outputs. A variety of outputs are generated as by-products of the product conversion cycle. In addition to the cost variance reports mentioned earlier, these outputs include summaries of production status and quantities completed. Reports to management regarding production costs and delays are very use-

[1] The details of actual and standard cost accounting systems are described in any cost accounting text. See, for instance, Charles T. Horngren and Gary Sundem, *Cost Accounting: A Managerial Emphasis*, 7th ed. (Englewood Cliffs, N.J.: Prentice-Hall, 1987).

ful; they often reveal the need for decisions concerning improvements in efficiency and productivity. If an on-line computer-based system is employed, displays of individual work-in-process and production order records and other specific information are also available.

Other related functions. Additional functions of interest include quality control, rework, scrap, and excess materials. We will discuss each function briefly, grouping related functions together.

Quality control is a matter of concern throughout the production operations. Adequate training of production employees, scheduled maintenance checks of machines, and frequent replacement of cutting tools help to assure that quality is "built into" products. In order to verify that quality specifications are being met and to detect defective units, inspections of work-in-process are made as necessary. Ideally, inspections of every unit of product would be conducted at every work center or department. However, this ideal can be approached only in the case of highly complex and critical product components, such as computer processor chips. For most products inspections are performed at one point: as the completed units emerge from the last production operation. Moreover, only a sample of the product units are generally inspected. The size of the sample depends in part on the type of inspection required. Inspections involving only visual checks can involve much larger samples than those involving destructive testing of the units. Where more units than expected are found to be defective, the samples are usually increased or the entire lots are inspected.

When units of product are rejected during quality control inspections, they are either reworked or scrapped. *Rework* of units takes place when the units do not meet design specifications but can be brought within

the specifications through additional efforts. Units to be reworked are returned to the work centers or departments where the defective work was performed. Added costs due to rework are charged to those work centers or departments. *Scrappage* of units takes place when the units are so spoiled that they cannot be reworked. Scrap costs are also charged to the work centers or departments that did the defective work, if they can be determined. Because scrappage represents waste and added production costs, scrap or spoilage reports are often prepared.

Excess materials are the units of raw materials remaining in a work center or department after the work on an order or job has been finished. These excess materials are returned to the storeroom, and the costs of the materials are deducted from the work-in-process records. Conversely, if added materials are needed for an order or job, they are issued by the storeroom in the same manner as the original materials were provided. In any transaction involving materials, of course, the raw materials records must be posted.

Relationships to the Organization

The product conversion cycle functions are typically achieved under the direction of the logistics management and finance/accounting organizational functions (units) of the firm. Although the logistics management function is also involved in the expenditure cycle, in a manufacturing firm it assumes a more complex structure.

Logistics. Figure 15-2 portrays the key units within a hypothetical manufacturing firm. In addition to the purchasing, receiving, and stores units found in a typical merchandising firm, it includes all of the production units, plus engineering design and sales order entry. The organizational structure shown in the figure reflects the view that **logistics man-**

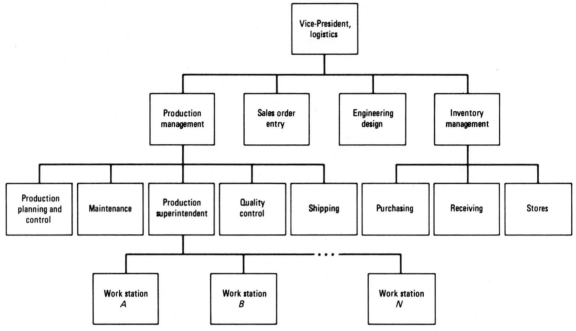

FIGURE 15-2 A partial organization chart that shows the logistics function for a manufacturing firm.

agement concerns the planning and control of the materials resource flows and transformations. (It should be noted that the latter two units and the shipping department are removed from the logistics management function in some manufacturing firms. Nevertheless, the remaining production and inventory management units encompass an imposing array of activities.)

Figure 15-3 depicts the relationships among the organizational units shown in Figure 15-2. Included in the figure are certain of the organizational units and documents that interface with the logistics function. The roles of several key organizational units within the function are described next. As a supplement to the descriptions, Figure 15-4 depicts the flows of documents among the organizational units.

Sales order entry is responsible for receiving the customers' orders, checking them for acceptability, and preparing formal sales orders. Orders for customized products then trigger the production activities, whereas orders for standard products lead to the release of finished goods from the warehouse for shipment.

Engineering design determines the specifications by which products (either those specially ordered or those needed to replenish inventories) will be manufactured. These specifications are embodied in two documents: a bill of materials that lists the needed quantity of each material and part and an operations list that shows the required sequence of labor and machine operations.

Production planning determines how many products are to be produced, when they are to be produced and with what facilities they are to be produced. The level of production is based on specific customer orders and sales forecasts; the timing of production is dependent on the estimated times required to perform specific operations; the production facilities are prescribed by design specifications. Two key documents gener-

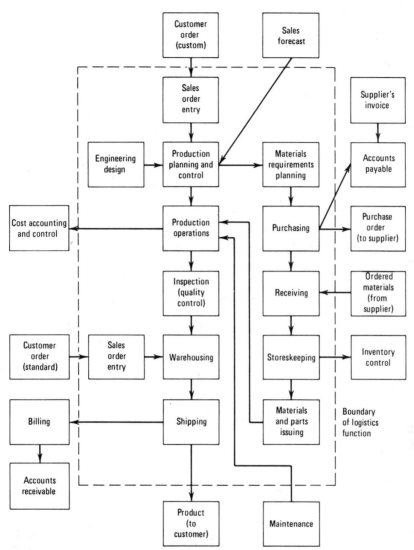

FIGURE 15-3 Organizational units that direct the functions involved in the product conversion cycle and the filing of customers' orders.

ated by production planning are the production schedule and the production order.

Inventory management, or a separate **materials requirements planning** department within the inventory planning function, is responsible for assuring that adequate quantities of materials will be available to use in manufacturing scheduled orders or jobs. Materials requirements planning begins with the "exploding" of materials requirements: that is, the multiplying of the number of units of product to be manufactured by the quantities of parts and materials needed per unit, as specified in the bill of materials. It continues with the requisitioning of the required parts and materials from the storeroom on the appropriate dates and with their assembly at the work stations where they are to be used.

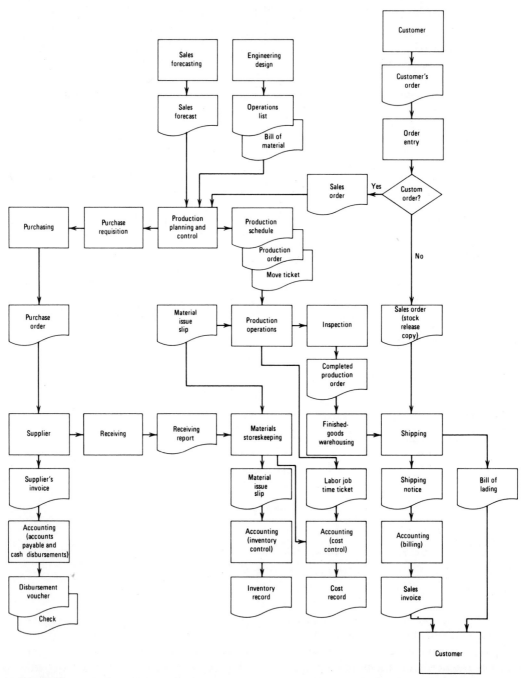

FIGURE 15-4 Flows of documents among the organizational units involved in product conversion and logistics.

It also consists of notifying the purchasing department when additional parts and materials must be ordered to fill specific orders or to replenish inventories.

Production control, which may be a part of production planning and control or a separate department, has several varied responsibilities. It dispatches (starts the actual production operations for orders or jobs), monitors actual operations, and suggests corrective actions when necessary. A key document involved in production control is the move ticket, which authorizes the movement of an order or job from one operation to the next.

Production operations, which are headed by a superintendent and include all the work centers or departments, performs all the actual work and rework on orders or jobs.

Quality control conducts inspections and tests of the products and either accepts or rejects units based on evaluations of product quality.

Maintenance performs scheduled and nonscheduled repair and maintenance of production equipment and other facilities.

Finance/accounting. The objectives and most of the units of the finance/accounting function have been discussed in earlier chapters. The cost accounting and control unit, however, appears for the first time. It accumulates material, labor, and overhead costs incurred in the production process and prepares cost variance reports. Cost accounting also may assist in developing labor and materials cost standards and assign values to work-in-process inventory.

Data Sources and Inputs

Sources

Data used in the product conversion cycle are mainly based on inputs from production operations and related to materials, labor, and production orders. However, other sources include the sales order department, receiving department, stores department, design engineering department, production planning department, and various product-oriented files.

Forms of Input

Manual systems. The product conversion cycle requires such source documents as bills of materials, operations lists, production orders, materials issue slips, labor job-time tickets, and move tickets. Other supporting inputs may include sales forecasts, sales orders, purchase requisitions, purchase orders, and receiving reports.

This relatively large number of inputs can be quite confusing. For greater clarity, each of the inputs just listed is briefly described in the context of a hypothetical manufacturing firm that produces such electrical products as motors, generators, resistors, and control instruments. The firm produces mainly for inventory, using the batch production approach. However, it also designs new electrical products or modifies standard products to meet customer specifications. It employs the logistics organizational structure shown in Figure 15-2.

The descriptions of the inputs, roughly in the sequence in which they might be prepared when special orders are received, are as follows:

Sales forecasts list the expected demand for the respective products over the coming periods. For instance, a particular forecast might indicate that sales of motor 5AX are expected to be 10 next week and 12 the following week.

Sales orders are the formal documents prepared from relatively informal customer orders. For instance, a particular order from Lipton Technology, Inc., may specify five generators, type PG21, 50 horsepower each, with customized shielding and added devices to maintain tight voltage regulation.

BILL OF MATERIALS		
Product Name and No. Generator PG 21	Authorization P D Q	Effective Date 1/1/90
Material or Part Number	Description	Quantity
18568	Casting for rotor shaft	1
32151	Salient poles	4
33592	Field windings	4
44276	Slip rings	2
98105	Ventilating fan	1

FIGURE 15-5 A bill of materials.

Bills of material specify the quantities of parts and materials to be used in specific products. Figure 15-5 shows a bill of material that pertains to the type of generator just noted, as established at a date prior to the order referenced. (Since the referenced order specifies custom features, the bill of material would be modified by engineering design before production begins.)

Operations lists specify the sequences of operations to be performed in fashioning and assembling the parts required for specific products. As Figure 15-6 shows, the list may include the work centers at which the operations are to take place, as well as machine requirements and standard time allowances.

Production orders incorporate data drawn from sales orders (or sales forecasts),

OPERATIONS LIST					
Product Name and Number Generator PG21		Authorization P.D.Q.		Effective Date 1/1/90	
Opera- tion Number	Description	Work Cen- ter	Machine Requirement	Standard Time (Hrs)	
				Set Up	Operating
G100	Machine rotor shaft	A	Lathe 75P RPM: 900 Tolerance: .0005	0.3	3.0
G200	Attach slip rings	B			0.9
G300	Mount salient poles	B			2.5
G400	Wrap windings on poles	C			1.8
G500	Mount fan	C			0.3

FIGURE 15-6 An operations list.

Receiving Report

Received from Baker Foundry No. 6313
Purchase order no. 7581 Date 10/10/90

Quantity	Unit	Description	Weight
40	ea.	Steel castings for rotors	8,000 #

Delivered by M. Olson, Westbound Freight Co.
Received by P. Woodson
Comments Good condition

FIGURE 15-7 A receiving report.

from the relevant operations list, and from the production schedule. Thus, a particular order might show a product number, the quantity to be produced, the customer order number, the list of operations, the start date for each operation, and the completion date.

Purchase requisitions request needed materials or parts. For instance, a requisition may specify that 40 castings for rotor shafts (material number 18568) are needed to replenish the materials and parts inventory. Apparently, the order placed by the customer noted earlier has caused the quantity on hand to drop below the reorder point.

Purchase orders specify needed materials and parts. They are addressed to specific suppliers.[2]

Receiving reports reflect the materials and parts received from suppliers. Figure 15-7 shows a receiving report that records the receipt of 40 castings.

Material issue slips, often called materials requisitions, direct the storeskeeper to issue materials or parts to designated work centers or authorized persons. Figure 15-8 shows a material issue slip for the five castings listed on the bill of materials for generator type PG21. The additional materials and parts, to be used at other work centers, will be issued on separate material issue slips. Costs are entered later by the inventory control department.

Labor job-time tickets record the elapsed times devoted by production employees to work prescribed by respective production orders. Figure 15-9 shows that Bill Smarts spent $3\frac{1}{2}$ hours machining a rotor shaft under production order number 8333.

Move tickets, also called travelers, authorize the physical movement of production orders from one work center to the next. A move ticket also records the quantity of items on an order and the date received at an incoming work center. Completed move tickets are used by production planning as the basis for posting work performance to production records, so that progress can be tracked. A move ticket pertaining to order number 8333 appears in Figure 15-10.

Several other documents are often needed. An *acceptance document* may be used to denote materials received at a work center or completed products received at the

[2]See Figure 13-5 for an example of a purchase order.

					No. 704
	Material Issue Slip				
	Issued to _Work Center A_ Date _10/22/90_				
	Charged to production order number _8333_				

Material or part number	Description	Quantity issued	Unit cost	Extended cost
18568	Casting for rotor shaft	5	500.00	2500.00

Authorized by _D. W. Munro_

Received by _F. J. Boswell_

Costed by _P. S. Johnson_

FIGURE 15-8   A material issue slip.

	Labor Job Time Ticket			
Employee no.	Employee name	Production order	Date
1368	Bill Smarts	8333	10/23/90
Work center	Operation number		Operation description
A	G100		Machine rotor shaft
Time started	Time finished		Elapsed time (hours)
8:30	12:00		3.50
Pieces finished	Hourly rate		Labor cost
1	10.00		35.00

Approved: _D. W. Munro_

FIGURE 15-9   A labor job-time ticket.

```
┌─────────────────────────────────────────────┐
│                  Move Ticket                  │
│                                               │
│  Move to _____ Work Center B _____   │
│                                               │
│  Operations _____ G200 _____   │
│                                               │
│  _____ G300 _____   │
│                                               │
│  Production order no. ____ 8333 _____   │
│                                               │
│  Start date of order ____ 10/23/90 _____   │
│                                               │
│  Date received _____ 10/24/90 _____   │
│                                               │
│  Quantity received _____ 5 _____   │
│                                               │
│                                               │
│  Received By       R. E. Green                │
│                    Le Roy Gainer              │
│  Posted By                                    │
└─────────────────────────────────────────────┘
```

FIGURE 15-10 A move ticket.

warehouse. Alternatively, copies of materials requisitions or move tickets may serve as acceptance documents. For instance, a move ticket may contain a collection of stubs that may be removed at the various work centers. A *work order* is used by a service department, such as repair and maintenance, to authorize the performance of specified tasks within the production area. A *quality control evaluation form or inspection report* records the results of inspections performed on products during or after production operations. Copies of the report are (1) attached to the move ticket and (2) forwarded to the production planning department. An *excess materials requisition* lists materials needed on a production order that exceed the quantities specified by the bill of material. It is handled in the same manner as a regular materials issue slip, except that it typically is printed on a form of a different color. A *returned materials form* reflects materials that remain after an order or job has been completed at a work center. A copy of the form is signed by the storeskeeper to acknowledge receipt, and other copies are used for posting to the work-in-process and raw materials inventory records.

Computer-based systems. All of the hardcopy documents listed for manual systems may also be used in computer-based systems. Preformatted screens can be devised that appear similar to the documents. They may be designed to handle individual transactions or batches of transactions. In some cases, the preformatted screens may be generated automatically upon the entry of key data via terminals or microcomputers. For instance, a move ticket or production order might appear automatically upon the entry of a production order number and work center number.

As Figure 15-11 shows, computer-based data entry can require numerous terminals or microcomputers, which are located in the various departments throughout a manufacturing firm. Each of the entry points accepts data concerning a particular type of transaction. Key documents can also be printed at appropriate points within the system. For instance, the order entry terminal is used to

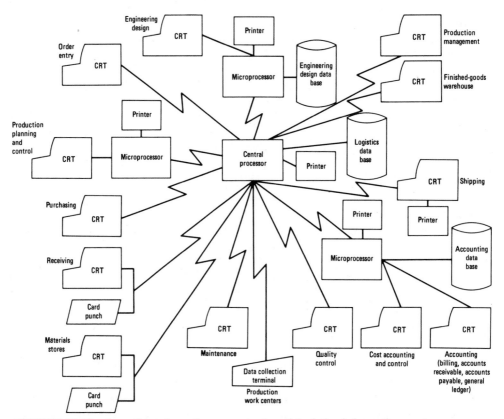

FIGURE 15-11 A configuration of a computer-based logistics information system.

enter sales order data, and production orders and move tickets based on these sales orders are generated on the printer in the production planning and control department. To take another example, data concerning issued materials are entered in materials stores, and hard-copy material issue cards are generated on a card punch. The system also can process entered data. Thus, direct labor hours devoted to production jobs are entered via the data collection terminals; the system then automatically records the start and stop times, computes the elapsed time, and stores this time.

Codes

A number of codes can be employed during production operations, including those pertaining to raw materials, orders, employees, work centers, and products. Perhaps the most difficult of these to code is a raw material. However, a well-designed material code can reduce the duplication among raw materials and increase production efficiency. Typically, a meaningful materials code in a fairly large manufacturing firm would contain several fields and nine or more numeric positions. Among the characteristics to be considered are raw materials class (e.g., steel, wood), subclass (e.g., bars, screws, strips), size dimensions, source (e.g., purchased, manufactured in house), shape, special machinings or features, relation to product (e.g., part, subassembly), and location in storeroom. Clearly, a wide variety of raw materials codes are in use.[3]

[3]See page 313 in Chapter 8 for an example.

Data Base

As a result of its very broad scope, the logistics function of a manufacturing firm maintains a large number of files. Figure 15-12 shows many of the files that could be included within the data base of the logistics function. Not included are certain files involved in inventory management, such as the receiving report file; certain document files, such as a material issues file; nor files in related data bases, such as the general ledger file, accounts payable master file, or a file containing engineering drawings of products. Moreover, the specific files that are encompassed by the logistics data base and their contents vary widely from firm to firm, since manufacturing environments are quite diverse. Also, the files may be stored on magnetic media (as shown in the figure) or on hard-copy cards or sheets. Furthermore, relationships among the files, if any, are dependent in large part on the extent to which a firm employs the data base approach, as discussed in Chapter 18.

Most files shown in Figure 15-12 are described in the following paragraphs. A more complete description would include a data dictionary and record layouts for all files.

Raw Materials Inventory Master File

Three inventory files are included in the product conversion data base. As the name implies, the **raw materials inventory master file** contains records of the raw materials, parts, and subassemblies required by a manufacturer. (Factory supplies are generally maintained in a separate file.) Each record reflects the receipts, issues, orders, and on-hand balances pertaining to a particular item. The primary key is normally the item (material or part number) number. In a manual system the file consists of cards, such as the card for item number 18568 shown in Figure 15-13. In the example the on-hand balances are maintained for amounts as well as quantities, so that the total of all amounts can be reconciled to the control account in the general ledger. Large manufacturing firms having multiple locations may maintain a separate raw materials inventory file at each location, perhaps with an overall file kept at the main office.

Work-in-Process Inventory Master File

The second of the three inventory files required by a manufacturer is the **work-in-**

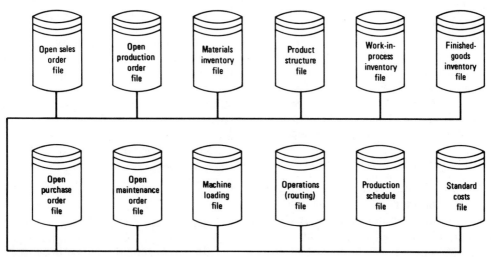

FIGURE 15-12 A logistics data base.

Materials Record Card										
Material or part no. 18568				Description Casting for rotor shaft						
Stores location Row 10 Bin A5				Supplier Baker foundry					Unit cost (std.) $500.00	
Reorder quantity 40				Reorder point 16						
Receipts			Issues			On order			On hand	
Date	Ref.	Qty.	Date	Ref.	Qty.	Date	Ref.	Qty.	Qty.	Amount
									20	10000.00
			10/22	704	5				15	7500.00
						10/24	7581	40	15	7500.00
11/12	6213	40							55	27500.00

FIGURE 15-13 A materials record card.

process inventory master file. It summarizes the raw materials, direct labor, and overhead costs pertaining to orders or jobs currently in production. Thus, it might be called a production order cost file. The primary key is usually the production order number.

In a manual system the costs for each production order are recorded on a separate card, such as the card for order number 8333 shown in Figure 15-14. The cards (records) for all of the orders or jobs in progress comprise a subsidiary ledger that supports the work-in-process inventory control account.

Finished Goods Inventory Master File

The third inventory file in a manufacturing firm, the **finished-goods inventory master file,** is in effect the merchandise inventory file of a merchandising firm. In a manual system the file may physically consist of completed production order cost cards. The pri-

mary key is usually the product number or code, rather than the production order number.

Open Production Order File

The **open production order file** consists of data related to production orders, except for the cost data contained in the work-in-process inventory file. It reflects the current status of orders being produced, both those based on customers' orders and those generated to replenish finished-goods inventory. As Figure 15-15 shows, records in this file track the progress of orders as they move through the various physical operations.

Product Structure File

In many manufacturing firms a bill-of-materials file would be maintained. How-

Production Order Cost Record									

Product _____ Generator PG21 _____ Product Order No. 8333

Quantity _____ 5 _____

Date Started _____ 10/23/90 _____

Date Finished _____

Material costs			Labor costs				Overhead costs		
Date	Issue number	Amount	Date	Work center	Operation	Amount	Date	Applied level	Amount
10/22/90	704	2500.00	10/23/90	A	G100	35.00	10/23/90	3.5 hrs.	70.00
Total material cost			Total labor cost				Total overhead cost		

FIGURE 15-14 A work-in-process ledger card.

Production order number (primary key)
Customer number (if a special order)
Customer name (if a special order)
Customer order number (if a special order)
Date of order
Date started (or to be started) in production
Date to be completed
Product number (or line number)
Product description
Quantity
Weight (if applicable)
Operation number[a]
Operation description[a]
Date scheduled[a]
Time started[a]
Time ended[a]
Machine number[a]
Special instructions (such as tools needed)[a]
Work center numbers[a]
Inspection results

[a] Repeated for each operation

FIGURE 15-15 Data items within a production center.

ever, a **product structure file** may replace the bill-of-materials file, thereby saving considerable storage space. In conjunction with relevant records from the raw materials inventory file, a structure (in effect, a record) in a product structure file can generate the needed bill of materials.

Assume that product A has the structure shown in Figure 15-16, consisting of the constituent raw materials. Codes appear that relate to the *lowest level* at which each raw material is to be found in the product. Thus, the code for materials B and E is 2, while the code for materials C and D is 1. By means of a data base software package called a bill-of-materials processor, a bill of materials would be generated that specifies the need for two units of B, one unit of C, and one unit of E in product A. (Data base software packages are discussed in Chapter 18.)

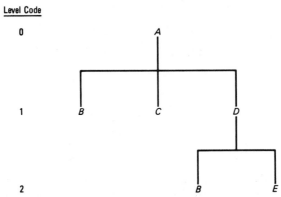

FIGURE 15-16 A product tree structure.

Machine Loading File

The **machine loading file** contains the status of each machine employed in production, showing the operations completed and scheduled for specific production orders. Usually the file is organized by work centers.

Other Files

Additional files that are needed include the production schedule, the operations list file, and the open sales order file. Reference files containing standard costs, overhead rates, and employee production quotas should also be accessible. Finally, a history file of past production orders, machine usage, work-center performances, and so forth should be available in summarized form.

Data Flows and Processing

Within the product conversion cycle the data flows and processing steps can be divided into the following phases: order entry, production and materials requirements planning, production operations, finished-goods dispositions, and cost accounting. Each of these phases can be examined through systems flowcharts for manual and computer-based processing procedures.

Manual Processing Systems

The manual processing procedures are flowcharted in three figures (Figures 15-17, 15-18, and 15-19).

Order entry. As Figure 15-17 shows, orders received from customers are first checked for accuracy and credit acceptability. Then formal sales orders are prepared in four copies. Two copies are sent to engineering design. By reference to the product specifications described in the sales order, engineering design pulls the appropriate bill of materials and operations list from the product file. If the order specifies new products or modifications, a new bill of materials and a new operations list are prepared.

Production and materials requirements planning. After receiving the bill of materials and the operations list, plus a materials inventory status or reorder report as prepared by inventory control, production and materials requirements planning does the following:

1. Prepares a production order and distributes copies, at the appropriate time, to production work centers and to accounting and control. A copy is also filed in the open production order file.

Part or Material	Quantity per Product	Number of Products Ordered	Gross Requirements
Casting for rotor shaft	1	5	5
Salient poles	4	5	20
Field windings	4	5	20
Slip rings	2	5	10
Ventilating fan	1	5	5

2. Explodes materials requirements and prepares a list to reflect the requirements, such as the list at the top of this page prepared from the order for five generators and the bill of materials in Figure 15-5.

3. Refers to the materials inventory status report to determine that sufficient parts and materials are currently on hand.[4]

4. Prepares material issue slips to request the issuance of the required materials and parts from stores.

5. Prepares move tickets to transfer the work-in-process from one work center to the next.

6. Enters the production order on the production schedule. Organized by calendar days and work stations, the schedule reflects for each open production order such details as beginning and ending times of each operation to be performed, machines to be used, and order priorities.[5]

7. Obtains approval from the customer for the production specifications and scheduled completion date of the ordered products. This approval may be routed through order entry, as shown in the flowchart, if time allows. Otherwise, approval may be obtained by telephone with telegram confirmation.

Production operations. Up-to-date production schedules are issued to the respective work centers. A copy of each production order is dispatched to the initial work center listed in the order. Materials and parts for each production order are issued to the production work centers according to the production schedule; accompanying material issue slips are signed by the receiving foremen. Employees and machines are assigned in accordance with the production schedule, unless departures from the schedule are necessary because of employee absences, machine breakdowns, or other causes.

Certain paperwork actions occur as work commences and progresses on each production order. Labor job-time tickets are prepared to record labor performed; these tickets are signed by each foreman and forwarded to cost accounting and control. One copy of each material issue slip is attached to the production order and accompanies the work in progress. Other copies of the material issue slip are forwarded to inventory control, where material costs are entered and the raw materials inventory file is updated; one costed copy is then sent to cost accounting and control. Move tickets, previously issued by production planning, are signed to reflect the transfers of work to succeeding

---

[4]If sufficient parts and materials were not on hand, it would be necessary to prepare a purchase requisition to request that the deficient quantities (not requirements) be ordered.

[5]The production schedule described here is the short-term, or detailed, schedule. Another type of schedule, the long-range production schedule, is also prepared as part of the strategic planning process.

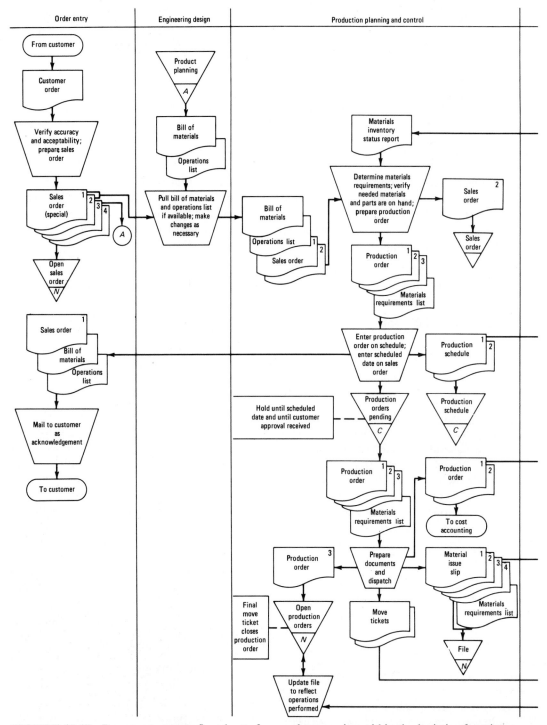

FIGURE 15-17 Document system flowchart of manual processing within the logistics function.

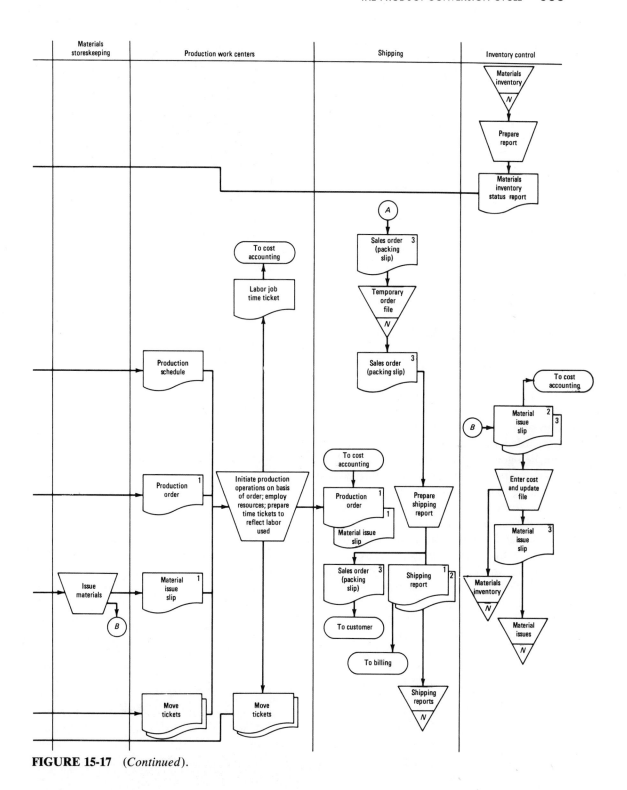

FIGURE 15-17 *(Continued).*

work centers; these signed move tickets are returned to production planning and control, which updates the open production order file to show the current status of work-in-process.

As each production order is completed, the work is inspected and an evaluation of the quality is expressed in an inspection report (not shown). The inspection report is returned to production planning. Any units of product that do not pass inspection are returned to appropriate work centers and scheduled for rework.

Dispositions of finished goods. When production orders are satisfactorily completed, the resulting finished goods are moved out of the production area. If the goods are produced for inventory, the finished goods are transferred into the warehouse. A move ticket signed by an employee in the warehouse signifies that the order is completed and notifies production planning and control to close the production order. The production order that has accompanied the work is forwarded to inventory control, where the finished-goods inventory file is updated. Then the production order is sent to cost accounting and control, which pulls the cost sheet from the work-in-process inventory file. Periodically, cost accounting and control transmits, via a journal voucher, a journal entry to general ledger.

If the goods have been produced in accordance with special customers' orders, the finished goods are transferred to the shipping dock. There a shipping clerk pulls the packing slip copy of the sales order from its pending file, ships the products, and prepares a shipping report. One copy of the shipping report is sent to billing, and the other copy is filed by shipping order number. The final move ticket, which transferred the work into shipping, is returned to production planning and control, thus giving notice that the production order can be closed. The production

order and material issue slips that accompanied the work are forwarded to cost accounting and control with a notation that the order is completed and shipped.

Cost accounting. To back up in time, a new cost sheet was opened by cost accounting and control on originally receiving each production order from production planning. Then, throughout the production process, the material and labor costs chargeable to the production order are posted to the cost sheet from material issue slips and labor job time tickets. Overhead costs are applied on the basis of direct labor hours. Periodically, cost accounting and control transmits to general ledger a journal voucher that summarizes the cost accumulations. Figure 15-18 portrays these processing steps.

When a production order is completed, the cost sheet is removed from the work-in-process inventory file. The costs are totaled, and the cost sheet, together with the production order and material issue slips, is forwarded to billing. Then the journal entry is transmitted, via a journal voucher, to general ledger. Figure 15-19 shows these processing steps.

Computer-Based Processing Systems

Manufacturing firms that are growing and changing are likely to experience problems when manual systems are employed. Increasing volumes of paperwork exert ever-heavier demands on clerks. Records tend to become out of date. Backlogs and delays occur during production operations. More and more promised delivery dates are missed, so that customer relations deteriorate. Overhead costs are not clearly traced to individual products. Overall costs of production climb higher and higher.

Computer-based systems can help manufacturing firms to overcome these problems. Batch-oriented processing systems can

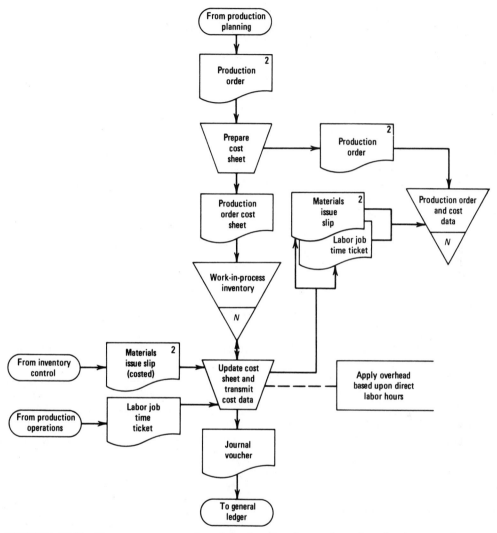

FIGURE 15-18 Document system flowchart showing the posting of production costs by cost accounting and control.

be used successfully. However, on-line production processing systems can offer such added benefits as the following:

1. Paperwork would be appreciably reduced; for example, labor job-time tickets could be eliminated.

2. Greater assistance would be provided by the system during the entry of data; since such relatively untrained persons as foremen would be entering much of the data, such assistance would help to minimize the introduction of errors.

3. Investment in inventory would be reduced, since the inventory records would be kept up to date and hence less safety

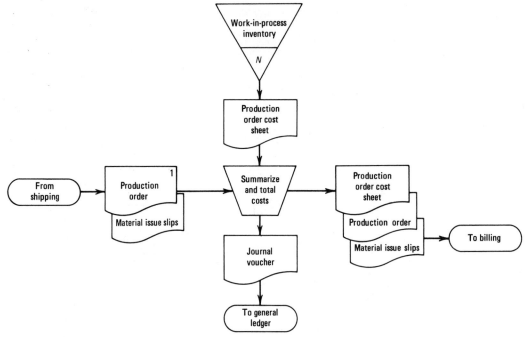

FIGURE 15-19   Document system flowchart showing the processing of completed production orders within cost accounting and control.

stock would be needed to prevent out-of-stock conditions.

4. Production records would be kept up to date and would be quickly accessible upon inquiry; thus, the progress of production orders could be tracked more effectively.

5. Changes in schedules would be effected quickly, since all relevant data files would be readily accessible.

6. Control over production operations and costs would be improved; for example, reports would be automatically triggered by such unfavorable conditions as (a) orders that have fallen too far behind schedule and (b) machines that have caused too many rejected parts or products.

7. Planning would be improved through better decision support to managers.

The following example procedure therefore assumes the presence of an on-line processing system.

Order entry. Orders received from customers are entered via order entry terminals, as shown in Figure 15-20. All orders are listed; those containing errors and those rejected by the credit check program are flagged. Acceptable orders are then placed in the open sales order file. Those orders involving standard product are also processed against the finished-goods inventory master file, with two possible actions: (1) if the ordered quantities are on hand, the balances in the file are reduced by those quantities and sales orders are prepared; (2) if the ordered quantities are not on hand, the affected quantities are listed on a back-order report and entered in the back-order field of the appro-

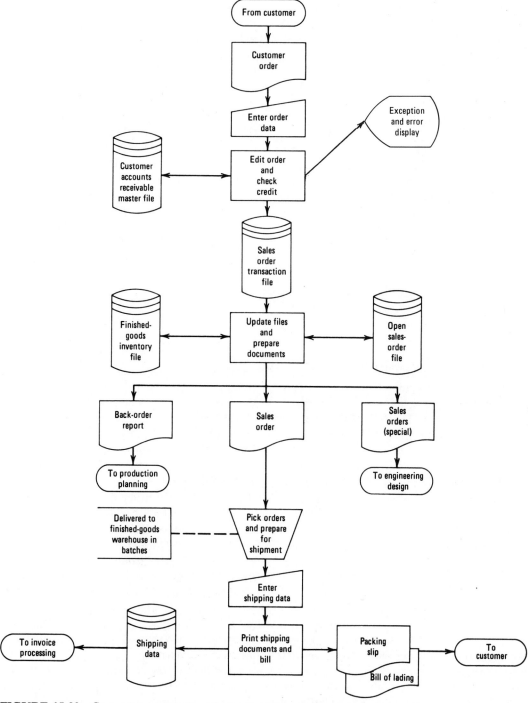

FIGURE 15-20 Computer system flowchart of order entry processing.

priate record within the file. Those orders involving specially manufactured products are sent to engineering design so that specifications can be prepared.[6]

The printed sales orders for standard products are delivered to the finished-goods warehouse in batches several times each day. There, the ordered products are obtained from the shelves and transferred to shipping. A shipping clerk enters necessary data concerning each shipment, such as sales order number and quantities and weights, via the shipping terminal.[7] The packing slips and bills of lading are printed, and the products are shipped. At the same time the data concerning the shipment are stored for the later preparation of sales invoices.

Production and materials requirements planning. Figure 15-21 shows the steps involved in computer-based production planning. Three key inputs flow into the planning process: specifications for special customer orders, sales forecasts, and back-order reports. The specifications for special orders update the product structure file and operations or routing file. The sales forecasts and back-order reports are used to determine the quantities of products needed to replenish the finished-goods inventory. Daily the special orders and other production requirements data are processed by complex production scheduling programs.

Several outputs are produced during the production planning process. (1) Prenumbered production orders are prepared, by reference to relevant input data and files, at the time the open production order file is updated. (2) Move tickets and material issue cards pertaining to each production order are printed. (3) A revised production schedule is printed, showing the assigned priorities for the respective production orders and their scheduled starting dates and work centers. (Priorities and scheduled starting dates are based in part on promised shipping dates of customers' orders.) (4) Bills of material and operations lists are printed for review by customers and production planning personnel. (5) A report is prepared, by means of a materials requirements program, to show the materials and parts needed to fill the production orders. This report also shows the quantities of materials and parts that must be ordered from suppliers.

When materials and parts must be ordered from suppliers, data from the materials requirements report are entered via the purchasing terminal. An ordering program reviews supplier performance data (i.e., relative prices, quality, past service) and selects the best supplier. Then it prepares a purchase order for the selected supplier, listing the economic order quantities for the materials and parts as shown in the materials inventory file. The order is then reflected in the open purchase order file, which is linked to the materials inventory file.

Upon receipt of ordered materials and parts, a receiving clerk enters the purchase order number from the packing slip. A receiving program verifies that an open purchase order is outstanding for the materials and parts. When a valid purchase order number is displayed, the clerk enters the counts or weights of the received items. The purchase order is then removed from the open purchase order file, the quantities are recorded in the materials inventory file, and a receiving card is punched. The receiving card accompanies the received materials and parts to stores, where it is initialed by the stores clerk and forwarded to accounts pay-

---

[6]Engineering design is aided by the computer system. Engineers use light pens to enter desired design features directly onto the screens of graphics terminals. The computer processor performs necessary design computations, based on these inputs, and displays the resulting product designs.

[7]All data are edited for errors, as shown in the upper portion of Figure 15-20. However, the edit step is not explicitly shown in the lower portion of the figure or in following flowcharts. It is omitted solely to conserve space.

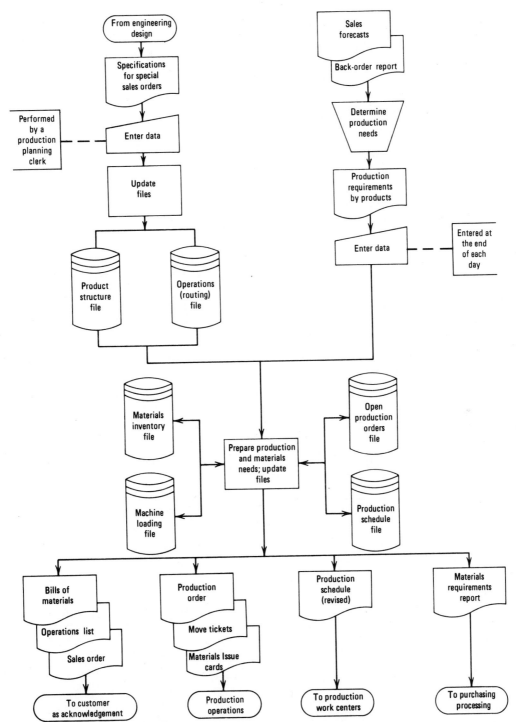

FIGURE 15-21 Computer system flowchart of production planning.

able. The stores clerk also enters the quantities in the stores terminal; the quantities received at stores are then compared by the computer program with the quantities reported by the receiving clerk.

Production operations and cost accounting. Orders are dispatched to work centers to begin production operations. Then, as Figure 15-22 shows, labor-time data and material issues are entered during production operations. Each employee enters data at the completion of each operation, and the com-

puter system time-stamps the transaction with the data and ending time. The stores clerk enters data concerning materials issues by inserting the material issues cards into the stores terminal and keying in the quantities issued to a particular order.

These entries affect the files in the figure as follows:

1. The status of the open production file is changed to show the completion of an operation of the affected production order.

2. The status of the machine loading file is

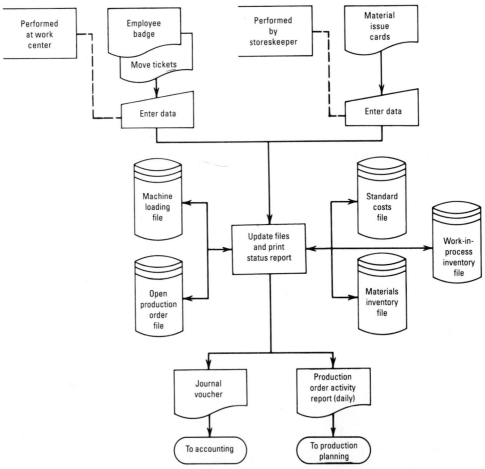

FIGURE 15-22 Computer system flowchart of processing steps during production operations.

changed to show that the affected machine is now free to perform the next scheduled operation.

3. The status of the materials inventory file is changed to show the issuance of materials to the affected order.

4. The status of the work-in-process inventory file is changed to show the addition of labor, materials, and overhead costs, so

that the file reflects the usage of labor and materials. The costs are computed by reference to the standard unit costs and overhead rates in the standard costs file.

As work is completed on each production order, the products are inspected and data concerning the results are entered into the production order record. (See Figure 15-23.) Accepted products are transferred to

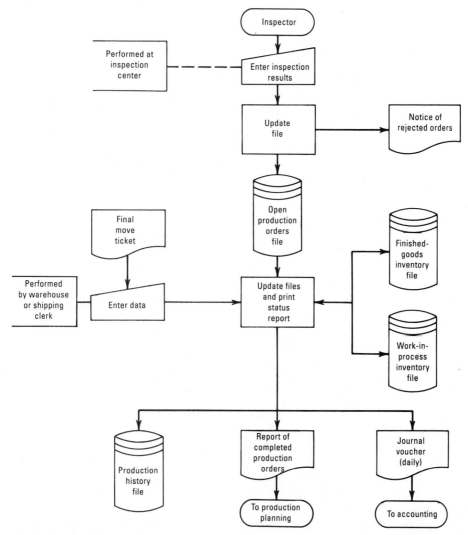

FIGURE 15-23 Computer system flowchart of processing steps after completion of production operations.

the finished-goods warehouse or to shipping, where data from the final move ticket are entered via a terminal. This notification causes the production order to be removed from the open production order file. It also results in the computation of the total cost for the production order, as well as the transfer of this total and all detailed costs from the work-in-process inventory file to the finished-goods inventory file. Rejected products are noted for rescheduling and moved to a hold area.

Two types of outputs are provided: (1) reports showing the status of production orders and (2) journal vouchers to be used by accounting in (a) charging production costs to work-in-process inventory and (b) transferring production costs from work-in-process inventory to finished-goods inventory.

Computer-Integrated Manufacturing

Computers have been applied within the production functions of manufacturing firms since the 1960s. A variety of computer-aided techniques have emerged, including computer-aided design, computer-aided manufacturing, robotics, and automated materials handling.

Computer-aided design (CAD) is the technology that employs a computer in creating, modifying, or documenting engineering designs. Generally it involves the use of an interactive computer graphics system. A CAD system enables a designer to develop a three-dimensional model of a product, expand or contract the size of the model, rotate the model for different views or perspectives, simulate performance of the product, develop product specifications, and prepare blueprints. The results can be stored and retrieved as desired. When effectively used, CAD greatly enhances the productivity of designers, improves the quality of products, and encourages the development and storage of complete documentation.

Computer-aided manufacturing (CAM) can be defined as the effective use of computer technology in planning and controlling activities in the production function. Included in CAM are such activities as estimating costs, preparation of operations lists, developing work standards, performing line balancing, performing materials requirements planning, maintaining quality control, and controlling machine tools.

Robotics involves the effective use of robots—programmable multifunctional devices that are designed to perform a variety of repetitious tasks. Robots consist of a series of assembled joints and links that are driven by electric, hydraulic, or pneumatic drives. Through various vertical, radial, and side-to-side motions they can accurately and consistently perform such tasks as welding, drilling, cutting, painting, assembling, and moving products and parts.

Automated handling of materials involves the use of computers to aid in the movement and stacking of materials within the production area and warehouse. A prime example of automated handling of materials is the automated guided vehicle system (AGVS), which uses computers to dispatch self-propelled vehicles to points in the warehouse and factory where they are needed. Then the vehicles are guided by the computer, or by built-in intelligence devices, to perform such tasks as moving goods to storage areas and loading pallets.

All of these computer-aided techniques are broadly encompassed by **computer-integrated manufacturing** (CIM). In effect, CIM involves the complete integration of the various computer-aided techniques within the manufacturing environment, ranging from the acquisition of materials through handling of materials to the distribution of products. Thus, CIM also includes such techniques as JIT systems and MRP systems. It focuses on the information processing functions, such as planning and control information pertain-

---

APPLICATION OF COMPUTER INTEGRATED MANUFACTURING
General Electric[a]

The Aircraft Engine Business Group of General Electric recently implemented the capabilities of computer-integrated manufacturing (CIM). The overall objective of this CIM is to optimize the yield from the manufacturing process while minimizing the lead time required for manufacturing specific engines. In addition, the system flexibly accommodates the constantly changing manufacturing requirements. These changes occur because of variations in product designs and fluctuating materials flows.

Encompassed with GE's CIM system are such activities as process planning, quality planning, and master computer operations. Several hundred linked numerical control machines are also involved. Product design data from remote CAD/CAM systems are teleprocessed to a central facility, where production plans and numerical control tapes are pre-

pared for specific aircraft engines. When the orders for these engines are put into production, the numerical control machines are coordinated by a central mainframe computer. Production control tracks parts, labor reporting, and status of each order as it moves through the manufacturing process. Quality planning and control develops the detailed inspection plan, performs the inspections, and maintains the quality histories. Maintenance monitors the operational status of all the machines involved in the process; when a machine exhibits troubling symptoms, computer diagnostics programs determine the source of the troubles. The CIM system even extends to such functions as long-term forecasting and finished-goods inventory management.

[a]Eric Teicholz, "Computer Integrated Manufacturing," *Datamation* (March 1984), pp. 169–174.

---

ing to the various orders and jobs. A related concept, called **flexible manufacturing systems,** focuses on the physical automation of the manufacturing and handling processes.

A variety of CIM applications are currently being developed or are already fully formed. Intel is developing a CIM for its plant in New Mexico. As of 1989 the project consists of several systems for materials handling and manufacturing, named COMETS, which have been interfaced (though not fully integrated).[8] Weyerhaeuser has a fully developed CIM, called Pro-smart, installed at its Longview, Washington, pulp and paper mill.[9]

[8]James R. Kellso, "CIM in Action: Microelectronics Manufacturer Charts Course Toward True Systems Integration," *Industrial Engineering* (July 1989), pp. 19–22.

[9]Willie Schatz, "Making CIM Work," *Datamation* (December 1, 1989), p. 19.

Accounting Controls

Several operational objectives pertaining to the product conversion cycle were stated at the beginning of this chapter. These objectives may be supplemented by control objectives such as the following:

1. To record the quantities of raw materials received, stored, and used in the proper accounts and accounting periods, and to reflect their costs in accordance with prescribed methods of valuation.

2. To assure that production orders are properly authorized and scheduled.

3. To record the resources assigned to production orders promptly and accurately, and to accumulate the related costs fully and in accordance with the established system of cost accounting.

4. To ascertain that the movements of production orders through the various opera-

tions and into the warehouse or shipping are reflected by acknowledgements at each center.

5. To value the completed products in the finished-goods inventory account in accordance with the established system of cost accounting.

6. To provide adequate safeguards for all inventories and production facilities.

Risk Exposures

In attempting to achieve these objectives, the product conversion cycle is exposed to a variety of risks. Typical risks are as follows:

1. Raw materials, finished goods, or scrap may be lost or stolen.

2. Production orders may be incorrectly costed.

3. Quantities of finished goods exceeding the quantities specified by production orders may be produced.

4. Recorded quantities of work-in-process or finished goods may be inaccurate.

5. Insufficient or excessive quantities of raw materials may be issued into production with respect to scheduled production orders.

6. Production orders may be lost during production operations.

7. Production costs may be expensed rather than capitalized as inventory costs.

8. Inventories may be incorrectly valued because of improper use of valuation methods or charges to wrong accounts.

9. Inventories may be inflated because obsolescent or slow-moving items have not been written down in value.

In order to counteract all such risks, a firm needs to incorporate relevant general and transaction controls.

General Controls

General controls that particularly concern the product conversion cycle include the following:

1. Within the organization the units that have custodial functions (the receiving department, materials stores, and finished-goods warehouse) are separate from those units that keep the records (the production planning and control department, inventory control department, cost accounting department, and data processing department).

2. Authorizations are required to issue production orders, to issue materials into production, and to begin production operations.

3. Complete and up-to-date documentation concerning the product conversion cycle, including copies of the documents, flowcharts, record layouts, and reports illustrated in this chapter, is available. In addition, details pertaining to the programs that perform materials requirements planning and production processing are organized into separate books or "packages" that are directed, respectively, to programmers, computer operators, and systems users.

4. Operating practices relating to processing schedules, reports, changes in programs, and other matters are clearly established.

5. Production policies are established by management concerning production scheduling, quality control inspections, cost controls, and other matters that affect the completion and accurate valuation of specified products.

6. Security is maintained (in the case of online systems) by such techniques as (a) requiring that clerks enter assigned passwords before accessing inventory and production order files, (b) employing terminals that are restricted solely to the

entry and access of production-related transactions, (c) generating audit reports (access logs) that monitor accesses of system files, and (d) dumping the inventory and production files onto magnetic tape backups. Security measures for manual and computer-based systems include the use of physically restricted production and stores and warehouse areas, in order to protect goods, materials, and production facilities.

Transaction Controls

Control points within the product conversion cycle include (1) the determined need for production orders, (2) the issuance of production orders, (3) the issuance of materials against production orders, (4) the initiation and movement of production orders through production operations, and (5) the completion and transfer of production orders to the warehouse or shipping department.

The following controls and control procedures are applicable to product conversion transactions and production orders:

1. Documents such as production orders, materials requisitions, and move tickets are prenumbered. They are also well designed; for instance, move tickets are designed to show the movement of work-in-process from work center to work center as they accompany the production orders.

2. Data on production orders and other documents relating to production are validated and edited as the data are prepared and entered for processing. In the case of computer systems the validation is performed by means of programmed edit checks as follows: validity checks of the production order number, operation number, work center number, material number, and product number; field checks of all numeric data fields; limit checks of the quantities of materials issued, hours worked by employees, and standard overhead rate; relationship check that compares the production order with the work center at which the order is scheduled to be; completeness checks on such data as operation times, in order to verify that all operations have been performed and reported.

3. Materials and parts are issued into production on the basis of quantities shown in production orders and copied onto requisition forms.

4. Errors detected during data entry or processing are corrected as soon as possible by means of an established error correction procedure. Figure 15-24 shows a listing of errors based on the editing of data.

5. Verifications are performed to ensure that all materials are issued into production, all production orders move from one work center to the next, and all completed orders are moved from the last work center or inspection point into the warehouse or to the shipping department. For instance, the production foreman at the first work center who receives materials from stores signs the materials requisition to acknowledge the receipt of the proper quantity.

6. All open transactions, such as partially completed production orders and rejected orders, are monitored, and all transactions missing one or more supporting documents are investigated.

7. Returns of excess materials, disposition of scrap, and write-downs of inventory values are subject to prior approval by the materials manager.

8. All accumulated costs on production orders are verified by a cost accounting clerk or computer program.

9. Account balances in the work-in-process

HARVIDELL, SCHAKINS & CO. INC.

ISSUANCES OF MATERIAL FOR PRODUCTION

ERROR REPORT

BATCH NUMBER	DOCUMENT NUMBER	DATE	PRODUCTION ORDER NUMBER	MATERIAL ID NUMBER	UNIT OF MEASURE	QUANTITIES		REASON FOR ERROR
						ITEM	DOCU	
2-1040	091443	1202XX	061939	102064	YARDS	2206	10796	UNIT OF MEASURE WRONG FOR MATERIAL ID
2-1040	091440	1302XX	061952				12920	DOCUMENT NUMBER IS NOT NUMERIC MONTH IS GREATER THAN 12
2-1040	09144	122XX	06J954				21792	DOCUMENT NUMBER DOES NOT CONTAIN 6 DIGITS DATE DOES NOT CONTAIN 6 DIGITS PRODUCTION ORDER NUMBER IS NOT NUMERIC
2-1040		1202XX	01197				9762	DOCUMENT NUMBER IS MISSING PRODUCTION ORDER DOES NOT CONTAIN 6 DIGITS
2-1040	091457						12425	DATE IS MISSING PRODUCTION ORDER IS MISSING
2-1040	091480	1202XX	061974	102376	YARDS	3500		QUANTITY IS MISSING
	091480	1202XX	061974	10186C	YARDS	1020		MATERIAL ID NUMBER IS MISSING MATERIAL ID IS NOT NUMERIC UNIT OF MEASURE IS MISSING
	091480	1202XX	061974	10769	EACH	K20	17975	MATERIAL ID NUMBER DOES NOT CONTAIN 6 DIGITS QUANTITY IS NOT NUMERIC

TOTAL OF REJECTED TRANSACTIONS 85670
TOTAL OF ACCEPTED TRANSACTIONS 623505
BATCH TOTAL 709175

BATCH NUMBER	DOCUMENT NUMBER	DATE	PRODUCTION ORDER NUMBER	MATERIAL ID NUMBER	UNIT OF MEASURE	ITEM	DOCU	REASON FOR ERROR
2-1044	091496	1202XX	061988	106996	YARDS	2210	13405	INVALID MATERIAL ID NUMBER

TOTAL OF REJECTED TRANSACTIONS 13405
TOTAL OF ACCEPTED TRANSACTIONS 130522
BATCH TOTAL 143927

FIGURE 15-24 A listing of data input errors. Copyright © 1980 by the American Institute of Certified Public Accountants, Inc.

and finished-goods subsidiary ledgers are periodically reconciled with the control accounts in the general ledger.

10. All inventories on hand are verified by physical counts at least once yearly under proper supervision, reconciled with the quantities shown in the inventory records, and adjusted when necessary to reflect the actual quantities on hand.

11. The valuations of all inventories are reviewed and adjusted when necessary to reflect losses of value, or to correspond to the established inventory valuation method and production period-end cutoff policies.

12. Budgetary control is established over production, preferably with the aid of standard costs, and periodic reviews are performed with respect to actual production costs and such key factors as scrap rates.

13. Labor-time tickets are approved by work center supervisors.

14. If processing is performed in batches, control totals are precomputed on quantities of materials issued or orders placed into production; these batch totals are compared with totals computed during postings to the production orders throughout the various production operations.

15. Copies of all documents pertaining to materials issues and production orders are filed by number, and the sequence of numbers in each file is periodically checked to see if gaps exist. If transactions are not supported by preprinted documents, as often is the case in on-line computer-based systems, numbers are assigned to generated documents and they are stored in transaction files.

16. In the case of computer-based systems, transaction listings and account summaries are printed periodically in order to provide an adequate audit trail. Sum-

mary reports are also prepared and the results therein reconciled to other reports. For instance, the quantities of spoiled units shown on production summaries are compared to scrappage reports.

Reports and Other Outputs

Outputs generated by the product conversion cycle include operational listings and reports, inquiry screens, and managerial reports. Many of these outputs are based on the various documents employed during logistics operations, as Figure 15-25 shows.

Operational Listings and Reports

Most of the listings relate to the inventories and production orders. Bills of material and operations lists, already noted, are two examples. The finished-goods reorder listing shows those items that have fallen below their planned replenishment levels and thus require new production orders. On the basis of the orders that are scheduled for production, the materials required for production must be listed and summarized in a materials requirements report. The **production activity report** lists all of the production orders currently outstanding and the work centers to which they have progressed. The **raw materials status report** shows the on-hand balances of all items and the quantities received and issued during the current week or month. The **finished-goods status report** shows the on-hand balances of all items and the quantities produced and sold.

Inquiry Screens

Inquiries may involve all aspects of production planning and operations, including the status and content of production orders, listings of outstanding purchase orders, production schedules, and so on. Figure 15-26

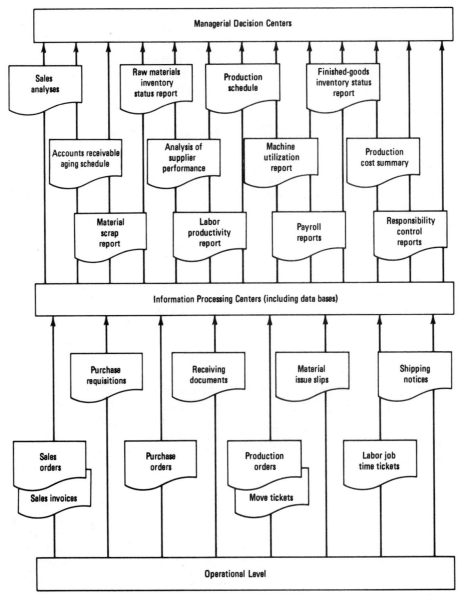

FIGURE 15-25 Reports based on documents generated during logistics-related operations.

shows two display screens based on inquiries. One reflects the composition of the current load at a particular work center. The other shows the costs pertaining to a raw material.

Managerial Reports

Because the scope of logistics management is so broad, numerous managerial reports are possible. Many are extensions of

```
INQUIRY    WORK CENTER SHORT TERM LOAD W/C 4002-847 VERTICAL MILL   DAY 207
-------    -------------------------- NO. OF MACH:  2  NO. OF SHIFTS: 2

TIME  START  PER  PLAN  * PRIMARY *  OVER  IDLE  *  SETUP  *
PER   DATE   LEN  CAP      LOAD      LOAD  TIME     TIME
             DAYS HRS   HRS   PERC   HRS   HRS    HRS   PERC
- - - - - - - - - - - - - - - - - - - - - - - - - - -

 1    207    5    150   136.0 90.7         14    24.0  16.0
 2    212    5    150   139.0 92.7         11     8.5   5.7
 3    217    5    150   151.0 100.7    1         15.2  10.1
 4    222    5    180   199.0 132.7   49         25.4  16.9

ORDER    ITEM    OPER   OPERATION     ORDER  *SCHEDULED*  MACH  RUN    SETUP
NO.              NO.    DESCRIPTION   QTY    START COMPL  NO.   TIME   TIME
- - - - -  - - - - - - - - - - - - - - - - - - - - - - - - - - - - -
205510 003204   0020   MILL SLOT     1000   207   211    1     60.0   7.5
205530 220121   0080   MILL KEYWAY    500   207   209    2     36.0   2.7
205509 003204   0020   MILL SLOT     1000   211   215    1     60.0   7.5
205526 003210-A 0060   MILL FLAT      400   210   215    2     70.1   6.3
205501 220121   0080   MILL KEYWAY    100   215   216    2      7.2   2.7
205515 103216   0060   MILL FLAT      400   216   220    1     72.0   3.0
205516 103217   0090   MILL FLAT      800   217   225    2    120.0   2.6
205571 104718   0070   MILL FLAT      7C0   221   227    1    105.0   7.5
```

a. A screen showing the composition of the current load at a particular work center.

```
                 --------DISPLAY ITEM INFORMATION--------        DATE: 402
      ITEM NO: 07694              DRAWING NO: L-11635   U/M: EA
  DESCRIPTION: WHEEL SPACER          E.C.NO: 0001  TYPE: 2
              ++++++++++++++++++++++++++++++++++++++++++++++      PDDC0220
              +  COST ACCOUNTING INFORMATION ON THIS ITEM   +
              ++++++++++++++++++++++++++++++++++++++++++++++

STANDARD COSTS. MATERIAL:        LABOR:          OVERHEAD:
ACTUAL COSTS. MATERIAL:          LABOR:          OVERHEAD:
DATE STANDARD COSTS INSERTED:
DATE ACTUAL COSTS UPDATED:
VALUE CLASSIFICATION:     A       UNIT PRICE:    $0.800
    COMMODITY CODE:               UNIT COST:     $0.150
    LOW LEVEL CODE:      1       SET-UP COST:    $0.110
    CARRYING RATE:     .5%


-----------------------------------------------------------
    PF05(N) GO TO NEXT ITEM
    PF01(R) RETURN TO PDDC MENU
```

b. A screen showing cost accounting information relating to a specified material or part.

FIGURE 15-26 Screens generated in response to inquiries. Courtesy of International Business Machines Corporation.

operational reports. For instance, a **production status and analysis report** lists the materials, direct labor, and overhead accumulated for each order currently in production, the variance of the actual costs from standards, and the percentage completion of each order. An open order status report shows those operations on production orders that are behind schedule. An employee efficiency report, shown in Figure 15-27a, reflects the percentage efficiency as well as ac-

tual production achieved by employees. A work center performance summary, shown in Figure 15-27b, indicates the utilization and efficiency achieved within the respective work centers. Other reports concern (1) equipment utilization, (2) usage of materials and labor on the respective orders, including spoilage, (3) percentages of scrap, rework, and rejects for the respective orders, and (4) past-due shipments of production orders.

EMPLOYEE EFFICIENCY REPORT		DEPT. NO. 60						EMPLOYEE NUMBER 197030		SHOP DATE 615

SHOP ORDER		OPER. NO.	QUAN. COMP.	ST'D. RATE	STD. HRS.	ACT. HOURS	EFFIC. %	REMARKS
PART NO.	LOT NO.							
0358117	040-0	1200	50	140	70	68	1029	
2103526	060-0	70	10	20	2	2	1000	
38264	100-0	50	50	22	11	10	1100	

a. A report of employee efficiency

WORK CENTER PERFORMANCE SUMMARY

SHOP DATE 615

MACH GROUP	NO. MCHS	CAP. HRS.	LOAD HRS.	ACTUAL HRS.	% UTILIZ.	% EFFEC.	TOT. IDLE HRS.	IDLE HOURS BY REASON CODE						
								1	2	3	4	5	6	7
0810	2	800	812	782	977	1038	18			15	3			
1930	1	400	338	398	995	849	2							2

IDLE TIME REASON CODES

1 No Operator   5 Other   (See Cards for Detail)
2 No Work   6 Set Up
3 Machine Breakdown   7 Re Set
4 Tool Trouble

b. A report of work center performance

FIGURE 15-27 Reports generated for use by logistics function managers. Courtesy of International Business Machines Corporation.

Summary

The product conversion cycle facilitates the conversion of raw materials into products or finished goods. Functions of the cycle are to undertake strategic planning, manage the raw materials inventory, initiate the production process, maintain and control production operations, accumulate work-in-process costs, complete and transfer finished goods, and prepare financial reports and other outputs. Related functions include quality control inspections, rework and scrappage, and return of excess materials. These functions are achieved under the direction of the logistics management and finance/accounting organizational units.

Most of the data used in the cycle arise from materials management, engineering design, and production planning and operations. Documents typically employed are bills of material, operations lists, sales orders, production orders, materials issue slips, labor job-time tickets, move tickets, and the documents involved in purchasing raw materials. Preformatted screens may be used to enter the various data related to engineering design, materials issues, and production operations. The data base includes such files as the raw materials inventory master, work-in-process inventory master, finished-goods inventory master, open production order, product structure, and machine loading files. Data processing consists of order entry, planning for production and materials requirements, production operations, dispositions of finished goods, and cost accounting. Processing may be feasibly performed by manual systems, but an increasing number of firms are employing on-line computer-based processing systems.

A variety of risk exposures exist in the processing of production-related transactions; these can be counteracted by means of adequate general and transaction controls. Among the outputs generated by the product conversion cycle are the bill of materials, operations list, production activity report, raw materials status report, finished-goods status report, production order inquiry screens, work center load inquiry screens, production status and analysis report, employee efficiency report, open order status report, and work center performance report.

Review Problem with Solution

Slick Signpainters

Statement

Stanley Fischer manages Slick Signpainters (SS), which is comprised of three painters and one secretary–bookkeeper. Customers consist of small business firms and other organizations, such as churches and towns, which place special orders. Since it acquires raw materials and supplies—boards, paints, brushes, turpentine—and produces finished signs, SS resembles a manufacturing firm. SS has a single microcomputer, which it uses to aid in processing its main transactions.

Required

Briefly describe the data sources and inputs, data base, procedures, controls, and reports that are likely to be involved in the process of converting the new materials into finished signs.

Solution

The process begins with a special order from a customer. Stanley plans the sign and determines the materials needed. If the materials are not on hand, he acquires the items from suppliers, either by preparing and mailing a purchase order or by calling the suppliers' stores and placing the orders. Upon receiving the materials and checking them in, he assigns the job to one of the painters and provides him or her the materials. Stanley also gives the painter the plan of the sign and provides notes (i.e., an operations list) concerning steps in completing and installing the sign. If the painter is currently busy on another job, he schedules the job in question. Stanley also estimates the overall cost of the job and the expected completion date.

The secretary–bookkeeper maintains the schedule and records the costs of the materials and time spent on each job. When the job is completed, the sign is delivered to the customer. She then applies an overhead charge to the job (based on the hours spent on the job), adds a markup percentage, and computes the total amount. After Stanley reviews the figures, she prepares an invoice for the customer.

The main files maintained, in addition to the production schedule, are a raw materials inventory file (in quantities only) and a job-cost file of orders currently in progress. Since the completed signs are immediately delivered to customers, no finished-goods inventory file is necessary. Another file not directly related to production is an order-invoice file, consisting of records of each customer special order and open invoice. All of these files are maintained on the hard disk of the microcomputer system and are updated via the microcomputer keyboard by the secretary–bookkeeper.

Many of the controls are maintained through the close supervision, planning, and reviews carried out by Stanley. He also keeps the raw materials locked in a storeroom, to which only he has a key. Only the secretary–bookkeeper and Stanley are allowed to use the microcomputer, which is located in her office. Order-invoices are assigned consecutive numbers and are reviewed by Stanley when he performs the monthly bank reconciliation.

At the end of each month Stanley receives listings of raw materials inventory and jobs in process, prepared by the secretary–bookkeeper. She also prepares reports that show actual costs for completed jobs versus the estimated costs, the jobs that were not completed on schedule, and the jobs currently in progress that appear to be behind schedule.

Note: This problem illustrates that many of the components of the product conversion cycle can be applied to a simple manufacturing situation. Even more could be added to this example. However, the problem also illustrates that the design should be adapted to the situation.

Review Questions

15-1 What is the meaning of each of the following terms?

Product conversion cycle
Inventory management
Materials requirements planning (MRP)
Just-in-time (JIT) system
Logistics management
Sales forecast
Sales order
Bill of material
Operations list
Production order
Material issue slip
Labor job-time ticket
Raw materials inventory master file
Work-in-process inventory master file
Finished-goods inventory master file
Open production order file
Product structure file
Machine loading file
Computer-aided (CAD)
Computer-aided manufacturing (CAM)
Robotics
Automated materials handling
Computer-integrated manufacturing (CIM)

Flexible manufacturing system
Production activity report
Raw materials status report
Finished-goods status report
Production status and analysis report

15-2 What are key objectives for the product conversion cycle?

15-3 What are the functions of the product conversion cycle?

15-4 What are several key decisions that must be made during strategic production planning?

15-5 What are four methods of physical production?

15-6 What are several key decisions that must be made with respect to the management of raw materials inventory?

15-7 What items of information are needed in making each of the decisions pertaining to inventory management?

15-8 How do materials requirements planning and just-in-time systems fit into inventory management?

15-9 What are several factors that determine the quantities of goods to be produced?

15-10 What types of control can be employed during the production process?

15-11 Briefly review the steps in recording the accumulation of costs during the production process.

15-12 Briefly describe the means of assuring quality in products.

15-13 How does the logistics management function relate to the product conversion cycle, and what are several organizational units within the function?

15-14 Identify several documents involved in the production process.

15-15 What are several characteristics of a material that can be built into a group code?

15-16 What are the key files needed in the product conversion data base?

15-17 Describe the procedural steps employed in a manual processing system that monitors and controls the conversion of raw materials.

15-18 Describe the procedural steps employed in an on-line computer-based processing system that monitors and controls the conversion of raw materials.

15-19 Briefly describe the several technologies that are encompassed by computer integrated manufacturing.

15-20 What are the exposures to risk that exist in the processing within the product conversion cycle?

15-21 Identify various general and transaction controls that concern the product conversion cycle.

15-22 Identify various reports and other outputs that may be generated from information provided by the product conversion cycle.

Discussion Questions

15-23 What changes are needed to adapt the product conversion cycle to a construction firm that engages in various projects for clients?

15-24 Contrast a computer-based processing system in a manufacturing firm using job order costing with a system in another manufacturer using process costing.

15-25 Author/critics such as Robert S. Kaplan have stressed that most modern cost accounting and information systems are deficient in several respects. One major deficiency relates to inadequate cost and productivity measures provided by the systems. Suggest several cost and productivity measures that should be provided by an ideal production information system.

15-26 Several emerging technologies were

described in the chapter. Describe the features and benefits of an "ultimate" computer-integrated manufacturing technology, one that might be in place in progressive firms in the year 2000.

Problems

15-1 The Hardmon Manufacturing Company produces metal products for industrial customers. Although some of the products are standard items (e.g., pistons), many are made in response to special orders. The firm therefore maintains a number of work centers, each with a particular type of machine or assembling equipment. It puts each order into the production process via a production order and accumulates the related costs on a work-in-process record. Standard unit costs are applied to material quantities and direct labor hours; standard work center overhead rates are applied on the basis of machine hours. When special orders are completed, they are delivered directly to the shipping area. Completed standard items are delivered to the finished goods warehouse.

Required

a. List the journal entries needed to record (1) the conversion of raw materials into finished goods, (2) the application of raw materials, direct labor, and various indirect costs to the production of the finished goods, and (3) the shipment of the finished goods. State how the actual expenses for such items as indirect labor and equipment maintenance are recorded and disposed of.

b. Briefly describe the various input documents that could suitably be used by Hardmon in this production situation.

c. Assuming that a computer-based system is approved for installation, describe the type of system (batch, on-line, or mixed) that appears most suitable for each of the following: (1) monitoring the production process, (2) preparing payrolls for the direct production employees, (3) managing the utilization and valuation records of the factory machines and equipment.

15-2 Draw the layout for a record of a work-in-process master file stored on magnetic disk. The file belongs to a manufacturing firm that accumulates costs by production orders. Enter data based on the following for production order 3569, started on February 16, 1989: direct materials issued, 40 units at $13 per unit; direct labor, 12 hours at $6.50 per hour and 20 hours at $8.30 per hour; overhead, applied on the basis of $7.00 per direct labor hour. Assume values for other data items that you include in the record layout. Ignore the lengths of the data fields.

15-3 Custom Woodcrafters is a small firm that manufactures custom-made home and office furniture. Its employees consist of 30 artisans (craftspersons), 7 master artisans, one scheduler, and several clerks. The owner is the sole manager. No salespersons are needed, since the quality of its products attracts more orders than the firm can handle. Each order is assigned to a master artisan, who designs the product, guides it through the production process, and approves the final result. At least two artisans are assigned by the scheduler to work on each other, depending on the complexity, requested date, and so on. After the product is completed, the price is determined by accumulating all related costs and then adding a percentage markup.

Required

a. List the data items that are needed in order to be able to plan, manufacture, and monitor the progress of an order.

b. List the data items that are needed in order to be able to price an order.

c. List the files that would store the data items in **a** and **b**.

d. Describe reports that would be useful to the scheduler and master artisans in performing their duties.

15-4 Refer to the hypothetical manufacturer of electrical products that has been used as an example in discussing the organization and input forms pertaining to the product conversion cycle. Figure 15-5 through 15-10, 15-13, and 15-14 contain data pertaining to an order from Lipton Technology, Inc., for five generators, type PG21, 50 horsepower each. The date of the sales order was October 19, 1990, and the customer order number was 28662.

Required

a. Design a production order form and insert the data just given and those provided on the various figures in the chapter. The date of the production order was Oct. 22, 1990. Assume that an order cannot be at a work center for less than a day, even though the work required at the center may not require more than an hour or two. Also, consider that an added day must be allowed for final inspection (Operation No. G900) at the QC center. The product is to be shipped the day following the inspection, provided that the quality is acceptable.

b. Design a record layout for an open production order file that is stored on magnetic disk. Insert the data pertaining to the order in **a** in the layout to reflect the progress of the order as of the end of October 24. Assume the start and ending times of operations; also assume that the record is variable in length. Use Figure 15-15 as a guide, but eliminate fields for which data are not provided.

15-5 Refer to the figures in the chapter pertaining to the hypothetical manufacturer of electrical products. Note that several materials are used in the production of generator type PG21, including part number 18568.

a. The current code for materials and parts has five numeric characters, which have been assigned rather randomly to the various materials. Suggest a revised code for materials and parts based in part on the data provided in the chapter concerning the hypothetical manufacturer. Make assumptions as necessary, and add other dimensions to the code that could render it more useful. Do not use more than eight characters in the code.

b. Prepare the materials requirements report that is based on production order 8333, prepared on October 19, 1990.

c. Prepare a material issue slip dated October 22, 1990, and prenumbered 705, and enter the materials needed at work center B for production order 8333. Unit costs are as follows: salient poles, $30 each; field windings, $55 each; slip rings, $68 each; ventilating fan, $84. Assume that all the parts except the casting are issued to work center B.

15-6 The Gem Manufacturing Company of Waltham, Massachusetts, employs a job order cost accounting system to record the costs of products manufactured. It charges costs into production from three types of source documents: materials requisitions, job-time tickets, and expense vouchers. Entries are recorded on journal vouchers. Subsidiary ledgers are maintained for raw materials, work-in-process, manufacturing overhead expense, and finished goods. Related control accounts appear in the general ledger.

Required

a. Prepare a diagram that shows the flow of production transactions through the accounting cycle.

b. Use sample journal entry formats to reflect the flows of costs from source documents into the financial statements.

c. Describe the contents of each of the foregoing subsidiary ledgers.

15-7 What error or fraudulent activity might occur if each of the following procedures is allowed?

    a. The work-in-process ledger is not periodically reconciled to the control account in the general ledger.

    b. Production supervisors do not observe factory employees as they clock in and out on production jobs.

    c. Scrapped materials are not maintained in a separate inventory and are not reported as they are generated during production.

    d. Overhead costs charged to various production jobs are based on the actual indirect production costs incurred during the current period.

    e. Products are manufactured at levels sufficient to utilize the production resources fully throughout the year.

    f. Raw materials are issued in quantities requested by the employees who will actually perform the production operations.

    g. Physical inventories of raw materials and finished goods are taken only when production activity is slow and factory employees are available to make the counts.

    h. The valuations of the raw materials inventory items are adjusted only to reflect receipts and issues.

15-8 What internal accounting control(s) would be most effective in preventing or detecting each of the following errors or fraudulent practices?

    a. A cost distribution clerk makes an arithmetic error in calculating the total costs allocated to all production jobs.

    b. An order that arrives at the final inspection station on the production line is missing 10 of the 100 units of product specified by the order; all of the work center supervisors protest that the units were missing when the order arrived at their centers.

    c. A production order is coded with an incorrect and nonexistent product number. The error is not noted until the order begins moving through the production process.

    d. The on-hand balance of a raw material shows a negative quantity.

    e. The manager of a production work center questions the direct materials cost and asks to see the materials requisitions. Personnel from the production planning department search for hours to find the requested documents.

    f. A raw materials storeskeeper takes certain expensive circuit boards home and covers the theft by submitting a write-off form to the accounting department that shows the boards to be obsolete and hence worthless.

    g. A small production order is laid aside when a rush job must be accommodated by a work center; the small order is then forgotten and never completed.

    h. As production orders are received, the production foreman requisitions the materials that he believes are needed for completing the job.

Often he overestimates the materials needed; the excess materials are then taken home by production employees.

i. A production planning clerk accesses the confidential salary file via an on-line terminal in the department.

15-9 What internal accounting control(s) would be most effective in preventing or detecting each of the following errors or fraudulent practices?

a. A production cost accounting program needs to be changed to reflect new standard costing procedures; however, the programmer who developed the program is no longer with the firm, and no one else understands the details of the program.

b. A production supervisor accesses the standard cost reference file and increases the standard overhead rate for her work center, so that the cost control reports will reflect favorable overhead cost variances.

c. A production employee enters a request for costly electronics parts on a material issue slip, using a nonexistent production order number, and then keeps the parts he receives from stores for personal use.

d. When entering the times pertaining to a particular job via a data collection terminal at a work center, an employee forgets to enter the job number to which they pertain.

e. At the end of a month it is discovered that the amount shown in the work-in-process inventory control account significantly exceeds the total of accumulated costs for all jobs in process.

f. The quantity of a raw material posted to a work-in-process ledger record is 450 units rather than 540 units; posting is performed by a cost accounting clerk who posts all of the materials issues once each day to the jobs in process.

g. The quantity of finished goods transferred into the warehouse for a production order was 100, but the warehouse clerk accidentally entered a quantity of 1000 into the computer system via the warehouse terminal.

h. A production employee keys an incorrect job number when entering his job hours, and the hours are posted to the wrong production order.

i. In entering data into an on-line terminal for a new production order, a production planning clerk keys a number for a product that is obsolete.

15-10 Munchen Manufacturing produces basic garden tools such as rakes and shovels. It maintains a large stock of raw materials in order to ensure that the production lines can operate at full capacity. Because the raw materials consist mainly of bulky wooden poles and steel plates, they are stacked next to the production areas as soon as received. No records are employed for their receipt. Production jobs are started each day on the basis of phone calls from the warehouse concerning which tools and sizes appear to be relatively low in stock. Since the warehouseman keeps the only records concerning finished goods, he is the best qualified to make such recommendations. Jobs are moved along the three production centers by an expediter. When completed, the finished goods are moved into the warehouse by a production employee. Then the warehouseman estimates the quantity received and enters the rough count on the materials records.

Management receives reports that reflect quantities produced and current levels (estimated) of finished goods on hand. The quantities produced have been gradually declining each month, even though the production lines are continually utilized. There often seem to be imbalances in the finished goods on hand, certain sizes of tools being in excessive supply and certain other sizes being quite low. Complaints are often received from customers (mainly garden shops) concerning inconsistent quality; when management investigates these complaints, it learns that all tools spoiled during production are discarded immediately. Employees are allowed to take any spoiled tools home for personal use.

Required

Discuss the problems in production management and weaknesses in internal accounting control. Recommend improvements.

15-11 Design formats for two reports that will provide needed information to enable the responsible managers to achieve the stated purposes:

   a. The first report should allow the evaluation of cost levels incurred in production. Costs relate to direct materials, direct labor, and overhead for the production orders that have been completed this month. The evaluation should consist of first comparing the actual (or applied) costs for these three elements with budgeted costs and then computing variances. No specific production numbers or cost values need to be entered.

   b. The second report should allow the daily evaluation of the use of materials in production operations, in order to control waste caused by the carelessness and inefficiency of employees. The report should pinpoint individual employees, by name, as well as specific materials and operations.

Enter onto the format the following identifying data: employees May Banks, Jerry Kimble, Robert Lambert, Judy Pierpoint, and Sandy Tempo; materials Delta and Omega; operations I, II, III, and IV. It is not necessary to enter numerical values for the actual quantities of materials used or for any comparative values.

15-12 Refer to Problem 10-8.

Required

List the features of the proposed report and related procedure that represent sound management control principles, as well as those that appear to be unsound.

Hint: Refer to the control reporting sections of a managerial or cost accounting textbook.

(CIA adapted)

15-13 Lecimore Company has a centralized purchasing department, which is managed by Joan Jones. Jones has established policies and procedures to guide the clerical staff and purchasing agents in the day-to-day operation of the department. She is satisfied that these policies and procedures are in conformity with company objectives and believes there are no major problems in the regular operations of the purchasing department.

Lecimore's internal audit department was assigned to perform an operational audit of the purchasing function. Their first task was to review the specific policies and procedures established by Jones. The policies and procedures are as follows:

• All significant purchases are made on a competitive bid basis. The probability of timely delivery, reliability of vendor, and so forth, are taken into consideration on a subjective basis.

- Detailed specifications of the minimum acceptable quality for all goods purchased are provided to vendors.
- Vendor's adherence to the quality specifications is the responsibility of the materials manager of the inventory control department and not the purchasing department. The materials manager inspects the goods as they arrive to be sure the quality meets the minimum standards and then sees that the goods are transferred from the receiving dock to the storeroom.
- All purchase requests are prepared by the materials manager on the basis of the production schedule for a four-month period.

The internal audit staff then observed the operations of the purchasing function and gathered the following findings:

- One vendor provides 90 percent of a critical raw material. This vendor has a good delivery record and is very reliable. Furthermore, this vendor has been the low bidder over the past few years.
- As production plans change, rush and expedite orders are made by production directly to the purchasing department. Materials ordered for canceled production runs are stored for future use. The costs of these special requests are borne by the purchasing department. Jones considers the additional costs associated with these special requests as "costs of being a good member of the corporate team."
- Materials to accomplish engineering changes are ordered by the purchasing department as soon as the changes are made by the engineering department. Jones is very proud of the quick response by the purchasing staff to product changes. Materials on hand are not reviewed before any orders are placed.
- Partial shipments and advance shipments (i.e., those received before the requested date of delivery) are accepted by the materials manager, who notifies the purchasing department of the receipt. The purchasing department is responsible for follow-up on partial shipments. No action is taken to discourage advance shipments.

Required

On the basis of the purchasing department's policies and procedures and the findings of Lecimore's internal audit staff:

a. Identify weaknesses and/or inefficiencies in Lecimore Company's purchasing function.

b. Make recommendations for those weaknesses/inefficiencies which you identify.

(CMA adapted)

15-14 The Prescott Manufacturing Company employs an on-line processing system to track its production orders. Each production order is first issued by the production planning department after a clerk enters data from a customer's order. In addition to three copies of the production order, which is automatically prenumbered and dated, the issuing program generates a move ticket for the initial work center and a materials requisition. The production data file (containing the schedule, machine loadings, bill of materials, and product structures), open production order file, work-in-process master file, and requisition file are accessed by this program.

The second step is to deliver a copy of the production order, move ticket, and requisition (the "package") to the initial work center. (The other copies of the order are filed numerically and sent to the sales order department.) Materials are delivered to the work center by the storeskeeper, who has received a copy of the requisition on his printer. The same program that generates the requisition for him reduces balances in the raw materials inventory master file to reflect their issuance. When materials are received, they are compared with the requisition already received.

Before and after the operation is performed at the initial work center, the involved employee enters the production order number and employee number into the work center terminal. The quantity completed is also entered upon completion. The computer system automatically records the start and completion times and dates. The program generates a move ticket for the next work center and enters the costs in a general ledger transaction file. The work-in-process is moved to the next center, together with the production order package. The files accessed by this program are the production order file, employee payroll file, work-in-process file, production data file, and general ledger file.

At the final work center, the employee who performs the last operation enters the same data as was entered at each previous center. The program recognizes, after accessing the production order file, that the order is completed. Then the program totals the work-in-process record, transfers it to the finished-goods inventory file, and enters the journal entry into the general ledger transaction file. It also removes the production order from the open file, transfers it to a completed order file, and enters time data into the employee payroll file. The production order package is returned to the production planning department.

At the end of each day a program posts the production transactions to the general ledger file and prints a summary of all completed production orders.

Required

a. Prepare a series of five system flowcharts that show the major steps in the preceding description. Assume that one operation is performed at each work center.

b. List programmed checks that should be performed by each program described and the data on which the checks are performed.

15-15 Industrial Builders of Austin, Texas, is a general building contractor specializing in shopping centers, office complexes, factories, hotels, and other large buildings. When the firm learns of a proposed project, it assigns an estimator to review the plans and prepare a bid quotation. Included within the quotation are estimates for materials, labor, subcontracted work, and such overhead items as building permits and supervision. The estimator draws on his or her experience, plus generally accepted cost guidelines and figures from the subcontractors, in developing these estimates. A profit margin then is added to the total estimated cost to arrive at the contract bid price.

If the contract is awarded to Industrial Builders, the project is assigned to a project manager. He or she has the responsibility for keeping costs within the total estimated cost and for meeting a scheduled deadline.

Unfortunately, most of the projects incur cost and time overruns. These overruns appear to be the cause of the firm's declining profitability during the past several years. The project manager blames these problems on the estimators and schedulers, saying that the estimated costs and scheduled deadlines are unrealistic. The estimators concede that cost estimates often tend to be low, since the inflation rate has been rather severe in recent years. However, they contend that the project managers are careless about watching costs and time schedules.

Required

a. Identify the sources that can provide Industrial Builders with the actual costs of projects pertaining to materials, labor, overhead, and subcontracted work.

b. Design formats for reports that will aid the firm in

    (1) Developing values for estimates.

    (2) Compiling the total estimated costs.

    (3) Controlling project costs and schedules.

15-16 The Sanders Manufacturing Company of Chapel Hill, North Carolina, custom-produces a variety of furniture products to customers' specifications. It employs a data collection and processing system to accumulate materials, labor, and overhead costs by job numbers. To perform these tasks, it utilizes a computer system that consists of a central processing unit, several data collection terminals, several magnetic tape drives, and two printers. It also employs a key-to-tape unit to convert materials data from documents to magnetic tape and a paper tape reader to convert employee time data to magnetic tape.

Data concerning the use of materials and parts are captured on material issues slips. These slips, which contain the number of each part or material issued as well as the quantity issued and the job number, are signed by production foremen as they receive the items from the storeskeeper.

Data concerning employee times devoted to jobs are captured by the data collection terminals located at stations on the production floor. As employees start or stop work on a job, they insert their employee badges into a terminal and key in the number of the job. The terminal automatically enters the employee number and job number, plus the time, onto punched paper tape within the terminal.

At the end of each day the material issues slips are batched and batch totals are computed of the quantities issued. Then the data are keyed onto magnetic tape and verified. They are edited during keying and also in a separate computer run. Transactions found to have errors or omissions are listed on an exception and summary report for cor-

rection and reentry the following day. Next, the materials transaction data are sorted by material (or part) numbers. Finally, the data are processed against the materials inventory master file, in order to reduce the on-hand quantities by the issued quantities. During this update run, three other actions occur: (1) the updated on-hand quantity in each record is compared with the reorder point quantity in the record; if the on-hand quantity is the smaller of the two quantities, it is listed together with the material or part number on a material reorder report. (2) The dollar amount represented by each material or part issue transaction is computed by multiplying the quantity issued by the unit price (one of the data items stored in each inventory record); the amounts then are written onto a new tape, together with the job numbers and the direct materials account code. (3) A batch total of quantities processed is computed and compared with the total originally computed; the result is printed on an exception and summary report.

At the end of each day, the punched paper tapes are also gathered from the data collection terminals and converted to the magnetic tape medium by a computer run. During this conversion run, the data are edited, the start and stop times are converted to hours expended, and a batch total is obtained of the total hours. Next, the time data are sorted by employee number. Then they are processed against an employee record file to achieve the following results: (1) The hours reported by each employee are added to accumulated hours worked during this pay period; at the end of the pay period the total will be compared with time attendance records for the employees. (2) The reported hours are converted into dollar amounts by multiplying the hours worked on each job during the day by the pay rate (one of the data items stored in each employee record); the amounts are then written onto a new tape, together with the job numbers and the direct labor account code. (3) A batch total of hours processed is computed and compared with the total originally computed; this result is printed on an exception and summary report.

The new magnetic tapes from the materials and labor time processing are then merged and sorted by job numbers during a single computer run. In the final computer run the dollar amounts for direct materials and direct labor are posted to the work-in-process inventory master file. This computer run also computes the added overhead charge for each job, multiplying the direct labor amount by the overhead percentage (one of the data items stored in each job record). Two outputs of this run are (1) a daily labor distribution summary by job number and (2) a job cost summary showing accumulated materials, labor, and overhead costs for each job compared to budgeted costs.

When new jobs are to be added to the work-in-process file or completed jobs are to be deleted, separate file maintenance runs are executed. These runs are necessary about every other day.

Required

a. Prepare a computer system flowchart of the present job cost procedure.

b. Suggest possible improvements in the data input and processing steps.

c. Draw a computer system flowchart that shows a revised on-line input and on-line processing procedure.

d. Design formats for the reports described in the foregoing problem statement.

15-17 Colorful Binding Materials, Inc., of Portland, Maine, produces bricks and concrete blocks for use in building homes and business facilities.[10] Most customers are

[10]Adapted from Ralph E. Struzziero, "Computer Application by a Concrete Block Manufacturer," *Management Accounting,* May 1971, pp. 34–38. Copyright © 1971 by National Association of Accountants, New York. All rights reserved. Reprinted by permission.

building contractors and brick and masonry suppliers. A wide variety of bricks and blocks are manufactured, both for inventory and for filling customers' orders. For each size, shape, and color there is a unique mix of raw materials. For instance, a particular variety of concrete block would contain an established mixture of cement, sand, silica, color, admix, and premix.

Production essentially consists of (1) mixing the ingredients for a batch, (2) feeding the mix into molding machines and applying heat, (3) removing the bricks or blocks from the machines and stacking them on pallets, and (4) storing in the yard or shipping to a customer. The production planning and control cycles involve

a. Production planning, which consists of forecasting sales and inventory needs, setting production levels, and preparing production orders to replenish needed inventory.

b. Order entry, which consists of receiving sales orders and either shipping from inventory or preparing related production orders.

c. Materials requirements planning, which consists of determining the quantities of materials needed to be purchased to cover planned production orders.

d. Machine loading and scheduling, which consists of projecting machine and labor loads and preparing short-range production schedules.

The production cycle for planning is a month, whereas the production cycle for short-range scheduling is a week in length. Most orders from customers are received with delivery due in seven days, although about 20 percent of orders are rush orders. Because of competitive conditions, the firm feels that it must handle all rush orders as soon as possible; however, it charges a premium price for such service. The typical orders received from a customer involve a variety of bricks and concrete blocks.

Files employed by Colorful include:

a. Bill of materials, showing quantities of materials used in one batch of a product.

b. Operations routing, showing the series of operations and corresponding times to manufacture a batch of a product.

c. Inventory file, showing on-hand quantities for all products, computed from beginning balances and quantities produced and sold.

d. Open production order file, showing the status of all production orders.

e. Materials file, showing quantities of raw materials on hand and on order.

f. Factory schedule, showing the starting and completion times, by operations, for all orders in production.

Currently, the firm maintains these files and prepares documents and reports without the assistance of computers. However, an investigation of these manual operations, prompted by difficulties in filling orders on time and high clerical and production costs, suggests that a computer-based system is feasible.

Required

a. Select and describe a computer-based logistics information system that would provide the most effective overall operational support for Colorful. Justify your choice, especially in view of the demands of the production process.

b. Draw a hardware configuration diagram of the selected system.

c. List key decisions that the selected information system can support.

d. Describe several reports that should be provided by the selected information system.

e. Assuming that the selected information system involves on-line input and processing, identify a set of general and transaction controls that should be adequate. With respect to the entry of data from sales orders, leading to the preparation of production orders, specify the programmed edit checks that would be desirable and the data items that each should check.

Suggested Readings

Blagg, R. Raymond, and Walton, Kenneth W. "Functional Time Reporting: Shortcut to Integrating Labor Data." *Management Accounting* (June 1984), pp. 34–38.

Davenport, Frederick J. "Financial Management Through MRP." *Management Accounting* (June 1982), pp. 26–29.

Dilts, David M., and Russell, Grant W. "Accounting for the Factory of the Future." *Management Accounting* (April 1985), pp. 34–40.

Gand, Harvey, and Cook, Milt E. "Choosing an MRP System." *Datamation* (January 1985), pp. 84–98.

Gerwin, Donald. "Do's and Don'ts of Computerized Manufacturing." *Harvard Business Review* (March–April 1982), pp. 107–116.

Groover, Mikell P. *Automation, Production Systems, and Computer-Integrated Manufacturing.* Englewood Cliffs, N.J.: Prentice-Hall, 1987.

Gunn, Thomas. "The CIM Connection." *Datamation* (February 1986), pp. 50–58.

Horngren, Charles T., and Sundem, Gary. *Cost Accounting: A Managerial Empha-*

sis. 6th ed. Englewood Cliffs, N.J.: Prentice-Hall, 1987.

Howell, Robert A., and Soucy, Stephen R. "Operating Controls in the New Manufacturing Environment." *Management Accounting* (October 1987), pp. 25–31.

Manufacturing Resource Planning. Atlanta Ga.: American Software, 1984.

McIlhattan, Robert D. "How Cost Management Systems Can Support the JIT Philosophy." *Management Accounting* (Sept. 1987), pp. 20–27.

Sadhwani, Arjan T., and Sarhan, M. H. "Electronic Systems Enhance JIT Operations." *Management Accounting* (Dec. 1987), pp. 25–30.

———, ———, and Kiringoda, Dayal. "Just-in-Time: An Inventory System Whose Time Has Come." *Management Accounting* (Dec. 1985), pp. 36–44.

Seglund, Ragnor, and Ibarreche, Santiago. "Just-in-time: The Accounting Implications." *Management Accounting* (August 1984), pp. 43–45.

Part IV

FLOURISHING DEVELOPMENTS IN COMPUTER-BASED SYSTEMS

Several developments concerning computer-based information systems have been emerging and expanding during the 1980s. These developments include microcomputers, computer-based auditing techniques, data base systems, computer-based communications networks, and decision support systems. Each of these five developing areas is expected to become even more important as we move toward the new century. Thus, a separate chapter is devoted to each developing area in this five-chapter part. Since the chapters are relatively independent, they may be "shifted" to other points within the textbook. For instance, Chapter 18 (Data Base Systems) may be read just after Chapter 8 (Files and Data Management), and Chapter 17 (Computer-Based Auditing) may be read just after Chapter 9 (Accounting Controls and Security Measures).

Chapter **16**

MICROCOMPUTERS IN BUSINESS SYSTEMS

Microcomputers have invaded the business world. Millions are being acquired each year, by small as well as large business firms and other organizations. In fact, microcomputers represent one of the fastest-growing segments of the computer market. Soon they are likely to be as plentiful, in the typical firm, as the familiar telephone.

Accountants, among others in the business world, are feeling the tremendous impact of microcomputers. These efficient and powerful machines expand the capacity of accountants and other professionals to handle complex undertakings. They reduce the necessity for time-consuming, repetitive, and mind-numbing operations. Thus, it is not surprising that new applications for micro-

computers are being discovered every day. Our survey of microcomputers includes their advantages, types, hardware, software, selection, management, controls, and applications. Most of the examples pertain to small business and professional firms, although we do give brief attention to the role of microcomputers in large firms.

Advantages of Microcomputers

Since microcomputers are miniature versions of mainframe computers, they offer all the basic capabilities of those computers. Their revolutionary impact, however, arises from four relative advantages that are intrinsic to microcomputers.

Low Cost

A typical microcomputer system can be acquired for only a few thousand dollars. For this relatively modest amount, the acquirer obtains a processor that rivals third-generation mainframe computers. Not only does the microcomputer process a greater number of instructions per second than such computers, but it has more primary storage capacity.

User Control

Most managers, accountants, engineers, and other key employees have an innate desire to control much of their own data processing and information retrieval. They prefer to draw on the firm's shared resource (i.e., large mainframe computer) only for high-volume transaction processing or other specialized computing tasks. By placing control in their hands, microcomputers enable managers, accountants, and other users to increase their productivity and effectiveness.

Versatility

Microcomputers are able to perform a wide variety of functions, ranging from information retrieval to word processing and financial modeling. Numerous software packages are currently available. Although mainframe computers can, of course, perform all of the same functions, microcomputers actually have greater versatility. They can (1) be dedicated to the processing needs of one or more users and also (2) be used to emulate terminals that connect directly to the mainframe computer.

Ease of Use

Because of their nature and setting, microcomputers are relatively easy to understand and put into use. The hardware configuration is basically simple, and the typical software package does not require the user to be a programmer. No waiting time or complicated sign-on procedure is necessary when a manager or employee needs to use his or her personal microcomputer. Moreover, an increasing number of microcomputers are lightweight and portable; these microcomputers may be easily carried from one work location to another or from work to home.

As might be expected, microcomputers also have disadvantages. From the point of view of users, their technology is changing so rapidly that by the time one model has been mastered, another has taken its place. From the point of view of larger firms, microcomputers are difficult to control and to incorporate into networks effectively. For instance, unauthorized persons have often been able to gain access to corporate data bases via networked microcomputers.

Types of Microcomputers

Microcomputers may be classified according to size, use, and method of handling inputs. However, we should note that these classification schemes overlap, and the types within each scheme tend to blur.

With respect to size, microcomputers range in both directions from the standard model. At the small end are the **portable computers,** which vary from suitcase models weighing 20 lb to hand-held models weighing less than 2 lb. Portable computers generally have a **liquid crystal display** (LCD) instead of the more common cathode ray tube (CRT) screen. At the other end are the supermicrocomputers, which in effect are small minicomputers. They provide greater primary storage capacity, word size, and processing speed than the standard microcomputer models.

With respect to use, microcomputers can be employed in a wide variety of applications and situations. They may be assigned to business applications such as general ledger accounting or to engineering applications such as product design. They may be employed as the sole computer within a small business firm or as a member of a network of computers within a large government agency. Most microcomputers currently in use are **dedicated** to a single task at a time. For instance, a particular microcomputer in a small firm may be used to handle sales orders during the morning and then to prepare the payroll that afternoon. Figure 16-1 shows a powerful microcomputer, the Apple Macintosh II, that can be dedicated to a wide variety of tasks. Other microcomputers enable more than one task to be performed *simultaneously*. In other words, they function in a multitasking mode. Figure 16-2 pictures a **multitasking microcomputer** processor to which 10 video display terminals

and two printers are connected. Figure 16-3 portrays a recent multitasking microcomputer, the IBM PS/2 Model 80-386, being employed within an architectural firm. (Only one video display terminal is pictured, although others can be in use at other locations in the firm.)

A third classification plan is according to the way inputs are handled. In **operator-oriented microcomputer systems** the transactions are entered manually by clerks through the keyboards or other devices. Each transaction is edited and processed completely before the next transaction is entered. Many operator-oriented microcomputer systems employ video display terminals for data entry. These terminals may be specialized to accommodate certain types of tasks, such as the small accounting computer system (portrayed in Figure 16-4) which handles postings

FIGURE 16-1   A dedicated microcomputer. Courtesy of Apple Corporation, Inc.

FIGURE 16-2 A multitasking microcomputer system. Copyright © 1987 by Contel Business Systems.

to accounts receivable ledger cards. A **file-oriented microcomputer system,** in contrast, feeds batches of data into the system via devices such as optical scanners or magnetic tapes. Thus, data entry is essentially under the control of the system itself.

Hardware

As a member of the computer family, a microcomputer consists basically of a central processing unit and input–output units. These units, or components, appear in Figure 16-3. Below and to the left of the user in

the figure is the central processing unit. In front of him is the keyboard (an input device) and the CRT screen (an output device for soft copy). To the left rear is the printer (an output device for hard copy). We shall explore these components more closely, as well as secondary storage media that are suitable for microcomputers and modems needed for communications.

Central Processing Unit

At the heart of the central processing unit is the **microprocessor.** It is constructed on a single silicon chip, which may measure

FIGURE 16-3 Components of a microcomputer system in action. Courtesy of International Business Machines Corporation.

FIGURE 16-4 A small accounting computer system. Courtesy of © Monroe Business Systems, Inc.

less than one inch square. Thanks to very-large-scale integration (VLSI), this chip contains several hundred thousand logic gates. Together with switches and a connected clock, it performs the control and arithmetic–logic functions. The chip also contains registers, called *cache memory,* that store relatively small quantities of data for very fast access. In addition, recently designed processor chips incorporate a math **coprocessor,** which can perform arithmetic computations 100 to 200 times faster than the principal microprocessor.

Microprocessors are designed by chip manufacturers. Two microprocessor chips found in many microcomputers in current use are the Intel 30386 and Motorola 68030 chips. However, new chips are continually under development; consequently, more powerful microcomputer chips—such as the Intel 30486 and Intel Reduced Instruction Set Computer (RISC) N10 chip—are being installed in newer microcomputers. The performance of microcomputer chips is measured by such factors as word size and clock frequency speed. For instance, the Intel 30486 has a word size of 32 bits and a clock frequency speed of 25 megahertz (million cycles per second). Because it also integrates both a math coprocessor and cache memory on the chip, it can execute software instructions several times faster than the most powerful Intel 30386 chip. The RISC microprocessor chip has a clock frequency speed of 50 megahertz, in addition to the ability to perform parallel processing and exhibit three-dimensional graphics.

The microprocessor chips are mounted on a main circuit board, often called a **motherboard,** planar board, or system board. Also on this board are primary storage (main memory) chips. In addition, the motherboard provides connection points (i.e., interfaces, ports, controllers) for a variety of input–output and storage devices. Figure 16-5 shows a motherboard for an IBM Personal System/2 microcomputer. Among the con-

nections which it provides are a **serial port** (i.e., a communications link), a **parallel port** (i.e., a printer or plotter link), a pointing device interface (i.e., a mouse or light pen link), and a disk controller (i.e., a link to a diskette drive). In addition, the motherboard usually contains modules for special capabilities, such as the graphics module shown in the figure. Furthermore, the board contains expansion slots (shown in the lower left-hand corner of the figure) and plug-in pins for such devices as add-in memory boards, terminal keyboards, timers, oscillators, accelerator cards, clock/calendars, and voice synthesizers.[1]

On the typical motherboard all of the various components receive their electrical power (in the form of digital electronic pulses) via one or more system bus bars or connectors. Figure 16-6 depicts a bus bar and a variety of likely components for a dedicated microcomputer having communications capability. Multiple buses are being increasingly used, since the newer microprocessor chips are designed to take advantage of their features. Two multiple bus architectures are the Extended Industry Standard Architecture (EISA) and Micro Channel.

The memory chips, which comprise the primary storage unit in a microcomputer, contain three types of memory: random-access memory, read-only memory, and erasable, programmable read-only memory. As in the case of mainframe computers, the *random-access memory* (RAM) accepts and stores data received from input devices or secondary storage units and generated from processing. Data are also transferred from RAM to output devices and secondary storage units. Because current RAM is a semiconductor storage medium, it is *volatile;* that

---

[1]Add-in memory boards provide additional primary or secondary storage; accelerator cards increase processing speed, clock/calendars keep track of the time and day, and voice synthesizers allow oral responses.

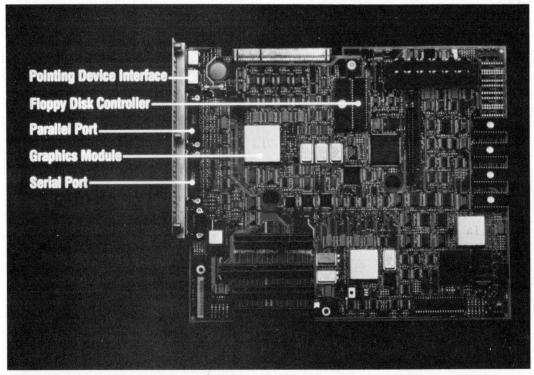

FIGURE 16-5 A view of the motherboard of a microcomputer. Courtesy of International Business Machines Corporation.

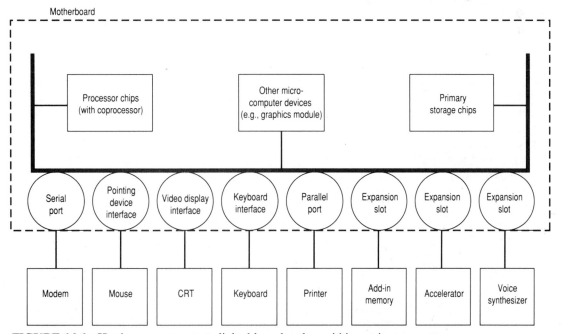

FIGURE 16-6 Hardware components linked by a bus bar within a microcomputer.

is, data stored in RAM are lost when the electrical power to the microcomputer is interrupted.[2] Current microcomputers provide one or more megabytes of RAM and often allow ten or more megabytes to be added if desired. *Read-only memory (ROM)* contains data that have been permanently written onto the medium by the microcomputer manufacturer. Thus, new data may not be written and existing data may not be changed; even a power interruption has no effect on data in ROM. **Erasable, programmable read-only memory** (EPROM) is read-only memory that may be programmed by the user of the microcomputer. The micro-instructions may not be erased or changed by the microprocessor; however, the user may employ a special ultraviolet process to erase the contents, after which he or she may insert new micro-instructions.

Input Devices

Data are typically entered into microcomputers by means of keyboards. Although key entry is slow, it has the advantage of allowing human users to interact directly with the microcomputer and the software that it executes. Also, current keyboard models include such features as 10-key numeric pads and special-function keys.

In addition to the keyboard, a variety of specialized input devices are now available for microcomputers. A hand-operated **mouse** allows users to point to and manipulate objects on the CRT screen. For instance, they can be used to open documents and files and to edit them easily and quickly. A **joystick** performs similar functions. A **light pen** allows users to draw lines and shapes on the screen. An **optical scanner** allows users to enter data by scanning bar and other character codes. A **voice-input device** allows users

to enter data in the form of speech. A **touch-input device** allows users to enter data (or instructions) by touching the CRT screen.

Three figures illustrate input devices. Figure 16-1 shows a mouse together with a keyboard, and Figure 16-3 portrays a user sitting at a keyboard. Figure 16-7 depicts the use of a user's finger to make a selection pertaining to a graph on a touch-sensitive screen.

The programs that process data and words, and also some of the data and words themselves, are entered via the secondary storage units. We will discuss this mode of entry in a later section.

Output Devices

Outputs from microcomputer systems are most often provided on CRT screens and by means of printers. The CRT screens display soft-copy outputs, such as the graph shown in Figures 16-1 and 16-7. If color display and graphics adapter cards have been added to the motherboard, the graphs would appear in color. Printers provide hard copy outputs on paper. Although printers are relatively expensive components in microcomputer systems, they are indispensible in today's paper-trail business world.

Three major types of printers used with the microcomputer systems are dot-matrix, daisy-wheel, and laser printers. The **dot-matrix printer** provides relatively high-speed printing (e.g., 100 to 900 characters per second) at the most reasonable cost. Printer characters from dot-matrix printers are lower in quality than those from the other types of printers, since the characters are formed of closely spaced tiny dots. However, the quality has been improving, since manufacturers have generally moved to the 24-pin printheads. The **daisy-wheel printer** produces letter-quality printing that is as sharp as that provided by the more expensive typewriters. It derives its name from print wheels that resemble daisies with petals

[2]When working with a microcomputer, a wise policy for a user to follow is to "save" the current work frequently to a nonvolatile storage medium, such as a hard disk or diskette.

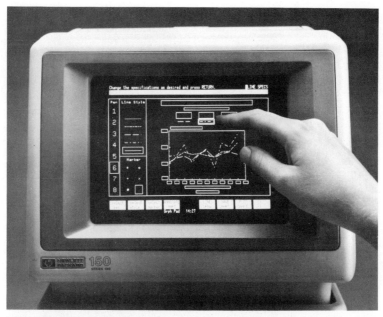

FIGURE 16-7   A terminal that combines touch input and graphics output. Courtesy of Hewlett-Packard Company.

radiating from a central hub. These print wheels may be changed very quickly to provide different typefaces as desired. The drawback of the daisy-wheel printer is the relatively slow rate (i.e., 30 to 60 characters per second) at which it types. The **laser printer** is a nonimpact printer that incorporates a laser device, a photosensitive drum, and a paper-handling mechanism. The printer operates by shining short bursts from a laser beam onto the drum, which thereby becomes sensitized. Next the drum is rotated through a toner bath to pick up the ink (toner) on the sensitized areas. This ink is then transferred to paper moving under the drum. A laser printer produces high-quality printing at relatively high rates of speed (e.g., 8 pages per minute). However, it is considerably more expensive than the other types of printers.

A large number of manufacturers provide printers to all conceivable specifications. Two popular printers are IBM's dot-matrix Proprinter (pictured in Figure 16-8) and Apple's LaserWriter (shown as part of a desktop publishing system in Figure 16-9).

Less common output devices for microcomputer systems include coded lights, plotters, and audio-response units. However, audio response is likely to become a more important mode of output in the future, since it is extremely user friendly.

Secondary Storage Media

The magnetic disk is the most widely used secondary storage medium. A disk controller allows a microcomputer to employ one or more disk drives, on which magnetic disks rotate. Two types of rotating magnetic disks are diskettes and hard disks.

The **diskette,** or floppy disk, consists of a circular piece of material coated with magnetic oxide and covered with a protective jacket. Diskettes are available in three sizes—8 in., $5\frac{1}{4}$ in., and $3\frac{1}{2}$ in.—as shown in

FIGURE 16-8 A dot matrix printer. Courtesy of International Business Machines Corporation.

Figure 16-10. Some diskettes are able to store data on both sides. Diskettes are inserted into the disk drives of microcomputers via slots in the microprocessors. (See Figure 16-11.) Although most microcomputers provide single disk drives for diskettes, some have twin disk drives for added convenience. Twin disk drives are labeled either as drives 1 and 2 or as A and B.

Diskettes offer several advantages. First, they allow direct access to data records. Second, they are convenient to store and transport. Third, they are quite inexpensive.

A magnetic **hard disk** for a microcomputer typically consists of a single platter, either $5\frac{1}{4}$ in. or $3\frac{1}{2}$ in. in diameter. It may be mounted on three types of drives:

1. A **Winchester drive,** which is mounted within the microprocessor housing, usually next to a diskette drive.

2. A **hard disk card** or board, which is inserted into an expansion slot within the microprocessor.

3. A **Bernoulli box,** which is attached externally to the microprocessor. In this arrangement the disk is in the form of a removable cartridge.

One advantage of a hard disk is that it rotates more rapidly than a diskette, thus allowing faster access to the data it stores. Another advantage is that its storage capacity is many times greater than that of a diskette. Common capacities for marketed hard disks are 10, 20, 40, 60, and 80 megabytes. Disk-

FIGURE 16-9   A laser printer, one component in a desktop publishing system. Courtesy of Apple Corporation, Inc.

ettes can store from $\frac{1}{2}$ megabyte to 2 megabytes of data characters.

Magnetic tape is also used as a storage medium with microcomputer systems. Mag-

FIGURE 16-10   Three sizes of diskettes. Reprinted with permission from Stephen A. Moscove and Mark G. Simpkin, *Accounting Information Systems,* 3rd ed. (New York: Wiley, 1987).

netic disks are used to store files and software while actively employed in processing, but magnetic tape is principally used as a backup medium. That is, periodically data on magnetic disks are (or should be) "dumped" onto magnetic tapes to provide security for file data. Two forms of magnetic tape are **tape cassettes** and **tape cartridges.** These tape forms can hold very large quantities of data and be loaded very quickly. For instance, a standard tape cartridge holds 60 megabytes of data and can be loaded in 12 minutes.

Optical disks represent the third medium for secondary storage. These disks, known as **CD ROM** (compact disk read-only memory), are inserted into externally attached optical disk drives. Available in 8-in. and $5\frac{1}{4}$-in. sizes, optical disks are generally

FIGURE 16-11 Insertion of a diskette into a microcomputer. Courtesy of International Business Machines Corporation.

used to store data bases of such reference matter as financial results and market analyses. Typical capacities of each side of optical disks are 400 and 600 megabytes.

Communications Devices

When microcomputers are linked to a mainframe computer or to each other, communications devices are needed. The main device of concern to a microcomputer user is the modem, which may be mounted internally (within the microprocessor casing) or attached externally. **Modems** transmit data at speeds (baud rates) up to 19,200 characters per second. Other devices that may be needed when microcomputers are

linked into networks include front-end processors, channel controllers, and emulation products.

Software

The advent of microcomputers has led to an explosion of software packages, for two major reasons: (1) microcomputers are being sold in huge volumes, and (2) most of the purchasers and users of microcomputers are not professional programmers and do not care to learn to program. Although game programs and personal-use programs receive much of the attention, many of the software packages are designed for business use. In order to provide this torrent of packages, a number of software vendors have come into existence. Among the more familiar names are Management Sciences of America, Microsoft, Cullinet, Lotus Development, and Digital Research.

Before surveying these software packages, we might recall that each microcomputer (like any type of computer) employs its own machine language. Thus, programming languages are necessary in order to develop the packages, as well as the operating system of the microcomputer system. Moreover, there are numerous occasions when programmers and users desire to develop their own special programs.

Although the operating system is generally written in a microcomputer's assembly language (for the sake of greater efficiency), many application packages and special programs are written in higher-level languages. For instance, BASIC is a popular procedure-oriented language used for many applications. It is easier to learn and apply than other procedure-oriented languages such as COBOL and FORTRAN. Well-tested compilers for BASIC source programs are available for virtually every business-oriented microcomputer. Moreover, other languages, especially C and PASCAL, are becoming increasingly popular.

The following survey of microcomputer software assumes that appropriate programming languages are employed. Included in the survey are operating systems, accounting applications, electronic spreadsheets, financial modeling systems, data base management systems, word processing systems, desktop publishing systems, and graphics systems.

Operating Systems

The **operating system** is the key system software that guides the operation of a microcomputer and all its components. Generally the operating system is provided on a diskette by the microcomputer manufacturer. In some cases the operating system is proprietary and unique to an individual manufacturer. An example is APPLE-DOS, which is used exclusively with an Apple microcomputer. In other cases the operating system is common to a variety of microcomputer models and makes. Examples of such operating systems in current use are UNIX (developed by American Telephone & Telegraph Company) and MS-DOS (developed by Microsoft Corporation). Any application software package written to comply with the MS-DOS operating system, for instance, will function on all IBM microcomputers and IBM-compatible microcomputers (e.g., Compaq, Zenith).

New operating systems are continually under development. The OS/2 operating system, recently developed by Microsoft Corporation, allows users to run applications designed for use with microprocessor chips having 32-bit word sizes. In particular, it is suited for IBM's PS/2 line of microcomputers. Since the UNIX and MS-DOS operating systems are designed for use with 16-bit microprocessors, the OS/2 operating system enables the performance of applications to be dramatically enhanced. Another operating system development relates to multitasking and multiprocessing. For instance, OS/2 allows multiple users to run applications concurrently on a microcomputer system and allows the processing of an application to be split among several processors.

The first step for a purchaser of a microcomputer is to "customize" the provided operating system to accommodate the particular hardware configuration of the microcomputer system. This customized operating system is either retained on the diskette or loaded onto the microcomputer's hard disk. Then, before each use the operating system is initiated or "booted" with the aid of its "bootstrap" program stored in ROM. The user is informed that a successful "boot" has occurred by means of a prompt or a message notifying him or her to take some action. For instance, a C> is a prompt that appears when the operating system has been booted from the hard disk.

Among the actions that may be taken by a microcomputer user when such a prompt appears are

1. Enter or "call up" an application package.
2. Enter or "call up" a programming language suitable to microcomputers, such as BASIC.
3. Specify a utility program.

An operating system does much more than initialize applications. For instance, it provides access to a variety of utility programs or routines. Typical utility programs include the following:

Command	Function of the Utility Program
COPY	Copies individual files from one disk to another
DIR	Provides a directory of all files on a specified disk
DEL	Deletes individual files from a disk

FORMAT	Prepares a disk to accept data or program files
DISKCOPY	Makes an exact copy of a disk
MD	Makes a new directory on a hard disk
CLS	Clears the monitor screen and moves the cursor back to the upper left corner of the screen

Microcomputers are currently affected by two problems that are traceable to operating systems. The first problem is software incompatibility, due to the lack of a standard operating system. That is, applications written for one operating system do not function with another operating system. Thus, when a person or a firm acquires a microcomputer, only those applications that are compatible with the microcomputer's operating system are available to the acquirer. The second problem relates to the security of the operating system. If appropriate measures are not incorporated into the operating system, serious adversities can occur. For instance, computer *viruses*—deliberate "bugs" written by pranksters—can be introduced into the microcomputer system and destroy files or cause other mischief.[3]

Accounting Application Packages

Most **accounting application packages** focus on common transactions. For instance, a typical set of packages covers transactions affecting the general ledger, accounts receivable, accounts payable, inventory, and payroll. Each of these packages verify and edit entered transaction data, process the data, update established master files, and produce various documents and reports. They normally include subsidiary ledgers for customers, suppliers, and employees. Designers of such packaged sets normally use a modular approach, the various transaction mod-

ules (e.g., accounts receivable) being integrated into the general ledger module. This design allows the subsidiary ledgers related to the various modules to be updated concurrently with the general ledger.

Microcomputer-based accounting application packages are used by firms of all sizes, from small business firms to large organizations having widespread operations. Since the users of these packages are typically data entry or accounting clerks, the designers attempt to render them as user friendly as possible. Menus, account prompts, forced balancing of transaction amounts, simplified reports, and thorough audit trails are among the accommodating devices employed. Tutorials and easy-to-understand manuals are often provided.

An enormous number of accounting packages are currently available from a variety of software vendors. These packages range from small business-oriented packages, such as Dac-Easy Accounting (developed by Dac Software, Inc.), to packages for larger organizations, such as MSA Accounting System (developed by Management Science America, Inc.). Figure 16-12 shows the main menu for the general ledger module of the MSA Accounting System. An appendix to this chapter describes the functioning of still another package, ACCPAC Plus (developed by Computer Associates).

Although accounting application packages have many similarities, they also differ in numerous respects. For instance, certain packages are designed with flexibility in mind; that is, they allow using firms to tailor the packages to the particular characteristics and needs of the firms. Other packages are specifically designed for specific types of firms, such as contractors, bankers, manufacturers, and certified public accountants. Thus, acquiring firms should carefully evaluate the available packages. Figure 16-13 lists a number of factors that are relevant to the consideration of accounting application packages. Certain publications, such as *Info-*

[3]See John J. Maher and James O. Hicks, "Computer Viruses: Controller's Nightmare," *Management Accounting* (October 1989), pp. 44–49.

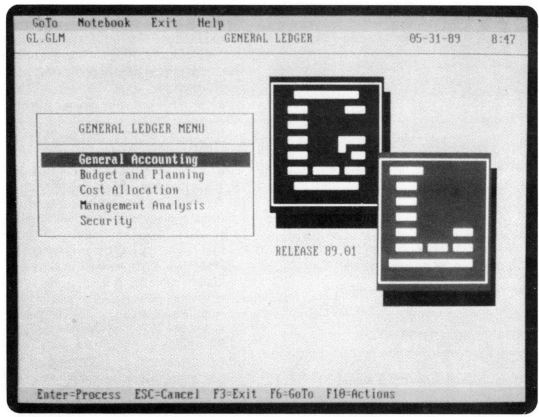

```
GoTo   Notebook   Exit   Help
GL.GLM                    GENERAL LEDGER          05-31-89    8:47



                 ┌─────────────────────────────────────┐
                 │  GENERAL LEDGER MENU                 │
                 │                                      │
                 │  General Accounting                  │
                 │  Budget and Planning                 │
                 │  Cost Allocation                     │
                 │  Management Analysis                 │
                 │  Security                            │
                 └─────────────────────────────────────┘

                            RELEASE 89.01



 Enter=Process   ESC=Cancel   F3=Exit   F6=GoTo   F10=Actions
```

FIGURE 16-12 A main menu for a general ledger accounting package. Courtesy of Management Science America, Inc., a division of Dun & Bradstreet Software, Inc.

world, Business Software Review, and *PC Week,* also provide reviews and comparisons of specific packages.

Electronic Spreadsheets

The software package known as an **electronic spreadsheet** has become the most popular accounting and business application since the first version, VisiCalc, burst on the scene in 1978. Since that date versions known as Lotus 1-2-3, SuperCalc, and Multiplan have appeared. (These names, and others to be mentioned in later sections, are registered trademarks.) An electronic spreadsheet is a multicolumn worksheet pro-

jected onto the CRT screen of a computer system. It allows accountants and others to work with a huge number of rows and columns, to perform powerful computer-aided functions, and to store the results in computer-readable files.

The electronic spreadsheet has four attributes that enable it to be an effective business planning tool:

1. It displays data in a form (i.e., columnar worksheet) that is familiar to accountants and other financially oriented persons. Figure 16-14 shows a spreadsheet display of accounting data. (Note the menu of options across the top, which allow the user to select actions or more detailed menus.)

Compatibility with currently-owned microcomputer hardware

Flexibility in making modifications to package specifications

Degree of integration with other modules in accounting system

Aids for interacting with package (e.g., menus, prompts)

Sufficiency of on-line data storage for files

Completeness and readability of user manuals

Degrees of reliability and rigor in detecting and correcting data errors

Ability to perform multiperiod processing (i.e., processing future periods without closing the current period)

Capability for producing managerial reports (e.g., budgets, cost variance reports)

Capability of fulfilling functional responsibilities (e.g., handling alternative cash payment methods in the case of accounts receivable modules)

Level and types of support provided by software vendor

Cost of package (or individual modules)

FIGURE 16-13 Criteria to consider when evaluating accounting software packages. *Sources:* Yair M. Babad and Kathryn M. Cullen, "Criteria for Selecting Accounting Software: Part I," *Journal of Accounting and EDP* (Spring 1986); and Charles R. Campbell, "Selecting and Evaluating Accounts Receivable, Accounts Payable, and General Ledger Software," *Journal of Accounting and EDP* (Spring 1985), pp. 47–54.

2. It eliminates the onerous chore of manual calculating, since it performs calculations such as footing, cross-footing, and extensions. At the same time, it does not require users such as accountants to act as programmers in order to gain desired results.

3. It allows accountants and other users to ask "what-if" questions and to obtain complete recalculations very quickly. Thus, an accountant who is preparing a forecast may change a sales estimate from an increase of 1 percent per month to 3

percent per month. The spreadsheet formulas will then automatically recalculate the expected sales levels. If the sales forecast is a part of a budgeted income statement, the spreadsheet formulas will also recalculate the expected net income amounts and all intervening expense amounts.

4. It enables templates to be constructed and repeatedly used in solving various problems. A **template** is a program that (a) models the relationships among factors, (b) details the procedural steps by which values are manipulated on the spreadsheet, and (c) expresses the format of the output. For instance, a template may be created by an accountant to prepare consolidated financial statements; this same template may be used at the end of each accounting period. Spreadsheet templates are extremely useful in planning and forecasting situations, since they allow users to ask "what-if" questions and obtain quickly recalculated answers. For instance, the accountant involved in preparing a budget forecast could change the estimate of sales growth to 5 percent per month (from the previous estimate of 3 percent). The spreadsheet program, or template, would then recalculate the expected sales amounts. Furthermore, if all expected costs have been entered, the expected net profit could also be recalculated. Figure 16-15 displays a template produced on a screen for verification by the user.

Financial Modeling Systems

Financial modeling software packages allow users to build customized models by employing powerful instructions and functions. A financial model has the primary purpose of enabling managers and other users to project future business activity or to aid in solving problems. Financial modeling software rep-

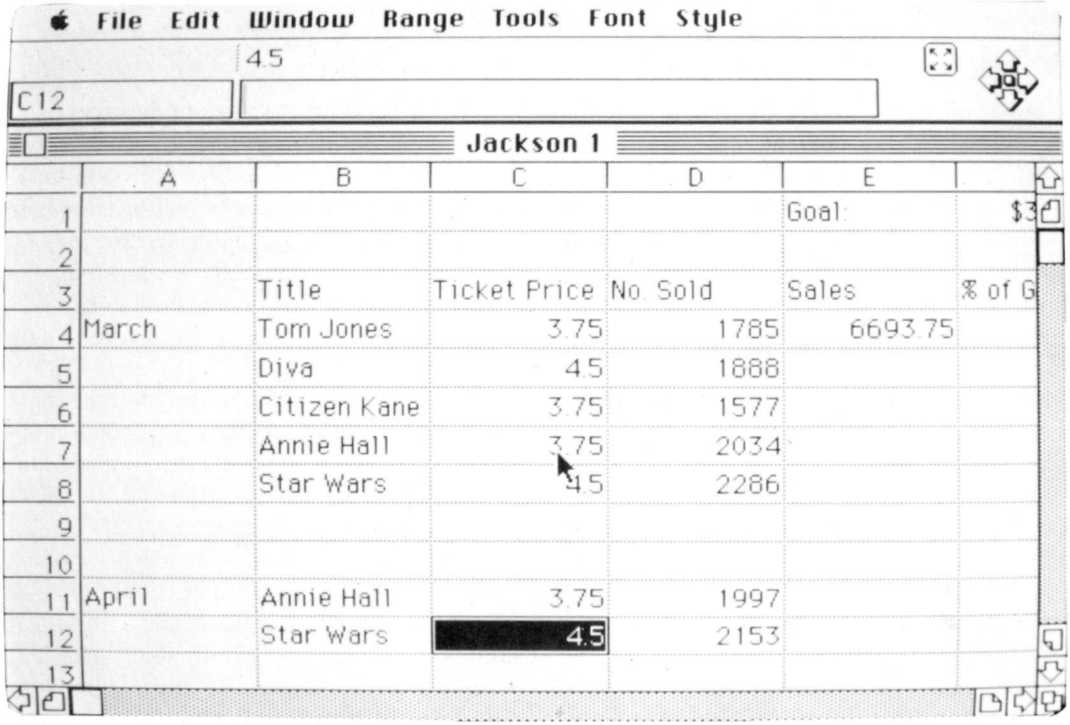

FIGURE 16-14 A columnar worksheet from an electronic spreadsheet. Courtesy of Apple Corporation, Inc.

	A	B	C	D	E	F
1	Account		Budget	Actual	Variance	Variance
2	Name		Amount	Amount	(Dollars)	(Percent)
3						
4	Sales		....	....	0	0
5	Cost of sales		....	....	0	0
6	Gross margin		0	0	0	0
7	Operating exp.		....	....	0	0
8	Nonoper. exp.		....	....	0	0
9	Total expenses		0	0	0	0
10	Net income		0	0	0	0
11						
12						
13						
14						

Notes: 1. Letters mark columns; numbers mark rows.
2. The spaces denoted by ..... indicate amounts to be entered, whereas the spaces marked by 0 indicate amounts to be computed by the spreadsheet software.

FIGURE 16-15 A spreadsheet template displayed on a screen. *Notes:* (1) Letters mark columns; numbers mark rows. (2) The spaces denoted by a row of dots indicate amounts to be entered, whereas the spaces marked by 0 indicate amounts to be computed by the spreadsheet software.

resents an alternative to electronic spreadsheets. Both allow calculations and other manipulations of data and clearly present the results in tabular or graphical forms. Both provide a programming language by which to provide instructions or to construct models. Both offer special functions and macro commands.

In many situations, however, financial modeling software packages are distinctly preferable to electronic spreadsheets. Financial modeling software enables decision makers and model builders to construct models with Englishlike statements. Not only do these statements provide more understandable documentation, but they also facilitate the logical development. Thus, fewer logic errors are found in financial models than in electronic spreadsheet programs. Also, financial models are more flexible and reusable, since the data are stored in files or data bases rather than in referenced cells. Finally, more manipulative techniques may be employed with the typical financial modeling software package. In addition to "what-if" statements, both goal-seeking commands and sensitivity analyses may be performed. Thus, financial modeling software is more suited to complex and recurring problems.

Certain microcomputer-based financial modeling software packages, such as EN-CORE! PLUS (developed by Ferox Microsystems, Inc.), emphasize the use of Englishlike commands. Other packages, such as IFPS/Personal (developed by Execucom Systems Corporation), provide a variety of user-friendly menus and built-in functions for developing models. Still others, such as JAVELIN PLUS (developed by Information Resources, Inc.), store both data and program logic in a multidimensional data base, from which a variety of two-dimensional views can be displayed for the user. Chapter 20 discusses the features of financial modeling languages in more detail.

Data Base Management Systems

From the viewpoint of a microcomputer user, an application is any data-oriented use to which the microcomputer system may be put. One such application is data management. A software package that enables users to manage data and files is known as a **data base management system** (DBMS). DBMS packages for microcomputers have become quite important, especially for small-business users, since they enable nonprogrammers to process and manage data without writing computer programs.

DBMS packages for the microcomputer environment range widely in capabilities. A simple, file-oriented package allows nonprogrammer users to develop mailing lists and keep track of records. A more complex, data-oriented package allows microcomputer users to build multiple files to desired specifications, keep the files up to date, sort records on desired keys, retrieve desired data items quickly from the files, summarize values of data items, and construct special reports according to desired formats.

Small businesses and professionals are becoming avid DBMS users. For instance, merchandising firms such as VCR movie rental companies maintain inventories by means of DBMS's. Doctors maintain patients' medical history records; lawyers prepare legal briefs and perform searches for case precedents; accountants maintain client records and prepare bills.

Currently popular data base management software packages include dBase IV (developed by Ashton-Tate), RBase for DOS (developed by Microrim), and Paradox (developed by Borland International). Each of these packages, as well as most other available packages designed for microcomputers, store data in tables in accordance with the *relational model*. (Concepts pertaining to DBMS models and other aspects of data management are discussed in Chapter 18.)

As in the case of electronic spreadsheets and other types of software packages, a number of factors should be considered during the selection process. For instance, the programming language provided by the package may be important, since it enables programmers or even informed users to develop their own menus, applications, and macro commands. Other factors include

1. The capacity of the primary storage unit for the microcomputer on which the package is to be used. Certain packages require 512 kilobytes or more of primary storage.
2. The speeds with which the operations are performed and data accessed.
3. The maximum size of files, in terms of records, fields, and bytes per field.
4. The processing capabilities, including sorting of multiple fields and mathematical functions.
5. User-friendly features, such as menus, prompts, and windows.
6. Report-writing capabilities, including flexible arrangement of formats, page breaks, allowance for numerous columns, and graphical formats.
7. Ability to transport data to spreadsheets or word processors.
8. Ability to download files from mainframe computers in a network.
9. The availability of such aids as tutorials, easy-to-read manuals, and so on.
10. The ability to apply password protection on selected files and fields.

Various periodicals (e.g., *Business Software Review, PC Week*) and services (e.g., *Data Pro*) provide evaluations of data base management software packages. In addition, evaluative articles appear on occasion. An example is "Data Base Programs as Tools for Better Management" by Victor J. Chorney, which appeared in the Summer 1988 issue of *Journal of Accounting and EDP*.

Word Processing Systems

Another widespread application of microcomputers is **word processing**—the preparation of letters and other textual materials (such as this textbook). Word processing software provides the ability to draft the text on a video screen and to make changes easily and quickly. It stores the results on a diskette, from which they may be printed as many times as desired. As the author can attest, after once using a word processor you will never willingly use a typewriter again. Currently available word processing systems include Word Perfect (developed by Word-Perfect Corporation), Microsoft Word (developed by Microsoft Corporation), Word-Star (developed by MicroPro International Corporation), and MultiMate (developed by Ashton-Tate Corporation).

The following list of available features suggests the value of word processing software:

1. Text previously typed may be edited at any time by powerful commands. Editing might consist of moving blocks of text to different locations, erasing lines, and inserting words.
2. Text may be reformatted. For instance, after a sentence in the middle of a paragraph is omitted, the paragraph can be reformatted by a single command. A heading can be centered by a single command.
3. Paragraphs may be typed without pause or the use of a return key. A word wrap feature automatically justifies the right margin and respaces each line as typed.
4. One word may be replaced by another throughout a text by the use of a single command.
5. Misspelled words are automatically corrected.

6. Backup copies of text are automatically created.

7. Help menus are displayed on single commands.

Recent upgrades of certain word processing packages enable users to prepare newsletters and perform other publishing tasks. For instance, they allow graphs to be integrated with text material. However, complex, high-quality publishing projects should normally be handled by desktop publishing systems.

Desktop Publishing Systems

A **desktop publishing package** enables users to format and print professional-quality newsletters and other textual materials. This type of software is particularly useful for projects that emphasize visuals such as pictures and graphs in color. Its use is also necessary when sophisticated typographical control and professional features such as registration and crop marks are involved.

The Apple Macintosh has been closely associated with desktop publishing since its introduction. Figure 16-9 shows a Macintosh-oriented desktop publishing system. Two desktop publishing packages for IBM-compatible microcomputers are PageMaker (from Aldus Corporation) and Ventura (from Xerox Corporation). These packages provide a variety of type fonts and style formats, a means of entering graphs by pointing at them on the screen and clicking a mouse, and the ability to retrieve text and graphics from other software packages such as word processors. One feature that facilitates the use of desktop publishing packages, as well as other types of microcomputer software packages, is known as split-screening or windowing. **Windows** are areas of a video display screen that are devoted to separate views. In the case of desktop publishing systems these views may be different documents, pages, or columns under development.

Graphics Systems

A **graphics system** displays financial and other information in graphical forms. It involves a wedding of microcomputer hardware and software. Graphics are best displayed on special graphics terminals or on color microcomputers containing graphics cards; they are transformed into hard-copy graphs by means of plotters, certain types of printers (e.g., laser, color ink-jet, dot matrix), or film-recording devices. Graphics software packages are needed to transform tabular data into such graphical forms as pie charts, bar graphs, line graphs, and flowcharts. Examples of microcomputer-based graphics packages are ChartMaster (from Ashton-Tate), 3-D Graphics (from Intex Solutions, Inc.), and PCcrayon (from PC-software).

Two major types of graphics packages are available. **Presentation graphics** generate high-quality graphs to be used in presentations and publications. The graphs are generally developed by transforming tabular data into the graphical forms. Often they appear in color, and some present three-dimensional views. **Freehand graphics** allow users to draw or "paint" pictures or graphs by means of light pens. These packages are pixel-oriented, in that the user can manipulate images bit by bit.

The hardware and software for graphics systems can be relatively expensive. However, the systems enable graphs to be produced in a very timely manner with little effort on the part of users. Since they can be operated by unsophisticated users, problems of communication do not arise. Also, if the systems are used frequently, the cost per graph can be dramatically reduced. Finally, as in the case of other microcomputer software packages, graphics systems can be shared by multiple users when the microcomputers are incorporated into the computer networks of automated offices. Graphics systems are also discussed in Chapter 20.

Other Software Packages

A variety of additional software packages are available for business firms. **Time-management packages** allow using firms to record the hours worked by employees and other data concerning their activities. **Electronic calendars** enable employees of firms to keep track of appointments, meetings, and other events. **Electronic mail** software transmits written messages via data communications networks to recipients who have electronic storage "mailboxes." **Voice mail** software transmits spoken messages to the telephones of recipients, provided that the telephones serve as terminals of a data communications network. **Videotex** software transmits data or images (e.g., documents, pictures, graphics) interactively to receiving points, which may be microcomputers, tele-

vision sets, or telephones. Firms can also receive data and images from other firms or from outside services, such as Dow Jones. **Decision support and expert system** software provides information that aids managers in making decisions concerning semistructured or unstructured problem situations. Chapter 20 discusses these types of software systems.

Integrated software packages do not fit into a single application category. Instead, they combine two or more functions and provide facilitating interfaces among them. Thus, users can easily switch from one application to another. Also, data can be easily transferred from one application to another. For instance, packages such as Symphony (from Lotus Development Corp.) and Framework (from Ashton-Tate) combine an electronic spreadsheet, a DBMS, a graphics

---

APPLICATION OF MICROCOMPUTERS
Continental Motor Inn[a]

Continental Motor Inn, a relatively small Cumberland, Maryland, firm, installed a microcomputer-based system several years ago to replace a manual system. The hardware configuration essentially consists of three Victor microcomputers plus two dot-matrix printers and one daisy-wheel printer.

Bob King, the president, did all the programming himself. His programs, which are menu-driven, pertain to the following applications.

1. General ledger processing, with daily balance sheets and income statements.
2. Payroll preparation, including quarterly payroll tax reports.
3. Liquor inventory recordkeeping.
4. Accounts receivable processing.
5. Accounts payable processing and check preparation.
6. Employee (e.g., waiters) scheduling.

As a result of these computerized accounting system applications, the inn has increased gross income by 50 percent, tripled the number of employees, and expanded to a second location.

This increased business has kept Bob so busy that he has not had time to write new programs. Thus, he is considering the acquisition of two programs to control the food inventories and room reservations. Since these programs operate only on IBM and IBM-compatible microcomputers, and because the current microcomputers are being used to their capacities, he is also considering the acquisition of an IBM PS/2.

[a]Carolyn Allen, "PC's Make It Better Inn-Side," *Modern Office Technology* (June 1985), pp. 129–134.

package, and a word processing package. The disadvantage exhibited by such integrated packages is that each function tends to have less power and flexibility than higher-quality packages that focus on a single function.

Approaches to Microcomputer Selection

With the advent of microcomputers, many small business firms have discovered that they are able to enter the computer age. However, selecting a particular computer is not an easy task. Hundreds of models of microcomputers are available. Other types of computers that might be considered add many more models.

Accountants are often involved in helping such firms to select computers that best meet their needs. It is therefore fitting to examine approaches to microcomputer selection. Our purpose in this section is not to explore the variety of concerns and steps necessary to analyze and design a new information system. These concerns and steps are the subject of Part V of this book. Instead, this section suggests approaches by which to develop answers to two questions: (1) Which of the many available microcomputers is best for this firm? (2) Is a microcomputer the best choice, or should some other type of computer be acquired?

Selection Criteria for Hardware

The first step after deciding that a microcomputer is needed is to specify exactly what those needs are. Is the microcomputer to be used primarily for transaction processing, for financial planning, or both? When the needs are settled, then the question should be: Which software package or packages will best satisfy these needs, and what are the requirements of the chosen software package(s)? What must be the capacity of primary storage and the processing speed of the processor to make best use of this software package?

This first step illustrates the maxim that the software "drives" the hardware. A business firm buys a microcomputer (or any computer) in order to meet certain data or information needs. It should not acquire a microcomputer in order to impress employees and customers with a state-of-the-art trophy.

The next step is to test a standard (unmodified) copy of the software package on various models of microcomputers, thereby, it is hoped, narrowing the choice to only a few likely models.

With respect to each model that passes the foregoing test, the following questions should be raised:

1. Does the model have sufficient capacity to meet anticipated future needs, or can the capacity be increased by the addition of storage modules?
2. Does the model (or the selected software package) incorporate adequate controls and security measures and provide clear audit trails?
3. Can reliable and timely maintenance be obtained from the manufacturer or other service network, and are backup systems conveniently available?
4. Does the manufacturer provide adequate documentation?
5. Does the dealer or manufacturer provide after-sales training?
6. Has the model been in use for a reasonable period, so that all "bugs" have likely been discovered?
7. Is the model reasonably priced compared to other possible models?
8. Will the manufacturer likely exist in the future and continue to support this product?

Selection Criteria for Software

Although fewer questions must be asked about each package under consideration, it is also necessary to comparison-shop for software. For instance, hundreds of general ledger accounting application packages are available, and each is unique in certain respects.

While each software package should be rated on performance and cost, equally important factors are:

1. User-friendliness.
2. Adequate and understandable documentation.
3. Adequate controls (e.g., editing controls, balancing controls, and audit trail features).
4. Report-generation capabilities.
5. Ability to transfer data to related applications or within a network.
6. Adequate software vendor support.

Outside advice should also be sought. Consultants such as those employed by public accounting firms can provide expert assistance in the evaluation of software as well as hardware. Other purchasers of microcomputer software and hardware are usually willing to share their experiences, negative as well as positive. Finally, information services can often be very helpful. Two services that provide evaluations in looseleaf notebooks are Datapro and Data Decisions; two on-line services are Datapro/Online and the Business/Professional Software Database.[4]

Management of Microcomputer Systems

Effective management of microcomputer systems begins with thorough planning and sound development. Planning includes such steps as clarifying the firm's objectives, preparing a long-range development plan, and devising microcomputer policies and standards. Planning should be performed by those who will be significantly affected by the presence of microcomputers. For instance, Syntex Corporation, a drug manufacturer based in Palo Alto, recently undertook planning and development of microcomputer systems for its inventory control function. Taking part were representatives from the information systems function, sales technical support, and major user departments.[5] Systems development consists of analyzing system and information needs, preparing designs of all system components, and implementing the designed system. Among necessary implementation activities are programming, installation, training, testing, and documentation. If software packages are acquired, the programming task is reduced; however, they usually must be modified to fit the firm's particular circumstances. Planning and systems development are discussed more fully in the chapters comprising Part V. While those chapters emphasize large system development, the process is similar for systems of all sizes.

Once they become operational, microcomputer systems require continued attention. How microcomputer systems are used, as well as how they should be managed, depends mainly on the business settings into which they are placed. These settings range from very small firms to firms having numerous departments and geographical locations.

---

[4]Datapro reference services, such as the *Datapro Directory of Software,* are products of Datapro Research Corporation, Delran, N.J. 08075; the *Data Decisions Software* reference notebook is a product of Data Decisions, 20 Brace Road, Cherry Hill, N.J. 08034; the Business/Professional Software Database is a trademark of Data Courier, Inc., 620 South Fifth St., Louisville, KY 40202.

[5]Jeff Moad, "The Second Wave," *Datamation* (February 1, 1989), p. 20.

APPLICATION OF MICROCOMPUTERS
Radio Corporation of America (RCA)[a]

During the early 1980s the controller's function of RCA collected financial information from the firm's operating units by means of the postal service, facsimile mail, telephone, and "dumb" terminals. Reliance on such diverse collection systems resulted in financial reporting that was unwieldly, prone to error, and incapable of timely responses to rapidly changing needs. Consequently, the controller commissioned the development of a new firmwide financial reporting system.

A project team was appointed that included a manager, four full-time systems analysts, and three part-time systems analysts. After investigation and analysis, the team recommended that common hardware and software units be linked to the mainframe computer by means of public telephone lines. Data would be entered via menus that were identical for all reporting units. Entered data would be uploaded to the mainframe computer; consolidated results would then be downloaded to microcomputers located in the offices of key managers.

The hardware configuration selected for each remote location consisted of an IBM PC XT, a Hayes modem, and an Epson printer. The software used to develop the input forms and output reports was Lotus 1-2-3. Upon being ordered and shipped, these hardware and software components were duly installed at the various locations. Previously designed menus, input forms, and output reports and graphs were tested. Field personnel were trained in the use of the new input systems. Documentation was also prepared and delivered to all locations. Conferences were held three times each year thereafter to evaluate the new systems and to discuss possible improvements.

[a]Bill Tomaskovic, "RCA Implements a Micro-based Corporate Financial Reporting Network," *Journal of Accounting and EDP* (Spring 1987), pp. 11–17.

Uses in Varied Business Settings

In a very small business firm a dedicated microcomputer may serve as the sole automated processing device. The office clerk may use packaged application programs to process a variety of transactions during the course of a day. At times when the clerk is not performing these transaction processing tasks, the manager might use the same microcomputer to prepare a budget or retrieve customer information.

In a very large firm a number of microcomputers (multitasking as well as dedicated) will likely be located in individual departments, sales offices, warehouses, accounting areas, and executive suites. Some may serve as **stand-alone microcomputers,** unconnected to other microcomputers. These stand-alone microcomputers are used to process data in the same manner as microcomputers in small firms. However, a large firm usually has larger computers, such as mainframe computers or minicomputers, that perform the processing tasks involving high volumes of transactions or complex computations. Often the outputs from these larger computers, or portions of the outputs, are used by one or another of the microcomputers as data for performing analyses or preparing summaries. These data from computer outputs must usually be keyed into the microcomputers. Since keying is a slow and error-prone process, an alternative means of transferring data would be highly desirable.

Many large firms have found such an alternative through the use of **micro-to-mainframe connections,** electronic links (together with special communications software) that enable data to be transferred between a microcomputer and a mainframe computer. Micro-to-mainframe connections allow data to flow either from the microcomputer to the mainframe computer (called uploading) or from the mainframe computer to the micro-computer (called downloading). Multiple micro-to-mainframe connections create a computer network; computer networks are discussed in Chapter 19.

As a member of a micro-to-mainframe connection, a microcomputer functions as a **terminal emulator.** That is, it imitates a terminal by providing a means of accepting data for transmission to the mainframe computer or receiving outputs from the mainframe computer. With appropriate software the microcomputer can serve as an intelligent terminal by also editing entered data and/or uploading entire files. A microcomputer within a computer network may alternatively serve in other roles. Thus, it may be a **workstation,** a center where processing tasks are performed. If it contains a hard disk, it may even function as a **file server,** in which role it provides application software and data files to multiple users in the network and also remains available for processing tasks (e.g., running spreadsheet applications). Microcomputers can therefore serve a variety of roles. When used appropriately within computer networks, they foster *cooperative processing,* the allocation of processing tasks so that the best capabilities of both microcomputers and the mainframe computer are employed.

Guidelines for Managing Large-Scale Microcomputer Systems

Microcomputer systems in large firms give rise to the same management problems caused by single microcomputers in very small firms. They also exhibit additional problems of a sticky nature, especially when computer networks are employed. Thus, the guidelines offered in this section pertain specifically to large-scale microcomputer systems, but they can be viewed as encompassing systems of all sizes.

A single person should be responsible for the use and management of all the micro-computers in a firm. Although the manager of a small firm can handle these responsibilities, a large firm should appoint a full-time microcomputer coordinator. This person, who might be responsible to the information systems director, would first assist in preparing a set of policies governing microcomputer use and management. If the policies are sound, they should ensure that the microcomputers are used effectively and efficiently in order to help achieve the firm's broad objectives.

Areas that should be addressed by policies include the following:

1. Limiting modifications of software by unsophisticated users.

2. Downloading files from and uploading files to a mainframe computer.

3. Sharing of applications between microcomputers and larger computers in a network.

4. Backing up microcomputer files.

5. Purchasing and using stand-alone microcomputers (i.e., those that are not directly tied into the computer network).

6. Training of microcomputer users and providing support through such services as information centers.

7. Maintaining microcomputer hardware and upgrading software.

8. Providing protection of microcomputer equipment.

9. Preventing unauthorized use of microcomputers and piracy of software.

10. Insuring security and privacy of data stored in files accessible via microcomputers.

11. Providing controls over the data handled by microcomputers.

All persons affected by microcomputers, from the users to the maintenance personnel, would be guided by detailed policies in these areas. The microcomputer coordinator would have the major responsibility for aiding those involved in implementing the policies.

Details concerning the policies will not be discussed here, since they appear elsewhere. Desirable policies with respect to networks are discussed in Chapter 19; those pertaining to the management of operational computer systems are discussed in Part V. Controls and security measures that are distinctive to microcomputer systems are surveyed in the following section.

Control and Security Framework

Problems Relating to Microcomputers

Microcomputers introduce severe control and security problems. These problems arise whether microcomputers serve as stand-alones or whether they are elements of a computer network. For instance, important data, such as a customer list, can be lost in either situation. Generally, potential breaches of security and losses of data are more serious in networks, however, since the data tend to be stored in central data bases.

One of the major problems is the physical location and accessibility of microcomputers. When placed at the desks of employees, they are often accessible by other employees. Any passing employee could use the microcomputer when the assigned employee is away from his or her desk. If the microcomputer is portable, the employee might take it home. There it could be available to his or her family. Also, the assigned employee might spill coffee or ashes on the equipment or on diskettes. Generally the microcomputer is plugged into the regular power supply. Thus, power outages or surges could cause loss of data or damage to the equipment.

A related problem is the lack of segregation of duties. Often one person performs the

functions of user, programmer, and operator. Furthermore, in a small firm one clerk may have access to all of the accounting application software packages and master files.

A third problem is an attitude of informality concerning the microcomputer. That is, employees tend to view microcomputers, especially stand-alones, as being outside the formal information system. An extreme, but not unusual, example of this attitude is reflected by the manager who brings his own microcomputer from home. This attitude is often reflected in an absence of formal change procedures and documentation pertaining to microcomputer programs. It also is seen in the lack of effective input and processing controls.

Other problems that arise when a computer network is employed are discussed in Chapter 19.

Specific Controls and Security Measures

Most of the controls and security measures needed in any computer-based system are suitable in the presence of microcomputers. Thus, our focus in this section will be on those controls and security measures that best counteract the listed problems.

Organizational and administrative controls. Management should develop policies that encourage the acquisition of standardized hardware and software. It should also specify a formal procedure for making changes to software packages; included in the procedure should be thorough testing and final approval of the changes by the key users.

Adequate segregation of duties among employees who use microcomputers should be established. All employees who are to use microcomputers should be trained *before* they are allowed to enter or access data.

Complete documentation of the hardware and software packages should be acquired from the suppliers, and thorough documentation of procedures and operating standards should be prepared. This documentation should be used in training and for general reference.

Security measures. Microcomputers should be installed in workstations or areas that are restricted to as few persons as feasible. They should be placed in locations that do not experience adverse temperatures or water leaks, and waterproof covers should be used when they are shut down. Power-surge suppressors should be installed to prevent high voltages in the power line. The delicate parts of the equipment (e.g., disk drives) should be cleaned periodically. Diskettes should be kept in protective sleeves and locked cabinets when not in use. They should also be kept away from potential electromagnetic forces (e.g., telephone ringers). Air-cleaning devices should be installed in the area where the microcomputers are located. The files and programs on all diskettes and hard disks should be indexed and copied. Backup copies of diskette and hard disk contents should be stored off-site. (The contents of a hard disk may be copied onto a cassette tape.) A disaster recovery plan should be devised concerning all microcomputers and stored data.

Access controls. Access to the data stored on hard disk in a microcomputer should be restricted in two ways: (1) by the assignment of passwords and (2) by locking the power source when the microcomputer is not in operation. Access to data stored on diskettes should be restricted by the use of a data librarian, who locks the diskettes in a cabinet and checks out the diskettes via a log. The data on diskettes may also be protected by

---

APPLICATION OF MICROCOMPUTERS
Holland Shipes Bennett Thrasher (HSBT), Certified Public Accountants[a]

HSBT is an Atlanta CPA firm that provides tax, auditing, and management advisory services to a diverse assortment of clients. It uses both a minicomputer system (IBM System 36) and a variety of microcomputers in such uses as the following:

1. Performing tax planning using spreadsheets.
2. Maintaining records concerning the firm's fixed assets.
3. Maintaining the firm's accounting records and printing monthly financial statements.
4. Projecting individual taxable incomes and cash flows.
5. Processing individual tax returns and maintaining detailed tax logs.
6. Calculating loan amortization payments and preparing schedules.
7. Entering journal entries and preparing all workpapers and trial balances and financial statements for clients.
8. Maintaining and controlling time records of auditors.
9. Applying audit sampling techniques to client data.
10. Preparing monthly bills for clients.
11. Planning assignments of staff personnel and analyzing results.
12. Preparing letters and audit reports.

[a]Thomas L. Jollay, "The Use of Computers in a Certified Public Accounting Firm: A Private Companies Practice Section Perspective," *Georgia Journal of Accounting* (Spring 1986), pp. 75–88.

the use of a security software package. This package "fingerprints" each diskette with a security code or password, which must be provided by a user. The same package can also prevent programs or data from being listed unless another password is provided. (These security features are built into certain operating systems.)

Application controls. Users should be aided in the entry of data by a menu, with easy-to-choose options. One of the options should be a help function that provides complete and clear directions concerning a processing step.

Application programs should contain a thorough set of programmed checks so that input data are adequately validated. A complete audit trail should be provided through such means as cross-references, transaction numbers, images of transactions, and before-and-after images of posted master file records. Reports and other outputs should be delivered only to specified recipients.

Summary

Microcomputers are having a tremendous impact on the business world. The impact is due to the low cost, user control, versatility, and ease of use of microcomputers. The heart of a microcomputer is a microprocessor plus the primary storage unit. The latter contains random-access, read-only, and erasable, programmable read-only memory units. Input devices include a keyboard, light pen, mouse, fingertip touch, and human voice. Outputs are provided by visual display screens and printers. Three types of available printers are the dot-matrix, daisy-wheel, and laser printers. Secondary storage generally consists of magnetic diskettes and hard disks. Packaged software is very important to the operation of microcomputers, although programming languages such as BASIC, COBOL, and PASCAL are often used by firms that develop their own application programs. A number of operating systems are employed with the various available microcomputer models, although some standardization is under way. The various types of software application packages include data base management systems, word processing systems, electronic spreadsheets, and accounting application packages for transaction processing.

In the selection of microcomputers, the software that best meets the needs of a firm should first be determined. Then microcomputers can be tested to find those on which the software performs best. Finally, features such as expandability, incorporated controls, maintenance, documentation, training, and price should be compared.

The management of a microcomputer system begins with planning and sound development. Once it becomes operational, the system should be guided by suitable policies and supervised by a microcomputer coordinator. Microcomputers may be used as stand-alones in all business settings; in computer networks they may serve as terminal emulators, workstations, or file servers.

A drawback to microcomputers is the set of control problems that they introduce, in both small-firm and network settings. The problems include easy accessibility to microcomputers, lack of segregation of data processing duties, attitudes of informality concerning microcomputers, and vulnerability of computer networks. A control framework for microcomputers should include adequate organizational segregation and administrative diligence, physical security measures, restricted access, editing of input data, and adequate audit trail.

APPENDIX TO CHAPTER 16

A Microcomputer-Based Accounting Application Package

Introduction

As noted in the chapter, microcomputer-based accounting application packages cover the spectrum of organizations, from the very smallest to multinational giants and from merchandisers to manufacturers and service-oriented firms. All packages provide certain basic features, such as posting to ledgers, checking transaction debits and credits, and generating income statements and balance sheets. However, additional features vary widely from package to package. For example, some packages contain relatively independent modules, whereas others are highly integrated. New features are being added in each new release that enters the marketplace. Recent features pertaining to user interfaces include pop-up windows, multiple layers of menus, context-sensitive on-line help, browse and search functions, artificial intelligence, and interactive tutorials. For instance, a search feature allows a user who is working in an accounts receivable module to call up a window that lists customer numbers and names. A help feature enables a user to click a mouse at an item, such as a customer name, and to obtain detail data concerning the item. A combined window and artificial intelligence feature presents a sentence broken into several windows, with options in each window; the user then selects the desired options that complete the sentence.

Space does not permit discussion of all the varieties of accounting application packages. Therefore, this appendix focuses on those packages that are integrated.

Integrated Accounting Packages

A packaged, integrated accounting system generally comprises several key subsystems, such as accounts receivable, accounts payable, purchasing, payroll, sales, inventory management, and general ledger. Each of these subsystems maintains interfaces or data links with the other subsystems, in order to ensure that query and reporting requirements are met. All of the subsystems provide flows to the general ledger, so that the general ledger accounts are posted in a reasonably direct and up-to-date manner.[6]

In reality, two levels of integration exist. At the lower level, a cross-reference file is created to facilitate interfile linkages. Figure 16-16 shows the use of a cross-reference file to enable users to post transactions to the general ledger, to retrieve detail data from ledger accounts, and to prepare reports involving ledger balances.[7] At a higher level of integration, direct links are created among the subsystems and the general ledger. In most current versions of fully integrated accounting packages, the integration is formed by means of relational data bases and the files are in reality normalized tables.[8]

---

[6]James A. Sena and Lawrence Murphy Smith, "Designing and Implementing an Integrated Job Cost Accounting System," *Journal of Information Systems* (Fall 1986), p. 103.

[7]Ibid, p. 103–104.

[8]F. E. Potter, "How to Integrate and Consolidate General Ledger Systems for Financial Control," *Journal of Accounting and EDP* (Spring 1987), pp. 4–6. Relational data bases and normalized tables are discussed in Chapter 18.

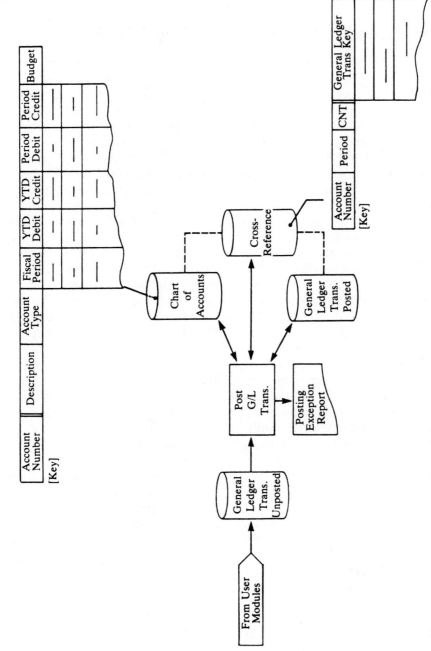

FIGURE 16-16 A cross-reference file related to the general ledger. Reprinted from the *Journal of Information Systems* with permission.

ACCPAC Plus: An Accounting Package

Overview of ACCPAC Family[9]

Computer Associates, a microcomputer products firm, has developed a family of accounting application packages. Called the ACCPAC products, this family consists of ACCPAC Easy, ACCPAC BPI, and ACCPAC Plus. ACCPAC Easy, a package designed for very small business firms, has two modules—General Accounting and U.S. Payroll. General Accounting is a fully integrated module containing the general ledger, accounts payable, and accounts receivable. The U.S. Payroll module can function alone or can be attached to the General Accounting module as a partially integrated module. ACCPAC BPI is designed for small and medium-sized business firms. The package consists of General Accounting, Accounts Receivable, Accounts Payable, U.S. Payroll, and Inventory Control modules. It allows departmental and divisional reports to be prepared. ACCPAC Plus is designed for medium-sized and large corporations. Its basic features are the focus of our concern.

Features of ACCPAC Plus

In addition to allowing departmental and divisional reporting, the ACCPAC Plus package enables intercompany consolidations to be performed. It can include part or all of the following modules: General Ledger and Financial Reporting, Accounts Receivable, Accounts Payable, Payroll, Inventory Control and Analysis, Order Entry, and Sales. The package also can incorporate special modules that pertain to specific types of business firms. For instance, a Retail Invoicing module provides a point-of-sale system for retail merchandisers; a Job Costing module provides a cost-tracking program for manufacturers, and a Time, Billing, and Client Receivables module provides service-oriented firms with the means of charging clients for time spent on their behalf. When tied to the General Ledger and Financial Reporting module, each of these modules becomes a part of a fully integrated system.

The following are recently developed features that may be incorporated within the ACCPAC Plus package:

1. A report writer that allows custom reports to be prepared from data stored in the files of any attached module.

2. A windowing system manager that allows up to 10 windows to be opened, so that as many as 10 tasks can be performed concurrently.

3. A network manager that allows users to share modules and data throughout a computerized local area network.

4. A graphics program that allows graphs of varied types (i.e., line, bar, stacked bar, pie, and exploded pie) and of three as well as two dimensions to be produced from stored information.

5. A decision support program that enables data to be transported to a spreadsheet and to be sorted and otherwise manipulated.

Other features will be noted during the following illustration.

An Illustration of ACCPAC Plus

For simplicity our illustration will be limited to the General Ledger and Financial Reporter module. However, we will refer to the Accounts Receivable module as a typical linking module.

Figure 16-17 diagrams the overall procedure involved in handling flows of data to the general ledger and reports. The first step is to

[9]This section concerning ACCPAC, including the several incorporated figures, appears with the permission of Computer Associates International, Inc.

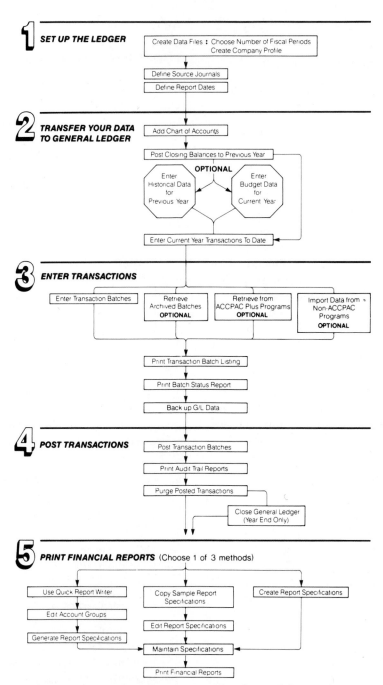

FIGURE 16-17 A procedure for handling flows of data to the general ledger.

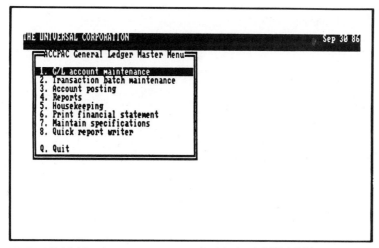

```
THE UNIVERSAL CORPORATION                                Sep 30 86
┌ACCPAC General Ledger Master Menu┐
│ 1. G/L account maintenance       │
│ 2. Transaction batch maintenance │
│ 3. Account posting               │
│ 4. Reports                       │
│ 5. Housekeeping                  │
│ 6. Print financial statement     │
│ 7. Maintain specifications       │
│ 8. Quick report writer           │
│                                  │
│ Q. Quit                          │
└──────────────────────────────────┘
```

FIGURE 16-18 A master menu used with the ACCPAC Plus accounting package.

set up the general ledger. This consists of specifying the fiscal periods, firm name, department codes, and chart of accounts (including account codes, descriptions, and account types). Then the data for the current and past years are transferred into the established account records. Budget data may also be prepared and entered. In addition, passwords can be assigned to the general ledger file.

General ledger maintenance and processing can be easily initiated by means of the master menu shown in Figure 16-18. For instance, option 1 is selected when an account is to be added or modified; option 2 is selected when transactions are to be entered; option 3 is selected when transactions are to be posted; and option 4 or 6 is selected when reports are needed. The last three options are described in the following paragraphs.

Entering transactions. Assume that the batch of transactions listed in Figure 16-19 is to be entered. The first step is to select option 2 (Transaction batch maintenance) from the master menu. Then select the "Enter/edit batch" option from the next appearing

menu. The screen input form shown in Figure 16-20 appears. The next step is to enter each transaction in turn, including the fiscal period, source code, and so forth. After all transactions of the batch have been entered, return to the master menu and select option 2 again. Then select the "Print batch" option. The entered batch of transactions is printed; it should clearly show any input errors, such as a transposition in a debit amount. To correct any discovered errors, select the "Enter/edit batch" again and reenter the incorrect items. Finally, print the Edit list and verify that all errors have been corrected and the batch totals are in balance.

Transactions do not need to be entered in batches. Transactions may be entered singly in an on-line manner.

Posting transaction batches. To post a verified batch of transactions, select option 3 (Account posting) from the master menu and then option 1 (Post general ledger) from the second-level menu that appears. The posting program displays the batch and transaction number as each transaction is posted. When subsidiary ledgers are maintained, such as

TRANSACTION REGISTER
Form GL 4

COMPANY: Universal Corp.
BATCH NO: 32 PAGE NUMBER: 1 OF 1

PERIOD	SOURCE	DATE MMDDYY	REF	DESCRIPTION	G/L ACC. CODE	DEPT. CODE	DEBIT	CREDIT
3	2	090386	JE69	XYZ SUPPLIES CK#593	752		57153.28	
3	2	090486	JE69	XYZ SUPPLIES CK#593	754			1143.06
3	2	090686		STANDARD GAS CK#594	815		2186.24	
3	2	091586	JE69	PRS SEPT REPORT CK#595	915		586.57	
3	2	091586	JE69	SEPT RENT CK#596	920		4295.00	
3	2	091786	JE69	STAPLER/SHRINKWRAP #597	945		693.21	
3	2	091786	JE69	PAPER/ENVELOPES CK#597	955		240.00	
3	2	093086	JE69	SEPT CKS #593 to 597	104			64020.24

BATCH TOTALS – Enter on transmittal ➔ 65163.30 65163.30

FIGURE 16-19 A batch of transactions for entry via ACCPAC Plus.

the accounts receivable ledger, the transactions are posted to both the subsidiary ledger and the general ledger.

The Account posting menu also provides such options as Close general ledger and Special posting (of transactions for the previous year).

Generating reports. After all the transaction batches for a day or period have been posted, various reports are normally printed. Selecting option 4 (Reports) from the master menu produces a menu that includes such options as Trial balance, G/L listing, and Source journals (among others). Selecting each of these listed options provides a report that facilitates the audit trail. The trial balance shows the balances of all general ledger accounts and aids in verifying that total debits equal total credits. The general ledger

```
THE UNIVERSAL CORPORATION                                   Date: Sep 30 86
Enter/Edit Batch of Transactions

     Batch Number [32 ] has      Transactions.
     ---------------------------------------------------------------

      Transaction Number [    ]

      Period       [ ]
      Source       [ ]
      Date         [ / / ]
      Reference    [      ]
      Description  [                    ]

      Account      [      ] Dept.[     ]
      Amount    Dr.[              ]     Cr.[              ]


Press ESCAPE to exit.
```

FIGURE 16-20 A screen form for entering batches of transactions via ACCPAC Plus.

```
THE UNIVERSAL CORPORATION                            Date: Sep 30 86
Create Report Specification

Please select from the following specifications:

    Balance Sheet                                            [N] Y/N
    Comparative Balance Sheet    (Current Year, Last Year)   [N] Y/N
    Comparative Balance Sheet    (Current Month, Last Month) [N] Y/N
    Income Statement                                         [N] Y/N
    Comparative Income Statement (Current Year, Last Year)   [N] Y/N
    Comparative Income Statement (Current Year, Budget)      [N] Y/N




    Press ESCAPE when entry complete.
```

FIGURE 16-21 A screen form that aids in creating reports via AC-CPAC Plus.

listing shows the details pertaining to all general ledger accounts and hence is the most important audit trail report. The source journal report shows the details of transactions entered into any specified journal (e.g., the accounts receivable journal).

To print financial statements, select option 6 (Print financial statement) or option 8 (Quick report writer) from the master menu. If the former is selected, specifications must previously have been designed and entered into the system. Then a wide variety of reports and schedules may be printed. If the latter is selected, the screen shown in Figure 16-21 appears. Then any of the reports listed in the figure may be printed. For instance, Figure 16-22 shows the initial portion of the balance sheet that is printed when Y is answered to the third option.

Comparison of Accounting Application Packages

As already noted, accounting application packages have differing features and capabilities. Packages designed for medium and large firms tend to have significantly more and stronger capabilities than packages for small firms. This statement can be supported by comparing ACCPAC Plus with a package such as Dac-Easy (from Dac Software, Inc.) or New Views (from Q. W. Page Associates, Inc.).

ACCPAC Plus exhibits the following added capabilities:

1. A greater variety of reports can be provided, including ad hoc reports that can be formatted by powerful report-writer software.

2. Consolidations of data from multiple divisions or subsidiaries can be performed.

3. Data can be easily transported to the control of other software packages, such as spreadsheets and relational data base management systems.

4. A variety of audit trail reports are provided, including source journals and general ledger listings. These reports aid in correcting data entry errors and must be printed for review before posting can occur. (In New Views the transactions are posted directly to the ledgers as entered,

```
                    THE UNIVERSAL CORPORATION
                         Balance Sheet
                       September 30, 1986

                            ASSETS
                            ......

                                        Curr. Mo.    Prev. Mo.
                                        .........    .........

    Current assets:
      Cash                                 12,906       13,874
      Accounts receivable                 503,852      514,882
      Inventory                           247,601      259,814
      Prepaid expenses                     11,737       12,968
      Investments                          98,000       98,000
                                         .........    .........
      Total current assets                874,096      899,538

    Fixed assets, at cost less depreciation:
      Land                                 65,000       65,000
      Buildings                           411,329      411,329
      Leasehold improvements                3,785        3,785
      Furniture & fixtures                 24,717       20,096
      Machinery & equipment               181,845      191,345
                                         .........    .........
                                          686,676      691,555
      Less accumulated depreciation       169,226      169,801
                                         .........    .........
                                          517,450      521,754
                                         .........    .........
                                        1,391,546    1,421,292
                                        =========    =========
```

FIGURE 16-22 A portion of the balance sheet printed via the use of the screen shown in Figure 16-21.

and no journals are maintained. Although this approach has the virtues of being simpler and faster, it can allow errors to be posted.)

5. Thorough edit checks, balance checks, and other controls are employed.

6. A greater quantity of data concerning past transactions can be stored and used for reference and for analysis.

7. Extensive documentation and user aids—including substantial manuals, on-line helps, and hierarchical menus—are available.

These added features and capabilities justify the added cost of a package such as ACCPAC Plus to many firms. On the other hand, it should be noted that packages such as Dac-Easy and New Views are quite inexpensive and very user friendly; they represent good investments for small firms.

Review Problems with Solutions

Computers Aplenty, Inc.
Problem 1 Statement

Computers Aplenty, Inc. (CAI), is a recently established computer retail store. It merchandises and services four makes of microcomputers and related components such as terminals, printers, magnetic tape casettes, and diskettes. It also carries a variety of business application software packages. Currently the store is managed by its owner, Jay Sparks, and employs 12 sales and service personnel.

Jay has high hopes that the store will grow rapidly in revenues and that more stores will be established. He recognizes the importance of an efficient and effective accounting information system (AIS) in achieving these hopes. Thus, he decides to utilize a microcomputer from his stock as the heart of the system. With the aid of a microcomputer he believes that the various transactions will be processed promptly, the files can be kept up to date, and needed information may be easily and quickly retrieved.

Required

a. Draw and label a hardware configuration diagram that reflects a suitable microcomputer system for CAI.

b. List several applications that would be suitable for CAI's microcomputer system.

c. Briefly describe software that would be suitable for use by CAI's microcomputer system.

d. Assume that CAI does grow rapidly so that two additional stores are established and a total of 50 employees comprise the work force. Discuss alternative ways in which the microcomputer system described in **a** might feasibly be augmented or replaced to accommodate this growth.

Solution

a. A suitable microcomputer system hardware configuration would likely consist of a microcomputer, plus a nonremovable hard disk drive, one diskette drive, a cassette tape drive, one video display terminal, and one printer. A labeled configuration diagram appears as follows.

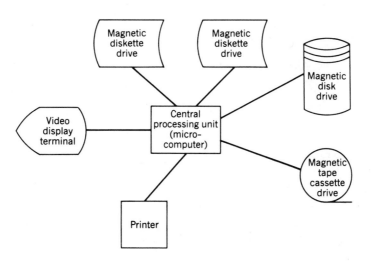

b. Applications that would be suitable for the microcomputer system include

    (1) General ledger accounting.

    (2) Accounts payable processing.

    (3) Accounts receivable processing.

    (4) Cash disbursements processing.

    (5) Cash receipts processing.

    (6) Payroll processing.

    (7) Service order processing.

    (8) Inventory record keeping and control.

    (9) Sales analysis and forecasting.

    (10) Cash forecasting and management.

    (11) Budgetary planning and control.

    (12) Capital investment analysis.

c. Software that would be suitable for the microcomputer system includes

    (1) An operating system.

    (2) Utility programs, such as text editors and directories.

    (3) Compilers for BASIC and COBOL.

    (4) An integrated package that includes an electronic spreadsheet, data manager, and word processor.

    (5) Application packages for general ledger accounting and the remaining applications listed under **b.**

d. When CAI consists of three stores and 50 employees, a single microcomputer system is not sufficient. Alternative systems that might be considered include

    (1) Separate microcomputer systems for each store.

    (2) A minicomputer system located at the main store, with terminals located at the other stores and tied by communications lines to the minicomputer.

    (3) A multitasking microcomputer system located at the main store, with terminals located at the other stores

and tied by communications lines to the supermicrocomputer.

    (4) A microcomputer at the main store, accompanied by the utilization of a commercial computer service bureau or time-sharing service.

Wu & Wright, CPAs

Problem 2 Statement[10]

The firm of Wu & Wright, CPAs, has just acquired an electronic spreadsheet package for use on its microcomputer. As their first application the partners decide to prepare an income statement template to enter data of a client firm into the income statement and to determine the effects on net income due to changes in certain factors.

They begin by inserting the diskette containing the spreadsheet package into disk drive A and turning on the computer. After obtaining the logo of the package, they strike the indicated key and obtain the control panel. This panel displays the rows and columns of the worksheet. (To be more precise, it displays a "window"—the first few rows and columns of the complete worksheet, plus a menu of commands.)

Then with the aid of the electronic spreadsheet manual and the menu, they develop the template shown at the bottom of page 757 for an income statement

Documentation for Template

a. Amounts indicated by .... are to be entered by user.

b. Amounts indicated by 0 are to be calculated by formulas that have been stored in

[10]This problem is adapted from an application in Frederick H. Wu, "Teaching Managerial (Cost) Accounting with Electronic Spreadsheet Software," published in *Issues in Accounting Education, 1984* (Sarasota, Fla.: American Accounting Association, 1984). Used with permission.

the memory of the spreadsheet software package.

c. The stored formulas are

(1) Cost of goods available for sale = beginning finished goods + cost of goods manufactured. (The formulas for this and the following relationships are expressed by the software in terms of cells—e.g., C12 is C9 + C10.)

(2) Cost of goods sold = cost of goods available for sale − ending finished goods.

(3) Gross margin = sales − cost of goods sold.

(4) Selling and administrative expenses = sales commissions + sales salaries + shipping expenses + administrative expenses.

(5) Net income = gross margin − selling and administrative expenses.

(6) Sales commissions = .05 × sales.

(7) Shipping expenses = $\frac{1}{30}$ × sales.

Required

a. Show the output that the software package would provide when the user entered the PRINT command, assuming that the following data were entered into the template just prior to the command: ABC Company; 1990; 1,200,000 (sales); 100,000 (beginning finished goods); 900,000 (cost of goods manufactured); 150,000 (ending finished goods); 100,000 (sales salaries); 100,000 (administrative expenses).

b. Show the bottom line of the income statement when the PRINT command is entered, assuming that the user changes the sales amount in the template to 2,000,000.

Template No. 1: Income Statement

Income Statement
For the Year Ended Dec. 31, ...

Sales		$.......
Less cost of goods sold:		
Finished goods, Jan. 1	$.......	
Cost of goods manufactured	....	
Cost of goods available for sale	$ 0	
Finished goods, Dec. 31	....	
Cost of goods sold		0
Gross margin		$ 0
Less selling and admin. expenses:		
Sales commissions	$ 0	
Sales salaries	....	
Shipping expenses	0	
Administrative expenses	....	
Net income		$ 0

Solution

a.

ABC Company
Income Statement
For the Year Ended Dec. 31, 1990

Sales		$1,200,000
Less cost of goods sold:		
Finished goods, Jan. 1	$ 100,000	
Cost of goods manufactured	900,000	
Cost of goods available for sale	$1,000,000	
Finished goods, Dec. 31	150,000	
Cost of goods sold		850,000
Gross margin		$350,000
Less selling and admin. expenses:		
Sales commissions	$ 60,000	
Sales salaries	100,000	
Shipping expenses	40,000	
Administrative expenses	100,000	300,000
Net income		$ 50,000

---

b. The bottom line that appears in the income statement as a result of a change of sales from $1,200,000 to $2,100,000 is

Net income $875,000

Review Questions

16-1 What is the meaning of each of the following terms?

Portable computer
Liquid crystal display (LCD)
Dedicated microcomputer
Multitasking microcomputer
Operator-oriented microcomputer system
File-oriented microcomputer system
Microprocessor
Coprocessor
Motherboard
Serial port
Parallel port
Erasable, programmable read-only memory (EPROM)
Mouse
Joystick
Light pen
Optical scanner
Voice-input device
Touch-input device
Dot-matrix printer
Daisy-wheel printer
Laser printer
Diskette
Hard disk
Winchester drive
Hard disk card
Bernoulli box
Tape cassette
Tape cartridge
CD ROM (compact disk read-only memory)
Modem
Accounting application package
Electronic spreadsheet
Template
Financial modeling software package
Data base management system
Word processing
Desktop publishing package
Window
Graphics system
Presentation graphics
Freehand graphics

Time-management package
Electronic calendar
Electronic mail
Voice mail
Videotex
Decision support and expert system
Integrated software package
Stand-alone microcomputer
Micro-to-mainframe connection
Terminal emulator
Workstation
File server

16-2 What are the major benefits of microcomputers?

16-3 In what ways may microcomputers be classified?

16-4 Describe the construction of a microprocessor.

16-5 What devices may be attached to a motherboard?

16-6 Contrast three types of memory used in microcomputers.

16-7 Identify several devices by which data may be entered into a microcomputer system.

16-8 Contrast the three types of printers used with microcomputers.

16-9 Describe the various types of secondary storage media for microcomputers.

16-10 Why have microcomputers led to a dramatic increase in software packages?

16-11 What programming languages are most commonly employed in microcomputer systems?

16-12 Describe the functions of an operating system in a microcomputer and how it is used to initialize operations.

16-13 Identify several utility programs provided by a current operating system.

16-14 Describe the desirable features of an accounting application package.

16-15 Describe several attributes of electronic spreadsheet packages.

16-16 What factors should be considered when selecting an electronic spreadsheet package?

16-17 In what ways are financial modeling software packages superior to electronic spreadsheet packages?

16-18 Describe several typical capabilities of data base management system software packages for microcomputers.

16-19 What factors should be considered when selecting a data base management system software package?

16-20 List several features available in a typical word processing system.

16-21 Identify several features that add value to a desktop publishing system.

16-22 Contrast two types of graphics packages.

16-23 What are the advantage and the disadvantage of an integrated software package?

16-24 What selection criteria should be applied by a firm that has decided to install a microcomputer?

16-25 In what ways might microcomputers be used in small and large business settings?

16-26 What areas should be addressed by policies pertaining to the management of operational microcomputer systems?

16-27 What are the major control and security problems that arise when microcomputers are used in business settings?

16-28 Identify a variety of controls and security measures that can largely overcome the foregoing problems.

Discussion Questions

16-29 In what ways does the electronic spreadsheet represent an improvement over the manual spreadsheet?

16-30 Discuss the advantages and disadvantages to a small firm of acquiring packaged software rather than writing its own application programs.

16-31 What sources might a small business owner draw on in deciding (a) whether or not to acquire a microcomputer and (b) which model would be best for her firm?

16-32 How are microcomputers likely to appear in 1995 and in what new ways might they be used then?

Problems

16-1 Microcomputers are widely used by a variety of firms. Identify several uses of microcomputers by the following types of firms. Be as specific as possible.

    a. Full-service bank that handles deposits, makes loans, and manages trusts.

    b. Engineering and construction firm that designs office buildings and various other projects for businesses and government organizations.

    c. Motorcycle chain that sells and services motorcycles and related two-wheel motorized vehicles.

    d. Full-service brokerage firm that handles investment and margin trades, performs investment research, and manages portfolios.

    e. University that performs teaching, research, and administration.

16-2 Microcomputers are widely used in public accounting firms. For instance, tax specialists use them to assist in preparing tax returns and in tax planning. Describe several specific problems encountered by management advisory services (MAS) consultants in which microcomputers may be of assistance.

 16-3 Co-op Sales of Dayton, Ohio, was established on June 1. Merchandise will be sold on credit, with payment due in 15 days. Inventory will be recorded by the periodic inventory method. The accounting records will consist of a general journal, sales journal, purchases journal, cash receipts journal, check register, general ledger, accounts receivable subsidiary ledger, and accounts payable subsidiary ledger. Within the general ledger will be the following accounts: Cash, Accounts Receivable, Merchandise Inventory, Supplies, Prepaid Expenses, Furniture and Fixtures, Accumulated Depreciation—Furniture and Fixtures, Accounts Payable, Notes Payable, Accrued Expenses Payable, FICA Taxes Payable, Income Taxes Payable, Capital Stock, Retained Earnings, Sales, Purchases, Purchase Discounts, Cost of Goods Sold, Salaries Expense, Depreciation Expense, Utilities Expense, Supplies Used, Rent Expense, Taxes Expense, Interest Expense, and Miscellaneous Expense.

Co-op's June transactions are

June 1 Capital stock is issued and sold for $50,000.

    1 Rent on a building for a year is paid in advance to the Monoco Realty Co., $2400. (Check number 1 is issued.)

    1 Furniture and fixtures are acquired in exchange for a 60-day, 15 percent note in the amount of $16,000.

    2 Merchandise inventory is acquired on 2/10, net/30 terms from Tenny's Wares; invoice 283 shows an amount payable of $8000.

    3 Supplies amounting to $800 are bought for cash from Vicor's Supply House. (Check number 2.)

4 Merchandise is sold to Loman's Outlet on invoice number S1, $1200.

5 Merchandise is purchased on 2/10, net 30 terms from Simon Manufacturing; invoice 101 shows an amount payable of $4500.

8 Bill is received from the city for building inspection, $50.

9 Merchandise is sold to Rustic Retailer, $2800. (Invoice number S2.)

10 Bill is received from the Bugle News for advertising, $220.

11 Check number 3 is mailed to Tenny's Wares for amount due.

12 Merchandise is sold to Sam's Stores, $4200. (Invoice number S3.)

15 Salaries are paid for the first half of June, $1600, less income taxes withheld of $240 and FICA taxes withheld of $110. (The payroll transaction is entered in the general journal, since special checks are issued to the employees. Normally a payroll register would support a payroll transaction, but it is omitted here to avoid excessive details.)

18 Remittance is received from Loman's Outlet for amount owed. (Remittance advice number R1 is prepared.)

19 Checks numbers 4 and 5 are mailed to the city and the newspaper for bills owed.

22 Merchandise is sold to Loman's Outlet, $3600. (Invoice number S4.)

24 Remittance is received from Rustic Retailer in the amount of $1000. (Remittance number R2.)

26 Merchandise is sold to Polly's Parlors, $1900. (Invoice number S5.)

29 Bill is received for utilities, $300.

30 Salaries are paid for the second half of June, $1600, less income taxes withheld of $240 and FICA taxes withheld of $110.

30 Adjustments are made based on the following:
   a. The ending merchandise inventory amounts to $3800. (The adjusting entry should involve debits to the Merchandise Inventory, Cost of Goods Sold, and Purchase Discounts accounts, with an offsetting credit to the Purchases account.)
   b. The interest on the note payable has accrued for one month.
   c. One month's prepaid rent has expired.
   d. The depreciation rate on furniture and fixtures is 12 percent per year, and the depreciation method to be used is straight-line.
   e. The amount of unused supplies at the end of the month is $200.
   f. The employers' contribution to payroll taxes must match the amount of the employees' contribution to FICA taxes.
   g. The losses resulting from

bad debts are estimated to be 2 percent of the balance of Accounts Receivable at the end of the month.

Required

Access the general ledger program (general accounting system package) via your school's microcomputer system, in accordance with directions provided by your instructor. Then perform the following:

a. Enter the listed accounts into the chart of accounts and assign numeric codes to the accounts.

b. Set up accounts receivable and accounts payable subsidiary ledgers.

c. Set up, or verify the availability of, a general journal, sales journal, invoice register (or purchases journal), and check register (or cash disbursements journal).

d. Enter all transactions listed, including the adjusting journal entries, into the appropriate journals and post the entries. Remember that all transactions that cannot be fitted into a special journal may be entered into the general journal.

e. Print an adjusted trial balance, income statement, and balance sheet.

f. Print all journals, ledgers, and schedules that the available general accounting system package will allow.

16-4   Refer to Review Problem 2.[11]

The partners of Wu & Wright, CPAs, decide to add supporting detail to their first spreadsheet application. A schedule of cost of goods manufactured is a

logical choice, since it provides supporting detail to a key line in the income statement. In the process of developing this schedule they list the following formulas:

a. Cost of direct materials available = beginning inventory + cost of purchases.

b. Direct materials used = cost of direct materials available for use − ending inventory.

c. Total indirect manufacturing costs = SUM (i.e., the sum of costs beginning with sandpaper and ending with fire insurance on equipment).

d. Manufacturing costs during the year = direct materials + direct labor + indirect manufacturing costs.

e. Manufacturing costs to account for = manufacturing costs during the year + beginning work in process.

f. Cost of goods manufactured = manufacturing costs to account for − ending work in process.

Required

a. Prepare a template for the schedule of cost of goods manufactured. Use the same conventions as in the Review Problem to indicate amounts to be entered and calculated.

b. Enter the following data into the template: ABC Company; 1988; 40,000 (beginning inventory); 400,000 (purchases); 50,000 (ending inventory); 300,000 (direct labor costs); 2000 (cost of sandpaper); 5000 (cost of lubricants and coolants); 40,000 (cost of materials handling); 20,000 (cost of overtime premium); 10,000 (cost of idle time); 40,000 (cost of indirect labor; 50,000 (cost of factory rent); 40,000 (cost of depreciation on equipment); 4000

---

[11]This problem is adapted from an application in Frederick H. Wu, "Teaching Managerial (Cost) Accounting with Electronic Spreadsheet Software," published in *Issues in Accounting Education, 1984* (Sarasota, Fla.: American Accounting Association, 1984). Used with permission.

(cost of property taxes); 3000 (cost of fire insurance on equipment); 10,000 (beginning work in process); and 14,000 (ending work in process). Print the schedule of cost of goods manufactured based on this data.

c. Change the amount of purchases from $400,000 to $600,000 and the amount of idle time from $10,000 to $30,000; print the resulting schedule of cost of goods manufactured and the income statement.

d. Change the beginning work in process from $10,000 to $0 and the ending work in process from $14,000 to $50,000; return all other amounts to those shown in **b**; print the resulting schedule of cost of goods manufactured and the income statement.

Note: In designing the template for this problem, be sure it is linked to the income statement in the same file. Otherwise, the changes in the cost of goods manufactured schedule will not be reflected in the income statement.

 16-5 The Wonderful Widget Co. has just completed its budget process for the coming year. On page 764 appears the resulting projection of operations and cash flow. A list of assumptions on which the projection was prepared appears on page 765.

Required

Access the electronic spreadsheet package available on your school's microcomputer system, in accordance with your instructor's directions. Then perform the following:

a. Set up the format for the projection shown on page 764, enter the relevant formulas based on the assumptions, then enter the estimated sales amount for January of 1000 (i.e., $1,000,000), and specify that the CALCULATE function be per-

formed. If all your formulas are correct, the display on your screen should appear exactly as the projection on page 764.

b. Print the projection of operations and cash flow.

c. Increase the estimated sales amount for January by 20 percent and calculate the remainder of the projected amounts; print the projection.

d. Reflect the following changes in assumptions: Materials cost 20 percent of sales, income taxes average 38 percent of net income from operations, the increase in accounts receivable equals the increase in sales for the month, the inventories remain the same from month to month, and the increase in accounts payable equals twice the increase in materials and marketing and administration expenses for the month.

e. Reenter an estimated sales amount for January of 1000, recalculate all amounts on the basis of these changed assumptions, and print the projection.

f. On the basis of the changed assumptions in **d**, view a pie chart that shows the proportions of cost of sales, total expenses, and income taxes for the year; prepare a hard copy of the chart on a plotter.

g. View a bar chart of the sales amounts for the 12 months of the year; prepare a hard copy of the chart on a plotter.

h. View a stacked bar chart of the net income after taxes and the gross profit for the 12 months of the year; prepare a hard copy of the chart on a plotter.

i. View a line graph of three types of operating expenses for the 12 months of the year; prepare a hard copy of the graph on a plotter.

j. View an *X–Y* graph of net sales versus gross profit; prepare a hard copy of the graph on a plotter.

WONDERFUL WIDGET CO.
PROJECTION OF OPERATIONS AND CASH FLOW
FOR THE YEAR 199X
(THOUSANDS OF DOLLARS)

	JAN.	FEB.	MAR.	APR.	MAY	JUNE	JUL.	AUG.	SEP.	OCT.	NOV.	DEC.	TOTAL FOR YEAR
SALES, NET	1000	1020	1040	1061	1082	1104	1126	1149	1172	1195	1219	1243	13412
COST OF SALES													
MATERIALS	250	255	260	265	271	276	282	287	293	299	305	311	3353
DIRECT LABOR	250	255	260	265	271	276	282	287	293	299	305	311	3353
FACTORY OVERHEAD	200	204	208	212	216	221	225	230	234	239	244	249	2682
TOTAL	700	714	728	743	758	773	788	804	820	837	853	870	9388
GROSS PROFIT	300	306	312	318	325	331	338	345	351	359	366	373	4024
EXPENSES													
MARKETING	100	102	104	106	108	110	113	115	117	120	122	124	1341
ADMINISTRATION	80	82	83	85	87	88	90	92	94	96	98	99	1073
INTEREST	20	20	21	21	22	22	23	23	23	24	24	25	268
TOTAL	200	204	208	212	216	221	225	230	234	239	244	249	2682
NET INCOME FROM OPERATIONS	100	102	104	106	108	110	113	115	117	120	122	124	1341
INCOME TAXES	50	51	52	53	54	55	56	57	59	60	61	62	671
NET INCOME	50	51	52	53	54	55	56	57	59	60	61	62	671
ADJUSTMENTS FOR CASH FLOW													
ACCOUNTS RECEIVABLE	0	-40	-41	-42	-42	-43	-44	-45	-46	-47	-48	-49	-487
INVENTORIES	0	-42	-43	-44	-45	-45	-46	-47	-48	-49	-50	-51	-511
ACCOUNTS PAYABLE	0	4	4	4	5	5	5	5	5	5	5	5	52
INCOME TAXES	0	0	0	0	0	0	0	0	0	0	0	0	0
NET ADJUSTMENTS	0	-78	-79	-81	-82	-84	-86	-88	-89	-91	-93	-95	-946
CASH FLOW FOR MONTH	50	-27	-27	-28	-28	-29	-29	-30	-31	-32	-32	-33	N/A
CUMULATIVE CASH FLOW	50	23	-4	-32	-60	-89	-118	-148	-179	-210	-242	-275	-275

*Assumptions for Projection of Operations
and Cash Flow*

(a) Net sales the first month are $1,000,000 and increase at the compound rate of 2 percent per month.

(b) Materials cost 25 percent of sales.

(c) Direct labor costs 25 percent of sales.

(d) Factory overhead is 80 percent of direct labor.

(e) Marketing expenses are 10 percent of sales.

(f) Administration expenses total 8 percent of sales.

(g) Interest averages 2 percent of sales.

(h) Income taxes average 50 percent of net income from operations.

(i) Cash flow is reduced by the increases in accounts receivable which equals two times the increase in sales for the month.

(j) Cash flow is reduced by the increase in inventories which equals three times the increase in cost of sales for the month.

(k) Cash flow is increased by the increase in accounts payable, which equals one-half the increase in materials and marketing and administration expenses for the month.

(l) Income tax payments will not differ significantly from the accrual, so no adjustment is necessary.

(m) No adjustments have been made for depreciation (a noncash expense) or equipment purchase (a cash requirement but not an expense) because it is assumed that they will be approximately equal during the year.

(n) Amounts having decimal remainders are rounded up.

 16-6 Smallshot & Sons, a small merchandising firm in Dubuque, Iowa, has just acquired a microcomputer and a financial modeling software package. The accountant decides to use the package to assist her in cash budgeting and planning. Using an analysis of past trends, she develops the following relationships:

a. Of monthly sales, 20 percent are for cash and 80 percent on credit.

b. Credit sales are collected over the following three months in the percentages of 10, 70, and 19, respectively. One percent of sales results in bad debts.

c. Beginning inventory each month has a value of $6000 plus 25 percent of budgeted sales (at cost) for the month.

d. Gross margin is equal to 40 percent of sales.

e. Of the inventory purchased each month, one-half is paid for in that month and one-half in the following month.

f. Dividends of $1500 are declared each quarter and paid in the last month of the quarter.

g. Operating expenses are equal to 40 percent of the gross margin each month plus $3210. Of these expenses, $1100 represents depreciation.

h. Miscellaneous expenses in addition to the foregoing operating expenses occur from time to time, but cannot be estimated by a formula.

i. A minimum cash balance of $6000 is required. If the projected balance is less than $6000, an amount must be borrowed to raise the balance to that level.

j. Interest on borrowed funds is charged at the rate of $1\frac{1}{2}$ percent per month. Borrowing occurs at the beginning of a month, and funds are repaid at the end of each month in which a balance in excess of $6000 is outstanding.

The budgeted time period is three months, and the forecasted sales amounts are separately estimated. Cash budgets are prepared for each *month* within the budgeted time period.

Required

a. Prepare templates for the schedule of cash collections from sales, the schedule of cash payments for merchandise purchases, the cash budget that includes these schedules, and the schedule of financing arrangements. Use a format for the cash budget that has beginning cash balance as the first line and ending cash balance as the final line. Include the formulas that reflect the relationships. (Note that IF–THEN statements are needed to express at least one relationship.)

b. Show the output that the software package would provide when the accountant entered the PRINT command, assuming that the following data were entered into the template just prior to the command: Smallshot & Sons; 1990; July; August; September; 18,000 (actual sales, April); 15,000 (actual sales, May); 16,000 (actual sales, June); 18,000 (budgeted sales, July); 24,000 (budgeted sales, August); 22,000 (budgeted sales, September); 4900 (cost of machinery overhaul, August); 6260 (beginning cash balance, July 1).

c. Show the bottom lines of the cash budget and the schedules if the sales in August were budgeted $2000 higher and the sales in September were budgeted $2000 lower.

16-7 The Gripper Brake Company is a small New Orleans manufacturer of brakes, brake linings, and other parts of braking systems. It sells approximately 100 different sizes and varieties of brake products to garages and retail outlets of motor vehicle products in 10 states. With a work force of 30 employees and three managers, Gripper generated sales revenues last year of $8 million.

Moreover, John Hartley, the owner and top manager of Gripper, foresees rapid growth in sales during the coming years.

Mr. Hartley, however, has become aware that the firm is already suffering growing pains. For instance, it is having difficulty in processing the increasing number of sales orders and in delivering orders to customers by promised dates. When customers inquire about the status of their orders, clerks often must spend hours tracking down the answers. Critical parts and materials needed in manufacturing ordered products are frequently out of stock. Losses from bad debts have been increasing at an alarming rate.

These problems lead Mr. Hartley to seek help from Jeff Harris, the firm's public accountant. After a careful investigation Jeff recommends that the firm acquire its own computer system. Upon agreement from Mr. Hartley, he investigates further and proposes three alternatives: (a) a minicomputer system, (b) a multitasking microcomputer system, and (c) three separate dedicated microcomputers.

Required

a. Describe the hardware components that appear to be suitable for each of the foregoing alternative computer systems and draw a hardware configuration diagram for each.

b. Contrast the benefits to Gripper of the three alternative computer systems.

c. List the types of software that should be acquired by Gripper, regardless of the alternative selected.

d. After installing the selected computer system, Gripper acquires software applications packages that perform general ledger accounting and that process sales orders. Briefly describe other software application packages that would aid Gripper in solving its current and future problems.

e. Assume that dedicated microcomputers having hard disks and single diskette drives are selected. Describe specific uses of diskettes and a hard disk with respect to data entry and storage for the inventory application. If a tape cartridge is included, what specific use would it have?

16-8 Prepare a comparative listing of several specific spreadsheet software packages and data base management system software packages that are currently available. Include for each package its major capabilities and features, as well as its current list price.

Hint: Refer to microcomputer journals such as *Byte Magazine* and *PC Week* and to such reports as those provided by *Datapro Research Corporation.*

16-9 On a monthly basis, a planning analyst computes several profitability indexes for the company's divisions and product lines. For the last six months, the analyst has used a microcomputer spreadsheet program for this purpose, manually entering data into the spreadsheet from printed listings of financial data. To improve the accuracy and decrease the preparation time of the indexes, the analyst suggested a micro-to-mainframe link (MML) for obtaining financial report data from the financial reporting data base system. The data base is maintained on the mainframe computer at the company's headquarters. The planning analyst works at a regional headquarters location in another city.

Required

For the MML application described, explain considerations for selecting, designing, implementing, and using

a. Hardware.

b. Software.

c. Controls.

Note: This problem cannot be fully answered until computer networks in Chapter 19 are covered. However, it may be discussed in this chapter to anticipate the network setting.

(CIA adapted)

Suggested Readings

Backes, Robert W., and Glowacki, Robert J. "Microcomputers: Successful Management and Control," *Management Accounting* (September 1983), pp. 48–51.

Bagranoff, Nancy. "Database Management Systems: Getting the Most from Your Database." *The Journal of Accountancy* (May 1988), pp. 122–128.

Borthick, A. Faye. "Good Software Choices Don't Just Happen." *CMA Magazine* (November 1988), pp. 48–52.

Bryan, Marvin. "Shopping for a PC DBMS." *Datamation* (March 15, 1989), pp. 25–35.

Callis, Melinda, and Skolnik, Sheryl. "Establishing and Controlling the Micro-Mainframe Link." *Journal of Accounting and EDP* (Summer 1985), pp. 4–13.

Chorney, Victor J. "Data Base Programs as Tools for Better Management." *Journal of Accounting and EDP* (Summer 1988), pp. 31–42.

Coon, Jennifer L. "Documenting Microcomputer Systems." *EDPACS* (October 1983), pp. 1–8.

Cummings, Steve, and Cummings, Marshall. "Financial Modeling: A Powerful Alternative." *PC Week* (April 3, 1989), pp. 97–100.

Dascher, Paul E., and Harmon, W. Ken. "The Dark Side of Small Business Computers." *Management Accounting* (May 1984), pp. 62–67.

"Desktop Publishing." *Supplement to PC Week* (August 21, 1989), pp. S/1–S/26.

Edwards, Chris. "Developing Microcomputer-Based Business Systems." *Journal of Systems Management* (April 1983), pp. 36–38.

Freeland, James R. "Can a Personal Computer Really Help You?" *Business Horizons* (Jan.–Feb. 1983), pp. 56–63.

Harper, Robert M., Jr. "Internal Control of Microcomputers in Local Area Networks." *Journal of Information Systems*. (Fall 1986), pp. 67–79.

Hurtado-Sanchez, Luis, and Horowitz, Robert J. "Developing and Implementing an Effective PC Policy." *Journal of Accounting and EDP* (Summer 1986), pp. 19–26.

Kahn, Beverly R., and Garceau, Linda R. "Controlling the Microcomputer Environment." *Journal of Systems Management* (May 1984), pp. 14–19.

Kliem, Ralph L. "Disaster Prevention and Recovery for Microcomputers." *Journal of Systems Management* (March 1984), pp. 28–29.

Leavitt, Don. "Integrated Software Tools for Today." *Datamation* (July 1, 1987), pp. 48–52.

Lees, John D., and Lees, Donna D. "Realities of Small Business Information System Implementation." *Journal of Systems Management* (Jan. 1987), pp. 6–13.

MacNichols, Charles, and Clark, Thomas. *Microcomputer-Based Information and Decision Support Systems for Small Businesses*. Reston, Va.: Reston Publishing, 1983.

Maher, John J., and Hicks, James O. "Computer Viruses: Controller's Nightmare." *Management Accounting* (October 1989), pp. 44–49.

Major, Michael J. "The Graphics Explosion." *Business Software Review* (June 1987), pp. 22–26.

Martin, James. "Strategic Uses for the PC in Business Environments." *PC Week* (Dec. 12, 1986), p. 38.

Moad, Jeff. "The Second Wave of PCs." *Datamation* (Feb. 1, 1989), pp. 14–20.

Nestor, James H. "An Introduction to the Micro-to-Mainframe Connection." *Journal of Accounting and EDP* (Winter 1989), pp. 4–9.

Petersen, Perry. "Branch Office Microcomputing." *Datamation* (November 15, 1984), pp. 104–109.

Rohm, Wendy Goldman. "The Overused, Underused, Betterused Micro." *Infosystems* (April 1987), pp. 60–63.

Romney, Marshall B., and Stocks, Kevin D. "How to Buy a Small Computer System." *The Journal of Accountancy* (July 1985), pp. 46–60.

Rose, Tawn A. "Microcomputers for Financial Consulting." *Management Accounting* (Feb. 1984), pp. 42–45.

Smith, L. Murphy, and Bain, Craig E. "Computer Graphics for Today's Accountant." *CPA Journal* (Feb. 1987), pp. 18–35.

Stanford, Eric. "Managing Control Risks in Microcomputing Systems." *Journal of Accounting and EDP* (Summer 1985), pp. 38–43.

Steinauer, Dennis D. "Security for Personal Computers: A Growing Concern." *Computer Security Journal* (Summer 1984), pp. 33–40.

Viator, Ralph E., and Poe, C. Douglas. "Building an Integrated Multiuser Accounting System with Micros." *The Journal of Accountancy* (July 1988), pp. 108–114.

Wayune, Robert C., and Frotman, Alan. "Microcomputer: Helping Make Practice Perfect." *The Journal of Accountancy* (Dec. 1981), pp. 34–39.

Wolfe, Christopher, and Wiggins, Casper E. "Internal Control in the Microcomputer Environment." *The Internal Auditor* (Dec. 1986), pp. 54–60.

Wu, Margaret S. "Choosing PC Software for Decision Making." *Journal of Systems Management* (December 1988), pp. 19–26.

Yoder, Steven E., and Knight, Sherry D. *Microaccounting.* Englewood Cliffs, N.J.: Prentice-Hall, 1985.

Zarley, Craig. "Corporate Users Turn to CD ROM for Business Applications." *PC Week* (Dec. 2, 1986), pp. 41, 49.

After studying this chapter, you should be able to do the following:

Discuss the impacts of computerization on audits.

Describe the various purposes and types of audits and auditors.

Identify the major standards of auditing.

Describe the several phases comprising the auditing process.

Discuss three major approaches to audits of computer-based information systems, as well as audit techniques that may be classified under each approach.

Describe currently emerging developments in auditing.

Chapter *17*

COMPUTER-BASED AUDITING

Users of an information system require reliable information from it. Managers, an important group of users, also are very concerned that the information system of their firm be both efficient and effective. **Audits** are examinations performed in order to evaluate such matters as (1) the reliability of information and (2) the efficiency and effectiveness of information systems.

The practice of auditing has become highly refined in North America, largely through the efforts of the American Institute of Certified Public Accountants (AICPA), the Institute of Internal Auditors (IIA), the EDP Auditor's Association, the Chartered Accountants of Canada (CAC), and the multitude of public accounting firms. Another influence on auditing has been the federal Foreign Corrupt Practices Act of 1977. Two products that reflect the refined state of auditing are (1) clearly stated sets of auditing

standards and (2) clearly stated multi-step auditing processes.

Students majoring in either accounting or systems analysis have roles to play with respect to auditing. A percentage of accounting majors will accept positions as auditors, and as such will be deeply involved in audit programs and processes. Those who become industrial or governmental accountants will need to rely on the information received from accounting information systems (AIS's). Thus, they will be interested in helping auditors to evaluate generated information and to detect control weaknesses in the systems. Those who become systems analysts (which could include some accounting majors) will be expected to design systems that provide reliable information. They will discover that they need to anticipate the problems and weaknesses that auditors frequently detect during their audits. In fact, systems analysts generally recognize the desirability of working closely with auditors during the analysis and design of an AIS. Doing so tends to ensure that adequate controls are built into the design, and thus to minimize costly revisions at later dates.

Impacts of Computerization on Auditing

As discussed in Chapter 9, computerization has significant impacts on the controls needed within a firm's information system. Computerization also often affects the audits of the information system, as the following quotation indicates:

The auditor should consider the methods the entity uses to process accounting information in planning the audit because such methods influence the design of the accounting system and the nature of the internal accounting control procedures. The extent to which computer processing is used in significant accounting applications, as well as the complexity of that processing, may also influence the nature, timing, and extent of audit procedures.[1]

The specific effects on auditing procedures and techniques will depend on the features of the computer-based processing system installed by the firm. However, one feature common to all computer-based systems is the absence of a visible audit trail; that is, the journals and ledger records are generally stored in computer-readable form on magnetic tapes or disks. Thus, an audit priority with respect to computer-based systems is the availability of frequent printouts of these records for review (or the ability to obtain such printouts on demand).

On-line processing systems generally have greater impacts on auditing procedures and techniques than do batch processing systems. As we recall, on-line processing systems write new data over existing data when updating records, thus eliminating the existing data. They often can function without the need for source documents, can involve complex processing and the updating of several files from individual transactions, can transmit data over great distances to remote terminals and microcomputers, must respond quickly to the information needs of users, and so forth. Since these conditions significantly affect the control framework, they also affect the conduct of audits.[2]

Although this chapter emphasizes the audits of computer-based systems, our attention cannot be *solely* focused on such systems. Very few, if any, present-day information systems are fully computerized, as we noted in an earlier chapter. An audit must encompass all controls and procedures comprising an information system, manual as well as computerized.

Types of Audits and Auditors

Audits that may be performed within a typical firm are classified as follows:

1. A **management audit** of the organization's structure, plans, policies, employee attitudes, and so forth.

2. An **operational audit** of the efficiency and effectiveness with which all resources are being used and the extent to which practices and procedures accord with established policies.

3. A **compliance audit** of the extent of compliance with laws, governmental regulations, contracts, and other obligations to external bodies.

[1]American Institute of Certified Public Accountants, *Statement on Auditing Standards No. 48: The Effects of Computer Processing on the Examination of Financial Statements* (New York: AICPA, 1984), Sec. 1.09.

[2]Gordon B. Davis and Ron Weber, "The Audit and Changing Information Systems," *The Internal Auditor* (August 1983), p. 36.

4. A **systems development audit** of the efficiency and effectiveness with which the various phases in a systems development project are being conducted.
5. An **internal control audit** of the adequacy of the internal controls and security measures.
6. A **financial audit** of the fairness with which financial statements present the firm's financial position and results of operations.

Other audits directly related to information systems include system development audits, system feasibility audits, system post-implementation audits, and computer operations and utilization audits. Certain of these audits overlap with or incorporate others. For instance, a financial audit incorporates an internal control audit.

Audits are generally performed by internal or external auditors. **Internal auditors** are employees of the firm being audited. In effect, they serve as management's in-house review function. **External auditors,** on the other hand, are public accountants who provide independent reviews for the owners of a firm. Internal or external auditors may also be **EDP auditors,** specialists in auditing computer-based information systems.[3] EDP auditors often work closely with other auditors who are not computer specialists. In addition to having a thorough knowledge of computer hardware and software, data bases, and computer networks, EDP auditors are expected to be familiar with a variety of computer-oriented controls and audit techniques.

Our focus in the following sections is on the financial audit, which is the most widely performed type of audit. We assume the presence of manual as well as computer-based processing. However, our main concern is with the latter, since computer-based processing creates the greatest auditing challenges.

Audit Standards

Being professionals, auditors are guided by standards. Internal auditors follow the Standards for the Professional Practice of Internal Auditing, whereas external auditors observe the Statements on Auditing Standards.[4] These two sets of standards have many more similarities than differences.

Content of Standards

Audit standards can be divided into two groups. One group specifies such professional characteristics as adequate technique training and proficiency, independent attitude, and due care during audits. Exhibiting due care involves planning the work adequately, supervising assistants properly, and gathering sufficient evidence.

Another group of standards pertains to the scope of audits performed. Internal auditors are enjoined to review all aspects of their firms' operations, controls, resources, and financial and operational information. In effect, the responsibilities of internal auditors (including those who specialize in EDP) lead them to perform most, if not all, of the types of audits we have described. External auditors, by contrast, have as their primary responsibility the performance of financial audits. As an integral part of such audits, one standard states that

there is to be a proper study and evaluation of the existing internal control as a basis for

---

[3]In public accounting firms they are often called management advisory services (MAS) specialists. For a survey of the various arrangements by which public accounting firms organize to conduct computer-based audits, see Richard S. Savich, "Organizing Audits in EDP Environments," *The CPA Journal* (August 1980), pp. 22–28.

[4]The Standards for the Professional Practice of Internal Auditing were promulgated by the IIA in 1978; the Statements on Auditing Standards were published by the AICPA in 1973 and later years.

reliance thereon and for the determination of the resultant tests to which auditing procedures are to be restricted.[5]

Each financial audit is to conclude with a report that expresses the external auditor's opinion concerning the financial statements of the firm being audited.

Effect of Computerization on Standards

As noted earlier, computerization does affect the audit procedures to be applied. On the other hand, computerization has *no* effect on the generally accepted standards of auditing. Auditors are expected to exhibit proper professionalism, which includes having adequate technical training and proficiency. They also are expected to follow the same thorough auditing process. This process must include the evaluation of all existing internal controls, including those that are computer oriented.

Auditing Process

Figure 17-1 portrays the steps that form the necessary **auditing process** for performing a financial audit. It is based on a description issued by the AICPA.[6]

Initiate Audit Planning

The first step to planning an audit is to understand the relevant matters concerning the firm being audited. A sound **audit plan** should be grounded in a knowledge of such aspects as management's philosophy and operating style, the organizational structure,

[5]American Institute of Certified Public Accountants, *Statement on Auditing Standards No. 1* (New York: AICPA, 1973), Sec. 320.01.

[6]AICPA, *Statement on Auditing Standards No. 55,* "Consideration of the Internal Control Structure in a Financial Statement Audit" (New York: 1988).

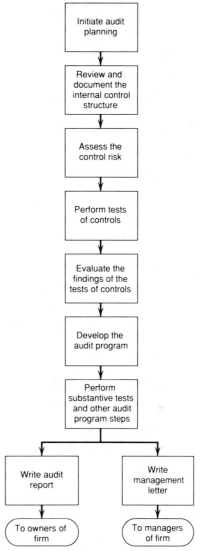

FIGURE 17-1 Steps comprising the process of conducting a finanical audit.

the personnel policies and practices, the accounting information system, and various external influences. An audit plan should also be based on a clear understanding of the objectives of the audit and its scope. For instance, the objectives of an audit involving a transaction processing system consist of determining that

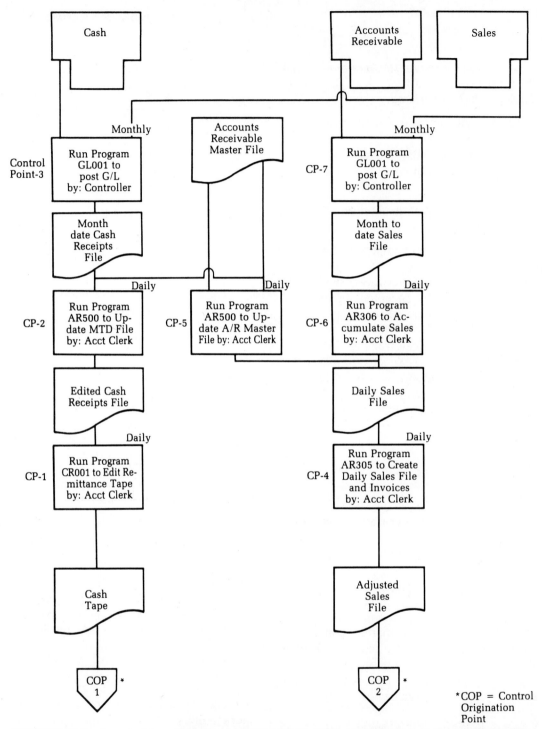

FIGURE 17-2 A control-type flowchart pertaining to the revenue cycle. Source: Frederick H. Wu and Randall L. Hahn, "A Control-Complexity and Control-Point Orientation to the Review of an Entity's Internal Control Structure in the Computer Environment," *Journal of Information Systems* (Spring 1989), p. 127. Reprinted with permission.

- All appropriate events are recorded as transactions.
- All recorded transactions are valid and properly authorized, valued, and classified.
- All transactions are recorded at the proper times and in appropriate subsidiary and summary records.
- Transactions are properly reflected in financial statements.

Review and Document the Internal Control Structure

As a continuation of the first step, the auditor gains an understanding of the internal control structure. That is, he or she reviews the policies and control procedures that are currently in operation. All control procedures related to the audit objectives are reviewed, including those that may be classified as general controls, transaction controls, preventive controls, detective controls, clerical controls, and computer-oriented controls. Strengths as well as weaknesses are noted. A variety of data-gathering techniques may be used during this review, including observation of activities, inspection of records and documents, and inquiries of key personnel.

The findings from the review should be documented by means of such data-organizing techniques as flowcharts and questionnaires. For instance, flowcharts that trace the flows of documents through transaction processing systems, as illustrated in Chapter 7, can be useful. Control-type flowcharts can also be quite informative. Figure 17-2 portrays a flowchart of this type for the revenue cycle of a firm. It specifies the control points where processing controls should be tested during the auditing process and contains such data as the processing frequency and authorizing personnel. Figure 17-3 shows an internal control questionnaire that may be used to document the presence or absence of

significant controls in a specific transaction processing system. When the internal control structure and/or information system is complex, the documentation should be relatively extensive. Figure 17-4 shows a questionnaire used to record interfaces between computer-based applications and the general ledger.

Assess the Control Risk

The first two steps in the auditing process provide an overall understanding (i.e., a macro view) of the existing internal control structure, including the control environment, accounting system, and control procedures. In turn, knowledge of the internal control structure points to the types of material misstatements that can occur in the financial statements.

Now the auditor is ready to form a preliminary assessment concerning the adequacy or inadequacy of the internal control structure and its operating effectiveness. This assessment is expressed in terms of the **control risk**—the risk that material misstatements, leading to significant errors in the financial statements, will fail to be prevented or detected by the current internal control structure. The level of control risk can vary from a maximum level to a minimum level, stated by a quantitative measure such as a percentage. A maximum level is assessed when the policies and control procedures within the internal control structure cannot be relied upon or cannot be tested in a cost-effective manner. A level below the maximum is assessed when the control procedures appear to be sufficiently sound and adequate to provide reasonable assurance that the transaction processing objectives can be achieved.

Perform Tests of Controls

If the control risk is assessed to be at a maximum level, the auditor must expand the

Question	Answer			
	Yes	No	Not Applicable	Remarks
1. Are customers' orders reviewed for accuracy and completeness before preparing sales invoices?				
2. Are customers' orders subject to approval by the credit department before being processed?				
3. Are sales invoices, shipping notices, and bills of lading prenumbered?				
4. Are employees in the sales order, inventory control, billing, and accounts receivable departments prevented from physical access to merchandise for sale?				
5. Are back orders prepared when sufficient merchandise is not on hand to fill orders?				
6. Are sales invoices compared with customers' orders and shipping notices?				
7. Are sales invoices checked for accuracy with respect to:				

FIGURE 17-3 Internal control questionnaire (partial) for sales transaction processing system.

tests to be performed within the audit program. On the other hand, if the control risk is judged to be below the maximum level, suitable tests of controls should be performed. **Tests of controls** (formerly called compliance tests) gather evidence concerning how well and consistently the current control procedures actually function. These tests may consist of observing the processing operations, reprocessing transactions, and so on. Their results document the basis for conclusions about the level of control risk. Several specific techniques for applying tests of controls within computer-based systems are discussed in later sections.

Evaluate the Findings of the Tests of Controls

After obtaining the results of the tests of controls, the auditor should have the means of evaluating the operational effectiveness of the internal control structure. Based on this evaluation, a specific level of control risk can be assessed. In turn, this determination should indicate the likelihood that the auditor will detect material misstatements that can arise in the financial statements. Finally, the auditor has the knowledge needed to construct a detailed audit program.

In effect, the evaluation ensuing from this climactic step represents the best judgment of the auditor concerning the adequacy of observed controls. It provides the foundation on which the audit program is constructed. If the controls are determined to be adequate, then the auditor is justified in relying on them to produce accurate financial statements. Thus, he or she need only perform the minimal number of substantive tests. If they are judged to be inadequate in one or more areas, then the auditor cannot fully rely on them. Instead, he or she must resort to additional tests of the underlying

Application	Automated Yes[a]	No	Programs Approx. Number	Language(s)	Does application have EDP integration with General Ledger	Other Systems	Any major changes since last year? (Y or N)	Any major changes planned? If so, when?
1. Payroll:								
a. Salary								
b. Hourly								
c. Distribution								
d. Taxes & benefits								
e. Other _____								
2. Sales and receivables:								
a. Sales orders & backlog								
b. Invoicing/billing								
c. Sales analysis								
d. Accounts receivable								
e. Cash receipts								
f. Other _____								
3. Cost and payables:								
a. Purchase orders								
b. Receiving								
c. Cost distribution								
d. Accounts payable								
e. Cash disbursements								
f. Other _____								
4. Inventory:								
a. Perpetual inventory								
b. Inventory control								
c. Other _____								
5. Production:								
a. Production orders								
b. Machine scheduling								
c. Status reports								
d. Efficiency reports								
e. Costs								
f. Material availability								
g. Other _____								
6. Forecasting:								
a. Sales								
b. Production								
c. Financial & accounting								
d. Other _____								

[a]Automated Method of Processing
B = Batch
RB = Remote Batch
OL/RT = On-Line/Real Time

FIGURE 17-4 Questionnaire used during the initial phase of an audit. Reprinted with permission from *Preliminary Review—Computer Audit Performance Guide Lines*. Copyright Arthur Young & Company, 1977.

records in order to develop a basis for evaluating the financial statements.

Making a sound evaluation of the control structure generally requires mature judgment and experience. It should take into account the concept of compensatory controls, that is, the toleration of relatively minor control weaknesses in one area if compensated for by control strengths in other areas.

Develop the Audit Program

An **audit program** is a list of specific tests and procedures needed to achieve the audit objectives. In addition to stating the nature of the tests and procedures, it also clarifies their extent and timing. The auditor refers to the evaluation of the level of control risk in establishing the tests and procedures. If the level of control risk is relatively low, for example, the tests may involve smaller samples of evidence and may be performed less frequently.

Perform Substantive Tests

Substantive tests constitute the bulk of the audit program. The purpose of substantive testing in a financial audit is to test assertions concerning account balances in the financial statements. During substantive testing evidence is obtained to the effect that transactions and account balances are valid and processed in accordance with generally accepted accounting principles. Typical tests confirm the existence of various assets (e.g., inventory) and analyze the trends of key factors (e.g., inventory turnover).

Communicate Audit Results

The final step is for the auditor to report the results of the audit to the proper parties. In the case of a financial audit performed by external auditors, the owners of the firm would receive the auditor's report. If serious control weaknesses are found in the present internal control structure, the auditor will also prepare a letter to management that details suggested improvements.

Auditing Approaches and Techniques

Among the techniques applied by auditors are counting cash on hand, tracing transactions through the accounting cycle, observing the taking of physical inventories, and confirming the existence of assets. These techniques are suitable for financial audits of either manual or computer-based information systems. Additional techniques are applicable only to those information systems which employ computer-based processing of transactions. Although no single audit would employ all these computer-oriented techniques because of the excessive costs entailed, each of the techniques can aid in tests of controls and/or substantive testing.

The techniques discussed are organized under three key approaches to computer-based auditing: auditing around the computer, auditing through the computer, and auditing with the computer. Our discussion presumes the prior and concurrent use of such review methods as interviews, observations, flowcharting, and questionnaires.

Auditing around the Computer

The **auditing-around-the-computer** approach treats the computer as a "black box." Instead of testing processing steps in a direct manner, it focuses on the inputs and outputs of the computer system. Underlying this approach is the following assumption: If the auditor can show that the actual outputs are the correct results to be expected for a set of inputs to the processing system, then the processing steps must be functioning in a reliable manner.

The key technique under this approach involves tracing selected transactions from source documents to summary accounts and records, and vice versa. As Figure 17-5*a*

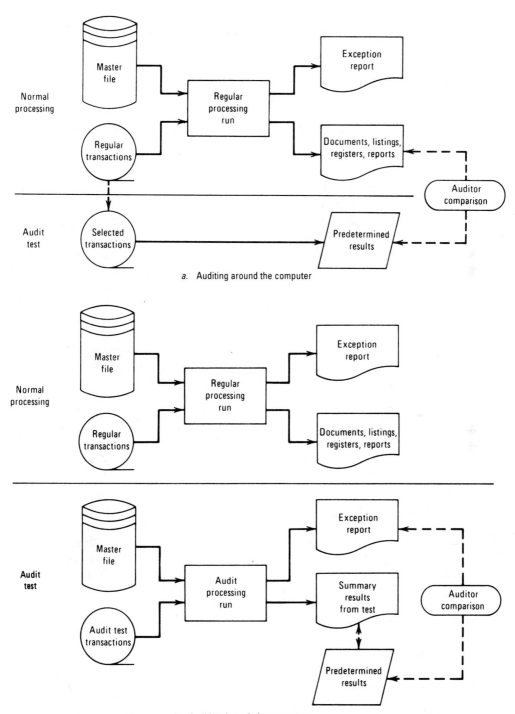

a. Auditing around the computer

b. Auditing through the computer

FIGURE 17-5 Auditing around the computer versus auditing through the computer.

shows, an auditor compares the actual results obtained by computer processing against those previously computed by hand. Any differences are likely to reflect control weaknesses. Because the controls are being tested, this technique is employed during the compliance testing step.

The auditing-around-the-computer approach is suitable only when three conditions are fulfilled:

1. The audit trail is complete and visible. That is, source documents are used for all transactions, detailed journals are printed out, and transaction references are carried forward from the journal to the ledgers and summary reports.

2. The processing operations are relatively straightforward and uncomplicated.

3. Complete documentation, such as systems flowcharts and record layouts, are available to the auditor.

These conditions are most likely to be found in independent batch processing applications, such as typical cash disbursements and payroll processing. Other types of applications, such as on-line sales order processing systems, often fail one or more of the conditions. They may dispense with source documents, receive individual transactions at random times, or involve complicated processing. Tracing transactions in such systems can be a very difficult task for auditors.

Since the auditing-around-the-computer approach ignores the computer and draws on a technique generally employed in manual system audits, the approach has an obvious appeal. Auditors do not need to understand computer processing. They apply a technique that is familiar to them and that they can perform efficiently and economically. Moreover, auditors can combine the tracing of selected transactions with such techniques as reviews of prenumbered source documents.

The major shortcoming of this approach is that it does not allow the auditor to determine exactly how all transactions will be handled by the computer processing programs, especially those transactions containing errors or omissions.[7] For instance, it does not indicate how an accounts payable program would process an invoice from a fictitious supplier. Thus, it does not reveal possible inadequacies in such controls as programmed checks.

Auditing through the Computer

An alternative approach for testing the effectiveness of controls in computer-based processing systems is known as **auditing through the computer.** This computer-oriented approach "opens the black box" and directly focuses on the processing operations within the computer system. It assumes that if the processing system is found to contain adequate controls, errors and irregularities are not likely to slip by undetected; as a result, the outputs can reasonably be accepted as reliable.

The through-the-computer approach should be employed when the around-the-computer approach is not suitable or sufficient. Thus, it should be applied when computer processing is complex and/or involves voluminous files, when the audit trail is fragmented or sketchy, or when documentation is poor. The approach may be applied in conjunction with the around-the-computer approach to provide greater assurance, unless the costs of the combined approaches are greater than the added benefits.

The auditing-through-the-computer approach embraces a family of techniques. Included in the family are the test data, inte-

---

[7]James I. Cash, Jr., Andrew D. Bailey, Jr., and Andrew B. Whinston, "A Survey of Techniques for Auditing EDP-Based Accounting Information Systems," *The Accounting Review* (Oct. 1977), p. 816. Of course, if a selected transaction happened to contain an error, the technique would indicate whether or not it was detected. However, the selected transactions are very unlikely to contain examples of all the various types of possible errors and irregularities.

grated test facility, parallel simulation, and embedded audit module techniques. As in the case of the transaction tracing technique, these techniques are most often employed in tests of controls.

Test data technique. The earliest technique developed within the through-the-computer approach, the **test data technique,** uses test or simulated transactions to audit computer processing. Its purpose is to determine the ability of application programs to process transaction data accurately and to detect possible errors and irregularities.

Figure 17-5*b* contrasts the test data technique with normal processing and also with the transaction tracing technique shown in part *a* of the figure. Simulated transactions are entered into the computer system. For instance, sales transactions may be entered from a magnetic tape in the same manner as they are entered during normal processing. The application program—the same program used during normal processing—edits the transaction data and then performs the usual file updating steps. As in the case of normal processing, test data processing generates outputs of two types: (1) listings of errors in transaction data, and (2) printed summaries and reports (e.g., a sales summary). At this point, however, the test data technique deviates from normal processing. Instead of being distributed to users, the outputs are closely inspected by the auditor. Both the detected errors and data in the summaries are compared with the results that the auditor has predetermined. This inspection is often performed manually by the auditor, although it may be programmed to be performed automatically by the computer system.

Figure 17-6 lists several test transactions prepared by the auditor for the test of a payroll application. The sheet also shows the results that the auditor expected. Below the sheet on the figure is the exception report that reflects the detected errors. Deviations between the expected results and actual

results would denote control weaknesses. (There are none in this example.)

Several conditions should be met if the test data technique is to be effective:

1. The test transactions, generally prepared by the auditor, should include both valid and invalid data. Invalid data should be complete, in that they test every possible input error, logical processing error, and irregularity. Hypothetical data, rather than actual data, should be used to allow the auditor to include all the test possibilities that he or she can envision. Preferably, the auditor should employ a **test data generator,** a utility software package available from a software supplier, to assist in developing the desired test data.

2. A test master file, or a copy of the actual master file, should be used during the testing. Otherwise, actual file records are likely to be contaminated by test data.

3. The auditor should maintain close controls over the testing procedure in order to preserve independence. He or she should observe the processing by the computer operator after personally handing him or her the test transactions. When the testing is completed, the auditor should immediately obtain the printed outputs. Also, the auditor should ascertain that the program being used is identical to the "production" program used in regular processing runs. To ensure that the computer operator does not slip in a "ringer," the auditor might time the test to take place, on a surprise basis, just after the program has been used in a scheduled processing run. If this procedure is not convenient, he or she might duplicate the production program and later observe the operator perform the testing of the data with this duplicate.

As a technique that embodies the through-the-computer approach, the test data technique has proven to be useful. It provides concrete evidence concerning the

Test Code	Condition Being Tested	Transaction Data				Expected Result	Actual Result
		Employee Number (1)	Employee Name (2)	Depart-ment No. (3)	Hours Worked (4)		
1	Valid transaction	13251	SMITH, JOHN	1	40.0	$200 gross pay $7800 earnings year-to-date	
2	Invalid check digit in field (1)	13629	BLACK, CHARLES	1	40.0	Exception	
3	Out-of-sequence in field (1)	13543	ADAMS, STEVE	1	40.0	Exception	
4	Invalid composition in field (2)	13658	BR67N, RODNEY	1	40.0	Exception	
5	Invalid relationship between fields (1) and (3)	13752	JONES, PAUL	2	40.0	Exception	
6	Out-of-limit in field (4)	24313	KRAUSE, KEN	2	60.0	Exception	
7	No matchup with master in field (1)	25000	TINGEY, SHERMAN	2	40.0	Exception	

Exception Report Messages   Explanation Code

EMPLOYEE 13629 HAS AN INVALID CHECK DIGIT	a
EMPLOYEE 13543 IS OUT-OF-SEQUENCE	b
EMPLOYEE 13658 HAS INVALID CHARACTERS IN NAME FIELD	c
EMPLOYEE 13752 DOES NOT CORRESPOND WITH DEPARTMENT	d
EMPLOYEE 24313 EXCEEDS ALLOWABLE HOURS WORKED	e
EMPLOYEE 25000 HAS AN INVALID EMPLOYEE NUMBER	f

a. Check figure is computed by computer to be a 7.
b. Employee number should be arranged in sequence.
c. Only alphabetic characters should appear in the name field.
d. The left-most digit of the employee number should correspond with the department number.
e. A maximum limit of 56 hours worked has been established.
f. No master record is found with number 25000 in the master file.

FIGURE 17-6 Test transactions and expected results for a payroll program test.

reliability with which a firm's computer programs screen and process transaction data. Its use requires minimal computer expertise on the part of auditors. Furthermore, it can be employed in a manner that does not interfere with the regular data processing activities of a firm.

However, this technique has several limitations:

1. In devising test transactions the auditor is very likely to overlook certain conditions that require testing. This is especially a likelihood if the processing system being tested is complex and the number of possible error conditions is large.

2. The test data can be quite expensive and time-consuming to develop, especially in the cases of complex programs that undergo frequent changes.

3. The technique is static in that it focuses on single points in time and does not provide continuing results. Because programs tend to be changed often, the results obtained rapidly become obsolete.

4. Attempts to maintain control over processing can be fraught with uncertainty. For instance, a knowledgeable computer operator may be able to substitute programs without being detected by an auditor who is barely "computer literate."

5. The technique focuses on individual applications; thus, it does not tend to provide comprehensive testing of the entire set of transaction processing systems.

6. The technique cannot be easily employed in the case of an on-line processing system. Not only may test data become commingled with live data in on-line files, but undesirable responses may be triggered. For instance, goods may be shipped on the basis of test sales transactions.

The fifth limitation above can be overcome by a variation of the test data technique. A **base case system** consists of a comprehensive set of test transactions that encompasses all of the transaction processing systems. While capable of providing a means by which to evaluate the processing reliability of the entire system, the base case system is very expensive to construct. In most cases it would be feasible to construct only as a by-product of system testing during the initial development of the information system.

Integrated test facility technique. Also called the minicompany technique, the **inte-** grated test facility (ITF) technique is an extension of the test data technique. It involves integrated data entry; that is, test transactions are entered into the computer processing system concurrently with the live (actual) transactions. Since they are processed by the same programs, the test transactions undergo the same processing steps as the live transactions. However, the test transactions are identified to the programs by means of a code, so that the results of their processing are shunted into a special test facility. Controlled by the auditor, this test facility consists of small-scale (i.e., minicompany) files pertaining to fictitious entities and events. When a test sales transaction is processed, for example, the results would be deposited in ITF files containing dummy accounts for customers and sales orders.

The auditor obtains printouts of the test facility records and the results of testing. By comparing these printouts with predetermined results, the auditor can evaluate how correctly the application programs process transactions and how effectively they detect errors. Figure 17-7 portrays the key features of the ITF technique.

Although the ITF technique employs test transactions that are very similar to those used in the test data technique, the ITF technique offers several relative advantages:

1. It allows test transactions to simulate live transactions more closely, since they are entered randomly and continually throughout the year. Because they are processed together with live transactions, the auditor has no doubts that the production programs are performing the processing. Because of the continuous feature, changes to the application programs are tested without undue delay as they become operational.

2. It is well suited for testing on-line processing programs, as illustrated in Figure 17-7. Since the test transactions are segregated from the live on-line files, they can-

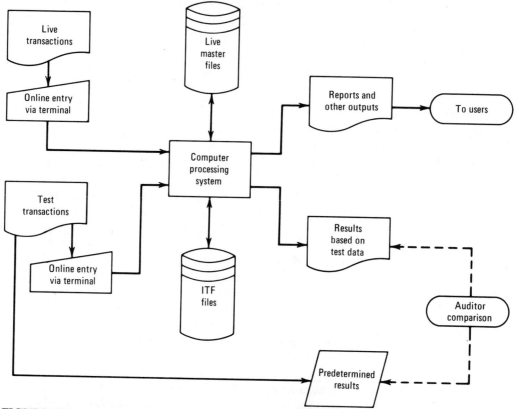

FIGURE 17-7 Integrated test facility technique.

not contaminate the live files or cause inaccuracies to appear in ledger totals.[8]

3. It enables all on-line applications within a computer system to be tested in an integrated manner. Thus, the technique allows a more comprehensive evaluation of input and processing controls.

Although these advantages have added to the popularity of the ITF technique, it does have significant drawbacks:

[8]An alternative version of the ITF technique allows test transactions to be entered into live files and later removed by adjusting entries. However, most managers would be quite uneasy if their live files were contaminated for even a short period; they also might fear (with some justification) that certain types of transactions would be difficult to reverse.

1. Although the continuing cost of testing is reasonably moderate, the initial cost of devising the test transactions is high.

2. The code required for the application programs to recognize the test transactions creates uncertainties. It would be possible, for instance, for a dishonest programmer employee to add instructions to the application programs, causing the programs to process the test transactions in a different manner from the live transactions. Therefore, the validity of the processing is always open to doubt.

Parallel simulation technique. The **parallel simulation technique,** also known as the audit simulation model technique, simulates the processing performed by the firm being

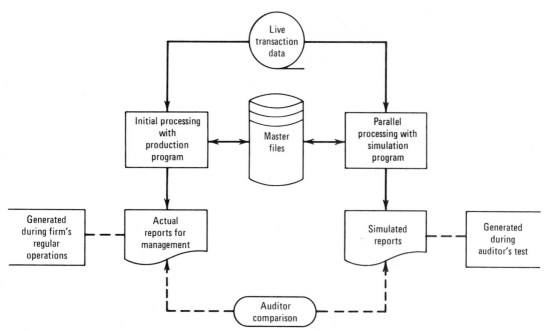

FIGURE 17-8 Parallel simulation technique.

audited. This simulation utilizes a program created by the auditor which, in effect, is a model of one or more of the production application programs used on a regular basis.

Figure 17-8 portrays the key features of parallel simulation. After developing the simulation program, the auditor enters the same data processed earlier by the firm. These actual data are then processed by the simulation program against the firm's actual master files. The reports generated during the simulation are then compared by the auditor with the reports generated by the firm's regular processing of the same data. Differences between the reports indicate that the production program is not processing the data in accordance with desired specifications.

The parallel simulation technique therefore verifies the processing accuracy of application programs. In addition, it enables the actual outputs from a firm's applications to be validated. Thus, the technique is as suited to substantive testing as it is to compliance testing.

However, the technique has severe drawbacks that prevent its widespread or comprehensive use. Developing the simulation program is likely to be a time-consuming and costly effort. Moreover, only an auditor with considerable computer expertise would be competent to undertake the effort. Furthermore, even an experienced auditor often has difficulty in tracing differences between the two sets of outputs back to differences in the programs.

As a consequence, the technique is typically limited to key segments of programs. For instance, only the portion of a fixed-assets application program that performs depreciation calculations might be simulated. To minimize the programming effort, auditors often resort to packaged software. (Packaged audit software is discussed in the next major section.)

A variation of parallel simulation is known as **controlled reprocessing.** To employ the reprocessing technique, the auditor obtains and verifies a copy of the firm's application program currently being used in processing. Then he or she reprocesses the actual transaction data for an earlier period by means of this copy. By comparing the outputs generated during the reprocessing with those generated earlier, the auditor can determine whether changes have been made in the program. If so, he or she can then investigate to see whether the changes have been properly authorized.

Embedded audit module technique. An **embedded audit module** is a programmed segment or module inserted into an application program to monitor and collect data for audit purposes. Figure 17-9 depicts the technique by which this module is commonly

used. As transactions enter the computer system, they are edited and processed by the appropriate application program. At the same time they are checked by the audit module embedded within the program. When a transaction meets certain conditions, it is selected by the module and copied onto an audit log. At periodic intervals the contents of the log are printed out for review and investigation by the auditor. (In fact, the audit log is formally called the system control audit review file, or SCARF.)

Among the conditions or actions that might be specified for listing on the audit log are

1. Unauthorized attempts to access a master file.

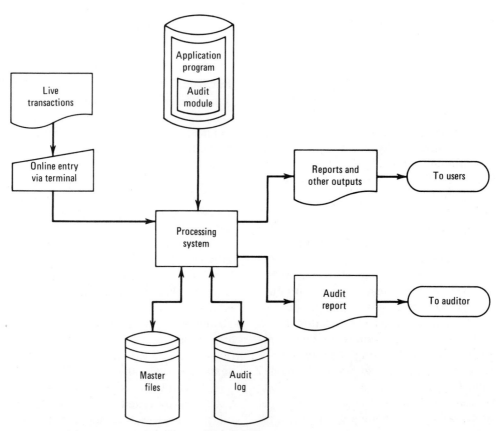

FIGURE 17-9 Embedded audit module technique.

2. Attempts to override processing parameters, such as established prices in a billing program.

3. Entry of unauthorized transactions.

4. Entry of transactions that exceed a certain dollar amount.

5. Entry of transactions affecting particular ledger accounts.

The embedded audit module technique is well suited for on-line computer processing systems. It enables the transactions of audit interest to be easily captured, even when the audit trail may be partially obscured. The technique can also be used for substantive testing. Transactions can be randomly captured according to a statistical sampling method throughout an accounting period. Moreover, processing can be monitored on a continuous basis. For instance, intermediate or final processing results pertaining to particular types of transactions (e.g., sales transactions) can be captured on the audit log.

Although this technique should gain in popularity with the increasing use of on-line processing systems, it does present certain difficulties and drawbacks:

1. Added time is required to process transactions, since all program instructions in the module must be executed for each transaction.

2. The design and implementation of the module can be costly, especially if the module is added after the application program is already in existence.

3. The security requirements are heightened, since the audit module and audit log must be kept secure from access by personnel within the firm being audited.

4. The criteria by which transactions are selected for audit review must be carefully established by the auditor. If the criteria are too tight, the number of transactions selected may become unwieldy. For instance, an auditor may decide that she wants to review all cash disbursements transactions in excess of $1000, and at the end of the first week of processing receives an audit report containing 500 such transactions. To counteract this problem, the audit module should be written to allow changes to criteria for selecting transactions.

Several features can be incorporated into the embedded audit module technique. Because each is costly and requires technical expertise on the part of auditors, certain of the features are omitted in many applications of the technique. However, each has been found to be useful in typical audit situations.

1. **Tagging** consists of attaching "tags," or special indicators, to selected transactions. These "tags" enable the transactions and related processing to be easily identified by the audit module.

2. **Snapshotting** (also called extended records) consists of capturing images concerning selected transactions and their processing. Snapshots are taken at various points during the processing, showing the contents of the primary storage areas at those points. These images are stored as records in the audit log and thus provide sufficient data to complete the audit trails.

3. **Tracing** consists of capturing data concerning the instructions that are executed during the processing of selected transactions. In addition to recording the executed instructions, this feature shows the points at which the program logic branches to succeeding instructions. Traces, which are often performed by system utility programs, assist the auditors in locating programming errors and in understanding the detailed functioning of application programs. Since traces show only those instructions actually executed, they are generally more useful than reviews of entire program listings.

4. **Real-time notification** involves the use of special auditor terminals. These terminals, which may be located in the auditor's offices, display the selected transactions or detected accesses at the moments they are actually captured by the audit module.

Auditing with the Computer

The third approach to auditing computer-based information systems consists of using the computer itself to aid in performing the audit steps, that is, in substantive testing. This computer-assisted approach has become increasingly important in the audits of firms which process voluminous transactions by means of computer-based systems.

Audit software. Auditing-with-the-computer techniques may be jointly described as audit software: computer programs used by auditors to aid in testing and evaluating the reliability of a firm's records and files.[9] Audit software programs are, in effect, audit "robots." That is, they essentially aid the auditor by performing the mechanistic audit functions that have been traditionally performed by junior auditors or clerical personnel. They are very useful, since they can perform these functions more quickly and accurately than a platoon of junior auditors. In fact, they are so fast that they are able to handle much larger samples of data (i.e., audit evidence).

Audit software may be classified as specialized and generalized. **Specialized audit software** is one or more programs custom designed by auditors to suit a particular audit situation. This type of software is seldom employed, for two reasons: (1) It is very time consuming and expensive to prepare, and (2) it requires considerable computer expertise

on the part of the auditor. One way to overcome these drawbacks, at least in part, is to adapt to audit purposes relevant programs that are currently in use by the firm being audited. **Generalized audit software** (GAS) is a set of programs that can be applied to a wide variety of firms and audit situations. GAS is typically developed by a software firm, computer manufacturer, or public accounting firm as a package. Thus, the using auditor need not be knowledgeable in programming. In fact, the typical GAS package is designed to be easy to use and is tailored to the language and needs of auditors. Because of its wide usage, GAS will be the focus of concern during the remainder of this section.

Functions of a GAS. Although functions may differ somewhat among the various available GAS packages, typical functions include

1. *Extracting or retrieving data* from the files of the firm being audited. A GAS package must have the ability to extract data from a variety of file structures, file media, and record layouts. The extracted data are edited and transferred to an audit work file from which they are available for use by the other programs in the package.

2. *Calculating with data* by performing addition, subtraction, multiplication, and division operations. Examples include the verification of the correctness of footings in journals and extensions on sales invoices.

3. *Performing comparisons with data* by using such logical operators as EQUAL, LESS THAN, and GREATER THAN. Comparisons may be performed in order to select for testing data items having certain features, to ascertain consistency between items, or to verify that certain conditions are met. Examples: an inventory file having 30,000 items might be searched and all items having balances in excess of

---

[9]Although embedded audit modules can be used in substantive testing, as we have noted, they are perhaps more useful in performing tests of controls. Thus, they are not considered in the discussion of this approach.

1000 items or $20,000 in value selected for review; the test counts of selected inventory items might be compared against the balances in the inventory records and differences listed for investigation; the credit limits of customers might be compared against the customers' account balances, with any account whose balance exceeds the credit limit being listed for follow-up.

4. *Summarizing data* in order to provide a basis for comparison. Example: detailed listings of salaries might be summarized for comparison with payroll reports.

5. *Analyzing data* in order to provide a basis for reviewing trends or judging likelihoods. Example: individual accounts receivable might be aged to provide a basis for judging the likelihood of their collection.

6. *Reorganizing data* by such operations as sorting and merging. Example: the various products sold by the firm might be resorted in ascending order of total sales quantities in order to facilitate analysis.

7. *Selecting samples* from an array of data. Example: a sample of customers might be selected randomly from the accounts receivable file, with the intention of confirming their account balances.

8. *Determining statistical measures* from an array of data. Example: the mean and median amounts of individual sales last month might be computed to aid analysis.

9. *Printing outputs,* such as reports, analyses, and forms. Example: the confirmation request forms and envelopes might be printed for those customers included in the sample mentioned in item 7.

Figure 17-10 illustrates the foregoing functions of a GAS package, together with typical inputs and outputs.

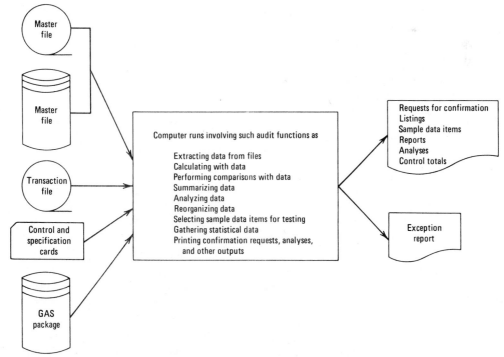

FIGURE 17-10 Applications of a generalized audit software package.

GAS packages have been developed by a variety of firms, including the larger public accounting firms. Examples are AUDITPAK II (developed by Coopers & Lybrand), STRATA (developed by Touche, Ross & Co.), and EDP AUDITOR (developed by Cullinet Corporation). Although each commercial package provides the various functions described earlier, each offers distinctive features. For instance, AUDITPAK II allows the auditor to retrieve data from records having an unlimited number of fields.

Steps in using GAS. The procedure for using the GAS package begins with the auditor planning the audit objectives and work program for a particular application. Next the auditor enters the details concerning the application on preprinted specification forms. These specifications are needed to inform the computer system of the characteristics of the file on which the application data are stored, the various functions and processing steps to be performed by the audit software, and the content and formats of the outputs.[10] Then the auditor obtains the firm's master and transaction files for the application and verifies their authenticity. Verification generally consists of accumulating control totals of key data fields and reconciling these totals to corresponding totals in general ledger accounts.

On the audit date the auditor submits the specification data for entry into the computer system. The specification data are then entered from some medium such as magnetic tape or disk or are keyed into a terminal. The auditor also provides the GAS package, which may be stored on magnetic tape, magnetic disk, or magnetic diskette. In order to maintain effective control over the processing, the auditor closely observes all computer operations pertaining to the audit tests. When the processing is completed, the audi-

tor takes immediate possession of all outputs, plus the GAS package.

Processing with the GAS package generally involves a number of runs. The first run extracts the data from the master and transaction files and stores the data in the audit work file. All later runs draw on data in the audit work file. The number and type of succeeding runs depend on the various functions that are specified in the audit program. For instance, a calculation run might be followed by a summarization and analysis run, which in turn is followed by a print run.

When the outputs are received from the computer operator, the auditor's work has just begun. Samples of items selected and listed must be reviewed and evaluated, summaries must be studied, confirmations must be mailed and answers investigated, totals must be verified against general ledger accounts, and so on. Thus, a GAS package does not relieve the need for professional experience and judgment on the part of auditors.

Advantages of a GAS package. To recapitulate several points mentioned earlier, the advantages of a GAS package are that it

1. Allows an auditor to access records stored in computer-readable form.
2. Enables an auditor to examine many more records than could be examined otherwise.
3. Performs a variety of essential auditing functions, including the statistical selection of samples.
4. Reduces the length, and hence the cost, of an audit if the firm is heavily computerized. (Alternatively, it reduces the dependence on nonauditing personnel for performing such routine tasks as summarizing data and preparing confirmation requests.)
5. Requires only a minimal amount of computer knowledge to use; also incorporates features to enhance ease of use.

[10]Some GAS packages require that a data dictionary (similar to that described in Chapter 18) be prepared in lieu of the specification forms described here.

6. Adapts to a wide variety of applications and record layouts, as well as to any type of organization.

Limitations of a GAS package. A major limitation is that a GAS package does not directly examine the application programs of a firm. Thus, it does *not* replace those techniques, such as the ITF technique, that audit through the computer.

Other limitations depend on the particular GAS package being considered. Two package-specific limitations relate to data retrieval and computer hardware compatibility. Certain packages cannot retrieve data easily from data bases containing data sets other than files (e.g., network structures). In such cases the data must be retrieved by the data base management system and then recast into file structures. This procedure causes the auditor to forfeit a degree of control. Moreover, certain packages can only be used directly with a limited range of computers (e.g., IBM computers). This limitation requires the auditors to translate data, by means of a standard software utility, from the format of the firm's computer system to the format with which it is compatible (e.g., the IBM format). Then an IBM computer, perhaps at a service center, would be used to execute the GAS functions. The added steps can substantially increase the time and cost of audits.

GAS packages are constantly undergoing improvements, so these limitations should disappear with time. For instance, certain GAS packages can now be used with a wide variety of computers, including microcomputers. GAS packages are also being made much easier to use, through the use of on-screen menus and other aids.

Selection of a GAS package. When choosing a GAS package, an auditor should, of course, consider the array of functions that each candidate provides. In light of the limitations already noted, the auditor should also ascertain (1) the variety of computers with which it is compatible, (2) the types of data structures that it can access, and (3) the ease of use that it offers. Another important consideration is the reputation of the audit software supplier and the level of support that will be provided, including documentation and training. Finally, the price of the GAS package is a significant factor; however, the total out-of-pocket costs, including documentation, training, and future enhancements, represent the most relevant monetary factors. Some suppliers bundle these additional elements into the quoted price, whereas others price each element separately.

Example involving a GAS package.[11] As a part of its annual audit of the BQ Merchandising Company, a public accounting firm decides to employ a GAS package to aid in auditing accounts receivable. The GAS package to be used is STRATA, which incorporates an array of functions that the auditors find appropriate to their needs.

The audit objectives pertaining to accounts receivable have previously been established. In summary, they consist of determining that all transactions affecting accounts receivable have been properly authorized, valued, classified, and recorded in the accounts receivable ledger and general ledger; that the transactions have been recorded in the proper accounting period; and that the effects of the transactions are properly reflected in the balance sheet and income statement.

After having completed several phases of the auditing process, including the evaluation of tests of controls, the auditors are now ready to develop and apply the audit program. When a GAS package is to be involved

---

[11]This illustration is based on a case copyrighted by Touche Ross & Co. and described in W. Thomas Porter and William E. Perry, *EDP Controls and Auditing*, 5th ed. (Boston: Kent Publishing Co., 1987), pp. 353–366. Used with permission.

in the audit, the steps consist of selecting the uses, designing the application of the package, preparing the specification sheets, and performing the audit processing.

1. *Selecting the Uses.* Among the tests and procedures that are to comprise the audit program, the auditors decide to use STRATA to
   a. Recalculate the current balance of each account in the accounts receivable subsidiary ledger, and sum all of the balances.
   b. Prepare an analysis of the aging of the accounts receivable records.
   c. Compare the current balance of each account with the credit limit for the customer, and identify any balances that exceed the credit limits or that are credits.
   d. Prepare a list of customer balances (with customer numbers and names).

   Each of these procedures is intended to further the achieving of the audit objectives. For instance, the first procedure should enable the auditors to confirm that the accounts receivable balance (at gross) in the balance sheet is properly valued; the second procedure should aid the auditors in determining whether the reserve for uncollectible accounts is sufficient; and the third should reveal possible irregularities in authorizing sales transactions. The list of account balances will be used to determine which accounts to confirm with customers, so that the validity of the accounts and their balances can be verified.

   The GAS package could be used in additional procedures if desired. For example, it could be used to obtain a random selection of accounts to be confirmed, to print the confirmation request forms, and to perform statistical analyses of the results of confirmations.

   Before deciding how to apply STRATA to the selected tasks, the audi-

tors must determine the specifics concerning the computer system of the BQ Merchandising Company. Accordingly, they ascertain the make and model of the computer, the capacity of its primary storage unit, the name of the operating system, the available input–output devices (e.g., magnetic tape, 9 tracks, density 1600 bytes per inch), the layouts of the accounts receivable records, and so on. On the basis of these facts, the auditors confirm that STRATA is compatible with the system and can be employed.

2. *Designing the Audit Application.* Next the auditors prepare a listing of the record layouts and the formats of the outputs. They describe in narrative form, and by means of a flowchart if suitable, the detailed steps to be performed and the calculations to be performed by the package.

   The accounts receivable detailed record layout contains the batch number, record code, division, customer number, invoice number, invoice date, original invoice amount, current open amount, date of last payment, and amount of last payment. The accounts receivable master record layout contains the customer number, customer name, address, zip code, and credit limit. (The field size and mode are also needed data.)

   The aging analysis is to be based on the invoice dates and will include subtotals for each customer of all open items invoiced in the past 30 days, 31 to 60 days, 61 to 90 days, and over 90 days. Totals of the aging categories are to be computed. The list of customer balances is to be arranged in a high-to-low sequence.

3. *Preparing the Specification Sheets.* STRATA requires the use of specification sheets that define (a) the general characteristics of the computer and input–output devices, (b) the format of the records in the auditor's work file, (c) the charac-

teristics of the files and records containing the data to be audited, (d) the functions to be performed by the GAS package, (e) the required calculations, and (f) the characteristics of the reports to be produced by the GAS package.

To illustrate, consider the data needed for the aging analysis. On a Data Field Selection sheet the auditors list the locations of the fields of data in the accounts receivable records. They also include the size, format, and name of each field, plus the number of work fields needed. Then they prepare a Work Record Specification sheet, such as the one shown in Figure 17-11, which defines the formats of the needed work fields. They also prepare a Print Specification sheet, which provides the details pertaining to the format and content of the aging analysis, and a Calculation Specification sheet, which states the method for calculating the amounts to appear in the aging columns, plus the totals of the aging columns.

4. *Performing the Audit Processing.* After the coding of the data has been adequately tested, the auditors schedule a

processing date. When the date arrives, the auditors obtain the files needed for auditing. Then the processing is performed and the audit outputs are obtained. The auditors review the outputs, such as the aging analysis, in order to verify that the audit objectives are met. For instance, the final total in the aging analysis is compared to the accounts receivable balance shown in the balance sheet. The aging totals are used to verify the accuracy of the aged trial balance of receivables prepared by the firm, as well as to judge the reasonableness of the reserve for doubtful accounts.

Emerging Developments in Auditing

Auditing is currently undergoing severe trials and dramatic changes. On the one hand, it is encountering difficulties in attempting to cope with advanced on-line information systems. On the other hand, it is gaining powerful support from new microcomputer-based audit tools and an enhanced sense of professionalism.

WORK FIELD NO.	WORK FIELD NAME	STORAGE FORMAT ALPHA-NUMERIC LENGTH	STORAGE FORMAT NUMERIC Decimal Places	STORAGE FORMAT NUMERIC Indicative Y Yes	REDEFINITION STARTING WORK FIELD	REDEFINITION STARTING LOCATION	DO NOT PUNCH	Do Not Punch LEFT-MOST BYTE LOCATION
5 6 8	9 22	23 25	26	27	28 30	31 33		Memo Only
2 W 0 1	C U S T O M E R N O	8						
2 W 0 2	U N D E R 3 0		2					
2 W 0 3	3 0 T O 5 9		2					
2 W 0 4	6 0 T O 8 9		2					
2 W 0 5	9 0 A N D O V E R		2					
2 W 0 6	C U S T O M E R B A L		2					
2 W 0 7	C U S T O M E R N A M E	1 5						
2 W 8								
2 W 9								
2 W 0								

FIGURE 17-11 Data concerning an accounts receivable audit as entered on a Work Record Specification sheet.

Auditing in Advanced On-Line System Environments

Two on-line system environments that can create difficult problems for auditors are computerized data base systems and computerized networks. Both are rapidly growing in number and complexity. In fact, the two environments are often combined by firms, thereby further increasing the complexity. The auditing implications of each will be separately discussed for convenience; however, the likelihood of encountering them in combined form should be kept in mind.

Data base systems. On-line systems that employ common data bases benefit auditors by clustering the data to be reviewed. Hence, many of the essential controls are focused around these clustered data. However, data base systems tend to complicate audits because they introduce data base software (the DBMS), complex data structures (the tree, network, and relational structures), on-line documentation (the data dictionary), and an additional organizational function (the data base administrator). An audit of a data base system must reckon with these added elements.

During the preliminary review step the auditor should examine the data base management system. If it is feasible, he or she might obtain a printout of the program code for the DBMS and compare it (at least roughly) against a printout obtained from the software firm that develops the DBMS. The auditor should also examine a printout of the data dictionary as well as other printed documentation. The procedure for maintaining the data dictionary, as well as the underlying data standards, should be reviewed.

During the detailed review step the auditor should examine specific general and application controls. Among these controls are the following:

1. Security measures pertaining to the data base (*e.g.*, passwords, backup and recovery procedures, data independence, boundary protection, and lockout provisions).

2. Organizational independence of the data base administrator as well as adequate authority to define data, maintain and approve changes to the data dictionary, maintain data base integrity, and monitor data base performance.

3. A transaction log, activity log, and console log.

4. A sound error-detection and -correction procedure.

5. An adequate array of programmed checks to validate input data.

During tests of controls several procedures might be performed. Most of these tests are likely to present difficulties to the auditor and certain of the tests may not be cost effective in all cases. However, tests such as the following must be performed to gain a basis for sound evaluation of the data base system:

1. Tracing selected transactions through the system, using a system software utility.

2. Reviewing the console log and investigating selected entries.

3. Entering test transactions for processing and deposit in an integrated test facility. (If the data base can be copied, test transactions may be processed against actual master files and data structures instead of the ITF.)

4. Monitoring transactions with an embedded audit module and entering selected transactions on an audit log.

Substantive testing must be conducted, as in the case of any audit. However, it may present even more difficulties for the auditor than tests of controls. The main problem is to retrieve data from the data base for testing and review. If the file structures are sequential, the data may be retrieved by the typical GAS package. However, if the structures are more complex, many GAS packages cannot gain access. Several other methods may be employed to gain access, although each has a drawback. The first method consists of using a generalized interface routine (utility) to convert the complex data structures into simple flat files, which may then be accessed by the GAS package. Although this may be achieved fairly easily if the utility is a part of the DBMS, the resulting flat files are distorted and awkward to use in later testing. The second method consists of adding a routine to the GAS package that is capable of accessing complex data structures. This solution is costly, since the routine must be modified each time the data base is changed. Also, the routine is difficult for the average auditor to apply. The third method is to use the DBMS itself to retrieve the data. This solution is often the best, although it requires a reasonable degree of computer expertise on the part of the auditor. The final method is to employ a GAS package that incorporates a generalized data structure access routine. Few GAS packages currently have such a routine, but more are likely to incorporate such routines in the near future.

Assuming that the data from the data base can be successfully transferred to the audit work file, the auditor may apply such tests as (1) reconciling batch totals to processed results and (2) verifying changes in account balances between successive closing dates.

Computer networks. Computer-based systems consisting of multiple computers connected by communication lines are known as computer networks or distributive processing systems. Although computer networks have not yet been discussed in this book, relevant audit considerations are briefly noted

here. Controls needed by networks are summarized in Chapter 19.

The distinguishing control problems of networks are caused mainly by the (1) communication lines and (2) the dispersed processing nodes. Each must be given added attention because of severe exposures to risk.

With respect to *communication lines,* the level of exposures should first be estimated. Threats may exist with respect to unauthorized access to transmitted data, lack of audit trails, transmission errors, and line noise and distortion. In estimating the level of exposure, the auditor might review performance reports to note volumes of traffic, security violations, hardware problems, software changes, and so on.

During his or her reviews of controls the auditor might examine such general controls as user manuals, software change procedures, hardware maintenance, system backup, transaction logs, and security precautions. Controls particular to the network, such as plastic debit cards and PIN numbers for electronic funds transfer systems, should be especially noted. Controls over messages (transactions) are also important. For instance, the auditor should determine whether each transaction is automatically assigned a sequential number and coded with the time, date, transmitting terminal number, and authorization number (e.g., merchant authorization number).

Tests of controls relative to communication networks might include (1) tracing a sample of transactions along the audit trail and (2) examining selected software changes for proper authorization, testing, and final approval.

With respect to *dispersed processing nodes,* the exposures to risk are greater than in a centralized computer processing center. Each processing point (e.g., a remote sales office) is smaller in personnel and resources, while the computer is more accessible to unauthorized persons. Most general controls—

documentation, password protection, operating system, change procedures—are pale imitations of those in a centralized processing center.

During the audit of a dispersed processing node, the auditor must perform all steps in the audit process. Thus, he or she begins with the preliminary and detailed reviews. Those controls that are present are identified. However, the auditor is likely to encounter difficulty in identifying control points as well as in evaluating the adequacy of those controls that are identified. After evaluating the controls, the auditor performs tests of controls and then substantive tests. Because of the complicated relationships between each dispersed processing node and the other processing nodes in the network, such tests are difficult to incorporate into computerized audit techniques. Thus, they often are performed around the computer at present. Within a few years, however, embedded audit modules are likely to be established throughout such networks. Auditors should then be able to view the results of network processing on a continuous basis.

New Auditing Techniques

As on-line processing systems and computer networks have blossomed, auditors have been urgently searching for new cost-effective techniques. One technique that has proven to be reasonably effective is **simulated attack.** Computer experts and hackers are employed to penetrate the security of a firm's computer system and to circumvent its controls. If their attempts are successful, the weaknesses in the computer system are pinpointed and added controls can be installed. Two other promising techniques are microcomputer audit-assist software and expert systems.

Microcomputer audit-assist software. The purpose of **microcomputer audit-assist soft-** ware is to move toward a paperless and pencilless audit through the use of microcomputers. To apply this technique, an auditor carries a portable microcomputer into the office where the audit is to be conducted. He or she then inserts a diskette containing templates into the disk drive of the microcomputer. With the aid of these templates the auditor performs audit tasks that formerly were done manually.

Templates are in effect programs that are constructed with the use of spreadsheet software packages. Templates are typically designed to aid in preparing trial balances, maintaining adjusting journal entries, evaluating sample results, scheduling and managing the time of auditors in field audits, performing reasonableness tests of expenses, and estimating interest expense. Figure 17-12 displays a worksheet prepared by Coopers & Lybrand, a large public accounting firm, to aid in summarizing and controlling accounts receivable confirmation requests. The template employed in this task has the name CONFIRM.

In some cases public accounting firms have grouped a collection of templates into a software package for use by auditors. An example is SeaCas (Systems Evaluation Approach—Computerized Audit Support), which is used by Peat Marwick Main & Co.

Microcomputer-based expert systems. An **expert system** is a computer model that incorporates the knowledge of human experts in order to aid in performing functions or making decisions. (Chapter 20 discusses the development of expert systems.) Expert systems are emerging as sound tools for auditors. In addition to serving as training devices and knowledge bases, expert systems can assist in developing audit programs, determining the size of test samples, assessing audit risks, performing analytical reviews, diagnosing errors in systems, and monitoring the effectiveness of controls. Examples of

```
***********************************************************************************
SUMMARY OF CONFIRMATION COVERAGE                                    VERSION 1.0
STORY SALES CO.                     PREPARER:JP
10/31/--                            RUN DATE:11/29/--
***********************************************************************************
CONFIRM  ACCOUNT   DESCRIPTION      WP     BK VALUE  BK VALUE  AUDITED   OVER/UNDER
NO.      NO.                        REF      SENT      RECD     VALUE      STATED
-----------------------------------------------------------------------------------
1        200-13    HART SUPPLY      50-40  1500000   1500000   1200000    -300000
2        200-24    JOHNSON LOCKS    50-41   980156    980156    980156          0
3        200-46    C&D CO.,INC.     50-42  2100450   2100450   2000000    -100450
4        200-58    VAL-MART         50-43   357456              357456          0
5        200-72    SMITHSON TECH. CO.50-44 2575100   2575100   2575100          0
                                                                               0
                                                                               0
                                                                               0
                                                                               0
                                                                               0
                                                                               0
                                                                               0
                                           -------   -------   -------   ----------
                                           7513162   7155706   7112712    -400450
                                           =======   =======   =======   ==========


RESPONSE RECAP                      # ITEMS   $ VALUE
--------------                      -------   -------
CONFIRMS MAILED                           5   7513162
CONFIRMS RECD                             4   7155706
RESPONSE %                            80.00     95.24

SUMMARY OF RESULTS                  # ITEMS   $ VALUE
------------------                  -------   -------
ACCOUNT TOTAL                           500  49852357
BOOK VALUE EXAMINED                       5   7513162
AUDITED VALUE EXAMINED                    5   7112712
% COVERAGE                             1.00     15.07
RATIO OF AUDITED TO BOOK VALUE                   .95
```

FIGURE 17-12 Microcomputer-assisted summary of accounts receivable confirmation request. Courtesy of Coopers & Lybrand. *Software News-letter,* Fall 1983, Coopers & Lybrand.

expert systems currently in use are audit-MASTERPLAN, AUDITPLANNER, and AY/ASQ.

The package named auditMASTER-PLAN was developed by the Institute of Internal Auditors. Although not truly an expert system, it contains a module that parallels the purpose of an expert system. The module in question identifies risk factors and assigns risk weights, in order to aid audit managers in planning audit activities. Audit managers actually develop the risk analysis model prior to its use, thereby validating the model. Other modules within the package set up the microcomputer files, define the audit universe, and aid long-term audit planning and budgeting. Marriott Corporation, one of several firms to employ auditMASTERPLAN, has found that it allows the audit managers more time to devote to audit management tasks.[12]

AUDITPLANNER is a rule-based expert system that aids auditors in making materiality judgments. Results of these judgments aid auditors in planning audit programs. In applying AUDITPLANNER, an auditor answers a series of questions about the system to be audited. After evaluating the answers, the expert system recommends a materiality level to be used in planning the extent of audit procedures.[13]

[12]David B. Dunmore, "Using auditMASTERPLAN," *Journal of Accounting and EDP* (Winter 1988), pp. 30–34.

[13]Grace T. Chu, "Expert Systems in Computer Based Auditing," *The EDP Auditor Journal* (Vol 1, 1989), pp. 29–30.

APPLICATION IN AUDITING
Peat Marwick Main & Co.[a]

As one of the very large public accounting firms in the United States, Peat Marwick Main & Co. has made strenuous efforts to integrate computer technology into its auditing activities. In 1982 it adopted Apple III as its standard support tool for auditors. When the Apple Macintosh appeared in 1984, the firm switched to this more portable, powerful, and user-friendly microcomputer. Several thousand Macintosh Plus microcomputers are currently in the hands of field auditors around the world. The firm also maintains a national computer group. This specialized group supports the auditors in a variety of ways. For instance, it develops software instruction manuals and other materials relating to the Excel spreadsheet package, which the auditors use in learning to apply the package. The group also develops training materials for such proprietary software as SeaCas and System 2190.

SeaCas and System 2190 provide the backbone of the computerized audit approach employed by Peat Marwick Main & Co. In brief, SeaCas automates the audit, while System 2190 aids in the audit of automated systems. SeaCas, the audit support and evaluation package, consists of five modules: (1) Financial Statement Subsystem—Basic Financial Statement Preparation (FFS—BFF), for the preparation of financial statements, (2) Financial Statement Subsystem—Consolidated Financial Statements (FFS—CFS), for the consolidation of entities maintained through FFS—BFF, (3) Sampling Subsystem, for the evaluation of statistical and nonstatistical plans, (4) SeaDoc, for the computer-assisted preparation of flowcharts and workpapers, and (5) Utilities Disk, for providing utilities to support the other SeaCas modules. System 2190, the generalized audit software package, enables auditors to extract and manipulate data from a client's computer system and to perform various statistical and sampling functions. Examples of command functions that the package provides to auditors are FOOT, MATCH/DIRECT, SAMPLE, AND SUMM.

[a]Gerald F. Hunter and Mark A. Poplis, "Computer Technology and Training: Yesterday, Today, and Tomorrow," *Georgia Journal of Accounting* (Spring 1986), pp. 15–30.

AY/ASQ (Arthur Young/Audit Smarter, Quicker) is a microcomputer audit-assist software package that contains five programs.[14] The cornerstone of this package is AY/Decision Support, an expert system that assists auditors in developing an overall audit plan and the detailed audit programs. It allows an auditor to enter the findings from a review of internal controls directly into an Apple Macintosh microcomputer. The expert system evaluates the internal control structure and assesses the risks due to control weaknesses. On the basis of these assessments, the system then generates printed detailed audit programs pertaining to the financial statement accounts. Other programs in the package allow auditors to create, modify, file, and retrieve audit workpapers; generate trial balances and draft financial statements; manage the time spent on audit engagements; and transfer data between the Macintosh and other computers.

Changing Roles of Auditors

As auditors have grown in number, their roles have undergone several changes. First, they participate more often in the development of new information systems. In such situations auditors generally serve as consultants to system design teams, ensuring that suitable controls are incorporated into

[14]Marketed by Arthur Young International, now Ernst and Young. The names of the software package and certain programs in the package have trademark protection.

the designs. When appropriate, they encourage the inclusion of embedded audit modules during the design stage. Second, auditors are gaining greater professional status. One sign of this enhanced status is the recent emergence of two professional examinations—the Certified Internal Auditor (CIA) examination and the Certified Information Systems Auditor (CISA) examination. These examinations are in addition to the Certified Public Accountant (CPA) and Certified Management Accountant (CMA) examinations, both of which are available to auditors as well as to other accountants. Third, larger numbers of auditors are specializing in the audits of computer-based information systems. This trend is evidenced by the growth in the EDP Auditors Association, which was formed in 1969. It now boasts thousands of members in scores of chapters throughout the United States and in foreign countries.

Auditors are likely to become even more involved with computer-based information systems in the future. They should be introduced to computer fundamentals and systems analysis early in their educational programs. Most will probably be trained in the use of computer-related auditing techniques at the beginnings of their careers. Many may develop skills in information systems design that rival those of professional systems analysts.

Summary

Audits of information systems evaluate the reliability of generated information and the efficiency and effectiveness of the systems themselves. Computerization has significant impacts on auditing procedures and techniques, although it has no impact on generally accepted auditing standards. Audits of information systems are performed by internal auditors and external auditors. A variety of audits may be performed by such auditors, including management audits, operational audits, compliance audits, internal control audits, financial audits, and systems development audits. The conduct of all audits should be guided by standards that relate to required professionalism, audit scope, and final reports.

The process of auditing a computer-based information system consists of (1) reviewing and documenting the internal control structure, (2) assessing the control risk, (3) performing tests of controls, (4) evaluating the findings, (5) developing the audit program, (6) performing substantive tests, and (7) communicating the audit results.

Three key approaches to computer-based auditing are auditing around the computer, auditing through the computer, and auditing with the computer. Auditing around the computer treats the computer as a "black box" and generally consists of tracing selected transactions via the audit trail. Auditing through the computer focuses on the processing operations within the computer system. Among the techniques suitable for this approach are the test data, integrated test facility, parallel simulation, and embedded audit module techniques. Auditing with the computer involves the use of audit software to aid in testing and evaluating the reliability of a firm's records and files. Generalized audit software packages perform such functions as extracting data from the firm's files, selecting samples from the extracted data, gathering statistics, calculating, summarizing, analyzing, making comparisons, sorting, and printing outputs. Using a GAS package should involve a series of steps that are carefully controlled by the auditor. GAS packages are quite popular, since they usually reduce the cost of an audit and require minimal computer knowledge on the part of the auditor.

Advanced on-line system environments are currently causing difficulties for auditors. Audits of data base systems, for instance, introduce complex data structures that cannot easily be handled by GAS packages. Computer networks introduce added threats because of communications lines and dispersed processing nodes. While the auditor does not yet have sufficient tools to ease these difficulties, the auditor does have new tools to aid in conducting the auditing process. Two very helpful and promising tools are microcomputer-based software and expert systems. On balance, auditors are growing in professionalism. Increasingly they are specializing in computer-based systems and are serving as control consultants during the development of new systems.

Review Problem with Solution

Statement

Merlin Distributors, Inc., of Normal, Illinois, provides a variety of home appliances to consumers through retailers located in most states. Although it markets the appliances under its own name, it acquires the merchandise from several manufacturers. Its major operations consist of purchasing, receiving, storing, and distributing the appliance products. These operations have been growing in volume since the firm's inception two decades ago. All of the operations are conducted at a single site.

As sales and related inventory activities grew in volume, management recognized the need for data processing assistance. Thus, it first installed a computer system 10 years ago. Although the system provided considerable assistance, it gradually became outdated. Consequently, last year it installed a late-model computer system. This new system includes a mainframe computer processor, magnetic tape and disk drives, high-speed printers, key-to-tape devices, and several terminals. It serves a redesigned information system that is organized around three processing areas: the revenue cycle (i.e., the sales and cash receipts systems),

the inventory control system, and the general ledger system. Transaction processing primarily affects these areas and is performed in batch mode. However, authorized personnel can directly access data in magnetic disk files via the terminals.

You have just been designated the auditor in charge of an impending financial audit of the computerized inventory control system. This will be the first audit involving the new computerized system.

Required

a. Outline the auditing process that you plan to follow, assuming you discover that the internal accounting controls relating to the computerized portion of the information system are sufficiently adequate to be relied on.

b. Identify several key general and application controls that you are likely to observe in your review of internal accounting controls, given the assumption listed under **a.** Include several programmed checks under application controls, and relate the programmed checks to affected data items via a matrix.

c. Describe audit techniques and procedures, especially computerized techniques, that will be useful in tests of controls. Assume that special audit instructions have been incorporated into the job costing program during its development.

d. List several specific audit objectives to be achieved during the substantive testing step.

e. Discuss how your firm's GAS package can be used with respect to each of the audit objectives listed in **d.**

Solution

a. The audit process to be followed consists of the following steps:

(1) Develop the audit objectives and scope, and then acquire adequate knowledge concerning management's philosophy and operating style, the organizational structure, the personnel policies and practices, the accounting information system, and relevant external influences.

(2) Perform a review of the internal control structure pertaining to the inventory transaction flows; document by means of such techniques as flowcharts and questionnaires.

(3) Assess the level of control risk.

(4) If the assessment in **(3)** indicates that the computer-oriented control structure can be relied upon, devise and perform tests of controls.

(5) Evaluate, on the basis of the tests of controls, the operational effectiveness of the portion of the internal control structure relating to the inventory control system.

(6) Develop the audit program, including the audit objectives relating to the inventory control application and the substantive tests and procedures needed to achieve them.

(7) Perform the substantive tests with the aid of the GAS package.

(8) Prepare a management letter in which any discovered control weaknesses are described, plus the auditors' report to the owners.

b. General controls likely to be observed include

(1) Adequate segregation of responsibilities among the user departments (e.g., inventory control department) and data processing departments.

(2) Adequate systems and program change procedure.

(3) Thorough and comprehensive documentation for systems personnel and users.

(4) A variety of logs, including a batch control log, data library log, console log, and error report.

(5) A variety of access restrictions, including the restriction of the computer facility to authorized personnel only, the restriction of terminals to the accessing of data only, and the requirement that passwords be used to access terminals.

(6) Adequate backup of the inventory master file and of computer equipment.

Application controls likely to be observed include

(1) Procedures that require approval of all inventory transactions.

(2) Prenumbered inventory transaction source documents.

(3) Key verification of data transcribed from the source documents to magnetic tape.

(4) Batch control totals on inventory quantities and on numbers of records, plus use of a batch transmittal sheet.

(5) Logging of totals in a batch input control log.

(6) Procedures for monitoring the correction of all input and processing errors.

(7) Run-to-run controls during processing.

(8) Programmed checks such as a limit check on quantities ordered and relationship check on quantities received. See the matrix on page 802.

(9) Distribution of outputs according to a report distribution manual or log.

(10) Review of processing results by originating departments.

c. Audit techniques and procedures that are suitable for tests of controls pertaining to the inventory control system include

(1) Reviewing evidence (e.g., signatures on system specifications) that the new system development of last year was

Programmed Check	Data Items						
	Inventory Item No.	Description	Supplier Number	Supplier Name	Quantity Ordered	Quantity Received	Unit Price
Validity	X		X				
Field	X	X	X	X	X	X	X
Limit					X		
Range							X
Relationship					X	X	
Completeness	X		X	X	X	X	X
Redundancy matching			X	X			

approved by management throughout the various phases; observing actual procedures followed in the computer operations (e.g., noting whether a data librarian maintains close control over data files).

Computer-oriented techniques may also be used in testing for unauthorized program changes. One technique consists of comparing current inventory processing programs with previous versions of the same programs and tracing changes to signed authorizations. Another technique is controlled reprocessing, in which the same data are processed by the current program and a previous version of the program.

(2) Observing computer operations to determine that systems personnel do not have unrestricted access to computer programs or data files, that only authorized personnel have access to the computer facilities, and that passwords are necessary in order to gain access to the system via terminals; examining several passwords to see that they do not allow the holders to access files other than those related to inventory, and that they do not allow files to be modified.

(3) Observing that selected source documents are properly authorized and prenumbered, that batch control totals are properly maintained and logged, that the control group is organizationally independent of the user departments and computer operations, and that key verification is carefully performed; tracing a sample of erroneous transactions listed on computer error reports to the original source documents and to the corrected inputs.

A computer-oriented technique that may be used in testing input controls is the test data technique. It consists of processing test inventory transactions in order to determine whether the programmed checks are comprehensive and operating properly.

(4) Observing the processing in computer operations, the transfers of data from the library to operations, and the movement of output results and error reports from the computer facility back to the control group; tracing selected inventory transactions from source documents to the output reports, and vice versa; reconciling batch control totals shown on batch transmittal sheets to the totals shown on exception and summary reports and in the control log.

Computer-oriented techniques

that might be used include (a) embedded audit modules to monitor transaction activity and (b) traces of selected transactions to observe the functioning of the inventory application programs. The use of these techniques, however, assumes that they are already built into the programs before the audit begins.

(5) Observing the distribution of output reports to the users, verifying that the distribution is in accordance with the distribution manual or log; reviewing the reports and tracing selected batches and file balances to their entries in the reports.

d. Audit objectives to be achieved via substantive testing include the following:

(1) To verify that the quantities shown in the inventory records agree with the physical quantities on hand.

(2) To verify that the prices and extensions for the inventory items are proper, and that the balance in the inventory general ledger account is correct.

(3) To verify that the value of the inventory on hand has been adjusted to allow for reduced salability due to obsolescence, etc.

(Other objectives might be listed, but the preceding objectives are most frequently encountered.)

e. The GAS package may be employed with respect to each of the foregoing objectives as follows:

(1) After the physical inventory is taken, the cards containing the counts of the various items can be keyed onto magnetic tape and the data sorted by inventory item number. This tape file can then be compared against the inventory master file by the GAS package; when the two quantities for an item are not equal, the difference is listed on a report. If a count is missing in either file for an item, that fact is noted on the report. The auditor then investigates the differences and makes necessary adjustments to equalize the quantities.

(2) In preparing the test of inventory prices, the statistical sampling routine of the GAS package can be employed to select a sample of inventory items (each of which lists a current price). Then the auditor can vouch the prices to the suppliers' invoices. The calculating function of the GAS package can be used to recompute the extension for each item, as well as the total amount of the inventory on hand. Any differences will be printed on a report, which will then be investigated by the auditor.

(3) To aid the auditor in analyzing the salability of the inventory, the GAS package can scan all inventory items in the master file and print an analytical report. This report could indicate (a) obsolescence, by listing all items for which no recent sales have been made; or (b) slow-moving inventory, by listing all items for which the quantity on hand appears excessive in relation to the quantities sold last year. Each item in the report could then be investigated by the auditor.

Review Questions

17-1 What is the meaning of each of the following terms?

Audit
Management audit
Operational audit
Compliance audit
Systems development audit
Internal control audit
Financial audit

Internal auditor
External auditor
EDP auditor
Audit standard
Auditing process
Audit plan
Control risk
Test of controls
Audit program
Substantive test
Auditing around the computer
Auditing through the computer
Test data technique
Test data generator
Base case system
Integrated test facility (ITF) technique
Parallel simulation technique
Controlled reprocessing
Embedded audit module
Tagging
Snapshotting
Tracing
Real-time notification
Specialized audit software
Generalized audit software (GAS)
Simulated attack
Microcomputer audit-assist software
Template
Expert system

17-2 Why has the auditing profession grown rapidly in recent years?

17-3 What features of a computerized on-line processing system affect audit procedures and techniques?

17-4 Contrast several types of audits, especially as they relate to information systems.

17-5 Contrast three types of auditors.

17-6 How are auditing standards affected by a change from a manual processing system to a computerized system?

17-7 Describe the sequence of steps comprising the auditing process.

17-8 Contrast tests of controls and substantive tests.

17-9 Contrast the three approaches to auditing computer-based information systems.

17-10 What conditions must prevail for auditing around the computer to be suitably applied, and what advantages does it offer?

17-11 Describe several techniques that may be classified as auditing through the computer. What feature do they have in common?

17-12 What conditions must be met for the test data technique to be effective?

17-13 In what circumstances is the ITF technique preferable to the test data technique?

17-14 What are the drawbacks to the test data and ITF techniques?

17-15 What are the benefit and the drawbacks of the parallel simulation technique? How does it differ from the controlled reprocessing technique?

17-16 What are the benefit and the drawbacks of the embedded audit module technique? How is it related to tagging and tracing techniques?

17-17 Describe the purpose of audit software.

17-18 Identify several functions that can be performed by the typical GAS package.

17-19 Describe the steps to be performed by an auditor in order to use a GAS package in a controlled manner.

17-20 What are the advantages of a GAS package?

17-21 What are the current limitations of a GAS package?

17-22 Describe the features that are unique to an audit of a data base system.

17-23 Discuss the problems that are encountered in the audit of a computer network with dispersed processing nodes.

17-24 Describe the uses of microcomputer audit-assist software.

17-25 Identify several uses of expert systems for aiding in conducting audits.

17-26 Identify three changes that are currently taking place with respect to the roles of auditors.

Discussion Questions

17-27 Contrast the level and types of computer-related knowledge needed by a general auditor with the level and types needed by an EDP auditor. Be as specific as possible.

17-28 Why is it becoming increasingly important for auditors to be consulted during the development phases of a new information system? Should the auditor ideally be a full-time member of the systems development team?

17-29 What are the advantages and drawbacks of an auditor relying exclusively on one technique, such as a GAS package or test data?

17-30 Why should an external auditor, whose primary responsibility is to express an opinion concerning the representations in financial statements, suggest improvements to the information system?

17-31 An internal auditor reviews and evaluates a portion of the information system of her firm once each year. This year she is to examine the sales order processing system, which has been significantly redesigned since the previous audit three years ago. Discuss the steps that she should perform in order to evaluate the effectiveness and efficiency of the new sales order processing system.

17-32 A few large public accounting firms have in certain of their offices computer terminals that are connected directly to the computer systems of major client firms. Discuss how these hookups can be beneficial to the external auditors in performing (a) tests of controls and (b) substantive tests.

17-33 Auditors currently are experiencing severe difficulties in auditing the most advanced on-line computer systems. Speculate on the auditing techniques that will be needed in a decade or so to audit information systems that (a) include completely automated offices, with microcomputers on every desk; (b) cut across company boundaries, such as linkups between firms and major suppliers; and (c) cut across national borders via satellites and other devices.

17-34 Discuss the ways that financial audits of computer-based information systems might affect the information systems organization, system development activities, computer operations, files, and other aspects of firms being audited.

17-35 Why do audit techniques always seem to lag behind the developments in computer technology? Can this lag be overcome in the future?

Problems

17-1 A large state agency maintains its own internal auditing staff. On occasion it also engages the services of auditors from a national public accounting firm. Currently the agency is involved in planning for the development and implementation of a new computer-based system.

Required

a. What types of audits might the internal auditors be assigned to perform?

b. What type of audit will the external auditors likely perform, and what role (if any) would the internal auditors likely have in this type of audit?

c. Assume that the head of the agency requests that (1) the internal auditors vouch invoices received from suppliers and approve them for payment, and (2) the external auditors design and implement needed internal accounting controls into the new computer-based system. How should the internal and external auditors respond to these requests?

17-2 Glazer Enterprises is a holding company that has acquired many companies in different industries in order to diversify. Glazer's most recent acquisition was Tanner Stores, a regional chain of department stores.

The audit committee of Glazer's board of directors has established a policy of having the internal audit department conduct a review of the operations of all new acquisitions. The primary purpose of this review is to determine the strength of each company's internal accounting controls.

Such a review was conducted for Tanner Stores. The internal audit department reported to Glazer's senior management and audit committee that it believed there were serious weaknesses in the controls over cash receipts. As a consequence of the suspected poor controls over cash receipts, and the fact that cash receipts are part of the revenue cycle, the audit committee directed the internal audit department to conduct an audit of the revenue cycle of Tanner Stores.

Required

a. What audit standards should be followed in performing the audit of the revenue cycle?

b. Discuss the means by which the internal auditors likely determined that serious weaknesses probably exist regarding cash receipts.

c. What are the audit objectives with respect to cash receipts?

d. The audit committee decided to expand the scope of the audit as a consequence of the suspected poor controls over cash.

What other course of action could have been taken?

(CMA adapted)

17-3 ToysGalore, Inc., a privately owned retail chain of toy stores operating in the Midwest, is having its financial statements audited for the first time by an external auditor. Management believes that the audited financial statements will help it to obtain the financing that will be needed for an expansion of operations.

The partner-in-charge of the audit engagement has suggested that the review and testing of the firm's internal control system be performed at an interim date. Tom Kodd, president, replied to this suggestion by asking, "What is the purpose of reviewing and testing internal accounting controls? Won't that take a lot of time and add significantly to the cost of the audit? What criteria would you use for evaluating our internal accounting controls, and what kind of evidence would you require?"

Required

a. Explain the purpose of the external auditor's study and evaluation of internal accounting control in connection with an audit of financial statements.

b. Identify the four criteria that would be used by the external auditor to determine whether the firm's internal accounting controls are adequate.

c. **(1)** Describe the review and evaluation steps or phases in the audit process.

(2) Explain what the external auditor reviews to gather evidence during each of these steps or phases of an internal accounting control study, assuming that the firm's information system is computerized.

(CMA adapted)

17-4 AndreCo is a growing manufacturer of subassembled components used in a variety of home appliances. Because sales have doubled in the past three years, management has decided to convert its manual system of information gathering and processing, which has evolved during the company's first 10 years in business, to a more efficient and effective system based on a planned integrated approach. AndreCo's chief financial officer, Robert Ganning, has been asked to present a plan for the development and implementation of the new system. Peter Martin, an internal auditor for AndreCo, has been asked to review the plan to assure its validity. Ganning indicated to Martin that as soon as the plan was ready, Martin would be given a copy to review and approve from the audit perspective.

"I think it would be better if we worked together throughout the process," said Martin. "I see three distinct review phases that should be handled as consecutive elements in the process of developing the new system: specification review, design review, and system review. Each phase should be completed and reviewed before the next is begun."

In the discussions that followed, Martin defined the three phases as follows.

  a. *Specification review:* a review of the system definition to determine whether the system provides for the internal control objectives of authorization, recording, safeguarding assets, and substantiation.
  b. *Design review:* a review of the detailed design to ensure that the system procedures and controls will accomplish the requirements established and approved in the specification review.
  c. *System review:* a trial run of the actual system during implementation to ascertain the presence of the original objective. Errors or omissions in translation of the de-

signed system to an actual, implemented system would be detected.

Ganning and Martin agreed that a three-phase review approach would be both effective and efficient, and they proceeded on that basis.

Required

Describe specific steps to be performed under each of the listed reviews, as well as the matters being reviewed.

(CMA adapted)

17-5 An internal auditor is preparing an audit program for a portion of her firm's computerized payroll application. She designates the scope of the audit to include *only* the following: payroll computation, labor cost distribution, and paycheck distribution.

Required

Indicate whether each of the following proposed audit procedures should or should not be included in the audit program. Justify any exclusions (e.g., this procedure is beyond the scope of the audit, this procedure does not provide useful audit evidence).

  a. Review the computer programming related to payroll computations.
  b. Determine whether checks are delivered to departmental timekeepers for distribution.
  c. Perform a review of workers' compensation claims.
  d. Perform a reconciliation of time-card hours to hours recorded on production time cards.
  e. Distribute checks to employees on a sample basis.
  f. Obtain a certificate from the timekeeper pertaining to employees who were absent when the auditor distributed paychecks

and who are to be paid later in the usual manner.

g. Review personnel files to verify documents in payroll files.

h. Review procedures related to the signing of paychecks.

(CIA adapted)

17-6 You are involved in the internal audit of accounts receivable, which represent a significant portion of the assets of a large retail corporation. Your audit plan requires the use of the computer, but you encounter the following reactions:

   a. The computer operations manager says that all time on the computer is scheduled for the foreseeable future and that it is not feasible to perform the work for the auditor.

   b. The computer scheduling manager suggests that your computer program be cataloged into the computer program library (on disk storage) to be run when computer time becomes available.

   c. You are refused admission to the computer room.

   d. The systems manager tells you that it will take too much time to adapt the computer audit program to the EDP operating system and that the computer installation programmers would write the programs needed for the audit.

Required

For each of the four situations described, state the action the auditor should take to proceed with the accounts receivable audit.

(CIA adapted)

17-7 Linder Company of Fresno, California, is completing the implementation of its new, computerized inventory control and purchase order system. Linder's controller wants the controls incorporated into the programs of the new system to be reviewed and evaluated. This is to ensure that all necessary computer controls are included and functioning properly. She respects and has confidence in the system department's work and evaluation procedures, but she would like a separate appraisal of the control procedures by the internal audit department. It is hoped that such a review would reveal any weaknesses or omissions in control procedures and lead to their immediate correction before the system becomes operational.

The internal audit department carefully reviews the input, processing, and output controls when evaluating a new system. When assessing the processing controls incorporated into the programs of new systems applications, the internal auditors regularly employ the approach commonly referred to as auditing through the computer.

Required

a. Identify specific application controls and programmed checks that should be incorporated in the programs of the new system.

b. Prepare a matrix that specifies the fields of data to be verified by the respective programmed checks listed in **a**, given that the following data items are entered relating to a purchase: transaction code, supplier name, supplier number, inventory item number, quantity ordered, unit of measure.

Hint: See the Review Problem.

c. Describe at least two techniques that can verify the proper functioning of controls by means of the through-the-computer approach.

(CMA adapted)

17-8 Refer to Problem 14-21 on page 657. You have been assigned as the external auditor in charge of a financial audit of the Vane Corporation's information system and financial statements. During your review of the payroll application you discover the facts listed in the problem.

Required

a. Indicate your preliminary assessment of internal accounting controls, based on the facts uncovered. What other facts would be helpful in arriving at your assessment?

b. Assuming that you assess the internal accounting controls to be inadequate, what step(s) in the audit process do you omit? What effect does this assessment have on your audit program?

c. Assuming that the uncovered facts, plus additional facts you discover, lead you to assess the internal accounting controls to be adequate, what types of tests might you perform? Be specific, noting tests based on the through-the-computer approach as well as on the around-the-computer approach.

d. Regardless of your assessment of the internal accounting controls, what are several audit objectives that your audit program would contain? Be specific with respect to the payroll application.

17-9 VBR Company has completed its implementation of the new on-line cash receipts–accounts receivable system. (See Problem 12-18, page 533.)

Required

a. Outline the steps in the process that an external auditor should follow when auditing this new cash receipts–accounts receivable application. Assume that the examination is a part of a financial audit of VBR's financial statements.

b. How would the process be affected if the auditor's overall evaluation, after tests of controls, is that the internal accounting controls are inadequate? Be as specific as possible in your answer.

17-10 The Northern Lights Co. of Fredericton, New Brunswick, maintains the following data items in its salary payroll master records.

> Social Security number.
> Plant code.
> Department code.
> Name.
> Address.
> Position or job code.
> Annual salary.
> Biweekly gross pay.
> Retirement rate.
> Bond deduction amount.
> Federal income tax exemptions.
> Provincial income tax rate.
> Pension plan deduction.
> Year-to-date earnings, gross.
> Bond balance.
> Year-to-date federal income tax withheld.
> Year-to-date provincial income tax withheld.
> Pension plan balance.
> Year-to-date earnings, net.

Required

Describe several ways that a generalized audit software package can aid in the audit of the payroll of the Northern Lights Co.

(SMAC adapted)

17-11 Solt Manufacturing Company of Honolulu, Hawaii, is undergoing an audit for the year ended June 30. During the course of the audit, Jim Peters, the auditor, plans to use a generalized computer audit software package. Solt's information systems (IS) manager has agreed to prepare special tapes

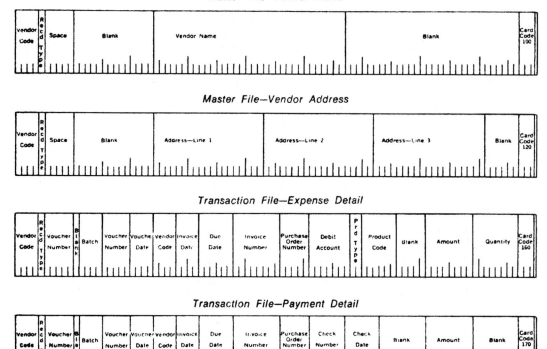

Master File—Vendor Name

Master File—Vendor Address

Transaction File—Expense Detail

Transaction File—Payment Detail

of data from the pertinent files whose record formats appear above.

In his review of the accounts payable and related procedures Mr. Peters learns that the following monthly outputs are prepared.

    a. Cash disbursements by check number.

    b. Outstanding payables.

    c. Purchase journals arranged by account charged and by vendor (supplier).

He also notes that vouchers and supporting invoices, receiving reports, and purchase order copies are filed by vendor code, whereas purchase orders and checks are filed numerically.

Required

a. Describe the controls that Mr. Peters should maintain over (1) preparing the special tape and (2) processing the special tape with the generalized computer audit software.

b. Prepare for the IS manager a schedule outlining the data that should be included on the special tape for examination of accounts payable and related procedures. This schedule should show (1) the client file from which the item should be extracted and (2) the name of the item of data.

c. Describe several ways the generalized audit software package can aid in the audit of the accounts payable and related procedures.

(CPA adapted)

17-12 Boos & Baumkirchner, Inc., of Montgomery, Alabama, is a medium-size manufacturer of products for the leisure-time activities market (camping equipment, scuba gear, bows and arrows, etc.). During the past year a computer system was installed, and inventory records of finished goods and parts were converted to computer processing. Each record of the inventory master file, which is stored on a magnetic disk, contains the following data items.

Item or part number.
Description.
Size.
Unit of measure code.
Quantity on hand.
Cost per unit.
Total value of inventory on hand at cost.
Date of last sale or usage.
Quantity used or sold this year.
Economic order quantity.
Code number of major supplier.

In preparation for the year-end physical inventory the firm prepares two identical sets of preprinted inventory-count cards. One set is for the inventory counts, and the other is for use in making audit test counts. Each card contains the following punched and interpreted data: the item or part number, the description, the size, and the unit of measure code.

In taking the year-end inventory, the firm's personnel will write the actual counted quantity on the face of each card. When all counts are complete, the counted quantity will be key-punched into the cards. The cards will be processed against the master file, and quantity-on-hand figures will be adjusted to reflect the actual count. A listing will be prepared to show any missing inventory-count cards and all quantity adjustments of more than $100 in value. These items will be investigated, and all required adjustments will be made. When adjustments have been completed, the final year-end balances will be computed and posted to the general ledger.

The auditor who will supervise the physical inventory and conduct an audit of inventory has available a general-purpose audit software package that will run on the firm's computer and can process both card and disk files.

Required

Describe several ways a general-purpose computer audit software package can be used to assist in all aspects of the audit of the inventory of Boos & Baumkirchner, Inc. (For example, the package can be used to read the inventory master file and list items and parts with a high unit cost or total value. Such items can be included in the test counts to increase the dollar coverage of the audit verification.)

(CPA adapted)

17-13 The Houston Manufacturing Company of Huntsville, Texas, stores its fixed-asset master file on magnetic disks. The layout of a fixed-asset record is as follows:

Field Size	Description of Data Item
5	Asset number
25	Description
1	Class of asset
3	Location of asset (i.e., plant, department)
6	Date of acquisition
2	Estimated useful life (years)
1	Depreciation method (e.g., straight line, sum-of-years)
3	Annual rate of depreciation (if needed)
9	Acquisition cost
9	Accumulated depreciation, beginning of month
8	Depreciation expense, year-to-date
6	Date of disposal (if appropriate)
9	Disposal amount (if appropriate)

During an annual audit the firm's external auditor decides to employ a GAS package to aid in the substantive testing. Among the objectives that the package should help achieve are: examining all changes since last year's audit, reconciling totals to the general ledger accounts, checking the accuracy of all calculated amounts, and performing suitable analyses.

Required

a. Describe, in terms of specific data items and functions, how the GAS package will assist in the audit of fixed assets.

b. Identify several audit procedures pertaining to fixed assets that cannot be performed, or can only be partially performed, by means of the GAS package.

Note: This problem requires a basic knowledge of auditing.

17-14 The Weimer Co. of Ames, Iowa, processes its payment transactions on a computer system. Batches of payment transactions are keyed onto magnetic tape from check vouchers, sorted by supplier number, and then checked by an edit run. Each payment transaction record contains the following data items. The size of the fields containing the data and sample data values appear to the right of the data item names.

Data Item	Size of Field (in characters)	Sample Value
Supplier number	4	4569
Voucher number	5	20310
Voucher date	6	060391
Invoice date	6	052891
Invoice number	5	68732
Purchase order number	5	10500
Due date	6	070391
Check number	6	530000
Check date	6	070291
Amount	9	5000.00

The edit program has been designed to verify the input data and processing by the use of the following types of programmed checks: field check, completeness test, sign check, sequence check, validity check, limit check, and relationship check.

Required

a. Prepare a matrix that specifies the particular data items to be verified by each of the programmed checks.

b. Prepare test transactions that each contain one error intended to determine that a programmed check is functioning properly. Each transaction should contain data in all the fields (except when the completeness of data is being tested). List the test transactions in the rows of a table that has columns pertaining to the ten fields of input data (with the column headings consisting of the data item names). In a separate table state the purpose of each transaction and show the expected result that should appear on an exception and summary report.

17-15 The Weimer Co. also processes its sales transactions on a computer system. Each sales order is entered via a terminal at a sales branch and stored on a magnetic disk at the home office to await further processing. As each sales order is entered, it is checked by an edit program. Each transaction involving a sales order should include the following data: user code, transaction code, customer number, sales branch number, salesperson number, expected shipping date, product number(s), and quantity (or quantities).

Required

a. Prepare test data that are to be used to check for the presence of needed programmed checks in the edit program. State the purpose of each test and show how an error detected by the test might be displayed on the screen of the auditor's terminal.

b. If the integrated test facility technique is employed in conjunction with the test sales transactions, describe the likely contents of the test facility and the report based on the contents.

17-16 Talbert Corporation hired an independent computer programmer to develop a simplified payroll application for its newly purchased computer. The programmer developed an on-line data base microcomputer system that minimized the level of knowledge required by the operator. It was based on typing answers to input cues that appeared on the terminal's viewing screen, examples of which follow.

New employees routine.

(1) Employee name?
(2) Employee number?
(3) Social security number?
(4) Rate per hour?
(5) Single or married?
(6) Number of dependents?
(7) Account distribution?

Current payroll routine.

(1) Employee number?
(2) Regular hours worked?
(3) Overtime hours worked?
(4) Total employees this payroll period?

The independent auditor is attempting to verify that certain input validation (edit) checks exist to ensure that errors resulting from omissions, invalid entries, or other inaccuracies will be detected during the typing of answers to the input cues.

Required

a. Identify the input validation (programmed edit) checks that the auditor should expect to find in the payroll edit program with respect to each input cue. Note that in the cases of certain cues more than one check is needed and that the same check may be applied to more than one cue. When a check requires that the data response to a cue be compared to another response, identify the data item being compared.

b. For each input validation (programmed edit) check identified in requirement **a**,

state the assurances that it should provide in the payroll application.

(CPA adapted)

17-17 Recently, the Central Savings and Loan Association of Jefferson City, Missouri, installed an on-line computer system. Each teller in the association's main office and seven branch offices has an on-line terminal. Customers' mortgage payments and savings account deposits and withdrawals are recorded in the accounts by the computer from data input by the teller at the time of the transaction. The teller keys the proper account by account number and enters the information in the terminal keyboard to record the transaction. The accounting department at the main office also has terminals. The computer is housed at the main office.

In addition to servicing its own mortgage loans, the association acts as a mortgage servicing agency for three life insurance companies. In the latter activity the association maintains mortgage records and serves as the collection and escrow agent for the mortgagees (the insurance companies), who pay a fee to the association for these services.

Required

Describe the ways an embedded audit module within the deposit/withdrawal processing program might be used to aid in performing tests of controls pertaining to Central's internal accounting controls.

(CPA adapted)

17-18 Ristan Enterprises manufactures and sells colored plastic bottles. Ristan's financial and manufacturing control systems are completely automated.

Christine Field, director of internal audit, is responsible for coordinating all of the operational and financial audits conducted by Ristan's internal audit department. She has been reading and has observed how external auditors use computers in their audits. She believes that Ristan should acquire computer audit software to assist in the financial audits that her department conducts. For instance, a generalized computer audit program would assist in basic audit work such as data retrieval of computer files for review. It would also extract samples, conduct other tests, and generate balances, all of which would be printed out so that conventional audit investigation techniques could be used. She also could use an integrated test facility (ITF), which uses, monitors, and controls dummy test data. This data would be processed with the regular data. The ITF and the test data would check the existence and adequacy of program data entry controls and processing controls.

She has also been aware of computer-assisted audit software, which can perform such functions as generating audit schedules and financial statements. Furthermore, she just read an article describing software called an auditor expert system.

Required

a. Identify the advantages and disadvantages to internal and external auditors of using various types of software to aid in conducting audits.

b. Contrast the purposes and features of the two audit techniques known as generalized audit software (GAS) and integrated test facilities (ITF).

c. Contrast the steps to be followed in using a GAS and those to be followed in using an ITF.

d. Contrast computer-assisted audit software and auditor expert system software, and state several possible uses of each in a firm such as Ristan.

(CMA adapted)

17-19 You have been assigned to review the internal controls of the credit department of a recently acquired subsidiary. The subsidiary imports several lines of microcomputers and sells them to retail stores throughout the country. The department consists of the credit manager (who was hired only six months ago to replace the previous manager, who retired), a clerk, and a part-time secretary.

Sales are made through 15 sales representatives—five at headquarters who handle large accounts with retail chains and the local area, and ten located throughout the country. Sales representatives visit the premises of current and prospective customers and, if a sale is made, prepare a customer order form, which consists of the original and three copies. One copy is retained by the customer, one by the sales representative, one is sent to the warehouse, and the original is sent to headquarters. For new customers, if the order is for more than $5000, a credit application is also completed and sent along with the order to headquarters. The credit application includes a bank reference and three credit references along with financial statements.

The purchase order sent to headquarters goes first to the credit department for approval. When the credit department receives the order, the clerk looks up the customer's name in a card file to determine whether it is a new or old customer. Only customers with "good credit" are listed in the file. If the customer is found, the clerk examines a monthly report which lists all accounts which have not been paid in 60 days. If the customer's account is not listed in the report, the clerk initials the purchase order as approved and sends it to accounting for recording and billing. Orders from new customers or from customers listed on the "60-day" report are held for review by the credit manager.

For orders greater than $5000 from new

customers, the credit manager reviews the credit application along with the financial statements and calls at least one of the credit references. If approved, the manager initials the order and gives it to the secretary to prepare a card for the clerk's "card" file and to file the credit application. If denied, the manager adds the customer's name to a list of past rejected credit applications and canceled accounts. For new customers with orders for less than the $5000 limit, the credit manager reviews the order and checks it against the list of past rejections. If not on this list, the order is initialed as approved and sent to accounting. For orders from customers with accounts 60 days past due, the manager reviews the details of the accounts and the original credit application. If approved, the order is initialed and sent to accounting.

If orders are not approved, the credit manager calls the warehouse to stop shipment. The order is marked "credit not approved" and given to the secretary who notifies the sales representative and the customer that the order has been rejected. The order and the credit application are then thrown away. Once each quarter, the credit manager requests that the accounting department provide a listing of all accounts over 90 days old with supporting detail of account activity for the last 12 months. The credit manager reviews this information and determines whether action should be taken. Action consists of first calling the sales representative who handles the account and asking him or her to contact the client about payment. If payment is not received in three weeks, the credit manager calls the customer and requests payment. At this time, the credit manager also has the clerk pull the customer's card from the clerk's "customer card" file. If payment is not made in two weeks, the account is turned over to a collection agency. When an account has been with a collection agency for two months without

receiving payment, the account is written off. The credit manager prepares the necessary adjusting entries.

Required

a. List four specific phases of an internal control evaluation and the appropriate audit steps needed to complete each phase in this situation.

b. Assuming that the foregoing description is correct, list four deficiencies associated with the credit function. Using the format suggested below, give the deficiency, associated risk, and a control that internal auditing should recommend to eliminate the deficiency.

Deficiency	Associated Risk	Recommended Control
(1)		
(2)		
(3)		
(4)		

(CIA adapted)

17-20 The Desmond Manufacturing Company of South Orange, New Jersey, recently installed an on-line computer system, primarily to monitor its production operations. Your public accounting firm performs the annual financial audit, and you have been assigned to audit the direct labor and materials collection and processing system.

Upon meeting with the production manager during your visit, you learn that the computer hardware used in this production system consists of a mainframe processor, terminals at the various production floor workstations and in the materials storeroom, magnetic disk drives, and a high-speed printer. The data collection and processing procedure is as follows: Data concerning labor hours worked on production jobs are entered via the production floor terminals by the production employees themselves. Data concerning direct materials charged into production are entered via the storeroom terminal by the storekeeper. Labor and materials data are edited when entered and then stored temporarily. Late each afternoon the data are processed by a job costing program, and the relevant files (i.e., materials inventory, labor expense, and work-in-process) are updated. Outputs from this processing include job cost reports, labor distribution reports, materials usage reports, cost variance reports, and exception and summary reports. Standard costs maintained in an on-line file are used to convert the labor times and material quantities to dollar values and to apply overhead costs.

Required

a. Outline the auditing process that you plan to follow, assuming that you discover that the internal accounting controls relating to the production labor and materials system are sufficiently adequate to be relied on.

b. Identify several key general and application controls that you are likely to observe in your review of internal accounting controls, given the assumption in **a**.

c. Describe audit techniques that will be useful in tests of controls. Assume that special audit instructions have been incorporated into the job costing program during its development.

d. List several specific audit objectives to be achieved during substantive testing.

e. Discuss specific functions that your firm's GAS package can perform during substantive testing.

Hint: Refer to the Review Problem and to any standard auditing textbook during the preparation of the solution.

Suggested Readings

American Institute of Certified Public Accountants. *Audit Approaches for a Computerized Inventory System.* New York: AICPA, 1980.

———. *Computer-Assisted Audit Techniques.* New York: AICPA, 1979.

———. *Considerations in Electronic Funds Transfer Systems.* New York: AICPA, 1978.

———. *Codification of Statements on Auditing Standards, Numbers 1 to 26.* New York: AICPA, 1980.

———. *Statement on Auditing Standards No. 48: The Effects of Computer Processing on the Examination of Financial Statements.* New York: AICPA, 1984.

———. *Statement on Auditing Standards No. 55: Consideration of the Internal Control Structure in a Financial Statement Audit.* New York: AICPA, 1988.

Borthick, A. Faye. "Audit Implications of Information Systems." *The CPA Journal* (April 1986), pp. 40–46.

Broad, Robert D. "The Audit of System Development Methodology." *Internal Auditor* (June 1986), pp. 47–49.

Carlow, Alan, and Johnson, Bart. "Overcoming the Mystique in EDP Auditing." *Management Accounting* (August 1984), pp. 30–37.

Cash, James I., Jr.; Bailey, Andrew D., Jr.; and Whinston, Andrew B. "A Survey of Techniques for Auditing EDP-Based Accounting Information Systems." *The Accounting Review* (Oct. 1977), pp. 813–832.

Davis, Gordon B.; Adams, Donald L.; and Schaller, Carol A. *Auditing and EDP.* 2d ed. New York: AICPA, 1983.

Dunmore, David B. "A Rule-Based Expert System for Auditors." *EDPACS* (Sept. 1987), pp. 1–5.

Edge, William R., and Wilson, Edward G. "A Prototype Expert System for Internal Auditors." *EDP Auditor* (1989), pp. 71–77.

Fields, Kent T.; Sami, Heibatollah; and Sumners, Glenn E. "Quantification of the Auditor's Evaluation of Internal Control in Data Base Systems." *The Journal of Information Systems* (Fall 1986), pp. 24–47.

Garsombke, H. Perrin, and Cerullo, Michael. "Auditing Advanced Computerized Systems in the Future." *The EDP Auditor* (2, 1984), pp. 1–11.

Grabski, Severin V. "Auditor Participation in Accounting Systems Design: Past Involvement and Future Concerns." *The Journal of Information Systems* (Fall 1986), pp. 3–23.

Groomer, S. Michael, and Murthy, Uday S. "Continuous Auditing of Database Applications: An Embedded Audit Module Approach." *The Journal of Information Systems* (Spring 1989), pp. 53–69.

Halper, Stanley D., et al. *Handbook of EDP Auditing*. New York: Warren Gorham & Lamont, 1986.

Holly, Charles L., and Reynolds, Keith. "Audit Concerns in an On-Line Distributed Computer Network." *Journal of Systems Management* (June 1984), pp. 32–36.

Hoar, Thomas. "How to Select an Audit Software Package." *Journal of Accounting and EDP* (Winter 1989), pp. 30–36.

Jancura, Elise G., and Boos, Robert V. *Establishing Controls and Auditing the Computerized Accounting System*. New York: Van Nostrand Reinhold, 1981.

Johnson, Robert C. "Microcomputers Help California's Auditors." *Internal Auditor* (April 1988), pp. 24–26.

Lampe, James C., and Kneer, Dan C. "Audit Implications of Distributed Data Processing." *The EDP Auditor* (1984), pp. 39–50.

Litecky, Charles R., and Rittenberg, Larry E. "The External Auditor's Review of Computer Controls." *Communications of the ACM* (May 1981), pp. 288–295.

Loebbecke, James K.; Mullarkey, John F.; and Zuber, George R. "Auditing in a Computer Environment." *The Journal of Accountancy* (Jan. 1983), pp. 68–78.

Mar, Steve. "Using Expert Systems to Enhance the PC Audit Program." *EDP Auditor* (1989), pp. 35–55.

Moeller, Robert R. *Modern Computer Security, Audit and Control*. New York: John Wiley, 1988.

Nadel, Robert B. "Computer Auditing—Has Its Time Come?" *The CPA Journal* (March 1987), pp. 24–29.

Pleier, Joseph R. "Computer-Assisted Auditing." *The Internal Auditor* (1984), pp. 13–20.

Porter, W. Thomas, and Perry, William E. *EDP Controls and Auditing*. 5th ed. Boston: Kent, 1987.

Sobol, Michael I. "Local Area Network: New Concern for Auditors." *Internal Auditor* (Feb. 1988), pp. 33–35.

Socha, Wayne J. "Practical Tips for Automating the Auditor." *Internal Auditor* (Feb. 1989), pp. 52–59.

Temkin, Robert H., and Winters, Alan J. "SAS NO. 55: The Auditor's New Responsibility for Internal Control." *The Journal of Accountancy* (May 1988), pp. 86–98.

Thomas, C. William, and Henke, Emerson O. *Auditing: Theory and Practice*. 2d ed. Boston: Kent, 1986.

Vallabhaneni, S. Rao. "Auditing Vendor-Developed Application Software." *Internal Auditor* (Oct. 1986), pp. 34–36.

Watne, Donald A., and Turney, Peter B. *Auditing EDP Systems*. Englewood Cliffs, N.J.: Prentice-Hall, 1984.

Weber, Ron. *EDP Auditing: Conceptual Foundations and Practice*. 2d ed. New York: McGraw-Hill, 1988.

Wu, Frederick H., and Hahn, Randall L. "A Control-Complexity and Control-Point Orientation to the Review of an Entity's Internal Control Structure in the Computer Environment." *The Journal of Information Systems* (Spring 1989), pp. 117–131.

After studying this chapter, you should be able to do the following:

Compare the file-oriented approach to data management with the modern data base approach.

Identify the components and functions of software used in the management of data base systems.

Contrast several logical data models that are currently employed in data base systems.

Describe the several sequential phases that are required in the design and implementation of sound data base systems.

Identify internal accounting controls and security measures that are particularly needed in data base systems.

Chapter **18**

DATA BASE SYSTEMS

In this information age the data resource has assumed increasing importance. When relevant data are uncollected or lost or inaccessible, a firm can suffer severe economic consequences. Consequently, the managements of many firms have recognized the vital need to devote careful attention to managing the data resource.

Chapter 8 discussed the fundamentals of data management, including the key functions, objectives, and underlying characteristics. It focused on the management of files and records, the traditional structures through which data have been organized and accessed for use. In recent years, however, the data base approach has enhanced the potential of data management. **Data base systems,** which combine the data base approach with suitable computer hardware and soft-

ware, enable firms to manage the data resource in an efficient manner while serving the information needs of users much more effectively.

This chapter emphasizes the aspects of data base systems with which accountants should become familiar. Thus, it begins with a thorough survey of the data base approach. Then it examines the functional components of data base management systems, contrasts the data models that provide extended structures for storing and accessing data, surveys the phased development of data base systems, and identifies controls and security measures that are particularly relevant to data base systems. The more technical and physical aspects of data base systems are de-emphasized, except when they bear directly on logical data base design.

Data Base Approach

All of the examples in prior chapters involving the management of data have been based on the file-oriented approach. Many firms continue to use this traditional approach with respect to some or all of their applications. With appropriate file and record structures this approach can be quite efficient. It can well serve the needs of the application and its users as long as the needs remain unchanged. However, an increasing number of firms have become dissatisfied with the file-oriented approach. Many such firms are moving toward or have fully adopted the data base approach.

Figure 18-1 presents the contrasting configurations of the two approaches. As described in Chapter 8, the file-oriented approach focuses on individual applications and provides separate sets of files for each. The **data base approach** assumes a broader perspective of a firm's information needs and treats data as a resource. Thus, it maintains the data for all applications in a central data base. The data base approach also interposes a data base management system, a special type of computer software, between the data base and the programs for each of the applications.

This description, while capturing essential differences, only scratches the surface. It does not mention several other significant distinctions, nor does it explain the critically important implications. A more complete description begins by highlighting the shortcomings of the file-oriented approach; then it identifies the key features, benefits, and drawbacks of the data base approach.

Shortcomings of the File-Oriented Approach

Data redundancy. Since each application within the file-oriented approach maintains its own files, those files needed by more than one application must be duplicated. Figure 18-2 shows duplicate inventory master files being maintained by sales and purchases transaction processing systems. Moreover, the same data items often appear in more than one file. Thus, the numbers of inventory items (and perhaps their descriptions) are likely to be repeated in the inventory master file, the open purchase order file, and the supplier file. Data redundancy exacts two costs: the cost of added storage space and the cost of increased file maintenance.

Data inconsistency. As a consequence of redundant files and data items, the characteristics of data items and their values are likely to be inconsistent. For example, the inventory item number may be assigned the name ITEM in the sales application program and INVNO in the purchases application program. The quantity on hand of inventory item B43 might appear as 100 in the file maintained by the sales application; however, the value for the same item may appear as 10 in the file maintained by the purchases application, if that file has not yet been updated to reflect a receipt of 90 units.

Inaccessibility of data. Information available under the file-oriented approach generally consists of reports that have been pre-programmed. An example of such a report is the inventory status report arranged according to the inventory item (i.e., the primary key). Ad hoc reports usually cannot be provided quickly upon request, especially if they are to be based on data from more than one application, for two reasons. Reprogramming is necessary to produce the reports, and files are not integrated across applications. Furthermore, information concerning particular activities or entities may be difficult to obtain, since each application or organizational function is considered to "own" the information it generates and stores.

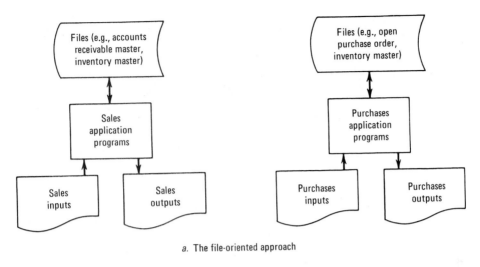

a. The file-oriented approach

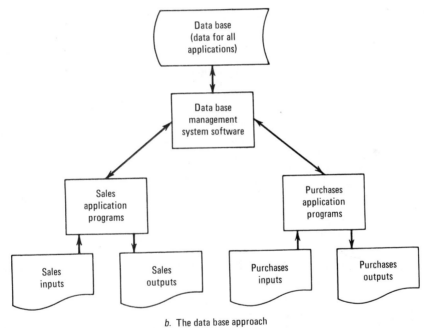

b. The data base approach

FIGURE 18-1 The two approaches to computer-based data management.

Inflexibility. Changes to current file-oriented applications and development of new applications are not easily made. They tend to be quite time-consuming and costly. The main reason for this inflexibility is that the application programs are closely dependent on (1) the data that they access and (2) the physical media on which the data are stored. Generally the programs directly incorporate the record structures and data names within the

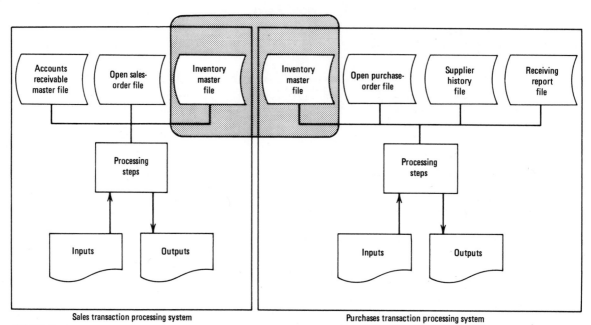

Sales transaction processing system   Purchases transaction processing system

FIGURE 18-2   Redundant files in file-oriented transaction processing applications.

files used in the applications. Programs must often be written with the nature of the physical storage media in mind, as well as the location of the records on the media and the file organization method being used. Thus, each change tends to involve extensive and detailed reprogramming. Since reprogramming is necessary each time a revision is made to a file (e.g., a lengthened field) and each time a new report is needed, the changes can become quite numerous. Furthermore, each change usually requires the attention of experienced programmers. These persons tend to be scarce resources in most firms.

Another reason for inflexibility is that the independent file represents the only type of data structure employed in the file-oriented approach. File structures are limited in their capacity to associate data that are related to each other. Although files may be consolidated, the larger records in such files are cumbersome to process and print.

Features of the Data Base Approach

The data base approach provides an array of features that overcome the redundancy, inconsistency, inaccessibility, and inflexibility of the file-oriented approach.

Data independence. Central to the data base approach is the feature of **data independence**—the separation of the data from the related application programs. Data independence is achieved by interposing a set of software known as a **data base management system** (DBMS) between the data base and the application programs. Figure 18-3 depicts this separation.

In addition to separating the data from application programs, the DBMS also isolates the logical view of data from the physical view. The **logical view** of data is the perspective that users have of the overall structure and relationships of data within the data base. This logical view, or "blueprint,"

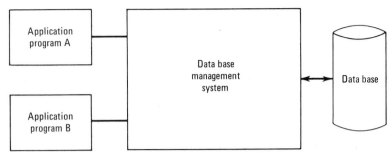

FIGURE 18-3 Data independence in the data base approach.

is generally called the **schema.** The term **physical view** refers to the actual arrangement and manipulation of data on the physical storage media.[1] Only the DBMS (apart from the data base administrator) has "knowledge" of both views.

Data independence enables changes to be made much more easily, quickly, and less expensively under the data base approach than in file-oriented systems. Changes affecting data need be made in the DBMS alone, rather than in all the application programs that use the data. Changes can be made to the physical storage of data without affecting the logical view or application programs. Thus, physical storage of data may be employed in the most efficient manner. Conversely, changes made to the logical view or to application programs do not affect the physical view. In fact, programmers and others can change application programs or develop new programs without being aware of how the data are physically stored.

Data standardization. Data items within a data base have standard definitions. For instance, the data item representing the

amount of a sale has only one name, meaning, and format. Thus, stored data are compatible with every application program that accesses the data base.

One-time data entry and storage. Individual values of data, such as the amount of a sales transaction, are entered into a data base from only one source. Entered data items are thus processed only once. Generally the entered and processed items are stored in only one location, unless duplicate items are needed to provide cross-references or faster retrieval. Consequently, redundancy is reduced and inconsistencies between data items are effectively eliminated. As a result, processing time is minimized, storage requirements are reduced, and data integrity is enhanced.

Data integration. Data are organized by means of flexible structures called **data sets.** Although data sets include files and records, they also encompass integrated groupings of logically related data. For instance, a data set might consist of the records from two or more files that are linked together. It might be a three-dimensional structure that consists of the income statements for a firm over ten years, segmented by the several divisions of the firm. Alternatively, it might be a collection of two-dimensional tables.

Data sets in the data base approach also

[1]We should note that the logical view, also called the conceptual view, and the physical view, also called the internal view, are similar to (but also somewhat different from) the logical and physical records discussed in Chapter 8.

integrate the data pertaining to a broad range of activities and entities. In some cases the data may consist of all the data needed by a firm, although more often a particular data base pertains to one or more broad functions or activities of a firm.

The integration of data sets has two useful effects. It enables all affected data sets to be updated simultaneously by entered data items. As a result, the data sets are synchronized and the data they contain are consistent and highly reliable. Integrated data sets also enable users to obtain needed data more easily and quickly from the data base. Because they often cut across broad areas of a firm, a wide variety of users' needs can be met from the same data base. Wide-gauged reports that require data from several areas, such as budgets and product analyses, can be provided more handily.

Shared data ownership. Related to data integration is the feature of shared data ownership. All data within a data base are "owned in common" by the users. Thus, users from the accounting function as well as those from marketing and production may draw upon the same data base.

Shared ownership does *not* mean, however, that every user's logical view extends to the overall schema of a data base. Instead, a typical user needs only a view of that portion of the schema that enables him or her to fulfill assigned responsibilities. The partial view of the schema that is of interest to a particular user is called a **subschema.** To use an analogy, a schema is like the map of a city, whereas a subschema is the portion of the map that shows an individual's neighborhood and other points of interest. Figure 18-4 illustrates the distinction between subschemas and the schema. Like the schema, the subschemas are maintained by the DBMS.

Shared ownership of data therefore prevents functions from blocking the free flow

of data to qualified users. At the same time, the subschema technique simplifies the logical view for each individual user and provides appropriate protection against unauthorized uses of the data base.

Centralized data management. As we have seen, data are controlled and maintained on a continual basis by the DBMS. It stands guard over the data base and presents the logical view to users and application programs. Moreover, the DBMS generally provides data security through such measures as passwords.

Data are managed at the most fundamental level by a centralized authority known as the **data base administrator** (DBA). The DBA has overall responsibility for the data resource and for maintaining the DBMS. Among the functions performed by the DBA are the definition of data requirements, the establishment of data structures, and the upholding of such features of the data base approach as standardized data items. The duties of the DBA are discussed more fully in Chapter 21.

Benefits of the Data Base Approach

Figure 18-5 summarizes the major benefits of the data base approach. It also correlates the positive effects with the features discussed in the previous section. In sum, most of the shortcomings of the file-oriented approach are overcome or significantly corrected. Redundancies are reduced through the one-time entry and processing of data, as well as by the integration of data sets. Inconsistencies are eliminated, since all data sites affected by transaction data are updated simultaneously. Increased flexibility is provided through data independence and standardization. Accessibility is improved, as a result of both the sharing of data by users and the extensive relationships among the data.

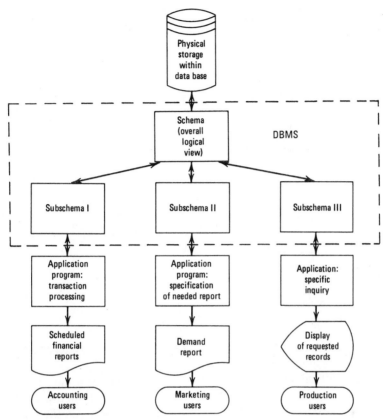

FIGURE 18-4 Three subschemas.

Each of these benefits enables the using firm to achieve the significant results listed in the figure.

Drawbacks of the
Data Base Approach

As might be expected, the data base approach exacts certain penalties. Consequently, it may not be the best choice for all firms or in all situations encountered by a single firm.

Costliness. The hardware and software required by the data base approach are very costly. Needed hardware usually includes a large primary storage unit, to contain the DBMS and operating systems, plus terminals for entering and receiving requests for information. Also, because all data in this approach must be stored on direct-access storage media, the storage cost per unit may be higher. Even more costly is the DBMS, usually a purchased software package that may cost in excess of $100,000. In addition, systems development personnel such as analysts generally need special training in the installation and modification of the DBMS and related software.

Initial inertia. Because it is radically different from the file-oriented approach, the data

Feature(s)	Benefit(s) Provided	Result(s) Achieved
Data independence Data standardization	Increased flexibility	Application programs can be changed more easily, more quickly, and less expensively.
One-time data entry Data integration	Reduced redundancy; eliminated inconsistencies	Storage space is conserved, processing time is minimized, and data are highly reliable.
Data integration Shared data ownership	Improved accessibility	Needed information can be obtained faster and more easily; a wider variety of users and their needs can be served.
Centralized data management	Improved data security and coordination	Unauthorized persons are prevented from accessing stored data; data resources are kept updated and available to meet specified requirements of users.

FIGURE 18-5   Correlation of data base features with the benefits they provide and the positive results the benefits achieve.

base approach generally creates complications and resistances. Systems development personnel encounter difficulties in working with an unfamiliar technology. Functional managers exhibit possessiveness with respect to "their" functional data and resist giving the data to a central data group. These reactions lead to considerable delays in putting the data base into operation.

Vulnerability.   Because a common data base is highly integrated, it is highly vulnerable. A breakdown in hardware or software has a much more severe effect than in a system having separate applications and files. If the data base becomes inoperable, none of the applications can operate.

Because of this vulnerability, the data base must be carefully protected. All data must be "backed up," so that the data base can be fully recovered if a malfunction occurs. The backup procedure, however, is complicated by the destructive nature of the overlay approach when updating data sets.

Data Base Management System

The heart of a data base system is the DBMS. As mentioned previously, it serves as the buffer between the physical storage of data and the logical views of the users. A DBMS must be both complex and powerful, since it implements the key features of the data base approach while managing the data base. Therefore, it deserves close attention at this point. This section explores the environment in which a DBMS operates and its functional components.

Environment of a DBMS

The environment of a DBMS ranges from users and their application software to the data base. To function properly, the DBMS must be compatible with the users' software, the operating system, and the computer hardware within which the various softwares operate. Figure 18-6 portrays these environmental factors and their relationship to three critical components of the

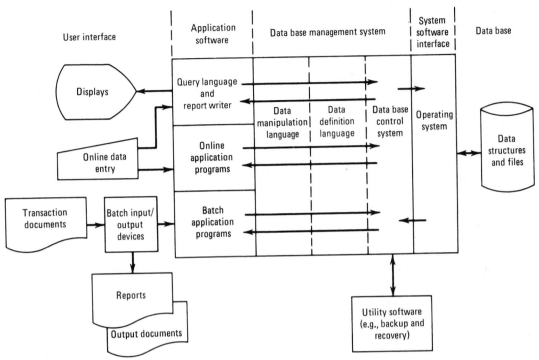

FIGURE 18-6 Environment of a data base management system.

DBMS. We can gain an understanding of this environment by observing the interactions of users, software, and hardware.

Initial interactions occur when users from throughout the firm access the computer system. Certain users (e.g., the payroll department) may enter transaction documents for batch processing. Other users (e.g., the sales order department) may enter transactions via on-line terminals or microcomputers, together with transaction codes or key words that specify the particular processing programs to be used. Still other users (e.g., cost accountants) may enter inquiries or ad hoc requests via on-line terminals.

Upon the entry of the data or inquiry/request (together with a transaction code or other designation), the operating system loads the appropriate software into primary storage and begins execution. An application

program is loaded in the case of transactions, whereas inquiry or report-writing software is loaded when an inquiry or request is entered.

As the application programs or other user-oriented software begin processing the transactions or inquiry/request, they need data from the data base. Transaction processing usually requires records from master files; inquiries and requests may also need master file records, or they may need data from history or open document or report files. The user-oriented software issues requests to the DBMS to acquire the needed data. Next the DBMS refers to the subschema of a requesting user, in order to ascertain the characteristics of the needed data. It also refers to the descriptions concerning the physical storage arrangements to determine the way to locate and access the data. The DBMS then provides specific instructions to the operating system (or to special access software in some systems), which directs the transfer of the data from the physical storage medium to the buffer of the primary storage unit. At this point the DBMS resumes control of the requested data, which it moves to the primary storage working area occupied by the requesting application program or other software. Finally, any processed data (e.g., updated master file records) are transferred back to the data base via the DBMS and operating system.

In addition to managing data, the DBMS may be requested by the user-oriented software to perform various processing steps. For instance, a batch application program may request that batched transactions be sorted. Other functions of the DBMS are discussed in the following section.

Functional Components of a DBMS

At present there is no uniform or "standardized" DBMS. The various available DBMS's vary widely in the set of functional components they incorporate. Often the marketing of a DBMS is similar to that of an automobile; it provides a set of basic or standard components and offers an assortment of "options." In line with this approach, the components that are standard to most DBMS's are a data base control system, a data definition language, and a data manipulation language. Optional components include a query language, report writer, screen formatter, host-language interface, utility software, and security software.

Data base control system (DBCS). The **DBCS,** or data base manager, controls the various components of the DBMS. It also communicates directly with the operating system. Thus, it is the key component that enables the DBMS to store, retrieve, and update data within the data base. Furthermore, it provides the capability for making changes to the data base as desired.

Data definition language (DDL). The **DDL** provides the means of completely describing the logical structure of the data base, including the schema and the subschema for each user. It also enables such physical aspects as the lengths of fields and character types to be defined. Thus, it serves in a manner similar to the Data Division in a COBOL-written application program.[2] Expressions written in DDL link the logical and physical views together, thereby providing an interface between the instructions in an application program and the data base. Rather than pertaining to a single application program, though, the DDL extends to all application programs and all data structures stored throughout an entire data base. The DDL also enables relationships among records and data items in complex data structures to be stated. Furthermore, it allows security measures such as passwords to be specified.

An example of a DDL used to express the structure of the data in portions of a schema pertaining to an accounts payable data base is shown below. Included are expressions that specify the name of the schema, a physical storage area, the data items in a record (including the primary key), a password, and the relationship between the supplier record and purchase order record. (Three dots indicate omitted expressions.)

```
. . .
SCHEMA NAME IS ACCTPAY
. . .
AREA NAME IS SUPP-AREA
    AREA CODE IS 2
    ALLOCATE 8 PAGES
    PAGES ARE 336 WORDS
. . .
RECORD NAME IS SUPPL
    RECORD CODE IS 10
```

[2]The Data Division in COBOL identifies the storage record layouts for inputs, outputs, and working storage. The division specifies the size to allot to each field, as well as its mode, placement of decimal points, and so on.

```
LOCATION MODE IS CALC DMSCALC
IN SUPP-AREA-NAME
USING SUPP-ID
DUPLICATES ARE NOT ALLOWED
05 SUPP-ID PIC X(6)
05 SUPP-NAME PIC X(30)
05 STREET-ADDRESS PIC X(30)
05 REMAIN-ADDRESS
      10 CITY PIC X(20)
      10 STATE PIC XX
      10 ZIP PIC X(9)

   . . .

PRIVACY LOCK IS AIOUZ

   . . .

SET NAME IS SUPPL-PO
   SET CODE IS 3
   MODE IS CHAIN
   ORDER IS FIRST
   OWNER IS SUPPL
   MEMBER IS PO AUTOMATIC
         SET OCCUR SELECTION THRU
         LOCATION MODE OF OWNER

   . . .
```

Data dictionary. Though not strictly a component of the DBMS, a **data dictionary** is a repository of data that is maintained by a DBMS or associated software. Normally organized around individual data items, it includes all pertinent aspects relating to the logical data structures and certain of the physical aspects. Thus, a data dictionary represents a duplication of the information contained in implemented DDL expressions. In fact, it may be used directly by the DBMS to locate the data needed to satisfy requests from application programs and other users' software.

A data dictionary, however, encompasses the totality of the data used by a firm in all applications. Even when a firm employs more than one data base and performs certain applications under the file-oriented as well as the data base approach, it usually maintains only one data dictionary. Consequently, a data dictionary serves as (1) one type of data documentation, (2) an aid in designing and changing the information system, and (3) a control device to prevent nonstandardized and unauthorized data. In serving these purposes it can provide a number of useful reports to the data base administrator, application programmers, and users such as accountants. Typical reports may list all programs or files in which a particular data item is used, all data items appearing in a particular application, and all users authorized to access a particular data item.

A definition in the data dictionary concerning each data item might include the following: the name and description of each data item, the length and character type of the field in which stored, the records or other data structures in which found, the outputs in which used, the application programs in which used, the authorized users and other security restrictions, and the sources of the data item. When complex data structures are employed in a data base, the relationships and linkages among data items are also included. Figure 18-7 shows segments of a data dictionary for a hypothetical manufacturer.

In some firms the data dictionary has been expanded to include broader aspects of information resource management. For instance, definitions concerning the key entities of a firm, such as customers and products, may be added. As we shall see, entities represent key building blocks in the schema or conceptual view of a firm. By their inclusion the data dictionary thus becomes a descriptor of the schema.[3]

Data manipulation language (DML). The **data manipulation language** (DML) provides the means of phrasing requests and inquiries. It enables data to be easily stored, manipulated, and retrieved from the data base by users. Most DML's provide those means

[3]Daniel S. Appleton, "The Modern Data Dictionary," *Datamation* (March 1, 1987), pp. 66–68.

Precise Manufacturing Co.

Data Dictionary

Item code	Item name	Item description	Field length	Character type	Records in which found	Source	Application programs	Outputs in which used	Authorized users
01	Customer order number	The code on the customer order that identifies the order	5	Numeric	Open order, sales history, back-order record	Customer order	AR14 SA04 SA12	Sales invoices, back orders, production orders, shipment records	Sales employees
02	Customer number	The code assigned to identify a customer	6	Numeric	Customer, open order record	Customer number list	AR04 AR14 SA04 SA12 CR02	Sales analysis by customer, list of outstanding orders, aging report, sales invoice	All employees
03	Customer name	The first name, middle initial and last name of a customer	25	Alphabetic	Customer record	Initial customer order	AR04 AR10	New business report, credit flash report, sales invoice, back order, shipment record	All employees
04	Credit limit	The maximum dollar amount that a customer may incur in outstanding	5	Numeric	Customer record	Credit record	CR02 AR04	Credit flash report	Credit manager

| 52 | Sales this month by salesperson | The dollar sales made by each salesperson in the current month | 8 | Numeric | Sales history record | Sales orders | SA04 SA06 | Sales analysis by salesperson | J. P. Morgan, S. C. Pierpoint |
| 53 | Scheduled delivery date | The date that a customer order is scheduled for delivery to | 8 | Alphanumeric | Open order, back order, production order record | Sales order acknowledgment or production order | SA04 PR08 | Unfilled order on hand, delayed orders, delayed invoices | T. Q. Adamly, M. U. Gump |

FIGURE 18-7 Segments within a data dictionary.

through the use of powerful verbs such as PRINT, DISPLAY, DELETE, ADD, SORT, and CALC. One or more may be used in an expression that the DML translates into executable commands. Included in the expressions are the names or codes of files, records, and data items. Thus, programmers and others who use DML verbs do not need to know the physical locations of the desired data. Furthermore, the expressions may be incorporated into application programs written in COBOL or other suitable language. Alternatively, the expressions may be entered by users who desire to manipulate or retrieve stored data. Examples of statements involving DML verbs might be

DELETE SALEREP (where SALEREP is an obsolete sale report file)

SORT ARFILE BY CUSTNO (where CUSTNO is the customer number in the accounts receivable file ARFILE)

Since many DBMS's are available, there has been concern regarding lack of standardized data base concepts and specifications. This concern includes both the DDL and the DML, because of their critical roles in a DBMS. For instance, DML verbs vary among DBMS's, causing unnecessary problems for programmers and users who may be involved with more than one DBMS. Thus, in 1971 a Data Base Task Group of the Conference on Data Systems Languages (CODASYL) proposed the adoption of standard DDL and DML specifications. No true standard yet exists. However, progress has been made in the related area of query languages, as we shall see.

Query language. A query language provides a variety of commands that allow interactive searches of a data base. It is designed to be user friendly, so that nonprogrammer users can obtain responses to their inquiries without assistance from professional pro-

grammers. For instance, the commands are in Englishlike form. Although a query language has similarities to DML expressions, it offers a wider set of commands that emphasize the retrieval function. Moreover, to enhance security, the users may be prohibited from using DML expressions.

Structured query language (SQL) is an example of a query language. Because it was developed by the largest computer manufacturer, IBM, for use on computers of all sizes, SQL appears likely to become the de facto standard query language.[4] SQL is being incorporated into numerous DBMS's that are based on the relational model (to be discussed later). In addition to being available to users via a terminal or microcomputer, SQL statements can be embedded into programs in COBOL and other languages used for writing application programs. An example of an inquiry phrased in terms of SQL expressions is

```
SELECT    SSN, NAME, GPA
FROM      STUD.FILE
WHERE     STANDING = SENIOR
          AND MAJOR = ACCOUNTING
```

Report writer. A report writer or generator, akin to a query language, aids users in obtaining responses to information requests. It provides ad hoc reports in accordance with specifications pertaining to the heading, columns in the body, totals, and so forth. Report writers are discussed more extensively in Chapter 20, which deals with decision support systems.

Screen formatter. A screen formatter aids programmers and users in developing preformatted screens and screen displays. Its pow-

[4]Robert M. Curtice and William Casey, "Database: What's in Store?" *Datamation* (December 1, 1985), p. 83.

erful features simplify the tedious details of spacing, inserting prompts, and so on.

Host-language interface.   A type of access software known as a host-language interface is included with many mainframe DBMS's. It enables the application programs, written in a language such as COBOL, to "talk" to the DBMS.

Utility software.   Several utilities are needed to perform such duties as loading new files and data structures, purging obsolete records and data, dumping data onto magnetic tape for backup, recovering data sets after power failures or other disasters, and interfacing with a data communications network.

Security software.   Various security measures can be provided by special security software. One measure already noted is to prevent access of data by unauthorized persons. Another needed measure is lockout, which prevents two or more users from attempting to access the same data at the same time.

Logical Data Models

The collection of data organized under the data base approach differs in certain respects from the files used in the file-oriented approach. Although files and records are usually retained in present-day bases, new data structures become available. These structures emphasize the logical view of data and the relationships among associated data items. Although an enormous variety of logical structures can be built to meet varied needs, most can be classified under three *logical data models:* the tree model, the network model, and the relational model.

The tree and network models are typically constructed from records, whereas the relational model consists of tables representing flat files. All three provide extensive linkages among the records or tables, so that as-

sociated data may be retrieved as needed. Much of our following discussions deal with the logical view of these linkages. However, we should be aware that the related data must be physically linked as well. Most of the access methods described in Chapter 8 are employed with the three data models.

Tree Model

The **tree model** expresses hierarchical relationships among the records or data items of two or more data sets. Its basic structure consists of nodes and paths. At the top of the structure is the **root node.** In using a tree model to access data, the only means of entry is through the root node. Extending downward from the root node are access paths that connect to nodes at one or more lower levels. Conversely, each lower-level node ties back to one (and only one) node at a higher level. Each lower-level node is known as a child; the upper-level node is called its parent.

Figure 18-8 presents three specific tree structures. Each is portrayed by means of a **data structure diagram,** also called a Bachman diagram, which diagrams the generalized relationships among nodes. These examples should clarify the foregoing logical concepts.

Figure 18-8a shows an example of a set, the simplest linked data structure. A **set** consists of nodes at two levels connected by an access path. The upper-level node is a parent, and the lower-level node is a child. In this case the upper-level node is also the root node; however, sets can be located at any two levels of a data structure.[5] The root node

---

[5]Terminology relating to data bases can be quite technical and variable. The term *set,* for instance, can be expanded to include a parent node and one *or more* children. Also, according to CODASYL conventions, the term *set* applies to networks only. The approach of this text is to introduce key concepts in as consistent and nontechnical a manner as possible. Thus, the main concept to be conveyed by the term *set* is that it is a building block for data structures such as trees and networks.

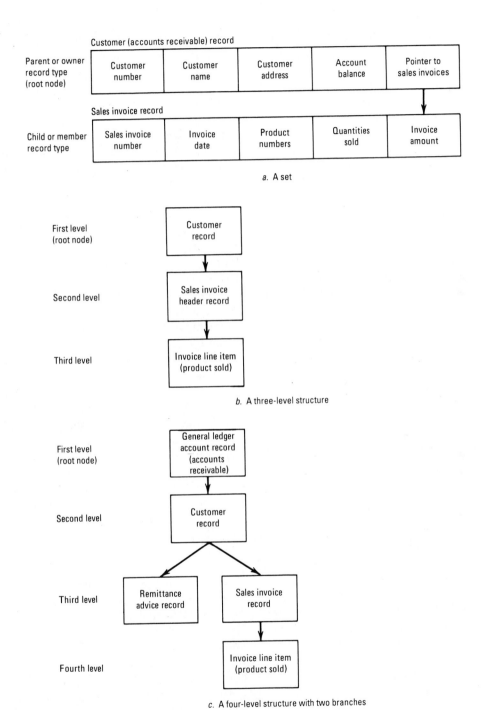

a. A set

b. A three-level structure

c. A four-level structure with two branches

FIGURE 18-8 Examples of tree structures.

in this example is a record in the accounts receivable master file (data set). The node at the lower level is a record in the sales invoice transaction file (data set). Both records shown in this diagram are actually *record types*, representing the category of records comprising their respective files. When record types appear in data structure diagrams, the term **owner record** may be substituted for parent and the term **member record** for child.

Another feature of a tree structure, as illustrated by Figure 18-8*a*, is a **one-to-many relationship.** In this type of relationship, one parent can have many children. Thus, any specific customer record may be associated with more than one sales invoice record (although in some instances there may be only one sales invoice). In a single occurrence, customer number 2356 of a firm may have been involved in three sales transactions this month and thus has received three sales invoices (children). However, each sales invoice belongs to only one customer (parent).

Figure 18-8*b* expands the set in Figure 18-8*a* to three levels, two sets, and three nodes. (In this and following data structure diagrams, the data items in the record types are omitted.) The customer record type now "owns" the sales invoice *header* record type, which in turn "owns" the invoice line-item record type. Thus, the sales invoice header record type, which consists of the sales invoice number and date, is an owner as well as a member record. It "owns" one or more line-item record types, where each line-item record includes one product number, the quantity of that product sold, and perhaps a description of the product. For instance, of the three sales invoices for customer 2356, one might own two line-item records and the other two might own three line-item records.

Figure 18-8*c* diagrams a structure consisting of four levels, four sets, five nodes, and two paths. The accounts receivable control account record type in the general ledger "owns" both the invoice and remittance ad-

vice record types. Thus, this data structure diagram expresses more relationships than do the two other diagrams in the figure. Again, the one-to-many relationship applies at all levels.

The main benefits of the tree model are that its logical structures are relatively simple and that requested data can be retrieved quite rapidly. The tree model is particularly suitable when the focus of concern is one entity, such as a customer or an employee. Thus, Manufacturers Hanover Trust Company, the fourth largest U.S. commercial bank, selected a DBMS based on a tree model because of its focus on bank customers.[6]

The particular DBMS software package selected by the bank was Information Management System (IMS), developed and marketed by IBM. IMS was introduced in 1968. Its use has been widespread, partly because its capabilities have been continually enhanced. One of its features is versatility in the physical access methods that it allows. For instance, the access from one record to another within a tree hierarchy can be achieved by means of embedded pointers, as shown in Figure 18-8*a*. IMS also allows related records to be stored together, so that sequential access is possible. In accessing the root node, IMS provides such methods as HISAM (i.e., via an index) and HDAM (i.e., via a hashing scheme).

Assume that a user wanted to retrieve data pertaining to customer 2356 and the sales invoices for that customer. Using HDAM (Hierarchic Direct Access Method), the IMS DBMS would first perform the calculations required by the hashing scheme to locate the disk address of the customer record. Next it would use the pointer in the customer record to locate and access the first sales invoice record. Then it would use a

---

[6]Marian Herman, "A Database Design Methodology for an Integrated Database Environment," *Data Base* (Fall 1983), p. 29.

pointer in that record (not shown in Figure 18-8a) to locate the next sales invoice record; this step would be repeated to find the last sales invoice record in the chain.

Network Model

The **network model,** also called the plex structure, expresses diverse relationships among records and data items of two or more data sets. Like the tree model, the network model establishes predefined access paths among the linked nodes. In contrast with the tree model, however, the network model (1) allows any node to be linked to any other node, (2) allows entry at more points than a

single root node, and (3) requires at least one member record type or data item to have two or more owners. Consequently, a network model offers a more realistic structuring of the complex relationships encountered by the typical firm. Figure 18-9 illustrates these general statements.

In Figure 18-9a an additional owner record has been imposed on the set shown in Figure 18-8a. The structure recognizes that the salesperson who makes a sale is related to the sales data. This relationship is perhaps due to a commission based on the amount of the sale. Thus, the salesperson record type also "owns" the sales invoice record type. Since the sales invoice record type has more

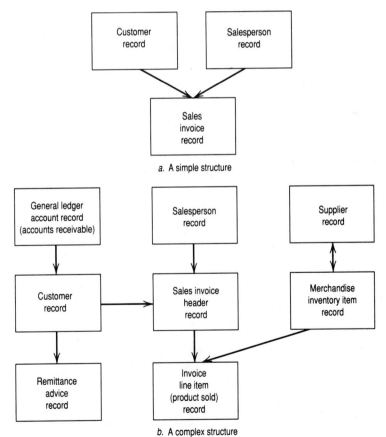

a. A simple structure

b. A complex structure

FIGURE 18-9   Examples of network structures.

than one owner record, the structure fulfills the criteria for a network. Also, as an owner record within a network the salesperson record type can serve as another entry point. Furthermore, it has a one-to-many relationship with the sales invoice record type. As a consequence, the structure would enable a user to inquire concerning recent sales made by salesperson 287. Upon accessing the record for salesperson 287, the network DBMS would then follow embedded pointers to access data from the four sales invoices reflecting recent sales.

Figure 18-9b shows a network structure that is an expansion of both the network structure in Figure 18-9a and the tree structure in Figure 18-8c. It is relatively intricate in several respects. First, it incorporates more record types (nodes), six of which are owner records. Entry into the network structure is now possible via the general ledger, supplier, and merchandise inventory records in addition to the two owner records in Figure 18-9a. Second, the network expresses more relationships, since more sets and access paths are available. Hence, a larger variety of reports and other outputs are possible, in order to meet the users' varied information needs. Third, the network includes a two-way relationship between the supplier record type and the merchandise record type. That is, the supplier record type can "own" the merchandise inventory record type, and the merchandise inventory record can "own" the supplier record type.

Let us explore this new type of relationship. A two-way relationship is described as a **many-to-many relationship,** since each of the record types involved can "own" multiple member records and also be "owned" by multiple owner records of the same type. A network that contains one or more many-to-many relationships is known as a **complex network.** In contrast, a network that contains only one-to-many (or one-to-one) relationships, such as the one in Figure 18-9a, is a **simple network.**

Figure 18-10a illustrates a many-to-many relationship in which only two record types are involved: a student record type and a class record type. Each student "owns" several classes, and each class "owns" a number of students. Figure 18-10b diagrams a simplified occurrence of this relationship. Many examples of many-to-many relationships appear in the area of business operations. For instance, consider the relationship between the finished goods and raw materials stocked by a manufacturer. Each product requires varied quantities of raw mate-

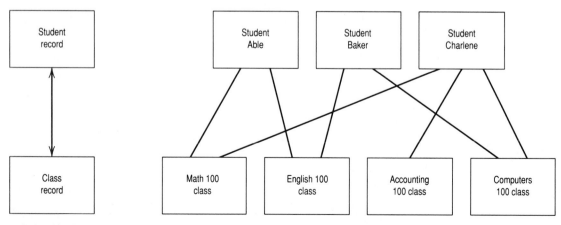

a. Student/class diagram

b. Student/class occurrence

FIGURE 18-10   Many-to-many relationships.

rials, and each raw material is likely to be used in more than one product.

Using suitable linkage, a many-to-many relationship in a network enables both record types to serve as owner records (and thus as entry points). Consequently, the two resulting sets increase the variety of possible information available to users. In the finished goods–raw materials example, reports are possible that (1) list all raw materials in each product (i.e., bills of materials) and (2) list all products in which each particular raw material and part is used (these are called "where used" reports).

Many-to-many relationships cannot be used by a DBMS as diagrammed in Figures 18-9b and 18-10a. They must be converted into equivalent one-to-many relationships. Figure 18-11 shows the conversion of the structure in Figure 18-10a. The new record, called the student/class record, is an example of an **intersection record.** It acts as the linkage between the two record types in a many-to-many relationship; thus, it allows either record type to serve as an owner record and to gain access to data in the other record. Stated another way, an intersection record is an index that provides cross-reference data. In this example, the student/class record would contain two columns, one for student identification number (e.g., 3456) and one for class code (e.g., ACC 100). The rows in this record could be quite numerous, since a student's number would appear as many times as the classes being taken. Thus, student Baker's number, 3456, would appear twice.[7]

Since intersection records convert all relationships to the one-to-many type, they have relevance to the tree model. That is, any network model can be converted into two or more tree models. If this is done, however, the same record types will appear more than once and new intersection records

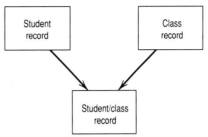

FIGURE 18-11   Two one-to-many relationships derived from the many-to-many relationship in Figure 18-10a.

will likely be introduced. Thus, the price for making this conversion is significant data redundancy.

The main benefit of the network model over the tree model is that it provides numerous relationships and entry points with minimum redundancy. Like the tree model, the network model enables requested data to be retrieved rapidly. On the other hand, the network model can be quite complex and thus difficult for programmers and users to understand.

The network model is particularly suitable when numerous transactions and routine requests for information occur and when the focus of concern is on several entities. Thus, Arizona State University (ASU) has employed the network model in developing its personnel data base, since such entities as students, faculty, staff employees, classes, and classrooms are all of concern. The particular DBMS software package selected by ASU was Integrated Database Management System (IDMS), developed by Cullinet Corporation and marketed by Computer Associates. IDMS employs embedded pointers to link related records together, including intersection records.

Relational Model

The **relational model** uses tables, rather than linked nodes, to structure the data in a data base. These tables, called **relations,** are two-dimensional data structures that resem-

---

[7]This example concerning a student/class relationship is continued in Review Problem 2 at the end of this chapter.

ble flat files. However, relations (which we will henceforth call tables to avoid confusion) are more sophisticated than files. Being constructed according to the rules of a branch of mathematics called relational algebra, tables can be manipulated in a variety of ways. They thereby enable a wider variety of information needs to be satisfied. In fact, the relational model is increasing its presence at the expense of the tree and network models, especially in microcomputer systems.

A table is constructed of rows (called **tuples** in relational algebra) and columns. All rows are of equal length, and each contains a unique occurrence of the entity to which the relation pertains. Each column contains the values of an attribute of the entity. The range of values that can appear in a column are called the **domain** of the attribute. In most tables the left-most column will contain a primary key.

Tables are designed according to a process known as **normalization.** They may be converted through this process from tree or network models, although a degree of redundancy is likely to be introduced. Alternatively, they may be designed from a conceptual model, to be discussed in the next section. Well designed tables (i.e., tables in the proper normalized form) will (1) pertain to a single entity or event and (2) be free of repeating groups. However, certain redundant columns are included, as an illustration will later explain.

Two features provide considerable flexibility to the relational model. First, each table is essentially independent, since no firmly established sets or other linked structures are predefined. Thus, each table can serve as a point of entry. Second, several powerful relational operators are available for manipulating the data in the tables. Perhaps the three most useful operators have the names SELECT, PROJECT, and JOIN.[8]

Each operator creates a new table. A SELECT operation does so by extracting the values of certain rows from a table. A PROJECT operation creates a new table by extracting the values of certain columns. A JOIN operation creates a new table by joining the values of rows and columns extracted from two or more tables. To perform a JOIN operation, the tables must have a column in common. Normally the common column is the primary key of one table and a nonprimary key, called a **foreign key,** of another table.

Example.[9] An illustration should clarify the concepts and features of the relational model. A manufacturing firm currently uses the network structure shown in Figure 18-12. It has been decided to change to a relational model. The four tables shown in Figure 18-13 have therefore been established. Two of the tables focus on two entities—employees and skills—and contain no repeating groups. Thus, they are in appropriate normalized form. In relational notation, the employee table may be described as follows:

EMPLOYEE(EMPLOYEE-NO.,
       EMPLOYEE-NAME, SSN, AGE)

The other two tables in the figure require an explanation. The employee/skill table is in effect an intersection table, since it provides cross-references between the employees and skills. The job table is a cross between a normalized table and an intersection table. Both the employee/skill and job tables represent redundant data. However, the redundancy is necessary in order to enable the data from the skill and employee tables to be brought together in new tables. Further redundancy is due to the situation. Thus, the employee/skill table repeats an employee

[8]Names of operators differ somewhat between specific DBMS packages. For instance, INTERSECT may replace or supplement JOIN in some packages.

[9]Based on an example in Dan C. Kneer and Joseph W. Wilkinson, ''DBMS: Do You Know Enough to Choose?'' *Management Accounting* (September 1984), pp. 34–38. Copyright © 1984 by National Association of Accountants, Montvale, N.J. All rights reserved. Reprinted by permission.

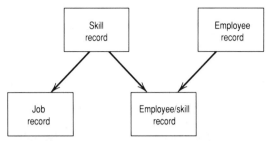

FIGURE 18-12 A complex network structure converted into a simple network structure with intersection record.

number in some cases, since an employee may have more than one skill. Another case of redundancy appears in the job table. This redundancy occurs because the table is not in proper normalized form. It should be split into two parts, a job table and a skill/job in-

tersection table. Job descriptions and accumulated costs would appear only in the job table, which would consist of only two rows with no redundancy.

Taken together, the four tables in Figure 18-13 reflect the relationships shown in the current network, even though firm predefined links are not present. By means of relational operators new tables can be created that contain the same data as provided through the predefined links of the network model. In fact, other new tables can be formed that are not represented by links in the network model.

The following inquiries, entered perhaps by the personnel manager, will illustrate the creation of new tables:

1. Which employees, identified by number, possess skill number 30?

Skill

Skill no.	Skill description	No. of vacancies
10	Lathe operator	0
20	Carpenter	1
30	Arc welder	0
40	Lab technician	0
50	Truck driver	2
60	Mechanic	0

Employee

Employee no.	Employee name	SSN	Age
1000	Brown	xxx-xx-xxxx	23
2000	Smith	"	26
3000	Kimble	"	30
4000	Jones	"	32
5000	White	"	45
6000	Green	"	39
7000	Black	"	37

Employee/skill

Employee no.	Skill no.
1000	30
2000	40
3000	50
3000	60
4000	10
5000	20
6000	60
7000	20
7000	30

Job

Job no.	Skill no.	Job description	Accum. cost
100	20	Lab facility	30000
100	40	Lab facility	30000
100	50	Lab facility	30000
100	60	Lab facility	30000
200	10	Filter system	14500
200	30	Filter system	14500
200	60	Filter system	14500

FIGURE 18-13 Tables in a skill-employee relational data base. Based on an example in Dan C. Kneer and Joseph W. Wilkinson, "DBMS: Do You Know Enough to Choose?" *Management Accounting* (September 1984), pp. 34–38. Copyright © 1984 by National Association of Accountants, Montvale, N.J. All rights reserved. Reprinted with permission.

2. Who are the firm's employees, identified by number and name?

3. Which employees, identified by number *and* name, possess skill number 20?

4. Which skills, identified by number and description, are assigned to job 200, identified by description?

5. Which skills, identified by description, are possessed by employee Kimble?

Figure 18-14 displays the new tables created by these inquiries. Each is discussed by reference to its inquiry number.

Inquiry 1: This table is created by the SE-LECT operator, which extracts the re-quested rows from the employee/skill table.

Inquiry 2: This table is created by the PRO-JECT operator, which extracts the re-quested first two columns from the em-ployee table.

Inquiry 3: This table is created by first using a JOIN operator to form a new table from the employee and employee/skill tables. This newly created table has nine rows (the number of the rows in the em-ployee/skill table) and five columns (i.e., employee number, skill number, employee name, SSN, and age). The two tables could be joined because the

New Table Based
on Inquiry 1

Skill no.	Employee no.
30	1000
30	7000

New Table Based
on Inquiry 2

Employee no.	Employee name
1000	Brown
2000	Smith
3000	Kimble
4000	Jones
5000	White
6000	Green
7000	Black

New Table Based
on Inquiry 3

Skill no.	Employee no.	Employee name
20	5000	White
20	7000	Black

New Table Based
on Inquiry 4

Job description	Skill no.	Skill description
Filter system	10	Lathe operator
Filter system	30	Arc welder
Filter system	60	Mechanic

New Table Based
on Inquiry 5

Employee name	Skill description
Kimble	Truck driver
Kimble	Mechanic

FIGURE 18-14 Responses to inquiries generated by using the data base in Figure 18-13.

employee number appeared in both tables; however, it appears only once in the new table. Using the new table, a PROJECT operator extracts the two relevant columns and a SELECT operator extracts the two relevant rows to create the brief table appearing in Figure 18-14.

Inquiry 4: This table is created by first using a JOIN operator to form a new table from the skill table and job table. The common column is the skill number, which is the primary key in the skill table and a foreign key in the job table. Using this newly formed table, a PROJECT operator extracts the three relevant columns and a SELECT operator extracts the three relevant rows for the new table in Figure 18-14.

Inquiry 5: This table is created by first using the JOIN operator twice to combine the skill and employee/skill tables and then to combine this newly formed table with the employee table. Using the *second* newly formed table, a PROJECT operator extracts the two relevant columns and a SELECT operator extracts the two relevant rows for the new table in Figure 18-14.

Advantages and drawbacks. The relational model offers several advantages to business firms. The tables are easy for programmers and such users as managers and accountants to use and understand. As we have seen, the model is extremely flexible, since any table can serve as an entry point for retrieving data and no relationships have been predefined. Thus, a larger variety of information requests from users can be satisfied, even if some of the requests were unanticipated when the tables were constructed. Finally, it is not necessary to rebuild portions of the structure to include new relationships, as is the case with tree and network structures.

The main drawback of the relational model is that current relational DBMS's are inefficient. Underlying physical structures consume huge quantities of storage space, and thus they cannot respond as quickly to inquiries as either tree or network structures. Moreover, more redundancy tends to appear in the logical structures, such as the common columns needed for joining tables together. Because these limitations become quite noticeable when large data bases are involved, the relational model has not become as dominant on mainframe computer systems as it has on microcomputer systems. In addition, because of slower access times the relational model tends to be less suitable for high-volume transaction processing applications.

Real-world application. Examples of relational DBMS's are Data Base 2 (DB2) from IBM, Oracle from Oracle Corporation, and DATACOM from Applied Data Research. Current users of DB2, for instance, include Sara Lee, Philip Morris, and Security Pacific Bank. Such users have selected a relational model primarily because of its ability to handle a multitude of information requests by diverse corporate users. They also believe that a relational DBMS such as DB2 will have improved performance as new upgrades are made.[10] Typically a relational DBMS uses indexes and inverted files as the physical means of accessing and reordering data in tables.

A Next-Generation Data Model

Although the relational data model has been implemented for scarcely more than a decade, an object-oriented data model may be on the horizon. An **object-oriented data model** consists of classes of classified objects. Examples of classes are vehicles, companies, and locations. Under each class would be specific instances. For instance,

[10]Tom McCusker, "Tracking the Wild Data Base," *Datamation* (July 1, 1989), p. 38.

under locations might be cities such as Detroit and Chicago. Class-hierarchy indexes facilitate the accessing of data needed to answer such inquiries as "List all vehicles that weigh more than 7,500 pounds and are manufactured by a company in Detroit."

Since object-oriented data models are semantic in nature, they must depend on knowledge-based and object-oriented programming. This type of programming, which is employed in expert systems, is still being developed.[11] Thus, no object-oriented data base management system is yet operational. An experimental system, called Orion, is currently in an experimental stage at the Microelectronics and Computer Technology Corporation.[12]

Development of Data Base Systems

Suggestions for designing files and records in the file-oriented environment were offered in Chapter 8. These suggestions pertain also to those data structures under the data base approach. In addition, though, more integrated analysis and design is needed for data base systems. This development activity involves four phases: definition of requirements, logical design, physical design, and implementation. Preceding these phases should be systems planning; during this period the undertaking is determined to be feasible, the project is scheduled, and so forth. (Planning of systems development is discussed in Chapter 21.)

Requirements Definition Phase

A firm's overall data base is the repository of all the data required by the firm's users to fulfill their responsibilities. Hence, the first step in developing a data base is to determine the data requirements—the overall collection of required data and the relationships among the various data items and sets.

Two contrasting approaches may be taken in defining data requirements. One approach begins by (1) analyzing the needs of each application and user in the firm and then (2) compiling these subcollections of data needs into a composite collection of data requirements. The other approach begins by (1) developing a **conceptual data model** for the entire firm and then (2) decomposing the various parts of the model into related data items and sets. Although each approach has been successfully applied, the latter is gaining increasing endorsement. It emphasizes the idea that a data base is a vital resource of a firm today and tomorrow, rather than a means of supporting current applications.[13]

At the heart of the conceptual modeling approach is the data-oriented conceptual data model, also called the enterprise model. This model reflects a broad view, sometimes called an external view, of a firm's real-world activities, functions, and setting. Included in this view are the firm's key and enduring entities, such as persons (i.e., customers), objects (i.e., inventory items), activities (i.e., production jobs), and events (i.e., sales transactions). Also included are the relationships among these entities. Although different types of models may portray these entities and relationships, perhaps the most suitable is the **entity-relationship diagram.**

Figure 18-15 depicts a portion of an entity-relationship diagram that pertains to the expenditure activity of a firm. Rectangles represent entities, and diamonds represent the relationships between entities. For instance, suppliers (an entity) provide inventory items (another entity). Cash amounts are drawn from bank accounts and flow to cash disbursements transactions. Three

[11]See Chapter 20 for a discussion of expert systems.

[12]Won Kim, "Defining Object Databases Anew," *Datamation* (February 1, 1990), pp. 33–36.

[13]Robert M. Curtis, "Getting the Database Right," *Datamation* (October 1, 1986), p. 100.

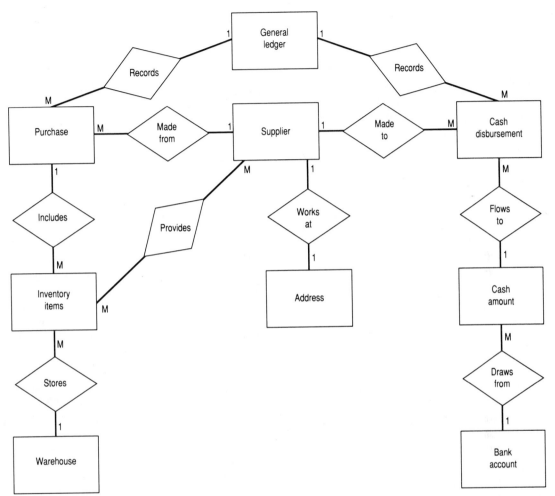

FIGURE 18-15 A partial entity-relationship diagram.

types of relationships are included: one-to-many (1 : M), many-to-many (M : M), and one-to-one (1 : 1). Most of the relationships shown in the figure are one-to-many. However, a many-to-many relationship appears between suppliers and inventory items. That is, a single supplier can provide more than one item and a single item can be provided by more than one supplier. The one-to-one relationship between a supplier and its work address also appears.

After the entity-relationship or other conceptual model is complete, the data base designers must include the needed data items. Data items are usually ascertained by interviews with users. In addition, structured analysis techniques may be employed, as described in Chapter 22. A cluster of determined data items is attached to each entity symbol in the entity-relationship diagram, as well as to relationship diamonds where appropriate. For instance, the data items relevant to an inventory item would likely include inventory item number, description, unit cost, quantity on hand, reorder quantity, and so on.

Logical Design Phase

Logical design consists essentially of converting the conceptual model into schema and subschemas. In terms of diagrams used in our discussions, this involves changing the entity-relationship diagram into a number of data structure diagrams. Another decision to be made concerns the particular data model to be employed.

The first step is to consider the schema, which provides the logical view of a data base. The schema can be shown by means of one or more data structure diagrams. If the conceptual model is in the form of an entity-relationship diagram, two major changes are necessary to convert to data structure diagrams: (1) the diamonds representing the relationships are omitted, and (2) the many-to-many relationships are decomposed into one-to-many relationships. To convert the partial entity-relationship diagram in Figure 18-15, for instance, nine diamonds would be removed. The many-to-many relationship between suppliers and inventory items would also be converted into two one-to-many relationships and a supplier/inventory item intersection record.

Another concern in developing the schema is the scope to be spanned. If a single data base is to span a firm's entire range of activities, then the data structure diagram will include the same rectangles shown in the entity-relationship diagram.[14] However, for most firms the schema will be complex or will involve more data than can be easily accommodated by available technology. Thus, several data bases or schemas will likely be needed. In such cases the multiple data bases should be based on integrated sets of activities or flows. For instance, data bases may logically be organized around (1) the major organizational functions, (2) the transaction cycles, or (3) the basic resources such as materials or cash.

The next step is to develop the subschemas. Users should again be consulted with respect to the included entities, relationships, and data items. After repeated consultations, the data base designers should produce an array of data structure diagrams and lists of relevant data items.

The final step in this phase consists of selecting the data model. This decision depends in large part on the mix of uses that the data base is expected to support. That is, what proportions of on-line transaction processing applications, batch processing applications, on-line inquiries, and ad hoc report writing are likely when the new data base is implemented? How is this mix likely to change over the next five years? Other questions related to use include the following: What transaction volumes are likely, and what peaks can be expected? How many changes to data structures are likely to occur each week? How many persons are expected to access the data base simultaneously? Answers to such questions can have an important bearing on the selection of the data model. In firms where more than one data base is to be developed, the selected type of data model may vary from data base to data base. Conversely, a firm may desire to employ more than one type of data model within the same data base.

These first two phases in data base development are of particular interest to accountants. Accounting expertise is beneficial with respect to modeling business activities as well as determining needed data.

Physical Design Phase

Although called the physical design phase, the third phase blends logical and physical concerns. Among the matters being considered are (1) the particular DBMS to select and (2) the structures of records or tables and related linkages.

---

[14] Within a few years DBMS developments may allow the conceptual model itself to serve as the schema. See Curtice and Casey, "Database: What's in Store?" *Datamation* (December 1, 1985), p. 83.

DBMS selection. Selecting a DBMS is a difficult but important decision. Numerous commercial DBMS packages are available. Figure 18-16 lists a sampling of packages designed for mainframe computers or minicomputers. Each particular DBMS has a distinctive set of features and capabilities. Although certain DBMS's are relatively popular, however, no single DBMS towers over the others in acceptance or possesses every desirable feature.

The first DBMS feature to consider is the data model. As figure 18-16 suggests, all the data models are supported by available packages. In some cases more than one data model can be employed, thereby increasing the versatility of the package. Moreover, DBMS's seldom support pure versions of data models; instead, they incorporate variations (e.g., a mixture of a tree or hierarchical model and a network model). Thus, sufficient variety exists for the data base designer to choose those DBMS's that offer the adaptations best harmonizing with the data model(s) selected in the preceding phase.

A number of other considerations affect the selection of the DBMS. Apart from price, these considerations include processing efficiency, timely responses to inquiries, built-in access control restrictions, ease of programming, compatibility with specific operating systems, incorporated utilities, and documentation.

Many of the selection considerations relate to aspects of physical storage. For instance, processing efficiency and timely responses to inquiries are affected by the ways a DBMS physically organizes and accesses data structures. If many batch processing applications are involved, a DBMS that allows sequential organization of records is desirable. If much on-line processing is involved, a DBMS that uses a random (hashing scheme) method of accessing records is preferable. When on-line inquiries predominate, a DBMS (such as Adabas) that structures data in inverted files is likely to be best. Recall that these physical aspects are different from the logical data models. Both must be considered in selecting a DBMS, even if the users will never be aware of the physical aspects. Chapter 24 discusses the procedural steps for selecting computer software such as a DBMS.

DBMS Package	Data Structures Provided	Supplier
IMS/VS	Hierarchical (tree)	IBM Corporation
SYSTEM 2000	Hierarchical, inverted files	SAS Institute
IDMS	Network	Computer Associates, Inc.
DBMS	Network	Digital Equipment Corp.
TurboImage	Network	Hewlett-Packard Co.
DB2	Relational	IBM Corporation
Ingres	Relational	Relational Technology, Inc.
Oracle	Relational	Oracle Corporation
dBase IV	Relational	Ashton-Tate
Ultra	Relational	Cincom Systems, Inc.
RBase for DOS	Relational	Microrim, Inc.
Adabas	Inverted files	Software AG of North America
DRS	Hierarchical, network, relational	Advanced Data Management, Inc.
Ramis II	Hierarchical, network, relational	On-Line Software International

FIGURE 18-16 A selective list of commercially available DBMS packages. Source: Philip Bronstein and Leon Hopkins, "Finding the Right Data Base," *Business Software Review* (June 1988), pp. 31–45.

Design of physical records and sets. The remaining aspects of physical design depend on the type of data model selected. In this section we consider record and set design for tree and network models. In the next section we consider the tables of relational models.

Record design begins with the listing of the data items to be included from the entity-relationship diagram. It then consists of applying the considerations discussed in Chapter 8. Thus, the included data items are named, grouped, and arranged in a suitable order; the field lengths are determined; primary and secondary keys are selected. The results are recorded in the data dictionary for each data item.

Set design begins by verifying the owner-member status between each pair of adjacent records from the data structure diagrams. The records serving as entry points (e.g., root nodes in the tree model) are marked and the physical access method specified. Next the method of physically linking the records in a set is specified. In the case of tree and network structures this method will often involve embedded pointers.

Because of their widespread use in data bases, we should look more closely at pointers. If we look back at the data structure diagram in Figure 18-8a, we see a pointer field in the customer record. Figure 18-17 shows a specific occurrence, in which two sales invoices are linked by embedded pointers to the record for customer number 10. The type of pointers used in this example are **forward pointers,** since the linkage is from the owner record to the first member record and then to the second member record. Since a pointer in the second sales invoice record points back to the owner record, this structure also forms a ring list or chain. (See Chapter 8 for the description of a ring list.)

Multiple pointer fields may be added to a record to provide the number of relationships specified by data structure diagrams. For instance, if customer records are associated with cash receipt records as well as sales invoice records, a second pointer field would appear in each customer record. This particular structure would facilitate the preparation of monthly statements to customers, since all the amounts affecting a customer's balance are linked together.

Additional pointer fields may also be

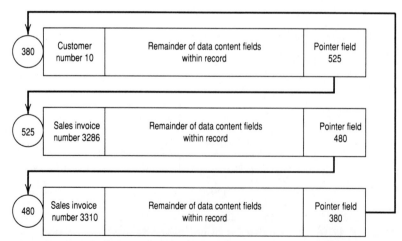

FIGURE 18-17 Embedded pointer chain for an occurrence involving a customer and two sales invoice records.

Customer number 10	Remainder of data content fields within record	Pointer to west territory list 120	Pointer to sales invoice list 260

FIGURE 18-18 A customer record that contains two pointer fields.

added to owner records to form attribute lists, as described in Chapter 8. As we recall, attribute lists enable reports to be prepared on the basis of secondary keys. To illustrate, let us reconsider the customer record in Figure 18-17. Assume that these records are maintained by a firm that has two sales territories—east and west. The territorial sales managers need frequent reports showing the details of sales made to customers in their territories. Figure 18-18 shows that an added

pointer field to link sales territories and customers is needed to prepare these reports. (This added linkage all takes place within the customer file, so no added record for sales territory would appear on the data structure diagram.) Figure 18-19 shows specific linkages for customers numbered 1 through 10 to sales territories, plus linkages of customer number 10 to the three sales made during a sales period. Upon accessing the index to the records in the customer file, the DBMS

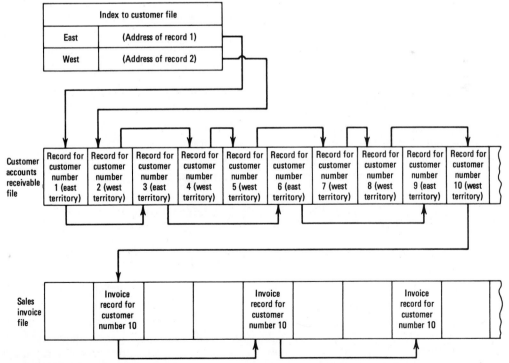

FIGURE 18-19 Embedded pointers used to link customer and sales invoice records and the sales territory attribute.

Sales Territory	Customer Number	Sales Invoice Number	Sales Amount[a]
East	1	xxx	xxx
	3	xxx	xxx
	6	xxx	xxx
	9	xxx	xxx
West	2	xxx	xxx
	4	xxx	xxx
	5	xxx	xxx
	7	xxx	xxx
	8	xxx	xxx
	10	xxx	xxx
		xxx	xxx
		xxx	xxx

[a] It is assumed that one sale has been made to each customer numbered 1 through 9 and that three sales have been made to customer 10.

FIGURE 18-20   A sales analysis report prepared with the aid of linked records and an attribute chain.

would traverse the customer records and the sales invoice records for the needed data. Then it would generate the desired report, shown in Figure 18-20.

Other variations of pointers are often employed. For example, **backward pointers** link an owner record to its member records in the opposite direction from forward pointers. **Parent pointers** point "upward" from each member (child) record to its owner (parent) record. If two or more of these pointers are included in the same set, they can enable requested data to be obtained more quickly, on the average. However, they should be used judiciously, since they (1) consume added storage space and (2) require added maintenance of pointers.

Relational table design.   Tables in the relational model involve some of the same design concerns as records. That is, the data items to be included must be ordered within the tables, the column widths (akin to field lengths) must be specified, and the primary key must be selected. On the other hand, the data content of each table is subject to the process of normalization. This process, introduced earlier, consists of decomposing tables through successive normal forms until the optimal form is reached. To be more specific, tables are reduced from first and second normal forms to the third normal form. In this optimal form each table should

1. Pertain to a single entity or event, such as inventory item, sale, purchase order, or job.

2. Contain unique rows.

3. Include a column that is designated as the **table key** (in effect, the primary key). In some cases, such as intersection tables, the table key may be a combination of two or more columns.

4. Be free of transitive dependencies, such as repeating groups.

Since the relational model does not entail the use of sets, set design is irrelevant. The only means of providing links is by means of common columns that are placed in tables. Each such common column must appear as a table key in one table.

APPLICATION OF DATA BASE DESIGN
Manufacturers Hanover Trust Company[a]

The Wholesale Banking Systems is one of four decentralized data processing functions within the Manufacturers Hanover Trust Company. Most of the applications of this function involve on-line, real-time processing, using mainframe IBM computers. During the early 1980s it was decided to convert the function to the data base approach. A Wholesale Data Administration function was established and assigned the development task. The project life cycle involved four phases. The first two design phases (called conceptual and detailed conceptual design) identified entities such as bank customers, relationships such as those between customers and their accounts and lockbox deposits, data items such as customer addresses and account balances, and

logical transactions such as "update account balance." The third phase (called the logical design phase) selected the IMS data base management system and the IBM DB/DC data dictionary and specified the record keys, the IMS segments, and the hierarchical data structures. The final phase (called the physical design phase) established the pointers, magnetic disk blocks, and other physical features. It also involved implementing the data structures, preparing documentation, and testing access of data via the logical structures.

[a]Marian Herman, "A Database Design Methodology for an Integrated Database Environment," *Data Base* (Fall 1983), pp. 12–27.

Implementation Phase

This final phase is of least concern, especially in this chapter. Implementation activities for general systems development projects are discussed in Chapter 24. In brief, however, activities related to data base implementation include (1) compiling the data base definitions via the DDL, (2) incorporating DML commands into application programs, (3) loading the data base with sample data and testing, (4) modifying the data base as necessary, and (5) loading production data into the data base.

Data Base Controls and Security Measures

Because of its importance to a firm's operations and decision making and also its vulnerability, a data base requires stringent controls and security measures. All those that are suitable for on-line processing systems,

as described in Chapter 9, also pertain to data base systems. The most relevant and critical of these controls and security measures are

- **Sound systems development procedures.** All changes to the data base, such as the addition of new data items and the modification of the DBMS, should be carefully controlled. Otherwise, the standardization and security of the data may be threatened, and data management procedures may become flawed.

- **Thorough documentation.** In particular, the data dictionary should be comprehensive and up to date.

- **Secure data accessing procedures.** The system of user codes and passwords should be sufficiently layered to provide precise protection over individual data sets and data items. For instance, certain sensitive data items could require as many as three passwords to access. Also, a lockout feature should prevent more than one user from accessing the same data simultaneously, causing possible loss of the data. A thorough data backup plan, including appropriate backup procedures for the data sets, should be developed.

- **Organizational addition of a data base administrator (DBA) and perhaps a security administrator.** The DBA should be responsible for the design and control of the data base. A primary function, therefore, is to establish and define the schema. This includes assigning standardized names to data items and sets, specifying data relationships, and compiling the data dictionary. Another function is to assign user codes and passwords and maintain other aspects of security (unless a security administrator is appointed). A third function is to control all changes made to data, as well as to software that operates the data base and programs that use the data therein. A final function is to administer the DBMS by preparing budgets, proposing policies, and communicating with programmers and users. To perform these functions effectively, the DBA should be organizationally separated from computer operations and the users.

Summary

The traditional file-oriented approach, discussed in Chapter 8, has severe shortcomings. Since the files are tied to individual applications, redundancy in files and data generally occurs. Redundancy leads to inconsistencies and hence to loss of data reliability. Other likely shortcomings are inflexibility and relative inaccessibility. An alternative approach, known as the data base approach, can reduce or overcome these shortcomings. It features data independence, data standardization, one-time data entry, data association and integration, shared data ownership, and centralized data management. Its benefits therefore include reduced redundancy, eliminated inconsistencies, increased flexibility, and improved accessibility. On the other hand, the drawbacks of the data base approach are increased cost, complexity, and vulnerability to loss of data.

A data base management system (DBMS) is a set of software that stores, maintains, and retrieves data from a central data base. It serves as a buffer between the application programs (and their users) and the data base, and it communicates directly with the operating system in accomplishing its purposes. Principal components of a DBMS are the data base control system, data definition language (with data dictionary), and data manipulation language. Optional components include a query language, report writer, screen formatter, host-language interface, utility software, and security software.

The three logical data models are the tree model, the network model, and the relational model. The first two may be depicted by data structure diagrams, whereas the third is portrayed by two-dimensional tables. The tree model forms hierarchical structures from root nodes and expresses one-to-many relationships. The network model forms interconnecting structures in which multiple nodes serve as entry points and at least one member record has two or more owner records. A complex version of the network model expresses many-to-many relationships as well as one-to-many relationships. The relational model does not explicitly predefine relationships among records and data items. Instead, the relationships are created as new tables upon entered requests by users. The tree and network models emphasize the rapid retrieval of data, whereas the relational model offers extreme flexibility and the familiarity of tables.

The development of data base systems involves four phases: definition of requirements, logical design, physical design, and implementation. The first two phases, which consist of developing a conceptual data model of a firm, determining needed data items, and selecting the most suitable logical data model(s), are of particular interest to accountants.

Controls and security measures relevant to data bases include sound systems development procedures, thorough documentation, secure data accessing procedures, and data base administration.

Review Problems with Solutions

Problem 1 Statement

The Phoenix Board of Realtors' Multiple Listing Service (MLS) publishes a weekly listing of houses for sale in the Phoenix metropolitan area. Each listing is based on a listing contract signed by the listing realtor and the owner. In the contract are specified all the details concerning the residence, including the address, asking price, number of bedrooms, number of baths, type of garage, mortgages pending, and special features. Upon being prepared, a copy of this contract is forwarded by the realtor to the MLS.

In the early years of the MLS, copies of the listing contract were distributed to member firms. However, about 1970 the data were transferred to computer-readable media; then, each Friday the listings were printed, bound into multiple-listing books, and distributed to the member firms.

The multiple-listing book actually consisted of two parts: (1) detailed descriptive data concerning each residence, arranged by MLS number; and (2) an index that referred to each detailed listing. Each index listing contained key summary data, such as the address, asking price, number of bedrooms, size of building, style and date of construction, nearest schools, and geographical area. With this summary data, realty associates

could scan the index for those houses that met a potential buyer's needs. If more data were needed or if a sale were consummated, the realty associate would use the MLS number in the index to locate the detailed description.

In the late 1970s, however, the book had grown to be a bulky 700-page volume containing an average of 9000 listings. Many of the listings were inaccurate, because of sales since the preceding Friday, and the new listings were not available until the next Friday. Searches for suitable listings sometimes required an hour or more. Furthermore, continued rapid growth in real estate transactions was expected in the Phoenix area.

Consequently, the MLS contracted with a computer consultant to develop a data base and retrieval system that would rectify the above problems. After careful study he proposed a system having the following features:

1. **Hardware** should include a visual display terminal and impact printer in the office of each of the 400 members. At the MLS office would be a central processor plus 800 megabytes of magnetic disk storage, magnetic tape backup, and a communication processor to interface with the terminals.[15]

2. **Software** should include a data base management system that allows tree structures and inverted files to be created, plus a command language that enables users at realtors' offices to enter new listings and to make inquiries. Other software should consist of an elaborate operating system for coordinating the various components, as well as utility routines for calculating

[15]These facts are based on a description of a computer system actually acquired by the Phoenix MLS and reported by Joe Cole in "Homes-for-Sale List Going Electronic," *The Arizona Republic* (April 23, 1978), pp. 13–14; and by Neal Savage in "Terminal Aid," *The Arizona Republic* (Jan. 30, 1983), p. SL2.

such real estate factors as amortization amounts.

Required

Design suitable data structures comprising a schema for this proposed system, and describe the steps involved in storing and retrieving data from the system.

Solution

The schema is depicted by the data structures shown on page 853.

The procedure for using the system is as follows: After a listing contract has been completed, a clerk in the realty firm enters the data via the office terminal. The data are stored in the two records, marked as the summary listing record and detailed data record. Pointers are established by the software as indicated, and the disk address of the summary record is added to each of the inverted files as applicable.

When a potential buyer enters the picture, a realty associate first determines the essential parameters, such as the top price that he or she would be willing to pay, the desired number of bedrooms, and the area. Next the realty associate keys these specifications into the terminal. The DBMS then employs the inverted files to locate those houses meeting all the specifications (if any) and displays the address and several other key facts concerning each.

For instance, assume that Ms. Betty Rowan, a realty associate with Mesa Realty, enters an inquiry concerning which homes are listed in Tempe having 1800 square feet or more, three bedrooms, an asking price of not more than $100,000, and a fireplace. The DBMS searches all the relevant inverted files and determines that houses at disk addresses 3810 and 6530 meet these specifications; it then moves to these disk addresses and displays the following data:

MLS 0721	1705 So. Beaver Dr.	$95,000
MLS 3782	2817 E. Coolidge Ave.	$98,500

If the potential buyer shows interest, the realty associate can request a hard-copy printout of the detailed descriptions of the two houses. Later, if one of the houses is sold, the realty associate enters that fact via the terminal; the house is then deleted from the file.

At any time a realtor can make a request for a printout of all houses listed with his or her firm. The DBMS will then follow the pointers that lead from the realtor record to each of the summary listing records in the realtor's chain.

Problem 2 Statement[16]

Rosebud College has a student/class data base, which is accessed by a DBMS that uses a network model. The data structure diagram that portrays the schema is like that shown in Figure 18-11, except that additional student and class data are kept in records that are "owned" by the student number and class code, respectively. That is, the student number and class code are record types that serve as entry points. The student data includes name, class standing, and GPA; the class data includes class title, time, days, classroom number, and instructor name.

The records are physically accessed by embedded pointers. For instance, the fields for the student number record type are as follows:

Student number	Pointer to student data	Pointer to student/class record

---

[16]This problem is based on James F. Smith and Amer Mufti, "Using the Relational Database," *Management Accounting* (October 1985), pp. 43–50, 54. Copyright 1985 by National Association of Accountants, Montvale, N.J. All rights reserved. Used with permission.

Pointer fields in the other record types are as follows: class code—pointers to student/class and class data record types; student data—pointer back to student number record type; class data—pointer back to class code record type; student/class —pointers to next record having the same student number, to next record having the same class code, back to student number record type, and back to class code record type.

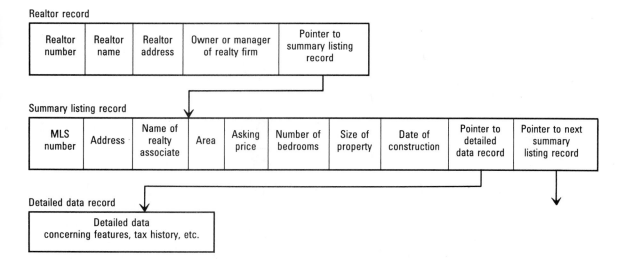

Realtor record

Realtor number	Realtor name	Realtor address	Owner or manager of realty firm	Pointer to summary listing record

Summary listing record

MLS number	Address	Name of realty associate	Area	Asking price	Number of bedrooms	Size of property	Date of construction	Pointer to detailed data record	Pointer to next summary listing record

Detailed data record

Detailed data concerning features, tax history, etc.

Inverted lists

Asking price range (000$)	Disk address
40–50	
50–60	
60–70	
70–80	
80–90	
90–100	
.	
.	
.	

Number of bedrooms	Disk address
1	
2	
3	
4	
5	
More than 5	

Building features	Disk address
Fireplace	
Pool	
Cul de sac	
Solar heat	
Spanish style	
.	
.	

Area	Disk address
North Phoenix	
West Phoenix	
East Phoenix	
South Phoenix	
Tempe	
Mesa	
.	
.	
.	

Size of building (square feet)	Disk address
1000–1600	
1600–1700	
1700–1800	
1800–1900	
.	
.	

Date of construction	Disk address
1989	
1988	
1987	
1986	
1985	
.	
.	

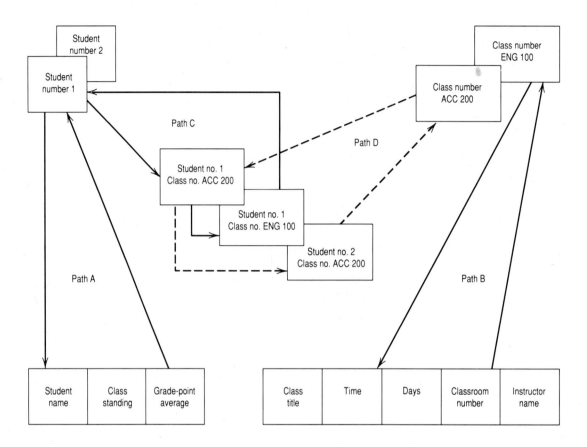

These pointers enable records to be accessed as desired. The diagram at the top of this page shows the access paths followed in retrieving various data during illustrative occurrences. Path A shows the retrieval of data for student number 1, path B the retrieval of data for class coded ENG 100, path C the retrieval of all classes taken by student number 1, and path D the retrieval of all students taking ACC 200.

Required

Rosebud plans to change to a DBMS based on the relational data model, so that retrieval of desired data will be easier for users in the various administrative offices and academic departments. Draw the tables that would be constructed by the relational DBMS. Explain how a class list would be prepared.

Solution

The columns in the tables would appear as shown.

Student table:

Student number	Student name	Class standing	Grade point average

Class table:

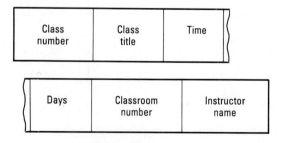

Class number	Class title	Time

Days	Classroom number	Instructor name

Student/class table:

Student number	Class number

To obtain a class list for ACC 200, a user would first enter the request via an Englishlike command. Then the DBMS would construct a new table by joining the three tables, projecting the desired columns (e.g., class code, student number, student name), and selecting the rows in which ACC 200 appears.

Review Questions

18-1 What is the meaning of each of the following terms?

    Data base system
    Data base approach
    Data independence
    Data base management system
      (DBMS)
    Logical view
    Schema
    Physical view
    Data set
    Subschema
    Data base administrator (DBA)
    Data base control system (DBCS)
    Data definition language (DDL)
    Data dictionary
    Data manipulation language (DML)
    Logical data model
    Tree model
    Root node
    Data structure diagram
    Set
    Owner record
    Member record
    One-to-many relationship
    Network model
    Many-to-many relationship
    Complex network
    Simple network
    Intersection record
    Relational model
    Relation
    Tuple
    Domain
    Normalization
    Foreign key
    Object-oriented data model
    Conceptual data model
    Entity-relationship diagram
    Forward pointer
    Backward pointer
    Parent pointer
    Table key

18-2 What are several shortcomings of the traditional file-oriented approach?

18-3 What are the benefits of the data base approach?

18-4 What features characterize the data base approach?

18-5 What are the drawbacks of the data base approach?

18-6 What are the relationships among the DBMS, operating system, data base, and users?

18-7 Describe the procedure by which the DBMS aids application programs in updating records in a data base.

18-8 Briefly describe several functional components of a typical DBMS.

18-9 Contrast the tree and network models.

18-10 In what ways does the relational model differ from the tree and network models?

18-11 What are the four phases in the development of data base systems, and what is achieved in each phase?

18-12 What is the relationship between an entity-relationship diagram and a data structure diagram?

18-13 What are the considerations in deciding on the data model to select for structuring data?

18-14 What are several factors to consider in evaluating DBMS packages?

18-15 What are the limitations of a typical DBMS package?

18-16 Contrast the design of physical records and sets for tree or network structures and the design of relational tables.

18-17 What are typical activities within the implementation phase of a data base development project?

18-18 Identify several controls and security measures that are pertinent to data base systems.

Discussion Questions

18-19 In what situations might a firm find the file-oriented approach preferable to the data base approach?

18-20 What improvements in data base systems are likely to occur in the next decade or so?

18-21 Very few firms develop their own data base management software. Instead, they buy commercial DBMS software packages. Discuss the advantages and disadvantages of this course of action.

18-22 What are the benefits and drawbacks to the development of a single overall data base that includes all of a firm's active data? What alternatives are feasible?

18-23 The input approach to data base design suggests that it is not possible to anticipate all user needs for information during the life of the data base. Therefore, the data base should be designed to provide any conceivable report requested by managers and other users. Discuss.

18-24 Why is the traditional file-oriented approach hampered in responding to such information requests as: Which salespersons who have been with the firm less than one year have sold product Q to customers who currently have overdue accounts in excess of $1000?

18-25 The controller of a firm requests that an accounting data base be established in conformity with the data base approach. Describe its features, especially as they would differ from the collection of flat files presently employed.

18-26 Briefly describe two accounting-related examples that could reasonably employ

    a. Tree structures.
    b. Network structures.
    c. Relational structures.

18-27 Does an accountant really need to
    a. Understand concepts underlying files and data structures?
    b. Be aware of the specific subschema of a data base that he is expected to use?
    c. Be aware of the specific pointers and indexes employed to implement the subschema in **b**?

18-28 Although the data base approach is inherently flexible, various techniques may be employed to enhance this attribute. For instance, a reporting hierarchy file may be established; contained within this file would be the responsibility reporting relationships within a firm. If the firm's organizational structure is changed at a later date (e.g., if the purchasing department is transferred from the production function to the administrative services function), the change can be effected by simply modifying the contents of the reporting hierarchy file; the cost center codes can remain unchanged. Hence, no reprogramming is necessary. Describe the contents of the reporting hierarchy file and illustrate the use of this technique by means of a simple organizational change. Also, describe the use of this technique with respect to product structures (i.e., the relationships between products and their constituent parts and assemblies).

Problems

18-1 The Bunting Construction Co. of Dayton, Ohio, is a building contractor and materials supplier. Its annual sales for last year were $105 million. For a number of years the firm has used computers to process transactions and prepare reports and documents. It currently employs a large mainframe computer to perform both batch and on-line processing. For instance, it processes most of the accounting applications, such as payroll, by the batch mode and maintains the relevant files on magnetic tape. On the other hand, it employs on-line processing, via terminals, to dispatch loads of materials to customers and to keep track of the status of construction projects.

Over the years the firm has developed and acquired over 150 application programs, and it maintains approximately 200 files. These programs and files are documented in a variety of styles; some documentation was prepared by programmers no longer with the firm, and some was acquired from software suppliers when packages were purchased. Many of the programs have not been changed significantly in several years. According to the information systems manager, the time required to make changes is very lengthy; he has not been able to spare programmers to spend this needed time in program maintenance, since he has been "pushed" to provide new programs. For instance, he has recently supervised the writing of several new engineering and bidding programs. As a consequence, the programs tend to be inefficient and unintegrated. In addition, many of the data items appear in several files and are used in a variety of programs. Often these data items (e.g., raw materials item numbers) are assigned a different name in each program.

The operations manager of Bunting recently raised a disturbing problem at a meeting of top managers. He complained that while he could make inquiries concerning individual projects via his terminal, he could not obtain certain reports—such as lists of overdue projects, cost overruns, and expected receipts of materials—in a timely manner. Other managers agreed that they likewise had difficulty in obtaining ad hoc demand reports from the information system. As a consequence of these comments, the president directed the controller to investigate the feasibility of moving to the data base approach.

Required

a. What benefits would Bunting gain by moving to the data base approach?

b. What steps should be taken in the process of converting to the data base approach?

c. How would a DBMS be selected, and what are several desirable components that it should contain?

d. If Bunting decides to convert only a portion of the files and programs to the data base approach initially, which areas of activity would be the best candidates?

(CMA adapted)

18-2. Mariposa Products, a textile and apparel manufacturer, acquired its own computer in 1980. The first application to be developed and implemented was production and inventory control. Other applications that were added in succession were payroll, accounts receivable, and accounts payable.

The applications were not integrated as a result of the piecemeal manner in which they were developed and implemented. Nevertheless, the system proved satisfactory for several years. Generally, reports were prepared on time, and information was readily accessible.

Mariposa operates in a very competitive industry. A combination of increased operating costs and the competitive nature of the industry have had an adverse effect on profit margins and operating profits. Ed Wilde,

Mariposa's president, suggested that some special analyses be prepared in an attempt to provide information that would help management improve operations. Unfortunately, some of the data were not consistent among the reports. In addition, there were no data by product line or by department. These problems were attributable to the fact that Mariposa's applications were developed piecemeal and, as a consequence, duplicate data that were not necessarily consistent existed on Mariposa's computer system.

Wilde was concerned that Mariposa's computer system was not able to generate the information his managers needed to make decisions. He called a meeting of his top management and certain data processing personnel to discuss potential solutions to Mariposa's problems. The consensus of the meeting was that a new information system that would integrate Mariposa's applications was needed.

Mariposa's controller suggested that the company consider a data base system that all departments would use. As a first step, the controller proposed hiring a data base administrator on a consulting basis to determine the feasibility of converting to a data base system.

Required

a. Identify the features that constitute a system under the data base approach.

b. List the benefits and drawbacks to Mariposa Products of converting to the data base approach.

c. What steps should be taken in converting to the new system?

d. What are several key duties of the data base administrator?

(CMA adapted)

18-3 Refer to Review Problem 1 in this chapter.

Required

Prepare a data dictionary that contains the data items explicitly shown in the realtor and summary listing records in the Solution. For each data item (other than a pointer) include the information shown in the chapter example (Figure 18-7); omit the outputs and application programs in which used. Assume values for field lengths and any other needed information not provided in the problem statement. Character modes may be numeric, alphabetic, or alphanumeric.

18-4 Memory King of Palo Alto, California, is a manufacturer of high-quality computer storage devices. It employs magnetic disks to store four of its major master files: the accounts receivable master file, the accounts payable master file, the inventory master file, and the personnel master file.

Records in each of these files are alike in three respects: They are fixed in length, arranged sequentially according to a primary key, and consolidated. For instance, each personnel record consists of 300 characters, is arranged by employee number, and incorporates relevant personnel data and job skills data. (Job skills data include the job skill codes and description pertaining to the employee; a single employee may possess as many as six job skills, although the average employee possesses three.) To take another example, each customer record consists of 450 characters, is arranged by customer number, and includes all sales and payment transactions that have occurred this current year. (As many as 20 sales may be recorded, although the average number of sales per customer this year is five.)

Required

a. If the firm uses the file-oriented approach, describe two alternative ways by which to organize the records and discuss the advantages of each.

b. If the firm uses the data base approach, describe the ways the data would be structured under (1) the network model and (2) the relational model.

18-5 Draw a data structure diagram for each described situation. Also, draw a linked list that represents an occurrence involving the record types, and include disk addresses in the pointer fields. Use one pointer field in each owner record of the linked list unless otherwise instructed. See the top of page 860 for the solution to part **a**.

    a. Customer records within the accounts receivable master file point to their sales invoice records maintained in a history file.

    b. Supplier records in the accounts payable file point to their purchase orders in the open purchase order file.

    c. Customer records within the accounts receivable master file point to their sales invoice records *and* to their remittance advice records maintained in separate transaction history files. (Use *two* pointer fields in the customer record.)

    d. Employee records within the employee master file point to their skills records in the skills inventory file.

    e. Skills records within the skills inventory file point to the employee records in the employee master file possessing such skills. (Note that the skills records are now the owner records and the employee master records are now the member records.)

    f. Skills records within the skills inventory file point to the employee records in the employee master file possessing such skills; department records within the department master file (containing such data items as the department number, department name, department manager, and responsibility center code) *also* point to the employees assigned to the departments. (Use *two* pointer fields in the employee record, one for the skill list and one for the department list.)

    g. Bank customer records within the bank customer master file point to their respective accounts (i.e., checking account, savings account, loan account) within three account master files; in turn, the respective accounts point to the transactions (i.e., deposits, withdrawals, loan contract initiations, payments) affecting the account balances. (Use *three* pointer fields in the bank customer record, one for each account link; use *two* pointer fields in each account record, one for each type of transaction list.)

    h. Product records within the product master file point to the relevant parts records in the parts inventory master file *and also* to the job order records in the work-in-process file; work center records in the work center file point to those job orders in the work-in-process file that are currently being processed at the respective work centers. (Use *two* pointer fields in the product record, one for the part list and one for the job order list; use *two* pointer fields in the job order record, one for the product list and one for the work center list.)

18-6 Draw a data structure diagram that models each of the following situations.

    a. Supplier records (the root node) have as members (children) the records in the open purchase order file, which in turn have as mem-

Solution to **a**.

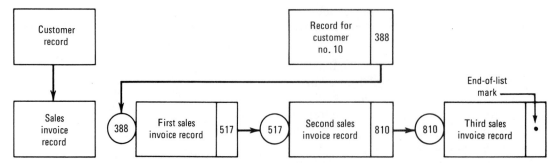

bers (children) the line items on order in each purchase order.

b. Convert the tree structure in **a** to a network structure by adding inventory records that also have the ordered items in purchase orders as members (children).

c. Product records (the root node) have as members (children) the parts inventory records, since parts are used in manufacturing the products. The product records also have as members (children) the production order records that pertain to the products being manufactured.

d. Convert the tree structure in **c** to a network structure by adding work center records that have as members (children) both (1) the production orders in process at the respective work centers, and (2) the machine loading records.

e. Convert the tree structure in **c** to a network structure, assuming that the parts records also have the product records as members (children). Also, show this complex network structure in a second diagram, in which an intersection record is added.

18-7   Refer to Figure 18-8c. Construct similar tree structures for each of the following entities, using the number of the records indicated. Note that records can be divided as suitable, as in the case of the sales invoice record shown in the figure.

a. A supplier, using five records with the general ledger account as the root node.

b. A raw material, using four records with the general ledger account as the root node.

c. An employee, using eight records with the employee number as the root node.

d. A production job, using five records with the general ledger account as the root node. *Hint:* A production job cost record type should appear at the second level.

18-8   The New West Department of Motor Vehicles (DMV) maintains two essential master files.

a. A vehicle-owner master file, which contains the owner's name, address, zip code, driver's license number, expiration date of license, date of birth, Social Security number, physical characteristics, and driving restrictions.

b. A motor vehicle master file, which contains the vehicle's identification number, make, year of manufacture, model or style, color, owner's name, and license number.

Currently, the files are organized sequentially and are independent of each other. However, the DMV has decided to acquire a data base management system, so that the data in the two files can be structured to answer key inquiries.

Required

a. Specify the schema needed to answer these questions: (1) If the owner's name is XXX, what vehicles are owned by him or her and what are their features? (2) If the vehicle's license number is YYY, who is the owner or owners and what are the details concerning the owner(s)? Use data structure diagram(s) as well as narrative description to specify the schema.

b. Prepare record layouts, including any fields that may be added by your design.

18-9 Refer to Figure 18-9*b*. Expand the network structure to include more relationships pertaining to the supplier, including the general ledger account and transactions involving purchase obligations and disbursements. Also, include a record for the general ledger itself, which links to each of its accounts. Furthermore, show in the expanded structure the conversion of the many-to-many relationship to two one-to-many relationships and an intersection record.

18-10 Cactus National Bank serves a state in the Southwest. Among the services that it provides to business and personal customers are checking accounts, savings accounts, and installment loans. Each customer may have one or more checking accounts, savings accounts, and installment loans. The checking and savings accounts have deposit, withdrawal, and adjusting (e.g., NSF check) transactions; the installment loans have loan and repayment transactions. The bank desires to integrate the data pertaining to individual business and personal customers. Therefore, it decides to convert to the data base approach.

Required

a. Draw a data structure diagram that represents a data base schema for these areas.

The schema should integrate all the data pertaining to an individual customer. The root node should be a record that contains the customer number, name, address, and other relevant background data. All the data pertaining to the accounts and loans should appear in separate records as members (children) to the root record. The transactions, in turn, should be members (children) of the accounts and loan records.

b. Bank tellers, who handle the checking and savings accounts, and loan officers, who administer the installment loans, are the most frequent users of the schema. Draw separate subschemas for the tellers and loan officers. The two subschemas should, in effect, split the schema into two parts, except that each should include the root node.

 18-11 Refer to the four tables in Figure 18-13, which comprise a relational data base. Assume that the following two tables are added to the data base and that the department table is completely filled with data.

Department

Dept. no.	Dept. name	Phone no.
1		
2		

Department/skill

Dept. no.	Skill no.
1	10
1	20
1	30
2	40
2	50
2	60

Required

a. Considering the data base *before* the addition of the two new tables, list three inquiries (other than those in the chapter example) that could be answered from the data. Then draw the newly created tables that provide the answers, and describe how the new tables were formed.

b. Using the added department and department/skill tables, develop the new tables to answer the following inquiries and describe their formation:

  (1) Which departments (by number) provide each of the required skills (by number and description)? Assume that skills 10, 20, 30, 40, 50, and 60 are required and that no employee has a skill used in both departments.

  (2) Which skills and employees (by number) are currently employed in department 2?

  (3) Which departments and skills (by number) are involved in job number 100?

c. Explain how the procedures for creating new tables are changed in **b (2)** and **b (3)** when employee names and skill descriptions, respectively, are needed.

18-12 The following three tables are maintained in a purchasing data base:

PARTS

PARTNO	PNAME
P107	BOLT
P113	NUT
P125	SCREW
P132	GEAR

SUPPLIERS

SUPPNO	SNAME
S51	ABC Co.
S57	XYZ Co.
S63	LMN Co.

PRICES

PARTNO	SUPPNO	PRICE
P107	S51	0.59
P107	S57	0.65
P113	S51	0.25
P113	S63	0.21
P125	S63	0.15
P132	S57	5.25
P132	S63	7.50

Required

Draw the new tables created by the following inquiries:

a. Which suppliers, by name, provide part 113?

b. Which suppliers, by name, provide gears?

c. Which suppliers, by name, provide more than three parts?

d. Which parts, by name, are provided by only one supplier?

e. Which suppliers, by name, have which parts (by name and number) that are priced below $0.50?

Specify for each inquiry a series of SELECT, PROJECT, and JOIN operators that will create the new relation.

(Courtesy of International Business Machines Corporation)

18-13 The data structure diagram at the top of page 863 represents the schema for an inventory management data base. Draw data structure diagrams that represent reasonable subschemas for the following users of this data base: (a) buyer, (b) receiving clerk, (c) accounts payable clerk, (d) inventory control clerk or supervisor. Certain record types will appear in more than one subschema.

18-14 Refer to Figure 18-15. Expand this entity-relationship diagram to include the sales and cash receipts activities. Begin by redrawing the diagram in the figure and then link the new activities directly to the diagram. If necessary, alter the positions of the present boxes and diamonds in order to accommodate the new activities.

18-15 Machinemade Shops, Inc., of Charleston, South Carolina, operates six machine shops throughout the Southeast. At the home office it maintains two master files of all owned machines. One file is arranged by machine ID numbers; two dozen records from this file appear on page 864. The other

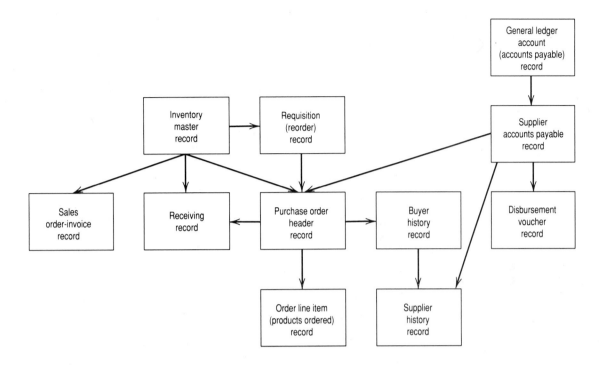

file is arranged by account number *and* machine ID number (a concatenated key) and contains a depreciation record for each machine. The firm stores its data under the control of a DBMS that enables the creation of tree structures and linked list structures.

Required

a. Assume that the records shown on page 864 constitute the entire machine file. Relist the disk addresses, machine ID numbers, and plant location numbers, *plus* a column that contains attribute chains pertaining to plant location numbers. Each attribute chain should form a ring structure.

b. Prepare a record layout showing all fields, including pointer fields, for the machine file whose records appear on page 864. Assume that all content fields in the record, except the primary key field, are secondary keys; attribute chains are formed on all secondary keys. In addi-

tion, the records in the file are owner records of the depreciation records. Ignore the field lengths and modes of data items.

c. List below the record layout in **b** the values that should appear in the machine with ID number 123, if a report showing the complete data for each machine and arranged by year of purchase is to be listed. Assume that the depreciation record for machine 123 is stored at disk address 6220. Ignore values for pointers pertaining to the account number and replacement cost attribute chains.

18-16 The following tables in a relational data base are not in a suitably normalized form. Specify the columns, using relational notation and assigned code names, of the two or more tables that represent suitable normalization in each case. Also underline the primary key for each table, as well as any foreign keys needed to provide common columns between tables. Include intersection tables when necessary, with both columns of each such table viewed as foreign keys.

 a. The job table in Figure 18-13. *Hint:* One of the two normalized tables should be specified as follows: JOB (JOB-NO*, JOB-DESCR, ASSUM-COST), where * represents the primary key field.

 b. An inventory table containing these columns: item number, item description, quantity on order, quantity on hand, supplier number, supplier name, supplier address. (Each inventory item may be supplied by more than one supplier.)

 c. A sales order table containing these columns: order number, order date, expected delivery date, customer number, customer name, customer billing address, customer shipping address, product number, product description, unit of measure, quantity of product, expected unit price. (More than one product can be included on a single order.) *Hint:* Begin with a customer table.

18-17 Jobs Not Sobs, a new nationwide job placement service, is planning to establish a computerized data base to match available jobs with job applicants' qualifications. The main users of the data base will be the clerks who enter and update the data concerning jobs and applicants, the service representatives who access the data base for information that helps place the applicants, and the

Disk Address	Machine ID No.[a]	Account Number	Year of Purchase	Plant Location Number	Replacement Cost
3600	113	1612	1980	3	$18,000
3640	114	1617	1980	6	12,800
3680	116	1619	1980	1	21,000
3720	117	1615	1981	2	16,500
3760	119	1618	1981	3	11,800
3800	120	1617	1981	4	22,200
3840	121	1613	1981	5	25,600
3880	123	1614	1982	3	17,000
3920	124	1612	1982	1	15,700
3960	125	1618	1982	6	14,700
4000	126	1611	1982	4	16,100
4040	127	1615	1983	2	23,800
4080	128	1613	1983	2	19,000
4120	129	1617	1983	1	21,600
4160	130	1614	1984	5	18,300
4200	131	1612	1984	6	15,000
4240	132	1619	1984	4	17,500
4280	133	1618	1984	3	28,000
4320	134	1617	1985	5	23,900
4360	135	1615	1985	3	18,800
4400	136	1613	1985	2	11,000
4440	137	1619	1986	1	23,900
4480	138	1611	1986	6	16,100
4520	139	1616	1986	4	27,300

[a]Machines 115, 118, and 122 have been sold.

service managers who access the data base for reports concerning placements.

Required

Describe the phases and steps required to develop the desired data base and make it operational. Include the critical decisions that must be made during the phases. Be as specific as possible in your discussion.

18-18 A medium-sized public accounting firm with 200 accountants provides audit, tax, and management advisory services to a variety of business and governmental clients. It decides to acquire a data base system. At present it is undecided concerning the choice of data model: tree, network, or relational. The areas to be included in the data base in the first year or so will be time recording and management of its professional and clerical staff, billing of clients, and project management of its engagements with clients. Thus, the processing mix will include some batch processing, although the majority of processing will involve on-line entry of time and engagement data and the access of data concerning engagements. All 200 accountants and the clerical staff of 20 will have access to terminals or portable microcomputers that can tie to the host minicomputer. Each engagement has an average duration of one month, and approximately 100 engagements are under way during the busy spring season.

Required

Describe the phases and steps in developing the desired data base. Be specific with respect to the decision concerning the type of data model and the related schema.

18-19 Compile a list of the factors that should influence the decision concerning the particular DBMS to acquire. As an aid in compiling this list, you might refer to a textbook concerning data base management or obtain the suggestions of a firm currently acquiring a DBMS.

18-20 Southeastern State University employs a DBMS based on the network model to integrate its data concerning students, classes, registration, and related matters. Among the reports and documents that the data base facilitates are class schedules for each student, class rosters (showing the list of students, by social security number, name, and major, for each class, plus the classroom number and professor), semester class schedules (showing the classes, plus times, rooms, and professors), and classroom schedules (showing the times each room is occupied and by which classes).

Required

a. Prepare a data structure diagram showing the portion of the schema that enables these reports to be generated. The result should be a network structure that contains several many-to-many relationships. Three entry points are needed, including the class and student records such as shown in Figure 18-10*a*.

b. Revise the data structure diagram in **a** to show all many-to-many relationships converted into one-to-many relationships with intersection records.

c. The class schedule for Melody Dunson, student number 684, is requested. Draw the linked list structure of the ring type that shows how the records are accessed, if the student's record is located at disk address 350 and the four classes she is taking (coded ACC221, CIS 302, ART 101, and MAT 201) are located at disk addresses 520, 260, 490, and 730, respectively.

d. Prepare an SQL expression similar to the one shown in the chapter to request a listing of the students who are majoring in accounting, have a grade-point average above 3.00, and either have senior standing or are older than 20. The student records are maintained in a data set called

STDREC and contain the student number, GPA, name, address, and related data.

18-21 The Bluegrass Plumbing Supply Co. of Lexington, Kentucky, wholesales a variety of plumbing supplies to plumbing contractors throughout several states.[17] To increase sales and improve profits, it feels that it needs to improve service in processing orders, to sharpen purchasing and receiving operations, and to reduce inventory investment. Thus, the firm designs a new system pertaining to purchasing and inventory control. To implement this new system, it acquires computer hardware, including terminals and magnetic disk storage. It also purchases a data base management system.

The newly designed system employs three key files: a product (finished-goods inventory) master file, a supplier master file, and an outstanding purchase orders file. These files are accessed via terminals by employees concerned with sales order processing, purchasing, and receiving.

When an order from a customer is received, a sales order clerk checks via a terminal to see whether the quantity shown in the inventory record is adequate to fill the order. If so, the quantity on hand is reduced to reflect the order; if not, the clerk checks to see if a purchase order is outstanding and when goods are due.

Each day, buyers in the purchasing department place purchase orders by entering (via terminals) the transaction code, the numbers of products being ordered, the order quantities, the anticipated unit prices, the supplier numbers, and the anticipated due dates. The computer system then retrieves the proper supplier record—which contains such data as the supplier name,

mailing address, and other header data that normally appear in a purchase order—and prepares the purchase order that has a computer-assigned number; finally, it places a copy of the order in the open purchase order file.

When ordered goods arrive at the receiving dock and have been counted, a receiving clerk enters the transaction code, the purchase order number, the product numbers, and the quantities received. The computer system then verifies that the purchase order is valid and that the quantities agree with those on the order. If the clerk enters an acceptance code, the system prepares a receiving report and also increases the quantity-on-hand balance in the inventory record to reflect the received goods.

Upon request of the purchasing manager, the system prepares a list of products that have fallen below their reorder points, together with their optimal reorder quantities. This list is used as the basis for making ordering assignments to the buyers.

Required

a. List the data items that should appear in each of the three files.

b. Prepare a data structure diagram that reflects a reasonable schema for the data base.

c. Prepare and discuss separate data structure diagrams that reflect the subschemas for (1) an order processing clerk, (2) a buyer, (3) a receiving clerk, and (4) the purchasing manager. In other words, isolate the portion of the schema that can satisfy the needs (e.g., to make an inquiry, to update a file, to prepare a report) of each of these four users. For instance, if the schema is in essence a structure involving three record types, a subschema may consist of two of these three record types. In fact, it may consist only of certain selected data items from the records.

[17] Adapted from *Information Systems in Management* by James A. Senn.© 1978 by Wadsworth Publishing Co., Inc. Reprinted by permission of Wadsworth Publishing Co., Inc., Belmont, Cal. 94002.

18-22 A preliminary survey of a firm's data base system and EDP (information system) department reveals the following:

a. There are no restrictions regarding type of transaction or access to the on-line terminals.

b. All users and EDP personnel have access to the extensive system documentation.

c. Before being entered in the user authorization table, user passwords and access codes are established by user management and approved by the manager of computer programming.

d. The manager of computer programming establishes and controls the data base directory. Users approve any changes to data definitions.

e. User requests for data are validated by the system against a transactions-conflict matrix to ensure that data are transmitted only to authorized users.

f. System access requires the users to input their passwords, and terminal activity logs are maintained.

g. Input data are edited for reasonableness and completeness, transaction control totals are generated, and transaction logs are maintained.

h. Processing control totals are generated and reconciled to changes in the data base.

i. Output is reconciled to transaction and input control totals. The resulting reports are printed and placed in a bin outside the EDP room for pickup by the users at their convenience.

j. Backup copies of the data base are generated daily and stored in the file library area, access to which is restricted to EDP personnel.

Required

a. List all effective controls and security measures that are currently installed.

b. Evaluate the relative adequacies of the general and application (transaction) controls, and indicate significant omissions.

(CIA adapted)

18-23 A systems analysis has just been completed for the Southwest Paper Co. of Tucson, Arizona, which manufactures and markets various types of paper for the printing industry.[18] This analysis initially was intended to identify the informational requirements related to the purchasing function, but it has subsequently been expanded to include the accounts payable function as well. The justification for expanding the investigation was based on the similarity of the data required in the data base to support both functions.

Analysis has identified the need for the purchasing department to maintain three files: (1) a supplier master file containing names, addresses, purchasing terms, and miscellaneous descriptive data; (2) an open purchase order file containing all the data related to purchase orders placed but not yet completed; and (3) a history file of purchases made in a two-year period, by product and suppliers. When purchase orders are closed upon receipt of invoices from suppliers, their data are transferred to the history file.

The accounts payable department, on the other hand, requires the following files: (1) a supplier master file containing all descriptive data necessary to produce and mail

---

[18] Adapted from John G. Burch, Jr., and Felix R. Strater, Jr., *Information Systems: Theory and Practice*, 2d ed. (New York: John Wiley, 1979). Used with permission.

checks for purchases received, (2) a file of invoices received from suppliers but not yet paid, and (3) a one-year history file of paid suppliers' invoices. Invoices are always paid nine days after receipt and transferred in a batch to the paid-invoice-history file.

Currently, these files are maintained on magnetic tape and processed by a tape-oriented computer system. However, after their analysis the firm decides to design an integrated purchasing and accounts payable system. This system is to be implemented on a medium-sized computer that has both magnetic tape and disk storage and can perform both batch and on-line processing.

Approximately 20 percent of all purchases are considered rebuys from an existing supplier. At any point in time there are 3000 active suppliers, 5000 open purchase orders, and 1500 open invoices. Annually the firm places 40,000 purchase orders.

Required

a. What files are needed in the integrated application system?

b. Prepare a matrix that shows the listed files across the top and that lists the data items in the respective files down the side.

c. How should each of the logical files be physically structured? Explain.

d. Assuming that a DBMS is acquired and all files are converted to magnetic disk storage, draw a data structure diagram that relates the records of files listed in **a** within a suitable purchasing/accounts payable schema. The DBMS can accommodate either the tree or network data model.

e. Expand the schema in **d** by linking other related record types, such as inventory records.

f. Develop a partial data dictionary for the purchasing/accounts payable schema of

d. List ten of the data items shown in the matrix of **b.** Assign item codes from 01 to 10 for the data items, and use reasonable values for field lengths. Use Figure 18-7 as a guide, but ignore the outputs and assume names for application programs and users. Also, include a column headed "Record(s) to which linked," and include the names of linked records for those items that are primary keys. For instance, if open sales invoice records are linked to the customer records, put "Open sales invoice" in the column when the item being listed is the customer number, a primary key.

g. Identify specific information requests that can be answered and reports that can be generated via the schema in **d.**

Suggested Readings

Anderson, Earl H., and Techavichit, Joseph V. "Data-base Systems and the Controller." *The Internal Auditor* (Feb. 1982), pp. 46–49.

Armitage, Howard, and McCarthy, William E. "Decision Support Using Entity-Relationship Modeling." *Journal of Accounting and EDP* (Fall 1987), pp. 12–19.

Bagranoff, Nancy, and Simkin, Mark G. "Database Management Systems: Getting the Most from Your Database." *The Journal of Accountancy* (May 1988), pp. 122–128.

Blanning, Robert W. "An Entity-Relationship Framework for Information Resource Management." *Information and Management* (1988), pp. 113–119.

Brackett, Michael H. *Developing Data Structured Databases.* Englewood Cliffs, N.J.: Prentice-Hall, 1987.

Briner, R. "Database Security." *Management Accounting* (Oct. 1981), pp. 28–30.

Burch, John G., Jr., and Grudnitski, Gary. *Information Systems: Theory and Practice.* 5th ed. New York: John Wiley, 1989.

CODASYL (Conference on Data Systems and Languages). *Data Base Task Group Report, 1971.* New York: Association for Computing Machinery, April 1971.

Curtis, Robert M., and Jones, Paul E., Jr. "Database: The Bedrock of Business." *Datamation* (June 15, 1984), pp. 163–166.

Everest, G. C. *Database Management: Objectives, System Functions, and Administration.* New York: McGraw-Hill, 1985.

Filteau, M. C.; Kassicieh, S. K.; and Tripp, R. S. "Evolutionary Database Design and Development in Very Large Scale MIS." *Information and Management* (Nov. 1988), pp. 203–212.

Gaydasch, Alexander, Jr. *Effective Database Management.* Englewood Cliffs, N.J.: Prentice-Hall, 1988.

Herman, Marian. "A Database Design Methodology for an Integrated Database Environment." *Data Base* (Fall 1983), pp. 20–26.

LeGore, Laurence B. "Smoothing Data Base Recovery." *Datamation* (January 1979), pp. 177–180.

McCarthy, William E. "An Entity-Relationship View of Accounting Models." *The Accounting Review* (Oct. 1979), pp. 667–686.

Merrett, T. H. *Relational Information Systems.* Reston, Va.: Reston Publishing, 1984.

Raine, Jesse, and Smith, Glenda E. "Building and Marketing a Commercial On-Line Database." *Journal of Systems Management* (Mar. 1987), pp. 22–34.

Severance, Jay, and Bottin, Ronald R. "Work-in-Process Inventory Control through Data Base Concepts." *Management Accounting* (Jan. 1979), pp. 37–41.

Smith, James F., and Mufti, Amer. "Using the Relational Database." *Management Accounting* (Oct. 1985), pp. 43–54.

Stern, Myles. "A Data Base Primer for Accountants." *Journal of Accounting and EDP* (Summer 1985), pp. 14–21.

CHAPTER OBJECTIVES

After studying this chapter, you should be able to do the following:

Discuss the fundamentals of data communications.

Describe the features and advantages of the two major wide-area network architectures.

Describe the features and uses of local area networks.

Identify various networking services available to firms.

Describe the range of controls and security measures that are pertinent to communications networks.

Describe a variety of specialized communications-based information systems based on network technology.

Discuss major considerations pertaining to the design of communications networks.

Chapter *19*

COMMUNICATIONS NETWORKS

Many modern firms conduct their affairs from more than one location. For instance, a typical manufacturing firm may have several plants, warehouses, and sales offices—all at locations removed from the central office. Communications between these remote locations have traditionally been conveyed by letters, telephone calls, telegrams, and interoffice messenger services. Most firms still communicate, at least in part, by these modes.

Currently, however, a geographically dispersed firm may electronically link its remote locations by means of a data communication system. This means of communication provides employees in remote locations with the same access to data, computing power, and managerial guidance that they would have if they were physically in the home office.

The purpose of data communications is therefore to bridge the distances between

users and key portions of the information system. A firm that installs a data communication system links together its data collection, processing, storage, and dissemination facilities into a geographically dispersed network. In such a firm the information system becomes a data/communication/information complex. This blurring or combining of data communications and data processing has been graphically illustrated by the movement of the American Telephone & Telegraph Company into the manufacturing and marketing of computer equipment.

Data communications networks have become increasingly common since the 1970s. Currently it is estimated that more than 90 percent of all computers (excluding microcomputers) in the United States are connected to data communications networks. The growth in data communications networks is due to two factors: (1) improvements in data communications technologies and (2) increased numbers of geographically dispersed firms with remote locations requiring close coordination and timely information.

To understand such networks, we need first to understand the data communications fundamentals that underpin the network structures. Then we can examine the more commonly encountered varieties of computer networks as well as several of the more significant applications of business-oriented networks. Finally we survey the key considerations that affect the sound design of an information system with a data communications sweep.

Accountants require a basic knowledge of data communications and the types of computer networks that can be structured. Not only are accountants called on to help select the options best suited to particular situations, but as auditors they are expected to evaluate the adequacy of security measures built into the resulting computer networks.

Fundamentals of Data Communications

Data communication networks vary enormously in patterns and options, as we shall see. However, the typical network consists of terminals, modems, communications control units, central processing units, and the communications channels that link them.

Figure 19-1 shows a relatively simple data communications network. For convenience we first consider the various hardware devices. Then we survey the communications channels that link together the devices as well as the various modes and means of transmitting data.

Hardware Involved in Data Communications

Terminals. The wide variety of terminals has already been discussed, in Chapter 5. Although a complete review is unnecessary, we should recall that terminals possess varying degrees of "intelligence."

A **"dumb" terminal** is essentially an input–output device. Appearing in the form of either a video display terminal or keyboard/printer terminal, it has few "intelligent" features. Generally it cannot communicate (without help) with a computer in the network, edit input data, or contain program instructions. Most "dumb" terminals currently are employed within networks to accept the entry of basic transaction data, to answer inquiries, or to monitor operations.

An **intelligent terminal** is, in effect, a small computer, often a microcomputer. Thus, it can communicate with other units in the network, edit and format data for transmission, process data against files, store transactions and results of processing, and so on. Although intelligent terminals very in degrees of brilliance, the common thread is

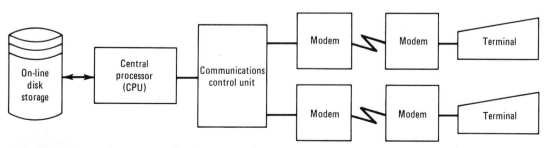

FIGURE 19-1 A data communications network.

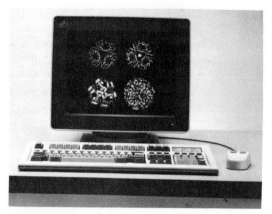

FIGURE 19-2 A terminal for use in a data communications network. Courtesy of International Business Machines Corporation.

programmability. Most intelligent terminals allow the stored programs to be modified, although in some the program instructions are hard-wired.

Figure 19-2 presents a video display terminal, also called a display station, that may serve as an input–output point within a data communications network. Although the model exhibited in the figure cannot perform processing operations, it contains a number of features for entering data and displaying and manipulating outputs (e.g., graphics) in full color. It also enables the screen to be split into as many as three areas for simultaneous entry and display.

Modems. Modulator–demodulator coupler units, known as **modems,** are devices that convert data for transmission over telephone lines. As Figure 19-3 shows, one modem is needed at the sending end to transform digital signals (i.e., 0s and 1s) generated by a device (e.g., a terminal) into analog signals (i.e., sine waves). The transformation is necessary because most voice telephone lines can handle only analog signals. When the signals are received at the other end (e.g., at the computer), they must be transformed back into digital signals, the only type that a pro-

cessor can handle. The two modems are connected to the sending and receiving devices (e.g., the terminal and computer) by interface cables that plug into ports.[1]

Modems look like small black boxes. However, they can vary in several respects. First, they may be connected onto communications lines in different ways. One way is by inserting a touch-tone telephone into couplers on the modems, thus forming an acoustical coupling to the public telephone lines. Another way is to hard-wire the modems directly to private communication lines. (Terminals using acoustical coupler modems are known as dial-up terminals, whereas terminals having directly wired modems are known as hard-wired terminals.)

Modems also vary with respect to **baud rates,** the number of data bits transmitted over communications lines per signal emitted. One baud is often (but not necessarily) equal to a bit per second (bps). Modems are commonly rated at 300, 1200, 2400, 4800, and 9600 baud, which generally means that they transmit at speeds of from 300 to 9600 bps. Modems with dial-up terminals transmit up to 2400 bps, while modems with hard-wired terminals generally transmit at higher speeds.

A third means of classifying modems is by mode of transmission. **Asynchronous modems** transmit by a ''start-stop'' operation, whereas **synchronous modems** transmit continuously. These modes of transmission are discussed further in a later section.

Modern-day modems provide, for a price, a number of optional features. Among these are built-in diagnostics, buffer storage, encryption, and data compression. Modems may also be built into terminals, so that terminals are easier to transport.

---

[1]A special type of communications line now available can transmit digital signals. Modems are not needed for such digital transmission lines; instead, simple devices known as data service units are employed.

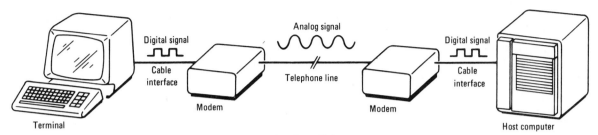

FIGURE 19-3 Use of modems in a data communications linkup.

Communications control units. A computer system consisting of a single central processor connected to single nonoverlapped input and output units at the same location is the simplest possible configuration. This system can easily be controlled by the operating system within the primary storage unit. As more input–output devices are added to the system, however, control mechanisms are also needed. As noted in Chapter 5, two control mechanisms—channels and controllers—aid communication within the system and accommodate overlapped processing.

When a computer-based system adds data communications to the above, other communications control units are often necessary. Three communications control units are communications processors, multiplexors, and concentrators.

A **communications processor,** also called a front-end processor, is a specialized, programmable device that relieves a central processor of certain communications burdens. In effect, it is a small computer. Among the functions that it performs for the processor are

1. Message switching, that is, asking (polling) terminals for messages, interrupting current processing by the central processor so that messages from terminals can receive high-priority processing, directing messages from the central processor to terminals, and routing messages among terminals.

2. Detecting and correcting errors in transmitted data.

3. Editing data, for example, translating data that have been coded for transmission into a form for processing, and vice versa.

4. Storing and moving data from the buffer into primary storage, and vice versa.

5. Keeping statistics concerning data messages received and sent and errors detected.

By relieving the central processor of these functions, the communications processor enables the former to perform its primary job of data processing more efficiently. It also helps the central processor to economize in the use of primary storage capacity. Also, communications processors often incorporate the devices known as channels, thereby eliminating their costs. On the other hand, communications processors are relatively costly devices and should be employed only when they save more than they cost.

A **multiplexor** is a communications control device that combines the data signals from multiple terminals into a composite signal for transmission to a single point. In other words, it enables the data (e.g., transactions, summary figures) from several terminals to be transmitted simultaneously over a single communication line and still to be received and handled as separate messages by the central processor. In fact, a multiplexor can handle a two-way simultaneous flow of messages.

Figure 19-4 contrasts a data communications system before and after a multiplexor has been added to collect the messages from five terminals. The effect has been to eliminate the need for four of the lines and eight of the modems. In this example system a communications processor has been placed at the front end of the central processor. If it were not present, a second multiplexor would be needed in its stead.

A multiplexor yields two major benefits. First, it increases the transmission speed overall, hence reducing the idle time of the central processor when waiting for the messages from the terminals. (On the other end, it also reduces the idle time of persons sitting at the terminals when waiting for responses from the processor.) This increase in speed occurs because the terminals operate at low speeds (e.g., 1200 bps), while the single line transmits at a high speed (e.g., 9600 bps). The other benefit of using the multiplexor is that it can provide significant savings in communication line costs. These savings, of course, are offset by the added cost of the multiplexor. Also, the single shared communication line between the multiplexor and the computer site is subject to higher charges than are the individual lines to separate terminals.

A **concentrator** is a line-sharing device, similar to the multiplexor, that incorporates certain functions of the communications processor. It can transmit several messages simultaneously over a single line. However, it allows messages from two or more terminals to share the same "path" or channel within the high-speed line. Thus, it more fully utilizes the line. For instance, if a particular multiplexor can control messages from four terminals, a similar concentrator might control messages from eight terminals (assuming that each terminal transmits only one-half the time). Alternatively, it can control the four terminals with a lower-grade line.

A **private branch telephone exchange** (PBX) is a switching device that controls the flow of incoming and outgoing telephone calls and data within the network of a firm. Most current PBX's control analog signals, but PBX's that control digital signals are now available.

Central processor. As in any computer system, the central processor within a network performs several key functions. It houses the operating system, performs various processing operations, and serves as the direct conduit to the centralized storage units. As a focal point within a network, however, a central processor has communications responsibilities. Thus, it must either (1) perform message switching and the other functions that are necessary in the network, or (2) coordinate the actions of a communications processor that performs the functions. Since these functions are incorporated within software known as **communications control programs** or teleprocessing monitors, the central processor therefore serves as the arena within which all the software are interlinked and controlled.

Central processors, also called host processors or computers, are often large-scale or mainframe computers. They may be minicomputers or superminicomputers, however.

Moving Data via Communications Channels

After our survey of hardware devices, we are ready to consider the dynamic aspect of data communications. The movement of data from one location to another involves such factors as the character of the link, grade of line, transmission types, transmission mode, protocol, and type of communications line service.

Medium. The communications link, or channel, may assume any of several forms. Apart from the postal service, the most common medium is the electrical line or cable.

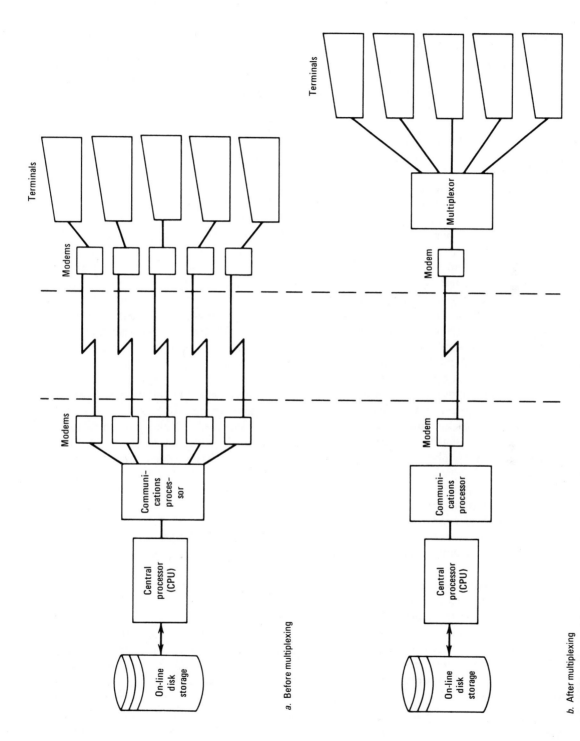

a. Before multiplexing

b. After multiplexing

FIGURE 19-4 A data communications network before and after multiplexing.

Traditional electrical lines are made of copper or aluminum. Each line consists of two insulated wires called a twisted pair. Although such lines typically link telephones and carry voice communications, they can also transmit data via analog signals. Perhaps the major benefit provided by these familiar *telephone lines* is their wide availability. *Coaxial cables* are also composed of copper or aluminum wires. They are better insulated to reduce interference, and they are designed to carry thousands of telephone calls over long distances and at high transmission volumes (i.e., millions of bits per second). Coaxial cables also can support a wider variety of devices and data than can telephone lines. However, they are not as widely accessible. *Fiber optics cables* consist of numerous glass or plastic filaments. They transmit data by means of concentrated light waves. Fiber optics cables have several advantages over metallic cables. Although less expensive and smaller, a single fiber optics cable can handle a volume of hundreds of millions of bits of data per second. Because of almost no interference from electrical sources, the data are transmitted with a high degree of reliability and security. Thus, fiber optics cables are being installed very rapidly.[2]

Other communications media include satellite transmission, microwave data transmission, and cellular radio. Future communications links are likely to include modulated laser light beams and helical waveguides. These means of transmission currently supplement and enhance the transmission of data via cables. Data can more easily be transmitted around the world, across continents, and to and from mobile vehicles. Although they allow data to be transmitted at high volumes, noncable transmission techniques are not likely to replace cables in the near future.

From the point of view of the user of a communications system, the type of link is transparent; that is, he or she is not concerned with the technical details, since any of the foregoing can accomplish the data communications mission. However, from the point of view of the system designer, the choice of link has a bearing on such critical factors as reliability, security, and cost.

Grade of line. Communications lines are graded according to their speed of transmission. **Narrow-band,** or subvoice, **lines** transmit at low rates (45 to 300 bps); **voice-band lines** transmit at higher rates (300 to 9600 bps), and **wide-band** or **broad-band lines** transmit at very high rates (up to several hundred million bps). The higher the speed, the greater the volumes of data transmitted. It should come as no surprise that higher-speed lines also involve higher communications charges.

Each grade of line is in active use today. Terminals operate in the narrow band, telephone lines in the voice band, and satellites in the wide band. Within the voice band, a further distinction may be observed. Regular dial-up telephone lines cannot transmit above the lower end of the band; only specially conditioned lines can transmit at the upper end.

Types of transmission. Several means of transmission are possible, given suitable communications equipment and lines. The choices are (1) simplex, half duplex, or full duplex, (2) analog or digital, and (3) serial or parallel.

Simplex, half duplex, and full duplex relate to the directions of transmission. **Simplex** allows transmission in one direction only. **Half duplex** allows transmission in both directions, but not at the same time. **Full duplex** allows transmission in both directions at the same time. Simplex transmission can be used to display information, such as airline arrivals and departures at airports; half du-

[2]Peter G. Balbus and Joseph L. Healey, "Out of the Labs and Into the Streets," *Datamation* (September 1, 1984), pp. 96–106.

plex is suitable for processing data in an on-line mode when immediate response is not necessary; full duplex should be used when real-time processing is necessary.[3]

Analog and digital relate to the form of transmissions. The wave form of **analog transmission,** as shown in Figure 19-3, is the type that most present-day communications lines are designed to carry. It must be converted to the digital pulsed form (also shown in Figure 19-3) by modems for use by computers. When **digital transmission** is employed along the communications lines, no modems are needed. It also allows data to be transmitted faster and more reliably. However, communications lines designed to transmit digital forms are relatively scarce and expensive. In future years they should become more common, so that digital transmission can be expected to increase.

Serial and parallel relate to the number of communication channels used to transmit a message. **Serial transmission** consists of sending an entire message over a single channel, one character after another. **Parallel transmission** consists of sending portions of the message over separate communications channels. The latter is faster but generally more expensive on a per-message basis.

Transmission mode. As noted earlier, the two basic transmission modes are asynchronous and synchronous. **Asynchronous transmission** involves a character-by-character transmission, since each character is preceded by a start bit and followed by a stop bit. Each character may be coded by a five-bit Baudot code, a six-bit binary coded decimal (BCD) code, or a seven- or eight-bit American Standard Code for Information Interchange (ASCII).

Synchronous transmission involves continuous transmission. Instead of marking

each character with start and stop bits, it transmits blocks of characters comprising entire messages. Thus, synchronous transmission allows much faster transmission. However, it requires that the sending and receiving modems be in synchronization throughout the transmission. Consequently, more expensive equipment is needed.

Protocol. A **protocol** prescribes the manner by which data are transmitted between data communications devices. It consists of the set of rules and procedures by which data, in the form of messages, are transmitted from one point to another within a data communications network or between two networks. Protocols can be extremely technical and complex. They span such matters as setting proper data formats and codes, matching speeds of communications devices, starting and stopping transmissions, and performing error-checking procedures.

Perhaps the clearest introduction to protocols is via the enclosures (i.e., envelopes) within which messages are transmitted. Each message requires such an envelope, so that it will not become intermixed with other messages. Thus, if the five terminals in Figure 19-4 each transmit a message to the central processor, the messages will travel in five separate envelopes. Each message will also carry identification that can be recognized by the various communications devices. In this situation, the communications processor will "read" the identifiers when it receives an envelope. In addition, it will check the message for errors and then route the message to the proper destination within the primary storage unit of the processor.

Figure 19-5 illustrates an envelope prescribed by a representative protocol for encasing messages. Note that the message is "buried" within several identifiers. The "header" and "end of message" are control markers to identify the beginning and ending of the message. The message number is a sequence number to provide an audit trail.

---

[3]Michael J. Cerullo, "Data Communications: Opportunity for Accountants," *CPA Journal* (April 1984), pp. 44–45.

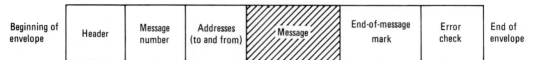

FIGURE 19-5   A typical protocol envelope.

Addresses specify where the message is directed (e.g., the sales program in the primary storage) and where it is coming from (e.g., terminal number 27). The error check is a character that enables the message to be checked for errors.

Since the envelopes containing messages are handled by the various devices in a data communications network, it is necessary that all of the devices accept the protocol chosen for the network. When devices do not conform to the protocol, **protocol converters** must be added to the network. Fortunately, the communications industry is progressing toward the universal adoption of a few standard protocols.[4]

Types of communications line service.
The three basic types of available service are private lines, public switched lines, and Wide Area Telephone Service (WATS) lines. **Private lines,** also called **leased lines,** are dedicated to the exclusive use of single customers for the duration of leased periods; their costs are fixed and depend on the lengths of the lines. **Public switched lines,** also called dial-up lines, employ the long-distance telephone service and thus are not exclusively available to individual customers. If a line is "busy" when a subscriber dials, he or she must wait until the line is free. As in the case of long-distance calls that we make to our parents or friends, the costs of switched lines depend on the lengths of time that the lines are used. **WATS lines** are also public switched lines; however, subscribers

pay service charges that include flat monthly rates for a minimum number of hours, plus (under many pricing plans) added charges for hours of service used beyond the minimum. Public switched lines (including WATS lines) offer easy accessibility; any telephone may be used to transmit data when connected to the terminal. However, these lines are less reliable than private lines in that the latter transmit data with the occurrence of fewer errors. Figure 19-6 compares the features and relative advantage of these three types of service.

In general, the key questions to ask when making a decision concerning line service is: How many hours will the line be used per day, and what is the distance between the sender and receiver? If it is likely to be used for only an hour or two each day, and the distance between points is great, the choice will probably be a public switched line. However, if it is likely to be used for several hours, and the distance is short, then the best choice will almost certainly be a private leased line. For the intermediate situations, the answer can be determined only by comparing the costs of the two options.

Public switched lines are increasingly being used, since telephone long-distance rates have been declining in recent years. Even where private lines are determined to be the more economical choice, public switched lines are sometimes used as back-ups.

Communications Network Architectures

A **wide-area communications network** consists of interconnected communications

---

[4]A full treatment of protocols is beyond the scope of this book. For an introduction to the complex protocols needed in extensive networks, see Eric D. Siegel, "Your Pocket Protocol Primer," *Datamation* (March 1984), pp. 152–154.

	Private line	Public switched line	WATS line
Use	Available only for use by paying customer	Employs public telephone lines; requires dialing for connection and service	Employs public telephone lines; requires dialing for connection and service
Rate	Fixed with respect to time used; variable with respect to distance	Variable with respect to time used	Fixed for a minimum number of hours per month; variable above the minimum
Advantages	Least expensive at high volumes and short distances	Least expensive at low volumes and relatively long distances	Tends to be least expensive at certain intermediate volumes and distances
	No waiting for service, hence generally faster transmissions	Flexible; can access system from any telephone	Flexible; can access system from any telephone
	Lower error rate		

FIGURE 19-6 Types of services in communications lines.

channels that link together two or more user locations. In order to be functional, the network must also incorporate necessary communications and information system devices, such as terminals, modems, and central processors. As we have already seen, networks may differ in many respects. In fact, it is scarcely an exaggeration to say that each specific network in the real world is unique. Nevertheless, networks (or portions of networks) may be classified in terms of their hardware/software structures, that is, their architectures or topologies.

The two contrasting architectures with respect to wide-area networks are centralized networks and distributed networks. Each warrants careful consideration. A third type of network, the local area network, receives attention in the next section.

Centralized Networks

A **centralized network** consists essentially of a single central computer processor and one or more linked terminals. For instance, a firm might locate a mainframe computer and on-line disk storage at its home office in Chicago; connecting to this centralized computer system might be terminals located at its four sales offices in Milwaukee, Des Moines, Pittsburgh, and Cincinnati.

The terminals that connect with the centralized computer system will normally be linked by devices such as described earlier. However, the terminals may assume a variety of forms. They may be dumb terminals or intelligent terminals, point-of-sale terminals or automated teller machines. They may be interactive terminals or remote job entry (RJE) stations. (Interactive terminals allow on-line interaction between a user and the system; RJE stations are terminals, perhaps accompanied by other input and output devices, that allow the entry of batched data.) Furthermore, the terminals may be located at remote points many miles from the computer system, or they may be located in the near vicinity.

Configurations. Centralized networks may be structured or configured by means of point-to-point lines, multidrop lines, multiplexed lines, or some combination of the foregoing. Figure 19-7 contrasts the three basic configurations when applied to the same set of terminals and central processor. (For simplicity, the figure ignores modems or assumes the use of digital transmission.)

A **point-to-point configuration** links each terminal separately to the central processor. Hence, this configuration provides the best service, since no terminal user has to wait his

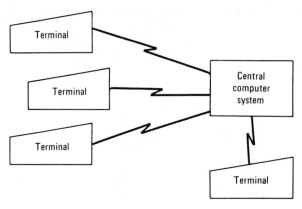

a. Point-to-point configuration

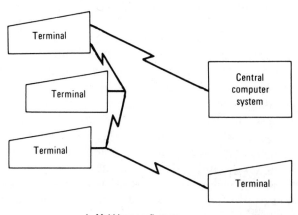

b. Multidrop configuraton

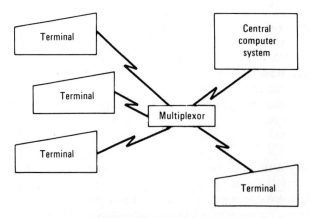

c. Multiplexed configuration

FIGURE 19-7 Centralized network configurations.

or her turn for a direct connection. A point-to-point configuration has three other advantages:

1. It is the simplest structure, since no line-sharing devices are generally needed.
2. It is flexible in that the communication lines may be public, private, WATS lines, or some combination of these.
3. It is the most reliable overall, since only one user is affected if a particular communication line fails.

The principal drawback of this configuration is that it involves the greatest communication line mileage of any of the three alternative configurations; hence, it is generally the most expensive, especially if most of the lines used are private lines.

A **multidrop configuration,** also called a multipoint configuration, links multiple terminals via ''drops'' to a single communication line, which in turn is connected to the central processor. The principal advantage of this configuration is economy, since the total communication line mileage normally is minimized. However, in relation to the point-to-point alternative the multidrop configuration has significant drawbacks:

1. A terminal user must typically wait for service, since only one terminal may send, or transmit, at a time. Generally, the waiting time (i.e., system response time) will increase as more terminals are added to a line.
2. It is inflexible in that only private leased lines may be employed.
3. It tends to be the least reliable overall, since all of the terminals beyond the point of a line failure will be out of service.

A final drawback is that the less expensive dumb terminals may not be used alone in multidrop configurations. Either terminals with a degree of intelligence or special added hardware must be employed, either of which

increases the overall cost of the configuration.[5]

A **multiplexed configuration** links a cluster of terminals to the central processor by means of a line-sharing device. The device may be either a multiplexor or a concentrator (the latter in reality a type of multiplexor).

This third configuration represents a compromise between the alternative configurations. For instance, it reduces the total communication line mileage below that required by the point-to-point configuration, but not as low as that required by the multidrop configuration. Thus, the overall cost of the configuration is likely to be less than the cost for the point-to-point configuration, although the saving is somewhat offset by the cost of the multiplexor. It also reduces the waiting time for service below the average waiting time required by a comparable multidrop configuration, because of the simultaneous transmission of messages via the single high-speed line to the central processor. Finally, the multiplexed configuration is flexible with respect to the type of service lines that connect to the terminals, but will permit only the use of a private line for the high-speed connection to the central processor.

Large centralized networks typically contain two or more of the basic configurations. Figure 19-8 portrays a network containing all three configurations.

Benefits. Centralized networks are utilized in such varied types of firms and other organizations as banks, utilities, merchandising chains, manufacturers, airlines, hospitals, and universities. They may constitute much of a firm's information system, such as a manufacturer's logistics network or a merchandiser's point-of-sale system. They may represent *dedicated systems,* such as an air-

[5]The added hardware will generally consist of small node controllers or concentrators at each remote point, plus a main data concentrator and multipoint modem (in place of the communications processor and ordinary modem) at the site of the central processor.

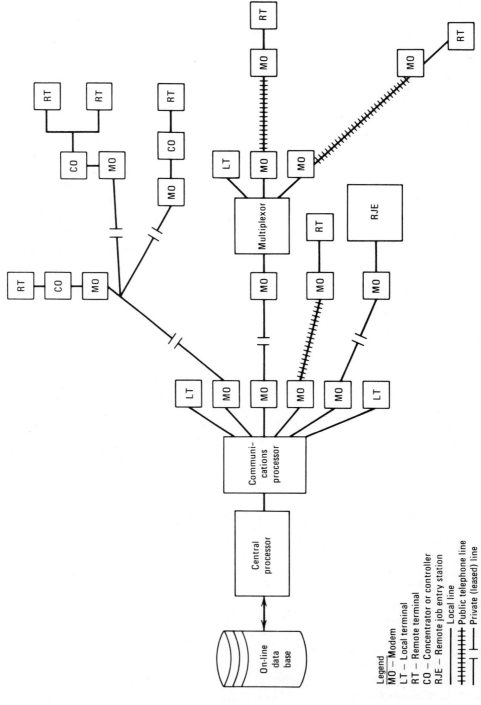

Legend
MO – Modem
LT – Local terminal
RT – Remote terminal
CO – Concentrator or controller
RJE – Remote job entry station
———— Local line
+++++++ Public telephone line
—|—|— Private (leased) line

FIGURE 19-8 A centralized network containing three basic configurations.

line reservation system that is set apart from the firm's accounting information system.

Centralized networks are in widespread use because they offer significant benefits that meet particular needs. These benefits hinge on their key features: a large central processor, an integrated data base, an elaborate control system, and a central staff of information systems personnel.

A large central processor provides concentrated raw computing power to the network. It thus can perform massive processing tasks, such as the manipulation of sophisticated financial planning models. It can also handle large processing volumes, such as those generated by numerous remote centers or branches. Furthermore, it can accomplish such processing at relatively low operating costs per transaction, thereby providing economies of scale.

A large processor is accompanied by a sophisticated operating system, which in turn facilitates the use of an integrated data base and elaborate control system. As described in Chapter 18, an integrated data base offers such benefits as reduced redundancy of stored data, simultaneous updating of all affected files, increased standardization of data items, better data documentation, and greater accessibility of data to meet managerial needs. An elaborate control system provides enhanced data security and reliability.

Centralized processing facilities encourage the establishment of a centralized corps of systems personnel. Because of its prominence and size, a centralized systems function can offer greater career opportunities. Hence, it can more easily attract the systems professionals currently in such short supply. Also, the supervision of systems personnel can be more effective, thus minimizing the coordination problems that generally plague decentralized staffs. Finally, centralized management of information system activities usually encourages a professional approach. This leads to optimal scheduling of data pro-

cessing runs, careful planning of systems development projects, consistent designing and programming of selected systems projects, and so on.

Drawbacks. Unfortunately, centralized networks have certain serious drawbacks. As in the case of the benefits, these drawbacks stem from the centralization of facilities and personnel.

The functioning of a centralized network, with its large central processor, is relatively complex. Thus, the network is difficult to design and costly to maintain. Consider, for instance, the tasks that must continually be directed and coordinated by the operating system. Transactions and inquiries from throughout the system must be edited and moved from the originating terminals through the communications channels to the processor. Application programs must be drawn from the on-line library for use in processing these transactions and inquiries. Then the transactions and inquiries, together with their programs, must be placed in partitions within primary storage. There they await their turns for processing and for accessing needed data from secondary storage. After being processed, they must enter a queue to await transmission back to the originating terminals or elsewhere. A priority rule must then be applied to decide which terminal is to receive the next outgoing message. Not surprisingly, an operating system having these responsibilities within a large network consumes many dollars and much primary storage. The communications costs are also likely to be relatively high. Furthermore, other elements of a centralized network are becoming increasingly costly. For example, the salaries of skilled computer system technicians and management have been rising dramatically.

Another major drawback of centralized networks is that they are rather inflexible and hence unresponsive to remote users. On the one hand, heavy transmission traffic may cause transactions and inquiries to be much delayed. On the other hand, the centralized staff may not be attuned to the needs and circumstances of remote users.

A third drawback is that centralized networks are vulnerable to disaster. If the processor fails, the entire network may be shut down.

Distributed Networks

A **distributed network** is a computer network in which the processing task, and possibly also the data management task, has been divided or distributed. Much of the processing load is generally assigned to smaller processors, such as minicomputers and microcomputers, which are under the direction of those who will use the processed data. In other words, a distributed network represents a user-oriented architecture.

Compared to decentralized systems. In the 1950s and 1960s data communications technology was still in its infancy. Computer networks were not technically feasible. Hence, firms that desired to employ computers for data processing had three choices: (1) subscribe to a computer service bureau, (2) install a single large computer, usually at the home office, or (3) install a variety of computers, usually at various locations. Those firms electing the third option created decentralized computer systems.

A decentralized computer system differs from a distributed network in that it has no communications links between the computers. A number of decentralized computer systems exist even today, since they have several significant advantages. First, they are less complex than computer networks, centralized or distributed. Second, decentralized computer systems are less costly, since they sharply reduce communications costs and allow the use of inexpensive microcomputers. Third, they enable managers to predict future processing costs more closely

and hence to budget more effectively. Finally, they provide the users greater control and are more responsive to users' needs than are centralized computers. As a consequence, many users and managers prefer decentralized computer systems over any type of network.

Movement toward distributed networks. In the early 1970s data communications networks became feasible options. Hence, the centralized networks already described began to dot the landscape. Somewhat earlier, the multiprocessing system had been developed. Consisting of two or more processors that shared the same primary storage unit, multiprocessing systems are able to process portions of the same program simultaneously. (See the discussion in Chapter 5.) Consequently, they represent the first application of shared or parallel processing.

The three aforementioned developments—decentralized computers, networking, and multiprocessing—led directly to the concept of distributed data processing. During the 1970s firms thus began to install distributed networks. Most of the networks were geographically dispersed. For example, the Celanese Company, a large textile manufacturer, located linked computers at its facilities in Charlotte, North Carolina, and Shelby, South Carolina.[6] When microcomputers emerged on the scene in the early 1980s, the growth of distributed networks accelerated. Because the capabilities of microcomputers are steadily increasing while their costs are decreasing, the number of distributed networks is likely to continue growing.

Processing by distributed networks. Distributed networks perform **distributed data processing,** a mixture of processing at various geographical locations and communica-

[6]Larry C. Brown, "Defining Distributed Data Processing," *Cost and Management* (November–December 1981), p. 7.

tion of data among the locations. All of the processors in the network share the total processing load over a period of time, although individual processors may act at times as though they are stand-alone decentralized computers. Distributed data processing assumes a variety of forms. Figure 19-9 portrays four of these forms; it is assumed that the distributed network consists of a host computer and four small, linked remote processors.[7]

The first two of these processing forms consist primarily of data entry functions. Transaction data are captured, checked for accuracy and completeness, batched and converted if necessary, and transmitted in detailed form to the mainframe for processing. After processing by the mainframe, the data are stored in a central data base. When needed, summary reports are prepared by the mainframe computer and transmitted to the remote processors. These processing forms differ only in degree from the functions performed by terminals in centralized networks. For instance, remote job entry from a specialized terminal of a centralized network may be quite similar to the entry of batched data via a remote processor. Perhaps the only difference is more thorough editing of data by the remote processor, so that all errors may be detected and corrected before transmittal. Another difference often encountered is the temporary storage of edited data at the remote site until a convenient processing time, say, 1 A.M.

The other two processing forms consist of complete data processing at the remote site, with summary data only being transmitted to the central data base. In one case, batch data are entered, converted, edited, sorted, and processed sequentially against master files in a local data base. In the other case, individual transactions are entered,

edited, and processed against the locally stored master files. In both cases, a printer at the remote site prepares needed managerial reports. These reports may be based on information either processed locally or centrally.

Distributed data bases. As noted earlier, data bases may be distributed to certain remote sites in a distributed network. Distributed data bases are particularly useful when large volumes of data need to be processed at remote locations or very fast access to data by local management is critical. Not only do they help meet the needs of local users, but they also can reduce the overall cost of data communications.

Data bases may be distributed by **replication** or by **partition**.[8] In the replicated approach, copies of files are stored at various remote locations. In the partition approach, segments of files are allotted to various locations in the network. The former approach creates redundancy throughout the system but retains the benefit of a centralized data base. The latter approach avoids redundancy but increases the complexity of transmitting needed data throughout the network.

The Ford Motor Company employs both approaches, as well as variations, throughout its several networks. Each district sales office maintains working files on the status of each vehicle ordered and the sales history of the district. These working files are copied from the master files in the home sales office. By contrast, the assembly division partitions the inventory files concerning vehicles (in-process and finished) to the various assembly plants. The parts division uses yet another approach: Each depot within the division maintains a parts file listing the parts it has on its premises, and the divisional home office maintains a master parts file. Each dealer's parts department accesses the depot's

---

[7]A communications processor and modems are normally employed in a distributed network. Modems have been omitted in this figure for the sake of simplicity.

[8]G. A. Champine, "Six Approaches to Distributed Data Bases," *Datamation* (May 1977), p. 70.

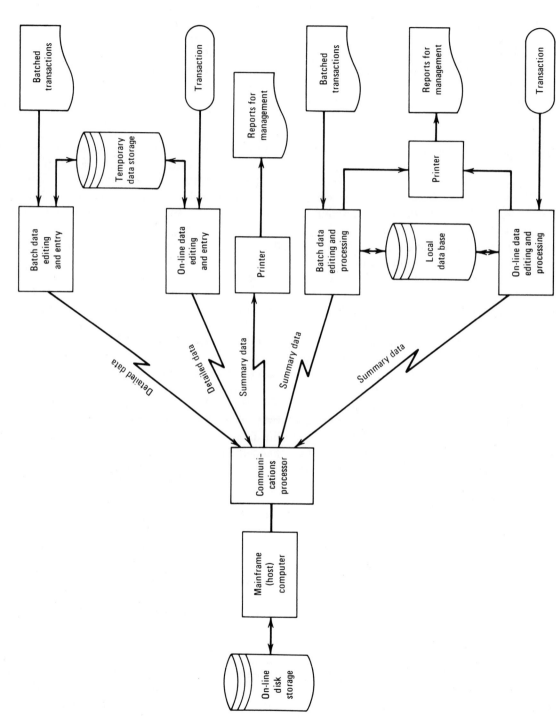

FIGURE 19-9 Distributed data processing functions.

parts file by terminal. Once a day the master file is updated to reflect the receipts by and shipments from each depot.[9]

Configurations. The two basic distributed network configurations are the star and ring. These configurations are contrasted in Figure 19-10. Like centralized network configurations, they may employ private, public, or WATS lines. Though not shown in the figure, they also normally incorporate communications control units and modems.

A **star configuration,** or network, consists of a central, or host, computer plus distributed computers that radiate from the center of the network like spokes from a hub. Each distributed computer must route all data, messages, and inquiries to or through the central computer. When an inquiry is to be transmitted from one outlying computer to another, the central computer functions as a switching device. A merchandising firm may form a star network by linking each branch sales office computer to the home office mainframe computer.

The chief advantages of the star network are its simplicity and flexibility; its main disadvantage is the lack of direct communications between remote locations.

In appearance the star network resembles a point-to-point centralized network. In fact, a point-to-point configuration can be easily converted into a star network by upgrading the terminals to microcomputers. If a portion of the processing is then shifted to the microcomputers, the network may truly be viewed as distributed.

A **ring configuration** consists of a closed loop of linked computers. No single computer dominates the network nor serves as a switching device. Instead, each computer communicates directly with its neighbors. The advantages of this configuration are its relative simplicity as well as the ability to

communicate directly with those computers at adjacent sites. The disadvantage is the lack of a central point that controls the flow of communications.

Because of the foregoing disadvantage, a ring network is most suited to units that are physically close to each other. For instance, a construction firm located in a major metropolitan area and having several independent divisions (e.g., concrete products, road construction, structures) likely qualifies as an apt application. A ring network would allow each division to maintain its own data processing facilities. At the same time, such matters as coordinating the flow of concrete to the two building divisions can be facilitated.

Numerous *hybrid* configurations based on the star and ring configurations are found in the real world. In fact, the star configuration just described is itself a hybrid between a centralized network and a decentralized collection of processors. A fully distributed star configuration would consist of a switching device in place of the host computer.[10] Other hybrid configurations might combine the star and ring configurations. An ultimate example is the *web configuration,* which adds links from each computer in the network to every other computer. The web configuration therefore eliminates the disadvantages of the two basic configurations, but it incurs the added costs of the new links.

Perhaps the most popular hybrid configuration is the **hierarchical network configuration.** As Figure 19-11 shows, a hierarchical configuration consists of several levels of computers that are tied in a tiered fashion to a host computer. The host computer at the top level is the largest computer, the computers at the second level are the next largest, and so on. Each higher-level computer

---

[9]R. G. Canning, "The Challenges of Distributed Systems," *EDP Analyzer* (August 1978), pp. 1–2.

[10]Some authorities classify a fully distributed network as a decentralized network. Our view is that a decentralized network has no communications links among the various remote sites.

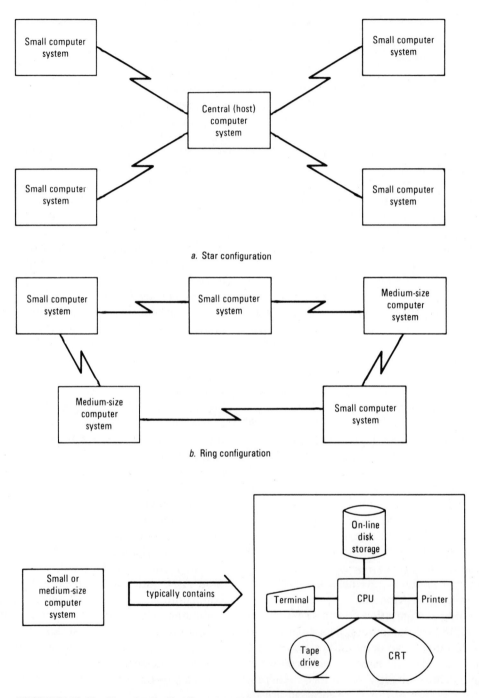

FIGURE 19-10 Two basic distributed network configurations.

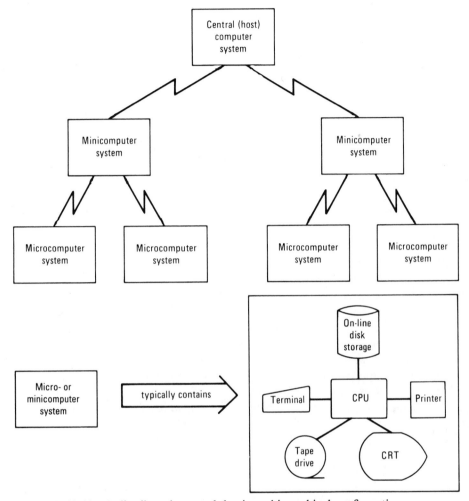

FIGURE 19-11 A distributed network having a hierarchical configuration.

downloads part of its processing task and files to computers at the next lower level. In turn, each lower-level computer can **upload** edited or processed data to the next higher level. The hierarchical configuration is well suited to many firms, since it mirrors the typical business organizational structure. For instance, the central computer can handle the processing needs of a home office, while the mid-level computers and lower-level computers serve the processing needs of regional offices and branch offices, respectively. The hierarchical configuration, like

any configuration, can be modified. For instance, a communication link could be added between the microcomputers shown in Figure 19-11 (e.g., between regional sales offices), thereby superimposing a ring upon the hierarchical configuration.

Benefits. Distributed networks have replaced centralized networks in such firms as manufacturers, merchandising chains, and insurance companies. Their success stems from significant benefits that offset certain deficiencies of centralized networks. (However, it should be stressed that centralized networks are "holding their own" in those circumstances where their advantages are overwhelming.)

Among the significant benefits provided by distributed networks are the following:

1. **Responsiveness to user needs.** A variety of hardware and processing options are available to the various users throughout the network. Managers located thousands of miles from the home office can employ those options that best suit their needs. The results are likely to be more efficient data processing, more timely reports, and more effective decision making at the remote sites throughout the network.

2. **Optimal use of facilities.** All of the sites within the network share the available facilities. Managers at remote locations, for instance, share the central processor and data base (if present in the configuration). Thus, if a manager at a remote location requires more computing power than his distributed processor can provide, perhaps to manipulate a large financial model, he can call on the central processor for assistance. Furthermore, the overall processing work load can be shared throughout the network. Assume, for example, that the work load temporarily overwhelms a microcomputer at a particular remote location. One or more jobs comprising the overload could be transmitted (with data and programs) to other computers in the network for processing. Hence, the overall processing work load of the network can be balanced and peaks can be more easily accommodated. Also, if various types and sizes of computers are tied into the network, opportunities for specialization exist. Processing tasks can be routed to those computers best suited to perform them. As a result, the performance of the overall network will be enhanced.

3. **Reliability of network operations.** If a particular computer within a distributed network fails, the remaining computers can generally handle the failed computer's processing load with only a slight loss in service. In other words, a distributed network possesses the attribute of "graceful degradation."

4. **Modularity and simplicity of processing facilities.** Each processing location within a distributed network represents a fraction of the overall network processing capacity. In effect, it is one module among many. Since additional modules can be added or deleted with ease, the network is extremely adaptable to growth and change. In certain respects it is also relatively free of complexity. For instance, each module (processing location) contains relatively simple processing hardware and software. Thus, it can be operated without a high degree of skill and experience.

5. **Reduction of certain costs.** Since much of the processing is performed at remote sites, only summarized results being transmitted, communications costs are significantly reduced. Also, if the distributed network contains a large central computer, economies of scale should be reaped. Although redundant processors are needed for the various remote sites, relatively inexpensive microcomputers can usually be employed.

Drawbacks. Perhaps the most serious drawback of distributed networks relates to adequate control and security. The tightly knit system of controls and security measures often found in centralized networks is extremely difficult to establish and maintain in distributed networks. One reason for this difficulty can be found in the less sophisticated operating systems employed in the relatively small computers of distributed networks. They cannot incorporate security measures and control features that are as elaborate as those in mainframe centralized computers. Another source of difficulty is the manager–user at each remote processing location who has sole authority over all operations and who is primarily responsible for "getting the work done." Typically he or she cannot establish adequate separation of organizational responsibilities, provide sufficient supervision of data processing activities, or maintain sound physical-security procedures. A third reason for control and security difficulties is the current lack of adequate audit techniques applicable to interactive systems and distributed networks. Because controls are so critical to the success of network operations, a later section reviews those controls and security measures that particularly apply to networks.

Distributed networks exhibit several other drawbacks. More computer hardware is necessary, since processors are operated by a number of users and separate data bases are normally maintained at the users' remote sites. When users are allowed to acquire their own hardware, they may choose equipment from different manufacturers. As a consequence, complex and expensive communications software may be needed to provide system compatibility and thus enable data to flow easily from point to point. Moreover, hidden costs are likely when users are allowed to develop their computer systems. Since users are inexperienced, the resulting systems will probably be less efficient than if they were designed by systems professionals. Furthermore, they may not be well documented nor standardized. Finally, uploading of data from users' sites to the central computer in a distributed network can contaminate the main data base if the data are not carefully edited and controlled.

Local Area Networks

Terminals and microcomputers are multiplying within the offices of the typical firm. Because their users are the managers and employees of the firm who are involved in related activities, communication among the terminals and microcomputers is highly desirable. Localized communications can be achieved most effectively via a **local area network** (LAN), a distributed network that functions within a single limited geographical area. The local area is usually a building or cluster of buildings. For instance, a LAN for a firm might be located within the confines of its home office building, linking together microcomputers in the executive suite, the accounting department, the marketing department, and so forth.

Components of a LAN

Being a computer network, a LAN comprises hardware, communications lines, and software. Although most of the components are common to all networks, certain components assume forms that are relatively peculiar to LAN's.

Hardware. Hardware in LAN's usually includes processors, terminals, magnetic disks, printers, facsimile devices, modems, and other devices needed to conduct business operations. At the heart of a LAN is the multifunction **workstation,** a desktop-oriented work area that consists of a processor and terminal and might include a printer and disk storage unit. Workstations may serve one person or a closely knit group of persons. Three levels of workstations can be identified: a microcomputer-based workstation, traditional workstation, and superworkstation. A microcomputer-based workstation consists of a basic microcomputer, such as an IBM PS/2 model or an Apple Macintosh model, together with video display screen and keyboard and perhaps mouse. The higher-level workstations are specifically designed for use in LAN's. In addition to providing more powerful processors and such features as windows and graphics displays, these workstations can be linked directly to such devices as graphics printers, word processing terminals, teleconferencing video screens and audio units, laser printers, added

FIGURE 19-12 A workstation for a data communications network. Courtesy of International Business Machines Corporation. *Note:* The computer shown is the IBM Personal/System 2, Model 70-386. Within the context of a data communication network it can serve as an intelligent workstation that may be placed at the upper end of the microcomputer-based category. Alternatively, it may serve either as a server or as a gateway, devices discussed in the following paragraphs.

disk storage units, and so on. Figure 19-12 shows a popular workstation for LAN's. LAN's are also characterized by a variety of devices, called **servers,** that enable services to be shared by several workstations. Among currently available servers are disk servers, print servers, processor servers, window servers, communications servers, and data base servers. Servers are usually specially dedicated microcomputers or minicomputers. For instance, a data base server used in a LAN by A. C. Scott Electric & Testing Co. is an HP 3000.[11]

Two additional hardware devices often

needed by LAN's are a network controller and a gateway. A **network controller,** also called a master station, is usually a dedicated computer or PBX. For instance, E. F. Hutton & Co. installed a Data General minicomputer as the network controller for each of its LAN's at 400 branch brokerage offices.[12] It controls the various workstations and assures that messages are properly routed. A **gateway,** or bridge, is a communications device that interfaces between a LAN and either another LAN or a wide-area network. It allows the LAN to send and receive messages from outside networks.

Software. The software needed within a LAN consists of operating systems, a network software server or controller, applications software, and possibly a data base management system. The operating systems are related to each workstation. While applications software packages may be available to all workstations, they must be accessed and used individually. The network software server, usually stored on a designated disk or file server, is communications software that transfers (downloads) application software to requesting workstations. It generally performs steps to ensure that the data and application software are secured from unauthorized persons and are transferred reliably. For instance, the communications software should have the ability to verify passwords, to apply edit checks, and in some cases to encrypt data. The data base management system performs the functions described in Chapter 18 for multiple workstations within the LAN.

Communications lines. Each workstation in a LAN should be able to communicate with every other workstation. Communications lines are used to link the stations. Most currently installed LAN's employ either

[11]Peter C. Coffee, "A 'Host' of Server Options Now Awaits Desktop PC Users," *Supplement to PC Week* (June 19, 1989), p. 1.

[12]Don Steinberg, "When E. F. Hutton Networks, Brokers Benefit," *PC Week* (May 5, 1987), p. C/1.

twisted pairs or coaxial cable, but fiber optics cable is being increasingly selected. Since a LAN is bounded by one or more privately owned buildings, the lines are privately owned. When coaxial or fiber optics cable is used, broad-band transmission is normally employed. Transmission rates of several million bytes per second are feasible.

The cabling for a LAN is usually installed within the walls of each building that is to house the LAN, preferably when the building is being constructed. The hardware devices comprising the workstations and servers can then be plugged into wall sockets.

Configurations

Three major types of configurations— star, ring, and bus—are currently available with respect to LANs. The star configuration has the network controller at its center. It is well controlled and relatively simple; however, the star configuration is limited in the number of workstations that can be supported. Moreover, if the network controller fails, the entire network becomes inoperable. The ring configuration has no network controller, since it is essentially a peer network. Its main drawback is that the loss of any workstation renders the network inoperable. The **bus configuration** consists of a common cable or bus, to which each workstation and each server is connected. Like the ring configuration, it is a peer network with no network controller. However, an inoperable workstation has no effect on the remaining workstations in the network. A fourth configuration, the **tree configuration,** is a cross between the star and bus configurations. Figure 19-13 portrays a simple tree configuration, which has a network controller, four workstations, and various servers. It connects to a mainframe computer and a wide-area network via a gateway. (No modems are shown, although they would be needed if the lines transmit analog signals.) Hence, the LAN

can send data to the mainframe computer for processing and can receive files downloaded by the mainframe.

Most firms that install LAN's do not construct the networks "from scratch." Instead, they purchase predeveloped network configurations from computer vendors. Examples of commercial networks are StarLAN (available from American Telephone & Telegraph Co.), Decnet (available from Digital Equipment Co.), and Ethernet (available from Xerox Corp.). Specialized communications networks such as these are described in a later section.

Messages are usually broken into packets of a standard size for transmission throughout the typical LAN. The protocol, or procedure for accessing and transmitting the packets, depends in part upon the type of configuration. For instance, in ring and bus configurations a popular procedure, known as token ring, involves the passing of a "token," a unique byte of data, from workstation to workstation within a network. Only a message packet containing the token is allowed to move through the network. This added feature is needed to avoid collisions between two messages being transmitted, since no controlling device is present.

In a star or tree configuration the procedure is somewhat simpler, since a network controller is in the LAN. Assume that workstation A desires to send a message consisting of several thousand characters to workstation D in Figure 19-13. The message is first divided by the controller into several packets and formatted into protocol envelopes. Then the workstation communications interface checks with the controller to see if the line is busy; when it is free, the first packet is transmitted. Other packets are transmitted between busy signals, until the entire message is sent. As the packets travel along the cable, they are checked at each station and each server device; when workstation D detects that it is the addressee, it intercepts the packets and reassembles them

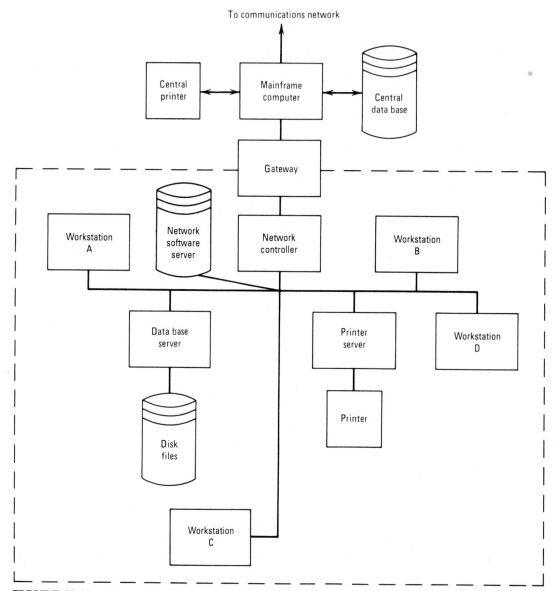

FIGURE 19-13 A local area network configuration.

into the message. It also sends an acknowledgment to workstation A.

Benefits of a LAN

A LAN is an effective means of enabling
a variety of users to share resources, including information. It tends to be less costly per
workstation than stand-alone systems. If
well designed, a LAN should result in improved employee productivity through enhanced communication (i.e., very fast transmission with low error rates). It is also quite
flexible, since new workstations and servers

can be easily added or removed from the network. Often equipment from a variety of different manufacturers are employed on a single LAN. Because of these benefits the LAN is the fastest-growing type of computer network. LAN's are expected to continue growing during the next few years at an average annual rate of 45 percent.[13]

Drawbacks of a LAN

Since a LAN is a distributed network, adequate controls and security are difficult to maintain. Also, currently available application software designed specifically for workstations in a LAN is lacking or inadequate. Furthermore, no single protocol is standard with respect to LAN's and their components; hence, workstations and servers from different manufacturers generally function according to different protocols and cannot be easily accommodated within the same LAN. At present, moreover, data often cannot be easily transmitted from a LAN to other networks because of incompatible equipment or protocols.[14]

Networking Services

The components comprising computer networks—hardware, software, and communications lines—are provided by a number of vendors. User firms either purchase the components to create their private networks, lease communications lines and spe-

cialized network devices for their private use, or "dial up" to public communications lines. Commercial networking services extend well beyond the familiar telephone calls, however. In fact, new developments in communications technology may be occurring at a greater pace than those in computer technology.

Commercial Communications Vendors

Communications carriers provide the public communications links or channels that transmit data and information. In addition to voice messages, these communications facilities carry business transaction data, electronic mail, facsimile, videotex (i.e., text and graphics images), and videoconferences (i.e., visual images of participants in long-distance phone conferences). Thus, communications facilities have truly become *multimedia* conveyors.

Among the more prominent communications carriers are AT&T, American Communications Co., General Telephone and Electronics Co., and MCI Communications Corp. They provide their services through voice-band and wide-band communications lines. The former are used mainly for telephone message traffic. The latter are usually incorporated with sophisticated technologies and special facilities to form **public data networks.** Each carrier markets its own public data network under copyrighted names. For instance, Accunet is marketed by AT&T Communications Co.; Telenet is marketed by General Telephone and Electronics Co. Other communications carriers, known as value-added carriers, lease communications facilities from the common carriers and provide enhanced services via their own public data networks to subscribers. For instance, McDonnall Douglas markets Tymnet.

Certain manufacturers of computer products have expanded their catalogs to include networking products. These proprie-

---

[13]Robert B. Fireworker and Hal Stewart, "Guidelines for Success with LAN's," *Journal of Systems Management* (May 1988), p. 37.

[14]Standards are slowly being developed with respect to the protocols of devices used in computer networks, however. For instance, Open System Interconnection (OSI), a framework for standardized protocols, has recently been endorsed by computer vendors. When implemented in the next few years, it should enable user firms to select a variety of network hardware without being concerned about incompatibility.

tary products, described as computer network architectures, are designed to be compatible with the computer products of each individual manufacturer. They provide the structures for the various configurations of wide-area networks discussed in an earlier section. Most allow a variety of dissimilar and normally incompatible devices, workstations, and other computers from multiple vendors to interchange data with each other (i.e., they foster an **open systems architecture**). Examples are Systems Network Architecture (SNA) from IBM Corporation and Digital Network Architecture (DNA/DECnet) from Digital Equipment Corporation. Usually these network architecture products are leased by firms for their private use, although more than one firm may be joined in a network. An example is the World Bank, which uses SNA to link IBM, DEC, and Unisys systems.[15]

Communications Services

The wide-area network architectures, as well as the commercial LAN network products mentioned earlier, can provide such services as follows:

1. Adaptability to one or more network configurations.
2. Effective error detection and correction techniques.
3. Interfaces that enable the interconnection of a variety of normally incompatible workstations and computers. The interfaces include special software that converts the protocols of the computers to that of the network.
4. Transmission of various types of data, including high-resolution graphics and videoconferencing images as well as text and voice, over the same cable.

[15]H. Clement Steyer, Jr., "The World Bank's Open Network," *Datamation* (Feb. 15, 1990), pp. 109–114.

5. Sharing of a central data base by various remote locations throughout the network.
6. Availability of high-speed digital transmission, thereby eliminating the need for modems.
7. Efficient and timely transmission of data via digital-oriented switching technologies such as message switching, packet switching, and time-division switching. **Message switching** involves the transmission of messages in their entirety as soon as communication lines become available (stop being "busy"). Unfortunately, the use of this technology results in considerable delays of time; thus, it is unsatisfactory when quick responses from the system are important. **Packet switching** involves the transmission of data in "packets." Since packets are smaller than full messages, they can be squeezed between other transmissions or routed over temporarily idle portions of the network. Thus, the delays are usually shortened. **Time-division circuit switching** involves the transmission of data in very small segments, usually single characters. Hence, the delays are shortened even more.
8. Interfaces to public data networks and the services that they provide. The main service is the means of transmitting data to almost any point in the United States and overseas, via such media as satellite communications links. Other services include processing data on large computers linked to the networks and accessing information bases. Both of these services can be obtained for fees based on the time and facilities used.

Public Information Bases

A variety of **public information bases** have been established by various vendor organizations. These information bases, which are in effect reference libraries, can be retrieved by subscribing firms and individuals. They contain specialized information on any of a multitude of subjects and are indexed for quick and precise access of specific facts needed by the user. Two examples are Dow Jones News/Retrieval Service and Compu-Serve. Information from these services can be accessed via any terminal, microcomputer, or other retrieval device attached to the network.

Integrated Services Digital Network (ISDN)

Although great strides have been made in improving computer networks, significant problems still remain. Most current networks employ analog transmission, which is relatively slow and requires modems. Each network is limited in the types of data that it can transmit, so that firms often have to acquire or lease several types of networks. Standardization of networks has not been fully achieved, so that linking of dissimilar computers can cause difficulties.

These problems should be overcome when the ISDN is approved and installed, probably in the 1990s. As its name implies, the ISDN will integrate all communications services in one standardized public data network. A user at any terminal or microcomputer attached to the network will be able to access data of any desired type from any point linked to the network. Information bases will be equally accessible. Requested data or information will be provided very quickly because they will be transmitted by extremely high-speed digital signals over wide-band fiber optics cables. All routing complexities will be easily handled by protocol conversion software available to the computers in the networks. Not only should this integrated network improve business communications, but it is likely to revolutionize communications

in the home. Individuals should be able to work, shop, and access vast data bases via home computers.

Another area of promise is software development. Most currently written software, from operating systems to application programs, pertains to individual computers. Now, integrated techniques are emerging to prepare software that must function in the environment of computer networks. Examples of commercial products are Systems Application Architecture (marketed by IBM Corporation) and Application Integration Architecture (marketed by Digital Equipment Corporation). Software developments such as these are discussed in Chapter 25.

Network Controls and Security Measures

A computer-based network generally exposes a firm's data to very serious threats of loss, unauthorized access, and inaccuracies. If the network involves distributed processing, these exposures are further heightened by the presence of remote processing sites. Furthermore, the threats of fraud and unreliability become more serious because of such sites.

To reduce such threats, careful attention must be paid to controls and security measures within the remote processing sites and throughout the network of communications channels. This section summarizes the needed controls and security measures, first for the remote sites and then for the network. Those pertaining to the network are classified under the headings of organizational controls, general security, system reliability, transmission controls, validation controls, and audit trail controls. These listings are very selective. For a more extensive discussion of general controls and security measures, see Chapter 9, particularly with respect to on-line data base systems. For a brief discussion of audit implications, see the last section of Chapter 17.

Controls for Remote Processing Locations

Because of the inherent problems of remote processing locations, the manager of each remote location should be strongly supported in the development and maintenance of adequate controls. For instance, a central information systems group should assist in the documentation of procedures and the training of employees. An internal audit group should periodically survey each remote location and recommend needed controls. The firm's architect should design the office area in a manner that provides appropriate physical restrictions with respect to the computer facility. Each remote location manager should be encouraged to provide close supervision, to segregate responsibilities for custody of assets from the record keeping of such assets, and so forth.

Organizational Controls

Organizational independence pertains in the presence of networks, just as it does in all types of information systems. The most distinctive organizational control is the need for managers in the information system who understand the particular concerns posed by computer networks. In firms of moderate size these managerial responsibilities may have to be assumed by the information systems director, perhaps with the aid of outside consultants. In large firms, however, positions such as network managers and/or security managers should be established. Responsibilities of a network manager might include

1. Establishing policies for the communications network, including those relating to security.
2. Evaluating the capabilities of available telecommunications devices and such

software as programming languages and operating systems.
3. Developing plans to assure adequate security, including passwords.
4. Creating interfaces between workstations and remote sites, in order to provide suitable connectivity of devices having different protocols.
5. Implementing connectivity standards.
6. Coordinating and maintaining (in conjunction with the director of communications) the physical aspects of the network.

General Security

A first step in establishing security is to implement the security plan developed by the network or security manager. For instance, one critical action is to assess the degree of risk that each specific exposure poses to the network. Then the actual security measures can be defined. With respect to physical security, the measures should specify that computer equipment and communications devices be placed in protected and restricted locations. Also, workstations should be locked when not in use. With respect to data security, transmitted messages of a confidential nature could be encrypted, transmitted at speeds too high to be tapped, or sent over relatively secure communications lines (e.g., coaxial cables). Satellite transmission should be avoided for such messages, since they may be intercepted by anyone having appropriate antenna.

Other security measures pertaining to data access include passwords and lockouts. Users can be assigned passwords that limit access to large blocks of data, such as the data stored on file servers. Alternatively, the passwords may restrict access to specific messages, such as the "mail" addressed to the user in a LAN. Where menus are employed, a user may be restricted to certain menus by a password. Passwords can also restrict access to certain functions, such as read data, write (copy) data, add data to files, and delete data. Passwords may be implemented via access tables. Lockouts are software techniques that prevent users from simultaneously accessing the same data within a data base stored in a network.

System Reliability

The communications devices and channels should be of high quality and incorporate reliability-enhancing features. Modems should reduce line noise, and hence errors, by a process of equalization. Concentrators that incorporate error-detecting codes, such as parity checks, can be employed. Communication facilities that transmit message packets by alternate routes, thereby increasing reliability, are available. As mentioned earlier, fiber optics cables should be used where feasible, since they provide high reliability.

System reliability is, of course, enhanced by the use of backup equipment. We have already noted the built-in backup feature of distributed networks. Centralized networks can incorporate backup processors, too. For instance, Figure 19-14 shows a duplexed network having a backup processor and a data base.

Transmission Controls

Transmission controls help to ensure that messages are sent and received correctly. One transmission control is the echo check, which consists of the transmitted message being returned and displayed on the screen of the source terminal. Another control is verification by system software that the source terminal code is valid. A third control is the dual transmission of messages. A fourth control is a standardized protocol, with control codes in the protocol being verified and acknowledged by each receiving device.

Validation Controls

Validation of input data should be performed by editing programs. In distributed networks these programs are generally developed centrally and downloaded from higher-level processors to the lower-level processors; this procedure ensures that input data are validated uniformly and that input errors are detected and corrected before being transmitted through the network.

Audit Trail Controls

To provide an adequate audit trail, each transaction or other message should be time and date coded. It should also be assigned a sequence number and tagged with the code number of the source terminal. (This identifying terminal code number may be provided by hard-wired instructions on a chip in each terminal.) In addition, a transaction history log should be automatically maintained by system software.

Examples of Specialized Networks

Numerous computer networks are currently in use. Many are employed by firms to collect varied transaction data from remote locations and process the data either locally or centrally. For instance, a firm might collect and process transaction data arising from sales, purchases, and production operations via its computer networks. Increasingly, however, firms are developing specialized computer networks that are dedicated to certain of their key functions. These specialized/dedicated networks are often designed to aid in either (1) processing key transactions or (2) communicating needed information. Often such networks are integrated, so that both of these purposes can be achieved.

A familiar example of a specialized/dedicated network is the airline reservation system. Available seats on airline flights are

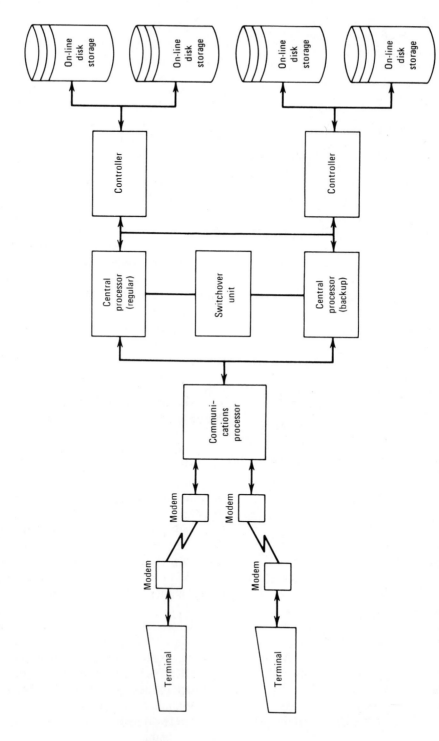

FIGURE 19-14 A duplex communications network.

maintained in on-line files. Reservation requests from customers are entered via terminals; if the requested seats are available, the records are updated to show the reservations and the customers are notified. Reservation clerks can also communicate with each other via the system. In addition, the system performs such processing as calculating fares and assigning boarding passes.

Airline reservation systems have been in existence for several decades. Several specialized/dedicated networks that have emerged more recently involve electronic mail systems, point-of-sale systems, electronic funds transfer systems, electronic data interchange systems, and automated office networks. Each type of network will be discussed and illustrated.

Electronic Mail Systems

An **electronic mail system** is a computer-based network that allows communications among individuals who have access devices attached to the system and storage locations (i.e., "mailboxes") for receiving the messages. Among the firms who are employing electronic mail systems is Domino's Pizza.[16] This fast food franchiser has installed a General Electric mainframe computer at Southfield, Minnesota. Connected to this host computer are Apple Macintosh Plus microcomputers located at each of its 30 distribution centers. Eighty Macintosh II CX's and several laser printers have also been placed within a LAN at its headquarters in Ann Arbor, Michigan, which is tied via a gateway to the wide-area network. All of the microcomputers can interchange electronic mail with any other workstations in the overall network. They also can receive data concerning financial performance and other matters from the central data base. In addition,

they are connected to outside data banks via CompuServe.

Point-of-Sale Systems

Computer-based **point-of-sale** (POS) **systems** are revolutionizing the information systems of retailing firms, especially those having numerous retail outlets. As customers, we have encountered such systems in grocery chains (e.g., Safeway Stores), department stores (e.g., Mervyn's), discount stores (e.g., Home Depot), and even university bookstores. Manual and electromechanical cash registers have disappeared in such retailers. In their places have appeared electronic cash registers, which in reality are intelligent terminals containing microprocessors. Figure 19-15 shows a POS terminal in a grocery store. POS terminals capture data, either through keying the product data or by optically scanning the Universal Product Code (bar code) on the products. In many POS systems the terminals then transmit the sales data via a centralized network to a central processor. Figure 19-16 portrays one POS terminal at a checkout station in a branch retail store. Through a communications device called a store controller all of the terminals in the branch are connected to the central processor.[17]

Most point-of-sale systems do more than simply collect and summarize sales data. In fact, their most important benefits derive from various support functions they perform. They may provide operational support in the form of credit checking. For instance, a customer who desires to pay by credit card will give the card to the cashier, who inserts it into a reader device attached to the terminal. The number of the credit card is then transmitted to the credit center maintained by a large bank. There the number is checked against the customer's credit

---

[16]"Towards an Electronically Democratic Workplace," *Modern Office Technology* (September 1989), pp. 57–62.

[17]Reprinted with permission from the *Journal of Systems Management*.

FIGURE 19-15 A point-of-sale terminal. Courtesy of International Business Machines Corporation.

record on centralized on-line files. If the check does not reveal a credit problem, the system accepts the sales data and flashes a green light at the terminal. If a problem exists, a red light is flashed and the data are rejected.

Another form of operational support pertains to merchandise prices. The prices, stored in on-line files at the central location or in the store controller, are automatically applied when the individual items are identified to the terminal. (In some systems the

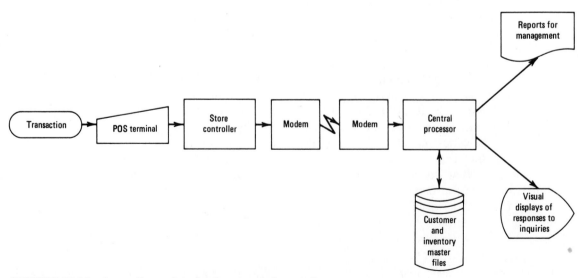

FIGURE 19-16 An on-line point-of-sale network for retailers.

prices are also called out by an audio response unit.) The amounts are then listed and identified in detail on register sales receipt slips.

A third form of support, both operational and decision oriented, consists of information developed by the system. Thus, the system updates the inventory master file to reflect sales of the various items. When the inventory level for an item reaches a predetermined reorder point for a particular store, the system automatically reorders the item for the store. Other information is available to managers through on-line inquiries or hard-copy reports. For instance, a manager may obtain information concerning sales during the past hour or day, broken down by merchandise classes; the average sales amount per customer this week; the number of customers who have checked out at each store today; and so forth.

Electronic Funds Transfer Systems

Financial institutions, such as commercial banks and savings and loan associations, have pioneered in the application of computer-based networks. On-line terminals are commonplace in most bank branches. Typically these terminals are connected via centralized networks to host computers. In turn, the networks are increasingly being employed as **electronic funds transfer (EFT) systems**—computer-based on-line systems that transmit and process the funds-related transactions of customers. EFT systems differ from traditional banking systems in that the transfers of funds are handled electronically rather than by means of paper checks.

A variety of transactions can be accommodated by EFT systems:

1. Deposits and withdrawals of funds by depositors.
2. Direct deposits of employees' payroll earnings by employer firms.
3. Payments of mortgage amounts, insurance premiums, utility bills, and other periodic expenses.
4. Transfers of amounts from checking accounts to savings accounts.
5. Payments for purchases at various retail establishments.

Most of these transactions can be made via terminals located at the teller windows of a bank, either at the main offices or at the branches. However, a terminal known as an automatic teller machine (ATM) is available at almost all bank branches, as well as in supermarkets and convenience stores. Accessing the system via an ATM requires the depositor to insert a bank card and to key in a PIN (personal identification number); these precautions provide considerable security against accesses by unauthorized persons.

POS systems are integrated with EFT systems when payments are made for purchases at retail establishments. When a customer buys merchandise at a retail establishment, he or she gives the merchant a bank debit card. The customer's identifying data are read from the card, either by means of a scanner or by keying the data into the POS terminal. In addition to entering the sales data into the retailer's data base, the retailer's POS system transmits the data to the bank's network. The latter then posts the transaction as a debit to the customer–depositor's account. Thus, the entire sales transaction and cash transfer is completed during the time that the customer is checking out.

The advantages of an EFT system—added convenience to customers and reduced transaction costs for banks (and retailers)—have led many banks to install ATM's and to issue debit cards. However, EFT systems have created several problems. They involve high initial costs, and they also introduce difficulties with respect to security. In addition, customers resist the immediate transfers of funds that debit cards entail,

---

APPLICATION OF COMPUTER-BASED NETWORKS
J. C. Penney Co.[a]

Telaction, an electronic home shopping interactive system, is currently being installed by J. C. Penney Co. It gives home customers access to an entire electronic mall, including 8500 supermarket items. By using push-button phones, shoppers can call up a wide variety of offerings via menulike displays. Shoppers then push the buttons pertaining to desired items. In the case of supermarket purchases the shoppers can even specify delivery times. Typical retailers (in addition to J. C. Penney) participating in the system include Neiman-Marcus Group, Inc., and Marshall-Field's.

Installation of the system has been slower than expected, since the technology is quite complex. The required computer network includes a host computer, a video–audio display system, a microwave dish, a trunk cable, and touch-tone phones. However, the resulting system is expected to be the "electronic shopping environment of the 1990s."

[a]Ann Hagedorn, "J. C. Penney's 'TV Mall' Humbly Arrives," *The Wall Street Journal* (February 16, 1988), p. 6.

---

since they lose the benefit of bank "float." Thus, integrated POS and EFT systems are growing more slowly than the systems involving electronic transfers alone.

Electronic Data Interchange Systems

An **electronic data interchange** (EDI) **system** is a computer-based network that facilitates the interchange of data from the computer system of one firm to the computer system of another. A network that integrates the POS system of a retailer and the EFT of a bank is an example of an EDI system. Most EDI systems, however, involve interchanges of data between an ordering firm and its key suppliers. For instance, Vanity Fair, a manufacturer of women's apparel, places orders with its suppliers via its EDI system. Then the suppliers send the invoice data via the same EDI system to the manufacturer. Vanity Fair in turn has EDI system links to about 20 of its key retail store customers, from whom it receives orders and to whom it sends acknowledgments and sales invoices.[18] An EDI system of this type can also be inte-

grated with a POS and/or an EFT system. Thus, Revco, a drug store chain, is considering an EDI system that is linked to its POS system, so that purchase orders will be automatically placed with key suppliers when the system determines that certain merchandise items have fallen below their reorder points.[19] If the EFT link were also included, the amounts of the invoices from such suppliers could be automatically transferred from the cash balance of Revco to those of the suppliers.

Figure 19-17 shows a network that integrates a retailer's POS system with an EDI system that interchanges data with its key suppliers and with an EFT system. When a customer makes a purchase, the amount is debited to his or her bank account and credited to the account of the retailer. The POS system reduces the inventory balances by the quantities sold; when the stock of a merchandise item falls below its reorder point, the system notifies the EDI system. The retailer's EDI system then prepares the data for a purchase order and transmits the data electronically to the appropriate supplier. After shipping the ordered merchandise, the

---

[18]Leila Davis, "Retailers Go Shopping for EDI," *Datamation* (March 1, 1989), pp. 53–54.

[19]Ibid, p. 54.

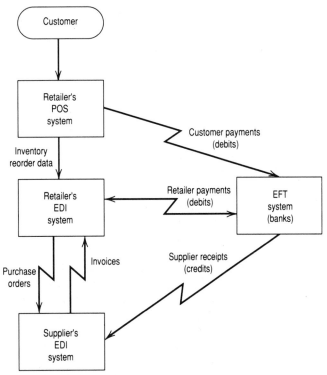

FIGURE 19-17 An integrated electronic data interchange system

supplier's EDI system prepares the data for a sales invoice and transmits the data electronically back to the retailer. Then the EDI system of the retailer transmits the amount to the EFT system, which debits the bank account of the retailer and credits the bank account of the supplier. Finally, the EFT system confirms the payment transactions, so that the correct balances will be reflected in the retailer's and supplier's records. Note that the EFT system could involve as many as three separate banks in these transactions.

EDI systems are growing rapidly among automobile manufacturers, retailers, pharmaceutical firms, transportation firms, and grocery chains. They not only reduce the paper flows but also can improve operations. EDI systems can reduce processing costs and delays, inventory levels, and outstand-

ing receivables. Furthermore, they can strengthen a firm's competitive position, since they enhance the speed with which the firm reacts to changing conditions and manages its business activities. Normally an EDI system can enable a firm to deliver its products in much shorter times and to use its labor force more efficiently.

Automated Office Networks

An **automated office** is an integrated network of multifunction workstations that support and facilitate the clerical and administrative management activities within an office complex. Among the activities that are performed in the typical automated office are word processing, data processing, desk top publishing, and information analysis. Data are communicated from workstation to workstation in the form of electronic mail, facsimiles, video images, and so on. Since communication is vital, a LAN underlies a true automated office. Also, an automated office may be connected to other wide-area networks and LAN's maintained by the firm.

A glimpse within a typical automated office may reveal the following sights: Secretaries are performing routine word processing duties, as well as posting the electronic calendar. Accountants are analyzing key financial information using spreadsheet packages. Marketing specialists are preparing graphics presentations. Managers are sending electronic mail to their counterparts and are revising sales forecasts by means of financial models.

Although they are very costly, automated offices can greatly improve the productivity of office employees and the effectiveness of managers. By reducing many of the mundane data-related tasks, they can improve the quality of employees' work lives. By integrating many work-related techniques and tools, they enable employees and managers to achieve results that have not been possible heretofore.

Citibank, a large New York-based banking firm, has developed a number of automated offices around the world. It uses a variety of hardware from IBM, Datapoint, Digital Equipment, and Tandem to equip the automated offices. Arcnet, marketed by Datapoint, provides the LAN bus configuration into which the hardware devices are plugged. The LAN's are linked together via SNA leased lines. Access to outside data services, such as Dow Jones and Newsnet, is provided by Telenet and Tymnet lines. Because of its banking activities, Citibank also integrates its LAN's and other networks with an EFT system.[20]

Network Design Considerations

All firms with multiple locations must resolve the following design questions: Should our firm utilize a wide-area data communications network? If so, should it be centralized, distributed, or a hybrid? Should local area networks be employed, and if so, should they be connected to the wide-area network? How should the network(s) be configured? What types of communications lines should be selected: private, public, WATS, voice-band, wide-band, public data networks? If a distributed network is selected, how should the data base be distributed?

These questions are fundamental to the design of an information system, since they are concerned with *what* is best to do *where* within the firm's physical boundaries. Certain of the decisions have already been considered. In this final section we focus on the choice of architectures and distributed configurations.

The preferable network architectures for a firm depend upon two major factors: its overall processing needs and its organizational philosophy. Often a firm finds that each architecture is best for certain applications. For instance, the Hewlett-Packard Company uses a centralized network to handle materials services, a distributed network to handle sales orders and accounts receivable, and a decentralized system to handle general and cost accounting.[21]

Overall Processing Needs

A centralized network is preferable when processing is relatively simple and can be met by a single mainframe computer and accompanying data base. If tight security is a critical concern, a centralized network may be necessary. A savings and loan associa-

---

[20]Don Tapscott, "OA Banks on Connectivity," *Datamation* (March 15, 1986), pp. 106–112.

[21]Cort Van Rensselaer, "Centralize? Decentralize? Distribute?" *Datamation* (April 1979), p. 90.

tion, which handles cash transactions from depositors at numerous branches, meets both of these conditions.

A distributed network is generally preferable under these conditions:

1. High and growing volumes of processing is necessary.
2. Much of the processing is interactive in nature.
3. Processing is widely dispersed geographically, often forming clusters of shared functions.
4. Physical operations and users' needs are diverse in nature.
5. Continuous availability of service is critical.

For instance, a distributed network should be favorably considered by a firm that is involved in production, warehousing, and distribution functions at a variety of locations throughout the United States, plus accounting and sales functions at other locations.

Hybrid networks are preferable when the processing conditions are mixed. For instance, a manufacturing firm that has 12 plants in the Midwest and 17 marketing/distribution centers across the United States, plus a main office in the Midwest, selected a hybrid network. It established a computer center near the main office, in which three interlinked mainframe computers were installed. One of these computers handles the functions in the main office, plus all engineering tasks and a central parts distribution center. Another computer supports the marketing/distribution centers, each of which has a middle-size computer. The third computer supports the manufacturing plants, which also have minicomputers, microcomputers, and factory floor terminals.[22]

22Devon D. Dietz and John D. Keane, "Integrating Distributed Processing within a Central Environment," *Management Accounting* (No. 1980), p. 44.

Organizational Philosophy

The organizational philosophy of a firm generally affects the selection of the network architecture. A firm that has a highly centralized organizational structure tends to prefer a centralized network. Conversely, a firm with a highly decentralized organizational structure usually selects a distributed network or even a decentralized system.

The relative dominance of the information systems function within the organization can also affect the selection. If the information systems function has sufficient influence with management, it may be able to effect a centralized network. In achieving this end, it may have stressed the benefits that a centralized staff can provide: professionalism, standardization, stricter security, and firmer control over data and applications. On the other hand, if the users have greater influence, they may be able to persuade management to install a distributed network.

Certain steps can be taken to create a better fit between the organization and the adopted computer network. For instance, a coordinating group can be appointed. This group, which could report to a high-level manager, might have such responsibilities as planning network developments, establishing standards, and monitoring hardware developments.

Distributed Network Configurations

When a distributed network is the preferred choice, a suitable configuration still needs to be developed. The following considerations are pertinent when designing the configuration:

1. Edit input data at the point of origin, so that errors are detected and corrected before the data are transmitted.
2. Move only summary data, if possible, through the network. To the extent possible, design hierarchical data flows that

send the summary data to the next-highest level.

3. Cluster the processing activities at remote locations to the greatest extent possible.

4. Distribute files to the points at which processing is performed. However, minimize redundancy of data throughout the network (i.e., use the partitioned data base approach if possible).

Summary

Data communications tie together a geographically dispersed information system. Accountants need to be aware of data communications and the types of computer networks that are generally encountered. The hardware involved in the communication of data includes terminals, modems, communications control units such as communications processors and multiplexors, and central processors. The communications channel may be metallic or fiber optics cable, or it may consist of transmission by satellite or microwaves. The grade of line may be narrow band, voice band, or wide band. The transmission type may be simplex, half duplex, or full duplex, while the mode of transmission may be synchronous or asynchronous. Each message is transmitted through the network in accordance with a protocol, which must be recognized by the various communications devices. The basic types of communications line service are private lines, public lines, and WATS lines. Each of the foregoing options has relative advantages for certain communications situations.

The two major architectures employed as computer networks are centralized and distributed. A centralized network consists essentially of a central processor and linked terminals. It may be configured by means of point-to-point lines, multidrop lines, or multiplexed lines. Its benefits are concentrated computing power, an integrated data base, a sophisticated operating system, an elaborate control system, and a professional staff. The drawbacks of a centralized network are that it is relatively complex and inflexible, unresponsive to the needs of remote users, and vulnerable to disaster. A distributed network consists of a number of processors linked into a unified structure. Although a distributed network often includes a central processor, at least some of the processing functions are performed by these distributed processors. The data base also may be distributed, either by a partitioned or a replicated approach. A distributed network may be configured as a star, ring, hierarchy, or some variation. Its benefits include responsiveness to user needs, optimal use of facilities, reliability of network operations, and modularity and simplicity of processing facilities. Its drawbacks include difficulties in maintaining adequate controls and security, relatively high hardware costs, and difficulties in coordination.

Recent developments in data communications technology include local area networks and various networking services. Local area networks consist of workstations, servers, network controllers, and other hardware. Possible configurations include the star, ring, bus, and tree. Networking services consist of public data networks, computer network architectures, public information bases, a proposed integrated services digital network, and open systems architecture.

Adequate controls and security measures are critical aspects of a computer network, since it is exposed to serious threats. Managers at remote locations of the network should be strongly supported in the maintenance of controls. Security should be based on a network security plan, and various measures such as encryption and backup equipment should be employed. Other controls relating to access, transmission, validation, and the audit trail should also be included.

Computer-based networks have been installed to meet a variety of specialized needs; such networks include electronic mail systems, point-of-sale systems, electronic funds transfer systems, electronic data interchange systems, and automated office networks. The preferable network architectures depend on such considerations as a firm's overall processing needs and its organizational philosophy.

Review Problem with Solution

Statement

The Mertz Wholesaling Company maintains a home office and two warehouses (A and B). It has decided to install a computer-based network that links the home office to the warehouses. The distances from the home office to warehouses A and B are 300 and 500 miles, respectively, and the distance between the two warehouses is 400 miles. The following cost data are available:

1. The monthly cost of leasing a suitable multiplexor is $500.

2. The monthly cost of leasing switching hardware for multidrops is $300.

3. The costs per minute for phone calls from the home office to warehouses A and B are $0.40 and $0.50, respectively.

4. The hours of message traffic between the home office and warehouses A and B are expected to be 40 and 30, respectively.

5. The monthly rates for private lines of a suitable grade are $5.00 per mile through the first 100 miles, $4.00 per mile for the next 100 miles, $3.00 per mile for the next 100 miles, and $2.00 per mile for all distances above 300 miles.

Required

If each of the two warehouses is provided a video display terminal:

a. Describe four alternatives, involving various network configurations and types of service, that may be employed in the network.

b. Compute the total monthly cost for each alternative in **a**.

c. Comment on the results obtained in **b**.

Solution

a. and **b. Alternative 1.** A point-to-point configuration that links the home office to each warehouse by separate private lines.
Monthly cost from home office to A:

$$(100 \text{ miles} \times \$5) + (100 \text{ miles} \times \$4) \\ + (100 \text{ miles} \times \$3) = \$1200$$

Monthly cost from home office to B:

$$\$1200 + (200 \text{ miles} \times \$2) = \$1600$$

Total monthly cost = $1200 + $1600 = $2800

Alternative 2. A point-to-point configuration that links the home office to each warehouse by separate public switched lines.
Monthly cost from home office to A:

$$\$0.40 \text{ per minute} \times 40 \text{ hours} \\ \times 60 \text{ minutes per hour} = \$960$$

Monthly cost from home office to B:

$$\$0.50 \text{ per minute} \times 30 \text{ hours} \\ \times 60 \text{ minutes per hour} = \$900$$

Total monthly cost = $960 + $900 = $1860

Alternative 3. A multidrop configuration that links the home office to warehouse B through warehouse A by private lines, as follows.

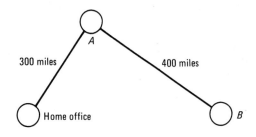

Total monthly cost:

$1200 + (400 miles × $2)
+ $300 for hardware = $2300

Alternative 4. A multiplexed configuration that links the home office to each warehouse via private lines and a multiplexor located at the midpoint between warehouses A and B, as follows:

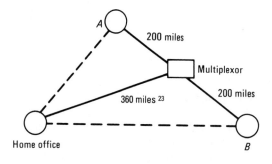

Monthly cost from home office to multiplexor:

(100 miles × $5) + (100 miles × $4)
+ (100 miles × $3) + (60 miles × $2) = $1320

Monthly cost from multiplexor to A and B:

2(200 miles × $2) = $800

Total monthly cost = $1320 + $800
+ $500 for multiplexor = $2620

[23] Since the distances among the home office, warehouse A, and warehouse B form a 300-400-500 right triangle, the distance to the midpoint of A and B is $\sqrt{300^2 + 200^2} = \sqrt{130,000} = 360$.

c. The computations show that the point-to-point configuration using private lines is the most costly alternative, followed by the multiplexed and multidrop configurations. The point-to-point configuration using public switched lines is the least costly. However, since a configuration employing public switched lines suffers the disadvantages of longer waiting times and less accurate transmissions than private lines, this least costly alternative may not be the best choice. Furthermore, if the hours of usage increase significantly in the future, public switched lines may become more costly. In other words, there is a break-even volume above which private lines become less costly than public switched lines.

Review Questions

19-1 What is the meaning of each of the following terms?

Intelligent terminal
"Dumb" terminal
Modem
Baud rate
Asynchronous modem
Synchronous modem
Communications processor
Multiplexor
Concentrator
Private branch telephone exchange
  (PBX)
Communications control program
Narrow-band line
Voice-band line
Wide-band line
Simplex transmission
Half-duplex transmission
Full-duplex transmission
Analog transmission
Digital transmission
Serial transmission
Parallel transmission

Asynchronous transmission
Synchronous transmission
Protocol
Protocol converter
Private line
Leased line
Public switched line
WATS line
Wide-area communications network
Centralized network
Point-to-point configuration
Multidrop configuration
Multiplexed configuration
Distributed network
Distributed data processing
Replicated data base
Partitioned data base
Star configuration
Ring configuration
Hierarchical network configuration
Download
Upload
Local area network (LAN)
Workstation
Server
Network controller
Gateway
Bus configuration
Tree configuration
Public data network
Open systems architecture
Message switching
Packet switching
Time-division circuit switching
Public information base
Electronic mail system
Point-of-sale (POS) system
Electronic funds transfer (EFT) system
Electronic data interchange (EDI) system
Automated office

19-2 Why have data communications networks grown in recent years?

19-3 Describe the various hardware devices that comprise a typical data communications network.

19-4 In what ways do modems differ?

19-5 Contrast three commonly employed communications control units.

19-6 Identify the options available with respect to

    a. The character of the communications link or channel.
    b. The grade of line.
    c. The type of transmission.
    d. The mode of transmission.
    e. Type of communication line service.

19-7 How does a communications protocol transmit data between communications devices?

19-8 Contrast a centralized network and distributed network.

19-9 What are three basic centralized network configurations, and what are the relative advantages of each?

19-10 What are the relative benefits and drawbacks of a centralized network?

19-11 What are three commonly employed distributed network configurations, and what are the relative advantages of each?

19-12 What are the relative benefits and drawbacks of a distributed network?

19-13 Describe the hardware, software, and communication lines that comprise a LAN.

19-14 Identify four configurations that may be employed by LAN's.

19-15 Describe the procedure by which a message is transmitted through a LAN.

19-16 What are the benefits and drawbacks of a LAN?

19-17 Discuss the networking services provided by commercial communications vendors.

19-18 Contrast three switching technologies for transmitting a message via a communications network.

19-19 What controls should be established for remote processing locations of a distributed network?

19-20 Identify several controls and security measures that pertain to communications networks.

19-21 Contrast an electronic mail system, a point-of-sale system, an electronic funds transfer system, an electronic data interchange system, and an automated office network.

19-22 What considerations are important in the choice between a centralized network and a distributed network?

19-23 What considerations should be designed into a distributed network?

Discussion Questions

19-24 Discuss likely impacts of a communications-based support system on a firm's data inputs, data processing files, reports, decision making, and organizational structure.

19-25 Describe applications of electronic data interchange systems in addition to those described in the chapter.

19-26 Describe a communications-based support system for a manufacturer that blends centralized and distributed networks.

19-27 To what extent does the configuration of a communications network affect decision making? For instance, does a centralized network require centralized decision making?

19-28 A centralized network requires a very lengthy design-and-implementation period. What difficulties may be encountered because of this lengthy period, and how might they be minimized?

Problems

19-1 A firm maintains a home office and six remote locations, geographically situated as follows:

A mainframe computer is installed in the home office, and each remote location houses a single terminal. The firm intends to establish a computer-based network.

Required

a. Connect the locations to form a centralized network having each of the following configurations:

   (1) Point-to-point.
   (2) Multidrop.
   (3) Multiplexed, with the multiplexor located at ④.
   (4) Point-to-point for three locations; multipoint for the remaining three locations.
   (5) Point-to-point for one location; multidrop for two locations; multiplexed for the remaining three locations. Select the points for each configuration, with an eye toward designing the most suitable combinations.

b. Assuming that microcomputers are placed in the remote locations, connect the locations to form a distributed network having each of the following configurations.

   (1) Star.
   (2) Ring, including the home office.
   (3) Combined star and ring.

19-2 A group of three small hospitals within a large metropolitan area decide to establish an on-line computer system to serve their data processing and retrieval needs. A central processor and on-line disk storage devices are located in a building in the downtown section of the central city. The hospitals are in the surrounding suburbs. Each is 15 miles from the computer site. The middle hospital is five miles apart from its neighbors.

Required

a. List the data communications components needed to connect the central processor to the middle hospital, assuming that the other two hospitals are not included.

b. Identify all the options available when selecting the communications channel in **a**.

c. Describe three possible configurations by which the three hospitals may be linked to the central processor.

19-3 Okefenokee, Inc., of Jacksonville, Florida, has branch offices in Orlando, Tampa, Fort Myers, Palm Beach, and Miami, plus a warehouse in Orlando. It has decided to install a computer-based network that will connect all branches and the warehouse to the mainframe computer located at the main office in Jacksonville. It plans to place one video display terminal in each of the branches and the warehouse, although it has not decided whether the terminals will be of the intelligent type or not. Before management decides on the final installation, it wants to see and compare the possible configurations.

Required

a. Using Ⓙ, Ⓞ, Ⓣ, Ⓕ, Ⓟ, Ⓜ, and W̄ to represent the various locations, draw point-to-point, multidrop, and multiplexed configuration diagrams for a centralized network. Assume that one multi-

plexor will be placed at Lakeland (between Orlando and Tampa) and another at Fort Lauderdale (between Palm Beach and Miami). Use ⊠ to represent a multiplexor.

b. Redraw each of the configuration diagrams to include all needed hardware, from the mainframe computer to terminals.

c. Assume that the main office and mainframe computer are moved to Tampa, with Jacksonville becoming a branch office. Redraw the point-to-point and multidrop configuration diagrams. Also, redraw the multiplexed configuration diagram in two versions: (1) using one multiplexor at Orlando, and (2) using two multiplexors at locations of your choice.

d. Using the same situation and symbols as in **a**, draw star and ring configuration diagrams for a distributed network.

e. If management decides to install a centralized network, which configuration diagram from requirements **a** and **d** appears to be the best choice? Why? Would some combined configuration appear to be even better?

Hint: Refer to a map of Florida in solving this problem.

19-4 The directors of Colorgraph Printing of Buffalo are reviewing a proposal to acquire Puball Publishers. Puball's operations are located in an urban area about 300 miles from Buffalo. Colorgraph's success in recent years, according to its management, is attributed in large part to its computerized information system. Puball, however, has used a computer only for financial accounting applications such as payroll and general ledger records.

In considering the acquisitions, Colorgraph's board of directors focuses on the possibilities of two options for expanding its information system to include Puball: (1) a centralized network or (2) a distributed network.

Required

a. Can terminals having only the capabilities of collecting, editing, transmitting, and receiving data be employed with both types of networks, or are they restricted to one of the types?

b. Compare the degree of detail likely to be transmitted from a remote location to headquarters by each of the two types of networks.

c. Explain briefly why Puball's management would be more likely to be involved in and concerned with data processing if a distributed network were installed. Assume that Puball would be organized as an independent profit center if acquired.

d. Explain why a distributed network would be less subject to a complete system breakdown.

(CIA adapted)

19-5 Which type of network—centralized, distributed, or local—would likely be most suitable in each of the following situations? Why?

  a. An airline reservation system with local offices in most larger cities.
  b. An integrated consumer-goods manufacturer that maintains close coordination among its plants, distribution centers, warehouses, and home office.
  c. A savings and loan institution with numerous branch offices throughout the cities of a state.
  d. A public utility that establishes automated offices throughout its headquarters facility.
  e. A New York stock exchange that maintains communications with brokers on the exchange floor and

brokerage offices in several northeastern cities.
  f. A department store chain that allows individual stores to handle credit sales and inventory, but that distributes paychecks from the home store.

19-6 For each of the following situations (1) identify the type of network described (e.g., a private centralized network having a point-to-point configuration) and (2) draw a configuration diagram of the network.

  a. An electric utility that serves a sizable southwestern city maintains a large host computer at its home office. Tied to this computer, through a communications processor, are a variety of interactive intelligent terminals. Several of these terminals are located in the accounting department at the home office. Others are located at two power plant construction sites, 100 miles and 170 miles distant and linked through microwave channels. Clerks at the home office and the remote sites enter data from suppliers' invoices. (Most of the suppliers to the construction sites are local contractors and subcontractors who expect prompt payments from the utility.) These entered accounts payable transactions are edited and matched against stored purchase and construction data by an accounts payable program which is called via the intelligent terminals. If the transactions are valid, they are transmitted to the home office and stored as disbursement vouchers. Once each day checks and reports are printed by the host computer, with the outputs appearing on printers in the accounting department or at the construction sites.

b. A large hospital in an eastern metropolitan area has installed a large mainframe computer to support its patient systems. Connected to this computer by coaxial cable are several dozen video display terminals, on-line disk files, and three printers. From the time a patient enters the hospital, he or she is monitored by means of the network. Terminals located in the admitting room, labs, operating rooms, central supply, nursing stations, and elsewhere record all actions and progress. When necessary the network triggers actions, such as the administering of medications. Reports and documents are printed as needed from the patients' files.

c. A group of small hospitals and clinics in a midwestern city share the services of a large central computer located in a downtown building. Essentially the same services are provided by this computer network as by the network described in **b**.

d. A large New York bank has installed 10 medium-size computers at several downtown and suburban locations. To each computer are tied several dozen intelligent terminals, which are located in a group of branches. An average of eight terminals are used in a branch, mainly by tellers and loan officers. The 10 computers, in turn, are linked to each other and to a mainframe computer in the bank's main office. A central data base of financial and operational data is maintained at the main office. In addition, files of depositors for each area are maintained at the location of each medium-size computer. The terminals are used to enter and edit depositor transactions, as well as to make inquiries concerning depositors' accounts. In some cases, for example, when depositors have bank accounts and loans in several branches, the inquiries must reach into the files of neighboring computers. A fairly common use of the terminals is to process a loan, including the determination of the loan repayment schedule.

e. A computer manufacturer located in a large western state has established an integrated and computerized logistics system. In its corporate office it maintains a large mainframe computer with a centralized data base. At each of its manufacturing plants and regional sales offices it has placed a medium-size computer together with a data base that contains files appropriate to the activities at the remote site. Within each plant a microcomputer is located in each department, and data collection terminals are placed on the factory floor. Within each regional sales office are installed a number of video display terminals and microcomputers; also, at each sales branch a number of terminals are installed. Each of the terminals and computers are tied to those at a higher level in the system. In addition, the computers at the plants are tied to those at other plants, while the computers at the regional sales offices are similarly linked to each other.

f. A rather small musical-entertainment firm is headquartered in Hollywood. However, it must maintain a large office in New York because its artists and agents often are in residence there. In addition to numerous telephone calls from coast to coast, it must transmit huge quantities of music-related and financial data. It employs a network that checks the transmitted data for accuracy and guarantees that the data will be transmitted in a very timely manner.

19-7 The Wunder Co. maintains a central computer system at its home office in Detroit. Its six sales offices are located in Milwaukee, Cleveland, Chicago, Minneapolis, Indianapolis, and Pittsburgh. Recently the firm decided to link these six sales offices together into a distributed network. Before it selects a particular configuration, however, the management would like comparative costs for two basic configurations: (1) a star configuration, with separate leased lines from the central computer to microcomputers at each of the sales offices; and (2) a ring configuration, with leased lines connecting Detroit to Milwaukee to Minneapolis to Chicago to Indianapolis to Pittsburgh to Cleveland back to Detroit.

The two types of costs that differ between the alternatives are for modems and data communications line charges. Each modem of the type needed rents for $50 per month. (Two modems are needed for each link.) Monthly rates to lease the needed wide-band communication lines are $10 per mile for the first 250 miles, $7 per mile for the second 250 miles, and $5 per mile for all miles over 500 miles. (These charges apply separately to each link.)

The mileages between affected cities are as follows:

Required

Calculate the total monthly communications cost for each of the configurations, on the basis of the figures given.

19-8 Electra Enterprises, Inc., is based in Los Angeles, where it maintains a relatively powerful minicomputer. At present it is considering the establishment of a centralized network that will tie its field offices to the main office. Its plans are to install video display terminals as follows: two in San Francisco, one in Denver, two in San Diego, and one in Phoenix. Three configurations are under consideration: (1) individual leased lines to each terminal; (2) point-to-point leased lines to each location, with concentrators used at those locations having two terminals; and (3) a multidrop leased line to the four locations, with a concentrator used at each remote location.

The leased lines for each of the alternative configurations may be voice-grade communications lines, which have a monthly pricing schedule as follows: $4 per mile for the first 25 miles, $3 per mile for the next 75 miles, and $1.50 per mile for all miles over 100 miles. (This schedule applies separately to each link.)

The mileages between affected cities are given at the top of page 917.

To From	Milwaukee	Cleveland	Chicago	Minn.	Indiana.	Pitts.
Detroit	353	170	266	671	278	287
Milwaukee		422	87	332	268	539
Cleveland			335	740	294	129
Chicago				405	181	452
Minneapolis					586	857
Indianapolis						353

From \ To	San Francisco	Denver	Phoenix	San Diego
Los Angeles	379	1059	389	125
San Francisco		1235	763	504
Denver			792	1108
Phoenix				353

The devices needed for the three alternative configurations are (1) 12 modems; (2) 8 modems, one front-end processor, two data concentrators; (3) 5 modems, one front-end processor, four multidrop concentrators. Monthly leased costs for the devices are $30 per modem, $300 per front-end processor, $100 per data concentrator, and $150 per multidrop concentrator.

Required

a. Calculate the total communications costs for each of the three alternative configurations.

b. Draw a hardware configuration diagram for each of the three alternatives.

19-9 The Riverfront Distributing Company of Cincinnati, Ohio, has distribution centers located in Dallas, St. Louis, Memphis, and Atlanta. It is interested in forming a centralized network between the home office in Cincinnati and the four distribution centers; that it, a central computer in Cincinnati will be linked to terminals in the centers. However, it has not yet decided on the most suitable configuration. To aid in making the final decision, it has gathered the following data.

    a. Distances between Cincinnati and Dallas, St. Louis, Memphis, and Atlanta are 924, 322, 473, and 474 miles, respectively. Distances from St. Louis to Dallas, Memphis, and Atlanta, are 661, 294, and 575 miles, respectively; and distances from Memphis to Dallas and Atlanta are 451 and 382 miles, respectively.

    b. Monthly rates per mile for private leased voice-grade communications lines are $3 per mile for the first 25 miles, $2 per mile for the next 75 miles, and $1 per mile for all miles over 100 miles. (This schedule applies separately to each line segment.)

    c. A multiplexor rents for $200 per month.

    d. Additional hardware (concentrators) needed for a multidrop configuration rents for a total of $300 per month.

    e. Conditioning necessary to upgrade a leased line segment between the central computer and the multiplexor costs $50 per month.

    f. Modems needed for each communications link in each of the configurations lease for $26 per month each.

    g. The average costs per minute for public calls between Cincinnati and the cities of Dallas, St. Louis, Memphis, and Atlanta are $0.70, $0.35, $0.50, and $0.50, respectively. The average costs per minute for public calls between St. Louis and the cities of Dallas, Memphis, and Atlanta are $0.60, $0.30, and $0.55, respectively.

    h. The average volume of message traffic between Cincinnati and each distribution center is 30 hours per month. There is no appreciable traffic among the various warehouses, since operations are coordinated by the home office.

Required

Compute the total monthly costs for the following configurations:

a. Point-to-point leased lines.

b. A multidrop voice-grade leased line through St. Louis, Memphis, and Dallas, with an offshoot from Memphis to Atlanta.

c. A conditioned voice-grade leased line from Cincinnati to St. Louis, where a multiplexor is located, with voice-grade leased lines to the other three centers.

d. A conditioned voice-grade leased line from Cincinnati to St. Louis, where a multiplexor is located, with public switched lines to the other three centers.

e. Point-to-point public switched lines.

Hint: Draw configuration diagrams and label.

19-10   The Greenleaf Company of Shreveport, Louisiana, has three plants for processing and canning fresh vegetables.[24] The three plants are located in Louisiana, Mississippi, and Alabama. Each plant has a warehouse where finished goods are stored and later shipped to food brokers and distributors throughout the nation. The home office performs most of the accounting and data processing tasks, including the maintenance of the "official" inventory files for the firm.

Under the owner-manager are three plant managers, one for each plant. Each plant manager has several dozen clerks, who maintain informal inventory records, perform various clerical duties, and periodically prepare sales and production performance reports. Each plant manager also has responsibility for purchasing raw produce for expected processing within his plant. Raw produce is supplied by a variety of local growers.

Since the firm has experienced problems related to production scheduling, quality control, inventory management, purchasing, and general reporting of performance information, the owner–manager ponders the installation of a computer-based information system. He hires an outside consultant to study the situation. After several days of analysis the consultant reports that a computer-based network does appear to be feasible.

Required

Assuming that you are the consultant, prepare a recommendation—complete with narrative description, diagram, and justification—concerning the particular communications-based configuration that appears to be the most suitable for the Greenleaf Company.

19-11   Contrast the controls and security measures needed in (a) a dedicated centralized airline reservations system with 300 terminals located in a variety of airports and interconnections to the reservations systems of three other airlines and (b) a distributed network maintained by a military aircraft manufacturer that links together its headquarters and four production plants.

19-12   Pinta Company is a regional discount chain headquartered in Montgomery, Alabama. Its stores, scattered throughout the Southeast, sell general merchandise. The firm is considering the acquisition of a point-of-sale (POS) system for use in all its stores. Of the various models available, the president believes that the type using a light pen to scan the universal product code on merchandise is the most suitable. However, it is quite expensive, so Charles Brenski, the president, asks the systems staff to prepare a report answering several questions.

Required

Prepare a report to the president that

a. Explains the functions and operation of a POS system, including its extension into

[24]Adapted from John G. Burch, Jr.; Felix R. Strater; and Gary Grudnitski, *Information Systems: Theory and Practice,* 2d ed. (New York: John Wiley, 1979), p. 118. Used with permission.

credit checking and electronic transfers of funds.

b. Identifies the advantages and disadvantages of the extended POS system described in **a**.

c. Identifies the special control and security problems that the extended POS system could present, together with suitable controls and security measures that should effectively counteract these problems.

Hint: Look in the Accountant's Index for a recent article describing POS systems.

(CMA adapted)

19-13 Imtex Corporation is a multinational company with approximately 100 subsidiaries and divisions, referred to as reporting units. Each reporting unit operates autonomously and maintains its own AIS. Each month, the reporting units prepare the basic financial statements and other key financial data on prescribed forms. These statements and related data are either mailed or telexed to corporate headquarters in New York City for entry into the corporate data base. Top and middle management at corporate headquarters utilize the data base to plan and direct corporate operations and objectives.

Under the current system, the statements and data are to be received at corporate headquarters by the twelfth working day following the end of the month. The reports are logged, batched, and taken to the data processing department for coding and entry into the data base. Approximately 15 percent of the reporting units are delinquent in submitting their data, and three to four days are required to receive all of the data. After the data are loaded into the system, data verification programs are run to check footings, cross-statement consistency, and dollar-range limits. Any errors in the data are traced and corrected, and reporting units are notified of all errors by form letters.

Imtex Corporation has decided to upgrade its computer communication network.

The new system would allow data to be received on a more timely basis at corporate headquarters and provide numerous benefits to each of the reporting units.

The systems department at corporate headquarters is responsible for the overall design and implementation of the new system. The systems department will utilize current computer communications technology by installing "smart" computer terminals at all reporting units. These terminals will provide two-way computer communications, and also serve as microcomputers that can utilize spreadsheet and other applications software. As part of the initial use of the system, the data collection for the corporate data base would be performed by using these terminals.

The financial statements and other financial data currently mailed or telexed would be entered by terminals. The required forms would initially be transmitted (downloaded) from the headquarters computer to the terminals of each reporting unit and stored permanently on disk. Data would be entered on the forms appearing on the reporting unit's terminal and stored under a separate file for transmission after the data are checked.

The data edit program would also be downloaded to the reporting units so that the data could be verified at the unit location. All corrections would be made before transmitting the data to headquarters. The data would be stored on disk in proper format to maintain a unit file. Data would either be transmitted to corporate headquarters immediately or retrieved by the computer at corporate headquarters as needed. Therefore, data arriving at corporate headquarters would be free from errors and ready to be used in reports.

Charles Edwards, Imtex's controller, is very pleased with the prospects of the new system. He believes data will be received from the reporting units two to three days faster, and that the accuracy of the data will be much improved. However, Edwards is concerned about data security and integrity during the transmission of data between the reporting units and corporate headquarters. He has scheduled a meeting with key personnel from the systems department to discuss these concerns.

Required

Imtex could experience data security and integrity problems when transmitting data between the reporting units and corporate headquarters.

a. Identify and explain the data security and integrity problems that could occur.

b. For each problem identified, list and explain a control procedure that could be employed to minimize or eliminate the problem.

Use the following format to present your answer:

Problem Identification and Explanation	Control Procedure and Explanation

(CMA adapted)

19-14 Vincent Maloy, director of special projects and analysis for Milok Company, is responsible for preparing corporate financial analyses and projections monthly and for reviewing and presenting to upper management the financial impacts of proposed strategies. Data for these financial analyses and projections are obtained from reports developed by Milok's systems department and generated from its mainframe computer. Additional data are obtained through terminals via a data inquiry system. Reports and charts for presentations are then prepared by hand and typed. Maloy has tried to have final presentations generated by the computer but has not always been successful.

The systems department has developed a package utilizing a terminal emulator to link a microcomputer to the mainframe computer. This allows the microcomputer to become part of the current data inquiry system

and enables data to be downloaded to the microcomputer's disk. The data are in a format that allows printing or further manipulation and analyses using commercial software packages, e.g., spreadsheet analysis. The special projects and analysis department has been chosen to be the first users of this new computer terminal system.

Maloy questioned whether the new system could do more for his department than implementing the program modification requests that he has submitted to the systems department. He also believed that his people would have to become programmers.

Lisa Brandt, a supervisor in Maloy's department, has decided to prepare a briefing for Maloy on the benefits of integrating microcomputers with the mainframe computer. She has used the terminal inquiry system extensively and has learned to use spreadsheet software to prepare special analyses, sometimes with multiple alternatives. She also tried the new package while it was being tested.

Required

a. Identify five enhancements to current information and reporting that Milok Company should be able to realize by integrating microcomputers with the company's mainframe computer.

b. Explain how the utilization of computer resources would be altered as a result of integrating microcomputers with the company's mainframe computer.

c. Discuss what security of the data is gained or lost by integrating microcomputers with the company's mainframe computer.

(CMA adapted)

19-15 For each of the following situations, describe desirable networks or combined networks. Identify the types of networks by name, and describe the characteristics of the data base where pertinent.

a. A nationwide brokerage firm, headquartered in New York City, has offices in most cities. In addition to providing prompt stock market information to its representatives and processing transactions at each office, the firm desires to allow its clients to access its securities data base.

b. An integrated steel manufacturer needs to coordinate the operations of its mills with those of its sales and service centers and with its headquarters. In addition, it desires to have close links to its key suppliers of raw materials and to its major customers, in order to reduce inventories and provide faster service.

c. A large grocery chain with numerous retail stores needs to check out its customers quickly and to maintain control over its pricing and stocking of merchandise. In addition, it desires to perform prompt credit checks on customers when necessary and to obtain payments from customers as quickly as possible.

d. A nationwide electronics products firm, with several plants and office complexes in separate cities, needs to maintain control over production and to increase efficiency in office operations. In addition, it desires to send memoranda from one site to another and to conduct videoconferences on a regular basis.

Suggested Readings

Buchanan, Jack R., and Linowes, Richard G. "Understanding Distributed Data Processing." *Harvard Business Review* (July–August 1980), pp. 65–75.

Caruso, Robert L. "Paying Bills the Electronic Way." *Management Accounting* (April 1984), pp. 24–27.

Cerullo, Michael J. "Data Communications: Opportunity for Accountants." *CPA Journal* (April 1984), pp. 40–47.

Copeland, Benny R., and Ramzy, Dave. "Office Automation: Selecting the Right Communication System." *Management Accounting* (July 1986), pp. 34–39.

Davis, Leila. "Retailers Go Shopping for EDI." *Datamation* (March 1, 1989), pp. 53–56.

Dietz, Devon D., and Keane, John D. "Integrating Distributed Processing within a Central Environment." *Management Accounting* (Nov. 1980), pp. 43–47.

Donovan, John J. "Beyond Chief Information Officer to Network Manager." *Harvard Business Review* (Sept.–Oct. 1988), pp. 134–140.

Fireworker, Robert B., and Stewart, Hal. "Guidelines for Success with LANs." *Journal of Systems Management* (May 1988), pp. 36–39.

Greenwood, Frank, and Greenwood, Mary M. "Principles of Office Automation." *Journal of Systems Management* (Feb. 1984), pp. 13–17.

Harper, Robert M., Jr. "Internal Control of Microcomputers in Local Area Networks." *Journal of Information Systems* (Fall 1986), pp. 67–80.

Hasz, Thomas W., and Boockholdt, J. L. "How Houston Lighting & Power Applied DDP." *Management Accounting* (March 1983), pp. 56–59.

Hirschheim, R. A. *Office Automation: Concepts, Technologies, and Issues.* Wokingham, Eng.: Addison-Wesley, 1985.

Jones, Del, and Lee, David R. "Managing Local Area Networks." *Journal of Systems Management* (July 1987), pp. 32–34.

Kneer, Dan C., and Lampe, James C. "Distributed Data Processing: Internal Control Issues and Safeguards." *EDPACS* (June 1983), pp. 1–14.

Kochar, Ips. "On-Line Security Strategies for Inter-Connected Computer Systems." *Journal of Systems Management* (Nov. 1984), pp. 32–35.

Liang, Ting-ping. "Local Area Networks: Implementation Considerations." *Journal of Systems Management* (January 1988), pp. 6–12.

Lowenthal, Eugene. "Database Systems for Local Nets." *Datamation* (Aug. 1982), pp. 97–106.

McCauley, Herbert N. "Developing a Corporate Private Network." *MIS Quarterly* (Dec. 1983), pp. 19–33.

McLeod, Raymond, Jr., and Jones, Jack Williams. "A Framework for Office Automation." *MIS Quarterly* (March 1987), pp. 87–106.

Moulton, Rolf T. "Network Security." *Datamation* (July 1983), pp. 121–124.

Musgrave, Bill. "Network Management: Keeping the Connection." *Datamation* (Sept. 1, 1987), pp. 98–107.

Nath, Ravinder. "Local Area Networks: The Network Manager's Perspective." *Information and Management* (April 1988), pp. 175–181.

Rushinek, Avi, and Rushinek, Sara. "Distributed Processing: Implications and Applications for Business." *Journal of Systems Management* (July 1984), pp. 21–27.

Siegel, Eric D. "Your Pocket Protocol Primer." *Datamation* (March 1984), pp. 152–154.

Sobol, Michael L. "Data Communications Primer for Auditors." *EDPACS* (March 1984), pp. 1–5.

Stallings, William. "Beyond Local Networks." *Datamation* (August 1983), pp. 167–176.

Tapscott, Don. "OA Banks on Connectivity." *Datamation* (March 15, 1986), pp. 106–112.

Vanecek, Michael T.; Zant, Robert F.; and Guynes, Carl S. "Distributed Data Processing: A New 'Tool' for Accountants." *The Journal of Accountancy* (Oct. 1980), pp. 75–83.

Woods, Larry D. "Understanding the Impact of Distributed Data Processing." *Journal of Accounting and EDP* (Spring 1986), pp. 27–34.

After studying this chapter, you should be able to do the following:

Describe the purposes and characteristics of the major types of support systems.

Identify the five levels of support that can be provided.

Discuss the various components of a computer-based decision support system, including the available options and criteria of effectiveness.

Identify the conditions under which effective decision support systems are designed and used.

Describe several applications of decision support systems to business situations.

Describe emerging types of decision support systems.

Discuss the characteristics, components, applications, and development cycles of expert systems.

Chapter **20**

DECISION SUPPORT SYSTEMS AND EXPERT SYSTEMS

A prime mission of an information system is to support managerial decision making. Recent developments in information technology and decision science have extended the capabilities of information systems to fulfill this mission. Two developments of critical importance are (1) interactive and high-powered computer-based systems and (2) business-oriented planning models. Thousands of business firms are currently using these developments to improve their strategic and tactical planning decisions.

Accountants have three reasons to exhibit interest in the development and maintenance of decision support systems. First, they are concerned with decision processes and related models, since accountants have the primary responsibility for providing rele-

vant decision-making information to managers. Second, they are knowledgeable about the inputs and outputs, since many needed data items are drawn from accounting transactions and outputs are expressed as financial reports. Third, they are often assigned the responsibility of evaluating the benefits of such systems against their high costs of development and maintenance.

This chapter begins with a description of operational and decision support systems. Next it identifies the several levels of support that can be provided by information systems. Then it analyzes decision support systems in terms of (1) the components that comprise the systems, (2) the criteria and conditions for designing effective systems, and (3) typical applications of decision support systems and the financial models they generally in-

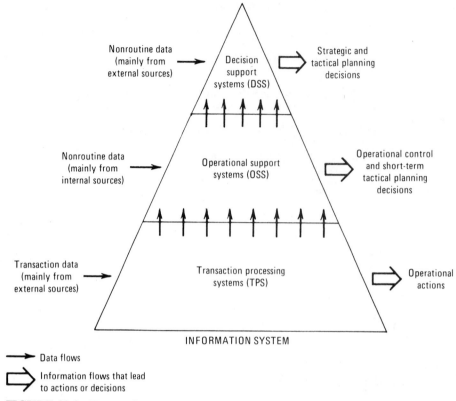

Nonroutine data
(mainly from
external sources) →

Decision
support
systems (DSS)

⇒ Strategic and
tactical planning
decisions

Nonroutine data
(mainly from
internal sources) →

Operational support
systems (OSS)

⇒ Operational control
and short-term
tactical planning
decisions

Transaction data
(mainly from
external sources) →

Transaction processing
systems (TPS)

⇒ Operational
actions

INFORMATION SYSTEM

→ Data flows

⇒ Information flows that lead
to actions or decisions

FIGURE 20-1 Types of support systems.

corporate. The chapter concludes with descriptions of other support systems, particularly those known as expert systems.

Types of Support Systems

In the first chapters of this book we observed that an information system may be viewed as consisting of multiple subsystems, such as the accounting information system and the management information system. We also noted that each such subsystem has one or more purposes and serves certain users. At this point we are ready to view the information system as consisting of three types of subsystems: the transaction processing system, the operational support system, and the decision support system. This revised classification plan does not in any way invalidate the previously described plans. It simply represents another useful view of the information system, a view that emphasizes the support missions of the information system.

Figure 20-1 portrays these three types of supporting systems as layers of the overall information system, represented by a triangle.[1] Since the information system mirrors

---

[1]Compare this figure with Figure 4-9, with which it has several points in common. Variations of the classification plan shown in this figure have been suggested. For instance, see Bart Johnson, "Why Your Company Needs Three Accounting Systems," *Management Accounting* (September 1984), pp. 39–46. Mr. Johnson identifies the three systems as the financial accounting system, the management accounting system, and the decision support system.

the organizational and physical features of a firm, the layers within the triangle also represent managerial and operational levels. Each supporting system receives flows of data; each supporting system also generates information outputs that further the objectives of the firm.

Transaction Processing Systems

At the lowest, or operational, level resides the basic **transaction processing system** (TPS). As we have noted earlier, the primary purpose of a TPS is not to aid the managerial decision making of a firm. The primary purpose of a TPS is to provide the framework through which the day-to-day routine data processing operations are conducted. On the other hand, a TPS does generate information as a by-product of the transaction processing. This information then (1) appears in scheduled reports or (2) flows into the operational or decision support systems.

Operational Support Systems

An **operational support system** (OSS) is an information processing system whose purpose is to aid the planning and control of operations. Its major impacts are on the structured tasks and problem situations with which a firm must deal in the short run. An OSS primarily focuses, therefore, on the short-term tactical planning and operational control decisions made by middle- and lower-level managers.[2] Examples of such decisions are the scheduling of production jobs and the approving of credit. The payoff from an improved OSS is increased operating efficiency, which may be reflected in greater responsiveness and lower costs.

[2]Operational support systems aid somewhat in the making of management control decisions. For instance, they provide the performance standards against which actual results are measured. However, since management control reports are issued on a regularly scheduled basis, the assistance of operational support systems is not fully needed.

Although difficult to define clearly, the scope of an OSS is roughly specified in Figure 20-1. On the lower end it merges with the transaction processing systems. On the higher side it blends into the higher-level decision support systems. It accepts both routine transaction data and nonroutine data, from both external and internal sources. These data are processed, often with the aid of decision models, to produce information for structured decision making.

The modern computer-based OSS generally possesses an array of attributes that enable it to provide very effective support. Since systems are often named for their attributes, a particular OSS may be described as interactive, time shared, and/or real time. Another particular OSS may be described as model based and/or dedicated.

Interactive. An interactive OSS incorporates interactive terminals that allow users to converse or interact directly with the system. It accommodates on-line processing of collected data and direct access of stored data. Consequently, users can obtain up-to-date and tailored information in a timely manner. For instance, a manager can receive an up-to-date status report of a particular order being produced for a customer. Figure 20-2 depicts the configuration of an interactive system.

Time-Shared. A time-shared OSS allows the system to be shared by a multitude of users. For instance a particular system may notify production employees when to expect upcoming job orders, may accept transaction data from storekeepers, and may interact with planners who develop this week's production schedule.

Real-Time. A real-time OSS provides real-time information to control a process or operation. In other words, it receives data concerning the process or operation, processes the data, and responds in a sufficiently timely

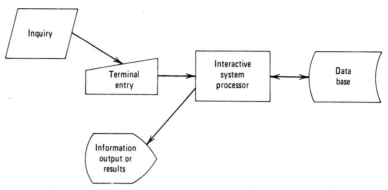

FIGURE 20-2 An interactive system.

manner to affect the decisions and actions necessary to control the process or operation. Refer to Figure 7-16 for a configuration of a real-time system.

The allowable response times for real-time systems vary, depending on the requirements of the process or operation being controlled and the context of the application. Continuous physical processes, such as steel-rolling and oil-refining, may require fractional-second response times for adequate control. Physical processes such as these, in fact, are generally controlled by specially designed process control computers. Discrete transaction-oriented business processes — such as credit control and production control — may accept response times of a few seconds or even of a few minutes or more.

A familiar example of a real-time system is a motel reservations system. A traveler requests a room, supplying such data as the specific motel at which the reservation is to be made, the dates needed, and the desired characteristics (e.g., a double bed plus rollaway bed). The motel clerk then enters the data via a terminal; within a few seconds she receives a response either confirming the reservation (and the nightly cost) or stating that no vacancies exist. The system controls the process by recording the room as being reserved (in the case of a positive confirmation), thus removing the room from the "in-ventory" for the desired dates and preventing other travelers from being assigned to the same room.

In certain real-time systems the control functions are triggered by built-in mechanisms rather than activated by inquiries. For instance, a real-time credit-checking system may automatically check a customer's current outstanding credit against his or her credit limit each time an order is placed for processing. If the credit limit is exceeded, the system itself may notify the order clerk that the order is rejected.

Model based. A model-based OSS is a computer-based support system that contains one or more **embedded decision models.** The decision models are applied automatically by the system to control some process or operation. The credit control system just described is an example. Another example is an inventory control system that automatically prepares a purchase order when the on-hand quantity of an inventory item falls below the reorder point.

The models in an OSS pertain only to structured decisions. Thus, they tend to be of the accept-reject type (e.g., the credit control model) or the optimizing type (e.g., the inventory control model). An appendix to this chapter reviews the features of a decision model and provides a more detailed example.

Dedicated. A dedicated OSS focuses solely on one particular use and type of user. The motel reservation system is an example of a dedicated system.

Conclusion. Operational support systems within a firm may be interactive, time-shared, real time, model-based, and dedicated. Drawing upon information from transaction processing systems and other sources, they aid managers in making decisions affecting operations.

Decision Support Systems

A **decision support system** (DSS) aids higher- and middle-level managers in making decisions that extend beyond the routine operations. Whereas the OSS is concerned with decisions involving short-term and well-structured problem situations, the DSS is concerned with decisions involving long-term and relatively unstructured problem situations. These decisions are often strategic in nature. However, certain tactical planning decisions with planning horizons of roughly one year may also be included. Whereas decisions involving an OSS are often made primarily by the system itself, decisions involving a DSS are never made solely by the system. That is, a DSS *always* requires the active participation of one or more managers. Thus, the payoff from a DSS is improved decision-making *effectiveness* of the affected manager.

Decision support systems have been used in a wide variety of problem situations in the real business world. Decisions resolved with the aid of a DSS include the following:

Shall a newly developed product be marketed?

Where shall new production facilities be located?

Shall a particular firm be acquired and incorporated into our operations?

What should be the budgeted net income and return on investment for each of our operating divisions?

How should we price our products for maximum sales and contribution to profits?

The concept of a DSS is not new. Managers have always been forced to make strategic and tactical decisions. They have always had assistance in doing so, usually from clerical assistants who have collected and analyzed the relevant data for decision making. Many managers in numerous firms still rely on the same type of assistance in their decision making. What is new is the array of capabilities provided to DSS by fourth-generation computer-based hardware, software, and techniques. Their incorporation into DSS have instilled added dimensions of support to strategic and tactical decision making.

Informational support is provided through both data collection and report generation. On the input side, nonroutine as well as transactional data are gathered, in large part from external sources. On the output side, ad hoc reports as well as scheduled reports can be made available. Thus, a manager using a DSS can obtain reports from a relevant reporting system, such as the profitability reporting system. However, he or she can also request ad hoc reports from the DSS, via a terminal or microcomputer. Furthermore, a manager using a DSS can employ models to experiment interactively with relevant data, perhaps by changing the values of certain factors and observing the results. Thus, a DSS enables a manager to gather a variety of perspectives concerning a complex problem situation and to explore the interactions of the significant factors. A manager can thereby discover and more soundly evaluate the alternative decision choices.

The key components of a DSS are pictured in Figure 20-3. A data base contains a variety of nonroutine data and planning data,

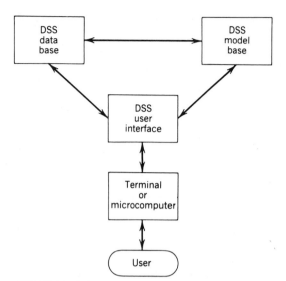

FIGURE 20-3 Key components of a decision support system.

plus summarized transactions that are relevant. A **model base** contains an array of decision models and statistical techniques, as well as the means to create new models. A **user interface** provides the managers or other users of a DSS with the means of interacting with the data and model bases. These components are described in more detail in a later section.

Although a DSS (like an OSS) is generally interactive, time shared, dedicated, and model based, it differs from an OSS in certain respects. Timeliness is not a critical factor to a DSS, so a DSS cannot be described as a real-time system. Also, the model base of a DSS contains different types of models from those found in the model base of an OSS. Examples of DSS-type models are financial planning models, corporate models, and portfolio models. These models tend to be utilized in simulations (experimentations) rather than in the optimizing procedures for which OSS-type models are designed. Finally, the data base for a DSS contains a larger portion of nonroutine data drawn from external sources.

In conclusion, a DSS is "an executive mind support system" in that it focuses on and enhances the decision-making abilities of the key managers of a firm.[3] As a formally established system, the DSS is a relatively new addition to the management information system of the typical firm. Nevertheless, it is appearing in an increasing number of firms and is being developed to higher levels of sophistication. In fact, some firms have several formal DSS's, each tailored to support one type of strategic or tactical planning process.

Levels of Decision Support

Not all computer-based support systems provide the same level or degree of decision support. At one extreme the decision maker receives very little assistance. At the other extreme the system *replaces* the human decision maker by actually making the decision and putting it into effect. Various reasons account for differences in support between two different support systems. One obvious reason is that the hardware and software may be more sophisticated in one of the systems. Another reason is that the type of decision supported by one system is better understood (i.e., structured) than the type of decision supported by the other system.

Even the same support system may not provide the same degree of support to different users. This is generally due to the fact that one manager has a greater capability for using the system than a second manager. The first manager may be better trained or may process information better than the second.

Because an objective in designing support systems is to maximize the support levels, we need to survey such levels before ex-

[3]P. G. Keen and G. R. Wagner, "DSS: An Executive Mind-Support System," *Datamation* (November 1979), p. 117.

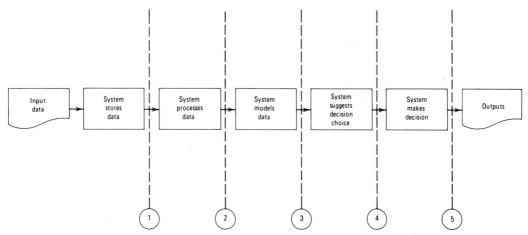

FIGURE 20-4 Levels of support provided by support systems. Adapted from Richard O. Mason, Jr., "Basic Concepts for Designing Management Information Systems," *AIS Research Paper #8* (Los Angeles: UCLA Graduate School of Administration, October 1969). Used with permission of the author.

amining support systems in detail.[4] Figure 20-4 portrays the several distinguishable levels of support.

Support Level I

At this lowest level of support the system collects data and stores the data in unprocessed form for later use. The decision maker identifies the problem requiring a decision, develops the appropriate decision (perhaps implicitly), retrieves the needed data from the system, processes the data via the model, selects the best alternative, and puts the decision into effect. An example is a decision concerning whether or not to market a new product. This system would collect the test-market data and the decision

maker would perform all the remaining steps.

Support Level 2

At this level the system collects data and processes or analyzes the data on demand. The decision maker performs all of the decision process steps listed earlier. However, the decision maker now has more usable information with which to work. For instance, the system may provide a manager with a cash-flow statement and a trend of past cash levels; on the basis of this information, the manager will decide whether or not to obtain a short-term bank loan.

Support Level 3

At this level the system employs a decision model to estimate the consequences of alternative courses of action. The decision maker then retrieves the results, compares the results for the respective alternatives, makes a decision choice, and puts the decision into effect. An example is the use of a

[4]For further discussion of the concepts discussed in this section, see Richard Mason, "Management Information Systems: What They Are. What They Ought to Be," *Innovation* (No. 13 1970), pp. 32–42; Steven Alter, "A Taxonomy of Decision Support Systems," *Sloan Management Review* (Fall 1977), p. 43; William R. King, "The Intelligent MIS—A Management Helper," *Business Horizons* (Oct. 1973), pp. 5–17.

pricing model to estimate the effects on sales of several proposed prices. On the basis of the resulting information the marketing manager can select the price that appears most suitable in the circumstances and then issue a new price list.

Support Level 4

At this level the system employs a decision model in the same manner as at support level 3. However, the system continues the process further, so that it points to the particular alternative that best satisfies the model criterion. The decision maker then retrieves this result and all underlying analyses, ratifies or rejects the suggested decision choice, and puts the decision into effect. For example, the decision model may suggest the best route by which to ship manufactured products to the southern-region warehouse. The decision maker may then elect to use this suggested route. However, he or she may judge a different route to be preferable, probably because of a factor that could not be taken into account by the model.

Support Level 5

At this level the system employs a decision model to make a decision and to put it automatically into effect. This level of support can be described as the **replacement level,** since the human decision maker has been fully replaced by the system. A likely candidate for this level of support is the inventory reorder decision. Using the economic order quantity (EOQ) decision model, the system determines the optimal quantities of items to reorder. Provided that adequate data concerning suppliers are accessible from the data base, the system can also prepare the necessary purchase orders for mailing.[5]

---

[5]Of course, when nonroutine situations occur for which the computer system has not been programmed, the human decision maker must be notified.

Conclusions

All of these support levels may be represented within the information system of a firm. Each level corresponds to a range of problems for which decisions are needed. Support only at the first level can be provided in the case of poorly understood (ill-structured) problems; the decision process is so hazy that no processing of collected data is possible. Level 2 support may be provided when certain of the problem relationships can be perceived. The support may be in the form of "heuristics," that is, rough problem-solving principles. Support at the third level can likely be provided when more of the problem relationships and likely consequences are understood. Support levels 4 and 5 can be provided only when the problem relationships and situations are well structured and clearly understood.

In line with its definition, decision support systems provide support at levels, 1, 2, or 3. Only operational support systems can provide support at levels 4 and 5, although such systems often provide support at the lower levels. For instance, an OSS provides level 1 support when an inventory manager inquires about the status of a particular item.

The level of support for particular types of problem situations is not necessarily fixed. With improvements in support system technology it may rise. For instance, a media selection problem may receive level 2 support today; with the installation of system improvements it may be capable of level 3 support next year.

Components of an Effective DSS

An effective DSS represents a sound blend of the major components portrayed in Figure 20-3. Designing an effective DSS is a difficult task, since each component involves multiple elements and activities. Figure 20-5, an expanded view of Figure 20-3, suggests the degree of complexity encompassed by a

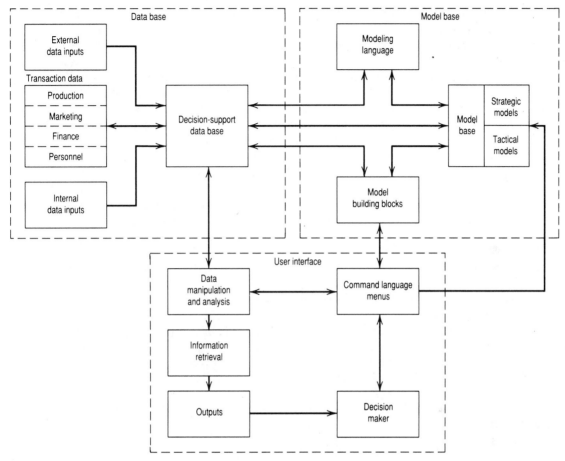

FIGURE 20-5   The structure of an effective decision support system.

DSS.[6] It also serves as the basis for discussing the criteria pertaining to an effective DSS. Illustrations are drawn from the Spire Corporation, a newly formed manufacturing firm that is currently developing a set of computer-based support systems.

Inputs

Data for use in a DSS are gathered from external sources and selected internal sources. Some, but by no means all, of the data from the external sources are based on transactions. If the DSS is to be effective, the data should be both relevant and accurate.

Relevant data.   The development of support systems begins with the identification of decisions to be supported. Based on the identified decisions, it is possible to specify much of the information needed by the decision makers. These information needs, plus the added data dictated by the human decision maker's style, establish the data to be acquired.

Assume that one key decision to be sup-

[6]Ralph H. Sprague, Jr., and Hugh J. Watson, "MIS Concepts, Part II," *Journal of Systems Management* (Feb. 1975), p. 37. Adapted with permission from the *Journal of Systems Management*.

ported by Spire's DSS is whether or not to manufacture a new product. It then follows that needed data will include the materials to be used, their sources, and their costs; the machines and labor needed in the production process, their availability, and their costs; the expected sales demand and price for which the product is to be sold; and so on. Certain of these data items will be obtained from external sources, while others will be obtained from various functions within the firm.

Accurate data. Sound decision making requires that the collected data be accurate. Therefore, the data should be validated by edit programs. If the data are entered via interactive terminals, special software may be employed to render the system user friendly and to ensure that erroneous data are corrected during the entry process.

Spire selects a suitable interactive entry system (actually a software package) to monitor data entry. The entry system will operate as follows: Upon being handed transactions (or other data) on coded documents, data entry clerks will first enter their user codes and the appropriate transaction codes. The system will then display preformatted screens on video display terminals. The clerks will key the data from the documents into the corresponding areas of the screens. Errors detected by the system will be brought to the attention of the clerks by means of clear messages. The clerks then will correct the errors. When the system has verified that all required data have been recorded and errors corrected, it transfers the data to the data base.

Data Base

Data for use in a DSS are stored in an easily accessible data base. For the data base to be effective, the stored and readily accessible data should be up to date and comprehensive.

Up-to-date storage. In most firms the data base for use by the DSS has been kept apart from the "live" data base that serves operational functions. As a result, the data needed by the DSS have had to be specially loaded from the operational data base. Not only has this procedure meant days or weeks of extra effort, but the loaded data have tended to become out of date. To overcome this deficiency, firms are beginning to link the "live" data base directly to the DSS. Although such system linkages increase the cost and complexity of the system, they enhance the up-to-dateness of the data.

Comprehensive storage. The stored data should be sufficiently comprehensive to provide support for all decisions that (1) lie within the scope of the system and (2) can reasonably be anticipated. Although specific items of data will differ substantially from situation to situation, they generally will include environmental data, internal planning data, data identified with specific models, and summary data based on past transactions. Figure 20-6 reflects these data categories and the specific data that Spire selects to be included in each category.

The data may be physically stored in one data base or multiple data bases. Regardless of the number of physical data bases, however, the overall set of data may conceptually be viewed as comprising planning-type data and operational-type data. These data should be organized into logical structures, so that they can be easily retrieved for use in the decision models.

Spire employs data base software that enables its varied operational and planning data to be stored in several structural forms. The operational data are stored in two-dimensional tables (relations). The environmental and internal planning data are stored in text files. The summary and certain of the model data are stored in multidimensional "cubes." An instance of a "cube" would be past sales data arranged according to time

Environmental data		Internal planning data		
(industry, market, economy, technology, re-source availability, demand–supply functions, and so forth)		(management policies and strategies, budgets, standards, capital projects, plans, cost–vol-ume–profit relationships, and so forth)		
Other model data		**Summaries**		
(sales forecasts, cost estimates, opportunity costs, and so forth)		(past sales trends, ratios, and so forth)		
Chart of accounts (including organizational cost and profit center breakdown)				
Customer data	Inventory data	Supplier data	Employee data	Property (fixed assets) data
Sales orders	Production and shipping records	Purchase orders	Time records	Disbursement vouchers

Planning data base / Operational data base

FIGURE 20-6 A comprehensive data base that spans a firm's decision and operational needs.

periods, products, sales territories, and customer classes.

Model Base

A variety of decision models are embedded in an on-line model base. The set of models resident at any point in time may be viewed as transitory; specific models are continually being expanded, revised, and replaced. In addition, the particular array of models comprising a model base will vary from firm to firm.

However, a reasonably complete model base would include models that aid (1) strategic and tactical planning, (2) the various major functions of a firm, and (3) the key decision makers of the firm. Figure 20-7 lists the variety of models that Spire selects for initial inclusion in its model base. Note that Spire's model base also includes decision models to be used by the operational support system.

Description of Model	Typical Function Aided
1. Regression model	Sales forecasting
2. Exponential smoothing model	Sales forecasting
3. PERT model	Engineering design
4. Linear programming model	Production scheduling
5. Line-of-balance model	Production routing
6. Economic order quantity model	Inventory control
7. Supplier evaluation model	Purchasing
8. Transportation model	Physical distribution
9. Discounted cash-flow model	Investment planning
10. Production cost variance model	Cost analysis
11. Cash-flow model	Financing
12. Budget model	Accounting control
13. Manpower planning model	Personnel planning

FIGURE 20-7 A variety of embedded decision models.

As a firm gains experience in modeling and higher-level managers gain confidence in the usefulness of DSS, broad-view models may be developed. This type of model can be very useful in strategic and longer-term tactical planning. Three versions of broad-view models are corporate models, financial planning models, and portfolio models.

A **corporate model** reflects the financial and/or physical relationships of a firm. It generally encompasses several functions or units; at its ultimate size it spans all aspects of the firm and even significant features of its environment, such as suppliers. A corporate model normally is employed by managers to predict future circumstances or values. This purpose is achieved through simulation (experimentation), usually over one or more time periods into the future. Thus, a manager might ask a corporate model to reflect the status of key factors (e.g., inventory level, net income) at the end of next year if certain strategies (e.g., price discounting) are adopted.

A **financial planning model** reflects a firm's formalized plans in financial terms. Also known as a budget model, it bears a close, or "shadow," correspondence to the accounting information system (AIS). That is, it accepts the same inputs as the AIS, employs an internal structure based largely on accounting relationships, and generates such outputs as income statements. A financial planning model is often used to simulate the flows of transactions over the budget planning period. It therefore enables managers to perceive likely financial consequences of possible decisions, so that they can develop the most suitable financial plans for the firm. Several variations of financial planning models are useful, including cash budget models, operational budget models, and capital budgeting models. From a global point of view financial planning models represent an important and heavily used subset of corporate models. As a group they bridge the firm's strategic planning and short-term tactical planning.

A **portfolio model** depicts in pictorial terms various key economic aspects of the business units (e.g., divisions) of a firm. For instance, a widely used portfolio model focuses on the relative growth of a "portfolio" of business units. In more specific terms, this model plots the relative market share of each product sold by a division versus its growth prospects. Another portfolio model reveals the variations in a key performance measure (i.e., return on investment) due to a variety of influencing factors (e.g., rate of growth, productivity.[7] By thus describing the current performance and status of the respective business units, a portfolio model can aid managers in deciding how to allocate resources. Another important value derives from the involvement of higher-level management in its construction. The involved managers are able to gain a better understanding of the critical factors underlying the success or failure of each business unit.

Modeling Tools

The decision models used in a DSS may be packaged or tailor made by members of the using firm. Most of the models listed in Figure 20-7 can be acquired as software packages. Even portfolio models are available from such organizations as the Strategic Planning Institute and Boston Consulting Group.[8] However, certain of the models will likely be tailor made. Only tailor-made models can fully respond to a firm's unique circumstances, and the process of designing a model provides a large portion of the benefits derived from modeling.

To be effective, a DSS should provide

[7]Richard A. Pappas and Donald S. Remer, "Status of Corporate Planning Models," *Managerial Planning* (March–April 1984), pp. 7–8.

[8]Ibid.

tools for developing tailor-made models and for managing all models in a model base. Three types of tools are model building blocks, model base management systems, and modeling languages.

Model building blocks. Blocks, or portions, of models should be available for use in the decision models. For instance, a corporate model may incorporate building blocks that forecast sales, compute economic inventory quantities, and determine break-even volumes. Examples of model building blocks that Spire will store include econometric models, standard management science models such as linear programming, and statistical routines such as time-series analysis and multiple regression. Most of these blocks will be software packages acquired from outside sources. However, some of the blocks will be routines developed by the firm's programmers.

Model base management systems. A **model base management system** (MBMS) is the modeling counterpart to a DBMS. In effect, it is software that operates under the control of the operating system. Its functions might consist of providing (1) links between models, (2) a model definition language, (3) mechanisms for modifying embedded models, and (4) a means of executing and manipulating models.

Modeling languages. The models that are tailor made must be programmed in a suitable language. Likewise, a programming language must be employed to link together the packages that form building blocks within larger models. In the past a procedure-oriented language such as BASIC, FORTRAN, or COBOL has generally been selected. However, such languages have severe limitations for modeling. They are difficult for the firm's programmers to modify, for nonpro-

grammers to understand, and for users to employ in necessary data manipulations.

In recent years more powerful, easier-to-use, and versatile **modeling languages** have been developed by commercial software firms. To facilitate the development and use of a DSS, one of these modeling languages should be selected. Currently over 70 languages are available. In effect, these languages are elaborate software packages that allow powerful instructions to be written.

Spire reviews the following modeling languages: CUFFS, IFPS, PLANR, EXPRESS, SIMPLAN.[9] It discovers that although these languages vary in certain respects, they all provide such features as

1. A variety of incorporated functions and statistical routines, including random-number generators, probability distributions, comparator routines, multiple regressions, and simultaneous equations.

2. A nonprocedural approach, which enables programmers to enter program changes *without* concern for the sequence in which they will be executed by the computer program.

3. A structured approach that facilitates the design of models as a linkage of interrelated modules.

4. A variety of model manipulative techniques, including sensitivity analysis, "what if" statements, and optimizing routines.

5. A report generator that enables customized reports to be specified and printed.

6. A set of easy-to-use commands, plus extensive diagnostics and interactive aids (such as responses to HELP messages en-

[9]CUFFS is available from Cuffs Planning and Models, Ltd.; IFPS is available from Execucom Systems Corporation; PLANR is available from Coopers & Lybrand; EXPRESS is available from Management Decision Systems; and SIMPLAN is available from SIMPLAN Group of Social Systems, Inc.

> **1.** The **time-based simulation** technique projects the states (values) of the key factors and criteria over future time periods, given current data values and expected rates of change.
> Example: A user might simulate the firm's budget over five years, with values of sales and net income being calculated each year.
> **2.** The **"what if" analysis** technique allows the user to ask "what if" questions in order to determine how key factors will respond to assumed changes or conditions.
> Example: A user might ask, "What will be the increase in my firm's labor costs next year if we grant a $2.00 per hour average increase in wage rates on January 1?"
> **3.** The **sensitivity analysis** technique, a special version of the "what if" analysis technique, reveals the sensitivity of the decision model criteria to changes in the values of key factors.
> Example: A user might ask, "What will be the effect on my firm's net income (the model criterion) if unit sales decrease by 10 percent next year?"
> **4.** The **goal-seeking analysis** technique allows the user to determine the levels of key factors needed in order to achieve a desired level in a model criterion.
> Example: A user might ask, "What volume (level) of sales units must my firm generate next year in order to achieve a 25 percent share of the market?"

FIGURE 20-8 Four model-manipulation or analysis techniques that may be used with a financial model.

tered by puzzled users and, in some cases, data entry and editing programs).

Data Manipulation and Analysis

It is not sufficient simply to plug data values into a decision model and determine values of the criteria. A decision maker should also be able to experiment with the data in order to gain greater insight into problem situations and consequences of decisions. An effective DSS therefore allows the use of the techniques described in Figure 20-8. Spire decides to acquire a modeling language that provides the capability of performing all of the listed techniques. In addition, the language that it selects allows the use of risk analysis, which involves the manipulation of factors having probabilistic values.

Information Retrieval Approaches

An effective DSS enables information to be processed and retrieved in an easy manner by users. The two "user-friendly" ap-

proaches currently employed are the command language approach and the menu approach.

Command language approach. This approach allows the decision maker to communicate by means of Englishlike commands. A suitable **command language** provides simple and descriptive words that are sufficiently powerful to generate reasonably complex processing sequences. Many of the key words are verbs—in effect, action codes. Thus, the word *DISPLAY* may retrieve data for use in answering an inquiry, whereas the verb *MODIFY* may update a stored record with new data.

The more advanced command languages allow users (such as managerial decision makers) to conduct a dialogue with the DSS in a natural manner, using a variety of ordinary words.[10] For instance, Spire selects a command language that allows such re-

---

[10] Among the few available "natural languages" are IN-TELLECT, marketed by Artificial Intelligence Corporation, and ON-LINE ENGLISH, marketed by Cullinet Corporation.

quests, prompting comments, and responses as follows:

Decision Maker: DISPLAY SALES IN BRANCH A FOR THE PAST THREE YEARS. *(The system then displays the requested information until the user taps a clear key.)*

System: DO YOU WANT TO MAKE ANOTHER REQUEST?

Decision Maker: YES.

System: WHAT TYPE OF REQUEST?

Decision Maker: A FORECAST FOR NEXT YEAR.

System: WHICH LINE OF OUTPUT?

Decision Maker: SALES FOR EACH OF THE BRANCHES, PLUS TOTAL SALES.

The command language can "call" the manipulation and analysis techniques that are available in the DSS system. Assume, for instance, that the decision maker would like the sales forecast for next year to be computed by the regression analysis technique. He or she would simply add the words *US-ING REGRESSION ANALYSIS* following *A FORECAST FOR NEXT YEAR.*

Menu approach. As noted earlier, this approach displays menus on CRT screens. The menus may include listings of stored data files, models, statistical techniques, and reports. They may also contain commands, such as Edit, Retrieve, Store, Whatif, Help, and Quit. Figure 20-9 displays a menu that is provided via a commercial modeling software package.

Spire considers the use of the menu approach for middle-level managers, who will be provided a modeling software package on microcomputers to support their decision making. A manager will first access a main menu that lists the various stored files for the decision areas being supported. Upon selecting the desired files (e.g., those pertaining to capital budgeting) by entering the corresponding number on the menu, the manager then obtains a second-level menu that shows various models, reports, and commands that are available.

The menu approach is more user

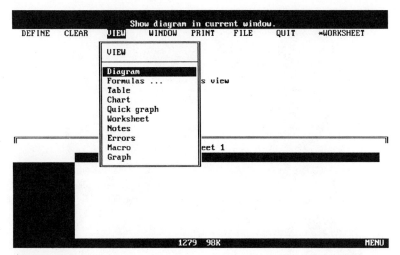

FIGURE 20-9 A menu of options for use in developing a financial model using the Javelin software package. Courtesy of Information Resources, Inc.

friendly than the command language approach; however, it is not sufficiently flexible for effective decision support. Thus, it must be supplemented by a dialogue technique, which prompts the decision maker by asking relevant questions. For instance, in the case of a capital budgeting decision it might ask such questions as: What is the desired rate of return on invested capital?

Outputs

An effective DSS should provide decision makers with information that is relevant, understandable, and timely. Spire considers all these attributes in the software packages that it plans to acquire.

Relevance is aided by means of a report generator, since it enables users to create the formats of desired reports. The users pinpoint the features of reports, either through coded specifications, through responses to system prompts, or through commands. The report generator then retrieves the needed data for the reports from the data base and presents the results in the format specified. Examples of report generators are Easytrieve Plus (from Pansophic) and Comprehensive Report Writer (from Software International). Report generators are often included as a feature of a multipurpose software package, such as FOCUS (from Information Builders).

To enhance understanding, outputs should appear in a variety of forms, from tabular layouts to graphical presentations. Graphs are particularly popular with users. For instance, they aid nonaccounting managers in interpreting accounting information and spotting trends. Color graphs, in either two or three dimensions, can be very impressive. Graphs can be displayed on screens, as in Figure 20-10, or they can be printed on plotters or laser printers. A graphics package can draw data from the data base and then translate the data into graphical outputs. When generated via mainframe computers, very-high-quality graphs can be produced in as many copies as desired. Examples of graphics packages are SAS/Graph (from the

FIGURE 20-10   A graphical display. Courtesy of Tektronix, Inc.

SAS Institute, Inc.) and Chartmaster (from Decision Resources).

Although systems that support decisions do not require real-time capabilities, they should present needed information in time to avoid penalties for delays; in other words, they should help to minimize the decision response delay. This type of delay consists of the intervals (1) from the time a problem arises until the time the manager is aware of the problem, (2) between the awareness of the problem and the decision, and (3) between the decision and the correction of the problem.[11]

From a behavioral point of view, the delay should be minimized in order to avoid irritating the decision maker and discouraging his or her use of the system. Either the requested information should be provided within a few seconds of a request or the system should respond to the decision maker that the information is not available. Spire specifies that the response time of its DSS must not exceed 10 seconds.

Human Interface

The key persons involved with a DSS are the model builders and the users/decision makers. Both types of persons should have an impact on the development of the DSS.

The **model builders** are the information processing specialists and programmers. Their responsibilities are to provide the technical expertise in designing the structures of the models, especially the integrated corporate and financial planning models. They also perform the detailed work in the implementation and revision of the designs. Furthermore, they provide close assistance to the users/decision makers.

The model builders can have a very beneficial effect on the DSS if their models are designed to be flexible and adaptable. Flexible models accommodate the various information needs of the respective using managers. Adaptable models are capable of being adjusted over time to new information needs and organizational constraints.

The **users/decision makers** are the managers who depend on the DSS for assistance in decision making. As we have seen, managers should have easy accessibility to and full understanding of the DSS and underlying models. Figure 20-11 illustrates this accessibility; it shows a manager in a hotel room many miles from his home office, who is able to access his DSS by means of a portable computer and modem. Another means of accessibility is via the information center (also called the infocenter). An **information center** is a service-oriented center in a firm where users/decision makers can receive assistance in using and developing DSS. Some information centers even help users to acquire microcomputers and to install DSS on them.

Users can also be aided by **groupware,** special software and associated technology services. Groupware enables decision makers to share needed information available in a data base. Thus, information relating to particular decisions can be selectively gathered and provided to one or more managers having responsibilities for those decisions. This information may be transmitted to the various users via either local or wide-area networks. Most firms using groupware employ such commercial products as Notes (from Lotus Development Corporation) and Apriori (from Answer Computer Inc.)[12]

Another user-oriented feature of a DSS is the incorporation of **human information processing** (HIPS) discoveries. According to HIPS, human decision makers have limitations and distinctive decision-making styles. To accommodate human limitations, a DSS should filter out irrelevant data, perform all

[11]Miles Kennedy, "Real Time Versus Exception Reports," *Journal of Systems Management* (April 1974), pp. 23–24.

[12]Esther Dyson, "Why Groupware Is Gaining Ground," *Datamation* (March 1, 1990), pp. 52–56.

FIGURE 20-11 A user of a DSS at a remote location. Courtesy of Hewlett-Packard Company.

necessary computations, highlight significant differences, and present information in easily understood formats. To suit differences in decison making, a DSS should support a variety of decision styles ranging from the intuitive to the analytical. For instance, Spire's DSS will allow random "browsing" among details and heuristic explorations of alternatives by those who employ the intuitive style. On the other hand, it will provide sequential search techniques and structured frameworks for those who desire a more analytical approach.

Design Considerations

Business firms have had over 20 years of experience in developing computer-based decision support models. Numerous man-

agement consulting firms have also worked with such firms, and many have developed their own decision support software packages. For instance, the large public accounting firms have developed financial planning software packages, which they have adapted to the design of budget and financial planning models for a variety of client firms. They have also used spreadsheet software packages to develop decision models for special situations, such as limited-partnership real estate investment offerings.

On the basis of this large body of experience in DSS development, including failures as well as successes, we can suggest several design considerations:

1. Involve higher-level management in the model-building activity. The most successful DSS is one that management understands and tailor-makes for its own use. Management participation is also necessary in order that the objectives of the models be clear and relevant to the firm's planning process.

2. Maintain full-time model builders who interact constantly with the managers. Although consultants are very useful, they are not sufficient. It is important that expert personnel be available to maintain the models and to coordinate the data processing personnel and DSS users.

3. Begin the model-building activity with a simple summary model and expand the detail gradually in a modular fashion. In this way management will understand and validate every step along the way. The modularity will also provide flexibility, so that the inevitable changes can be made more easily.

4. Structure the DSS and embedded models to accord with the firm's organizational structure and information system architecture. For example, Figure 20-12 shows the major features of decision support and financial planning systems that generally accord with a decentralized organization and distributed processing network.[13]

5. Include the various attributes of effective models, as discussed in the preceding sections.

6. Document the developing model fully, so that users and future model builders can refresh their memories concerning its construction, use, and limitations.

Applications of Decision Support Systems

A large number of DSS applications have been reported in articles and professional meetings. Three real-world examples will illustrate the wide variety of such applications.

A Strategic-Level DSS

The L. D. Shrieber Cheese Company of Green Bay, Wisconsin, provides an example of decision support at the strategic level. During a recent year it needed to make decisions concerning the size and layout of a major new production plant. A study team consisting of the prospective plant manager and several other managers was formed. The team was to develop a proposal concerning its recommended decision choices, accompanied by appropriate supporting information and a list of alternative choices. The proposal was to be submitted to top management, which would make the final decisions. After several attempts to develop the proposal on the basis of manual calculations, the team developed a family of decision models called GYMJAC. These models, which involved risk analysis techniques, were programmed by means of the IFPS modeling language. They were then used in an interactive computer-based support system to develop the final proposal. Top management expressed confidence in the results.[14]

A Financial Planning DSS

The Tanner Companies, a Phoenix-based multidivisional firm, undertakes construction projects throughout Arizona and also sells construction materials. It employs a financial planning model in its budgeting process. The model, which is linked to and fed by marketing and production models, provides timely forecasts for as far as five years into the future.

The financial planning model consists of

[13]Reprinted from Joseph W. Wilkinson, "Financial Modeling within Distributed Systems," *Journal of Systems Management* (March 1984), pp. 33–37.

[14]Keen and Wagner, "DSS: An Executive Mind-Support System," *Datamation* (November 1979), pp. 120–121.

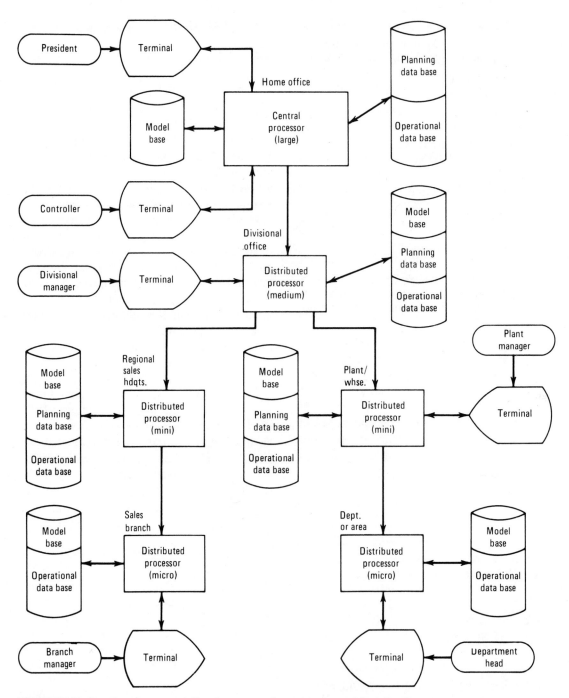

FIGURE 20-12   Corporate modeling for a manufacturing firm with a distributed processing network.

three modules. The first module generates financial statements at the divisional level. The second module produces a consolidated balance sheet and income statement, and the third module provides a funds flow statement. All of these outputs represent forecasts and are based on planned strategies and assumptions concerning upcoming economic conditions and company operations.

A powerful feature of the model is its ability to answer "what if" questions posed by managers. It enables the managers to evaluate how changes in key factors will affect critical criteria. For instance, the model enables the treasurer to evaluate how refinancing a loan will affect the net income and the cash balance.

The top managers of the Tanner Companies are enthusiastic about the benefits of their financially oriented DSS. They are certain that better planning has led to a more precise definition of the firm's needs, which in turn has resulted in improved cash management and reduced borrowing rates.[15]

An Operation-Based DSS

Frito-Lay, the snack food division of Pepsico, Inc., gathers data concerning its sales by means of hand-held computers carried by its route sales force. At the operational level the sales data are used to determine which stores need replenishments, where products are collecting dust, and how to arrange the next day's delivery schedules.

The sales data are also fed into the computer system via microcomputers and uploaded to the mainframe computer located at Plano, Texas. Summary and analyzed sales information, in graphical formats, is then available to managers throughout the firm via computer networks (both WAN's and

LAN's). This information can aid managers in making a variety of tactical decisions, ranging from sales planning to production scheduling and plant expansion.[16]

A Cash Budgeting Model Involving Uncertainty

A final example concerns the Nalani Company, a hypothetical retailer of Hawaiian dresses called muumuus.[17] In the interest of obtaining more realistic cash forecasts, the firm develops the financial planning model shown in Figure 20-13. This cash-flow model, which is written in the fourth-generation financial modeling language known as Interactive Financial Planning System (IFPS), specifies several of the variables in the form of probability distributions. For instance, expected unit sales and expected collections are assumed to be distributed normally around mean values, while the interest rate on borrowings has a triangular distribution.

Two contrasting solutions, based on given data, appear in Figures 20-14 and 20-15. Figure 20-14 displays the deterministic solution based on the most probable values of the distributions. In other words, it presents the results under the condition of assumed certainty. Figure 20-15 portrays the probabilistic solution, including a normal distribution table, frequency table, selected statistics, and selected histogram. The probabilistic solution, pertaining only to the variable called BORROWINGS, provides additional information for use by the treasurer in making cash-related decisions. For instance, the

[15]Joseph W. Wilkinson, "Financial Models: Helping Top Managers Plan," *Arizona Business* (First Quarter 1984), p. 10.

[16]Bob Francis, "Frito Lays a New IS Bet," *Datamation* (February 15, 1989), pp. 75–78.

[17]Dennis F. Togo, "Risk Analysis for Accounting Models Utilizing an Advanced Electronic Spreadsheet Software," *Journal of Information Systems* (Spring 1988), pp. 61–72. The software, IFPS, is copyrighted © 1988, by EXECUCOM Systems Corporation, Austin, Texas.

IFPS CASH FLOW MODEL

```
1    COLUMNS ACT1, QTR1, QTR2, QTR3, QTR4, QTRA, YEAR
2    * SCHEDULE 1: SALES BUDGET
3    *
4    EXPECTED UNIT SALES = 3100, NORRANDR (3000, 200)
5    EXPECTED UNIT PRICE = 35, T1090RANDR (33, 35, 40)
6        TOTAL SALES = EXPECTED UNIT SALES * EXPECTED UNIT PRICE
7    *
8    CASH SALES = TOTAL SALES * UNIRANDR (.55,.65)
9    CREDIT SALES = 42000, TOTAL SALES - CASH SALES
10   *
11   * SCHEDULE 2: CASH COLLECTIONS
12   *
13   CASH SALES COLLECT = CASH SALES
14   CURRENT AR COLLECT = CREDIT SALES * NORRANDR (.80, .05)
15   PRIOR AR COLLECT = 0, 9000, PREVIOUS CREDIT SALES - PREVIOUS CURRENT AR
         COLLECT
16       COLLECTIONS = CASH SALES COLLECT + CURRENT AR COLLECT + PRIOR AR
         COLLECT
17   COLUMN 7 FOR L4, L6, L8, L9, L13, L14, L15, L16 = SUM (C2 THRU C5)
18   *
19   * SCHEDULE 3: PURCHASES BUDGET
20   *
21   COST OF GOODS SOLD = TOTAL SALES * (1/(1 + .50))
22   COLUMN 7 FOR L21 = SUM (C2 THRU C5)
23   DESIRED END INVENT = 8000, FUTURE COST OF GOODS SOLD * .10
24   COLUMN 7 FOR L23 = C5
25   INVENT NEEDS = COST OF GOODS SOLD + DESIRED END INVENT
26   COLUMN 7 FOR L25 = L21 + L23
27   BEG INVENT = PREVIOUS DESIRED END INVENT
28   COLUMN 7 FOR L27 = C2
29       PURCHASES = INVENT NEEDS - BEG INVENT
30   COLUMN 7 FOR L29 = L25 - L27
31   *
32   * SCHEDULE 4: DISBURSEMENTS FOR PURCHASES
33   *
34   CURRENT PURCH DISB = 0, PURCHASES * TRIRANDR (.35, .40, .50)
35   PRIOR PURCH DISB = 0, 35000, PREVIOUS PURCHASES - PREVIOUS CURRENT PURCH
         DISB
36       PURCHASES DISBURSE = CURRENT PURCH DISB + PRIOR PURCH DISB
37   COLUMN 7 FOR L34, L35, L36 = SUM (C2 THRU C5)
38   *
39   *
40   * CASH FLOW STATEMENT
41   *
42   BEGIN CASH = 0, PREVIOUS END CASH
43   COLUMN 7 FOR L42 = C2
44   * CASH RECEIPTS:
45       COLLECTIONS = L16
46   COLUMN 7 FOR L45 = SUM (C2 THRU C5)
47   CASH AVAIL = BEGIN CASH + COLLECTIONS
48   COLUMN 7 FOR L47 = L42 + L45
49   *
```

Continued

FIGURE 20-13 A financial planning model containing probability distributions.

944

IFPS CASH FLOW MODEL

```
50  * CASH DISBURSEMENTS:
51      PURCHASES DISBURSE = L36
52      OPERATING EXPENSES = NORRANDR (30000, 2000)
53      CAPITAL PURCHASES = 0, 40000, 0
54  COLUMN 7 FOR L51, L52, L53 = SUM (C2 THRU C5)
55  TOTAL DISBURSEMENTS = L51 + L52 + L53
56  COLUMN 7 FOR L55 = L51 + L52 + L53
57  MINIMUM CASH = 10000
58  COLUMN 7 FOR L57 = 10000
59  CASH NEEDS = TOTAL DISBURSEMENTS + MINIMUM CASH
60  COLUMN 7 FOR L59 = L55 + L57
61  *
62  CASH DIFF = CASH AVAIL – CASH NEEDS
63  COLUMN 7 FOR L62 = L47 – L59
64  *
65  * FINANCING:
66      BORROWINGS = IF CASH DIFF .LT.0 THEN – CASH DIFF ELSE 0
67      REPAYMENTS = IF (CASH DIFF – INT PAID) .LE. 0 THEN 0'
68        ELSE IF (CASH DIFF – INT PAID) .LE. CUMUL BORROW THEN CASH DIFF – INT
            PAID'
69          ELSE CUMUL BORROW
70      INT PAID = IF CASH DIFF .LE. 0 THEN 0'
71        ELSE IF CASH DIFF .LE. CUMUL INT THEN CASH DIFF'
72          ELSE CUMUL INT
73  COLUMN 7 FOR L66, L67, L70 = SUM (C2 THRU C5)
74  TOTAL FINANCING = BORROWINGS – INT PAID – REPAYMENTS
75  COLUMN 7 FOR L74 = L66 – L67 – L70
76  *
77  END CASH = 12000, CASH AVAIL – TOTAL DISBURSEMENTS + TOTAL FINANCING
78  COLUMN 7 FOR L77 = L47 – L55 + L74
79  *
80  * SUPPORTING COMPUTATIONS:
81  CUMUL BORROW = PREVIOUS CUMUL BORROW + BORROWINGS – PREVIOUS
        REPAYMENTS
82  INT EXPENSE = ROUND (CUMUL BORROW * TRIRAND (.025, .03, .04))
83  COLUMN 7 FOR L82 = SUM (C2 THRU C5)
84  CUMUL INT = PREVIOUS CUMUL INT + INT EXPENSE – PREVIOUS INT PAID
```

FIGURE 20-13   (*continued*).

10 percent value for borrowings during the year indicates that 90 percent of the expected values are less than $37,245 and only 10 percent were larger. Hence, borrowings of $37,245 will have a 90 percent chance of covering cash needs for the year. If only $25,000 were borrowed, as suggested by the deterministic solution, the cash needs are not likely to be met. Frantic borrowing may then be necessary, perhaps at higher-than-optimal rates.

The risk analysis illustrated by this example employs the technique known as Monte Carlo simulation. It involves a number of iterations (1000 in this case), in which values are randomly selected from the probability

	QTR1	QTR2	QTR3	QTR4	YEAR
SCHEDULE 1: SALES BUDGET					
EXPECTED UNIT SALES	3000	3000	3000	3000	12000
EXPECTED UNIT PRICE	35	35	35	35	
TOTAL SALES	105000	105000	105000	105000	420000
CASH SALES	63000	63000	63000	63000	252000
CREDIT SALES	42000	42000	42000	42000	168000
SCHEDULE 2: CASH COLLECTIONS					
CASH SALES COLLECT	63000	63000	63000	63000	252000
CURRENT AR COLLECT	33600	33600	33600	33600	134400
PRIOR AR COLLECT	9000	8400	8400	8400	34200
COLLECTIONS	105600	105000	105000	105000	420600
SCHEDULE 3: PURCHASES BUDGET					
COST OF GOODS SOLD	70000	70000	70000	70000	280000
DESIRED END INVENT	7000	7000	7000	7000	7000
INVENT NEEDS	77000	77000	77000	77000	287000
BEG INVENT	8000	7000	7000	7000	8000
PURCHASES	69000	70000	70000	70000	279000
SCHEDULE 4: DISBURSEMENTS FOR PURCHASES					
CURRENT PURCH DISB	27600	28000	28000	28000	111600
PRIOR PURCH DISB	35000	41400	42000	42000	160400
PURCHASES DISBURSE	62600	69400	70000	70000	272000
CASH FLOW STATEMENT					
BEGIN CASH	12000	10000	10000	10000	12000
CASH RECEIPTS:					
COLLECTIONS	105600	105000	105000	105000	420600
CASH AVAIL	117600	115000	115000	115000	432600
CASH DISBURSEMENTS:					
PURCHASES DISBURSE	62600	69400	70000	70000	272000
OPERATING EXPENSES	30000	30000	30000	30000	120000
CAPITAL PURCHASES	40000	0	0	0	40000
TOTAL DISBURSEMENTS	132600	99400	100000	100000	432000
MINIMUM CASH	10000	10000	10000	10000	10000
CASH NEEDS	142600	109400	110000	110000	442000
CASH DIFF	−25000	5600	5000	5000	−9400
FINANCING:					
BORROWINGS	25000	0	0	0	25000
REPAYMENTS	0	4100	4373	4504	12977
INT PAID	0	1500	627	496	2623
TOTAL FINANCING	25000	−5600	−5000	−5000	9400
END CASH	10000	10000	10000	10000	10000
SUPPORTING COMPUTATIONS:					
CUMUL BORROW	25000	25000	20900	16527	
INT EXPENSE	750	750	627	496	2623
CUMUL INT	750	1500	627	496	

FIGURE 20-14 A deterministic solution using the cash-flow model.

NORMAL APPROXIMATION TABLE

PROBABILITY OF VALUE BEING GREATER THAN INDICATED

	90	80	70	60	50	40	30	20	10
BORROWINGS									
QTR1	13636	17051	19513	21616	23583	25549	27652	30114	33529
QTR2	−2388	−1213	−365	359	1036	1713	2438	3285	4461
QTR3	−2511	−1254	−347	428	1152	1877	2651	3558	4816
QTR4	−2246	−1132	−328	358	1000	1642	2328	3132	4246
YEAR	16297	19893	22485	24701	26771	28842	31057	33650	37245

FREQUENCY TABLE

PROBABILITY OF VALUE BEING GREATER THAN INDICATED

	90	80	70	60	50	40	30	20	10
BORROWINGS									
QTR1	13141	17421	20016	22116	24055	26041	28043	30175	33001
QTR2	0	0	0	0	0	0	0	540	4292
QTR3	0	0	0	0	0	0	0	1055	4654
QTR4	0	0	0	0	0	0	0	438	4304
YEAR	16172	19828	22535	25142	27115	29195	31066	33294	36588

SAMPLE STATISTICS

	MEAN	STD DEV	SKEWNESS	KURTOSIS	10PC CONF	MEAN 90PC
BORROWINGS						
QTR1	23583	7761	−.3	3.0	23268	23897
QTR2	1036	2672	3.3	14.8	928.1	1144
QTR3	1152	2859	3.0	11.9	1037	1268
QTR4	1000	2533	3.0	12.7	897.5	1103
YEAR	26771	8173	−.1	3.0	26440	27102

HISTOGRAM FOR COLUMN   YEAR OF BORROWINGS

```
131-140                                   *
121-130                                   *
111-120                               *   *   *
101-110                           *   *   *   *
 91-100                   *   *   *   *   *   *
 81-90                    *   *   *   *   *   *   *
 71-80                    *   *   *   *   *   *   *
 61-70                    *   *   *   *   *   *   *
 51-60                    *   *   *   *   *   *
 41-50                *   *   *   *   *   *   *   *
 31-40            *   *   *   *   *   *   *   *   *   *
 21-30        *   *   *   *   *   *   *   *   *   *   *
 11-20    *   *   *   *   *   *   *   *   *   *   *   *   *
  1-10  * * * *  *  *  *  *  *  *  *  *  *  *  *  *  *  *  *  *
       ----------------------------------------------------------
                     1       2       3       3       4
           1    8    6       4       1       9       7
           2    9    5       2       8       5       1
           7    2    7       2       7       2       7
           5    5    5       5       5       5       5
```

FIGURE 20-15 A probabilistic solution using the cash-flow model.

distributions of the input variables. Monte Carlo simulation is slowly gaining acceptance by the managers of business firms.

Emerging Support Systems

Additional types of systems that support decision making have emerged in recent years. In this section we introduce two such systems: executive information systems and strategic support systems. These support systems can be viewed as variant forms of a DSS, although each differs from a DSS in certain respects.

Executive Information Systems

An **executive information system** (EIS) is the tailored information support system for the chief executive officer (CEO) of a firm. Its purpose is to provide the information that its user needs to guide his or her firm, including information for making strategic planning and management control decisions and for overseeing firm-wide operations. Thus, it focuses more on information relating to a set of managerial responsibilities than on information for specific ad hoc decisions.

Like a DSS, an EIS consists of three major components: a data base, a model base, and a user interface. Since the chief executive officer has very broad responsibilities, the data base of an EIS typically contains data pertaining to competitors, products, markets, organizational units, key success factors, and so on. For instance, data may be stored in multidimensional forms, with separate dimensions for the major income statement and balance sheet accounts, time periods, product lines, customer classes, and divisions of the firm. Thus, the amount of product line A sold to customer class 2 during the past three years would be accessible. Stored models might relate to the industry and economy as well as

the firm itself. The models would allow the chief executive to perform simulations and analyses pertaining to future conditions. An effective EIS also provides considerable assistance via the user interface, ranging from tailored menus and prompts to mouses and touch screens. Many of the outputs consist of analyses and trends presented in graphical form.

An EIS can be constructed by the firm's information system analysts and model builders. Alternatively, software packages can be acquired to provide the "shells" around which to assemble the EIS components. These "shells" provide data base structures, graphics, report generators, and user interface features. They may provide other interfaces, such as links to external data banks and teleconferencing connections. Examples of software packages suitable as EIS "shells" are FOCUS (from Information Builders) and RAMIS II (from Mathematica, Inc.).

Strategic Support Systems

A **strategic support system** (SSS) is an outgrowth of the DSS and EIS. It focuses on strategic concepts, such as those pertaining to a firm's markets, competitive situation, and value chain. An SSS has become increasingly desirable for many firms, especially those faced by global competition, short product life cycles, and growing investment costs.

A suitable strategic model within an SSS may provide five dimensions: (1) key financial variables, (2) products, (3) markets, (4) competitors, and (5) future time periods. Analyses and forecasts involving all five dimensions can enable users to gain realistic views of possible future scenarios.[18] The users of an SSS may be the board of directors,

---

[18]Peter Fredericks and N. Venkatraman, "The Rise of Strategy Support Systems," *Sloan Management Review* (Spring 1988), pp. 48–50.

higher-level managers, or the firm's planning group.

Norton-Villiers-Triumph (NVT), a British firm, presents a case in which an SSS was sorely needed. During the 1970s the firm had continuing losses due to Japanese competition. After a strategic survey, performed by a consulting group, the firm discovered that it had not been sufficiently aware of market segmentation (with respect both to products and to geography), of pricing and cost strategies, and of market growth. The Japanese firms (Honda, in particular), which had apparently studied the strategic conditions closely, were able to gain increased market share and a long-term competitive advantage.[19]

All types of support systems can be expected to multiply in the near future, with respect both to types of applications and to number of installations. For instance, certain decisions that are too unstructured to be well supported today will be attacked successfully by future support systems. Support systems will also be more effectively designed for group decision making. This development should be warmly welcomed, since strategic decisions are rarely considered by only one manager, even when that manager is the CEO. A related development will be the increasing use of computer networks to enhance the effectiveness of support systems. Thus, managers in New York and Chicago will be able to employ a DSS and/or SSS via their firm's computer network to cooperate in making sound and timely choices relating to difficult problems. A final development that relates to support systems is the rise of expert systems.

Expert Systems

Artificial intelligence (AI) is "the part of computer science concerned with designing intelligent computer systems, that is, systems that exhibit the characteristics we associate with human behavior—understanding language, learning, reasoning, solving problems, and so on."[20] Three major areas in which artificial intelligence has been applied are natural language, robotics, and expert systems. Natural languages are being employed in the development of extremely friendly user interfaces. Robotics is being used in the development of robots that perform key physical functions in factories, laboratories and other workplaces.

In contrast to natural languages and robotics, expert systems process and analyze information. The following sections survey the characteristics, components, applications, and development of expert systems.

Characteristics

An **expert system** is a knowledge-based computer software model that simulates the behavior of one or more human experts in solving a difficult problem or making a decision. It utilizes a type of knowledge engineering in order to incorporate the specialized knowledge and symbolic reasoning of the human experts.

Expert systems are increasing in popularity within organizations of all types. Their major benefits are that they generally improve the quality of decisions and the timeliness of decision making. They also enhance the productivity of manager-decision makers and preserve critical expertise.

In a sense typical expert systems are variations of DSS's, since they are designed to cope with the same type of relatively unstructured problem situations. However, they can differ significantly, as illustrated by the game of chess. When a chess champion is said by a popular newspaper to have played

[19]*Ibid.*, pp. 50–51.

[20]A. Barr and E. Feigenbaum, *The Handbook of Artificial Intelligence,* Volume 1 (HeurisTech Press, 1981).

the "computer," an expert system is involved. When the chess champion uses a computer program to aid him or her in learning chess or to suggest moves to be made against a human opponent, a DSS is involved. Other differences between an expert system and a DSS are as follows:

1. An expert system makes judgments and recommends particular decision choices to the user, in much the way that hired human experts would. Although the user and an expert system often interact, as when the user provides added facts requested by the expert system, the user is more passive than when employing a DSS.

2. An expert system relies on special computer languages that allow logical inferences to be drawn and heuristic techniques to be applied. Furthermore, these languages enable the logic paths used in solving a particular problem to be retraced; through this retracing procedure the user can analyze the "thinking process" performed by the expert system.

3. Expert systems are adaptive, in that they can learn. One type of learning occurs when the human experts add new knowledge that they have acquired. A more intriguing form of learning occurs when the expert system itself learns from past mistakes. For instance, an expert system used to recommend audit programs may propose a sales audit program that omits a minor but important task. Upon being informed by the auditor–user of the omission, the expert system can modify its logic.

4. Expert systems are more limited, in that they serve a narrower range of problem situations than do DSS's. To be suitable, the situations must require a high degree of scarce expertise, entail frequent decisions with high payoffs, and remain relatively stable (unchanged).

Components

An expert system also differs from a DSS with respect to the components of which it is composed. The key components of an expert system are a knowledge base, a task-specific data base, an inference engine, and a user interface. Figure 20-16 depicts the relationships among these components. The user initiates the expert system by providing necessary specific data to the task-specific data base via the user interface. In turn, the task-specific feeds the facts to the knowledge base, which then interacts with the inference engine in tracing the steps through the computer program. Recommendations resulting from this process are provided through the interface. Let us consider each major component more closely.

The **knowledge base** incorporates the knowledge of the experts that pertains to the domain of the problem situation. Two techniques for expressing the knowledge are (1) production rules and (2) semantic networks. **Production rules** are simple "if–then" rules that represent the specific consequences of given conditions or actions. An instance is as follows: *If* (1) a patient was caught unprepared in a sudden rainstorm and (2) the patient has developed a fever, *then* the patient likely has a cold. **Semantic networks** are decompositions of objects, such as a breakdown of a product into its parts and subassemblies. As the term implies, the networks appear as hierarchies linked through words. Figure 20-17 shows a simplified semantic network pertaining to the broad object called ASSET. Each node in the network is called a frame.

The **task-specific data base** contains the facts relevant to a specific application of the expert system. For a tax-planning expert

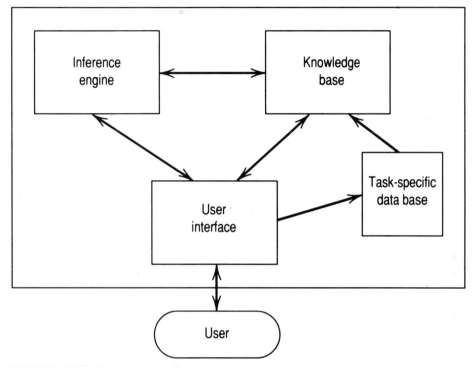

FIGURE 20-16 Components of an expert system.

system it might contain the dollar values and characteristics of the various assets and other accounts for a firm involved in tax planning. As noted earlier, these data are fed into the system through the user interface at the beginning of an application.

The **inference engine** contains the heuristic reasoning procedures that simulate the decision-making processes of the human experts. It "drives" the expert system; that is, it determines the sequence in which to apply the production rules or to trace through the semantic networks of the knowledge base. Two types of sequences are called forward chaining and backward chaining. *Forward chaining* consists of moving through the rules or networks to reach conclusions, that is, to develop specific recommendations. *Backward chaining* consists of beginning

with a conclusion or recommendation and moving back through the rules or networks to discover whether it is logically sound. Backward chaining is as important as forward chaining. It allows users to evaluate the validity of conclusions or recommendations.

The user interface, as in a DSS, is the means by which the user communicates with the system. An effective means of initiating the session is to have the expert system ask questions that need to be answered by the user.

An additional component not shown is the *development engine*. This component provides the means by which the knowledge and inference processes of the experts are encoded and embedded in the expert system. It also allows the rules or semantic networks to be modified.

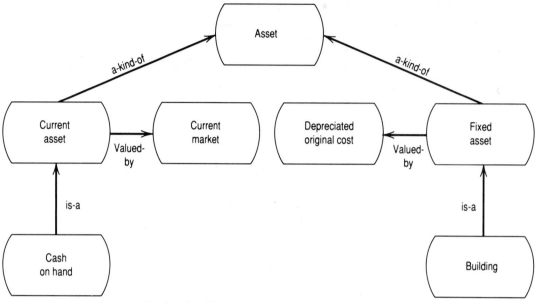

FIGURE 20-17 An example of a simplified semantic network making up part of a knowledge base.

Applications

An increasing number of expert systems are appearing in firms of all types. An early expert system developed by Digital Equipment Company, named XCON, enables the manufacturer to specify the needed components and their arrangements for computer systems ordered by customers. ExperTAX is an expert system developed by Coopers & Lybrand to aid accountants in providing tax-planning advice. Other specific expert systems are listed in Figure 20-18.

In some cases expert systems can be incorporated into the information systems of firms to aid with daily decision making. American Express has a very successful expert system that is being employed to detect fraudulent credit card activity. Each time an authorization request is received, the expert system "looks" into the data base to see the pattern of recent expenditures. If the previous requests this week relating to a particu-lar card, for instance, have been entered from Paris, Hong Kong, and Chicago, the system would alert the credit clerk that the card might be stolen.[21]

Developmental Considerations

Building an expert system requires the services of experts, knowledge engineers, and users. The **knowledge engineers,** akin to systems or information analysts, are the architects of the system's development engine. They first determine from users the purposes and applications of the proposed expert system. Then the knowledge engineers extract relevant information from the experts. This process may take months or even years,

---

[21]Harvey Newquist, "The Real Thing: How Artificial Intelligence Is Changing Business," *Business Software Review* (March 1988), p. 58.

Name	Purpose	Developer
Loan Probe	To aid banks in assessing commercial loan portfolios	Peat Marwick Main & Co. (See box below.)
MYCIN	To aid physicians in diagnosing bacterial infections	Stanford University
MUDMAN	To aid in determining the suitable composition of mud for oil well drilling	N. L. Baroid
CONSULTANT	To aid field service representatives in pricing bids during competitions for computer system engagements	IBM Corporation
Mentor	To aid in diagnosing problems in air conditioning systems	Honeywell Bull
Mass Storage Advisor	To diagnose errors detected in mass storage systems	Chevron Information Technology Co.
INTERNAL CONTROL ANALYZER	To evaluate the quality of internal control in the revenue cycle	Graham Gal
AUDIT PLANNER	To aid in making materiality judgments during the planning of audits	Paul Steinbart

FIGURE 20-18 Expert system applications.

APPLICATION OF AN EXPERT SYSTEM
Peat Marwick Main & Co.[a]

Loan Probe is the name given to an expert system developed by Peat Marwick Main & Co. (PMM), one of the Big Six public accounting firms. Loan Probe is designed to aid banking clients in assessing the probable losses in their commercial loan portfolios, as well as to help bankers in calculating their loan-loss reserves. This expert loan evaluation system contains more than 6000 rules derived from those used by experts in PMM's financial services department. It was tested with banking clients whose assets ranged between $200 million and $1 billion.

In order to use Loan Probe, a user gathers data concerning both the borrower and the loan. Relevant data include the loan amount, types of collateral guarantees, and the key financial facts pertaining to the borrower. By asking a series of questions, the expert system assures that needed data are entered. When Loan Probe is satisfied that it has sufficient facts, it then produces a recommendation. It might suggest that the lending bank set aside a loan-loss reserve within a certain range. Alternatively, it might indicate that no reserve is necessary.

[a]Grace T. Chu, "Expert Systems in Computer Based Auditing," *The EDP Auditor Journal* (Vol. 1, 1989), pp. 31–32.

since it taps the accumulated knowledge and experience of the experts. From such extracted information the knowledge engineers construct (1) the production rules or semantic networks that will comprise the knowledge base and (2) the reasoning mechanisms to guide the inference engine.

After the foregoing specifications are assembled, they are encoded in a programming language. It is possible to code by means of languages such as COBOL or C. However, languages that embody reasoning and manipulate symbols are more suited to expert systems than are procedural languages that employ algorithms and perform computations. The two most commonly used reasoning-based languages are Lisp and Prolog. Lisp links lists of data stored in the knowledge base; it can perform such list manipulations as matching, sorting, summarizing, and decomposing. Prolog analyzes logical statements, determining whether they are true or false on the basis of rules and facts provided by the knowledge base.

Writing programs from scratch with the use of such languages can be very time consuming. Expert system shells have been developed to reduce the development times. An **expert system shell** is a commercial software development package that is suited for use in constructing a variety of expert systems. In effect, it is an inference engine generator. An example of an expert system shell to be used on mainframe computers is EMYCIN (a derivative of MYCIN, listed in Figure 20-18). It can generate inference systems that apply the production rules in rule-based expert systems. Microcomputer-based expert system shells include KnowledgePro (developed by Knowledge Garden), Personal Consultant (developed by Texas Instruments), and VP Expert (developed by Paperback Software).[22]

Expert systems are in their infancy. They are likely to expand greatly in sophistication in coming years and decades. One avenue of improvement lies in the movement toward computer hardware and software that imitate the cerebral neurons and networks of the human brain. These **neurocomputers** and **neural networks** should enable expert systems to combine rational problem solving with pattern recognition and other functions that involve intelligence.[23]

Summary

An information system has the purpose of supporting decision making. To do so, it employs two systems—the operational support system (OSS) and the decision support system (DSS)—to accompany the transaction processing systems (TPS). The TPS resides at the operational level and provides the framework for the routine data processing operations. In contrast, the OSS focuses on the short-term decisions made by the middle- and lower-level managers. A modern computer-based OSS exhibits interactive, time-shared, and real-time capabilities. Some OSS's also include embedded decision models and serve one particular use. The DSS focuses on the long-term strategic and tactical planning decisions made primarily by the higher-level managers. A computer-based DSS exhibits the capabilities of the OSS except for the real-time capability; on the other hand, it incorporates more complex models and other elements. Decision support may be viewed as consisting of five levels, ranging from collecting and storing data

---

[22]For examples of additional expert system shells, see William P. Martorelli, "PC-Expert Systems Arrive, *Datamation* (April 1, 1988), p. 66.

[23]James Martin, an extremely prolific computer-age author, predicts that a large neurocomputer will possess as many neurons by the year 2020 as the cerebral cortex of the human brain. See his article entitled "The State of Technology in the Second Decade of the 21st Century," in *PC Week* (November 21, 1988), p. 41.

(level 1 support) to making the decision for the manager (level 5 support). An OSS is capable of providing support at any of these levels; however, because of the unstructured nature of its decision situations, a DSS cannot provide support at the highest levels.

An effective computer-based DSS contains a variety of elements. Inputs consist of relevant and accurate data from external and internal sources. A data base consists of up-to-date and comprehensive data. A model base consists of models pertaining to all decisions within the scope of the DSS plus broad-view models of the corporate, financial planning, and portfolio types. Modeling tools include model building blocks (e.g., statistical routines) and model-based management system software. Also included are one or more modeling languages that are powerful, easy to use, and versatile. The data manipulation and analysis element includes such techniques as time-based simulation, "what if" analysis, sensitivity analysis, and goal-seeking. The information retrieval element includes a command language and assorted menus. Outputs include tailor-made (on request) hard-copy and soft-copy reports in graphical as well as tabular and textual forms. The human interface element includes model builders and users/decision makers.

Their influence is reflected by a model design that is flexible and adaptable and that accommodates differing human information processing styles. Other design considerations suggest that users should be fully involved in the design process, that the initial models should be simple, that the expanded models should be modular, that the models should accord with the firms' organizational structure and information system architecture, and that the models should be fully documented.

Other support systems are emerging. They include executive information systems and strategic support systems, which support decision making at the highest management level within firms. Expert systems are also being introduced into numerous firms. Although they are employed in managerial decision making, they differ in significant ways from the several types of support systems. Moreover, the components which they comprise include knowledge bases and inference engines rather than data bases and model bases. Expert systems are developed by drawing on the knowledge of experts, which is coded by means of special reasoning-based languages. In most cases this coding is facilitated by the use of expert system shells.

APPENDIX TO CHAPTER 20

Decision Models

This appendix reviews the various ways models can be classified. Then it focuses on models used in decision making. Decision models employed by both operational support systems and decision support systems are broadly encompassed in the discussion. Factors and relationships pertaining to decision models are illustrated by means of an optimizing model, of the type often found in operational support systems. Decision models suitable for decision support systems are illustrated applications on pages 941–948.

Classifications of Models

Models used in the business world can be classified according to their form. Engineering drawings, maps, flowcharts, and miniature versions of a firm's products are models that can be described as physical (iconic) or pictorial. Other models are symbolic or mathematical in form. An example is the general model of the accounting process, which can be stated as follows:

$$\text{Assets} = \text{Equities}$$

Decision models are generally symbolic in form, although they sometimes appear in pictorial form (e.g., the break-even chart).

A second way to classify models is by purpose. Three purposes are to describe, to predict, and to prescribe. A map, for instance, is descriptive in purpose. The accounting model may be either descriptive or predictive. When used to generate historical accounting statements, it is descriptive in purpose; when used to generate a budget, it is serving a predictive purpose. Some decision models, such as financial planning models, have predictive purposes; other decision models, such as optimizing operational models, have prescriptive or normative purposes.

Models can also be classified according to the certainty/uncertainty dimension. Models may be **deterministic**, with inputs and outputs expressed as single or point values. Deterministic models are appropriately used when values can be determined with certainty. Models may alternatively be **probabilistic**, with inputs and outputs expressed in the form of probability distributions. Probabilistic models recognize the uncertainty of future conditions. Most decision models in current use are deterministic, although instances of probabilistic decision models are beginning to appear.

Model Construction

A model is a representation of reality. In the case of a decision model, the reality represented is a real-world problem situation. As noted in Chapter 4, a decision model describes the relationships of factors that are relevant and significant to the problem situation. To develop a decision model, therefore, it is necessary first to identify (1) the factors and (2) the relationships among the factors.

Factors

The factors in a decision model consist of decision variables and parameters. **Decision variables** are factors controllable by a manager making a decision. In the case of an inventory reorder decision model, the quantity to reorder would be the key decision variable. **Parameters** are factors that are fixed or ''given'' when computations are to be performed with a model. Parameters in the case of the inventory reorder decision model include the expected demand for the inventory item in question, the cost of carrying a unit of the inventory item in stock, and the cost of placing each reorder of the inventory item with a supplier.

Relationships

One or more relationships tie together the decision variables and parameters. In the inventory reorder decision model the key relationship is as follows:

$$T = \frac{D \times O}{Q} + \frac{Q \times C}{2}$$

where
  T = the total inventory cost
  D = the expected annual demand in units
  C = the annual carrying cost per unit

O = the incremental cost to place an order

Q = the quantity to be ordered

Purpose

After the relationships have been established, the purpose of the model must be established. This purpose determines how the model will be used. As mentioned earlier, decision models have the purpose either of predicting future conditions or of indicating optimal decisions. Some decision models, such as our inventory-reorder decision model, can serve both purposes.

To use the model as a **predictor,** a manager might assume various values for the decision variable Q and observe the predicted total inventory cost for each value. He or she could also vary the values of one or more parameters in the relationship, such as the expected demand, and observe the effects on total inventory cost. By using the model in this way, the manager would gain information for planning decisions.

To use the model as a **decision selector,** the manager would focus on the decision that would minimize the total inventory cost (the criterion). Therefore, he or she would transform the model into an expression of the optimizing solution as follows.

$$EOQ = \sqrt{\frac{2 \times D \times O}{C}}$$

EOQ denotes the economic order quantity, the reorder quantity that minimizes the total inventory cost.[24] Since the expression states the means of achieving the desired objective, it is known as the **objective function** of the inventory-reorder model. The manager then would either use this objective function to decide on the quantity to reorder or allow the

[24]This computation, derived by means of differential calculus, consists of solving for the derivative of T with respect to Q and setting the expression equal to zero.

computer to make and to implement the choice.

Benefits and Limitations

A decision model such as the inventory reorder model can be very beneficial to the managers of a firm, especially when it is embedded in the firm's information system. Three key benefits of an embedded decision model are that it

1. Provides an explicit and structured representation of a problem situation.

2. Enables managers to experiment with the problem situation, so that they can gain a greater understanding of (a) the relative influence of the respective factors in the situation and (b) the decision process itself.

3. Relieves managers of personal involvement in the decision process each time certain recurring decisions must be made, so that the managers can devote their time to more complex decisions.

However, difficulties in constructing specific decision models often limit the full realization of these benefits:

1. Many decision situations involve more than one objective. In such cases it is difficult to formulate an objective function that represents suitable trade-offs among the multiple objectives.

2. Many decision situations are so complex that the relationships cannot be determined fully or the alternative courses of action cannot be identified completely.

3. Even when decision models can be expressed fully, there are many cases in which no computationally feasible procedure exists for finding optimal solutions.

4. In many situations there are factors whose values cannot easily be forecast, perhaps because of inadequate past data

or because the factors are mainly qualitative in nature.

Review Problem with Solution

Problem Statement

The Nielsen Sales Company of Youngstown, Ohio, is interested in developing a financial planning model. It intends to begin with a very simple overall model and then progress to more detailed and complex versions. Upon analyzing the basic financial trends and relationships, it discovers the following:

1. Sales have increased by about 10 percent each year for the past several years.

2. The contribution margin percentage has remained rather constant at 30 percent.

3. Fixed expenses consist of selling, administrative, and financial expenses. Selling expenses for a coming year are budgeted as 20 percent of sales for the first six months of the current year. Administrative expenses have remained constant. Financial expenses have averaged 15 percent of outstanding debt.

4. Income taxes have averaged 18 percent of profit before taxes.

Required

a. Construct a financial planning model that generates the expected sales, contribution margin, total expenses, and net profit after income taxes for a standard planning period (i.e., the coming year).

b. Compute values for the foregoing factors if the following values are assumed for the current year.

Actual sales, first six months	$1,000,000
Estimated sales, second six months	900,000
Administrative expenses	217,000
Average outstanding debt	800,000

Solution

a. Expected sales = 1.10 (sales, first six months + sales, second six months)
Expected contribution margin = 0.30 × expected sales
Expected total expenses = 0.70 × expected sales + 0.20 × sales, first six months + administrative expenses + 0.15 × outstanding debt
Expected profit before income taxes = expected sales − total expenses
Expected net profit after income taxes = (1 − 0.18) × profit before income taxes

b. Expected sales = 1.10 × ($1,000,000 + $900,000) = $2,090,000
Expected contribution margin = 0.30 × $2,090,000 = $627,000
Expected total expenses = 0.70 × $2,090,000 + 0.20 × $1,000,000 + $217,000 + 0.15 × $800,000 = $2,000,000
Expected profit before income taxes = $2,090,000 − $2,000,000 = $90,000
Expected net profit after taxes = (1 − 0.18) × $90,000 = $73,800

Review Questions

20-1   What is the meaning of each of the following terms?

Transaction processing system
Operational support system
Embedded decision model
Decision support system
Model base
User interface
Replacement level
Corporate model
Financial planning model
Portfolio model
Model-based management system
Modeling language
Time-based simulation
"What if" analysis

Sensitivity analysis
Goal-seeking analysis
Command language
Model builder
User/decision maker
Information center
Groupware
Human information processing
Executive information system
Strategic support system
Artificial intelligence
Expert system
Knowledge base
Production rule
Semantic network
Task-specific data base
Inference engine
Knowledge engineer
Expert system shell
Neurocomputer
Neural network

20-2 Why are decision support systems of particular interest to accountants?

20-3 Contrast the characteristics of transaction processing systems, operational support systems, and decision support systems.

20-4 Contrast the purposes of operational support systems and decision support systems.

20-5 What capabilities does a computer-based operational support system typically possess? A decision support system?

20-6 Identify several decisions that can be aided by (a) an operational support system and (b) a decision support system.

20-7 Contrast the five levels of decision support.

20-8 Identify the components of a decision support system.

20-9 What attributes should the input data for a decision support system possess? The data base? The outputs?

20-10 Describe the variety of models that are likely to be found in the model base of an effective decision support system.

20-11 Identify several attributes of a typical modeling language.

20-12 Contrast four data manipulation and analysis techniques.

20-13 Contrast the command language and menu information retrieval approaches.

20-14 Discuss the roles of model builders and users/decision makers in designing models, as well as the type of relationship they should foster.

20-15 Identify the array of attributes that should be possessed by a decision support system.

20-16 Describe several key considerations that pertain to the design of a decision support system.

20-17 Contrast four types of emerging support systems.

20-18 What are the key components of an executive information system?

20-19 What are the key components of an expert system?

20-20 In what significant ways does an expert system differ from a decision support system?

20-21 What are typical examples of expert systems?

Discussion Questions

20-22 Should decision support systems be real-time systems?

20-23 Can the accounting information system be viewed as a collection of integrated models?

20-24 Can a small firm justify the use of a decision support system?

20-25 Describe examples (other than those in the chapter) of systems that provide support at each of the five levels of support.

20-26 Reports on demand have become more common with the development of computer-based support systems. Ideally, should all reports be provided only on demand?

20-27 Select a strategic decision that is the joint responsibility of several vice-presidents and describe how they might be aided by a computer-based decision support system.

20-28 Discuss the problems likely to be encountered during the development and installation of a computer-based decision support system.

20-29 Discuss possible impacts of a communications-based support system on a firm's data inputs, data processing, files, reports, decision making, and organizational structure.

20-30 Although computers have been used in business applications for more than a quarter of a century, computer-based decision support systems are just now appearing in many firms. Why have they been so slow to be developed and used?

20-31 What are the objections, if any, to providing "real-time" (say, hourly) financial reports to higher-level managers?

20-32 A popular magazine has proposed that interactive terminals will appear on every manager's desk within a few years. Discuss the likelihood that this forecast will be realized and the impacts on managerial decision making if it is.

20-33 Discuss the relative advantages of optimization decision models and simulation models.

20-34 The economic order quantity model can be used to aid in making inventory reordering decisions. The linear programming model can be used to aid in making production mix decisions. Describe how the integration of these two decision models can aid in making better overall decisions within the production-inventory area of a manufacturing firm.

20-35 A multidivisional firm decides to develop a large-scale corporate model for use in budget planning and reporting. Discuss the various options that must be weighed in the design of such a model. One set of options, for example, concerns the scope of the outputs: Should reports be prepared pertaining to each division? Should corporationwide reports be prepared? Or both?

20-36 Select a strategic decision that is the responsibility of the president of a firm and describe the ways he or she might be aided by a computer-based executive information system.

Problems

20-1 For each of the following situations, identify a suitable support system and the level of support that is required or can reasonably be expected:

    a. Making of reservations by an airline.

    b. Checking of credit by a discount store.

    c. Maintaining of control over accounts receivable by a home appliance retailer.

    d. Maintaining of close control over sales and inventory by a department store.

    e. Maintaining of controls over the physical flows of job orders by a manufacturer that has a complex production process involving numerous parts and materials, labor inputs, machining operations, and inspections.

    f. Maintaining of controls over its freight cars by a railroad that carries cargo across the country.

    g. Maintaining of controls over the times and costs incurred on construction projects currently in progress by a contractor.

    h. Providing of nationwide after-sales service by a manufacturer of computer-related equipment.

i. Providing of electronic transfer of funds service by a statewide bank whose depositors can have bills debited directly from their accounts into the accounts of creditors such as utilities.

j. Providing assistance to a manufacturer in making plant location decisions.

k. Providing assistance to an architect in designing a new special-purpose building.

l. Helping a manufacturer that has alternative uses for its available production space to decide whether to make or to buy parts.

m. Providing assistance to a hospital in selecting the most suitable capital expenditure projects to undertake during the next five years.

n. Providing assistance to a drug chain in establishing pricing policies.

o. Assisting an investment counselor in managing a securities portfolio.

p. Assisting a consumer goods firm in evaluating proposals for new products.

20-2 The Industrial Savings and Loan Association of Akron, Ohio, has 50 branches throughout Ohio. It has experienced several gradually worsening problems in recent years. One problem is obtaining daily prompt summary information concerning total transactions conducted at all branches. Another problem pertains to a check-cashing service provided by the association for the purpose of attracting new depositors; occasionally a "patron" will cash bad checks at several branches in a single day, and the fact will not be discovered until the next day. A third problem has been a difficulty in developing sound appraisal values quickly when potential borrowers apply for loans on real estate. A fourth problem pertains to a poor service pattern: almost twice as many customers are serviced at a typical branch between 10:00

A.M., and 11:00 A.M. and also between 2:00 P.M. and 3:00 P.M. as during the noon hour.

Required

Describe, with the aid of diagrams, the *support systems* that could help overcome these problems. Note that a single system will likely *not* be the best solution and that a computer-based system is not the best solution to every problem. Assume that the home office currently has a medium-size computer and that each branch has a programmable calculator.

20-3 The Balboa Company of Northridge, California, is a relatively small soft-drink distributor. It recently acquired an integrated disk-oriented minicomputer system with packaged software. Interactive processing can be performed and inquiries made via any of the system's three terminals. Data within the system are retrieved by means of menus.

The first application that the firm decides to implement is the general ledger application. With the provided software package, the main menu for this application appears as the following screen:

```
        GENERAL LEDGER

          MAIN MENU
    1. JOURNAL PROCESSING
    2. FINANCIAL STATEMENTS
    3. YEAR-END CLOSING
    4. FILE MAINTENANCE
ENTER NUMBER OR COMMAND CODES
```

Number 1 is employed to enter transactions affecting general ledger accounts; number 3 is employed to process year-end closing entries; and number 4 is used to enter changes in permanent data, such as a change to an account title, into the general ledger records.

Number 2 is of particular interest to the manager, since it displays information pertaining to the financial statements. Before this type of information (and the remainder of the general ledger application) can be implemented, however, it is necessary to specify the financial statements, the chart of accounts, and the detailed data items in each general ledger account. When these specifications are provided to the software, the manager will be able to "reach" within the general ledger data base and "pull out" displays of any financial statement, or even the details of any account.

Required

Design separate menu screens that will display the following:

a. A list of the financial statements that are to be stored and available for display upon appropriate command.

b. A format of the income statement, together with general ledger account numbers. (For the purposes of this problem, the income statement may be in summarized form and employ generalized descriptions.)

c. A format of a specific asset account within the balance sheet, showing the account number, description, balance at beginning of period, debits and credits to the account (including journal reference numbers), and the current balance.

 20-4 *Note:* This problem can be solved on a microcomputer by means of an electronic financial modeling package such as Javelin or IFPS/PC.

Refer to the Review Problem. Solve for the expected net profit after taxes if each of the following changes is made. In each part return to the "base" model formula and values given in the Review Problem.

a. Sales are expected to increase by 20 percent in the coming year.

b. Actual sales for the first six months were $800,000.

c. Administrative expenses are expected to increase by $83,000 during the coming year.

d. Financial expenses are expected to average 20 percent of outstanding debt in the coming year (and debt is expected to remain at the present level).

20-5 The Speedy Bike Company of Cambridge, Massachusetts, sells bicycles to bike shops, department stores, and discount stores throughout the country. It employs eight salespersons, each of whom covers several states. Because sales trends are extremely important to its success, the firm carefully records considerable data concerning each sale and stores the data, in coded form, within a sales data base. Any manager can retrieve desired data, via interactive terminals, from this data base by means of Englishlike commands. Software within the system can select data, arrange data, and compute totals as specified by the commands.

Each sales transaction, broken down according to product characteristics, is stored according to the following format. (The transaction code is omitted.)

Product number 1a	Wheel size 2–3	Color 4	Style 5	Sales territory 6–7

Outlet 8–10	Salesperson number 11	Date 12–16	Blank 17	Quantity 18–20

aDigit position(s) pertaining to each field.

Codes, on a selected basis, are as follows.

Product number: 1, single speed; 2, three-speed; 3, five-speed; 4, ten-speed standard; 5, ten-speed deluxe

Color: 1, blue; 2, red; 3, green; 4, tan; 5, black; 6, orange; 7, yellow.

Style: 1, male; 2, female.

Salesperson: 1, Jake; 2, Julie; 3, Sam; 4, Cindy; 5, Mac; 6, Marsha; 7, Rick; 8, Trish.

Following is the set of transactions for the first day of May:

```
2262214310705012 005
4261114310705012 021
3263108181205012 010
4275108181205012 003
4262222057405012 090
4261110263105012 030
3263110571105012 020
1244116208605012 004
5262116208605012 006
4261216433605012 012
```

Required

On the basis of this very limited sample, specify the responses that the system would provide to a manager who enters the following commands:

a. NAME PRODUCT THAT HAD MOST UNIT SALES.

b. NAME WHEEL SIZE THAT HAD LEAST UNIT SALES.

c. LIST COLORS THAT HAD NO UNIT SALES.

d. LIST TWO TOP SALESPERSONS IN ORDER OF UNITS SOLD AND UNIT SALES OF EACH.

e. LIST UNIT SALES BY TERRITORY AND TOTAL.

20-6 You are the sales manager of the recently-formed Vega Corporation, which sells two products in three sales territories. The contents of two files of keen interest to you contain the up-to-date information shown at the bottom of the page. Vega has installed an interactive decision support system for use by you and the other managers. The system includes a command language, a relational data base, and a report generator.

Sales File

Date of Sale	Sales Invoice No.	Customer Name	Sales Terr.	Product Name[a]	Quantity Sold	Amount of Sale
Jan. 2	1	D. Smith	B	Alpha	3	30.00
Jan. 3	2	F. Brown	A	Omega	8	160.00
Jan. 5	3	M. Mosley	C	Omega	5	100.00
Jan. 8	4	G. Dane	C	Omega	10	200.00
Jan. 8	5	O. Lamm	A	Alpha	6	60.00
Jan. 9	6	P. Piper	A	Alpha	10	100.00
Jan. 10	7	S. White	B	Omega	7	140.00
Jan. 12	8	H. Rosner	C	Alpha	12	120.00

[a]Only one product may be recorded on a single invoice.

Product File

Product Name	Description	Unit Cost	Unit Price	Supplier Name	Quantity on Hand
Alpha	Whirl	7.00	10.00	Cody	150
Omega	Swirl	16.00	20.00	Barker	80

Required

Show the report that the system would provide if you enter each of the following command statements:

a. REFER TO SALES FILE
PRINT DATE AND NAME AND
AMOUNT
BY TERRITORY

b. REFER TO SALES FILE
PRINT AMOUNT AND NAME
BY TERRITORY
RANKED BY AMOUNT
IF AMOUNT LESS THAN $100, OMIT

c. JOIN SALES AND PRODUCT FILES
PRINT CENTERED HEADING
"SALES SUMMARY"
SUM UNIT SALES AND AMOUNTS
BY PRODUCT
PRINT TOTALS AFTER NAME AND
DESCRIPTION AND SUPPLIER
PRINT GRAND TOTALS, UNIT
SALES AND AMOUNT

20-7 The Saferoads Auto Insurance Co. of Dallas, Texas, sells automobile insurance throughout the southern and southwestern states. A regional sales and claims office is located in each of the states serviced. Each regional office is headed by a regional manager; a regional sales manager and a claims manager report directly to the regional manager. These managers, plus the key managers in the home office, need a variety of timely and relevant information to aid in decision making.

Required

a. For each of the following, identify two key decisions that could be aided by a support system.

(1) President.
(2) Regional manager.
(3) Regional sales manager.

(4) Regional claims manager.
(5) Insurance agent.

b. Describe, with the aid of diagrams, two separate computer-based support systems (an OSS and a DSS) that would be useful to Saferoads. Include system structures, levels of support, and design features in your descriptions.

20-8 The Fast Track Racing Association of Tallahassee, Florida, intends to establish an information service.[25] Subscribers to the service will be able to obtain information about racehorses, jockeys, and trainers. Data will be collected concerning the breeding and age of a horse, plus its form, starting odds, jockey, and trainer in each previous race and the upcoming races in which it has been entered. Other data to be collected will include the training, experience, and track history for each jockey and trainer, as well as the track conditions for the major tracks throughout the country during the racing days of the past two years. Up-to-the-minute data will also be provided concerning the latest official bookmaking prices and odds on each horse in upcoming races. Several thousand horses, several hundred jockeys and trainers, and several dozen tracks will be involved.

Required

a. Identify the key decision to be supported by this service, and design outputs that contain information useful to the subscribers.

b. Describe and justify a suitable decision support system for this information service, including the level of support that it should provide and the design features that it should incorporate.

---

[25]Based on a problem given in a Master of Science examination by the University of London and published in R. I. Tricker, *Management Information and Control Systems* (New York: John Wiley, 1976), p. 290. Used with permission.

20-9 For several years the Programme Corporation of Urbana,
Illinois, has encountered difficulties estimating its cash flows. The result has
been a rather strained relationship with its
banker.

Programme's controller would like to
develop a means by which he can forecast
and plan the firm's monthly operating cash
flows. The following data was gathered to
facilitate cash forecasting and planning.

a. Sales have been and are expected
to increase at 0.5 percent each
month.

b. Of each month's sales, 30 percent
are for cash; the other 70 percent
are on open account.

c. Of the credit sales, 90 percent are
collected in the first month following the sale and the remaining 10
percent are collected in the second
month. There are no bad debts.

d. Gross margin (profit) on sales averages 25 percent.

e. Sufficient inventory purchases are
made each month to cover the following month's sales.

f. All inventory purchases are paid
for in the month of purchase at a 2
percent cash discount.

g. Monthly expenses are payroll,
$1500; rent, $400; depreciation,
$120; other cash expenses, 2 per-
cent of that month's sales. There
are no accruals.

h. Ignore the effects of corporate income taxes, dividends, and equipment acquisitions.

Required

a. Construct a financial planning model that
generates the monthly operating cash inflows and outflows for any specified
month.

b. If sales for the current month are $10,000,

compute the cash inflows and outflows for
the next two months.

c. "What if" the sales are expected to increase at 1.0 percent per month in the future? Determine the changes in the
amounts of the cash inflows and outflows
for the next two months, assuming that
sales for the current month remain at the
level of $10,000.

d. "What if" monthly inventory purchases
are changed to cover the average of one-
half the current month's sales and one-
half the following month's sales. Show
the change to the financial planning model
and determine the changes in cash outflows for the next two months, assuming
the conditions specified in **a** above.

e. Often a cash forecast is used to determine
the expected level of cash at the end of
each month. Assume that this model is
expanded to include the calculation of the
expected level of cash. Assume further
that the forecast for a following month
shows that the cash balance is $2000
lower than desired but that the firm prefers not to borrow money to raise the cash
balance to the desired level. Describe a
type of analysis that can aid in determining other means by which to raise the cash
balance to the desired level.

(CMA adapted)

 20-10 The Star Manufacturing
Company of Memphis, Tennessee, produces plastic mouldings.[26]
It has recently been considering whether it
should introduce a new product. Before a decision to introduce the product can be made,
a sales price and an appropriate level of marketing expenditures must be determined. On
May 1 the marketing vice-president receives
a market research report on the product,

[26]Adapted from John Dearden and F. Warren Mc-
Farland, *Management Information Systems: Text and
Cases* (Homewood, Ill.: Richard D. Irwin, 1966), pp.
368–369. Copyright © 1966. Used with permission.

which provides the following information about anticipated demand, assuming that the product is introduced on January 1 of next year.

a. No sales will be generated if the product is sold at a price as great as $5 per unit. Since the product's variable costs of manufacture will be $1 per unit, prices below this cost will not be feasible.

b. If no marketing expenditures are undertaken, 100,000 units should be sold in January at a price of $1. It is further estimated that a linear relationship will exist between prices and monthly sales volumes. Thus, at $2 the volume will be 75,000 units; at $4 the volume will be 25,000 units (still assuming no marketing expenditures).

c. Marketing expenditures will increase the product's sales by $0.1 \times M/(0.001M + 5)$ percent over what they will be if no expenditures are made, where M stands for marketing expenditures in dollars. Hence, $10,000 of marketing expenditures will be expected to generate a percent increase in sales **units** of

$$\frac{0.1 \times 10,000}{0.001 \times 10,000 + 5} = \frac{1000}{10 + 5}$$

$$= \frac{1000}{15}$$

$$= 66.6$$

d. The demand is subject to seasonal effects, as reflected by the following indices: Jan., 1.0; Feb., 1.2; Mar., 1.4; Apr., 1.6; May, 1.4; June, 1.2; July, 1.0; Aug., 0.8; Sept., 0.6; Oct., 0.4; Nov., 0.6; Dec., 0.8. Thus, in March, 140,000 units can be sold at a price of $1, assuming no marketing expenditures.

e. Fixed costs related to the product will be $30,000 per month.

f. Ignore the effects of corporate income taxes.

Required

a. Construct a financial planning model for use by the Star Manufacturing Company in evaluating the new product decision.

b. Determine by simulation the expected profit that would be received in January and February if the product is introduced and the sales price is set as $2 and if marketing expenditures are to be $6000 per month.

c. "What if" the sales price is set as $3? Determine the change in the expected profit for January, assuming that other factors remain the same.

d. "What if" marketing expenditures are to be $10,000? Determine the change in the expected profit for January, assuming that other factors remain the same.

e. Forecasted sales cannot be known with certainty. Assume that the market research report indicated that at a sales price of $1 and with no marketing expenditures, the probabilities for January's sales are as follows:

(1) Probability of 0.2 that 80,000 units will be sold.

(2) Probability of 0.4 that 100,000 units will be sold.

(3) Probability of 0.4 that 130,000 units will be sold.

Using a table of random numbers, perform five simulations for the month of January, list the resulting profits, and compute the average (expected) profit. Explain the results.

20-11 Meesar Company manufactures a variety of products for the consumer market. One of these is a lawn sprinkler for use by homeowners.

The company has developed guidelines that it attempts to follow for inventory levels and production quantities of lawn sprinklers. Jon Yoon, manager of planning in Meesar's accounting department, believes that these guidelines can be captured in a financial model that would aid in planning and controlling operations. If a financial model for lawn sprinklers can be developed successfully, then similar models could be developed for Meesar's other products as well.

The guidelines that Meesar generally has been following are

- Finished-goods inventory at the end of a month should be equal to 25 percent of the next month's expected sales.

- Work-in-process inventory at the end of a month should be equal to 40 percent of the next month's expected sales. The work-in-process inventory should be 100 percent complete as to direct materials and 80 percent complete as to conversion costs.

- Direct materials inventory at the end of a month should be equal to the quantity needed to complete the coming month's expected sales plus the direct materials required to meet the finished-goods inventory requirement at the end of the coming month.

- Direct materials are purchased during a month to meet all inventory and production requirements for that month.

- Production for a month should generate enough units to meet the expected sales for the month.

- During the year, the direct material purchase and production requirement for a month are adjusted for any differences between the expected and actual sales of the prior month.

On the basis of these guidelines, Yoon has developed the components of the following lawn sprinkler financial planning model. The only component Yoon has not yet developed is the formula for the equivalent production

in lawn sprinkler units for the conversion costs (M_n). The explanations of the notation used follow the formulas.

Formulas:

$$ES_n = \sum_{i=1}^{3} S_{ni}p_i$$
$$FG_n = .25\ ES_{n+1}$$
$$WIP_n = .40\ ES_{n+1}$$
$$DM_n = .35\ ES_{n+1} + .25\ ES_{n+2}$$
$$P_n = .75\ ES_{n+1} + .25\ ES_{n+2}$$
$$P'_n = .75\ ES_{n+1} + .25\ ES_{n+2} + (AS_{n-1} - ES_{n-1})$$

Notation:

n = current month (1 = January, 2 = February, etc.).

i = one of three probability levels (i.e., optimistic, average, pessimistic).

S_{ni} = one of three estimated sales volume levels for a month.

p_i = one of three probability levels for estimated sales volume levels for a month.

ES_n = expected sales volume in lawn sprinkler units for month n.

FG_n = finished-goods inventory in lawn sprinkler units at the end of month n.

WIP_n = work-in-process inventory in lawn sprinkler units at the end of month n.

DM_n = direct materials inventory in lawn sprinkler units at the end of month n.

P_n = lawn sprinkler units of direct material that should be purchased in month n (no adjustment factor included because prior month's actual sales are not known).

P'_n = lawn sprinkler units of direct material that should be purchased in month n when actual sales from prior month are known (adjustment factor included).

AS_n = actual sales in lawn sprinkler units for month n.

$(AS_{n-1} - ES_{n-1})$ = adjustment factor for month n when actual sales differ from expected sales in month $n - 1$.

M_n = equivalent production in lawn sprinkler units for conversion costs during month n.

Meesar's estimated sales of lawn sprinklers for the first six months of 1991 and the standard cost for a lawn sprinkler follow.

Estimated Sales Volume in Units

	Optimistic ($p = .2$)	Average ($p = .5$)	Pessimistic ($p = .3$)
January	20,000	18,000	15,000
February	25,000	20,000	18,000
March	26,000	22,000	20,000
April	24,000	20,000	17,000
May	21,000	18,000	14,000
June	16,000	15,000	10,000

Standard Cost:

Direct material		
Aluminum	.8 lb @ $2.50/lb	$ 2.00
Plastic	.4 lb @ $7.50/lb	3.00
Direct labor	.6 hr @ $12.50/hr	7.50
Manufacturing overhead	.6 hr @ $2.50/hr	1.50
Total standard cost		$14.00

Required

a. Using the formulas that Jon Yoon has developed, calculate the following items for March 1991:

(1) The number of lawn sprinklers that should be in the finished-goods inventory at the end of March.

(2) The number of lawn sprinklers that should be in the work-in-process inventory at the end of March.

(3) The pounds of aluminum that should be in the direct materials inventory at the end of March.

b. Assume that Meesar Company would actually sell 16,000 lawn sprinklers in January and 22,000 in February. Calculate the number of pounds of plastic Meesar would purchase in March in this situation.

c. Develop the formula in terms of expected sales that would be used to determine the equivalent production in lawn sprinkler units for conversion costs during a month without regard to any adjustment factor for the difference between actual and expected sales (i.e., the formula for M_n).

(CMA adapted)

20-12 Identify which of the following problem situations are most suitable for the application of expert systems. Briefly describe the construction of the expert system in each such case.

a. Determining whether an order from a customer should be accepted.

b. Determining whether the internal control structure of a firm is adequate.

c. Determining whether the balance of a general ledger account is material.

d. Determining the amounts to allocate to a firm's organizational units via an operational budget.

e. Determining the variety of activities to be undertaken by a manager during the course of a workday.

f. Determining the stocks to select for an investment portfolio.

g. Determining the particular computer system to select for a firm's business data processing applications.

h. Determining the quantity of an inventory item to reorder.

i. Determining whether the financial position of a firm is sound.

20-13 As a knowledge engineer, you have been consulted about the construction of an expert system to aid in personal investing. You begin by investigating the variety of factors that influence the investment environment for individuals. Some of the factors you discover are income level, amount of savings, amount of insurance coverage required, amount of emergency funds required, marital status, and investment objectives. Then you consider the various investment options, such as money market fund, bond fund, and stock fund.

Required

Describe how you would continue in developing a rule-based expert system, including in your description (1) typical questions that the system should ask the potential investor in order to develop the task-specific data base, (2) typical rules that might be found in the knowledge base, and (3) several suggested recommendations that the expert system might provide to the potential investor.

20-14 Citizens' Gas Company is a distribution firm that provides natural gas service to approximately 200,000 customers in Louisiana. The customer base is divided into three revenue classes. Data by customer class appear in the following table:

Class	Customers	Sales in Cubic Feet	Revenues
Residential	160,000	80 billion	$160 million
Commercial	38,000	15 billion	25 million
Industrial	2,000	50 billion	65 million
		145 billion	$250 million

Residential customer gas usage is primarily for residence heating purposes, and consequently it is highly correlated to the weather (i.e., temperature). Commercial and industrial customers, on the other hand, may or may not use gas for heating purposes, and consumption is not necessarily correlated to the weather.

The largest 25 out of the total of 2000 industrial customers account for $30 million of the industrial revenues. Each of these 25 customers uses gas for both heating and industrial purposes and has a consumption pattern governed almost entirely by business factors.

The company obtains its gas supply from 10 major pipeline companies. The pipeline companies provide gas in amounts specified in contracts and extending over periods ranging from 5 to 15 years. For some contracts the supply is in equal monthly increments, whereas for others the supply varies in accordance with the heating season. Supply over and above the contract amounts is not available, and some contracts contain take-or-pay clauses—that is, the company must pay for the volumes specified in the contract, whether or not it can take the gas.

To assist in matching customer demand with supply, the company maintains a gas storage field. Gas can be pumped into the storage field when supply exceeds customer demand; likewise, gas can be obtained when demand exceeds supply. There are no restrictions on the use of the gas storage field except that the field must be filled to capacity at the beginning of each gas year (September 1). Consequently, whenever the contractual supply for gas for the remainder of the gas year is less than that required to satisfy projected demand and replenish the storage field, the company must curtail service to the industrial customers (except for quantities that are used for heating). The curtailments must be carefully controlled, so that an oversupply does not occur at year's end. Similarly, care must be taken to ensure that curtailments are adequate during the year, to protect against the need to curtail commercial or residential customers in order to replenish the storage field at year's end.

In recent years, the company's planning efforts have not provided a firm basis for the establishment of long-term contracts. The current year has been no different. Planning efforts have not been adequate to control the supply during the current gas year. Customer demand has been projected only as a function of the total number of customers. Commercial and industrial customers' demand for gas has been curtailed excessively. This has resulted in lost sales and caused an excess of supply at the end of the gas year.

In an attempt to correct the problems of Citizens' Gas, the president has hired a new director of corporate planning and has instructed the director to present him with a conceptual design of a system to assist in the analysis of the supply and demand of natural gas. The system should provide a monthly gas plan for each year for the next five years, with particular emphasis on the first year of the plan. The plan should provide a set of reports that will assist in the decision-making process and that will contain all necessary supporting schedules. The system must provide for the use of actual data during the course of the first year to project demand for the rest of the year and the year in total. The president has indicated to the director that he will base his decisions on the effect on operating income of alternative plans.

Required

a. Identify the criteria on which this executive information system (or strategic support system) is to be based.

b. Describe the design features of the system that the new director should propose to aid in planning the firm's natural gas needs, including the user interface.

c. Identify key information that should be incorporated into the system; explain why each item is important to the decision situation.

d. Design the format of at least one report that can aid the decision-making process.

(CMA adapted)

20-15 Ace Corporation has been a leading manufacturer of cash registers and accounting and proofing machines for almost 50 years. Much of Ace's success can be attributed to an extensive and excellent marketing organization and its reputation for reliable business machines within the retailing and banking industries.

Until the 1960s Ace's equipment was primarily mechanical with minimal electronic components. However, many of the mechanical components in business machines were replaced by electronic counterparts in the 1960s; these electronic components were cheaper and more efficient and provided additional machine flexibility. Ace's management has been reluctant to switch from its old-line mechanical machines to new electronic systems because of the heavy investment in engineering development and manufacturing facilities for mechanical systems. Competitive pressure from new electronic machines has caused a rapid deterioration in Ace's market share and profit margins. Consequently, management has decided to initiate a program to introduce new lines of electronic business machines as replacements for its current mechanical machines.

Although this new electronic equipment will be introduced several years after the competitor's electronic equipment, management believes that further deterioration in Ace's market position can be prevented by capitalizing on some of Ace's strong points. Ace has a superior sales force, which has maintained good relations with the retail and banking industries. Traditionally, Ace's customers have replaced or upgraded their old equipment with Ace equipment. Ace's new line could incorporate unique features that the competition lacks, thereby making it more attractive to customers.

Developing new products at Ace has been primarily the responsibility of the development and engineering research department (DER) in conjunction with the marketing and manufacturing departments. DER primarily is responsible for developing product specifications, building and field testing prototype products, and evaluating any changes in manufacturing facilities which may be required. Once a product is approved for sale and production, it is released to the manufacturing department for production.

Numerous changes have to be made in all three departments. For example, DER needs additional strengths in electronics engineering. Marketing needs to reorient its sales force. Manufacturing needs to retool extensively and retrain its maintenance and service personnel. Much of the present manufacturing equipment and inventory of unfinished goods would become obsolete.

Another option available to Ace's management would be to approach an outside equipment manufacturer to produce part or all of the new equipment. In this case Ace would determine the specifications for the new equipment and then have it engineered and/or manufactured, in whole or in part, by outside firms. The equipment would be marketed under the Ace label.

Management has asked its staff to recommend a suitable strategy for transforming Ace Corporation from a supplier of primarily mechanical machines to a company offering electronic systems. The staff specifically has been asked to study the ramifications of Ace (1) developing and manufacturing new equipment in house or (2) approach an outside manufacturer to produce equipment according to Ace's specifications which would then be marketed under the Ace label. Management has instructed its staff to consider the broad financial, technological, organizational, and market conditions and constraints in developing its strategy.

The current statement of financial position for Ace Corporation is presented below. Selected five-year averages for the most recent five years are as follows:

Operating margin (before taxes)	12%
Annual increase in net income	11%
Return on sales	5%
Return on investment	7%
Return on equity	16%

Ace Corporation
Statement of Financial Position
May 31, 1990
(in millions of dollars)

Current assets	
Cash and equivalents	$ 15
Accounts receivable (net)	148
Inventories	
Materials and supplies	25
Work in process	14
Finished goods	56
Prepaid expenses and deposits	10
Total current assets	$268
Plant and equipment	
Land	4
Buildings	69
Machinery and equipment	140
Construction in progress	5
Accumulated depreciation	(101)
Equipment on rental (net)	8
Other assets (net)	18
Total assets	$411
Current liabilities	
Notes and loans payable	$ 15
Accounts payable	42
Accrued payroll and other expenses	37
Current maturities of long-term debt	3
Income taxes	14
Total current liabilities	$111
Long-term debt	
9¼% sinking fund debentures (due in 10 years)	25
8½% senior notes (due in 14 years)	60
Other long-term debt	36
Deferred income taxes	15
Total liabilities	$247
Stockholders' equity	
Common stock (par value, $1.00)	$ 9
Additional paid in capital	11
Retained earnings	144
Total stockholders' equity	$164
Total liabilities and stockholders' equity	$411

Required

a. Describe the features of a computer-based strategic support system that might be constructed to aid in developing and updating strategies for transforming the product orientation of Ace.

b. Identify information to be incorporated into the strategic support system. Include information relating to technological, financial, organizational, and market considerations.

c. Describe the features of a computer-based decision support system that can be constructed to aid in developing the recommendation concerning the specific make-or-buy decision.

(CMA adapted)

20-16 Colorful Building Materials, Inc., of Portland, Maine, produces bricks and concrete blocks for use in building homes and business facilities.[27] Most customers are building contractors and brick and masonry suppliers. A wide variety of bricks and blocks are manufactured, both for inventory and for filling customers' orders. For each size, shape, and color there is a unique mix of raw materials. For instance, a particular variety of concrete block would contain an established mixture of cement, sand, silica, color, admix, and premix.

Production essentially consists of (1) mixing the ingredients for a batch, (2) feeding the mix into molding machines and applying heat, (3) removing the bricks or blocks from the machines and stacking them on pallets, and (4) storing in the yard or shipping to a customer. The production planning and control cycles involve

a. Production planning, which consists of forecasting sales and inventory needs, setting production levels, and preparing production orders to replenish needed inventory.

b. Order entry, which consists of receiving sales orders and either shipping from inventory or preparing related production orders.

c. Materials requirements planning, which consists of determining the quantities of materials needed to be purchased to cover planned production orders.

d. Machine loading and scheduling, which consists of projecting machine and labor loads and preparing short-range production schedules.

The production cycle for planning is a month, whereas the production cycle for short-range scheduling is a week in length. Most orders from customers are received with delivery due in seven days, although about 20 percent of orders are rush orders. Because of competitive conditions, the firm feels that it must handle all rush orders as soon as possible; however, it charges a premium price for such service. The typical orders received from a customer involve a variety of bricks and concrete blocks.

Files employed by Colorful include

a. Bill of materials, showing quantities of materials used in one batch of a product.

b. Operations routing, showing the series of operations and corresponding times to manufacture a batch of a product.

c. Inventory file, showing on-hand quantities for all products, computed from beginning balances and quantities produced and sold.

d. Open production order file, showing the status of all production orders.

e. Materials file, showing quantities of raw materials on hand and on order.

f. Factory schedule, showing the starting and completion times, by operations, for all orders in production.

Currently, the firm employs on-line computer-based transaction processing systems to maintain these files and prepare the outputs. However, the computer-based systems are not designed to provide needed information for decision making (other than the status reports and production schedule).

Required

a. List decisions pertaining to logistics that must be made by managers.

b. Describe the features of a decision support system that could aid managers in making needed tactical and strategic planning decisions relating to logistics. Include descriptions of useful outputs.

c. Describe the features of an executive information system that could aid the president in developing strategies and policies concerning markets and products.

d. Contrast the information needs for the decision support system and executive information system.

Suggested Readings

Akers, Michael D., and Porter, Grover L. "Expert Systems for Management Accountants." *Management Accounting* (March 1986), pp. 30–38.

Applegate, Lynda A.; Konsynski, Benn R.; and Nunamaker, Jay F. "Model Management Systems: Design for Decision Support." *Decision Support Systems* (March 1986), pp. 81–91.

Andersen, Anker V. *Graphing Financial Information: How Acountants Can Use Graphs to Communicate.* New York: National Association of Accountants, 1983.

Barbary, Clifton L. "A Database Primer on Natural Language." *Journal of Systems Management* (Feb. 1987), pp. 12–17.

Benson, Beth A. "Computer Graphics for Financial Management." *Management Accounting* (January 1984), pp. 46–49.

Borthick, A. Faye, and West, Owen D. "Expert Systems—A New Tool for the Professional." *Accounting Horizons* (March 1987), pp. 9–16.

Chandrasekaran, G., and Ramesh, R. "Microcomputer-Based Multiple Criteria Decision Support System for Strategic Planning." *Information and Management* (April 1987), pp. 163–172.

Crescenzi, Adam D., and Kocher, Jerry. "Management Support Systems: Opportunity for Controllers." *Management Accounting* (March 1984), pp. 34–37.

Dahn, Richard L., and Coleman, John R. "A Computerized Financial Planning Model for a HMO." *Omega* (No. 3, 1982), pp. 267–278.

Davenport, Thomas H.; Hammer, Michael; and Metsisto, Tauno J. "How Executives Can Shape Their Company's Information System." *Harvard Business Review* (March–April 1989), pp. 130–134.

Davis, Gordon B., and Olsen, Margrethe H. *Management Information Systems: Conceptual Foundations, Structure, and Development.* 2d ed. New York: McGraw-Hill, 1985.

Davis, Michael W. "Anatomy of Decision Support." *Datamation* (June 15, 1984), pp. 201–208.

Donnelly, Robert M. "Keep Up with Decision Support Systems." *Financial Executive* (August 1983), pp. 44–46.

El-Badawi, Mohamed H. "A Computerized Corporate Financial Model." *Cost and Management* (March–April 1984), pp. 22–27.

Ford, F. Nelson. "Decision Support Systems and Expert Systems: A Comparison." *Information and Management* (1985), pp. 21–26.

Fredericks, Peter, and Venkatraman, N. "The Rise of Strategy Support Systems." *Sloan Management Review* (Spring 1988), pp. 47–54.

Gallagher, John P. *Knowledge Systems for Business: Integrating Expert Systems & MIS*. Englewood Cliffs, N.J.: Prentice Hall, 1988.

Head, Robert V. "Information Resource Center: A New Force in End User Computing." *Journal of Systems Management* (February 1985), pp. 24–29.

Iyer, Raja K. "Information and Modeling Resources for Decision Support in Global Environments." *Information and Management* (Feb. 1988), pp. 67–73.

Johnson, Bart. "Why Your Company Needs Three Accounting Systems." *Management Accounting* (September 1984), pp. 39–46.

Kaplan, S. Jerrold, and Ferris, David. "Natural Language in the DP World." *Datamation* (August 1982), pp. 114–120.

Kleim, Richard. "Computer-Based Financial Modeling." *Journal of Systems Management* (May 1982), pp. 6–13.

Leigh, William E., and Doherty, Michael E. *Decision Support and Expert Systems*. Cincinnati: South-Western Publishing Co., 1986.

Leonard-Barton, Dorothy, and Sviokla, John J. "Putting Expert Systems to Work." *Harvard Business Review* (March-April 1988), pp. 91–98. McCartney, Laton. "The New Info Centers." *Datamation* (July 1983), pp. 30–46.

Liang, Ting-peng. "Expert Systems as Decision Aids: Issues and Strategies." *Journal of Information Systems* (Spring 1988), pp. 41–50.

Luconi, Fred L.; Malone, Thomas W.; and Scott Morton, Michael S. "Expert Systems: The Next Challenge for Managers." *Sloan Management Review* (Summer 1986).

McKee, Thomas R. "Does Your Practice Have a Place for an Expert System?" *The CPA Journal* (January 1988), pp. 114–118.

Murry, John P. "How an Information Center Improved Productivity." *Management Accounting* (March 1984), pp. 38–44.

Necco, Charles R., and Tsai, Nancy W. "Use of Fourth Generation Languages: Application Development and Documentation Problems." *Journal of Systems Management* (August 1988), pp. 26–33.

Neumann, Seev, and Hadass, Michael. "DSS and Strategic Decisions." *California Management Review* (Spring 1980), pp. 77–84.

Pappas, Richard A., and Remer, Donald S. "Status of Corporate Planning Models." *Managerial Planning* (March–April 1984), pp. 4–16.

Ramesh, R., and Sekar, G. Chandra. "An Integrated Framework for Decision Support in Corporate Planning." *Decision Support Systems* (No. 4, 1988), pp. 365–375.

Rector, Robert L. "Decision Support Systems—Strategic Planning Tool." *Managerial Planning* (May–June 1983), pp. 36–41.

Rockart, John F., and Treacy, Michael E.

"The CEO Goes On-Line." *Harvard Business Review* (Jan.–Feb. 1982), pp. 82–88.

Rodenbeck, Julia M. "Financial Modeling on the Micro." *Managerial Planning* (Nov.–Dec. 1983), pp. 26–29.

Seilheimer, Steven D. "Current State of Decision Support System and Expert System Technology." *Journal of Systems Management* (August 1988), pp. 14–19.

Sheil, Beau. "Thinking about Artificial Intelligence." *Harvard Business Review* (July–August 1987), pp. 91–97.

Sprague, Ralph H. "A Framework for the Development of Decision Support Systems." *MIS Quarterly* (December 1980), pp. 1–26.

Sprague, Ralph H., and Carlson, Eric D. *Building Effective Decision Support Systems*. Englewood Cliffs, N.J.: Prentice-Hall, 1982.

Summer, Mary, and Benson, Robert. "The Impact of Fourth Generation Languages on Systems Development." *Information and Management* (Feb. 1988), pp. 81–92.

Thierauf, Robert J. *User-Oriented Decision Support Systems: Accent on Problem Finding*. Englewood Cliffs, N.J.: Prentice Hall, 1988.

Wagner, G. R. "Decision Support Systems: Computerized Mind Support for Executive Problems." *Managerial Planning* (Sep.–Oct. 1981).

Watkins, Paul R. "Perceived Information Structure: Implications for Decision Support System Design." *Decision Sciences* (January 1982), pp. 38–59.

Part **V**

SYSTEMS DEVELOPMENT LIFE CYCLE

An information system undergoes *system life cycles*—that is, it passes through stages that begin with conception, lead to birth, progress through adolescence to maturity, and end in death. Out of death usually emerges the conception for a new system generation, and thus the cycle begins again. Of particular interest is the period from conception to birth, during which the new system is developed. Generally this developmental period is subdivided into several phases for closer study and management control. Chapters 21 through 25 span these developmental phases, which include systems planning, systems analysis, systems design, systems justification and selection, and systems implementation. Two other topics are also included in these chapters. The organization of the systems function is discussed in Chapter 21, and the operational stage is discussed in Chapter 25.

After studying this chapter, you should be able to do the following:

Survey the organization of the information systems function, including its location within the overall organizational structure as well as its own internal structure.

Discuss the dynamic management perspective known as information resource management.

Describe the major considerations pertaining to the development of new or revised information systems, including the underlying reasons, approaches to development, levels of development, and development sequence.

Identify the key steps in the planning phase of a systems development.

Identify the key steps involved in the definition and initiation of a project to develop a module within an information system.

Chapter *21*

SYSTEMS ORGANIZATION AND PLANNING

Information systems are playing an increasingly important role in typical modern firms. They are being called on to process ever-larger volumes of transaction data. Often they are designed to maintain up-to-date records that can be accessed from many miles away. Moreover, as outlined in the last chapter, they are being used more than ever before to support managerial decisions of all types.

This growing importance of information systems is reflected in various ways. For instance, the budget for the information systems function has mushroomed in many firms. Also, the job activities of most employees and many managers have been significantly affected.

Because the typical information system has assumed a greater importance, all related

facets have taken on added importance. Two matters of particular concern are (1) the organization of the information systems function and (2) the orderly planning of information systems development. This chapter will explore both of these matters. Furthermore, our exploration of the respective phases of systems development will continue throughout the remaining chapters of the book.

Organization of the Systems Function

Four major questions must be answered concerning the organization of the systems function:

1. To whom should the information systems manager report within the organization?

2. What should be the nature of the information systems function, with respect to size, structure, and responsibilities?

3. To what extent should the organizational structure of the information systems function be centralized or decentralized?

4. What should be the interactions between the information systems function and groups such as the accounting function and outside consultants?

Location of the Systems Function

Traditionally, the responsibility for providing information to the managers of a firm and to outside parties has fallen within the province of the accounting or the controllership function. In order to fulfill this responsibility, the controller generally has supervised the activities related to the development and operation of the information system.

Since the advent of computers and the emergence of new functional information systems, however, this responsibility has been shifting. In many firms the information systems function has been organizationally relocated. Instead of being under the jurisdiction of the controller, it has been placed in such firms under the responsibility of a non-accounting manager. In many cases this non-accounting manager is on a higher managerial level within the organization than the controller.

On the other hand, this trend has not become an avalanche. A number of firms still retain the controller as the overseer of the systems function. Thus, the traditional organizational arrangement must offer advantages that compete with those provided by the newer arrangements.

The controller as the overseer.   Figure 21-1, a partial organization chart, portrays the traditional arrangement. The information systems manager (the actual title may differ) reports to the controller, who in turn is under the jurisdiction of the vice-president of finance.

This arrangement has several advantages. First, because it is traditional and ac-

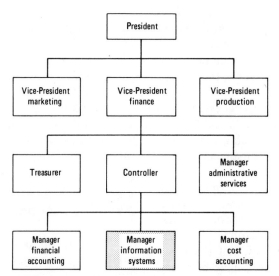

FIGURE 21-1 An organizational structure in which the controller oversees the information systems function.

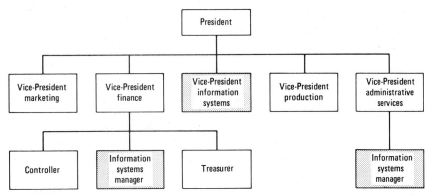

FIGURE 21-2   Three possible overseers of the information systems function and its managers.

cepted, it avoids the trauma of a severe organizational change. Second, and more
important, this arrangement reflects the central role of the accounting function in transaction processing and financial reporting.
The accounting function is responsible for
most of the transactions to be processed; it
also has the task of providing financial information to managers in functions throughout
a firm and to persons outside the firm. Third,
since many of the earliest and most successful computer applications concerned such
accounting activities as payroll, accounts receivable, and inventory control, the accountants who were responsible for, or at least
involved in, such applications have solid experience in systems development.

The controller is perhaps the crucial factor in such an arrangement. If the controller
fully understands the information needs of
managers in all of the nonaccounting functions, and if he or she has a solid grounding
in the fundamentals of modern information
technology, then the arrangement may be
satisfactory.

Nonaccounting managers as overseers.
Figure 21-2, another partial organization
chart, shows three other possible locations
of the information systems function. Instead
of reporting to the controller, the information
systems manager might report to (1) the vice-

president of finance, (2) the vice-president of
administration, or (3) the president.[1] Instead
of being at the fourth managerial level, as
shown in Figure 21-1, the information systems manager now resides at either the third
or the second managerial level. There are important advantages to be gained by each of
these alternatives.

By moving to a higher managerial level,
the information systems manager attains
more status or "clout." He or she can deal
on a more equal basis with the managers of
user functions; furthermore, he or she can
obtain a broader perspective of the firm's
overall information needs.

By moving out from under the controller's jurisdiction, the information systems
function can gain the advantage of greater
independence. This is especially the case if
the shift completely severs the ties to the finance function.

To grasp this point, we need to consider
the possible constraints under the accounting
or finance function. In such a situation the
information systems function may be required to favor accounting or financially oriented applications or requests. Even if the

[1]Other alternatives are to have the information systems
manager report to (1) an executive vice-president or to
(2) a chief information officer. The latter possibility is
described on page 982.

function is not in fact required to show such favoritism, the managers of other functions may *perceive* favoritism to exist. These managers, such as the production and marketing managers, might therefore harbor ill feelings toward the information systems function. As a result, they likely would not make the best use of the information services. (Note that these arguments would also apply if the information systems function were under the production or marketing function.)

Independence of the information systems function, on the other hand, helps to assure fair and equal service to all functions. It allows the function greater freedom to cross organizational lines and therefore to develop more effective integrated systems. It also enables the function to resist pressure tactics.

Independence thus can best be achieved when the information systems manager reports to the president (or his executive vice-president) or to a nonpartisan function such as administration. Which of these locations is preferable depends largely on the organizational philosophy of a firm and the perceived importance of the information systems function.

Growth of the Systems Function

As the information systems function moves to a higher level within the organization, it generally grows in size. This growth may be measured in its organizational form, its budgeted dollars, and its responsibilities. At a relatively low level the function is likely to be a department, whereas at a higher level it may become an independent office or larger unit. Its budget is likely to follow a roughly S-shaped curve, with increases in the steeply rising portion sometimes equal to 50 percent per year.[2] The responsibilities are likely to swell from routine transaction pro-

cessing to include strategic systems planning, end-user support, data communications support, and decision support.

Even in those cases in which the information systems function has not moved to higher organizational locations, the function has grown in size. (However, the growth is likely to be slower.) The prime reason for growth is best explained by the stage hypothesis.[3] Firms that introduce computers into their information systems progress through several stages. Each succeeding stage witnesses the implementation of new applications, exposes managers to new information processing possibilities, and requires higher degrees of control and integration. These ever-greater information system developments in turn call for greater amounts of resources and responsibilities.

Structure of the Systems Function

As discussed in Chapter 5, a firm's organizational structure is affected when computers and other aspects of information technology are introduced. Since the information systems function of the firm is responsible for incorporating and managing the activities related to information technology, its organizational structure is particularly affected.

Three basic organizational structures appear to be suitable with respect to the information systems function. Two of these structures employ hierarchies to arrange information systems activities, whereas the third structure is more fluid. The hierarchical structures may arrange activities according to (1) functions or (2) products. Thus, as described in Chapter 9, the information systems function may be organized into two major functions: the data processing function and the systems development function. Under the data processing function would be such minor functions as data control, data preparation, and computer operations. Within the systems development function

---

[2]Richard L. Nolan, "Managing the Computer Resource: A Stage Hypothesis," in Richard L. Nolan, ed., *Managing the Data Resource Function*, 2d ed. (New York: West Publishing, 1982), p. 11.

[3]Ibid., pp. 10–17.

the systems analysis and programming functions could be organized into separate minor functions. Alternatively, they could be organized by products, with each product group or division having its own systems analysis–programming unit.

The third type of structure, which is relatively flexible and dynamic, might assume any of several forms. It could involve a matrix form, in which systems employees are attached to functional units and also assigned to product work groups. Matrix forms are suitable for employees who provide support to users concerning specialized skills.[4] Another organizational form consists of a cluster, or a small work group, which might focus on a project. When the current project is completed, the group disbands and the employees are assigned to another project. For example, systems analysts may be assigned to a systems development project that involves a sales order processing system. Such projects often cut across functions within the firm. Thus, Xerox Corporation assigned systems personnel to projects that involved the development of automated office systems for all its functions.[5] A variation of the cluster form is the "starship model," in which industrious individuals with leadership qualities (star performers) are identified and assigned temporarily to projects. For instance, the brokerage firm Merrill Lynch employed this form to stimulate the development of upgraded computer-based financial reporting systems.[6]

Responsibilities of the Systems Function

As noted earlier, two major functional responsibilities of the information systems

function are data processing and systems development. Since the various responsibilities of the data processing function were discussed in Chapter 9, our concern in this section will be limited to the systems development function. Figure 21-3 presents a feasible organizational structure for the information systems function. Innumerable variations and elaborations are possible, as suggested in the previous section. However, the positions shown in the figure are representative of those found in numerous organizations. Responsibilities that might be assigned to such positions are described in the following paragraphs.

Information systems manager. As the head of the information systems function, the **information systems manager** (also called the director of information systems) provides overall leadership. He or she helps to set the objectives for the function, takes part in the long-range planning of systems development, and provides guidance in controlling systems development activities. The information systems manager also (1) supervises and evaluates the performances of the key managers and staff personnel within the function and (2) hires and trains new managers when necessary. Furthermore, he or she justifies the overall level of costs incurred by the function, keeps abreast of new technological developments in the systems field, and stays alert for new ways of improving the information system.[7]

Staff. Various staff groups are needed in larger organizations. A *planning staff* aids in developing long-range systems plans, in coordinating with the corporate strategic planning group, and in establishing information-related policies. A *technical staff* aids in monitoring technological developments, evaluating the potential for applying new technologies within the firm, and planning

[4]Robert W. Zmud, "Design Alternatives for Organizing Information Systems Activities," *MIS Quarterly* (June 1984), p. 83.

[5]Jeff Moad, "Navigating Cross-Functional IS Waters," *Datamation* (March 1, 1989), p. 75.

[6]John Kirkley, "No Magic, Just Hard Work," *Datamation* (May 15, 1989), p. 68.

[7]In some firms a chief information officer performs certain of these functions. See page 989.

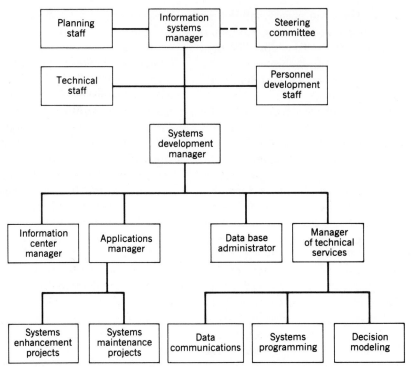

FIGURE 21-3 A partial organizational structure of the information systems function, with emphasis on systems development.

the diffusion of new hardware and software throughout the firm. A *personnel development staff* aids in recruiting and training systems professionals.

Steering committee. The **steering committee,** generally composed of major users of the information system, provides overall guidance in systems development. Its responsibilities are discussed later in this chapter.

Systems development manager. Direct responsibility for systems development activities rests with the **systems development manager,** who provides overall direction of new systems projects, specialized developmental activities, data base administration, information system management, and hardware and software maintenance.

Applications manager. The primary responsibility of the **applications manager** is to develop information system applications. The work concerning these applications may be organized by project (as shown in Figure 21-3). Typical purposes of a project are to analyze, design, and implement new or enhanced systems applications. Often a firm has several projects under way concurrently. One project may consist of improving a transaction processing system; another may pertain to the development of a decision support system. Projects are headed by **project managers,** who take part in overall project planning, obtain needed resources, and direct and control the activities of project teams. Project teams in turn comprise of systems analysts, application programmers, and other personnel (such as accountants) who understand the project areas. **Systems ana-**

lysts analyze the present system (if any), devise the broad design, and provide specifications to the programmers. An important part of their duties is to work closely with users of the system in order to define information needed from the new or improved application. **Application programmers** prepare program flowcharts or other logical diagrams and then write the computer programs that are to direct the new or improved applications. They also are responsible for testing and debugging the programs. Both the systems analysts and the programmers prepare documentation pertaining to the applications.

Applications development may be organized by functions instead of by projects. Thus, a firm might have a systems analysis unit, a systems design unit, a programming unit, and an implementation unit. This approach works well, however, only when no major development projects are necessary. If new projects must be introduced in an established, functional organization, it is best to employ a matrix approach. Each project would be headed by a project manager, but the members of the project team would remain under the jurisdiction of the functional managers.[8]

A less glamorous but still vital responsibility of the applications manager concerns the maintenance of currently operational systems. As in the case of the developmental function, systems maintenance can be organized according to projects. Systems analysts and application programmers would be assigned, on a full- or part-time basis, to projects within this function. Their primary duty in systems maintenance is to make necessary design modifications to existing systems applications. Although the modifications should preferably be planned, certain

changes will always be necessary on a unplanned and even "crash" basis.

Manager of technical services. A variety of responsibilities may be assigned to a **manager of technical services,** including those related to data communications, systems programming, and decision modeling. If the organization includes a security manager, he or she may also report to this manager. Another specialist, not shown in Figure 21-3, is a coordinator of users or systems integrator. This specialist serves as a coordinator between the information systems function and the user departments of the firm. His or her value derives from a knowledge of both the technical aspects and the business features of the systems applications.

Information center manager. Since the position is relatively new, the responsibilities of an information center manager are not clearly established. However, in a typical firm they may consist of providing internal consulting service and support facilities for end-user applications. For instance, services may involve assistance to users in developing special applications and acquiring an understanding of microcomputer-based software packages (e.g., spreadsheet packages).

Data base administrator. As noted in Chapter 18, a data base administration function is responsible for the design and control of a firm's data base. Headed by a **data base administrator** (DBA), the function manages all aspects of the data resource. One primary responsibility is to establish and define the schema of the data base. Fulfilling this responsibility consists of assigning standardized names to items and records; specifying their contents, formats, primary keys, and relationships; and compiling the results into a data dictionary. Another responsibility of the function is to control the use of the data base by assigning user codes and maintaining other security measures. A third responsibil-

---

[8] Thomas R. Gildersleeve, "Organizing the Data Processing Function," *Datamation* (November 1974), pp. 47–48.

ity, related to the first two, is to control all changes in data and in programs that use the data base.

Since the data base function and the DBA are rather new to the information systems scene, these responsibilities should be viewed as rough representations only. In some firms the DBA has sufficient authority to resolve data disputes among major users; in other firms he or she is mainly a data technician.[9]

Centralization versus Decentralization

Large firms with multiple divisions, products, and facilities must decide whether to centralize or decentralize the information systems function. Often this decision is tied to the decision concerning centralized versus distributed systems facilities, as discussed in Chapter 19. It is likely also to be influenced by a firm's general philosophy concerning the extent to which decision making should be decentralized within the circle of higher-level management.

Centralization consists of grouping all systems development and data processing activities in one central location under the line authority of the information systems manager. The benefits of centralization structure parallel those for centralized computer facilities: the need for fewer systems personnel and related resources; the ability to attract (and have available for assignment) more highly qualified systems professionals; and the ability to provide better overall management control, coordination, and standardization. For instance, centralization should assure that all divisions and other organizational units acquire compatible computer hardware and software and develop standardized applications. Centralization is particularly suitable in the presence of centralized computer networks that emphasize on-line transaction processing.

Decentralization consists of dispersing the systems personnel and activities throughout the organization. Figure 21-4 portrays a decentralized structure for a firm having two divisions and two production plants. The dashed lines represent functional (rather than line) authority exerted by the information systems manager and his much-reduced central group. Line authority is exercised by the decentralized division, plant, and functional managers. The benefits of a decentralized structure are significant. By being closer to the actual users of the information system, the systems analysts and other personnel can more precisely determine particular localized needs of the users. A spirit of participation and harmony can be fostered more easily than if the systems personnel are located far away in a central office. Direct, face-to-face communication can prevent the many misunderstandings and errors often caused by long-distance communication and remoteness. Faster service generally can be provided when users request system changes. Decentralization is particularly suitable for firms having wide geographical dispersion and a distributed data base that is heavily drawn upon for decision making information.

Decentralization, of course, is a matter of degree. Some large firms believe that they should maintain a sizable central or corporate group as well as decentralized units. They feel that the added benefits of a central group outweigh the added personnel costs. Not only can a larger central group maintain more specialists for assistance to the decentralized units, but it can provide sounder long-range systems planning and foster greater standardization of data and procedures.

---

[9]See Edward K. Yasaki, "The Many Faces of the DBA," *Datamation* (May 1977), pp. 75–79.

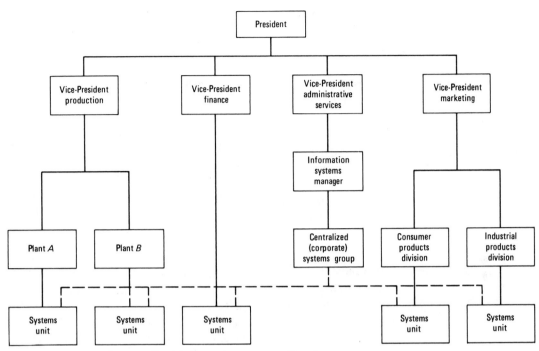

FIGURE 21-4   A decentralized information systems function.

Interactions between the Systems Function and Others

The information systems function interacts with a wide variety of parties, both inside and outside the firm. In addition to individual employees and managers, these parties include top management, user groups (e.g., accountants), suppliers of hardware and software, and consultants. Since the interactions with individual employees and managers (including top management) are discussed throughout Part V, the present discussion will be limited to the last three parties just mentioned.

Accounting function.   One of the largest and most significant user groups within a firm is the accounting function. Because it is so dependent on the information products provided by the information system, the ac-

counting function must maintain extremely close ties with the information systems function. Furthermore, these ties are doubly important in firms that have organizationally removed the information systems function from under the wing of the controller.

Fortunately, several means are available by which to maintain close relationships between the two functions. They include

1. Assigning both the controller and information systems manager to a steering committee that has long-range planning responsibilities.

2. Assigning accountants to project teams responsible for developing new or revised systems applications.

3. Assigning persons who are grounded in both accounting and information technology to serve as coordinators between the

accounting departments and the information systems function.

4. Establishing an internal audit group, staffed by accountants and systems-oriented auditors, that is responsible for evaluating the performance of the information system, including its internal controls and its outputs.

5. Establishing data control groups within departments of the accounting function. For instance, a payroll control section may be installed to control the flow of payroll data into the data processing department.

Hardware and software suppliers. Firms that decide to acquire computer systems suddenly find that they have created a number of new relationships. During the process of investigating the feasibility of new hardware and software, they come into contact with various manufacturers' representatives. Once they select the particular hardware and software, they continue these contacts with the chosen suppliers, usually throughout the lives of the hardware and software.

Most of the day-to-day interactions with hardware and software suppliers are conducted by the information systems manager. However, many of the employees within the information systems function encounter from time to time the suppliers' sales representatives, maintenance engineers, and assorted specialists. Ideally, all such contacts with suppliers are friendly and professional.

On the other hand, close personal relationships should not be encouraged, since it is desirable to maintain an objective viewpoint with respect to the array of competing hardware and software. Moreover, the sales representatives should not be used as consultants; they obviously are biased toward particular brands of hardware or software and typically are not as well informed about information needs as trained consultants are.

Consultants. Many firms do need occasional outside assistance with their systems development activities, however. Preferably, they acquire the services of experienced systems professionals, often from major private consultant firms or the large public accounting firms, for periods ranging from less than a day to several years or more. These consultants may aid in any aspect of systems development, from planning to installation and operation. Thus, audit consultants often are hired to provide advice concerning needed internal accounting controls during a system design phase. By using such consultants the information systems function receives the benefits of objective viewpoints and the accumulated experiences of prior system engagements. Also, consultants can usually gain the attention and approval of higher-level management for needed system changes; often, they have freer access to the president, for instance, than does the information systems manager.

On the other hand, the information systems function should not lean unduly on consultants. For instance, the information systems manager should not allow consultants to make decisions or to do detailed systems development tasks.

Information Resource Management

We have just discussed the organization of the information systems function. In the next sections we will survey the activity of systems planning. A bridge between these topics is the management of information system development and operations. The currently accepted conceptual basis for such management is known as information resource management.

Information resource management (IRM) views information as a resource, requiring the same careful management as any valuable asset. It emphasizes that an output orientation should be maintained by the management of a firm, including the information systems manager. Instead of focusing primarily on data processing, management should be at least as concerned with information processing—processing that serves managerial decision making.

IRM is closely affiliated with the systems approach described in Chapter 2. It suggests that the broad information needs of a firm are holistic, in that they are largely guided by the objectives and planning strategies of that firm. With respect to control, it also suggests that information is "the cohesive element that holds the organization together. In doing so, it cuts across departmental and divisional and (functional) lines."[10]

Firms that endorse the IRM view may appoint a **chief information officer** (CIO), normally at the vice-presidential level. The CIO has key responsibilities with respect to the firm's information and information system. He or she develops policies that govern the standardization, generation, and dissemination of information throughout the firm. The CIO also provides overall direction of the information system, including its continued development, operations, and coordination among the various organizational units. (Thus, the information systems manager in such firms reports to the CIO, unless the positions are combined.)

In performing his or her responsibilities, the CIO should

1. Effectively blend the emerging and converging technologies of word processing, data communications, and artificial intelligence with those of data processing, data retrieval, and report generation.

2. Integrate the processing of formal and informal information to meet the specific needs of managers throughout the organization.

3. Plan in a careful and thorough manner the appropriate development of new transaction processing and decision support systems.

4. Provide due attention to behavioral considerations, such as the relocation of employees affected by new system developments.

5. Exhibit flexibility in adjusting to rapid changes in information technology.

6. Administer in an efficient and effective manner the allocation and use of resources within the organizational units of the information systems function.

These attributes of effective information management are translated into specific guidelines in the discussion of the systems development cycle in the remaining chapters of this book.

Overview of Systems Development

Assume that a newly established firm designs and installs an information system that exactly meets its needs. Can this firm's management then ignore further systems planning and development? The answer is a resounding NO. An information system should continually be monitored for needed improvements and redevelopments throughout the life of the firm that it supports. When the need for redevelopment becomes apparent, suitable development approaches and procedures should be employed.

Need for Systems Development

Existing information systems need to undergo redevelopment when causal factors

[10]Eileen Trauth, "Research-Oriented Perspective on Information Management," *Journal of Systems Management* (July 1984), p. 14.

arise. These causal factors in turn are discovered or recognized by means of certain "triggers."

Causal factors. Three major causal factors are internal or environmental changes, developments in technology, and shortcomings in the existing information system.

Firms and their environments change. They grow in size, revise their strategies, introduce new accounting practices, market new products, restructure their organizations, encounter new competitors, and face new governmental regulations. Since such changes generally affect the information required by the firms, the information systems need to be realigned to accord with the changed business conditions. Assume, for instance, that a firm which has traditionally sold high-quality and sophisticated products determines that it needs to increase its sales volume significantly in order to meet its profit goals. To do so, however, it must appeal to customers who demand products having lower prices and faster deliveries. In order for this changed marketing strategy to succeed, the firm must modify its information system. One likely change would be to install more on-line processing features.

Information technology is expanding at a rapid pace. Computer hardware, software, and applications are mushrooming across all lines, from input–output devices to data base techniques. Firms that make effective use of new information technology can become more competitive and reap other benefits. For instance, retailing firms are using point-of-sale systems to provide better service to customers. Firms of all types are applying information technology to develop new decision support systems and expert systems, thereby enabling them to make better and faster decisions.

Many current information systems exhibit severe shortcomings. Certain of these systems are *ineffective* in that they do not fully meet management's information needs. Perhaps the information they provide is too limited, in that it does not include estimates of lost sales or the sales prices of competitors; perhaps it is too general in that it does not analyze sales by products, classes of customers, and so on. Perhaps the systems do not provide needed reports in a timely manner; or they too often generate too much irrelevant information, causing busy managers to waste precious time wading through reams of detailed reports to find key facts. Often deficient information systems are *inefficient*. Perhaps they process transactions in too costly a manner or do not maintain a reasonably high level of throughput.

Triggers. The need for new or improved systems is generally quite apparent. For instance, when a division is created to produce and market a new product, it is not difficult to spot the need for an accompanying new divisional information system. However, needed changes to existing information systems may not be so obvious. Triggers therefore are often necessary.

Perhaps the most common trigger is the request or complaint from a user, such as a department manager, who might ask that a report be prepared. Such a request might be symptomatic of a shortcoming in relevant information for decision making. Or the department manager may complain that there seem to be too many rush jobs followed by slack periods. This situation may be symptomatic of poor production scheduling, which in turn is related to poor forecasting and order processing procedures.

The need for changes may also be revealed by more systematic means. Thus, accounting and information systems managers may check reports for symptoms, such as high data processing costs or excessive delays in deliveries. An even more thorough approach is the periodic systems or management audit. For instance, the internal audit

Customer complaints
Delayed deliveries or shipments
Late payrolls
Delinquent reports
Unclear or overlapping responsibilities
Excessive overtime
Cash shortages
Low labor productivity
Idle employees
High ratio of indirect labor costs to direct labor costs
Information needed for making decisions unavailable or out of date
Duplication of activities
Excessive bad debts
Slow response to customer inquiries
High employee turnover
Loss of many competitive bids
Production and data processing bottlenecks
Unreasonably large peaks in data processing
Numerous clerical errors
Materials and inventory shortages or excesses
High operating or clerical costs
Excessive processing of data
Redundant files
Paperwork lost or unaccounted for
Untidy work areas
Complaints from vendors about delayed payments
Cost or time overruns on contracts
Accumulations of back orders
Excessive investment in inventories
Very inaccurate sales and production forecasts
Use of expeditors to speed up urgent orders
Inability to explain yearly changes in operating results
Large, unexplained cost variances
Excessive idle production capacity
Excessive homework by managers
Bootlegging of information by managers

FIGURE 21-5 Symptoms of shortcomings in information systems.

group may thoroughly review the operations of one major subsystem, such as materials management, each year.

Figure 21-5 lists various symptoms of shortcomings that may be discovered either casually or by systematic means. Since they often are symptomatic of serious deficiencies in the information system, they normally lead to careful investigations. If deficiencies subsequently are uncovered, a systems development effort should be undertaken.

Approaches to Systems Development

Several approaches to systems development are available. Since each approach has a counter approach, they may be paired as follows:

1. The piecemeal approach versus the systems approach.
2. The bottom-up approach versus the top-down approach.

3. The total-system approach versus the modular approach.

4. The "great leap forward" approach versus the evolutionary approach.

Piecemeal approach versus systems approach. The **piecemeal approach** consists of developing the information system without waiting for an overall plan to be devised. When this approach is followed, the focus at any point in time is on a single activity, such as sales order or accounts payable processing. The selected activity is developed without regard for its setting within the information system or for the firm's overall objectives.

Although the piecemeal approach has resulted in successful individual applications, it is unnecessarily restrictive and has resulted in the development of subsystems that have not meshed smoothly with adjoining subsystems. It also often has dealt with symptoms rather than the deeper and broader underlying problems—that is, it has focused on "putting out fires." Furthermore, because planning is often inadequate even within the individual project, the resulting system applications tend to be behind schedule and over budget. To overcome such shortcomings, the systems approach has been adopted by many firms.

The *systems approach,* as described in Chapter 2, has two emphases: (1) an overall perspective and (2) step-by-step planning. Thus, the systems approach suggests that in developing an information system, it is highly desirable to view the system as a whole and to define its overall objectives. Furthermore, the developmental steps should be carefully planned, preferably as a part of the firmwide long-range planning process. If the systems approach is fully realized, the newly developed or revised portions of the information system should be well integrated and in tune with the overall objectives of the firm.

Bottom-up approach versus top-down approach. Assuming that planned overall systems development is preferable to a "firefighting" approach, should it begin at the bottom or at the top?

The **bottom-up approach** begins at the bottom, or operational, level, where the transaction processing systems are located. After these systems, such as the payroll and accounts payable systems, have been fully developed and made operational, the approach moves to the next stage. In the second stage the transaction processing systems are tied together into larger systems. For example, the purchases and accounts payable systems may be tied into the materials management functional system. This linking process continues by succeeding orderly stages. In the third stage, for instance, the materials management, production, and distribution functional systems may be integrated into a logistics system. At each successive stage the resulting systems would be headed by managers at higher levels within the organizational structure. In addition to processing data for use in operations, the systems would provide decision-making information for such managers. However, this decision-making information would be viewed as a *by-product* of the data processing activity.

In contrast to the bottom-up approach, the **top-down approach** begins at the top of the organization. The approach consists first of clearly establishing *objectives and policies,* both of the firm and the information system. To perform this task, the participants must analyze the firm's environment and major internal activities. As discussed in Chapter 2, this process generally consists of reviewing the firm's key success factors, industry, markets, resources, physical activities, organization, and so on.

The next step in the top-down approach is to perform an information-needs analysis, which consists of identifying the decisions made by managers and then analyzing each decision in terms of needed information. (Chapter 4 detailed the relationships between decisions and information needs.)

After information needs have been determined, the top-down approach leads "downward" to needed reports, data bases, processing procedures, and inputs. These component needs lead in turn to specifications concerning needed system equipment and other system-related resources.

In essence, the top-down approach is a refined application of the systems approach, whereas the bottom-up approach is an orderly version of the piecemeal approach. Both approaches contribute to sound systems development, and neither is sufficient alone. Following the top-down approach leads to a well-planned overall system and stresses the all-important information needs for decision making. However, it does not provide clear guidance to the identification and designing of the also important transaction processing systems and related files. A firm needs workable transaction processing systems right away; it cannot afford to wait for the top-down approach to "filter down" to the operational level. Following the bottom-up approach provides these needed transaction processing systems and integrates them to achieve operational efficiencies. However, it virtually ignores the vital informational needs of managers. Consequently, the concurrent employment of both approaches often may be the best solution.

Total-system approach versus modular approach. The **total-system approach** views the firm as a completely integrated set of flows and procedures—in effect, a monolithic structure. In accordance with this viewpoint, the approach then suggests that all of the flows and procedures should be analyzed together. Following on this analysis, all parts of the information system should be developed simultaneously.

Although the total-system approach represents in a sense the ultimate systems approach, it is generally unworkable. All except the smallest firms are so complex that they defy simultaneous analysis and design at a detailed level. Therefore, a less ambitious but more feasible approach is necessary.

This alternative approach has been labeled the modular, or building-block, approach. Modules or building blocks are identified within an overall plan; then they are analyzed, designed, and installed one by one. Each fits into the niche assigned to it by the plan and links to adjoining modules. Figure 21-6 shows several linking modules within an overall information system of a manufacturing firm.

The **modular approach,** which resembles the later stages of the bottom-up approach, overcomes the major drawback of the total-system approach. It allows the information system to be viewed as a network of "black boxes," one "black box," or module, being opened and developed at a time. As a result, each module can be developed within a reasonable period of time and thus made available for operational use. Moreover, since modules are considered to be more independent (i.e., less tightly coupled to their neighbors) than they are under the "total system," the modular approach is more adaptable. Thus, necessary changes can be made more quickly. However, a warning is in order: The interfaces or links among modules must be constantly kept in mind during the developmental period if the piecemeal approach is to be avoided.

Examples of the modular approach can be drawn from Figure 21-6. Assume that the production planning and control module is selected as the first to be developed. A project team would undertake the sequence of phases needed to develop a new or improved production planning and control system, perhaps using both the top-down and the bottom-up approaches. The next module

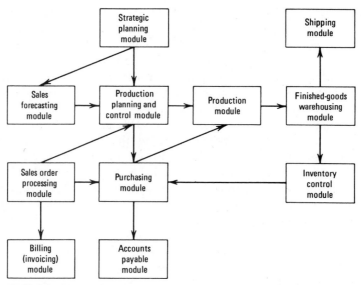

FIGURE 21-6 Modules comprising a portion of an information system.

to be developed might be the purchasing module, and then the production module. Perhaps it might be desirable to divide this last module into two or more projects, since it spans a wide scope of activities. For instance, it may be divided into production operations and cost accounting projects. During the development of each module, its links to the other modules (e.g., production planning and control to production, sales forecasting, sales order processing, and purchasing) need to be carefully incorporated into the design.

"Great leap forward" approach versus evolutionary approach. As noted in Chapter 5, computer hardware, software, and applications have progressed through several generations during the past 40 years. Some firms have kept pace with this technological progress, so that their current information systems have reached an advanced stage of development.

Consider the case of many firms, how-

ever. When their managements decide changes are needed, their information systems are likely to be relatively unsophisticated and primitive. A choice is open: Either (1) take a "great leap forward" from their present stage to the most advanced "state-of-the-art" stage or (2) move toward this advanced stage in an evolutionary manner.

The **"great leap forward" approach** is appealing, since it promises to provide advanced capabilities *now* rather than *later*. For example, for a manufacturing firm it might mean a highly integrated logistics system that is fully on line. For a bank it might mean a completely integrated depositor data base. For a wholesaling firm it might be a sophisticated set of marketing-oriented decision models.

However, the "great leap forward" approach entails severe risks. Attempting to move too far too fast can lead to costly failure. The leap may be too complex for the systems analysts and programmers to handle successfully. Or the leap may provide a sophisticated system that unsophisticated users are not prepared to accept and use effectively.

For these reasons the **evolutionary,** or stage-by-stage, **approach** has been widely adopted. Under this approach, a firm progresses through a series of stages over time, developing in each stage a somewhat more advanced system. Although it means more development cycles, or iterations, the evolutionary approach produces systems that can be more easily "digested" by both designers and users.

A variation of the evolutionary approach is **prototyping.** This approach, like any evolutionary approach, incorporates a learning process into systems development. However, prototyping spans a much shorter time span (months rather than years) and does not involve several changes in system technology. It consists of devising a prototype design in a relatively short time during an initial iteration. This prototype, which represents a crude approximation of the final design, is then put into operation by users. As experience is gained with the prototype and additional information needs are determined, the design is refined. This fine tuning may continue through several reiterations. When a design revision is fully satisfactory to the users, the process ceases. Although relatively costly in time and money, prototyping is becoming more popular. It is especially suited to those system situations which are unstructured and in which the information needs cannot be precisely stated at the beginning.

Levels of Systems Development Applications

As we have stressed earlier, an information system cannot be realistically viewed as a monolithic structure. It consists of numerous subsystems with varying characteristics, demands, and users. Figure 21-7, a compos-

ite of several other figures already presented, illustrates the diversity of subsystems. It also indicates that the supporting subsystems can be developed at various levels of support. Furthermore, the figure suggests that these subsystems may be integrated to a greater or lesser degree. Finally, the figure reminds us that all subsystems must draw on a data base or data bases.

Additional figures might recast the information system in somewhat different terms. For instance, the higher levels of subsystems may be termed advanced management information systems or fully integrated management information systems. However, Figure 21-7 emphasizes that formal systems (1) must be developed at differing levels and in differing degrees of complexity and (2) generally evolve over time to higher levels of operational and decision support.

A number of problems hinder the successful development of more complex and higher-level computer-based applications. These problems range from lack of support by top management to poor project planning and control by the information systems function. Overcoming these problems requires sound strategies on the part of the information systems manager.

Among the sound strategies that might be employed are the following:

1. Prepare a careful and thorough sequence of systems development activities. Adapt this sequence of activities to fit the most suitable development approach for each systems development project. For instance, adapt the sequence to fit the bottom-up approach when a transaction processing system is the subject of a project. (Also, apply the prototyping approach where appropriate, as in the development of unstructured decision support systems.)

2. Assess the current environment, in order to determine the (a) current position and

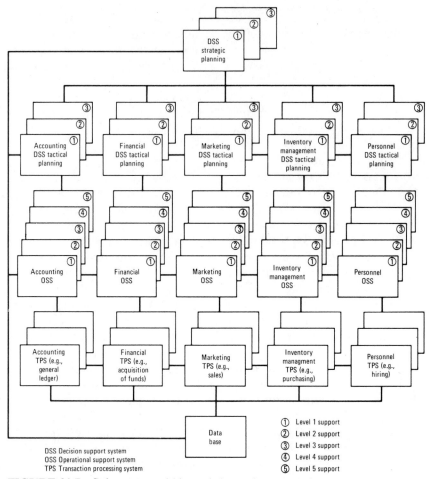

FIGURE 21-7 Subsystems within an information system.

condition of the firm within its industry, (b) current business opportunities, (c) new technology, (d) stage of the information system's maturity, (e) current capabilities of the information system, and (f) current information system resources.[11]

3. Undertake careful and appropriate systems planning. This planning should include the consideration of subsystems at all levels (e.g., decision support systems as well as transaction processing sys-

tems). Although one type might be given priority over another, all types should be included in the overall planning process.

Systems Development Sequence

Figure 21-8 lists a sequence of activities pertaining to the development of a new or improved information system or subsystem. Under each of the five major phases of the sequence are listed several steps. The remainder of this chapter discusses the systems planning phase. The other phases are discussed in Chapters 22 through 25. (The

[11]Brent Bowman, Gordon Davis, and James Wetherbe, "Modeling for MIS," *Datamation* (July 1981), p. 160.

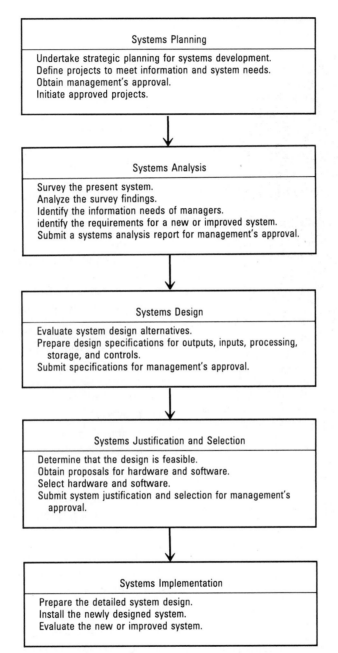

FIGURE 21-8   The systems development sequence.

operational phase, not shown in the figure, is also discussed in Chapter 25.)

Before beginning the discussion, however, we need to insert a disclaimer. Figure 21-8 does not portray the precise way systems development takes place in the real world. For one thing, every firm (and textbook author, for that matter) has its own unique sequence of phases and steps. For another thing, the real world cannot be as orderly as the sequence suggests. Often it is necessary for those in the systems development to repeat the same step several times. For instance, during the design phase it may be necessary to iterate or to "loop back," perhaps to refine the objectives or to gather more facts concerning the present system. Also, since several persons often are involved in the systems development sequence, two or more phases and steps may be performed concurrently.

Other factors that may affect the sequence of system development activities are

1. The experience of the prospective users of the information system. If the users are very familiar with computer-based systems, certain steps may be eliminated.
2. The degree of structure in the system being developed. A transaction processing system is very structured and thus amenable to a carefully sequenced approach.
3. The technological level of the system being developed. An extremely innovative design will likely require an extensive sequence.
4. The scope of the systems project. A project of broad scope will also likely require an extensive sequence.
5. The importance of the systems project. A project of minor importance will likely require fewer steps than a very critical project.[12]

Nevertheless, Figure 21-8 serves two useful purposes. It provides (1) a picture of a reasonable typical sequence and (2) a framework for guiding our discussion of systems development.

Systems Planning

The first phase of formal systems development involves planning on two levels. It begins with overall long-range strategic planning.[13] It then leads to the detailed definition, approval, and initiation of manageable systems projects.

Strategic systems planning is recognized by an increasing number of firms as especially important. There are several reasons for this growing recognition.

1. Changes are buffeting the systems area more vigorously than ever.
2. Systems hardware and software needed to fulfill system designs often require long lead times and hence orderly planning procedures.
3. Systems-related costs are absorbing larger shares of available resources.
4. The integration of hastily designed and unplanned transaction processing systems into larger modules has proven to be very difficult and costly.[14]

Certain features frequently characterize strategic systems planning in participating firms. First, the planning is conducted on a continuing basis. Second, the planning for systems development is incorporated into

---

[12]Brandt Allen, "An Unmanaged Computer System Can Stop You Dead," *Harvard Business Review* (Nov.–Dec. 1982), pp. 76–87.

[13]It will always be necessary to respond quickly to requests by users for relatively small system changes, such as revised reports. These are viewed as a part of systems maintenance, however, and therefore do not require strategic systems planning.

[14]Robert V. Head, "Strategic Planning for Information Systems," *Infosystems* (Oct. 1978), p. 46; F. Warren McFarlan, "Problems in Planning the Information System," *Harvard Business Review* (March–April 1971), p. 76.

the firm's overall long-range capital budgeting processes. Third, the plans resulting from strategic systems planning are revised periodically to reflect changed priorities and new conditions.

As Figure 21-9 shows, several steps are involved in strategic systems planning. Each merits brief discussion and illustration.

Obtain Support of Top Management

The most critical step in successful systems planning is the first one: obtaining the full support of top management.[15] The president as well as the vice-presidents must warmly endorse planning efforts aimed at developing an improved information system. If they do so, middle- and lower-level managers will take their cues from above and respond favorably.

Furthermore, top management must participate in systems development. Among the actions that it should take are

1. Setting specific directions and priorities with respect to systems development.
2. Clarifying the objectives of the information system and the firm, as well as the constraints with respect to systems development.
3. Approving the strategic systems plan and system projects.
4. Monitoring the progress of systems development.
5. Making the key appointments, such as the information systems manager.

Organize Steering Committee

Top management participation can be facilitated by means of one or more advisory or steering committees for systems development. Such committees generally are composed of higher-level representatives of the major users of information systems. Thus, they typically would include the functional vice-presidents and other major general managers, such as division managers. Often a committee of this type is headed by the firm's president.

A number of firms, including the American Can Company, feel that this "advisory committee approach provides . . . an excellent vehicle for insuring the right level of

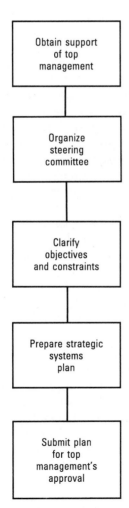

FIGURE 21-9 Steps in strategic systems planning.

[15]Several studies bear out this statement. See, for instance, Michael J. Cerullo, "MIS: What Can Go Wrong?" *Management Accounting* (April 1979), p. 43; and Richard F. Powers and Gary W. Dickson, "MIS Project Management: Myths, Opinions, and Reality," *California Management Review* (Spring 1973), p. 153.

management participation, guidance, and control.''[16] Not only does it inform the major users of all systems development and coordinate their viewpoints, but it serves as an effective conduit between top management and the working level of the information systems function.

Although the exact functions of a steering committee vary from firm to firm, they generally include most of the following:

1. Reviewing and either approving or making recommendations concerning its firm's strategic systems plan, systems projects, and major hardware and software acquisitions.
2. Coordinating the orderly and logical undertaking of systems projects within the strategic systems plan.
3. Monitoring the progress of systems projects.
4. Reviewing the performance of the information systems function.

In order to fulfill these functions effectively, the steering committee needs to be closely involved with the strategies as well as the plans concerning the information system. Example strategies might specify that

1. All acquired computer hardware and software must be compatible with existing systems.
2. The data base should foster effective decision-making information rather than technical efficiency. Typically the steering committee would review and approve such strategies. However, if the information systems manager is a member (or even the chairman) of the steering committee, the committee itself might formulate the strategies.

---

[16]William S. Woodside, ''Gearing the Information System for Rapid Change,'' *Infosystems* (March 1979), p. 72.

Clarify Objectives and Constraints

Clear, sound, and explicit objectives are necessary for effective planning. Three sets of objectives require consideration: the overall objectives of the firm, the overall objectives of the information system, and the narrower objectives pertaining to each systems project.

A firm's objectives are often stated in general terms, such as to maximize long-run profits, to provide a high level of customer service, and to increase the share of the market. However, the overall objectives must also be stated in more specific terms if they are to be operationally useful. For instance, a specifically stated objective might be to achieve a 5 percent sales growth next year.

Objectives of the information system should be consistent with the firm's objectives. Like the firm's objectives, they are sometimes expressed in general terms. A number of objectives so expressed have appeared in earlier chapters, including the objectives of processing efficiency, timely information, and system flexibility. However, they also must be stated in specific terms if they are to be useful for planning. Two specifically stated objectives are to increase transaction capacity by 10 percent next year or to reduce the error rate by 20 percent within two years.

Objectives pertaining to systems projects are narrower in scope than the overall system objectives, but they also should be quite specific. Objectives of a production control project might include (1) a savings in production costs of $20,000 next year, (2) an increase in on-time deliveries to customers from 70 percent to 90 percent within two years, and (3) a 25 percent reduction in materials spoilage next year.

Strategies, policies, and key success measures follow from objectives. A merchandising firm with a growth objective may adopt a strategy of price discounting and a policy of late store hours; it may select as key success measures the annual percentage change in dollar sales and share of the market. With respect to the firm's information system, the objective pertaining to economical operations might translate into a batch processing strategy and a policy that requires all system designs to be justified in terms of cost savings. A related key measure of effectiveness might be the percentage of data processing costs to total sales.

Similarly, a firm's strategies may be translated directly into its information system strategies.[17] For instance, strategies to improve credit practices and manufacturing productivity may translate into operational support system strategies to monitor credit and production performance. A strategy to diversify the firm's products may translate into a decision support system strategy to evaluate new product ideas.

Constraints on the strategic systems plan should also be identified. In addition to externally imposed requirements by governmental agencies and the economy, relevant constraints include restrictions on the scopes and budgets of systems projects and upon the availability of resources. A particular constraint often felt by firms is the limited availability of experienced systems analysts. Another constraint often imposed by a firm's management is that the organizational structure not be significantly altered by systems development activities.

Prepare Strategic Systems Plan

The tangible product of strategic systems planning is a written plan. This plan observes a basic rule of systems development: *document thoroughly* during each phase of the systems development sequence.

[17]William R. King, "Strategic Planning for Management Information Systems," *MIS Quarterly* (March 1978), pp. 27–37.

If the strategic systems plan is grounded soundly on the objectives previously discussed and if it reflects the firm's environmental opportunities and problems, it should provide several benefits:

1. A broad blueprint for systems development in the coming years, pointing out a clear and orderly course of action.
2. A vehicle for coordinating systems planning with other strategic plans of the firm, so that management can determine the appropriate shares of overall resources to allot to each major category of investment.
3. A documented assurance that every portion of the information system has been considered and evaluated against the other portions and that wasteful duplications have been minimized.
4. A standard against which to evaluate the performance of the information systems function.
5. A device for preparing employees for changes and for instilling realistic expectations in users.

Although the contents of the plan will vary from firm to firm, they likely will include

1. Objectives, policies, and constraints related to the information system.
2. Planned systems projects and their relative priorities.
3. Tentative resources needed for systems development, including costs, personnel, and equipment.
4. Tentative timetables for specific system development and projects.

The plan may also include an appendix that describes the relationships of the firm's information system to its operational functions, to its organizational structure, and to its environment and needed resources.

Chapter 2 considered such relationships in detail.

Often the strategic systems plan consists of two parts: a one-year operational plan and a multiyear long-range plan. (A five-year long-range planning horizon is typical.) The short-range plan provides the necessary details for budgetary control, and the long-range plan provides the broader perspective. Included as support for the long-range plan should be projections that show expected technology, work loads, system capacities, and system configurations. Both parts of the plan should span all aspects of the information system. In addition to the transaction processing systems, the plan should include telecommunications, decision support systems, office automation, and such industry-specific applications as computer-integrated manufacturing systems.

As the basis for preparing the strategic systems plan, higher-level management (including the information systems manager) performs a strategic analysis. In essence, this analysis peers into the future. It attempts to determine future problems and opportunities for the firm and the roles of the information system in meeting these future challenges. If the vision is clear, sound future directions can be plotted. A dramatic example is American Airlines' Sabre reservation system. On the basis of a strategic analysis, it decided to install computer on-line terminals in every travel office. Although very costly and difficult, this new system enabled American Airlines to leap ahead of its competition.

Submit Plan for Approval

As with other strategic plans, the strategic systems plan requires the approval of top management. The approval process serves two major purposes: (1) to supply a prior control over expenditures and actions; (2) to signal future directions of systems development to the managers throughout the firm.

Project Definition and Initiation

According to the modular approach, the systems project is the critical focus of concern in systems development. Prior to its undertaking, however, a systems project must be well defined. Project definition consists of such steps as identifying likely project areas, undertaking a preliminary investigation, determining the priority of the project, preparing a formal project proposal, and obtaining approval for the proposed project. After approval gives birth to a project, several initiating steps are needed to put the project in motion. Figure 21-10 shows this sequence of steps.

Identify Likely Projects

Since systems projects must be identified before they can be included in the strategic systems plan, this step is actually initiated during the overall systems planning activity. However, it is included under project definition, since it is the first step toward a clear and detailed definition of what is to be done.

Identification begins with a description of the major problem or problems, such as poor management of inventories. It continues with the objectives or expected improvements, such as "to provide inventory status information within two minutes of an inquiry." Objectives are necessary identifiers, since they provide the specifications against which the resulting system is to be judged. Identification also includes the scope and depth of the project. Is its scope, for instance, a transaction processing system for sales, a transaction processing system for sales *and* accounts receivable, or a marketing decision support system? When identifying the scope, depth within the project area is also relevant. Its depth may range from a small modification of a manual system to a complete changeover to an on-line computer-based system. It is also important

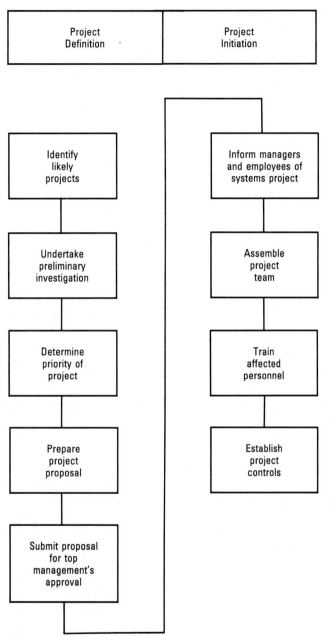

FIGURE 21-10   Steps in project definition and initiation.

when identifying a project to denote the interfaces or relationships with other projects.

Undertake Preliminary Investigation

A thorough definition of a project, however, consists of many more facts and estimates: costs, benefits, time schedules, work details, and so on. Therefore, a survey, also called a **feasibility study** or high-point review, usually is undertaken. Its purpose is to gather in the space of a few days or weeks the facts needed either (1) to prepare a formal proposal, if the project appears to be feasible; or (2) to reject the project, if it appears not to be feasible.[18]

Determine Priority of Project

At some point in the systems planning phase it is necessary to assign priorities to the respective projects. They often are assigned very early in the planning process, so that tentative schedules can be reflected in the strategic systems plan. If so, they will either be confirmed or revised on the basis of additional data gathered during preliminary investigations.

Assigning priorities is a difficult but extremely important step, since it determines the order in which the modules comprising a new or improved system will be completed. For instance, a sales forecasting project might be assigned a higher priority than an inventory management project, perhaps because current sales forecasts are quite inaccurate. In this case, a new sales forecasting system would be completed ahead of a new inventory management system. Often a data base project is assigned the highest priority,

since stored data provide the basis for conducting operations and making decisions.

Both rational and nonrational criteria are applied in the process of assigning project priorities. Rational criteria include (1) expected cost savings or profit improvement, (2) expected acceptability and effective use by users, (3) expected long-term viability, (4) logical relationship to other projects being planned, and (5) urgent need to correct intolerable conditions. Nonrational criteria include (1) interest on the part of a powerful manager and (2) desire for a "showpiece" (e.g., a state-of-the-art electronic office or a sophisticated data communications network).

A formal methodology can be applied to identify the projects having the greatest net benefits or strategic impacts. Two such methodologies are *Business Systems Planning* and *Information Engineering*.[19]

Prepare Project Proposal

The key document supporting a systems project is the **project proposal**, also called a problem definition statement or a project development plan. Its detailed description of the proposed project serves two purposes: (1) to enable top management to evaluate the worthiness of the project and (2) to provide a blueprint and standard for the later phases of analysis, design, and implementation.

The content of a project proposal generally consists of details concerning such items as the following: identified problems and objectives, the scope of the project and its relationships to other projects, the tentative time schedule for the respective systems development phases, the resources estimated to be required, and the benefits versus the costs of

---

[18]The term *feasibility study* is employed to cover a wide variety of undertakings. For instance, a feasibility study may be used for the express purpose of determining that a computer should be acquired. Feasibility studies of this type are much more extensive than the preliminary survey mentioned. They generally require longer than a few days or weeks and often span all the operations of a firm.

[19]See International Business Machines Corporation, *Business Systems Planning—Information Systems Planning Guide,* Publication No. GE20-0527 (New York: IBM, 1978), and Arthur Young Information Technology Group, *The Arthur Young Practical Guide to Information Engineering* (New York: John Wiley & Sons, 1987).

the project. It likely will break down the resource requirements, such as man-hours, into categories such as the phases of systems development. It may also analyze the costs by such categories as personnel, equipment, and supplies. Furthermore, both the man-hours and the costs usually will be projected period by period over the expected duration of the project.

A thorough project proposal might additionally incorporate such data as

1. A work plan specifying in detail what is to be done, how it is to be done, and who is to do it.
2. A description of system-related requirements, such as the expected volume of transactions or messages and special input–output features.
3. The expected impacts of the project upon the organizational structure, managers, and employees.

Submit Proposal for Approval

Each project should be approved by managers at the highest level of a firm. Although approvals will be needed at later points in the systems development cycle, this first approval is perhaps the most critical. An approval at this point will usually lead to major expenditures of time and money.

Thus, while top management will scrutinize all aspects of the proposal carefully, it will take an especially close look at the comparison of benefits versus costs. Although estimated benefits and costs must necessarily be fairly rough at this point, they nevertheless provide one of the most relevant gauges of ultimate success.

Inform Employees and Managers

Employees and managers are vitally important to the success of a systems project.

After all, *people*—not computers—will operate a new or improved system. Also, *people* will use the information outputs of a new or revised system.

Furthermore, employees and managers often are directly affected by systems projects, because of changes that generally accompany new or improved systems. These changes may be reflected in work and social relationships, in job content, and even in status. Being human, employees and managers tend to view such changes as adverse to their interests. They strongly favor their present jobs and job relationships, to which they have developed emotional attachments.

Consequently, these vital cogs in the operation and use of a firm's information system generally will resist any contemplated changes in the system. In fact, they often will become quite upset and possibly hostile when they even hear rumors of possible changes.

Behavioral reactions such as these render imperative the *immediate* announcement of an approved systems project. Informing the employees and managers at the earliest possible time achieves two benefits: (1) It quells the "rumor mill" and hence the misinformation generally dispensed via rumors; (2) it gives those who will be affected the maximum time to adjust mentally to the impending changes.

In addition to the bare facts concerning the systems project, the announcement should tell *why* the changes are desirable and *how* the affected employees and managers will benefit. (Often these reasons will differ in certain respects from those used to gain acceptance by top management.) If these reasons are understandable and appear cogent, the employees and managers could well be motivated to accept the impending changes. Furthermore, if assurances concerning job security and other personal concerns are provided, those affected should remain relaxed and productive during the period of transition.

APPLICATION OF SYSTEMS PLANNING
Weyerhaeuser Company

Weyerhaeuser, a timber products firm, introduced an information systems planning methodology in 1981. This methodology, which was devised by the advanced systems planning group in the information systems department, results in the preparation of a plan of action for the current year and a long-range systems plan for the next five years. These plans are based on a decision-oriented approach, which begins with the statement of companywide and information systems objectives. One stated objective, for instance, is to "increase profitability through improved access to information for trade-off decisions related to raw materials, products and customers in manufacturing, marketing and logistical operations." Then the plan focuses on specific application systems. For each application system area, the plan defines the information strategies, scope, operational flows, functional responsibilities, critical success factors, planning team, and schedule. On the basis of this planning activity the planning team then defines information system requirements and proposes plans of action for developing new systems.

This approach was first applied in a project involving the pulp business (division). By means of a series of interviews of affected managers, as well as other techniques, the team prepared a well-documented plan of action. This plan was enthusiastically approved by higher-level management.[a]

In 1986 the firm realigned its information systems function. First, it reorganized the function as a profit center. As such it "sells" its services to the various business units inside the firm. Since the business units have the option of looking outside the firm for their computer-related services, the information systems function must provide greater value in order to succeed. Second, information systems personnel were decentralized throughout the firm, in order to serve each of the business units more effectively.[b]

[a]Pran N. Wahi, Kenneth A. Popp, and Susan Stier, "Applications Systems Planning at Weyerhaeuser." *Journal of Systems Management* (Mar. 1983), pp. 12–21.
[b]Thomas M. Lodahl and Kay Lewis Redditt, "Aiming IS at Business Targets," *Datamation* (Feb. 15, 1989), p. 97.

Assemble Project Team

As noted earlier, systems projects are usually conducted by teams. **Project teams** enable persons with differing areas of expertise and experience to pool their ideas. Although project teams will differ in their composition, three areas of expertise and experience are often represented by the following:

1. Computer systems analysts and programmers, who understand the technical aspects of systems design, hardware, and software.

2. Managerial accountants, who understand such systems aspects as transaction processing, coding, and controls, as well as the general reporting needs of management.

3. Users, who understand the firm's specific operations and needs. For instance, production employees and/or managers should be on a project team dealing with the production area, since they best understand production operations and needs.

Participation by users also is beneficial for another reason. The users thereby feel that the new or improved system is truly theirs, rather than a creation imposed on them by outsiders. Therefore, they can help to gain acceptance for the new or improved system from other affected employees and managers in the area.

Train Affected Personnel

Systems development generally is enhanced by prior training of project team members. Of course, the level of training should accord with the current knowledge of each member. Members who represent users, as well as accountants and junior systems analysts, probably require training in systems analysis and design at a basic level. Experienced systems analysts, on the other hand, likely will benefit from advanced training in those areas or from training in a related area such as accounting. In addition to improving their technical skills, such training will enable the members to communicate with each other more effectively.

Managers who will be affected by new or improved systems should also receive training or indoctrination sometime during the development cycle. They should learn the basics of systems technology and sound approaches to systems development and application. This background should then enable managers to evaluate the potential of computer-based systems and to control their use more effectively. For instance, they should be less likely to acquire "computeritis," an affliction that causes the sufferer to be blinded by the mystique and glamour of computers.

Training can be provided by in-house programs if the firm is sufficiently large. Most firms, however, take advantage of courses offered by such organizations as the American Management Association, the National Association of Accountants, and the larger computer-hardware manufacturers.

Establish Project Controls

The key standards against which project progress will be measured are the time schedule and cost projections. Control over times and costs can be exercised through such techniques as Gantt (bar) charts and PERT networks, plus periodic review meetings and progress reports.

Summary

When establishing an information systems function within the organizational structure of a firm, it is necessary to decide (1) where it will be located within the structure, (2) how the responsibilities will be structured and divided, (3) whether the structure will be centralized or decentralized, and (4) what the interactions with other groups and functions will be. Three likely locations are within the finance/accounting function, within an administrative services function, and as one of the equally independent major functions of the firm. Responsibilities of the information systems function are generally divided among systems development and data processing activities, with a variety of projects and specialized units being located within the systems development activity. Both centralization and decentralization offer advantages. Some firms attempt to achieve the advantages of both by blending a central group with decentralized units. Continuing relationships must be maintained by the information systems function with key users such as the accounting function and with hardware and software suppliers; occasional relationships with consultants are also desirable.

Information resource management bridges the information systems organization and systems management. This concept views information to be a resource, focuses on information processing, and reinforces the principles of the systems approach. Systems development, one function of information resource management, begins with the recognition of a need. This recognition may be triggered by the emergence of serious problems or significant changes. After a need is recognized, the firm must select from among such developmental approaches as the piecemeal, systems, top-down, bottom-up, total, modular, "great leap forward," and evolutionary approaches.

The development of new or improved

systems consists of such phases as systems planning, systems analysis, systems design, systems justification and selection, and systems implementation. Systems planning involves three subphases: strategic planning, project definition, and project initiation. Strategic planning consists of obtaining the support of top management, organizing a steering committee, clarifying objectives and constraints, preparing a strategic systems plan, and obtaining top management approval for the plan. Project definition consists of identifying likely projects, undertaking a preliminary investigation, determining the priority of the project, preparing a project proposal, and obtaining top management approval for the project proposal. Project initiation consists of informing employees and managers of the approved systems project, assembling a project team, training the affected personnel, and establishing project controls.

Review Problem with Solution

Statement

History The Precise Manufacturing Company (which we will call Precise) is a well-established business corporation. It was started by three friends in Chicago during 1950. These friends—John Curtis, Tom Wilson, and Chim Yu—had served in the armed forces together and were impressed with the scarcity of quality light machine tools. In the initial organization they occupied the three key managerial positions. John was designated as president because of his military leadership experiences; he also assumed responsibility for financing and accounting. Tom took charge of production and engineering because he had earned a degree in engineering. Chim assumed direction of the marketing effort because of his previous sales experience and his outgoing nature.

The firm did well from the beginning. In part this stemmed from a spurt in demand created by the Korean War, but mainly it was the result of the hard work and abilities of the founders. As a consequence, the firm has grown steadily over the four ensuing decades. The single original building that housed both the Chicago offices and the plant in 1950 has blossomed into three new separate buildings: a home office building, a plant, and a warehouse. The plant has several production lines and materials storerooms. Sales branches have sprouted in 10 cities throughout the United States. This growth in facilities has been matched by a growth in equities. Several issues of capital stock have been sold publicly. Twenty-year bonds were issued in 1973. The organization has also expanded. Four additional managers have been added at the vice-president level alone. Chim (marketing) and Tom (engineering) have been joined by Jack Hemp (production), Violet Apley (finance), Sue Harold (accounting), and Mark Andrews (administration). Finally, the range of products has been broadened. A line of portable electric power tools for use by homeowners and light contractors was added in 1983 and has quickly established a niche.

Over the years the firm has built a reputation for quality precision products. Its engineers consistently have provided excellent designs and have designed new tools in accordance with customers' special orders. On several occasions the engineers have developed new machine tools with such superior features that they have been described in trade magazines. Although the power tools are not as precisely engineered, they are clearly in the quality end of their markets.

Current status. Currently (1990), therefore, the firm is fairly sizable, with 10,500 customers and expected net sales for the year of about $95 million. Of these sales, approximately 90 percent involve precision machine tools, replacement parts, accessories, gauges, and pneumatic power tools marketed directly to industrial manufacturing firms and indirectly through machine tool distributors and parts distributors. About 10 percent of the total sales involve the new line of portable electric-powered tools, which are marketed through jobbers, industrial and home supply distributors, and wholesalers.

Roughly 200 standard products, plus several hundred parts, are produced for inventory and stocked in finished-goods warehouses. The remaining production involves custom-designed products, including variations of the standard products, that are based upon special orders and instructions from industrial manufacturers. These custom-designed products, representing about 15 percent of total sales, are, of course, higher priced than the standard products. Their prices are determined on the basis of accumulated labor, material, overhead, and design costs. Cost of sales for all products averages 40 percent for direct materials, 40 percent for direct labor, and 20 percent for manufacturing overhead.

In order to produce this wide variety of products, Precise acquires 7500 parts and raw materials from 300 suppliers and subcontractors.

Precise has 1500 employees and managers and 5000 stockholders. A six-person board of directors, representing the stockholders, includes the three founders, an investment banker, a large stockholder, and the president of one of the firm's largest customers.

Current problems. Although Precise's sales have continued to grow, certain disturbing signs have appeared. For the past couple of years the *rate* of sales growth has been declining, and the amount of net income has fallen from $3.1 million last year to an estimated $2.3 million this year. Another drop in net income is expected next year. Although these declines can be attributed in part to the recent softness in the overall economy, they are also directly traceable to problems within the firm. Both the cost of sales and operating costs have been rising faster than sales, the latter rather rapidly. Also, the average time required to fill a sales order for standard products or parts has become so lengthy that many promised delivery dates are being missed. (As a result, the firm receives numerous complaints from customers.) These increases in costs and delivery times are particularly surprising, since certain automated equipment has been installed in recent years for the express purpose of decreasing costs and speeding up operations.

One reason for these problems appears to be the long-continued growth of the firm to its present size and complexity. For instance, the 500 sales orders received during an average day this year are a bit overwhelming. Clerks are so busy and confused by the mass of paperwork that they cannot satisfactorily inform customers concerning the status of their orders. Often they make errors in processing sales orders and preparing monthly statements. Of course, these clerical shortcomings lead to more customer complaints.

Other signs point to management problems. Inventory levels are rising; nevertheless, materials and parts and products are often found to be out of stock, necessitating back orders and delays. Cash balances have become lower than desirable, requiring emergency short-term bank loans at high rates of interest. Sales forecasts have been quite inaccurate, leading to poor estimates of needed materials and parts in production.

Stirrings of concern. These problems have increasingly concerned John Curtis, the president. He feels that major changes may be necessary. Furthermore, these changes may need to be initiated rather soon. Not only does the decline in profits threaten to become precipitous, but the firm's market share is being challenged. A couple of machine tool competitors recently have introduced new lines of high-quality machine tools, and another competitor in portable electric power tools has initiated an aggressive television advertising campaign to expand its share of the market.

After discussing these problems with his vice-presidents, John decides to obtain help. He contacts Alice Renolds, a partner in the CPA firm that audits Precise's accounting records each year. Ms. Renolds recommends that John talk to a manager of the CPA firm named Tod Stuart. In an ensuing interview, Tod describes his background to John. He has an accounting education and several years of experience in the management advisory services department of the CPA firm. Many of his assignments have involved the analysis of business problems. Several have led to major redesigns of accounting and information systems and the installation of computers. In short, Tod seems to be qualified to help. So John engages his services and describes his firm's problems.

Tod begins the consulting engagement by examining Precise's financial statements and records, by observing activities throughout the firm, and by talking to a wide cross section of employees and managers. At the end of two weeks he prepares a written report to John.

In his report Tod states the following: "Some of the problems faced by the firm are caused by the volatile nature of the machine tool industry, which currently is experiencing a slight recession. However, many of the underlying problems currently experienced by the firm are traceable to an inadequate and antiquated information system. The present system appears to have grown throughout the life of the firm with no overall or consistent direction; at present it is a patchwork of paperwork procedures that is costly to operate and nonproductive of needed information. For instance, the information system for the relatively new portable power tool division apparently has been hastily devised, with little planning, and has not been integrated with the larger preexisting information system. Managers through-out the firm do not receive the facts that they need to plan and control the activities of the firm. Consequently, I recommend that a comprehensive systems development program be commenced, with a view to developing an improved information system. This more effective information system should help to reverse the alarming trends in the financial condition and operating results of the firm, as well as to alleviate the other serious problems that exist. In large part the new information system will achieve these results by providing managers with the information that they need, when they need it, for making better planning decisions and for taking necessary corrective actions."

Management concurrence. Upon reading this report, John becomes convinced of the need for early action. He therefore calls a meeting of his vice-presidents. Tod is invited to explain the desirability of the proposed systems development program. Not unexpectedly, his proposal gives rise to varied concerns. Violet Apley wonders about the likely cost of the program, saying that "a systems development program will probably result in our buying a lot more expensive computer equipment." Chim, the vice-president of marketing, adds that "a new system, with its new ways of doing things, may take so much time to learn that my salesmen won't have time to be making sales." Mark, the vice-president of administrative services, points out that when the program becomes known, "rumors will spread via the grapevine to the effect that employees will be laid off; the resulting uncertainty and confusion might play havoc with the efficiency of operations."

A lengthy discussion follows. Tod responds to Violet's concern by stating that "judgment should be reserved concerning the acquisition of new equipment; in fact, no new equipment should be acquired unless its benefits outweigh its costs." He answers Chim with the comment that "any new system should be designed to operate as simply as possible; brief special-training sessions can quickly teach them what they need to know to use the system. Also, an improved information system can really help in the marketing area. Not only can it help to meet promised delivery dates, but it can show you ways to increase sales." John promises Mark that he will announce that "no employees will be laid off because of a new system. Instead, affected employees will be transferred and retrained. Normal attrition will provide the cost savings that we expect from the new system over the long run." The president then goes on to assure all of the managers present that "you will participate in and have substantial control over the planning and development of an improved information system. Also, none of you will suffer any loss of authority due to any new system. It will be there to serve you, not to reduce your status."

After another meeting, and repeated reassurances such as the foregoing, the vice-presidents vote to commence a systems development program as soon as possible. Then the president takes the idea to the board of directors, which after another discussion concurs with the proposed program.

Organizational additions. The president next makes two major appointments, which the board of directors ratifies. His first appointment is an information systems steering committee to oversee the systems development program. This committee, which is to report directly to him, will consist of the six vice-presidents and be chaired by Mark Andrews. His second appointment is an information systems manager. Tod Stuart agrees to accept this position and to resign from the CPA firm. Tod, who is to report to the vice-president of administration, will organize and direct an information systems department.

Tod's first step after his appointment is to find two key managers—the systems de-

velopment manager and the data processing manager. He reaches into the accounting function for both managers. As the systems development manager he selects Eric Peter, who is currently the assistant chief cost accountant. Eric has an analytical mind, works well with all the managers of the firm, and has a broad and deep understanding of the firm's activities. As the data processing manager he selects Cynthia King, who is currently performing the same role within the accounting function. She is familiar with the computer equipment currently in use and with such accounting-oriented applications as payroll and inventory recordkeeping.

Figure 21-11 portrays a selected portion of Precise's organizational structure, including these additions.

Systems planning. The steering committee beings meeting weekly. (Later, after the initial planning is completed, it will meet monthly or when the need arises.) At the first two meetings the members discuss the objectives and policies relative to the information system. Their deliberations result in the preparation of a memorandum, which the president issues to all managers. The first page of the memorandum (which appears as Figure 21-12) presents the objectives. The remaining pages present more specifics concerning the objectives and policies. For example, acceptable sales growth is specified to be 10 percent annually, with at least one new product introduced each year. A high level of customer service means 99 percent of all orders are to be delivered on time. One of the policies states that a strategic systems plan is to be prepared and revised at least once each year and lists steps comprising the planning process.

During the next several meetings the committee reviews drafts of a strategic systems plan prepared by Tod. After several rewrites a plan emerges that is acceptable to the committee. Since the entire plan totals 50 pages, it cannot be reproduced here. How-

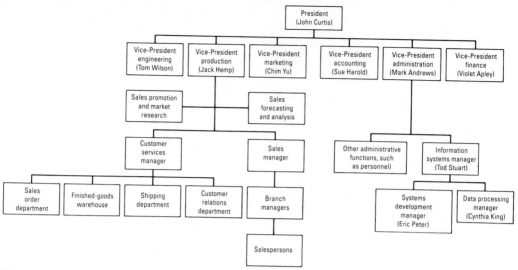

FIGURE 21-11 A partial organization chart for the Precise Manufacturing Company.

PRECISE MANUFACTURING CO.

Memorandum

To: All Managers
From: John Curtis, President
Subject: Objectives and Policies Pertaining to the Information System
Date: October 1, 1990

As our firm grows over the years in size and complexity, it is necessary that the information system grow and adapt to provide the information needed for planning and control purposes. This statement lists the objectives that the companywide information system should meet in the years ahead and issues the initial policies that are to aid in implementing the objectives. The objectives and policies are the result of considerable thought on the part of our Information System Steering Committee and should lead to a greatly improved information system.

Objectives:

1. To foster continued growth in sales by providing information regarding product demand, market trends, competitors' actions, new products, state of the economy, and technological developments.

2. To develop and maintain a high level of customer service by providing appropriate information that enables shipments to be delivered when promised and in good condition.

3. To conserve resources and reduce operating costs by providing information for controlling the productivity of employees, the levels of inventories, the utilization of equipment, and the percentage of production-line rejects.

4. To maintain financial soundness by providing information regarding the flow of and need for working capital and long-term funds.

5. To adapt the information system to future changes encountered, in order to continue to provide managers at all levels with all the information that they need, when they need it, for making effective decisions.

6. To incorporate new techniques and equipment into the information system when they show promise of providing information benefits that exceed their costs.

FIGURE 21-12 A statement of information system objectives for Precise.

PRECISE MANUFACTURING CO.

Strategic Systems Plan
for the five years from 1991 through 1995

I. Summary of the plan

II. Objectives of the redesigned information system

III. Assumptions and constraints

IV. Schedule of personnel requirements (person-months)

V. Schedule of cost requirements (dollars)

VI. Schedule of equipment requirements (dollars and units)

VII. Systems projects
   a. Title
   b. Problems and objectives
   c. Scope and relationship to other projects
   d. Estimated time schedule
   e. Estimated personnel, equipment, and other needed resources
   f. Justification, or expected benefits versus costs

Appendix A. Summary of data processing equipment currently in use

Appendix B. Forecast of hardware and software developments

FIGURE 21-13   An outline of the strategic systems plan for Precise.

ever, an outline of the plan appears in Figure 21-13. Parts IV, V, and VI are the essence of the plan. Together they reflect the resource requirements for the planning period, broken down by quarters. Their totals have been obtained by summing the data estimated for the projects identified in part VII.

The steering committee forwards the plan to the president. John notes his agreement and submits it to the board of directors with a recommendation for approval. On January 4, 1991, six months after John took the first step toward planning, the board gives full approval to a comprehensive systems plan. The only major constraint specified is that the annual budgeted amounts for information system development and opera-

tions should not exceed 1 percent of net sales.

Project investigation and ranking. Now system development projects can be selected and commenced. At the next meeting of the steering committee, Tod Stuart therefore reviews the various projects identified in the plan, such as the projects concerning inventory management, production management, purchasing and quality control, distribution management, general ledger and financial reporting, operational budgeting, financial management, and sales order processing and management.

After considerable discussion the steering committee selects three possible projects for further study at this time: the inventory management project, the financial management project, and the sales order processing and management project. Tod therefore asks Eric Peter, the recently appointed systems development manager, to undertake this assignment. Eric in turn assigns Renee Irvine, the firm's most experienced systems analyst, to conduct a preliminary investigation. Renee accordingly spends a week in each of the three areas. After observing operations, interviewing key personnel, and gathering facts, she concludes that all three areas warrant extensive systems development.

Tod carries this news to his superior, Mark Andrews. At a February meeting of the steering committee they therefore jointly recommend that project proposals be prepared. They also suggest priority rankings for these three likely projects, as well as for all the others that have been identified.

Their nomination for highest priority goes to the sales order processing and management project (henceforth called the sales project). Several reasons are given for this choice. Sales order processing represents an activity that triggers other key activities, such as production and purchasing. Improvements to the activity are needed because of rising clerical costs, numerous billing errors, and complaints about delayed deliveries. Substantial payoffs in cost savings and customer relations should result. Furthermore, the better sales information provided as a result of this project should foster competitive advantages.

The second highest priority is recommended for the financial management project, with the inventory management project receiving the third-place ranking.

Detailed project definition. Since he performed the preliminary surveys, Renee is assigned the task of drafting project proposals. She begins with the proposal for the sales project. Within a few days she submits a draft copy to Eric. Key sections of this draft

proposal are summarized in the following paragraphs.

The **objectives** (and hence expected benefits) from the project are to:

1. Shorten the average time between the receipt of a sales order and the shipping of the ordered products, so that at least 99 percent of promised delivery dates are met.

2. Improve the up-to-dateness of information regarding the status of any particular sales order and the availability of finished goods, so that no record is out-of-date by more than eight hours.

3. Reduce the average time required for responding to customer inquiries concerning the status of orders to less than one minute.

4. Reduce the billing error rate from one error per 12 transactions to one error per 1000 transactions.

5. Reduce the costs of processing sales orders and of billing by 25 percent.

6. Improve the information needed for making decisions concerning sales.

The **scope** of the project extends through all systems development phases; it will even carry into the operational phase until the users are satisfied that the improved system is functioning properly. With regard to breadth, the project extends from the point at which the sales order is obtained from the customer until the shipment and invoice leave for the customer. The organizational units to be included are the branch sales offices, the data processing section, the finished-goods warehouse, and the sales order, credit, shipping, and billing departments. Functions having close relationships include finished-goods inventory control, sales analysis, production planning and control, general accounting, and accounts receivable. Therefore, it will be necessary to coordinate design efforts pertaining to the sales project with design efforts directed at such functions.

The scope of the project extends beyond the operational level; it also includes the information needs of the several managerial levels within the function responsible for sales-related decisions.

Two major **constraints** of the project are the time schedule and the cost budget. Two additional constraints (imposed by Chim, the marketing vice-president) are that

1. The organizational structure within the marketing function is not to be altered.
2. Customers are not to be disturbed in any way by the project.

Resources needed for the project include personnel, supplies, and equipment. The key personnel will be the members of the project team. (In the course of preparing this proposal, Renee checked with Eric Peter about members for the team. Eric then "recruited" three current employees: Steve Randle, a section head in the sales order department; Patsy Meyers, a management trainee with an MBA degree; and Ralph Scott, an experienced accountant in the internal audit department. Although their superiors did not like to lose these valued persons, the president's strong support for the systems development program exerted powerful persuasion.) Other personnel include programmers, typists, and clerks, who will be assigned to assist the team as needed. Supplies will consist mainly of paper and notebooks. Equipment will include purchased calculators and leased computer terminals.

The **time schedule** is summarized by means of a Gantt chart. Initiating and organizing activities are to start April 1, 1991, and the project is slated for completion on November 30, 1992. More detailed charts accompany this schedule. Work plans are also included within the proposal, showing who is to do what.

The values of **expected benefits** are estimated as follows:

Reduction in clerical salaries (7 clerks @ $16,000)[20]	$112,000
Savings in supplies because of reduced errors and back orders	3,000
Savings in data processing equipment because of more efficient usage	9,000
Added profits from more sales (and less lost sales) because of better customer service	40,000
Total expected annual benefits	$164,000

In addition, there should be such intangible benefits as more timely and relevant information for employees and managers. However, no values have been assigned to these benefits at this time.

The estimated **costs** can be classified as project-related costs and added costs pertaining to the improved system when operational. Project costs are summarized as follows.

	1991	1992
Team members' salaries	$ 95,500	$116,700
Programmer's salary		32,800
Salaries for typists and clerks	9,000	11,000
Supplies and miscellaneous	2,000	3,000
Equipment	1,500	2,500
Total project costs	$105,000	$166,000

Added costs pertaining to the improved system, which will begin in 1993, are estimated to be $50,000 in the first year of operation and to increase by $8000 in each following year. These costs, presumably arising from new up-to-date data processing equipment and additional systems support personnel, are highly uncertain at this point. However, they provide the basis for a rough cost-benefit comparison. More-refined fig-

[20]Although no employees will be discharged when the new sales system is installed, normal attrition should enable this reduction to be realized.

ures will become available as the system takes shape.

Project approval. After making certain minor revisions to the draft proposal, Eric has a final copy typed. The proposal then follows channels, going first to Tod and then to Mark. At a March meeting the steering committee approves the proposal. Then, in the last week of March, the project proposal receives final approval from the president.

Initiation of project. Several events take place after the final project approval. Eric immediately appoints Renee to be the project manager. They both meet with the team members, who will be assigned on a full-time basis to the project. The following day the president meets with Chim, the marketing vice-president, plus his sales managers and department heads. He informs them of the project and asks them to tell their employees. That same day the president issues a formal announcement of the project; as a part of the announcement he states that no one will be discharged or demoted. Those no longer needed in sales order processing and management activities will be transferred elsewhere and trained for new positions.

Shortly thereafter, Renee completes her proposals for the other two projects and turns the drafts over to Eric. Then she organizes the sales project by obtaining supplies, working space, and needed calculating equipment. She also reserves spaces in a ba-sic systems analysis course, offered in downtown Chicago, to which she dispatches his three team members. Finally, she arranges for monthly progress review meetings to be held with Tod and Eric. Progress reports are to be prepared quarterly and submitted to the steering committee.

Required

a. Prepare a project summary page for the sales project as it might appear in the strategic systems plan.

b. Prepare a Gantt chart for the sales project, if the respective phases are expected to end on the following dates: initiation, April 30; analysis, July 31; design, December 15; justification and selection, January 31; and implementation, November 30, 1992. All phases are expected to begin immediately at the conclusion of the preceding phase except for the justification and selection phase, which is expected to begin one-half month earlier.

c. Prepare a summarized work plan for the selected project. Make assumptions concerning the various tasks to be performed, the persons assigned to each task, and the estimated man-days assigned to each task.

d. Prepare a comparison of expected benefits and costs for the five-year life of the improved sales information system.

e. Comment on the soundness of the systems planning steps.

Solution

a. Project Summary for the Sales Project:

Project: Sales Order Processing and Management Module
Problems: Rising clerical costs, numerous billing errors, and complaints about delayed deliveries.

Project Scope: Survey the present procedures and reports relating to sales orders, shipping, and billing; analyze the operating, planning, and control needs related to branch sales offices, sales order section, finished-goods warehouse, credit department, shipping department, and billing department; develop a detailed design of an improved sales information system; integrate the designed system with such other systems as the inventory management system, the production planning system, and the accounts receivable system; install, test, and put into operation the designed information system.

Project Objectives:
   To improve the sales order processing and management system so that it provides needed information regarding sales levels and flows to other systems and to managers; to enhance sales processing efficiency with respect to processing and shipping times and costs; to improve accuracy of processing and billing.

Estimated Time Schedule: Beginning on April 1, 1991, and ending on November 30, 1992.

Estimated Resources:

   Person-Months: 80.   Cost: $271,000.
   Equipment: Purchased calculators and leased computer terminals.

Expected Benefits:
1. Shortened average time between the receipt of a sales order and the shipping of the ordered products, so that at least 99 percent of promised delivery dates are met.

2. Reduced average time to respond to customer inquiries concerning the status of orders, so that 100 percent of inquiries are answered within one minute.

3. Reduced billing error rate to one error per 1000 transactions (from a current rate of one error per 12 transactions).

4. Reduced costs of processing sales orders and billing, by at least 25 percent.

5. Improved up-to-dateness of information regarding the status of any particular sales order and the availability of finished goods, so that no record is out of date by more than eight hours.

6. Better information for making decisions concerning sales.

b. Gantt Chart:

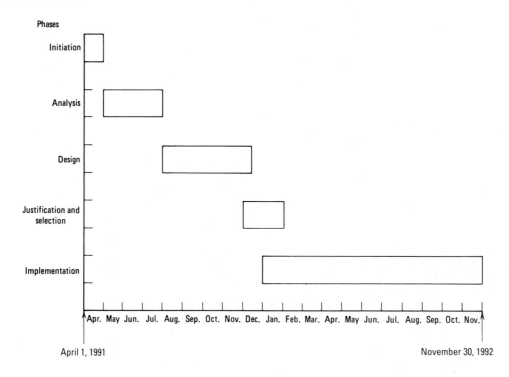

c. Summary work plan:

Project: Sales Order Processing and Management

Task	Assigned To	Estimated Person-Days
I. *Project Initiation*		
1. Organize resources and establish controls	RI	11
2. Obtain training	All	62
3. Obtain overview of information system environment	PM, SR, RS	15
II. *Systems Analysis*		
1. Survey present sales order processing system	PM, SR, RS	140
2. Perform work measurement techniques	RI	20
3. Analyze gathered data and determine system requirements	All	52
4. Determine information needs of managers	RI, RS	50
5. Prepare analysis report	RI	10
III. *Systems Design*		
1. Define alternative designs	All	80
2. Design reports	All	50
3. Design data base	RI, SR	70
4. Design data processing and inputs	PM, RS	100
5. Design controls and security measures	PM, RS, SR	30
6. Prepare systems design report	RI	10

(Table continued)

Task	Assigned To	Estimated Person-Days
IV. *Justification and Selection*		
1. Prepare feasibility analyses	PM, RS	62
2. Evaluate hardware and software proposals	RI, SR	60
3. Prepare recommendation for selection	RI	16
V. *Systems Implementation*		
1. Prepare detailed design, including programs		300
2. Train personnel, document procedures, install system		440
3. Test and convert to improved system		218
Total person-days		1796

Note: No assignments are indicated during the systems implementation phase, since the project team members will likely be replaced (at least in part) by others such as programmers and training personnel.

d. A comparison of expected benefits and costs appears in the table below.

e. The Precise Manufacturing Company has generally followed a sound series of systems planning steps. The reactions of the various managers are to be expected. An alternative approach that could have been considered would be to conduct an extensive feasibility study *before* deciding upon specific projects. The purpose of the feasibility study would be to determine if a new mainframe computer system is feasible. Under the described procedure, this determination must be made at some point during the sales project.

	1991	1992	1993	1994	1995
Benefits	0	0	$164,000	$164,000	$164,000
Costs	$105,000	$166,000	50,000	58,000	66,000
Net, yearly	($105,000)	($166,000)	$114,000	$106,000	$ 98,000
Net, cumulative	**($105,000)**	**($271,000)**	**($157,000)**	**($ 51,000)**	**$ 47,000**

Review Questions

21-1 What is the meaning of each of the following terms?

Information systems manager
Steering committee
Systems development manager
Applications manager
Project manager
Systems analyst
Application programmer
Manager of technical services
Information center manager

Data base administrator (DBA)
Information resource management
Piecemeal approach
Top-down approach
Bottom-up approach
Total-system approach
Modular approach
"Great leap forward" approach
Evolutionary approach
Prototyping
Strategic systems planning
Feasibility study
Project proposal
Project team

21-2 Discuss the likely managers to whom the information systems manager might report.

21-3 Discuss the internal structure of the systems development group within the information systems function.

21-4 What are the advantages of a centralized information systems function?

21-5 What are the advantages of a decentralized information systems function?

21-6 How may close relationships be maintained between the accounting and information systems functions?

21-7 What views of importance to information systems managers are embodied in the information resource management concept?

21-8 What are the causal factors that lead to a need for systems development?

21-9 Describe several types of triggers that may initiate systems development activity.

21-10 Discuss the several approaches to systems development.

21-11 In what situations is prototyping likely to be a preferred approach?

21-12 Identify the major types of subsystems that are candidates for systems development.

21-13 What strategies can be employed to ensure sound systems development?

21-14 List the phases in the systems development cycle.

21-15 What factors may affect the systems development cycle?

21-16 What are the reasons for the growing recognition of strategic planning as a needed process?

21-17 Discuss the steps needed for sound strategic planning.

21-18 What are the typical functions of a steering committee?

21-19 What are the benefits of a strategic systems plan?

21-20 Describe the likely contents of a strategic systems plan.

21-21 What are the steps leading to a project proposal?

21-22 Describe the likely contents of a project proposal.

21-23 What criteria can be employed to establish the priorities of competing projects?

21-24 What initiating steps should be taken prior to the actual commencement of a systems project?

21-25 Why is it important to inform employees and managers as soon as possible of an approved systems project, and what should an announcement contain?

21-26 Describe the composition of a project team that will be involved in a project affecting the marketing function.

21-27 Why is training important for those who will be involved in or affected by systems development projects?

Discussion Questions

21-28 Describe prevailing conditions within a firm that might necessitate the assumption by the president of immediate authority over the information systems functions, so that the information systems manager reports directly to him or her.

21-29 Discuss the trade-offs involved in deciding the extent to which the information systems function of a large firm should be decentralized.

21-30 Why is the accounting function decentralized in many firms? Does this situation parallel the decentralization of the information systems function?

21-31 What are the roles of the external auditor in a firm's systems development?

21-32 A consultant comments to the president of a manufacturing firm, ''Your firm's financial health is declining because your picture of your business has become blurred.'' What are the implications of this comment with respect to the information system?

21-33 Suggest symptoms that could reflect the following underlying problems:

    a. Inadequate internal control system.

    b. Inefficient procedures.

    c. Insufficient information provided to managers.

    d. Poorly motivated employees.

    e. Lack of easily accessible and up-to-date information.

    f. Poorly integrated operations and procedures.

    g. Weak organizational structure.

    h. Inadequate decision processes.

    i. Inadequate processing equipment.

21-34 Should a small business firm emphasize the bottom-up or the top-down approach to systems development?

21-35 Which systems development approaches are best for each of the following types of system applications?

    a. Decision support system

    b. Transaction processing systems.

    c. Operational support systems.

21-36 Identify several pitfalls of systems development and indicate how each may be circumvented.

21-37 Discuss the difficulties that can arise when one portion of an information system has been newly designed and installed, while the remainder of the system is relatively obsolete and problem-ridden.

21-38 Is it possible for any except the smallest firms to achieve ''fully realized'' information systems that are completely up to date and sound throughout? If not, what are the implications for systems development in such firms?

21-39 In which systems development phases would each of the following positions likely be actively involved, and why?

    a. Systems analyst.

    b. Managerial accountant.

    c. Auditor.

    d. Information systems manager.

    e. Higher-level manager.

    f. Programmer.

    g. Data preparation clerk.

21-40 Discuss the relationship of the strategic systems plan to the overall budgeting and planning process of a firm.

21-41 Should the strategic systems plan incorporate new projects if the need for the systems to be developed via the projects has not yet become manifest?

21-42 How can the strategic systems plan accommodate changes that take place inside and outside the firm?

21-43 How can a steering committee reduce conflicts between the information systems function and user departments?

21-44 In what ways do projects currently in progress affect decisions concerning upcoming projects?

21-45 State one or more quantitative objectives that might pertain to each of the following systems projects undertaken by a manufacturing firm:

a. Payroll processing system.
b. Accounts payable—cash disbursements processing system.
c. Cash receipts—accounts receivable processing system.
d. Cash management system.
e. Production management system.
f. Personnel management system.
g. General ledger—financial reporting system.

21-46 Two ways to establish the scopes of systems projects are according to (1) transaction processing systems and (2) operational functions. Discuss other schemes by which to define the scopes of systems projects.

21-47 What are the advantages in having a systems project team headed by

a. a systems analyst?
b. a manager who will use the system?

21-48 Suggest three overall objectives and three key success factors for each of the following types of firms:

a. Automobile manufacturer.
b. Bank.
c. Public utility.
d. Wholesale grocer.
e. Contractor.
f. Jobbing printer.
g. Commercial airline.
h. Hardware manufacturer.
i. Life insurance company.
j. Department store.
k. Cosmetics goods manufacturer.
l. Food manufacturer.
m. Computer manufacturer.
n. Hospital.

Problems

21-1 The Bryan Trucking Company of Newark, Delaware, has four major functions: operations, sales, finance, and administration. Each function is headed by a vice-

president. Three managers report to the vice-president of finance: the controller, the treasurer, and the budget director. In turn, four managers report to the controller: the chief financial accountant, the tax manager, the cost analysis and reports manager, and the EDP (electronic data processing) manager.

Recently the president has received several complaints. The operations and sales vice-presidents have complained that they do not receive adequate reports to help them in planning trucking operations or in analyzing sales trends; they also say that the reports they do receive are often a week or so late. In fact, they say, the financial statements and accounting reports always seem to take precedence over other reports. They feel that this situation is not only unfair; it is also hazardous to the firm's financial health, since sales and operations are the primary contributions to the firm's profits. The EDP manager complains (more softly and indirectly) that she is short of staff and hardware, since the systems budget is too restrictive. She must contest with the other accounting managers for budget resources; after all, she has been told by the controller, there are only so many dollars available for finance and accounting activities. Currently the dollars available to her are being used to maintain generally sound transaction processing systems and financial reporting; as a result, few dollars are available to provide other key management information.

The president is concerned about these complaints. He feels that relevant, adequate, and timely information is vital to the firm's well-being. Therefore, he calls on a consultant from a local management consulting firm to aid him in resolving this problem.

Required

Prepare a report from the consultant to the president of the Bryan Trucking Company. The report should identify and weigh the alternative courses of action available to him and suggest a preferable course of action.

21-2 The Quaker Public Service Company of Philadelphia requires a sizable information systems function to maintain its extensive computer-based information system. Heading the function is a director of information systems, who reports to the executive vice-president. Among the managers and organizational units comprising the information systems function are the following:

> Assistant director of information systems.
> Data processing manager.
> Systems development manager.
> Data control supervisor.
> Data base administrator.
> Technical staff.
> Planning staff.
> Personnel development staff.
> Data preparation supervisor.
> Data librarian.
> Operations supervisor.
> Manager, systems programming.
> Program maintenance manager.
> New systems design manager.
> First-shift operations supervisor.
> Second-shift operations supervisor.
> Third-shift operations supervisor.
> Hardware maintenance manager.
> Manager, special services.
> Project manager, billing and customer accounting.
> Project manager, work order and expense accounting.
> Project manager, accounts payable and disbursements.

Required

Prepare an organization chart of the information systems function in good form.

21-3 The Chem Products Corporation of Lafayette, Indiana, has employed automated data processing for a number of years. Furthermore, the manager of EDP, Mike O'Dell,

has headed the data processing activities since the days when punched-card equipment was in use. Now he supervises an information system that incorporates the latest-model Burgen computer. As in the days of punched-card equipment, he reports to the controller (who in turn reports to the vice-president of finance).

Mike O'Dell has organized his department so that three managers report directly to him: the manager of data preparation, the manager of systems analysis and design, and the manager of operations and programming.

Susan Hazelbaker, the manager of data preparation, supervises the data entry clerks. In addition, she maintains the data library and documentation books.

Doug White, the manager of systems analysis and design, supervises five systems analysts. They are each assigned systems design tasks, pertaining either to new systems or to systems maintenance, that they are expected to undertake on their own. In the case of most assignments their outputs consist of flowcharts and forms layouts, from which the programmers are expected to develop new or modified programs. Often, however, the systems analysts must coordinate their efforts with the procedures and reports section, which has the responsibility of developing procedures, forms, reports, the chart of accounts, and documentation pertaining to noncomputerized operations. This procedures and reports section is headed by Dorothy Hines, who reports to the chief accountant, a manager on the same level as Mike O'Dell.

Bill Ferrell, the manager of operations and programming, has responsibility for three activities: computer operations, computer programming, and data control. However, the computer operators and programmers in effect form one group, since they assist each other in their respective duties and even substitute for each other when an employee is sick or on vacation. Also, of course, the computer programmers work closely with the systems analysts, since the latter provide the specifications from which the former must prepare programs. The data control clerks and the computer operators also assist each other; for instance, a computer operator may check the control totals to the batch input control sheet or may distribute the outputs to the user departments.

Required

Critique the organizational structure of the Chem Products Corporation.

21-4 The Saltwater Shipwares Company of Bridgeport, Connecticut, manufactures and sells a variety of small products for marine craft. It maintains an inventory of almost 12,000 separate items, many of which are low-volume sellers. Most of the sales are made through a catalog distributed to retail outlets of marine supplies throughout many of the 50 states.

The current information system is a mixture of manual and computer-based processing, with an emphasis on the former. From time to time the president has considered further computerization; however, the firm has reaped sizable profits every year during the past decade, so she has not pursued the matter.

Added growth and a consequent stepped-up pace in operations, though, have put almost intolerable strains on the data and information processing activities. These strains can be observed in the following comments made at a recent meeting of several key managers convened by the president:

Inventory Manager: Our firm's enduring objective of customer service is very commendable and has gotten us where we are. However, it means that we must keep all of the inventory items in stock at all times. Because our record keeping for inventory transactions is swamped, this policy requires, in effect, that we continually must be restocking in order to guarantee an adequate supply on hand.

Production Manager: To keep inventory fully stocked in every item, we are making one short production run after another. Short production runs are very costly,

and they require a lot more paperwork overall. My foremen can't get anything done because they are always filling out forms. When they do get a moment free, another rush order comes along.

Treasurer: Our desire never to be out of stock of course increases our inventory investment and hence our cash needs. However, there is another problem. Summer is our peak season, whereas winter is a trough. This seasonal effect complicates my cash planning; one season I'm hustling to raise enough cash to finance our replenishment of inventory, which has been depleted by peak sales; in another season I have large amounts of inactive cash lying around. If I could forecast better, I could do a better cash-planning job; however, I usually can't get the sales and inventory data fast enough to anticipate our needs.

Distribution Manager: More and more deliveries to customers are late. In the past we've been able to promise delivery in a week. Now we are lucky to deliver in two weeks, although we can reduce the time to 10 days by working overtime. One reason for the delays is the added number of shipments, but another reason is that we don't receive the ordered goods as soon from the warehouse. Also, many of the orders are improperly filled, and we must send them back to be redone. The warehouse pickers claim that they are being run ragged because the items on the orders are listed without regard to their warehouse locations.

Sales Manager: These late deliveries have caused serious difficulties with our customers. Many have griped about our deteriorating service, and some have switched to competing lines. Another problem that concerns me is our catalog. It has been published late the last two years and contains too many errors. For instance, certain dropped items have not been excluded, and many price changes have had to be handled by supplement sheets. Customers expect the catalog to be on time and accurate.

Required

a. Relate the symptoms mentioned in the foregoing comments to underlying problems with the information system.

b. Suggest objectives for a revised information system. (At least two of the objectives should include quantitative factors, based on assumed levels of desired efficiency or effectiveness.)

21-5 The president of the Reckers Manufacturing Company of Bozeman, Montana, has become increasingly concerned with apparent weaknesses in the firm's information system. Data processing costs are rising, records are out of date and often incorrect, reports contain conflicting and inadequate information, customers often receive ordered products several weeks later than promised, and so on.

As the problems seem to be worsening, the president decides to get the views of a consultant. The selected consultant performs a preliminary survey and reports back that the information system does indeed exhibit signs of ineffectiveness and inefficiency. Each function is in effect operating its own data processing system. Certain of the systems, such as the production and inventory transaction processing systems, mainly employ manual procedures. Other systems, such as the accounts receivable and payroll transaction processing systems, employ batch-oriented computer-based procedures. All of the systems lack adequate controls and are poorly designed. Duplicate files are maintained between systems. Although each system generates large quantities of documents and reports, the information is not useful for controlling operations or for making decisions that cut across two or more functional areas.

Because of the seriousness of the problem, the president calls a meeting of his top managers. In attendance are the controller, the production manager, the purchasing manager, the treasurer, the personnel manager, and the sales manager. After hearing the report of the consultant, they agree that definite steps need to be taken. However, when the president proposes that the information system be completely overhauled, he receives the following comments:

Controller: Who will be in charge of such an extensive project? The accounting function has a key role in the information system, and our people do not want some outsider or nonaccountant messing with the chart of accounts or telling us how to process accounting transactions or to prepare financial statements for our stockholders.

Production Manager: Since production and inventories are the heart of our operations, we should have the biggest say in any design effort. However, I don't see how you can computerize production scheduling, since the schedule changes so frequently because of rush orders.

Purchasing Manager: I agree with the production manager. Computerizing the purchasing or inventory procedures doesn't make sense, since human judgment often must be applied. For instance, if a particular material is found to be out of stock, we don't just automatically order that item. We look at the status of other materials acquired from the same supplier and place a larger order for several items. In that way we get a bigger discount. A computer can't do that job.

Treasurer: I don't see how we can afford a costly and lengthy study; our financial position is not healthy enough to allow us to spend recklessly.

Personnel Manager: Such a massive effort as you describe would be extremely traumatic to our employees. Many would become upset and quit or would try to obstruct changes.

Sales Manager: Do we *really* need a new information system? After all, our sales are doing well and I have a better "feel" for the market than any thick, fancy reports can give me.

The president begins his rejoinder with this statement: "I appreciate your concerns. However, something must be done. I don't receive the information I need to manage this firm, and there are too many other problems to ignore. Also, I believe that we can make the change in just a few months' time. We'll just contract with our consultant friend here; he can bring in enough manpower to design and install a total, modern computer-based system."

Required

Respond to the comments of each of the managers, including the president. Suggest suitable steps, if any, that should be taken by the management of the Reckers Manufacturing Company to rectify the problems related to the information system.

21-6 The Sunbelt National Bank of Baton Rouge, Louisiana, is a full-service bank: It not only offers checking and savings account services, but also makes loans for personal and business endeavors.

The bank's information system is a combination of automated and manual procedures, but on balance it appears rather inadequately to serve the needs of the bank and its managers. For instance, checks are processed by means of special sorter equipment and a centralized computer. However, many data processing activities are performed manually. Moreover, information concerning depositors and borrowers is difficult to access and information for managerial decision making is scant.

At this month's management meeting the bank's data processing manager describes to the president and other key officers the various sophisticated data processing devices available. He cites, as examples, the availability of terminals and data bases. After a full discussion, the management decides to undertake an extensive revision of the bank's information system.

Required

a. Discuss the approaches to systems development from which the bank's management may select.
b. Describe the combination of approaches suitable for developing a revised information system for the Sunbelt National Bank.

21-7 Marvin Grey is the president of the Grey Manufacturing Company, a firm located in St. Paul, Minnesota. After returning from a business equipment convention, he calls in Denise Ballard, the director of information systems, and expresses his enthusiasm for what he has just seen. He further states that he has decided the Grey Manufacturing Company should have the most advanced equipment and systems concepts available. All the warehouses, plants, and sales offices are to be tied by a communications network to the home office and to each other. Each remote site will maintain its own miniprocessors and terminals that can perform remote processing and also transmit data to the home office and to all other re-

mote sites. A sophisticated data base with a company wide schema, plus distributed data bases at the remote sites, will store all active data.

Denise Ballard mentions in response that she has not been associated with system development programs involving the features mentioned by Grey. In fact, the present system at Grey is a basic, uncomplicated batch-oriented computer-based system that focuses on the more routine accounting transactions.

Marvin Grey responds that the system he described is essentially simple and straightforward. Thus, it should not be unduly difficult to design and implement. Denise can learn whatever else she needs to know on the job. He, for one, wants to "get the jump" on his competitors. Denise is therefore to present a systems development plan in three weeks.

Required

Discuss the pros and cons of Mr. Grey's approach to systems development.

21-8 The Book Chain, Inc., is a chain of 10 retail bookstores scattered throughout Alaska. Headquartered at Anchorage, the chain specializes in outdoor recreational, technological, and trade books, as well as fictional books of all types. The firm has been successful for many years, because reading helps people to endure the long, hard winters. Its sales received an especially strong stimulus a few years ago when legions of construction workers and professional personnel poured into the state to build the long pipeline from the North Slope oilfield. Each new year, however, brings in ever more potential customers as cities such as Anchorage undergo population explosions.

Partly because of its phenomenal sales growth, the Book Chain has overlooked certain inefficient operations and poor management practices. For example, payroll procedures contain several significant control weaknesses that have led to the overpayment of employees or the preparation of paychecks for nonexistent employees. Also, book ordering is not carefully controlled; many orders contain errors in quantities, which result in back orders. Because of the great physical distances involved, a back order may require 8 to 10 weeks to fill. Furthermore, the ordering manager makes ordering decisions based on inadequate information, leading to the gross overstocking of certain books and to understocking of currently popular books.

Such inefficiencies and weak decision making have led to higher operational costs and poor customer service. Although the firm still makes substantial profits in spite of these weaknesses, the competition in book retailing is growing. In the next year or so, sales and hence profits could suffer severely.

In view of this contingency, the owners of the Book Chain have decided that a thorough revision of procedures, practices, and the information system is highly desirable. A systems development effort should lead to changes in all operational and management activities at each of the 10 stores, as well as in the accounting, ordering, receiving, personnel, and planning activities at the main office.

Required

Describe the phases and major steps that should comprise the development of an improved information system at the Book Chain, culminating with the installation and operation of the improved information system. Limit your description to roughly two pages, but be sure to incorporate references to specific circumstances of the Book Chain.

21-9 Most firms that undertake extensive systems developments of their information systems likely will organize systems projects that focus on payroll, cash receipts, cash disbursements, and other basic transactions. However, each type of firm likely will organize projects that reflect its unique operations and management activities. Suggest project areas that are unique and suitable to the following types of firms or organizations:

    a. Bank.
    b. Hospital.
    c. University.
    d. Municipality.
    e. Contractor.
    f. Public utility.

21-10 Kids Incorporated is a medium-size toy manufacturer headquartered in Oakland, California. The firm manufactures three lines of toys: plastic, metal, and electric. Each line consists of approximately 30 individual toy products. Although all the toys are manufactured in the same plant, each line is separated organizationally from the others. However, all three lines are sold by all members of the sales force, who are assigned to the five regional sales territories covering the continental United States.

The president of Kids Incorporated, Ms. Uno, has become increasingly dissatisfied with the firm's information system. She and her fellow managers can obtain information from the system only at the end of the month. Because of the present highly competitive conditions in the toy-making industry, such infrequent reports put the firm at a disadvantage. Upon questioning the controller, the president learns that the information system also has serious weaknesses at the operational level.

Thus, Ms Uno informs Mr. Moni, the controller, that he is to study and develop a redesigned information system. She states that the only constraint is "to leave the organizational structure untouched. Otherwise, you have free rein." However, she insists that the study must be completed within four months, as conditions have become intolerable.

Mr. Moni realizes that he does not have the time or expertise to undertake such a systems study. Therefore, he hires Berry Low, a recent MBA graduate, as a special staff assistant. Berry is assigned the system study as his first project; he is to report to Mr. Moni when the study is completed and again when the revised system design is prepared.

Berry Low goes to work. He researches what other firms are doing and talks to computer manufacturers. He follows their ideas and approaches as closely as possible. He designs forms to aid in maintaining better control over production and marketing operations. He designs reports to provide more timely sales and competitive information to managers. He chooses a computer that is the most modern version available. In fact, it will not be on the market for another two months, although he is assured that it can be delivered within the four-month deadline.

At the end of four months Mr. Moni, together with Berry Low, attends a meeting of the president and top managers of the firm. Berry presents the design for the new system. All of the managers are impressed. They enthusiastically approve the acquisition of the computer system and the entire system design.

One month later the new computer-based information system is in place, thanks to the efforts of Berry Low and several sales engineers from the computer manufacturer. The employees, operating managers, and foremen then see the system for the first time. They had not been told about it earlier, so that they would not become upset. Some respond to this surprise with grumbles and mumbles; some are even overheard to say that they had guessed something like this was in the works. The grumbles, mumbles, and comments are suppressed, however, when Ms. Uno announces that no one will be fired because of the new system.

Three months pass. To the surprise of the managers, as well as of Ms. Uno and Berry Low, the complaints come rolling in. More time goes by, and the complaints become a crescendo. Finally, when it is evident that the system is not working but instead is causing dissatisfaction, the computer and

system are scrapped. The firm returns to the old way of doing things. The only feature retained is the more timely preparation of managerial reports.

Required

a. Critique the approach to systems development employed by Kids Incorporated.

b. Describe the phases and steps that should have been taken, from the planning phase to the implementation phase.

21-11 Audio Visual Corporation manufactures and sells visual display equipment. The company is headquartered near Boston. The majority of sales are made through seven geographical sales offices located in Los Angeles, Seattle, Minneapolis, Cleveland, Dallas, Boston, and Atlanta. Each sales office has a nearby warehouse to carry an inventory of new equipment and replacement parts. The remainder of the sales are made through manufacturers' representatives.

Audio Visual's manufacturing operations are conducted in a single plant, which is highly departmentalized. In addition to the assembly department, there are several departments responsible for various components used in the visual display equipment. The plant also has maintenance, engineering, scheduling, and cost accounting departments.

Early in 1988, management decided that its management information system (MIS) needed upgrading. As a result, the company ordered an advanced computer in 1988, and it was installed in July 1989. The main processing equipment is still located at corporate headquarters, and each of the seven sales offices is connected with the main processing unit by remote terminals.

The integration of the new computer into Audio Visual's information system was carried out by the MIS staff. The MIS manager and the four systems analysts who had the major responsibility for the integration were hired by the company in the spring of

1989. The department's other employees—programmers, machine operators and keypunch operators—have been with the company for several years.

During its early years, Audio Visual had a centralized decision-making organization. Top management formulated all plans and directed all operations. As the company expanded, some of the decision making was decentralized, although the information processing was still highly centralized. Departments had to coordinate their plans with the corporate office, but they had more freedom in developing their sales programs. However, as the company expanded, information problems developed. As a consequence, the MIS department was given the responsibility of improving the company's information processing system when the new equipment was installed.

The MIS analysts reviewed the information system in existence prior to the acquisition of the new computer and identified weaknesses. They then redesigned old applications and designed new applications in developing the new system to overcome the weaknesses. During the 18 months since the acquisition of the new equipment, the following applications have been redesigned or developed and are now operational: payroll, production scheduling, financial statement preparation, customer billing, raw materials usage in production, finished-goods inventory by warehouse. The operating departments of Audio Visual affected by the systems changes were rarely consulted or contacted until the system was operational and the new reports were distributed to the operating departments.

The president of Audio Visual is very pleased with the work of the MIS department. During a recent conversation with an individual who was interested in Audio Visual's new system, the president stated, "The MIS people are doing a good job and I have full confidence in their work. I touch base with the MIS people frequently, and they have encountered no difficulties in do-

ing their work. We paid a lot of money for the new equipment and the MIS people certainly cost enough, but the combination of the new equipment and new MIS staff should solve all of our problems."

Recently, two additional conversations regarding the computer and information system have taken place. One was between Jerry Adams, plant manager, and Bill Taylor, the MIS manager; the other was between Adams and Terry Williams, the new personnel manager.

Taylor–Adams Conversation

Adams: Bill, you're trying to run my plant for me. I'm supposed to be the manager, yet you keep interfering. I wish you would mind your own business.

Taylor: You've got a job to do, but so does my department. As we analyzed the information needed for production scheduling and by top management, we saw where improvements could be made in the work flow. Now that the system is operational, you can't reroute work and change procedures, because that would destroy the value of the information we're processing. And while I'm on that subject, it's getting to the point where we can't trust the information we're getting from production. The mark-sense cards we receive from production contain a lot of errors.

Adams: I'm responsible for the efficient operation of production. Quite frankly, I think I'm the best judge of production efficiency. The system you installed has reduced my work force and increased the work load of the remaining employees, but I don't see that this has improved anything. In fact, it might explain the high error rate in the cards.

Taylor: This new computer costs a lot of money, and I'm trying to be sure that the company gets its money's worth.

Adams–Williams Conversation

Adams: My best production assistant, the one I'm grooming to be a supervisor when the next opening occurs, came to me today and said he was thinking of quitting. When I asked him why, he said he didn't enjoy the work anymore. He's not the only one who is unhappy. The supervisors and department heads no longer have a voice in establishing production schedules. This new computer system has taken away the contribution we used to make to company planning and direction. We seem to be going way back to the days when top management made all the decisions. I have more production problems now than I used to. I think it boils down to a lack of interest on the part of my management team. I know the problem is within my area, but I thought you might be able to help me.

Williams: I have no recommendations for you now, but I've had similar complaints from purchasing and shipping. I think we should get your concerns on the agenda for our next plant management meeting.

Required

a. Apparently the development of and transition to the new computer-based system has created problems among the personnel of Audio Visual Corporation. Identify and briefly discuss the apparent causes of these problems.

b. How could the company have avoided the problems? What steps should be taken to avoid such problems in the future?

(CMA adapted)

21-12 *Datacruncher Office Equipment, Inc. (Continuing Case)*

Required

a. Prepare a brief memorandum from the president announcing the need for a systems development program and the composition of the steering committee. (Do not include information system objectives or policies in this memorandum.)

b. Outline a strategic systems plan and include the details of the following:

   (1) Objective of an improved information system.

   (2) Priorities for identified systems projects (as suggested by your instructor).

   (3) An organization chart (appendix to the plan).

   (4) A coded chart of accounts (appendix to the plan).

c. Prepare a proposal for one of the identified systems projects, including objectives, scope, constraints (if any), needed resources, time schedule, expected benefits and costs, and work plan.

d. Prepare a memorandum listing the steps necessary to initiate the project proposed in **c.**

e. Draft a policy statement concerning the treatment of employees and managers to be affected by the project proposal in **c.**

f. Prepare a memorandum suggesting desirable changes, if any, to the organizational structure.

Suggested Readings

Ahituv, Niv; Neumann, Seev; and Hadass, Michael. "A Flexible Approach to Information Systems Development." *MIS Quarterly* (June 1984), pp. 69–78.

Allen, Brandt. "An Unmanaged Computer System Can Stop You Dead." *Harvard Business Review* (Nov.–Dec. 1982), pp. 76–87.

Applegate, Lynda M.; Cash, James I. Jr.; and Mills, D. Quinn. "Information Technology and Tomorrow's Manager." *Harvard Business Review* (Nov.–Dec. 1988), pp. 128–136.

Biggs, Charles L.; Birks, Evan G.; and Atkins, William. *Managing the System Development Process.* Englewood Cliffs, N.J.: Touche Ross & Co. and Prentice-Hall, 1980.

Bowman, Brent; Davis, Gordon B.; and Wetherbe, James C. "Three Stage Model of MIS Planning." *Information and Management* (February 1983), pp. 11–25.

Boynton, Andrew C., and Zmud, Robert W. "Information Technology Planning in the 1990's: Directions for Practice and Research." *MIS Quarterly* (March 1987), pp. 59–72.

Corbin, Darrell S. "Strategic IRM Plan: User Involvement Spells Success." *Journal of Systems Management* (May 1988), pp. 12–16.

Davenport, Thomas H.; Hammer, Michael; and Metsisto, Tauno J. "How Executives Can Shape Their Company's Information Systems." *Harvard Business Review* (March–April 1989), pp. 130–134.

Davis, Leila. "Initiating Systems Projects." *Datamation* (October 15, 1989), pp. 81–84.

Doll, William, and Ahmed, Mesbah U. "Objectives for Systems Planning." *Journal of Systems Management* (December 1984), pp. 26–31.

Er, Meng C. "Prototyping, Participative and Phenomenological Approaches to Information Systems Development." *Journal of Systems Management* (August 1987), pp. 12–15.

Gremillion, Lee L., and Pyburn, Philip. "Breaking the Systems Development Bottleneck." *Harvard Business Review* (March–April 1983), pp. 130–137.

Hanks, George F. "Rx For Better Management: Critical Success Factors." *Management Accounting* (October 1988), pp. 45–49.

Hax, Arnoldo C. "Planning a Management Information System for a Distributing and Manufacturing Company." *Sloan Management Review* (Spring 1973), pp. 85–98.

Head, Robert V. "Information Resource Planning." *Journal of Systems Management* (October 1983), pp. 6–9.

Henderson, John C., and Sifonis, John G. "The Value of Strategic IS Planning: Understanding Consistency, Validity, and IS Markets." *MIS Quarterly* (June 1988), pp. 187–200.

Horton, Forest Woody, Jr. *Information Resources Management: Concept and Cases.* Cleveland: Association for Systems Management, 1979.

King, William R. "Integrating Computerized Planning Systems into the Organization." *Managerial Planning* (July–August 1983), pp. 10–13.

Lederer, Albert L., and Mendelow, Aubrey L. "Information Systems Planning: Top Management Takes Control." *Business Horizons* (May–June 1988), pp. 73–78.

Lederer, Albert L., and Sethi, Vijay. "Pitfalls in Planning." *Datamation* (June 1, 1989), pp. 59–62.

Leifer, Richard. "Matching Computer-Based Information Systems with Organizational Structures." *MIS Quarterly* (March 1988), pp. 63–73.

Lodahl, Thomas M., and Redditt, Kay Lewis. "Aiming IS at Business Targets." *Datamation* (Feb. 15, 1989), pp. 93–100.

Melone, N. Paule, and Wharton, T. J. "Strategies for MIS Project Selection." *Journal of Systems Management* (February 1984), pp. 26–33.

Meyers, Kenneth D. "Total Project Planning." *Datamation* (April 1, 1984), pp. 143–148.

Mockler, Robert J. "Computer Information Systems and Strategic Corporate Planning." *Business Horizons* (May–June 1987), pp. 32–37.

Nolan, Richard L. *Managing the Data Resource Function.* 2d ed. New York: West Publishing, 1982.

Raghunathan, Bhanu, and Raghunathan, T. S. "Impact of Top Management Support on IS Planning." *Journal of Information Systems* (Spring 1988), pp. 15–23.

———— and ————. "MIS Steering Committees: Their Effect on Information Systems Planning." *Journal of Information Systems* (Spring 1989), pp. 104–116.

Reck, Robert H., and Reck, Virginia P. "Steering IS Committees Straight." *Datamation* (October 15, 1989), pp. 89–92.

Selig, Gad J. "Approaches to Strategic Planning for Information Resource Management (IRM) in Multinational Corporations." *MIS Quarterly* (June 1982), pp. 33–45.

Sethi, Narendra K. "MIS and the Planning Process." *Managerial Planning* (Nov.–Dec. 1983), pp. 46–51.

Shore, Edwin B. "Reshaping the IS Organization." *MIS Quarterly* (December 1983), pp. 11–17.

Sprague, Ralph H., Jr., and McNurlin, Barbara C. (eds.) *Information Systems Management in Practice*. Englewood Cliffs, N.J.: Prentice-Hall, 1986.

Sullivan, Cornelius H., Jr., and Smart, John R. "Planning for Information Networks." *Sloan Management Review* (Winter 1987), pp. 39–44.

Tripp, Robert S., and Filteau, Mark C. "Blueprints: Adopting a Construction Trade Approach in Designing Large Scale Management Information Systems." *Information and Management* (September, 1987), pp. 55–70.

Venkatakrishnan, V. "The Information Cycle." *Datamation* (September 1983), pp. 175–180.

Wahi, Pran N.; Popp, Kenneth A.; and Stier, Susan M. "Applications Systems Planning at Weyerhaeuser." *Journal of Systems Management* (March 1983), pp. 12–21.

Willoughby, T. C. "Project Selection Top Priority for MIS Executives." *Journal of Systems Management* (December 1983), pp. 9–11.

Zmud, Robert W. "Design Alternatives for Organizing Information Systems Activities." *MIS Quarterly* (June 1984), pp. 79–93.

Chapter **22**

SYSTEMS ANALYSIS

Systems analysis follows systems planning and precedes systems design. It is a critical phase, since effective systems analysis clearly defines what is needed from a new or improved information system. It defines not only the requirements of the system but also the information needed by the users of the system. By reference to these sets of requirements the features of the new or improved system can be precisely specified in the systems design phase.

Accountants have an essential role in the systems analysis phase, since they are vitally concerned with information for managerial decision making. In addition, they are familiar with techniques for collecting and organizing data, interpreting the information derived from data, and evaluating the systems that provide the information.

Steps in the Analysis Phase

As discussed in Chapter 21, the preferable approach is to conduct each phase of the systems development cycle with respect to individual modules of the information system. The objectives pertaining to each system module (i.e., subsystem) are defined in an approved project proposal, which has been prepared on the basis of a feasibility study.

Five key steps in the analysis of a system module are to survey the present system, to analyze the survey findings, to identify the information needs of managers, to identify the system requirements, and to submit a report of the requirements for management's review. These steps are shown in Figure 22-1. Each step is discussed in turn.

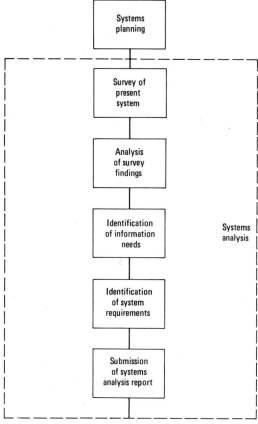

FIGURE 22-1   The steps in the systems analysis phase.

Survey of Present System

Reasons for surveying.   Before discussing such matters as the scope of a **system survey** and the sources of data, we need to answer the question: Why should the present information system be surveyed at all? After all, the survey step is time-consuming and expensive. Also, preoccupation with the innumerable details of what presently is being done may distract from what should be done; that is, focusing attention on the present system may obscure the vision of an *ideal* information system.

Although these arguments are beguiling, several excellent reasons can be offered in favor of a survey. First, it informs those conducting the analysis of the firm's essential operations, data and information flows, and interrelationships. Second, a survey confirms that the present system really does need to be improved. It may also bring to light undetected weaknesses and problems, such as duplicated operations and bottlenecks. Third, a survey gathers the data needed for comparisons. It compiles, for example, actual cost data that can be contrasted with the estimated cost for an improved system. Cost comparisons are needed both (1) for determining the feasibility of an improved system and (2) for justifying the acquisition of new equipment such as computers.

Last, but not least, a survey can gain the participation of those who will use the new or improved system. Involving the users at this early stage can nourish a feeling that they are helping to develop "their own" system. This feeling can lead to greater user acceptance and more effective use of the final product. For example, a manager of a southern newspaper that installed an advanced, computerized classified-advertising system credits its success to the involvement of advertising personnel in its design.[1]

Scope of survey.   Assuming that a firm has adopted the modular approach, the focus of a survey is on the module (i.e., subsystem) described by the project proposal. For example, the purchases transaction-processing system might be the focus of concern. In this instance the survey would consist of looking quite intently at the data and information flows pertaining to purchases. Facts would be gathered concerning

1. Information system elements (i.e., inputs, files and data bases, outputs, controls, and processing procedures).

[1]Dave Mollen, "Narrowing the Gap," *Datamation* (May 1980), p. 198.

2. Information system resources (i.e., personnel, equipment, and supplies).

Much of the gathered data would consist of measurements, such as *volumes* of transactions processed, *times* of key processing operations, *costs* of resources, and *numbers of errors* made in processing transactions.

The scope of a survey, however, is more intensive and extensive than may first be apparent. It delves into the pertinent aspects of physical operations, resource flows, and organizational structures. It ranges outward to the interfaces with adjoining modules; not only must the object module fit smoothly with its neighbors, but in time the module may be integrated with them. The scope even extends to aspects of the firm's environment, such as relationships with suppliers and levels of market prices.

Finally, the scope of the survey ranges upward from the operational level, in accordance with the bottom-up approach. It necessarily touches on managerial decision making, since a by-product use of transactional and operational data is to provide summarized reports for managers.[2]

Sources of facts. Where are the facts or data in a survey to be found? As already suggested, they are located in a variety of sources, both internal and external to the firm.

Internal sources consist of documents and records, paperwork and physical operations, and employees and managers. Documents and records of interest include policy statements, corporate minutes, charts of accounts, job descriptions, organization charts, procedures manuals, budgets, financial statements, files and managerial reports. Paperwork and physical operations supplement such documents and records, since

they reveal what is currently being done on a day-to-day basis. Interviews with employees and managers help to fill in data not provided by the above. They can provide knowledge of the historical development, of informal relationships within the firm, of information needed but not now generated.

External sources can be extremely varied. They include parties with which the firm has dealings, such as customers, industry trade associations, and relevant government agencies. They also include trade and professional journals, such as *Moody's*. In addition, they include firms that have information systems similar to the one being surveyed. During our discussion of data gathering techniques later in this chapter, we will revisit some of these sources.

Behavioral considerations in surveys. A survey involves numerous contacts with people. The systems analysts conducting the survey should therefore employ sound principles of human relations. In essence they should continually consider the feelings and reactions of those persons affected by the survey.

As already noted, an appropriate step is to communicate openly and early with the affected persons. They should be informed at the outset concerning key aspects of the survey—its purpose, scope, and expected duration. In addition, the systems analysts should become acquainted with the affected employees and managers as soon as possible.

The systems analysts should encourage participation throughout the survey. For instance, when discussing aspects of the system with employees and managers, the analysts should encourage questions and suggestions. Good suggestions should be incorporated into the systems design, with credit fully given to the suggesters.

Participative analysis and the team approach can be aided by packaged techniques. Two such packages are Rapid Analysis (marketed by Computers & Engineering

---

[2]On the other hand, the scope of the survey does *not* include a review of available computer hardware and software. This review occurs later in the systems development sequence.

Consultants) and Joint Application Design (marketed by IBM). These techniques provide guidelines that specify the relative roles of the analysts and users. They enhance the productivity of all members of the team and usually result in sounder analyses and designs.[3]

From the beginning the systems analysts should be solicitous of the welfare of the affected employees and managers, reassuring them concerning the possible repercussions. Thus, the purposes of the survey can be expressed in a positive way, such as to help employees and managers to be "more effective in their jobs." Stating the purpose as "cutting clerical costs," on the other hand, is to be avoided. Moreover, the systems analysts can publicize those personnel policies that are intended to benefit employees and managers in such situations. For instance, the firm may have a policy that no employee will lose his or her position because of a change in the system; instead, he or she may transfer to another position and receive training at no cost if it is needed. (Obviously, the system analysts cannot set such personnel policies, but more and more firms have found such enlightened policies to be sound in the long run.)

By following sound human-relations practices such as these, the systems analysts can improve the chances that the information system being developed will be accepted and hence successful.

Analysis of Survey Findings

A survey consists essentially of asking such questions as: What is done? How is it done? Who does it? Where is it done? An analysis, on the other hand, consists of asking and attempting to answer such searching questions as: Why is it done? How well is it done? Should it be done at all? If so, is there a better way to do it?

When the questioning is carried on in a skeptical but open-minded manner, and is complemented by experience and creative intelligence, significant answers should be forthcoming. Such answers can point toward a new or improved system design.

Of course, the questions to be asked need to be more specific than those listed above. Figure 22-2 lists a number of specific questions that can aid in analyzing the findings of a particular survey. Many questions could be added to the list. In fact, public accounting firms have compiled lengthy lists of questions pertaining to internal accounting controls alone.

In addition to a questioning attitude and checklists such as shown in Figure 22-2, sound systems analysis requires criteria by which to judge the present system. Suitable criteria are provided by the objectives for an effective and efficient information system. A list of broad objectives appears in Figure 22-3. The list has been compiled from objectives pertaining to data conversion, data management, and data controls and security. To this list has been added the objective of *simplicity,* which applies to all aspects of an information system. A simple system is easy to use and understand; hence *people* (e.g., employees and managers) are able to operate the information system effectively and are motivated to do so.

Guided by appropriate objectives and aided by specific questions, systems analysts are better able to perform thorough analyses. They are more likely to see beyond the symptoms described in Chapter 21 and the faulty diagnoses of others. Consequently, they are more likely to discover the underlying problems, deficiencies, and weaknesses in information systems.

These desired results can be illustrated by two examples. (1) A systems analyst observes that duplicate records concerning the progress of production orders are maintained by the sales order and production control departments. Upon further investigation she

[3]Don Leavitt, "Team Techniques in Systems Analysis," *Datamation* (November 15, 1987), pp. 78–86.

1. Are tasks and responsibilities clearly defined and assigned?
2. Are tasks and responsibilities distributed effectively among employees and organizational units?
3. Are the policies and procedures understood and followed?
4. Does the productivity of clerical employees appear to be satisfactorily high?
5. Do the various organizational units cooperate and coordinate well in maintaining smooth flows of data?
6. Does each procedure achieve its intended objective?
7. Are redundant processing operations being performed?
8. How necessary is the result accomplished by each operation?
9. Do unnecessary delays occur in obtaining or processing data?
10. Do any operations cause bottlenecks in the flow of data?
11. Are the number of errors that occur in each operation minimized?
12. Are physical operations adequately planned and controlled?
13. Is the capacity of the information system (in terms of personnel, equipment, and other facilities) sufficient to handle the average volumes of data without large backlogs?
14. Are the peak volumes of data handled adequately?
15. How easily does the system adapt to exceptional occurrences and growth in use?
16. How necessary is each document?
17. Is each document suitably designed for efficient use?
18. Are all of the copies of documents necessary?
19. Can reports be prepared easily from the files and documents?
20. Do unnecessary duplications occur in files, records, and reports?
21. Are files easily accessible and kept up to date?
22. Are sound performance standards developed and kept up to date?
23. Is data processing equipment being used effectively?
24. Is the system of internal control adequate?
25. Do the informal flows of data and information harmonize with the formal flows?

FIGURE 22-2   A checklist for analyzing information systems.

- Efficient and hence economical operations.
- Adequate capacity for expected growth.
- Timeliness in responding to inquiries and providing reports.
- Reliability of system hardware and software.
- Accurate, up-to-date, and relevant information.
- Security of the data and system facilities.
- Flexibility and adaptability to changes and new demands.
- Simplicity and hence user-friendliness.

FIGURE 22-3   A list of information system objectives.

unearths the basic problem: The production control department does not keep its records up to date and furthermore is reluctant to share its information with other departments. A solution to this problem must therefore involve a method of keeping records up to date and making their contents easily accessible to those who have a "need to know." (2) Another systems analyst hears from a manager that the major problem in his department stems from the heavy workloads imposed upon his employees. The manager adds that computers are the only solution. Upon investigation, however, the analyst discovers that the underlying problems are (a) lack of adequate supervision, reflected by poor employee productivity; and (b) uneven work flows, which cause valleys as well as peaks in the workload.

Identification of Information Needs

Although an analysis of the operational weaknesses and problems is necessary, it is not sufficient. It does not deal adequately with the prime purpose of the information system, which is to supply decision-oriented information to managers.

Analyzing managerial information needs is therefore an important part of the analysis phase. Firms with poorly defined information needs are usually plagued by unsound decision making. Managers in such firms often receive too many bulky reports containing too much irrelevant information; the result is information overload. On the other hand, these same managers often do not receive certain key information that they do need.

Information needs analysis. A sound analysis of information needs is based on the top-down approach. Figure 22-4 diagrams the sequence of actions embodied in an **information needs analysis.** Provided that the modular approach to systems development has

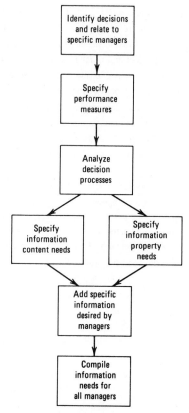

FIGURE 22-4 The steps in an information needs analysis.

been adopted, the information needs analysis would span those managers whose responsibilities fall within the scope of the systems project being conducted.

Much of the background pertaining to an information needs analysis has been presented in Chapter 4, which discussed the range of decisions made by typical firms as well as content and properties of needed information. Therefore, a brief discussion of Figure 22-4 will suffice.

In order to determine information needs, it is first necessary to identify the various decisions to be made. These decisions tend to be grouped by decision centers or decision points. Each decision center or point can be associated with a manager who has the responsibility for making the decisions.

After each manager is identified with a particular decision center or point, he or she would be asked to aid in specifying his or her (1) decision responsibilities and (2) information needs. Knowing the decision responsibilities is the key to determining information needs. For instance, decisions related to the hiring and retaining of needed personnel are the responsibility of the personnel manager. To judge how well these decisions are being made, the personnel manager and his or her superior need information that pinpoints their effect on the firm's welfare. One such piece of information is the performance measure known as employee turnover.

Most information needs follow only after a close analysis of each decision. Answers are needed to such questions as

What is the decision process followed by the manager?

What factors are incorporated within the decision model used (either explicitly or implicitly) in the process?

How often is the decision made?

A decision analysis should enable a systems analyst to specify both the content and properties of needed information. Such specifications are not easily compiled, but the endeavor can be aided by pinpointing the key dimensions through such questions as

To what types of managerial activity (e.g., strategic planning, management control) are the decisions directed?

At what managerial level are the decisions being made?

Which operational functions will be affected by the decisions?

What is the personal background of the manager making the decisions?

Answers to these questions can be helpful in specifying information needs, since each cat-

egory within such dimensions has a distinctive pattern of information needs.

Now that the information needs for the individual decisions have been specified, what next? To these information needs should be added other information that each manager *perceives* he or she needs. Although this information may not directly aid in making particular decisions, it may be desired as a means of monitoring areas of activity within which the manager has an interest.

A final step in an information needs analysis is to compile and correlate the information needs for all the managers of a firm. Information needs that are common to several managers should also be noted. The resulting compiled set of needs can serve as the basis for developing reports, data bases, and data sources during the design phase.

Information needs methodologies. The managers who are to use the information are vital to information needs analyses. No one else understands their areas of responsibility as well as they do. However, managers often have difficulty in identifying the information they need or even all the decisions they make.

Systems analysts should consider the use of proven methodologies to aid managers in overcoming these difficulties. Three such **information needs methodologies** are known as Business Systems Planning (BSP), Business Information Analysis and Integration Technique (BIAIT), and Critical Success Factors (CSP).[4] Each of these methodologies provides a systematic approach to the development of information needs; each uses the

[4]For details concerning these methodologies, see International Business Machines Corporation, *Business Systems Planning—Information Systems Planning Guide,* Publication No. GE20-0527 (New York: IBM Corp., 1978); D. C. Burnstine, *BIAIT: An Emerging Management Discipline* (New York: International, Inc., 1980); J. F. Rockart, "Chief Executives Define Their Own Data Needs," *Harvard Business Review* (March–April 1979), pp. 115–126.

technique of asking the affected managers a number of structured questions. However, they differ in certain respects. For instance, BSP asks open-ended questions about the firm's processes and the managers' felt needs. BIAIT asks a few closed-ended questions that focus on key activities of the firm (e.g., Do you bill customers or accept cash?).

Methodologies such as these can be quite useful. However, they are less than perfect in that they seldom detect all information needs or reconcile conflicting needs lists. Where information needs are felt to be significantly lacking, a firm might consider using the prototyping approach to systems development.

Identification of System Requirements

At this point the systems analysts will have completed their analyses of the present operational system and the information needs. By reference to these findings, plus the previously stated objectives for the module being studied, they can now identify the requirements concerning system performance. Often these requirements will consist simply of a revision and refinement of the project objectives, although in some cases they might detail all required processes and outputs.

The exact nature of **system requirements** will vary from module to module, but typical requirements would include

1. Required capacity or throughput in terms of number of transactions per time period.

2. Required response time in number of seconds or minutes.

3. Maximum allowable number of errors per 1000 transactions.

4. Required number of file accesses per time period.

5. Maximum allowable delay in preparing reports after an event such as the end of an accounting period.

6. Contents and frequencies of required documents and reports.

7. Required processor features, such as multiprogramming and interactive processing.

8. Required security features, such as password protection at multiple data levels and lockout provisions on data sets.

When establishing system requirements, it is important to remember the relationships with adjoining modules. For instance, a required report may require the use of certain data generated within another module.

Submission of Systems Analysis Report

The systems analysis phase is brought to a conclusion with the preparation of a **systems analysis report.** This report is essentially a summary of findings, supported by extensive documentation. In part the report will repeat much of the project proposal, although revisions and additions are likely. For instance, the cost and time budgets likely will be updated to reflect more current and well-grounded estimates.

To be specific, the systems analysis report, also called the *requirements report,* will typically include

1. Objectives and constraints of the project.

2. Scope of the project.

3. Summary of the problems.

4. Summary of the information needs.

5. Summary of the system performance requirements.

6. Time schedule.

7. Cost budget.

A number of appendixes may provide details, utilizing such techniques as flowcharting, work measurement, and decision flow diagramming. (The latter two of these techniques are discussed in the following sections.)

The systems analysis report has two purposes. In addition to documenting the findings of the analyses, it provides the basis for review by higher management levels within the firm. After being prepared, the report will usually be sent to the steering committee. If this body approves the report, it is then forwarded to the president or board of directors. After careful evaluation, the report either is given final approval or is disapproved. If the report receives approval, the systems project team has the "green light" to move into the systems design phase.

Techniques for Gathering Facts

Systems analysts employ a variety of tools or techniques when performing system analyses. Certain techniques are employed primarily to gather facts. Other techniques help to organize gathered facts for analysis. In this and the following section several of the major techniques in each category will be displayed.

Techniques for gathering facts include reviews of documents and records, interviews, observations, and questionnaires.

Reviews of Documents and Records

A wealth of documentation is available concerning a firm and its information system. As noted earlier, this documentation ranges from the chart of accounts to financial data pertaining to the firm's industry. Systems analysts should obtain copies of such documentation for review.

By reviewing such documentation, systems analysts can gain considerable insight into the operations of the present information system and the firm. They can learn through the chart of accounts, for instance,

how the present accounting information system has been structured. They can learn by studying the industry data where the firm stands within the industry.

Reviews of documents and records should precede most of the other data gathering techniques. In addition to presenting an overview, they provide a basis for comparison. Charts of accounts and procedures manuals, for instance, show how the present system should work. This information can then be compared with facts gained by other techniques concerning how the system really does function. Differences between how a system is supposed to function and how it really does function can point to possible problems. Prior knowledge of features of the present system can also increase the effectiveness of other techniques. By being aware of the source documents and reports, for example, systems analysts can conduct more effective interviews with managers and employees.

Interviews

Interviewing is perhaps the single most important data gathering technique. Interviews with managers provide the means by which the information needs are discovered and problems are uncovered. Interviews with employees as well as managers help to reveal differences between what the present system design shows and what is actually being done. Even more important, interviews provide a natural means of involving managers and employees in the systems development process. The systems analysts can thereby build acceptance and support for a new or improved system.

Good interviewing is an art that can be learned. In essence, it is a combination of sound planning, good manners, and friendliness. Among the guidelines to be followed are those listed in Figure 22-5.

Interviews are critical to systems surveys, but they contain two major pitfalls.

1. Ascertain the interests, background, and responsibilities of the person to be interviewed *before* the interview.
2. Gather facts concerning the matters to be discussed *beforehand.*
3. Prepare a list of the questions to be asked during the interview.
4. Obtain approval from the interviewee's superior for the interview.
5. Make an appointment that is convenient with the interviewee and be on time.
6. Notify the interviewee beforehand of the purpose of the interview and of the matters that it will cover.
7. Open the interview by explaining the interviewer's role in the study, then draw out information by pertinent questions, especially concerning the interviewee's knowledge of the situation, needs for information, and ideas for improvements.
8. Listen carefully to the interviewee's answers without interruption.
9. When conversing do not resort to jargon, broad generalizations, personal opinions, or irrelevant comments.
10. Be natural, but businesslike, so that the interview flows easily.
11. Maintain a courteous, respectful, tactful, and friendly manner throughout the interview.
12. Ask permission to take notes or use a tape recorder during the interview.
13. End the interview with a summary of the discussion, a thank you, and a prompt exit.
14. Shortly after the interview, review and complete the notes taken or conversation recorded; send a copy of the notes to the interviewee for review and correction.

FIGURE 22-5 A list of guidelines for interviewing.

One pitfall is that the interviewee may provide information that is misleading. For example, an interviewee's bias may cause his or her facts to be distorted. Or the interviewee may say what he or she thinks the interviewer (the systems analyst) wants to hear. On the other hand, the interviewee may not cooperate at all. To circumvent this latter pitfall, the systems analyst must resort to other interviewees and employ other data gathering techniques.

Observations

Observing activities related to information systems is a technique that serves two purposes. The technique helps to familiarize a systems analyst with the setting, relationships, and constraints of the system. Often he or she can spot weaknesses, especially if the observations are unannounced. For instance, a walk through the production area may reveal that a low level of productivity exists and that employees are careless in performing procedures. The act of observing

also provides verification. For example, assertions made by interviewees or descriptions provided in documents may be verified firsthand.

Questionnaires

A standardized list of questions represents an efficient technique for surveying specific aspects of information systems. For instance, questionnaires customarily are employed when surveying the controls incorporated in the system.

Questionnaires (or checklists) may be used in various ways. They may be used to guide the discussion during interviews, as already noted. Alternatively, they may be employed when personal interviews are not possible. For instance, if information is needed from several branch sales managers located at distant points, identical questionnaires may be mailed to them for answering.

Questionnaires are also a useful aid during the analysis step, as Figure 22-2 suggests. Questionnaires used for this purpose usually are constructed to enhance their analytical capability. For instance, questionnaires such as those used in the survey of internal accounting controls have questions phrased in a standard way. "No" answers to questions suggest specific control weaknesses. (See Figure 17-3.)

The major shortcoming of questionnaires or checklists is the restricted nature of the questions. Typically they request brief objective answers, such as "yes" or "no" or choices among multiple entries. They do not enable in-depth answers to be provided easily. For this reason, questionnaires should be viewed as generally less useful than interviews.

Traditional Systems Analysis

Survey of Analysis Techniques Already Seen

An information system consists of numerous data items, complex relationships, and involved flows. In order to organize these facts, systems analysts employ a variety of techniques. Most of the techniques involve diagrams or graphic representations. One technique, the system flowchart, has appeared frequently in earlier chapters. Other techniques that have been introduced, and the figure in which they first appeared, are as follows:

- Business activity overview diagram (Figure 3-1).
- Hardware configuration diagram (Figure 5-7).
- Preformatted screen (Figure 7-6).
- Form analysis sheet (Figure 7-19).
- Control-oriented flowchart (Figure 7-22).
- Record layout (Figure 8-7).
- Display screen format (Figure 10-10).
- Data flow diagram (Figure 11-2).
- Internal control questionnaire (Figure 17-3).

- Data dictionary (Figure 18-7).
- Data structure diagram (Figure 18-8).
- Entity-relationship diagram (Figure 18-15).

Classification of Systems Analysis Techniques

Fact-organizing techniques may be categorized in various ways. Certain techniques are analytical, in that they present conceptual and logical views of the information system and its components. Other techniques are design oriented, in that they present relatively detailed and physical specifications of an information system. Another division of fact-organizing techniques is between traditional and structured techniques. Traditional techniques that are suited for systems analysis are discussed in this section; structured techniques are covered in the following section.

Organized information systems development dates roughly from the post-World War II era. Systems flowcharts were among the first techniques to be devised, being offshoots from engineering-oriented process charts. Other techniques, such as work measurement analyses, also were adapted from techniques devised and employed by industrial engineers. Certain techniques, such as work distribution charts, were adapted from office systems and methods. Taken together, these adaptations comprise the set of classical or **traditional systems analysis techniques.** Most of the techniques are applicable to manual as well as computer-based information systems.

Specific Traditional Techniques

Although all of the traditional systems analysis techniques cannot be identified, the following descriptions pertain to decision flow diagrams, work distribution charts, work measurement analyses, input–output matrices, and space layout diagrams.

Decision flow diagrams. Information needs are based on the decisions to be made by managers, as previously discussed. Decisions must therefore be identified, and the relationships between decisions and key needed information must be traced. **Decision flow diagrams,** such as the example shown in Figure 22-6, can aid in achieving these purposes. (Figure 22-6 exhibits similarities with the decision chain appearing in Figure 4-10, although their purposes and production situations are somewhat different.)

The compilation and correlation of information needs can be a complex task. Not only must lists of needed information be gathered, but key relationships among managers and their respective information needs and sources should be clarified. An information flow diagram, another useful technique, (1) identifies the key information requirements of managers throughout an organization and (2) shows the flows of needed information from their sources to the recipient managers. (The sources of information may be governmental agencies or other points outside the firm, by-products of transaction processing, or other managers inside the firm.)

Work distribution charts. Work distribution analyses are related to work measurement analyses in that they employ time measurements. Rather than using the measurements to compute productivities or set standards, however, work distribution analyses reflect the distribution of times among respective clerical tasks. They make use of **work distribution charts,** which portray in matrix format the times worked by each employee on each task within an activity. For instance, a work distribution chart may reflect the average hours spent by billing department employees upon the various billing tasks. By analyzing the data portrayed in a work distribution chart, a systems analyst often can determine a more equitable and efficient allocation of tasks. Figure 22-7 shows a work distribution chart for a shipping department.

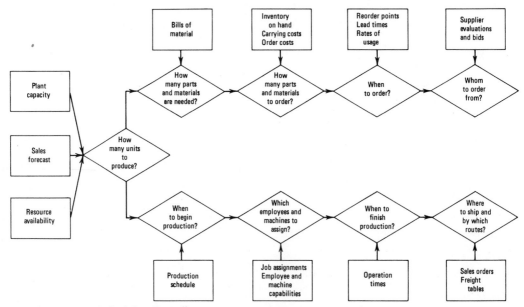

FIGURE 22-6   A decision flow diagram.

No.	Activity	Hours per week	M. T. Sullivan — supervisor — Task	Hours per week	Terry Frank & Jim Williams — shipping clerks — Task	Hours per week	Ralph Johnson — traffic clerk — Task	Hours per week	Paul Emerson — expeditor — Task	Hours per week	Linda Dent & Sandra Pyle — typists — Task	Hours per week
1	Controlling sales orders	35	Spot-checking shipping order file against outstanding order report from sales order department	2	Date-stamping and checking packing slip copies from warehouse to shipping copies; noting unshipped items on shipping copies	33						
2	Preparing shipping forms and reports	102	Reviewing summary report of shipments	1	Proofreading typed bills of lading for accuracy and completeness; preparing summary report of shipments from bills of lading copies	30 3					Typing bills of lading from packing slip copies; typing summary report of shipments	60 8
3	Scheduling, routing, and dispatching shipments	60	Preparing work assignments for shipping handlers	2	Collecting packing slips and spot-checking weights of packed shipments against weights noted on packing slip copies by handlers	8	Maintaining file of shipping rates; entering shipper, schedule, route, and charges for shipments on packing slip copies	1 37	Delivering bills of lading to shipper's representatives for signature	12		
4	Supervising shipping activities	25	Training employees and observing their performances; checking employees' attendance; answering employees' questions	12 2 2					Helping speed shipments and eliminating bottlenecks.	9		
5	Following status of sales orders and shipments	25	Handling customers' inquiries regarding shipments	8	Handling customers' inquiries regarding shipments	2	Answering inquiries of shippers regarding routes and charges	1	Following progress of special orders through production and into shipping area	14		
6	Performing miscellaneous activities	33	Preparing letters and memos; conferring with vice-president of marketing and other department heads	3 8	Collating bills of lading and shipping orders to be sent to billing department	4	Preparing special instructions for shippers	1	Picking up and delivering papers dealing with rush orders; filing	2 3	Typing correspondence and packing labels; filing	4 8
	Totals	280		40		80		40		40		80

FIGURE 22-7   A work distribution chart for a shipping department.

Work-measurement analyses. Numerous measurements are needed to analyze flows related to the information system. Examples include the number of source documents, such as sales orders received daily and the number of back orders created this month. Often the measurements can be expressed in the form of analyses, such as the analysis of sales orders received this week by size.

Various techniques are available for measuring quantitative data, ranging from simple counts to statistical techniques such as regression analysis. One useful set of techniques is collectively known as work measurement analysis.

Work measurement essentially consists of (1) measuring volumes of work performed and the required times and then (2) computing such measures as rates of output and levels of productivity. For example, if a clerical employee spends 20 hours processing 400 purchase orders, his or her rate of output is 20 purchase orders per hour.

In addition to specifying productivity levels, work measurements can also be used as the bases for evaluating the performances of routine clerical tasks such as keypunching, sorting, posting, and checking documents. Assume, for instance, that a posting standard of 30 invoices per hour is established. This standard can then be used to compare and evaluate the performance of posting clerks. A clerk who posts 33 invoices per hour would exceed the standard by three invoices, thus achieving an efficiency of 110 percent of standard.

Developing clerical work performance standards can be quite expensive, since they usually involve detailed studies of performance times and motions. On the other hand, productivity analyses can be much less expensive. Since they do not require a high degree of precision, they can be based on sampled data. **Work sampling,** a work measurement technique that consists of observing employee activity at random time intervals, has therefore become an increasingly popular technique of analysis. On the basis of the sampling of observations, the work sampling technique provides a measure of productivity for an average day (or other period of time) in a particular department or work area.

Figures 22-8, 22-9, and 22-10 contain the worksheets and graph used in the work sampling technique. On the basis of the daily observations in Figure 22-8, which are summarized weekly as shown in Figure 22-9, an analyst could prepare a graphical profile of average productivity throughout the hours of a workday. The graph in Figure 22-10 suggests that average productivity is significantly below the desirable level.

Matrix-oriented analyses. A matrix, also called a grid chart, reflects the relationships between two factors. Since relationships are important in systems analysis, a number of matrices are employed by systems analysts. The work distribution chart, for instance, is a matrix that shows the relationships between tasks and employee times. Other systems-related matrices show relationships between (1) users and the reports they receive, (2) data elements and files in which they are stored, and (3) decision makers and their decision responsibilities.

One of the most widely used matrices shows the relationships between inputs (data items) and the outputs in which they appear. Figure 22-11 shows an example of an **input–output matrix** pertaining to the purchases procedure of a retailing firm. The data items that appear in the left-hand column are captured from such sources as purchase requisitions, suppliers' invoices, receiving reports, and cost accounting records. The X's in the matrix indicate the outputs from the purchasing and receiving departments in which the above data items are reflected.

Input–output matrices aid the systems analysts by highlighting reports that are redundant or that may be combined with other reports. In Figure 22-11, for instance, the listed receiving register in effect duplicates the listed receiving report; it may therefore be replaced by a copy of the receiving report. On the other hand, input–output matrices do *not* aid the analysis of data processing operations or information flows.

Space layout diagrams. Floor-plan-like drawings, called **space layout diagrams,** can aid in arranging the physical and paperwork flows. For purposes of analysis, the current flows can be superimposed onto the space layout. Then proposed flows can be drawn onto another copy of the space layout. Figure 22-12 presents a space layout diagram with current flows in a three-dimensional format. Scaled cutouts of desks, machines, and other fixtures are helpful in trying different arrangements on a scaled two-dimensional layout drawing.

		Daily Observation Worksheet Sales Order Department		June 10, 1991		
Observation		**Productive**		**Nonproductive**		**Total**
No.	Time	At desk	Away from desk	Personal	Idle	
1	8:21	⊞ ⊞ I ⊞ ⊞	⊞ II	⊞	⊞ II	40
2	9:08	⊞ II ⊞ ⊞	⊞ ⊞	III	⊞ ⊞	40
3	9:49	⊞ III ⊞ ⊞	⊞ I	⊞ III	⊞ III	40
4	10:30	⊞ ⊞ ⊞ ⊞ ⊞ ⊞ ⊞ ⊞				40
5	11:09	⊞ ⊞ ⊞ II ⊞ ⊞ ⊞ ⊞			III	40
6	1:52	⊞ ⊞ II ⊞ ⊞	⊞ IIII	III	⊞ I	40
7	2:20	⊞ II ⊞ ⊞	⊞ IIII	⊞ I	⊞ III	40
8	2:39	⊞ ⊞ ⊞ II ⊞ ⊞ ⊞ ⊞		III		40
9	3:57	⊞ IIII ⊞ ⊞	⊞ III	⊞ I	⊞ II	40
10	4:47	III ⊞ ⊞	⊞ IIII	II	⊞ ⊞ ⊞ I	40
	Totals	241	58	36	65	400
		299		101		

Productive   299/400 = 75%
Nonproductive   101/400 = 25%

FIGURE 22-8   Daily observation worksheet for work sampling.

Structured Systems Analysis

During the past two decades a new body of systems analysis techniques has emerged. These techniques, applied within the framework of **structured systems development,** represent a disciplined approach to systems analysis. Structured systems development provides three major benefits: (1) higher-quality system designs, (2) greater efficiency in the systems development process, and (3) better communication between systems analysts and the prospective users of designed systems.

Time Periods	Mon. P[a]	Mon. N[b]	Tues. P	Tues. N	Wed. P	Wed. N	Thurs. P	Thurs. N	Fri. P	Fri. N	Total P	Total No.[c]	Percent Productive
8:00– 8:30	28	12					26	14			54	80	67%
8:31– 9:00			29	11	29	11			30	10	88	120	73%
9:01– 9:30	27	13			23	17			24	16	74	120	62%
9:31–10:00	24	16	21	19	19	21	22	18			86	160	54%
10:01–10:30	40	0	36	4			33	7			109	120	91%
10:30–11:00			32	8	33	7			35	5	100	120	83%
11:01–11:30	37	3			28	12	29	11	21	19	115	160	72%
11:31–12:00			21	19			23	17	23	17	67	120	56%
12:01–12:30													Lunch
12:31– 1:00													Lunch
1:01– 1:30			23	17							23	40	57%
1:31– 2:00	31	9			29	11	30	10	30	10	120	160	75%
2:01– 2:30	26	14	25	15	25	15			24	16	100	160	63%
2:31– 3:00	37	3			31	9	34	6			102	120	85%
3:01– 3:30			30	10							30	40	75%
3:31– 4:00	27	13			25	15	24	16	20	20	96	160	60%
4:01– 4:30			61	19					28	12	89	120	74%
4:31– 5:00	22	18			22	18	41	39	15	25	100	200	50%
Totals	299	101	278	122	264	136	262	138	250	150		2000	

[a]Productive.
[b]Nonproductive.
[c]Number of observations.

FIGURE 22-9 Weekly work sampling summary.

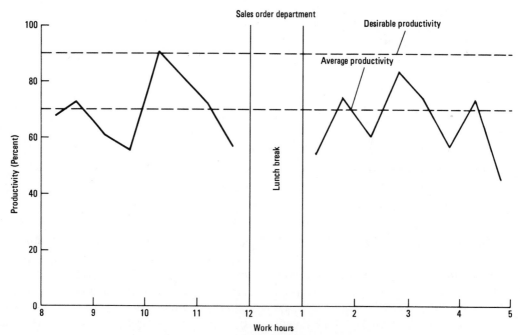

FIGURE 22-10 Productivity graph based on work sampling.

Data Item and Source	Sales order—invoice	Bill of lading	Back order	Shipment record	Delayed order report	Inventory flash report	Sales flash report	Sales analysis by salesperson	Sales analysis by product
Date of event or output	X	X	X	X	X	X	X	X	X
Customer order number (sales branch)	X								
Name of customer (customer's order)	X	X							
Address of customer (customer's order)	X								
Place to be shipped (customer's order)	X	X							
Quantities ordered (customer's order)	X				X		X		
Product numbers (customer's order)	X	X	X	X		X	X	X	X
Product descriptions (product file)	X	X	X						
Unit prices (pricing file)	X		X						
Scheduled delivery date (production control department)	X								
Priority (sales order dept.)	X								
Sales order—invoice no. (sales order dept.)	X		X	X	X				
Credit terms (credit dept.)	X								
Salesperson number (customer's order)	X							X	
Sales branch number (customer's order)	X						X		
Channel of distribution code (sales branch)	X								
Special delivery instructions (customer's order)	X	X							
Freight charges (shipping data file)	X	X							
Bill of lading number (shipping data file)		X		X					
Where shipped from (shipping data file)		X							
Products shipped (shipping dept.)		X							
Quantities shipped (shipping dept.)		X		X					
Routing (shipping data file)	X	X							
Method of shipment (shipping data file)	X	X							
Carrier (shipping data file)	X	X							
Weight of shipment (shipping dept.)		X							
Packaging data (shipping dept.)		X							
Back order number (finished-goods whse.)			X						
Quantities backordered (finished-goods whse.)			X						
Availability date (production control department)			X						
Dates of shipments (shipping dept.)			X	X					
Cost of order (cost acctg. dept.)	X								
Total sales amount (billing dept.)	X						X	X	X
Status of orders (production control department or finished-goods whse.)					X				
Units forecasted to be sold (sales forecasting dept.)							X		
Number of days delayed (production control department)					X				
Percent of orders delayed (production control department)					X				
Units below reorder points (inventory control department)						X			
Units forecasted to be ordered (inventory control department)							X		
Units actually sold (sales analysis department)							X		
Salesperson's quotas (sales branch)								X	
Contribution margins (sales analysis department)									X
Percent of total market (sales analysis department)									X

FIGURE 22-11 An input–output matrix.

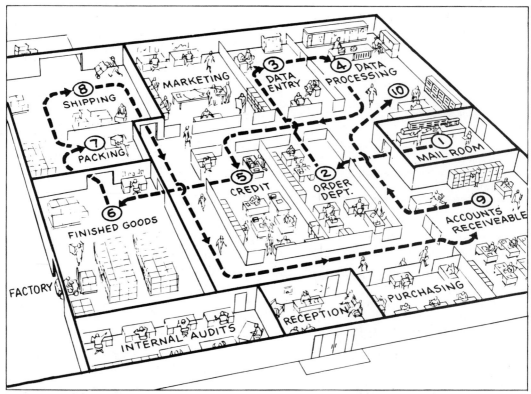

FIGURE 22-12 A space layout diagram showing flows of a form through the departments of a manufacturing firm. *Source:* Leslie H. Matthies, "The Physical Side of a Management System," *Journal of Systems Management* (October 1984), p. 10. Reprinted with permission.

Characteristics of structured systems development include

1. An integrated view of the portion of the information system to be developed (called the systems project span).
2. A systematic decomposition of the systems project span into smaller, more manageable modules.
3. A focus on the conceptual and logical aspects of the system, that is, on the data, information, events, entities, flows, and their relationships.
4. A variety of diagrams that are easy to understand and that interrelate closely with each other.

Among the diagrams that have been devised for structured systems development are hierarchy charts, data flow diagrams, entity-relationship diagrams, decision trees, decision tables, program flowcharts, HIPO diagrams, state-transition diagrams, Warnier–Orr diagrams, and data dictionaries. Two diagrams from this list, hierarchy charts and data flow diagrams, serve to illustrate the characteristics of structured techniques. Certain of the remaining diagrams have been discussed in previous chapters, and others will appear in Chapter 25.

Hierarchy Charts

A **hierarchy chart,** also known as a function chart or a structure chart, describes the hierarchical levels and relationships within a system or partial system. Each successive lower level of a hierarchy chart provides a

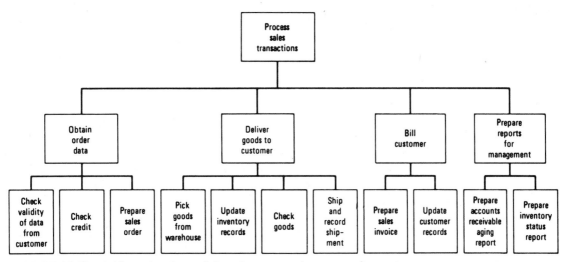

FIGURE 22-13 A hierarchy chart of the sales transaction processing system.

more detailed (decomposed) view of the activity at the next higher level. For instance, Figure 22-13 presents a three-level hierarchy chart for a key activity—the sales transaction processing system—of a firm. Modules at the second level represent four key subactivities involved in the sales activity. In turn, modules at the third level represent sub-subactivities involved in each subactivity. Each module at the third level can be further decomposed into further details. For instance, the module labeled "prepare sales invoice" can be broken into detailed processing steps.

Each lower-level module (such as "prepare sales invoice") can be annotated with related input data and output information as well as the processing steps. When this is done, the module then becomes a HIPO (Hierarchy plus Input, Process, and Output) diagram.

Data Flow Diagrams

Flow-type diagrams are familiar to systems analysts and accountants through the example of system flowcharts. In recent years the flow-type diagram known as the data flow diagram (also called the bubble chart or SADT diagram) has become increas-

ingly popular. In contrast to the system flowchart, the **data flow diagram** presents purely logical views of systems activities. That is, it excludes such physical features as computer processing, on-line disk files, and paper outputs.

Both the system flowchart and data flow diagram have valid roles in systems development. The major role of the system flowchart is to document the particulars of a current processing system or the specifications of a new or improved system. On the other hand, the data flow diagram is better suited for use in analyzing a processing situation or need. It enables systems analysts to visualize the essential aspects of a systems activity without the distraction of physical constraints.

Data flow diagrams and hierarchy charts represent alternative means of portraying a systems activity, since both techniques provide integrated and decomposing views. Thus, each level of a hierarchy chart can be paralleled by one or more separate data flow diagrams. All of the data flow diagrams relating to a hierarchy chart articulate; that is, they interlock in a manner similar to the modules in the hierarchy chart.

The construction of articulated data flow diagrams can be seen in Figures 22-14, 22-15,

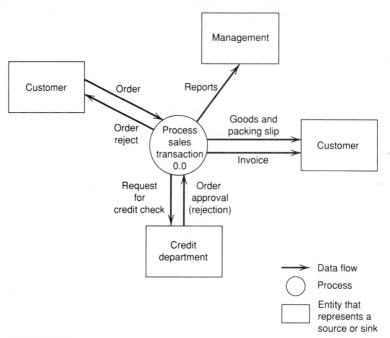

FIGURE 22-14 A context diagram, the top-level data flow diagram that parallels the top module in Figure 22-13.

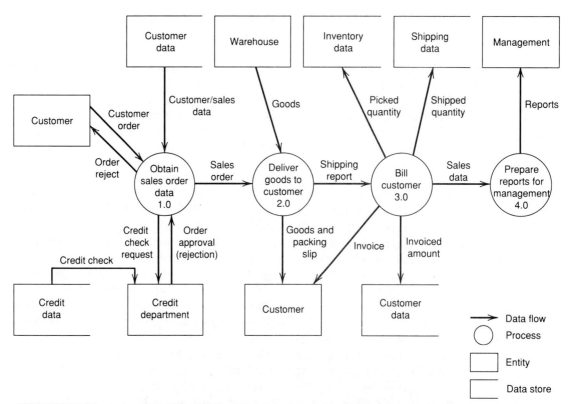

FIGURE 22-15 A data flow diagram (level 1) of the four major subactivities in processing sales transactions.

APPLICATION OF STRUCTURED SYSTEMS ANALYSIS
Exxon Corporation[a]

An integrated oil company, Exxon, developed a technique that defines the information and system requirements of a department or other business unit. Called Structured Systems Analysis (SSA), this technique consists of the following integrated set of models and diagrams:

1. Global business model, which shows the overall relationships among the functions of the business firm under study.

2. Functional matrix, which relates the responsibilities for each function identified in the global model.

3. Data flow diagrams.

4. Detailed activity models, (similar to the diagram shown in Figure 22-13).

5. Data structure diagram, which shows the logical structure (e.g., a hierarchy) of data items listed in the data dictionary.

6. Glossary, which lists the various business terms used in the various operations.

SSA has been employed by Exxon to analyze the requirements of such business units as central purchasing and refinery blending. It has also been used to develop a multipurpose financial modeling system. Those who have employed the technique believe that it improves the quality of analysis, facilitates communication between analysts and users, increases the productivity of analysts, and provides a useful tool for project management.

[a]Kathleen S. Mendes, "Structured Systems Analysis: A Technique to Define Business Requirements," *Sloan Management Review* (Summer 1980), pp. 51–63.

and 22-16.[5] Figure 22-14 shows a **context diagram,** the top-level data flow diagram that parallels the top-level module in the hierarchy chart in Figure 22-13. The context diagram consists of a single circle (process), plus all of the sources and dispositions (sinks) that are external to the process. The 0.0 appearing inside the circle indicates that the top level is also called the zero level. Figure 22-15 shows a data flow diagram that parallels the second level of the hierarchy chart. (As a matter of convention, however, this data flow diagram is described as a level 1 diagram.) The number of processes equals the number of modules on the hierarchy chart. Each process is numbered, in order to relate it to lower-level data flow diagrams.

[5]Note that these data flow diagrams differ from the data flow diagram shown in Figure 12-2. The latter diagram was provided to introduce the general appearance of a data flow diagram and was not intended to illustrate the articulation property.

Figure 22-16 shows level 2 and 3 data flow diagrams. The level 2 diagram is based on the subactivity "deliver goods to customer"; thus, the processes are coded as 2.1, 2.2, 2.3, and 2.4. As the figure indicates, the level 3 diagram is a decomposition of the sub-subactivity "ship and record shipment"; thus, the processes are coded as 2.41 and so on.

Structured Systems Analysis Methodologies

A number of methodologies have been devised to aid systems analysts in applying systems analysis and design techniques. Several such methodologies were listed earlier in the chapter. Recently methodologies that employ structured techniques have become available. A typical example is Structured Analysis and Design Techniques (SADT) from Softech, Inc.

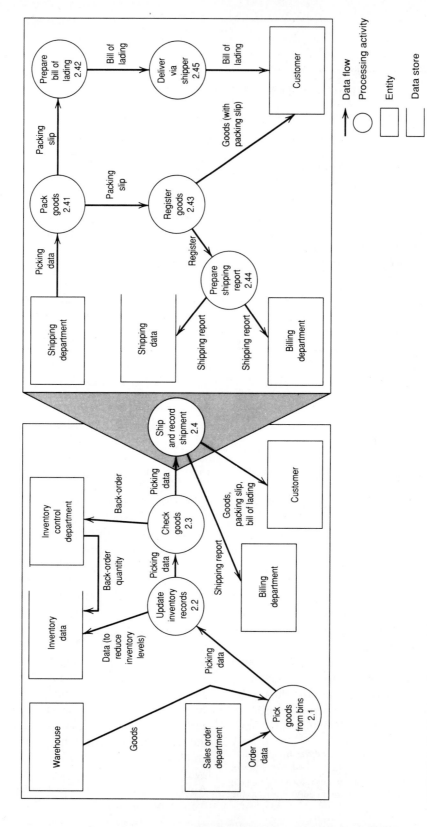

FIGURE 22-16 Two levels of data flow diagrams, based on a hierarchy diagram.

Summary

Systems analysis is a critical phase in systems development, since it defines the needs of a new system. Steps in systems analysis include surveying the present system, analyzing the survey findings, identifying the information needs, identifying the system requirements, and submitting the systems analysis report. Techniques for gathering facts include reviews of documents and records, interviews, observations, and questionnaires. Traditional systems analysis techniques for organizing facts include decision flow diagrams, work distribution charts, work measurements, matrix-oriented analyses, and space layout diagrams. Structured systems analysis techniques provide an integrated view of the conceptual and logical aspects of a system, using diagrams that generally decompose the system into ever-smaller modules. They include hierarchy charts and data flow diagrams.

Review Problem with Solution

Statement

Overall review. The Precise Manufacturing Company (introduced in the review problem for Chapter 21) has initiated a systems project that is to focus on sales order processing and management. A project team, consisting of a project head and three members, begins the project with a review of the firm's environment, financial status, operations, and organization. During this review the team identifies key success measures for the machine tool industry, such as share of the market, product engineering and quality, production efficiency, on-time delivery, and after-sales customer service. The team also confirms that significant improvements are needed in such areas as sales and market planning and production scheduling.

System survey within the project area. Early in May the team members begin their survey of sales order processing and management. To gather necessary data, they interview managers and key employees, observe the various operations, and examine various records and manuals. For example, the team members visit the departments involved in the sales order and billing operations, watch the flow of forms through the offices, and observe the products moving into and through the warehouse and to the shipping area. They note the employees performing their assigned tasks within the working areas; they look particularly for delayed flows, peak volumes, patterns in productivity, and other significant features. They also employ a variety of fact-organizing techniques, including the following:

1. **Overview diagram,** as shown in Figure 22-17.

2. **List of source documents, reports, and files,** as shown in Figure 22-18. In addition, the team collects copies of all documents, reports, and file record formats.

3. **Structured analysis diagrams,** as shown in Figures 22-13 through 22-16. In addition, the team prepares detailed input–process–output diagrams based on the hierarchical activity diagram in Figure 22-13 and the copies of documents and reports.

4. **Work distribution charts** for the shipping department, as shown in Figure 22-7, and for the sales order department.

5. **Productivity graph** for the sales order department, as shown in Figure 22-10. This graph, which is based on the data in the work sampling worksheets shown in Figures 22-8 and 22-9, indicates that the high costs incurred by the sales order department are partly due to substandard productivity.

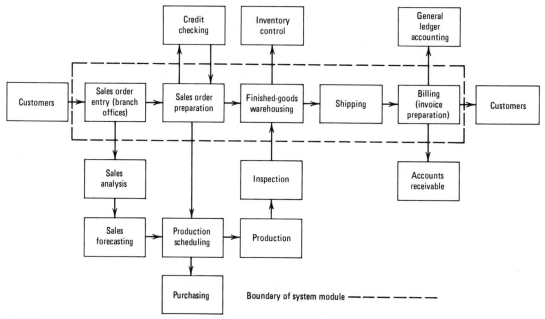

FIGURE 22-17 An overview diagram of the sales order processing and related systems at Precise.

6. **System flowcharts** of the present sales order processing. These flowcharts in effect provide details of the broad-level processing depicted in the overview diagram. In addition to showing the conversion of customers' orders into sales invoices (similar to the procedure shown in Figure 12-17), they illustrate two relatively unusual situations: (a) the preparation of special orders for custom-made products and (b) the preparation and processing of back orders.

7. **Lists of decisions** made by the key managers in the marketing function. For instance, Figure 22-19 shows the decisions made by the vice-president of marketing. In addition, the head of the project team prepares decision flow diagrams similar to Figure 22-6.

Analysis of operations and information needs. In July the team analyzes the gathered facts. It concludes, for instance, that only minor weaknesses exist in the distribution of work within the shipping department. On the other hand, major weaknesses are discovered in the sales order and billing departments. Tasks appear to be poorly distributed among the order and billing clerks; as a result, some clerks are idle much of the day and others are constantly busy. This finding reinforces the results of the work sampling technique, which shows that productivity is significantly below par in the sales order department. Upon reflection, the team concludes that two causes lie at the root of these problems. Overall low productivity stems from the fluctuating inflows of sales orders. The sales order department is staffed to handle the morning peaks, so that during the rest of the day certain clerks are idle. The imbalance in work is largely the fault of the supervisor, who apparently does not assign work in a fair and equitable manner.

The team also concludes that certain

Source and generated documents

    Customer order
    Sales order
    Sales invoice
    Bill of lading
    Production request (back order)
    Production order
    Sales return form

Files

    Product
    Master list of order numbers
    Open orders
    Closed orders
    Customer accounts receivable
    Credit history
    Warehouse, pending sales orders
    Shipping, pending shipping orders
    Billing, pending sales orders
    Shipping data
    Bill of lading
    Production request
    Back-order tickler
    Sales invoice

Reports

    Sales by product analysis (monthly)
    Sales by salesperson analysis (monthly)
    Products shipped and sold (daily, by total weight and dollars)
    Outstanding orders (monthly)

Related reports

    Sales forecast (monthly)
    Production schedule (weekly)
    Finished-goods inventory status (monthly)
    Accounts receivable aging schedule (monthly)

FIGURE 22-18 A list of source documents, reports, and files related to Precise's sales order processing and management system.

source documents (e.g., the production order and sales order) are poorly designed, files contain redundant and noncurrent data, and reports provide unreliable and insufficient customer and product information. Other weaknesses pertaining to the sales order processing and billing procedure are listed in Figure 22-20.

The team thus determines that the sales system contains a number of weaknesses. Although the system is not likely to collapse, it can be expected to worsen with time. For instance, rising administrative costs, caused in part by the swollen clerical force in the sales order department, can be expected to continue rising with sales growth. Inquiries can be expected to consume more clerical time and to be accompanied by longer response times. Overcoming these problems, the team concludes, will require extensive changes in the information system.

Report approval. Early in August, Tod Stuart presents a systems analysis report to

Specific Decision	Type of Decision
Introducing new products	Strategic planning
Eliminating current products and adjusting product mix[a]	Strategic planning
Establishing pricing, discounting, and profit policies	Strategic planning
Approving individual product price changes	Strategic planning
Selecting new channels of distribution[a]	Strategic planning
Researching and developing new markets	Strategic planning
Locating new warehouses[a]	Strategic planning
Devising customer service, advertising, and sales promotion strategies	Strategic planning
Counteracting competitors actions[a]	Strategic planning
Increasing sales and share of market[a]	Strategic planning
Minimizing marketing costs	Management control
Revising the marketing organization and sales branch territories	Strategic planning
Approving sales forecasts[a]	Strategic planning
Undertaking major resource investments (facilities, special planning studies, advertising campaigns, etc.)[a]	Strategic planning
Setting profit margins allowed to distributors	Tactical planning
Maintaining relations with large customers	Tactical planning
Setting employment standards and hiring middle-level and staff department managers[a]	Strategic planning
Evaluating and improving middle-level and staff department manager performance	Management control
Coordinating budget control for marketing function	Management control

[a]Decisions made jointly with other managers.

FIGURE 22-19   A list of decisions made by the vice-president of marketing.

1. Orders are sometimes overlooked at sales branches, since no registers are maintained.

2. Orders are slow in reaching the home office when mailed from the sales branches.

3. Credit checks cause excessive delays in processing.

4. Sales order files are not up to date.

5. Sales orders are not prenumbered.

6. Excessive numbers of back orders are necessary.

7. Back orders are not cross-referenced to original sales orders; hence, there are gaps in the audit trail.

8. Sales orders are not adequately controlled within the finished-goods warehouse.

9. Sales orders are poorly designed. For instance, ordered items are not arranged according to warehouse locations; thus, warehouse pickers lose time in filling orders.

10. Orders awaiting shipment are not physically protected, so that considerable pilferage occurs.

11. Shipments are not logged in a register, so that inquiries lead to laborious searches of shipping papers.

12. Sales prices and discounts allowed customers are not carefully checked in the billing department; this practice leads to numerous errors.

13. Batch control totals are not run on batches of sales orders prior to their entry into the billing operation.

14. Computer runs to prepare sales invoices are not carefully scheduled.

15. Data entry clerks and computer operators are not adequately trained; thus, they make numerous errors.

16. Inventory records are usually not up to date, since they are updated by periodic computer runs.

17. Production scheduling is unreliable; thus, often there are delays in filling special orders and backorders.

18. Sales forecasts are highly inaccurate, in part because of weak analysis of past sales trends. (This weakness is related to weakness number 17.)

FIGURE 22-20   Weaknesses detected in Precise's sales order processing and billing procedure.

the steering committee. This report, which had been prepared during the last few days of July, contains the findings discussed in the preceding sections, plus a list of system requirements, a list of information needs, and a revised cost-versus-benefits analysis. In the letter of transmittal, signed by Tod Stuart, this recommendation appears: "It is my opinion that the findings justify a continuation of the sales project essentially as originally proposed." After a lengthy discussion, the steering committee concurs. One week later the president gives final approval for the systems design phase to begin.

Required

a. Prepare a list of requirements for an improved sales order and management system and related activities. Assign arbitrary but reasonable values to the various requirements.

b. List typical information needs of the vice-president of marketing.

Solution

a. List of system requirements:

Capacity: average of 800 sales orders daily, with a peak of 1000.

Backlog: not in excess of two hours equivalent processing time.

Average processing time: 24 hours for orders received for standard products; three days for special orders, except when designing is required.

Response time for telephone or in-person inquires: one minute or less.

Accuracy: no more than one processing error per 1000 sales transactions.

Reports: concise but adequate information to enable managers to fulfill their decision responsibilities (per lists of needed information).

Reporting delay: less than 30 minutes for specially requested reports (except for strategic planning decisions); less than two days after the end of the reporting period for scheduled reports.

Delivery reliability: 99 percent of promised delivery dates are to be met.

File accesses: average of 2000 daily, including file maintenance and inquiries.

In addition, the following requirements pertain to related modules which affect sales order processing operations:

Back orders: to be reduced from 15 percent to 2 percent of received orders within two years.

Sales forecasting: error to be reduced to plus or minus 3 percent of sales within one year.

Sales analyses: seven analyses and other reports to be prepared to meet the preceding requirement and to provide needed information for marketing managers.

b. A list of information needed by the vice-president of marketing appears on page 1060.

Review Questions

22-1 What is the meaning of each of the following terms?

System survey
Information needs analysis
Information needs methodologies
System requirements
Systems analysis report
Traditional systems analysis techniques
Decision flow diagram

Marketing policies
Current unit price by product
Unit cost to unit price by product
Expected unit price by product
Expected marginal costs and revenues at various price levels
Expected unit contribution margin by product
Amount of sales and sales returns by product line, daily
Amounts of sales for this month and past five years by product, type of customer, sales
　branch, salesperson, and channel of distribution
Amounts of gross profit and contribution margin for past five years by same segments
Amounts of marketing expenses, variable and nonvariable, for past five years
Ratio of marketing expenses, variable and nonvariable, to sales for past five years
Variances from budget of actual expenses for marketing services, machine tools, power
　tools, sales forecasting and analysis, and market research for each month this year
Variances of actual sales, gross profits, contribution margin, and marketing expenses from
　budget for past five years and for each month this year
Decline or growth in sales from last month to this month
Expected sales by product for next month, quarter, and year
Expected contribution margin by product, sales branch, and channel of distribution for next
　month and quarter
Current profit margins for each distributor
Percentage change in sales, from last year to this year, for each large customer
Advertising effectiveness
Market conditions and trends
Availability of resources: marketing personnel, equipment, facilities
Actions of competitors
New construction by competitors and by Precise during past five years, by location and
　type of marketing facility
Price structures of competitors
Strengths of competitors: sales territories, terms, product quality, service, salespersons
Industry sales for past 10 years
Precise's share of market for past 10 years
Value of capital goods production in the United States by state for past 10 years
Expected value of capital goods production for next year
Expected amount of disposable income in the United States for next year
Expected value of construction in the United States for next year
Expected new technological developments
Status of all marketing research projects currently conducted by Precise
Percentage of Precise's customers not ordering any products for last three years
Ratio of new customers to all customers for last three years
Solicited customer opinions of Precise's product lines and service
Solicited public opinions of Precise's advertising, packaging, public image
Budget requests for coming year for each reporting manager
Justification for marketing budget requests from each reporting manager, especially
　concerning discretionary costs and new salespersons
Attitude and motivation of each reporting manager and salesperson

Work distribution chart
Work sampling
Input–output matrix
Space layout diagram
Structured systems development
Hierarchy chart
Data flow diagram
Context diagram

22-2 What are the typical steps in the systems analysis phase?

22-3 What are the reasons for conducting a survey of the present system?

22-4 Discuss the scope of a system survey.

22-5 Describe the sources of data in a system survey.

22-6 Discuss the behavioral aspects to be considered during a system survey.

22-7 Contrast the questions that should be asked during a system survey and during a systems analysis.

22-8 What are the general objectives that serve as criteria when asking analytical questions?

22-9 Why is an information needs analysis an important part of the systems analysis phase?

22-10 What is the sequence of actions embodied in an information needs analysis?

22-11 What questions should be answered in the course of identifying the decisions made by managers?

22-12 How do decisions relate to the information needs of managers?

22-13 What techniques may be used to aid managers in identifying their information needs?

22-14 What are several system requirements that should be specified during the systems analysis phase?

22-15 What are several sections that might appear in a systems analysis report?

22-16 What is the purpose of reviewing documents and records?

22-17 Discuss the guidelines for interviewing.

22-18 What are interviewing pitfalls?

22-19 What is the purpose of observing system activities?

22-20 How may questionnaires or checklists be used?

22-21 In what ways may fact-organizing techniques be classified?

22-22 Identify several traditional systems analysis techniques.

22-23 How may a decision and information analysis be aided?

22-24 What is the purpose of a work distribution analysis?

22-25 For what purposes may work measurement techniques be used?

22-26 Describe the process by which productivity of a department may be measured.

22-27 Identify several types of systems-related matrices.

22-28 How do structured systems analysis techniques differ from traditional systems analysis techniques?

22-29 What are the benefits of structured systems development?

22-30 Identify several structured systems analysis techniques.

22-31 Describe the similarities and differences between hierarchy charts and data flow diagrams.

Discussion Questions

22-32 Discuss the reasons *against* analyzing the present information system.

22-33 What difficulties are likely to be encountered in attempting to specify the information needs for decisions that are made jointly by two or more managers?

22-34 Discuss the advantages and disadvantages of (a) stopping all reports and (b) requiring that each manager explicitly request the continuation of any report that he or she feels is really needed.

22-35 Discuss key decisions and information needs pertaining to each of the following functions within the specified types of firms:

  a. Loan function within a savings and loan institution.
  b. Sales function within a discount department store.
  c. Production function within a farm equipment manufacturer.
  d. Patient care function within a hospital.
  e. Construction function within a building contractor.

22-36 When managers leave a firm and are replaced by other managers, the information needs often change even though the decisions remain unchanged. What difficulties, if any, does this situation pose for a systems analyst during the systems analysis phase?

22-37 If a systems analyst attempts to be concerned both with the people who will be affected by systems analysis and design and the technical elements of the information system, will not one or the other be slighted?

22-38 For each of the following systems projects, what key facts are needed and what are their sources likely to be?

  a. Payroll processing system.
  b. Accounts receivable processing system.
  c. Inventory management system.
  d. Purchases processing system.

22-39 Consider a four-person systems project team in which (a) the inputs, (b) the outputs, (c) the processing, and (d) the data base have each been assigned to one member. Each member is to analyze and design his or her assigned element. Is this a reasonable division of responsibilities?

22-40 Describe the steps involved in analyzing the information system of a small firm of your choice.

22-41 List the questions that should be asked in analyzing each of the following problem situations, which have occurred within a manufacturing firm:

  a. Production costs have risen significantly because of increased overtime, idle time waiting for materials, and reworking of products.
  b. Credit losses have increased because of a heightened delinquency rate.
  c. Late shipments of orders have increased because of bottlenecks in production and the warehouse.
  d. Customer complaints have increased because of poor quality of products.
  e. Finished-goods inventory levels have fluctuated widely because of large errors in forecasting sales.

22-42 Discuss the proposed changes in the following situation. A firm that manufactures small, specialized lift-and-delivery vehicles employs a manual cash disbursements processing system. However, the volume of checks written each month has become so large that the treasurer has proposed the conversion to a computer-based cash disbursements processing system.

During an analysis of the present system the following facts emerge:

  a. 16,000 suppliers have been paid this year.
  b. Of these 16,000 suppliers, 12,000 have received one order from the firm.
  c. A few suppliers receive in excess of 100 orders per month from the firm.
  d. Each order is paid by a separate check.

Problems

22-1 List the questions that should be asked in analyzing each of the following problem situations, which have occurred within a manufacturing firm.

    a. Production costs have risen significantly because of increased overtime, idle time waiting for materials, and reworking of products.

    b. Credit losses have increased because of a heightened delinquency rate.

    c. Late shipment of orders has increased because of bottlenecks in production and the warehouse.

    d. Customer complaints have increased because of the poor quality of products.

    e. Finished-goods inventory levels have fluctuated widely because of large errors in forecasting sales.

22-2 Which fact-gathering technique(s) appear to be most appropriate in each of the following cases? Why?

    a. Determining the procedure that should be followed by the cashier in preparing the bank deposit.

    b. Determining the information needs of the personnel manager.

    c. Determining the average number of work orders processed during a typical day.

    d. Determining how the sales order processing procedure is actually performed.

    e. Investigating the general level of productivity in the finished-goods warehouse.

    f. Surveying the general adequacy of internal accounting controls in the cash disbursements procedure.

    g. Surveying the opinions of all employees concerning the possible change to flextime.

    h. Investigating the complaint that ordered products are frequently out of stock.

    i. Determining the extent to which transaction documents are miscoded.

22-3 The Snowqueen Cleansing Products Company of Madison, Wisconsin, has undertaken a comprehensive long-range systems development program. After several preliminary planning sessions, the steering committee has identified a number of modules comprising the information system. Included among these modules are order processing and billing, shipping, finished-goods warehousing, raw-materials storeskeeping, accounts payable, accounts receivable, inventory management, production planning and control, quality control, purchasing, sales forecasting and analysis, production operations, payroll, cash receipts, cash disbursements, labor distribution and job costing, property and plant, personnel, administration, stockholder transactions, financial accounting and reports, general ledger, budgeting, and strategic planning.

After careful deliberations, the steering committee decides that four systems projects will be started concurrently. Two of these systems projects affect the purchasing and general ledger modules. Purchasing has been selected because of severe problems currently being experienced in that area, whereas general ledger has been selected because of its key role in the accounting processing cycle. The third and fourth systems projects are to be selected on the basis of your recommendation, since you are a systems consultant with wide experience.

Required

a. Select the third and fourth systems projects and justify. (Since few details are provided in the problem, your justification must necessarily be expressed in general terms.)

b. For one of the selected projects, plan a survey of the present information system module. The plan should include

(1) A description of the scope of the survey, including the incorporated transaction processing system (if any), physical operations, and organizational units, as well as interfaces with (a) adjoining systems modules, (b) relevant aspects of the firm's environment, and (c) managerial decision making.

(2) A description of the various sources of facts and fact-gathering techniques to be employed.

22-4 George Morrill is the purchasing manager for Tolliver Electronics, Inc., an Amherst, Massachusetts, manufacturer of high-quality electronics products. Before becoming purchasing manager, he was an electronics technician and quality control supervisor.

George will be making decisions with regard to

a. Selecting the suppliers from whom to buy parts and subassemblies (tactical planning decisions).

b. Establishing purchasing policies (strategic planning decisions) to be made together with higher-level managers within the firm.

c. Hiring and evaluating supervisors, buyers, and other purchasing department personnel (management control decisions).

d. Negotiating purchase contracts (tactical planning decisions).

Required

a. Describe the analysis that should be performed to determine George's information needs.

b. List several information items needed for making each of these decisions.

c. List the properties of information needed for the second and fourth decisions.

d. Describe two key reports that George should receive.

22-5 Rasher's Grocery Stores is a local chain of 10 stores in Tampa, Florida. Each store has an average of four cash registers and serves 600 customers daily. However, growth trends indicate that 800–900 customers likely will be served daily at each store within three years.

For several years the management of Rasher's has been watching developments in computerized POS systems. It has become convinced that the benefits of such systems—increased productivity, more effective use of checkout stations, improved control over inventories, and automatic verification of customer credit—will have a healthy effect on the firm's slim profits.

Recently, therefore, management requested the information systems manager to undertake an analysis and feasibility study. After several weeks of investigation the information systems manager concludes, on the basis of a rough comparison of benefits and costs, that a centralized computer with disk files and POS terminals in each store is the most likely configuration. However, this determination depends on the ability of the POS system to accomplish certain feats.

Thus, the system should reduce the average checkout time from 4 minutes to 2.5 minutes. It should enable a credit check to be performed in 10 seconds or less, and the response to each keyed-in grocery sale should not exceed 2 seconds. No more than one error in 1000 transactions should be caused by the system, and the system should reduce human checkout errors by 25 percent.

In addition to aiding the checkout procedure, the POS system should provide inventory reorder reports and other daily management information within one hour after the stores close at 9:00 P.M. It should also have the capacity of storing all the price data, plus inventory records and sales history data; all these data might require as much as 100 million bytes of storage.

Required

a. List several objectives of the POS systems project.

b. Describe the fact-gathering techniques that were likely employed during the analysis and feasibility study, and associate at least one fact with each technique.

c. List questions that should have been asked during the analysis of the survey findings.

d. List the system requirements and information needs for the proposed POS system. Be as specific as possible.

22-6 Refer to Problem 14-22, pertaining to the Rose Publishing Company.

Required

a. List sources of the facts that were gathered during the analysis of the current payroll system.

b. Briefly describe techniques that likely were used to gather facts; specify at least one fact that was likely gathered by each technique.

c. List questions that likely were asked during an analysis of the facts uncovered during the survey of the current system.

d. Describe underlying weaknesses and problems that appear to exist in the current system.

e. The items listed in the box represent many of the system and information requirements for a new payroll system. List other requirements, both system and in-

formational, that are desirable in a new system. (Some of these requirements, such as timeliness, may be implied in the statements in the box.)

f. The departmental supervisors and project managers are both allowed in the proposed system to have access to labor distribution data on a limited basis. Discuss the reasons for allowing each of the parties to have access to the data specified. The limitations on data may cause conflicts between the parties. Discuss behavioral actions that could be taken by the systems consultant to reduce or eliminate these possible conflicts.

(CMA adapted)

22-7 Jack Ladd has recently joined the Wexler Home Products Company of Long Beach, California. His title is Systems Analyst I, a position for which he is qualified by virtue of receiving a degree in business systems analysis from the local university. He has performed exceedingly well in his first several assignments. Thus, his supervisor feels confident in assigning Jack to perform an interview. He gives Jack the assignment late Thursday afternoon.

The interview is to take place with the manager of inventory, Colin Blunt. Jack's task is two-fold: (1) to uncover facts that can aid in correcting problems that have been traced to the inventory management function, and (2) to gain Blunt's cooperation in an analysis and redesign of the inventory management system.

Jack resolves to deal with these tasks in an expeditious manner. Therefore, he appears bright and early Friday morning at Blunt's office. He explains that his business is urgent, so Blunt cancels his scheduled staff meeting to talk with Jack.

Jack opens the interview by telling Blunt that top management is "concerned about serious problems in the inventory management function." He continues by explaining that he is there to help correct these problems. "In fact," he says, "our systems group can completely redesign your inventory procedures without bothering you at all. All we need is your story concerning the problems, and we can get started. We'll even keep mum during our study so that the employees won't know what is going on. That way, they can keep on with their work and won't be worried about possible layoffs when the new system is installed."

Jack continues by offering suggestions concerning several small problems pertaining to inventories that he had noted while walking through the area that morning. He also explains the workings of scientific inventory order models, including their ability to "minimize the array of inventory expenditures and optimize return on investment." Jack feels that this will show Blunt that he "knows his stuff."

After Jack has completed this exposition, he asks Blunt if he is willing to cooperate. "After all," as Jack added, "it's to your benefit to clear up these problems before more are uncovered." Blunt replies (as Jack clicks on his tape recorder) that he will have to discuss the matter with his superior, the production manager.

Jack feels that this reply is a rebuff to his efforts. Therefore he states that he has another meeting to attend, gets up, and leaves. When he sees his supervisor later that morning, Jack repeats what Blunt had said and ends by exclaiming, "I don't think that Mr. Blunt wants to cooperate. He certainly didn't offer any facts, and he seemed to be stalling when I put the question to him."

Required

Critique the interviewing approach of Jack Ladd.

22-8 The Funtime Novelty Company of Sioux Falls, South Dakota, is a small manu-

facturer of varied novelties and toys. It sells this wide line of standardized products to retail stores in the Midwest, shipping goods from its finished-goods warehouse as orders are received. The firm is organized according to four major functions: production, marketing, finance, and administrative services. Each major function is headed by a vice-president who reports to the president.

In recent years Funtime has experienced rapidly rising costs and declining profits, even though sales have remained relatively stable. Earlier this year the president became sufficiently concerned that she initiated a long-range systems development program. After consultation with the four vice-presidents, she decides that the production area warrants the earliest attention. Therefore, she directs the information systems manager to analyze the operations and information needs of the production function.

Upon performing a preliminary survey, the information systems manager becomes convinced that inadequate information may be the most serious deficiency. Thus, he assigns the most experienced systems analyst, Allan Adler, to analyze the information needs of the production function.

Allan begins his analysis by interviewing the respective managers within the production function. In each interview his aim is to identify the objectives and key decisions for which the manager is responsible. Later interviews will attempt to discover the less obvious decisions, to delve into decision processes, and to pinpoint information needs that relate to the managers' personal desires. The following facts are based on his first set of interviews:

The vice-president of production has the overall responsibility for production activities. In addition to overall budgetary planning and the establishment of yearly and monthly production levels, he supervises the engineering manager, purchasing manager, production planning manager, receiving department manager, stores manager, and production superintendent.

The engineering manager is responsible for designing the various products, maintaining their bills of materials, and specifying quality levels for materials.

The purchasing manager is responsible for obtaining needed materials at the specified quality levels, at the lowest possible prices, and at the times needed for production.

The production planning manager is responsible for scheduling production to meet the levels specified by the production vice-president. She maintains perpetual inventory records for all raw materials, work-in-process, and finished goods. Therefore, she initiates (1) production orders to maintain adequate levels of finished goods and (2) purchase requisitions to replenish the raw materials needed to produce the various products. An equally important responsibility is to minimize the investment in inventories.

The receiving department manager is responsible for receiving ordered materials, including the verification of their condition and quantity.

The stores manager is responsible for receiving raw materials from receiving and finished goods from production, storing the materials and finished goods, issuing the materials to production as needed, and transferring the finished goods to shipping as specified by sales orders.

The production superintendent is responsible for completing production operations on job lots specified in production orders. Satisfactory completion means that a job lot is delivered to the finished-goods warehouse on the scheduled date, that the production costs are as low as possible, and that the products all pass quality inspections. Aiding the production superintendent in these responsibilities are various workstation foremen and quality inspectors.

Required

a. Identify the objectives that each of the managers should strive to achieve and the key decisions that he or she must make.

b. List several key items of information needed by each manager to meet his or her stated responsibilities.

c. Expand the decision flow diagram shown in Figure 22-6 to include additional decisions identified in **a** above.

d. Describe the decision processes employed by the production planning manager in

 (1) Deciding on the scheduled dates for a particular job lot.
 (2) Deciding when particular materials need to be replenished.

22-9 Six employees comprise the accounts payable department of the Hubbard Sales Company, a Stillwater, Oklahoma, firm. They perform the following sets of tasks for the designated number of hours daily:

Supervisor (Alice Whitespan)

Supervise employees	4 hours
Aid in verifying invoices	2 hours
Approve disbursement vouchers	$\frac{1}{2}$ hour
Aid in preparing checks	$\frac{1}{2}$ hour
Other activities, such as correspondence	1 hour

Accounts Payable Documentation Clerks
(Jackie Culver and Susan Lynch)

Handle purchase order copies	2 hours
Handle receiving report copies	2 hours
Process suppliers' invoices	$10\frac{1}{2}$ hours
Assemble disbursement voucher packets	$1\frac{1}{2}$ hours
Other activities, such as filing	1 hour

Freight Bill Clerk (Joyce Itel)

Prepare, verify, and post freight bills	$4\frac{1}{2}$ hours
Assemble and review disbursement vouchers	$1\frac{1}{2}$ hours
Other activities	1 hour

Disbursement Control Clerk (Pat Chase)

Assemble, review, and approve disbursement vouchers	4 hours
Prepare and review checks	3 hours
Other activities	1 hour

Typist–clerk (Betty Bush)

Type checks (and accompanying voucher stubs)	5 hours
Other activities, such as typing correspondence and filing	2 hours

Required

a. Prepare a work distribution chart, using such tasks as supervision, purchase order processing, and voucher processing.

b. Identify weaknesses in the distribution of tasks, such as illogical assignments of tasks and assignments that appear to violate internal control concepts.

22-10 The Quinn Company of Flagstaff, Arizona, has received from customers numerous complaints that ordered merchandise is arriving later than promised. A systems analyst in the firm, Kim Scott, is therefore assigned the task of determining the cause of the late shipments. She begins by listing several possible causes, including inefficient processing of sales orders, an inefficient warehouse picking procedure, and low productivity in the shipping department.

After observing the warehouse operations, Kim feels reasonably confident that the picking procedure is satisfactory and that ordered merchandise is delivered promptly to the shipping dock. Before investigating the sales order processing procedure, she decides to ascertain the level of productivity in the shipping department. If it is considerably below the norm, then she will recommend improvements in that area. Perhaps such improvements will eliminate the need to study sales order processing at this time. Since Kim has other high-priority projects "wait-

ing in the wings," both she and her supervisor would welcome such an outcome.

Kim therefore considers how best to determine the shipping department productivity. She realizes that simply observing the work for an hour or so would not yield sufficiently valid or complete results on which to base a conclusion. However, she doesn't have time to sit around for a week and observe, since other duties call. After deliberation, she decides to employ the work sampling technique, which only requires that she make brief observations randomly throughout the week. She then uses a random-number table to select the random times. At each of the times she records productivity data on a worksheet. The data on page 1069, for instance, were recorded on Monday.

Observations during the remaining days of the week approximate the data recorded in the table; that is, the daily profile is representative of the long-term productivity pattern in the shipping department.

Required

a. Compute the productive and nonproductive percentages for the day pictured.

b. Prepare a productivity graph for a representative day in the shipping department. Use hour blocks (e.g., 8:00 A.M. to 9:00 A.M., 9:00 A.M. to 10:00 A.M.) to determine points for the graph.

22-11 Masters Merchandising, Inc., of Worcester, Massachusetts, acquires and sells a wide variety of housewares. Inventory management is therefore a critical function. Recently the firm studied the inventory management function for the purpose of redesigning the key inputs, processing steps, and outputs. It began the study by defining the various activities and subactivities that are encompassed within the inventory management function. The results follow:

Activities

Store and record additions to merchandise.

Replenish inventory.

Prepare reports for management.

Monitor inventory usage.

Receive ordered merchandise.

Subactivities

Prepare supplier evaluation report.

Prepare shipping record and ship merchandise.

Prepare purchase requisition.

Determine quantity of merchandise received.

Determine quantity of merchandise moved to storage.

Prepare inventory status report.

Prepare receiving report.

Calculate quantity to reorder.

Prepare and transmit purchase order.

Update inventory records to show reduction of inventory on hand.

Prepare inventory aging report.

Determine supplier with whom to place order.

Match receipts with orders or returns with credit memos.

Update inventory records to show additional quantity on hand.

Update inventory records to show quantity ordered.

Required

a. Prepare a hierarchy chart for inventory management.

b. Prepare a context diagram.

c. Prepare a data flow diagram for the activity "replenish inventory."

d. Prepare a lower-level data flow diagram for the subactivity "prepare purchase order."

22-12 Refer to Problem 14-22.

Required

a. Prepare a context diagram of the timekeeping–payroll–labor-distribution procedure of Rose Publishing Company, as described in the problem.

b. Prepare a level 1 data flow diagram of the major subactivities in the procedure.

c. Prepare a level 2 data flow diagram that details the "collect and record employee time data" subactivity.

22-13 Wekender Corporation of San Diego owns and operates 15 large departmentalized retail hardware stores in major metropolitan areas of the southwestern United States. The stores carry a wide variety of merchandise, but the major thrust is toward the weekend "do-it-yourselfer." The company has been

Daily Observation Worksheet
Shipping Department (16 employees) May 5

Observations		Productive		Nonproductive	
Number	Time	In Area	Out of Area	Personal	Idle
1	8:36	8	4	2	2
2	9:05	10	4	1	1
3	10:01	8	3	1	4
4	10:29	12	1	1	2
5	11:42	11		2	3
6	1:47	14		1	1
7	2:18	12	2		2
8	3:04	10	1	4	1
9	3:52	11	3		2
10	4:48	6			10

successful in this field, and the number of stores in the chain has almost doubled since 1983.

Each retail store acquires its merchandise from the company's centrally located warehouse. Consequently, the warehouse must maintain an up-to-date and well-stocked inventory to meet the demands of the individual stores.

The company wishes to hold its competitive position with similar-type stores of other companies in its marketing area. Therefore, Wekender Corporation must improve its purchasing and inventory procedures. The company's stores must have the proper goods to meet customer demand, and the warehouse, in turn, must have the goods available. The number of company stores, the number of inventory items carried, and the volume of business all are providing pressures to change from basically manual processing to computer-based processing procedures.

Top management has determined that the following items should have high priority in the new system.

a. Rapid ordering to replenish warehouse inventory stocks with as little delay as possible. (Approximately 2500 vendors are on the active list.)

b. Quick filling and shipping of merchandise to the stores. (This involves determining whether sufficient stock exists.)

c. Some indication of inventory activity. (Approximately 1000 purchase orders are placed weekly.)

d. Perpetual records in order to determine inventory level by item number quickly. (Approximately 10,000 separate items of merchandise are active.)

A description of the current warehousing and purchasing procedures follows:

Stock is stored in bins and is located by an inventory number. The numbers generally are listed sequentially on the bins to facilitate locating items for shipment. However, this system frequently is not followed; as a result, some items are difficult to locate.

Whenever a retail store needs merchandise, a three-part merchandise request form is completed. One copy is kept by the store and two copies are mailed to the warehouse the next day. If the merchandise requested is on hand, the goods are delivered to the store, accompanied by the third copy of the request. The second copy is filed at the warehouse.

If the quantity of goods on hand is not sufficient to fill the order, the warehouse sends the quantity available and notes the quantity shipped on the request form. Then a purchase memorandum for the shortage is prepared by the warehouse. At the end of each day, all the memos are sent to the purchasing department.

When the purchase memoranda are received from the warehouse, purchase orders are prepared. Vendor catalogs are used to select the best source for the requested goods, and the purchase order is prepared and mailed. Copies of the order are sent to the accounts payable department and the receiving area; one copy is retained in the purchasing department.

When ordered goods are received, they are checked at the receiving area, and a receiving report is prepared. One copy of the receiving report is retained at the receiving area, one is forwarded to the accounts payable department, and one is filed at the warehouse with the purchase memorandum (if a purchase memorandum had been prepared).

When the receiving report arrives in the accounts payable department, it is compared with the purchase order on file. Both documents are also compared with the vendor's invoice before payment is authorized.

The purchasing department strives periodically to evaluate the vendors for financial soundness, reliability, and trade relationships. However, because the volume of requests received from the warehouse is so great, this activity currently does not have a high priority.

Each week a report of the open purchase orders is prepared to determine whether any action should be taken on overdue deliveries. This report is prepared manually by scanning the files of outstanding purchase orders.

Required

a. Describe in specific terms, with the aid of flowcharts if desired, the computer-based processing system that best suits the stated needs of the warehousing and purchasing procedures; justify your choice.

b. Sketch a configuration of this system that identifies the needed hardware components.

c. Identify the needed files and the data items in each file.

d. Prepare a hierarchy chart of the purchasing, inventory, and payables procedure.

e. Prepare a context diagram of the purchasing, inventory, and payables procedure.

f. Prepare a level 1 data flow diagram of the major subactivities in the purchasing, inventory, and payables procedure.

g. Prepare a level 2 data flow diagram that details the "order retail store merchandise from warehouse" subactivity.

h. Design the formats of three useful managerial reports pertaining to warehousing and purchasing activities, and indicate the purpose of each report.

i. Devise a code for identifying inventory items.

j. Devise a record layout for purchase transactions.

k. Without prejudice to the answer in requirement **a**, assume that Wekender Corporation acquires a data base management system.

(1) Draw a data structure diagram that would portray a schema for the data base, assuming that a network model is selected.

(2) Draw the tables that would contain the data if the relational model is selected. Include appropriate foreign keys (common columns) in the tables to reflect (at least implicitly) the linkages shown in the schema for the network model.

(3) Specify the physical access and organization methods that could likely be used if the network model is selected; how would they differ if the relational model is selected?

(4) Specify several inquiries and reports that might be aided by the structures under either of the data models, including the reports described in **h**.

(CMA adapted)

22-14 Wright Company of Binghamton, New York, employs a computer-based data processing system for maintaining all company records. The present system was developed in stages over the past five years and has been fully operational for the last 24 months.

When the system was being designed, all department heads were asked to specify the types of information and reports they would need for planning and controlling operations. The systems department attempted to meet the specifications of each department head. Company management specified that certain other reports be prepared for department heads. During the five years of systems development and operation there have been several changes in the department head positions because of attrition and promotions. The new department heads often made requests for additional reports according to their specifications. The systems department complied with all of these requests. Reports were discontinued only on request by a department head, and then only if it was not a standard report required by top management. As a result, few reports were in fact discontinued. Consequently, the data processing system was generating a large quantity of reports each reporting period.

Company management became concerned about the quantity of information that was being produced by the system. The internal audit department was asked to evaluate the effectiveness of the reports generated by the system. The audit staff determined early in the study that more information was being generated by the data processing system than could be used effectively. They noted the following reactions to this information overload:

a. Many department heads would not act on certain reports during periods of peak activity. The department head would let these reports accumulate with the hope of catching up during a subsequent lull.

b. Some department heads had so many reports that they did not act at all on the information or they made incorrect decisions because of misuse of information.

c. Frequently, action required by the nature of the report data was not taken until the department head was reminded by someone who needed the decision. These department heads did not appear to have developed a priority system for acting on the information produced by the data processing system.

d. Department heads often would develop the information they needed from alternative, independent sources, rather than utilizing the reports generated by the data processing system. This was often easier than trying to search among the reports for the needed data.

Required

a. Indicate which of the observed reactions are functional behavioral responses and which are dysfunctional behavioral responses. Explain your answer in each case.

b. Assuming one or more of the responses is dysfunctional, recommend procedures the company could employ to eliminate the dysfunctional behavior and to prevent its recurrence.

(CMA adapted)

22-15 *Datacruncher Office Equipment, Inc. (Continuing Case)*

Required

a. Prepare a report that surveys the environment of the firm, including relevant data concerning the office equipment industry, the major resources needed, and the principal legal requirements. (Use library sources in compiling this report.)

b. Prepare a financial analysis of the firm by reference to the financial statements in Exhibit A-2. (See pages C-8–C-9).

c. Prepare a plan of analysis for the selected systems project(s), specifying (1) the techniques to be employed in gathering and organizing facts concerning the present system, (2) the areas in which each technique is to be used, and (3) the nature of results that each technique can be expected to provide.

d. Prepare an outline of questions to ask one key manager (within the scope of the selected systems projects[s]) during an interview that pertains to his or her information needs.

e. Prepare a decision flow diagram for a function within which the selected systems project(s) is (are) located.

f. Prepare an analysis of the present system (within the scope of the selected systems project[s]), with particular emphasis upon significant problems.

g. Prepare a hierarchy chart and data flow diagram (within the scope of the selected systems project[s]). Include three levels for both techniques.

h. Prepare a list of requirements for an improved system (within the scope of the selected systems project[s]). Assign reasonable, though arbitrary, values to system requirements involving capacities, timeliness, accuracy, and so on. Also, include a set of information needed by the sales manager or branch manager.

Suggested Readings

Aktas, A. Ziya. *Structured Analysis and Design of Information Systems.* Englewood Cliffs, N.J.: Prentice-Hall, 1987.

Burch, John G., Jr., and Grudnitski, Gary. *Information Systems: Theory and Practice.* 5th ed. New York: John Wiley, 1989.

Collard, Albert F. "Sharpening Interviewing Skills." *Journal of Systems Management* (Dec. 1975), pp. 6–10.

Davis, William S. *Systems Analysis and Design: A Structured Approach.* Reading, Mass.: Addison-Wesley, 1983.

Finneran, Thomas R., and Henry, Shirley J. "Structured Analysis for Data Base Design." *Datamation* (Nov. 1977), pp. 99–113.

Fitzgerald, Jerry. "Data Flow Diagrams for Auditors." *EDPACS* (October 1987), pp. 1–11 and *EDPACS* (November 1987), pp. 1–7.

Highsmith, Jim. "Structured Systems Planning." *MIS Quarterly* (September 1981), pp. 35–54.

Mendes, Kathleen S. "Structured Systems Analysis: A Technique to Define Business Requirements." *Sloan Management Review* (Summer 1980), pp. 51–63.

Mosard, Gil. "Problem Definition: Tasks and Techniques." *Journal of Systems Management* (June 1983), pp. 16–21.

Plenert, Gerhard. "The Basics of a Successful System." *Information and Management* (December 1988), pp. 251–254.

Rockart, John F. "Chief Executives Define Their Own Data Needs." *Harvard Business Review* (March–April 1979), pp. 81–93.

Rudkin, Ralph E., and Shere, Kenneth D. "Structured Decomposition Diagram: A New Technique for System Analysis." *Datamation* (Oct. 1979), pp. 130–140.

Sibley, Edgar H. "System Analysis: A Systemic Analysis of a Conceptual Model." *Communications of the ACM* (June 1987), pp. 506–521.

Stanga, Keith G., and Benjamin, James J. "Information Needs of Bankers." *Management Accounting* (June 1978), pp. 17–21.

Wetherbe, James C. *Systems Analysis for Computer-Based Information Systems.* New York: West Publishing, 1979.

Whitten, Jeffrey L.; Bentley, Lonnie D.; and Ho, Thomas I. M. *Systems Analysis and Design Methods.* St. Louis: Mosby, 1986.

Yourdon, Edward. *Modern Structured Analysis.* Englewood Cliffs, N.J.: Prentice-Hall, 1989.

Chapter *23*

SYSTEMS DESIGN AND APPLICATION DEVELOPMENT

Systems design, the creative phase in the systems development cycle, consists of synthesizing the requirements into a cohesive and focused information framework. The design activity is not a simple task, since numerous design alternatives are usually available. The optimal design is the one that best fits the particular set of circumstances at hand while meeting several tests of feasibility.

This design chapter, like the other chapters that concern systems development, has intentionally been placed in the last part of the book. We cannot fully understand the concepts and processes of design without a basic knowledge of all aspects of information systems. On the other hand, the considerations related to design should integrate and reinforce our overall comprehension of information systems.

Accountants can play important roles in the design phase. Because of their knowledge of information needs and transaction processes, they can aid in the design of reports, source documents, files, processing procedures, and controls. With the increasing availability of powerful design techniques, they can personally become involved in the development of applications within the accounting information system.

Steps in the Design Phase

Authorities in systems development agree that the systems design phase follows the systems analysis phase. However, they tend to disagree on almost every other point regarding the role of systems design. For instance, they disagree concerning the point at which the systems design phase begins and concerning what steps comprise the phase. Some authorities say the design phase begins with a determination of system requirements; others take the position that it begins with the identification of system design alternatives. Some say that it includes such steps as developing a logical design, developing a physical design, adding detailed features to these designs, and determining the feasibility of the selected design. Others take a more restricted view, saying that the design phase concentrates on developing reasonably specific but not overly detailed design specifications.

These disagreements should not be unsettling. All of the steps must be performed at some point during the systems development sequence. Hence, for the purpose of discussing the systems design phase, we will simply take the following view: The systems design phase begins with an evaluation of the system design alternatives, leads to the preparation of specific user-oriented design specifications, and concludes with their submission to top management. These steps are shown in Figure 23-1.

Evaluation of Design Alternatives

An effective systems design corrects the weaknesses and problems that led to the systems development project. Expressed more positively, the design fulfills the objectives of the project, which have been converted into specific systems and information requirements during the systems analysis phase.

Generally, a wide variety of **design alternatives** confronts the systems analyst/designer at the beginning of the design phase. Some of these alternatives can quickly be discarded. Perhaps they do not fit the particular set of circumstances at hand. Maybe

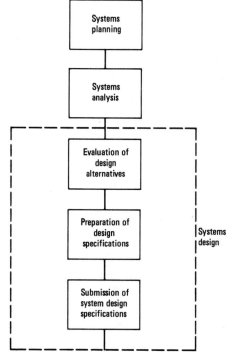

FIGURE 23-1 The steps in the systems design phase.

they would consume a disproportionate share of resources. Other alternatives may represent plausible possibilities. However, only one of these alternatives represents the best choice. The role of the systems analyst/designer is to work with users to narrow the alternatives until the best choice is found.

Range of alternatives. We might view the alternative design possibilities in two ways: (1) by the extent to which they differ from the present design (if any) and (2) by the features that they exhibit.

According to the first viewpoint, alternative designs range from a very slight modification of the present system to a radically new design. Consider the alternative designs available when the present information system involves manual processing. At one extreme, the manual processing features would be retained, but perhaps with a new control added or a source document revised. At the other extreme, the system might be transformed into a real-time computer-based system with operational and decision support capabilities.

The second viewpoint sees design alternatives as combinations of system features. Figure 23-2 presents a panorama of selected features, which have been gleaned from discussions in earlier chapters. Other features, such as controls and security measures, could have been included. However, the figure graphically suggests the large number of combinations available in this modern era of information technology.

Descriptions of alternatives. Each identified design alternative should be described in terms of such features as shown in Figure 23-2. Its differences from the present system

may also be denoted, if desired. The description of a design alternative at this stage, however, should be relatively broad and undetailed. It will be rendered in more detail later if found to be a promising possibility.

Let us consider two plausible design alternatives for a sales order processing system. Each alternative will be described by an overview diagram and a brief narrative.

The first alternative, shown in Figure 23-3, involves the use of a centralized computer at the home office. Each order is received by a salesperson from a customer and delivered to the appropriate sales branch. The branch mails the order to the home office, where clerks process the order and deliver a copy to the warehouse. After the goods are picked, they are shipped to the customer. Then the shipping copy is batched with other notices of shipped orders and processed daily on the centralized computer.

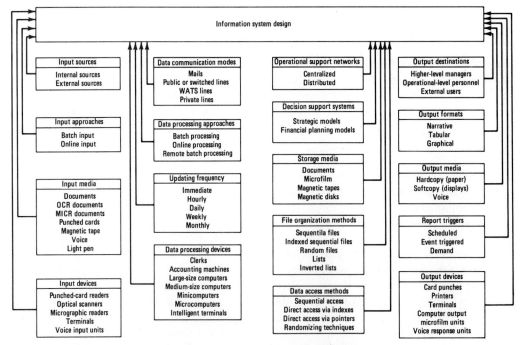

FIGURE 23-2 Range of alternative features from which information system designs may be formed.

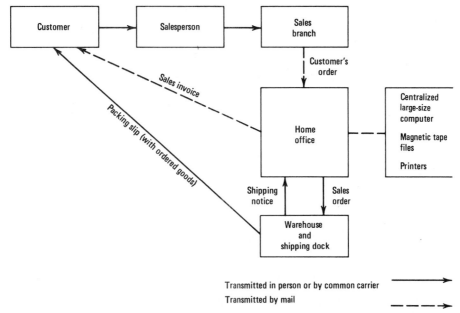

FIGURE 23-3 A broad-level diagram showing a design of a sales order management system: centralized computer alternative.

The resulting sales invoices are mailed to the respective customers.

The second alternative, shown in Figure 23-4, involves the use of terminals and a data communications network. Upon receiving an order from a customer, the salesperson transmits the order to the sales branch via his or her portable terminal. At the sales branch the order is checked for completeness and accuracy and then transmitted to the home office. The computer system automatically prints a copy of the sales order on a terminal at the warehouse. After the goods have been picked and shipped, the shipping department clerk uses a terminal to transmit shipping data back to the home office. By reference to on-line customer accounts receivable files, the centralized computer prepares a sales invoice and stores it on the disk. The stored invoices are printed hourly; then they are mailed to customers.

These descriptions clearly reflect the key differences between the two alterna-tives. Although broad and undetailed, these descriptions provide enough facts to enable a reviewing group to make meaningful com-parisons.

Narrowing of alternatives. After identify-ing those alternative designs that appear to be plausible for a particular situation, the de-sign participants must narrow the list. This narrowing process begins with attempts to answer the following questions concerning each design alternative:

1. Does it satisfy the *objectives* for the sys-tem? That is, does it meet the information needs and system requirements specified during the analysis phase?

2. Is it *technically feasible?* That is, is the existing state of technology adequate for the system to be achievable?

3. Is it *operationally feasible?* That is, can and will the system be used by the person-nel for whom it is designed?

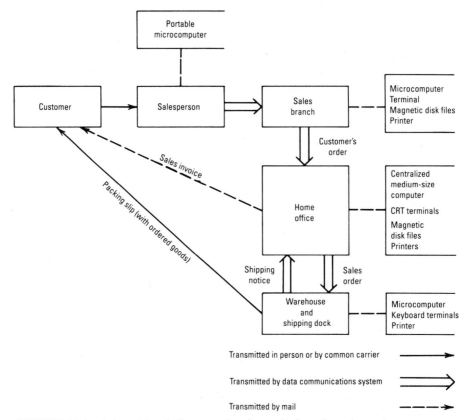

FIGURE 23-4 A broad-level diagram showing a design of a sales order management system: communications-based alternative.

4. Is it *economically feasible?* That is, can the economic benefits be expected to exceed the economic costs of the system?

These criteria, which can be considered as early as the preliminary study, are difficult to apply. The design participants, however, can gain assistance from a variety of sources. For instance, in evaluating the first question they can refer to various diagrams and other documentation prepared during the analysis phase. They can talk to equipment manufacturers and other firms with similar equipment when evaluating **technical feasibility.** They can talk to the prospective users themselves when evaluating **operational feasibility.** Fi-

nally, they can compare specific cost and benefit values when evaluating **economic feasibility.**

On the other hand, the design participants should not attempt to apply the feasibility criteria fully during the systems design phase. Time is reserved later in the systems development sequence for the detailed evaluation of feasibility, especially economic and operational feasibility.[1] Furthermore, an excessive concern with feasibility during this phase may inhibit the creative act of design,

[1]Chapter 24 discusses economic feasibility, and Chapter 25 discusses operational feasibility.

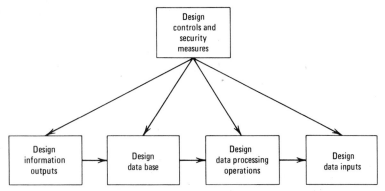

FIGURE 23-5 The sequence in designing system components.

with the consequence that certain promising design alternatives may not be carefully explored.

Thus, the final narrowing process is often left in the hands of higher-level managers. That is, the several most promising design alternatives are presented to the steering committee, and from these alternatives the committee selects one or two as worthy of detailed attention.

Preparation of Design Specifications

What happens to the one or two (or perhaps even more) design alternatives that pass the screening? The answer is that each becomes a nucleus for reasonably specific **design specifications.** Usually, these design specifications are grouped around the components of an information system: the data inputs, data processing, data base, information outputs, and controls and security measures.

Design sequence. However, the sequence in which these specifications are prepared does not follow the order listed earlier. Instead, the preparation of design specifications begins with the information outputs. As the final products of the information system, the outputs are the key determinant of the remaining system components. After the output specifications usually come the data base specifications, followed by the data processing and the data input specifications. The system controls and security measures should be specified in conjunction with the specifications for each of the other elements. Figure 23-5 shows this desired sequence for designing system components.[2]

Content of specifications. The design specifications typically consist of the features listed in Figure 23-6. In sum, they provide an explicit outline of the capabilities and peculiarities of a specific system design.

Other specifications are added as needed. For example, if the system design involves changes to the chart of accounts or coding schemes, these changes would be described. If the system being designed includes or consists of a structured data base, the schema would be designated. If the system being designed includes a decision support system, the types of decision models would be specified.

[2]Reprinted with permission from Joseph W. Wilkinson, "Guidelines for Design Systems," *Journal of Systems Management* (Dec. 1974), p. 38.

System Components	Features
Output	Name
	Purpose
	Distribution to users
	Contents (information items)
	General format
	Frequency (or trigger)
	Timeliness (response time or delay after an event occurs)
	Output medium
Data base	File name (or data structure name)
	File type
	File size (number of records)
	Content of record (data items)
	Record size and layout
	File organization method
	Storage medium
	Data characteristic (e.g., numeric)
	Updating frequency
	Data structures
Data processing	Sequence of steps or runs
	Processing modes, cycles, volumes
	Modes of data communication
	Processing capabilities at each physical location
Data input	Name
	Purpose
	Source
	Method of collecting data
	Volume (peak and average)
	Contents (data items)
	General format
	Data entry method
Control and security	Type
	Purpose
	Specific system component affected
	Method of correcting error or establishing security

FIGURE 23-6 Typical features included within design specifications.

Submission of System Design Specifications

The system design specifications should be submitted for a thorough review and approval at a high management level. In most cases the president or board of directors should give the final approval, since project development costs will rise dramatically beyond this point.

The design specifications should be well documented within a formal **systems design proposal** or report, so that top management can

1. Decide among competing designs (if two or more designs are still being studied at this point).
2. Determine the extent to which the design specifications accord with the objectives, as reflected in information needs and system requirements.
3. Participate more fully in the design process and communicate more clearly with the designers.

A systems design proposal should begin with a cover letter that summarizes the findings of the design phase. Figure 23-7 suggests several of the items that might appear in the cover letter. The body of the proposal would contain the detailed design specifications, together with the various system flowcharts and other diagrams prepared during the phase. In addition, the proposal would show a detailed cost-versus-benefits analysis and a plan for implementing the selected design. It would clearly state all underlying assumptions and constraints. In short, the design proposal should provide all information needed by management to make a sound decision.

(Date)

Dear Mr. (President or other top manager)

Summary of recommended design(s)
Objectives to be achieved by design(s)
Expected benefits to be attained
Summarized needs in hardware and software
Summarized cost estimates
Expected impacts of design(s) on information system
Expected impacts of design(s) on organization

(Signed)

FIGURE 23-7 Suggested contents of a cover letter for a design proposal.

System Design Considerations

Although a sound system design depends heavily on creativity, several guidelines are available. Most of the guidelines have been offered in earlier chapters with respect to various systems components. We have already noted in this chapter a guideline concerning the proper sequence for designing systems components. Nevertheless, the following checklist provides a useful summary of systems design principles.

1. **Rigorously apply system criteria.** All three types of feasibility should be examined, as noted earlier. Furthermore, the objectives pertaining to a new or improved system, as stated in the systems plan and project proposal, should be achieved to the greatest extent possible. For example, the system should provide ample capacity to meet current peak demands and allow added reasonable capacity for growth. It should have built-in reliability and dependability. It should be flexible in order to adjust easily to future changes. Each major system activity should be designed to enhance appropriate attributes, as illustrated in Figure 23-8 for the data processing activity.

2. **Incorporate reasonable trade-offs.** Since certain objectives conflict with each other, trade-offs are necessary. For instance, it may be desirable to gain a faster response time at the expense of economy. If the added benefits realized from enhancing one objective exceed the losses from sacrificing another objective, the trade-off is viewed as reasonable.

3. **Focus on functional requirements.** Design specifications should be expressed in terms of capabilities and needs; that is, they should be functional rather than specific to hardware and software. One might specify that the primary storage should have a designated level of capacity, rather than that the MAXI 460 computer is needed.

4. **Serve multiple purposes.** Most designs should be multidimensional, thereby enabling the system to serve more than a single purpose or a single type of user. Generally a system module should aid in processing transactions as well as providing decision or control information; it

---

Data processing should include a careful mixture of manual and automated operations that are

1. Smoothed, in order to reduce peaks and backlogs. For instance, department stores and public utilities often prepare bills on a cyclical basis rather than once a month.

2. Simplified, in order to minimize backtracks and bottlenecks.

3. Standardized, in order to achieve consistency in performance.

4. Customized, in order to fit the characteristics of the data to the process. For instance, large volumes of transaction data dictate the use of the batch processing approach, whereas smaller volumes of data and the need for up-to-date information dictate the use of the on-line processing approach.

5. Integrated, in order to improve efficiency and reduce redundancies. For instance, the integration of payroll accounting and labor distribution accounting represents a logical design, since the two activities share a common resource (manpower) and provide a means of crosschecking a key data item (hours worked).

FIGURE 23-8 Design considerations pertaining to data processing operations.

should serve employees as well as managers (and also perhaps outside parties).

5. **Relate to users' concerns.** A system design should be as simple as possible so that the resulting system is easily usable by employees and managers. It should reduce the load on human users through prompts, menus, on-line helps, preformatted screens, and so on. The design should also provide all information that the employees and managers need to fulfill their responsibilities. For instance, as many of the informal information flows as feasible should be converted to formal information flows.

6. **Provide a tailored product.** A system design should fit the particular circumstances of a firm. Thus, a general ledger system for a steel manufacturer should be quite different from a general ledger system for a university. With respect to the firm's environment, the system should reflect such aspects as resource inputs and competitors' activities. With respect to internal activities, the physical operations should dictate the formats of source documents and managerial reports.

7. **Integrate system modules.** A system design for a single module should link the module to other modules within the overall information system. The design should be relatively standardized so that the system will perform consistently throughout and maintenance is simplified.

8. **Avoid design excesses.** Although a system design should allow for anticipated growth and change, it should not be too high powered. For instance, a design should not specify complete automation if a mix of machines and people can achieve the same result at lower cost.

9. **Apply sound methodologies.** Although the methodologies or approaches used in creating a system design are not a part of the specifications, they are important in achieving desired results. A system de-

sign has a better chance of being sound when the methodology includes top management support, careful planning and analysis, full user involvement, appropriate approaches (i.e., top-down, modular, evolutionary), and thorough documentation. Furthermore, the methodology should be fitted to the nature of the systems being developed. For instance, decision support systems generally thrive on development cycles that are relatively short and iterative as compared to the development cycles for operational support systems.

User-Developed Applications

Information systems have traditionally been developed and operated by information system professionals. However, in recent years the users of information systems have become more involved. In the activity called **end-user computing** the users work directly ("hands on") with computers. They also have participated in **user-developed applications.** In fact, the number of user-developed applications is growing rapidly throughout many firms. As a consequence, the domination by information systems professionals has lessened. This trend is expected to continue.

Reasons for Increased User Development

To a large degree user-developed systems have grown because of the delays and high costs of traditional systems development. Often users have been forced to wait months or years after they have submitted requests before their new systems are ready for use. These delays are due to a scarcity of experienced systems analysts, to large backlogs of planned systems projects, and to the lengthy nature of traditional systems development. Since systems development activities tend to be labor intensive, the lengthy processes translate into higher costs. Furthermore, the salary levels of systems professionals have been rising at an above-average rate. In order to satisfy their work-related needs, users have been forced to become "do-it yourselfers."

Another problem with traditional systems development has been miscommunication and changing needs. Professional systems analysts tend to misunderstand the needs of users, and users often have difficulty in anticipating their needs and expressing them clearly. Moreover, the needs of users generally change during the lengthy periods of systems development.

User-developed systems have also been influenced by information technology. Improvements in microcomputers, fourth-generation languages, and automated offices have hastened the growth of user development. Users have become familiar with microcomputers through their workplaces and also through academic courses. They have become more facile in their use through user-friendly software, such as menu-driven spreadsheet and word processing packages.

User-developed systems can be very successful. They tend to fit the needs of the users more closely. Often users can develop systems that are quite innovative in dealing with the application situations. Furthermore, users are more likely to make effective use of systems that they have been involved in developing.

Problems of User Development

Rampant user development can, however, cause serious losses and inaccuracies. Users often do not fully appreciate the need for adequate controls and security measures. Thus, they tend to omit adequate programmed checks in the programs that edit input data. Consequently, erroneous data are likely to be entered into the files. In a network any uploaded data can contaminate the central data base. Users also may omit such security measures as password protection and file backups. They usually fail to document adequate any systems developed. Consequently, systems analysts and/or auditors should, as a minimum protection, review all systems developed by users. In many cases professional systems personnel can assist users in the development of their systems.

Characteristics of User Development

Suitable applications. Not all applications are suitable for user development. Applications that demand processing efficiency and adequate control structures should be developed by professional systems personnel. Included in this category are large transaction processing systems (e.g., payroll, sales order) and dedicated operational support systems (e.g., airline reservation systems, inventory control systems). Commercial software applications, such as accounting and manufacturing packages, are clearly the province of professionals.

Those types of systems that are well suited for user development include specialized reporting systems, decision support systems, and specialized operational support systems. For instance, an accounting manager may develop reports that compare key ratios for his firm with ratios that reflect industry averages; a marketing manager may develop a sales forecasting system; a treasurer may develop a system that tracks her firm's cost of capital and borrowing trends. These systems are normally intended to serve only the user/builders and their immediate staffs.

An example of a user-developed system can be found in the purchasing department of a subsidiary of Chrysler Corporation. The administrative manager of the department needed to have a new management reporting system designed for use with the department's new minicomputer-based data base management software. With the approval of the data processing department the purchasing administrative manager and her secretary attended a programming class for two weeks. Using the skills acquired, they programmed applications pertaining to buyers' reference files, engineering changes, and so on.[3]

Development approach. Users require considerable assistance when developing systems. One type of assistance is via powerful software tools, to be discussed in the following section. Another type of assistance can be provided by professional systems personnel, as discussed in the next section. A third type of assistance is available through the development approach.

A basic approach in user-developed systems is, of course, participative designing. Participation by users enables systems to be designed from the user's perspective. It also reduces the chances for miscommunication. A companion approach is prototyping, which was introduced in Chapter 21. Prototyping combines the analysis and design phases, since it consists of devising a rough-cut design (working model) as soon as the requirements are stated. Elaborate design specifications are ignored. The rough-cut design is put to use as soon as possible. As the users employ the system, they identify needed improvements and implement these into revised system designs.

Prototyping provides several benefits. It minimizes the development time for new systems and incorporates needed changes more easily. It improves the productivity of the user/designers, since they learn through experience. It also tends to reduce the development costs.

User-development tools. Until the 1980s systems development software was difficult

to understand and apply. Consequently, applications were developed only by systems professionals. In recent years software that is directed primarily to the users of information systems has become available. This software, known collectively as **fourth-generation languages** (4GLs), can be employed by users to develop the types of applications discussed in an earlier section. It can be applied either with the assistance of professional systems personnel or by the users alone. It can also increase the productivity of systems professionals when used to develop transaction processing systems and other applications.

Fourth-generation languages span a variety of user-friendly software. The category includes the modeling languages that are well designed for developing decision support systems and financial models. These modeling languages, such as IFPS, were described in Chapter 20. Fourth-generation languages also include **application generators,** powerful software packages that allow users to develop complete applications. Application generators typically include a number of generalized programmed modules or routines; each module performs a function such as accepting inputs interactively, validating inputs, updating data sets, and generating ad hoc reports. Examples of application generators are RAMIS II (from Mathematica, Inc.) and Nomad2 (from D & B Computer Services). Fourth-generation languages may be attached to other software packages. For instance, Application-By-Forms is a type of language that enables a user to define a desired application by filling in forms provided by the software. It is attached to the relational data base management system known as Ingres.

The features that should be provided by user-development tools, such as an application generator, are as follows:

1. A nonprocedural programming language by which the user can specify the desired

[3]Ralph H. Sprague, Jr., and Barbara C. McNurlin, *Information Systems Management in Practice* (Englewood Cliffs, N.J.: Prentice-Hall, 1986), pp. 281–282.

result, rather than the procedural actions for achieving the result.

2. A data base management system, preferably employing the relational model.

3. A report writer that enables users to specify the formats of ad hoc reports.

4. A CRT screen definition and management facility.

5. An ad hoc query language with English-like commands or a set of menus.

6. A business graphics package for presentation graphs.

7. A variety of software support utilities that enable interfacing with other packages (e.g., spreadsheets), backing up of files, and so on.

Information centers. With an increase in user-developed systems, firms have employed various means to assist them in their endeavors. One of the most successful approaches has been the establishment of information centers. An **information center** is a physical location, operated by the information systems function, where users can receive adequate support. Among the computer system-oriented services that may be offered are training in the use of computers (including microcomputers) and in system development tools, selecting computers and software, consulting on system development problems, and assisting in user-development projects. Assigned to the information center may be systems analysts, model builders, software specialists, and application specialists. These centers are likely to expand, both in numbers and in services offered, in coming years.

Hughes Aircraft Company is an example of a firm that has had an information center for several years. In one service activity, systems analysts assigned to the center wrote 12,000 lines of FOCUS code in order to help the controller's department develop an on-line financial reporting system. They included sufficient documentation to enable the controller's personnel to maintain the system thereafter.[4]

Exxon Corporation has a multigroup information center in its New York corporate headquarters. The Client Support Center is the largest group; it provides consulting, training, and technical assistance in the application of end-user computing tools. Three other groups, which serve users through the Client Support Center, provide assistance with decision support system development, office systems development, and technical evaluation of new hardware and software.[5]

Systems Design Methodologies

Systems design techniques aid in developing and documenting the specifications for new or improved information systems. They consist of diagrams (e.g., systems flowcharts), matrices, layouts, and specification sheets. An instance is a list of file specifications, such as shown in Figure 23-9. All of the fact-organizing techniques suited to systems analysis can also be employed as systems design techniques. Both the traditional and the structured techniques may be reviewed by referring to the appropriate sections in Chapter 22.

As we have noted earlier, various methodologies relating to systems design and development are increasingly being used. Their advantage is that they guide a systems analyst through the analysis and design phases of the systems development cycle. In effect, systems methodologies provide a disciplined, step-by-step approach that increases the productivity of systems analysts.

[4]Ralph H. Sprague, Jr., and Barbara C. McNurlin, *Information Systems Management in Practice* (Englewood Cliffs, N.J.: Prentice-Hall, 1986), pp. 374–375.

[5]Richard T. Johnson, "The Infocenter Experience." *Datamation* (Jan. 1984), p. 137.

```
Title of the file
Purpose of the file
Average and peak volumes of data affecting the file
Number of file accesses per period of time
Source of each data item
Updating cycle
Number of records in the file
Type of file
Relationship to other files
File organization method
File storage medium
File access time (average)
Reports prepared from file
```

FIGURE 23-9 A list of items comprising a file specification.

They also aid analysts in spotting inconsistencies and omissions. Many of the methodologies incorporate structured techniques, thereby enhancing these advantages.

Systems methodologies can be classified in various ways. One meaningful classification plan divides methodologies between those that are noncomputerized and those that are computerized.

Noncomputerized Methodologies

Traditional noncomputerized methodologies can be quite informal. One approach sometimes employed by small firms is to tape all of the firm's reports on a wall in a closed room. The firm's assembled key managers are then asked to justify each report in turn. If a report cannot be justified, it is ripped off the wall. The remaining reports are then assembled as the new system's set of outputs. Another approach, called "storyboarding," consists of building a storyboard, an array of colored index cards. Taken together, the cards reflect the varied features of a systems project. Included might be current problems, system requirements, hardware features, software features, alternative design configurations, financing considerations, and so forth. By reference to the cards, the analysts compile the components of the new system.[6]

More formalized and structured (but noncomputerized) methodologies that are available commercially include

1. Accurately Defined Systems (ADS), developed by National Cash Register Corporation.
2. Analysis, Requirements Determination, Design, and Development (ARDI), developed by Philips, a Netherlands-based firm.
3. Business Information System Analysis and Design (BISAD), developed by Honeywell Information Systems, Inc.
4. Structured Analysis and Design Technique (SADT), developed by Sof Tech, Inc.

Each of these packaged techniques provides an integrated approach to systems analysis and design. ADS, for instance, employs five standardized and interrelated forms to define and specify a system design. Outputs and inputs are defined on the first form and second form, respectively. Computations to be performed and the rules of computational logic are stated on the third form. Data to be retained (stored) for subsequent use are noted on the fourth form. Finally, the logic definitions are expressed on the fifth form. All the items of data listed on ADS forms are assigned specific tags, so that they can be linked throughout the five forms.

Computerized Methodologies

Developing new information systems in large firms is a tremendous task. Consequently, methodologies that elicit the aid of computers are helpful and even necessary.

---

[6]Arnold D. Shiflett, "How We Automated Our Accounting Department," *Management Accounting* (June 1983), pp. 34–38.

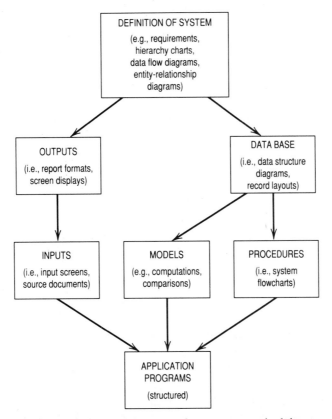

FIGURE 23-10 Components of a systems methodology.

In some cases methodologies have been devised by individual firms and tailored to their particular needs. As an example, the U.S. Air Force Logistics Command devised a unique methodology to develop a Requirements Data Bank system.[7] Working within the framework of the Information Engineering methodology, it determined the functional requirements for the new system. Then it employed a variety of computerized tools, such as Excelerator from Intech Corporation, to prepare the structured diagrams that defined the needed system. From this definition the analysts designed the specifica-

tions ("blueprints") relating to outputs, data base, inputs, procedures, and models. Finally, they prepared (with the aid of computerized tools) the programs that comprise the desired new system. Figure 23-10 shows the steps from the system definition to the final application programs.

For most firms customized systems methodologies are too expensive to develop. Thus, a variety of packaged computerized methodologies have evolved. Among the earlier methodologies of this type were Automated Data Systems Analysis Technique (developed by RAND Corporation), Time Automated Grid System (developed by IBM Corporation), and Structured Systems Development and Requirements Definition (developed by Ken Orr and Associates).

[7]Robert S. Tripp and Mark C. Filteau, "Blueprints: Adopting a Construction Trade Approach in Designing Large Scale Management Information Systems," *Information and Management* (1987), pp. 55–70.

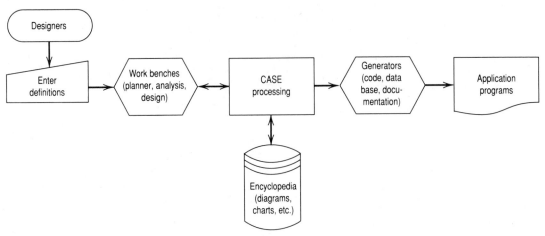

FIGURE 23-11   Components of an integrated CASE tool.

Many of the recently developed packages, however, are members of the **Computer-Aided Software Engineering (CASE)** family of systems development tools. While a variety of CASE tools are available, the integrated CASE packages support all phases of systems development. They also incorporate various software modules called workbenches and generators. The **CASE workbenches** accept definitions of a new system from human analysts; next they convert the definitions into various structured diagrams and charts (e.g., entity-relationship diagrams, data flow diagrams, hierarchy charts). These diagrammatic descriptions are stored in a centralized repository called a **CASE encyclopedia.** The **CASE generators** then draw particular system descriptions from the encyclopedia and prepare suitable coded application programs. The generators also develop the specifications for outputs, data base, and other components of the new system. Figure 23-11 portrays the components of an integrated CASE package.

The benefits of an integrated and computerized systems development package such as CASE are significant. New systems are developed faster and placed into operation sooner. The productivity of each analyst is thereby increased. Usually the new systems incorporate better designs, especially if the users are involved. Because the package standardizes the process and eliminates any inconsistencies, the systems tend to reflect a higher level of quality. Moreover, the documentation for the new system is automatically provided as a by-product of the development process.

Limitations of Methodologies

Methodologies, especially when computerized, are proving to be a boon to systems development. However, they are not panaceas. Perhaps their greatest limitation is that they do *not* eliminate the need for human analysts to define the requirements for new systems. They also do not clarify the key decisions concerning system architectures, especially when computer networks and on-line processing are needed. For instance, they cannot deal explicitly with response-time delays and geographic dispersion of processing facilities.[8] Furthermore,

---

[8]Dwight F. Townsend, "Systems Analysis: Key to the Future," *Datamation* (October 1980), p. 147.

APPLICATION OF SYSTEMS DESIGN
Chase Manhattan Bank[a]

Chase Manhattan Bank is a large financial services institution whose major activities involve corporate lending, consumer lending, investment banking, and demand deposit banking. Of these activities, consumer lending in the early 1970s was the least profitable. Upon investigation it was determined that several critical problems existed:

1. The consumer lending department was small and buried in the organizational structure.
2. The management accounting system was weak, in that the managerial control reports were inadequate.
3. Data processing for all banking functions involved batch processing on a pooled basis, using large mainframe computers and service bureaus.

A systems project to develop new management accounting systems for consumer banking was approved. Two organizational changes were quickly made to enhance the success of the project: (1) A new consumer group was established at a high level in the organizational structure, with all consumer-related activities (e.g., ATM's, Visa bankcards, consumer loans) assigned to it, and (2) all branch banks and consumer services were set up as profit centers. Then the project was assigned to the MIS controllership group within the firm.

After surveying the situation, the project team first determined that one primary information need concerns profitability—analyzed by branch, service, and consumer. With respect to systems requirements, the team determined that the systems should provide interactive capability, allow downloading from mainframe computers to workstations, process all requests from managers promptly, summarize detailed production data and upload, and incorporate adequate security measures.

Various alternative system designs were considered, including the continuation of the then-current centralized networks. The design alternative that was selected involves a three-tier architecture. The top tier, called the backbone, links the information system services on a corporation-wide basis. It includes mainframe computers, minicomputers, and a number of terminal emulators. The middle tier, called community-of-interest services, consists of linking minicomputers and high-speed communications lines and shared resources such as local area network servers. These connector networks tie the backbone tier to the bottom tier. This bottom tier, called personal services, consists of the workstations employed by users in automated offices and branch banks. These workstations allow end users to do their own computing and to develop applications as needed.

After selecting the system architecture, the team then developed the design specifications and selected the specific hardware and software to be installed. Finally, the designed system was implemented.

[a]Michael Robin, "The Evolution of Management Accounting Systems at Chase Manhattan Bank," *Journal of Accounting and EDP* (Winter 1988), pp. 15–29.

all of the methodologies (but especially the computerized versions) require extensive training of analysts.

Summary

Systems design, the creative phase of the development, consists of three steps: identifying and evaluating design alternatives, preparing design specifications, and submitting the specifications for approval. Each design alternative should be described clearly so that it can be evaluated properly. A sound alternative must satisfy the objectives for the system and appear to be technically, operationally, and economically feasible. After pinpointing the most plausible alternatives, it is necessary to develop specifications pertaining to the outputs, data base, data processing operations, data inputs, and control and security. Then the specifications should be submitted within a systems design proposal for approval by top management.

A sound system design requires the application of such principles as incorporating reasonable trade-offs, focusing on functional requirements, serving multiple purposes, considering user concerns, providing a tailored product, integrating system modules, avoiding design excesses, and applying sound methodologies.

User-developed systems applications are increasing as a result of the inadequacies of traditional systems development, changing users' needs, and developments in information technology. However, user-developed systems are subject to such problems as inadequate controls and security measures. To improve the chances for success, user-developed systems should focus on specialized reporting and support systems, employ the prototyping approach, and apply such tools as fourth-generation languages and application generators.

Systems design methodologies can aid in developing and documenting design specifications. Although traditional noncomputerized methodologies are still in use, various computerized methodologies are being increasingly employed. The most promising computerized methodology, CASE tools, incorporates such components as workbenches, generators, and centralized encyclopedias. Methodologies, however, cannot substitute for the creativity provided by human systems analysts.

Review Problem with Solution

Statement

Overall review. The Precise Manufacturing Company (introduced in the review problem for Chapter 21) has initiated a systems project that focuses on sales order processing and management. The project team completes its survey and analysis of the project area, submits its systems analysis report, and obtains approval to commence the systems design phase.

Evaluation of alternative designs. The systems design phase begins early in August. After considerable discussion the team prepares, in broad terms, the following list of alternative designs for a new system:

Alternative I. Processing would be performed by means of a new, more powerful *centralized* computer located at the home office. Orders would be delivered to the sales branches by salespersons and telephoned to the home office via WATS lines. After orders are processed, they would be batch-processed on the central computer to produce sales invoices.[9] In effect, this alternative consists of retaining the present processing approach, except that orders would be mailed only for the purpose of confirming telephone orders and controls would be significantly strengthened. The advantages are that the added cost outlays and procedural changes should be *relatively* small, processing delays would be reduced, clerical productivity would be increased, and processing efficiency would be maintained at a high level.

Alternative II. Processing would be performed on *decentralized* small computers located at the sales branches. This alternative would consist of the same procedure as in alternative I, except that the shipping notices would be returned to the sales branches. The sales branches would then prepare sales invoices, using customer and product data maintained on magnetic disk files in the sales branches. The advantage of this alternative is based on the fact that the sales branches

---

[9]See Figure 23-4 and the accompanying narrative for more details concerning this alternative. Note that since this alternative allows limited processing apart from the centralized computer, it may be described as a hybrid distributed network.

are closer to the customers. By maintaining the customers' records, the sales branches can provide better service to customers, such as answering inquiries. Also, by having their own computers, the sales branches can perform other local processing, such as the preparation of branch payrolls and reports.

Alternative III. Processing would be performed on a *centralized* computer that links to the sales branches via a data communications network. Intelligent terminals would be located at the sales branches, a microcomputer would be placed in the warehouse, and "dumb" terminals would be located in key departments.[10] Its advantages include more up-to-date data, greater system flexibility, greater capability in answering inquiries and preparing special reports, and greater savings in clerical costs.

Alternative IV. Processing would be performed on small computers located at the sales branches, each computer being linked to all other computers to form a *web-distributed network*. The alternative combines the features of alternatives II and III, but with the large centralized computer replaced by a relatively small computer. Its advantages are those listed for alternatives II and III; however, it offers greater flexibility, backup, and load-balancing capability than either, although its cost would be greater.

The four preceding alternatives are presented at an August meeting of the steering committee. After considerable discussion, alternatives II and IV are discarded. Although both would be technically feasible, their operational and economic feasibility are questionable. Both require personnel in the sales branches to become heavily involved in data processing operations. Some of these personnel likely will resist the significant changes in their job activities. Also, the added costs will be relatively large, since a new computer is required for each branch

and the sales branch personnel must be trained. Furthermore, splitting the customers' files among the branches will make various sales-oriented reports and analyses more difficult to prepare. Alternative IV has the added disadvantage of being risky. It represents a "great leap forward" in technological complexity as compared with the existing system. It also introduces problems in data control and security that are more severe than those encountered with the other alternatives.

Alternatives I and III appear to be more promising. Each offers several advantages with lower risk of operational infeasibility. Each can presumably prove to be economically feasible, since the projected benefits seem relatively large vis-à-vis the expected added cost outlays. Finally, each alternative seems to solve the more serious problems uncovered during the analysis.

However, there does not seem to be a clear-cut case favoring one alternative over the other. Although alternative III obviously offers certain benefits not provided by alternative I, it will also be more costly than alternative I. Therefore, the steering committee requests that more detailed design specifications be prepared for *both* of the alternatives.

The steering committee also requests that alternative IV be filed away for future reference. At the time of the next systems development project in this area (perhaps five years in the future), alternative IV might well be a logical next stage. This is particularly the case in light of certain expected future developments. Data communications and small-computer costs should decline in the coming years, and distributed data bases are expected to become more viable Moreover, the firm plans to build decentralized warehouses adjacent to the sales branches in the next few years, thus increasing the need for distributed data processing.

Preparation of design specifications. In accordance with the directive from the steer-

---

[10]See Figure 23-3 and the accompanying narrative for more details concerning this alternative.

Descriptive title / Key characteristics	Purpose of report					Frequency	Distribution of report									
	I	II	III	IV	V		A	B	C	D	E	F	G	H	I	J
1. Sales analysis by salesperson (actual sales amounts and contribution margin vs. quotas; broken down by product)		X				D				X						
2. Sales analysis by product (sales amounts; percent of total market)			X			W	X		X	X						
3. Sales analysis by sales branch (actual sales amounts vs. quotas; trend; broken down by product)		X				W			X							
4. Sales analysis by channel of distribution (amount and percentage)			X			M	X									
5. Sales analysis by size of customer (large, medium, and small groupings; showing percentage changes)			X			M	X		X							
6. Sales analysis by size of order, including average size			X			M			X							
7. Sales analysis by customer (grouped by sales branch and salesperson)	X					Q			X	X						
8. Analysis of sales returns and allowances by product (showing causes, percent of sales of each product)			X			W	X									
35. Production schedule, showing status of special orders being produced	X					D	X		X					X		X
36. Department overtime report, showing hours and percentage change from past week			X			W					X	X	X	X	X	
37. Projected stock-outs of finished goods for coming weeks, by product			X			D		X				X				X
38. Inventory flash report, showing status of products below reorder points				X		T						X				
39. Delayed invoices, showing number of days past scheduled dates and percent of total orders				X		T		X							X	
40. Comparative performance of common carriers	X					M								X		
41. Stock status report	X					M							X			
42. Credit flash report, showing customers who exceed credit limits or who have excessive activity				X		T						X				
43. Shipments flash report, showing late shipments				X		T		X								
44. Accounts receivable aging schedule	X					W						X				
45. Analysis of uncollectible accounts			X			M						X				
46. Credit statistics, including percentage of orders approved and collected	X					M						X				
47. Salesperson commission report	X					M				X						

FIGURE 23-12 List of scheduled reports for managers within the sales order processing and management system. See the key on page 1093.

KEY FOR FIGURE 23-12

1. The codes are as follows.

Purpose of report:
I Operational or historical
II Control (detailed, periodic)
III Planning
IV Control, key factors only
V Control, exception

Frequency:
D Daily
W Weekly
M Monthly
Q Quarterly
T Triggered

Distribution:
A Vice-president of marketing
B Customer services manager
C Sales manager
D Branch manager
E Sales order department manager
F Credit department manager
G Finished-goods warehousing manager
H Shipping department manager
I Billing department manager
J Other manager(s)

(Salespersons receive copies of report numbers 1, 2, and 7, plus their own performance reports.)

2. The timeliness of reports is as follows:
a. Daily reports are to be in the hands of users by 8:00 A.M. the following day.
b. Weekly reports are to be available on Mondays at 8:00 A.M.
c. Monthly and quarterly reports are to be available within two days after the end of the reporting period.

3. The output media are as follows:
a. Printed or hard-copy form for all scheduled reports.
b. Printed or hard-copy form for all triggered reports, unless alternative III is selected. In the latter case the triggered reports would be displayed on appropriate CRT screens at the end of each working day in which the exceptional conditions occur.

ing committee, the project team begins to prepare design specifications. Its first step is to specify the documents and reports needed from whichever design is selected. Then it prepares twin sets of specifications pertaining to the data base, data processing, data inputs, and controls. The specifications for alternatives III are as follows:

1. *Scheduled reports* to be provided by the redesigned system are listed in Figure 23-12. Accompanying this list is a set of justifications for the reports. For instance, report 1 will enable the sales manager and branch managers to judge salesperson effectiveness, and it might also serve as the basis for compensation. Report 29 (contribution analysis by product) will aid in making decisions concerning the retention of products, the setting of prices, and the direction of sales efforts. Reports 10, 11, and 30 (sales branch performance reports, and product-line income statements) represent the compo-

nents of responsibility and profitability reporting systems. Also included in these specifications are the formats of newly designed reports.

2. *Output documents* consist of those listed in Figure 22-18 plus a newly designed shipping record. The sales order is redesigned to array the ordered products in "picking order" and to provide the respective warehouse location numbers. The production order is redesigned to combine key facts from the operations list, sales order, production schedule, and back order; it consequently can be employed for all orders and thus eliminate the need of the current back-order and special-order documents.

3. *Data base* specifications begin with the list of files in Figure 22-18. To this list are added files of shipping records, salespersons, sales histories, and sales prices. Each file is supported by a file analysis sheet that states the purpose and charac-

Data Item	Customer	Finished goods (product)	Salesperson	Open orders	Closed orders	Back orders	Shipment record	Shipping data
Customer number	X			X	X			
Name of customer	X							
Address of customer	X							
Place to be shipped	X			X				
Date account opened	X							
Class of customer	X							
Credit limit	X							
Credit terms	X							
Date of last order	X							
Special discounts	X							
Balance of account	X							
High balance, last 3 months	X							
High payment, last 3 months	X							
Aged amount due	X							
Collection status	X							
Quantity on order	X							
Sales this month	X							
Sales, year-to-date	X							
Order-invoice number	X		X	X	X	X	X	
Product number		X		X	X	X	X	
Product description		X						
Finished-goods warehouse number		X						
Unit price		X						
Standard unit cost		X						
Quantity on hand by warehouse		X						
Quantity on order by warehouse		X						
Date ordered		X						
Discount code		X						
Bill-of-material number		X						
Economic reorder quantity		X						
Reorder point		X						
Minimum balance		X						
Quantity shipped this month, by whse.		X						
Sales this month, by sales branch		X						
Sales year-to-date, by sales branch		X						
Salesperson number			X	X				
Sales commission rate			X					
Sales branch number			X	X				
Sales this month, by salesperson			X					
Sales year-to-date, by salesperson			X					
Date of order				X	X		X	
Scheduled delivery date				X	X	X		
Priority				X	X	X		
Customer order number				X	X	X		
Stock item or order code				X	X			
Where shipped from				X	X	X	X	
Quantities ordered				X	X	X		
Total sales amount				X				
Back-order number				X		X		
Availability date						X		
Date shipped					X		X	
Quantities shipped					X		X	
Bill-of-lading number							X	
Route								X
Freight rate by carrier								X
Special shipping instructions				X				X
Production order number						X		

FIGURE 23-13 A data-item-versus-file matrix for sales transactions.

Customer Number (6)ᵃ	Customer Name (25)	Customer Billing Address			
		Street (25)	City (20)	State (2)	Zip (5)

Customer Shipping Address				Date Account Opened (6)	Class (2)	Credit Limit (5)	Credit Standing (4)	Credit Terms (2)	Date of Last Order (6)	Special Discount (1)
Location (25)	City (20)	State (2)	Zip (5)							

Account Balance (8)	High Balance, Last 3 Months (8)	High Payment, Last 3 Months (8)	Aged Amounts Due				Collection Status (2)
			Current (8)	0–30 Days Past (8)	30–60 Days Past (8)	Over 60 Days Past Due (8)	

Quantity on Order (3)	Sales This Month (8)	Sales Year-to Date (8)	Pointer to Open Orders (6)	Pointer to Closed Orders (6)

ᵃNumber of positions in field.

FIGURE 23-14 Record layout for Precise's accounts receivable master file.

teristics. Other data base specifications include

a. A matrix of data items versus files in which they appear, as shown in Figure 23-13.

b. A list of the key features pertaining to each file proposed for the redesigned system.

c. A record layout for each file proposed for the redesigned system. For in stance, Figure 23-14 shows a record layout for the accounts receivable master file, including a field containing the pointers to the relevant order-invoices in the open and closed order-files.

d. A proposed schema of logical data relationships.

e. A data dictionary. Figure 23-15 illustrates a segment consisting of six data items among the several hundred to be employed by Precise. (It does not show all of the fields even for the six displayed items. Not shown are such features as the primary users of each data item, the security level of the item, the programs in which the item is used, and the linkages among the item and other items and files in the data base.)

4. *Data processing* specifications consist primarily of system flowcharts plus accompanying notes. (See Figure 12-21 and related narrative for details.)

5. *Data input* specifications consist of (a) the input–output matrix shown in Figure 22-11 and (b) preformatted screens. The input–output matrix pinpoints the need for a new document called a salesperson's call report. Since this report (actually a document) is to provide data for the salesperson's performance report, it should contain the salesperson's name and number, the date of a call, the customer called on, the class of customer, and whether or not the customer placed an order. The preformatted screens provide assistance in the entry of sales orders, production orders, sales returns, and shipments. They are preceded by a main menu that

Precise Manufacturing Co.

Data Dictionary

Item Code	Item Name	Item Description	Field Length	Character Type	Records in Which Found	Source	Number of Appearances	Outputs in Which Used
01	Customer order number	The code on the customer order that identifies the order	5	Numeric	Open order, sales history, back-order record	Customer order	500–600 daily	Sales invoices, back orders, production orders, shipment records
02	Customer number	The code assigned to identify a customer	6	Numeric	Customer, open order record	Customer number list	10,500–12,000	Sales analysis by customer, list of outstanding orders, aging report, sales invoice
03	Customer name	The first name, middle initial and last name of a customer	25	Alphabetic	Customer record	Initial customer order	10,500–12,000	New business report, credit flash report, sales invoice, back order, shipment record
04	Credit limit	The maximum dollar amount that a customer may incur in outstanding credit sales	5	Numeric	Customer record	Credit record	10,500–12,000	Credit flash report
52	Sales this month by salesperson	The dollar sales made by each salesperson in the current month	8	Numeric	Sales history record	Sales orders	200	Sales analysis by salesperson
53	Scheduled delivery date	The date that a customer order is scheduled for delivery to customer	8	Alphanumeric	Open order, back order, production order record	Sales order acknowledgment or production order	500–600 daily	Unfilled orders on hand, delayed orders, delayed invoices

FIGURE 23-15 A segment of a data dictionary for Precise.

lists the available data entry screens and other interactive functions.

6. *Control and security* specifications consist of lists of needed application controls and security measures.

Submittal of systems design proposal. The foregoing specifications are compiled into a systems design proposal and submitted under a cover letter. At a December letter meeting of the steering committee the proposed system design for alternative III is approved, subject to the submission of benefit and cost data that affirm the economic feasibility of the project.

Required

a. Prepare a cover letter pertaining to the design proposal for an improved sales order and management system, using alternative III as the design to be recommended.

b. Prepare the following selected design specifications for an improved sales order and management system:

(1) A format for a key factors report to be provided to the vice-president of marketing. The report should include relevant and key information in narrative, graphical, and tabular forms.

(2) A format of the newly designed production order.

(3) A listing of each file specified for the newly redesigned system, together with the needed or preferable storage medium, file organization method and updating frequency.

(4) A schema for the sales data base, consisting of (a) a network structure in which the general ledger account, salesperson, and finished-goods inventory records are the entry records, and (b) a set of inverted lists arranged on class of customer, credit standing, state codes, and dates of last order.

(5) A list of inquiries that can be satisfied by the preceding schema.

(6) A preformatted data entry (input) screen for sales orders.

(7) A list of desirable application controls for the newly redesigned system.

Solution

a. See the letter that follows.

(Date)

Mr. John Curtis, President
Precise Manufacturing Company
Chicago, Illinois

Dear Mr. Curtis:

Enclosed is a proposal pertaining to a redesigned sales order and management system. This design proposal is based on a thorough survey and analysis of the present system, together with a careful consideration of the objectives to be achieved.

Summary of Recommended Design. We propose that the sales order and management system be redesigned to employ on-line input and processing and reconfigured to be a computer network. A mainframe computer would be installed in the home office, a microcomputer in the warehouse, and intelligent terminals in the sales branches. These distributed processors would be linked by a data communications network consisting of leased lines. In addition, "dumb" terminals would be located in the key departments (i.e., sales order, credit, billing, shipping, warehouse) and linked to the computers. Each salesperson would transmit orders to the appropriate sales branch via a portable terminal. Sales and inventory files would be stored on magnetic disks and backed up on magnetic tapes. Sales orders, sales invoices, plus managerial reports and other documents, would be generated on printers located in the home office, warehouse, and sales branches. In addition, key managers would be provided with portable microcomputers for use in accessing the data base and retrieving desired sales information.

Objectives to Be Achieved. This redesigned system should achieve the following objectives stated in the initial project proposal:

1. To improve the processing of sales orders, so that needed information is available to managers and interfacing systems.
2. To enhance sales processing efficiency, especially with respect to times, and the benefit-cost ratio.
3. To reduce sales processing and billing errors.

Expected Benefits to Be Attained. The recommended system design can easily meet all system requirements. Since the requirements have been derived by reference to observed weaknesses in the present system, the redesigned system is expected to overcome all such weaknesses. In specific terms, the redesigned system is expected to

1. Provide adequate capacity to meet sales volumes during the next five years.
2. Reduce the time needed to process sales order transactions, so that almost all promised delivery dates are met and backlogs are minimized.
3. Provide greater efficiency and effectiveness in processing and maintaining finished-goods inventories, so that sufficient goods are available to fill most orders and so that back orders are minimized.
4. Establish adequate controls over sales order transactions, so that transaction data are not lost and input and processing errors are almost completely eliminated.
5. Maintain up-to-date records pertaining to the status of open sales orders and finished-goods inventory, as well as sufficient backup records and audit trails.
6. Render greater accessibility to stored data, so that inquiries by clerks, managers, and customers can be quickly answered.
7. Provide more timely, accurate, and relevant information (e.g., sales forecasts, sales analyses, profitability reports) for managerial decision making. (Although all information needed by the vice-president of marketing cannot be satisfied by his system, a large proportion can be.)
8. Provide tangible and intangible benefit values that exceed the relatively high level of one-time and recurring costs. (Although savings in operating costs—as listed in the project proposal—are not likely to be realized, the larger-than-expected benefits should more than offset the added costs.)

Summarized Resource Needs.[a] Hardware needs consist of one medium-size current-model computer with 1-megabyte primary storage capacity, and one microcomputer with 1MB primary storage capacity, 10 intelligent terminals, three portable microcomputers, 12 "dumb" terminals, approximately 80 portable terminals, 24 impact and nonimpact printers, 22 modems, and one front-

---

[a]Certain data included in this section are assumed.

end processor. Software needs consist of an operating system, a data communications software system, a network data base management system, a sales application software package (including a credit-checking model), an inventory control package, a report generator, a sales forecast package, and a financial modeling package. Additional personnel needs include a data base administrator, a systems programmer, and an applications programmer. Costs are expected to be approximately $2 million for systems development, hardware, software, plus the following for annual recurring operations:

Computer operations	$ 15,000
Maintenance contract	120,000
Communications lines	160,000
Information system maintenance	40,000
Data and information control	30,000
Information system administration	25,000
Total recurring costs	$390,000

These costs, however, should be offset by roughly $1,000,000 in annual benefits due to clerical savings, inventory carrying cost savings, savings in stock-out costs, savings in interest charges on working capital and other funds, savings from reduced errors, and increased contribution margins from greater sales arising from better customer service and managerial decisions. Also, certain of the above costs (including all one-time costs) are to be allocated to the inventory and financial management projects, since the hardware and part of the software should benefit those areas.

Expected Impacts. With respect to the information system, the mode of data input and processing will change from batch to on-line. More editing and processing and routine decision-making steps will be performed by the computer system. With respect to the organization, fewer clerks will be needed. On the other hand, the remaining clerks and managers will need intensive training in the use of the newly implemented system. This training should help to offset expected resistance from those affected.

We will be pleased to discuss this recommendation with you at your convenience.

Sincerely,

Tod Stuart
Information Systems Manager

b. (1) Format for a key factors report:

Precise Manufacturing Co.

To: Vice-President of Marketing

Subject: Report of Key Factors

As of: _____

(*Brief narrative explanation* of marketing possibilities, status of major marketing programs and activities, new programs and advantages of competitors, new sales branch managers, significant economic events)

(*Trends,* in graphed form, of the following:
  Percentage shares of market for Precise and competitors
  Net profit to sales percentages for Precise and competitors
  Return on total assets for Precise and competitors
  Marketing employee turnover)

Current measures

Total backlog of unfilled orders	$
Total canceled orders this week	$
Number of customer complaints	
Change in number of new customers	±
Percentage change in total customers	±

Significant deviations from plan

	Product no.	Variance
Product sales		

	Product contribution margins	
Product contribution margins		

	Prices	
Prices		

	Marketing expenses	
Marketing expenses		

(2) Format for a combination production order:

Precise Manufacturing Co.
Production Order

Product or Part No. _____			Order No. _____					
Quantity _____			Customer Order No. _____					
Description _____			Back Order No. _____					
Bill of Material No. _____			Date Issued _____					
			Date Required _____					

Operation No.	Dept. No.	Machine No.	Description of Operation	Tools Required	Std. Oper. Time	Start Date	Comments

(3) Listing of file features:

File Name and Type	Primary Key	Storage Medium	File Organization	Updating Frequency
Accounts receivable master file	Customer number	Magnetic disk	Indexed sequential	As received
Finished-goods inventory (product) master file	Product number	Magnetic disk	Indexed sequential	As received
Salesperson master file	Salesperson number	Magnetic tape	Sequential by number	Twice weekly
Open orders file	Order number	Magnetic disk	Random	As received
Sales history file (closed orders)	Order number	Magnetic disk	Sequential by number	Twice weekly
Back-order transaction file	Back-order number	Magnetic disk	Random	As received
Shipment records history file	Shipment date	Magnetic tape	Sequential by date	Daily
Shipping data reference file	—	Primary storage	—	As changes occur

(4) Schema for the sales data base:

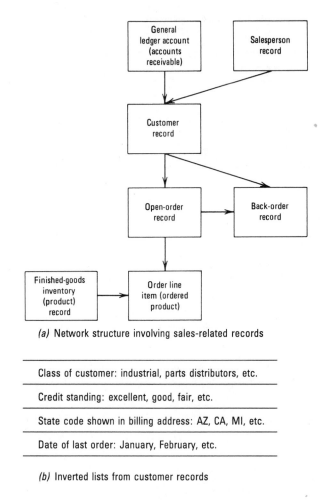

(a) Network structure involving sales-related records

Class of customer: industrial, parts distributors, etc.

Credit standing: excellent, good, fair, etc.

State code shown in billing address: AZ, CA, MI, etc.

Date of last order: January, February, etc.

(b) Inverted lists from customer records

(5) Examples of inquiries satisfied by a structured sales data base:

What is the status of order number XXX placed with customer ZZZ?
Which back orders are outstanding with customer ZZZ?
Which products are on order by customer ZZZ, and in what quantities?
How many units of product YYY are on order?
Which customers have been sold products by salesperson WWW?
Which industrial customers have a credit standing of excellent?
Which customers in state VV have not ordered products this year?
Which five salespersons have made the greatest amount of sales this year, and what
   are the amounts?

(6) For a preformatted data entry screen for sales orders, see Figure 7-6.

(7) For a list of application controls pertinent to an on-line sales application, see Chapter 12.

Review Questions

23-1 What is the meaning of each of the following terms?

> Design alternative
> Technical feasibility
> Operational feasibility
> Economic feasibility
> Design specification
> Systems design proposal
> End-user computing
> User-developed application
> Fourth-generation language
> Application generator
> Information center
> Computer-Aided Software Engineering (CASE)
> CASE workbench
> CASE encyclopedia
> CASE generator

23-2 What are the steps in the systems design phase?

23-3 In what two ways may alternative system designs be viewed?

23-4 Discuss some of the features that make up design alternatives and the ways that they might differ.

23-5 Discuss how design alternatives may be evaluated.

23-6 Discuss the variety of features likely to appear in design specifications.

23-7 Why is it desirable for top management to review and either approve or disapprove a systems design proposal?

23-8 Discuss briefly the design considerations pertaining to the overall systems design.

23-9 What are the reasons for the increasing number of user-developed systems in recent years?

23-10 What are the inherent problems when users develop their own systems?

23-11 Which types of applications are most suitable for development by users?

23-12 Describe the most suitable approach when users develop their own systems.

23-13 Identify the features that should be provided by user-development tools.

23-14 What types of services should be available in information centers?

23-15 What are the benefits of systems design methodologies?

23-16 Describe the use of integrated CASE tools in developing application programs.

23-17 What are the limitations of design methodologies?

Discussion Questions

23-18 Discuss the relative importance of each of the following components of an information system:

> **a.** Inputs.
> **b.** Outputs.
> **c.** Data base.
> **d.** Central processor.
> **e.** People.

23-19 If designing an information system is essentially a creative process, why attempt to teach systems design in a formal course?

23-20 Considering the great variety of automated devices available for collecting, processing, and storing data—as well as the numerous variations in documents and reports—how can a systems designer narrow the range of possible system design alternatives to a manageable number?

23-21 Discuss the following: "The physical operating system should drive the accounting system."

23-22 Assume that you have been assigned the responsibility of designing for a bank the portion of the information system pertaining to depositor transactions and depositor-oriented management reports. The bank, which has a main office and a dozen branches, currently employs an information system that essentially involves manual processing of transactions. It generates very few reports that focus on depositor activity. Your first task is to specify alternative system designs (say, six) that consist of various combinations of system elements and capabilities. Include in each alternative such aspects as data processing, input modes, data base features, output characteristics, and decision support levels.

23-23 Discuss the impacts of each of the following aspects on the design of an information system and its various elements:

- a. Organizational structure.
- b. Managerial styles.
- c. Customized products made to customers' orders.
- d. Keen competition requiring high level of customer service (e.g., prompt deliveries, generous repair warranties).
- e. Extensive regulation (e.g., as experienced by a public utility).
- f. Wide geographical dispersion of the home office, plants, warehouses, and sales offices.

23-24 Discuss the likely effects, if any, of each of the following changes on the design of an information system:

- a. Addition of a new product.
- b. Expansion into a new market area.
- c. Significant reduction of prices by a major competitor.
- d. Significant reduction by top management of the budget for the information systems function.
- e. Significant improvements in the available computer hardware.

23-25 What course of action should be followed when the potential users of an information system refuse to participate in its design?

23-26 Suggest key design specifications for each of the following systems:

- a. A nationwide on-line motel reservations system.
- b. A budgetary system for high-level management planning and control.

23-27 What added difficulties, if any, are encountered when designing an information system for a not-for-profit organization instead of for a profit-oriented firm?

23-28 Discuss specific design principles that pertain to each of the following system elements:

- a. Outputs.
- b. Inputs.
- c. Data base.
- d. Controls and security measures.

23-29 Discuss the particular concerns that a systems designer faces when designing an information system for a firm faced with a dynamic environment and other rapidly changing internal conditions.

23-30 Assume that your firm utilizes a centralized computer-based network which links several remote points to the home office. One day the president requests that the response time for sending and receiving data via the network be significantly reduced. What alternative steps can be taken to satisfy this request?

23-31 The president of your firm learns that another firm, which happens to be in a different industry, has a very successful purchases and accounts payable transaction processing system. He immediately calls you (since you are the information systems manager) and tells you to install the same system. What is your response?

23-32 A manufacturer is faced with sharp fluctuations in orders from the retail stores which comprise its major customer base. These fluctuating orders tend to be magnified, because of time delays, into wide oscillations in production levels. As a result, excessive overtime may be required in one week, followed by excessive idleness in the next week. What revisions in the information system design might alleviate this problem?

23-33 A distributor discovers that 50 percent of the orders it receives from customers involve sales of $10 or less. However, each order, regardless of size, requires approximately $10 to process. What revisions in the information system design might reduce total processing costs?

Problems

23-1 For each of the following described systems, propose an alternative system design and sketch overview diagrams of both the present and proposed systems.

   a. A department store employs a point-of-sale system to process its sales transactions. The cash registers on each floor are in effect stand-alone intelligent terminals. Transactions are processed by each register and then captured on optically scannable paper tape. At the end of each day the tapes are carried to the accounting department, read into the store's computer, and processed to update magnetic disk files and print sales and cash summaries.

   b. A distributor employs a centralized data preparation section to key data concerning shipped orders onto magnetic tape. Then the transactions are processed to update magnetic disk files and to produce sales invoices.

   c. A retail chain with 10 outlets employs a centralized order-filling system. Each store prepares replenishment orders when stocks run low. These orders are mailed to the warehouse, which fills the orders and ships the merchandise to the ordering store. When warehouse stocks need to be replenished, the warehouse sends a purchase requisition to the purchasing department. Purchase orders are then prepared and mailed to suppliers. Copies of the orders filled by the warehouse and the purchase orders are sent to the computer data processing department, where they are keyed to magnetic tape and processed against files stored on magnetic disks.

   d. A catering service employs a service bureau to process its accounts payable and cash disbursements. As invoices are received from suppliers, they are checked and keyed onto magnetic tape cassettes. These cassettes are delivered to the service bureau, which prepares checks and such other outputs as a check register and a list of expenditures by account number. The checks and outputs are returned by messenger to the firm, which mails the checks to the suppliers.

   e. A manufacturer with a factory and local warehouses employs a decentralized order-processing system. Minicomputers are located at each warehouse, whereas larger computers are located at the factory and the home office. All these computers utilize magnetic disk files. Orders are received from customers at the home office. Formal sales orders are prepared and mailed to the warehouse, which maintains an inventory file on magnetic disk. Next, the home office prepares sales invoices, which are mailed to customers. Periodically the home office initiates production orders to the factory. The factory maintains production records via its computer. It ships the finished goods directly to the warehouses according to pre-established proportions and provides information to the home office.

23-2 Assume that you have been assigned the responsibility of designing for a bank the portion of the information system pertaining to depositor transactions and depositor-oriented management reports. The bank, which has a main office and a dozen branches, currently employs an information system that essentially involves manual processing of transactions. It generates very few reports that focus on depositor activity. Your first task is to specify alternative system designs (say, six) that consist of various combinations of system components and capabilities. Include in each alternative such aspects as data processing, input modes, data base features, output characteristics, and decision support levels.

23-3 American Sterilizer Co., a manufacturer of hospital equipment, maintained a centralized computer network during the first half of the 1980s.[11] The network included two IBM mainframe computers plus 700 terminals that were linked by leased lines. Increased end-user computing, however, drained the mainframe resources. Response times became unreasonably lengthy, system reliability declined, and computing costs escalated. In 1986, therefore, the information systems director proposed an alternative system architecture based on microcomputers.

Required

By reference to the source article cited, describe the features of the new (in 1986) alternative system design, the benefits gained from the new system architecture, and the lessons learned by the firm in making the conversion to the new system architecture.

23-4 Refer to Problem 7-19, in which it is mentioned that Auto Barn is considering the acquisition of a computer system. Its current manual system can no longer handle the increasing sales and inventory transactions. Also, the managers are not receiving the information they need to make planning and control decisions. To foster the change, the president has just hired Lynn Barton, an accountant who has several years of experience as a systems consultant with one of the larger local public accounting firms. She has been appointed as manager of information systems, with the responsibility of directing the development of a new computer-based system.

Required

Describe the major steps that should be taken in the planning, analysis, and design phases of this systems development.

23-5 The Auto Rite Corp. of St. Paul replaces mufflers, transmissions, brakes, and other key automobile parts. Its dozen shops throughout the city service a total of about 200 car owners on an average day and 300 car owners on a busy day. Each shop maintains a standard inventory of 1000 different

[11]Based on an article by Mark W. Doll and William J. Doll entitled "A Productive PC Operation," *Datamation* (October 15, 1989), pp. 77–78.

types and sizes of mufflers and other parts. A manager and an average of four mechanics staff each shop. All shop managers report to a shop operations superintendent.

After a thorough analysis by the firm's controller, the president decides that a minicomputer system is needed to handle the various transactions at the shops and to prepare such outputs as shop orders for the mechanics, itemized receipts of work done for customers, and daily analyses of jobs performed for managers. The minicomputer system will have terminals at the respective shops, with the processor and disk files and printer located at the main office. The selected system should provide features that aid data entry, foster data control and security, and enable users to access specific shop orders. It should be capable of operating 12 hours per day, processing 60 transactions per hour, and responding to 90 percent of all data requests within 10 seconds. It should also accommodate a data base management system which the president plans to acquire next year.

Required

Prepare specific conceptual design specifications for the shop order processing system, based on the foregoing description, and an analysis of the needed inputs, files, and outputs. Make assumptions concerning quantitative values (e.g., that the average data record consists of 300 characters).

23-6 Hawkeye Hobby Shops is a chain of four stores located in Des Moines, Iowa. Each store carries a full line of hobby products; in addition, two of the stores specialize in radio control modeling. In 1990 the combined sales volume for the stores exceeded $2 million.

Each of the stores specializing in radio control modeling has a staff of four persons, and each of the remaining stores has a staff of three. In addition, Adele Tush, the owner,

and three bookkeeping clerks reside at the flagship store.

Because the hobby market is very competitive, Ms. Tush places the highest priority on customer service. One key aspect of customer service, she feels, is the maintenance of adequate inventory on hand at all times. When the firm consisted of only one store and did not specialize, she was able to achieve this objective. With multiple stores and a much larger number of items sold, however, her control over inventory has slipped. As a result, stock-outs and lost sales frequently occur. Reordering of merchandise is consuming much of her time and the time of the clerks.

Other related problems are also being experienced. Processing of transactions such as accounts payable and cash disbursements is becoming burdensome. Suppliers often complain that payments are received late, and many purchase discounts are lost. Moreover, Ms. Tush is becoming buried in masses of data and, consequently, has had increasing difficulty in finding or preparing information she needs for managing.

Another problem area is internal control. For instance, each cashier—the only nonsales employee in each outlying store—reconciles the cash receipts and the cash register tape at the end of each day and delivers them to the main store. The processing duties in the main store are inadequately divided, and Ms. Tush does not have time to provide close supervision. For instance, the one clerk handles both the general ledger and cash receipts.

Required

Propose a computerized solution to the problems experienced by the Hawkeye Hobby Shops. Include in your solution the following:

a. A description of the revised information system, including procedures and controls.

b. A hardware configuration diagram of the computer-based system to be installed.

c. A list of benefits that should be obtained from the revised information system.

d. Assuming that the revised information system is computerized and employs on-line processing, (1) prepare a menu that lists needed functions pertaining to purchasing, inventory receipts, payables, and disbursements, and (2) draw preformatted screens for entering cash disbursements.

e. Briefly describe several reports that can be useful in helping Ms. Tush to manage the four stores.

23-7 Harold Seymour is a management accountant with XLB Company. He is serving on a project team that is responsible for recommending a new regional sales distribution system. Although the project team has approved the draft for the final report of the project team, which is to be submitted to top management, Seymour is not pleased with the approved report.

Jane Bier of the marketing department was appointed the leader of the team because she had experience with sales distribution systems. Seymour was assigned to the team for his expertise in budgets and cost analysis and because of his involvement in a similar project with a previous employer.

The project team worked well together, identifying the positive and negative factors of the various alternatives. These factors were considered as the proposed regional distribution system was molded and designed. Seymour used his prior experience to explain the impact some of the negative factors could have on the volume and cost estimates for the proposed system.

The sales volume, costs, and cost savings estimates are very optimistic. The major negative factors and their impact have been discussed in the meetings but are not mentioned in the report or in the supporting financial data. Seymour knows from his previous experience that some of the negative factors could easily occur and could have a significant influence on the estimated financial benefits of the system to the company.

In other words, Seymour believes that the final report lacks a proper balance. He argues that the potential negative factors and their financial impact should be identified and discussed in the report for top management. The project team as a whole does not think the report needs to be revised because the system as designed is good, and the final conclusions will be the same.

The draft of the final report was composed by Bier. Seymour agrees with the proposed system and the overall conclusions of the report, but he does not believe the report is complete. Bier strongly favors the proposed system even though she has not developed the basic design. Bier's strong positive attitude for the proposed system is reflected throughout the report.

Required

a. Discuss the need to include negative factors in the system design report.

b. Discuss the bases, other than financial, on which the proposed system alternative should be evaluated.

c. If the proposed system alternative is approved by management, what behavioral actions should be taken by the project team to help ensure its successful implementation and use?

(CMA adapted)

23-8 The Public Employees Credit Union of Albuquerque, New Mexico, has grown to a membership of 2000. Its key transactions consist of cash receipts (largely via payroll deductions) from members, plus cash disbursements (mainly in the form of loans to members).

Currently the credit union employs calculators, one programmable electronic calculator, and two accounting machines to aid in the processing of these transactions. However, the daily transactions are so numerous that the clerks are unable to process all transactions on the day received. Furthermore, other processing must also be performed periodically. In addition to payroll processing, the clerks must (1) prepare statements for members after each semiannual dividend payment and (2) prepare new membership cards and new member ledger cards at the end of each year.

These heavy processing requirements cause several problems. The clerks must often work overtime to catch up. Also, it is necessary to close the office to loan business for several days after January 1. In spite of these efforts, the membership records are frequently out of date.

Consequently, the board of directors instructs the manager to investigate the feasibility of alternative processing approaches. After careful study, she selects three alternatives for consideration:

   a. Batch processing at a nearby service bureau at a cost of $0.50 per member per month. Transactions would be sent by bus express service to the bureau each Friday evening, with updated member records being returned on Monday morning. Statements would be printed quarterly.
   b. On-line processing at the same service bureau, at a cost of $0.25 per member per month, plus the acquisition cost of an on-line keyboard/ printer terminal (approximately $5000). The information provided would be essentially the same as in alternative **a**, except that files would be continually on line and accessible for inquiries. Transactions would be processed daily.
   c. Acquisition of a microcomputer with magnetic diskette files, terminal, and printer for approximately $10,000. (Software packages can also be acquired for $2000, or programs can be written by the credit union.) The information provided would be the same as in the second alternative given.

Required

Prepare a summary systems design proposal that the manager might present to the board.

23-9 The Reddy Watts Public Service Co. provides electric service to 40,000 residents and businesses in the Cheyenne, Wyoming, area. For a number of years it has prepared its customers' monthly bills with the aid of a small punched-card-oriented computer system. Data (i.e., meter numbers and meter readings) are transcribed from meter reading documents onto punched cards. These cards are then read into the computer, which accesses the customer records and other necessary records stored on magnetic tape, computes the quantities of kilowatts consumed and the amounts due, and prints the bills on punched cards. Customers then return the stubs of these bills with their payments, which are processed in the cash receipts procedure.

Because of the steady growth in customers and the increased need for managerial information, the management of Reddy Watts has decided to upgrade its customer billing system. When giving you this assignment, the president indicates that although the meter reading should still be done by human meter readers, the rest of the system should employ modern input and output devices. It should also enable managers and accountants to access customer records when desired and should provide improved information for managers.

Required

a. Develop design specifications for the new customer billing system, to the extent that data in the problem permit.

b. Design the bill for **residential** customers, and identify in an adjoining list the source of each item in the bill.

c. Design the record formats for all files needed by the customer billing system.

d. Prepare a system flowchart for the customer billing system.

e. Design at least two reports that would provide useful billing information to the management of Reddy Watts.

23-10 Mighty Good Photography, Inc., of Detroit is a prestige portrait photography firm with seven studios. It also maintains a processing laboratory, which is physically located at the home office.

During the past couple of years the firm has converted such applications as payroll and accounts payable to a small computer system. Now the president asks you, as the firm's systems analyst, to analyze the present billing and cash collection system.

Upon investigation, you gather the following facts:

a. Each studio daily sends copies of sales tickets (unnumbered) to the home office, together with cash and checks received and the portrait negatives. Each sales ticket references a sitting number corresponding to the negatives. Occasionally, two or more sales tickets refer to the same portrait, as when copies are desired by grandparents as well as parents. In these cases, single checks may total the amounts on the multiple sales tickets.

b. At the home office a cashier clerk first compares the sales tickets, monies, and negatives. Then she reviews the sales tickets for completeness. When inconsistencies or omissions are discovered, she phones the studio to straighten out the errors. Next she checks extensions on sales tickets and runs an adding machine tape of monies received, prepares a daily remittance list, and then fills out the daily deposit slip. Finally, she posts the total cash received to the cash receipts book and prepares the entry for the general ledger.

c. After completing these steps, the cashier clerk forwards the sales tickets, negatives, and a copy of the daily remittance list to the billing section. Three billing clerks in the section perform several steps. (They share the work, so that we can describe these steps by use of the collective "she.") First, she writes job tickets for the laboratory, using the sitting numbers and customer names as references. Then she forwards the negatives to the laboratory for processing, accompanied by the job tickets. Next she prepares, on an accounting machine, three-part invoice-statements. The machine simultaneously posts the transaction data to the customers' ledger cards, enters the sales on the studio sales register, and prepares a punched paper tape. She also posts the collections to the individual customers' ledger cards from the remittance list copy. Finally, she (a) files the invoice-statements and customer ledger cards in the back of the open accounts receivable file, for each studio, until notification that the ordered portraits have been mailed to the customers; and (b) sends the punched paper tape to a service bureau for processing and the preparation of sales reports.

d. The processing laboratory returns the stubs of job tickets to the billing section to confirm the mailing of the ordered portraits. One of the billing clerks pulls the invoice-statements and customers' ledger cards from the file and stamps the latter with the mailing date. Then she mails the first copy of the invoice-statement to the customer. The remaining copies are refiled with the ledger cards for use as follow-up if payments are not received within 30 days.

e. Daily studio sales registers are totaled in the billing section at the end of the month; the totals are compared by the service bureau. After the totals are confirmed, they are posted to the general ledger to reflect monthly sales.

f. At the end of the year the orders in process are backed out of these sales totals, in order that the financial statements will properly reflect only completed sales.

g. Processing in the billing section has been falling more and more behind. For instance, 30 days often pass between the time when the stubs are received in the section and the time when invoice-statements are mailed. Collection follow-up also lags, so that 30-day follow-up often becomes 50-day follow-up. The last aging of accounts receivable, prepared seven months ago by the firm's auditors, showed that 35 percent of the receivables were 90 days or more old; moreover, the total

amounts on the detail customer ledger cards differed from the balance in the general ledger control account by $100,000.

Required

a. Analyze the findings of the investigation pertaining to the present billing and cash collection system of Mighty Good Photography, Inc.

b. Assuming that the present computer system is capable of employing disk-oriented files, describe (1) changes needed to convert the described activities to computer-based processing, and (2) benefits that should result from these changes.

23-11 Metropolitan Hospital, a 400-bed facility averaging 80 admissions and 80 discharges per day, has been experiencing a severe backlog in billing patient accounts. Currently, there are 2720 unbilled patient accounts. Mike Ridgeway, billing supervisor, has prepared an analysis of the unbilled accounts for Jane Blough, controller, and Eli Fernandez, hospital administrator. The analysis, which includes discharged patients only, appears at the top of page 1112.

Metropolitan utilizes a unit-record billing system. A billing record card is prepared for each patient at the time of admission. The admissions department is responsible for entering insurance information on this card and then forwarding the card to the billing department. The billing department keeps records for patients occupying beds in an in-process file; records for discharged patients are kept in either a pending file or a ready-to-bill file. Discharges are documented in the Daily Hospital Census Report filled out by Nursing Services.

The pending file of unbilled accounts contains discharged patient records that have either an incomplete diagnosis, unspecified benefits, or are awaiting additional charges. Diagnoses can only be provided by

Metropolitan Hospital
Report of Unbilled Accounts
May 31, 1990

Principal Payor	Account Status			
	Ready To Bill	Diagnosis Incomplete	Benefits Not Specified	Awaiting Charges
Medicare	576	78	172	84
Medicaid	234	62	174	34
Blue Cross	288	104	152	52
Commercial insurance	394	76	62	53
Self-pay	108	0	0	17
Total	1600	320	560	240

the patient's physician. Specific charges are provided by the various hospital departments (surgery, pathology, pharmacy, etc.). An average of three days after discharge is required for all charges to be posted to a patient record. Once all charges are posted, an average of one day is required to prepare bills. More complete insurance information is, in most cases, provided by the patient. Only when the records are complete is the account moved to the ready-to-bill file.

Required

a. Using the Report of Unbilled Accounts for Metropolitan Hospital, prepare an analysis by account status that reflects the number of days of

- total unbilled accounts.
- expected average unbilled accounts.
- excess unbilled accounts.

On the basis of your analysis, identify the account status that has the most serious backlog problem, and explain why you selected that account status.

b. Identify and explain two possible causes of the billing backlog for each account status that has a backlog problem.

c. Recommend immediate measures that Metropolitan Hospital could take to alleviate the current billing backlog. Be specific as to the effects on the backlog.

d. Recommend long-run changes that could be implemented by Metropolitan Hospital to prevent a backlog of unbilled accounts from recurring.

(CMA adapted)

23-12 *Datacruncher Office Equipment, Inc. (Continuing Case)*

a. Describe two alternative designs for an improved system (within the scope of the systems project); include an overview diagram with each description; identify the relative benefits and drawbacks of each design alternative and the likely impacts on operations and the organization.

b. Prepare a menu that contains a variety of data entry and retrieval choices, including several key transactions. Then draft a preformatted screen display, which is to aid in the entry of data pertaining to one key transaction.

c. Prepare a list of documents and reports to be provided by the improved system, including the purpose, frequency, distribution, and medium of each output.

d. Sketch the formats for (1) two key reports and (2) one key document.

e. Prepare a list of the files in **a**, showing for each file its most desirable storage medium, organization method, updating frequency, and primary key.

f. Devise a schema that reflects useful linkages among part or all of the files listed in **e**; display the schema by means of a data structure diagram and suggest several complex inquiries that could be answered more promptly because of the linkages.

g. Draw a system flowchart to portray the processing steps in the preferable design alternative.

h. Prepare a list of suitable application controls and security measures for the improved system.

i. Prepare the cover letter of the design proposal that pertains to the preferable system design alternative.

Suggested Readings

Bernheim, Richard C. "The Right Way to Design a Cost Accounting System." *Management Accounting* (Sept. 1983), pp. 63–67.

Burch, John G., Jr., and Grudnitski, Gary. *Information Systems: Theory and Practice.* 5th ed. New York: John Wiley, 1989.

Cerullo, Michael J. "Designing Accounting Information Systems." *Management Accounting* (June 1985), pp. 37–42.

Closs, David J. "Designing Computerized Inventory Management Systems." *Journal of Accounting and EDP* (Summer 1985), pp. 22–29.

Cobb, Richard H. "In Praise of 4GLS." *Datamation* (July 15, 1985), pp. 91–96.

Cook, Mark G. "Control and Audit of Host-Based End-User Computing." *Internal Auditor* (August 1987), pp. 36–40.

Davis, Richard K. "New Tools and Techniques to Make Data Base Professionals More Productive." *Journal of Systems Management* (June 1984), pp. 20–25.

Gibson, Michael L. "A Guide to Selecting CASE Tools." *Datamation* (July 1, 1988), pp. 65–66.

Gibson, Michael L.; Synder, Charles A.; and Rainer, R. Kelly, Jr. "CASE: Clarifying Common Misconceptions." *Journal of Systems Management* (May 1989), pp. 12–19.

Giovinazzo, Vincent J. "Designing Focused Information Systems." *Management Accounting* (Nov. 1984), pp. 34–41.

Grossman, Theodore, and Palvia, Shailendra. "The Design and Implementation of a Multidimensional Retail Merchandising Information System." *Journal of Information Systems* (Fall 1988), pp. 119–131.

Hammer, William E. "Systems Design in a Data Base Environment." *Journal of Systems Management* (Nov. 1982), pp. 24–29.

Harrison, Ralph. "Prototyping and the Systems Development Life Cycle." *Journal of Systems Management* (August 1985), pp. 22–25.

Hodge, Robert D. "Integrating Systems." *Journal of Systems Management* (August 1989), pp. 18–20.

Kaplan, Robert S. "Accounting Lag: The Obsolescence of Cost Accounting Systems." *California Management Review* (Winter 1986), pp. 174–199.

Klein, Gary, and Beck, Philip O. "A Decision Aid for Selecting among Information System Alternatives." *MIS Quarterly* (June 1987), pp. 177–186.

Lauer, Joachim, and Stettler, David M. "New Directions for Information Centers." *Journal of Systems Management* (Oct. 1987), pp. 6–11.

Martin, Merle P., and Fuerst, William. "Communications Framework for Systems Design." *Journal of Systems Management* (March 1984), pp. 18–25.

Oglesby, John N. "How to Shop for Your Information Center." *Datamation* (June 1, 1987), pp. 70–76.

Robin, Michael. "The Evolution of Management Accounting Systems at Chase Manhattan Bank." *Journal of Accounting and EDP* (Winter 1988), pp. 15–29.

Rowe, Lawrence A. "Tools for Developing OLTP Applications." *Datamation* (August 1, 1985), pp. 73–82.

Schussel, George. "Application Development in the 5th Generation." *Datamation* (Nov. 15, 1987), pp. 94–102.

Sena, James A., and Smith, Lawrence Murphy. "Designing and Implementing an Integrated Job Cost Accounting System." *Journal of Information Systems* (Fall 1986), pp. 102–112.

Sprague, Ralph H., Jr., and McNurlin, Barbara C. (eds.) *Information Systems Management in Practice.* Englewood Cliffs, N.J.: Prentice-Hall, 1986.

Srinivasen, C. A., and Dascher, Paul E. "Information Systems Design: User Psychology Considerations." *MSU Business Topics* (Winter 1977), pp. 51–57.

Swift, Michael K. "Prototyping in IS Design and Development." *Journal of Systems Management* (July 1989), pp. 14–23.

Tripp, Robert S., and Filteau, Mark C. "Blueprints: Adopting a Construction Trade Approach in Designing Large Scale Management Information Systems." *Information and Management* (1987), pp. 55–70.

Wilkinson, Joseph W. "Guidelines for Designing Systems." *Journal of Systems Management* (Dec. 1974), pp. 36–40.

Wysong, Earl M., Jr. "Using the Internal Auditor for System Design Projects." *Journal of Systems Management* (July 1983), pp. 28–33.

After studying this chapter, you should be able to do the following:

Describe a suitable procedure for determining that an information system design is feasible.

Outline the steps required to select the specific resources, especially computer hardware and software, that are to implement a feasible information system design.

Discuss considerations involved in developing an economic feasibility analysis for a proposed information system design.

Identify the array of options available when selecting the needed system resources.

Contrast several methods of evaluating proposals from suppliers of computer hardware and software.

Chapter **24**

SYSTEMS JUSTIFICATION AND SELECTION

Anew or improved information system should be based on a sound design. However, a sound design is not enough. The system design also must be justified (shown to be feasible). If the new or improved system is not feasible, it will have scant chance for success.

Feasibility, though, can seldom be determined in an easy and straightforward manner. Often, judgment plays a large role. Thus, the higher-level management of a firm must make the final feasibility determination.

After a system design is justified, it must be realized. Accordingly, the resources required to make it operational must be selected and acquired. In the case of computer-based information systems, these resources include system hardware, system software, and skilled personnel.

Higher-level management needs assistance in making resource decisions, since systems justification and resource selection involve highly technical considerations. It must draw on the advice of persons who have expertise in these areas. Systems designers can, of course, provide assistance concerning technical feasibility of specific types of computer hardware and software, and accountants are particularly qualified to assist in the area of economic feasibility.

This chapter focuses on the procedures and problems involved in justifying system designs and selecting computer hardware and software. First, steps in the systems justification and selection phase will be reviewed. Next, the considerations underlying economic feasibility will be explained. Then, major options and useful evaluation techniques available when selecting computer hardware and software will be surveyed.

Steps in Systems Justification and Selection

The systems justification and selection phase, like the systems design phase, is clouded by disagreements. Certain authorities say that a system must be justified prior to the systems design phase. Others say that systems justification is an integral part of the systems design phase. Still others say that a system cannot reasonably be justified until after design specifications have been prepared and approved.

These disagreements are more apparent than real, however. The feasibility of a proposed system must be considered from the inception of the project, as noted in Chapter 21. Feasibility should continue to be tested during the systems analysis and design phases. If a proposed system design alternative is found to be infeasible, it should be discarded, or at least deferred. At the end of the systems design phase, the outlines of one or more likely system design alternatives will have at last been fully delineated; costs and benefits can then be better estimated than before. At that point, management has a clearer vision and sounder basis for judging feasibility than at any previous point.

Consequently, it is reasonable to conclude that the acid test of feasibility should follow hard on the heels of the design specifications. For convenience, however, it is equally reasonable to assign systems justification to a separate phase.

Once feasibility is proven, it is usually necessary to select such system resources as computer hardware and software. This selection process consists of preparing system resource specifications, of soliciting proposals from suppliers of hardware and software, of evaluating the received proposals, and of selecting the best combination of hardware and

software to meet the feasible system design. Figure 24-1 lists these steps within the systems justification and selection phase.[1]

Determination of Design Feasibility

Feasibility is closely related to usability. As pointed out in Chapter 23, three types of feasibility pertain to information systems: technical feasibility, operational feasibility, and economic feasibility. A feasible information system design may not violate any of these types of feasibility. Thus, it may not specify equipment beyond the bounds of current technology, it may not include system features unacceptable to the intended users, and it may not require expenditures that exceed the projected benefits.

A **feasibility study** is a careful examination of the feasibility of a system design. The result of the examination is a determination that the system design is or is not feasible technically, operationally, or economically. Because feasibility concerns arise from the beginning of a systems project, a feasibility study often is viewed as embracing the systems planning, analysis, and design phases as well as the systems justification phase.

As noted in Chapter 23, several alternative systems designs usually emerge in the search for ways to satisfy systems and information requirements. Often the respective system designs entail the acquisition of new resources. For instance, if the present system is manual, one alternative design might propose the acquisition of desk calculators, whereas a second alternative design might propose the acquisition of a new computer system and related software. If the present system is computer-based, one alternative

---

[1]These steps may be performed by a system project team or by a special *feasibility committee*. Whichever of these groups undertakes the listed steps may also perform the follow-up step: devising a plan to implement the selected hardware and software within the system design specifications.

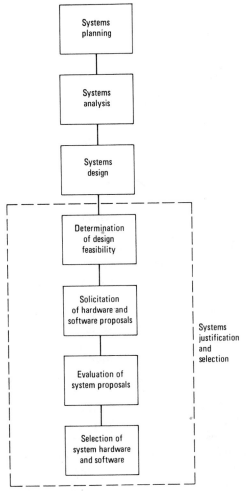

FIGURE 24-1   The steps in the systems justification and selection phase.

design might propose a larger replacement computer, whereas another alternative design might propose that the system be upgraded with a new data base and data communications network.[2]

[2]The term *system,* as used here, might pertain to an application area such as sales order processing or logistics management in the large or moderate-size firm, whereas it might pertain to the entire information system in a small firm.

As might be expected, a feasibility study focuses on the new resources that are proposed in each alternative system design. If the proposed resources can (1) fulfill the system requirements in a technical sense, (2) satisfy the users' needs and expectations, and (3) meet management's economic criteria, then the design alternative should be judged feasible.

If more than one alternative design is judged to be feasible, management should decide which is preferable. It might attempt to spot the alternative that provides the highest ratio of benefits to costs. However, it must also take into account subjective considerations. For instance, the relative advance, or "leap forward," in information technology must be considered. Management may choose a more conservative design alternative over a more innovative or sophisticated design alternative in order not to "leap too far." Or it may decide that a sophisticated design alternative is preferable but that its most risky aspects should be deferred.

This step of determining feasibility pertains mainly to systems designed by systems professionals. Systems that are developed by individual users seldom involve the acquisition of new hardware and software. Moreover, since they generally follow the prototyping approach, complete design specifications are not prepared.[3]

Solicitation of Proposals

Once an alternative system design has been decided on, the sources of the needed resources become the paramount concern. Numerous hardware suppliers and software suppliers, as well as varied suppliers of computer-related services, are available.[4] Thus, an important question to answer is: By what means can the most suitable suppliers be located?

Resource specifications. The best solution is to begin by specifying the firm's resource needs in detail. These **resource specifications,** which would evolve from the systems design specifications, should state technical capabilities that selected resources must meet and the support requirements that the suppliers of the resources must provide.

Figure 24-2 lists a typical set of specifications prepared by a firm to indicate its computer system needs. Included are specifications pertaining to the system design, the needed hardware, the needed software, and the required level of system support.

Design specifications incorporated within resource specifications should span all applications to be served by selected resources. Adequate detail should be provided. For instance, specimen source documents and reports, record layouts, diagrams of physical locations, and forecasts of expected sales volumes are all highly desirable. Selected data concerning the present information system may also be usefully included.

The hardware specifications provide the basis for a proposed configuration. They tell the suppliers who receive them what capabilities are needed, so that the suppliers can match specific hardware items to the system design. For instance, a specification of on-line input and output capabilities at certain physical locations likely will lead to a configuration that includes remote terminals.

The software specifications indicate what instructional capabilities are needed to operate the hardware configuration and to generate the desired outputs. Also included in the software specifications are the particular programming languages desired. For example, COBOL typically is specified when business applications are included within a system design.

The system support specifications dictate what support a selected supplier must provide. Among the support services specified may be assistance in developing application programs, in training employees to use the new system, in testing programs during

---

[3]On the other hand, a feasibility study *should* be performed when a new information center is being considered, or when new fourth-generation software packages are being proposed for use within the center.

[4]These varied suppliers of hardware, software, and services are surveyed later in this chapter.

System Design Specifications

Output specifications
Data base specifications
Processing specifications
Input specifications
Control and security specifications

Hardware Specifications

Processor speeds and capabilities
Secondary storage capacities and access capabilities
Input–output speeds and capabilities
Compatibility features
Modularity (expandability) features
Error detection and correction techniques
Data communications capabilities
Special features, such as multiprogramming and virtual storage
Maximum allowable downtime (as a percentage of total time)

Software Specifications

Programming languages and compilers
Utility packages
Application packages
Operating system capabilities
Data management packages

System Support Specifications

Programming assistance
Training programs
Test facilities and time available
Backup facilities
Maintenance assistance

FIGURE 24-2   A typical list of resource specifications.

their development periods, in maintaining the hardware during its operational life, and in obtaining access to backup facilities when the proposed system fails.

Completing the specifications would be a cover letter that offers more data concerning the firm and requests additional data from the suppliers. It might state, for instance, the objectives for the firm's information system and the ceiling on system expenditures. It might also request such data as hardware and software prices; other charges, such as overtime use fees; service locations; existing users; expected delivery dates and installation schedules; electric power requirements; and suggested weekly processing schedules.

Request for proposal procedure. The cover letter and resource specifications together represent a **request for bid or proposal** (RFP). The next action, ideally, is to send the RFP to each promising supplier. A typical RFP, however, consists of over 100 pages (and often several hundred pages) of text and exhibits. Thus, practicality requires that the number of solicited firms be narrowed. The usual procedure is as follows:

1. Screen the numerous suppliers with the aid of consultants, catalogs, and computer industry publications such as *Datamation* and *Auerbach's Infotech Reports.*

2. Pick several (e.g., three to six) reputable suppliers whose products or services appear capable of satisfying the resource specifications.

3. Contact each selected supplier and request that a bid or proposal be submitted by a specified deadline date, perhaps 30 to 60 days after the RFP is received.

Evaluation of Proposals from Suppliers

Upon following the procedure just detailed, a soliciting firm likely will receive several proposals. Each proposal worthy of attention responds directly to all specifications. Thus, it contains data concerning one or more proposed hardware configurations, software packages and systems, support services, purchase and/or rental prices, installation dates, and so on. It also details the use of the resources within the specified system design.

When all of the proposals are on hand, the next step is evaluation. Several evaluation techniques should be employed in this critical step, as described later in this chapter.

To assure that the evaluation step is conducted in a professional manner, the feasibility committee or project team may be temporarily augmented. Computer hardware specialists and system software programmers, for example, are professionals whose presence can be invaluable. If such professional assistance is not available inside the firm, it often will be desirable to obtain advice and assistance from such outside sources as consulting firms and public accounting firms. On the other hand, represen-

tatives from hardware and software manufacturers should *not* be assigned to a feasibility committee, since their advice is likely to be biased.

Selection of System Resources

The selection of specific resources follows on the heels of the evaluation process. This selection process involves three actions.

First, the feasibility committee or project team weighs the evaluation results to determine specific resources from whichever supplier or suppliers seem most suitable. For instance, it might conclude that hardware proposed by supplier A and software proposed by supplier X best satisfy the specifications.

Second, the feasibility committee or project team prepares a report for presentation to higher-level management. This report might be termed a **feasibility report,** since it clearly presents the justification for the preferred system design (and consequently for the specified resources). In addition, the report summarizes the proposals received from suppliers and ranks them in order of preference. It lists the strengths and weaknesses of each proposal. For the recommended proposal or proposals the report indicates personnel requirements, implementation plans, and anticipated problems. In effect, the feasibility report is an expanded or final version of a systems design report. Certain firms, in fact, use the feasibility report in lieu of a systems design report or proposal.

Third, management makes the final decision concerning the system resources. Its decision may be (1) to approve the recommendation of the feasibility committee or project team; (2) to disapprove the recommendation; (3) to defer approval, perhaps to allow time for other system applications to be added to the design; or (4) to approve the recommendation, subject to revisions in the system design, in suggested suppliers, or in the implementation schedule. Management likely will weigh all of these options carefully, since such decisions may commit the firm to extensive expenditures and generate organizational problems for an extended period into the future.

Example of Systems Justification and Selection[5]

The experience of XYZ Leasing, a small (and hypothetical) automobile-leasing firm, will provide an example of the systems justification and selection phase. Although the procedures followed by XYZ are less formal than those suggested in the preceding discussion, they are generally sound and appropriate to a small firm.

In recent years a local service bureau has been satisfying the data processing needs of XYZ. However, an increase in service charges and a steep growth trend in sales convince XYZ's management to investigate the acquisition of its own computer.

Accordingly, XYZ gathers information concerning the parameters of a needed system. For instance, it determines that the number of rental automobiles to be accounted for during an average period is 1200, whereas 900 entries (on the average) are posted each month to the 133 general ledger accounts. Next, the firm's managers explore the benefits. They ascertain that a new computer-based system will be necessary to enable the present clerical staff to handle growing transaction processing and financial reporting requirements during the next few years. They also discover that this same computer-based system can significantly improve profits through better profitability information—for example, the relative profitabilities of rental locations, various pricing strategies, various mixes of automobiles. These benefits, the managers believe, will exceed the cost of a new minicomputer system. Thus, management makes considered judgments that (1) a new computer-based system is economically feasible and (2) a minicomputer (especially a relatively powerful type) is technically feasible.

Management next prepares an RFP to solicit proposals from prospective suppliers of hardware and software for minicomputers. It first provides overall information concerning XYZ, such as the number of employees (60) and number of locations (eight). Then it specifies the requirements of the new system. For example, the new system must provide the following technical features:

1. On-line interactive processing.
2. Menu selection and program prompting for data entry, inquiry, file update, and report generation.
3. Multiprogramming capabilities.
4. Printer spooling, concurrent with other functions.
5. Program prompting for such functions as paper changing and file mounting.
6. Preparation of special reports by users through report-writing software.
7. Multiple security levels to limit access to authorized individuals.[6]

Most of the 200 pages in the RFP, however, consist of detailed specifications concerning six applications: general ledger and financial reporting, rental revenue, cash payment and bank reconciliation, fixed assets (i.e., the fleet of rental automobiles), unap-

---

[5]Adapted from Germain B. Boer and Sam W. Barcus III, "How a Small Company Evaluates Acquisition of a Minicomputer," *Management Accounting* (March 1981), pp. 13–23. Copyright © 1981 by National Association of Accountants, New York. All rights reserved. Reprinted by permission.

[6]Ibid., p. 17.

plied cash and items billable, and payroll. For each application the RFP contains a system flowchart, a narrative description of the processing to be performed by the new system and the scope of the application, relevant statistics pertaining to the application, master file data, input descriptions and screen formats, and output descriptions and report formats.

For instance, several key facts abstracted from the section pertaining to the fixed-assets application are as follows: The application's scope spans the processing of all transactions affecting rental automobiles against a fixed-assets master file. These transactions, including inquiries, are to be entered via CRT terminals and with the assistance of menu screens. Outputs are to include an active fleet inventory report (on request) and monthly reports concerning vehicle deletions and extraordinary depreciation.

Proposals are received by XYZ from several suppliers and are first screened for acceptability. Those proposals that do not respond fully to instructions and questions stated in the RFP are dropped. The remaining proposals are listed on a spreadsheet and compared with respect to such features as word size (in bits), size of primary storage, cycle time, arithmetic precision, number of concurrent tasks that can be performed, virtual memory capability, minimum response time, time to sort a 3000-record file, available disk storage, expandability of the system, training assistance provided, and maintenance service provided. Costs are also listed for each supplier, broken down by both hardware and software components.

On the basis of these cost and noncost comparisons, the manager in charge of the evaluation procedure prepares a feasibility report for the president. In the report he ranks the suppliers in order of preference. The president therefore has a clear-cut and soundly supported basis for making the final choice.

Considerations of Economic Feasibility

Economic feasibility is a key concern when evaluating proposed system changes. The resources needed in a new or improved information system involve expenditures, as do all other resources needed by a firm. Thus, their acquisition must be justified on economic grounds. Since such resources normally will have expected lives of longer than a year, capital budgeting methods should be employed in the justification process.

This section first reviews basic economic concepts pertaining to information. Then it examines the criteria for judging feasibility, the costs and benefits pertaining to the economics of information systems, the means of estimating such costs and benefits, and the computational methods that provide the values for the criteria.

Information Economics Concepts

Information, being a resource, has both values (benefits) and costs. For example, a piece of information has value if it is relevant to a decision situation and it is unknown to the decision maker when presented to him or her. (Such information is often said to have "surprise value.") The same piece of information also has a cost attached, since expenditures are involved in its collection and processing.

Information economics is the study of values and costs of information and their trade-offs. A fundamental tenet of information economics is that additional information should be gathered and provided for any purpose, such as making a decision, so long as the value of the next piece of information exceeds the costs of its collection, processing, storage, and reporting. Another way of expressing this principle is to say that information should continue to be gathered and provided so long as its marginal value ex-

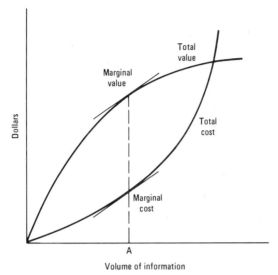

FIGURE 24-3 Components of the cost and value of information.

ceeds its marginal cost. When the marginal cost equals the marginal value, the optimal volume of information has been reached. In Figure 24-3 the optimal volume is marked by point A.[7] As we can see, the net value (total value less total cost) is maximized at that volume.

An example of information economics appears in the problem of scrapped units during a production process. Each scrapped unit results in one fewer unit being produced and sold. To combat these lost sales, we might prepare a daily scrap report that shows the scrap rate in each production process. This report can be said to have value if it enables management to reduce scrappage and hence the sales losses. If the payoff in dollar savings exceeds the costs of providing the information, the report is economically worthwhile. On the other hand, an addition to the report that shows the exact time each unit is

scrapped may not be economical. The added value from this piece of information likely will not exceed the cost of its collection.

Since costs and values attach to all the resources and attributes of information systems, concepts of information economics are central to information system design. In other words economic considerations underlie every design decision. In addition to decisions concerning whether or not to prepare more reports, information economics concepts aid in making decisions concerning needed controls, hardware features, and so forth. Assume, for example, that we are concerned about the number of internal accounting controls to design into a particular system. Our design decision should be based on a trade-off between (1) the added accuracy (value) gained from each additional control and (2) the direct cost of that control plus the indirect cost resulting from loss in processing efficiency. To take another example, consider the decision concerning the appropriate number of terminals for a new on-line computer-based system. In this case, our design decision should be based on a trade-off be-

[7]Adapted with permission from John G. Burch, Jr.; Felix R. Strater, Jr.; and Gary Grudnitski, *Information Systems: Theory and Practice*, 2d ed. (New York: John Wiley, 1979), p. 18.

tween the cost of each added terminal and the value of the added service to users.

As might be expected, information economics provides the underpinning for economics feasibility determinations. The next section discusses a major concern of economic feasibility: the criteria for judging whether or not a proposed cost outlay is economically feasible.

Criteria of Economic Feasibility

The key criterion of economic feasibility can be stated broadly as follows: A proposed investment in information-related resources is economically feasible if the benefits or values derived from the use of the resources exceed the initial cost of the investment plus all related expenditures. Thus, an investment in computer hardware and software should be made only if the benefits derived, such as savings in clerical salaries and payoffs from better decisions, are greater than the added costs of the hardware and software plus the salaries of newly hired computer operators and other related costs.

From an economic point of view, this criterion incorporates the same considerations as does any capital investment situation; that is, an investment in information system hardware and software is no different, economically speaking, from an investment in a delivery truck, a sales promotion campaign, a new office building, or an executive training program. In fact, information system investments compete with these other investments for available funds within a firm's capital budgeting program.

The broad criterion of economic feasibility must be applied within the framework of a specific decision model. Four currently employed models will be briefly discussed. Each model is labeled to reflect its adaptation of the broad criterion.

Net present value criterion. As mentioned earlier, key information system resources

such as computer hardware and software usually have economic lives exceeding one year. Therefore, a discounted cash flow model should normally be employed when determining economic feasibility. Future cash outflows, such as those pertaining to expected year-to-year expenditures, and future cash inflows, such as cost savings expected over the life of an acquired computer, should be discounted to the present time. The total present value of all costs should then be compared to the total present value of all cost savings and other benefits. If the **net present value** is positive—that is, if the total present value of cash inflows is greater than the total present value of cash outflows—the investment in the resources can be expected to provide a satisfactory return. Thus, it may be described as being economically feasible.[8]

To apply the net present value criterion, we need to measure or estimate the following:

1. The invested cost in resources to be acquired, plus operating costs and other cash outflows over the lives of the resources.
2. The benefits to be derived from the resources during their lives.
3. The economic lives of the resources.
4. The salvage values of the resources at the end of their economic lives.
5. The salvage values of resources to be replaced (if any), including both (a) their current salvage values and (b) their salvage values at the ends of their economic lives.
6. Tax-related facts such as the depreciation method and the tax rate.

---

[8]Often, however, certain factors affecting economic feasibility cannot be quantified. Therefore, the numerical computation of economic feasibility by the foregoing procedure is subject to modification of the impact of such nonquantifiable factors.

7. The required rate of return on invested capital, which is to be used in discounting future cash flows to the present time.[9]

Later sections will examine the types of costs and benefits pertaining to information system resources and apply these factors in illustrative computations.

Other criteria. Although the net present value criterion is sound, it is not sufficient in certain situations. Other useful criteria (and related models) include the payback period, the cost-effectiveness measure, and the benefit–cost ratio.

The **payback period** criterion measures the number of years required to recover the initial costs invested in resources. Although it does not reflect a return on the investment, the payback period can represent a useful screening criterion, especially when an investment is risky.

The **cost-effectiveness** criterion provides a means for comparing two or more alternative system designs. For instance, it may be used to compare the respective costs over the next five years of processing sales orders manually versus processing the same sales orders by means of a computer system. Its drawback is that it does not take benefits into account. However, it can be a useful criterion when the benefits are difficult to estimate quantitatively but can reasonably be viewed as roughly equal under the respective alternatives.

The **benefit–cost ratio** criterion, also called the profitability ratio, is a modification of the net present value criterion. Since it measures the benefits received or effectiveness gained from each invested dollar, the benefit–cost ratio enables competing investment opportunities to be ranked. This criterion provides a sound basis not only for

choosing among alternative system designs and competing systems applications but also for choosing between improving the information systems and, say, expanding the production facilities.

Costs Related to Information System Resources

The relevant costs for determining the economic feasibility of an information system design are those that are directly related to (1) the acquisition of resources, (2) the development of the new or improved information system, and (3) the operation and maintenance of the information system during the lives of the acquired resources. At the time when the feasibility determination is made, most of these costs represent added future cash outflows and hence must be estimated.

One-time costs. Costs related to the initial acquisition of resources and the development of the new or improved information system represent in total the amount of the initial investment. Since they generally are incurred only once during the life of a particular set of information system resources, they may also be described as **one-time costs.**

Figure 24-4 lists a typical set of one-time costs for a new or improved computer-based information system. For convenience these have been categorized as costs related to system design, system installation and conversion, system site preparation, system hardware, and system software.

Most of the costs in the first two categories are for salaries of the project team and newly hired systems personnel. Also included, however, are costs for supplies, storage media, equipment rentals, and salaries needed to carry out such activities as designing, testing, converting files, and retraining displaced employees. The majority of these costs are incurred during the implementation phase, as discussed in Chapter 25.

[9]Theoretically, the required rate of return is the cost of capital. However, since the latter is very difficult to determine, most firms use a judgmental approach to determine the rate of return.

System Design Costs

Detailed design
Programming

System Installation and Conversion Costs

System and program testing
File conversion
Retraining of displaced employees
Training of newly hired analysts, programmers, and operators
Inefficiencies caused by learning new equipment and procedures

System Site Preparation Costs

Construction of wiring and piping systems
Construction of electrical power supply
Construction of air conditioning system
Construction of sprinkler system
Construction of other miscellaneous facilities, such as false flooring,
    file storage vault, and special lighting

System Hardware Costs

Central processing unit
Additional processors
Secondary storage devices
Input–output devices
Data communications equipment
Terminals
Peripheral equipment, such as key-to-tape devices
Transportation of equipment

System Software Costs

Operating system, utility routines, compilers
Data communications software
Application program packages
Data management software packages
Decision model software packages
Outside computer time-sharing rentals

FIGURE 24-4 One-time costs for a new or improved computer-based information system.

Costs in the remaining three categories, on the other hand, consist mainly of physical equipment: sprinkler systems, computers, software packages, and so on. (However, the site preparation costs sometimes include significant amounts of wages for construction workers.)

Incidentally, all costs pertaining to a new or improved computer-based information system do not appear in Figure 24-4. Certain of these costs "which may not be easily measured should nevertheless be considered. For example, the installation of a new . . . system usually causes upheaval and disruption of routine, changes in employee morale, obsolescence of employee skills, changes in organization structure, and other phenomena. Management functions may be drastically revised, and some routine management functions may be replaced by programs in the data processing system. These and similar changes will result in costs that should be included"[10] in some manner in the justification process.

Levels of the aforementioned array of one-time costs can vary from a few thousand dollars up to several million dollars. At the lower end of the cost scale might be a simple transaction processing computer system for a small retailer. At the higher end of the cost scale would likely be a sophisticated support system for a large manufacturer, including numerous computers, elaborate data communications equipment, powerful data base management systems, and complex embedded financial planning models.

One-time costs, however, are influenced not only by the type and scope of the designed system but also by the financing arrangements. Thus, if the hardware and software are purchased outright, all of their costs fall under the category of one-time costs. However, if the same hardware and software are leased, the outlays are classified as recurring costs.

Recurring costs. All relevant costs not classified as one-time costs can be described broadly as **recurring costs.** Typical categories of recurring costs include those pertaining to data preparation and handling, computer operations and maintenance, information system maintenance, data and information control, and information system administration. Figure 24-5 lists these categories of recurring costs. Under each category appear examples of specific recurring costs.

Recurring costs alternatively may be categorized and computed by object classes. With respect to information systems, the major object classes for recurring costs include labor costs, supplies costs, hardware or equipment costs, and overhead costs.

[10]Committee on Managerial Decision Models, *Committee Reports: Supplement to Vol. XLIV of the Accounting Review* (Evanston, Ill.: American Accounting Association, 1969), p. 59.

Assume, for instance, that a firm has the following monthly costs:

3 data processing employees	$2000 each
1 central processing unit, rental charge	600
1 printer, rental charge	500
1 disk drive, rental charge	700
1 tape drive, rental charge	550
Utilities	300
Space, rental charge	$1 per square foot
Paper, magnetic tapes, etc.	350

Then, if the data processing facilities occupy 400 square feet of space, the recurring costs categorized by object classes would be as follows:

Labor (3 × 2000)	$6000
Hardware ($600 + $500 + $700 + $550)	2350
Supplies	350
Overhead ($300 + $400 × $1)	700
Total monthly costs	$9400

Recurring cost levels vary widely with respect to individual system projects. Such factors as volumes of transactions and response times significantly affect the cost levels. Thus, it is usually necessary to estimate such underlying factors prior to estimating costs.

Moreover, recurring cost levels for complete information systems can vary considerably from firm to firm and from industry to industry. For instance, grocery firms tend to spend about 1 percent of their revenues for information system operations and maintenance, whereas firms in the banking industry tend to spend around 5 percent of their revenues for the same purpose.

Benefits Related to Information System Resources

A new or improved information system can provide benefits by streamlining opera-

---

Data Preparation and Handling Costs

Wages and salaries for data preparation clerks, tape librarian, and others; supplies; peripheral equipment rentals or obsolescence

Computer Operations and Maintenance Costs

Wages and salaries for computer operators, custodians, technicians, and supervisors; supplies; repair parts; utilities; equipment service contracts; space rentals; freight; data transmission fees; computer-related equipment rentals or obsolescence; taxes; insurance; building occupancy

Information System Maintenance Costs

Salaries for programmers and system analysts

Data and Information Control Costs

Wages and salaries for internal auditors, control clerks, and others; printing fees applying to programming manuals and other documentation; security systems

Information System Administration Costs

Salaries of system managers, data base administrator, secretaries, and others

---

FIGURE 24-5 Recurring costs for a new or improved computer-based information system.

tions, reducing asset levels, and improving the quality of management planning and control. In economic terms these benefits may be classified as either cost savings or revenue increases. With regard to measurability they may be classified as tangible benefits or intangible benefits.

Cost savings versus revenue increases. **Cost savings** are the measurable amounts by which operating and maintenance costs are reduced when a new or improved information system is installed. Also called displaceable costs or avoidable costs, such cost savings are most often achieved by reducing the number of required employees. A new computer-based information system, for instance, will generally displace clerks who formerly performed the operations that are now automated. Cost savings can also be generated by reducing required investments in assets. For example, investment in inventory can be reduced by the use of automated record keeping and inventory control techniques. Reduced inventory levels in turn yield savings in such carrying costs as insurance and interest on borrowed funds. Still other savings can result from reduced materials waste and spoilage in production and related operational areas.

Certain of these cost savings, however, will be offset by the added needs of a new system. For instance, a new computer-based information system requires that computer operators, data preparation clerks, and other computer-related personnel be employed. Changing from a tape-oriented computer system to a disk-oriented computer system produces savings in tape costs but requires added costs for disks.

Revenue increases can be achieved through added processing capacity and the more efficient use of resources. For instance, a computer-based information system that can handle more customer orders each day and can process each order more speedily will help to create satisfied customers. These satisfied customers likely will give the firm their continued business; in time, others will learn of the high level of customer service and will also give the firm their business, thus increasing the firm's revenues. To take another example, computerized reservations systems have enabled the airlines to accommodate more passengers on a typical flight. Fuller flight loadings have a positive effect on airline revenues.

Tangible versus intangible benefits. A **tangible benefit** is a cost saving or revenue increase that is sufficiently "concrete" to be readily measurable in dollars. Certain of the examples provided earlier would reasonably be classified as tangible benefits. Displaced personnel cost savings can be measured by the salaries of the displaced persons; fuller flight loadings can be measured by the fares of the additionally accommodated passengers.

Intangible benefits, on the other hand, are those whose values are not easily measurable. A number of recognizable and significant benefits fall into this category, as Figure 24-6 shows. For instance, the increase in revenues stemming from speedy sales order processing (cited earlier) might be quite large. However, it is far from easy to estimate what proportion of added revenues stems from speedier order processing and what portion stems from the desirability of the products.

Approaches for Estimating Values

As the preceding comments suggest, estimating values can be difficult. How many dollars, for instance, is more relevant or more timely information worth to a decision maker? An answer to this question requires a knowledge of the likely payoff from each decision and the expected effectiveness with which the decision maker will employ the information.

Other factors also render estimation difficult. The rapid technological developments

Reduced input and processing errors

Better and more selective information for decision making

Improved control over managerial performance

More timely reporting to all managerial levels and geographical points

Greater capacity for converting data into information

Greater flexibility in responding to changes

Better product design and quality control

Improved logistical scheduling, leading to better use of personnel

Smoother operations, with fewer fluctuations, less overtime, and fewer materials shortages

Increased labor productivity

More efficient use of space

Better utilization of equipment

Up-to-date records and files

Increased cash flow

More-integrated and -standardized activities and operations

Fewer stock-outs of products (and hence fewer lost sales)

Faster billing of customers (and hence faster collections)

Higher level of customer service with respect to deliveries and answers to inquiries

Greater ability to compete and to locate potential customers

Simpler preparation of budgets and managerial reports

FIGURE 24-6 Intangible benefits attainable by information systems.

in computer hardware increase the uncertainty concerning the obsolescence of a newly installed computer-based information system. The integrated nature of an information system, especially one that employs a common data base, causes many costs and benefits to be jointly applicable to several applications; a reasonable basis of allocation to individual applications generally cannot be determined.

In spite of such difficulties, estimates of costs and benefits must be developed to the greatest extent possible; otherwise, management will be required to substitute considerable judgment for sound analytical procedures. For instance, if the intangible benefits related to improved managerial decision making are not estimated, at least roughly, management may make serious misjudgments. Thus, it might reject a high-cost system design in favor of a lower-cost design, even though the high-cost system could yield much greater long-term benefits. Data base system designs often can be justified only on the basis of intangible benefits; however, such benefits have "far outweighed the costs" in most firms that have installed such systems.[11]

Various approaches may be employed to estimate intangible benefits. For instance, rough estimates may be made concerning the value levels of the total intangible benefits, probabilities can be assigned to each level, and the expected values can be computed. A simpler approach avoids any attempt to quantify the intangible benefits. Instead, the net annual cost (total annual cost minus tangible benefits) is computed; then this net cost is compared to the intangible benefits. Consider the example of a system involving computer-integrated manufacturing.[12] Suppose that the net annual cost is $100,000. Management would then compare the intangible benefits (i.e., greater flexibility in making product changes, shorter production times, better customer service) against the $100,000. If management believes that the intangible benefits are likely to exceed $100,000, then it should judge the investment to be economically feasible.

[11]Gabrielle K. Wiorkowski and John J. Wiorkowski, "Does a Data Base Management System Pay Off?" *Datamation* (April 1978), p. 114.

[12]Robert S. Kaplan, "Must CIM Be Justified by Faith Alone?" *Harvard Business Review* (March–April 1986), pp. 87–95.

Economic Feasibility Computations

Data for example. A simplified example should clarify the use of economic feasibility models. The following data are available for Smalltime, Inc., a small firm that is considering the acquisition of a small computer system:

Purchase price of the hardware and software, together with systems development costs (i.e., the amount of the investment)	$45,000
Annual recurring operating costs of the present accounting information system	240,000
Expected annual recurring operating costs of the newly proposed computer system	220,000
Salvage value of the present data processing equipment (equal to its book value)	5,000
Expected salvage value of the computer hardware in four years	10,000
Expected salvage value of the software in four years	0
Expected economic life of the computer system if acquired	4 years
Required after-tax rate of return	14 percent

We will first compute the net present value while ignoring the effects of income taxes to simplify the computations. Then we will compute the net present value, benefit–cost ratio, and payback period, taking into account an assumed marginal income tax rate of 34 percent.

Net present value (taxes not included). Figure 24-7 shows the computations for the net present value model. (Note that the present value factors are found in the appendix to this chapter on page 1142.) The cash inflows are found to exceed the cash outflow, at present value, by $24,200. Since the cash inflows exceed the cash outflow, the investment can theoretically be viewed as economically feasible. However, since the income tax rate may not realistically be ignored, this computation is suspect.

One-time costs	($45,000)	
Less: salvage value of present equipment	5,000	
Net investment (cash outflow)		($40,000)
Annual operating costs, present system	$240,000	
Annual operating costs, proposed system	220,000	
Annual savings in operating costs	$ 20,000	
Total cost savings, at present value (PV):		
(PV of $20,000 for 4 years at 14% =		
$20,000 × 2.914)		58,280
Salvage value of proposed computer		
system at PV:		
(PV of $10,000 to be received in 4		
years = $10,000 × 0.592)		5,920
Total cash inflows, at PV		$64,200
Excess of returns at PV		$24,200

Note: Outflows are shown in parentheses.

FIGURE 24-7 Computations using the net present value model; the effects of income taxes are ignored.

Net present value (effects of taxes included). Figure 24-8 shows the revised computations for the net present value, with the effects of taxes taken into account. Now the cash inflows exceed the cash outflows, at present value, by only $13,054. Although the amount is smaller than computed previously, it represents a more valid solution.

The difference in the net present values is due to the effect of income taxes on the

Net investment (cash outflow)		($40,000)
Before-tax annual cost savings = $20,000		
After-tax annual cost savings: $20,000 × (1 − 0.34) =	$13,200	
Depreciation tax shield[a] =	2,975	
After-tax annual cash inflows	$16,175	
Total cost savings at present value (PV): (PV of $16,175		
for 4 years at 14% = $16,175 × 2.914)		47,134
Salvage value of proposed computer system at PV: (PV of		
$10,000 to be received in 4 years = $10,000 × 0.592)		5,920
Total cash inflows, at PV		$53,054
Excess of returns at PV		$13,054

$$^a \text{ Depreciation expense per year} = \frac{\$45,000 - \$10,000}{4} = \$8,750$$

Depreciation tax shield per year = depreciation expense × tax rate = $8,750 × 0.34 = $2,975

Note: Outflows are shown in parentheses.

FIGURE 24-8 Computations using the net present value method; the effects of income taxes are included.

savings in operating costs. Each year's after-tax savings drop from $20,000 to $16,175 when the marginal income tax is increased from 0 percent to 34 percent. In computing the savings, we have assumed that the entire net invested cost of $40,000 is depreciated over the four-year life of the computer equipment and that the straight-line method is employed. Thus, the depreciation tax shield each year is $2,975. The other amount making up the $16,175 is $13,200, which is determined by reducing the $20,000 by the amount of added taxes.

No other tax effects are reflected in Figure 24-8 for the following reasons:

1. Since the book value of the present data processing equipment equals its salvage value, no gain or loss exists on the disposal.

2. Since the salvage value of the proposed computer will be a return of capital, it is not taxable.

Benefit–cost ratio. To provide a basis for comparing the investment in a computer system against competing capital investments, we should compute the benefit–cost ratio by the formula

Benefit–cost ratio

$$= \frac{\text{Total present value of cash inflows}}{\text{Present value of net investment}}$$

$$\text{Benefit–cost ratio} = \frac{\$53,054}{\$40,000} = 1.33$$

Since the value of the ratio exceeds 1.00, the investment may be viewed as economically feasible.

Payback period. The payback period may be computed by the formula

Payback period

$$= \frac{\text{Net investment}}{\text{Annual after-tax cash inflow}}$$

$$\text{Payback period} = \frac{\$40,000}{\$16,175} = 2.47 \text{ years}$$

This result shows that the amount of the investment is expected to be recovered well before the end of its economic life. If it is desired to show the payback (payoff) trend more clearly, a **payoff analysis graph** may be prepared.

Difficulties in Justification

Justifying an information system design is often an extremely difficult task. The difficulties encountered in estimating costs and benefits were noted earlier. The other key factors, such as economic lives and required rates of return, are scarcely less difficult to estimate. Moreover, the computational techniques used in determining economic feasibility may be difficult to apply, especially when hardware and software are to be acquired in phases or when several alternative system designs are being compared.

Furthermore, difficult choices often must be made during the justification process. For example, what if a proposed information system design does not prove to be economically feasible, even though an improved computer-based information system seems to be clearly needed? In such a case it may be necessary to pursue one of the following avenues of recourse:

1. Omitting less critical but expensive features of the designed system in order to reduce costs more than benefits.[13]

2. Considering other options, such as acquiring a second-hand computer or obtaining computer capability from a commercial service, in order to reduce costs without significantly affecting benefits.

---

[13]Bankers Trust found that by omitting on-line access from tellers' terminals to customer files, it was able to transform an infeasible design into an economically feasible one. See Robert Chapman, "Facing Financial Realities in Banking," *Datamation* (June 1978), p. 153.

3. Increasing the scope of the system design: for example, adding such applications as inventory control and sales analysis to a sales order processing system design, in order to raise the level of expected benefits.

Part of the difficulty in justifying system designs can be traced to the decision makers. The higher-level managers who have the final decision responsibility often exhibit biases against the acquisition of computer systems. Because they likely have had no academic courses involving computers, such managers tend to minimize their value to the firm. Moreover, managers frequently demand relatively short payback periods and hence tend to reject certain investments that may otherwise be feasible.

Options for System Acquisition

The example involving Smalltime, Inc., tacitly assumed that the resources would be purchased from a computer equipment manufacturer. Other options are available, such as leasing the needed hardware and software or subscribing to a service that provides the needed hardware and software capabilities. Because of their importance, the major options will be surveyed and their relative advantages and disadvantages assessed.

Purchasing versus Leasing

Determining that a new or improved system is economically feasible does not settle the question of financing. It is still necessary to decide whether the resources are to be purchased or leased on a long-term financing contract. The decision is not obvious, since each choice offers one or more significant advantages. On the one hand, purchasing generally requires a smaller cash outlay in the long run. On the other hand, leasing requires a relatively small initial cash outlay, provides greater flexibility, lessens such

risks as equipment obsolescence, and in some cases provides added tax benefits.

In order to make a sound financing decision, such factors as the following should be considered:

1. Past experience with similar data processing equipment. For instance, a firm normally should not purchase its first computer, since it could make a serious, irreversible mistake through inexperience.

2. Expected economic life of the equipment. The longer a firm expects to use equipment such as a computer, the greater the difference between cash outlays for purchasing and for leasing. If a firm plans to retain a computer longer than about four years, it should carefully consider the purchase option.[14]

3. Life of a long-term financing lease contract. The expected length of a financing contract under the lease option also affects the financing decision. If the contract life is at least three years, the difference between the cash outlays for the two options (mentioned in item 2) is generally reduced. On the other hand, the risk of obsolescence is increased, since the lease contract cannot be canceled during its life.

4. Expected intensity of use. If a firm plans to use a new computer for two or three shifts, it will be inclined to purchase, since additional shift usage often involves higher leasing costs.

5. Availability of funds. If funds are not readily available or if interest rates are relatively high, the leasing option is likely to be preferred.[15]

6. Expected resale value of equipment (if purchased). The higher the expected re-

---

[14]Neil D. Kelley, "The Impact of Buying or Leasing," *Infosystems* (May 1980), p. 78.

[15]Ibid.

sale value, the more advantageous the purchase option.

A third financing option is renting. A rental contract, also called an operating lease contract, is similar to a financing lease contract, except that the former can be terminated on fairly short notice (usually 90 days). Because of this privilege, rental payments typically are higher than lease payments. Rental contracts also can be quite restrictive; for instance, they usually provide for extra charges when the hardware is used beyond a specified number of hours per month. Furthermore, they do not allow the using firm to apply payments toward the purchase of the hardware, whereas many lease contracts do provide this opportunity.

In-House System versus Outside Computing Service

It is not necessary that information system resources physically reside on a firm's premises. A firm may instead acquire computer capabilities from outside commercial computing services. To make intelligent choices between in-house systems and outside services, however, a firm's management needs to be aware of the spectrum of options available under each category.

In-house systems are provided by a variety of firms. Perhaps the best-known firms are the large general-purpose manufacturers such as IBM, Honeywell, Bull, Unisys, National Cash Register, and Control Data Corporation. However, the computer equipment field abounds with hundreds of smaller manufacturing and service firms having more-limited product lines.

These less well-known firms may roughly be classified as follows:

1. Small computer manufacturers that specialize in minicomputers, microcomputers, small accounting computers, process computers, and the like.
2. Peripheral equipment manufacturers that produce terminals, storage devices, optical scanners, voice-response systems, and so on.
3. Firms that produce business forms and supplies such as paper forms and magnetic tape.
4. Software product firms that provide packaged application programs, data base management systems, and other types of computer software.

Two types of nonmanufacturing firms also represent options when considering in-house systems. **Computer-leasing firms** acquire computer systems for leasing to user firms. Generally, their rates are below those charged by the manufacturers. **Used-computer brokers** bring sellers of used computers together with those firms that are in the market for used computers; in effect, they are agents and are paid fees for their services. Both of these types of firms help to make hardware more easily available to firms that perhaps cannot justify the higher prices charged by manufacturers.

Outside computing services are mainly provided by two types of firms: service bureaus and time-sharing utilities. A **service bureau** is a firm that provides batch data processing services at a remote location. A subscribing firm prepares the source data records, such as time cards and sales orders, and then transports these records to the site of the service bureau; when the desired outputs are prepared, they are returned to the subscriber's location. A **time-sharing service center,** also called an on-line computing services supplier, is a firm that provides batch or on-line data processing service through one or more on-line (remote job entry) terminals located on a subscriber's premises. The subscribing firm prepares the source data records and enters them via the terminals; after processing takes place within the center's computer system, the outputs are produced on the subscriber's terminals. Thus, the subscriber does not need to transport data, as is the case with a service bureau. Generally the subscribing firm's files are stored on-line within the center's computer system.

Both types of outside computing service firms provide their services to a wide variety of firms. Many of the subscribing firms are small. However, a number of subscribers are large firms that have their own in-house computers but also require supplemental computing capability. Subscribing firms include manufacturers, distributors, banks, hospitals, and laboratories.

Outside computing services offer several advantages.[16] Perhaps the most frequently cited advantage is economy. Computing service firms charge fees that are related to the extent of usage; thus, a subscriber pays only for what it uses. Many subscribers, especially smaller firms with fairly low transaction volumes, find an outside computing service cheaper than an owned or leased minicomputer. For instance, H. P. Hood, Inc., of Charlestown, Massachusetts, a producer of dairy products, finds that a time-sharing utility in Wellesley, Massachusetts, serves its data processing needs most economically.[17]

Another important reason for using an outside computing service is the availability of professional data processing and data base assistance, so that the subscriber does not need to hire professional systems personnel. Computing service firms provide generalized software packages for such applications as payroll and general ledger processing; most will also develop tailor-made application programs for a fee. In addition, a number of computing service firms are specialists in particular industries and business areas. For instance, one firm may specialize in the insurance and transportation industries, whereas another may specialize in engineering and scientific problem-solving services. Certain computing service firms also provide access to specialized data bases containing such data as financial trends economic statistics, and credit records.

More services are continually being added. For example, Automatic Data Processing, Inc. (ADP), provides microcomputers on subscribers' premises for use in processing transactions. It also provides information-based services such as real-time collision repair estimates for insurers and body shops. Andersen Consulting, a division of Arthur Andersen & Co., offers advice concerning the operation and management of subscribers' information systems.[18]

A third reason for using outside computing services is to obtain reliable added capacity or backup quickly, either (1) to handle new or peak processing loads or (2) to maintain normal processing loads during a system conversion or malfunction. Reputable outside computing services perform extensive maintenance on their systems in order to provide very reliable service.

Outside computing services do have disadvantages, however. Perhaps the most important disadvantage is the loss of control over transaction records and files, which *may* result in reduced data security. A subscribing firm cannot always be assured that adequate controls and security measures are being applied. An added disadvantage of a service bureau is a longer average turnaround time for job processing. Not only are outputs delayed, but vital files and data are inaccessible during the processing periods. Added disadvantages of a time-sharing service center are additional charges for (1) transmitting data to and from the remote service center and (2) providing the on-site terminals. Also, the variable cost of processing

[16]Herbert A. Seidman, "Remote Computing Service or In-House Computer?" *Datamation* (April 1978), p. 95.

[17]Jonathan Davis, "Hood Chooses MIS for Its Frogurt," *Management Accounting* (May 1979), pp. 38–41.

[18]Sidney Shepherd, "Up from Payroll: New Age for the Service Bureau," *Business Software Review* (March 1988), pp. 59–60.

each transaction is often higher than in the case of an in-house system. Thus, when transaction volumes are large, the in-house option is generally cheaper.

A third type of service firm, known as a **facilities management** firm, manages the in-house computer facilities of a subscribing firm for a fee. The main advantage provided by a facilities management firm is convenience. As in the case of the other types of service firms, it minimizes the need for an information systems function in the subscribing firm. It also brings into the firm professionals who have data processing experience and knowledge. On the other hand, the facilities management option puts control of the information into the hands of outsiders. Consequently, conflicts often arise between representatives of the outside firm and the subscribing firm's management. Thus, this option should normally be considered only when a firm "has a serious need and there doesn't seem to be any other way. You don't know how to solve your data processing problems and it's occupying a major portion of a management's time."[19]

Facilities management can apply to the communications network as well as (or instead of) the computer hardware. For instance, H. J. Heinz Co. recently signed a three-year contract with Genix Corporation, a facility management firm, to operate its computer network and its data processing operations. This move allows Heinz to dispense with a communications group in its information systems function.[20]

Single versus Multiple Suppliers

When selecting resources for a new or improved information system, a firm might decide on a single supplier. Alternatively, it might decide to obtain the computer itself from one supplier, the peripheral equipment from a second supplier, and the computer software from a third supplier. The latter alternative has both advantages and disadvantages.

Employing multiple suppliers often results in initial cost savings. A firm can compare costs and pick each item with the lowest price tag. By choosing multiple suppliers it also serves notice that it is not "locked in" to one supplier. Thus, the firm can reasonably expect solicitous attention and service from competing suppliers who hope to be selected in the future.

Two major drawbacks attend the use of multiple suppliers, however. The first is the inconvenience of multiple dealings. Multiple contracts must be drawn and signed, for instance. A second disadvantage is the possibility that long-term costs will be greater. Extensive modifications and relatively frequent maintenance, for instance, may be needed if the hardware items from different manufacturers are not fully compatible.

Large versus Small Computers

Another consideration is whether to acquire large computers or small computers to achieve a required level of computing capacity. Although this is in part a design problem, it is significantly affected by economics.

To visualize the problem, assume that two alternative system designs have been developed: a distributed processing design and a centralized processing design. On the basis of a painstaking feasibility study, both alternatives have been shown to be economically feasible when compared to the present system. Which design is preferable? The answer depends on the relative cost levels of the alternative designs as well as on key noneconomic factors. The distributed processing design, involving the use of small, dispersed computers, is likely to be less costly when a firm has a number of geographically scat-

[19]Steven Stibbens, "Facilities Management: A Difficult Business to Manage," *Infosystems* (Jan. 1979), p. 56.

[20]Susan Kerr, "Cutting through Network Control," *Datamation* (October 15, 1989), pp. 30–32.

APPLICATION OF SOFTWARE DEVELOPMENT
Aetna Life & Casualty[a]

A growing number of firms have tired of waiting for software vendors to develop software application packages that meet their particular needs. Thus, certain larger user firms have decided to develop their own custom packages. The Investment Management Group within Aetna Life & Casualty of Hartford, Connecticut, recently decided to follow such a course. It is currently developing a new investment management and accounting system, in order to process its transactions more efficiently. The resulting program, named Aetna Distributed Assets Management (ADAM), will be designed for the securities environment of the 1990s. The package will have two functions: (1) securities accounting and (2) portfolio management. The stakes are rather high, since the group manages $75 billion in assets for the firm and outside investors and processes more than $500 billion worth of transactions each year.

A software development of this size is imposing even to a large insurance firm. To ensure that the software package will be sound, Aetna has hired Andersen Consulting and Digital Equipment Corp. to provide consulting assistance. To recoup part of its software development costs, the firm has contracted with Andersen Consulting to market the software package to other insurance firms and financial institutions. Andersen Consulting was selected partly because it specializes in insurance practices (as well as in numerous other areas) and because of its worldwide operations. Also, Andersen has agreed to develop all future upgrades of the package.

[a]Leila Davis, "Initiating Systems Projects," *Datamation* (October 15, 1989), pp. 81–82.

---

tered sites at which processing results are needed. Processing of data on small computers at the various sites can lead to data communications cost savings. On the other hand, the centralized processing design very likely will be less costly in a firm in which numerous users are grouped within a single or a few major locations.[21] Moreover, if the firm intends to make use of financial planning models and large data base management systems, these can be better accommodated at present by large computers.

General versus Custom Software

A growing number of software service firms are producing a vast array of software packages. These packages of "canned software products" range from application programs to operating systems and data base management systems.

Two questions arise when a firm is considering the acquisition of software resources for a new or improved information system:

1. Should a software package be purchased from a software products firm or some other outside supplier, such as a general-purpose computer manufacturer, or should the software be written by the firm's own programmers?

2. If a software package is to be acquired, should it be a general package written for use by a large number of users, or should it be a custom package tailored expressly for the use of the firm in question?

General software packages are less expensive initially, and they tend to reduce the time needed to put them into operation. However, extensive modifications may be required to adapt them to a firm's particular features. In-house programs and custom packages generally perform tasks more effi-

[21]Kenneth M. Sullivan, "Does Distributed Processing Pay Off?" *Datamation* (Sept. 1980), pp. 192–196.

ciently than general software packages. Moreover, in-house programs can be more easily modified as demands change.

When the hardware as well as the software is packaged, the resulting system is known as a **turnkey system.** All the acquiring firm needs to do is "turn the key" to start the system operating.

Techniques of System Evaluation

When proposals are received from several suppliers, not all can be accepted. How can the respective proposals be soundly evaluated? The first step is to check each proposal carefully for offered capabilities and features. If a proposal responds satisfactorily to each specified requirement, it will have passed its initial screening. At this point, the proposed hardware or software can be viewed as being technically feasible.

Evaluation must extend well beyond this initial screening, however, since no single proposal will likely be superior in every respect. For instance, one proposal may offer hardware having the fastest processing speed, another the lowest cost, and a third the greatest after-sale service and support. Thus, the application of several evaluation techniques is usually necessary. Three commonly employed evaluation techniques are the benchmark problem, the simulation model, and the weighted-rating analysis.

Benchmark problem. Hardware or software performance can be evaluated by means of **benchmark problems.** These problems usually represent typical batch processing applications or system functions. For instance, a problem might consist of updating the inventory master file to reflect receipts and issues of materials.

If a hardware benchmark is specified, the prepared benchmark problem, such as an inventory updating program, would be run on each of the computer systems being eval-

uated. The times required to process a test data set on the respective computer systems would be compared; the computer system having the lowest time would "win" the benchmark test.

If a software benchmark is specified, the various competing software packages would be run on the same computer system. Thus, two operating systems might be tested on the firm's present computer system or on a computer system that it plans to acquire.

Benchmark problems can be useful in showing how well proposed hardware or software can be expected to perform in typical circumstances. Their results can also provide the basis for developing cost–performance ratios, a useful measure. Assume, for example, that computer system B requires twice as much time to perform a benchmark task as computer system A. Computer system A can therefore be said to have a performance value of 2, whereas computer system B has a performance value of 1. If the cost of computer system A is $1 million, and the cost of computer system B is $0.6 million, their cost–performance ratios per million dollars of investment are 2.00 and 1.67, respectively.

The benchmark problem, however, is a limited evaluation technique. It does not accurately reflect the overall performance of hardware, since the work load of a computer system normally consists of a variety of applications. It also ignores certain factors that are critical to the success of a new system, such as the level of support provided by a supplier.

Simulation model. A second evaluation technique involves the simulation of a mathematical model. The first step in applying this technique is to build a model of the proposed computer system. Included in the model would be descriptions of the processing steps, transaction volumes, files, output volumes, and such equipment features as access methods and storage capacities. Then the model is "stepped through" the processing activities that the proposed system will be required to handle, and various operating results are measured. These results likely will include access times, response times, run times, throughputs, equipment utilization percentages, and cost levels.

The simulation model, therefore, provides a wide variety of data by which to evaluate a proposed system design. It is particularly useful in evaluating real-time system designs. For instance, by using a model of a real-time system involving a network of remote sites, the systems analysts can observe the effects of expected peak transaction volumes on response times. Consequently, they can ascertain the number and type of needed data communications lines.

The simulation model technique has four disadvantages: (1) It is expensive to apply, (2) its results are difficult for management to absorb, (3) the validity of its results is subject to question, and (4) it ignores nonquantifiable and subjective factors that may be critical to the success of a new system. These disadvantages can be overcome to some extent, however. A firm can employ a simulation model package such as **SCERT** (Systems and Computers Evaluation and Review Technique) to reduce the cost of building and executing a model. To overcome the problem of validity, the firm can first build a model of the existing processing system and then compare its results with the actual results achieved by the present system.

It should be recognized, though, that the disadvantages just cited render the simulation model technique unsuitable in many situations. Therefore, it is used less frequently than the third evaluation technique, the weighted-rating analysis.

Weighted-rating analysis. A **weighted-rating analysis** provides the means of incorporating relevant factors not evaluated by other techniques. Applying this technique involves the construction of a table such as the one

shown in Figure 24-9. The table arrays all factors considered relevant to the selection of system resources.

As Figure 24-9 suggests, these factors include not only those pertaining to hardware and/or software but also those pertaining to the support by a supplier of the system resources that it provides. System support can be a very important consideration, since a firm that acquires hardware and software is also acquiring a long-term relationship with a supplier.

Let us examine more closely the construction of the table shown in Figure 24-9. In essence it contains a comparative evaluation of proposals from A and B, two prospective suppliers of hardware and software required by a system design. (Proposals from additional suppliers could be included, if desired.) On the basis of the best available information or judgment of the evaluators, raw scores are listed in the suppliers' columns for all of the relevant factors. (A raw score of 5 is excellent; a raw score of 1 is poor.) For instance, scores for hardware performance may be based upon the results of the benchmark tests; scores for a factor such as hardware **modularity** (the ease with which hardware capacity can be expanded to accommodate future growth) may be based on discussions with other firms that currently use each supplier's hardware.

Weighted scores are next computed. To find these weighted scores, the evaluators must first specify the weights for the respective factors; that is, a total of 100 points must be distributed to the factors according to the relative significance of each. Each factor weight is then multiplied by the raw scores for the two suppliers to determine the weighted scores for that factor. For instance, the weight of 10 points assigned to hardware performance is multiplied by supplier A's raw score of 5 and by supplier B's raw score of 3, to obtain weighted scores of 50 and 30, respectively.

Finally, all of the weighted scores for

Factor	Weight	A's Proposal		B's Proposal	
		Raw score	Weighted score	Raw score	Weighted score
Hardware					
Performance (e.g., response time)	10	5	50	3	30
Compatibility with existing hardware and software	10	4	40	3	30
Modularity	5	3	15	4	20
Reliability	5	4	20	5	25
Ability to deliver on schedule	5	2	10	5	25
Special features (e.g., control features, security packages)	5	5	25	3	15
Hardware subtotals	40		160		145
Software					
Range of capabilities	10	3	30	4	40
Efficiency in use	8	5	40	3	24
Ease in making changes	7	4	28	3	21
Advanced features (e.g., firmware)	5	5	25	2	10
Software subtotals	30		123		95
Support					
Assistance, training, and documentation	5	2	10	5	25
Test arrangements	5	3	15	4	20
Backup facilities	5	3	15	5	25
Maintenance and service	7	3	21	5	35
Reputation, experience, and financial condition	8	3	24	5	40
Support subtotals	30		85		145
Totals	100		368		385

FIGURE 24-9   A weighted-rating table for hardware and software selection.

each supplier are totaled. In Figure 24-9 the total weighted scores of the proposals from suppliers A and B are 368 and 385 points, respectively. Thus, this technique indicates that the proposal from supplier B is slightly preferable to the proposal from supplier A.

Weighted-rating analysis offers significant advantages. It provides a structured means of including intangible but important factors in the evaluation process. The technique is also widely applicable. It may be used to evaluate software packages as well as hardware products and combined computer systems. For instance, it is suited to the evaluation of data base management systems and operating systems.

The technique is often difficult to apply, however. It requires the evaluators to make a series of subjective judgments. The weights for the various factors must be assigned, and then the points for each alternative must be estimated. Although outside assistance is available, from consultants or such services as Datapro Research Corporation, the evaluators must make the final choices. Another difficulty is that differences in total point values (as in Figure 24-9) are often quite narrow. In such cases other techniques must provide the discrimination among proposals.

Conclusion. All of the three evaluation techniques discussed can contribute to the final selection of system resources. However, none of the three can usually be relied on alone. An ideal technique would be one that incorporates the three techniques into a single methodology, so that an overall index can be computed for each competing proposal. A methodology that meets this requirement is known as requirements costing.[22] A discussion of this methodology is beyond the scope of this book; however, we can gain a glimpse of its usefulness by making a simple computation.

Assume in the example given above that the total costs for the hardware and software of suppliers A and B have been quoted as $1 million and $1.1 million respectively. Then an overall index, based on the totals listed in Figure 24-9, can be computed as follows:

$$\text{Index for supplier A: } \frac{368}{\$1,000,000}$$

$$= 0.368 \text{ per } \$1000$$

$$\text{Index for supplier B: } \frac{385}{\$1,100,000}$$

$$= 0.350 \text{ per } \$1000$$

Thus, the proposal from supplier A appears to provide greater value for the required cost than does the proposal from supplier B.

Summary

A newly designed system must be justified, and the resources to make it operational must be selected and acquired. Systems justification and selection—which normally follow closely upon the specification of the system design—consist of determining that a design is feasible, circulating resource specifications among prospective suppliers, evaluating proposals from responding suppliers, and selecting the most suitable system resources.

Feasibility pertains to technical capability, operational acceptability, and economic value. Although all three types of feasibility are important, economic feasibility is a central concern of management. The information generated by an information system should provide benefits at least equal to the cost required to generate the information. Thus, a proposed investment in an information system can be viewed as economically feasible if the benefits derived from the investment exceed the cost of the investment. Various criteria may be employed to ascertain economic feasibility, including the net present value of cash flows, the payback period, cost-effectiveness, and the benefit–cost ratio. Costs used to determine economic feasibility include one-time costs and recurring costs; benefits include cost savings, revenue increases, and various intangible benefits. Both costs and benefits must be estimated; often this is a difficult task. Feasibility computations preferably employ the discounted cash flow method, although the payback period method also provides useful information. If economic feasibility is not proven, it may be necessary to revise the system design, to defer the project, or to take other actions.

Selecting the needed resources, such as computer hardware and software, requires that resource requirements be specified carefully and fully. Sound selection procedures also dictate that all feasible options be considered. Acquisition options include purchasing the resources, leasing the resources, and subscribing to outside computing services such as service bureaus and time-sharing service centers. Other options include obtaining the resources from a single supplier or several suppliers, acquiring small computers or large computers, and acquiring

[22]For an extensive description of the requirements costing methodology, see Edward O. Joslin, *Computer Selection* (Reading, Mass.: Addison-Wesley, 1968).

general packaged software or customized software.

When proposals are received from prospective suppliers, various techniques may be employed in their evaluation. One technique is to prepare and run a benchmark problem. Another is to examine the proposed systems by means of a simulation model. A third technique is to compare alternative proposals by means of weighted ratings of relevant factors. Two or more of these techniques may be needed to evaluate satisfactorily the resources required by certain system designs.

APPENDIX TO CHAPTER 24

Present Value Tables

TABLE 1 Present Value of $1

Years	5%	6%	8%	10%	12%	14%	15%	16%	18%	20%	22%	24%	25%
1	0.952	0.943	0.926	0.909	0.893	0.877	0.870	0.862	0.847	0.833	0.820	0.806	0.800
2	0.907	0.890	0.857	0.826	0.797	0.769	0.756	0.743	0.718	0.694	0.672	0.650	0.640
3	0.864	0.840	0.794	0.751	0.712	0.675	0.658	0.641	0.609	0.579	0.551	0.524	0.512
4	0.823	0.792	0.735	0.683	0.636	0.592	0.572	0.552	0.516	0.482	0.451	0.423	0.410
5	0.784	0.747	0.681	0.621	0.567	0.519	0.497	0.476	0.437	0.402	0.370	0.341	0.328
6	0.746	0.705	0.630	0.564	0.507	0.456	0.432	0.410	0.370	0.335	0.303	0.275	0.262
7	0.711	0.665	0.583	0.513	0.452	0.400	0.376	0.354	0.314	0.279	0.249	0.222	0.210
8	0.677	0.627	0.540	0.467	0.404	0.351	0.327	0.305	0.266	0.233	0.204	0.179	0.168
9	0.645	0.592	0.500	0.424	0.361	0.308	0.284	0.263	0.225	0.194	0.167	0.144	0.134
10	0.614	0.558	0.463	0.386	0.322	0.270	0.247	0.227	0.191	0.162	0.137	0.116	0.107

TABLE 2 Present Value of $1 Received Annually for N Years

Years (N)	5%	6%	8%	10%	12%	14%	15%	16%	18%	20%	22%	24%	25%
1	0.952	0.943	0.926	0.909	0.893	0.877	0.870	0.862	0.847	0.833	0.820	0.806	0.800
2	1.859	1.833	1.783	1.736	1.690	1.647	1.626	1.605	1.566	1.528	1.492	1.457	1:440
3	2.723	2.673	2.577	2.487	2.402	2.322	2.283	2.246	2.174	2.106	2.042	1.981	1.952
4	3.546	3.465	3.312	3.169	3.037	2.914	2.855	2.798	2.690	2.589	2.494	2.404	2.362
5	4.330	4.212	3.993	3.791	3.605	3.433	3.352	3.274	3.127	2.991	2.864	2.745	2.689
6	5.076	4.917	4.623	4.355	4.111	3.889	3.784	3.685	3.498	3.326	3.167	3.020	2.951
7	5.786	5.582	5.206	4.868	4.564	4.288	4.160	4.039	3.812	3.605	3.416	3.242	3.161
8	6.463	6.210	5.747	5.335	4.968	4.639	4.487	4.344	4.078	3.837	3.619	3.421	3.329
9	7.108	6.802	6.247	5.759	5.328	4.946	4.772	4.607	4.303	4.031	3.786	3.566	3.463
10	7.722	7.360	6.710	6.145	5.650	5.216	5.019	4.833	4.494	4.192	3.923	3.682	3.571

Review Problem with Solution

Statement

The Adams Transportation Company, a medium-sized bus line of Durham, North Carolina, utilizes a manual information system in the conduct of such basic operations as scheduling bus lines, selling tickets, purchasing supplies, and paying drivers and other employees. However, the firm's management recognizes the need for a revised information system. Upon being assigned the task, the firm's systems analyst designs a new computer-based information system. He then asks the chief accountant to aid him in determining that the newly designed system is economically feasible. The chief accountant suggests that they employ three criteria: net present value, benefit–cost ratio, and payback period.

To apply these criteria, they first gather data concerning the expected costs and benefits. Then they investigate the experiences of other firms to determine a reasonable economic life. On the basis of the composite experiences of several firms, they estimate the economic life for both hardware and software to be five years.

	Year 0	Year 1	Year 2	Year 3	Year 4	Year 5	Total
One-time costs							
System design	$90,000						$90,000
System installation and conversion	80,000						80,000
System site preparation	30,000						30,000
System hardware	400,000						400,000
System software and services	300,000						300,000
Total investment	$900,000						$900,000
Recurring costs—proposed system							
Data preparation and handling		$50,000	$55,000	$65,000	$75,000	$80,000	$325,000
Operations		60,000	70,000	80,000	100,000	120,000	430,000
Maintenance, facility and system		70,000	75,000	85,000	100,000	130,000	460,000
Administration and control		20,000	20,000	20,000	25,000	30,000	115,000
Total costs		$200,000	$220,000	$250,000	$300,000	$360,000	$1,330,000
Recurring costs—present system							
Data preparation		$150,000	$160,000	$170,000	$180,000	$190,000	$850,000
Operations, clerical		280,000	300,000	340,000	375,000	420,000	1,715,000
Maintenance, system		50,000	60,000	70,000	80,000	90,000	350,000
Administration		20,000	20,000	20,000	25,000	30,000	115,000
Total costs		$500,000	$540,000	$600,000	$660,000	$730,000	$3,030,000
Savings in recurring costs		$300,000	$320,000	$350,000	$360,000	$370,000	$1,700,000
Benefits of proposed system							
Profits from added sales		$90,000	$90,000	$90,000	$140,000	$140,000	$550,000
Savings from reduced inventory investment		10,000	10,000	10,000	10,000	10,000	50,000
Total other benefits		$100,000	$100,000	$100,000	$150,000	$150,000	$600,000
Added cash inflows resulting from proposed system		$400,000	$420,000	$450,000	$510,000	$520,000	$2,300,000

At this point they are able to prepare the table on page 1143, which contains relevant data and computations over a five-year horizon. The first set of costs, the one-time costs, are all incurred at the time when the new system is first installed (year zero). The next two sets of costs are the expected recurring operating costs for the present manual system and for the proposed computer-based system. The difference between these two recurring-cost sets represents the differential costs, or cost savings, resulting from reduced operating costs. Most of these cost savings are due to reduced clerical salaries. The final set in the table consists of two additional benefits expected from the proposed system: added contribution margins from added sales and savings resulting from reduced investments in inventory. In year 1, for instance, the added sales are expected to be $300,000 and the reduction in inventory investment to be $100,000. If the contribution margin is 30 percent and the carrying cost percentage per dollar of investment is 10 percent, the amounts of the benefits are $90,000 and $10,000, respectively.

The bottom line in the table reflects the total year-by-year inflows to be expected from the change to the computer-based information system. Each total amount is the sum of the recurring cost savings and other benefits. The amounts are larger in succeeding years because of the expected growth in the firm's operations and hence the ever-greater advantage of a computer-based system.

Other data needed in the economic feasibility computations are determined by consultation with the president and treasurer. These data are (1) the rate of return required to cover the cost of capital and to compensate for the uncertainty of attaining estimating benefits, 16 percent; (2) the marginal income tax rate, 34 percent, (3) the salvage value of presently owned systems resources, as well as the salvage value of the hardware and software to be acquired, zero dollars.

Required

a. Compute the net present value of the proposed investment.

b. Compute the benefit–cost ratio of the proposed investment.

c. Compute the payback period of the proposed investment.

d. Prepare a payoff analysis graph of the proposed investment.

Solution

a. The computations needed to determine the net present value are shown in the table on page 1145. They begin with the values from the bottom line of the previous table, which are arrayed in the second column. Then they consist of the following steps:

(1) Computing the amount of the added income tax due to the added cash flow generated by the investment. For year 1 this amount will be

$$\$400,000 \times 0.34 = \$136,000$$

(2) Computing the amount of the depreciation expense on the investment, assuming that the straight-line method is to be used. For each year the amount will be

$$\$900,000 \times \frac{1}{5} = \$180,000$$

(3) Computing the amount of the tax saving which is due to depreciation expense. For each year this amount will be

$$\$180,000 \times 0.34 = \$61,220$$

(4) Computing the net amount of added income tax, represented by the difference between the added income tax

Year	Cash Inflow (from previous table)	Depreciation Expense	Net Added Income Tax	After-tax Cash Inflow	Decimal Equivalent of Discount Factor	Present Value of After-tax Cash Inflow
1	$400,000	$180,000	$136,000	$325,200	0.862	$280,322
2	420,000	180,000	142,800	338,400	0.743	251,143
3	450,000	180,000	153,000	358,200	0.641	229,606
4	510,000	180,000	173,400	397,800	0.552	219,586
5	520,000	80,000	176,800	404,400	0.476	192,494
	Total present value of cash inflows					$1,173,151

Expected economic life = 5 years.
Required rate of return = 16 percent.
Depreciation based on straight-line method.

caused by a greater cash flow generated by the investment (from step 1) and the tax saving stemming from the depreciation tax "shield" (from step 3). For year 1 this amount will be

$136,000 − $61,200 = $74,800

(5) Computing the amount of the after-tax cash inflow, represented by the difference between the cash inflow resulting from the investment (from the table) and the net amount of added income tax (from step 4). For year 1 this amount will be

$400,000 − $74,800 = $325,200

(6) Computing the present value of the after-tax cash inflow. For year 1 this amount will be

$325,200 × 0.862 = $280,322

(7) Computing the total present value of after-tax cash inflows over the economic life of the investment. This amount is $1,173,151. From the last computation it follows that the net present value is

$1,173,151 − $900,000 = $273,151

Thus, the investment in the new computer-based information system appears to be economically feasible.

b.

$$\text{Benefit–cost ratio} = \frac{\text{Total present value of cash inflows}}{\text{Present value of investment}}$$

$$\text{Benefit–cost ratio} = \frac{\$1,173,151}{\$900,000} = 1.30$$

c. The payback period is based on the comparison of after-tax cash inflows, listed in the fifth column of the table shown above, with the investment amount of $900,000. Its value is somewhat less than three years, since

($325,200 + $338,400 + $358,200) = $1,021,800.

d. A payoff analysis graph appears on page 1146. It shows an initial negative cash flow of $900,000 but an accumulated net positive flow after five years of $924,000. (This net flow is computed algebraically by adding all flows as follows: $325,200 + $338,400 + $358,200 + $397,800 + $404,400 − $900,000.)

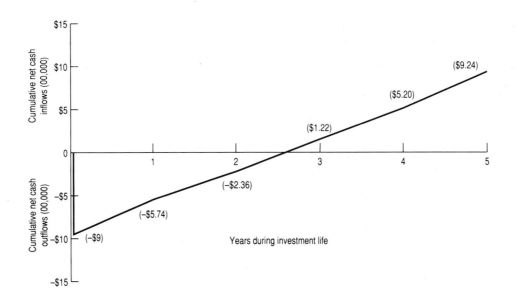

Review Questions

24-1 What is the meaning of each of the following terms?

Feasibility
Feasibility study
Resource specification
Request for proposal
Feasibility report
Information economics
Net present value
Payback period
Cost-effectiveness
Benefit–cost ratio
One-time cost
Recurring cost
Cost saving
Revenue increase
Tangible benefit
Intangible benefit
Payoff analysis graph
Computer-leasing firm
Used-computer broker
Service bureau
Time-sharing service center
Facilities management
Turnkey system
Benchmark problem
SCERT
Weighted-rating analysis
Modularity

24-2 Distinguish among the three types of feasibility.

24-3 Discuss the steps involved in the systems justification and selection phase.

24-4 Describe the content of resource specifications.

24-5 What are management's options upon receiving a final feasibility report?

24-6 Discuss the pertinence of information economics to the design of information systems.

24-7 Identify four possible criteria for evaluating economic feasibility.

24-8 Identify the major one-time costs pertaining to new or improved computer-based information systems.

24-9 Identify several recurring costs pertaining to new or improved computer-based information systems.

24-10 Contrast cost savings and revenue increases related to computer-based information systems.

24-11 Contrast tangible and intangible benefits related to computer-based information systems.

24-12 Describe the factors and steps involved in determining the economic feasibility of system resources by means of the discounted cash flow approach.

24-13 What are several approaches by which estimation difficulties can be minimized or circumvented?

24-14 What may be done if a system design cannot be shown to be economically feasible?

24-15 What factors should be considered in deciding whether to purchase or to lease the resources relating to a new or improved computer-based information system?

24-16 How does renting differ from leasing?

24-17 What types of firms are available from which computer hardware or software may be acquired?

24-18 Contrast the services provided by a service bureau and a time-sharing service center.

24-19 What are the advantages and disadvantages of obtaining computer services from an outside computing services firm?

24-20 What are the advantages and disadvantages of obtaining needed resources from more than one supplier?

24-21 Contrast the conditions under which small distributed computers are preferable to large-scale centralized computers, and vice versa.

24-22 What questions should be weighed when considering the use of general software or custom software?

24-23 Contrast the three evaluation techniques, including their relative advantages and disadvantages.

24-24 Describe several features that may be included under the category of "systems support provided" when evaluating the proposals of suppliers.

Discussion Questions

24-25 Discuss the respective contributions that a systems analyst and an accountant can make in the procedure that determines whether or not an information system design is feasible, as well as the desirability of having them closely coordinate their efforts during the procedure.

24-26 Describe the similarities and differences (if any) in (a) the procedure for determining that a proposed computer-based information system is economically feasible and (b) the procedure for determining that a proposed turret lathe for the production function is economically feasible.

24-27 How may the discounted cash flow model be best applied when two or more new alternative system designs are to be examined for economic feasibility?

Hint: Remember that retaining the present information system is one of the alternatives being considered during the application of the discounted cash flow model.

24-28 Discuss various intangible costs as well as benefits that management must weigh when determining whether or not a proposed information system design is economically feasible.

24-29 According to the procedure described in this chapter, a proposed information system design is first determined to be economically feasible and *then* the resources (e.g., computer hardware and software) are selected. Should this sequence be reversed, so that the resource costs are precisely known when feasibility computations are made?

24-30 In what ways may information gain value?

24-31 How does the concept of the value of information influence the design of an information system?

24-32 Information value can be estimated in some situations. Consider the situation in which certain information that completely eliminates the uncertainty concerning future conditions becomes available. How can the value of this "perfect information" be established?

24-33 Describe several methods by which the risks and uncertainties related to a proposed information system design may be accommodated during the application of the discounted cash flow model.

24-34 Discuss (1) benefits to be derived from and (2) costs associated with each of the following reports:

    a. Sales forecast.
    b. Exception report to a production department manager concerning exceptional costs incurred on specified job orders.
    c. Cash flow projection.
    d. Income statement.

24-35 Contrast the intangible benefits that can be expected from an improved purchases transaction processing system with those to be expected from a budgetary control system.

24-36 How can the benefits from reducing a clerical work force, as provided by a new computer-based processing system, be compared with the cost of fearful and less-productive clerks who know they may be released?

24-37 Assume that a firm proposes to install the facilities for a new computer-based information system in several rooms of its home office which are vacant and have no other foreseeable use. How much should be charged for the space occupied by the new system in the feasibility computations, if this space represents $\frac{1}{100}$ of the overall usable space in the home office building and the annual depreciation on the building is $100,000?

24-38 Discuss the trade-offs involved in evaluating each of the following proposals:

    a. To incorporate an additional internal accounting control in the sales transaction procedure.
    b. To provide direct access, via audio response, to depositors who desire to check the current balances in their accounts.
    c. To replace a magnetic tape drive with a magnetic disk drive.
    d. To split the present sales account into several sales accounts subdivided according to product lines.
    e. To install in the main factory a new-model minicomputer that can perform calculations significantly faster than the present minicomputer.

24-39 Discuss the advantages and disadvantages of hiring an outside consultant to help evaluate proposed hardware, rather than accepting the advice of a sales representative of a computer hardware manufacturer.

24-40 In what respects is the acquisition of software similar to a make-or-buy decision concerning key subassemblies?

24-41 What criteria should apply to the selection of decision support software?

24-42 Assume that a sales representative describes a new OCR input device that is superior to any other input device on the market. Discuss the steps that you would take to evaluate the possibility of installing this device as a part of your information system. Currently, you employ key-to-tape input devices exclusively.

24-43 Describe one situation in which each

of the following alternatives would be appropriate for a specific firm:

- a. Owner of minicomputers located at all remote sites.
- b. Owner of a single large computer located at the home office.
- c. Subscriber to a service bureau.
- d. Subscriber to a time-sharing service center.
- e. Subscriber to a facilities management firm.

Problems

Note: When necessary for solving the following problems, refer to present value tables on page 1142.

24-1 The Pence Company of Ellensburg, Washington, a local grower and distributor of produce, is investigating the economic feasibility of acquiring a small computer system to aid in processing transactions and providing information for managers. It has gathered the following data:

Purchase price of hardware and software	$85,000
Other one-time costs, such as costs pertaining to design and implementation	$40,000
Annual savings in operating costs	$38,000
Salvage value of the computer system in five years	$22,000
Salvage value of presently owned processing devices	$0
Expected economic life of the computer system	5 years
Required after-tax rate of return	18 percent

Required

- a. Compute the net present value of the returns from the proposed investment in the computer system, ignoring the effects of taxes.
- b. Compute the payback period, ignoring the effects of taxes.
- c. Compute the benefit–cost ratio, ignoring the effects of taxes.
- d. Compute the net present value of the after-tax returns, assuming that (1) the marginal income tax rate is 34 percent, (2) all one-time costs are depreciated over the economic life according to the straight-line method, and (3) the book value of the presently owned processing devices is zero.
- e. Compute the payback period under the assumptions stated in **d**.
- f. Compute the benefit–cost ratio under the assumptions stated in **d**.
- g. Evaluate the economic feasibility of the proposed investment in the computer system, based on the results obtained in the preceding parts.

24-2 Newton Enterprises of Morgantown, West Virginia, is considering the installation of a new-model computer-based processing system to replace the various accounting machines and earlier-model computer equipment presently used for processing. The purchase price of the computer hardware and software is expected to total $475,000, with an additional $100,000 required for the analysis, design, and implementation of the new system. The new system is expected to have a five-year economic life, at the end of which the resale value of the computer hardware is estimated to be $50,000.

Annual operating and maintenance costs for the present manual information system have averaged $370,000 over the past two years and are not expected to change in the foreseeable future. By contrast, the operating costs of the proposed computer-based system, if installed, would not be expected to exceed $170,000 in each of the first two years and $120,000 in each of the last three years. In addition, maintenance expenses are expected to average $30,000 per year over the life of the system.

Management has specified that at least a 16 percent rate of return (after income taxes) must be earned on all investments. The presently owned processing equipment can be sold for $25,000, its book value.

Required

a. Compute the net present value of the returns from the proposed investment in the computer-based processing system, ignoring the effects of taxes.

b. Compute the payback period, ignoring the effects of taxes.

c. Compute the benefit–cost ratio, ignoring the effects of taxes.

d. Compute the net present value of the after-tax returns, assuming that (1) the marginal income tax rate is 34 percent, and (2) all one-time costs are depreciated over the economic life according to the straight-line method.

e. Compute the payback period under the assumptions stated in **d**.

f. Compute the benefit–cost ratio under the assumptions stated in **d**.

g. Evaluate the economic feasibility of the proposed investment in the computer-based processing system, based on the results obtained in the foregoing parts.

 24-3 The I. M. Reliable Company of Hamilton, Ontario, sells bicycles through various retail outlets and handles its own parts inventory in one large warehouse. Annual company sales exceed $3 million, with daily savings averaging more than $15,000. The company has experienced a recent overall growth of 5 percent and is projecting an annual growth of 10 percent.

The existing computer system for handling inventory is tape oriented. It is being taxed to the limit of its capacity. Management believes that conversion to a modernized computer-based inventory control system will provide greater flexibility, speed, and continued growth potential. As a result, management authorizes a feasibility study.

As the analyst doing the study, you obtain data concerning the costs of the present system and projected costs for two new alternative systems, called A and B. (See the tables on page 1151.)

Additional gathered data indicate that alternative A will provide for an eventual growth greater than the 10 percent projection and would take 21 months to implement. Moreover, this alternative will provide updated status reports, automatic invoicing, and preprinted customer statements.

Alternative B will provide for the projected 10 percent growth only and requires redesigning if further growth is to be accommodated. Although this alternative will meet the basic requirements of the company, it will not allow interrelation of the various programs; that is, the output of one program cannot be used as input to another program.

Required

a. Compute the annual savings and the net cumulative annual savings of each alternative as compared with the costs of the current system.

b. Draw a payoff analysis chart comparing the costs and savings for each of the alternatives to the existing system.

c. Which alternative would you recommend

Current Costs

Type of Cost	Year 1	Year 2	Year 3	Year 4	Year 5
Personnel	$42,000	$55,000	$68,000	$80,000	$100,000
Equipment rentals	30,000	34,000	38,000	42,000	45,000
Supplies	20,000	22,000	24,000	26,000	28,000
Overhead	18,000	20,000	22,000	24,000	28,000
	$110,000	$131,000	$152,000	$172,000	$201,000

Alternative A

Type of Cost	Year 1	Year 2	Year 3	Year 4	Year 5
Systems development costs					
Systems design	$80,000	$10,000			
Programming	65,000	10,000			
Training	6,000				
Physical planning	4,000				
Conversion and test	5,000	8,000			
Recurring costs					
Personnel		30,000	$35,000	$40,000	$45,000
Rentals		30,000	33,000	36,000	39,000
Supplies		25,000	27,000	29,000	31,000
Overhead		20,000	25,000	30,000	35,000
	$160,000	$133,000	$120,000	$135,000	$150,000

Alternative B

Type of Cost	Year 1	Year 2	Year 3	Year 4	Year 5
Systems development costs					
Systems design	$30,000				
Programming	25,000				
Training	3,000				
Conversion and test	5,000				
Recurring costs					
Personnel	7,000	$30,000	$35,000	$40,000	$45,000
Rentals	5,000	22,000	25,000	28,000	31,000
Supplies	4,000	20,000	22,000	24,000	26,000
Overhead	3,000	12,000	17,000	22,000	27,000
	$82,000	$84,000	$99,000	$114,000	$129,000

to management? Discuss the intangible benefits as well as the results shown in **b**; also, describe other data that could aid you in developing your recommendation.

(SMAC adapted)

24-4 Northland Conglomerate Company of Niagara Falls, Ontario, has completed a feasibility study to upgrade its computer system. Management has asked for a detailed schedule of the benefits of this new system. The document on page 1152 is provided.

BENEFITS TO BE DERIVED FROM THE NEW SYSTEM

a. Production

  (1) Sales forecasting is presently expressed in dollars per product line. Calculation of units by product line takes an estimated two man-days, a total of $130. This saving would be repeated each time the sales forecast is updated, presumably monthly. The program to calculate the forecast in units would also be more accurate than the present method of applying factors to dollar values. $1,560

  (2) More effective inventory control would permit an overall reduction in inventory. The ability to establish total requirements quickly would help to overcome stock-out situations. For this calculation we estimate a 10 percent inventory reduction. The cost of capital for our firm approximates 20 percent, and the benefit then approximates 20 percent of $100,000. $20,000

  (3) Evaluation of changes to plans will be possible in detail. This is not so under our present system. Parts explosions are time-consuming and can only be done monthly. The effect would be increased production flexibility and the reduction of sales losses caused by finished-goods stock-outs. We estimate that this benefit can be valued as the equivalent of hiring two clerks. $17,000 $38,560

b. Engineering

  (1) Use of the computer in filling and updating bills of material would save 40 percent of the industrial engineer's time. $12,000

  (2) The improved updating of files, which includes the bills of material and product structure files, should save at least 25 percent of one clerk's time. $3,000

  (3) Estimated clerical savings in labor calculations, rates, and bonus details approximate two man-days per week, or 40 percent of one person's time. $4,800 $19,800

c. Sales

  Improved reporting will enable sales personnel and management to react more quickly to prevailing conditions. The implied benefit would be sales increases, especially during promotions, and a better sales–expense ratio. We are assuming an improvement in sales of $1000 per salesperson, for a total of $5000. $5,000

d. Marketing

  Revised reports and an improved forecasting system will help in establishing sales trends and will help production department flexibility and inventory control.

e. Accounting

  (1) Standard costing of all bills of materials, as well as the side effect of being able to cost new products quickly, can be expressed as the equivalent of saving 30 percent of the plant accountant's time. $7,500

  (2) A revised incentive earnings and payroll system installed on the computer should reduce the payroll department clerical labor from roughly three days to one day; the benefit is roughly equivalent to 40 percent of one clerk's time. $4,000 $11,500

         TOTAL $74,860

Required

As the firm's controller, which of the foregoing benefits would you accept as relevant to the economic justification of the system and as reasonably capable of being quantified? Explain your reasoning with respect to each benefit.

(SMAC adapted)

24-5 The Jarvon Company of Lincoln, Nebraska, is a distributor of cosmetics. Because of continued growth and the need to compete effectively, the management has assigned you to conduct a feasibility study. Your first step is to gather data concerning the present processing system, which consists of manual processing and limited processing on a tape-oriented computer system. For instance, payroll, the general ledger accounting, and inventory record keeping are handled by the computer system.

You next study the needs of the firm in the areas of purchasing, billing, and inventory management. On the basis of your investigation you specify a particular system design. After management approves the overall design, you estimate the costs and benefits that are to be expected from its installation.

Your design contemplates the purchase of a modern disk-oriented computer system (software as well as hardware) for approximately $140,000. The system is expected to have a $50,000 salvage value at the end of its five-year economic life. However, maintenance costs for the computer system will be $9000 per year higher than those for the present computer system.

Several significant benefits are expected to be achieved with the new computer system. Purchasing costs are expected to be reduced from current levels by $20,000 in each of the first three years and by $30,000 in the last two years. Savings in billing costs are expected to be $10,000 in the first year and to increase by $5000 in each of the following years. Improved inventory management is expected to reduce processing and stock-out costs by $10,000 in each of the next five years. In addition, the reduction in inventory is estimated to average about $100,000 over the five-year period.

The controller provides you with the following figures: a 20 percent required rate of return (after income taxes); a 34 percent marginal income tax rate; and a 10 percent inventory carrying cost rate. He also tells you that the salvage value (and also the book value) of the current computer system is $20,000 and that all costs related to the study and installation of the new system should not exceed $30,000. The straight-line method of depreciation is employed with respect to newly acquired assets.

Required

Compute (1) the net present value and (2) the benefit–cost ratio of the proposed new computer system. Be careful to include tax effects, such as (1) the savings stemming from the depreciation tax "shield," (2) the added taxes, if any, resulting from the gain on the sale of the present computer system, and (3) the added taxes resulting from net yearly savings. Assume that the cost for design and installation is to be amortized over the economic life of the investment.

 24-6 The Jackson Lumber Company of Santa Rosa, California, is a wholesale lumber distribution firm. It purchases carload lots of lumber and millwork and delivers individual orders to contractors and lumber yards. The firm has experienced rapid growth and presently operates from three warehouses with a fleet of leased trucks. Its success has stemmed in large part from competitive pricing and fast service, backed by an extensive inventory. However, several problems have plagued the firm in recent years, including rising overhead costs, considerable overtime charges incurred by truck drivers, and periodic inventory outages. Consequently, the profit margin has been shrinking. Since stiff competition prevents significant increases in prices, the president recognizes that the operating costs must be reduced and sales growth must be continued.

Mr. Jackson, the president, therefore requests assistance from the firm's public accounting firm. After studying the firm's operations, the consultants from the public accounting firm recommend that the Jackson

Lumber Company acquire a computer-based information system. Mr. Jackson agrees with the recommendation, subject to findings that suggest it would be economically feasible. Therefore, the consultants gather the following estimates:

Purchase price of computer hardware, including needed terminals, data collection devices, magnetic disk drives, and printer	700,000
Purchasing price of software packages	75,000
Cost of training employees	40,000
Detailed designing and programming costs	40,000
Preparation of computer site	25,000
Conversion of files to magnetic disk storage	10,000
Testing of hardware and software	10,000
Annual cost of leased communication lines	80,000
Annual cost of contract for hardware maintenance	45,000
Added annual salaries for computer-related personnel	85,000
Added annual electric power consumption	10,000
Added supplies, such as paper, needed annually	5,000
Annual cost savings from reduced number of trucks required	85,000
Annual cost savings from reduced number of truck drivers and overtime	120,000
Annual cost savings from reduced inventory investment	90,000
Annual cost savings from reduced errors in order processing	15,000
Annual cost savings from more efficient purchasing procedures and advantageous orders	20,000
Average annual added sales from better customer service	200,000
Annual cost savings from reduced number of clerks	120,000
Sale value of presently owned data processing machines	0
Estimated economic life of computer hardware and software	5 years

Depreciation method	Straight-line
Marginal income tax rate	34 percent
Required after-tax rate of return	14 percent
Salvage value of new computer hardware	$100,000
Contribution margin percentage	30 percent

Required

a. Determine whether the recommended computer-based information system is economically feasible. Ignore the investment tax credit; assume that all one-time costs are to be amortized over the economic life of the hardware and software.

b. Discuss the specific intangible benefits that could have a bearing on the economic feasibility of the recommended computer-based information system.

24-7 Many small and medium-size firms have decided that computerized data processing would be beneficial to their needs. They are confronted with several alternatives, however. They may buy or rent a small or medium-size computer system, they may subscribe to a commercial time-sharing service, or they may utilize a local service bureau. Discuss which of these alternatives appears to be suitable to each of the following firms:

a. A small but rapidly growing contractor that needs consolidated financial statements pertaining to the operations of its several divisions.

b. An independent automotive supply house that needs to maintain an inventory consisting of over 50,000 parts by placing weekly orders with suppliers.

c. An engineering research center ("think tank") that needs to keep track of costs incurred against various contracts, to prepare periodic cost reports, and to provide computational facilities for its engineers.

d. A medium-size public utility that needs to prepare customers' bills on a daily basis (known as cycle billing), as well as to prepare payrolls, maintain the general ledger, keep track of costs incurred in new construction and maintenance operations, and provide monthly reports to managers.

 24-8 The Jacob J. Cohen Company avoided the use of computers for many years because J.J. disliked them. J.J. recently expired suddenly, and his successor (and daughter), Sheila J. Cohen, has an open mind with regard to computers. She has decided to conduct a cost–benefit analysis of various systems for a period of three years and has established the following facts:

a. Four alternatives are to be considered:

(1) To keep on with the present manual system.

(2) To use the services of Sharecomp, the only computer service bureau providing local service.

(3) To purchase a minicomputer from the C.B.M. Corporation and to modify the software to suit Cohen Co.

(4) To contract with Advanced Data Products for the provision of a suitable in-house system.

b. The present manual system uses four accounting machines that rent for $300 per month each and employs six clerks at an annual average salary of $15,000. The predicted expansion of the firm will require one extra accounting machine and one extra clerk in year three. The cost of the accounting machines and the salaries of the clerks will increase by at least 10% each year. If the manual system is replaced, $5000 per clerk will be needed for severance pay.

c. Sharecomp has simplified the Cohen business information needs to a series of transactions. It is prepared to sign a three-year contract to process all transactions at a fixed price of $1.50 per transaction. There will be about 40,000 transactions in the first year, increasing by 20% for each of the following two years. One clerk would be needed to provide the necessary interaction with Sharecomp.

d. C.B.M. (a very large firm) will sell a suitable system for $90,000 at the beginning of the first year. Maintenance for the first year will be $9000 and is expected to increase by 12% per year. All initial software will be included in the purchase price.

One programmer-operator at a salary of $30,000 per year, rising by 10% each year, will be needed, as will two clerks. This system will accommodate the expected expansion of Cohen Co. and allow for some new developments.

e. Advanced Data Products (a small firm) will lease a suitable system to the company and develop the software needed. It will agree to a three-year contract at a fixed price of $40,000 per year, including software maintenance, and a development charge of $50,000 to be paid during the first year. The system will also accommodate the expected expansion and would require two clerks but no operator. It also would allow for some new developments.

Required

a. Compute the total net cost of the four alternatives, given that the cost of capital is

12 percent. Assume that all costs are incurred at the beginning of the respective years.

b. Discuss the intangible benefits that are likely to be available as well as the inherent risks if each of the alternatives is adopted.

c. Which of the alternatives seems to be the best choice? Justify your decision.

(SMAC adapted)

24-9 Fritz and Meyer, a medium-size brokerage firm in Bloomington, Indiana, has determined that a new computer-based information system is economically feasible and has selected the best specific computer system for its needs. Now it needs to decide how the acquisition of the new system is to be financed. It accumulates the following data:

a. The purchase price of the computer system is $400,000. If the purchase option is chosen, it will be necessary to contract for maintenance separately at an annual cost of $30,000. On the other hand, the computer system is estimated to have a resale value of $50,000 at the end of its five-year economic life. The straight-line method of depreciation may be employed.

b. An annual rental charge for the new computer system is $130,000. This amount restricts use to 40 hours per week; however, it provides for all necessary maintenance. The terms of the operating lease also (1) allow the firm (the lessee) to cancel the lease at the end of one year with no penalty, and (2) allow the lessor to adjust the leasing charge if inflation exceeds 10 percent in that year.

c. The marginal income tax rate is 34 percent. If the computer system is leased (i.e., rented), the amount of

the purchase price can be otherwise invested at an 18 percent rate of return.

Required

a. Compute the annual and cumulative costs for each of the financing alternatives over the five-year economic life; show each set of computations in a table and state all assumptions.

b. Compute the present values of each set of future annual costs determined in **a,** and state which financing alternative is more financially attractive.

c. Discuss the reasons why management *may* logically choose the alternative method of financing that is more costly.

Note: This problem requires knowledge of matters not illustrated in the chapter. Refer to a managerial accounting text for aid.

24-10 Yellow Jacket Corporation of Fort Worth, Texas, is a land developer and home builder. Currently it employs a service bureau to process its payrolls, accounts payable, and general ledger. However, it is considering a conversion to an in-house computer system. Accordingly, the president of the firm asks the controller to find the computer system that will best serve Yellow Jacket's needs.

With the assistance of the firm's internal auditor, the controller prepares a request for proposals (RFP), which she mails to approximately 25 suppliers of small computer systems. The RFP consists of the following information:

a. General background of Yellow Jacket Corporation, especially with respect to current development and building activities.

b. Descriptions of current computerized applications, including system flowcharts, file formats, report contents, and general data such as number of general ledger accounts.

c. Specifications of data to be proposed by each supplier, including the characteristics of the most suitable processor, the number, type, and speed of input–output units, the characteristics of secondary storage devices, the programming languages and compilers available for the recommended processor, the most suitable application software packages, the estimated time needed for installation, the floor space requirements, the electric power requirements, the itemized costs, and the support services available.

Required

Evaluate the foregoing procedure and the contents of the RFP.

24-11 Tarabini Technics has grown to a firm having several dozen employees and several hundred transactions per week. It believes that computer-based transaction and information processing would be extremely helpful to its further growth and prosperity. Thus, the president explores the possibility with her two key managers.

Required

Discuss the various options that the managers should consider with respect to computer-based processing.

24-12 Five years ago, Black Motors, an international auto maker, contracted with Blue Computer Company for minicomputers to support the data processing for its 30 largest U.S. dealers. Black Motors has 1400 dealers in the United States. Three years ago the dealers began using the Blue computers under long-term leases. The Black Motors Computer Support Group (CSG) is responsible for applications software. Altogether,

each dealer spends about $5000 a month on hardware and software rental.

When the Blue systems were first proposed, CSG sent the dealers specifications of what the systems would and would not do. The dealers were pleased with the proposed capabilities and agreed that the proposed system would serve their needs.

The dealers gradually came to realize, however, that the Blue computer systems did not live up to CSG's promise. At a meeting two years ago, the dealers formed a committee composed of dealer representatives to address the problems. The software problems seem to have begun three years ago, when Black Motors moved its corporate staff, including CSG, from the East Coast to the Midwest. Many of its programmers declined to move, so that CSG's ability to support the Blue systems was impaired.

Two years ago, CSG began upgrading the computer systems used by all but the 30 largest dealers with minicomputers from Green Computer Company. To support these systems, most CSG personnel work on software for the Green computers. Software for the Green and Blue Computers are incompatible but perform similar functions.

Three months ago, CSG sent the 30 largest dealers a letter assuring support for the Blue systems for the next four years and promising a decision about long-term support. The dealers remained skeptical and have been talking about legal action to force CSG to comply with its original agreement.

Required

Given the difficulties described, explain what CSG should do to improve computer system support for the 30 largest dealers. Include in your explanation the reasons for the actions you suggest.

(CIA adapted)

24-13 The following are results of benchmark problems run on configurations A, B, and C.[23] The benchmark problems run on each configuration are representative sample workloads, which test for both input–output and internal processing capabilities of each configuration. The monthly rental, based on projected usage of at least 176 hours per month, is $30,000 for configuration A, $34,000 for configuration B, and $32,000 for configuration C.

Benchmark Results: CPU Times (in Seconds) for Compilation and Execution of Different Programs

	Type of Problem		
Vendor	Process-Bound Problem	Input–Output-Bound Problem	Hybrid Problem
A	400.5	640	247.5
B	104.9	320	260.3
C	175.4	325	296.8

Required

a. On the basis of the three benchmark problems, decide which vendor's (supplier's) configuration is preferable.

b. Compute cost-effectiveness indices by dividing the total benchmark time of each configuration by that vendor's monthly payments. How do these computations affect the results?

 24-14 The Kenmore Company has determined that a new interactive computer system is economically feasible with respect to its accounting transaction processing applications. It has requested and received proposals from three suppliers of hardware and software. The system evaluation team assigns the following weights and ratings to the relevant factors:

		Supplier		
Factor	Weight	X	Y	Z
Hardware performance	20	8	7	9
Software suitability	15	9	6	7
Hardware features	10	7	8	7
Software features	10	8	6	5
Overall price	15	7	9	8
Support by supplier	20	8	10	8
System reliability	10	10	9	10

Required

a. Compute the total evaluations of the suppliers, using the weighted-rating analysis technique, and explain the results.

b. Describe the uncertainties involved in using the data provided.

c. What other techniques might aid in making the final selection?

 24-15 The Labrador Company is a manufacturer located in Winnipeg, Manitoba. Recently the firm introduced a new product line and a job costing system. The president prudently decides, as a consequence, that the current manual operations should be evaluated in order to determine their ability to cope with the expanding work load. He further decides that a feasibility study should be conducted by a group of key managers, with the help of any outside organization who his executive committee feels might provide insight to the problems being faced. After being appointed, the study committee carries out a thorough feasibility study. On the basis of its findings, the committee reports to him these three alternatives:

a. Introduce a large, general-purpose computer capable of incorporating an integrated management information system and encompassing many firm activities.

b. Introduce a minicomputer capable of handling only the order en-

[23] Adapted from John G. Burch and Gary Grudnitski, *Information Systems: Theory and Practice*, 4th ed. (New York: Wiley, 1986). Used with permission.

try, inventory, and job costing systems.

    c. Continue with the present manual operations.

When questioned regarding his own ranking of the relative importance of each of the various selection criteria, the president indicates that the level of annual operating costs is his prime concern. He also mentions that he considers the cost of new system development and the payback period of each of the alternatives important. The president also points out that any good system should provide timely and accurate information concerning the operations of the company and should also provide the internal controls necessary to satisfy both the internal and the external auditors. Since the board of directors has actively been pursuing new product opportunities through diversification and mergers, he feels that the ability of a system to handle an increasing work load is likewise of concern.

    Since the firm is located in a small city, about two hours' driving time from the nearest major city, he feels that the recommended system should provide a degree of reliability. Any hardware problems would mean the system would be down for at least two hours before a service technician could arrive from the city. The recommended system should provide enough flexibility to eventually support new applications and should have sufficient storage capacity to meet current data storage requirements and provide the capacity to expand with the new applications.

    Toward the end of the feasibility study the committee develops the alternative evaluation matrix shown at the top of page 1160. The various evaluation criteria that the president had indicated as important are listed down the left-hand side of the matrix and numbered 1 through 10. The committee's findings concerning the relative ability of each alternative to meet these criteria are shown in columns I, II, and III.

Required

a. On the basis of the information given on page 1160, assign weighting factors and explain your assigned value for each of the evaluation criteria. Most important factor(s) should be given a weight of 10, important criteria a weight of 5, and less-important criteria a weight of 3.

b. Rank each alternative on the basis of its ability to meet each of the criteria by assigning a rating from 1 to 5. The ratings are as follows:

Very poor	1
Poor	2
Fair	3
Good	4
Very good	5

For example, in considering the speed of each alternative, the manual system, being the slowest of the three, might be given a rating of 1; the minicomputer might be next at 4; and the large computer, since it is the fastest, might be rated at 5.

    Finally, by multiplying the weighting factor of each selection criterion by the rating of each alternative, establish the weighted ratings for each component. On the basis of the total rating value for the system, recommend the system that best meets the overall needs of the firm.

c. Assume that proposals from specific suppliers are to be evaluated. How would a weighted rating table developed for that purpose differ from the alternative evaluation matrix?

(SMAC adapted)

24-16 The Tootle Corporation of Newark, New Jersey, has decided to acquire a data base management system. After receiving proposals from three suppliers, the feasibility study team employs a weighted-rating analysis as

Alternative Evaluation Matrix

Alternative	I	II	III
Evaluation Criteria	**Large Computer**	**Minicomputer**	**Manual System**
Performance			
1. Accuracy	Very good	Very good	Fair
2. Control capability	Very good	Very good	Poor
3. Flexibility	Very good	Good	Fair
4. Growth potential	Very good	Limited to three years without degradation	Very poor
5. Reliability	Good	Good	Fair
6. Speed	Very good	Good	Poor
7. Storage capacity	Good	Good	No problem
Costs			
8. System development	$60,000	$40,000	0
9. System operation	$10.00 per product	$8.50 per product	$19.00 per product
10. Payback	15 months	12 months	Not applicable

its chief means of evaluation. In preparing to apply this evaluation technique, it assigns weights to the relevant factors to be considered and then rates each supplier on each of the factors on a scale from 1 to 10. The results are listed in the table below, with the numbers in parentheses being the weights.

Required

Complete the weighted-rating analysis and explain the results.

		Supplier		
Factor	**Weight**	**Able**	**Baker**	**Charlene**
Ease of use	(12)	10	8	10
Compatibility to variety of hardware	(10)	7	9	8
Software support by supplier	(10)	7	10	8
Price of package	(9)	8	10	6
Reliability	(8)	9	6	10

		Supplier		
Factor	**Weight**	**Able**	**Baker**	**Charlene**
Query language facility	(8)	8	9	8
Training provided by supplier	(6)	6	8	8
Performance	(6)	10	8	10
Documentation	(5)	5	9	7
Data definition facility	(5)	10	7	8
Reputation of supplier	(5)	8	8	10
Enhancements	(4)	7	5	9
Ease of installation	(4)	7	5	9
CODASYL compatibility	(4)	10	8	10
Flexibility to accommodate changes	(4)	5	6	8

24-17 The Troy Company of Saskatoon, Saskatchewan, has gross yearly sales of $20 million. The firm conducts all of its business activities from one location. Presently, the office workers perform all clerical operations in such basic business applications as accounts payable, accounts receivable, general ledger, and invoicing. The amount of work that the office staff performs is increasing each year, and the staff, which now numbers 10 people, is finding it difficult to keep up with the excess work load. Additional clerical help is not the solution, and the manager recognizes that automation of the firm's procedures is essential.

In the existing system orders are received through the mail. Clerks pull customers' records to check for poor credit risks and delinquent accounts. These are then referred to the manager, who decides how to handle them.

Each customer record is updated manually, and an entry is made in the summary of sales. An invoice and bill of lading are made up, and the latter is sent to the warehouse for assembly of the order. The products are picked from the inventory, and product cards are changed to reflect the change in inventory. If a product is not in stock, the office is notified and the invoice is adjusted. The return of a copy of the bill of lading to the office to advise that the order has been filled serves as authorization for sending the invoice to the customer.

At present, there are 5000 customers for whom records are kept (200 characters of data per customer) and 400 products for which product ledger cards are kept (150 characters of data per product).

The design objectives are that the proposed system must be able to handle the existing order entry and invoicing applications as well as an improved inventory control function. It would also be desirable if some other basic functions could be handled.

Moreover, the system must be designed to operate without a team of computer-oriented personnel. No in-house programming or operation talent is available, and training of such a staff is not planned.

After a study of the system requirements and the potential benefits, two alternative system designs are proposed. One approach is to use a small business computer system that handles the several applications. The applications will be handled sequentially, and no internal processing interfaces are needed between applications. All essential functions can be handled, although some cannot be handled as completely as desired. The back-order and future-order functions, for example, cannot be satisfactorily handled automatically, and so they will be maintained manually. Commissions and accounts payable will not be handled initially. Also, there is no possibility of handling the sales analysis requirements of the company.

In this first alternative, magnetic ledger cards are used as the storage medium. There is a magnetic ledger card for each customer and for each product. Processing is performed one application at a time. When the accounts receivable or invoicing program is loaded into the computer, only that application can be run. Input to the program is provided by the magnetic ledger cards and by transaction data keyed in at the keyboard. Output is produced on the printer as the magnetic ledger cards are processed (e.g., updated). The supplier provides developed basic business programs with this machine and charges $5 per instruction when deviations from the standard program are required. It appears that approximately 2220 instructions will need to be modified in these programs. The hardware configuration has a purchase price of $32,450. On a five-year purchase plan the monthly payments are $725. Monthly maintenance is $100. Installation can be accomplished in three months. The supplier will supply four additional weeks of programmer training for the user, at any time the user desires. This system requires 100 square feet of space.

The other proposed system uses a relatively sophisticated minicomputer with disk files. In this system orders will be entered via a series of keyboard CRT display units. When an order arrives at a CRT unit, the operator enters the customer's identification. The program will validate this identification, check the customer's credit, and then notify the input clerk at the CRT whether to proceed with the first product ordered or to take the order to the manager to be handled manually. If the customer has a good credit rating, the operator will then enter the product number and the quantity desired, wait for the program to check whether enough inventory is available to fill the order, and then enter the next product ordered. This procedure is repeated until the entire order is entered. The input clerk is notified if special action is required (such as excluding an item from the order because of insufficient inventory). Items that must be reordered are output on a printer. Invoicing for all deliverable items is performed automatically, as is the preparation of shipping documents. The preceding procedures initiate other functions, such as the processing of salespersons' commissions.

The proposed minicomputer system includes the processor, three CRT units, two printers, and a disk drive. This hardware costs $36,000 or $790 per month on a five-year monthly installment plan. Maintenance is $280 per month. Application software will have to be developed in its entirety to make the integrated approach work. This cost is estimated to be $75,000, despite the use of much of the manufacturer's software. It is estimated that the installation time for such a system would be nine months. Also, this minicomputer would require 200 square feet of space.

The manufacturer of the small business computer provides, at a $300 charge, the means to convert Troy's customer and product files to magnetic ledger card media. With respect to the minicomputer system, the software developed for processing the sales data also can be used to convert the data to disk storage. (However, the data in the present files will still need to be keyed into the computer system via the CRT units.)

Current space costs are $3 per square foot per month. Data entry keying and key-verifying rates are $8 per hour at a rated speed of 10,000 keystrokes per hour.

Required

a. Develop the costs associated with each of the proposed systems over the first two years, assuming that hardware will be purchased using monthly payments and ignoring the salaries for all in-house personnel.

b. Compare, in qualitative terms, the benefits of each proposed system.

c. Which alternative system should the manager choose? Justify your answer.

(SMAC adapted)

24-18 *Datacruncher Office Equipment (Continuing Case)*

Required

a. Prepare a feasibility analysis for the preferable design alternative, and summarize the justification for the design alternative.

b. By reference to manufacturers' brochures and other available information, list specific hardware and software systems that appear suitable for the preferable design alternative.

Suggested Readings

Bennett, Robert E., and Hendricks, James A. "Justifying the Acquisition of Automated Equipment." *Management Accounting* (July 1987), pp. 39–46.

Borthick, A. Faye, and Scheiner, James H. "Selection of Small Business Computer Systems: Structuring a Multi-Criteria Approach." *Journal of Information Systems* (Fall 1988), pp. 10–29.

Buss, Martin D. J. "How to Rank Computer Projects." *Harvard Business Review* (Jan.–Feb. 1983), pp. 118–125.

Buss, Martin D. J., and Herman, Elaine. "Packaged Software: Purchase or Perish." *Financial Executive* (Jan. 1983), pp. 26–33.

Compton, Ted R. "A Cost-Effective Internal Control System—Management's Dilemma." *Journal of Systems Management* (May 1985), pp. 21–25.

Davis, Gordon B., and Olson, Margarethe H. *Management Information Systems: Conceptual Foundations, Structure, and Development*. 2d ed. New York: McGraw-Hill, 1985.

Gand, Harvey, and Cook, Milt E. "Choosing an MRP System." *Datamation* (Jan. 1983), pp. 84–98.

Ghandforoush, Parviv. "Model for Mini Computer Selection." *Journal of Systems Management* (June 1982), pp. 11–13.

Guimaraes, Tor, and Paxton, William E. "Impact of Financial Analysis Methods on Project Selection." *Journal of Systems Management* (Feb. 1984), pp. 18–22.

Held, Gilbert. "Choosing the Lease or Purchase Option." *Journal of Accounting and EDP* (Spring 1986), pp. 22–26.

Kaplan, Robert S. "Must CIM Be Justified by Faith Alone?" *Harvard Business Review* (Mar.–Apr. 1986), pp. 87–95.

Keim, Robert T., and Janaro, Ralph. "Cost/Benefit Analysis of MIS." *Journal of Systems Management* (September 1982), pp. 20–25.

Ladd, Eldon. "How to Evaluate Financial Software." *Management Accounting* (January 1985), pp. 39–43.

Lay, Peter M. Q. "Beware of the Cost/Benefit Model for IS Project Evaluation." *Journal of Systems Management* (June 1985), pp. 30–35.

Litecky, Charles R. "Intangibles in Cost/Benefit Analysis." *Journal of Systems Management* (Feb. 1981), pp. 15–17.

McFadden, Fred R., and Seever, James D. "Costs and Benefits of a Data Base System." *Harvard Business Review* (Jan.–Feb. 1978), pp. 131, 139.

Mahmood, M. A. "Choosing Computer Services for Small Businesses." *Journal of Systems Management* (July 1982), pp. 22–24.

Myers, Edith. "Here Come the Super Service Bureaus." *Datamation* (Oct. 15, 1984). pp. 110–118.

Palvia, Prashant, and Palvia, Shailendra. "The Feasibility Study in Information Systems: An Analysis of Criteria and Contents." *Information and Management* (1988), pp. 211–224.

Sassone, Peter G., and Schwartz, A. Perry. "Cost-Justifying OA." *Datamation* (Feb. 15, 1986), pp. 83–88.

Smith, Robert D. "Measuring Intangible Benefits of Computer-Based Information Systems." *Journal of Systems Management* (Sept. 1983), pp. 22–27.

Sussman, Philip N. "Evaluating Decision Support Software." *Datamation* (Oct. 15, 1984), pp. 171–172.

Vaid-Raizada, Vishist K. "Incorporation of Intangibles in Computer Selection Decisions." *Journal of Systems Management* (Nov. 1983), pp. 30–36.

Vanecek, Michael. "Computer System Acquisition Planning." *Journal of Systems Management* (May 1984), pp. 8–13.

CHAPTER OBJECTIVES

After studying this chapter, you should be able to do the following:

Install systems control and management techniques such as Gantt charts and critical-path network diagrams.

Describe the activities involved in implementing an information systems project.

Employ techniques related to the detailed design of information systems.

Identify appropriate responses to people affected by the implementation of a new or improved information system.

Discuss several major concerns and activities of the operational phase of an information system.

Evaluate several methods for charging the costs related to services provided by an information system and the information systems function.

Describe several techniques for evaluating and controlling the effectiveness and efficiency of systems-related personnel and other resources.

Chapter **25**

SYSTEMS IMPLEMENTATION AND OPERATION

Systems designs, feasibility computations, and accepted resource proposals reside on paper. A new or improved information system comes alive only through a series of implementation steps. Generally, these implementation steps engage the efforts of many persons, introduce complex jumbles of activities, and entail extensive costs. Furthermore, these steps typically span a longer time period than all the preceding phases combined. Thus, the implementation is worthy of careful attention.

Both systems analysts and accountants should participate in this realization phase. Systems analysts can assure that the designs are fully realized in computer programs and detailed layouts. They can also aid in a variety of the other implementation steps.

Accountants can be particularly useful in establishing controls and standards over implementation and operational activities, as well as in evaluating the newly installed information system.

At the end of the implementation phase a new or improved information system achieves full operational status. Although many of the developmental problems and difficulties are over, certain concerns remain partially unsettled. For instance, the problems of operational and economic feasibility must be tracked well into the operational phase. Other concerns arise, even after the new system moves safely through its early shakedown period. Among these concerns are (1) the method of accounting for systems-related costs and (2) the means of evaluating the continuing effectiveness and efficiency of systems-related resources.

This chapter surveys the steps and activities of both phases. It also examines several techniques that are widely employed in project management and detailed design.

Management of Systems Implementation Projects

Implementing a newly designed information system involves a variety of activities during and after the implementation phase. These activities are likely to be more successfully conducted when they are carefully planned and controlled. Figure 25-1 shows the major subphases pertaining to systems implementation and their relationship to the preceding phases.

Establishing Implementation Plans and Controls

Plans were formulated and controls established at the outset of the systems project. Additional planning of implementation activities very likely was included in a systems design report. However, detailed plans and precise controls pertaining to implementation activities can be developed only after management has approved the design specifications and the selection of hardware and software. Not until this time do the planners generally have certain key facts, such as the beginning date of the implementation period, the exact list of implementation activities, and the dollar amount authorized for implementation.

The implementation phase therefore begins with the completion of an **implementation plan.** Included in the plan will be cost budgets, time schedules, and details concerning the respective implementation activities.

A sound implementation plan requires careful preparation. First, the activities are

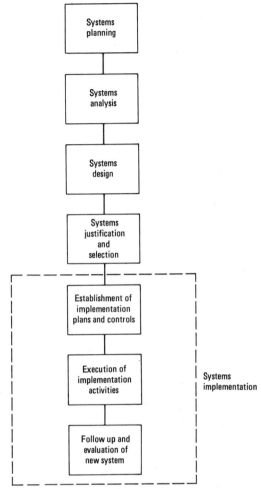

FIGURE 25-1 The steps in the systems implementation phase.

subdivided into specific tasks of relatively short duration. For instance, an activity called "train personnel" may involve such tasks as "arrange training site" and "provide orientation to users." The time needed for each task is next estimated. Estimated times should be realistic, allowing for such factors as breaks, travel, and orientation sessions. Upon setting the estimated task times, the completion dates for the tasks can be determined. Finally, the times must be translated into personnel costs by means of hourly

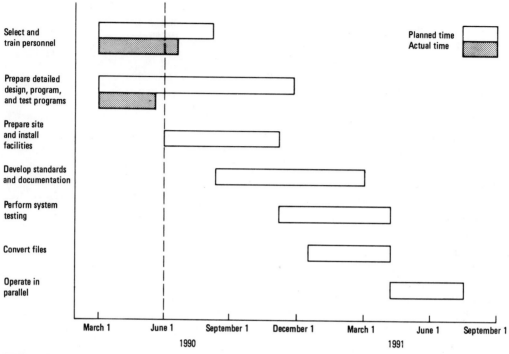

FIGURE 25-2 A Gantt chart of systems implementation activities.

rates. These rates are assigned on the basis of skills possessed by the individuals who are to perform the tasks.

The plan is preferably developed with the full participation of persons who are to use the newly implemented systems. Users should concur in the time estimates, for instance.

The control process consists of comparing actual costs incurred and actual time expended against the preestablished budgets and schedules. These comparisons can be provided to managers in various ways. *Periodic exception reports* may be prepared. *Exhibit boards* may be maintained. *Progress review meetings* may be held periodically, perhaps at the times the respective milestones are reached. Corrective actions may be taken when such monitoring activities bring significant deviations to light.

Two of the most widely used devices for scheduling and controlling projects (espe-

cially project times) are known as Gantt charts and network diagrams.

A **Gantt chart** is a bar chart with a calendar scale. Figure 25-2 presents a Gantt chart that contains several major implementation activities.[1] Each planned activity appears as a bar that marks the scheduled starting date, ending date, and duration. Below each planned activity bar appears a bar that represents actual progress to date. The appeal of the Gantt chart is that it clearly reflects the current status at a glance. For instance, on June 1 it can be quickly seen that the activity labeled ''Select and train personnel'' is ahead of schedule, whereas the activity labeled ''Test programs'' is behind schedule.

[1]Note that the activities in the Gantt chart are *not* broken down into tasks, as suggested in an earlier paragraph so that the chart will have a simple appearance. The concepts being discussed are valid for any level of detail.

The major drawback of the Gantt chart is that it does not show relationships among the various activities. For instance, Figure 25-2 does not show that the installation of the physical facilities is related to the activity of testing the system, even though the latter will not normally begin until the former is completed. Although relationships such as this might be inferred in relatively simple and clear-cut projects, they are more difficult to visualize in complex projects.

A **network diagram** explicitly portrays the relationships among the activities comprising a project. Figure 25-3 presents a network diagram of the activities comprising a systems implementation project. When prepared according to a quantitative methodology, network diagrams can facilitate the planning and control of complex systems implementation projects. An appendix at the end of the chapter describes the methodology of network diagrams.

Other Preliminary Actions

The execution of implementation activities is guided by the implementation plans and controls. Two preliminary actions not appearing on the schedule, however, should set the stage for implementation.

One preliminary action is to inform the employees and managers. An announcement might specify any new computer hardware being acquired and the impact of the information system change on the affected organizational units. Disseminating this information should reduce the uncertainty inherent in such a situation and thus reduce the rumors that are bound to fly.

The other preliminary action is to reorganize the project team. During the earlier systems development phases, the tasks have been largely technical in nature. Therefore, the project manager during those phases would most suitably have been a systems

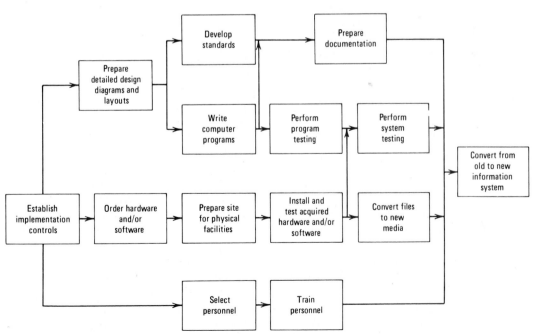

FIGURE 25-3 A network diagram of systems implementation activities.

professional. However, the task of implementing a new system is essentially managerial in nature. Thus, the project manager during this period would more suitably be drawn from personnel assigned to the function being redesigned. For example, a project pertaining to inventory control should probably be headed by a materials manager. In addition, it may be desirable to assign specialists in such implementation activities as system testing to the team.

If the project is large and unique, the information systems manager might consider engaging an outside *systems integrator* to head the project. Systems integration services are available from such firms as IBM and Martin Marietta, which have personnel who are experienced and knowledgeable in systems technology.[2]

Implementation Activities

After these preliminary actions are completed, the project team is ready to begin the implementation. It will then proceed to execute the initial activities, as shown in the schedule. They may be the same activities as those appearing in Figure 25-3, or they may be others. We should recognize that system development projects are widely varied. Certain projects involve a change to new computer hardware, for instance, whereas other projects consist simply of adapting applications to presently available computer hardware. Thus, the sequence and relative importance of implementation activities necessarily will vary. In some cases the writing of computer programs will precede the installation of hardware, whereas in other cases this sequence will be reversed. In some cases physical preparation is important, whereas in other cases it is a trivial matter.

[2]Christopher Keene, Peter Jessel, and John Hagel, "Solving the Systems Puzzle," *Datamation* (Nov. 1, 1988), p. 120.

Because of such variations among projects, those activities that appear to be important to most projects are examined briefly below. This order of presentation is necessarily arbitrary.

Personnel selection and training. Newly implemented information systems usually require new people to operate and maintain them. Thus, personnel selection is an early concern. Candidates for new positions should be selected by careful procedures. For instance, they should be tested for aptitude and interviewed for attitude.

Newly created positions might be filled from two sources: the present employees and the outside labor market. Present employees should be given prior consideration, for several reasons: (1) Transferring present employees to new positions usually costs less than recruiting new employees from the outside; (2) present employees already understand the firm's operations, whereas new employees need time to learn the firm's way of doing things; (3) employee morale is enhanced by a fill-from-within policy, especially if the employees considered for transfers are to be displaced by the new system. On the other hand, it generally will not be possible to utilize present employees in all newly created positions. For those positions requiring a high degree of computer expertise, it may be necessary to recruit outside the firm. For instance, systems programmers and hardware specialists usually are brought in from the outside.

Employees in new positions should be fully trained in the areas in which they are unfamiliar. Those employees who are transferred to new system-related positions, such as computer operations, must learn new skills. Those employees who possess the requisite skills but are new to the firm must learn the firm's procedures and practices. In addition, all of the clerks and managers who will use the new system must be indoctrinated in (1) the procedures that govern its use and (2) the information that the system can provide to them.

Training programs can be very costly and time consuming; however, they provide very desirable benefits. Consider the experience of Huntington Memorial Hospital (HMH) when it converted to a real-time patient information system a few years ago:

Formal training programs for more than 1,000 employees provided eight hours of hands-on experience during an eight-week period before the system was brought on-line in nursing and ancillary departments.

Each trainee received an initial three hours of training on operating the keyboard/ display and printer terminals. This was followed by another three hours of studying departmental procedures, and classes concluded with two hours on terminal operations and procedures.

By the time training classes were over, not only were all new users throughout HMH thoroughly familiar with the system, but their comments and suggestions had led to useful changes and additions to display and printed formats, input techniques, and more. As a result, before the system went live in nursing and ancillary services, it had the full support of its users. They knew the system was designed to make their jobs easier, and they wanted to begin using it.[3]

As noted in Chapter 21, training may be conducted either by outside organizations or by the firm itself. In-house training is often less formal than outside courses and seminars, but it can be very effective. For example, users of new on-line systems have received in-house training via the following means.[4]

1. User manuals or handbooks.
2. Slide presentations.
3. Tape-recorded narratives.
4. Seminars.
5. Simulations.
6. Personalized tutorials for viewing via CRT screens.
7. Computer-assisted instructions available via HELP commands to interactive terminals.

Physical preparation. When a system design requires the installation of new hardware, the facilities to house the equipment must be carefully prepared. Physical facilities may range from a desktop for a microcomputer or a terminal to a complete data center. Although the latter is an extreme case, it illustrates the possible impact that this activity can have on the implementation.

A **data center** is generally a centralized site for data storage, processing, and retrieval. It often houses one or more mainframe computer configurations and in some cases includes additional minicomputers. The center must incorporate air conditioning, raised floors, uninterruptible power supplies, and fire detection and prevention systems. In this age of data communications it must be able to accommodate numerous data and voice lines. Furthermore, offices and space must be provided for operators, clerks, technicians, and supervisors—who may number in the hundreds—and for disk and tape files and supplies.

The expected delivery date of ordered hardware will affect the scheduling of physical preparation and installation activities. Usually, this date will be specified in the contract negotiated with the supplier, together with other requirements such as acceptance tests to be performed prior to final acceptance of the delivered hardware. However, experience has shown that this delivery date may be missed. Thus, the exact dates of the

[3]Robert Spaziano, "A Hospital's Cares," *Datamation* (June 1980), p. 162.

[4]Phillip G. Elam, "On-Line Training: Brief, Simple, Direct," *Infosystems* (Nov. 1978), pp. 65, 68; Robert Chapman, "Facing Financial Realities in Banking," *Datamation* (June 1978), p. 160.

installation activity are subject to some degree of uncertainty. Often the installation activity, and hence later activities, must be rescheduled.

Detailed system design. A computer-based information system cannot be made operational until all design details have been filled in. Inputs, files, and outputs must be precisely and minutely specified. Computer programs must be written line by line to specify each processing action to be performed, each file field to be updated, each information item to be reported, and each programmed check to be applied.

Computer programs will either be written "from scratch" or be converted from other programs. Newly written programs are, of course, needed when a firm acquires a computer for the first time and does not buy packaged software. They may also be necessary when the design for a new system is a significant departure from the present system (e.g., when an on-line processing system is designed to replace a batch processing system). Program conversions are necessary when a firm acquires a newer-model computer to replace its present computer; they are also usually necessary when it acquires software packages, since the packages typically require modifications to fit the particular needs of the firm.[5]

Various detailed design aids are available. **Layout forms,** such as gridded spacing charts and record layouts, aid in the detailed design of documents, reports, and file records. An example of a spacing chart appears in Figure 25-4. **Logic diagrams,** such as program flowcharts and decision tables, aid in the preparation of computer programs. In effect, logic diagrams are the bridges be-tween system flowcharts, a key element of design specifications, and the detailed codes comprising computer programs. (A later section in this chapter discusses logic diagrams more fully.)

Program and system testing. Thorough testing is necessary before a new computer system is ready for operation. Testing consists of two stages: program testing and system testing.

Program testing, which checks the reliability of each program, should begin as soon as each program has been completed. Since programs generally are written early in the implementation phase, program testing likewise can begin early. Logic errors can thereby be spotted and corrected before the time for system testing arrives.

Careful testing of program code is usually a far-from-simple task. It should therefore be conducted in a systematic manner. Each program should first be manually *desk-checked* by the programmer. Next, the programmer should devise **test data.** Sufficient data should be devised to test all possible conditions ("branches") that may be encountered, including those representing error conditions. Expected results from the use of the test data should be predetermined. These results should include error messages as well as valid outputs, since the test data will incorporate errors to check the branches containing programmed controls. Then the programmer should execute the program with the test data until he or she is convinced that it is free of bugs (i.e., fully "debugged").

Several approaches can enhance the program testing process, including the following:

1. A top-down approach in which (a) each program is first checked to see that the subroutines function properly within the calling or main routine and (b) each subroutine is then checked to see that the detailed instructions are proper.

---

[5]In some cases *emulators* (hardware devices used in conjunction with special software) can be employed to enable computer programs to operate on newer-model computers. However, programs executed with the aid of emulators are less efficient than rewritten or converted programs.

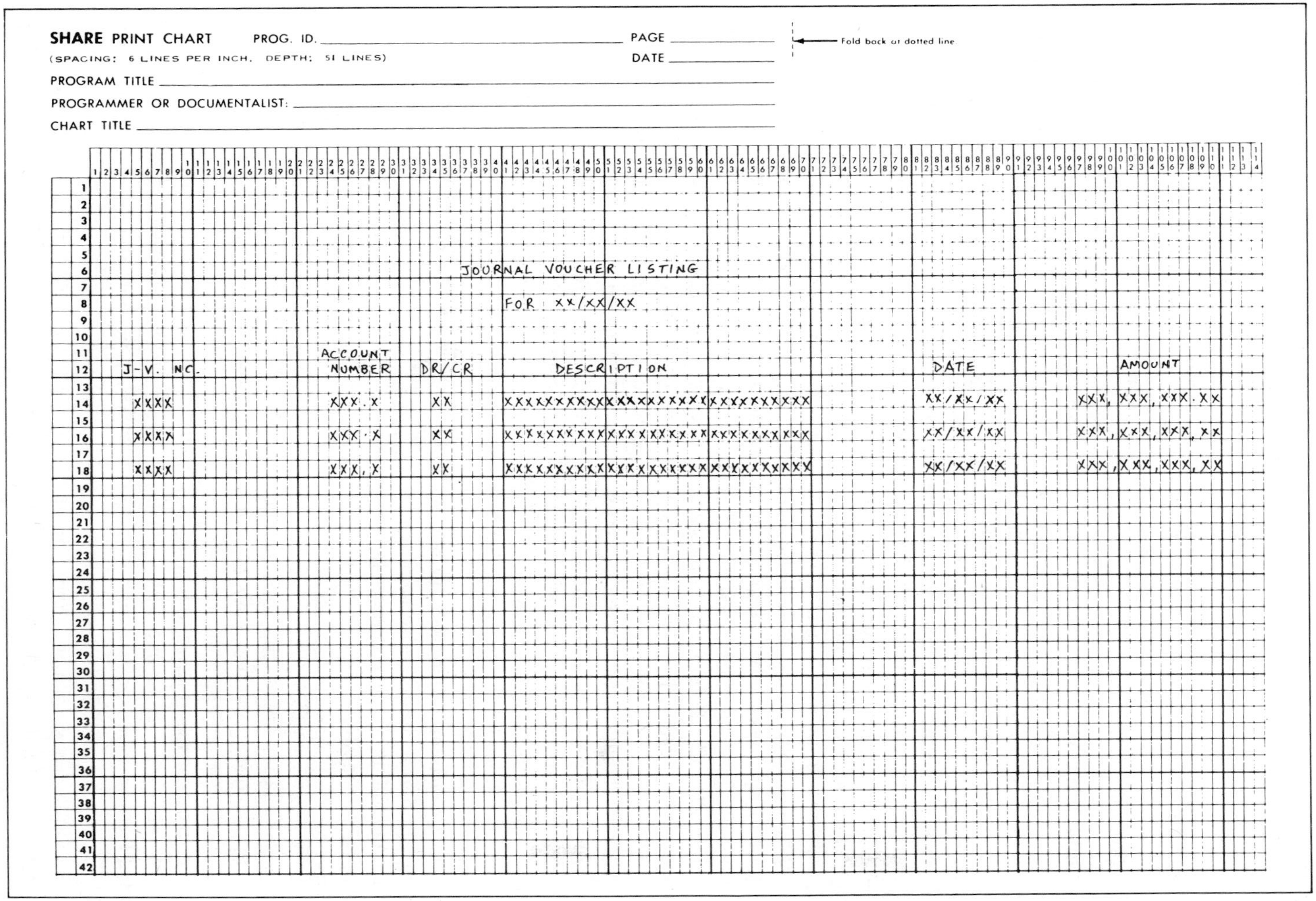

FIGURE 25-4 A report layout on a spacing chart.

2. A series of debug routines that print a message each time a module or subroutine is entered or exited.

3. Interactive testing via visual display terminals.

4. A **walkthrough,** or informal trace, of the program logic and steps by the members of a program test team.

System testing examines the compatibility of the various software elements with the hardware on which they are to be operated. Its main purpose is to verify that the application programs, system software, data base management system, and other software packages function effectively with the central processor(s), the data base, the communication units, and other hardware devices. Thus, tests should be performed to uncover errors resulting from faulty interfacing and integration of the respective elements into the complete system. For instance, test transactions that affect several programs and files of a newly designed on-line data-managed system should be entered.

The tests should be as thorough as possible. Every likely type of transaction should be entered for processing. Every system attribute, such as transaction processing capacity and response time, should be strained to the maximum.

Complex systems, such as real-time operational support systems, pose severe system-testing difficulties. Two approaches that have been successfully employed in such systems are

1. An accumulative approach. For instance, two application programs may be combined and tested. Then a third program is added to this string of two and tested, and so on. This type of testing is known as **string testing.**

2. A prototype approach. In this approach a scaled-down, or simplified, model of the designed system is constructed and tested by the actual users as well as designers;

on the basis of the results of these tests, the full-scale, or complete, version in constructed and then tested.

An example of a complex system is an electronic data interchange (EDI) system. A large consumer-goods manufacturer recently developed an EDI system involving more than 30 key trading partners (customers). Testing of this system was conducted on a pilot basis with eight of the customers. Test data were keyed into the system by a salesperson, and the resulting document (e.g., a sales order/picking list) was checked by a user (e.g., a stock picker in the warehouse). After this pilot testing was completed, parallel testing was performed with all of the customers until the "bugs" were worked out.[6]

System testing necessarily follows program testing, and it is not completed until near the end of the implementation phase. However, it may begin fairly early. For instance, testing of key programs and files need not wait for the arrival of the newly acquired computer. Instead, the firm's programmer may travel to the site of an identical computer, perhaps at the premises of the computer manufacturer, and perform this initial system testing.

Standards development. Well-conceived standards provide useful yardsticks. Most well-managed firms have established standards in various areas of operation. For instance, a typical manufacturing firm has standards respecting the quality and price of raw materials that it purchases.

Major changes planned by a firm, however, generally give rise to the need for new standards. Thus, a firm that radically alters its information system, perhaps by the acquisition of its first computer, must develop a

---

[6]Robert A. Payne, "EDI Implementation: A Case Study," *Journal of Systems Management* (March 1989), pp. 14–17.

variety of new standards. These standards may pertain to such aspects as

1. System elements (e.g., standardized data items, standardized codes).
2. Performance (e.g., standardized employee productivity rates, standardized equipment utilization levels).
3. Documentation (e.g., standardized flow-charting symbols and techniques).

Standards affecting a newly designed information system should be completely developed during the implementation phase. Otherwise, problems likely will occur when it becomes operational.

Documentation. A sometimes slighted implementation activity is the preparation of descriptive documentation. As outlined in Chapter 9, documentation consists of narrative descriptions, program listings, operating instructions, sample documents, report and file layouts, flowcharts, and other descriptive materials pertaining to the features and operations of an information system.

Adequate documentation is extremely useful, since it

1. Helps new employees learn their duties and responsibilities.
2. Guides computer operators during processing runs.
3. Provides systems analysts and programmers with vital reference material when program changes are necessary.
4. Provides auditors with starting points during evaluations of internal accounting controls.
5. Facilitates communication among all of the aforementioned parties and the users of the information system.

In order for documentation to serve these purposes well, it should be viewed as an integral and important part of the implementation phase, be performed in a professional manner with "tender loving care," and be based on standards applied consistently.

Documentation is likely to improve in upcoming years, since powerful computerized tools have become available. These packages aid systems analysts in developing structured diagrams (e.g., data flow diagrams), data dictionaries, and documentation features via microcomputer screens. Examples of computer-aided documentation packages are Excelerator (from Index Technology Corporation), Information Engineering Workbench (from KnowledgeWare, Inc.), and Problem Statement Language/Problem Statement Analyzer (developed at the University of Michigan). In addition to providing documentation, these packages check the completeness and consistency of the structured diagrams.

File conversion. Every system design specifies changes or conversions in one or more components. For instance, a particular design may specify that manual processing procedures are to be converted to computer programs and that source documents are to be converted from plain-paper stock to OCR forms. Such conversions occur as a part of the detailed design activity.

Another type of conversion often required during the implementation phase concerns the data base. Generally, files must be converted from one medium to another. For instance, they may need to be converted from file folders in a manual system to magnetic tapes in a computer-based system. Or they may need to be converted from magnetic tapes to magnetic disks. The former situation normally will be more difficult than the latter, but a data base conversion is seldom easy. In fact, a conversion of an active file from magnetic tape to magnetic disk can be a pressure-packed experience if the file must remain in active use.

To appreciate the difficulties involved in

file conversion, consider the following necessary actions:

1. The files must first be "cleaned up" by validating each needed item of data, deleting each item no longer needed, and filling in each missing item.

2. Special programs may need to be written to transfer data from the current storage medium to the new storage medium, as well as from the current file structure to the new file or data structures.

3. The data must be physically loaded into the new files or data structures.

4. The data in the new files or data structures must be reconciled with the data in the current files.

5. Backup copies of the current files must be retained, in case discrepancies appear in the converted data.

Final system conversion. The time when a newly designed system replaces a current system and becomes fully operational is known as the **cutover point.** Cutover may take place as soon as such activities as system testing and file conversion have been completed; that is, a firm can convert directly and with no further ado from its present system to the newly designed system. This *direct approach* saves the time and cost of further testing. However, it represents a risky "sink or swim" approach, since the firm cannot be sure that the newly designed system will function adequately under real-world operating conditions. Thus, except in the cases of entirely new systems or minor system changes, a firm will prudently perform a final system checkout during a trial period. Two major checkout approaches are available.

Parallel operation involves the concurrent operation of both the present system and the new system for a reasonable period of time. This checkout approach enables the outputs from both systems, such as reports

and account balances, to be compared and their differences reconciled. When the results indicate that the new system is able to perform satisfactorily under actual operating conditions, cutover can safely take place. The primary purpose of parallel operation, therefore, is to avoid failure or serious problems in a new system and the adverse effects (e.g., losses of data) that problems would entail.

Parallel operation has drawbacks. It is costly and burdensome, since dual staffs are usually needed to operate the two systems. The project team often must work overtime when trouble-shooting problems and reconciling differences in operating results. So there is a natural tendency and desire to minimize the period of parallel operation. Nevertheless, several operating cycles should be checked (when parallel operation is felt to be the best checkout approach) in order to minimize the risk of later problems and possible failure.

As we have implied, parallel operation is likely not to be the best checkout approach in certain situations. Among these situations are

1. A new system for a newly organized function of a firm.

2. An improved system whose outputs are not compatible with the outputs of the present system.

3. An improved system that is to be installed in numerous locations throughout a firm.

In such situations, final checkout must be adapted to fit the circumstances. Perhaps a variety of hypothetical transactions can be devised to test the new system. A more likely adaptation, however, is an approach labeled modular conversion (also known as a pilot operation or a phase-in conversion approach). A **modular conversion** approach involves the checkout and cutover to a new or improved system in modules or segments. It often accompanies the modular approach to systems development.

Thus, a firm might convert by organizational segments (e.g., product lines, departments, sales territories, plants) or by information system segments (e.g., outputs, data base, transaction types). Consider, for instance, the situation in which a bank has developed an on-line transaction processing system for its numerous branches. The bank likely will employ the pilot operation approach, checking out and cutting over to the new system one branch at a time. It can thereby discover and correct problems under simpler and more localized conditions than would prevail if it attempted to check out all branches at once. These benefits, attainable from any application of the modular conversion approach, more than offset the accompanying drawback—a greatly extended checkout period.

Follow-up and evaluation of new system. Cutover marks the point at which the operational phase begins. However, the newly implemented system should not be viewed as being in its final form. Typically, a new system must undergo a "shakedown" period. Undiscovered quirks need to be ironed out, so that the system runs smoothly. The system design requires fine-tuning. Users must

---

APPLICATIONS OF MODULAR CONVERSION IMPLEMENTATIONS

Heinz-U.K.'s Conversion[a]

The British subsidiary of the H. J. Heinz Company has been developing a computer-integrated manufacturing system. This highly automated system is designed to integrate manufacturing with its finance/accounting and sales/marketing activities. As the first phase of the implementation Heinz-U.K. acquired mainframe computers from IBM and minicomputers from Digital Equipment Corporation and installed data base management systems. After these functioned properly as separate installations, the second phase involved linking the computers together in a local area network and incorporating microcomputers. The third phase, to be completed in 1989, consists of installing the materials requirements planning software. Later phases will include applications software that tracks cost of work in progress, that records finished goods transfers, and that aids in production management, engineering, maintenance control, and asset management. In time similar integrated systems will be installed at other Heinz plants in the United States and other countries.

[a]Tom McCusker, "Heinz Embarks on IS Course to Handle a Growing Variety," *Datamation* (Feb. 1, 1988), pp. 36–37.

Georgia-Pacific's Conversion.[b]

The wood-products firm known as Georgia-Pacific also decided to improve its manufacturing systems. Its currently established distributed computer network, which links its 166 production facilities to its corporate offices in Atlanta, will serve as the foundation for the new systems. Eventually the firm intends to have such functions as sales forecasting and master production scheduling performed centrally from its corporate offices and such functions as inventory control and materials planning performed by each plant. In its first phase the basic materials planning application was installed in the tissue paper products plants at Bellingham, Washington, and four other sites. Phase two will consist of adding shop floor control and other production applications at these same five plants. Phase three will link the full materials-production systems at the five plants to the corporate offices and the master scheduling application to the five plants. Later phases will add the applications at the remaining plants and expand the applications to include sales order entry and warehouse distribution.

[b]Chris Sivula, "Georgia-Pacific's MRP II Test," *Datamation* (Nov. 15, 1989), pp. 95–101.

learn how to operate the system and become reconciled to the "new way of doing things." To assure that these results are achieved, members of the project team should observe operations, provide assistance, and make necessary adjustments.

An example will suggest the value of this continued surveillance. An order clerk was reassigned and trained to operate an on-line terminal, and did well for several weeks. Then, one day, a rare type of order transaction occurred for which she had not been trained. A systems analyst quickly was able to explain the procedure for entering the transaction and to reassure her concerning other new types of transactions that she might encounter. He explained that built-in controls would catch and display any keying errors—that is, that she had complete control over the entry of correct data. After this explanation she had a better understanding of and a greater appreciation for the new system.

After a reasonable period of time the new system should achieve a stabilized operating condition. At this point the users may formally "accept" the system in writing, thus agreeing that it meets their objectives and needs.

One last task, however, remains. The new system needs to be evaluated. A **postinstallation evaluation** enables the project team and the information systems manager to (1) assess the extent to which the preestablished objectives are being met, (2) spot significant modifications that are needed, (3) evaluate the performance of the project team, and (4) improve decisions concerning future systems development projects. Thus, it serves as the final link in the control of systems projects.

A postinstallation evaluation should be analytical in nature. For instance, it should induce an analysis of the differences between projected costs and actual costs, as well as the reasons for these differences. It should provide a similar analysis of anticipated benefits, such as improved processing efficiency

and ease of use. In addition, it should examine (1) the extent to which the system fulfills the information needs of managers, and (2) the possibility that an alternative system design might have more fully satisfied these information needs. Furthermore, it should attempt to judge the degree to which the new system has gained acceptance by the users.

The postinstallation evaluation should culminate in a written report to management. The report will contain a summary of the preceding assessments. It might also include a historical record of the implementation activities.

Detailed System Design Techniques

Detailed system design consists, in large part, of preparing logic diagrams and writing (or customizing) the computer programs. The program flowchart was the first logic diagram to receive wide usage. It is still the best example of a classical detailed design technique. A variety of diagrams reflecting the structured systems development approach at a detailed level have been devised in recent years. Included in this category are the decision table, decision tree, bubble chart, data hierarchy diagram, Warnier–Orr diagram, hierarchical input process output (HIPO) diagram, structured English, and pseudocode. These structured techniques differ mainly in degree of detail from the structured techniques described in Chapter 22.[7] They offer the same benefits as provided by all structured techniques.

Several of the aforementioned logic diagrams are briefly discussed and illustrated in the following paragraphs. Then the process of developing software is described.

---

[7]Certain of the techniques are listed both here and in Chapter 22, since they overlap the systems analysis and detailed design phases.

Logic Diagrams

Program flowcharts. A **program flowchart** portrays the sequential and logical operations to be performed by a computer when carrying out a program's instructions. Known also as a block diagram, a program flowchart encompasses the detailed steps needed to perform a major processing step, such as sorting the records in a file or updating a master file.[8] Pictorially, a program flowchart is a "blowup" of a rectangular computer processing symbol on a system flowchart. The several processing symbols that typically appear in a system flowchart therefore represent a series of coordinated program flowcharts.

Program flowcharts are prepared by using standard symbols connected by flowlines. Figure 25-5 shows four standard flowcharting symbols and their meanings. The program flowchart shown in Figure 25-6 illustrates the use of these symbols. It portrays the detailed steps necessary to update a master file. In order to understand the construction and advantages of program flowcharts, let us examine the circumstances pertaining to and logic embodied in the figure.

Figure 25-6 portrays an accounts receivable processing application. Two files are involved: (1) a transaction file, consisting of sales and cash receipts transactions; and (2) an accounts receivable master file. Each record in the transaction file contains a transaction code (*1* means a sale, and *2* means a cash receipt), a three-digit customer number, and the amount of the transaction. The transaction records have first been transcribed from source documents onto a magnetic medium; then they have been sorted in customer number order to accord with the records in the master file. Following the last record in the transaction file is a record con-

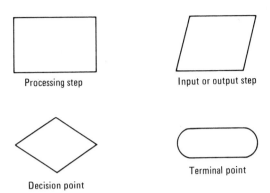

FIGURE 25-5 Standard program flowcharting symbols.

taining a "dummy" 999 customer number—a number larger than any actual customer number. At the end of the master file is an end-of-file indicator. The master file is considerably larger than the transaction file, since the activity ratio ranges from 20 to 30 percent.

The initial step in the processing application is to instruct the computer's input devices to read the first transaction and master records. The next step is to check to see whether the end-of-file indicator has been encountered. Since the master file consists of more than one record, it will not yet be encountered (although it will be at some later time). Therefore, the third step is to compare the customer numbers on the transaction and master records. One of three conditions will be discovered upon this comparison: The customer number on the transaction record will be (1) larger, (2) equal to, or (3) smaller than the customer number on the master record. If the second condition occurs, the master file record is to be updated by the transaction. Then the next transaction record is to be read.

Since records in the master file greatly outnumber transaction records, however, often the first or third condition will occur. If the first condition occurs (e.g., the customer number on the transaction record is 105 and

---

[8] In practice, two levels of program flowcharts often are used, one at a macro level and one at a more detailed, micro level. However, this distinction will be ignored in our relatively brief discussion.

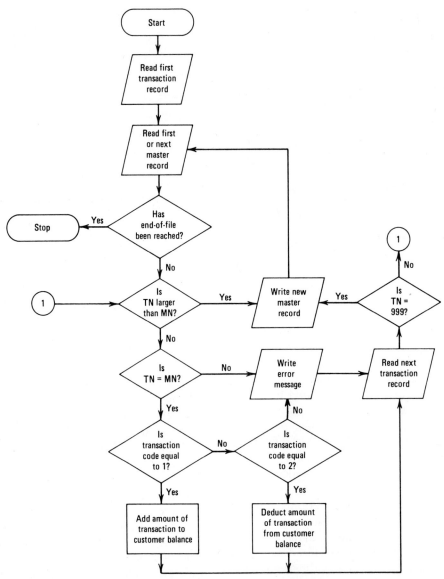

Note: TN refers to the customer number on a transaction record. MN refers to the customer number on a master record.

FIGURE 25-6 A program flowchart.

the customer number on the master record is 100), the master record at hand is no longer needed in the processing run. Either (1) none of the transactions pertain to that particular master record or (2) all transactions pertaining to that master record have already been reflected in the master record. Thus, it is necessary to read (access) the next master record containing a larger customer number. First, however, the master record at hand must be written onto the new file medium, such as a new magnetic tape. If the third condition occurs (e.g., the customer number on the transaction record is 110 and the cus-

Condition	Rule 1	2	3	4	5	6
C1. Has end-of-file indicator been reached?	N	N	N	N		Y
C2. Is customer number on transaction record larger than number on master record?	Y	N	N	N		
C3. Is customer number on transaction record equal to number on master record?		N	Y	Y		
C4. Is transaction a sale?			Y			
C5. Is transaction a payment?				Y		
C6. Is customer number the dummy 999?		N	N	N	Y	
Action						
A1. Read transaction record.		X	X	X		
A2. Read master record.	X				X	
A3. Write new master record.	X				X	
A4. Write error message.		X				
A5. Add amount of transaction to customer balance.			X			
A6. Deduct amount of transaction from customer balance.				X		
A7. Stop processing.						X

Note: Y means yes, N means no.

FIGURE 25-7 A decision table.

tomer number of the master record is 107), apparently an error condition exists. Perhaps a transaction record is out of sequence, a customer number is incorrectly keyed, or a master record is missing. Whatever the cause, an error message is to be written onto an exception report and the next transaction record is to be read.

The processing is to continue until all transaction records have been read and dealt with as described earlier. Then the record containing the number 999 will be encountered. Since this number should be larger than every customer number appearing on master records, a looping procedure is to be set in motion. That is, each remaining master record is to be read and written onto the new file medium (e.g., new magnetic tape) until the end-of-file indicator is reached. At that time the program is to cease execution.

Decision tables. A **decision table,** another commonly used logic diagram, focuses on the "decision choices" inherent in many

data processing and decision support applications. By means of a matrix format it identifies sets of actions that accompany alternative sets of conditions. It does *not,* however, specify the sequence in which processing actions are to be performed or conditions are to be tested.

Figure 25-7 presents a decision table that corresponds to the program flowchart shown in Figure 25-6.[9] Each decision point (represented by a diamond in the program flowchart) appears as a separate condition in the decision table. Each processing step and input–output step appears as an action. Each logic path through a program flowchart, consisting symbolically of diamonds, rectangles, and parallelograms, appears as a rule in the decision table. For instance, the conditions and actions reflected in rule 3 correspond to the logic path that (1) begins with the dia-

[9]The decision table in Figure 25-7 represents an example of the limited entry form, since conditions must be answered by either *Y* (yes) or *N* (no).

mond labeled "Has end-of-file indicator been reached?" (2) progresses downward through three more diamonds, (3) executes the processing action to "Add amount of transaction to customer balance," and (4) executes the input action to "Read next transaction record."

Because a decision table shows all of the rules—the logical relationships—pertaining to a data processing or decision situation, it can replace or supplement a program flowchart. A useful approach is to prepare a decision table first, since the sequencing of steps can be ignored. Then the decision table can be used to guide the preparation of a program flowchart.

To construct a decision table of the limited-entry form, begin by developing a clear statement of the problem or processing situation. Next, identify and list the conditions and actions, without regard to order, along the left-hand portions of the table format. Then complete the total number of possible rules (i.e., responses to sets of conditions) by means of the formula 2^R, where R is the number of independent conditions. Enter all possible rules into the columns of the table, thereby forming a "full" decision table. Finally, combine rules where possible and eliminate irrelevant rules to form a "collapsed" decision table.

Consider the application of this approach to the construction of the "collapsed" decision table appearing as Figure 25-7. The accounts receivable processing application is first described in writing. From the description, the six conditions and seven actions are abstracted and listed. Then the total number of possible rules is computed to be $2^6 = 64$. These rules are next inserted into columns across a (very wide) spreadsheet. Each rule is reflected by a combination of six N's and Y's in the condition portion and by one or more X's in the action portion of the table. For instance, six of the rules would appear as follows:

C1	Y	Y	Y	Y	Y	Y
C2	N	Y	Y	Y	Y	Y
C3	N	N	Y	Y	Y	Y
C4	N	N	N	Y	Y	Y
C5	N	N	N	N	Y	Y
C6	N	N	N	N	N	Y
A7	X	X	X	X	X	X

However, only one of these rules is needed. When C1 ("Has the end-of-file indicator been reached?") is Yes, the other conditions are irrelevant and the action remains the same ("Stop processing"). Thus, these six rules can be collapsed to the single rule appearing as rule 6 in Figure 25-7. The remaining possible rules can be likewise collapsed into rules 1 through 5 in Figure 25-7.

Data hierarchy diagrams. Similar in appearance to the hierarchy chart, a **data hierarchy diagram** reflects the details pertaining to a collection of related data. Figure 25-8 presents a data diagram that shows four levels of detail pertaining to the data in a sales invoice. This particular structured diagram can aid in the design of a file layout of a sales transaction record or in the writing of a sales invoicing application program.

Another diagram that is more closely related to the hierarchy chart is the hierarchy, plus input, process, and output (HIPO) diagram. A **HIPO diagram** shows the key input data needed by a single process box and the output information generated by the process. For instance, in Figure 22-13 the process "Check credit" might be expanded into a HIPO diagram. One of the input data would be the quantity of ordered items, whereas an output would be either a credit approval or a rejection. The process box would list the series of steps required to generate the output.

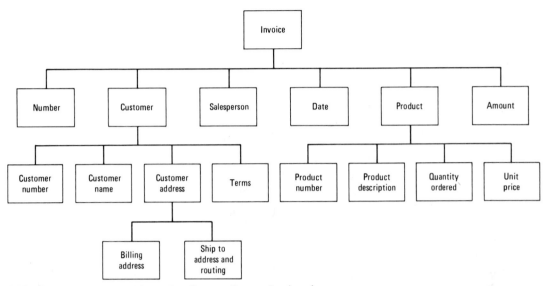

FIGURE 25-8   A data hierarchy diagram for a sales invoice.

Warnier–Orr diagrams. Jean-Dominique Warnier and Ken Orr developed a structured technique that employs the **Warnier–Orr diagram.** This diagram is used to represent in graphical format a processing sequence, data structure, or structure of a document or report. Figure 25-9 shows the data structure of a sales invoice. Each bracket indicates a grouping of data; as the brackets move to the right in the diagram, the data items become more detailed (i.e., at lower levels in the hierarchy). As is apparent, a Warnier–Orr dia-

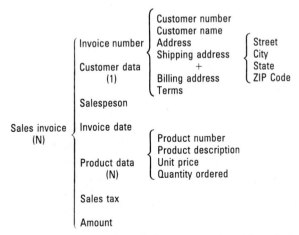

Note: (a) Number or letter in parentheses indicates the number of times the item occurs.
(b) The + means that either or both of the items may appear.

FIGURE 25-9   A Warnier–Orr diagram of the data hierarchy within a sales invoice.

gram is an alternative technique to the data hierarchy diagram. It provides easy-to-read documentation that can aid in writing structured computer programs.

As mentioned, the Warnier–Orr diagram can be used to describe a process. However, **pseudocode** and *structured English* represent very desirable alternatives. Both describe processes by means of informal languages that are not bound by the constraints of specific programming languages. They are also known as program design languages (PDL's). An example of a PDL is Context Free Grammar, which uses free-form English statements within a loose structure of text segments, flow segments, and data segments.[10]

Software Code Development

Computer programs. Detailed sets of instructions, known as **computer programs,** are prepared from logic diagrams. As noted in Chapter 5, these software products serve various purposes. Application programs process transactions, retrieve stored data, prepare reports, and solve problems. Since they provide the details that enable computer-based system designs to be realized, application programs are of prime importance to systems analysts and accountants. Programs known as operating systems control the various processing operations of central processing units and their attached input and output devices. Programs comprising data base management systems control the processing and retrieval of data in data base environments.

Each program must be written in a specific programming language. The most widely employed language for business applications is **COBOL,** a highly structured and well-documented procedure-oriented

[10]Csaba J. Egyhazy, "Technical Software Development Tools," *Journal of Systems Management* (Jan. 1985), pp. 10–11.

language. Figure 25-10 presents a program written in COBOL. Various other languages are used, however, in situations in which their advantages are compelling. An assembly or symbolic language generally is used when processing efficiency is important, as in the cases of utility routines and operating systems. **FORTRAN,** an algebraic-type procedure-oriented language, is well suited to engineering and management science applications. **BASIC,** an easy-to-learn language designed for use via interactive terminals, is attractive to occasional users such as accountants. Fourth-generation languages, such as FOCUS and Interactive Financial Planning Systems (IFPS), are nonprocedural languages that can be even more easily learned and used by nonprofessional programmers. Figure 20-13 listed a complete program written in IFPS.

Coding is the act of writing instructions comprising a program. Coding is normally the final step in developing a detailed system design. When performed manually it is also one of the most time-consuming activities in the entire systems development cycle. Besides the innumerable details posed by the procedure being coded, a programmer is confronted by the rules and constraints of the language being used. Furthermore, he or she often faces a complex programming environment. For example, the programmer must deal with randomly arriving and departing transactions when coding an on-line processing program to be employed within a distributed computer network.

A disciplined approach to program development and coding therefore is essential. A top-down approach known as **structured program design** has been gaining in popularity among programmers because it provides a high degree of discipline. It begins with the development of a relatively broad logic diagram. From this top-level diagram are prepared other logic diagrams at several levels, with each successive level presenting more details. Any of the logic diagrams we have described can be employed in structured pro-

```
IDENTIFICATION DIVISION.
PROGRAM-ID. WEEKLY SALES EARNINGS REPORT.
AUTHOR. MARK.
INSTALLATION. ASU COMPUTER CENTER.


ENVIRONMENT DIVISION.
CONFIGURATION SECTION.
SOURCE-COMPUTER. E425.
OBJECT-COMPUTER. E425.
INPUT-OUTPUT SECTION.
FILE-CONTROL.
    SELECT DATA-FILE ASSIGN TO 0100.
    SELECT REPORT-FILE ASSIGN TO 0300.


DATA DIVISION.
FILE SECTION.
FD  DATA-FILE, LABEL RECORD IS OMITTED, DATA RECORD IS CARD-IMAGE.
01  CARD-IMAGE, PICTURE X(80).
FD  REPORT-FILE, LABEL RECORD IS OMITTED, DATA RECORD IS LINE-IMAGE.
01  LINE-IMAGE PICTURE X(132).
WORKING-STORAGE SECTION.
77  TOTAL-SALES, PICTURE 99999V99, VALUE ZERO.
77  COMMISSION, PICTURE 9999V99.
77  TOTAL-COMMISSION, PICTURE 9999V99, VALUE ZERO.
01  HEADING.
    02 FILLER, PICTURE X(35), VALUE SPACES.
    02 FILLER, PICTURE X(29), VALUE 'WEEKLY SALES EARNINGS REPORT'.
01  HEADING-ONE.
    02 FILLER, PICTURE X(26), VALUE SPACES.
    02 FILLER, PICTURE X(23), VALUE 'SALESMAN        SALES'.
    02 FILLER, PICTURE X(27), VALUE '        COMMISSION
01  HEADING-TWO.
    02 FILLER, PICTURE X(26), VALUE SPACES.
    02 FILLER, PICTURE X(24), VALUE 'NUMBER        AMOUNT'.
    02 FILLER, PICTURE X(2), VALUE SPACES.
01  SALES-REPORT-DATA.
    02 SALESMAN-NO, PICTURE 999999.
    02 SALES-AMOUNT, PICTURE 99999V99.
    02 FILLER, PICTURE X(3), VALUE SPACES.
01  DETAIL-LINE.
    02 FILLER, PICTURE X(25), VALUE SPACES.
    02 SALES-NO-OUT, PICTURE ZZ9999.
    02 FILLER, PICTURE X(11), VALUE SPACES.
    02 SALES-OUT, PICTURE ZZZ99.99.
    02 FILLER, PICTURE X(12), VALUE SPACES.
    02 COMMISSION-OUT, PICTURE ZZZ9.99.
    02 FILLER, PICTURE X(10), VALUE SPACES.
01  TOTALS-LINE.
    02 FILLER, PICTURE X(26), VALUE SPACES.
    02 FILLER, PICTURE X(6), VALUE 'TOTALS'.
    02 FILLER, PICTURE X(10), VALUE SPACES.
    02 TOTAL-SALES-OUT, PICTURE $ZZ99.99.
    02 FILLER, PICTURE X(12), VALUE SPACES.
    02 TOTAL-COMMISSION-OUT, PICTURE $ZZ9.99.
    02 FILLER, PICTURE X(11), VALUE SPACES.

CONSTANT SECTION.
77  TEN-PERCENT, PICTURE V99, VALUE .10.

PROCEDURE DIVISION.
START.
    OPEN INPUT DATA-FILE AND OUTPUT REPORT-FILE.
    WRITE LINE-IMAGE FROM HEADING AFTER ADVANCING TO TOP OF PAGE.
    WRITE LINE-IMAGE FROM HEADING-ONE AFTER ADVANCING 1 LINES.
    WRITE LINE-IMAGE FROM HEADING-TWO BEFORE ADVANCING 1 LINES.
READ-SALES-DATA.
    READ DATA-FILE INTO SALES-REPORT-DATA, AT END GO TO FINISH.
    ADD SALES-AMOUNT TO TOTAL-SALES.
    COMPUTE COMMISSION = SALES-AMOUNT • TEN-PERCENT.
    ADD COMMISSION TO TOTAL-COMMISSION.
    MOVE SALESMAN-NO TO SALES-NO-OUT.
    MOVE SALES-AMOUNT TO SALES-OUT.
    MOVE COMMISSION TO COMMISSION-OUT.
    WRITE LINE-IMAGE FROM DETAIL-LINE.
    GO TO READ-SALES-DATA.
FINISH.
    MOVE TOTAL-SALES TO TOTAL-SALES-OUT.
    MOVE TOTAL-COMMISSION TO TOTAL-COMMISSION OUT.
    WRITE LINE-IMAGE FROM TOTALS-LINE AFTER ADVANCING 1 LINES.
    CLOSE DATA-FILE AND REPORT-FILE.
    STOP RUN.
```

FIGURE 25-10 A computer program written in COBOL.

gram design, since all embody this necessary top-down approach.

The structured program design approach results in the formation of independent but interconnected program modules within an integrated framework. Incorporating such modules, called subroutines, enables significant benefits to be realized. A programming task can be spread among several programmers. Programming errors (called *bugs*) can be isolated more quickly, and thus the time required to test programs is reduced. Changes in programs can also be effected more quickly.

Computer-aided tools. Because manual coding is so tedious, computer-aided code generation tools have been devised. As in the case of all computer-aided system development tools, these **application code generators** increase the productivity of programmers. Manyfold increases (e.g., 30 to 1) in productivity are not uncommon.

Application code generators are in effect a subset of fourth-generation languages. However, they vary in certain respects. Some code generators accept specification statements that describe the logic of an application. Then they generate code in the form of a third-generation procedural language, such as COBOL. Others, such as the CASE packages described in Chapter 23, accept definitions of the desired application. Then they convert the definitions into structured diagrams, charts, and a data encyclopedia. From these specifications the CASE package generates either a procedural language or a special high-level code. Some application code generators function separately. Others are components of complete application generator packages that include data base management systems, query software, report generators, and graphics.

An example of an application generator is Application Factory (from Cortex Corporation). It generates on-line production programs that are compatible with VAX mini-computers from Digital Equipment Corporation. Recently DuPont Corporation used Application Factory to generate software code in the Bulk Continuous Filament project, a part of the inspection and packing system at one of its textile plants. DuPont's managers were pleased with the results, since the project was completed ahead of schedule, under budget, and with greater-than-expected functionality.[11]

Integrated software architectures. An increasing number of information systems employ integrated computing environments. These environments include wide-area networks, local area networks, and often electronic data interchange networks. In many cases such multiple networks include computer hardware and software from various manufacturers. Also, a wide variety of users are served by these networks. Developing new application programs under such conditions can be awesomely difficult. Consequently, the larger computer manufacturers are currently devising application development architectures for integrated computing environments. IBM Corporation has proposed Systems Application Architecture (SAA), Hewlett-Packard has introduced Distributed Application, and American Telephone & Telegraph has offered Application Operating Environment.[12] In effect, these architectures are specifications that describe how applications are to be built. When applications software is written according to the specifications, it should provide common access to all qualified users. That is, a user who accesses the system at any point should be able to process transactions or employ needed software packages easily and freely.

[11]Carma McClure, "Software Automation," *Business Software Review* (September 1987), pp. 30–31.
[12]Gary McWilliams, "Integrated Computing Environments," *Datamation* (May 1, 1989), pp. 18–21.

People Concerns During Implementation

Much of this chapter has dealt with the numerous steps and activities—the mechanics—involved in successfully implementing information systems. However, mechanistic concerns are considerably less important than people concerns. In fact, the president of a high-technology manufacturer estimates that "implementation is 10 percent mechanics, 30 percent education [training] and 60 percent [people] acceptance."[13]

Uncertainties and Fears

Since people will use and operate a new information system, as noted earlier, their concerns must be kept in mind throughout the implementation phase. These concerns mainly consist of (1) uncertainties about the impending changes in the information system and (2) fears that the changes will disturb their familiar and comfortable work patterns, will break up their work and social groups, and may cause the loss of status and even of job security.

Forms of Resistance

Because of such uncertainties and fears, the affected employees and managers will tend to resist the changes being implemented. Their resistance may take varied forms of aggressive or evasive behavior. For instance, production-line employees may intentionally enter incorrect time data into the system, thereby distorting the reported labor costs. Salespersons may blame the system for errors that they make in recording customers' orders. Data processing clerks may revert to the old way of processing transac-

[13]"Software Package Leads to Modular On-Line System," *Infosystems* (Nov. 1980), p. 92.

tions, thus bypassing the controls and processing capabilities of the new system. Managers may obtain information for decision making from informal sources, thus ignoring the reports of the new system.

Significant resistance can be fatal to the success of a newly implemented system. In other words, it can cause the system to be operationally infeasible and hence to fail to achieve its stated objectives.

Desirable Actions

Several positive actions fortunately are available to counteract such resistance. As described in Chapters 21 and 22, these actions should begin early in the systems development sequence and should continue through the implementation phase.

The first positive action, previously stressed, is to keep both managers and employees *fully informed* concerning the impending changes. They should be told not only *what* changes are being made but also *why* the changes are being made.

Another positive action is to solicit the *active participation* of both managers and employees. Managers can be asked to express their support for the changes, to assist in screening the array of needed information, and to make key decisions concerning implementation activities. Employees can be asked to make suggestions concerning improvements in the system design and to provide data for use in program testing. Participation is especially important when the system is relatively complex, as in the case of decision support systems. However, participation in all situations should provide such benefits as

1. Helping the users to understand the workings of the new system.
2. Committing the users to the notion of change.

3. Giving the users a feeling that the new system is theirs, rather than a creation imposed by outsiders.
4. Giving the users a sense of security and satisfaction in their jobs.
5. Assuring that the system will be well integrated into the employees' work environment and is consistent with the social values of the work groups.

A third positive action is to provide reassurances to both the managers and employees. They should be told and shown how the new system will benefit them in their jobs. For instance, they might be reassured that the new system will provide greater job satisfaction, relieve them of the onerous aspects of their responsibilities, and provide increased opportunities for advancement. Affected managers and employees can also be reassured, through announced personnel policies, that they will be treated fairly. For example, the policies might state that managers and employees displaced by the new system will be either (1) relocated in jobs of equal pay and status or (2) aided in finding comparable jobs outside the firm.

Still other desirable actions include those that provide assistance to the users, such as

1. Designing the system to be as easy to operate by the employees as possible.
2. Assigning assistants to high-level managers who are knowledgeable concerning the use of interactive terminals and other elements of decision support systems.
3. Setting implementation deadlines that are reasonably met and not inconvenient to the affected employees and managers.
4. Keeping all employees informed and educated through the use of newsletters, meetings, seminars, and so forth.

Limitations

The preceding actions can help to assure that a soundly designed system will be operationally feasible. However, it should be noted that the reactions of the employees and managers can definitely place limits on the system design. For instance, a design that causes severe changes within the power structure of a firm is likely to be doomed to failure; the affected managers can be expected to resist the system so fiercely that it will not have a chance to work effectively.

Activities During the Operational Phase

Figure 25-11 shows the relationship of the operational phase of a new information system to the preceding developmental phases. It also presents several key activities that generally take place on a *continuing* or *recurring* basis during the operational phase. Each will be briefly reviewed in turn.

Routine Operations

The most visible activity, of course, is the series of routine operations performed on a daily basis. Data are collected concerning various transactions, prepared in computer-sensible form, and entered for processing; outputs are generated periodically or on demand. Computer operators mount tapes for a processing run and dismount them after the run is completed. Accountants and engineers access stored data via terminals. Although specific activities vary in accordance with the particular system configuration, they revolve around the familiar information system tasks observed in Chapter 1.

Accounting for System-Related Costs

The services provided by an information system—collecting transaction data, storing the data, delivering useful information to us-

ers, and so on—can be very expensive. They often depend not only on the operation of complex hardware and software but also on the informed actions of numerous professional systems personnel. The substantial costs for such system-related resources should periodically be established within a firm's overall operating budget. Then the actual incurred costs must be reflected in some manner in the firm's financial records and statements. For various reasons, which will be discussed later, a firm may well decide to charge many of these costs, especially those identified with routine operations, to the users of services. Therefore, another important activity during the operational phase is the accounting for system-related costs.

Control of System-Related Resources

Accounting for system-related costs is part of a larger time and cost control framework. The mission of this larger framework is to assure that all resources devoted to the information system are used effectively and efficiently. Therefore, a third activity (related to the first two) is the evaluation and control of system-related resources. It consists essentially of establishing standards and comparing actual results (e.g., utilization of equipment and personnel performances) against these standards.

Audits of System Operations, Controls, and Outputs

Evaluation should not be limited to the effectiveness and efficiency of system-related resources, however. Systems and higher-level managers are also concerned with the efficiency and effectiveness of the information system itself. Thus, still another key activity consists of auditing the information system, including its operations, controls, and outputs.

Obviously, the auditing activity is closely related to the two previous activities.

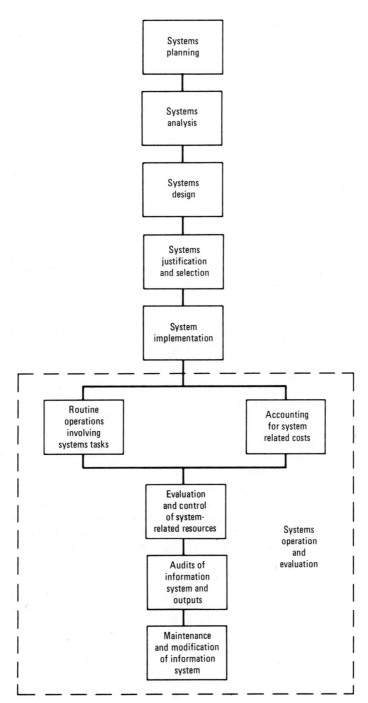

FIGURE 25-11 Key activities in the systems operational phase.

In fact, it may be combined with the activity concerned with controlling system-related resources and administered by the same organizational unit. The organizational unit generally concerned with audits and controls is the internal audit department.

System Maintenance and Modifications

An information system does not stay in its initial operating condition indefinitely. In fact, maintenance is a continuing activity throughout its operating life. Significant modifications typically are necessary from time to time. An essential aim of audits and evaluations is to spot the need for changes.

Maintenance or modifications may be needed for any of a number of reasons. A design weakness necessitating correction may be discovered, for instance. A manager may insist on an added report, or top management may revise a major policy of the firm. Conditions may change in the firm's environment; for example, new government regulations may be issued, economic factors may shift sharply, or new technology may become available.

This restorative activity serves two important functions. First, it keeps the information system in an up-to-date, effective, and efficient state. Second, it signals, via increasing levels of required modifications, the need for a new development cycle. However, it consumes as much as 80 to 90 percent of overall systems work schedules.

Role of Accountants in Operational Activities

Accountants often become involved in all of these operational activities. With respect to routine operations and system modifications, their roles may be limited to those of users; however, at times they become active participants in the modification of reports and controls and perhaps the related processing steps. With respect to three of these activities, they generally have quite active roles. Their expertise assists them in devising suitable methods of charging system-related costs, in evaluating system-related resources, and in conducting audits.

Because of the active involvement of accountants in these latter activities, we shall examine accounting for system-related costs and control of system-related resources at greater length. The audit activity is not discussed further, since it was described in Chapter 17.

Accounting for System-Related Costs

Several questions arise with respect to costs incurred in processing data and providing other services related to the information system: Should such costs be charged to users? If they should be charged, on what basis should the chargeout rates be established? If a cost basis is selected, what factors should be considered? How and under what conditions should established chargeout rates be modified? Figure 25-12 portrays the various decision branches that may be followed.

Establishing Need for Charging Costs

System-related costs include those pertaining to computer hardware and software, data communications, supplies, operational personnel, maintenance personnel, and systems analysts and programmers. In previous decades many firms simply absorbed all such costs into general overhead accounts. This practice avoided the sticky problems that arise when costs are to be allocated among the various users. It also encouraged managers to make use of newly acquired computers. Since computing power was in effect a "free good," managers drew on it extensively. Computer-based applications mushroomed. Not surprisingly, system-related costs also grew rapidly.

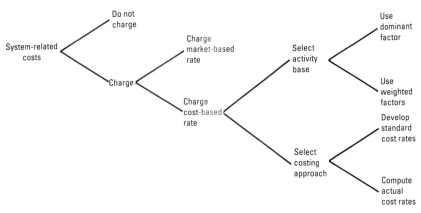

FIGURE 25-12   A decision tree for system-related costs.

The managements of such firms soon realized the need to control the growth of these system-related costs. Most rejected the use of arbitrary budget ceilings to restrain such costs, since they recognized that this approach might stifle the growth of their firms. Instead, they generally settled on the use of *chargeouts:* charges of system-related costs to users on the basis of soundly established *chargeout rates*.

Chargeouts are widely accepted today as the most suitable means of accounting for and controlling system-related costs, since their use helps

1. To ensure that the resources of the systems function will be shared efficiently and effectively in accordance with each user's needs.
2. To stimulate the involvement of the benefiting users in information system developments.
3. To provide cost data by which to evaluate the efficiency and effectiveness of the information systems function.
4. To provide reliable usage data by which to plan future expansions in information system services.

In order to set up a chargeout system, management first must budget the amounts that the respective users (responsibility centers) within a firm can spend for system-related services. The next step is to establish rates to charge for the use of system resources. These rates should then be translated into prices for such services as processing sales orders and cash payments, printing statements and reports, and handling information inquiries and other requests. By reference to these prices, each user can decide whether the benefits from particular services exceed their costs. If so, he or she can request such services rationally and have the resulting costs charged against his or her budget.

Not all system-related costs need be included within a chargeout system, however. Consider system development projects, such as the design and installation of a data base, which affect more than one using function. If the costs of such interrelated projects are designated as general overhead, three benefits should be reaped. Potential users likely will support the projects more actively, cost allocation headaches will be avoided, and system development will proceed in a more planned manner.

Establishing Chargeout Rates

The heart of a chargeout system is the schedule of rates charged for system-related services. Thus, considerable care should be taken in selecting chargeout rates for use in a particular system. To the greatest extent possible, the resulting chargeout rates should be

1. Fair, in that they reasonably measure the quantity of resources used.
2. Understandable, in that they are or can be expressed in terms familiar to users.
3. Consistent, in that similar services under similar circumstances are comparably priced.

In addition to possessing these attributes, the chargeout rates should encourage the economical use of systems resources, minimize conflicts among users, and generate realistic planning information. Furthermore, the rates should be relatively inexpensive to determine and apply.

Chargeout rates may be market based or cost based, as denoted by the two branches leading from the "Charge" fork in Figure 25-12.

Market-based rates. A **market-based rate** is directly related to prices charged in the marketplace. It is appropriate when the information systems function is established as a profit center. In such a case the information systems manager has profit responsibility, and the systems function is allowed to charge rates that are comparable to those charged by the "market"—that is, the commercial data processing services. At the same time, users are allowed to acquire system-related services from the source with the lowest prices, even if that source may be *outside* the firm. As a consequence of this competition, the systems function cannot charge at a rate higher than the market rate; thus, users will be assured of reasonable rates. Moreover, the systems function will be highly motivated

to be efficient, so that it will earn a profit at this market-based rate.

Although market-based rates generally meet the criteria stated earlier, their use can pose dangers for a firm. For instance, the systems function might incur a loss in providing service at the market rate; it would then be tempted to advocate the use of a negotiated "transfer price or rate."[14] If such a negotiated rate is allowed, the user would be less motivated to employ the resources in an efficient and economical manner. Moreover, considerable animosity might then develop between the systems function and the users. Because of such dangers, the profit center approach and market-based rates are most suitable in forms that (1) have a solid commitment to the decentralized organization structure and (2) have previously gained considerable experience in the use of cost-based chargeout rates.

Cost-based rates. A **cost-based rate** is directly related to the costs that are or should be incurred by the systems function. Cost-based chargeout rates are intended to provide returns that cover the costs of a service-oriented cost center (in this case, the systems function). Either actual costs or standard costs may be used as the basis in determining the chargeout rates.

Actual cost rates, also known as average cost rates, are computed by dividing the actual total system-related costs by an activity base such as actual processing hours. Rates determined in this manner are understandable to users. They are also likely to be lower than market-based rates and thus to encourage the fuller use of system resources.

Actual cost rates, however, fail with respect to the consistency criterion. Inconsistency occurs because the rates must be recomputed periodically (perhaps each month

---

[14]A *transfer price* is the amount charged to a user for a good or service supplied by a function or organizational unit within the same firm.

or quarter) and their values depend on the activity levels achieved. When total activity is low, the rate is high; when total activity is high, the rate is low. Motivation to achieve processing efficiency is also lacking, since actual rates enable all costs to be recovered, regardless of their levels. Actual cost rates therefore may even tend to encourage inefficiencies. Furthermore, they provide no means by which to evaluate the efficiency of the systems function.

Standard cost rates are determined on the basis of careful studies. Instead of reflecting actual cost and activity levels, they express cost levels and activity levels attainable in the circumstances, given reasonably efficient operations. Normally, they are held constant for reasonably long periods, such as a year or longer.

Although standard cost rates are not quite as understandable and easily determined as actual cost rates, they more fully satisfy the remaining stated criteria. Not only are they fairer and more consistent, but they provide greater motivation toward efficiency. Motivation is provided by measuring the differences between standard and actual costs and reporting these differences as efficiency variances.

Figure 25-13 contrasts the methods of computing chargeouts by means of the two cost-based chargeout rates. It also shows the determination of chargeout costs when the market-based rate is used. In all cases the activity level is assumed to be measured by computer processing hours.

Modifying Chargeout Rates

In complex computer systems the established chargeout rates may need to be modified. For instance, computer systems with multiprogramming capabilities are designed to serve multiple users simultaneously. Often they are also characterized by rather wide fluctuations in use. Such systems may require chargeout rates that are multifaceted and adjustable in nature.

Multifaceted chargeout rates explicitly incorporate usage of the major components of the computer-based system. Instead of a single rate based on the overall productive time of the central processor, a multifaceted rate is in essence a series of rates built into a formula or algorithm. A separate chargeout rate is computed for each component, on the basis of either actual or estimated usage of that component. The overall charge to a particular job is then calculated by using the algorithm that applies these rates to the times that the respective components are used in completing that job.

To illustrate, we will assume that a particular computer system that operates in a multiprogramming mode consists of four components: a central processor, a disk

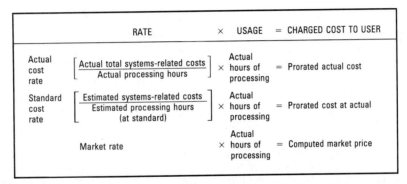

FIGURE 25-13 Three methods of computing chargeout costs.

drive, a terminal, and a printer. A chargeout algorithm based on these components might be as follows:

$$\text{Charge} = \{Cr_1 + Pr_2 + Tr_3 + Dr_4\}$$

where

C is the central processor time used.
P is the number of lines of printed output.
T is the terminal connect time.
D is the disk time used.
r_i is the individual chargeout rate of the ith component.[15]

Adjustable rates can be varied to achieve specific objectives of the systems function. For instance, rates may be varied to provide multiple levels of service. Thus, a user desiring fast response might be charged a higher rate than a user who is satisfied with an overnight response. Alternatively, rates may be varied to achieve the objectives of minimizing peak operating levels and balancing loads. Thus, a user who requires service during a peak period might be charged a higher rate than a user who is willing to receive service during a period of low usage; or, a user whose job requires a heavily used component (say, a high-speed nonimpact printer) may be charged a higher rate than a user whose job can be handled on a less heavily used component (such as a slower-speed impact printer).

Examples Involving Chargeout Rates

Firms such as Pacific Bell Telephone Co. and Seafirst Bank have experimented with varying types of chargeout systems before deciding upon the best systems for their firms. For instance, Northwestern National Life Insurance Co. developed computer programs to accumulate and allocate systems-related costs to users. However, management felt that the chargeout system should provide better control by measuring indirect as well as direct systems-related costs and by providing more detailed bills to users. It investigated software packages that perform such tasks, such as PACS Plus (from Signal Technology, Inc.) and MICS (from Morion Associates). After selecting and installing a package such as these, the manager of computer management and evaluation made the following comments: "User demands have leveled off significantly as their recognition of systems usage and how to do things more efficiently has increased. Correspondingly, IS costs have reached a plateau and are no longer growing. Overall, (he) is satisfied, as he believes that chargeback has met its objectives."[16]

Complex configurations and new services, such as information centers, can present challenges to chargeout systems. A suggested approach in the case of a newly installed information center is as follows: During the early phase, encourage use of the center by charging all costs to general overhead. As the center expands its services, charge users only for a portion of the services (e.g., for use during peak periods). When the center has reached the desired size and is fully known to users, charge users for all services.[17]

Control of System-Related Resources

Figure 25-14 portrays the time and cost framework of steps involved in controlling the use of system-related resources. One

---

[15]For more complete examples, see John J. Andersen, "Direct Chargeout of Information Systems Services Costs?" *Management Adviser* (March–April 1974), p. 31.

[16]Jeanne Buse, "Chargeback Systems Come of Age," *Datamation* (Nov. 1, 1988), pp. 52–53.

[17]Leon B Hoshower and Anthony A. Verstraete, "Accounting for Information Center Costs," *Journal of Accounting and EDP* (Winter 1986), pp. 7–8.

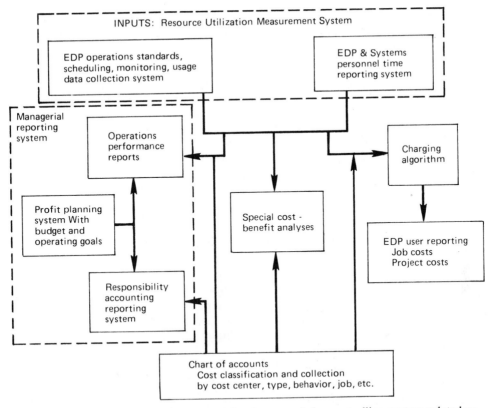

FIGURE 25-14 A time and cost accounting framework for controlling system-related resources.

step encompassed within this framework is charging costs to users. Other included steps are measuring the use of the resources, preparing periodic managerial reports, and performing special analyses.[18]

Measuring Resource Usage

To determine how effectively and efficiently resources are being used, it is first necessary to measure and record their usage. Certain of these usage measurements may be

the same as those employed to determine charges to users.

Measurements pertaining to computer facilities should include the times that the various components (e.g., central processor, terminal, printer) are devoted to various productive *and* nonproductive tasks. For instance, measurements may in a particular computer installation indicate that the central processor, two disk drives, and a printer were devoted to the preparation of sales commission statements for one hour this morning. Other measurements might reflect the time required to execute particular program instructions and the percent of time spent by the central processor in waiting for input-output operations to be completed. Measurements pertaining to personnel include the quantities of (1) documents typed per hour, (2) errors committed per 1000 keystrokes, and (3) debugged program instructions written per day.

Measurement data may be collected by either manual or automated methods. Manual methods involve the preparation of personnel time reports and computer logs. Automated methods include the use of hardware monitors and software monitors.

Personnel time reporting systems involve the manual preparation of time sheets by programmers, systems analysts, and other systems personnel. Each completed time sheet reflects hours worked. These times may be coded according to either or both of the following breakdowns:

1. By tasks, such as programming, testing, preparing documentation, and analyzing the present system.

2. By projects or jobs, such as the development of a new inventory control system and the maintenance of the general ledger system.

Computer logs are records of productive and nonproductive uses of computer facilities. A separate log, such as shown in Figure 25-15, may be prepared by each computer operator during his or her shift. In addition to showing data pertaining to the various jobs processed, a computer log reflects time periods required for preventive maintenance, program testing, and other necessary activities.

Hardware monitors are electronic or electromechanical devices having probes that attach to various components of computer systems. They count the signals emitted by the components and record these counts on some medium such as magnetic tape. A particular monitor, for instance, may count the number of times that disk accesses occur and the duration of each access.

Software monitors are programs or software packages residing within computer systems. They can record the same signal counts as hardware monitors; in addition, they can perform other monitoring actions, such as taking "snapshots" of internal conditions and indicators at designated times.

Reporting Equipment Performance

A systems manager is vitally concerned with the proper utilization of computer-related equipment. Inadequate utilization can result in operational ineffectiveness and degraded levels of service. Thus, a systems manager (and his or her superiors) needs an-

				Equipment			Operation Time		
Job No.	Usage Code	User Charge No.	Program No.	Tape Drives	Disk Drives	Printers	Start	End	Elapsed
268	01	10	756-5	1, 4	3		7:56	8:10	14 min.
268	01	10	783-4		3	1	8:12	8:14	2 min.
269	10	06		1, 2, 4			8:16	8:20	4 min.
269	02	06	825-3	1, 2, 4	1, 2,	1, 2	8:21	8:58	37 min.
	12						9:00	10:00	60 min.

COMPUTER LOG
Date ___11/23___ Shift ___2___ Operator ___B.P.___

FIGURE 25-15 A computer log of data processing operations.

swers to such questions as: How many hours of computer time were employed in productive uses last month? Is the total time devoted to productive uses as large as planned? Were sufficient hours devoted to preventive maintenance, so that the equipment will avoid undue downtime?

Answers to such questions should be provided by the equipment utilization report illustrated in Figure 25-16. Not only does this report provide a detailed breakdown of equipment uses, separated between chargeable and nonchargeable uses, but it also reflects the variances of actual hours from standard hours. It therefore provides the basis for effective planning and control by helping systems management to identify problem areas, to schedule next month's processing operations, and to estimate future needs for additional capacity.

Other reports pertaining to equipment performances are also needed. For instance, reports should be prepared for the systems manager that reflect performance with respect to throughput (e.g., jobs processed per hour), response times, and multiprogramming levels. Furthermore, reports should be prepared for each user that reflect the charges assigned to him or her that month on the basis of equipment usage.

Reporting Personnel Performance

Systems personnel should be utilized as efficiently as systems-related equipment. Accordingly, a systems manager needs answers to such questions as: How productive were the data entry clerks this week? Did the computer operators maintain processing jobs on schedule this week? Have the programmers

		Actual		Standard		Variance in hours
Usage Code	Use	Hours	%	Hours	%	Favorable (Unfavorable)
01	Production runs, regular	260	43.1	255	43.3	(5)
02	Production runs, special	4	0.7	5	0.8	1
03	Reruns	10	1.7	15	2.5	5
04	Compilations	42	7.0	40	6.8	(2)
05	Tests	80	13.3	85	14.4	5
	Total chargeable hours	396	65.8	400	67.8	4
10	Set ups	120	20.0	100	17.0	(20)
11	Equipment failure	10	1.7	15	2.5	5
12	Preventive maintenance	40	6.7	40	6.8	—
13	Idle time	12	2.0	10	1.7	(2)
14	Training	15	2.5	15	2.5	—
15	Other	8	1.3	10	1.7	2
	Total noncharge-able hours	205	34.2	190	32.2	(15)
	Total hours	601	100	590	100	(11)

Equipment Utilization Report

Month: March

FIGURE 25-16 An equipment utilization report.

written and tested as many instructions this week as their experience levels would dictate? Are the systems analysts performing the analysis, design, and installation steps for their respective projects in accordance with established schedules?

Questions such as these can be answered by the following performance evaluation reports:

1. A report that compares the performances of data entry clerks, perhaps in terms of keystrokes per hour, against standard output rates and/or keying errors per 1000 transactions against standard error rates.

2. A report that compares the actual processing times of jobs handled by computer operators against scheduled processing times for those jobs.

3. A report that compares the performances of programmers, perhaps in terms of instructions written per day, against standard daily quotas.

4. A report that compares the actual progress made by systems analysts assigned to projects against milestones established within those projects. A report of this type may show that work is two days behind schedule in the systems analysis phase but three days ahead of schedule with respect to the systems design phase.

These performance evaluation reports reflect variances in terms of counts or time measurements. In addition, cost-related measurements can be reported. Examples include costs per transaction processed and project cost overruns or underruns. Periodic responsibility reports can be prepared that show the variances between costs budgeted by the systems function and actual costs incurred by the systems function, as well as the variances between actual costs incurred and costs charged to users. If the systems function is a profit center, profit variances should also be reported.

Analyzing System Effectiveness

A systems manager is concerned with the effectiveness of the information systems function as well as its efficiency. Questions such as the following must therefore be answered: Is the systems function satisfying all legitimate needs of users? How soon will additional resources be needed to prevent service levels from degrading?

Answers to these questions are not easy to obtain. One approach is to poll users and to monitor measures that reflect their satisfaction. One quantitative measure is the number of complaints received. Qualitative measures might include employee attitudes concerning the user-friendliness of computerized applications and working conditions. A second approach is to analyze trends of such effectiveness measures as response times and time delays in correcting specific systems problems. A third approach is to develop models of the information system and its tasks. Because they can incorporate a variety of system-related tasks, ranging from routine processing to new project developments, such simulation models enable the mix of tasks to be evaluated.[19] Because they can also incorporate the variables that affect growth, the models can predict the dates when new capacity will be needed. Various model packages are currently available, including PLAN IV (marketed by IBM) and BEST/1 (marketed by BGS System).[20]

Summary

Systems implementation consists of such major steps as the establishment of

[19]Donald D. Scriven and Stephen F. Hollam, "New Approaches to Computer Performance Evaluation," *Infosystems* (Oct 1976), pp. 52–54.
[20]John R. Hansen, "Getting a Handle on Computer Performance," *Infosystems* (June 1978), p. 88.

plans and controls over implementation, the execution of implementation activities, and the performance of a postinstallation evaluation. Control techniques such as budgets, Gantt charts, and network diagrams should be employed to control the costs and times expended during the implementation phase. Implementation activities include personnel selection and training, physical preparation, detailed system design, program and system testing, standards development, documentation, file conversion, and final system effectiveness. At the end of all implementation activities, cutover from the present system to the newly designed system takes place. After the new system has been operational for a reasonable period, a postinstallation evaluation should be performed.

Logic diagrams such as program flowcharts and decision tables are prepared as a part of the detailed design activity. By reference to these diagrams, programmers code the computer programs which instruct the computer.

The concerns of people who will use and operate the new system are important. In fact, they are more important than the mechanics of implementation, since severe resistance to a new system can cause it to fail. It is therefore vital that those who implement a new system take positive behavioral actions that have the effect of gaining acceptance for the system.

The operational phase of an information system involves such activities as performing routine operations, accounting for system-related costs, evaluating and controlling system-related resources, auditing the information system and its outputs, and performing systems maintenance and modifications.

Accounting for system-related costs consists of determining whether the costs are to be charged to users or to general overhead and whether the chargeout rates are to be market based or cost based. If the chargeout rates are to be based on costs, it is also necessary to determine (1) whether they are to be computed using actual costs or standard costs and (2) whether they are to be adjusted to reflect varying levels of service and usage of computer facilities.

The evaluation and control of system-related resources is necessary to ensure their effective and efficient use. Hence, each application of a resource should be measured and recorded, employing such techniques as personnel time reporting systems, control logs, hardware monitors, and software monitors. Then the actual measured values, expressed in such terms as processor times required to complete data processing tasks and personnel productivities per time periods, are compared with standards. The resulting variance and ratios are reflected in equipment utilization reports, performance reports, and effectiveness analyses.

APPENDIX TO CHAPTER 25

Network Diagrams

Large, complex projects, such as those involved in the implementation of information systems, can be difficult to plan and control. Network analysis techniques were developed in the 1950s to deal with the difficulties posed by such projects. In essence, a network analysis technique generates a network diagram that reflects the relationships among the various activities encompassed by a specific project.

Two major network analysis techniques currently used to plan and control projects are PERT (Program Evaluation and Review Technique) and CPM (Critical Path Method). These two techniques differ in certain respects. For example, PERT employs three estimates for the time required to complete each activity within a project; CPM requires only one time estimate. PERT emphasizes the planning and control of time, whereas CPM also incorporates the planning and control of dollar resources.[21] Furthermore, the terminology differs somewhat between the two techniques.

The discussion in the following sections will focus on time budgeting. Since this focus is closer to that of PERT than CPM, we will tend to employ the terminology ascribed to PERT. However, for the sake of simplicity we will assume single time estimates for the respective activities.[22]

Nomenclature

Figure 25-17 presents a simple network diagram for a hypothetical project. The key features of the diagram are

1. **Activities:** tasks to be completed in the course of the project. Nine activities (labeled A, B, C, E, F, G, H, I, and J) appear in the figure, together with the "dummy" activities labeled D and K. Each activity requires an estimated time for completion (e.g., four weeks in the case of activity A).

2. **Events:** milestones (points in time) representing the completion of one or more activities *and* (except for the terminal event)

the beginning of one or more following activities. Seven events, numbered from 1 through 7, appear in the figure.

3. **Paths:** routes through the network from the initial event to the terminal event (i.e., from event 1 to event 7). Six paths can be traced through the figure: *A-G-K; A-H; A-F-I; B-E-I; B-D-J;* and *C-J.*

4. **Critical path:** the path with the greatest overall total time. In this example, *A-F-I* is the critical path, since 4 + 4 + 5, or 13 weeks, is the greatest time required to complete the project by any path shown.

5. **Overall project time:** the time required to complete all activities within the project. The time along the critical path (13 weeks in this example) is equal to the overall project time.

Diagram Development

Developing or constructing a network diagram involves two basic steps: estimating activity times and linking activities together. Both steps usually are difficult to perform in complex real-world projects.

Estimating activity times requires knowledge of such factors as the available resources and the exact nature of the activities. It is also necessary to judge the productivity of each resource in achieving the tasks involved in each activity. Consider, for instance, the activity of testing computer programs. The network developer or planner must judge how many program instructions can be tested each day by each programmer, must determine how many instructions will comprise the computer programs (which may not yet be written), and must decide how many programmers will be involved in the program testing activity.

Linking activities together requires close knowledge of their relationships. The planner needs to be aware of those activities that necessarily precede other activities,

---

[21]This distinction is rather minor, since an extension of PERT (known as PERT/COST) is concerned with dollar resources.

[22]In effect, we will assign expected values to the time estimates. By not dealing with three estimates we ignore the possibility of using probability concepts to measure relative dispersions of completion times.

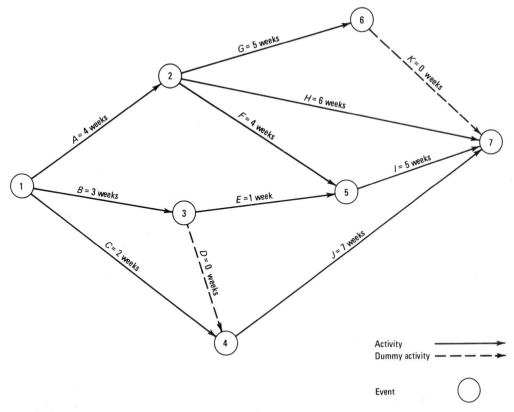

FIGURE 25-17 A network diagram of a simple project.

those activities that necessarily follow other activities, and those activities that can be performed concurrently. Thus, the planner might ascertain that personnel selection, preparation of physical facilities, ordering of selected equipment, and detailed design can be performed simultaneously. Then these four activities would be drawn as emerging from a single event. Next, he or she would determine that personnel training follows personnel selection; equipment installation follows physical preparation; *and* the arrival of ordered hardware and software, plus programming and standards development, follows preparatory detailed design activities. These subsequent activities would be attached to their predecessor activities. This procedure would be continued until all activ-

ities comprising a project have been fully linked to related activities. In a complex project the resulting diagram may resemble a tangled maze of arrows and numbered circles.

Computational Procedure

After developing a network diagram, the next objective is to compute the overall project time and critical path. Although the values of these key factors are readily apparent in a simple diagram such as Figure 25-17, they are not so apparent in the more complex diagrams usually encountered in real-world projects. A systematic procedure is therefore desirable.

One suitable procedure consists of these steps:

1. Determine the earliest time when each event in the network can take place.
2. Compute the overall project time.
3. Determine the latest time when each event can occur within the constraint of the overall project time.
4. Compute the critical path.

Figure 25-18 shows the application of this procedure to the network portrayed in Figure 25-17. The specific values derived by each of the above steps are discussed next.

Determine the Earliest Times

Each event has an earliest time (ET). An ET for a particular event may be defined as

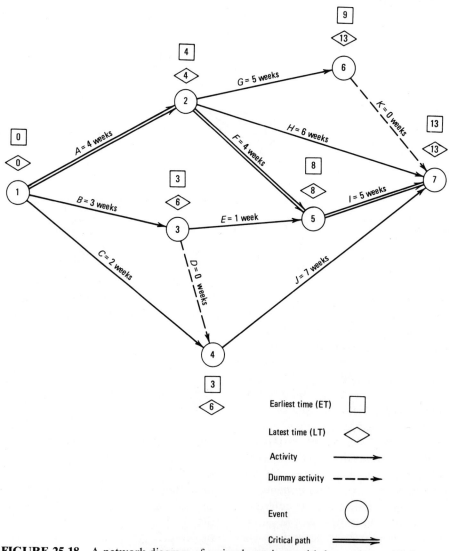

FIGURE 25-18 A network diagram of a simple project, with key values added.

the sum of activity times along a path from the beginning point of a project to the event. When more than one path leads to an event, the ET is the *largest* time required by any of the paths.

Consider event 5 in Figure 25-18. Two paths, *A-F* and *B-E,* lead to the event. Path *A-F* is comprised of 4 weeks + 4 weeks = 8 weeks. Path *B-E* is comprised of 3 weeks + 1 week = 4 weeks. The larger time of 8 weeks is thus the ET for event 5, as denoted by the *8* in the square symbol.

A question that might be asked at this point is, Why not allow a particular event to have an ET for each path leading to the event? For instance, why not assign 4 weeks as a second ET as event 5, since path *B-E* only requires 4 weeks to complete the *B* and *E* activities? The answer is as follows: Each event in a network diagram represents a termination point as well as a commencement point; progress cannot begin on any activities *beyond* an event until *all* preceding activities have been completed. Thus, activity *I* cannot begin until activities *A* and *F* as well as *B* and *E* are completed; 8 weeks after the project begins is therefore the earliest time that activity *I* can begin.

Dummy activities, such as activities *D* and *K* in Figure 25-18, also must be considered when determining earliest times. A *dummy activity* is a constraint or imaginary activity rather than a real activity; that is, it requires *zero* time and use of resources. However, a dummy activity is needed to show more fully the relationship between activities and to allow the proper ET to be determined at a particular event. For instance, a dummy activity is needed to constrain the beginning of the equipment installation until after the ordered hardware and software arrive, even though the physical preparation activity will be completed at an earlier date. Similarly, in Figure 25-18, activity *J* cannot begin until after activity *B* is completed. Thus, dummy activity *D* is drawn between activity *B* and event 4, with the result that

the ET at event 4 will be 3 weeks + 0 weeks = 3 weeks, rather than 2 weeks.

Compute the Overall Project Time

The overall time to complete all of the activities within a project is the ET of the terminal event. In Figure 25-18 the overall project time is 13 weeks, the ET of event 7.

Determine the Latest Time

Each event has a latest time (LT). An LT for a particular event may be defined as the latest time that an event can take place without delaying the completion of the overall project. When more than one path leads from a particular event toward the terminal event, the LT is the *smallest* of the LT values for the respective paths.

Let us consider the LTs for events 4, 3, and 2 in Figure 25-18. To determine each of these LT's we begin by setting the LT for event 7, the terminal event, at 13 weeks, the overall project time. Then, to find the LT for event 4, deduct 7 weeks from 13 weeks, thereby obtaining 6 weeks. Since only one path leads back to event 4, 6 weeks is the only possible LT. To find the LT for event 3, next deduct 0 (the time for activity *D*) from 6 weeks, thereby obtaining 6 weeks. However, this is not the only possible LT for event 3, since the path *E-I* also leads back to the event. For this path the LT is 13 weeks − 5 weeks − 1 week = 7 weeks. Because 6 weeks is *smaller* than 7 weeks, the LT for event 3 should be 6 weeks. Finding the LT for event 2 means comparing the LT's for three paths.

LT via path *G-K* is 13 − 0 − 5 = 8 weeks.

LT via path *H* is 13 − 6 = 7 weeks.

LT via path *F-I* is 13 − 5 − 4 = 4 weeks.

Since 4 weeks is the smallest value, it represents the LT for event 2.

Compute the Critical Path

The critical path of a network is the path whose activity times equal the overall project time. For Figure 25-18 the critical path is *A-F-I,* as seen earlier. In a complex network, however, the critical path seldom can be spotted by knowledge of the overall project time alone. Thus, a more operational definition for the critical path is as follows: The critical path is the path formed by events at which the ET's are equal to the LT's.

In Figure 25-18 the ET equals the LT at events 5 and 2. Conversely, the ET and LT at events 3, 4, and 6 are not equal. Thus, the critical path ranges from event 1 to event 2 to event 5 to event 7.

The critical path is so named because the activities it encompasses are critical or bottleneck activities. If any of these activities is delayed (i.e., its time is lengthened), the overall project time will be lengthened. On the other hand, activities not on the critical path are not critical. Any such noncritical activity might be delayed (up to a point) without the overall project time being affected. For instance, in Figure 25-18, activity *G* might be delayed for up to 4 weeks without affecting the overall project time of 13 weeks.

The notion of *slack time* is generally introduced into network computations to denote the extent of allowable delay. The slack time of a noncritical event is the difference between its ET and LT.[23] For instance, the slack times for events 3, 4, and 6 in Figure 25-18 are 3, 3, and 4, respectively. Incidentally, the slack times for events along the critical path are zero, since the ET and LT for each event are equal. Thus, the critical path may alternatively be defined as the path along which the slack times are zero.

---

[23]Slack times may alternatively be measured in terms of activities if the ET's and LT's are determined for activities rather than events.

Benefits

A network diagram aids in both planning and controlling the progress of a project. In the planning phase it forces managers to analyze the various activities necessary to complete the project and the relationships among the activities. It directs attention to the critical or bottleneck activities that are most likely to delay the project. By also revealing those activities that are less critical, a network diagram suggests possibilities for reallocating personnel and equipment resources to the critical activities. In some cases such reallocations can reduce overall project times.

Throughout the course of a project the network diagram can provide effective means of control. First, it keeps managers informed of progress, including the most likely completion date. Second, it points to those activities that are behind schedule. Third, it provides the basis for making revisions as circumstances change during the course of the project.

Packaged computer programs are of great assistance in implementing the use of network diagrams. In fact, the network diagram truly can be called a "child of the computer," since network diagrams for complex projects could not be employed without computer assistance.

Applications

Network diagrams are applicable to all types of projects. They have limited usefulness in recurring types of activities. Examples of successful applications, in addition to the implementation of information systems, include the construction of buildings, the development of new products, and the auditing of financial records and accounts.

Review Problem with Solution

Problem Statement

On April 30 the steering committee of the Precise Manufacturing Company approves the final feasibility report of the sales order processing and management project. The information systems manager then establishes the implementation period, which is to extend for a full 52 weeks. He divides the overall phase into such major activities as detailed design and training. These activities are reflected in the accompanying network diagram. Activity times appear in parentheses after the activity labels and are stated in weeks. Events appear at the beginning and end of each activity, starting with event 1 and finishing with event 11. Event 11 marks the cutover point. By means of this network diagram, the project leader guides and controls the activities of her project team during the next year. The work of the project generally progresses in a smooth manner. Only one significant delay is encountered:

the ordered hardware and software arrive a month late. Consequently, the equipment installation activity is not completed until October 25, approximately a month behind schedule. However, since adequate slack time is available, the overall project time is not lengthened.

Required

Verify the critical path shown in the network diagram and compute the slack times for the various events.

Solution

The critical path shown in the diagram is equal to the project time of 52 weeks, or the cumulative times of the activities along the path $(3 + 16 + 17 + 8 + 8 = 52)$. This total time is greater than the time along any other path from event 1 to event 11. For instance, the total time along path $1-2-5-11$ is computed as $3 + 4 + 14 = 21$ weeks.

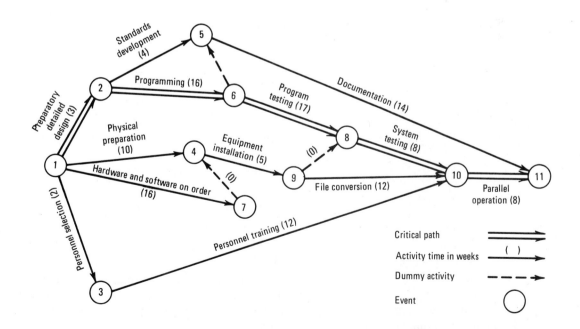

The "slack" times are as follows:

Event	ET (weeks)	LT (weeks)	Slack Time (weeks)
1	0	0	0
2	3	3	0
3	2	32	30
4	16	27	11
5	19	38	19
6	19	19	0
7	16	27	11
8	36	36	0
9	21	32	11
10	44	44	0
11	52	52	0

Review Questions

25-1 What is the meaning of each of the following terms?

Implementation plan
Gantt chart
Network diagram
Systems integrator
Data center
Layout form
Logic diagram
Program testing
Test data
Walk through
System testing
String testing
File conversion
Cutover point
Parallel operation
Modular conversion
Postinstallation evaluation
Program flowchart
Decision table
Data hierarchy diagram
HIPO diagram
Pseudocode
Warnier–Orr diagram
Computer program

COBOL
FORTRAN
BASIC
Coding
Structured program design
Application code generator
Chargeout rate
Market-based rate
Cost-based rate
Adjustable rate
Personnel time reporting system
Computer log
Hardware monitor
Software monitor

25-2 How can accountants be useful in the implementation of an information system?

25-3 Describe the various plans and controls that should be established at the beginning of the implementation phase.

25-4 Contrast the Gantt chart and network diagrams.

25-5 What two preliminary actions are often necessary just prior to the execution of implementation activities?

25-6 What are the major activities involved in implementing an information system?

25-7 Identify several means of providing training to users of information systems.

25-8 Discuss the features that must typically be installed in the physical facilities that are to house a computer.

25-9 Describe the sequence of actions required to develop and test a computer program.

25-10 Contrast program testing and system testing.

25-11 What are the purposes of documentation?

25-12 What actions are necessary during file conversion?

25-13 Contrast the parallel operation and modular conversion approaches that may be employed during a final system-checkout period.

25-14 Why should a newly implemented system be evaluated at some point during the operational phase?

25-15 Contrast a program flowchart and a decision table.

25-16 Contrast a data hierarchy diagram and a Warnier–Orr diagram.

25-17 What are the relative advantages and suitable uses of such programming languages as assembly languages, COBOL, FORTRAN, BASIC, and fourth-generation languages?

25-18 What are the advantages of the structured design approach?

25-19 In what ways can application code generators be used to produce computer code?

25-20 Describe the nature and purpose of integrated software architectures.

25-21 In what ways can employees and managers cause the failure of a newly implemented information system that is unacceptable to them?

25-22 What positive actions can be taken to help assure the acceptance, and hence the operational feasibility, of a newly implemented information system?

25-23 What benefits are gained through the active participation of managers and employees in the implementation of a new information system?

25-24 Briefly describe several major activities that generally take place during the operational phase of an information system.

25-25 Why is systems maintenance necessary?

25-26 Why should system-related costs be charged to users?

25-27 What criteria should be employed when establishing chargeout rates?

25-28 Contrast the use of market-based rates and cost-based rates.

25-29 In what ways might chargeout rates be modified?

25-30 Identify several measurements appropriate in determining the use of system-related resources.

25-31 What data collection methods are employed in recording data concerning the use of system-related resources?

25-32 Describe several reports that provide the basis for evaluating and controlling system-related resources.

Discussion Questions

25-33 Does a firm ever complete the design and implementation of a new information system?

25-34 How may the various activities of an implementation phase be kept from disrupting the services provided by the present system?

25-35 Discuss the variety of standards that should be developed during the implementation phase, including standards pertaining to the operation of a computer-based system. Give examples of standards that fall within the various categories identified.

25-36 A division of a large manufacturing firm has recently decided to install a logistics data base containing very complex data structures. Discuss alternative approaches to the implementation of the data base.

25-37 Describe all the matters that should be examined during a postinstallation review and evaluation of a recently implemented communications-based real-time information system.

25-38 A systems analyst has just devised a design for a new production information system. She is justly proud of the design, since it is innovative and well structured. However, the production manager and his employees are very critical of the new system and refuse to use it properly. Discuss.

25-39 A new marketing information system has just been put into operation. Although the information systems manager believes that it is a definite improvement over the previous system, and the president agrees, the marketing managers and salespersons complain loudly about the "red tape" the new system requires. However, an objective observer says that the input steps are simpler and the required input data items are fewer than with the previous system. Discuss.

25-40 Contrast the varieties of fears and uncertainties likely to be experienced by (1) managers and (2) employees during the implementation of an information system.

25-41 Discuss the hidden costs traceable to employee fears and uncertainties.

25-42 Contrast the types of resistance likely to be exhibited at (1) the middle managerial level and (2) the lower managerial level during the implementation of an information system.

25-43 Identify the variety of subactivities that might be included under the following major implementation activities:

    a. Preparation of physical facilities.
    b. Testing.

25-44 Identify activities likely to be required during the operational phase of an information system, other than those described in the chapter.

25-45 What are the respective responsibilities of the information systems manager and the user managers for systems maintenance?

25-46 Discuss the problems that a poorly established and administered chargeout system might create for the information systems function and the firm of which it is a part.

25-47 In what situations might a user department be charged with system development costs?

25-48 Compare the use of a chargeout rate based on standard costs with a manufacturing overhead rate.

25-49 Describe the way that a chargeout system can motivate a marketing manager to request that unnecessary sales reports be eliminated.

25-50 Discuss the problems that can arise when the information system function is established as a profit center but users are not allowed to patronize outside commercial processing services under any circumstances.

25-51 Discuss the procedure by which the president of a firm can judge whether the expenditures for the computer-based information system are too high, too low, or about right.

25-52 Identify the several weaknesses in the routine operations of a computer-based information system that an evaluation team or internal auditors should watch for.

25-53 Discuss drawbacks to the use of such single measures as keystrokes per hour and instructions written per day when attempting to evaluate the performances of data entry clerks and programmers, respectively.

Problems

25-1 A savings and loan association has decided to undertake the development of an in-house computer system to replace the processing it currently purchases from a time-sharing service. The internal auditors have suggested that the systems development process be planned in accordance with the systems development life cycle concept.

The following nine items have been identified as major systems development activities that will have to be undertaken:

    a. System test.
    b. User specifications.
    c. Conversion.
    d. System planning study.
    e. Technical specifications.
    f. Postimplementation review.

g. Implementation planning.
h. User procedures and training.
i. Programming.

Required

a. Rearrange these nine items to reflect the sequence in which they should logically occur. If certain items would likely occur roughly at the same time, bracket those items.

b. An item not included in the list is file conversion. List the key steps involved in this activity.

c. Describe the results that the postimplementation review should achieve.

d. Describe the ways that the three final system conversion approaches would be applied in this situation.

(CIA adapted)

25-2 Artists' Delights, Inc., of Lawrence, Kansas, is a manufacturer of paints, brushes, and other art supplies. Although the firm has prospered for a number of years because of its quality products, it currently is experiencing several problems. For instance, it is having difficulty in keeping its catalog up to date, in conducting low-cost and efficient production operations, in maintaining adequate inventories, and in making prompt deliveries of ordered goods. Since the president recognizes that most, if not all, of these problems are related to the firm's information system, he has authorized the director of information systems to undertake a systems development investigation.

The director forms a steering committee, which in turn establishes several project areas. It assigns the highest priority to the inventory area and approves the organization of a project team. After analyzing inventory operations and management, the team recommends that a computer-based system be considered as a replacement for the present manual information and processing system. Upon the concurrence of the steering committee, a feasibility study then is undertaken. Based on costs and benefits developed during this study, a computer-based information system is found to be feasible.

At this point the steering committee asks the director to prepare plans that reflect the activities necessary to acquire a computer-based system and to put it into operation. If the plans appear reasonable, the steering committee likely will give its approval to proceed.

The director thus sits down and ponders. He is aware that the present information system has many deficiencies, including weak standards and documentation. He also recognizes that no one in the firm has experience with computers. Because of these deficiencies he intends to acquire well-documented software packages for the first applications to be implemented on the anticipated computer system. However, he does want to develop the programs for the other applications, which he hopes can be in process later this year.

Required

Prepare an appropriate list of implementation activities for the director to submit to the steering committee. Arrange the activities in approximate chronological order.

25-3 Thrift-Mart, Inc., is a chain of convenience grocery stores in Washington, D.C. Elvira Jones, the development manager for the chain, has been assigned the project of finding a suitable building and establishing a new store. Her first step is to enumerate the specific activities to be completed and to estimate the time required for each activity. She then asks you to develop suitable planning and control mechanisms, based on the data listed at the top of page 1208. She tells you that the activity designations refer to the bounding events for each activity. For in-

Activity Designation	Description of Activity	Expected Activity Time (weeks)
1 to 2	Find building	4
2 to 3	Negotiate rental terms	2
3 to 4	Draft lease	5
2 to 5	Prepare store plans	4
5 to 6	Select and order fixtures	1
6 to 4	Accept delivery of fixtures	6
4 to 8	Install fixtures	3
5 to 7	Hire staff	5
7 to 8	Train staff	4
8 to 9	Receive inventory	3
9 to 10	Stock shelves	1

stance, event 1 refers to the beginning of the search for a building and event 2 refers to the completion of the search.

Required

a. Prepare a network diagram to aid in coordinating the activities.

b. Determine the overall project time and the critical path of the project.

c. Prepare a Gantt (bar) chart to monitor and control the progress of the 11 activities listed, assuming that the project will begin on March 1. Use the diagram prepared in **a** as a guide.

d. Verify that the ending date on the Gantt chart reconciles with the overall project time determined in **b**.

e. Elvira would like to finish the project two weeks earlier than the schedule indicates. She believes that she can persuade the fixture manufacturer to deliver the fixtures in four weeks instead of six weeks. Would this step achieve the objective of reducing the overall project time by two weeks?

f. The project cannot be implemented successfully unless the required resources are available as needed. What information does Elvira need to administer the project in addition to that shown by the diagrams prepared in the previous requirements?

(CMA adapted)

25-4 Davison, Tricker & Co., a public accounting firm in Nashville, Tennessee, has decided to obtain a new computer system. Not only will the new system enable the firm to prepare tax returns more accurately and quickly, but it will also enable internal recordkeeping to be processed more quickly. Furthermore, it will allow the firm to offer a financial modeling service to its small and medium-size clients.

After the analysis and design phases have been completed, the partners review the computer systems that appear to be suitable to the firm's needs. Finally, they agree upon a particular computer system. Before pursuing the matter further, however, they ask you to plan the many activities necessary to place the selected computer system into operation. As a first step, you develop the following list of activities and the expected time for each activity:

Activity Code	Description of Activity	Expected Activity Time (weeks)
A	Prepare implementation plans	2
B	Select personnel	4
C	Develop training materials	6
D	Train personnel	9
E	Develop detailed design	6
F	Write computer programs	10
G	Develop test data and test programs	5
H	Prepare documentation	4
I	Negotiate contract and order computer system	3
J	Prepare computer site	4
K	Receive and install computer system	2
L	Test computer system	7
M	Convert files	6
N	Conduct parallel operation	12

You then prepare the following key, which relates the activities and the events by which they are bounded:

Activity Code	Bounding Events
A	1 → 2
B	2 → 4
C	2 → 3
D	4 → 12
E	2 → 5
F	5 → 6
G	6 → 7
H	7 → 12
I	2 → 8
J	8 → 9
K	9 → 10
L	10 → 12
M	10 → 11
N	12 → 13

You also note the need for two dummy activities having these bounding events: O, 3 → 4; P, 11 → 12.

Required

a. Prepare a network diagram based upon the foregoing activities.

b. Determine the expected overall project time and the critical path.

c. Prepare a table which lists the earliest time (ET), latest time (LT), and slack time for each event (or, alternatively, each activity).

25-5 Whitson Company, of Vancouver, B.C., has just ordered a new computer for its financial information system. The present computer is fully utilized and no longer adequate for all of the financial applications Whitson would like to implement. The present financial system applications must be modified before they can be run on the new computer. Additionally, new applications which Whitson would like to have developed and implemented have been identified and ranked according to priority.

Sally Rose, manager of data processing, is responsible for implementing the new computer system. Rose listed the specific activities which had to be completed and determined the estimated time to complete each activity. In addition, she prepared a network diagram to aid in the coordination of the activities. The activity list and the network diagram are presented on the next page.

Required

a. Determine the number of weeks which will be required to implement fully Whitson Company's financial information system (i.e., both existing and new applications) on its new computer and identify the activities which are critical to completing the project.

b. The term slack time is often used in conjunction with network analysis.

   (1) Explain what is meant by slack time.

   (2) Identify an activity which has slack time and indicate the amount of slack time available for that activity.

c. Whitson Company's top management would like to reduce the time necessary to begin operation of the entire system.

   (1) Which activities should Sally Rose attempt to reduce in order to implement the system sooner? Explain your answer.

   (2) Discuss how Sally Rose might proceed to reduce the time of these activities.

d. The general accounting manager would like the existing financial information system applications to be modified and operational in 22 weeks.

   (1) Determine the number of weeks which will be required to modify the existing financial information system applications and make them operational.

Activity	Description of Activity	Expected Time Required to Complete (in weeks)	Variance in Expected Time (in weeks)
AB	Wait for delivery of computer from manufacturer	8	1.2
BC	Install computer	2	.6
CH	General test of computer	2	.2
AD	Complete an evaluation of manpower requirements	2	.8
DE	Hire additional programmers and operators	2	1.6
AG	Design modifications to existing applications	3	1.2
GH	Program modifications to existing applications	4	1.4
HI	Test modified applications on new computer	2	.4
IJ	Revise existing applications as needed	2	.6
JN	Revise and update documentation for existing applications as modified	2	.4
JK	Run existing applications in parallel on new and old computers	2	.4
KP	Implement existing applications as modified on the new computer	1	.6
AE	Design new applications	8	3.2
GE	Design interface between existing and new applications	3	1.8
EF	Program new applications	6	2.6
FI	Test new applications on new computer	2	.8
IL	Revise new applications as needed	3	1.4
LM	Conduct second test of new applications on new computer	2	.6
MN	Prepare documentation for the new applications	3	.8
NP	Implement new applications on the new computer	2	.8

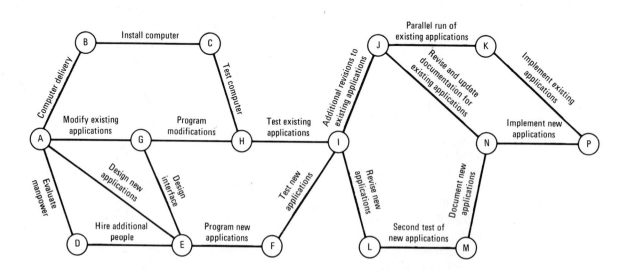

(2) What is the probability of implementing the existing financial information system applications within 22 weeks?

Table of Areas Under the Normal Curve

Z	Area	Z	Area	Z	Area
0.1	.540	1.1	.864	2.1	.982
0.2	.579	1.2	.885	2.2	.986
0.3	.618	1.3	.903	2.3	.989
0.4	.655	1.4	.919	2.4	.992
0.5	.692	1.5	.933	2.5	.994
0.6	.726	1.6	.945	2.6	.995
0.7	.758	1.7	.955	2.7	.997
0.8	.788	1.8	.964	2.8	.997
0.9	.816	1.9	.971	2.9	.998
1.0	.841	2.0	.977	3.0	.999

Hint: Refer to a statistics text or description of the PERT techniques for aids in doing **d** (2).

(CMA adapted)

25-6 The Reddon Company of Provo, Utah, manufactures and sells plastic products. The company management believes a successful firm should have formally stated objectives. Financial and output goals have been established for all departments, and they are evaluated against those goals. In addition, the company aggressively seeks new products to support its goal of growth.

Early in 1989 Cupot, Inc., offered to sell its design and preliminary engineering studies for a plastic sewing machine housing to Reddon. Cupot management had concluded that the product was too remote from its normal product lines and, equally important, would require manufacturing expertise not possessed by Cupot.

Reddon management asked the marketing department to research the sales potential of the housing. The product development department, a department of the product division, studied the production problems of the product. Both departments concluded that it was feasible to add the housing to the company's product line. However, each observed that problems could be encountered because this was a new market for Reddon and a modification of current manufacturing techniques and processes would be required. In spite of these warnings, Reddon management purchased the idea from Cupot and authorized the project late in 1990.

The management concluded that the marketing and manufacturing requirements were of sufficient complexity to require a project team to bring the product into being. This was a new management technique for Reddon. George Aldon, an experienced sales manager with a strong manufacturing background, was chosen to head the project team. He was selected to head the team because he had been with the company for many years, was well known, and was well liked by most people in the company. This was important because the project team had no resources of its own and would have to rely on regular departments to get the work completed.

Aldon was permitted to select one person from each of three departments—sales, manufacturing, and financial management—to make a four-person project team. The project team was charged with the planning, coordination, and successful introduction of the housing. The three team members were responsible for developing the schedule of services needed, serving as liaison with their former areas and evaluating the work done by the regular departments. All members of the team would return to their departments when the team completed its task of guiding the new product through its first year of sales.

The project team developed a list of major events and activities leading to the introduction of this new product, such as the development of a sales program, the modification of the manufacturing facilities, and the performance of a sample production run. Financial requirements in broad terms were also prepared.

The product was not ready for introduction in late 1990 as planned. The sales program was not yet finalized, nor were the manufacturing modifications complete. The departments had worked on the project whenever time was available in the regular work schedules. The department heads stated that they were unable to do more because no adjustment in the available resources had been made. Although the project team had prepared a financial requirement schedule, it was not ready when the company budget was adopted. Consequently, the financial requirements were not incorporated in the budget.

George Aldon was disappointed that the team was unable to meet the planned introduction date. This was the first assignment he had failed to complete successfully. He attributed the lack of success to the departmental managers who regularly failed to meet the deadline in the original timetables. The other members of the project team worked hard but, in his opinion, were not forceful enough when dealing with their former departments.

Required

a. Describe the potential advantages of the project approach to the development of a new product.

b. Discuss the likely reasons why the project was late.

c. Suggest improvements in the foregoing procedures and circumstances.

(CMA adapted)

25-7 The B&B Company of Boone, North Carolina, manufactures and sells chemicals for agricultural and industrial use. The company has grown significantly over the last 10 years but has made few changes in its information gathering and reporting system. Some of the managers have expressed concern that the system is essentially the same as it was when the firm was only half its present size. Others believe that much of the information from the system is not relevant and that more appropriate and timely information should be available.

Dora Hepple, chief accountant, has observed that the actual monthly cost data for most production processes are compared with the actual costs of the same processes for the previous year. Any variance not explained by price changes requires an explanation by the individual in charge of the cost center. She believes that this information is inadequate for good cost control.

George Vector, one of the production supervisors, contends that the system is adequate because it allows for explanation of discrepancies. The current year's costs seldom vary from the previous year's costs (as adjusted for price changes). This indicates that costs are under control.

Vern Hopp, general manager of the Fine Chemical Division, is upset with the current system. He has to request the same information each month regarding recurring operations. This is a problem that he believes should be addressed.

Walter Metts, president, has appointed a committee to review the system. The charge to this System Review Task Force is to determine whether the information needs of the internal management of the firm are being met by the existing system. Specific modifications in the existing system or implementation of a new system will be considered only if management's needs are not being met. William Afton, assistant to the president, has been put in charge of the task force.

Shortly after the committee was appointed, Afton overhead one of the cost accountants say, "I've been doing it this way for 15 years, and now Afton and his committee will try to eliminate my job." Another person replied, "That's the way it looks. John and Brownie in general accounting also think their positions are going to be eliminated or at least changed significantly." Over the next few days, Afton overheard a middle manager talking about the task force, saying, "That's all this company thinks about, maximizing its profits—not the employees." He also overheard a production manager in the mixing department say that he believed the system was in need of revision because the most meaningful information he received came from Brad Cummings, a salesperson. He stated, "After they have the monthly sales meeting, Brad stops by the office and indicates what the sales plans and targets are for the next few months. This sure helps me in planning my mixing schedules."

Afton is aware that two problems of paramount importance to be addressed by his System Review Task Force are (1) to determine management's information needs for cost control and decision-making purposes and (2) to meet the behavioral needs of the company and its employees.

Required

a. Discuss the behavioral implications of having an accounting information system that does not appear to meet the needs of management.

b. Identify and explain the specific problems B&B Company appears to have with regard to the perception of B&B's employees concerning:

(1) The accounting information system.

(2) The firm.

c. Assume that the initial review of the System Review Task Force indicates that a new accounting information system should be designed and implemented.

(1) Identify specific behavioral factors that B&B's management should ad-

dress in the design and implementation of a new system.

(2) For each behavioral factor identified, discuss how B&B's management can address the behavioral factor.

(CMA adapted)

25-8 The Pine Cone Merchandising Company of Fayetteville, Arkansas, sells novelties and souvenirs on credit to gift shops and department stores. Currently, it processes sales and cash receipts transactions by a computer program whose logic is similar to that shown in Figure 25-6.

Assume that on a particular day the following data pertaining to ten sales and/or cash receipts transactions constitute the transaction file to be processed by the program:

Customer Number	Transaction Code	Transaction Amount
101	1	$30.00
123	2	60.00
156	1	55.00
210	1	46.00
210	2	72.00
265	2	36.00
318	1	17.00
612	2	39.00
526	2	51.00
840	1	28.00
999		

The transactions have presumably been sorted in customer number order, and the "dummy" record has been inserted at the end of the transaction file.

Required

a. Complete the table shown on page 1214 (headings as well as columns), which shows the actions that the program takes

Number of pass	TN at start of pass	MN at start of pass	Read first transaction record (TN)	Read first master record (MN)	Has end of file been reached?	Is TN larger than MN?	Write new master record	Read next master record (MN)	Is TN equal to MN?	Is transaction code equal to 1?	Add transaction amount to customer balance	Read next transaction record (TN)	
1	—	—	101	100	No	Yes	Yes	101	—	—	—	—	
2	101	101	—	—	No	No	No	—	Yes	Yes	+$30	123	
3	123	101	—	—	—								

during successive processing passes. Assume that the master file contains records sorted by the following customer numbers: 100, 101, 120, 123, 155, 170, 200, 210, 243, 265, 312, 318, 475, 526, 612, 771, 840, 876, 913. An end-of-file indicator follows the last record.

b. The computer program whose logic is shown in Figure 25-6 can detect certain types of errors in the transaction data (e.g., an out-of-sequence transaction record). Identify at least one type of transaction data error that the program would not detect.

25-9 The Pine Cone Merchandising Company, which currently processes its accounts receivable transactions by means of a computer program, would like to process its inventory transactions in a similar manner. It therefore devises the following procedure:

Inventory transactions involving receipts and issues will continue to be captured on suitable source documents. Then, selected data from these transactions will be transcribed, via key-to-tape devices, onto magnetic tape. The data items to be transcribed will consist of the inventory item number, the transaction code (1 means receipt; 2 means issue), the source document number, and the quantity of the item involved. Next, the transactions will be sorted by inventory item number and also by transaction code. Then the transaction file will be processed against the inventory master file, which is arranged in inventory-item-number

sequence. During the processing run the quantities received will be added to the quantity balance of each item in the master file, while the quantities issued will be deducted from the quantity balance. An updated master file will be written onto a new magnetic tape. Errors will be listed on an exception report during processing. Errors include out-of-sequence transactions, transactions that cannot be matched with master file records, and quantity balances that are negative after updating.

Two printed outputs are to be prepared: (1) the exception report, which is to contain the errors indicated earlier, plus totals of quantities received, quantities issued, and quantity balances (but with negative balances excluded from the last total); (2) an inventory status report, which lists for each inventory item the item number, description, quantity balance before updating, transaction quantities (if any), and quantity balance after updating.

Required

a. Draw a system flowchart to reflect the entire inventory transaction processing described above.

b. Prepare a program flowchart to reflect the necessary logic for processing the inventory transaction file against the inventory master file.

25-10 The Greenspray Company of St. Johns, Newfoundland, is a retailer of fishing supplies. Recently it acquired a minicomputer system. One of the high-priority applications is to be a program that evaluates wholesalers from whom Greenspray might purchase supplies for resale. The criteria that the program is to apply are as follows:

a. A quality rating from 1 to 3 for each wholesaler, in which 1 represents the highest rating.
b. Percentage of times each wholesaler has been late in delivering orders in the past.
c. Whether each wholesaler's prices have been stable or unstable.
d. Whether each wholesaler is in an economically undepressed ("well-off") area or a depressed area.
e. Whether or not each wholesaler has suggested new products from time to time.

The decision rules according to which actions are to be applied by the program are as follows:

a. If the quality rating is 1, award the wholesaler 20 percent of the business.
b. If the quality rating is 2, and the wholesaler is not more than 10 percent late, award it 15 percent of the business.
c. If the quality rating is 2 and the wholesaler is more than 25 percent late, reject it.
d. If the quality rating is 2 and the wholesaler is between 10 percent and 25 percent late, award it 10 percent of the business, but only if prices have been stable.
e. If the quality rating is 3 and the wholesaler is not more than 5 percent late, award it 10 percent of the business, but only if it is in a depressed area and if it has been good at suggesting new products.

Required

a. Compute the total number of possible rules that would be listed within a "full" decision table of the limited entry form.
b. Prepare a "collapsed" decision table that shows the logic needed to write a program for the selection of wholesalers by the Greenspray Company.

(SMAC adapted)

25-11 The Sunset Wholesaling Company of Hayward, California, distributes imported beers and fine wines to retail stores throughout the state. Because many of the products are in limited supply, often the company must impose limits on ordered items in order to accommodate as many customers as possible. Recently it acquired a small computer system with terminals, disk storage, and printers. One of the major applications is to be the processing of customers' orders. As each order is received, the customer's number and the product number and quantity ordered are to be entered via one of the terminals. Then a computer program is to process the order on the basis of the following conditions:

If a quantity ordered does not exceed the order limit and credit is approved, prepare a shipment release and deduct the quantity from the inventory records. However, if the quantity on hand is not sufficient to fill the order, prepared a back order and enter the quantity back-ordered on the inventory records. (Do not ship *any* of the quantity ordered in this case until the back order is received, unless the customer has marked the order "Urgent." In that case, ship as much as is on hand and the remainder when the back order is received.) If the quantity ordered exceeds the order limit, ship only the quantity up to the order limit and notify the customer that he may submit another order next week. If credit for the customer is not approved, reject the entire order. If no inventory record or customer record is found in storage, print a notice to that effect on an exception report and hold the order until the record is found.

Required

Prepare "full" and "collapsed" decision tables that show the logic needed to write a program for processing orders from customers. Assume that (1) only one product is ordered on a single customer order and (2) a credit checking subroutine will be available within the computer system for the sales order program to query.

25-12 David Sadfoss is a systems analyst for the Brookside Manufacturing Company of Boulder, Colorado. Since David is a hardworking and intelligent graduate of a nearby university, he was recently given a challenging assignment: developing a new purchase-ordering system for the firm.

Having been exposed to the latest forecasting techniques (in a senior-level course he took two years ago), he decided that they should provide the foundation for his design of the purchasing system. Consequently, he developed a sophisticated ordering model that incorporated exponential smoothing forecasts, economic order quantities, quantity discount analysis, and supplier evaluation features. As a result the system would automatically produce a purchase order that needed only to be approved by a buyer and the purchasing manager before being mailed to the supplier.

Upon presenting his new design to his superior and then to higher management he was accorded a puzzled reception. However, after he pointed out such benefits as reduced inventory costs and fewer stock-outs, the reception became quite warm and approval was granted.

He then turned to the implementation of his new purchase-ordering system. After writing the necessary programs and conducting extensive tests, he presented the system to the buyers at a special meeting. (The purchasing manager could not attend, since he was out of town. However, he had been informed the previous week by the president that the new system had the approval of top management and that he was to allow David complete freedom in putting the new system into effect.) At the meeting, several buyers were impressed, especially since the new system involved the use of computer terminals. A few buyers seemed a bit dubious, but David assured them of the benefits described above.

When the new system was completely installed, David met again with the buyers to explain the use of new forms and the sequence of steps necessary to operate the installed terminals. He also left some operating instructions, which he had written the previous weekend, consisting of about 20 typed pages. (He had meant to develop some diagrams and other instructional aids to show at the meeting, but the implementation schedule was rather tight and he did not have time.) At the end of the same day the president issued a bulletin in which he stated that the new system would require the services of one-half the current number of buyers. For the present all buyers would be kept; however, at the end of the month only those buyers who appeared to have adjusted most easily and enthusiastically to the new system would be kept in their positions. Others would be transferred to new positions (if available) and completely retrained in their duties or would be helped to find employment outside the firm.

Required

Discuss people-related problems caused by actions taken and not taken by David and the president during the development and implementation of the new purchase-ordering system. Suggest specific steps which, if taken during this period, would have rendered the new system more operationally feasible.

25-13 Wagstaff Pharmaceuticals of Milwaukee is a drug manufacturer. Its several divisions are served by a corporate headquarters and staff functions that are centralized and located at the home office. Information System Services (ISS) is one of these staff functions. Its services range from the data processing of routine transactions to the development (i.e., analysis, design, implementation) of information systems at the department, division, or functional level.

ISS provides its services on request to the various departments and functions within the several divisions, as well as to other corporate staff functions. The systems manager assigns priorities to the various requests, usually on a first-come, first-served basis.

However, he tries to give due consideration to rush requests. The users are not charged for these services; instead, all costs related to the system are absorbed as corporate overhead.

Despite the simplicity of this approach, many managers within the firm have complained about it. They say, for instance, that often they must wait for quite a while before their requests are filled. Also, they complain, other managers seem to receive service before they do, even though they (the complaining managers) had entered their requests earlier.

Because such complaints have been increasing, the president of the firm has decided to change the approach. Henceforth, he states, the recipients of services from ISS will be charged for services they receive. At the end of each month the systems manager will compute a chargeout rate, based on actual costs for the past month and the actual number of hours the central processor was in use. This chargeout rate will then be multiplied by the number of hours required by each user's job; the resulting amounts will then be charged against each user's budget. If the services requested by a user are quite sizable or are expected to be of long duration, however, the systems manager will

have authority to negotiate a lower chargeout rate for that user. On the other hand, if any user is dissatisfied with the services provided by ISS or with the rates, that user has permission to utilize outside commercial processing services.

The system's manager's performance will be evaluated according to the extent that the charges to users "cover" his budgeted costs. Thus, he is expected to be energetic in stimulating usage for the services provided by ISS. (Currently, the systems manager is evaluated according to the extent that actual costs compare with budgeted costs. He prepares his budget semiannually on the basis of his estimate of user demand; this budgetary procedure will remain unchanged under the new approach.)

Required

a. Discuss the weaknesses of the current approach for accounting for system-related costs.

b. Discuss the advantages of the proposed accounting approach over the current approach.

c. Discuss problems that the proposed approach will likely create and describe means of overcoming these problems.

24-14 The Lagoon Company of Gainesville, Florida, utilizes a centralized computer installation to provide data processing and information services to its various operational functions. It treats the computer installation and all system-related activities as a single cost center. Once each year a budget is prepared and a single chargeout rate is computed. This chargeout rate is then used to allocate system-related costs to users for services provided.

At the beginning of this year the system-related costs for the coming year were budgeted as follows:

Payroll (including salaries, benefits, and taxes)	$210,000
Equipment rental (including mainte-nance)	350,000
Supplies (variable)	24,000
Utilities (includes a variable compo-nent of $10 per hour)	70,000
Miscellaneous (including insurance and security)	30,000

The time of computer operations during the current year was expected to total 3000 hours.

During the year, four functions utilized system-related services for the following time periods:

Accounting-finance	1000 hours
Marketing	800 hours
Administrative services	600 hours
Purchasing	500 hours

Required

a. Compute the chargeout rate for the year, if all of the system-related costs are fixed in behavior except for those explicitly designated to be variable.

b. Determine the amounts to be charged each of the four functions during the year.

c. If actual system-related costs during the year are $700,000, compute a cost variance that can help higher-level management to evaluate the performance of the systems manager.

Hint: Apply flexible budgeting concepts in computing the cost variance.

25-15 Tyler Enterprises, Inc., of College Park, Maryland, charges its operating and staff departments for computer-based processing and information services. The chargeout rate is determined by the total budgeted costs for the information systems department, divided by the available hours for processing productive jobs on the central processor. For the current year the total costs have been budgeted at $2 million, and 5000 hours of central processor time have been projected.

In recent months, however, the systems manager has received complaints from the market research and production planning departments. They feel that they are being treated unfairly by the current chargeout rate. A substantial portion of the budgeted costs of $2 million includes rental costs for printers, terminals, and disk storage units. However, their jobs essentially require the use of the central processor alone; the other hardware is primarily available for such jobs as processing accounting transactions.

As a result of these complaints the systems manager proposes that the charges to users be computed on the basis of a chargeout algorithm. (The algorithm that she proposes is identical to the one appearing on page 1192.)

The following month the systems manager's proposal is put into effect. Two of the first jobs processed under the new charging scheme exhibit the following usages according to the monitors:

	Job #761	Job #762
Central processor time	2 hours	1 hour
Number of lines of printed output	200	5000
Terminal connect time	0	1 hour
Disk time	30 minutes	1 hour

Job #761 involved the preparation of the monthly production schedule by the use of a linear programming model.

Job #762 involved the processing of sales orders, with shipping notices being printed on the terminal at the remote warehouse and sales invoices being printed at the home office.

Required

a. Compute the charges for jobs #761 and #762 by using the chargeout rate based solely on central processor time used.

b. Compute the charges for jobs #761 and #762 by using the chargeout algorithm. Assume that the rates established for the various components are as follows:

$$r_1 = \$300 \text{ per hour}$$

$$r_2 = \$1 \text{ per 25 lines}$$

$$r_3 = \$25 \text{ per hour}$$

$$r_4 = \$30 \text{ per hour}$$

c. Compare the results obtained in **a** and **b,** above, and comment on the apparent desirability of each charging approach.

25-16 The Malone Corporation of Corvallis, Oregon, installed a computer-based information system several years ago. The quality of information has improved and growth in transaction volumes has been handled with ease, but system-related costs have also risen in an alarming fashion. Consequently, the president recently asked the firm's public accounting firm for assistance in pinpointing the problems. In response to this request, a specialist in management advisory services (MAS) from the public accounting firm visited the Malone Corporation and observed the activities within the systems department.

In her report, submitted today, the MAS specialist offers these observations:

a. No written policies or procedures concerning information systems development or operations can be found.

b. Systems projects are assigned verbally, with target completion dates being suggested casually. Projects are undertaken only upon requests of users and the concurrence of the systems manager.

c. Jobs from users are processed as received. Turnaround time for an average job is three days; however, jobs marked "rush" are given top priority and processed within one day, even if overtime is required.

d. Systems personnel are evaluated casually. Personnel turnover is high, partly because the job market is excellent but also because many employees feel that the systems manager plays favorites.

e. Reports concerning equipment utilization and personnel performance are non-existent.

f. Documentation is scant, consisting primarily of manufacturers' publications.

Required

a. Describe the relationships between the observations by the MAS specialist and the problem of high system-related costs.

b. Discuss the likely state of relationships between the systems manager and (1) systems personnel and (2) users.

25-17 Spiffy Software, Inc., of Waco, Texas, specializes in the development of software packages for sale to small and medium-size firms. Its professional personnel consist primarily of programmers. Each programmer is assigned at any time to a single programming project, consisting of the development of a particular software package. Five major tasks are involved in the development of a package: logic diagramming, coding, desk checking, program testing, and documentation. A programmer is evaluated with respect to each task, since he or she stays with an assigned project until its completion.

The evaluation process begins with the establishment of performance standards by the programming supervisor. In planning a particular programming project, he estimates its level of difficulty; next, he schedules the appropriate number of days for each task, broken down according to the several programs comprising the software package. Then the assigned programmer reports, on weekly time sheets, the times spent on the respective tasks. At the end of each month, programmer performance summaries are prepared, showing the differences between scheduled and actual times and the percent efficiencies.

The data in the table below are available concerning the performance last July of Erin Jones, a programmer assigned to the accounts payable package.

Required

a. Prepare a programmer performance summary for Erin Jones.

Hint: The percent efficiency for the logical diagramming of program AP1 would be computed as

$$\frac{4}{3\frac{1}{2}} \times 100 = 114 \text{ percent.}$$

b. Discuss other factors by which programmers of Spiffy Software, Inc., might be evaluated.

25-18 The Lybrand Co. of Bowling Green, Ohio, last year installed a computer system that includes a large-scale central processor, eight disk drives (on two selector channels), and four tape drives (on one selector channel). The system has multiprogramming and overlap capabilities. Unfortunately, the new system does not provide the performance that was promised by the equipment manufacturer. So an outside computer consultant is engaged to determine the cause of the poor performance.

The consultant first installs a hardware monitor on the computer system. After two weeks he summarizes the measurements, which show that the CPU was active 40 percent of the time, one disk channel was active 70 percent of the time, the other disk channel was active 30 percent of the time, and the tape channel was active 10 percent of the time. Furthermore, the CPU was waiting for one of the disk drives to complete some processing action 50 percent of the time.

Next the consultant turns to the computer log. From the entries for the past month he prepares the following summary (in hours):

Processing jobs	150
Setup of jobs	30
Testing and debugging programs	80
Downtime for maintenance	20
Idle time	40

Programming Task	Program AP1		Program AP2	
	Scheduled	**Actual**	**Scheduled**	**Actual**
Logic diagramming	4[a]	3½	5	4
Coding	6	7	10	6 (½ completed)
Desk checking	2	2	3	
Program testing	5	4	6	
Documentation	4	4½	4½	

[a] The numbers represent days scheduled and days actually worked.

Required

Discuss the preceding findings and suggest recommendations that the consultant might offer to the Lybrand Co.'s management. What other data, if any, would you like to have if you were the consultant?

25-19 The Weimer Co. of Ames, Iowa, processes its payment transactions on a computer system. Batches of payment transactions are keyed onto magnetic tape from check vouchers, sorted by supplier number, and then checked by an edit run. Each payment transaction record contains the following data fields:

Data Item	Number of Characters
Supplier number	4
Voucher number	5
Voucher date	6
Invoice date	6
Invoice number	5
Purchase order number	5
Due date	6
Check number	6
Check date	6
Amount	8

Required

Prepare a test deck that is to be used to check for the presence of the following types of programmed checks in the edit program: field check, completeness test, sign check, sequence check, check-digit verification, and relationship check. State the purpose of each test and show how an exception and summary report might reflect an error detected by the test.

25-20 The Weimer Co. also processes its sales transactions on a computer system. Each sales order is entered via a terminal at a sales branch and stored on a magnetic disk at the home office to await further processing. As each sales order is entered, it is checked by an edit program. Each transaction involving a sales order should include the following data: user code, transaction code, customer number, sales branch number, salesperson number, expected shipping date, product number(s), and quantity (or quantities).

Required

Prepare test data that are to be used to check for the presence of needed programmed checks in the edit program. State the purpose of each test and show how an error detected by the test might be displayed on the visual display screen of the terminal.

25-21 The Snyder Company of Bethlehem, Pennsylvania, processes its payroll weekly by means of a computer-based processing system. Payroll transaction records are keyed from time cards to magnetic tape. Then they are processed to prepare paychecks, updated the payroll master file, and print a payroll register.

The data items appearing in each transaction record consist of the transaction code, employee number, employee name, department number, pay category (hourly or salaried), and the hours worked (if an hourly employee).

The data items appearing in each record of the payroll master file consist of the employee number, employee name, Social Security number, department number, regular hourly wage rate (if an hourly employee), number of exemptions, other deduction factors, total gross earnings year-to-date, total deductions year-to-date (various), and total net pay year-to-date.

In addition to preparing the various outputs noted above, the update processing program performs the following checks:

  a. A field check on each numeric and alphabetic field on the transaction record.

  b. A relationship check to see that the first digit of the employee number agrees with the department number on the transaction record.

c. A relationship check to see that if the pay category code specifies a salary employee, there is no number appearing in the hours-worked field on the transaction record.

d. A limit check to see that the number of hours worked does not exceed 80.

e. A sequence check to see that the employee number on each succeeding transaction record is larger than the number on the previous record.

f. A sign check to see that the computed net pay is not negative.

g. A cross-footing balance check to see that gross pay less deductions equals net pay.

The processing program also

a. Prints all errors on an exception report (including multiple errors found in a single transaction record), together with identifying data for the erroneous transactions, then bypasses the erroneous transactions.

b. Accumulates a hash total on employee numbers, a quantity total on hours worked, and a record count of the transactions records (including erroneous transactions); prints the control totals on the exception report at the end of the processing run.

c. Lists erroneous transactions on a suspense tape.

d. Writes a new payroll master file on magnetic tape.

Required

a. Prepare a broad, or macro, program flowchart of the update and paycheck prepara-

tion run using "Edit," "Pay Computation," "Net Pay Programmed Checks," and "Output" processing modules or subroutines. Assume that both transaction and master records have been sorted in employee number sequence.

b. Prepare a detailed, or "micro, program flowchart of the "Edit" module.

25-22 The Independent Underwriters Insurance Co. (IUI) of Hartford, Conn., established a systems department two years ago to implement and operate its own data processing system. IUI believed that its own system would be more cost effective than the service bureau it had been using.

IUI's three departments—claims, records, and finance—have different requirements with respect to hardware and other capacity-related resources and operating resources. The system was designed to recognize these differing needs. In addition, the system was designed to meet IUI's long-term capacity needs. The excess capacity designed into the system would be sold to outside users until needed by IUI. The estimated resource requirements used to design and implement the system are shown in the following schedule:

	Hardware and Other Capacity Related Resources	Operating Resources
Records	30%	60%
Claims	50	20
Finance	15	15
Expansion (outside use)	5	5
Total	100%	100%

IUI currently sells the equivalent of its expansion capacity to a few outside clients.

At the time the system became operational, management decided to redistribute total expenses of the systems department to the user departments on the basis of the actual computer time used. The actual costs for the first quarter of the current fiscal year were distributed to the user departments as follows:

Department	Percentage Utilization	Amount
Records	60%	$330,000
Claims	20%	110,000
Finance	15%	82,500
Outside	5%	27,500
Total	100%	$550,000

The three user departments have complained about the cost distribution method since the systems department was established. The records department's monthly costs have been as much as three times the costs experienced with the service bureau. The finance department is concerned about the costs distributed to the outside-user category because these allocated costs form the basis for the fees billed to the outside clients.

James Dale, IUI's controller decided to review the distribution method by which the systems department's costs have been allocated for the past two years. The additional information he gathered for his review is reported in Tables 1, 2, and 3.

Dale has concluded that the method of cost distribution should be changed to reflect more directly the actual benefits received by the departments. He believes that the hardware and capacity-related costs should be allocated to the user departments in proportion to the planned long-term needs. Any difference between actual and budgeted hardware costs would not be allocated to the departments but remain with the systems department.

The remaining costs for software development and operations would be charged to the user departments based on actual hours used. A predetermined hourly rate based on the annual budget data would be used. The hourly rates that would be used for the current fiscal year are as follows:

Function	Hourly Rate
Software development	$ 30
Operations	
Computer related	$200
Input/output related	$ 10

Dale plans to use first-quarter activity and cost data to illustrate his recommendations. The recommendations will be presented to the systems department and the

TABLE 1 Systems Department Costs and Activity Levels

| | Annual Budget | | First Quarter | | | |
| | | | Budget | | Actual | |
	Hours	Dollars	Hours	Dollars	Hours	Dollars
Hardware and other capacity-related costs	—	$ 600,000	—	$150,000	—	$155,000
Software development	18,750	562,500	4,725	141,750	4,250	130,000
Operations						
Computer related	3,750	750,000	945	189,000	920	187,000
Input–output related	30,000	300,000	7,560	75,600	7,900	78,000
		$2,212,500		$556,350		$550,000

TABLE 2 Historical Utilization by Users

	Hardware and Other Capacity Needs	Software Development		Operations			
				Computer		Input–Output	
		Range	Average	Range	Average	Range	Average
Records	30%	0–30%	12%	55–65%	60%	10–30%	20%
Claims	50	15–60	35	10–25	20	60–80	70
Finance	15	25–75	45	10–25	15	3–10	6
Outside	5	0–25	8	3–8	5	3–10	4
	100%		100%		100%		100%

TABLE 3 Utilization of Systems Department's Services in Hours (First Quarter)

	Software Development	Operations	
		Computer Related	Input–Output
Records	425	552	1580
Claims	1700	184	5530
Finance	1700	138	395
Outside	425	46	395
Total	4,250	920	7,900

user departments for their comments and reactions. He then expects to present his recommendations to management for approval.

Required

a. Calculate the amount of data processing costs that would be included in the claims department's first-quarter budget according to the method James Dale has recommended.

b. Prepare a schedule to show how the actual first-quarter costs of the systems department would be charged to the users if James Dale's recommended method was adopted.

c. Explain whether James Dale's recommended system for charging costs to the user departments will

   (1) Improve cost control in the systems department.

   (2) Improve planning and cost control in the user departments.

   (3) Be a more equitable basis for charging costs to user departments.

(CMA adapted)

25-23 *Datacruncher Office Equipment, Inc. (Continuing Case)*

Required

a. Draw a network diagram that shows the relationships and times for the activities pertaining to the implementation of the preferable design alternative; compute the total project time and the critical path.

b. Draw a program flowchart and decision table for one processing step (preferably a file processing step) in the preferable design alternative.

c. Write a computer program (in COBOL or other suitable language) that relates to the logic diagrams in **b.**

Suggested Readings

Allen, Brandt. "Make Information Services Pay Its Way." *Harvard Business Review* (Jan–Feb. 1987), pp. 57–63.

Andersen, Anker V. *Budgeting for Data Processing*. New York: National Association of Accountants, 1983.

Bartholomew, John J. "Implementing a Change in the Accounting MIS of a Bank." *Cost and Management* (March–April 1981), pp. 14–20.

Berliner, Harold I., and Golland, Marvin. "Minicomputer Systems: A Practical Approach to Computer Implementation." *Financial Executive* (Nov. 1980), pp. 24–29.

Biggs, Charles L.; Birks, Evan G.; and Atkins, William. *Managing the Systems Development Process*. Englewood Cliffs, N.J.: Prentice-Hall, 1980.

Carlyle, Ralph. "Leaping Ahead in Software Productivity." *Datamation* (Dec. 1, 1989), pp. 21–32.

Carroll, Archie B. "Behavioral Aspects of Developing Computer-Based Information Systems." *Business Horizons* (Jan.–Feb. 1982), pp. 42–51.

Casimir, Rommert J. "Characteristics and Implementation of Decision Support Systems." *Information and Management* (Jan. 1988), pp. 1–7.

Chubb, Timothy D. "Why Computer Systems Conversions Are Tricky." *Management Accounting* (Sept. 1983), pp. 36–41.

Collins, Frank, and Morres, Tom. "Microprocessors in the Office: A Study of Resistance to Change." *Journal of Systems Management* (Nov. 1983), pp. 17–21.

DeGroff, William J. "Accounting for Computing Costs." *Journal of Accounting and EDP* (Spring 1985), pp. 25–32.

Edelstein, Lee, and Aird, Susan. "Commitment: The Key to Successful Accounting System Implementation." *Management Accounting* (Dec. 1988), pp. 50–51.

Egyhazy, Csaba Ja. "Technical Software Development Tools." *Journal of Systems Management* (Jan. 1985), pp. 8–13.

Faerber, Leroy G., and Ratliff, Richard L. "People Problems behind MIS Failures." *Financial Executive* (April 1980), pp. 18–25.

Green, Gary I., and Keim, Robert T. "After Implementation What's Next? Evaluation." *Journal of Systems Management* (Sept. 1983), pp. 10–15.

Gremillion, Lee L., and Shea, Timothy P. "COBOL Application Code Generators." *Journal of Systems Management* (Dec. 1985), pp. 30–33.

Hamilton, Scott, and Chervany, Norman, L. "Evaluating Information System Effectiveness—Part I: Comparing Evaluation Approaches." *MIS Quarterly* (Sept. 1981), pp. 55–67.

Hoffman, Michael J. "DP Cost Allocation: A Management Perspective." *Journal of Systems Management* (Jan. 1984), pp. 16–19.

Isaacs, P. Brian. "Warnier–Orr Diagrams in Applying Structured Concepts." *Journal of Systems Management* (Oct. 1982), pp. 28–32.

Khan, M. B., and Martin, Merle P. "Managing the Systems Project." *Journal of Systems Management* (Jan. 1989), pp. 31–37.

Kolle, Michael. "Going Outside for MIS Implementation." *Information and Management* (Oct. 1983), pp. 261–268.

Lederer, Albert L.; Stubler, William F.; Sethi, Vijay; and Ryan, John C. "The

Implementation of Office Automation." *Interfaces* (July–Aug. 1987), pp. 78–84.

Lees, John D., and Lees, Donna D. "Realities of Small Business Information System Implementation." *Journal of Systems Management* (Jan. 1987), pp. 6–13.

Lin, Chien-Hua M. "System for Charging Computer Services." *Journal of Systems Management* (Nov. 1983), pp. 6–10.

London, Keith R. *Decision Tables*. Princeton, N.J.: Auerbach Publishers, 1972.

Martin, Merle P., and Trumbly, James E. "Measuring Performance of Automated Systems." *Journal of Systems Management* (Feb. 1986), pp. 7–17.

Matthews, Mark D. "Interfaces and Implementation of an Automated Project Management Network Planning System." *Journal of Systems Management* (May 1985), pp. 34–40.

Multinovich, J.S., and Vlahovich, Vladimir. "A Strategy for a Successful MIS/DSS Implementation." *Journal of Systems Management* (August 1984), pp. 8–15.

Newman, Michael. "User Involvement— Does It Exist, Is It Enough? *Journal of Systems Management* (May 1984), pp. 34–37.

Nolan, Richard L. "Controlling the Costs of Data Services." *Harvard Business Review* (July–August 1977), pp. 114–124.

———. *Managing the Data Resource*. 2d ed. New York: West Publishing, 1982.

Rajarman, M. K. "Structured Techniques for Software Development." *Journal of Systems Management* (March 1983), pp. 36–38.

Rizzuto, Christine, and Rizzuto, Ralph. "Chargeouts: A Perspective for Change." *Datamation* (Dec. 1978), pp. 125–128.

Sen, Tarun, and Yardley, James A. "Are Chargeback Systems Effective? An Information Processing Study." *Journal of Information Systems* (Spring 1989), pp. 92–103.

Singleton, John P.; McLean, Ephraim R.; and Altman, Edward N. "Measuring Information Systems Performance: Experience with the Management by Results System at Security Pacific Bank." *MIS Quarterly* (June 1988), pp. 325–337.

Srinivasan, C. A., and Dascher, Paul E. "Performing a Management Audit of EDP Operations." *Financial Executive* (Nov. 1980), pp. 30–37.

Walsh, Myles E. "What is a Data Center?" *Journal of Systems Management* (Jan. 1984), pp. 20–29.

Wheelock, Alton R. "Service or Profit Center?" *Datamation* (May 1982), pp. 167–176.

Zawacki, Robert A. "Performance Standards, Goals and Objectives for DP Personnel." *Journal of Systems Management* (Jan. 1984), pp. 12–15.

Part VI

COMPREHENSIVE CASES

Learning to develop information systems is not a simple task. It is not sufficient to become familiar with terminology, concepts, techniques, and the several phases of the systems development cycle. It is also necessary to *experience and apply* these materials in settings that are realistic and comprehensive. This final part of the book, therefore, presents seven comprehensive cases that, it is believed, approximate situations found in real-world firms.

Case A concerns Datacruncher Office Equipment, Inc., a continuing case with requirements at the ends of Chapters 21 through 25. It provides the materials for a term project that simulates the development of an improved information system. Cases B through F provide the basis for designing components of improved information systems. These design specifications may, if desired, be incorporated into formal system design proposals and preceded by cover letters to management. Case G, Representative Distributing Company (RDC), may be used for extended assignments involving electronic spreadsheet and data base management software packages.

CASE A

Datacruncher Office Equipment, Inc.

Statement

Datacruncher Office Equipment, Inc., of Dallas, Texas, is a manufacturer of varied machines and devices for the modern office. Among its products are desk calculators, terminals, printer units, key-to-tape units, microfilm readers, word processing systems, time-stamping machines, and addressing devices. The firm distributes it products nationwide through 150 franchised dealers who also handle the products of competitors. In addition, the firm sells direct to large and medium-size business firms and other organizations having substantial data processing requirements. The firm also provides service to its customers. About 600 customers receive statements at the end of a typical month for sales or service.

Datacruncher was started in the late 1960s. The founders were four employees—two salespersons and two engineers—from a long-established office machines manufacturer. They foresaw the growing importance of the office in the modern firm. Their vision has been amply rewarded, since their firm has enjoyed an explosive growth. Of course, vision alone was not sufficient to generate this growth. A sound knowledge of the office equipment market and skillfully designed products were the essential ingredients.

The firm's growth is reflected by several measures. Sales have reached $70 million during this year just ended; this amount represents a 20 percent increase over last year's sales. The number of managers and employees has climbed to almost 1100 as of this year-end. Approximately 500 suppliers provide materials and parts for the 120 products that the firm manufactures. The physical facilities consist of the home office building and production plant, located just off an express parkway in Dallas, plus three regional sites in San Francisco, St. Louis, and Philadelphia. Each regional site contains a sales office and a warehouse. A finished-goods warehouse is attached to the plant in Dallas.

Besides growth in sales the firm's founders have emphasized the need to increase the firm's share of the office equipment market and the return on total assets. To achieve these objectives, they have stressed aggressive salesmanship, new-product development, prompt deliveries of ordered products, minimized production and inventory costs, and prudent cash management.

Organization

Datacruncher is organized as a corporation and has 2500 stockholders. The board of directors consists of the four founders plus four outside directors. The four founders occupy top positions in the firm: Bill Dixon is the president, Bert Sanders is the vice-president of marketing, Judy Hollis is the vice-president of engineering, and Jim Marshall is the vice-president of production. The first two were formerly salespersons; the last two were engineers. Other high-level managers include Harry Myler, vice-president of administration; Charles Dauten, vice-president of finance; Barbara Fulton, controller; and Tim Baker, director of information systems. (A more detailed enumeration of the firm's managers and employees appears in Exhibit A-1.)

Financial Status

The income statements for the last two years (as shown in Exhibit A-2) reflect the

EXHIBIT A-1 Selected Data Concerning Personnel and Organization
1. Numbers of Managers and Employees

Organizational Unit	Number	Organizational Unit	Number
FINANCE FUNCTION		**Data processing**	
Cost accounting		System analysts	3
Senior clerks	2	Programmers	5
Junior clerks	2	Operators	4
Accountants	2	Data entry clerks	14
Secretary/typist	1	Secretary/typist	1
Manager	1	Supervisors	2
		Manager	1
Billing			
Senior clerks	2	**Other**	
Junior clerks	3	Senior clerks	10
Secretary/typist	1	Junior clerks	9
Manager	1	Accountants	5
		Financial planners	3
Accounts receivable		Secretary/typists	6
Senior clerks	4	Managers	4
Junior clerks	3		
Secretary/typists	2	**ADMINISTRATION FUNCTION**	
Manager	1	**Information systems**	
		Project leader	1
Accounts payable		System analysts	2
Senior clerks	2	Staff assistants	4
Junior clerks	3	Secretary/typists	2
Secretary/typist	1	Manager	1
Manager	1		
		Personnel	
Payroll		Senior clerks	15
Senior clerks	2	Junior clerks	20
Junior clerks	3	Secretary/typists	4
Secretary/typists	2	Staff assistants	4
Manager	1	Supervisors	4
		Manager	1
Cash receipts			
Senior clerks	4	**Other**	
Junior clerks	2	Senior clerks	12
Secretary/typists	2	Junior clerks	11
Manager	1	Secretary/typists	3
		Staff assistants	6
Cash disbursements		Supervisors	2
Senior clerks	3	Managers	2
Junior clerks	3		
Secretary/typist	1	**MARKETING FUNCTION**	
Manager	1	**Sales order**	
		Senior clerks	10
Credit		Junior clerks	15
Senior clerks	3	Secretary/typists	3
Junior clerks	4	Supervisors	3
Secretary/typist	1	Manager	1
Manager	1		

Organizational Unit	Number	Organizational Unit	Number
Dealer sales		**PRODUCTION FUNCTION**	
Senior clerks	8	**Production operations**	
Junior clerks	9	Secretary/typists	4
Secretary/typist	1	Fabricators	45
Sales coordinators	4	Assemblers	54
Manager	1	Supervisors	12
		Managers	2
Large customer sales			
Senior clerks	6	**Purchasing**	
Junior clerks	5	Senior clerks	4
Secretary/typist	1	Junior clerks	2
Sales coordinators	3	Secretary/typists	4
Manager	1	Buyers	16
		Manager	1
Service		**Production planning**	
Senior clerks	12	**and control**	
Junior clerks	16	Senior clerks	8
Secretary/typists	3	Junior clerks	10
Service representatives	30	Secretary/typists	2
Manager	1	Production planners	2
		Manager	1
Sales offices (3)		**Receiving**	
Senior clerks	30	Senior clerks	2
Junior clerks	20	Junior clerks	3
Secretary/typists	6	Receivers	10
Supervisors	6	Supervisor	1
Salespersons	100	Manager	1
Managers	3		
		Data processing	
Warehouses (4)		System analysts	2
		Programmers	3
Senior clerks	10	Operators	4
Junior clerks	8	Data entry clerks	10
Secretary/typists	4	Secretary/typist	1
Order pickers	60	Supervisors	2
Managers	4	Manager	1
Shipping		**Other**	
Senior clerks	4	Senior clerks	11
Junior clerks	3	Junior clerks	10
Secretary/typist	1	Secretary/typists	3
Packers/shippers	12	Maintenance workers	10
Supervisors	2	Inspectors	4
Manager	1	Storeskeepers	3
		Managers	3
Other		**Engineering function**	
Senior clerks	12	Senior clerks	5
Junior clerks	16	Junior clerks	8
Secretary/typists	2	Secretary/typists	4
Staff assistants	10	Senior engineers	15
Market planners	3	Junior engineers	25
Managers	2	Managers	3

EXHIBIT A-1 (*Continued*)
2. Payroll Costs (Average)

Senior clerks	$22,000 per year
Junior clerks	$17,000 per year
Secretary/typists	$12,000 per year
Accountants	$25,000 per year
System analysts	$27,000 per year
Programmers	$20,000 per year
Operators	$10.00 per hour
Data entry clerks	$7.00 per hour
Financial planners	$29,000 per year
Project leader	$33,000 per year
Staff assistants	$22,000 per year
Market planners	$28,000 per year
Sales coordinators	$20,000 per year
Service representatives	$25,000 per year
Salespersons	$15,000 per year
	plus 6% of sales
Other pickers	$7.00 per hour
Packers/shippers	$8.00 per hour
Fabricators	$9.00 per hour
Assemblers	$9.00 per hour
Buyers	$24,000 per year
Production planners	$29,000 per year
Receivers	$7.00 per hour
Maintenance workers	$9.00 per hour
Inspectors	$20,000 per year
Storeskeepers	$8.00 per hour
Junior engineers	$30,000 per year
Senior engineers	$38,000 per year
Supervisors	$35,000 per year
Managers (department level)	$40,000 per year
Managers (middle level; e.g., director of information systems, controller, cashier)	$50,000 per year
Managers (vice-president level)	$70,000 per year
President	$100,000 per year

Notes: a. Fringe benefits are equivalent to 15 percent of the above salaries or wages.

b. Overtime pay, at 1½ times regular rate, is authorized only for hourly production line employees. An average of one hour of overtime per week is worked by each production employee.

sales growth mentioned earlier. They also show, however, that net income has grown less rapidly than net sales. In fact, net income for this year has declined from last year's net income. There are indications that this decline stems from two factors: (1) rising costs in production, inventory, and other areas; and (2) necessary reductions in the prices of certain products to combat the new products of competitors.

The balance sheets for the last two years (also shown in Exhibit A-2) indicate that the firm's financial position is basically sound. However, there are certain adverse signs, such as a shrinking cash balance.

Procedures

Four broad activities at the operational level can be identified as the revenue cycle, the production cycle, the expenditure cycle,

EXHIBIT A-1 *(Continued)*

3. Organizational Relationships

Function	Middle-Level Managers	Departments
Finance		Data processing Billing Cost accounting Accounts receivable Accounts payable Inventory control Payroll General ledger
	Controller	
	Cashier	Cash receipts Cash disbursements Credit Cash management
Administration	Director of information systems	Information systems
	Internal affairs manager	Personnel Taxes and insurance Office operations
Engineering		Product design and development Industrial engineering
Production		Purchasing Production planning and control Receiving Raw materials stores Data processing Maintenance Quality control
	Production superintendent	Fabrication Assembly
Marketing		Market research Advertising
	Sales manager	Dealer sales Large customer sales Service Sales order Sales offices (3)
	Distribution manager	Shipping Warehouses (4)

Notes: a. Each function is headed by a vice-president.

b. Those departments for which no middle-level managers are shown report directly to the vice-presidents.

and inventory management. Other activities include engineering design, market research, personnel and payroll, cash management, and general ledger accounting. Processing of transactions pertaining to the first four preceding activities, plus payroll and general ledger accounting, is aided by two computers. One of these computers is located within the accounting function, the other within the production function. The following sections describe briefly the current processing, including key documents, outputs, and files. (In addition, Exhibit A-3 contains measures of activity relating to the following procedures.)

Revenue cycle.   Salespersons periodically visit the dealers and prospective business firms and other organizations in their sales regions. As they obtain orders, they mail or phone in the orders to their regional sales offices. Each sales office then records the orders on a register and prepares formal sales orders in quadruplicate. The original of each order is mailed to the customer, whereas the last copy is filed by customer name. At the end of each day the batch of orders (consisting of the middle two copies of all orders prepared that day) is mailed to the home office.

When received in the sales order depart-

EXHIBIT A-2

Datacruncher Office Equipment, Inc.
Statement of Income
For the Years Ended December 31, 1989 and 1990

	1990	1989
	(thousands of dollars)	
Revenues		
Sales, dealers	$35,812	$30,654
Sales, direct	27,343	21,870
Service	7,327	6,236
Total revenues	$70,482	$58,760
Cost of goods sold	49,934	39,375
Gross profit on sales	$20,548	$19,385
Operating expenses		
Selling and distribution expenses	$11,284	$ 9,532
Administrative (including accounting and data processing) expenses	2,302	1,875
Research and engineering expenses	1,346	1,473
Interest expense	1,372	1,013
Other expenses, including depreciation	741	733
Total operating expenses	$17,045	$14,626
Net income before income taxes	$ 3,503	$ 4,759
Provision for income taxes	1,191	1,618
Net income	$ 2,312	$ 3,141

EXHIBIT A-2 (*Continued*)

Datacruncher Office Equipment, Inc.
Statement of Financial Position
December 31, 1989 and 1990

	1990	1989
	(thousands of dollars)	
Assets		
Current assets		
Cash	$ 516	$ 2,178
Accounts receivable, net	12,022	9,518
Inventories		
Raw materials and parts	5,674	4,852
Work-in-process	6,923	5,107
Finished goods	9,547	7,321
Prepaid expenses	547	695
Total current assets	$35,229	$29,671
Fixed assets	$12,184	$11,380
Less: Accumulated depreciation	7,132	5,939
Net fixed assets	$ 5,052	$ 5,441
Other assets	$10,636	$ 6,991
Total assets	$50,917	$42,103
Equities		
Current liabilities		
Notes payable	$ 5,731	$ 1,880
Current maturities of long-term debt	682	595
Accounts payable	4,619	3,751
Accrued expenses and taxes	6,978	4,826
Total current liabilities	$18,010	$11,052
Long-term debt	$ 7,100	$ 6,400
Stockholders' equity		
Common stock, no par value		
Authorized 1,000,000 shares;		
outstanding 650,000 shares	$ 9,858	$ 9,858
Capital surplus	2,610	2,610
Retained earnings	13,339	12,183
Total stockholders' equity	$25,807	$24,651
Total equities	$50,917	$42,103

EXHIBIT A-3 Measures of Activity

DOCUMENT VOLUMES PER MONTH

Sales orders	2000
(with an average of 6 items per document)	
Cash receipts	1950
Purchase requisitions	1000
Purchase orders	1000
(with an average of 8 lines per document)	
Back orders	260
Production orders	105
Shipping reports	1980
Bills of lading	1980
Materials requisitions	475
Move tickets	355
Stock transfer notices	240
Receiving reports	960
(with an average of 7 lines per document)	
Disbursement vouchers	1010
Check vouchers (other than payroll)	830

NUMBERS OF ACTIVE RECORDS IN KEY FILES

Accounts receivable	1850
Accounts payable	517
Finished-goods inventory	120
Work-in-process inventory	170
Raw-materials and parts inventory	11,960
Bills of material	120
Employee earnings	1098
General ledger	92

OTHER MEASURES OF ACTIVITY

Number of new customers per month	20
Number of inquiries from customers per day	70
Number of adjustments (e.g., sales returns, purchases returns, write-offs) per month	160
Number of days (on the average) between the time that a purchase order is mailed and materials or parts are received	15
Number of days (on the average) required to process a sales order	12
Percentage of products rejected during production inspections during current year	5
Number of dealers accounting for 75% of sales by all dealers	40

ment, the orders are reviewed for completeness and accuracy by sales order clerks and numbers are assigned. The orders are then forwarded to the credit department for a credit check. When credit is approved for the amounts of the orders, one copy of each order is sent to the inventory control department, the orders are reviewed for completeness and accuracy by sales order clerks and numbers are assigned. The orders are then forwarded to the credit department for a credit check. When credit is approved for the amounts of the orders, one copy of each order is sent to the inventory control department and the other copy to the billing department.

By reference to computer printouts of product status, inventory control clerks determine whether or not sufficient inventory is available to fill each order. If sufficient inventory is available at the warehouse in the region where the customer resides, one copy of the order is mailed there. If sufficient inventory is not available in the regional warehouse but is available in the main finished-goods warehouse in Dallas, the copy of the order is routed there instead. In either case the goods are picked and readied for shipment, based on the order. A shipping report and bill of lading are prepared and the order is shipped. A copy of the shipping report is enclosed with the shipment as a packing slip, and another copy is returned to the billing department. If sufficient inventory is not available to fill the order in its entirety, the inventory control clerk prepares a back order, which he or she routes to the production planning and control department.

Upon the receipt of a shipping report, a billing clerk pulls the department's copy of the sales order from a file, verifies that the product numbers and quantities match, and notes the shipping date and prices on the order copy. Next he or she sends the order copy (together with the other orders processed that day) to the data preparation section in the accounting data processing department. The orders then are keyed onto magnetic tape, edited, sorted, and processed against the accounts receivable and finished-good inventory (product) master files. Sales invoices are generated as outputs from this processing, together with an open sales invoice file on magnetic tape.[1] Two copies of each sales invoice are mailed to a customer, two other copies are sent to the sales order department and the appropriate regional sales office, and a fifth copy is filed alphabetically.

All cash receipts from customers are received in the mailroom at the home office. There they are opened and listed on a special form. Then the checks are routed to the cashier, together with a copy of the list. The cashier prepares a bank deposit slip in duplicate, endorses the checks, and delivers the deposit to the bank the next morning. A copy of the deposit slip is returned to a file in her office. Another copy of the listed receipts is sent to the credit department, where a clerk enters the customer numbers that correspond to the listed names and addresses. The clerk forwards the list to the data preparation section, which keys the receipts data onto magnetic tape. The transaction data are then sorted and processed against the accounts receivable master file once each day. At the end of the month the accounts receivable master file is processed to produce an accounts receivable aging schedule, which is sent to the credit manager, and statements, which are mailed to customers.

Production cycle. Products are manufactured either for inventory or to fill back orders. The overall production level generally is based on a sales forecast made by the marketing function. However, back orders occur because of out-of-stock conditions, and they must be fitted into the schedule. In fact, back orders are given priority in order to pacify unhappy customers.

Production operations are triggered when the production planning and control department receives production authorizations or back orders. The production authorizations are prepared by comparing forecasted sales levels with current levels of finished-goods inventory on hand and are issued jointly by the production superintendent and the inventory control manager.[2] Back orders are prepared, as described earlier, on the basis of orders that cannot be filled. The production planning and control

---

[1]Sales due to services rendered are also reflected in sales invoices. The service details, including amounts, appear on service reports forwarded to billing by the service department. The amounts charged to customers must of course be processed against the accounts receivable master file.

[2]Needed levels of product are related to the rates at which products are being sold, which in turn are tied to the sales forecast.

department then obtains the bills of material from the engineering function and explodes the production requirements to determine materials and parts requirements. With the materials and parts requirements in hand, a production planning clerk checks a computer printout of materials and parts inventory on hand. If the materials and parts on hand are adequate for a particular product, the clerk schedules a production run (based on available labor and machines). As each scheduled date nears, the clerk sends the affected production authorizations and back orders to the data preparation section of the production data processing department. There the production requirements data are keyed onto magnetic tape, sorted by product number, and processed to produce numbered production orders, materials requisitions, and move tickets. Files used in this processing run are the bill-of-materials file, the operations list file, the open production order file, and the work-in-process inventory master file.

Copies of the materials requisitions are sent to the materials storeroom, which then delivers materials and parts to the designated production departments. Copies of the production orders and the move tickets are sent to the first production department involved in the manufacturing process (usually the fabricating department). Copies of production orders are also sent to the cost accounting department, and copies of materials requisitions are kept in the data processing department for inventory processing. As work is completed on an order in a department, a move ticket is returned to the production planning and control department. At the end of each day, all returned move tickets are batched and forwarded to the data preparation section. There the move ticket data are keyed onto a magnetic tape, sorted by production order number, and processed to produce a daily production status report. The open production order file is updated during the processing.

In separate daily processing steps the materials requisitions are batched, keyed onto a magnetic tape, sorted by material-part number, and processed to update the raw-materials inventory master file. Then the materials requisitions are resorted by production order number and processed (together with labor job-time tickets forwarded from work centers and sorted in a like manner on a separate magnetic tape) to update the work-in-process inventory master file.

When a production order has progressed through the fabrication and assembly departments, the units of completed product are inspected. Those units that pass inspection are released to the finished-goods warehouse, and copies of the order release are sent to the production planning and control department and the cost accounting department. From the central warehouse the finished products are shipped, via stock transfer notices, to the three remote warehouses as needed to replenish stocks. The production planning and control department records the completion and then sends the releases to the data preparation section. There they are keyed onto a magnetic tape, sorted by product number, and processed against the finished-goods and work-in process inventory master files, as well as the open production orders file. A completed production orders report is also printed; it includes the costs charged to each order.

When the materials and parts needed to manufacture particular products are not available, the production planning and control clerk prepares purchase requisitions. These requisitions are sent to the purchasing department.

Expenditure cycle. A wide variety of expenditures, ranging from utilities to insurance, are necessary. Expenditures for raw materials and parts, as well as subassemblies, are particularly significant, since the products manufactured by the firm require a high level of precision. Thus, the procedure pertaining to the purchases of such items and the disbursements for them is another of the critical transaction cycles within Datacruncher.

Purchases are initiated by either production planning and control clerks or inventory control clerks. The former clerks issue purchase requisitions when they note that materials and parts are not adequate for upcoming production runs, whereas the latter clerks issue similar documents when their experience suggests that the on-hand quantities of particular items have declined to reorderable levels. On the basis of these purchase requisitions, buyers in the purchasing department select suppliers who are known to be reliable and enter their codes on the requisitions, together with acceptable prices for the items to be ordered. The requisitions are then forwarded to the data preparation section in the production data processing department. There they are keyed onto a magnetic tape, sorted by supplier number, and processed to produce purchase orders. During subsequent runs, the raw-materials inventory master file and the open purchase order file are updated. The purchase orders are then signed by the purchasing manager and mailed to the suppliers. Copies of the purchase orders are forwarded to the receiving department and the accounts payable department, and a fourth copy is filed by supplier name in the purchasing department.

When ordered materials and parts arrive at the receiving dock, receiving clerks pull the purchase order copies from their file. Then they count or weigh the items and prepare receiving reports. The items are next transferred to the materials storeroom and the initialed copies of the receiving reports are sent on to the accounts payable department and filed. Another copy of each receiving report is sent to the data preparation section of the data processing department, and a

third copy is filed numerically in the receiving department. In the data preparation section the receiving reports are keyed onto a magnetic tape, sorted by material-part number, processed to update the raw-materials inventory master file, resorted by purchase order number, and processed to update the open purchase order file.

When suppliers' invoices arrive in the accounts payable department, clerks pull the receiving reports and purchase orders from the file and compare the documents. After completing their vouching of the invoices, they prepare disbursement vouchers, record them in a voucher register, and file all the documents together by payment due date.

Each day other clerks pull the vouchers due for payment that day and send them to the data preparation section of the accounting data processing department. There the payment data are keyed onto magnetic tape, sorted by supplier account number, and processed to produce check vouchers and a check register. The accounts payable master file is also updated during this run; in effect, each affected supplier's account is credited to reflect the obligation and debited to reflect the payment.

Inventory management. Three inventory files are maintained by the firm. The raw-materials inventory master file is updated to reflect orders for materials and parts, as well as receipts from suppliers and issues into production. The finished-goods inventory master file is updated to reflect the newly manufactured products and the sales of products to customers. The work-in-process inventory master file is updated to reflect the start in production of each production order, the issues of materials into production, the charges of labor (from job-time records) into production, the application of overhead to production, and the completion of production.

Problems

A number of specific problems have become apparent. Some of these problems relate to the procedures described earlier, whereas other problems arise from weaknesses in the organizational structure and in financial planning. Many of these problems stem from the fact that the founders have focused on selling and engineering. They have not given as much attention to the areas of accounting, finance, production, and inventory management. Most of the problems also arise from the rapid growth in sales.

Some of the more significant problems, in addition to those noted earlier, should be mentioned. Interest costs are relatively high, as are costs in production and distribution. Back orders are fairly numerous, even though inventory levels have been rising. Promised delivery dates on customers' orders are often missed, even though lead times of two weeks or more often are allowed. Processing backlogs are sustained in several of the accounting departments. These backlogs lead to a variety of ill effects; for instance, purchase discounts are frequently lost and numerous errors are introduced into the transaction data. The percentage of products that do not pass inspection is rather high, perhaps at least in part because of fairly obsolete production equipment and a high labor turnover. Production schedules are difficult to keep up to date, and production jobs often fall behind their schedules. In fact, production clerks keep extremely busy "pushing" jobs, monitoring their progress, and answering phone calls from concerned customers and salespersons. Also, production rates tend to fluctuate, so that production employees are idled at times and required to work overtime at other times. This problem stems in part from rush back orders; however, it also arises from sales forecasts that prove to be quite inaccurate and from planning procedures that are relatively weak. For instance, the budget process is fairly rudimentary. Budgets are not tied to carefully established cost standards, are not developed in detailed formats, and are not revised to reflect changed conditions. Finally, the reports provided to managers are rather inadequate; most are of the status variety, such as the weekly materials-and-parts status report, the daily product-status report, and the monthly report of budgeted costs versus actual costs.

Initiation of Systems Development

These problems, and their effects on the firm's financial status, have been of concern to the founders for some time. Their view is that at least some of the problems are aggravated by an inadequate information system. Recently, in fact, they created the position called director of information systems and hired Tim Baker, because they strongly felt that corrective measures were necessary. Perhaps, they thought, he could harmonize and update an information system that is rather uncoordinated and somewhat obsolete at present.

After hearing the news concerning the decline in net income for this year, the founders decide to take further action. They appoint a steering committee and announce a long-range systems development program. They ask the committee to develop a strategic systems plan, in which a number of systems projects are identified. Within a couple of months the committee develops the requested plan. Among other features the plan includes the projected time periods for several identified systems projects, plus rough values pertaining to the expected benefits and required resources for each (see Exhibit A-4). A high-priority systems project is duly commenced and progresses through the analysis and design stages. Then more detailed costs and benefits are developed for a preferable design alternative (shown in Exhibit A-5), and the economic feasibility of the alternative is examined. After ascertaining that the alternative is indeed feasible, and thus that new computer hardware and software should be acquired, an implementation plan is developed (based on the activity times shown in Exhibit A-6). Finally, after several more months of intense effort, an important module of the new information system is in place and operational.

Notes:

1. Exhibits A-4, A-5, and A-6 will be provided by your instructor when this case is assigned.
2. Requirements for this case appear as the last problems in Chapters 21 through 25.

CASE B

Microcomputer Merchandise Mart

Statement

Microcomputer Merchandise Mart (MMM) is a St. Louis merchandiser of microcomputers and related equipment. Among the products that it sells are video display terminals, printers, modems, hard disk drives, diskettes, and business software packages. The firm sells these products through retail stores that are located in shopping centers within the St. Louis metropolitan area. It also provides limited product service to customers, who consist primarily of small businesses, professionals, and other individuals.

Bill Princeton and Jill Harvard, two members of the sales force of a large microcomputer manufacturer, established MMM in 1980. They still own a significant portion of the outstanding stock of the firm. During its several years of existence MMM has done very well. Not only have sales grown fairly rapidly, but the product lines have been expanded and the employees have increased in number. This growth has occurred in spite of the fact that several new competitors have started operations in every year since 1980.

This case is reprinted from *Accounting Information Systems: Essential Concepts and Applications,* by Joseph W. Wilkinson, with permission of John Wiley & Sons, Inc.

Currently, the firm handles five brands of microcomputers, as well as several brands of terminals, printers, and other peripherals. To sell these products, it maintains three retail stores, plus one warehouse attached to a main office. It employs 70 persons, ranging from the president to a janitor.

Organization and Functions

The president of MMM is Bill Princeton. Reporting to him are seven managers: Tod Dartmouth, Betsy Stanford, Bob Brown, Jack Yale, Paul Cornell, Jill Harvard, and Tom Carnegie. Tod is in charge of purchasing activities and supervises several buyers who specialize in the various product lines. Betsy oversees clerks and bookkeepers who process transactions and maintain the accounting records. Bob directs the operations of the several retail stores. Each store, together with its salespersons and clerks, is under the day-to-day control of a store manager. An assistant to Bob handles the advertising. Jack serves as administrative manager, with responsibilities for personnel, insurance, budgeting, cost analysis, and systems and procedures. Paul is in charge of servicing activities and the crew of servicepeople. Jill performs the duties of treasurer. Reporting to her is a credit manager, cashier, and finance clerks. Tom maintains the warehousing operations, which include receiving, storing, shipping, and customer delivery.

Operational and Financial Aspects

The company sells its products for cash or on credit. It has about 2000 credit customers. The firm acquires products for sale from 100 suppliers. In most cases MMM receives a purchase discount from a supplier, if paid within 10 days, although in certain cases full payment is due in 30 days. Usually freight and sales tax are added to the invoices by suppliers. Most suppliers allow returns.

MMM maintains its cash in two bank accounts. There is one account for general funds and one for payrolls. The company also has petty cash and change drawer funds. Among the resources that it owns are the office building, warehouse, and retail stores; the land on which these buildings are located; the furniture and fixtures in each of the buildings; cash registers and other office equipment; and vehicles in the warehouse and vehicles for delivering ordered merchandise. All the buildings currently have mortgages that are being paid off, and certain vehicles are being financed by short-term notes.

MMM is capitalized as a corporation, solely by means of $100 par common stock. The stock was sold at a premium. It earns revenues by sales of microcomputers and other computer equipment, and by servicing the equipment. Most products are sold at established prices, but trade discounts are allowed on occasion to small businesses and professional firms. The firm allows returns and allowances within a specified period from the dates of sales. It does not finance any sales; instead, it refers customers to banks and consumer finance companies. It allows cash discounts on sales if paid in full within 10 days; otherwise, it expects full payment within 30 days.

The perpetual inventory method for recording purchases is employed by MMM. The firm prefers to record managerial salaries separate from clerical salaries and wages. Commissions are paid to the salespersons in the various retail stores. Other expenses include utilities, supplies, donations, dues and subscriptions, advertising, insurance, repairs and maintenance, in addition to those arising from credit sales and fixed assets and loan transactions. It prefers to provide separate expense accounts for major operating activities, although it groups all office-related expenses (e.g., accounting, credit) under the category of office expenses. It also records all purchase discounts lost as an expense.

Accounting Records

The following journals and ledgers are employed by MMM for processing transactions through the accounting cycle:

General journal.
Sales journal.
Purchases journal.
Cash receipts journal.
Cash disbursements journal.
Payroll register.
General ledger.
Accounts receivable subsidiary ledger.
Accounts payable subsidiary ledger.

All credit sales are entered in the sales journal. All purchases of merchandise, supplies, and fixed assets, plus all related expenses, are entered into the purchases journal. All checks other than paychecks are entered in the cash disbursements journal. Paychecks, written on a payroll bank account, are entered in the payroll register. Amounts equal to the total payroll are written on the general bank account.

The accounting records are entered and posted manually. Betsy supervises the posting to the general ledger; she prepares and posts the adjusting journal entries herself. Then she prepares a trial balance and financial statements with the aid of an electronic spreadsheet package to compute key financial ratios and to print hard copy financial reports for the other managers.

Sales-Related Procedures*

Sales orders are received by salespersons either in person or by phone. Customers may come into a retail store, see demonstrations, and select the preferred microcomputers and related equipment. Or they may visit several competing stores and call the salespersons when they have made their decisions. In some cases salespersons go to the premises of prospective customers and demonstrate the use of computers in their businesses or professions.

Regardless of how received, sales orders are recorded by salespersons on order forms. Three copies of each order are prepared—the original for the customer, the second copy for the salesperson, and the third copy for posting. If cash in full is paid by the customer at the time of the sale, his or her copy is marked paid, and the sale is rung up on a cash register. (The customer also receives the cash receipt tape.) If no cash or if only a partial payment (i.e., a deposit) is received at the time of the sale, the sale is treated as a credit sale.

Credit sales must be approved prior to processing by the salespersons, who initial the posting copy. After approval is granted for a sale, the posting copy is sent to the warehouse. There the ordered items are assembled and checked off the posting copy. Any out-of-stock items are noted on the copy. Then the assembled goods are forwarded to the shipping department, together with the posting copy. The shipping depart-

ment prepares the goods for shipment, completes a bill of lading, and ships the order. It also returns to the accounting department the posting copy, which has been marked to reflect the quantities actually shipped. In addition to the original bill of lading given to the carrier, one copy accompanies the goods and another is filed.

A billing clerk in the accounting department prepares a sales invoice from the posting copy. He or she refers to a pricing sheet in the preparation of the sales invoice. Then the clerk enters the sale in the sales journal. The original of the sales invoice is mailed to the customer, the second copy is sent to the credit manager, the third copy is sent to the warehouse to post the disposition of goods to the inventory ledger cards, and the fourth copy is given to a bookkeeper (together with the posting copy of the order) to post to the accounts receivable ledger records. After the accounts receivable ledger record is posted, the fourth copy is used by the bookkeeper to post to the general ledger; then each fourth copy of the invoice and the posting copy of the order are filed together by customer name.

If an order cannot be completely filled because there is an insufficient quantity of an item on hand, the warehouse clerk uses the copy of the sales invoice to prepare a back order and sends it to the purchasing manager.

The mail received each day is opened by the cashier. Each letter containing a cash remittance is set aside. After all mail is opened, the cashier verifies that each cash remittance is accompanied by the top portion of the sales invoice or by a letter stating the amount mailed. If a cash amount is unaccompanied, the cashier prepares a cash remittance advice. She then prepares a deposit slip, combining the cash received in the mail with the cash from the three cash registers of the retail stores for the previous day. Next she sends the pile of remittance notifications and advices (together with a copy of the deposit

*Note: Service procedures are excluded in this description.

slip) to the bookkeeper for entry into the cash receipts journal, for posting to the accounts receivable and general ledgers, and for filing. Finally, she takes the deposit to the bank and returns with a bank-stamped duplicate deposit slip, which she files chronologically.

The cash received each day via the cash registers is checked at the end of the day by each store manager. He or she balances the amount received against the total shown on the cash register tape, using a cash sales summary sheet; he or she files the tape for possible future reference. Then the manager delivers the cash and summary sheet to the cashier at the main office by 9 A.M. the following day. The cashier verifies that the total amount of cash agrees with the total shown on the summary sheet; then she adds the cash to the amount received by mail that day (as already noted). She files the summary sheets with the returned deposit slip.

Plans for Systems Development

During the past year MMM has become increasingly aware that it needs to modernize its information system. Not only are its clerks and bookkeepers having difficulty in processing the growing volume of transactions, but its physical operations and management are becoming less efficient and less effective. For instance, it processes numerous back orders, thereby signifying that merchandise levels are not being adequately controlled. It often ships ordered products later than promised. Its budgets are often wildly unrealistic and its profit margins are shrinking.

Thus, MMM decides to develop a computer-based information system. Preliminary investigation indicates that the benefits from such a system will significantly exceed the expected costs. The first area that it decides to computerize is the revenue cycle and related decision support activities. Although the managers agree that they should not se-

lect the specific computer models until further development, they strongly believe that the system should employ microcomputers. An added advantage from developing such a system is that it can serve as the basis for demonstrations to potential customers who are also considering the computerization of their information systems.

Design Features for the New Computer-Based Revenue System

In order to ensure that the new computer-based system is soundly designed, the president hires Mark Anders, an experienced information systems consultant from the St. Louis office of a large public accounting firm. After a careful analysis of the present revenue system and its problems, Mark proposes the following conceptual design.

Processing steps. The computer-based system is to utilize on-line entry and processing of sales-related transactions. Cash sales (in full or in part) will be entered via point-of-sale terminals, whereas credit sales will be entered by data entry clerks (in the sales department) on the basis of sales order forms prepared by the salespersons. As in the present system, customers will receive receipts for cash, sales orders to acknowledge orders placed, and the ordered goods (together with packing slips). Salespersons also receive copies of system-generated sales orders. When the orders have been entered and edited, they are stored in an on-line sales order file. These order data are employed in the processing steps leading to the updating of relevant files (i.e., sales file, merchandise inventory file, accounts receivable file, general ledger file). A picking order is generated for the warehouse, which assembles the ordered items and transmits them to the shipping department. (Any items not available are placed on a back order, which is automatically generated when the merchandise inventory file shows the on-hand quantities to be less than the ordered quantities.) When the goods for an order are shipped, the shipping clerk enters the data, and a bill of lading and packing slip are generated; a shipping file is updated. Also, the computer system prepares a sales invoice for the customer and stores a copy in an online sales invoice file. At the end of each day, a program prints replenishment reports from the merchandise inventory file. These reports show the items (and related quantities) whose on-hand balances have fallen below preestablished minimum points for each of the retail stores. These reports are used by the warehouse to pick the needed items and to forward the items to the shipping department for delivery to the stores.

With respect to cash received through the mail in payment of accounts, the mailroom clerk daily endorses the checks received with restrictive endorsements and prepares a remittance listing of amounts received. These remittances, together with related batch totals, are entered by the clerk into a terminal. The receipts data are edited by the computer system and then posted to the accounts receivable master file. The mail clerk then forwards the cash to the cashier and the remittance advices to the accounts receivable bookkeeper. (Cash from the stores is delivered, together with the cash register receipt tapes, to the cashier at the end of each day.) The computer system prepares a deposit slip in duplicate, plus listings of customer account activity and the cash receipts journal. The cashier compares the checks and deposit slip and takes them to the bank. The bookkeeper compares the remittance advices, the activity listing, and the cash receipts journal; if they agree, the hard copies are filed chronologically and a copy of the journal is sent to the cashier. The computer system automatically updates the general ledger to reflect the total cash received and the reduction in the accounts receivable balance.

Data entry. The computer system will be programmed to provide assistance to clerks during data entry. When a clerk first accesses the system, a master menu appears. The clerk enters the appropriate number for the desired item from the menu. Then a preformatted screen display appears. The clerk enters data items onto the screen display, usually working from a previously completed form (e.g., a sales order form prepared by the salesperson or a remittance advice generated earlier by the system as a part of the sales invoice.) The entered data are edited by a program. If the clerk indicates that the data are acceptable (by responding with a YES when the system asks, "Are all entered data correct?"), the system accepts the data for further processing and storage.

Data base. The files needed by MMM with respect to the revenue cycle include a sales transaction file, cash receipts transaction file, shipping file, accounts receivable master file, pricing file, general ledger file, open sales orders file, sales invoice file, deposit slip file, cash remittance file, merchandise inventory master file, and back order file.

These files will be included in a data base under the control of a data base management system (DBMS) of the network type. Records in the following files are to be linked because of associations that are relevant to the needs for operational and decision-making information: accounts receivable, merchandise inventory, cash receipts, sales, back order, general ledger, and sales invoice.

Controls and security measures. Emphasis will be placed on controls and security measures. The procedures, for instance, include a sounder segregation of duties. A number of programmed checks will be employed. Clerks will be aided in the entry of data via the use of menus and preformatted screens. Security measures will be sufficiently comprehensive to assure the privacy and integrity of data and the protection of facilities and assets. Documentation will be thorough. A variety of application controls, in addition to programmed checks, will be incorporated into each of the transaction processing systems.

Auditing of the new computer-based system will involve approaches that trace transactions "around the computer," that examine the way edit programs handle a variety of input errors that are intentionally introduced via test transactions, and that aid the auditors in performing substantive tests of MMM's data inputs, outputs, and files.

Networking features. Because MMM has several retail stores, the design encompasses the use of a data communications network. This computer network will be relatively simple, but it requires a number of design choices (e.g., the type of network and the type of configuration).

Required

a. Prepare a description of the small computer industry, including the competition, markets, needed resource inputs, technological developments, and legal obligations.

b. Prepare a diagram of the operational functions.

c. Draw an organization chart.

d. Design or obtain a source document pertaining to one of the basic transactions handled by the firm.

e. Devise a coded chart of accounts that would be suitable for MMM. List all expense accounts under the categories "Operating Expenses" and "Nonoperating Expenses."

f. Devise group coding structures that will accommodate revenue and expense transactions for MMM.

g. Draw suitable formats for the purchases journal and the accounts payable subsidiary ledger.

h. Prepare a segment of an internal control questionnaire for the revenue cycle.

i. List the control weaknesses in the current procedure and recommend improvements.

j. Complete the document system flowchart of the current sales and cash receipts procedure whose beginning appears on page C-21.

k. Draw a hardware configuration diagram that portrays the key components of the new computer system; ignore the data communications network devices.

l. Prepare a system flowchart of the procedure for the proposed computer-based revenue cycle.

m. Draw data entry screens that illustrate the use of (1) a menu for the revenue cycle, and (2) a preformatted screen display relating to the cash receipts transaction.

n. Draw record layouts for the accounts receivable and the open sales order files, indicating the sequence of the data items, the length of each field, and the mode of data.

o. Prepare a table that lists the storage medium, primary key, and organization/access method for each file, assuming that the files are not physically linked.

p. Prepare a data structure diagram showing a network-type schema for the data and records needed in the revenue cycle of MMM; also, identify the subschemas needed for sales and cash receipts processing and reporting preparation. (Note that *all* identified files do not need to be included in the schema and subschemas.)

q. Prepare the logical views of several key relations needed in revenue cycle processing, assuming that a relational data base model is selected.

Salesperson at retail store

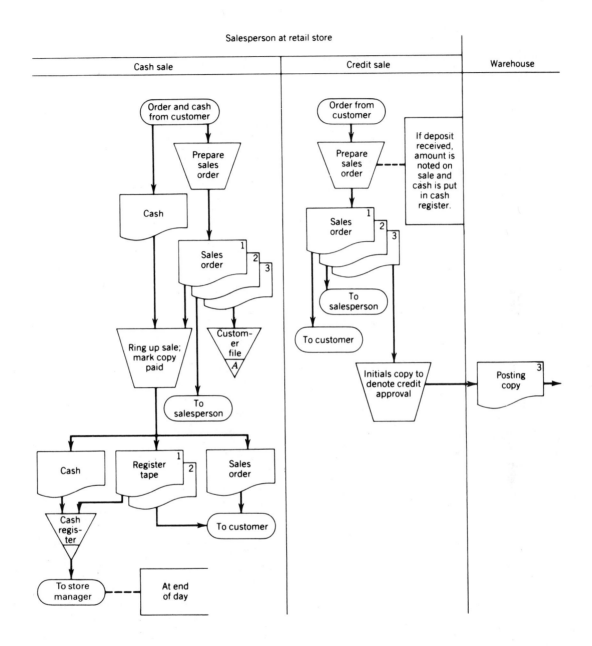

r. List several key decisions related to product sales that must be made by MMM. Identify in each example the type of decision and the responsible manager.

s. Select a strategic decision and operational control decision from the list of

key decisions. For each of these two decisions identify the needed information and key properties.

t. List several reports that can aid managers in planning and controlling revenue-generating activities; describe the purpose of each.

u. Design the formats of two reports that will aid MMM in profit planning and control of key profit centers, respectively.

v. List the security measures needed with respect to MMM's revenue cycle.

w. List the application controls that are suitable for cash receipts transaction processing; also prepare a list of programmed edit checks that should be employed by an edit program for sales order entry, and indicate the fields of data being verified by each check.

x. Prepare a list of test transactions that may be performed during compliance testing of the sales transaction processing system.

y. Describe the uses of a GAS package in performing substantive tests of the sales transaction processing system.

z. Describe a suitable computer network for MMM, including type, configuration, communications line service, and grade of lines. Also, draw a configuration diagram that portrays the described network.

CASE C

XYZ Company

Statement

The XYZ Company of Seattle, Washington, is a large West Coast distributor that sells a variety of merchandise on credit. Sales orders are phoned in by salespersons and recorded on special coding forms by sales clerks. Data preparation clerks then key the data onto a magnetic medium for entry into the firm's computer-based processing system.

Each sales order contains the following data items:

1. Customer number.

2. Customer name and address.

3. Shipping address, if different.

4. Date ordered.

5. Date to be shipped.

6. Salesperson number.

7. Sales territory number.

8. Products ordered, by number.

9. Quantities ordered of the preceding products.

Assume that C. James (customer number 1158) ordered 12 units of product number 2001 from salesperson number 315, sales territory 20, on August 10, 1990, for shipment on August 14. The coded sales transaction is portrayed in the accompanying record layout. Preceding the transaction data is the code for credit sales, CRS, which identifies the type of transaction and thus specifies the application program that is to process the transaction data.

CRS	1158	C. James	113 Main St.	Portland, Ore.	97132	800 Front St.

Portland, Ore.	97131	81090	81490	315	20	2000	12

Entered sales ordered are edited and stored on an open sales order disk file. As ordered goods are shipped, shipping records are prepared. (On the average 6000 orders are shipped daily.) After conversion to magnetic tape, a batch of these records is sorted in customer-account-number order. (For convenience an average of 40 change records pertaining to new or deleted customers are included with the shipping records.) Then all the records in the batch are processed by a file updating program.

The updating program

1. Updates the 20,000-record accounts receivable master file stored on magnetic tape. Each record in this file is variable in length and contains data as follows: customer account number, name, address, credit limit, balance at the beginning of the year, current account balance, and data for each transaction this year (transaction code, date, document number, and amount).

2. Updates the 400-record inventory master file stored on magnetic disk. Records are organized sequentially and accessed directly via an index.

3. Updates a sales history file stored on magnetic disk, in order to provide a historical record of sales and shipments.

4. Updates the open sales order file by deleting the sales order if the order is completely filled, or by noting the quantity shipped if the order is partially filled.

5. Adds a record to a back-order file on magnetic tape for each order in which shipped quantities were less than ordered quantities.

6. Creates a sales invoice tape on the basis of data drawn from several of the files.

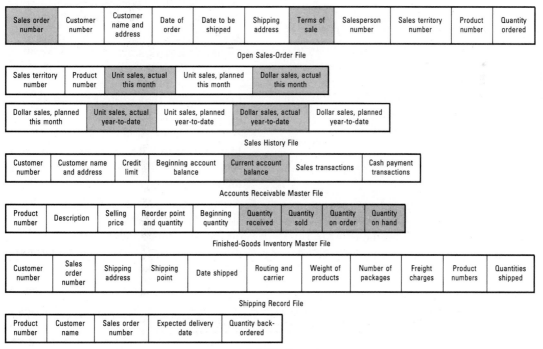

Sales order number	Customer number	Customer name and address	Date of order	Date to be shipped	Shipping address	Terms of sale	Salesperson number	Sales territory number	Product number	Quantity ordered

Open Sales-Order File

Sales territory number	Product number	Unit sales, actual this month	Unit sales, planned this month	Dollar sales, actual this month

Dollar sales, planned this month	Unit sales, actual year-to-date	Unit sales, planned year-to-date	Dollar sales, actual year-to-date	Dollar sales, planned year-to-date

Sales History File

Customer number	Customer name and address	Credit limit	Beginning account balance	Current account balance	Sales transactions	Cash payment transactions

Accounts Receivable Master File

Product number	Description	Selling price	Reorder point and quantity	Beginning quantity	Quantity received	Quantity sold	Quantity on order	Quantity on hand

Finished-Goods Inventory Master File

Customer number	Sales order number	Shipping address	Shipping point	Date shipped	Routing and carrier	Weight of products	Number of packages	Freight charges	Product numbers	Quantities shipped

Shipping Record File

Product number	Customer name	Sales order number	Expected delivery date	Quantity back-ordered

Back-Order File

Note: Data items in shaded fields are computed or generated from tables by the computer program, either at the time the record is created or at the time the record is updated.

The record layouts for these six files are shown on page C-23. All data items shown are based on the following sources: (1) inputs from transaction records (e.g., sales orders and shipping records), (2) tables accessed by the updating program (e.g., sales order number table and sales terms table), (3) transfers from other files (e.g., the sales order number in the shipping record file from the open sales order file), and (4) results of processing steps performed by the updating program (e.g., current account balance).

Among the outputs generated from the data in the aforementioned files are the following:

a. Sales invoices and a sales journal. The diagram on page C-25 details the preparation of these outputs from the sales invoice tape, which in turn consists of data extracted from the open sales order, accounts receivable, inventory, and shipping transaction files.

b. Monthly statements and an aging analysis. The diagram on the top of page C-26 shows the formats of these outputs, which are based on data shown from the accounts receivable master file.

c. Sales analyses, such as the analysis of sales by sales territory and product line shown on the bottom of page C-26.

Required

a. Complete the layout of an accounts receivable record for C. James as of August 15, on the basis of the data in the sales order record layout and the monthly statement. Assume that this customer has a credit limit of $10,000 and that this is the first transaction by the customer.

b. Prepare a computer system flowchart to reflect the generation of the sales invoices and sales journal, beginning just after the shipping records and change records have been sorted. Also, state the number of

tape drives and disk drives and printers that are needed by XYZ Company's computer installation to accommodate this sales application, assuming that each direct access file requires its own disk drive.

c. Justify the use of magnetic tape as the storage medium for the accounts receivable master file, as well as the use of magnetic disk as the storage medium for the inventory master file.

d. Suggest changes to the accounts receivable master file that should improve processing efficiency.

e. Describe the steps by which the actual dollar sales amounts are computed by the program. Include in your answer the sources of the data items used in the computations.

f. Explain, with the aid of a computer system flowchart, the computer runs needed to prepare the illustrated sales analysis from data in the sales history file.

g. XYZ converts all files in this application to magnetic disk storage. It then acquires a DBMS that can accommodate tree and network data models. Draw a data structure diagram that portrays a schema for facilitating the preparation of all the described outputs.

h. Identify specific information requests and other reports that can be generated via the schema in g.

i. Assume that XYZ trades in its first DBMS for another DBMS that is based on the relational model. Identify the relations that are needed to implement the schema in g, including the columns in each relation (except the sales history relation).

j. Give examples of information requests that can be satisfied by single SELECT, PROJECT, and JOIN commands to this relational data model when the schema described in g is implemented.

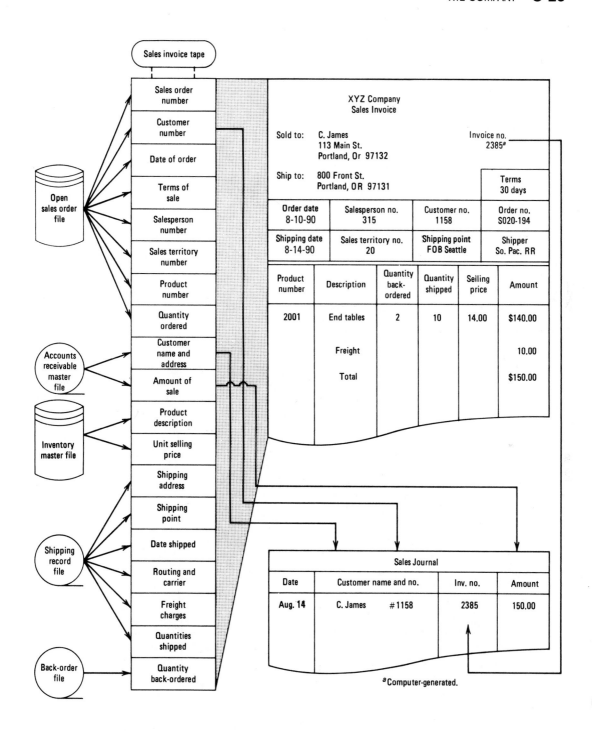

Computer-generated.

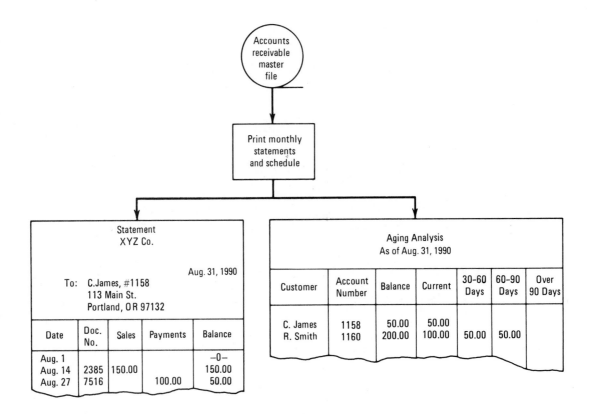

Accounts receivable master file

Print monthly statements and schedule

Statement
XYZ Co.

Aug. 31, 1990

To: C.James, #1158
113 Main St.
Portland, OR 97132

Date	Doc. No.	Sales	Payments	Balance
Aug. 1				–0–
Aug. 14	2385	150.00		150.00
Aug. 27	7516		100.00	50.00

Aging Analysis
As of Aug. 31, 1990

Customer	Account Number	Balance	Current	30–60 Days	60–90 Days	Over 90 Days
C. James	1158	50.00	50.00			
R. Smith	1160	200.00	100.00	50.00	50.00	

Sales Analysis by Sales Territory and Product Line
For month ending August 31, 1990
(000's of units and dollars)

Sales territory number	Product	Actual sales for month Units	Actual sales for month Dollars	Variance from budget— month	Actual sales year-to-date Units	Actual sales year-to-date Dollars	Variance from budget— year-to-date
01	1000	315	$5,985	($155)	2560	$48,640	$250
	2000	105	1,470	20	912	12,768	176
	3000	726	7,986	382	5685	62,535	425
	4000	227	4,540	(177)	1704	34,080	(310)
	Total	1373	$19,981	$130	10861	$158,023	$541
02	1000	520	$9,880	$360	4654	$88,426	$1,340
	2000	316	4,424				

CASE D

Delmo, Inc.

Statement

Delmo, Inc., of Harrisburg, Pennsylvania, is a wholesale distributor of automotive parts that serves customers in the states east of the Mississippi River. The company has grown during the last 25 years from a small regional distributorship to its present size.

The states are divided into eight separate territories in order to service Delmo customers adequately. Delmo salespersons regularly call on current and prospective customers in each of the territories. Delmo customers are of four general types:

1. Automotive parts stores.
2. Hardware stores with an automotive parts section.
3. Independent garage owners.
4. Buying groups for garages and service stations.

Because Delmo, Inc., must stock such a large variety and quantity of automotive parts to accommodate its customers, the company acquired its own computer system very early and implemented an inventory control system first. Other applications, such as cash receipts and disbursements, sales analysis, accounts receivable, payroll, and accounts payable, have since been added.

Delmo's inventory control system comprises an integrated purchase ordering and perpetual inventory system. Each item of inventory is identified by an inventory code number; the code number identifies both the product line and the item itself. When the quantity on hand for an item falls below the specified stock level, a purchase order is automatically generated by the computer. The purchase order is sent to the vendor after approval by the purchasing manager. All receipts, issues, and returns are entered into the computer daily. A printout for all inventory items within product lines, showing receipts, issues, and current balances, is prepared weekly. Current status for a particular item carried in the inventory can be obtained daily if desired, however.

Sales orders are filled within 48 hours of receipt. Sales invoices are prepared by the computer the same day that the merchandise is shipped. At the end of each month several reports are produced that summarize the monthly sales. The current month's and year-to-date sales by product line, territory, and customer class are compared to the same figures from the previous year. In addition, reports showing only the monthly figures for product line within territory and customer class within territory are prepared. In all cases the reports provide summarized data. In other words, detailed data such as sales by individual customers or products are not listed. Terms of 2/10, net 30 are standard for all of Delmo's customers.

Customers' accounts receivable are updated daily for sales, sales returns and allowances, and payments on account. Monthly statements are computer-prepared and are mailed following completion of entries for the last day of the month. Each Friday a schedule is prepared showing the total amount of accounts receivable outstanding by age—current accounts (0–30 days), slightly past-due accounts (31–90 days), and long-overdue accounts (over 90 days).

Delmo, Inc., recently acquired Wenrock Company, a wholesale distributor of tools and light equipment. In addition to servicing the same type of customers as Delmo, Wenrock also sells to equipment rental shops. Wenrock's sales region is not so extensive as Delmo's, but the Delmo management has encouraged Wenrock to expand the distribution of its products to all of Delmo's sales territories.

Wenrock Company uses a computer service bureau to aid its accounting functions. For example, certain inventory activities are recorded by the service bureau. Each item carried by Wenrock is assigned a product code number that identifies the product and the product line. Data regarding shipments received from manufacturers, shipments to customers (sales), and any other physical inventory changes are delivered to the service bureau daily, and the service bureau updates Wenrock's inventory records. A weekly inventory listing showing beginning balance, receipts, issues, and ending balance for each item in the inventory is provided to Wenrock on Monday morning.

Wenrock furnishes the service bureau with information about each sale of merchandise to a customer. The service bureau prepares a five-part invoice and records the sale in its records. This processing is done at night, and all copies of each invoice are delivered to Wenrock the next morning. At the end of the month, the service bureau provides Wenrock with a sales report classified by product line showing the sales in units and dollars for each item sold. Wenrock's sales terms are 2/10, net 30.

The accounts receivable function is still handled by Wenrock's bookkeeper. Two copies of the invoice are mailed to the customer. Two of the remaining copies are filed—one numerically and the other alphabetically by customer. The alphabetic file represents the accounts receivable file. When a customer's payment is received, the invoice is marked "paid" and placed in a paid invoice file in alphabetic order. The bookkeeper mails monthly statements according to the following schedule:

10th of the month	A–G
20th of the month	H–O
30th of the month	P–Z

The final copy of the invoice is included with the merchandise when it is shipped.

Wenrock has continued to use its present accounting system and supplies Delmo management with monthly financial information developed from this system. However, Delmo management is anxious to have Wenrock use Delmo's computer and information system because that would reduce accounting and computer costs, make the financial reports of Wenrock more useful to Delmo management, and provide Wenrock personnel with better information to manage the company.

At the time Delmo acquired Wenrock, it also hired a new marketing manager with experience in both product areas. The new manager wants Wenrock to organize its sales force using the same territorial distribution as Delmo, to facilitate the management of the two sales forces.

The new manager also believes that more useful sales information should be provided to individual salespersons and to the department. Although the monthly sales reports currently prepared provide adequate summary data, the manager would like additional details to aid the sales personnel.

Required

a. Identify and briefly describe the additional data Wenrock Company must collect and furnish in order to use the Delmo information system. Also, identify the data, if any, currently accumulated by Wenrock that no longer will be needed because of the conversion to the Delmo system.

b. Devise codes for identifying inventory items and customers.

c. Design data entry screens for capturing data pertaining to the sales and cash receipts transactions, assuming that data are entered by the on-line method.

d. Draw suggested layouts of Delmo's inventory and accounts receivable master records, based on the descriptions of their uses in processing.

e. On the basis of the data currently available from the Delmo information system, what additional reports could be prepared that would be useful to the marketing manager and the individual salespersons? Briefly explain how each report would be useful to the sales personnel.

f. List the general and application controls that would be appropriate for the combined system, assuming that online processing is performed.

g. Largely because of the acquisition of Wenrock and the expansion of the overall sales territory, cash management has become an important concern to Delmo. The treasurer therefore needs a weekly report that estimates cash receipts for the following week. To develop the data for the report, he suggests that the timing of payments by credit customers against their accounts be monitored week by week. Other reporting needs have been recognized, such as sales analyses and the reports described in **e**. Thus, the president of Delmo is considering the desirability of implementing the data base approach. Describe, with the aid of a data structure diagram, a schema that spans the sales and cash management activities of Delmo. Identify three related reports whose preparation can be aided by the use of data structures in this schema, and illustrate their preparation by means of an example.

(CMA adapted)

CASE E

Grind and Cast Corporation

Statement

The Grind and Cast Corporation of Las Vegas, Nevada, produces grinding balls and castings for use by mining and other heavy industries in the western United States. Although both products are manufactured in the same plant, the production process is quite different. Grinding balls are manufactured in a continuous high-volume process with a high degree of mechanization. Castings are manufactured in small numbers according to job orders and with a considerable amount of labor.

Although the firm is firmly established in the sales of grinding balls, it is still struggling with respect to the production and sales of castings. Production is inefficient and costly, cost estimates are quite inaccurate, and a high percentage of casting orders are shipped late.

It has become quite clear to the management of Grind and Cast that the production information system requires an extensive redesign. Better information is needed to aid in estimating costs, planning production, tracking castings as they flow through the production process, and controlling direct materials and labor costs.

After a thorough analysis of operations, as well as of benefits and costs, the management decides to install an on-line production information system that supports both operations and decision making. Although the system will improve the production of grinding balls as well as castings, its principal focus will be on the latter.

Accordingly, a system is designed that

begins with the on-line entry of each sales order as received. As each sales order is entered, it updates the customer's master file and adds a record to the castings job order file. At the end of each day an open casting job order register is printed. At the beginning of each week the production planning department reviews the production schedule prepared the previous week and the five open casting job order registers for the previous week. It then makes up a new production schedule and enters the schedule data into the system via its visual display terminal. The system then automatically prints a release-to-moulding work center report and a multipart job card. The multipart job card has a perforated section for each work day and is preprinted to show all needed information concerning the job.

Job cards are issued to the moulding work center on the date that production is to begin. The cards accompany the job as it moves through the various work centers. At the end of each day the work center foreman writes onto the perforated section the quantity of good castings completed, the number scrapped, and the work center number; then he or she returns the section to the production planning department. At the beginning of the next day the production planning department enters the progress of each job via its terminal. Daily reports, showing production in each work center broken down by job number, are produced from these data.

The major files consist of

1. A *work center file,* showing for each work center the work center number and all jobs in progress, including quantities on hand and completed each day.

2. A castings *open job order file,* showing for each job the job order number, casting number, ordered quantity, order date, promised date, on-hand quantity, quantity scrapped, and priority code.

3. An *engineering file,* showing the details concerning each type of casting.

4. A *master schedule file,* showing for each job the job order number, casting number, ordered quantity, scheduled production date, estimated shipping date, quantities currently in all of the work centers (i.e., moulding, pouring, shake out, heat treat, finishing, and shipping), quantity scrapped, actual starting date, actual date moved to shipping, quantity shipped, actual shipping date, and price.

Required

a. Prepare system flowcharts to portray the online entry and processing of job orders through production, including the updating of all the previously listed files except the engineering file.

b. Design a data entry screen for the input of data concerning progress of production jobs at each work center.

c. Design the formats for the daily open order register and the daily production report by work center. Note that the former simply reflects the new job orders created during a particular day, whereas the content of the latter is described in the problem statement.

d. Assume that the designed system allows on-line inquiries. Design two screens that display information of interest concerning casting jobs.

e. Draw a record layout of the open job order file.

f. From the description of the files, it is apparent that certain files are closely related to others and that there are data redundancies. Sketch a diagram that shows a useful schema (i.e., a plan of data structures, or linkages among related types of records) for the casting production data base.

g. Devise a code for identifying raw materials.

h. List the general and application controls that would be appropriate for the new computer-based system, including programmed edit checks and fields of data verified by the checks.

i. No provision is made in the previously delineated production information system for the collection and control of costs. Design an on-line work-in-process cost accounting system to collect and store direct materials and direct labor costs both for castings and for grinding balls. Include in your design (1) input data items, (2) system flowcharts, (3) record formats for the master files, and (4) formats of cost reports. Assume that standard cost data and predetermined manufacturing overhead rates are stored in one of the master files. Also, assume that the cost accounting system is separate from the production information systems for tracking castings and grinding balls, but that those systems feed production data to the cost accounting system as daily inputs.

CASE F

TLC Hospital

Statement

A hospital is a health care facility that provides various services to patients, whether they be admitted on an overnight status or whether they visit on an outpatient basis. Patients can be viewed as akin to raw materials when they enter for service and as finished goods when they complete their treatments. Among the services provided to patients are X-ray examinations, laboratory tests, diagnoses, therapeutic treatments, nursing care, meals, room accommodations, and counseling. The organization is capital intensive, fixed costs being from 65 to 85 percent of total costs. Typical fixed costs are depreciation on land, buildings, and medical equipment; insurance; interest on loans; taxes; repairs and maintenance; emergency power plant operation; hospital security; and public relations. The full capacity of a hospital is about 90 percent, the remaining bed spaces being reserved for emergency situations.

Hospitals face certain sticky problems. Although they are expected to provide high-quality medical services, they cannot repossess goods in the case of nonpayments. Moreover, they are expected to accept emergency cases, even when the parties are not likely to pay. In addition, they must often collect from third parties (e.g., Blue Cross, Medicare, Medicaid) when eligible members of reimbursement programs are involved. Finally, hospitals must often depend on part of their revenues from grants, bequests, and nonrelated operations.

TLC Hospital has been recently established in Orange County, California, because of its rapidly growing population. The hospital facilities, which will provide 150 beds and be equipped to accommodate as many as 3000 outpatients per month, are nearing completion. The chief administrator, Dr. Townsend Applewaite, has made all the necessary arrangements with Medicare, Medicaid, and the California state health care reimbursement program. Other administrators, clerical personnel, and nurses have been hired. Contractual agreements have been negotiated with physicians. Now the most urgent task is to develop planning and information systems for the hospital.

Organization

The organization consists of a central administrative office and three major functions: business, patient care, and medical services. The business office includes billing, accounts receivable, general ledger, purchases, accounts payable, payroll, claims, and customer relations departments. Patient care includes the admitting and discharge department, nursing stations, outpatient clinics, food service, laundry, and emergency room. Medical services include laboratory, radiology, operating room, and medicines. All of the departments and other units represent responsibility centers to which direct costs can be assigned and indirect costs allocated. The centers that provide patient care and services also generate revenues through charges to patients' bills.

Operational Procedures

A person who enters the hospital as an overnight patient must be admitted. The patient is assigned a room. Each group of rooms is controlled by a nursing station. Nurses are provided all the information needed to care for the patients under their care, including diets, medications, wake-up times, and so forth. Physicians specify medical services to be provided patients, including examinations and tests, operations, medications, and radiology treatments. When a physician determines that a patient is well enough to leave, the patient must be discharged.

Accounting Considerations

The information system of a hospital must maintain the collection of costs and billing of patients, as noted earlier. Costs incurred for patients are charged to each department. In the case of departments and administrative units for which the costs cannot be easily charged directly to specific pa-

tients, the costs are allocated to those departments providing direct patient services. Billing rates for patients are established to cover all direct and indirect costs, plus allowances for debt service and future growth.

In addition, the accounting information system generates financial statements as well as managerial information for hospital planning and control. These financial statements should comply with the chart of accounts established by the American Hospital Association. Statements must also be prepared and sent to third parties for reimbursement. Each third party has its own requirements with respect to forms, types of coverage, and methods and levels of payment. Collection of amounts due requires diligence and systematic follow-up in the case of many individual patients and even some third parties.

The major planning and control activities are to be fostered through a participative budgeting process. Townsend, as chief administrator, will send to the middle-level administrators and all department heads a memorandum on budget guidelines. It will include a "statement of conditions," which identifies the external and internal conditions having significant impact on hospital operations, a projection of basic hospital units of service for each month of the upcoming fiscal year and for the two subsequent years, and a budget calendar. The units of service include the number of inpatient admissions, outpatient visits, patient days, average daily bed occupancy, and emergency room cases. Unit costs are based on diagnosis-related groups (DRG's), where a DRG represents a bundle of services provided to a typical patient at standard charging rates.

Required

a. Describe the features of a suitable in-house on-line information system for TLC Hospital. Include the key aspects of the needed local area network, such as the configuration, hardware, and controls.

b. Design a charge of accounts for TLC Hospital, and describe two alternative group coding schemes for patients.

c. Draw a master menu for the on-line system that relates to the various accounting transactions and other key activities (e.g., word processing, financial modeling) that could be available to users with general accounting area passwords. Also, prepare a master menu for users involved in patient care. Then prepare a second-level menu when the option entitled Patient Records is chosen from the latter master menu. Finally, draw a data entry screen that would appear when the option entitled Establish New Patient File is chosen from the second-level menu.

d. Describe a procedure for alerting a nursing station to the need to provide specific medication to a specific patient at a particular time. Include the menus and display screens that could be involved in this procedure.

e. List various information items that are important to the managing of TLC Hospital, including critical success factors as well as operating and financial factors.

f. Describe reports that would be useful in planning and controlling the activities of TLC Hospital (1) from month to month and (2) over the next several years.

g. Describe the steps in the participative budgeting process that should follow the issuance of the high-level administrator's guideline memorandum. Assume that the middle-level administrators and department heads have access to terminals within the local area network and that the hospital employs financial modeling software.

CASE G

Representative Distributing Company (RDC)

A case designed for use with "hands-on" microcomputer
projects involving electronic spreadsheet and data base
management system packages

Statement

The Representative Distributing Company (RDC) is a Phoenix wholesaler of office equipment. Among the 16 products that it distributes are desks, chairs, bookcases, tables, filing cabinets, sofas, and safes. The firm sells on credit to 30 Arizona customers,

This case is reprinted from *Accounting Information Systems: Essential Concepts and Applications,* by Joseph W. Wilkinson, with permission of John Wiley & Sons, Inc.

mainly retail office furniture and/or supply stores. It purchases the products on credit from 12 office furniture manufacturers. Terms of both sales and purchases are net invoice amount if paid within 30 days, or 2 percent discount if paid within 10 days of the invoice date.

The firm was founded in 1982 as a corporation by Jack Pollard, who serves as president and chairperson of the board. Other officers of the firm include a vice president, a controller–treasurer, a sales manager, a purchasing manager, and a distribution manager. All these managers, plus three outside directors, comprise the board of directors. All stock is owned by the directors. During its several years of operation the firm has grown steadily in sales volume. Although this growth has been funded in part by bond issues, it has mainly been supported by yearly net earnings. As the financial statements for the most recent year indicate, the firm's net earnings and current financial condition are generally satisfactory.

RDC operates from a single office building and adjacent warehouse, which are leased. Roughly a dozen employees (other than the managers listed) comprise the work force. All the employees are salaried. These employees use an accounting information

---

Representative Distributing Company
Statement of Financial Position
As of December 31, 1989

ASSETS

Current Assets	
Cash	$ 2,960,000.00
Accounts Receivable	1,100,000.00
Merchandise Inventory	6,270,000.00
Supplies	150,000.00
Prepaid Expenses	820,000.00
Total Current Assets	$11,300,000.00
Fixed Assets	
Furniture and Fixtures (net of depreciation)	$ 2,720,000.00
Equipment (net of depreciation)	3,030,000.00
Delivery Vehicles (net of depreciation)	580,000.00
Total Fixed Assets	$ 6,330,000.00
Other Assets	$ 1,810,000.00
Total Assets	$19,440,000.00

LIABILITIES

Current Liabilities	
Accounts Payable	$ 1,620,000.00
Salaries and Wages Payable	380,000.00
Income Taxes Payable	1,570,000.00
Sales Taxes Payable	290,000.00
Other Accrued Payables	310,000.00
Total Current Liabilities	$ 4,170,000.00
Bonds Payable (2,000 bonds of $1,000 each @ 10%, due on December 31, 1999)	$ 2,000,000.00
Total Liabilities	$ 6,170,000.00

OWNERS' EQUITY

Capital Stock ($10 stated value, 800,000 shares authorized, issued, and outstanding)	$ 8,000,000.00
Additional Paid-In Capital	400,000.00
Retained Earnings	4,870,000.00
Total Owner's Equity	$13,270,000.00
Total Equities	$19,440,000.00

system (AIS), which was computerized two years ago. At the heart of the system is a multitasking microcomputer. Attached on-line to this computer are four terminals, two printers, a 60-megabyte hard disk, and a tape cartridge backup storage unit. Among the available applications software are integrated accounting packages (e.g., general ledger, accounts receivable, accounts payable modules), an electronic spreadsheet package with graphics capabilities, and a relational data base management system (DBMS) package.

Requirements Pertaining to a Spreadsheet Package

a. Enter on a spreadsheet the financial statements listed on this page and on page C-34; omit the dollar signs and commas within amounts, but include the decimal points and cents. Print the entered financial statements, and then save them in a file (e.g., FIN).

b. Enter the heading "SELECTED FINANCIAL RATIOS" on the spread-sheet just below the financial statements. Then set up labels for the following ratios and enter on the spreadsheet appropriate formulas into cells within column G:

(1) Current ratio.

(2) Return on net sales (where return is net income before taxes).

(3) Return on owners' equity (where return is net income after taxes).

(4) Return on total assets (where return is net income after taxes, plus bond interest times the complement of the tax rate).

(5) Average accounts receivable collection period.

(6) Debt/equity ratio (where debt is total liabilities and equity is total owners' equity).

Print only the section of the spreadsheet showing the calculated results of the financial ratios. *Hint:* The formulas for the ratios should refer to the cells where the appropriate financial statement values reside. Also, expand column G on the spreadsheet to a width that can easily accommodate the formulas.

Representative Distributing Company
Income Statement
For the Year Ended December 31, 1989

Net Sales	$27,400,000.00
Cost of Sales	14,200,000.00
Gross Margin	$13,200,000.00
Expenses	
Selling Expenses	$ 560,000.00
Warehousing and Shipping Expenses	2,800,000.00
Other Operating Expenses	1,340,000.00
Administrative Expenses	4,140,000.00
Nonoperating Expenses, including Interest	250,000.00
Total Expenses	$ 9,090,000.00
Net Income before Taxes	$ 4,110,000.00
Income Taxes	1,315,200.00
Net Income after Taxes	$ 2,794,800.00

c. Print a display of the underlying formulas, including the spreadsheet border in the printout (if the spreadsheet package in use allows the border to be printed).

d. Develop a template for the income budget for the firm using the formula mode. The template should have the following heading:

REPRESENTATIVE DISTRIBUTING COMPANY
INCOME BUDGET
FOR THE NEXT TWO YEARS
(Thousands of Dollars)

ITEM   Estimates
[   ] [   ]

Follow these procedures in developing the template:

(1) Use side headings that parallel the income statement already entered in **a**.

(2) Add this statement after the Net Sales item: Based on current sales of $____. [The ruled space following the dollar sign should occupy a specific cell (e.g., E14).]

(3) Enter formulas to compute the value of each line item in the income statement for two years, and place these formulas in cells in two adjoining columns below the heading "Estimates" (e.g., columns G and H). In setting up formulas use cell references, such as the cell where the current sales value is located (e.g., E14).

(4) Derive the formulas from the Budget Assumptions listed in the accompanying box.

(5) Save the template in a new file (e.g., BUDTEMP).

Hint: To save time in preparing the template, load the financial statements and copy the portion pertaining to the income statement side headings onto a new space on the worksheet.

Representative Distributing Company
Budget Assumptions

1. Net sales are expected to increase 10 percent each year over the sales of the previous year.

2. Cost of sales averages 55 percent of net sales.

3. Selling expenses average 3 percent of net sales.

4. Warehousing and shipping expenses average 8 percent of net sales, plus a fixed portion of $1 million.

5. Other operating expenses average 2 percent of net sales, plus a fixed portion of $800,000.

6. Administrative expenses are expected to average 13 percent of net sales, plus a fixed portion of $2 million.

7. Nonoperating expenses are expected to remain fixed at $250,000 per year for the foreseeable future.

8. Income taxes average 32 percent of net income before taxes.

---

e. Load the budget template and switch to the values mode. Then enter the two budget years (e.g., 1990 and 1991) in the brackets below the heading "ESTI-MATES" and the current net sales value in the cell on the Net Sales line. If formulas have been correctly entered on the template, the two years of estimated values should promptly appear for all the income statement items through the Net Income After Taxes. Save the resulting budget in a new file (e.g., BUDG), with the values appearing in the integer display format or mode.

f. Reload the budget template. Assume that the value of current net sales is expected to increase by $3 million. Make this change on the budget template (i.e., perform this "what if") and observe the results. Save these results in a new file (e.g., BUDG2).

g. Reload the budget template. Switch to the formula mode. Then make changes in the formulas based on these revised assumptions.

(1) Net sales are expected to increase by only 3 percent each year over the sales of the previous year.

(2) The cost of sales is expected to average 60 percent of net sales for the next two years.

(3) The selling expenses are expected to rise to 5 percent of net sales for the next two years.

(4) The nonoperating expenses are expected to rise to a fixed level of $500,000 for the next two years.

After these changes are made, save the template in a new file (e.g., BUDREV). Then reload the file and enter the current net sales and two budget years (e.g., 1990 and 1991). Save the results as *integer* values in a new file (e.g., BUDG3).

h. Reload the revised template just saved in **g**. Now consider a "worst case"—an increase of cost of sales to 70 percent of net sales for the next two years. Make this change and recalculate the expected net incomes after taxes for the next two years. Do the values of net incomes and income taxes appear to be correct? If not, revise the template by modifying the formula for income taxes. This formula should include a logical function that has the IF–THEN format. Each statement in the function should be set off by commas (e.g., A,B,C, where A is an IF, B is a THEN, C is an ELSE). The statement for the first budget year should begin as IF (G30 > 0 . . .), where G30 is assumed to be the cell on the Income Taxes line. For convenience the logical function can be placed in another cell below the income budget (e.g., A38) and referenced by the cells on the Income Taxes line. After modifying the template by means of this logical function and saving the template in a new file (e.g., BUDWST), enter the current net sales and observe the results. Save the results as integer values in a new file (e.g., BUDG4).

i. Reload the original template (e.g., BUD-TEMP). Change the side label pertaining to Net Sales to read Break-even Sales. Calculate on a separate sheet of paper the level of break-even sales for the first budget year, using the formula

Break-even sales = fixed expenses
+ variable expenses

where variable expenses equal the variable expense percentage times the break-even sales amount. Enter the calculated amount of break-even sales in the sales cell for the first budget year, and verify that the amount of net income is zero. Repeat the process for the second budget year. Save the results for the second year in a new file (e.g., BESALES).

j. Print each of the saved files. In the case of templates, include the border (if the spreadsheet package in use allows the border to be printed).

(1) Budget template named BUDTEMP in d (formula display format).

(2) Budget estimates named BUDG in e (integer display format).

(3) Budget estimates based on "what ifs" and named BUDG2 in f (integer display format).

(4) Revised budget template named BUDREV in g (formula display format).

(5) Budget estimates based on revised budget template and named BUDG3 in g (integer display format).

(6) "Worst-case" budget template named BUDWST in h (formula display format).

(7) Budget estimates based on "worst-case" budget template and named BUDG4 in h (integer display format).

(8) Break-even sales for the second budget year and named BESALES in i (integer display format).

k. Reload the file containing the original budget results (see e). View a simple bar graph of net sales for the two budget years. Use "Net Sales" as the main heading. Add labels for the time axis, but ignore labels for the Y-axis. Plot the graph.

l. Assign number 2 to the next graph, a stacked-bar graph of cost of sales, total expenses, and net income before taxes for the two budget years. Use a main heading of "MAJOR COMPONENTS OF SALES," which should be typed in a cell below the budget template before beginning the graph. Add time labels, but ignore labels for the Y-axis. Then plot the graph.

m. Assign number 3 to the next graph, an X–Y graph of NET SALES versus NET INCOME AFTER TAXES for the two budget years. Use a subheading that states, "In Thousands of Dollars." Use

"Net Sales" as the *X*-axis label and "Net Income after Taxes" as the *Y*-axis label. Use the actual years (e.g., 1990 and 1991) as point values. Plot the graph.

Requirements Pertaining to a Data Base Manager Package

a. Review the background facts concerning RDC. Then examine the tables within the relational data base maintained by the firm on pages C-40 and C-41. Draw a data model that shows the relationships among these tables, on the basis of the key data items shown for the tables.

b. Open a new data base called CUSTDB in the data base package that is available to you. Then establish the five tables described in **a** and enter the data they contain. Note that the table names and column names listed in the legend should be used for identification when storing the data.

c. Obtain printed outputs of the complete Sale table and Product table.

d. Obtain a printed output of these columns from the Customer table: CUSTNO, NAME, CITY, ZIP, CUSBAL. Sort the output by zip codes.

e. Search the appropriate tables for the following specified characteristics, and obtain printed outputs of the indicated columnar data:

  (1) All customers who are located in Tempe; print customer number, city, and current balance.

  (2) All products for which the quantity on hand is less than 40 units; print product number, description, and quantity.

  (3) All sales made during the first half of July; print customer number and sales amount.

  (4) All amounts received between July 10 and July 25 that were larger than $2000; print the receipt number, date of receipt, and amount.

  (5) All customers having a current balance in excess of $1000; print customer name, zip code, and current balance (and sort by zip code in ascending order).

f. Design a form, entitled PRODFORM, to be used in entering product-related data. Then enter the following data for a new product:

No. 72   SAFE, WALL

Cost: $310.00   Price: $428.00

Quantity on hand: 3 units

Supplier No.: 358

Obtain a printed copy of the product data entry form by entering a command that is provided by the software package you are using.

g. Design a report that is entitled "Inventory Valuation Report as of July 31" and that has a data base name of PRODRPT. This report has the following column headings:

Number

Description

Unit Cost

Quantity on Hand

Valuation

The valuation column is to be computed (by the software package) as the product of unit cost times quantity on hand. Also, include a footing section that shows the total valuation. Obtain a printed output of the report.

h. Use suitable commands to form new tables that can answer the following inqui-

Legend

CUSTNO: customer number	CRELMT: credit limit	PRICE: unit price of product
NAME: name of customer	CUSBAL: account balance	QOH: quantity on hand
ADDRESS: address of customer	PRODNO: product number	RECNO: cash receipt number
CITY: city	DESCR: description of product	DATE: date of transaction
ZIP: Zip Code	SUPNO: supplier number	RECAMT: amount of cash receipt
PHONE: telephone number	COST: unit cost of product	SALENO: sale number
		SALAMT: amount of sale

Table: CUST

CUSTNO	NAME	ADDRESS	CITY	STATE	ZIP	PHONE	CRELMT	CUSBAL
1010	BROWN'S OFFICE MART	109 W. YALE ST.	TEMPE	AZ	85282	967-0012	$5,000.00	$2,240.00
1015	SILVERFIELD FURNITURE	56 E. ARKWAY DR.	FLAGSTAFF	AZ	86001	921-5917	$7,000.00	$6,810.00
1020	THE FURNITURE SUPERSTORE	303 N. ROBSON AVE.	MESA	AZ	85201	969-1565	$3,000.00	$1,780.00
1025	MORTON'S FURNITURE	10 SPENCE RD.	TEMPE	AZ	85282	945-4888	$5,000.00	$800.00
1030	CROWN'S CASUAL FURNITURE	101 N. MCTELLIPS ST.	PHOENIX	AZ	85068	934-0114	$8,000.00	$1,500.00
1035	THE FURNITURE PLACE	1028 E. CAPTAIN DR.	GLENDALE	AZ	85311	991-8810	$6,500.00	$1,360.00
1050	THE FURNITURE WAREHOUSE	13 N. EXTENSION RD.	MESA	AZ	85202	834-8181	$7,000.00	$1,412.00
1055	DRIGHTON'S SECURITY SERVICES	89 E. TELLA DR.	SCOTTSDALE	AZ	85253	945-9601	$8,000.00	$2,370.00
1060	COSTLESS FURNITURES, INC.	1861 E. KELLA ST.	GLENDALE	AZ	85314	922-1867	$7,000.00	$2,300.00
1070	BUDGET FURNITURE STORE	161 N. 61ST ST.	MESA	AZ	85606	892-6001	$8,000.00	$0.00
1080	FURNITURE UNLIMITED	333 S. EVEN AVE.	CHANDLER	AZ	85230	963-2077	$8,000.00	$0.00
1085	THE FURNITURE GALLERIES	2200 N. GOODY DR.	SUN CITY	AZ	85375	861-6610	$9,000.00	$0.00
1090	THE CHAIR EXPERTS	593 E. BECK ST.	FLAGSTAFF	AZ	86003	952-3210	$5,000.00	$2,407.00
1095	THE SOFA CONNECTIONS	9321 HAITS ST.	PHOENIX	AZ	85020	933-6391	$7,000.00	$0.00
1105	THE BOOKCASE, INC.	1886 N. COLUMBUS ST.	MESA	AZ	85821	899-5122	$7,000.00	$0.00
1110	MITCHELL'S HOUSE OF LAMPS	1095 E. ELAY DR.	GLENDALE	AZ	85317	867-6243	$8,000.00	$0.00
1115	P & P FURNITURES	63 E. MEDIA ST.	PHOENIX	AZ	85021	956-7771	$6,000.00	$0.00
1120	A-1 FURNITURES, INC.	115 S. LOYD ST.	TEMPE	AZ	85281	967-7791	$5,000.00	$3,600.00
1130	REGESTER HOME FURNISHINGS	283 E. DADY ST.	TEMPE	AZ	85283	968-4425	$6,000.00	$0.00
1135	KIPPER'S BUSINESS INTERIORS	77 W. TOY DR.	PHOENIX	AZ	85023	861-6774	$5,000.00	$1,905.00
1140	THE SHOWROOM	1111 W. SHEILA DR.	SCOTTSDALE	AZ	85256	890-3335	$6,000.00	$2,335.00
1150	MESA FURNITURE SHOPPE	838 N. CONNELL WAY	MESA	AZ	85201	834-1551	$4,000.00	$0.00
1155	THE AFFORDABLE FURNITURES	1000 W. WARREN RD.	CHANDLER	AZ	85224	963-6161	$9,000.00	$2,800.00
1160	THE WOODWORK, INC.	2021 S. STELLAR PKWY.	CHANDLER	AZ	85224	963-2000	$7,000.00	$550.00
1165	RICHIE'S FURNITURE MART	5106 E. FALCON DR.	MESA	AZ	85205	981-3838	$5,000.00	$0.00
1170	RELIABLE OFFICE FURNISHINGS	40 E. BASELINE AVE.	MESA	AZ	85204	934-7799	$4,000.00	$3,310.00
1175	VALUE FURNITURE CO.	20 WILLIAMS RD.	MESA	AZ	85207	891-0001	$8,000.00	$560.00
1185	PST FURNITURE SHOWCASE	2107 E. FRYE RD.	SCOTTSDALE	AZ	85254	977-4321	$7,000.00	$850.00

Table: PRODUCT

PRODNO	DESCR	SUPNO	COST	PRICE	QOH
10	DESK, STANDARD	352	$170.00	$240.00	114
11	DESK, EXECUTIVE	366	$210.00	$295.00	30
20	CHAIR, STANDARD	354	$80.00	$113.00	140
21	CHAIR, EXECUTIVE	354	$156.00	$218.00	50
22	CHAIR, FOLDING	364	$40.00	$56.00	310
25	SOFA	362	$370.00	$520.00	25
30	TABLE, COMPUTER	370	$80.00	$112.00	47
31	TABLE, CONFERENCE	372	$350.00	$490.00	10
32	TABLE, FOLDING	364	$80.00	$114.00	169
40	LAMP, TABLE	360	$60.00	$84.00	90
41	LAMP, FLOOR	360	$80.00	$116.00	78
50	BOOK CASE	368	$98.00	$138.00	30
60	FILE CABINET, 4 DRAWER	356	$134.00	$188.00	60
61	FILE CABINET, 2 DRAWER	356	$65.00	$91.00	28
62	STORAGE CABINET	350	$120.00	$170.00	120
70	SAFE, FLOOR	358	$280.00	$395.00	12

Table: SALE

SALENO	CUSTNO	DATE	SALAMT
5109	1120	07/03/89	$3,600.00
5110	1035	07/04/89	$1,360.00
5111	1130	07/05/89	$2,000.00
5112	1095	07/07/89	$4,160.00
5113	1170	07/09/89	$3,310.00
5114	1115	07/11/89	$2,360.00
5115	1010	07/14/89	$2,240.00
5116	1140	07/17/89	$2,335.00
5117	1085	07/20/89	$7,200.00
5118	1055	07/24/89	$2,370.00
5119	1015	07/28/89	$6,810.00
5120	1155	07/31/89	$8,500.00

Table: PROD/SL

PRODNO	SALENO	QUAN
10	5109	15
62	5110	8
40	5111	10
41	5111	10
25	5112	8
20	5113	10
21	5113	10
11	5114	8
30	5115	20
60	5116	10
61	5116	5
10	5117	30
70	5118	6
50	5119	5
25	5119	8
31	5119	4
22	5120	50
32	5120	50

Table: RECPT

RECNO	CUSTNO	DATE	RECAMT
3285	1160	07/04/89	$1,000.00
3286	1105	07/04/89	$4,200.00
3287	1025	07/10/89	$2,400.00
3288	1165	07/10/89	$1,780.00
3289	1150	07/12/89	$1,800.00
3290	1130	07/14/89	$2,000.00
3291	1095	07/17/89	$4,160.00
3292	1115	07/21/89	$2,360.00
3293	1070	07/24/89	$5,120.00
3294	1080	07/25/89	$1,000.00
3295	1110	07/28/89	$900.00
3296	1085	07/31/89	$4,200.00

ries, and obtain a printed output of each table.

(1) To which customers (by numbers and names) were sales made in July, and what were the dates and amounts of the sales?

(2) Which products (by numbers and descriptions) were sold to which customers (by numbers and names) in July, and in what quantities?

(3) To which Mesa customers (by names) were sales made in July, which products (by descriptions) did these customers buy, and what were the sales dates?

(4) Which customers (by numbers and names) were involved in both a sale and a cash payment in July, and what were the dates, transaction numbers, and amounts?

INDEX